Cross and Tapper
on Evidence

Cross and Tapper
on Evidence

Ninth edition

Colin Tapper, MA, BCL,

of Gray's Inn, Barrister, Professor of Law
and Fellow of Magdalen College, Oxford,
Special Consultant to Masons (Solicitors)

Butterworths
London, Edinburgh, Dublin
1999

United Kingdom	Butterworths, a Division of Reed Elsevier (UK) Ltd, Halsbury House, 35 Chancery Lane, LONDON WC2A 1EL and 4 Hill Street, EDINBURGH EH2 3JZ
Australia	Butterworths, a Division of Reed International Books Australia Pty Ltd, CHATSWOOD, New South Wales
Canada	Butterworths Canada Ltd, MARKHAM, Ontario
Hong Kong	Butterworths Asia (Hong Kong), HONG KONG
India	Butterworths India, NEW DELHI
Ireland	Butterworth (Ireland) Ltd, DUBLIN
Malaysia	Malayan Law Journal Sdn Bhd, KUALA LUMPUR
New Zealand	Butterworths of New Zealand Ltd, WELLINGTON
Singapore	Butterworths Asia, SINGAPORE
South Africa	Butterworths Publishers (Pty) Ltd, DURBAN
USA	Lexis Law Publishing, CHARLOTTESVILLE, Virginia

© Reed Elsevier (UK) Ltd 1999

A CIP Catalogue record for this book is available from the British Library.

First edition	1958
Second edition	1963
Third edition	1967 (reprinted 1969, 1970, 1972, 1973)
Fourth edition	1974 (reprinted 1975, 1977)
Fifth edition	1979 (reprinted 1982, 1983, 1984)
Sixth edition	1985 (reprinted 1987)
Seventh edition	1990 (reprinted 1994)
Eighth edition	1995

ISBN 0 406 90413 8

Printed and bound in Great Britain by The Bath Press, Bath

Visit us at our website: http://www.butterworths.co.uk

Preface to the ninth edition

It was with typical prescience, equanimity and optimism that Professor Cross looked forward to the day when the law of evidence would be rendered redundant by the liberalisation of the rules for the admissibility of evidence. There can be no doubt but that some such liberalisation has taken place, for example in the increasingly relaxed attitude to the admission of hearsay, and to the competence of children. He could not have appreciated the force of countervailing tendencies which have subsequently emerged, for example in the shape of restrictive rules designed to protect the vulnerable, such as those connected with the incorporation of the European Convention on Human Rights, or those proposed in the Youth Justice and Criminal Evidence Bill 1999. The clash of these factors has complicated the exposition of the law of evidence attempted in this edition.

There can be no doubt that the law of evidence is in a state of flux. It is well illustrated by the different states of reform in different areas. Thus some major measures have been enacted and come into force since the last edition, for example the provisions of the Civil Evidence Act 1995 accomplishing the liberalisation of the admission of hearsay in civil proceedings; others have been enacted, but not yet come into force, such as the Human Rights Act 1998 (although in some respects it is treated as if it were already in force); others have been drafted and introduced, but have not yet been enacted, such as the Youth Justice and Criminal Evidence Bill 1999; others have been proposed and approved by the government, but not yet introduced in the form of a bill, such as the Law Commission's proposals to reform the law of hearsay in criminal proceedings; and others are still at the stage of consultation awaiting final approval, such as the Law Commission's preliminary proposals for the reform of the law relating to the admissibility of evidence of bad character in criminal proceedings. It might also be mentioned that the context of the law of evidence in civil proceedings has been revolutionised by the new Civil Procedure Rules which came into force four days before the manuscript for this edition was delivered to the publishers. These rules employ new terminology, and have been drafted in a deliberately loose form so as to promote their objective of increasing the powers of judges over the civil procedure, including procedure at trial, and it cannot be pretended that it has been possible to assimilate them and to anticipate their effect with any certainty at this stage. It was for reasons such as this that the gap between editions of this book has been reduced for this edition from five years to four, and may result in the adoption of other means to keep the text current between editions.

Vigorous efforts have been made to simplify the exposition of the law to reflect the liberalising tendencies of the modern law. Thus reform of the law of hearsay has permitted the jettisoning of two complete chapters from previous editions, and a drastic curtailment of detail in those that remain. One other major simplification is represented by the elimination from this edition of the more substantive aspects of estoppel, limiting exposition here to cause of action and issue estoppel. By contrast, some aspects of the law have been dealt with in a more detailed fashion, for example the law relating to the admissibility of improperly obtained evidence.

The general strategy of previous editions has been maintained. English law is largely expounded in the text, and foreign comparison and illustration restricted to the footnotes. An attempt has been made to balance exposition with evaluation, in a way which can satisfy the requirements of practitioners and students alike. An attempt has been made to expound English law as at 30 April 1999, subject to reservation as to the assimilation of the Civil Procedure Rules mentioned above; treatment of overseas law has been truncated at an earlier point, varying between jurisdictions, but more often terminating as at the end of 1998.

As always my grateful thanks for assistance of many kinds must be extended to my students and colleagues at Oxford for their help and encouragement in many different ways, especially to Roderick Bagshaw, Katharine Grevling and Peter Mirfield who regularly contribute to the B.C.L. seminar on the law of evidence, and to those students whose participation in that seminar makes it so enjoyable.

Colin Tapper
Magdalen College

1 May 1999

Extract from the preface to the first edition

In the preface to the first edition of his *Law of Evidence*, the late S L Phipson said that he had endeavoured to supply students and practitioners with a work which would take a middle place between 'the admirable but extremely condensed *Digest [of the Law of Evidence]* of Sir James Stephen, and that great repository of evidentiary law, *Taylor on Evidence*'. Those words were written as long ago as 1892, and Phipson's book now has claims to be regarded as *the* great English repository of evidentiary law. I realise therefore that I am flying high when I say I hope to have supplied students and practitioners with a work which will take a middle place between those of Stephen and Phipson. The needs of students and practitioners are not, of course, identical; but I have catered for the students by including a good deal more theoretical discussion in the text than is customary in the case of a book designed solely for the practitioner, and I have catered for the latter by including many more cases in the footnotes than any student could conceivably wish to consult. Nearly all the decisions that are really important from the student's point of view are mentioned in the text. Though I have primarily borne in mind the requirements of those who are working for a law degree, I trust that the book may not prove too long for those working for the professional examinations. The long book may often be tedious, but it is sometimes more digestible than the shorter one.

I have adopted the growing practice of citing a number of decisions of the courts of the Commonwealth. My citations are not intended to be exhaustive. I have, in the main, chosen Commonwealth decisions in which English cases have been discussed or which provide a neat illustration of what is pretty clearly English law.

I have laid myself open to the charge of having quoted at too great length from English judges and American writers. My answer is that I have endeavoured to meet the undoubted need for an up-to-date account of the theory of the subject – a need that is made plain by the fact that, in nine cases out of ten, any advocate can say whether evidence is admissible or inadmissible, but he is frequently at a loss to explain why this should be so. It is impossible to give a satisfactory account of the theory of our law of evidence without frequent reference to the ipsissima verba of the judges and the work of such great American exponents of the subject as Thayer, Wigmore, Morgan and Maguire.

Rupert Cross

January 1958

Contents

CHAPTER I

Introduction   1

CHAPTER II

Matters not requiring proof and judicial findings as evidence   66

Chapter III

Burdens and proof   106

Chapter IV

The functions of the judge and jury   157

Public policy   472

Opinion   510

CHAPTER XIII

Hearsay in general   529

CHAPTER XIV

Hearsay in civil proceedings   563

CHAPTER XV

Hearsay in criminal proceedings   580

CHAPTER XVI

Documentary evidence   638

CHAPTER XVII

Proof of frequently recurring matters 666

Table of statutes

References in this Table to *Statutes* are to Halsbury's Statutes of England (Fourth Edition) showing the volume and page at which the annotated text of the Act may be found.

Page references printed in **bold** type indicate where the section of the Act is set out in part or in full.

Table of cases

C

PAGE

D

G

H

I

J

N

R

PAGE

PAGE

CHAPTER I

Introduction

The evidence of a fact is that which tends to prove it—something which may satisfy an inquirer of the fact's existence. Courts of law usually have to find that certain facts exist before pronouncing on the rights, duties and liabilities of the parties, and such evidence as they will receive in furtherance of this task is described as 'judicial evidence'. After mentioning the development of the law of evidence in section 1, the extent to which it applies to all of the different stages and matters considered by the courts, and to other tribunals, will be considered in section 2. The main purposes and categories of evidence will be considered and exemplified in section 3 together with the question whether any broad general rules can usefully be elaborated. The chief such rule is that of relevancy and is discussed in section 4.

SECTION I. THE DEVELOPMENT OF THE LAW OF EVIDENCE

Although some of the modern rules of evidence can be traced to the middle ages, the story of their development really begins with the decisions of the common law judges in the seventeenth and eighteenth centuries. Those decisions were responsible for a complex and now almost defunct body of law concerning the competency of witnesses and the exclusion of all but the best evidence, together with other rather less defunct rules such as the rule against hearsay with its numerous exceptions, the rule excluding evidence of opinion and the rudiments of the modern law of character evidence. The nineteenth and twentieth centuries have witnessed a number of statutory reforms, but it is the older decisions of the common law judges which dictate the form in which much of the law of evidence must be stated, for this law still consists to a large extent of exclusionary rules, rules declaring that certain matters which might well be accepted as evidence of a fact by other responsible inquirers will not be accepted by the courts, rules declaring, in other words, what is not judicial evidence. There are however also signs of an increasing tendency, especially in civil cases, to develop guidelines relating to the weight of such evidence[1] and to elaborate rules relating to the circumstances in

---

1   Eg Civil Evidence Act 1995, s 4, though the tendency was first discerned long ago, 'People were formerly frightened out of their wits about admitting evidence lest juries should go wrong. In modern times we admit the evidence and discuss its weight.' (Cockburn CJ in *R v Birmingham Overseers* (1861) 1 B & S 763, at 767). See also for a modern recommendation of such an approach in Scotland, *L v L* 1997 SCLR 866, at 871D.

which its disclosure can be compelled.[2] Three factors which have contributed to the largely exclusionary character of the law of evidence are the jury, the oath and the common law adversary[3] system of procedure.[4] Allowance must also be made for a deep-seated fear that evidence will be manufactured by or on behalf of the parties.[5]

> [T]he presumption ... is, that no man would declare anything against himself, unless it were true; but that every man, if he was in a difficulty, or in the view to any difficulty, would make declarations for himself.

No doubt it was this fear which lay at the root of the extraordinary common law rule that the parties to litigation were unable to give evidence. It was abolished for civil cases by the Evidence Act 1851, but not until the Criminal Evidence Act 1898 came into force was the accused allowed to give evidence for himself in all criminal cases. Changes such as those mentioned are climacteric, and have a bearing upon other rules of evidence.

Thus it was the removal of many of the restrictions and disqualifications upon other witnesses by the Evidence Act 1843 which paved the way for the competence of parties under the Evidence Act 1851, and the anomalies thereby created between civil and criminal proceedings provided much of the impetus towards making the accused generally competent in 1898. A policy of piecemeal reform is liable to have particularly unfortunate results in relation to a subject so highly integrated as this department of the law.

The persistent application of the policy led one commentator to speak of the law of evidence in the following terms:[6]

> Founded apparently on the propositions that all jurymen are deaf to reason, that all witnesses are presumptively liars and that all documents are presumptively forgeries, it has been added to, subtracted from and tinkered with for two centuries until it has become less of a structure than a pile of builders' debris.

Yet it must not be supposed that all assessments of the modern law of evidence are equally critical. In *A-G v Horner (No 2)*[7] Hamilton LJ consoled himself with the following reflections:

> I yield to authority on the law of evidence without reluctance, because I am satisfied that in the main the English rules of evidence are just, and I am satisfied also that there is no portion of the English law which ought more rigidly to be upheld. My experience is that the public have in the result derived great benefit from their strict application.

Most lawyers would, however, probably have agreed that the time had come for a comprehensive survey of the whole field when, in September 1964, the Lord Chancellor

---

2 See ch X below.
3 Some of the worst effects of this on the modern law of evidence, especially in criminal cases, may be alleviated by the modern pressure towards discussion between counsel for both sides and the judge as to the proper terms in which the jury should be directed, see eg *R v N* [1998] Crim LR 886, and by the increasing use of model forms of direction, although it would be better if these were made more readily accessible, see Munday [1996] Crim LR 296.
4 Modern scholarship suggests that judicial control of lawyers also played its part. Langbein (1978) 45 U Chi LR 263.
5 *R v Hardy* (1794) 24 State Tr 199, at 1093 per Eyre CB.
6 Harvey *The Advocate's Devil* (1958) 79.
7 [1913] 2 Ch 140, at 156.

and Home Secretary referred the law of evidence in civil and criminal cases respectively to the Law Reform Committee and the Criminal Law Revision Committee. The terms of reference were: To review the law of evidence in civil [criminal] cases and to consider whether any changes are desirable in the interests of the fair and efficient administration of justice, and in particular what provision should be made for modifying rules which have ceased to be appropriate in modern conditions.

The Law Reform Committee produced a series of reports which resulted in the Civil Evidence Acts of 1968 and 1972.[8] The Criminal Law Revision Committee made practically all its recommendations in 1972 in one highly controversial report, the 11th Report, 'Evidence (General)',[9] and although it met with a frosty reception at the time, many of its recommendations have subsequently been enacted.[10] The result of the references of 1964 was to increase the pre-existing differences between the rules of evidence in civil and criminal cases. Some disquiet was expressed by the Roskill Fraud Trials Committee Report[11] about the extent of such divergence, especially in view of the more radical approach adopted in civil cases as a result of the enactment of the Civil Evidence Act 1968.[12] The force of the law of evidence has been weakened in criminal cases by restriction of the grounds upon which an appeal may be allowed to cases in which the conviction is unsafe,[13] with the result that where the rules prescribe the inadmissibility of evidence on grounds other than irrelevance or unreliability, failure to observe those rules will no longer lead to the conviction being quashed. Deprived of any incentive to appeal against such decisions, it may be that such rules will begin to decay. It remains the case that there are still many differences between the rules applying to criminal and to civil proceedings.[14] Nor does their removal seem necessarily imminent despite the current tendency to refer evidential reform to the Law Commission.[15] The common law rules of evidence were evolved for jury trial, a procedure which is obsolescent in civil cases although it is still the mode of trial for serious criminal charges and, even in the case of less serious ones, the fact that they are for the most part heard by lay magistrates may be thought to justify a greater restriction of the area of admissible evidence than is suitable in proceedings before a legally qualified judge sitting alone. Subject to the solution of the vexed problem of the right extent of the difference between the rules governing civil and criminal cases, the law of evidence is a fit subject for codification. If this task is ever undertaken in England, there will be some useful precedents which are mentioned from time to time in this book. There is the Indian Evidence Act 1872, drafted by Sir James Stephen, which still forms the basis of a number of Evidence Ordinances in the Commonwealth. In both Canada[16] and Australia[17] the respective Law Reform Commissions have undertaken extensive work in this field at the Federal

---

8   Hearsay Evidence in Civil Proceedings, Cmnd 2964 (1966); The rule in *Hollington v Hewthorn & Co Ltd*, Cmnd 3391 (1967); Privilege in Civil Proceedings, Cmnd 3472 (1967); Evidence of Opinion and Expert Evidence, Cmnd 4489 (1970).
9   Cmnd 4991. Its earlier 9th Report, Cmnd 3145 (1966) also contained recommendations on evidence now embodied in ss 9–11 of the Criminal Justice Act 1967.
10 Principally in the Police and Criminal Evidence Act 1984, the Criminal Justice Act 1988, and the Criminal Justice and Public Order Act 1994.
11 (1986), paras 5.7 and 5.8.
12 Now superseded by the Civil Evidence Act 1995.
13 Criminal Appeal Act 1995, s 2, substituting new sub-s (1) in Criminal Appeal Act 1968, s 2.
14 The principal differences are that in criminal proceedings the standard of proof is higher; the accused is incompetent as a witness for the prosecution, unsworn evidence may be given by young children, special rules govern the competence and compellability of the accused's spouse, there is no issue estoppel, and the reception of hearsay and opinion evidence is governed in part by the common law.
15 References to which often remain limited either to civil or to criminal proceedings.
16 See draft Code of Evidence published by Law Reform Commission of Canada in 1976 and the Report of the Federal and Provincial Task Force on the Uniform Rules of Evidence (1982).
17 See Law Reform Commission of Australia Report No 38 'Evidence' (1987).

level, but, as yet, it has not proved possible to enact comprehensive legislation to implement the various proposals.[18] In the United States the Federal Rules of Evidence, approved by Congress in 1975, does not amount to a complete code, nor is it, in itself, binding upon the separate States, but it has been widely adopted by them, and in some constitutes part of a code.[19]

Despite the best efforts of the Law Commission, reform of the law of evidence in criminal cases has been obstructed by the refusal of the legislature to authorise comprehensive and systematic empirical research into the operation of the jury system.[20] It is likely that further comprehensive reform will[1] result from the incorporation of the European Convention of Human Rights[2] into English law.[3] It cannot be excluded that a painful, and confusing, process of adjustment of the law of evidence will now take place.[4]

The advent of the new Civil Procedure Rules may have an enormous impact upon the operation of the rules of evidence in civil proceedings, since the whole aim of the new rules is to simplify and expedite the administration of justice, and far-reaching powers have been conferred upon the courts to exclude admissible evidence[5] and to limit cross-examination[6] in order to achieve those ends. Given the strategic emphasis upon increasing judicial flexibility, and the deliberate drafting of the rules in less technical language than in the old Rules of the Supreme Court so as to encourage purposive interpretation, it is, at this stage, impossible to be sure precisely how these rules will affect the law of evidence.

---

18   Although far reaching Evidence Acts, incorporating much of the thinking of the Law Reform Commission, have been enacted for New South Wales and Commonwealth courts. Reference will most often be made in this work to the Evidence Act 1995 (Commonwealth). Even there however the new legislation builds on the old concepts: see *O'Brien v Gillespie* (1997) 41 NSWLR 549. For an appraisal from an English point of view, see Dennis [1996] Crim LR 477, and from an Australian, Smith (1995) 18 UNSWLR 1; for comprehensive analysis, see Odgers *Uniform Evidence Law* (2nd ed, 1997).

19   Comparison with the law of evidence in the United States is complicated, especially in criminal cases, by the impact of the provisions there of constitutional provisions, though, somewhat paradoxically, it has been argued that in some respects the modern interpretation of these provisions has led to greater convergence with English law, see Imwinkelreid [1990] Crim LR 790.

20   Despite the fact that such a proposal was the very first recommendation of the Report of the Royal Commission on Criminal Justice (Cm 2263, 1993).

1   Before the passage of the Human Rights Act 1998 it was held that proceedings could not be stayed awaiting such incorporation: *Secretary of State for Trade and Industry v Hinchcliffe* (1998) Times, 2 February; and that its provisions could not be applied by a court in anticipation: *R v Staines and Morrissey* [1997] 2 Cr App Rep 426; since its passage, but before it has been brought into force, there may be means of achieving such anticipation, see *R v DPP, ex p Kebilene* [1999] 3 WLR 175.

2   It should be noted that outside the strict province of community law, the authoritative source for construction of this Convention is the European Court of Human Rights, and not the European Court of Justice: *Kremzow v Austria* [1997] 3 CMLR 1289.

3   Human Rights Act 1998.

4   As has been the case in Canada, New Zealand and South Africa where similar schemes of incorporation of human rights have been introduced. For some anticipation see articles in [1999] Crim LR 251 et seq.

5   Rule 32.1(2).

6   Rule 32.1(3).

SECTION 2.   RANGE OF THE LAW OF EVIDENCE[7]

The most cursory glance at the table of contents of this, or of any other, general work on the law of evidence reveals a wide diversity of topics and rules.[8] Some rules deal with essentially procedural matters, such as those relating to the ability to secure the disclosure of relevant evidence, and the validity of reasons for not doing so, or rules about the form in which questions may be put to a witness; some deal with witnesses, such as the rules relating to their competency and the extent to which their evidence requires corroboration; some deal with the admissibility of particular sorts of evidence, such as rules relating to the use which might be made of evidence of the previous discreditable conduct of the accused or of potentially unreliable evidence such as hearsay or opinion; and some deal with questions of proof, such as rules about judicial notice or the amount of proof required. These various categories overlap and interlock. The interesting thing is that they can be fitted together into so many different patterns. There is no type of proceeding to which all of the rules of evidence apply. There are a number of ways of dividing the rules up, into those which apply to different types of proceedings, civil and criminal for example. Yet cutting across this is a division between the rules applying in the higher and in the lower courts. These two cross-cuts alone manage to yield three quite different versions of the rule against hearsay, applying variously to civil cases in the higher courts, to criminal cases in the higher courts and to civil cases in the lower courts. It is worth a brief glance at some of the more important patterns. The most significant difference is probably that between the rules which apply to judicial proceedings in the courts, and those which apply to the determination of facts in other tribunals.

A.   PROCEEDINGS IN COURTS

It is to be expected that the fullest range of the rules of evidence will apply to proceedings in courts, but there are still important variations in the precise mixture of rules which apply to different types of jurisdiction, to different types of court, and at different stages in the proceedings. Something will be said of each of these in turn.

1.   Different types of jurisdiction

Notwithstanding many assertions of the common character of the law of evidence in civil and criminal proceedings, it is obvious, even to those making such assertions, that many of the rules are different, and that those that are the same are often applied differently.[9] Thus in *R v Christie*[10] Lord Reading having stated the theoretical similarity went on to say that in practice 'it is desirable in certain circumstances to relax the strict application of the law of evidence.' He had in mind the need to temper the strictness of the law when it was applied to the accused in a criminal case, and in particular the need

---

7   For elaborate statutory recognition of the need for different rules in different situations see in Australia, Evidence Act (Cwth) 1995, ss 4,5, 8 and 9; and for exegesis *Epeabaka v Minister for Immigration and Multicultural Affairs* (1997) 150 ALR 397.

8   For a more detailed appraisal of the complexity of this situation, see Tapper in Birks (ed) *Pressing Problems in the Law 1 Criminal Justice and Human Rights* (1995).

9   See eg *Halford v Brookes* [1992] PIQR P175 where civil proceedings were brought for damages for murder and Rougier J rehearsed a number of differences between the proceedings before him and earlier criminal proceedings which had resulted in the acquittal of one of the defendants.

10   [1914] AC 545, at 564.

to preserve the accused from the effect of admitting evidence more prejudicial to the accused than probative of the prosecution case. This factor undoubtedly underlies many of the differences between the rules applied in the two types of proceeding. It has, in some areas, been implemented by statutory provisions. Thus the Criminal Evidence Act 1898 imports a special regime to apply to the accused as a witness, different from that applying to other witnesses, just because of his greater vulnerability. Even here the matter is not straightforward, for strictly such a consideration should lead not to discrimination between civil and criminal proceedings, but rather between rules applying to the accused in criminal proceedings, and those applying to others. This can lead to difficulty when the true adversary is not the prosecutor, but a co-defendant, for whom similar consideration must be shown, leading to further modification in the rules.[11] Another factor which contributes, perhaps even more strongly, to the differences between the rules applying in criminal and civil proceedings is the difference between the form of procedure and method of trial. In criminal cases pleading is generally oral, and there are commonly no interim applications. In civil cases there is hardly ever a jury. Here too the consequences of such differences find statutory expression, for example in the different methods of reforming the hearsay rule to be found in the Civil Evidence Act 1995 and the Criminal Justice Act 1988.[12] It cannot be maintained that all of the differences stemmed from such considerations. For many it is hard to find any rational explanation, for example, why the admissibility of dying declarations by way of exception to the hearsay rule should have been limited not only to criminal cases, but to those involving the trial of the accused for the homicide of the declarant. Many statutory differences are equally puzzling. It is not at all obvious why the admissibility of the unsworn evidence of children should ever have been confined to criminal cases by s 38 of the Children and Young Persons Act 1933,[13] nor why in South Africa the hearsay rule should not apply to Admiralty proceedings.[14]

In general the courts are concerned with a lis, a dispute between the parties before them,[15] which is resolved by the adversarial process so typical of the common law. There are other aspects of their jurisdiction which are of a different character. Interim applications often have to be heard urgently without recourse to the full panoply of evidential rules, often admitting hearsay, and even when such an application is treated as the trial of the claim still the more relaxed rules to the admission of hearsay may be applied.[16] Though if interim proceedings, for example such a care order in respect of a child, involve making serious allegations against a party, and may lead to important consequences for that party, it seems that he is entitled to have the matter determined by evidence tendered on oath.[17] In proceedings for judicial review cross-examination on affidavits is allowed only when there is an issue of jurisdictional fact.[18] In *Scott v Scott*[19] Viscount Haldane singled out the paternal jurisdiction exercised in relation to

11   See eg *Murdoch v Taylor* [1965] AC 574, [1965] 1 All ER 406.
12   And only to a slightly extent more similar, that proposed by the Law Commission in Law Com 245 *Evidence in Criminal Cases: Hearsay and Related Topics* (Cm 3670, 1997).
13   See now Children Act 1989, s 96(2).
14   See Admiralty Jurisdiction Regulation Act 1983, s 6(3), and *Cargo Laden and Lately Laden on Board the MV Thalassini Avgi v MV Dimitris* 1989 (3) SA 820.
15   In principle the same rules apply to class actions as to those involving only the parties before the court: *Syndicat National des employés et al v Public Curator* [1996] 3 SCR 211.
16   Cp *Rose v Information Services Ltd* [1987] FSR 254 (where they were) with *Re A Debtor (No 87 of 1993)* [1996] 1 BCLC 55 (where they weren't).
17   This accounts for the refusal to permit hearsay in summary contempt proceedings: see *R v Shokoya* (1992) Times, 10 June. But see in Canada *R v Budreo* (1996) 104 CCC (3d) 245 for relaxation of the rules relating to standard of proof in relation to a preventive order against a paedophile.
18   *R v Arts Council of England, ex p Women's Playhouse Trust* (1997) Times, 20 August.
19   [1913] AC 417.

wards of court and lunatics. In *Official Solicitor of the Supreme Court v K*[20] the House of Lords considered how far the ordinary principles of judicial inquiry were to apply to such proceedings. In particular the House considered whether it was open to the judge to find facts relevant to the exercise of his discretion upon a basis of hearsay.[1] Lord Devlin distinguished between those rules which may vary and those which are so fundamental that they have to be observed by everyone who acts judicially, and which constitute the rules of natural justice. He was quite clear that many of the rules of evidence fell into the former category:[2]

> There are also rules of less importance designed to aid in the administration of justice and to regulate procedure. They are rules of convenience rather than of principle; and the rule against hearsay ... is among them. No one would suggest that it is contrary to natural justice to act on hearsay.

The particular application to hearsay has been overtaken by statute, but the general principle remains, that the precise mixture of rules is not fixed, but determined by the nature of the jurisdiction. As Lord Evershed said[3] in the same case:[4]

> [I]t [is] not enough to say that the proceeding is a judicial proceeding. It is necessary to define or to have in mind what is the true character of this judicial proceeding and what is its end or purpose.

This view has now prevailed in relation to the rules of evidence to be adopted in all those proceedings where the welfare of a child is paramount, for example under the provisions of the Children Act 1989.[5] It may still be the case that special care is required in evaluating hearsay emanating from a child in a pre-trial interview.[6]

Many administrative functions involving the finding of facts used to be performed by the ordinary courts. Most of these have now been transferred to special administrative tribunals, but some are still considered by the ordinary courts. In the performance of some of these the courts also apply a different set of rules of evidence, including at least one set permitting the admission of hearsay, whether in the Crown courts,[7] or before magistrates.[8] Similarly when magistrates act in committal proceedings the rules of evidence differ from those which apply when they are conducting a

---

20 [1965] AC 201, [1963] 3 All ER 191.
1 The same principle leads to modification of the ambit of legal professional privilege in wardship proceedings, *Re A* [1991] 2 FLR 473.
2 At 238, 208.
3 With whom Lord Reid expressly agreed.
4 At 217, 195.
5 *Re L (a minor)* [1997] AC 16, [1996] 2 All ER 78, but see also the minority view of Lords Nicholls and Mustill at 33B, 91A (in relation to immunity claimed on the grounds of legal professional privilege); *Re B (minors) (care proceedings) (evidence)* [1997] Fam 117, [1997] 2 All ER 29 (in relation to relaxation of rules relating to issue estoppel). For the position in Australia see Dickey (1993) 67 ALJ 614.
6 See *C v Minister of Community Welfare* (1989) 52 SASR 304.
7 *Kavanagh v Chief Constable of Devon and Cornwall* [1974] QB 624, [1974] 2 All ER 697. The position with regard to cross-examination was less certain, but in *R v Crown Court at Aylesbury, ex p Farrer* (1988) Times, 9 March it was held that the court had no power to order a licensing authority to call a witness to give oral evidence as opposed to the admission of hearsay. The position is the same in Canada, see *R v Zeolkowski* [1989] 1 SCR 1378.
8 *Westminster City Council v Zestfair Ltd* (1989) 88 LGR 288.

summary trial.[9] Even in extradition proceedings where the evidence must be such as would, according to the law of England, justify the accused's committal for trial,[10] the magistrate is justified in not applying rules of practice, which would apply in an English trial.[11] Forfeiture proceedings fall sufficiently outside the general rules as to entitle magistrates not to give a prior acquittal the weight to which it would otherwise be entitled.[12] It has been said that in conducting judicial proceedings which have a strong administrative element a judge is entitled to take into account material of the type which would be accepted by a responsible administrator.[13]

2.   Different types of court

It has already been noted that different courts often apply different mixtures of rules of evidence. This is sometimes accomplished by explicit legislation in the statute establishing the court. Thus the legislation establishing the new County Courts in 1846 for the first time made the parties competent witnesses, and not until 1851 was the position in the High Court brought into line. Occasionally legislation establishes totally new courts, and sometimes explicitly abridges the rules of evidence to be applied in them. Thus when the Industrial Court was set up under the Industrial Relations Act 1971, it was provided that 'it should not be bound by any enactment or rule of law relating to the evidence which is admissible in proceedings in other courts.'[14] Such provisions are however to be construed narrowly, and it has been said in Australia that:[15]

> the rules of evidence should not be treated as excluded from the proceedings of a court unless the words are clear or the context compelling.

A similarly cautious approach has also been adopted in that jurisdiction to a more general authorisation of relaxation in Ord 33, r 3 of the rules governing the Federal Court of Australia, where the Court has said that it will be slow to apply the rule to admit hearsay in respect of a central issue.[16]

It is perhaps surprising that so little formal recognition is given to the difference in the practical approach to the law of evidence in criminal proceedings between

9   Compare *R v Horsham Justices, ex p Bukhari* (1982) 74 Cr App Rep 291 (no discretion to exclude admissible evidence in committal proceedings) with *R v Sang* [1980] AC 402, [1979] 2 All ER 1222 (discretion at summary trial affirmed); *R v Crown Prosecution Service, ex p Warby* (1994) 158 JP 190 (magistrates not entitled to consider claim to public policy immunity at committal proceedings) with *R v South Worcestershire Magistrates, ex p Lilley* [1995] 4 All ER 186, [1995] 1 WLR 1595 (so entitled at summary trial). They are not however at liberty simply to disregard the rules of evidence, and a decision to commit so doing will be liable to be quashed on judicial review: *R v Bedwellty Justices, ex p Williams* [1997] AC 225, sub nom *Williams v Bedwellty Justices* [1996] 3 All ER 737.

10   Extradition Act 1989, s 9. *R v Governor of Brixton Prison, ex p Levin* [1997] AC 741, [1997] 3 All ER 289.

11   *R v Governor of Pentonville Prison, ex p Schneider* (1981) 73 Cr App Rep 200 (rules of practice relating to competence of co-accused as witness for the prosecution); *R v Governor of Pentonville Prison, ex p Voets* [1986] 2 All ER 630, [1986] 1 WLR 470 (rules of practice excluding identifying photographs of accused clearly indicating possession of a police record).

12   *Customs and Excise Comrs v T* [1997] CLY 1107.

13   *R v Sanghera* [1983] 2 VR 130, at 131, per McGarvie J.

14   Industrial Relations Act 1971, Sch 3, para 18(5).

15   *Geschke v Del-Monte Home Furnishers Ltd* [1981] VR 856, at 863, construing Market Court Act 1978, s 13(2) providing that 'the Court may inform itself in such a manner as it thinks fit and is not required to conduct any proceedings in a formal manner.'

16   *Pearce v Button* (1986) 65 ALR 83, at 90, 97 and 102.

magistrates courts, especially those comprising lay magistrates, and the higher criminal courts.[17]

3. Different stages of proceedings

Even if judicial proceedings in the ordinary higher courts alone are considered, deviations are still to be found between the rules which apply to the finding of facts at different stages[18] within those proceedings. This may be illustrated by considering some of the variations which apply, before trial, to issues of fact which arise in relation to a plea in a criminal case or to those which arise in relation to the admissibility of evidence, and, after trial, to those which arise on questions of sentence or on appeal.

(i) Pre-trial

At the pre-trial stage such scanty authority as exists conflicts as to whether the courts should try to follow the rules, which apply at the trial stage as far as possible.[19] In relation to affidavits in civil proceedings it is uncertain how far inadmissible evidence can be relied upon as a source of belief.[20] In criminal proceedings it seems that the judge is bound by no rules at all in in determining the facts relevant to the question of disclosure of evidence to the defence.[1] Then in *R v Podola*[2] a full Court of Criminal Appeal overruled *R v Sharp*,[3] in favour of the view that the burden of proving unfitness to plead was, like the substantive defence of insanity, on the accused who raised it rather than on the prosecution.[4] If raised by the prosecution it must be proved by them beyond reasonable doubt.[5] So far as issues of fact relevant to the admissibility of evidence are concerned the general rule is that such questions should be tried by the judge on the voir dire,[6] at a trial within the trial.[7] It would however be unrealistic for

17 See Darbyshire [1997] Crim LR 105, 627.
18 For example even the test of relevancy may apply differently to an issue at the stage of discovery and at trial, see *The Captain Gregos* (1990) Times, 21 December.
19 Powers to compel the production of evidence may not apply, see *R v Manchester Crown Court, ex p Brokenbrow* (1991) Times, 31 October. For discussion of the situation in Australia see *Casley-Smith v FS Evans & Sons Pty* (1988) 49 SASR 314.
20 Contrast *Savings and Investment Bank Ltd v Gasco Investments (Netherlands) BV* [1984] 1 All ER 296, [1984] 1 WLR 271 (where material inadmissible at the trial was disregarded) and *Deutsche Ruckversicherung v Walbrook Insurance Co Ltd* [1994] 4 All ER 181, [1995] 1 WLR 1017 (where it was allowed).
1   *R v Law* (1996) Times, 15 August.
2   [1960] 1 QB 325, [1959] 3 All ER 418. In this case expert witnesses were called on each side and cross-examined, and the accused also testified and was cross-examined. In the Scottish case of *Russell v HM Advocate* 1946 JC 37, a similar issue of fact was determined by the judge, and not by the jury. See also *Jessup v Mahon* 1989 SCCR 600.
3   (1958) 41 Cr App Rep 197.
4   This was regarded as a suitable analogy for other pre-trial issues such as autrefois convict or autrefois acquit in *R v Martin Coughlan* [1976] Crim LR 631, where an accelerated procedure for reading statements was also approved. In the United States such an allocation has been held not to violate the constitutional guarantee of due process of law, *Medina v California* 112 Sup Ct Rptr 2572 (1992).
5   *R v Robertson* [1968] 3 All ER 557, 52 Cr App Rep 690.
6   Or in the case of committal proceedings by the bench of magistrates engaged upon that task, *R v Ormskirk Magistrates, ex p Davies* (1994) 158 JP 1145. It seems to be within the discretion of the court whether or not reasons for the decision are pronounced: *Wallace and Fuller v R* [1997] 1 Cr App Rep 396, PC.
7   In the United States only the rules of privilege apply at this stage: see Federal Rules of Evidence, rr 104(a), 1101(d)(1); *Bourjaily v US* 483 US 471 (1987).

such evidence to be considered in total isolation from that already adduced at the trial proper.[8] Most such trials have dealt with the admissibility of confessions, and it is well-established in such cases that the prosecution bears the burden of proving the issue of admissibility beyond reasonable doubt,[9] and that witnesses, including the accused,[10] can be called,[11] and cross-examined. Where the burden of satisfying a preliminary question is borne by the accused in criminal proceedings the standard of proof is the balance of probabilities just as it is on issues at the trial proper.[12] The general question of the range of rules which does apply at this stage of judicial proceedings has been examined very thoroughly in the United States.[13] While it appears that in general the rules here relating to evidence are more similar to those governing the trial, there are some indications of a few differences. Thus in one case[14] the court took the view that the proponent of the evidence, there the prosecution, need make out only a prima facie case to show that a tape-recording satisfied the condition of originality. A similarly reduced onus has been applied in relation to jurisdictional questions.[15] It must also often be the case just because the purpose of the preliminary issue is to determine the admissibility of a disputed piece of evidence, or the competency of a witness, that the rules at the preliminary stage must be different from those operating at the trial so as to allow the piece of evidence to be perused, or the witness examined.[16] How much further the rules are different is obscure in the modern English law.[17] It is sometimes suggested that a distinction is required between preliminary issues of authenticity which require only a prima facie case to be established in advance, and those of admissibility which require proof at least on the balance of probabilities at

8   *R v Tyrer* (1989) 90 Cr App Rep 446.
9   Now as a result of Police and Criminal Evidence Act 1984, s 76(2), in this respect re-enacting the common law, see *R v Sartori, Gavin and Phillips* [1961] Crim LR 397. The position is the same in Canada, (*Horvath v R* [1979] 2 SCR 376); and in New Zealand (*R v McCuin* [1982] 1 NZLR 13, there uniquely among evidentiary matters, see *R v Dobler* [1993] 1 NZLR 431, at 438). In the United States (*Bourjaily v US* above) the standard is merely proof on the balance of probabilities, as it is generally believed to be in Australia (*Wendo v R* (1963) 109 CLR 559), though there is also some support for an intermediate standard, see *R v Askeland* (1983) 8 ACR 338.
10   *R v Cowell* [1940] 2 KB 49, [1940] 2 All ER 599.
11   Under cl 54(4) of the Youth Justice and Criminal Evidence Bill 1999 it will be for the party calling the witness, including the prosecution, to establish competency on the balance of probabilities.
12   *R v Mattey and Queeley* [1995] 2 Cr App Rep 409.
13   See Maguire and Epstein (1927) 36 Yale LJ 1101; Saltzburg (1974) 27 Stan LR 271. Rule 104(a) of the US Federal Rules provides that the judge is not bound by any of the rules of evidence except those relating to privileges in deciding such questions.
14   *R v Robson and Harris* [1972] 2 All ER 699, [1972] 1 WLR 651.
15   In England see *Vitkovice Horni a Hutni Tezirvisto v Korner* [1951] AC 869, at 883, and in Australia *Empire Shipping Co Inc v Owners of the Ship 'Shin Kobe Matu'* (1991) 104 ALR 489.
16   A procedure endorsed, though not implemented, in *R v Yacoob* (1981) 72 Cr App Rep 313, at 317, in relation to calling the witness on the preliminary question of her competency at the trial. It was pointed out in *R v Ferguson* (1996) 112 CCC (3d) 342, at 361c, that as witnesses could be called in criminal trials either by prosecution of defence it would be odd to have a different burden of proof of facts relating to competency depending upon which it was to be.
17   In *Duke of Beaufort v Crawshay* (1866) LR 1 CP 699 an affidavit which would have been inadmissible at the trial seems to have been admitted at this preliminary stage. There is also some suggestion that the rules permitting expert evidence of mental condition may apply less stringently on a preliminary issue than at the trial proper, see *R v Ward* (1992) 96 Cr App Rep 1, at 66, and *R v Heaton* [1993] Crim LR 593.

that stage.[18] Different considerations may also apply when the rules for the inadmissibility of evidence are discretionary.[19]

(ii)   Post-trial

There are also significant differences in relation to the mixture of rules which apply to issues of fact which arise to be determined after the trial has concluded, either in relation to the order of the court, or at the appellate stage.

(a)   Order

In criminal cases issues of fact often arise in relation to the basis for sentencing the accused,[20] or making some other order.[1] If there is a contested trial, to the extent that the relevant matters have emerged during the hearing, sentencing may be conducted on the basis of the judge's assessment of those matters.[2] If the accused pleads guilty,[3] then there may be some discrepancy between the basis for that plea, and the pre-sentence report submitted by the prosecution.[4] This is intended to be used at the sentencing stage, though it is clear that many of the statements in it will amount to hearsay.[5] It seems that this is immaterial so long as the facts are not disputed,[6] but that if they are, it is necessary to prove them by evidence admissible under the rules for the

---

18   Eg its canvassing by the Supreme Court of Canada in *R v Evans* [1993] 3 SCR 653, citing McCormick (4th ed, 1992) Vol 2 p 54.

19   See *R v Sparkes* (1996) 88 ACR 194 (evidence obtained during hypnosis).

20   See Thomas [1970] Crim LR 80 and *Principles of Sentencing* (2nd edn, 1978) ch 12. In Canada the Supreme Court has pronounced it commonplace that the strict rules which govern at the trial do not apply at a sentencing hearing (*R v Gardiner* (1982) 140 DLR (3d) 612, at 648), and that there is no difference between the situation in Australia, Canada and England, *R v Brown* [1991] 2 SCR 518, at 522.

1   *R v Thompson and Smith* [1997] 1 Cr App Rep (S) 289, the Criminal Justice Act 1993 explicitly applies the civil standard of proof in respect of confiscation orders in drug trafficking cases, and implements statutory assumptions, ss 7 and 9 (amending the Drug Trafficking Offences Act 1986). See also *DB Deniz Nakliyati TAS v Yugopetrol* [1992] 1 All ER 205, [1992] 1 WLR 437 applying the trial rules to a post-trial application for inspection of a third party's bank account under the Bankers' Book Evidence Act 1879, s 7. In *Re Westmid Packing Services Ltd, Secretary of State for Trade and Industry v Griffiths* [1998] 2 All ER 124 Lord Woolf deplored the development of special evidential rules to deal with the issue of disqualification of a director found unfit to direct a company.

2   The prosecution should not advert in opening to any facts which are not to be proved by evidence, even if their only relevance is as to sentence: *R v Hobstaff* (1993) 14 Cr App Rep (S) 605.

3   The prosecution should not agree to an unreal set of facts as part of a plea-bargaining arrangement with the defence, without reference to the judge: *R v Beswick* [1996] 1 Cr App Rep (S) 343.

4   In cases tried on indictment where the accused has a criminal record, a statement of his previous convictions and antecedents is prepared by the police in the form of a proof of evidence: *Practice Note* [1993] 4 All ER 863. In *R v Butterwasser* [1948] 1 KB 4, [1947] 2 All ER 415, Lord Goddard CJ drew attention to the practice of substituting for the normal trial oath the special voir dire oath for such evidence given at the sentencing stage.

5   In the analogous case in domestic proceedings in the magistrates' courts of a report by a probation officer on the means of the parties, received to help in determining the amount of an order, after a decision on the merits, it is expressly provided by statute that the ordinary exclusionary rules of evidence do not apply. See Magistrates' Courts Act 1980, s 72(5). The position is the same in Canada: see *Albright v R* [1987] 2 SCR 383 explicitly approving this work, and permitting the proof of previous convictions by hearsay.

6   *R v Marquis* (1951) 35 Cr App Rep 33.

trial,[7] and if they are not, that this cannot be remedied on appeal.[8] Issues may also arise which are relevant to sentence but not, or insufficiently relevant, to any issue before the jury.[9] In such cases[10] a special Newton hearing,[11] taking its name from the leading case, should be held.[12]

Although it is clear that the accused is entitled to testify at such a hearing,[13] it is perhaps superfluous to note that little consideration appears to have been given to questions such as the compellability of an accomplice of the accused at this stage, any need for the corroboration of such evidence, the extension of rules relating to the protection of victims of sexual offences,[14] or the permissible range of cross-examination.[15] So too if an inference is to be drawn as to the facts of the offence either from the facts as stated by the prosecution on a plea of guilty, or from the evidence at the trial, any matters upon which it is proposed to rely for the purposes of sentencing should be indicated to the accused in advance,[16] and supported by evidence, including the calling of witnesses,[17] if the facts are disputed. Recent legislation appears to have restricted the circumstances under which anything other than offences for which the accused has been previously convicted, or those which the accused has asked to be taken into consideration can be used to assess the appropriate sentence,[18] thus avoiding anything like the application of the similar facts rule at the sentencing stage.[19] It is

7   In the somewhat similar situation of a report by a court welfare officer to a court considering a family matter relating to children hearsay may be included, but any critical issue should be decided by original evidence, see *Thompson v Thompson* [1986] 1 FLR 212n, approved by the Court of Appeal in *H v H and C, K v K* [1990] Fam 86, [1989] 3 All ER 740. See also Children Act 1989, s 7.

8   *A-G's Reference (No 95 of 1998)* (1999) Times, 21 April.

9   This may increasingly be the case in offences of strict liability after *R v Sandhu* [1997] Crim LR 288 (holding evidence of mental state irrelevant to guilt); see commentary by Thomas to *R v Hill* [1997] Crim LR 459.

10   *R v Tolera* [1999] 1 Cr App Rep 29 (discrepancy with basis for plea of guilty); *R v Finch* (1993) 14 Cr App Rep (S) 226 (different sentencing issues). See also *R v Winter* [1997] 1 Cr App Rep (S) 331 (discrepancy between basis for pleading guilty and evidence in contested trial of co-accused).

11   It is, for example, not treated as a contested hearing for legal aid purposes: *R v Legal Aid Board, ex p Graham Dobson & Co* [1996] 40 LS Gaz R 25.

12   *R v Newton* (1982) 77 Cr App Rep 13. This procedure applies equally to appeals to the Crown Court, *R v Williams* (1983) Times, 26 April. See in Canada *R v Gauthier (No 2)* (1996) 108 CCC (3d) 231.

13   *R v Jenkins* (1990) 12 Cr App Rep (S) 582, even where he has already testified at the trial as he may wish to add to that testimony on the different issues relevant to sentence, although in Australia it was held in *R v Ford* (1994) 75 ACR 398 that the court should not admit self-serving hearsay inconsistent with the verdict at trial.

14   But see *R v Ashmeil* (1988) 10 Cr App Rep (S) 126 where the court discouraged even the taking of a statement of the effect of a rape upon the victim, despite this being a consideration relevant to sentence.

15   It seems clear that the provisions as to cross-examination in the Criminal Evidence Act 1898, s 1(f) are inappropriate for proceedings after verdict, notwithstanding its terminology. It is generally inappropriate for the judge to cross-examine the accused on the matter, *R v McGrath and Casey (*1983) 5 Cr App Rep (S) 460. It may also be impolitic for the accused to cross-examine his victims on their impact statements, and appropriate allowances should be made: *R v H (indecent assault)* (1999) Times, 18 March.

16   *R v Lester* (1975) 63 Cr App Rep 144.

17   *R v Robinson* (1969) 53 Cr App Rep 314; *R v Hearne* [1976] Crim LR 753.

18   Criminal Justice Act 1991, ss 2(2)(a) and 29, as amended by Criminal Justice Act 1993, s 66. Doubts have even been expressed about the application of these provisions to cases where there are specimen counts: *R v Perkins* [1994] Crim LR 141, *R v Kidd* [1998] 1 All ER 42, [1998] 1 WLR 604.

19   It must surely be the case that if such offences have not been admitted by the accused they must be proved according to the ordinary rules and under the ordinary conditions: see *Anderson v DPP* [1978] AC 964, sub nom *DPP v Anderson* [1978] 2 All ER 512; *R v Marshall* [1989] Crim LR 819.

immaterial that the evidence relied upon for sentencing was erroneously admitted at the trial, and this applies even though it favours the accused.[20] Another disputed question relates to the burden and standard of proof required to establish facts at this stage of the proceedings. In Canada the Supreme Court has rejected the American view,[1] that a lesser standard is appropriate, in favour of adherence to the ordinary criminal standard of proof beyond reasonable doubt, resting upon the prosecution, on the basis that, in the words of Stephen, the question of sentence is the gist of criminal proceedings, being to them as the bullet is to the powder.[2] In England it is now quite clear that the incidence and onus of proof in a *Newton* enquiry apply as at the trial both in relation to matters of aggravation which the prosecution must prove,[3] and to matters of mitigation which the defence must establish.[4] It has been held in Australia that statistical material is more readily admissible at this stage than at the trial proper.[5]

(b) Appeal

The final situation[6] to be mentioned here is that concerned with the rules to be applied to evidence adduced on an appeal.[7] There are provisions on both civil[8] and criminal[9] appeals for allowing fresh evidence to be heard. In each case the relevant provisions narrow, rather than broaden, the range of material which may be adduced compared with that admissible in the court below.[10] There are however some differences between the extent to which the courts are prepared to limit the ambit of the fresh evidence to be received in the two types of proceedings. The reason for this appears to be that in criminal proceedings the need to avoid inflicting injustice upon the accused may more readily override the need to achieve finality in litigation.[11]

20 *Flewitt v Horvath* [1972] RTR 121, where the evidence admitted at the trial was hearsay, and wrongly taken into account by the magistrates in determining not to disqualify the accused driver; see also *James v Morgan* [1988] RTR 85 where hearsay evidence that the accused's drink had been 'laced' by his friends was rejected on the same issue. By contrast the Supreme Court of the United States has held it an unconstitutional denial of due process of law to exclude hearsay favouring the accused at the sentencing stage, *Green v Georgia* 442 US 95 (1979).

1   In *Williams v New York* 337 US 241 (1949). A disturbing side-effect is that the discrepancy permits American courts to sentence on the basis of guilt in respect of crimes for which the accused has been acquitted at the very same trial, *US v Watts; US v Putra* 519 US 148 (1997), cp *R v Gillespie* [1998] Crim LR 139.

2   *R v Gardiner* (1982) 140 DLR (3d) 612, quoting Sir James Fitzjames Stephen (1863) Cornill Magazine 189.

3   *R v Kerrigan* (1992) 14 Cr App Rep (S) 179.

4   *R v Carroll* (1992) 13 Cr App Rep (S) 99. Indeed in cases to which the provisions relating to the making of assumptions under the Drug Trafficking Offences Act 1986 apply, there is some counterpart to the rules which apply at trial in relation to the operation of presumptions, *R v Redbourne* (1992) 14 Cr App Rep (S) 162, and to the rules for the distribution of evidential and persuasive burdens: see *R v Tolera* [1998] Crim LR 425.

5   *Morris v East* (1988) 91 FLR 23.

6   The two may overlap, and in Canada it has been held that the rules relating to fresh evidence on appeal are more relaxed when the appeal is against a sentencing determination (*R v Riley* (1996) 107 CCC (3d) 278) though they still do not extend to adducing evidence as to the basis for a plea bargain: *R v K(S)* (1995) 99 CCC (3d) 376.

7   Similarly restrictive principles have been applied to discovery for the purposes of an appeal: *R v Secretary of State for Home Department, ex p Gardian* [1996] Imm AR 6; and in Queensland to setting aside a judgment obtained by fraud: see *Brough v Abel* [1987] 1 Qd R 138.

8   Old RSC Ord 59, r 10(2), preserved in the Civil Procedure Rules, Sch 1.

9   Criminal Appeal Act 1968, s 23.

10 Although r 10(2) contains no such explicit limitation to evidence which would have been admissible at the trial as does s 23(2)(a), such limitation may be implied. As it may in relation to s 23(1), see *R v Lattimore* (1975) 62 Cr App Rep 53, at 56.

11 *Braddock v Tillotson's Newspapers Ltd* [1950] 1 KB 47, at 54, [1949] 2 All ER 306, at 311.

Civil cases. The rules of evidence are often relaxed in civil cases by agreement between the parties. Thus in one case no objection was taken to the admission of a hearsay report in a local newspaper to show what had taken place at the trial, no proper note having been taken.[12] In civil cases the same rules apply whether or not the issue arises on an appeal from a summary judgment,[13] a hearing with, or without a jury, or in deciding whether or not to re-open a trial,[14] but not on an appeal by case stated on a question of law,[15] nor in the case of an appeal against an ancillary order in family proceedings,[16] or against a refusal to set aside a statutory demand.[17] If the appeal is by way of rehearing, the appellate court may take into account evidence of events between the original trial and the appeal being heard,[18] as it may if the subsequent events have destroyed the whole common basis on which the trial was conducted.[19] Special grounds are still[20] needed before fresh evidence is admitted after a trial on the merits,[1] and the classic statement of the conditions[2] to be applied in such cases was made by Denning LJ in *Ladd v Marshall:*[3]

> [F]irst, it must be shown that the evidence could not have been obtained with reasonable diligence for use at the trial: second, the evidence must be such that, if given, it would probably have an important influence on the result of the case, although it need not be decisive: third, the evidence must be such as is presumably to be believed, or in other words, it must be apparently credible, though it need not be incontrovertible.

The first condition will normally not be satisfied if the evidence could have been secured before the trial through disclosure,[4] though the court may permit fresh evidence to be taken to replace that contained in a note which has been lost by accident.[5] This condition also covers a case where a witness who can be found could not reasonably

---

12   *Re Cowburn, ex p Firth* (1882) 19 Ch D 419, at 424.
13   *Langdale v Danby* [1982] 3 All ER 129, at 137, [1982] 1 WLR 1123, at 1132.
14   *Sincroflash Ltd v Trusthouse Forte plc* (1983) Times, 7 January, but not when reviewing a discretionary decision taken on an interim application, *Hadmor Productions Ltd v Hamilton* [1983] 1 AC 191, at 220, [1982] 1 All ER 1042, at 1046.
15   *Brady (Inspector of Taxes) v Group Lotus Car Companies plc* [1987] 2 All ER 674, at 688, as approved by the Court of Appeal, [1987] 3 All ER 1050.
16   *Marsh v Marsh* [1993] 2 All ER 794, [1993] 1 WLR 744 where an intermediate standard applied whereby the judge could temper the rigour of *Ladd v Marshall* as he felt fit without being bound to admit fresh evidence as on a rehearing de novo.
17   *Salvidge v Hussein* (1998) Times, 11 November.
18   *Rushmoor Borough Council v Richards* (1996) 160 LG Rev 460.
19   *Mulholland v Mitchell* [1971] AC 666, [1971] 1 All ER 307. In such a case there is an obligation of disclosure to the other side: *Vernon v Bosley (No 2)* [1999] QB 18, [1997] 1 All ER 614.
20   The wording of the old Order 59, r 10(2) is retained by Sch 1 to the Civil Procedure Rules.
1   See *AIB Finance Ltd v Debtors* [1997] 4 All ER 677; *Canada Trust Co v Stolzenberg (No 4)* (1998) Times, 14 May. A summary judgment under the Civil Procedure Rules, Part 24 seems like one under the old RSC Ord 14 to remain a decision on the merits: see *Ramanathan Rudra v Abbey National plc* (1998) 76 P & CR 537.
2   In *Lattimer v Cumbria County Council* [1994] PIQR P395 Staughton LJ suggested absence of delay as a fourth implicit condition.
3   [1954] 3 All ER 745, at 748, [1954] 1 WLR 1489, at 1491. Expressly approved by the House of Lords in *Skone v Skone* [1971] 2 All ER 582, at 586, [1971] 1 WLR 812, at 815, and in *Langdale v Danby* [1982] 3 All ER 129, at 137, [1982] 1 WLR 1123, at 1133.
4   *Turnbull & Co v Duval* [1902] AC 429, though this will not necessarily bar admissibility in a case where a party has been misled into believing that disclosure would be ineffective, *Skone v Skone* [1971] 2 All ER 582, at 587, [1971] 1 WLR 812, at 816.
5   *Re Cowburn, ex p Firth* (1882) 19 Ch D 419, at 426.

have been expected to testify to the desired effect, but a court will be slow to accept fresh evidence upon this basis.[6]

The second condition represents a compromise between two formulations suggested in *Brown v Dean*, the stronger expressed by Lord Loreburn LC, that 'if believed it would be conclusive',[7] the weaker by Lord Shaw, that it be 'so gravely material and so clearly relevant ... that it should have been before the jury.'[8] It will be hard to satisfy if the evidence relates to a matter already taken into account hypothetically in the assessment of damages.[9] The test is even more stringent when the fresh evidence relates solely to credit,[10] but it may nevertheless be admitted even then in an exceptional case if the court has been deceived and the evidence may reasonably have tipped the scales.[11]

The third condition relates to the cogency of the evidence and is really implicit in the second. In particular it seems that fresh evidence is unlikely to be admitted if it amounts to no more than a witness wishing to renege on the evidence he gave at the trial.[12]

The rule in *Ladd v Marshall* is designed to ensure that litigation is not unduly prolonged, but as such, it is subservient to the principle that a litigant should not succeed by fraud, and in such a case fresh evidence may be admitted notwithstanding the restrictions imposed by the rule,[13] thus avoiding the need to institute fresh litigation to set aside the judgment.[14]

Criminal cases. In criminal cases the situation is different, first because of the importance of securing justice for the accused,[15] and second, because of the width of the power to order a new trial.[16] Thus the relevant section of the Criminal Appeal Act 1968[17] contains two separate provisions for the adduction of fresh evidence[18] on a criminal appeal, s 23(1) conferring a wide discretionary power,[19] and s 23(2) imposing a more circumscribed duty to do so. Even so the court will not normally,[20] even under s 23(1),

6   See *Williams v Reason* [1988] 1 All ER 262.
7   [1910] AC 373, at 374.
8   At 376.
9   See *Hunt v Severs* [1993] QB 815, [1993] 4 All ER 180 referring to dicta of Lord Wilberforce in *Mulholland v Mitchell* [1971] AC 666, [1971] 1 All ER 307.
10   *Braddock v Tillotson's Newspaper Ltd* [1950] 1 KB 47, at 57, [1949] 2 All ER 306, at 313.
11   *Meek v Fleming* [1961] 2 QB 366, at 379, [1961] 3 All ER 148, at 154, per Holroyd Pearce LJ. Willmer LJ thought it enough that such evidence be of vital significance, and Pearson LJ that it merely be material.
12   *Pursell v Railway Executive* [1951] 1 All ER 536.
13   See *Meek v Fleming* above, endorsed by *Brady (Inspector of Taxes) v Group Lotus Car Companies plc* [1987] 3 All ER 1050.
14   *Zincroft Civil Engineering Ltd v Sphere Drake Insurance plc* (1996) Times, 13 December.
15   Said in *Hughes v Singh* (1989) Times, 21 April to be the overriding consideration. The rule is nevertheless available also to the prosecution: *R v Gilfoyle* [1996] 3 All ER 883, [1996] 1 Cr App Rep 302.
16   Criminal Appeal Act 1968, s 7.
17   As amended by Criminal Appeal Act 1995, s 4.
18   This will normally be evidence of fact rather than of opinion, as suggested by the wording of the provision, because the issue should normally have been raised at the trial, and because experts are more fungible: *R v Jones* [1997] 1 Cr App Rep 86.
19   So wide as to justify its reception in exceptional cases even after a plea of guilty: *R v Foster* [1985] QB 115, [1984] 2 All ER 679, or on the factual basis for a sentence: *R v Frankum* (1983) 5 Cr App Rep (S) 259. It extends to evidence which had been held inadmissible at the trial if the appellate court believes it to be admissible: *R v Gilfoyle* [1996] 3 All ER 883, [1996] 1 Cr App Rep 302, and at 899, 321 was said 'to be confined only by the requirement that the court must be satisfied that it is necessary or expedient in the interests of justice to require the evidence to be given.'
20   For an exceptional case when it did, see *R v Ahluwalia* (1992) 96 Cr App Rep 133.

admit evidence which could not have been adduced at the trial, such as hearsay,[1] nor will it admit fresh expert evidence in rebuttal, preferring to order a new trial.[2] It will also insist upon the observance of the procedural requirements which apply by statute to the admission of evidence at the trial.[3] Section 23(2) provides that if the fresh evidence is capable of belief[4] and would have been admissible at the trial,[5] it should be received on appeal unless the court is satisfied that it would afford no ground for allowing the appeal[6] or that there was no reasonable ground[7] for failing to adduce it at the trial. This provision seems to be accorded the same generous interpretation as that given to the predecessor of s 23(1), and to permit the reception of fresh evidence going to credit whether it relates directly to evidence adduced by the relevant witness at the trial,[8] or to the previous convictions, previous inconsistent statements, or other matter of discredit of an important witness on an important matter.[9] It does not extend to expert evidence on issues of mental impairment not raised at the trial,[10] at least without any explanation for failure to do so.[11]

B.   PROCEEDINGS IN OTHER TRIBUNALS[12]

There is a very wide variety of proceedings of a quasi-judicial, administrative and legislative nature in which issues of fact require authoritative determination. Many of

1   *R v Dallas* [1971] Crim LR 90; *R v Lattimore* (1975) 62 Cr App Rep 53, at 56, though hearsay may be used to determine what fresh evidence should be produced, *R v Callaghan* [1988] 1 All ER 257, [1988] 1 WLR 1. See also in Australia *R v Scoullar* (1995) 76 ACR 487.

2   *R v Merry* (1970) 54 Cr App Rep 274.

3   *R v Conway* (1979) 70 Cr App Rep 4, where the procedure of first putting an inconsistent statement to a witness before contradicting him, prescribed by the Criminal Procedure Act 1865, s 4, was insisted upon.

4   Amended from the old form 'likely to be credible' on the basis of being more generous, but see Smith [1995] Crim LR 920, at 928 for a convincing counter-argument. See *R v Miller* [1997] 2 Cr App Rep 178 where this factor was decisive.

5   Inadmissible evidence cannot be relied upon to render a conviction unsafe: *R v Thomas* [1996] Crim LR 654, disapproving of *R v Beckford and Daley* [1991] Crim LR 833 to the extent of any inconsistency. But see *R v D* [1996] 1 All ER 881, [1996] 1 Cr App Rep 455 where a judgment in a related case was admitted under s 23(1) although it would not have constituted admissible evidence; see also *R v Loughran* [1999] Crim LR 404 where inadmissible expert evidence seems to have been relied upon.

6   In Australia it must be such as would be likely to have affected the result: *Mickelberg v R* (1989) 167 CLR 259.

7   Failure to call expert evidence has been held to be reasonable where the field was 'arcane': *R v Latte* [1996] CLY 1388 (experts on lighting and facial recognition at distance); see also *R v Cassidy* [1995] 3 NZLR 184 where reasonable not to have sought overseas supporting expert (only local expert on behaviour during sleep unexpectedly reneged on his witness statement under cross-examination). In Scotland the Criminal Procedure (Scotland) Act 1975, s 228(2) more stringently requires the evidence to have been unavailable: *Elliott v HM Advocate* 1995 SCCR 280.

8   *R v Hamilton* (1917) 13 Cr App Rep 32. In Canada subsequent recantation has been accepted as fresh evidence, but to justify a retrial rather than an acquittal: *R v H(H)* (1996) 108 CCC (3d) 447; cp *R v Teneycke* (1996) 108 CCC (3d) 53 where such evidence was rejected.

9   *R v Parks* [1961] 3 All ER 633, 46 Cr App Rep 29; *R v Williams*; *R v Smith* (1994) Times, 27 January; *R v Austin* [1996] CLY 1427. For discussion of the cogency required of fresh evidence in criminal cases, see: in Australia, *Gallagher v R* (1986) 160 CLR 392, *Mickelberg* above; in Canada, *Palmer v R* [1980] 1 SCR 759, *Stolar v R* [1988] 1 SCR 480; and in New Zealand, *R v Dunsmuir* [1996] 2 NZLR 1.

10   *R v Arnold* (1996) 31 BMLR 24; *R v Lewis* [1996] Crim LR 260.

11   Some forms of mental illness might themselves inhibit forensic reliance upon them.

12   See generally E Campbell in Waller and Campbell (eds) *Well and Truly Tried* (1982) p 36, and for the position in the United States see Davis and Pierce 2 *Administrative Law Treatise* (3rd edn, 1994) ch 10.

them are susceptible of control by courts of law. It is sometimes a matter of dispute how far and how many of the rules of evidence apply, or should apply, in such proceedings.[13] It is largely because the concerns and purposes of these bodies vary so widely that few general principles can be discerned.[14] In any given tribunal the rules may, as in the case of courts, vary according to the gravity of the issue involved.[15] Conversely even the same issue may be decided upon a different basis when it is before a tribunal rather than a court.[16] Even when the formal rules of evidence apply to a non-judicial tribunal, to an arbitration for example, a more tolerant attitude to the enforcement of the rules is likely to be exhibited.[17]

Many of the bodies charged with these functions are set up by statute, and it is not uncommon in such cases for some express provision to relate to the procedure to be applied.[18] In some cases where the inquiry is of a formal nature the statute may expressly import rules of evidence as they apply in the ordinary courts.[19] Thus the Race Relations Act 1976 regulates compulsory provision of information and disclosure of documents by reference to civil proceedings in the High Court.[20] It is however more common for the provision to exclude the strict application of the rules of evidence which apply in ordinary courts,[1] although this may still leave their application optional.[2] Sometimes the statute contents itself with bestowing a power to prescribe the rules of evidence which are to apply.[3] In *R v Deputy Industrial Injuries Comr, ex p Moore*[4] where there was such a power, no regulations had been made under it. It was said that the existence of the power indicated that Parliament did not intend the strict rules of evidence to apply.[5] It would however be rash to construe the non-existence of such a power as indicating any intention in the matter at all. The precise pattern of rules depends upon a very wide range of factors defining the nature of the proceedings.[6]

13 Sometimes a general revision of the rules of evidence will provide explicitly for its application outside the ordinary courts, thus the Civil Evidence Act 1995, s 11 applies its provisions relating to hearsay to civil proceedings before any tribunal in which 'the strict rules of evidence apply'; see also in Scotland, Civil Evidence (Scotland) Act 1988, s 9.
14 It is exacerbated by divergence between tribunals of a given type when the power to determine the rules which apply is given to the tribunals themselves, without a power in the national presiding officer to prescribe rules of practice: see *Eurobell (Holdings) plc v Barker* [1998] ICR 299.
15 In *R v Wolverhampton Coroner, ex p McCurbin* [1990] 2 All ER 759, [1990] 1 WLR 719 it was held that in the Coroners' Court unlawful killing must be established beyond reasonable doubt, but death by misadventure only on the balance of probabilities; for a slightly different approach to this issue in Australia see *Anderson v Blastriki* [1993] 2 VR 89.
16 As in *R v Maidstone Crown Court, ex p Olson* (1992) 136 Sol Jo LB 174 where a licensing authority need determine an allegation of indecent assault only on the balance of probabilities, and was not bound by the applicant's acquittal of that very offence.
17 See *Re Enoch and Zaretzky, Bock & Co's Arbitration* [1910] 1 KB 327.
18 For example, the Building Societies Act 1986, ss 48(3), 52(8), 57(4) and 57(5).
19 In Canada a reference simply to 'all relevant evidence' has been held to exclude hearsay: *R v Zeolkowski* [1989] 1 SCR 1378.
20 Section 50(3)(a). See also Osteopaths Act 1993, s 26(3) where the procedure of the place where the tribunal sits is to be applied; cp *McAllister v General Medical Council* [1993] AC 388, [1993] 1 All ER 982 where the Privy Council determined that the law of England applied to proceedings of the Council wherever it sat.
1 See eg CCR Ord 19, r 5(3) governing reference to arbitration, and Town and Country Planning (Enforcement) (Inquiries Procedure) Rules 1981, SI 1981/1743, r 11(4).
2 See in Australia, *General-Motors-Holden's Automotive Ltd v Kalogerinis* (1994) 62 SASR 492.
3 Occasionally overlaid by a few compulsory rules, see Social Security Act 1998, s 16(5) (privilege against self-incrimination).
4 [1965] 1 QB 456, [1965] 1 All ER 81.
5 At 474, 85.
6 *R v Commission for Racial Equality, ex p Cottrell and Rothon* [1980] 3 All ER 265, [1980] 1 WLR 1580. Proceedings are not converted from judicial to administrative just because the tribunal dismisses a claim without consideration of the merits: *Barber v Staffordshire County Council* [1996] 2 All ER 748.

[T]here are degrees of judicial hearing, and those degrees run from the borders of pure administration to the borders of the full hearing of a criminal cause or matter in the Crown Court. It does not profit one to try to pigeon-hole the particular set of circumstances either into the administrative pigeon-hole or into the judicial pigeon-hole. Each case will inevitably differ, and one must ask oneself what is the basic nature of the proceeding.

Flexibility is the essence of the matter. The precise concatenation of rules of evidence and procedure should be adapted to the purposes of the proceedings, and to their circumstances. Where the procedure is in some sense judicial it is common to invoke the rules of natural justice, but this carries the matter little further:[7]

Natural justice requires that the procedure before any tribunal which is acting judicially shall be fair in all the circumstances, and I would be sorry to see this fundamental general principle degenerate into a series of hard and fast rules. For a long time the courts have, without objection from Parliament, supplemented procedure laid down in legislation where they have found that to be necessary for this purpose.

Even if it were possible, it would not be appropriate to specify here all of the various mixtures of rules of evidence which apply in all of the different tribunals which have to decide issues of fact. It is however worth drawing attention to some of the main rules which have been controverted, and to give a few examples of the approaches adopted by the courts in order to resolve them. The rules involved have principally been those dealing with the calling of witnesses, the administration of an oath, the right to cross-examine, the admissibility of hearsay and the need to disclose.

It is clear that the nature of the issues of fact to be decided and the consequences of a finding must have an important bearing on the nature of the rules which govern that finding.[8] Thus in *R v Board of Visitors of Hull Prison, ex p St Germain (No 2)*[9] where the board of visitors were adjudicating upon allegations of very serious offences, guilt of which would involve substantial loss of liberty, the requirements were very stringent. Nevertheless they differed quite substantially from those which would have operated in a court. Thus while the court thought it necessary to allow the accused to call witnesses and to cross-examine, it nevertheless permitted discretion to the chairman to limit the number of witnesses upon proper grounds, and to insist upon cross-examination being channelled through himself.[10] In view of the notorious difficulty of some of the issues involved, questions of identification at a distance for example, the court was reluctant to permit disposal simply on the basis of hearsay,[11] but here too its

---

7   *Wiseman v Borneman* [1971] AC 297, at 308, [1969] 3 All ER 275, at 277, per Lord Reid. In Australia in *Hempel v A-G* (1987) 77 ALR 641 it was held to be consistent with natural justice in extradition proceedings to cast the onus of proof upon the party resisting extradition, and not allow him to cross-examine witnesses, or even an oral hearing.

8   In *R v Milk Marketing Board, ex p Austin* (1983) Times, 21 March, QB, where a tribunal decision could deprive a man of his livelihood the full criminal standard of proof was required.

9   [1979] 3 All ER 545, [1979] 1 WLR 1401.

10   This course was also required by the Court of Appeal in *Chilton v Saga Holidays plc* [1986] 1 All ER 841, where although the rules for the arbitration of small claims authorised an informal and equal approach to be adopted they were nevertheless held not to permit the Registrar to disallow cross-examination by a legally represented party, the other party not being so represented.

11   The United States has now abandoned its old rule that such an issue could not be decided solely on the basis of hearsay: *Johnson v US* 628 F 2d 187 (1980), at 190.

solution was not exclusion, as it might have been at common law, but rather to give the accused an adequate opportunity to deal with it.[12] This decision may be compared with that in *R v Commission for Racial Equality, ex p Cottrell and Rothon*[13] where questions of the right to cross-examine and to rely upon hearsay were also raised. Here however the point arose in relation to the issue of a non-discrimination notice by the Commission for Racial Equality within the statutory framework of the Race Relations Act 1976. The allegations did not involve the commission of a criminal offence, nor did an adverse determination involve loss of liberty, or, at least in the absence of a series of further steps, interference with the discriminator's business. It was for these reasons that the court distinguished the prison visitors' case, and decided that the scheme of the Act neither required to be supplemented by an automatic right to cross-examine, nor excluded the admission of hearsay. Indeed since the statute made it proper for the commission to delegate its investigatory functions, the court thought it right for the commission to act upon the basis of the hearsay necessarily contained in reports by those carrying out such functions. Such statutory support is not however necessary. In cases where the statute provides little more than a requirement that a tribunal shall act upon the basis of evidence, the general view is that this entitles it, in the absence of special considerations, to act upon any material, including hearsay, which is logically probative:[14]

[T]echnical rules of evidence form no part of the rules of natural justice. The requirement that a person exercising quasi-judicial functions must base his decision upon evidence means no more than that it must be based on material which tends logically to show the existence or non-existence of facts relevant to the issue to be determined, or to show the likelihood or unlikelihood of the occurrence of some future event the occurrence of which would be logically probative. It means that he must not spin a coin or consult an astrologer; but he may take into account any material which as a matter of reason, has some probative value in the manner mentioned above. If it is capable of having any probative value, the weight to be attached to it is a matter for the person to whom Parliament has entrusted the responsibility of deciding the issue. The supervisory jurisdiction of the High Court does not entitle it to usurp this responsibility and to substitute its own view for his.

Disciplinary proceedings seem close to the model of a criminal trial,[15] normally require proof beyond reasonable doubt,[16] require similar identification warnings;[17] and are subject to a similar approach to the use of fresh evidence at the appellate stage;[18] but

---

12 A similar approach was taken to hearsay in the form of a scientific certificate in *R v Governor of Swaleside Prison, ex p Wynter* (1998) Times, 2 June.

13 [1980] 3 All ER 265, [1980] 1 WLR 1580; see also *R v Haringey London Borough Leader's Investigative Panel, ex p Edwards* (1983) Times, 22 March.

14 *R v Deputy Industrial Injuries Comr, ex p Moore* [1965] 1 QB 456, at 488, [1965] 1 All ER 81, at 94, per Diplock LJ. See also *Minister for Immigration and Ethnic Affairs v Pochi* (1980) 31 ALR 666.

15 Although in Australia in *McCarthy v Law Society of New South Wales* (1997) 43 NSWLR 42 held to be comprehended within the description 'civil proceedings' for the purpose of admitting an inspector's report into evidence.

16 *Re A Solicitor* [1993] QB 69, [1992] 2 All ER 335; see also Police (Discipline) (Senior Officers) Regulations 1985, SI 1985/519, r 18(2)(b); Code of Conduct of the Bar of England and Wales, cl 10.

17 *R v Cardinal Newman's School, Birmingham, ex p S* (1997) Times, 26 December.

18 *Thomson v Scottish Solicitors Discipline Tribunal* (1999) Times, 13 May.

application of the civil standard of proof has been approved,[19] the use of confessions which would there be inadmissible has been allowed, facts have been permitted to be proved by reference to criminal convictions otherwise inadmissible at law,[20] and there is even no absolute entitlement to cross-examine,[1] though in some cases the rule excluding evidence of similar facts seems to have been applied.[2] As the issue departs further and further from the model of a criminal prosecution[3] so the likelihood of importing rules of evidence which apply there diminishes. Thus the wholly inquisitorial procedure before a coroner is inimical to the application of the rules of evidence, which accordingly do not apply to such proceedings.[4] Indeed in the case of local inquiries in planning matters Lord Diplock has refused even to adopt the terminology of natural justice as suggesting that 'the prototype is only to be found in procedures followed by English courts of law.'[5] Instead he referred simply to the need for the procedure to be fair. Indeed so far from finding that rights to cross-examine constitute one of the ingredients of a fair procedure he suggests that they might make it unfair:[6]

To 'over-judicialise' the inquiry by insisting on observation of the procedures of a court of justice which professional lawyers alone are competent to operate effectively in the interests of their clients would not be fair.

He also drew attention to the totally different conditions of a planning inquiry in relation to the nature of the issues, the number of interested parties, and of their witnesses, and the length of the proceedings.[7] He felt that in determining even so apparently

19   *R v Hampshire County Council, ex p Ellerton* [1985] 1 All ER 599, [1985] 1 WLR 749, disapproving remarks in *R v Police Complaints Board, ex p Madden* [1983] 2 All ER 353, [1983] 1 WLR 447. In Australia different standards are sometimes applied to very similar issues on identical wording within the same state, cp *T v Medical Board (South Australia)* (1992) 58 SASR 382 (proof beyond reasonable doubt of unprofessional conduct of doctor) and *Versteegh v Nurses Board of South Australia* (1992) 60 SASR 128 (balance of probabilities of unprofessional conduct of nurse), and in the case of federal police disciplinary proceedings the burden has been reduced by statutory provision, see *R v O'Connell* (1994) 76 ACR 140; in Canada, Charter guaranties of non-compellability and the presumption of innocence do not apply automatically to them, *Starr v Houlden* (1990) 64 DLR (4th) 285.
20   *Re Del Core and Ontario College of Pharmacists* (1985) 19 DLR (4th) 68; cp *Hill v Clifford* [1907] 2 Ch 236.
1   *Shakespeare v British Coal Corpn* (1988) Times, 5 April; *R v Governor of Swaleside Prison, ex p Wynter* (1998) Times, 2 June.
2   *Lanford v General Medical Council* [1990] 1 AC 13, [1989] 2 All ER 921; *Re College of Physicians and Surgeons of Ontario and K* (1987) 36 DLR (4th) 707.
3   Though the seriousness of the consequences may require some evidential safeguards, see in Ireland, *Gallacher v Revenue Comrs (No 2)* [1995] 1 IR 55, where an internal enquiry into an employee's conduct was prevented from relying on hearsay for this reason.
4   *R v West London Coroner, ex p Gray* [1988] QB 467, [1987] 2 All ER 129; *McKerr v Armagh Coroner* [1990] 1 All ER 865, [1990] 1 WLR 649; *R v Lincoln Coroner, ex p Hay* (1999) Times, 30 March. See in Canada, Ontario Law Commission *Report on Law of Coroners* (1995), at 89; and *Hurd v Hewitt* (1994) 120 DLR (4th) 105 applying the distinction more generally between adjudicative and investigative inquiries (rule in *Browne v Dunn* (1893) 6 R 67 not applying in latter). This may cause problems where the two forms overlap, see *Phillips v Nova Scotia* [1995] 2 SCR 98. In Australia different rules of evidence have been applied to investigative and adjudicative functions of the same Commission: *Re An Application Under The Criminal Justice Act* [1994] 2 Qd 581.
5   *Bushell v Secretary of State for the Environment* [1981] AC 75, at 95, [1980] 2 All ER 608, at 612.
6   At 97, 614.
7   In Scotland in *Errington v Wilson* 1995 SC 550 even in so administrative a matter as ordering the destruction of food unfit for human consumption, cross-examination was required because there was no special urgency, the owner's rights would be affected, and the issue depended entirely on the evaluation of expert evidence.

straightforward a matter as the fairness of allowing cross-examination a multitude of factors needed to be considered, such as, in the case of an expert opinion witness, the nature of the topic on which the opinion was expressed, the qualifications of the witness and competence of the cross-examiner, and the inspector's view of whether his report would be more useful if cross-examination were allowed.

In general, powers to compel attendance and to administer an oath require to be endowed by statute,[8] though it is possible for a tribunal recognised by law, even though not set up by statute, to secure a subpoena to secure the attendance of a witness.[9] The power to administer an oath does not preclude the reception of unsworn testimony, if appropriate.[10] The application of spousal immunities may depend upon how close the issues are to an accusation of crime.[11] In principle, public policy immunity applies to tribunals,[12] but in some cases it has been thought desirable to make explicit provision.[13] In those cases where a witness can be compelled to give evidence, the normal range of privileges will presumably apply in the absence of specific statutory provision,[14] since it would be odd for a court to be in a weaker position than a tribunal in securing relevant evidence.[15] It may however be preferable to save any desired exclusionary privilege when the ordinary rules are relaxed. It may finally be noted that the nature of the issue before a tribunal may dictate the application of different, and more restrictive, rules as to the admissibility of fresh evidence on appeal.[16]

It need hardly be added that the purposes and position of legislative committees are so far removed from those of a court, that quite different sets of rules apply,[17] including some abrogating protection so well-established in the ordinary courts as that of the privilege not to disclose communications between solicitor and client.

It may also be the case that where the inquiry is essentially governmental, for example, in England under the Tribunals of Inquiry (Evidence) Act 1921, there may be no need to claim immunity on the basis of public policy.[18]

---

8   It has however been held in New Zealand that there is no necessary objection to the use of video linkage by tribunals just as by courts: *B v Dentists' Disciplinary Tribunal* [1994] 1 NZLR 95.

9   *Currie v Chief Constable of Surrey* [1982] 1 All ER 89, [1982] 1 WLR 215, QB.

10   *General Medical Council v Spackman* [1943] AC 627, [1943] 2 All ER 337.

11   See *Australian Federal Police Comr v McMillan and Hordes* (1987) 24 ACR 278.

12   See eg *Sharples v Halford* (1991) Times, 9 October.

13   Town and Country Planning (Enforcement) (Inquiries Procedure) Rules 1981, SI 1981/1743, r 11(4).

14   *AM & S Europe v EC Commission* [1983] QB 878, at 896, [1983] 1 All ER 705, at 720; but see *Parry-Jones v Law Society* [1969] 1 Ch 1, at 9, [1968] 1 All ER 177, at 180. See further p 439 below.

15   See *New Victoria Hospital v Ryan* [1993] ICR 201 for effective acknowledgement of legal professional privilege in the Employment Appeal Tribunal.

16   *R v Immigration Appeal Tribunal, ex p Weerasuriya* [1983] 1 All ER 195, distinguishing *Hadmor Productions Ltd v Hamilton* [1983] 1 AC 191, [1982] 1 All ER 1042.

17   See May *Treatise on the Law, Privileges and Usages of Parliament* (20th edn, 1983), *First Report of Select Committee on Procedure* (1978); for Australia see *Parliamentary Committees; Powers Over and Protection Afforded to Witnesses* (Parl Pap No 168, 1972); and for Canada see *Witnesses Before Legislative Committees* (Ontario Law Reform Committee, 1981). See also Harders (1993) 67 ALJ 109.

18   For a general discussion of the evidential rules relating to such bodies see Hallett *Royal Commissions and Boards of Enquiry* (1982). The evidential rules relating to inquiries by bodies like Royal Commissions have been much debated in the Commonwealth, see eg *Bisaillon v Keable* [1983] 2 SCR 60; *Bercove v Hermes (No 3)* (1983) 51 ALR 109.

SECTION 3.   PURPOSES AND CATEGORIES OF JUDICIAL EVIDENCE

Judicial evidence is used to prove either facts in issue, or facts from which facts in issue may properly be inferred. It comprises the testimony of witnesses, documents and things. The first part of this section will consider the main categories of facts in issue, and will categorise and give examples of different sorts of circumstantial evidence. The second part will explain and give examples of the different types of judicial evidence.

A.   OBJECTS OF PROOF

The objects of proof are either facts in issue or facts, relevant to facts in issue, of which circumstantial evidence is the clearest example.

I.   Facts in issue

There are two principal types of facts in issue, those which are in issue as a matter of substantive law, and those which are in issue as a matter of the law of evidence itself.[19]

The main facts in issue are all those facts which the claimant[20] in a civil action, or the prosecutor in criminal proceedings, must prove in order to succeed, together with any further facts that the defendant or accused must prove in order to establish a defence. A few examples will show that the main facts in issue in a particular case can only be ascertained by reference to the substantive law and statements of case.

Suppose the claimant is seeking damages for personal injuries which he alleges were caused by the negligent driving of a motor car by the defendant. The question whether the defendant owed a duty of care to the claimant is the concern of the law of tort; the respects in which the claimant contends that the duty was broken are to be gathered from the allegations of negligence set out in his particulars of claim; and, if negligence is denied in the defendant's defence,[1] the law of evidence indicates how the claimant may substantiate, or the defendant disprove, the allegations of negligence. If negligence is not denied in the defence, and there is no claim of contributory negligence, the only issue between the parties will most probably concern the amount of damages to which the claimant is entitled; thus the sphere of the law of evidence may be restricted to one issue by the statements of case.

Most cases involve more than one issue. Even the simplest claims for damages for assault or breach of contract normally give rise to disputes about the amount of damages to be awarded as well as to questions whether the defendant inflicted the blows, or made the agreement, as the claimant contends; while further issues may be raised by the defendant by means of such pleas as those of self defence and contractual incapacity. In criminal cases:[2]

---

19   In *R v Robertson; R v Golder* [1987] QB 920, at 927, [1987] 3 All ER 231, at 236 the Lord Chief Justice characterised the former as the 'restricted meaning' and the latter as the 'extended meaning'.

20   This term must be taken to include the applicant or petitioner where appropriate, and the word 'defendant' must be taken to include the respondent.

1   Under the Civil Procedure Rules, r 16(5) the defendant is required to deny, admit or state that he is not in a position to do either to all of the allegations in the particulars of claim, including those of the claimant's statement of value, under r 16(3), (4) the defendant is taken to deny any allegations inconsistent with his statement of case, and any allegation as to amount unless it is admitted.

2   Per Lord Goddard CJ, in *R v Sims* [1946] KB 531, at 539, [1946] 1 All ER 697, at 701.

whenever there is a plea of not guilty, everything is in issue, and the prosecution has to prove the whole of their case, including the identity of the accused, the nature of the act and the existence of any necessary knowledge or intent.

Failure to discriminate clearly between different issues is one of the most potent, and least recognised, sources of confusion and difficulty in the law of evidence. It is especially acute in criminal proceedings just because no formal pleadings are made or required in advance.

As Thayer has shown,[3] failure to recognise the dependence of the law of evidence on the substantive law and rules of procedure has led to the inclusion in textbooks of much that is not comprised in the subject. For example, formal admissions, and some branches of estoppel belong to the heading of procedure, while other branches of estoppel and the rules governing the admissibility of evidence of character in civil cases are based on the substantive law. These matters are briefly discussed in this book for the sake of completeness and conformity with tradition, but every endeavour is made to avoid reference to decisions that turn exclusively on the substantive law or questions of procedure.

Subordinate or collateral facts which may be in issue are those affecting the competence or credibility of a witness and those affecting the admissibility or cogency of certain items of evidence; they may be in issue in a particular case on account of the law of evidence itself, and not on account of the substantive law or statements of case.

An illustration of such a fact in relation to competency occurred in *R v Yacoob*[4] where the competence of the witness depended upon whether or not she was married to the accused. Similarly it may be relevant to know of the existence of a relationship which would tend to make a witness biased in favour of a party calling him. He may thus be asked about the relationship in cross-examination and, if it is denied, the relationship may be proved by the opposite party.[5]

An example of a fact relating to the admissibility of an item of evidence is furnished by the normal requirement that a document be shown to be genuine before being produced to the jury.[6] The cogency of a piece of evidence may also become a subordinate fact, for example, when a challenge is mounted to the accuracy of a new device for measuring the speed of a motor car.[7]

2.   Facts as evidence of other facts: circumstantial evidence

If the only evidence which could be adduced were that directly of facts in issue, or direct evidence, many claims would fail for lack of adequate proof. At some stage, resort almost always has to be had to 'circumstantial evidence' which may be defined as any fact (sometimes called an 'evidentiary fact', 'factum probans' or 'fact relevant to the issue') from the existence of which the judge or jury may infer the existence of a fact in issue (sometimes called a 'principal fact' or 'factum probandum'). A typical instance is afforded by the statement of a witness at a trial for murder that he saw the accused carrying a blood-stained knife at the door of the house in which the deceased was found mortally wounded. The prosecutor invites the jury first, to assume that the witness is speaking the truth, and secondly, to infer that the accused inflicted the mortal wound with the knife.

3   *Preliminary Treatise on Evidence at the Common Law* passim.
4   (1981) 72 Cr App Rep 313.
5   *Thomas v David* (1836) 7 C & P 350.
6   See *R v Wayte* (1982) 76 Cr App Rep 110.
7   *Kent v Stamps* [1982] RTR 273.

Evidentiary facts may be proved by testimony, admissible hearsay, documents, things and other evidentiary facts. An example of the proof of one such fact by another is afforded by the statement of a witness at a trial for murder that he saw blood on the coat pocket in which the accused's knife was found. The jury is asked, first, to assume that the witness is telling the truth, secondly, to infer that the blood on the pocket came from the knife, and finally to infer that the blood was on the knife because the accused stabbed the deceased with that weapon. This process might be prolonged still further, but as the number of steps which have to be taken from the first evidentiary fact to the ultimate inference of a fact in issue increases, the weaker becomes the former as a means of proving the latter and the opportunities of adducing evidence in favour of a contrary conclusion are increased.[8]

The common fear of manufactured evidence applies, perhaps even more strongly, to circumstantial evidence: 'Circumstantial evidence may sometimes be evidence, but it must always be narrowly examined, if only because evidence of this kind may be manufactured to cast suspicion on another.'[9]

No useful purpose is served by a comparison of the merits of direct and circumstantial evidence. Although, in legal parlance, circumstantial evidence does not mean a detailed account of what happened (as it formerly did in popular speech), the phrase retains an important element of its original meaning when used by lawyers because circumstantial evidence derives its main force from the fact that it usually consists of a number of items pointing to the same conclusion. The blood on the accused's knife may not be of much significance, but additional facts, such as the accused's animosity towards the deceased, benefits to be derived by the accused from the death of the deceased, and the accused's efforts to conceal the knife may give it a very damning complexion.[10]

3.   Examples of circumstantial evidence

This section adopts one of the classifications of circumstantial evidence devised by Wigmore.[11] His division of the subject into 'prospectant', 'concomitant' and 'retrospectant' evidence involves the use of strange words, but it has the merit of stressing the main types of argument by which the relevance of one fact to another may be established. When considering some of the illustrations given in the following paragraphs, the reader would do well to bear in mind that the number of witnesses allowed to give evidence at common law trials was greatly restricted down to the middle of the nineteenth century. Those who had any interest in the outcome of the proceedings were generally unable to testify before the Evidence Act 1843 came into force, parties in civil cases, and their spouses, were made competent only by the Evidence Acts of

---

8   'Arguments upon evidence are generally arguments from effects to causes; and in proportion as the number of possible causes of a given effect increases, the force of the argument is diminished. It is impossible to fix the precise point at which the argument becomes so weak as not to be worth noticing' (Stephen *General View of the Criminal Law* (1st edn) 307).

9   *Teper v R* [1952] AC 480, at 489.

10   'It has been said that circumstantial evidence is to be considered as a chain, and each piece of evidence as a link in the chain, but that is not so, for then, if any one link break, the chain would fall. It is more like the case of a rope comprised of several cords. One strand of the cord might be insufficient to sustain the weight, but three stranded together may be quite of sufficient strength. Thus it may be in circumstantial evidence—there may be a combination of circumstances, no one of which would raise a reasonable conviction or more than a mere suspicion; but the three taken together may create a conclusion of guilt with as much certainty as human affairs can require or admit of' (per Pollock CB in *R v Exall* (1866) 4 F & F 922, at 929). See also *Thomas v R* [1972] NZLR 34.

11   Wigmore *A Treatise on the Anglo-American System of Evidence* (Tillers revn, 1983) vol 1A para 43.

1851 and 1853 respectively, and, as a general rule, the accused and his spouse were unable to give evidence at a criminal trial before the Criminal Evidence Act 1898 came into force.[12] The result was that circumstantial evidence was often all that was available on points upon which direct evidence would probably be given nowadays.

(i)   Prospectant evidence

In its most general form, the argument for the reception of this kind of evidence is that the occurrence of an act, state of mind or state of affairs in the past justifies an inference that the act was done, or state of mind or affairs existed at the moment of time into which the court is inquiring.

(a)   Continuance

If the speed at which someone was driving at a particular time is in issue, evidence of the rate at which he was travelling a few moments earlier is admissible;[13] in cases turning on the existence of a partnership, evidence of its existence at a time earlier than that with which the court is concerned is likewise admissible.[14] Evidence has been received of a person's theological opinions four years before the time at which their nature was in issue;[15] while the fact that someone was alive at an antecedent date may support an inference that he was alive at a subsequent date.[16] Evidence of this sort is given so frequently that it is sometimes said that continuance in general, and the continuance of life in particular, is the subject of a rebuttable presumption of law; but the question is simply one of relevance, depending on the common experience of mankind, and it would be best to avoid the use of the word 'presumption' altogether in this context, or, if that term must be employed, it should be qualified by the use of some such expression as a 'presumption of fact' or a 'provisional presumption'.[17]

It is important to remember that there are degrees of relevance when this kind of evidence is being considered. Proof of the theological beliefs entertained by a man thirty years earlier, would not support a reasonable inference concerning his beliefs at the time which the court was examining,[18] and neither law nor logic can specify the stage at which such evidence ceases to be of any weight—everything depends upon the facts of the particular case. If it were proved that a husband was in good health the day before his wife married someone else:[19]

---

12   During the previous 25 years the total exclusion of this evidence had been relaxed by sundry statutes applying to specific offences.
13   *Beresford v St Albans Justices* (1905) 22 TLR 1. Compare *R v Horvath* [1972] VR 533; and see *R v Martin* (1981) 4 ACR 302.
14   *Brown v Wren Bros* [1895] 1 QB 390.
15   *A-G v Bradlaugh* (1885) 14 QBD 667, at 711.
16   In *Chard v Chard* [1956] P 259, [1955] 3 All ER 721, Sachs J inferred the continuance of life of a woman of 26 for a further 16 years.
17   'Nothing can be more absurd than the notion that there is to be any rigid presumption of law on such questions of fact, without reference to accompanying circumstances, such, for instance, as the age or health of the party. There can be no such strict presumption of law. I think that the only questions in such cases are, what evidence is admissible? and what inference may fairly be drawn from it?' (per Denman CJ in *R v Harborne Inhabitants* (1835) 2 Ad & El 540, at 544–5).
18   *A-G v Bradlaugh* (1885) 14 QBD 667, at 711; nor, in Australia, that a man with a craving for drugs on a given day had one 12 days earlier, *R v Hawes* (1994) 35 NSWLR 294.
19   Per Lush J in *R v Lumley* (1869) LR 1 CCR 196, at 198.

the inference would be strong, almost irresistible, that he was living on the latter day, and the jury would in all probability find that he was so. If, on the other hand, it were proved that he was then in a dying condition, and nothing else was proved, they would probably decline to draw the inference.

(b)   Course of business

To prove postage, evidence may be given that a letter was copied in an office letter book, and that, according to the practice of the office, all letters dealt with in this way were posted immediately.[20] Similarly, if delivery of a document to a particular individual must be proved, the jury may be invited to infer it was handed to him by his servant on proof that it was delivered to the latter although he was not authorised to receive the document on behalf of his master.[1] It seems however that these two steps cannot be combined and proof of a practice of postage accepted as evidence of receipt by the intended recipient.[2]

(c)   Habit[3]

The fact that someone was in the habit of acting in a given way is relevant to the question whether he acted in that way on the occasion into which the court is inquiring. Thus, in *Joy v Phillips, Mills & Co Ltd*[4] a claim was made for workmen's compensation in respect of the death of a stable boy caused by a kick from a horse. The deceased was found near the horse, holding a halter which there was no occasion for him to use at that time of day. It was held that the defendant might call evidence of the boy's practice of teasing the horse as tending to negative the applicant's claim that the accident arose out of and in the course of the deceased's employment. Phillimore LJ said:[5]

> wherever an inquiry has to be made into the cause of the death of a person and, there being no direct evidence, recourse must be had to circumstantial evidence, any evidence as to the habits and ordinary doings of the deceased which may contribute to the circumstances by throwing light upon the probable cause of death is admissible, even in the case of a prosecution for murder.

There is no rule against the reception of relevant evidence prejudicial to the character of the deceased when his death, its cause, or the state of mind of the person who brought

---

20   *Trotter v Maclean* (1879) 13 Ch D 574; cf *Hetherington v Kemp* (1815) 4 Camp 193 (proof letter put on office table where letters for posting usually put insufficient). Proof of postage is evidence of delivery to addressee (*Watts v Vickers* (1916) 86 LJKB 177). See Interpretation Act 1978, s 7 as to service by post.

1   *Macgregor v Keily* (1849) 3 Exch 794. Cf *Tanham v Nicholson* (1872) LR 5 HL 561, which turned on substantive law.

2   *Bogdal v Hall* [1987] Crim LR 500 (though this decision may merely express scepticism of the efficiency of the computerised operation of public bureaucracy, at least to the prejudice of the accused).

3   This section was explicitly approved in *R v Watson* (1996) 108 CCC (3d) 310, at 325a.

4   [1916] 1 KB 849; *Lahrs v Eichsteadt* [1961] Qd R 457. It is not always easy to distinguish between the proof of isolated acts and of habit; the fact that the evidence amounted to no more than the former may have accounted for its exclusion in *Manenti v Melbourne Tramways* [1954] VLR 115.

5   [1916] 1 KB 849, at 854.

it about is in issue,[6] but, when the evidence of habit refers to the practice of a party to the dispute, the prohibition on evidence which merely goes to show that his disposition is that of a man likely to do the wrongful act in question must always be borne in mind.

(d)   Motive or plan

Facts which supply a motive for a particular act, such as the impending discovery by the deceased that the man accused of his murder had procured loans from him by means of forged documents,[7] or the impecuniosity of an alleged forger,[8] are among the items of circumstantial evidence which are most often admitted. Further examples are afforded by more or less any murder trial at which proof is given of facts supplying a motive for revenge, financial or amatory[9] gain, or the removal of someone who was in a position to disclose unpleasant information concerning the accused.[10] Conversely, facts which tend to show a total absence of motive may be adduced, as where the lack of pecuniary embarrassment on his part is proved by someone accused of arson with intent to defraud an insurance company.[11] It is, however, easy to attach too much weight to evidence of motive: 'Almost every child has something to gain by the death of his parents, but rarely on the death of a parent is parricide even suspected'.[12] So far as lack of motive is concerned, 'there is a great difference between absence of proved motive and proved absence of motive'.[13]

Facts, such as the purchase of poison by someone who is accused of murder,[14] which suggest the existence of a plan or design, or preparation for a given course of action may always be proved, and this evidence is of considerable weight because it calls for an explanation of his conduct from the person against whom it is given. When it consists of declarations of an intention to act in a particular way, the hearsay rule has to be borne in mind. If the declarations are made by a party, they may often be brought within the category of admissions and thus be received under a well-recognised exception embodied in s 76 of the Police and Criminal Evidence Act 1984 in criminal cases, and in civil cases by virtue of s 1 of the Civil Evidence Act 1995. Even if the declarations are not those of a party they are certainly admissible in civil cases under the Act of 1995, and possibly in criminal cases under an ill-defined exception to the hearsay rule; but, assuming that such remarks are admissible, the judges seem to have taken different views about the relevance of the intention to the question whether an act said to have been intended was, in fact, performed. If the statement was that of the accused, and the conclusion that it was carried out would be favourable to his case, it may be excluded on account of the ease with which the evidence could have been manufactured.[15] When there is no such obvious risk, some cases suggest that the statement is admissible as tending to establish the performance of the act said to have

---

6   The prosecution unsuccessfully contended that such a principle existed in *R v Hector* [1953] VLR 543. Cf *R v Biggin* [1920] 1 KB 213, and Criminal Justice and Public Order Act 1994, s 31.
7   *R v Palmer* (1856) 5 E & B 1024; Stephen *History of Criminal Law* ch III, 389.
8   *Russell v Hawes* (1863) 3 F & F 322.
9   *Plomp v R* (1963) 110 CLR 234, refuting the suggestion that evidence of motive is relevant only to mens rea.
10   *R v Clewes* (1830) 4 C & P 221.
11   *R v Grant* (1865) 4 F & F 322.
12   Best *Principles of the Law of Evidence* (12th edn) 384.
13   Per Channell J in *R v Ellwood* (1908) 1 Cr App Rep 181, at 182.
14   *R v Palmer*, above.
15   *R v Petcherini* (1855) 7 Cox CC 79.

been intended,[16] while others are against admitting it for this purpose.[17] The question whether evidence is sufficiently relevant to be admissible is pre-eminently one on which different views may be taken, and, assuming that a person's present declaration of his intention is admissible as evidence of that fact, it is probably best not to try to lay down any general principle on the subject of its relevance to the performance of a subsequent act by the declarant.

(e)   Knowledge or capacity

Facts which tend to prove or negative a person's capacity to do an act into which the court is inquiring may be highly relevant. Thus, the accused's knowledge of the effects of certain drugs, his skill in their application, and his ability to procure them, would be admissible evidence at his trial for murder by means of their use, and the absence of any of these factors would likewise be admissible on his behalf.[18] The most frequently cited case in which this type of evidence was discussed is, however, a civil suit. In *Dowling v Dowling*[19] the claimant claimed repayment of money lent, and evidence of his consistent impecuniosity extending over a period of seven years up to the date of the alleged loan was received in support of the defendant's denial that it was ever made. An unusual decision relating to the knowledge of the accused occurred in *R v Potamitis*[20] where the accused was charged with an elaborate fraud to which his defence was that, although he was the person to whom the money was passed, he had been acting as the innocent dupe of a third party fraudster. It transpired that all of the detail of the fraud had previously occurred in crimes for which the accused's cousin had been convicted, and who had been subsequently visited by the accused in the prison. Despite the apparent relevance of such evidence it was excluded, it is submitted mistakenly, because of the danger of inference of guilt by association.

(ii)   Concomitant evidence

The general argument for the reception of evidence of this type is that circumstances existing contemporaneously with the transaction into which the court is inquiring render the facts alleged by one or other of the parties more or less probable. It is best illustrated by what is usually described as evidence of opportunity, but reference must also be made to the reception of evidence as part of the res gestae and the general question of the use of standards of comparison.

---

16 *Johnson v Lyford* (1868) LR 1 P & D 546 (declaration of intention to execute copy will, evidence that will which was in fact executed was in terms of copy); *R v Buckley* (1873) 13 Cox CC 293 (declaration by police officer to superior that he would go in search of accused after dark admitted as evidence that he did so).

17 *R v Wainwright* (1875) 13 Cox CC 171 (declaration by deceased that she was going to accused's premises inadmissible because intention might not have been carried out); *R v Thomson* [1912] 3 KB 19 (declaration by deceased that she intended to perform illegal operation on herself inadmissible, but no attempt made by Court of Criminal Appeal to distinguish between these statements and statements that she had in fact operated on herself; both treated as inadmissible hearsay); see further below, p 553

18 In the United States such knowledge is often subsumed under a broadened category of opportunity, see *US v Green* 648 F 2d 587 (1981), at 592.

19 (1860) 10 ICLR 236. For discussion, see Glass (ed) *Seminars on Evidence* 83.

20 [1994] Crim LR 434.

(a) Opportunity

The presence of the accused at the time and place of an alleged crime is something which must be proved by the prosecution on practically every criminal charge, and the establishment of an alibi[1] is conclusive in favour of innocence.[2] Any evidence which tends to prove either of the above facts is therefore admissible, and, if the defence consists of an allegation that other named persons committed the crime, their alibis in turn become relevant and admissible as part of the case for the prosecution.[3] It is however regarded as too remotely relevant that such persons advance a false alibi.[4] Because of the difficulties which an alibi defence sprung for the first time at the trial could create, special rules providing for advance notice were devised.[5] Section 5(7) of the Criminal Procedure and Investigation Act 1996 now requires advance disclosure of the names and addresses of alibi witnesses if known and, if not, any information in the possession of the defence which might help to find them.[6]

If a false alibi is tendered the judge should direct the jury in accordance with the standard Judical Studies Board terms, which stress that a false alibi may be advanced in support of a true defence. Failure so to direct does not however necessarily lead to the conviction being quashed, since all will depend upon the rest of the evidence.[7]

Opportunity is an important feature in many cases in which adultery is alleged. In *Woolf v Woolf*[8] the Court of Appeal decided that the fact that a couple occupied the same bedroom must be treated as clear evidence of adultery in all but the most unusual circumstances. There is, however, no irrebuttable presumption of law to this effect, even if the evidence of opportunity is accompanied by evidence of inclination arising from the previous association of the parties.[9]

(b) Res gestae

A fact may be relevant to a fact in issue because it throws light on it by reason of proximity in time, place or circumstance. This is frequently expressed by the statement that the relevant fact is part of the res gestae, although it is difficult not to sympathise with Sir Frederick Pollock when he described this as an unmeaning term which 'merely

---

1 An unsupported denial of presence at the scene of the crime does not amount to an alibi: *R v Mussell and Dalton* [1995] Crim LR 887. See also Criminal Procedure and Investigation Act 1996, s 5(8).
2 On the whole subject see Gooderson *Alibi*. The fact that the defence of alibi is raised does not mean that a judge should never leave some other defence such as self-defence to the jury *(R v Bonnick* (1977) 66 Cr App Rep 266).
3 *R v Dytche* (1890) 17 Cox CC 39.
4 *R v Steel* as reported in (1981) 73 Cr App Rep 173, at 186.
5 First by the Criminal Justice Act 1967, s 11.
6 For cases on the construction of the earlier provision see *R v Hassan* [1970] 1 QB 423, [1970] 1 All ER 745; *R v Lewis* [1969] 2 QB 1, [1969] 1 All ER 79; *R v Sullivan* [1971] 1 QB 253, [1970] 2 All ER 681; *R v Cooper* (1979) 69 Cr App Rep 229; *R v Fields and Adams* [1991] Crim LR 38. See also *R v Stephens* [1997] 3 NZLR 716 construing the identically worded New Zealand provision. Whether or not the prosecution should be permitted to put in an alibi notice as part of its case will depend upon the circumstances, see *R v Rossborough* (1985) 81 Cr App Rep 139. See also Tosswill [1978] Crim LR 276, in Canada, *R v Witter* (1996) 105 CCC (3d) 44; and in Australia, *R v Hunt* (1994) 76 ACR 363.
7 *R v Lesley* [1996] 1 Cr App Rep(S) 39, setting out the specimen direction at 46F.
8 [1931] P 134; but see *Ross v Ross* [1930] AC 1, as applied in *Webster v Webster* [1945] NZLR 537.
9 *England v England* [1953] P 16, [1952] 2 All ER 784.

fudges the truth that there is no universal formula for all the kinds of relevancy'.[10] The doctrine is mainly concerned with the admissibility of statements made contemporaneously with the occurrence of some act or event into which the court is inquiring, and it is best discussed later, but this seems to be the proper place to illustrate the part which contemporaneity may play in the relevance of one fact to another. In *R v Moore*[11] the accused were charged with obtaining two pounds by false pretences in consequence of a card trick practised on the prosecutor in a railway train. As he alighted, the prosecutor said he would fetch the police, and he caused the accused to be arrested almost immediately. His evidence was that a total stranger handed him two pounds forthwith, and the Court of Criminal Appeal held that this fact was rightly admitted because 'it related to part of the res gestae and an inference might fairly be drawn from it'.[12] The fact's relevance to the issue is obvious enough. If someone is handed the exact sum of which he says he has been defrauded shortly after making a complaint to this effect, the two events are probably connected with each other. It is likely that the person who handed the money over was acting on behalf of the person against whom the complaint was made, and the payment suggests that the complaint was justified. If the prosecutor had received two pounds from an anonymous donor two days after his railway journey, that fact might still be regarded as relevant to the question whether he was defrauded in the train, but the relevance of such a payment would become more and more remote with the passage of time until it lapsed into insignificance so far as the guilt of the accused was concerned. The relevant degree of contemporaneity may depend upon the particular issues raised by the parties. Thus in *Ratten v R*[13] it was the fifteen-minute period during which the deceased must have been shot, within which the accused denied that the telephone call in question had been made.[14] It is questionable whether anything is gained by using such phrases as 'pars rei gestae' to describe relevancy due to contemporaneity, but the terminology is in constant use in the courts.

(c)   Standards of comparison

Whenever it is necessary to determine whether someone's conduct complies with some objective standard, as where negligence is alleged, evidence is admissible to show how others might be expected to behave in similar circumstances. This, in appropriate cases, may comprise evidence of moral standards or of professional practice. Thus in *Fraser v Thames Television Ltd*[15] witnesses were allowed to testify that they would never use ideas for programmes without the consent of their originators. Similarly in *G & K Ladenbau (UK) Ltd v Crawley and de Reya*[16] a number of solicitors testified to their individual practice in conducting searches of registers during the course of

---

10   Pollock-Holmes *Correspondence* vol 2, 285. Lord Tomlin suspected it of being 'A phrase adopted to provide a respectable legal cloak for a variety of cases to which no formula of precision can be applied' (*Homes v Newman* [1931] 2 Ch 112, at 120). 'If you wish to tender inadmissible evidence, say it is part of the res gestae' (Lord Blackburn). Stone speaks of the law as to res gestae as 'the lurking place of a motley crowd of conceptions in mutual conflict and reciprocating chaos' (55 LQR 66).
11   (1914) 10 Cr App Rep 54.
12   At 56.
13   [1972] AC 378.
14   Though in *Teper v R* [1952] AC 480, it might be thought that insufficient attention was paid to the fact that the accused's alibi was inconsistent not only with his presence on the scene at the time of setting the fire, but also with his presence there at the time at which the utterance in question was made.
15   [1984] QB 44, [1983] 2 All ER 101.
16   [1978] 1 All ER 682, [1978] 1 WLR 266.

conveyancing transactions. In *Banque Keyser Ullmann SA v Skandia (UK) Insurance Co Ltd*[17] the evidence related to the practice in the London insurance market when an underwriter learned of deception practised by a broker upon his principal. Where the practice of a particular branch of a trade is in question, evidence may be tendered of the practice in closely related branches.[18]

No special rules apply to such cases beyond those which require the evidence tendered to be more than remotely relevant to the issue, and unlikely to raise a number of collateral questions. It is, however, essential that the point in dispute should concern some matter as to which the argument from analogous situations to the situation under inquiry is likely to be of real assistance to the court. For instance, if it becomes necessary to determine whether a book is obscene, ie whether it is likely to corrupt the morals of its readers, the court must answer this question by reading the book itself. It has been said that no useful purpose would be served by a perusal of other books in order to compare them with the one under consideration, and that if such other books are tendered in evidence, the evidence will be rejected because it is collateral, i e irrelevant, or insufficiently relevant to the issue.[19]

The courts are frequently asked to apply standards of comparison when the identity of handwriting is in issue, but this question is best considered in connection with documentary evidence.

(iii)   Retrospectant evidence

(a)   In general
In its most general form, the argument for the reception of this kind of evidence is the converse of that which demonstrates the relevance of prospectant evidence: the subsequent occurrence of an act, state of mind or state of affairs justifies an inference that the act was done, or the state of mind or affairs existed, in the past. Thus, a driver's excessive speed may be proved to support the conclusion that he was going too fast a short distance further back.[20] A classic and simple example is provided by *Gumbley v Cunningham*[1] where the House of Lords permitted an inference to be drawn from the proportion of alcohol in the accused's blood some four hours after an accident to what it must have been at the time of the accident, given the normal rate of elimination. A person's anterior intention may also be proved by his subsequent acts, although this general principle of relevancy has often had to give way to precedent based on the dread of manufactured evidence as in advancement cases.[2]

Similarly, the court may be invited to infer that an event occurred from subsequent events which followed it in the ordinary course of business, as when an indorsed cheque is produced by the drawer to show that a payment was made.[3] Servants usually claim arrears of salary shortly after their employer has defaulted, so failure to make such a claim is some evidence that no salary was due.[4] Quite apart from any question of the

---

17   [1990] 1 QB 665, [1987] 2 All ER 923, expressly approving the statement in Cross.
18   *Noble v Kennoway* (1780) 2 Doug KB 510 (practice in Labrador trade to prove practice in Newfoundland trade); *Fleet v Murton* (1871) LR 7 QB 126 (evidence of practice in colonial fruit trade to prove practice in London fruit trade).
19   *R v Reiter* [1954] 2 QB 16, [1954] 1 All ER 741; cf *Dalton v Higgins* (1964) 43 DLR (2d) 574 (evidence of other provinces' fire prevention regulations excluded in claim concerning a fire).
20   *R v Dalloz* (1908) 1 Cr App Rep 258. Cf *Beresford v St Albans Justices* (1905) 22 TLR 1.
1   [1989] AC 281, [1989] 1 All ER 5.
2   See *Warren v Gurney* [1944] 2 All ER 472, at 473.
3   *Egg v Barnett* (1800) 3 Esp 196.
4   *Sellen v Norman* (1829) 4 C & P 80. But see *Bogdal v Hall* [1987] Crim LR 500 where failure to complain of non-receipt of social security cheques was not accepted as proof of their receipt.

course of business, delay in taking action may always have to be explained in order to prevent the conclusion that the circumstances of which complaint is ultimately made did not justify such action.

(b)   Omnia praesumuntur rite esse acta

Proof that someone acted as holder of a public office is evidence of his title to do so.[5] On a charge of assaulting a police officer in the course of his duty, formal proof of his appointment is not essential as evidence that he acted as a police officer will suffice.[6] Similarly, if a solicitor claims damages for words spoken of him in the way of his profession, it is unnecessary for him to produce his practising certificate, or an extract from the roll of solicitors, provided there is evidence that he acted as a solicitor.[7]

The principle applies to corporations, so proof that a company has acted as such is evidence that it was duly incorporated.[8] In short, there is a rebuttable presumption of law establishing due appointment and capacity to act—'omnia praesumuntur rite ac solemniter esse acta'.[9]

So far as its application to the validity of appointments is concerned, the presumption is confined to those affecting the public at large. Although the fact that a man is a solicitor may be proved by his having acted in that capacity, retainer by a particular client cannot be proved in this way,[10] a letter in his handwriting relating to the client's affairs will not suffice,[11] any more than the appointment of other private agents can be proved by the fact that they purported to act on behalf of named principals. On the other hand, if a statute provides that trustees of public property shall take an oath before acting, proof of their having acted as trustees dispenses with the necessity of showing compliance with this provision.[12] The distinction can be justified on the ground that absence of a right to act in a certain capacity is more likely to be discovered if the capacity is public than if it is private, but the matter has never been fully considered by the courts, and there is no doubt that private authorisation may sometimes be inferred from retrospectant circumstantial evidence. For example, if A is injured by B's car, B's ownership of the car is some evidence that it was being driven by his servant or agent, and this is because those who drive other people's cars are, more often than not, authorised to do so.[13]

As has been truly said 'The wheels of business will not go round unless it is assumed that that is in order which appears to be in order'.[14] Much trouble and expense is saved when the courts act on this assumption, as when they hold that the fact that speed limit signs were erected is prima facie evidence that the local authority had carried out the duties imposed upon it by the Road Traffic Acts.[15] The maxim omnia praesumuntur rite esse acta must, however, be used with care in criminal cases. It cannot be relied

---

5   For a full citation of authorities see Phipson Law of Evidence (14th edn) para 5.15.
6   R v Gordon (1789) 1 Leach 515.
7   Berryman v Wise (1791) 4 Term Rep 366. See now Solicitors Act 1974, s 18 and s 63, rendering authorised Law Society lists admissible evidence.
8   R v Langton (1876) 2 QBD 296. As to companies incorporated under the Companies Acts, see s 15 of the Companies Act 1948.
9   The judgment of Lord Ellenborough in R v Verelst (1813) 3 Camp 432 is strong authority for treating the presumption as a rebuttable presumption of law.
10   Bright v Legerton (1861) 2 De GF & J 606.
11   Such evidence might now be admissible to prove the relationship of solicitor and client under the Civil Evidence Act 1995 or under the Criminal Justice Act 1988.
12   Pritchard v Walker (1827) 3 C & P 212.
13   Barnard v Sully (1931) 47 TLR 557; Manawatu County v Rowe [1956] NZLR 78.
14   Per Lord Simonds in Morris v Kanssen [1946] AC 459, at 475, [1946] 1 All ER 586, at 592.
15   Gibbins v Skinner [1951] 2 KB 379, sub nom Boyd-Gibbons v Skinner [1951] 1 All ER 1049.

upon to prove the existence of facts central to an offence.[16] Nor should it be relied upon to presume a fact contrary to the liberty of the subject, such as that a prisoner is being held in lawful custody.[17] The presumption cannot be invoked to support the conclusion that a breathalyser was approved by the Secretary of State in accordance with statutory requirements from the mere fact that an instrument of that type was issued to the police.[18]

Those who are concerned to establish that things were done in the right order in the absence of affirmative evidence to that effect may be able to rely on an extension of the principle *ut res magis valeat quam pereat* even when it is clear that the maxim *omnia praesumuntur rite esse acta* is inapplicable because the evidence shows that at least one act was performed prematurely. Thus, in *Eaglehill Ltd v J Needham (Builders) Ltd*[19] a notice of dishonour of a bill of exchange which plainly could not be met because it was drawn on a company which had since gone into liquidation was mistakenly posted on 30 December, the day before, instead of the day after, the bill was presented. The notice was received on 31 December and it was presumed that the bill had already been dishonoured on that day because, if two acts are done, one of which ought to be done after the other, it is presumed that they were done in the right order.[20]

(c) Mechanical instruments
A presumption which serves the same purpose of saving the time and expense of calling evidence as that served by the maxim *omnia praesumuntur rite esse acta* is the presumption that mechanical instruments were in order when they were used. In the absence of evidence to the contrary, the courts will presume that stopwatches and speedometers[1] and traffic lights[2] were in order at the material time. The court will be reluctant to limit the range of evidence admissible to challenge the reliability of such an instrument in the absence of clear statutory authority to do so.[3] Although in *Castle v Cross*[4] the court omitted the qualification that the instrument must be one of a kind as to which it is common knowledge that they are more often than not in working order, it is submitted that some such qualification is necessary. As Lord Griffiths observed in *Cracknell v Willis*[5] 'trial by machine' is an entirely novel concept and should be introduced with a degree of caution. Such caution is accorded by not applying this presumption to instruments in respect of which there is no common knowledge that they are more often than not in working order. If there is no such knowledge, evidence

16 *R v Willis* (1872) 12 Cox CC 164; *Scott v Baker* [1969] 1 QB 659, [1968] 2 All ER 993; *Dillon v R* [1982] AC 484, [1982] 1 All ER 1017.
17 *Dillon v R*, above.
18 *Scott v Baker*, above, though there were then so many cases that formal proof of approval of that device was no longer required, *R v Jones* [1969] 3 All ER 1559, [1970] 1 WLR 16.
19 [1973] AC 992, [1972] 3 All ER 895.
20 In *Cooper v Chief Comr of Land Tax* (1988) 12 NSWLR 660 this was restricted to cases where the order of events was necessary to the efficacy of the acts.
1 *Nicholas v Penny* [1950] 2 KB 466, sub nom *Penny v Nicholas* [1950] 2 All ER 89; *Skalde v Evans* [1966] SASR 176; *Re Appeal of White* (1987) 9 NSWLR 427; *R v Amyot* [1968] 2 OR 626.
2 *Tingle Jacobs & Co v Kennedy* [1964] 1 All ER 888n, [1964] 1 WLR 638n. See also *S v Lund* 1987 (4) SA 548.
3 *Cracknell v Willis* [1988] AC 450,[1987] 3 All ER 801, overruling *Hughes v McConnell* [1986] 1 All ER 268,[1985] RTR 244. Conversely the Court will allow oral evidence as to the correct operation of a machine to compensate for a technical failure to comply with the statutory procedure for putting an automatic print-out into evidence, *Greenaway v DPP* [1994] RTR 17.
4 [1985] 1 All ER 87, [1984] 1 WLR 1372.
5 At 459, 806.

should be adduced,[6] though in the case of commonly used instruments, it may come from a regular operator, and not necessarily from a technical expert,[7] and is not required if the output of the machine is not itself put in evidence. [8]

(d)   Possession as evidence of ownership

A further rebuttable presumption of law is that of lawful origin. It lies at the root of the substantive law of acquisitive prescription:[9]

> Modern possession and user, being prima facie evidence of property and right, the judges attached to them an artificial weight, and held that uninterrupted, uncontradicted, and unexplained, they constituted proof from which a jury ought to infer a prescriptive right, coeval with the time of legal memory.

Quite apart from any question of prescriptive right, possession is always treated as prima facie evidence of ownership of real[10] or personal[11] property. As Wills put it in a well-known passage:[12]

> The acts of enjoyment from which the ownership of real property may be inferred, are very various, as for instance, the cutting of timber, the repairing of fences or banks, the perambulation of boundaries of a manor or parish, the taking of a wreck on the foreshore, and the granting to others of licences or leases under which possession is taken and held; also the receipt of rents from tenants of the property; for all these acts are fractions of that sum total of enjoyment which characterises dominium.

Moreover, in disputes concerning the title to a small piece of land, the claimant's possession of other parts of the same property is admissible evidence of his right to possession of the strip in question, as in *Jones v Williams*[13] where the claimant averred that he was the owner of the entire bed of a river at a certain spot, and his possession of the bed lower down the river was admitted to rebut the presumption of law that the defendant, the owner of land on the bank opposite to the claimant's land, owned the bed up to the middle of the stream. In these cases there must be such a common characteristic of locality as would raise an inference that the place in dispute belonged to the claimant if the parts over which he is proved to have exercised possession belonged to him, and, in modern times, questions of the admissibility of such evidence will normally arise only where the title deeds are not clear. In most cases, the matter is, in the first instance, governed by some such rebuttable presumption of law as that

---

6   As required by s 69 of the Police and Criminal Evidence Act 1984 in the case of computers, affirmed in *R v Shephard* [1993] AC 380, [1993] 1 All ER 225, at 386, 230. See also *Leonard v Newell* [1983] Tas R 78 (requirement of expert evidence of operation of local radar); *Chiou Yaou Fa v Morris* (1987) 46 NTR 1 (requirement of expert evidence of operation of satellite navigation system; *State Insurance Comr v Whyatt* (1984) 37 SASR 454 (breathalyser not sufficiently reliable). But see *Crosthwaite v Loader* (1995) 77 ACR 348 (presumed accuracy of scallop measuring devices).

7   *R v Shephard*, above.

8   *Prince v DPP* [1996] Crim LR 343 (breathalyser output used as justification for securing blood test).

9   Best *Principles of the Law of Evidence* (12th edn) 322.

10   *Doe d Graham v Penfold* (1838) 8 C & P 536.

11   *Robertson v French* (1803) 4 East 130.

12   *Law of Evidence* (3rd edn) 62.

13   (1837) 2 M & W 326; *Doe d Barrett v Kemp* (1835) 2 Bing NC 102.

riparian owners have the right to the bed of a river up to midstream, or that, where two properties are separated by a hedge and ditch, the ditch is the boundary.

(e) Silence: failure to explain, to give evidence or to call a witness[14]

General considerations. As a matter of everyday lay reasoning the evidence against a man may be greatly strengthened by his failure to give a prompt explanation of conduct proved or alleged against him, or by the inadequacy of the explanation which he does give; those negative facts can therefore be regarded as a species of retrospectant evidence. There are at least two reasons why a belated explanation should be suspect. First the delay in giving it may have been due to the fact that it had to be contrived; second it may have impeded investigation by the opposite party.

However people react to charges in very different ways and this means that all inferences from silence must be made with caution. The silent party may have been confused or taken by surprise, he may have considered the allegation to be unworthy of an answer, or he may have wished to conceal matters concerning himself or others which are irrelevant to the case before the court. He may also have wished to have legal advice before speaking; or if he has received legal advice not to speak, to act upon it. Reflections of this nature suggest that before a person's silence is allowed to count against him the circumstances must have been such that an explanation was called for, and there must have been no apparent reason, apart from a consciousness of guilt, for its absence.[15]

These conflicting considerations have caused particular concern in criminal cases, and have led to the development of special rules in relation to police investigation, including the necessity to explain the nature of the offence under investigation, and to give a warning of the effects of the suspect's response or lack of it. Such warnings may then themselves have second order effects in determining the inferences to be drawn from silence after they have been given.[16]

It is proposed here to consider first the inferences which may be drawn in civil cases, where there has been less direct statutory intervention than in criminal, distinguishing failure to explain from failure to testify or to call witnesses at trial. The position in criminal cases will then be considered, taking into account the greater degree of statutory intervention,[17] distinguishing similarly between the two sorts of failure.

Civil cases: failure to explain. A thin stream of civil cases has adhered to the proposition that failure to answer an allegation is capable, depending upon the circumstances, of amounting to evidence against the silent party.[18] As an illustration,

14 Heydon (1974) 1 Monash ULR 53. The diversity of situations compendiously lumped together under the rubric 'the right to silence' was emphasised by Lord Mustill in *R v Director of Serious Fraud Office, ex p Smith* [1993] AC 1, at 30, 31, sub nom *Smith v Director of Serious Fraud Office* [1992] 3 All ER 456, at 463, 464, who distinguished no fewer than six.

15 See *Weissensteiner v R* (1993) 178 CLR 217 where the High Court of Australia analysed similar factors in relation to the failure of the accused to testify; see also *R v Demeter* (1995) 77 ACR 462.

16 See *Bruce v R* (1987) 74 ALR 219 where the High Court of Australia pointed out that an explanation could have been given before the accused was cautioned; but see also *R v McCarthy* [1992] 2 NZLR 550 explaining that the accused may often be in a similar position, even though not yet formally cautioned.

17 Though full consideration of the most important provisions is postponed until later chapters.

18 *Hayslep v Gymer* (1834) 1 Ad & El 162 (failure to deny claim of gift); *Bessela v Stern* (1877) 2 CPD 265 (failure to deny oral claim of promise to marry). Failure to answer isolated letters is less likely to have the same effect: *Wiedemann v Walpole* [1891] 2 QB 534 (letter alleging promise of marriage); *Thomas v Jones* [1921] 1 KB 22 (letter alleging paternity).

if two cars are involved in a collision, and a passenger in one of them claims damages from both drivers, it has been said that 'proof of the collision is held to be sufficient to call on the two defendants for an answer'.[19] The principle underlying the cases in which reliance has been placed on the maxim res ipsa loquitur is based on the importance of the absence of an explanation. In *Ellor v Selfridge & Co* for instance, the claimants were hit by a van which mounted the pavement, and Scrutton LJ said:[20]

> The fact that in the present case the van appeared upon the pavement, where it had no business to be, and injured the plaintiffs on the pavement, and the further fact that the defendants offered no explanation why their van was there seem to be more consistent with negligence than with the exercise of reasonable care.

In cases of racial discrimination it is rarely possible to prove more than discrimination and difference of race, if this is done, then in the absence of any credible explanation it is permissible to infer that the discrimination was made upon racial grounds.[1]

Civil cases: failure to testify. In *McQueen v Great Western Rly Co*[2] the claimant claimed that his goods had been lost owing to the crime of one of the defendant's servants. All he could prove was that the goods were delivered to the company, and placed on a truck in a siding to which the public had access, after which they disappeared. It was held that the defendant's failure to explain the loss did not make the plaintiff's evidence sufficient to sustain his case. As Cockburn CJ said:[3]

> If a prima facie case is made out, capable of being displaced, and if the party against whom it is established might by calling particular witnesses and producing particular evidence displace that prima facie case, and he omits to adduce that evidence, then the inference fairly arises, as a matter of inference for the jury and not a matter of legal presumption, that the absence of that evidence is to be accounted for by the fact that even if it were adduced it would not displace the prima facie case. But that always presupposes that a prima facie case has been established; and unless we can see our way clearly to the conclusion that a prima facie case has been established, the omission to call witnesses who might have been called on the part of the defendant amounts to nothing.

Very soon after the parties were enabled to testify in most civil cases by the Evidence Act 1851, Alderson B recognised that the failure of one of them to deny a fact which it is in his power to deny 'gives colour to the evidence against him'.[4] Parties were made

---

19   *Baker v Market Harborough Industrial Co-operative Society* [1953] 1 WLR 1472, at 1476, per Denning LJ. See also *Bray v Palmer* [1953] 2 All ER 1449, [1953] 1 WLR 1455 and *France v Parkinson* [1954] 1 All ER 739, [1954] 1 WLR 581. The effect of these decisions is that if two cars are in collision on cross-roads of equal status, and there is no further evidence, the correct inference is that both parties were negligent. *Hummerstone v Leary* [1921] 2 KB 664 is a decision to the same effect; but it was pointed out in *Nesterczuk v Mortimore* (1965) 115 CLR 140 that all these decisions are explicable on narrower grounds and the High Court of Australia held that the trial judge had rightly dismissed both claim and counter-claim where one of the two cars involved in a collision must have swerved and there was no evidence which. An inference of joint negligence may not be justified where the collision was not head-on but between rear portions of two vehicles (*Wotta v Haliburton Oil Well Cementing Co Ltd* [1955] 2 DLR 785).
20   (1930) 46 TLR 236, italics supplied.
1   See *North West Thames Regional Health Authority v Noone* [1988] ICR 813.
2   (1875) LR 10 QB 569.
3   At 574. See also *Hughes v Liverpool City Council* (1988) Times, 30 March.
4   *Boyle v Wiseman* (1855) 10 Exch 647, at 651.

compellable as well as competent by that legislation, and it might have been argued that in those circumstances it was incumbent on a party to call his opponent, rather than to rely on inferences from his silence; but in *Halford v Brookes*[5] it was argued that the effect was rather to make it clear that a party to civil proceedings enjoyed no right of silence, and that inferences could be drawn even more readily in civil proceedings. The strength of such inference was examined by the House of Lords in *R v IRC, ex p TC Coombs & Co*:[6]

> In our legal system generally, the silence of one party in face of the other party's evidence may convert that evidence into proof in relation to matters which are, or are likely to be, within the knowledge of the silent party and about which that party could be expected to give evidence. Thus, depending on the circumstances, a prima facie case may become a strong or even an overwhelming case. But, if the silent party's failure to give evidence (or to give the necessary evidence) can be credibly explained, even if not entirely justified, the effect of his silence in favour of the other party may be either reduced or nullified.

This makes it clear, first, that a prima facie case must be established;[7] second, that it applies to partial as well as total failure to testify; and third, that the inference may be rebutted by a plausible explanation. for silence.[7a] The effect can be to convert a prima facie case into proof of even the most serious matter, such as murder.[8]

There does not appear to be much discussion in the English authorities of the effect of the failure of a party to a civil case to call a witness who might have been expected to give evidence favourable to him. A variety of explanations could be given for such a failure but, subject to these, it is difficult to believe that an English judge would dissent from the following observations in a joint judgment delivered in the Supreme Court of Victoria on an appeal in a civil case tried with a jury:[9]

> [W]here a party without explanation fails to call as a witness a person whom he might reasonably be expected to call, if that person's evidence would be favourable to him, then, although the jury may not treat as evidence what they may as a matter of speculation think that that person would have said if he had been called as a witness, nevertheless it is open to the jury to infer that that person's evidence would not have helped the party's case; if the jury draw that inference, then they may properly take it into account *against the party in question* for two purposes, namely (a) in deciding whether to accept any particular evidence, which has in fact been given, either for or against that party, and which relates to a matter with respect to which the person not called as a witness could have spoken; and (b) in deciding whether to draw inferences of fact, which are

---

5 [1991] 3 All ER 559, [1991] 1 WLR 428, CA.
6 [1991] 2 AC 283, at 300, [1991] 3 All ER 623, at 636. See also Privy Council in *Gibbs v Rea* [1998] AC 786.
7 Cp the dissent of Dixon CJ in *Insurance Comr v Joyce* (1948) 77 CLR 39, at 61. Much more attention has been paid to this question in Australia where it is referred to as the rule in *Jones v Dunkel* (1959) 101 CLR 298, and appears to have survived non-reference to it in the Evidence Act (Cwth) 1995: see *Australian Securities Commission v AS Nominees* (1995) 133 ALR 1.
7a In *Killick v Pountney* (1999) Times, 30 April, the possibility of alternative explanations was sufficient to displace any adverse inference.
8 As in *Halford v Brookes* above, and *Francisco v Diedrick* (1998) Times, 3 April.
9 Newton and Norris JJ in *O'Donnell v Reichard* [1975] VR 916, at 929. An adverse inference need not necessarily be drawn: *Flack v Chairperson, National Crime Authority* (1997) 150 ALR 153.

open to them upon evidence which has been given, again with respect to matters to which the person not called as a witness could have spoken.

Criminal cases: failure to explain at common law. As long ago as 1820 Abbot CJ said:[10]

> No person is to be required to explain or contradict until enough has been proved to warrant a reasonable and just conclusion against him, in the absence of explanation or contradiction; but when such proof has been given, and the nature of the case is such as to admit of explanation or contradiction if the conclusion to which the prima facie case tends to be true, and the accused offers no explanation or contradiction, can human reason do otherwise than adopt the conclusion to which the proof tends?

In those days the accused was incompetent to give evidence on his own behalf, but the explanation might have been given by other witnesses, or it might have been advanced out of court.[11] Much depended upon the circumstances, and in particular whether a denial of an accusation was to be expected.[12] If it was, then silence might be regarded as demeanour indicating acceptance of the charge.[13] Such an inference was much less eligible when the parties were not on equal terms, and especially in the case of police interrogation.[14] Arcane distinctions were drawn between the use of silence to indicate acceptance of an allegation,[15] directly to show consciousness of guilt,[16] to strengthen other prosecution evidence,[17] and to weaken other defence evidence.[18]

A particularly common situation arises when one suspected of handling is found in possession of recently stolen goods. If he fails to give a credible explanation of the manner in which he came by them, the jury is entitled to infer that he was either the thief or else guilty of dishonestly handling the goods, knowing or believing them to have been stolen, contrary to s 22 of the Theft Act 1968. The absence of an explanation is equally significant whether the case is being considered as one of theft or handling, but it has come into particular prominence in connection with the latter because persons found in possession of stolen goods are apt to say that they acquired them innocently from someone else. Where the only evidence is that the defendant on a charge of handling was in possession of stolen goods, a jury may infer guilty knowledge or belief (a) if he offers no explanation to account for his possession, or (b) if the jury are satisfied that the explanation he does offer is untrue. If, however, the explanation offered is one which leaves the jury in doubt as to whether he knew or believed the goods were stolen,[19] they should be told that the case has not been proved, and therefore the verdict should

---

10   *R v Burdett* (1820) 4 B & Ald 95, at 120. See also *Purdie v Maxwell* [1960] NZLR 599; *Sanders v Hill* [1964] SASR 327; *R v Lepage* [1995] 1 SCR 654.

11   Though an English court would almost certainly agree with the decision of the Cape Provincial Court in *S v Kibido* 1988 (1) SA 802 that the failure of an unrepresented defendant to put his defence to particular witnesses in cross-examination should ground no adverse inference.

12   See *R v Cramp* (1880) 14 Cox CC 390 (where it was); *R v Mitchell* (1892) 17 Cox CC 503 (where it was not).

13   *R v Christie* [1914] AC 545.

14   *Hall v R* [1971] 1 All ER 322 (even though before caution); *R v Chandler* [1976] 3 All ER 105, [1976] 1 WLR 585 (where the presence of the suspect's solicitor at a police interview was regarded as evening the terms).

15   As in *Parkes v R* [1976] 3 All ER 380, [1976] 1 WLR 1251.

16   As in *R v Ryan* (1964) 50 Cr App Rep 144, but see the criticism of this reasoning by the High Court of Australia in *Petty and Maiden v R* (1991) 173 CLR 95.

17   As in *R v Sullivan* (1966) 51 Cr App Rep 102.

18   As in *R v Gilbert* (1977) 66 Cr App Rep 237.

19   Or that they were stolen at all: *R v Irwin* [1997] CLY 1110.

be not guilty.[20] It goes without saying that what constitutes recent possession within the meaning of the above doctrine is a question of fact depending on the circumstances of the particular case,[1] but it must be emphasised that, even if no explanation is given by the handler, 'the jury are entitled, but not compelled to convict'.[2] In the absence of further incriminating circumstances, an inference is not warranted that someone in possession of goods obtained by means of blackmail or deception[3] knew of the unlawful obtaining, even if no explanation is forthcoming. On the other hand the mere fact that a reasonable explanation is forthcoming does not mean that the jury must be directed to acquit.[4] The inference of guilty knowledge is warranted in the case of recently stolen goods because theft is by far the most common means of unlawful acquisition.[5] Now that theft and handling, unlike the former larceny and receiving, are not mutually exclusive offences because most handlers by receiving become thieves through a later appropriation, it is probably safer to convict of theft, where both offences are charged and the evidence justifies the conclusion that one or other of them was committed.[6]

Criminal law: the effect of statutory provision upon failure to explain. Where the law imposes a duty to provide an explanation, as in some statutory offences, the inference to be drawn from failure to reply may be strengthened.[7] As noted above the particular problems of alibis advanced for the first time at the trial was dealt with by statutory intervention, and more general recommendations allowing adverse inference from failure to mention when questioned matters later relied upon in evidence were made by the Criminal Law Revision Committee,[8] though its recommendations in this respect led to the jettisoning of the Committee's whole report at that time. Nevertheless the recommendations were as ultimately accepted, and constitutes the substance of s 34 of the Criminal Justice and Public Order Act 1994.[9] The Act also permits adverse inference from failure to explain ostensibly incriminating real evidence[10] or presence in a particular place.[11] In this way statute has intervened to supplement common sense in the two common situations, of late excuses and late explanations. It should be noted

20 *R v Aves* [1950] 2 All ER 330, this is the effect of *R v Schama, R v Abramovitch* (1914) 84 LJKB 396 (the leading case); see also *R v Garth* [1949] 1 All ER 773; *R v Raviraj* (1986) 85 Cr App Rep 93.
1 *R v Marcus* (1923) 17 Cr App Rep 191. The circumstances of the receipt may be relied on as proof that the goods were stolen (*R v Sbarra* (1918) 87 LJKB 1003; *R v Fushillo* (1940) 27 Cr App Rep 193; *R v Guidice* [1964] WAR 128). The accused's demonstrably false testimony is evidence to the same effect (*R v Young* (1952) 36 Cr App Rep 200). The circumstance of statements by third parties that the goods were stolen, even though believed and acted upon by the accused, is inadmissible to show that the goods were in fact stolen, but it is admissible to show that the accused believed that they had been, *R v Hulbert* (1979) 69 Cr App Rep 243; *R v Korniak* (1983) 76 Cr App Rep 145. It might in some circumstances be very difficult to draw the inference against a particular one of two co-habiting spouses, see *R v Myall* (1986) 43 SASR 258.
2 Per Lord Goddard CJ in *R v Cohen* [1951] 1 KB 505, at 508, [1951] 1 All ER 203, at 206.
3 Theft Act 1968, s 24(4).
4 *R v Ately* (1985) 9 NSWLR 226.
5 *DPP v Nieser* [1959] 1 QB 254, [1958] 3 All ER 662, where it was said that one way of supporting an inference that the accused knew of the unlawful obtaining would be to prove an association with the obtainer showing that they were in each other's confidence.
6 *Stapylton v O'Callaghan* [1973] 2 All ER 782.
7 *Elliot v Loake* [1983] Crim LR 36.
8 In its 11th report Evidence (General) Cmnd 4991 (1973) paras 28–52.
9 Discussed in more detail at p 624 below. Preceded in Northern Ireland by the Criminal Evidence (NI) Order 1988 (SI 1988/1987 (NI 20)); see Jackson [1991] Crim LR 404; (1993) 44 NILQ 103. See generally Pattenden (1998) 2 E & P 141, Mirfield *Silence, Confessions and Improperly Obtained Evidence* (1997) pp 238–281.
10 Section 36.
11 Section 37.

that it also supplements,[12] rather than supplants, the common law, which may still be invoked in these situations.

Criminal cases: failure to testify at common law. The Criminal Evidence Act 1898 both permitted the accused to testify for himself generally in criminal cases, and regulated permissible comment.[13] It gradually became established that if comment was to be made, it had to take a particular form,[14] though the judge could refrain from making any comment.[15] The position was summarised in *R v Martinez-Tobon:*[16]

(1) The judge should give the jury a direction along the lines of the Judicial Studies Board specimen direction based on *R v Bathurst* [1968] 2 QB 99 at 107, [1968] 1 All ER 1175 at 1178. (2) The essentials of that direction are that the accused is under no obligation to testify and the jury should not assume he is guilty because he has not given evidence. (3) Provided those essentials are complied with, the judge may think it appropriate to make a stronger comment where the defence case involves alleged facts which (a) are at variance with prosecution evidence or additional to it and exculpatory, and (b) must, if true, be within the knowledge of the defendant. (4) The nature and strength of such comment must be a matter for the discretion of the judge and will depend upon the circumstances of the individual case. However it must not be such as to contradict or nullify the essentials of the conventional direction.[17]

Here too new statutory provisions have been enacted to extend the range of such comment.[18] There is no intrinsic reason not to rely on the tender of false testimony in earlier proceedings as indicative of guilt, in the same way as pre-trial lies may be equated with pre-trial silence.[19]

It has been held in Australia to amount to a ground for appeal that counsel failed to call credible and available witnesses for the defence, contrary to the accused's interests, and without specific instructions.[20]

Criminal cases: the effect of lies. In *R v Nash,*[1] the appellant was charged with the murder of her child whose body was found in a well. She had been seen near the well with the child for whom she could not find a home, and she also told lies concerning the child's whereabouts. When affirming the conviction Lord Coleridge CJ said 'the

---

12   Criminal Justice and Public Order Act 1994, ss 34(5), 36(6) and 37(5).
13   Section 1(b). For the position in Canada in the light of the Charter on failure to testify, see *R v Noble* [1997] 1 SCR 874; and on failure to call witnesses, *R v Dupuis* (1995) 98 CCC (3d) 496, *R v Carey* (1996) 113 CCC (3d) 74, *R v S(G)* [1995] 2 SCR 411.
14   As set out in *R v Bathurst* [1968] 2 QB 99, [1968] 1 All ER 1175.
15   *R v Harris* (1986) 84 Cr App Rep 75, though by 1993 the *Bathurst* direction seems to have become mandatory, see *R v Taylor* [1993] Crim LR 223, *R v Fullerton* [1994] Crim LR 63.
16   [1994] 2 All ER 90, [1994] 1 WLR 388, at 98, 397C.
17   [1994] 2 All ER 90, at 98.
18   Criminal Justice and Public Order Act 1994, s 35, discussed in more detail in ch IX below. There is here no explicit preservation of the pre-existing common law. See generally Pattenden (1997) 2 E & P 141. As in the case of comment on silence, it followed prior experiment in Northern Ireland. For exposition see *Murray v DPP* [1994] 1 WLR 1, 99 Cr App Rep 396; and for excoriation see Jackson (1993) 44 NILQ 103.
19   In *Broadhurst v R*, above, Lord Devlin had been referring to lies told in court. See also *R v Binham* [1991] Crim LR 774.
20   *R v D* (1996) 86 ACR 41. Where there are good reasons not to call witnesses for the prosecution, no adverse inferences can be drawn, *R v Martelli* (1995) 83 ACR 550; and a fortiori no favourable inferences, *R v Yaari* (1995) 101 CCC (3d) 401.
1   (1911) 6 Cr App Rep 225.

facts which are proved call for an explanation, and beyond the admittedly untrue statements, none was forthcoming'.[2] There the effect of silence as to the true explanation was magnified in its significance by the fact of advancing a false one. This important consideration was elaborated by Lord Devlin delivering the decision of the Privy Council in *Broadhurst v R:*[3]

> There is a natural tendency for the jury to think that if an accused is lying, it must be because he is guilty, and accordingly to convict him without more ado. It is the duty of the judge to make it clear to them that this is not so. Save in one respect, a case in which an accused gives untruthful evidence is no different from one in which he gives no evidence at all. In either case the burden remains on the prosecution to prove the guilt of the accused. But if on the proved facts two inferences may be drawn about the accused's conduct or state of mind, his untruthfulness is a factor which the jury can properly take into account as strengthening the inference of guilt. What strength it adds depends, of course, on all the circumstances and especially on whether there are reasons other than guilt that might account for such untruthfulness.

This dictum appears to apply outside the area of evidential support[4] and identification,[5] and to permit, if not require, some explicit direction as to the strength of any such inference in the light of the circumstances of the case.[6] One such circumstance may be that where the alternative charges are murder and manslaughter, the lies may be explicable by reference to either, and will thus be unhelpful in relation to a charge of murder.[7]

In many cases where the prosecution seeks to rely upon inferences from silence, lies may come into play either because the accused alleges that he had mentioned a relevant fact at an early stage, and the prosecution contends that the allegation is a lie;[8] or where the accused supplements or amends his initial account to accommodate subsequently established facts about which he had hitherto been silent, and it is alleged that the later account is a lie.[9] The latter situation does not require a specific direction since it will be central to the issues in the case,[10] but the former may require a special direction that there are more reasons for lying than consciousness of guilt.[11]

(f) Fingerprints, bodily samples and tracker dogs

Fingerprints.[12] An expert witness informs the court, often with the aid of photographs, that he took the fingerprints of the accused and found them to be identical with those on some object with which the case is concerned. This is very strong retrospectant circumstantial evidence, and convictions have been upheld when there was no other

2   At 228.
3   [1964] AC 441, at 447, [1964] 1 All ER 111, at 119, 120.
4   Below p 238
5   Below p 686.
6   *R v Bey* [1993] 3 All ER 253, [1994] 1 WLR 39; *R v Sharp* [1994] QB 261, [1993] 3 All ER 225; *R v Goodway* [1993] 4 All ER 894, 98 Cr App Rep 11.
7   *R v Richens* [1993] 4 All ER 877, 98 Cr App Rep 43; *R v Taylor* [1998] Crim LR 822.
8   As in *R v Robinson* [1996] Crim LR 417.
9   As in *R v Hill* [1996] Crim LR 419.
10   But even there it has in Australia been held to be fortified by failure to testify to explain the lie, *Murphy v R* (1994) 62 SASR 121.
11   See the analysis in *R v Burge and Pegg* [1996] 1 Cr App Rep 163.
12   See Campbell [1985] Crim LR 195.

evidence of identity.[13] The expert must point out the resemblances which lead him to say that the fingerprints are identical but the jury has to decide whether his conclusion is correct.[14] It has been held in Victoria that a statement by the expert to the effect that it is impossible for two people to have the same prints is inadmissible.[15]

Subject to this point it seems that no special rules apply to the admissibility of fingerprint evidence. In *Callis v Gunn*[16] such evidence was held to be admissible although the accused had not been cautioned when asked by a police officer for his prints. The ordinary principles governing the judge's discretion to exclude evidence at a criminal trial would of course apply to such a case. The procedure for taking fingerprints is now governed by the Police and Criminal Evidence Act 1984.[17]

Bodily samples. Scientific advance has supplemented the possibility of identification by comparison of fingerprints with newer methods. First, blood testing was employed to help determine paternity. Although it gradually became more refined, this technique suffered from defects. It involved what some regarded as a peculiarly objectionable intrusion upon their bodily integrity,[18] and in most cases it operated only negatively to rebut a purported identification. Its use in paternity cases was thus often controversial, since it might seem capable only of bastardising, but not of legitimising, a child. Nevertheless its usefulness was recognised, and its use regulated, by the Family Law Reform Act 1969.[19]

The situation has been transformed by the further development of DNA testing of bodily samples.[20] This technique has the advantage that it can use any tissue carrying the relevant genetic code, that the sample need be neither large nor recent, and, most significantly of all, that it furnishes effectively[1] conclusive positive proof of identity, or of family relationship. On the other hand it has the disadvantage that at present it is a complex matter to perform the test, and there are plenty of opportunities for errors of evaluation[2] and calculation, though the technology is constantly improving.[3] The statistical significance of the evidence has proved difficult to explain to a jury,[4] and has been far from clarified by attempts to employ Bayesian analysis,[5] resulting in some

---

13 *R v Castleton* (1909) 3 Cr App Rep 74; cf *R v Court* (1960) 44 Cr App Rep 242 (fingerprints on car windscreen insufficient evidence of possession on receiving charge). See also in Canada, *R v Lepage* [1995] 1 SCR 654.
14 In *R v Buisson* [1990] 2 NZLR 542 it was emphasised that such comparison could not be made by the jury alone.
15 *R v O'Callaghan* [1976] VR 676.
16 [1964] 1 QB 495, [1963] 3 All ER 677.
17 Section 61.
18 See *S v S* [1972] AC 24, [1970] 3 All ER 107; and after the advent of DNA testing, *Re F (a minor)* [1993] Fam 314, [1993] 3 All ER 596. Cp *JPD v MG* [1991] IR 47.
19 Sections 20–25.
20 An enormous literature has been created dealing with this problem. The technique is continually being developed so it is best to concentrate on the most recent contributions which, at the time of writing, are well evaluated in Redmayne [1998] Crim LR 437.
1   Given the virtual certainty of there being some supporting non-statistical evidence, see *R v Doheny and Adams* [1997] 1 Cr App Rep 369, at 373E.
2   For problems where the potential suspects all come from an unusual and isolated racial group see Hunter [1998] Crim LR 478; and for an Australian example, *R v Pantoja* (1996) 88 ACR 554. In *R v Dougherty* [1996] 3 NZLR 257 an appeal was allowed after fresh evidence showed that earlier scientific evidence had been flawed.
3   In Canada a voir dire may be held to resolve such problems, *R v Johnston* (1992) 69 CCC (3d) 395. Its use was deprecated in Australia in *R v Jarrett* (1994) 62 SASR 443.
4   See *R v Deen* (1994) Times, 10 January where the equation of the odds against an innocent person having the relevant string of DNA with the odds against the accused, who has the string, being innocent was described as the prosecutor's fallacy.
5   In *R v Adams* [1996] 2 Cr App Rep 467 it was decisively rejected in favour of a direction in terms of the random occurrence ratio. For the position in Australia see *R v Mitchell* (1997) 130 ACTR 48; in Canada, see *R v Legere* (1994) 95 CCC (3d) 139.

disarray in the admission of such evidence.[6] The Family Law Reform Act 1969 has now been amended[7] to allow for the use of this new technique.[8] The new provisions permit tests to be ordered not only upon the application of the parties, but also by the court of its own motion. The amended s 20 now recognises the possibility of obtaining a positive result, and the establishment of maternity as well as paternity. While s 21 still prevents a blood test from being taken without the consent of the subject,[9] and this will remain the normal case, it is less clear that consent is required for tests of other substances. Probably where any taking would involve an assault the common law would dictate a similar result, at least in the absence of explicit authorisation by the court.[10] It is however possible, in some circumstances, to secure testable tissue without an assault, and in such a case there seems to be no obstacle to using it, even without the consent of the subject. If the court's direction to submit to such a test is refused, s 23 permits the court to draw any inference from such refusal as seems proper in the circumstances.

These provisions apply only to civil proceedings in which parentage is in issue, but there seems no reason why such tests should not be used with the consent of the parties in other civil, or in criminal, proceedings. The Royal Commission on Criminal Justice considered the question of DNA matching techniques, and recommended the reclassification as 'non-intimate' of samples taken by plucking hair[11] or by oral swabbing. It recommended also the retention of DNA records of those convicted of criminal offences for investigative processes,[12] and of a wider group for the purposes of statistical matching.[13] An attempt to implement these recommendations is to be found in the Criminal Justice and Public Order Act 1994.[14] The wider group consists of those who provided samples which were processed for the purpose of the same investigation as one resulting in another's conviction.

Tracker dogs.[15] If, after being taken to the scene of a crime, a dog picks up a scent and leads those in charge of him to the accused, a useful piece of retrospectant circumstantial

6   It was accepted in *JPD v MG* [1991] IR 47 and *Welch v HM Advocate* 1986 JC 13; but rejected in *R v Tran* (1990) 50 ACR 233 and *R v Lucas* [1992] 2 VR 109.

7   By s 23 of the Family Law Reform Act 1987. For the position in Scotland see *Cameron v Carr* 1997 SCLR 1164, construing the relevant legislation.

8   In *F v Child Support Agency* [1999] 2 FCR 385 an adverse inference from refusal of such a test together with hearsay evidence from the mother was enough to rebut the presumption of legitimacy.

9   *Re H (a minor) (blood tests: parental rights)* [1997] Fam 89, [1996] 4 All ER 28. But the greater readiness to draw an adverse inference from refusal is likely to discourage refusal. See *Re GW (blood tests)* [1994] 2 FCR 908 where the mother was having intercourse with three men at the approximate time of conception, and sought a blood test from only one for the purposes of DNA examination. Under the old elimination technology his refusal to be tested, unless the other two were also tested, might well have been capable of yielding little adverse inference, but given the greater discrimination of DNA testing it is submitted that the Court of Appeal was justified in inferring paternity from his refusal.

10   See *R v Borden* [1994] 3 SCR 145.

11   Other than pubic hair. See also *R v Cooke* [1995] 1 Cr App Rep 318. In Canada legislation authorising blood and buccal testing was held consistent with the Charter, but, in the then current state of the technology, hair plucking was not: *R v F(S)* (1997) 153 DLR (4th) 315.

12   It has already been held that DNA samples taken for the purposes of one investigation may be used in another (*R v Kelt* [1994] 2 All ER 780, [1994] 1 WLR 765) but not where the accused has been given an assurance that the sample will be destroyed if he is acquitted of the crime for which the sample was taken, and in error the sample was retained and used in a trial relating to a quite separate and much earlier incident: *R v Nathaniel* [1995] 2 Cr App Rep 565. For a similar result in Canada see *R v Borden* [1994] 3 SCR 145.

13   Cm 2263 (1993) paras 2.25–2.38, recommendations 13, 14, and 19–21.

14   Section 57, inserting a new sub-s (3A) into s 64 of the Police and Criminal Evidence Act 1984.

15   See McCormick [1985] Crim LR 202. In *Pierce v Minister of Community Welfare* (1987) 27 ACR 119 evidence derived from observation of the manipulation by a child of anatomically explicit dolls was analogised to that obtained from the observation of tracker dogs.

evidence may have been brought into existence. The South African Appellate Division regard it as too unreliable to be received on account of the danger of misunderstanding the dog's behaviour.[16] Such evidence has, however, been received in Scotland,[17] Northern Ireland,[18] New Zealand,[19] Canada[20] and the United States,[1] but rejected in Mauritius.[2] In *R v Pieterson and Holloway*[3] the Court of Appeal in this country also accepted the principle of admitting such evidence. In each such case however it is necessary to lay an adequate foundation by way of adducing sufficient evidence of the training, skills and habits of the particular dog and its handler. Evidence or judicial notice of the fact that each human being has a different scent which is liable to be picked up by a well-trained dog might be desirable. The person giving such evidence must not express his opinion about what the dog was thinking at the material time.[4] It is also necessary to direct the jury to the special need for care, given that the dog cannot be cross-examined.[5]

(g)   Corpus delicti[6]

Every contested criminal case raises two questions, although there may often be no dispute about the first. The questions are was the crime charged committed? and was it committed by the accused? The first is often said to be concerned with the 'proof of the corpus delicti'.

On a trial for murder, for example, the courts will be loath to convict unless someone deposes to the death of the deceased, or this fact is admitted by the accused who either denies malice aforethought[7] or withdraws his confession[8] at the trial. It was once thought that there could not be a conviction of murder or manslaughter in the absence of some direct proof of death. Great caution is obviously required before there can be a conviction of homicide without a corpse but people have been convicted of murder in the absence of such evidence,[9] when the facts were such as to render it highly probable that the accused killed the deceased and disposed of his body. DNA fingerprinting has enhanced the chances of convicting in these circumstances by enabling such things as bloodstains to be attributed to the offspring of particular parents.[10]

---

16   *R v Trupedo* [1920] AD 58.
17   *Paterson v Nixon* 1960 JC 42.
18   *R v Montgomery* [1966] NI 120.
19   *R v Lindsay* [1970] NZLR 1002; *R v McCartney* [1976] 1 NZLR 472.
20   *R v Haas* (1962) 35 DLR (2d) 172.
1   *Roberts v Maryland* 469 A 2d 442 (1983).
2   *Dulip v R* [1990] Maur 149. I am indebted for this reference to Mr David Kell.
3   [1995] 1 WLR 293, [1995] 2 Cr App Rep 11.
4   *R v Te Whiu and Buckton* [1964] NZLR 748.
5   Although absence of a formal warning may not be fatal to a conviction if the dog's reliability has been established, and the need for caution is implicit in other more general directions: *R v Sykes* [1997] Crim LR 752.
6   See Norval Morris in 68 LQR 391, and Delaney in 68 LQR 560 (Irish cases).
7   As in *R v Camb* (1947). Notable British Trials (admission corpse pushed through porthole, though death alleged to have been accidental).
8   As in *R v Davidson* (1934) 25 Cr App Rep 21.
9   *R v Onufrejczyk* [1955] 1 QB 388, [1955] 1 All ER 247. See also *R v Horry* [1952] NZLR 111, and case note by Northey, 15 MLR 348; *R v Chamberlain* (1984) 51 ALR 225. After such a decision in *Weissensteiner v R* (1993) 178 CLR 217, there were credible reports of sightings of one of the alleged victims.
10   A conviction of murder upon such a basis was reported in (1989) Times, 15 March.

In *R v Burton* the accused was seen to come out of a warehouse with a quantity of pepper. As there was a great deal of pepper inside the warehouse, none was proved to be missing, but the accused was nevertheless convicted of stealing pepper. In fact he made statements amounting to confessions of guilt, but Maule J said: 'If a man go into the London docks sober, without means of getting drunk and come out of one of the cellars very drunk wherein are a million gallons of wine, I think that would be reasonable evidence that he had stolen some of the wine in the cellar though you could not prove that any wine was stolen, or any wine was missed'.[11]

B. MEANS OF PROOF

1. Testimony

To revert to the principal items of judicial evidence, 'testimony' is the statement of a witness in court[12] offered as evidence of the truth of that which is stated. Many of the rules of evidence, such as those concerned with the oath, the competency of witnesses and their cross-examination, are designed to ensure that testimony shall be as reliable as possible. There is a sense in which testimony is the only item of judicial evidence. A hearsay statement, if oral, has to be narrated to the court; if it is contained in a document, the document has usually, though not invariably, to be produced to the court and identified by a witness. The same is true of things.[13] In all the above cases, however, testimony is used for a widely different purpose from that of inducing the court to accept the witness's direct statement concerning a relevant fact, and that is why hearsay statements, documents, and things, though normally proved by a witness,[14] may properly be regarded as separate items of judicial evidence.

The general rule is that a witness can give evidence only of facts of which he has personal knowledge, something which he has perceived with one of his five senses. The only exception to the general rule is the expert witness testifying to matters calling for expertise. Parts of his testimony may be based on information derived from textbooks or on what he has learnt from other people. The party against whom testimony is given has a right to cross-examine the witness and this right, coupled with the personal knowledge rule, lay at the root of the ban on hearsay evidence. The probative value of a statement is diminished if it is not made by a witness when giving evidence in the proceedings.

2. Hearsay

A litigant may endeavour to prove a fact in issue by direct testimony, that is by swearing to it himself, or calling a witness to swear to it, but it sometimes happens that the best he, or his witness, can do is to depose to what someone else was heard to say on the subject, and the rule against hearsay must then be borne in mind. In spite of the etymological ineptitude the rule applies to what people wrote as well as to what they

---

11 (1854) Dears CC 282, at 284. See *R v Joiner* (1910) 4 Cr App Rep 64, on the need for caution where the accused is in possession of goods in suspicious circumstances, but there is no evidence that they were stolen.
12 Or through a video-link.
13 See *R v Forrester* [1985] 2 NZLR 85 where the jury was not entitled to take into account real evidence which it discovered for itself in an exhibit handed to it in the course of a trial.
14 The only exception is a public document which proves itself, ie may simply be handed to the judge.

were heard to say, and to what the witness himself said out of court as well as to what he proves to have been said by others whether they are or are not called as witnesses.

It is ironic that the first statutory formulation of the hearsay rule appeared in the legislation designed[15] to abolish it in civil proceedings, the Civil Evidence Act 1995. Section 1(2) accordingly states:

In this Act—
(a) 'hearsay' means a statement made otherwise than by a person while giving oral evidence in the proceedings which is tendered as evidence of the matters stated; and
(b) references to hearsay include hearsay of whatever degree.

It should be noted that the definition applies only for the purposes of civil proceedings, but the Law Commission has proposed a similar formulation for the purposes of criminal proceedings,[16] where it is to be retained. The definition conflates two historically different rules, the first relating to statements made by non-testifying third parties, and the second to previous statements of a testifying witness.[17] In both cases the aim of the rule was to prevent reliance upon such statements as proof of the truth of any matter asserted by them. Where it was not intended to use them for that purpose but merely because of the circumstantial relevance of the fact of their having been made, then they were untouched by the exclusionary rule. So, if the issue were whether or not a third party had threatened one accused of crime, for the purposes of establishing a defence of duress, evidence of such a threat was held not to fall within the rule.[18] Similarly if a previous inconsistent statement were to be tendered not to prove the truth of what it asserted, but to discredit contrary testimony from its maker, once again it was held to be admissible, but for that purpose only.[19] As may be imagined admissibility for one purpose, but not for another, created serious analytic problems relating to the scope and effect of the rule.[20]

Unfortunately the question of the scope of the rule has not been entirely solved by the definitions proposed by the Law Commission since they refer to statements *made*, and one of the more obscure areas of the old law related to the application of the rule to statements, when *implied* either from conduct[1] or from other uses of language.[2] It is significant that the Law Commission itself envisages 'reference to the existing case-law in cases where the boundary of the definition is unclear'.

It remains the case that hearsay will be admissible to a greater or lesser extent in both civil and criminal proceedings.[3] It is however often regarded as less convincing in principle on account of the lack of opportunity to cross-examine a non-testifying third party, or in the case of a consistent out of court statement, on account of the ease

---

15   Law Com No 216 *The Hearsay Rule in Civil Proceedings* (Cm 2321, 1993).
16   Law Com No 245 *Evidence in Criminal Proceedings: Hearsay and Related Topics* (Cm 3670, 1997). Draft Bill, cl 1, with marginal note *The Hearsay Rule*, '(1) In criminal proceedings a statement not made in oral evidence in the proceedings is not admissible as evidence of any matter stated....'
17   Sometimes described as the rule against narration, or the rule against self-corroboration.
18   *Subramaniam v Public Prosecutor* [1956] 1 WLR 965.
19   *R v Golder, Jones and Porritt* [1960] 3 All ER 457, [1960] 1 WLR 1169.
20   Eliciting from Lord Reid in *Myers v DPP* [1965] AC 1001, [1964] 2 All ER 881, at 1019, 884 the lament that 'it is difficult to make any general statement about the law of hearsay which is entirely accurate'.
1   Explored by Parke B in a graphic series of examples in *Wright v Doe d Tatham* (1837) 7 Ad & El 313.
2   Hotly disputed in *R v Kearley* [1992] 2 AC 228, [1992] 2 All ER 345.
3   See further below chs xiv-xv.

of fabrication and multiplication. Such considerations lead to expedients such as greater discretion in relation to admission, and special rules relating to the assessment of weight.[4]

3. Documents

The contents of a document may be incorporated in the evidence of a witness who swears, for instance, that he entered into a written contract, and the court may be referred to them because they contain admissible hearsay statements, as when an entry made by a registrar of births, deaths and marriages is produced to prove one of these occurrences. Strictly speaking, the contents of a document need not be treated as a separate item of judicial evidence, although it is convenient to do so because they are governed by special rules.

A document may be put in evidence either as a chattel—a substance such as a paper or parchment bearing an inscription, or else as a statement—the inscription on the substance. This distinction was very clearly expressed by Hoffmann J in *Huddleston v Control Risks Information Services Ltd*[5] in distinguishing between the application of the Supreme Court Act 1981 to 'property' and to 'documents':

> a written instrument or any other object carrying information such as a photograph, tape recording or computer disk can be both 'property' for the purposes of s 33(1) and a 'document' for the purposes of s 33(2). Whether for the purposes of a particular case it is the one or the other depends on the nature of the question which it is said may arise.

When treated as a chattel, there is no doubt that it constitutes real evidence, as when a deed alleged to have been stolen is produced to the court in order to show that it bears the finger-prints of the accused. When treated as a statement, a document constitutes testimonial evidence in the vast majority of cases; but it may be used as circumstantial evidence, as when ancient leases are tendered to prove that the lessor, through whom the claimant seeks a prescriptive title, was in possession of the locus in quo:[6]

> Ancient documents coming out of proper custody, and purporting on the face of them to show exercise of ownership, such as a lease or licence, may be given in evidence ... as being in themselves acts of ownership and proof of possession.

Although it is produced and identified by a witness, the document is not incorporated in his testimony as having been written or read by him, neither are its contents tendered as proof of anything they may assert. It is offered to the court as the kind of document which would only have been executed by someone in possession. In other words, its existence is a relevant fact proved by real evidence—the production of a material object for examination by the court.

---

4   Existing law: see Civil Evidence Act 1995, s 6(2)(a) (discretion), s 4 (weight); Criminal Justice Act 1988, ss 24, 25 (discretion), Sch 2 (weight). Law Commission draft bill, cll 9, 15 (discretion), cl 13 (weight).
5   [1987] 2 All ER 1035, at 1037, [1987] 1 WLR 701, at 703.
6   *Malcomson v O'Dea* (1863) 10 HL Cas 593, at 614, per Willes J.

4. Things or real evidence

Things are an independent species of evidence as their production calls upon the court to reach conclusions on the basis of its own perception, and not on that of witnesses directly or indirectly reported to it. If a witness swears that he saw a knife, and that it bore blood-stains, the court is asked to assume that both statements are true; but, if the witness swears that the bloodstained knife he produces is the one he saw on a particular occasion, only one assumption has to be made by the court in order to reach a conclusion as to the condition of the knife.

Although it was devised by Bentham and adopted by Best, 'real evidence' is not a term which has received the blessing of common judicial usage. There is general agreement that it covers the production of material objects for inspection by the judge or jury in court, but it is debatable how much further the term should be extended.

(i)   Material objects

If the condition of a material object is among the facts in issue, as where it is alleged that a suit made by a tailor does not fit his customer,[7] or the defendant's dog is vicious,[8] the object may be produced to the judge and jury to enable them to form their own opinion on the matter.[9] Indeed, failure to produce such an object may be the subject of observation by the judge,[10] and, if its value is in issue, a presumption adverse to his case operates against a party who fails to produce the thing.[11] In exceptional circumstances the court will accept secondary evidence of real objects rather than requiring their physical production, for example photographs of aircraft parts.[12] If an object is fungible replicas may be examined, but they must be identical in all relevant respects.[13]

Real evidence may be used as a means of proving facts in issue, it may also be used in an endeavour to establish relevant facts, as when a knife found in the hands of a person accused of murder is produced in order to show the jury that it bears the stains of blood. But, although the production of exhibits is a common enough occurrence, the above example shows that real evidence is of little value unless accompanied by testimony identifying it as the object the qualities of which are in issue, or relevant to the issue. It is of great value so far as it goes, but it rarely goes very far.

(ii)   Appearance of persons

A person's physical characteristics are frequently included among the possible items of real evidence, and these may often serve as a valuable means of proof. For instance, the fact that the accused is left-handed, tall or short, strong or weak, has a distinctive

---

7   Thayer 263 (n).
8   *Line v Taylor* (1862) 3 F & F 731.
9   Though any experiment to be performed upon it must be conducted in the presence of the parties, so that they may make submissions: *R v Higgins* (1989) Times, 16 February.
10   *R v Francis* (1874) LR 2 CCR 128, at 133, per Lord Coleridge CJ.
11   *Armory v Delamirie* (1722) 1 Stra 505.
12   *R v Uxbridge Justices, ex p Sofaer* (1986) 85 Cr App Rep 367. See also *Tudhope v Stewart* 1986 JC 88; *Dyk v Protec Automotive Repairs* (1997) 151 DLR (4th) 374.
13   *R v Devichand* [1991] Crim LR 446 where the weight of tins of paint was relevant, but the tins shown to the jury bore a different price tag from those in issue, and because this might have influenced the jury the conviction was quashed.

voice,[14] may frequently render it more or less probable that he committed the crime charged; a physical deformity such as a rupture may lead almost inevitably to the conclusion that a man was not guilty of rape;[15] and the resemblance which a child produced to the court bears to its alleged father or mother may be some, though very weak, evidence of parentage.[16] If, at the hearing of a claim for damages for personal injuries, the court examines those injuries or their effects, it may be said to be receiving real evidence,[17] but great caution is exercised in allowing wounds to be exhibited owing, no doubt, to the prejudice which might be excited.[18] Again, the court is acting on real evidence when it determines the age of a child by inspection,[19] which may include inspection of photographs.[20]

(iii)   Demeanour of witnesses[1]

Nokes included the demeanour of witnesses among the items of real evidence. If a witness gives his evidence in a forthright way, unperturbed by cross-examination, the court will no doubt be more disposed to believe him than would be the case with a halting and prevaricating witness. So far as its bearing on the facts in issue is concerned, this type of demeanour is analogous to the answers given by a witness who is being cross-examined as to credit, and may rightly be regarded as evidence in the case.[2]

When the court acts on the remarks or behaviour of a witness as constituting a contempt, it may be said to accept real evidence because it is not asked to do more than act on its powers of perception in determining the existence of a fact in issue—the contemptuous conduct.

14   *Bulejcik v R* (1996) 185 CLR 375.
15   1 Hale, PC, 635–6.
16   *Burnaby v Baillie* (1889) 42 Ch D 282; *Slingsby v A-G* (1916) 33 TLR 120, at 122, where Lord Loreburn regarded such evidence as of some weight, and Lord Shaw regarded it as worthless except where there was a difference in colour between the alleged parent and child (see *MacLeod v Hill* [1976] 2 WWR 593); *Russell v Russell and Mayer* (1923) 129 LT 151, at 153, where the evidence was admitted, but spoken of as unsafe and conjectural; *C v C and C* [1972] 3 All ER 577, [1972] 1 WLR 1335 (photographic evidence of resemblance of child to alleged father admissible).
17   And where the court proposes to rely upon such observations they should be drawn to the attention of counsel so as to permit representations to be made, see *Angaston and District Hospital v Thamm* (1987) 47 SASR 177.
18   See *Gray v La Fleche, Saskatchewan Power Corpn* (1962) 31 DLR (2d) 189, showing that the fact that liability is admitted makes a difference. In *Niznik v Johnson* (1961) 28 DLR (2d) 541 motion pictures were shown to the court in order to establish the fact that the claimant's manifestations of pain in court were faked. See also *Stevens v William Nash Ltd* [1966] 3 All ER 156, [1966] 1 WLR 1550 and *Draper v Jacklyn* [1970] SCR 92.
19   Children and Young Persons Act 1933, s 99. In *R v Colgan* [1959] SRNSW 96, it was held that, subject to the judge's discretion, it was proper to allow the jury to see a girl alleged to be mentally defective with whom the accused was charged with having had intercourse, although the girl was not called as a witness.
20   *R v Land* [1998] 1 Cr App Rep 301.
1   For a sceptical appraisal see Stone [1991] Crim LR 821. Evidence of demeanour out of court was rejected in *R v Keast* [1998] Crim LR 748.
2   If the inference might be controversial there is something to be said for drawing the matter to the attention of the parties in case they wish to make submissions about it, see *Newell v Cronje* 1985 (4) SA 692; *In the Marriage of Zantiotis* (1993) 113 FLR 182.

(iv)   View

A view is an observation undertaken out of court during the course of a trial. When that which is shown at the view is something that might have been produced as an exhibit had it been convenient to do so, as when omnibuses are examined in the yard of the court,[3] or the tribunal visits a place so that witnesses can show where they were standing at the relevant time,[4] the court is being asked to act on real evidence. Although in *Goold v Evans & Co*[5] Hodson LJ regarded a view of a factory to observe the reconstruction of an accident as no more than a means of interpreting evidence given in court,[6] Denning LJ regarded it as a species of real evidence, a view subsequently endorsed by the Court of Appeal. In *Buckingham v Daily News Ltd*[7] it held that the trial judge had rightly taken into account his opinion of the working of the machine formed at a view. Parker LJ said that the occurrences at the view were part of the evidence; it was as if the machine had been brought into the well of the court and the claimant had there demonstrated what had occurred on the occasion under inquiry. It is for this reason essential that such a demonstration[8] should take place in the presence of judge,[9] parties,[10] accused,[11] and, where there is one, jury. Such a demonstration may be distinguished from a visit to a relevant public place to appreciate better the evidence adduced in court. Even in such a case however it has been said to be better for the judge to give prior warning to the parties of any such proposed visit.[12] The purpose of such a warning is to give the parties an opportunity to suggest possibly misleading features such as a change since the events in question, or allow the parties to answer points raised by the judge at such a view.[13] Such a visit by the jury in the absence of the judge is also undesirable since it is so highly likely that questions will be asked and things said transforming the character of the visit into something more akin to a demonstration.[14] In some cases a demonstration may be too graphic, and justice better served by the use of expert evidence, informed outside the court by experimentation.[15]

As with other types of real evidence, there is no intrinsic objection to the reception of photographs, or in the case of demonstrations, film or video recordings. Thus the recording of the route taken by a car was admitted in *R v Thomas*.[16] The main consideration is relevancy. In the case of inanimate objects it is important to film them as close to the relevant happening as possible, so as to minimise the possibility of material change. In the case of demonstrations involving animate bodies, such as an

---

3   *London General Omnibus Co Ltd v Lavell* [1901] 1 Ch 135 where, however, the Court of Appeal regarded the evidence as insufficient; too much importance has been attached to the dicta of Lord Alverstone CJ in this case, see *R v De Grey, ex p Fitzgerald* (1913) 109 LT 871. Where relevant, musical or dramatic performances may be given in or out of court.

4   *Karamat v R* [1956] AC 256, [1956] 1 All ER 415, where the view was treated as a substitute for, or supplementary to photographs and plans. See also Megarry J in *Tito v Waddell* [1975] 3 All ER 997, at 1002, [1975] 1 WLR 1303, at 1307.

5   [1951] 2 TLR 1189.

6   A view also held in Australia, see *Railways Comr v Murphy* (1967) 41 ALJR 77.

7   [1956] 2 QB 534, [1956] 2 All ER 904; see also *Webster v Burns* [1964] NZLR 749.

8   See *R v Harbour* [1995] 1 NZLR 440 for an apt illustration of the fine line between a simple view and a demonstration.

9   *Tameshwar v R* [1957] AC 476, [1957] 2 All ER 683; *R v Hunter* [1985] 2 All ER 173, [1985] 1 WLR 613.

10   *Salsbury v Woodland* [1970] 1 QB 324, [1969] 3 All ER 863.

11   *R v Ely Justices, ex p Burgess* (1992) 157 JP 484.

12   Lord Widgery in *Salsbury v Woodland* at 344, 874.

13   See *Parry v Boyle* (1986) 83 Cr App Rep 310.

14   *R v Hunter*, above.

15   *R v Sutherland* (1996) 112 CCC (3d) 454 (preferred to computer simulation of the trajectory of a bullet).

16   [1986] Crim LR 682.

allegedly obscene dance, it is exceedingly unlikely that a sufficiently accurate or trustworthy reconstruction can be made, because,[17]

> it would be almost impossible to analyse motion by motion those slight differences which may in the totality result in a scene of quite a different character from that performed on the night in question.

No such objection would apply to a film of the very dance that was the subject of the charge.[18]

If considered, not as real evidence, but as a species of testimony by conduct, the evidence is equally objectionable as hearsay.[19] Such an objection can, however, be overcome if such a reconstruction can be brought within an exception to the hearsay rule, as in *Li Shu-ling v R*[20] where the accused's re-enactment of his crime could be considered to come within the exception for confessions.

(v)   Automatic recordings

Recordings have become increasingly important on account of the increased use of electronic apparatus for such purposes as recording interviews with suspects by the police, and with victims of abuse by social workers, monitoring telephone calls, conducting continuous video surveillance,[1] and generally conducting business. Most discussion once centred on the admissibility of tape-recordings,[2] but this has been supplemented by a burgeoning stream of authority[3] on the admissibility of other media such as film, video-tape and computer output.[4] The relevance of what was recorded, and the operation of other exclusionary rules may determine ultimate admissibility. Thus if a recording were obtained illegally[5] or in breach of public policy[6] it might be rejected on these grounds, but not because it was a recording. If the matter recorded is itself in issue,[7] then the recording is capable of constituting real evidence of it.[8] It is incumbent

---

17   *R v Quinn and Bloom* [1962] 2 QB 245, at 259, [1961] 3 All ER 88, at 93.
18   As in *S v W* 1975 (3) SA 841.
19   This was the essence of the objection to the admission of a video recording of an interview between a child and a social worker in a sexual abuse case involving the use of anatomically accurate dolls, *Re E; Re G* (1986) 136 NLJ Rep 843.
20   [1989] AC 270, [1988] 3 All ER 138. See also Children Act 1989, s 7.
1   This practice has become sufficiently common to have elicited judicial requests for authoritative regulation to govern the procedure: *R v Caldwell, R v Dixon* (1993) 99 Cr App Rep 73, *R v Roberts* [1998] Crim LR 682.
2   Many of the relevant authorities were cited in *R v Maqsud Ali; R v Ashiq Hussain* [1966] 1 QB 688, [1965] 2 All ER 464.
3   And commentary, see eg Goldstein [1987] Crim LR 384, Munday (1995) 159 JP 547, and Elliott [1998] Crim LR 159.
4   A concern is that the transition from analogue to digital technology increases the possibility of undetectable interference, see further 5th Report of the House of Lords Committee on Science and Technology, *Digital Images as Evidence* (3 February 1998).
5   See *R v Senat, R v Sin* (1968) 52 Cr App Rep 282.
6   *R v Migliorini* (1981) 38 ALR 356.
7   This should be distinguished from the situation where the recording is testimonial, for example in the case of child witnesses, see further below. For an unusual intermediate situation see *Bulejcik v R* (1996) 185 CLR 375 where the identity of a participant in a recorded conversation was in issue, and the jury wished to have for comparison in the jury room, a recording which had been made of the accused's unsworn statement made before them in the courtroom.
8   *R v Governor of Brixton Prison, ex p Levin* [1997] AC 741, [1997] 3 All ER 289. In *R v Nikolovski* [1996] 3 SCR 1197 the trial judge's identification of the accused from a video-recording of the robbery was upheld over failure by the victim to make a dock identification.

on the prosecution to account satisfactorily for failing to adduce at the trial[9] any video recording which may be relevant.[10] If only part of the original recording has been retained, a court may treat that as a very material factor influencing the exercise of any discretion to exclude the part which is tendered.[11]

At a trial by jury, the party relying on a recording or film must satisfy the judge that there is a prima facie case that it is authentic, and it must be sufficiently intelligible to be placed before the jury.[12] The evidence must define and describe the provenance and history of the recording up to the moment of its production in court.[13] There is no need to account for the absence of the original if the copy is shown to be authentic.[14] Where it is helpful, a copy in the shape of a transcript of a sound recording,[15] or even of a summary,[16] may be adduced in evidence to help the jury.[17] It should be noted that while a literal transcription of a tape in a language understood by the jury may sometimes help it to understand the sounds recorded on the tape,[18] it is more common to permit the jury to receive a written translation in cases where a foreign language was used.[19] If such a transcript is put in evidence the court will, of course, have to be satisfied of its accuracy. Such a translation cannot help the jury to understand the sounds, and experts must testify to its accuracy.[20] Provided that this has been done there is no objection to the receipt of such translations by the jury.[1] In such a case the judge has a discretion to permit the jury to be supplied with the transcript, but solely to help it to

9   It is permissible to withhold information about it from the accused, or even from his solicitor, during the process of investigation: *R v Imran and Hussein* [1997] Crim LR 754, despite ss 34–38 of Criminal Justice and Public Order Act 1994.

10   So to fail might amount to abuse of process: *R v Birmingham* [1992] Crim LR 117; but credible testimony that the video contained nothing relevant may be accepted: *R v Reid* [1997] CLY 1172.

11   *R v Curran and Torney* [1983] 2 VR 133.

12   A technically enhanced version of a tape has been held admissible in New Zealand: see *R v Taylor* [1993] 1 NZLR 647; and, it seems, in Australia: *R v Buckett* (1995) 132 ALR 669, at 697.

13   *R v Robson and Harris* [1972] 2 All ER 699, [1972] 1 WLR 651; *Butera v DPP* (1987) 164 CLR 180, at 184. It is not however necessary in every case to prove every part of the recording authentic in every detail to the standard of scientific certainty: *R v Chen* [1993] 2 VR 139.

14   *Kajala v Noble* (1982) 75 Cr App Rep 149.

15   It is acceptable for such a transcript to be authenticated not by the typist, but by a police officer who was present at the interview, and who has compared the transcript with the recording.

16   This appears to have occurred by agreement in *R v Aitken* (1991) 94 Cr App Rep 85, and was approved in *R v Riaz, R v Burke* (1991) 94 Cr App Rep 339. Although the use of a summary may avoid the tedium of listening to a full recording, it is dangerous to rely upon it when there is a suggestion of ambiguity, as in *R v Brown* [1995] Crim LR 494 where much depended upon whether the absence of punctuation in the summary reflected the sense of the breaks in the recorded speech.

17   This applies equally to the sound-track of a video recording: see *Re G* [1987] 1 WLR 1461, at 1472. The use of video recording and transcript is likely to shorten the presentation of the relevant evidence significantly.

18   As in *Hopes and Lavery v HM Advocate* 1960 JC 104, where a typist who prepared a transcript after familiarising herself with the contents of the recording by playing it over many times was permitted to testify to the authenticity of her transcription.

19   In *R v Duffy* [1999] 1 Cr App Rep 307 this analogy was used to admit evidence from his social worker of the meaning of sounds made by a disabled person in seeking to express himself in English, which no one else could understand; cp *R v Imrie* (1916) 12 Cr App Rep 282. This problem is dealt with in Part II Ch 1 of the Youth Justice and Criminal Evidence Bill 1999.

20   Expert evidence of the nature of non-verbal sounds is also admissible: see *R v Chan* (1993) 87 CCC (3d) 25.

1   *R v Maqsud Ali, R v Ashiq Hussain* [1966] 1 QB 688, [1965] 2 All ER 464. The same view has prevailed in Australasia, see *Butera v DPP* (1987) 164 CLR 180; *R v Menzies* [1982] 1 NLZR 40, and in Canada, see *Papalia v R* [1979] 2 SCR 256.

understand the tape recording, which itself remains the only evidence of what was said.[2] For this reason the jury may be permitted recourse to the tape during its deliberations at the discretion of the judge,[3] but not normally to a transcript, least of all over the objection of the defence.[4] Such use should normally take place in open court, certainly if that is the first occasion on which the tape is actually played, but access to the tape in the jury room may sometimes be allowed.[5] Where a video recording has been received under the provisions of s 32(A) of the Criminal Justice Act 1988[6] it is a matter for the discretion of the judge whether it should be replayed to the jury.[7] In exercising that discretion the judge should consider any possible distortion occasioned by hearing part of the evidence twice in what might well be an especially dramatic form, and in particular should not normally allow a replay at the instance of the prosecution, in the absence of a request from the jury.[8] Any such replay should normally be in court,[9] the jury should be specially warned not to accord the evidence disproportionate weight, and should be reminded of the cross-examination and re-examination of the complainant.[10] Since the rule allowing jury access to recordings has also been extended to those which have not been tendered in evidence, but merely referred to by the defence to demonstrate impropriety in initial interviewing, and inconsistency with evidence in court, it is even more important in such cases to ensure that the jury is directed clearly of the limited purposes for which such recordings can be used.[11]

While the use of such transcripts is clearly a great convenience to the jury some doubt has been expressed as to how far the recording may be supplemented by evidence explaining it. In the case of video-tapes a number of cases have accepted the principle of permitting a witness to testify to the identity of the accused and the person shown on the film.[12] This seems correct in principle since evidence is readily admitted when required to supplement the production of an exhibit, and in these cases the testimony of a witness who knows the accused well and has observed his personal characteristics

2   *R v Rampling* [1987] Crim LR 823; see also *R v Rowbotham* (1988) 41 CCC (3d) 1, at 48. There seems to be no objection to a witness using a tape to help refresh his memory in an appropriate case, see *R v Sitek* [1988] 2 Qd R 284.
3   *R v Riaz, R v Burke* (1991) 94 Cr App Rep 339. An exception occurs however if the prosecution and defence have agreed on a summary of the tape which omits a disputed passage; it is not then open to the jury by listening to the full tape to make its own determination of what it contains, *R v Hagan* [1997] 1 Cr App Rep 464.
4   *R v Coshall* [1995] 12 LS Gaz R 34, CA; *R v Boakes* [1996] CLY 1393.
5   *R v Tonge* (1993) 157 JP 1137, and even though there the judge felt that he had to impose the condition that the jury should not attempt to decipher passages regarded as indecipherable for the purposes of preparing the transcript.
6   As substituted by s 54 of the Criminal Justice Act 1991.
7   This discretion may be exercised to prevent a video recording from being played as part of the closing address of the defence, *R v Eldridge and Salmon* [1999] Crim LR 166.
8   *R v M* [1996] 2 Cr App Rep 56.
9   This applies equally to cases where the recording is of the events in issue: *R v Hagan* [1997] 1 Cr App Rep 464; *R v Imran and Hussein* [1997] Crim LR 754.
10 *R v Rawlings; R v Broadbent* [1995] 1 All ER 580, [1995] 2 Cr App Rep 222. This applies even if the video has not been replayed, but lengthy extracts read out by the judge from the transcript: *R v McQuiston* [1998] 1 Cr App Rep 139. It seems however that it is not fatal not to remind the jury of cross-examination in such a case if in the judge's view no purpose would be served by it, and the jury does not request it: *R v Saunders* [1995] 2 Cr App Rep 313; cp *R v O* [1996] 3 NZLR 295 , requiring the jury to be provided with transcripts of cross-examination relating to the video, if provided with a transcript of it.
11 *R v Atkinson* [1995] Crim LR 490 (though failure to do so as not there fatal).
12 *Kajala v Noble* (1982) 75 Cr App Rep 149; *R v Caldwell; R v Dixon* (1993) 99 Cr App Rep 73 See also *R v Smith* (1983) 33 SASR 558; *R v Sitek*, above (where the issue was not the identity but the actions of the accused); *Steele v HM Advocate* 1992 JC 1.

and body movements in everyday life[13] is likely to be helpful to the jury which will only have seen the accused at the trial. In *Taylor v Chief Constable of Cheshire*[14] this was taken a step further in allowing evidence of the commission of an offence by the accused to be tendered by witnesses who had seen a video recording of an incident, even though the video recording had been accidentally erased before the trial. The court took the view that their evidence was just as much direct evidence of the commission of the offence as would have been that of someone observing an event through binoculars; in other words the recording was simply an extension of the human senses.[15] It should perhaps be remembered that in *Maqsud Ali* the actual recording was unintelligible to the jury, and it is perhaps not going too far to assimilate a situation in which the actual recording is unavailable. Although objection to the evidence in *Taylor* contended that it was hearsay, this cannot be sustained since the recording was automatic, and the only human mind through which the information passed was that of the witnesses, who were present and available for cross-examination.[16] The argument that such cross-examination might be less effective in the absence of the recording seems speculative, and to be, in principle, a consideration going more to weight than to admissibility.

Exactly the same principles apply to more complex automatic recordings, such as those of a radar trace of the movements of a ship.[17] In the case of statements contained in documents produced by computers compliance with the special statutory conditions set out in s 69 of the Police and Criminal Evidence Act 1984 must be proved,[18] whether the statement is hearsay, or no more than a form of automatic recording.[19] It might be supposed that in the case of any new and unfamiliar form of automatic recording the court will require more in the way of foundation testimony to prove the ordinary working of the device.[20] Thus in *R v Cochrane*[1] it was not enough to produce witnesses who knew nothing at all about the working of the relevant computer, or even where it was located. On the other hand once a device has become familiar, and is widely regarded as reliable, the testimony of an operator may well be sufficient.[2]

---

13   In *R v Clare, R v Peach* [1995] 2 Cr App Rep 333 this was extended to the case of a police witness testifying to the identity of the accused where his familiarity was derived from another, and clearer, video recording taken elsewhere the same day.

14   [1987] 1 All ER 225, [1987] 1 WLR 1479.

15   It has even been held in Scotland in the case of tape-recorded interviews with suspects at police stations that the evidence of the recording and of the memory of those present are equally primary evidence of what was said, *HM Advocate v Swift* 1983 SCCR 204, at 207.

16   Evidence of what appeared on the visual display of a breath-testing device was accepted as being real evidence in *Owen v Chesters* [1985] RTR 191, and in *Gunn v Brown* 1987 SLT 94.

17   *The Statue of Liberty* [1968] 2 All ER 195.

18   Though Law Com No 245 *Evidence in Criminal Proceedings: Hearsay and Related Topics* (Cm 3670, 1997) has recommended repeal of any special additional condition, para 13.23, rec 50.

19   *R v Shephard* [1993] AC 380, [1993] 1 All ER 225. Though these will be little, if at all, more difficult to satisfy than the conditions for admissibility at common law (see further below p 592).

20   But see *Castle v Cross*, above, and compare *Mehesz v Redman* (1980) 21 SASR 569; *Holt v Auckland City Council* [1980] 2 NZLR 124.

1   [1993] Crim LR 48.

2   As in *Shephard* above, see also *Marac Financial Services v Stewart* [1993] 1 NZLR 86.

SECTION 4.   RELEVANCE, ADMISSIBILITY AND WEIGHT OF EVIDENCE[3]

The main general rule governing the entire subject is that all evidence which is sufficiently relevant to an issue before the court is admissible and all that is irrelevant, or insufficiently relevant,[4] should be excluded.[5]

The affirmative aspect of this rule (the exceptions to which constitute much of the law of evidence) and its negative aspect (to which there are no exceptions at common law)[6] must be considered separately. When this has been done the distinction between the relevancy, admissibility and weight of evidence will be examined.

A.   THE ADMISSIBILITY OF RELEVANT EVIDENCE

I.   Definition of 'relevance'

It is difficult to improve upon Stephen's definition of relevance when he said that the word 'relevant' means that:[7]

> any two facts to which it is applied are so related to each other that according to the common course of events one either taken by itself or in connection with other facts proves or renders probable the past, present, or future existence or non-existence of the other.

Elsewhere the same writer suggested as a test for determining whether one fact should be regarded as evidence of, or relevant to another, that the matter under discussion should be cast into the form of a syllogism of which the alleged evidentiary fact constitutes the minor premise; it is then necessary only to consider whether the major premise is a proposition the truth of which is likely to be accepted by the person who has to draw the conclusion—in the case of a lawsuit, a reasonable man.[8] For example, suppose that goods were found in the possession of the accused shortly after they were missed, and he was unable or unwilling to give an adequate explanation of the manner in which he came by them. These would be relevant facts on a charge of stealing because, if the matter were cast into the form of a syllogism, it could be stated in the following way: men found in possession of goods which have recently been missed are frequently guilty of stealing them if they do not give an adequate explanation of their possession (major premise); the accused was found in possession of the goods

---

3   See Eggleston *Evidence, Proof and Probability* (2nd edn, 1983), especially ch 6, together with the same author's earlier papers in Glass (ed) *Seminars on Evidence* ch 3; and 4 Melb ULR 180; ALRC Res Paper No 7 'Relevance'; see also James in (1940) 29 Cal LR 689.

4   See *R v Yaeck* (1991) 68 CCC (3d) 545, at 565 citing and applying this passage.

5   See per Goddard LJ in *Hollington v F Hewthorn & Co Ltd* [1943] KB 587, at 594, [1943] 2 All ER 35, at 39.

6   Some statutory rules provide for the admission of evidence of dubious logical relevance, for example s 6 of the Criminal Procedure Act 1865 (permitting any criminal conviction to be put to a witness in cross-examination with a view to attacking credibility), see further below, p 315; Theft Act 1968, s 27(3) (inferring guilty knowledge from previous convictions), see further, below, pp 377–8. See also the proposal of the Royal Commission on Criminal Justice Cm 2263 (1993) para 8.34 and rec 194 to admit evidence of the accused's previous convictions even though he has not testified, and the evidence is inadmissible in chief, and hence at least as prejudicial as probative.

7   *Digest of the Law of Evidence* (12th edn) art 1.

8   *General View of the Criminal Law* (1st edn) 236.

in question shortly after they were missed, and he gave no adequate explanation of this fact (minor premise); therefore the accused may have been guilty of stealing the goods (conclusion). As the validity of the major premises on which courts are invited to act can usually be taken for granted, the deductive method outlined above is seldom used in practice, but the test of the syllogism may be found useful whenever there is any doubt about the relevance of evidence.

In applying the test care may have to be taken with regard to the selection of the appropriate major premise. For example no one knows whether a majority of those who plan to kill a particular person actually do so, but no one doubts the relevance in a murder case of the accused's plan to kill the deceased. The appropriate major premise is not 'those who plan to kill a particular person usually do so,' but 'those who plan to kill a particular person are more likely to do so than those who have no such plan.' The whole point of a lot of circumstantial evidence is to establish the accused's membership of a number of different classes of persons more likely than non-members to have done or omitted to do some act, purchasers of poison, those with a grudge against a certain person and those standing to gain by his death, for instance.[9]

In this sense relevance is an absolute concept, either proof of one fact makes the existence of another more probable, or it does not. It is however often regarded as variable, and evidence regarded as more or less relevant. This seems to relate more to the cogency of the evidence,[10] given its relevance, but it secures a place in the exposition of the subject because the qualification of sufficiency appears to relate to it. As explained in *R v Wilson* this often allows a balancing process to be performed:[11]

> [L]ack of relevance can be used to exclude evidence not because it has absolutely no bearing on upon the likelihood or unlikelihood of a fact in issue but because the connection is considered to be too remote. Once it is regarded as a matter of degree, competing policy considerations can be taken into account. These include the desirability of shortening trials, avoiding emotive distractions of marginal significance, protecting the reputations of those not represented before the Courts and respecting the feelings of a deceased's family. None of these matters would be determinative if the evidence in question were of significant probative value.

2.   Exceptions

The general rule that all relevant evidence is admissible is subject to numerous exceptions because: our law ... undoubtedly excludes evidence of many matters which anyone in his own daily affairs of moment would regard as important in coming to a decision.[12] The following four exceptions are frequently stressed, but there are many others.

9   Eggleston *Evidence, Proof and Probabilty* (2nd edn, 1983) 80.
10   In Canada in particular it is stressed that relevance is independent, and requires no minimum threshold, of cogency, see eg *Morris v R* [1983] 2 SCR 190, at 203.
11   [1991] 2 NZLR 707, at 711.
12   Per Darling J in *R v Bond* [1906] 2 KB 389, at 410. See also the remarks of Hamilton LJ, p 2 above.

(i)   Hearsay

Hearsay which is highly relevant on account of the contents of the statement and because the circumstances in which it was made greatly enhance the probability of its truth is often excluded, as when an attesting witness's death-bed confession of having altered a deed was rejected in a claim based on the document.[13]

(ii)   Opinion

Witnesses are generally not allowed to inform the court of the inferences they draw from facts perceived by them, but must confine their statements to an account of such facts.

It frequently happens that a bystander has a complete and full view of an accident. It is beyond question that, while he may inform the court of everything which he saw, he may not express an opinion on whether either or both of the parties were negligent.[14]

Opinion is often said to be excluded because it is irrelevant, but something more will have to be said on this subject in ch XII; expert witnesses may testify to their opinion on matters involving their expertise.

(iii)   Character

An accused person's reputation among his neighbours as a man likely to have committed the offence charged is usually inadmissible evidence of his guilt, although it might be regarded as a relevant fact, and witnesses' opinions about a person's disposition to act in a particular way are generally excluded.

(iv)   Conduct on other occasions

It might be thought that the fact that someone behaved in a particular way on one occasion is relevant to the question whether he behaved in a similar fashion on the occasion which is being considered by the court, merely by reason of the general tendency of human behaviour to repeat itself. Nevertheless, evidence may generally not be given of a party's misconduct on other occasions if its sole purpose is to show that he is a person likely to have conducted himself in the manner alleged by his adversary on the occasion which is under inquiry. 'You must not prove, for example, that a particular engine driver is a careless man in order to prove that a particular accident was caused by his negligence.'[15]

---

13   *Stobart v Dryden* (1836) 1 M & W 615. The confession could now be proved under the Civil Evidence Act 1995, but it would still be inadmissible in a criminal case as evidence that the deed was forged.

14   Per Goddard LJ in *Hollington v F Hewthorn & Co Ltd* [1943] KB 587, at 595, [1943] 2 All ER 35, at 40.

15   Per Stephen J in *Brown v Eastern and Midlands Rly Co* (1889) 22 QBD 391, at 393. The context makes it plain that Stephen J was concerned with conduct on other occasions as proof of disposition. See also *R v Westfield Freezing Co* [1951] NZLR 456.

3. Multiple relevance and admissibility

An item of evidence may be relevant for more than one reason. In other words, the major premise of a syllogism may be altered, although the minor premise and conclusion remain the same. To enlarge upon an example cited in an old case,[16] suppose that A is charged with stealing a shirt from B's house, that shortly before the alleged theft a shirt was stolen from C's house, and that C's shirt was found in B's house in circumstances suggesting that it had been inadvertently left there by the person who stole B's shirt. Evidence tending to show that A stole C's shirt might be regarded as relevant on either of the following grounds: (a) people who steal one thing frequently steal another, A stole C's shirt, therefore A probably stole B's shirt; (b) the man who stole B's shirt probably had C's shirt in his possession, A stole C's shirt, therefore A probably stole B's shirt. The first argument is of a general nature and is based on the tendency of thieves to repeat their conduct; the second is more specific and is based on the particular facts of the case. The evidence would be inadmissible on the first ground because it would merely show bad disposition, but it would be admissible on the second ground as tending to identify the thief of B's shirt. If evidence is admissible for one purpose, it cannot be rejected on the ground that it is inadmissible for some other purpose. It is desirable that in such circumstances the two purposes are kept clearly distinguished in the mind of the trier of fact. In criminal cases tried by a jury the judge should be particularly careful in his direction. Thus if evidence of the previous convictions of the accused should be admissible in the course of cross-examination for the purpose of impugning his credibility as a witness, it is necessary for the judge to instruct the jury that it must not take the evidence into account as showing the accused's guilt directly.[17] Some scepticism may reasonably be expressed as to how effectively such directions can prevent the evidence from being used for the wrong purpose.[18] Indeed in some cases the danger is recognised as being so great as to require the principle of multiple admissibility to be overridden, and the evidence excluded altogether, though only as a matter of discretion.[19] These remarks must also be understood to be subject to the operation of some rules, such as that excluding evidence the admission of which would be likely to damage the interests of the state, which override arguments for admission based on any type of relevancy.

Wigmore described the principle involved as one of 'multiple admissibility'.[20] The term is not particularly well chosen, because it suggests that evidence may be admissible for more than one purpose. This is undoubtedly true, but the point of the rule under consideration is that evidence may be admissible for one purpose although it is inadmissible for another. It is, however, difficult to suggest anything better, and,

16   *R v Whiley* (1804) 2 Leach 983, at 985. Cf *R v O'Meally (No 2)* [1953] VLR 30 (proceeds of robberies left at scene of murder, accused's participation in the robberies could be proved); *R v Sims* [1967] Qd R 432 (prison clothing found near house broken into by escaped prisoner).
17   The desirability of giving this sort of guidance was emphasised by Lord Pearce in *Selvey v DPP* [1970] AC 304, [1968] 2 All ER 497, at 528. For examples of such directions see p 410 below.
18   Some of the strongest expressions have been made by American judges. Justice Jackson described it as 'unmitigated fiction' in *Krulewitch v US* 336 US 440 (1949), at 453; Judge Learned Hand as 'a mental gymnastic' in *Nash v US* 54 F 2d 1006 (1932), at 1007, Judge Jerome Frank as 'a judicial lie' in *US v Grunewald* 233 F 2d 556 (1956), at 574, while Traynor CJ remarked that a jury 'cannot segregate evidence into separate intellectual boxes', in *People v Aranda* 407 P 2d 265 (1965), at 272.
19   *R v Shepherd* (1980) 71 Cr App Rep 120; *R v Watts* [1983] 3 All ER 101, at 104, 77 Cr App Rep 126, at 129, where Lord Chief Justice Lane said that the jury was required 'to perform difficult feats of intellectual acrobatics' which were 'practically impossible'.
20   I Wigmore para 13.

although the term is not employed by English judges, the doctrine it embodies is mentioned in numerous dicta. The application of the doctrine is fraught with danger, but the total exclusion of the evidence could be productive of even greater injustice.[1]

B. THE INADMISSIBILITY OF IRRELEVANT AND INSUFFICIENTLY RELEVANT EVIDENCE

1. Illustrations

A few illustrations may be given of the exclusion of evidence which is irrelevant, or insufficiently relevant, to any issue before the court.

(i) Remoteness

In *Hart v Lancashire and Yorkshire Rail Co*[2] the fact that the defendant's method of changing the points was altered after an accident was held to be inadmissible as evidence that the accident was caused by the defendant's negligence. According to Bramwell B:

> People do not furnish evidence against themselves simply by adopting a new plan in order to prevent the recurrence of an accident. Because the world gets wiser as it gets older, it was not therefore foolish before.

In *Hollingham v Head*,[3] the defence to a claim for the price of guano was that an express condition in the contract of sale provided that the goods should be equal to Peruvian guano. The defendant wished to call witnesses to swear that the claimant had entered into contracts with other customers containing a term similar to that for

---

1 'No doubt it renders the administration of justice more difficult when evidence which is offered for one purpose or person, may incidentally apply to another; but that is an infirmity to which all evidence is subject, and exclusion on such a ground would manifestly occasion greater mischief than the reception of the evidence' (Tindall CJ in *Willis v Bernard* (1832) 8 Bing 376, at 383). 'It often happens, both in civil and criminal cases, that evidence is tendered on several alternative grounds, and yet it is never objected that if on any ground it is admissible, that ground must not prevail, because on some other ground it would be inadmissible and prejudicial. In such cases it is usual for the judge (not always very successfully) to caution the jury against being biased by treating the evidence in the objectionable sense' (per Jelf J in *R v Bond* [1906] 2 KB 389, at 389). There is, however, no rule of practice requiring such a warning to be given, the matter is entirely one for the judge's discretion (see per Murray CJ in *R v Kennewell* [1927] SASR 287, at 302). For an application in the context of statutory rules, see *R v Wall* [1983] NZLR 238.
2 (1869) 21 LT 261, at 263. Cf *State Electricity Commission of Victoria v Gray* [1951] VLR 104, at 116 (change in lighting system after accident admissible to show warning could have been given before accident) and *Anderson v Morris Wools Pty Ltd* [1965] Qd R 65 (evidence of alteration of machine after accident admissible to show precaution which might have been taken). The US Federal Rules, r 407 reads: 'When, after an event, measures are taken which, if taken previously, would have made the event less likely to occur, evidence of the subsequent measures is not admissible to prove negligence or culpable conduct in connection with the event. This rule does not require the exclusion of evidence of subsequent measures when offered for another purpose, such as proving ownership, control, or feasibility of precautionary measures, if controverted, or impeachment.' Such evidence is also admissible in Canada: *Winsor v Marks & Spencer Canada Ltd* (1995) 129 DLR (4th) 189.
3 (1858) 27 LJCP 241.

which he contended, but the Court of Common Pleas held that he was not entitled to do so:[4]

It may be often difficult to decide upon the admissibility of evidence, where it is offered for the purpose of establishing probability, but to be admissible it must at least afford a reasonable inference as to the principal matter in dispute.

In *Holcome v Hewson*,[5] a brewer claimed damages for breach of a publican's covenant to buy beer from him. The defence was that the claimant had supplied bad beer, and evidence to the effect that he had supplied other publicans with good beer was rejected. He 'might deal well with one and not with the others'.[6]

Relevancy is a matter of degree and it is as idle to enquire as it is impossible to say whether the evidence was rejected in the above two cases because it was altogether irrelevant, or merely because it was too remotely relevant. It may also, on occasion, require a balance to be struck between the probative force of the evidence and external pressure vitiating its use,[7] such as the time likely to be taken in resolving collateral issues, the danger of manufacture, and sensitivity to private and public sentiment. These will be considered in turn.

(ii)   Multiplicity of issues[8]

The judgment of Willes J in *Hollingham v Head* contains a timely reminder that litigants are mortal, and Rolfe B once pertinently observed that:[9]

if we lived for a thousand years instead of about sixty or seventy, and every case was of sufficient importance, it might be possible, and perhaps proper ... to raise every possible inquiry as to the truth of statements made ... In fact mankind finds it to be impossible.

Evidence which might even be highly relevant in a protracted academic investigation is treated as too remote from the issue in a forensic inquiry because the body which has to come to the conclusion is controlled by the time factor, not to mention considerations such as the danger of distracting the jury,[10] and the undesirability of pronouncing upon matters which are not being litigated. Thus, in *Agassiz v London Tramway Co*[11] the claimant, a passenger on a tram, claimed damages for personal injuries caused by a collision which she contended was due to the negligence of the driver. She said that she heard a fellow passenger tell the conductor that the driver ought to be reported, only to be met by the disconcertingly frank reply 'he has already been

---

4   Per Willes J at p 242.
5   (1810) 2 Camp 391. Cf *R v Whitehead* (1848) 3 Car & Kir 202, where, on a charge of manslaughter against a doctor, evidence of his skilful treatment of other patients was excluded.
6   Per Lord Ellenborough CJ.
7   In *Ashmore v Corpn of Lloyd's* [1992] 2 All ER 486, at 493, [1992] 1 WLR 446, at 454 the House of Lords encouraged judicial intervention upon these lines.
8   The extent to which the rules of relevance may be moulded to meet the exigencies of other facts has been examined quite independently in two modern essays: from a theoretical point of view by Dworkin in Tapper (ed) *Crime, Proof and Punishment* (1981); and from a more practical point of view by Mr Justice Fox in Waller and Campbell (eds) *Well and Truly Tried* (1982).
9   *A-G v Hitchcock* (1847) 1 Exch 91, at 105.
10   'The fewer and simpler the issues left to the jury, the less chance there is of a miscarriage of justice' (per Byrne J in *R v Patel* [1951] 2 All ER 29, at 30).
11   (1872) 21 WR 199.

reported, for he has been off the line five or six times today—he is a new driver'. Kelly CB rejected the evidence, not because it infringed the rule against hearsay, but because it would have given rise to many collateral issues as to whether the driver had been reported, and whether he had been off the points five or six times or was a new driver.

From time to time the courts have admitted evidence of particular instances to show that wherever A has occurred B has followed in support of an argument that A caused B, but generally only when a striking coincidence would have to be assumed if A did not cause B. In *Hales v Kerr*,[12] for instance, the claimant alleged that he had contracted barber's itch from the implements used by the defendant, a hairdresser, and he was allowed to prove that two other customers of the defendant contracted the same disease in the previous month after he had cut their hair. It certainly would have been a coincidence of some magnitude if three customers of the same barber had not contracted a disease connected with hairdressing from the same source.

(iii)   Danger of manufactured evidence

The courts rightly take the view that the degree to which an item of evidence is relevant to an issue diminishes in proportion to the likelihood of its having been manufactured, but it is open to question whether people are as prone to manufacture evidence as some judgments suggest,[13] and the bogey has led to certain exclusionary rules, the mechanical application of which may lead to the rejection of evidence of real probative value.

It has certainly played a large part in the development of the rule excluding hearsay, and especially the rule excluding evidence of previous consistent statements of a witness. The dread of manufacture has retarded and complicated reform of this branch of the law to no small extent.[14] The major inroads made by common law were mainly confined to statements made by deceased persons;[15] the first major statutory reform, the Evidence Act 1938, excluded from its ambit statements made by a person with an interest of his own to serve,[16] and even the fresh and liberal approach adopted by the Civil Evidence Act 1968 applied special rules in the case of previous statements made by witnesses whom it was proposed to call.[17]

This spectre still haunts attempts to reform the hearsay rule in criminal proceedings. The Criminal Law Revision Committee admitted that '[t]he need to provide for safeguards against the use of manufactured evidence caused ... more difficulty than did any of the other questions relating to hearsay evidence.'[18] In order to meet this danger the Committee proposed an even more elaborate provision relating to the admissibility of proofs of evidence than that made by the Civil Evidence Act 1968,[19] insisted on a strict notice procedure,[20] and wished to bar altogether any statement said[1] to have been made after the accused had been charged. This final provision reveals

12   [1908] 2 KB 601; see also *Akerele v R* [1943] AC 255, [1943] 1 All ER 367.
13   See the remarks of Eyre CJ, p 2 above.
14   The House of Lords has suggested that such caution has proved justifiable in the light of cases of miscarriages of justice, see *R v Kearley* [1992] 2 AC 228, at 258, [1992] 2 All ER 345, at 366.
15   See further ch XV below.
16   Section 1(3).
17   Section 2(2).
18   11th Report on Evidence (General) Cmnd 4991, para 240, see also para 229.
19   Draft Bill, cl 32(3).
20   Clause 32(3) and (4).
1   Para 237(iv). But see Police and Criminal Evidence Act 1984, Sch 3, para 2.

the absurd straits into which the cause of reform of the laws of evidence can be driven by the fear of manufacture. The reasoning appears to assume that there are some who are prepared to manufacture everything about a document except its date.

A slightly less timorous approach was adopted by the Roskill Committee[2] which felt that the exposure of fabrication was likely to be so devastating as to operate as an adequate deterrent. Even so it felt constrained to require documents prepared specifically for the purposes of legal proceedings to be admitted only with the leave of the court.[3]

(iv)   Sensitivity

In *Vernon v Bosley*[4] the trial judge disallowed cross-examination of a divorced woman about an extra-marital affair of her ex-husband when she was to be called as a witness by him in a claim in which one of the elements was the collapse of their marriage. He took the view that the distress and embarrassment would outweigh its value. While reversing him on its application in that case, the Court of Appeal nevertheless enunciated as a general principle that:

> the degree of relevance needed for admissibility is not some fixed point on a scale, but will vary according to the nature of the evidence and in particular the inconvenience, expense, delay or oppression which would attend its reception …. For example, having to answer a question may involve a witness in breaking a confidence imposed by his religion, profession or conscience.

Control of such weighing was equated for appellate purposes with that applicable to the exercise of discretion by the trial judge.[5]

2.   Apparent exceptions

A few exceptions to the general prohibition on irrelevant evidence have been suggested, but it is submitted that none of them is substantial so far as English law is concerned.

(i)   Facts affecting the admissibility of evidence

Phipson said that Thayer was inaccurate when he asserted that 'without any exception, nothing that is not logically relevant is admissible', because numerous facts are legally admissible although they have no logical bearing on the issue the court has to decide.[6] He referred to such facts as that a witness was not sworn in a particular way, that a hearsay declarant was dead at the date of the trial, and that due search had been made for a lost document. It seems, however, that the criticism is a purely verbal one, because it assumes that by 'logically relevant' Thayer meant relevant to the main facts in issue.

2   *Fraud Trials Committee Report* (1986) para 5.36.
3   This requirement effectively putting the burden of showing non-fabrication upon the party tendering the document was enacted as s 26 of the Criminal Justice Act 1988.
4   [1994] PIQR P337.
5   See further below p 176.
6   *Manual of Law of Evidence* (7th edn) 28; Thayer *Preliminary Treatise on Evidence at the Common Law* 266. The view taken in the text is followed by the editor of *Phipson's Manual* (12th edn) p 25.

His statement might equally well be taken to mean that nothing is admissible which is not relevant, either to the main facts in issue, or else to such subordinate facts as those relating to the credibility and admissibility of evidence, in which case the relevance of the facts mentioned by Phipson is obvious enough.

(ii) Curative admissibility[7]

It is sometimes said that, if irrelevant evidence is adduced by one party, his opponent may seek to dispel its effect by calling irrelevant evidence himself. Whatever the position may be in certain American jurisdictions, this principle (which Wigmore described as one of 'curative admissibility') is not recognised by the English courts. Thus, in *R v Cargill*,[8] on a charge of unlawful intercourse with a girl between thirteen and sixteen, the prosecutrix swore that she had been chaste before the accused seduced her. This was irrelevant, because absence of consent and hence the girl's character, is immaterial in such a case, but it did not entitle the accused to call evidence concerning the girl's behaviour with other men because the court was not prepared to say that, if the prosecution introduced a matter irrelevant to the issue, the defence was entitled to call evidence with regard to that irrelevant issue.

(iii) Conditional admissibility[9]

One fact may only be relevant to another if it is taken together with some further matter, and it may well be the case that this can be proved only by a witness who will be called after the one who testifies to the fact the relevancy of which is being considered. In such circumstances, the court allows the evidence to be given conditionally on its turning out to be relevant. If it proves to be irrelevant, the judge will tell the jury to disregard it. An excellent example is provided by the rules governing the admissibility of statements made in the presence of a party. These only have probative value in the light of the conduct of the person to whom they were made. If A confronts B and alleges that he has committed a crime against him, and B is later tried for that offence, evidence of what A said will usually be relevant only if B's conduct is something other than a stalwart denial of the charge; but there is no doubt that A's statement may always be proved in the first instance, although the judge may subsequently be obliged to tell the jury to disregard it altogether.[10] Such a state of affairs is better regarded as a concession to the fact that the evidence in a case often emerges slowly, and from the mouths of many witnesses, rather than an exception to the rule prohibiting the reception of irrelevant, or insufficiently relevant, matter.

---

7 I Wigmore para 15.
8 [1913] 2 KB 271. See also *Ready v Brown* (1968) 118 CLR 165. On the other hand in *Barry v News Group Newspapers Ltd* 1999 SLT 590 it was held in Scotland that if irrelevant evidence were adduced cross-examination to show it was a lie was permitted in an effort to discredit the witness's testimony as to relevant matters; for a similar rule in Australia see *R v Maslen and Shaw* (1995) 79 ACR 199.
9 I Wigmore para 14; Phipson *Law of Evidence* (14th edn) para 7.05, citing *Haig v Belcher* (1836) 7 C & P 389. The same notion is involved in the statement that evidence will be received de bene esse for the origin of which see FDM in 62 LQR 38, and Plucknett in 68 LQR 130.
10 *R v Christie* [1914] AC 545. Such a direction may be exceedingly difficult to phrase, see *Hoch v R* (1988) 165 CLR 292.

(iv)   Inextricable matter

In a few cases relevant and admissible evidence is so closely linked to irrelevant evidence that it is impracticable to sever the irrelevant evidence from the relevant, and in such a case the irrelevant evidence is admitted so long as its admission is unlikely to be harmful.[11] Thus evidence is frequently given of, say, the colour of a person's hair, even though it is irrelevant to any issue in the case. If however the irrelevant evidence may cause harm, such as evidence of the accused's mens rea in an offence of strict liability, and can be severed, then it must be excluded.[12]

C.   RELEVANCE AND ADMISSIBILITY

Although there are no real exceptions to this rule, the existence of important exceptions to the rule that all sufficiently relevant evidence is admissible renders it essential to draw a sharp distinction between the relevancy and admissibility of evidence. The former is a concept arrived at inductively from experience, and its applicability can be tested deductively by the construction of a syllogism. It is not primarily dependent on rules of law.[13] The admissibility of evidence, on the other hand, depends first on the concept of relevancy of a sufficiently high degree, and secondly, on the fact that the evidence tendered does not infringe any of the exclusionary rules that may be applicable to it.[14] To quote Wigmore:[15] 'Admissibility signifies that the particular fact is relevant and something more,—that it has also satisfied all the auxiliary tests and extrinsic policies.' It is especially important not to smuggle new rules of inadmissibility into the law under the guise of axioms of relevance. The facts of every case are always complex, and it is inherently unlikely that any absolute general rules of relevance will be of legal significance. Thus a purported rule that evidence of the 'lifestyle' of the accused is never relevant to a charge of possession of drugs, but only to one of possession with intent to supply, has had to be rejected.[16] Although the distinction between relevancy and admissibility is expressly recognised in many English judgments, an over-simplification of Stephen's has exercised a somewhat baneful influence, and, by way of reaction perhaps, demands are sometimes made for the recognition of further basic concepts in the law of evidence.

---

11   Even in the case of inextricable inadmissible evidence a conviction will not necessarily be quashed if it is left in, so long as a sufficiently firm direction is given to the jury: *R v Flicker* [1995] Crim LR 493 (impossible to edit out from a vital statement an incidental reference to the accused's previous record).

12   *R v Sandhu* [1997] Crim LR 288.

13   Thayer sometimes wrote as though the doctrine of precedent was wholly inapplicable to questions of relevance (see (1900) 14 Harv LR 139, answering Fox 14 Harv LR 39). Wigmore, on the other hand, said 'So long as courts continue to declare in judicial rulings what their notions of logic are, just so long will there be rules of law which must be observed' (I Wigmore (Tillers revn) 691). For once the truth really does lie between the two views and Thayer conceded as much when he said decisions concerning relevance may 'stand as a precedent to half settle other cases'.

14   In the United States it has been held constitutional for states to draft legislation making relevant evidence inadmissible, even in the case of evidence relevant to the defence in a criminal case, *Montana v Egelhoff* 116 S Ct 2013 (1996) (evidence of voluntary drunkenness).

15   I Wigmore (Tillers revn) 689.

16   *R v Guney* [1998] 2 Cr App Rep 242, at 267A disapproving of dicta in *R v Halpin* [1996] Crim LR 112.

1. Stephen's terminology

In his *Digest of the Law of Evidence* Stephen attempted to state the rules concerning the matters that may be proved in court wholly in terms of relevancy. The result was that he had to explain the rejection of hearsay on the ground that it was irrelevant or deemed to be irrelevant, while its reception under exceptions to the hearsay rule was based on the fact that it was relevant or deemed to be so. Other exclusionary rules were likewise said to involve the rejection of evidence which is irrelevant or deemed to be irrelevant. The objection to this mode of expression is that much of the evidence which English law rejects is highly relevant, and no one would now wish wholeheartedly to adhere to the terminology of the Digest, although its influence has been considerable.

2. The demand for more basic concepts

It is sometimes said that, in addition to recognising the separate concepts of relevancy and admissibility, we should allow for the two further concepts of 'materiality' and 'receivability'.[17] If this were done, 'relevant' would imply that the evidence tendered tends to prove the fact it purports to establish, 'materiality' would mean direct relevance to a fact in issue, 'admissibility' would denote that the evidence did not infringe an exclusionary rule, while 'receivability' would mean that the evidence was relevant, material and admissible. All that need be said here is that the additional concepts are not employed in practice, and it is by no means certain that their adoption would render the exposition of the law any clearer.

3. Admissibility and weight of evidence

Questions concerning the admissibility of evidence must be distinguished from those relating to its weight. The former is a matter of law for the judge (although it may sometimes depend upon a preliminary finding of fact by him); the weight of evidence, on the other hand, is a question of fact, although, in cases tried with a jury, the summing-up frequently contains observations on the cogency of certain matters, and the judge can always withdraw an issue from the jury because the proponent has not adduced sufficient evidence in support of his claim. The distinction between admissibility and weight does not require further elaboration, but it is not clear-cut. The weight of evidence may affect its admissibility as this is to some extent dependent on the degree of relevancy of the matter under consideration.[18] The tendency of the modern law is in favour of a broad basis of admissibility.[19]

---

17 Montrose (1954) 70 LQR 527. The concept of materiality is employed by Wigmore, that of receivability is canvassed by Professor Montrose.
18 *R v Quinn and Bloom* [1962] 2 QB 245, [1961] 3 All ER 88. This is a complicating factor in the modern law relating to the admissibility of 'similar fact' evidence in criminal cases, see further below p 357.
19 'People were formerly frightened out of their wits about admitting evidence lest juries should go wrong. In modern times we admit the evidence and discuss its weight' (Cockburn CJ in *R v Birmingham Overseers* (1861) 1 B & S 763, at 767).

Chapter II

Matters not requiring proof and judicial findings as evidence

The general rule is that all of the facts in issue or relevant to the issue in a given case must be proved by evidence—testimony, hearsay statements, documents or things. While the question of which facts are in issue in any given proceedings is really a matter of substantive law it should be noticed that such rules occasionally masquerade as rules of evidence. This is the case with so-called irrebuttable presumptions of law, as for example s 50 of the Children and Young Persons Act 1933[1] which says that it shall be conclusively presumed that no child under ten can be guilty of any offence. Similarly it is not uncommon for a statute to dispense with proof of a matter which it might be expected would be in issue, for example s 79(1) of the Animal Health Act 1981 dispenses with proof of the appointment or handwriting of certain officials for the purposes of the Act.

If, in a moment of forgetfulness, the claimant or prosecutor fails to prove an essential fact, his opponent may well succeed on a submission that there is no case to answer although the evidence was readily available, for the court only rarely exercises its discretion to allow a witness to be recalled.[2] There is a number of exceptions to this general rule. In some cases the judge, or trier of fact, is entitled to find a fact of his own motion. He may take judicial notice of it. In others, a party may make a formal admission of a relevant matter. Even if he does not go so far, a matter may still be determined against him as a result of certain circumstances which the law treats as preventing him from contesting it. In such circumstances he is said to be estopped. One example of such a circumstance is when the same matter has been determined against him and in favour of his opponent by a binding and conclusive judgment of a court. It is thus convenient to consider also in this chapter the whole question of the status of judicial findings in other proceedings. Each of these topics, judicial notice, formal admissions, estoppel and evidence of judicial findings will be considered in turn, the second of them very briefly indeed.

---

1   As amended by Children and Young Persons Act 1963, s 16.
2   See *R v Pilcher* (1974) 60 Cr App Rep 1; *R v Gainsborough Justices, ex p Green* (1984) 78 Cr App Rep 9; and in Australia *Bulecjik v R* (1997) 185 CLR 375, at 408. For one of the rare exceptions see *James v South Glamorgan County Council* (1994) 99 Cr App Rep 321.

SECTION I.   JUDICIAL NOTICE[3]

When a court takes judicial notice of a fact, as it may[4] in civil and criminal cases alike, it declares that it will find that the fact exists, or direct the jury to do so, although the existence of the fact has not been established by evidence. If, for instance, the date of Christmas should be in issue, or relevant to the issue, it will not be necessary for the party who desires to establish that fact to call a witness to swear that the relevant date is 25 December, because this is a matter of which judicial notice is taken. There are two classes of case in which the court will act in this way, for, to quote Lord Sumner:[5]

> Judicial notice refers to facts which a judge can be called upon to receive and to act upon either from his general knowledge of them, or from inquiries to be made by himself for his own information from sources to which it is proper for him to refer.

From time to time statute has provided that judicial notice shall be taken of certain facts. It will therefore be convenient to illustrate the application of the doctrine by reference to facts which are judicially noticed without inquiry, facts judicially noticed after inquiry, and those of which notice must be taken under various statutory provisions. Certain theoretical questions are raised at the end of the section.

A.   FACTS JUDICIALLY NOTICED WITHOUT INQUIRY

It would be pointless to endeavour to make a list of cases in which the courts have taken judicial notice of facts without inquiry. The justification for their acting in this way is that the fact in question is too notorious to be the subject of serious dispute.[6] Familiar examples are provided by the rulings that it is unnecessary to call evidence to show that a fortnight is too short a period for human gestation,[7] that the advancement of learning is among the purposes for which the University of Oxford exists,[8] that cats

---

3   For theoretical discussion see Thayer *Preliminary Treatise on Evidence at the Common Law* ch 7; Morgan *Some Problems of Proof Under the Anglo-American System of Litigation* 36; McConville (1979) 1 Liverpool LR 62; Carter in Waller and Campbell (eds) *Well and Truly Tried* (1982).

4   The court has a discretion, and if the facts to be noticed would, for example, go a long way towards establishing a major part of the prosecution's case, may decline to take notice and instead require evidence to be called, see *R v Zundel* (1987) 35 DLR (4th) 338.

5   *Commonwealth Shipping Representative v P and O Branch Services* [1923] AC 191, at 212. Morgan (*Some Problems of Proof* p 61) says the party who asks that judicial notice be taken of a fact 'has the burden of convincing the judge (a) that the matter is so notorious as not to be the subject of dispute among reasonable men, or (b) the matter is capable of immediate accurate demonstration by resort to readily accessible sources of indisputable accuracy'. Davis (see for example (1955) 55 Columbia LR 945) has promoted a distinction between the judicial notice of adjudicative and legislative facts which was accepted by the Canadian Law Reform Committee in its draft code, though it is more common to restrict judicial notice to adjudicative facts. See US Federal Rule 201; Report of Canadian task force on Uniform Rules of Evidence s 4.4(c); Australian Law Reform Commission, Research Paper 10 'The Judge—Adducing Evidence and Judicial Notice' Part C proposal 5.

6   Care needs to be taken where some aspect of the situation is beyond dispute but the purported notice goes beyond that to others which are disputable, for example not only that an Indian Reserve is on a lake, but that therefore water is available for domestic purposes, *Tsawwassen Indian Band v Delta Corpn* (1997) 149 DLR (4th) 672.

7   *R v Luffe* (1807) 8 East 193.

8   *Re Oxford Poor Rate Case* (1857) 8 E & B 184 (a decision that university premises came within special rating provisions).

are kept for domestic purposes,[9] that the streets of London are full of traffic and that a boy riding a bicycle in them runs a risk of injury,[10] that young boys have playful habits,[11] that criminals have unhappy lives,[12] and that the reception of television is a common feature of English domestic life enjoyed mainly for domestic purposes.[13] The court may be taken to know the meaning of any ordinary expression in the English language,[14] and that the value of money has declined since 1189.[15] Judicial notice will also be taken of the fact that a post card is the kind of document which might be read by anyone,[16] but not that husbands read their wives' letters.[17] These conclusions have been reached without reference to any extraneous sources of information, but there is a number of cases in which judicial notice has been taken only after such reference has been made.

B.   FACTS JUDICIALLY NOTICED AFTER INQUIRY

Foremost among these are cases in which the court acts on information supplied by a Secretary of State with regard to what may loosely be described as political matters; but other illustrations are provided by cases concerning inquiries into historical facts, questions concerning the existence of various customs and matters of professional practice. It is sometimes said that the judges take judicial notice of the common law, but there is no need to deal separately with this aspect of the subject.

The sources consulted by the judge may include reports of previous cases, certificates from various officials, works of reference[18] and oral statements of witnesses.

What was once a notorious fact to be noticed without further ado may become one of which notice will only be taken after the court's memory has been refreshed. In *Hoare v Silverlock*[19] for instance, the claimant had applied to a benevolent society for assistance, and she alleged that the defendant had defamed her by saying her friends would realise the truth of the fable about the frozen snake. Erle J said:[20]

> I may take judicial notice that the words 'frozen snake' have an application very generally known indeed, which application is likely to bring into contempt a person against whom it is directed.

If such a point were to come before a jury today, they would require a good deal of instruction in the mysteries of Aesop's fables.

---

9   *Nye v Niblett* [1918] 1 KB 23 (cats protected by the Malicious Damage Act 1861).
10   *Dennis v AJ White & Co* [1916] 2 KB 1, at 6, [1917] AC 479, at 492.
11   *Clayton v Hardwicke Colliery Co Ltd* (1915) 85 LJKB 292.
12   *Burns v Edman* [1970] 2 QB 541, [1970] 1 All ER 886.
13   *Bridlington Relay Ltd v Yorkshire Electricity Board* [1965] Ch 436, [1965] 1 All ER 264.
14   *Chapman v Kirke* [1948] 2 KB 450, at 454, [1948] 2 All ER 556, at 557. See in Australia *Bendixen v Coleman* (1943) 68 CLR 401.
15   *Bryant v Foot* (1868) LR 3 QB 497. See in Australia *In the marriage of Monticone* (1989) 98 FLR 460.
16   *Huth v Huth* [1915] 3 KB 32.
17   *Theaker v Richardson* [1962] 1 All ER 229, [1962] 1 WLR 151.
18   Such works must be 'authoritative', see *Casley-Smith v FS Evans & Son Pty (No 4)* (1988) 49 SASR 339; and may not be consulted by the jury in its own initiative, *R v Wallace* [1990] Crim LR 433 (though there consultation of a dictionary was not sufficiently material on the facts to justify allowing the appeal).
19   (1848) 12 QB 624.
20   At 633.

1.   Political matters

In *Duff Development Co Ltd v Government of Kelantan*[1] the government of Kelantan applied for an order against the enforcement of an arbitration award on the ground that Kelantan was an independent sovereign state. The Secretary of State for the Colonies in reply to an inquiry from the Master wrote that Kelantan was a sovereign state and the Sultan ruler thereof. The House of Lords held that this concluded the matter because:[2]

> It has for some time been the practice of our courts, when such a question is raised, to take judicial notice of the sovereignty of a state, and for that purpose (in case of any uncertainty) to seek information from a Secretary of State; and when information is so obtained the court does not permit it to be questioned by the parties.

The source of information to which the court resorts is treated as one of indisputable accuracy for reasons of public policy—the undesirability of a conflict between the courts and the executive. As in all cases in which the courts renounce their powers of determining facts on the basis of evidence, the practice may be represented as something like a submission to official dictatorship, but, in this instance, it is difficult to see how else a judge should act when confronted with such questions as the sovereignty of a foreign state, the membership of a diplomatic suite, the extent of territorial waters or the existence of a state of war.[3] Moreover the courts form their own opinion of the effect of the Secretary of State's answer and they may differ inter se on this point.[4]

2.   Historical facts

In *Read v Bishop of Lincoln*[5] the question was whether the mixing of communion wine with water and various other practices were contrary to the law of the church. It was held, against an objection to their doing so, that the courts might consider historical and ritualistic works on the subject. In the course of his speech in the House of Lords Lord Halsbury made it clear that the judge can rely on his own historical learning in such a case, although 'where it is important to ascertain ancient facts of a public nature

---

1   [1924] AC 797. See also *Taylor v Barclay* (1828) 2 Sim 213 (judicial notice of non-recognition of South American republic after consultation with Secretary of State); *The Fagernes* [1927] P 311 (Admiralty's statement of extent of territorial waters conclusive); *Engelke v Musmann* [1928] AC 433 (Secretary of State's letter as to membership of diplomatic suite conclusive); *R v Bottrill, ex p Kuechenmeister* [1947] KB 41, [1947] 2 All ER 434 (judicial notice of continuance of war with Germany after consultation with Secretary of State).
2   Per Lord Cave at 805.
3   See cases cited in n 21 above and *Preston v Preston* [1963] P 141, at 149, [1962] 3 All ER 1057, at 1060 f. Judicial notice will not be taken of a particular event, such as the date of a military operation, in a modern war; *Commonwealth Shipping Representative v P and O Branch Services* [1923] AC 191.
4   *Carl-Zeiss-Stiftung v Rayner and Keeler Ltd (No 2)* [1967] 1 AC 853, [1966] 2 All ER 536. In *A-G v Tse Chu-Fai* (1998) 153 ALR 128 where the High Court of Australia was faced with a difficult question relating to the effects of the transition of sovereignty in Hong Kong it explicitly affirmed its own ultimate right to decision, but found the view of the government helpful in determining the question of construction.
5   [1892] AC 644.

the law does permit historical works to be referred to'.[6] If questions concerning the tenets of a political creed were to arise, the English courts would no doubt do what Australian courts are prepared to do and consult the appropriate literature.[7] A similar practice would no doubt be adopted with regard to general scientific or aesthetic questions. The courts will also take notice of what people must have believed at a given time about such contemporary matters as the likelihood of a war.[8]

3. Custom

As a general rule a court cannot treat a fact as proved on the basis of the evidence in a previous case,[9] but this rule does not apply to the proof of custom, for it has been recognised that a time must come when the courts, having had the question of the existence of a custom before them in other cases, are entitled to say that they will take judicial notice of it and will not require proof in each case.[10] This recognition was made by Bray J in the Divisional Court when upholding a County Court judge's right to take judicial notice of the custom whereby a domestic servant might terminate her employment within the first month of her engagement by less than a full month's notice but the doctrine he enunciated lies at the root of the court's recognition of a vast number of mercantile customs.[11] It is not always easy to say when a custom has been recognised with sufficient frequency to become the subject of judicial notice. Whereas the courts were not prepared to recognise that it was the usual practice of a hotel-keeper to be in possession of furniture under hire purchase agreements in 1875, they were prepared to do so in 1881.[12]

4. Professional practice

In *Davey v Harrow Corpn*,[13] Lord Goddard CJ said:[14]

> Where a boundary hedge is delineated on an ordnance survey map by a line, that line indicated the centre of the existing hedge. That is in accordance with the practice of the ordnance survey and courts can take notice of that practice as at least prima facie evidence of what a line on the map indicates.

Judicial notice will likewise be taken of the practice of conveyancers.

6   At 653; *Evans v Getting* (1834) 6 C & P 586 (history of Breconshire not received on question
      of boundaries of Welsh parishes because of possible prejudice of author); *Darby v Ouseley* (1856)
      1 H & N 1.
7   *Australian Communist Party v Commonwealth* (1951) 83 CLR 1.
8   *Monarch S S Co Ltd v Karlshamns Oljefabriker A/B* [1949] AC 196, at 234, [1949] 1 All ER
      1, at 20, per Lord Du Parcq.
9   *Roper v Taylor's Central Garages (Exeter) Ltd* [1951] 2 TLR 284.
10   *George v Davies* [1911] 2 KB 445, at 448.
11   *Brandao v Barnett* (1846) 12 Cl & Fin 787.
12   *Re Matthews, ex p Powell* (1875) 1 Ch D 501; *Crawcour v Salter* (1881) 18 Ch D 30.
13   [1958] 1 QB 60, at 69.
14   *Re Rosher* (1884) 26 Ch D 801.

C.   STATUTORY PROVISIONS[15]

The doctrine of judicial notice can be made to render assistance in connection with the proof of documents. We shall see in ch XVIII that, subject to the presumption of due execution arising from the production of a document more than twenty years old from the proper custody, the due execution of a document, i e, the fact that it was signed or sealed by the person by whom it purports to be signed or sealed, must be proved before the court will receive it in evidence. This would lead to endless trouble in the case of various documents in constant use, and there are numerous statutes which provide that judicial notice shall be taken of the signatures of various persons attached to official documents.[16] Difficulties formerly experienced with regard to the proof of statutes, i e, showing that the document before the court corresponded with those of the Act duly passed by both Houses of Parliament, have been resolved by what is now s 3 of the Interpretation Act 1978. Its effect, when read together with the second schedule and s 9 of the repealed Interpretation Act 1889, is that every Act passed after 1850 shall be a public Act and judicially noticed as such in the absence of an express provision to the contrary. Judicial notice has always been taken of a public Act of Parliament, ie, no evidence has ever been required concerning its passage through Parliament and its contents, but, before 1850, such evidence was required in the case of private Acts unless, as was often the case, they contained some special provision about judicial notice. Even now, if reliance is placed upon a private Act passed before 1850, it may be necessary to produce a Queen's Printer's copy of the statute.[17] Local byelaws must be formally proved.[18]

It is unfortunate that there is no express provision for the taking of judicial notice of statutory instruments because, even in modern times, the courts have varied in their insistence on the production of a Stationery Office copy[19] and it is not even clear that proof by this method is authorised in the case of all statutory instruments.[20] It is however clear that proof of a statutory instrument is not required once constant reliance upon it has made it a matter of which judicial notice may be taken.[1] It has been suggested that no objection should be taken to informal proof of such instruments, unless there is some reason to doubt its accuracy.[2]

D.   THEORETICAL QUESTIONS

The principal theoretical questions raised by the practice of taking judicial notice concern its relationship to the reception of evidence, the use which a judge can make of his personal knowledge, the rationale of the practice and its scope.

---

15   See European Communities Act 1972, s 4(2), for judicial notice by the English courts of community treaties and decisions of community courts, and Patents Act 1977, s 91, for judicial notice of the European Patent Convention.
16   E g, the Evidence Act 1845, s 2.
17   Evidence Act 1845, s 3. Before this statute it might have been necessary to call someone to prove that a private Act was duly passed. Now it is sufficient that a copy of any such statute passed before 1850 should purport to be that of the printer to the King or Queen. By the Documentary Evidence Act 1882, a Stationery Office copy is made equivalent to a Queen's Printer's copy.
18   See *Donnelly v Carmichael* 1995 JC 215.
19   See *Palastanga v Solman* [1962] Crim LR 334.
20   But see *R v Clarke* [1969] 2 QB 91, [1969] 1 All ER 924.
1   *R v Jones* [1969] 3 All ER 1559, 54 Cr App Rep 63; the same is true in Scotland, see *Valentine v McPhail* 1986 JC 131.
2   *R v Tang* [1995] Crim LR 813.

I. Judicial notice and the reception of evidence

No problem arises with regard to the distinction between receiving evidence and taking judicial notice of a fact when the subject of judicial notice is a matter of common knowledge with regard to which no inquiry is made by the judge. In such a case the judge is acting on his own knowledge and that is a completely different procedure from the reception of evidence. The processes begin to approximate when the judge makes inquiries before deciding to take judicial notice. If learned treatises are consulted, it is not easy to say whether evidence is being received under an exception to the rule against hearsay or whether the judge is equipping himself to take judicial notice.[3] When the certificate of a Minister is sought on the question of the sovereignty of a foreign state, Law Lords have said both that evidence is not being taken and that the best evidence is being received.[4] Speaking of the class of case in which assessors may be consulted under statutory powers, Lord Denning said:[5]

> The court must possess itself of necessary information. Some judges may have it already because of their previous experience. Others may have to acquire it for the first time, but in either case the information they glean is not evidence strictly so-called. When an assessor explains the technicalities, he does not do it on oath, nor can he be cross-examined, and no one ever called the author of a dictionary to give evidence. All that happens is that the court is equipping itself for its task by taking judicial notice of all such things as it ought to know in order to do its work properly.

The approximation of taking judicial notice to the reception of evidence is even more marked when sworn testimony is heard before judicial notice is taken. In *McQuaker v Goddard*[6] the trial judge held that, in the absence of any evidence of scienter, those in control of a zoo had no case to answer when a claim for personal injuries was made in respect of a bite from a camel because camels are mansuetae naturae. He reached this conclusion after consulting books about camels and hearing witnesses, some of whom spoke of the wild habits of camels but the more expert of whom deposed to the tameness of these animals. The judge's decision was affirmed by the Court of Appeal, Clauson LJ being careful to point out that, when hearing the witnesses, the judge had not been taking evidence in the ordinary sense. The witnesses were simply assisting him in 'forming his view as to what the ordinary course of nature in this regard in fact is, a matter of which he is supposed to have complete knowledge'.[7] It seems that, even where the processes of taking judicial notice and receiving evidence approximate most closely, they remain essentially different, firstly, because, when the judge decides to take judicial notice of a fact after hearing witnesses, he may withdraw that fact from the

---

3   The distinction can be of practical importance only in a case tried with a jury. If evidence is being taken, the judge must place it before the jury. If judicial notice is taken he can direct the jury to find the fact judicially noticed.

4   Contrast Lord Finlay and Lord Sumner in *Duff Development Co Ltd v Government of Kelantan* [1924] AC 797, at 813 and 824 respectively.

5   *Baldwin and Francis Ltd v Patent Appeal Tribunal* [1959] AC 663, at 691. In *R v HM Coroner for Surrey, ex p Wright* [1997] QB 786 it was held that an assessor sitting with a coroner could cross-examine witnesses, but could not tender evidence.

6   [1940] 1 KB 687, [1940] 1 All ER 471; cf *Turner v Coates* [1917] 1 KB 670. These cases were decided under the common law concerning liability for animals.

7   [1940] 1 KB 687, at 700. The ambiguity of this distinction between taking judicial notice and receiving evidence has been reflected in the need to give alternative bases for judgment in *Tutin v Mary Chipperfield Promotions Ltd* (1980) 130 NLJ 807.

jury although the witnesses do not speak with one voice. Secondly, the judge's decision constitutes a precedent.

If the processes of taking judicial notice and receiving evidence of a fact are essentially different, no evidence should be admissible in rebuttal of a fact which is judicially noticed. It appears that this is the case in spite of occasional remarks suggesting that taking judicial notice is merely the equivalent of prima facie proof of a fact. These remarks turn on the extreme generality of the facts of which judicial notice may be taken. Judicial notice that the seal or signature on a document is that of a particular court or official merely means that the seal or signature is recognised as similar to that of the court or official, and evidence of forgery in a particular case, though plainly admissible, does not rebut the fact of which judicial notice is taken.[8] Similarly, evidence that a particular practice was not followed on a particular occasion would not rebut the existence of the practice of which judicial notice is taken, nor, strictly speaking, would evidence of a change of practice for judicial notice is simply taken of the current practice at a particular time. There are of course many cases of judicial notice in which there can be no question of evidence in rebuttal, as when judicial notice is taken of the facts stated in the certificate of a government department.

There is something to be said for a practice under which a judge could state that he proposed to take notice of the existence of certain facts within his personal knowledge, subject to anything urged upon him to the contrary,[9] but this raises the whole question of the extent to which a judge can make use of his personal knowledge.

2. Personal knowledge[10]

The general rule is that neither a judge nor a juror may act on his personal knowledge of facts,[11] even if it is acquired only from previous cases heard in the same court.[12] Nor may the court take steps to acquire such knowledge in private, and in cases where the jury is permitted to disperse during a trial, it should be warned not to do so.[13] If the jury defies the judge's instruction not to visit the site of a crime to conduct its own observations, it may be enough to invalidate a conviction.[14] Justices may not apply scientific instruments[15] to exhibits in private,[16] nor may jurors conduct experiments in the jury room,[17] and if there is a serious possibility that they may, it has been suggested

8   *Holland v Johns* (1917) 23 CLR 149, at 154.
9   Cf *Thomas v Thomas* [1961] 1 All ER 19, [1961] 1 WLR 1, where the magistrates did not give the defendant an opportunity of urging them to take contrary action; *In the marriage of Dean* (1988) 94 FLR 32; US FRE 201(e) reading in part as follows: 'A party is entitled upon timely request to an opportunity to be heard as to the propriety of taking judicial notice and the tenor of the matter noticed'. See also Australian Law Reform Commission Research Paper 10, 'The Judge—Adducing Evidence and Judicial Notice', Part C proposal 2(b) (iii).
10   See Manchester (1979) 42 MLR 22.
11   *Palmer v Crone* [1927] 1 KB 804.
12   *Jarvis v DPP* [1996] RTR 192 (that a particular police station had only one breath-testing device).
13   *R v Oliver* [1996] 2 Cr App R 514.
14   *R v Morrison and Sutton* [1997] CLY 1331, although if a juror visits the scene of the crime in private the irregularity will not be fatal provided it is unrelated to any issue in the case: *R v Smyth* (1998) Times, 16 September.
15   Though the use of such things as magnifying glasses or rulers is not excluded: *R v Maggs* (1990) 91 Cr App Rep 243.
16   *R v Tiverton Justices, ex p Smith* [1980] RTR 280.
17   *R v Stewart and Sappleton* (1989) 89 Cr App Rep 273.

that they be warned not to do so.[18] This rule has reference to particular facts.[19] When taking judicial notice a judge frequently makes use of his general knowledge,[20] and justices can certainly make use of their knowledge of local conditions[1] though in *Bowman v DPP*[2] this was distinguished from judicial notice, and warning recommended so as to facilitate comment by an opponent, absence of which may lead to a conviction being quashed.[3] Distinction from the private reception of evidence is not always easy to draw. In *R v Field Justices, ex p White*,[4] for instance, the issue was whether cocoa must necessarily contain a quantity of foreign ingredients. This is not a matter of general notoriety or even something which can be put beyond dispute by reference to the appropriate sources of information. Nevertheless, some of the justices had acquired knowledge of the subject in the navy, and the Divisional Court did not dispute the propriety of their making use of it. Wills J, a distinguished mountaineer, said:

> In the nature of things, no one in determining a case of this kind, can discard his own particular knowledge of a subject of this kind. I might as well be asked to decide a question as to the sufficiency of an alpine rope without bringing my personal knowledge into play.

In *Reynolds v Llanelly Associated Tinplate Co* in which the Court of Appeal held that the county court judge had gone too far in making use of his personal knowledge of the prospects of employment of a workman of a particular age and skill, Lord Greene said:[5]

> The practice of county court judges of supplementing evidence by having recourse to their own local knowledge and experience has been criticised, praised as most beneficial, objected to and encouraged in different decisions.

This case was cited in *Wetherhall v Harrison*[6] in which a Divisional Court held that a distinction should be drawn between the use of their private knowledge by judges and arbitrators on the one hand and by justices and jurors[7] on the other hand. The

---

18   *R v Taka* [1992] 2 NZLR 129, at 132.
19   Though the distinction is sometimes hard to draw, and it is difficult to reconcile the result in *Jarvis* above with that in *Mullen v Hackney London Borough Council* [1997] 2 All ER 906, [1997] 1 WLR 1103 where the court was prepared to take judicial notice of the past behaviour of the defendant in relation to undertakings to the court, even though there was no evidence to that effect, and indeed some evidence to the contrary.
20   But in *Donnelly v Carmichael* 1995 JC 215 it was held improper for a judge to supplement partial evidence of a location, which should have been fully proved, with his local knowledge about it.
1   *Ingram v Percival* [1969] 1 QB 548, [1968] 3 All ER 657 (extent of tidal water); *Kent v Stamps* [1982] RTR 273 (topography of road); *Paul v DPP* (1989) 90 Cr App Rep 173 (residential character of area).
2   [1991] RTR 263.
3   As in *Norbrook Laboratories (GB) Ltd v Health and Safety Executive* (1998) Times, 23 February.
4   (1895) 64 LJMC 158; cf *R v Tager* [1944] AD 339.
5   [1948] 1 All ER 140, at 142 where a number of the relevant authorities are cited. See also *DPP v Curtis* [1993] RTR 72 (Justices not to use 'knowledge' of physical and mental human condition to determine whether refusal of breath test reasonable); *R v Wood* [1982] 2 NZLR 233 (New Zealand court not entitled to take judicial notice that 'supertoms' grafted); *Cronk v Canadian General Insurance Co* (1995) 128 DLR (4th) 147 (Canadian court not entitled to take judicial notice of time differential required to find employment at various levels).
6   [1976] QB 773, [1976] 1 All ER 241.
7   The extent to which the issue can be ventilated in relation to jurors is limited by the strict restriction on evidence of what has taken place in the jury room: Contempt of Court Act 1981, s 8; see in Australia *R v Myles and Myles* (1995) 83 ACR 519.

latter are not trained to exclude certain matters from their consideration and, in any event, as a cross-section of the community they should pool their general knowledge. The issue had been whether a motorist whose roadside breath test had proved positive had simulated a fit in order to prevent a specimen of his blood being taken. One of the justices was a doctor and he communicated his views about the possible effects of the prospect of having his blood taken on the accused to the other members of the bench. They also made use of their wartime experience of the effect of innoculations on certain people. The accused was held to have had a reasonable excuse for not providing a specimen and the Divisional Court held that the conduct of the justices had been proper for there had been no question of one of their number giving evidence to the others.[8] Similarly in *R v Blick*[9] the Court of Criminal Appeal upheld the conviction of the accused after the reception of evidence in rebuttal precipitated by a note passed to the judge by a juror, based upon the juror's personal knowledge of the locality in question.

Nor should it be forgotten that some judges, like those in the Patent Court, are selected just because they have some technical expertise, and they may probably take notice of a wider range of matters, though their not having such expertise does not mean that they can take notice that there is none.[10] All that can be said is that, within reasonable and proper limits, a judge, and, to a greater extent, a justice or juror, may make use of his special knowledge of general matters, but no formula has yet been evolved for describing those limits.[11]

3. Rationale

There are at least two reasons why we should have a doctrine of judicial notice. In the first place, it expedites the hearing of many cases. Much time would be wasted if every fact which was not admitted had to be the subject of evidence which would, in many instances, be costly and difficult to obtain. Secondly, the doctrine tends to produce uniformity of decision on matters of fact where a diversity of findings might sometimes be distinctly embarrassing. It was used to promote such consistency in the application to flick-knives of the definition of offensive weapons in *R v Simpson*.[12] It has been said that the basic essential is that the fact judicially noticed should be of a class that is so generally known as to give rise to the presumption that all persons are aware of it.[13] No doubt this is the justification for taking judicial notice in the vast majority of cases, but it is not always so. It would be idle to pretend that the particulars with regard to the behaviour of camels of which the court heard evidence in *McQuaker v Goddard* could be presumed to be generally known.[14]

---

8   Cf *Mangano v Farleigh Nettheim* (1965) 65 SRNSW 228 (juror with special knowledge should give evidence).
9   (1966) 50 Cr App Rep 280.
10   *Hauni-Werke Korber & Co KG's Application* [1982] RPC 327.
11   They are however clearly exceeded when argument is supplemented not by expert evidence, but by handing up a technical article from a journal, *Dawson v Lunn* (1984) 149 JP 491 (justices). See also *R v Wood* [1982] 2 NZLR 233 (jurors).
12   [1983] 3 All ER 789, citing this passage. Followed in relation to butterfly knives in *DPP v Hynde* [1998] 1 All ER 649, [1998] 1 WLR 1222.
13   *Holland v Jones* (1917) 23 CLR 149, at 153, per Isaacs CJ; *Auckland City Council v Hapimana* [1976] 1 NZLR 731.
14   That they require help in the act of copulation.

4. Scope

Thayer spoke of judicial notice as 'an instrument of great capacity in the hands of a competent judge ... not nearly as much used in the region of practice and evidence as it should be'.[15] This is an exaggeration for there cannot be a much greater scope for the doctrine of judicial notice than there is at present, but perhaps the cases do indicate an excessive caution on the part of the courts, although the caution is often more apparent than real.

In *Brune v Thompson*[16] the question was whether an undertaking to call evidence from London (made under the old procedure) had been satisfied by production of a document from the Tower, and the court refused to take judicial notice of the fact that the building is in London. Thayer pointed out that this was correct because part of the Tower was in Middlesex, as opposed to the County of London.[17] The courts may be thought to have been over cautious in refusing to take judicial notice of the time of sunset on a particular day as they had been referred to an almanac,[18] assuredly a source of indisputable accuracy. But allowance must be made for borderline cases in which the time of sunset in a place at some distance from any of those mentioned in the almanac is in issue. In such circumstances the safest course may be to require the evidence of an astronomer.[19] An example of caution which can be described as excessive is provided by *Deybel's* case[20] where the question was whether an arrest had been effected between Beachy Head and the North Foreland in Kent. The arrest took place eight leagues from Orford Ness in the county of Suffolk, but the court would not take judicial notice of the fact that this spot was outside the specified area because parts of Suffolk might have been in Kent. Lest it should be thought that such caution merely represents the timid approach of a past period, a further reference must be made to *Preston-Jones v Preston-Jones*.[1] In that case the only fact of which the House of Lords would take judicial notice was that the duration of the normal period of gestation is about nine months. Only Lord Morton of Henryton was prepared to follow Denning LJ in inferring from that fact that a child born to a woman 360 days after she last had intercourse with her husband could not be his child. As is so frequently the case, the problem is where to draw the line between the realm of facts which will be judicially noticed and those which must be

---

15   *Preliminary Treatise on Evidence at the Common Law* 309.

16   (1842) 2 QB 789.

17   Thayer pp 310–311. Cf the same author's explanation of *Kearney v King* (1819) 2 B & Ald 301, sometimes erroneously cited for the proposition that judicial notice will not be taken of the fact that Dublin is in Ireland, when in fact it decided only that an allegation that a bill was drawn in Ireland was not proved by showing that it was drawn in Dublin for non constat that there was not a place called Dublin outside Ireland (there are in fact at least four towns of that name in the United States). See also *Thorne v Jackson* (1846) 3 CB 661.

18   It has been held in South Africa that times of sunrise and sunset cannot be proved satisfactorily from a diary, *S v Sibuyi* 1988 (4) SA 879.

19   *Collier v Nokes* (1849) 2 Car & Kir 1012; *R v Crush* [1978] Crim LR 357; *R v Trawick* (1972) 8 CCC (2d) 471; cf *Dugas v Leclair* (1962) 32 DLR (2d) 459.

20   (1821) 4 B & Ald 243. It has even been said that the courts cannot take judicial notice of the relative distance of places (per Wilde J arg. in *Kirby v Hickson* (1850) 14 Jur 625). The question was whether Russell Square was within 20 miles of Grosvenor Square in London. A South Australian court has taken judicial notice of the fact that a suburb of Adelaide is less than 100 miles away from that city (*Blatchford v Dempsey* [1956] SASR 285). But see *R v Dodd* [1985] 2 Qd R 277 where it was held, it is submitted correctly, that even though judicial notice might be taken of geographical locations, it would not necessarily extend to the time needed to drive from one to another, since this might require evidence of likely traffic conditions at different times.

1   [1951] AC 391, [1951] 1 All ER 124 (above). See McConville (1979) 1 Liverpool LR 62, at 74.

proved by evidence. But there appears to be no more enthusiasm for a bold application of the doctrine of judicial notice now than there was in the past.

5. Tacit applications

The tacit applications of the doctrine of judicial notice are more numerous and more important than the express ones. A great deal is taken for granted when any question of relevance is considered or assumed. For example, evidence is constantly given that persons accused of burglary were found in possession of jemmies or skeleton keys, that powder puffs and pots of vaseline were found on the premises of those charged with homosexuality, and that the accused became confused when charged; these facts are relevant only provided there is a common practice to use such things in the commission of the crime, or provided that guilty people tend more than innocent ones to become confused when charged, but no one ever thinks of calling evidence on such a subject.

SECTION 2.   FORMAL ADMISSIONS

A party may admit facts for the purposes of the trial, thus saving his adversary the trouble and expense of proving them. In a civil case he may be induced to do this by the possibility that he will be made to bear the cost of proving such facts if he does not admit them. These formal admissions which cannot be contradicted by the person who makes them, and which are binding only for the purposes of the particular case in which they are made, must be distinguished from the informal admissions that are received under an exception to the rule against hearsay discussed in ch XV. Unlike formal admissions, informal admissions are an item of evidence. Their maker may endeavour to explain them away at the trial at which they are proved.

Under s 10 of the Criminal Justice Act 1967, a formal admission of any fact of which oral evidence may be given[2] may be made by or on behalf of the prosecution or defendant before or at any criminal proceedings, and may, with the leave of the court, be withdrawn.

The procedural details, with regard to formal admissions in civil and criminal cases, are beyond the scope of this book.

SECTION 3.   ESTOPPEL

When an estoppel binds a party to litigation he is prevented from placing reliance on or denying the existence of certain facts. This justifies the treatment of estoppel as an exclusionary rule of evidence. So regarded, it is less rigorous than the rules governing the exclusion of evidence on the ground of public policy because estoppels operate only if they are pleaded, but, like the exclusion of evidence on that ground, and unlike the exclusion of evidence under the rule relating to similar facts, estoppels operate without reference to the purpose for which reliance is placed on a particular fact. From the point of view of the party in whose favour they operate, estoppels can be regarded as something which renders proof of certain facts unnecessary. The only form of estoppel which needs to be discussed in a work on the law of evidence is estoppel by record.

2   So not if the evidence would be inadmissible: see *R v Coulson* [1997] Crim LR 886.

The principles underlying estoppel by record[3] are '*Interest rei publicae ut sit finis litium*'—it is for the common good that there should be an end to litigation, and '*Nemo debet bis vexari pro eadem causa*'—no one should be sued twice on the same ground. The practical consequence is that, generally speaking, the order of a court of competent jurisdiction[4] is conclusive.[5] An application may be made to have it set aside if it was obtained by fraud,[6] and fraud or collusion in the obtaining of a judgment may be proved by a stranger to the proceedings.[7] These matters belong to the law of procedure, but the conclusive effects of judgments on the whole world as well as the parties to civil litigation have some bearing on the law of evidence. After they have been considered, reference will be made to the somewhat specialised question of estoppel by record in matrimonial causes and the position in criminal cases.

It is important to stress the point that we are at present concerned with the extent to which judgments constitute an estoppel and thus prevent any evidence from being given to contradict them. There is a wholly different problem of the extent to which they can be regarded as prima facie evidence of the facts upon which they were founded (discussed in the next section of this chapter). This distinction, together with that between the effect of a judgment on parties and strangers respectively, may be illustrated by a hypothetical case in which A has obtained judgment for a thousand pounds, damages against B on account of the negligence of C, B's servant, acting in the course of his employment. If B seeks to recover this sum from C, C will be estopped from denying that a thousand pounds was the sum which B was ordered to pay A because the judgment is conclusive as to its terms, even against strangers to the proceedings in which it was pronounced, but at common law it was not even admissible as evidence that C was, in fact, negligent. If, as would hardly be likely to be the case, the question of C's negligence were to be raised again in litigation between A and B, B would be estopped from denying it because, as between parties to the proceedings in which they were obtained, judgments are conclusive so far as their grounds, as well as their terms, are concerned. It should be noted that an estoppel can be raised on a foreign judgment, whether national[8] or supranational,[9] even one itself denying fraud in obtaining a prior foreign judgment.[10] However it may sometimes be more difficult to discern the precise issues in such cases.[11] In the case of two inconsistent foreign judgments each pronounced by a court of competent jurisdiction, the earlier prevails.[12]

---

3   Spencer-Bower *Res Judicata* (2nd edn, 1969, by Sir Alexander Turner). Letters patent may constitute estoppel by record between the Crown and the Grantee (*Cropper v Smith* (1884) 26 Ch D 700), but the only estoppel of this nature which is worth any discussion in a work of this sort is estoppel by a judgment or res judicata. Estoppel by record is a misnomer because the doctrine applies to judgments which are not those of a court of record (see Lord Guest in *Carl-Zeiss Stiftung v Rayner and Keeler Ltd (No 2)* [1967] 1 AC 853, at 933, [1966] 2 All ER 536, at 564).

4   *R v Hutchings* (1881) 6 QBD 300 shows that there is no estoppel where the justices exceeded their jurisdiction by declaring that a road was a highway.

5   Even if made only because a claim has been withdrawn, rather than litigated out: see eg *Barber v Staffordshire County Council* [1996] 2 All ER 748.

6   In *R v Calcedo* [1986] VR 499 an acquittal obtained by a plea bargain from which the accused subsequently resiled failed to ground an estoppel.

7   *R v Duchess of Kingston* (1776) 20 State Tr 355.

8   *DSV Silo—und Verwaltungsgesellschaft mbH v Owners of the Sennar* [1985] 2 All ER 104, [1985] 1 WLR 490 (Dutch Court).

9   *Iberian (UK) Ltd v BPB Industries plc* [1997] ICR 164 (European Court).

10   *House of Spring Gardens Ltd v Waite* [1991] 1 QB 241, [1990] 2 All ER 53. More readily on substantive than purely procedural decisions, especially if interim *Desert Sun Loan Corpn v Hill* [1996] 2 All ER 847.

11   The matter is fully treated in textbooks on the Conflict of Laws; see, for example, Dicey and Morris *Conflict of Laws* (12th edn, 1993).

12   *Showlag v Mansour* [1995] 1 AC 431, [1994] 2 All ER 129.

A. CONCLUSIVE EFFECT OF JUDGMENTS ON THE WHOLE WORLD—JUDGMENTS IN REM

A judgment is conclusive as against all persons of the existence of the state of things which it actually effects when the existence of that state is in issue or relevant to the issue.[13] Obvious examples are provided by an action for malicious prosecution in which the record of the Criminal Court would be conclusive of the acquittal of the claimant,[14] or an action by a surety against the principal debtor in which a judgment obtained against the surety by the creditor would be conclusive of the fact that it was obtained and the amount for which it was pronounced.[15] These examples may seem somewhat trivial, but the conclusiveness of a judgment with regard to the state of things which it actually effects is of great importance if it is in rem.

A judgment in rem is:[16]

> A judgment of a court of competent jurisdiction determining the status of a person or thing, or the disposition of a thing (as distinct from a particular interest in it of a party to the litigation).

Allen v Dundas[17] is a simple illustration of the effect of such a judgment so far as the whole world is concerned. The defendant was indebted to P, and, on P's death, X obtained probate of what purported to be P's will. The defendant paid X the amount of P's debt, and, when the grant of representation was set aside in favour of the claimant because the will was a forgery, it was held that the defendant was not liable to pay the debt over again to the claimant. Everyone was bound to give credit to the probate (a judgment in rem) until it was vacated, which meant that the claimant was estopped from denying X's executorship at the material time. Other examples of judgments in rem are provided by the condemnation of a ship by a Prize Court which precludes everyone from denying the non-neutral nature of the cargo,[18] a determination that a street is a highway,[19] and a decree of nullity or divorce.[20] Just occasionally difficulty may be experienced in determining exactly what matters the judgment comprises.[1]

B. EFFECT OF JUDGMENTS ON PARTIES TO CIVIL CASES

Whether a judgment is in rem within the meaning of the above definition or in personam—a term which can be taken to comprise all judgments that are not in rem, its effect on the parties and those claiming through them is much wider than its effect in

---

13 Stephen *Digest of the Law of Evidence* (12th edn) art 41. This article was adopted by Lord Goddard CJ in *Hollington v Hewthorn & Co Ltd* [1943] 2 All ER 35, at 39.
14 *Purcell v Macnamara* (1807) 9 East 157.
15 *Re Kitchin, ex p Young* (1881) 17 Ch D 668, at 673.
16 17 *Halsbury's Laws of England* (4th edn) 194, as adopted in *Lazarus-Barlow v Regent Estates Co Ltd* [1949] 2 KB 465, at 475, [1949] 2 All ER 118, at 122, by the Master of the Rolls who added 'such a judgment is conclusive evidence for and against all persons whether parties, privies or strangers, of the matters actually decided'.
17 (1789) 3 Term Rep 125.
18 *Geyer v Aguilar* (1798) 7 Term Rep 681.
19 *Wakefield Corpn v Cooke* [1904] AC 31.
20 *Salvesen v Austrian Property Administrator* [1927] AC 641; *Callaghan v Hanson-Fox* [1992] Fam 1, sub nom *Callaghan v Andrew-Hanson* [1992] 1 All ER 56.
1   See *Neil Pearson & Co Pty Ltd v Comptroller of Customs* (1995) 127 FLR 350 (whether previous decision established that goods dutiable or that persons importing them liable to pay duty for doing so) where there is extensive discussion of the principles of estoppel generally.

litigation between strangers. This is because the rule is that parties and their privies[2] are estopped from denying not merely the state of affairs established by the judgment, that A has been adjudged liable to B in the sum of a thousand pounds, for example, or that C is divorced, but also the grounds upon which that judgment was based, that A broke a contract with B, or that C committed adultery.

1.   Cause of action estoppel[3]

Estoppel by record inter partes, or '*estoppel per rem judicatam*' as it is usually called, is of two kinds. The first, now generally coming to be known as 'cause of action estoppel', is dependent on the merger of the cause of action in the judgment. Although its bearing on the substantive law is of great importance, this kind of estoppel does not call for detailed consideration here. Once it appears that the same cause of action was held to lie or not to lie in a final judgment between the same parties, or their privies, litigating in the same capacity, there is an end of the matter: 'If one party brings an action against another for a particular cause and judgment is given on it, there is a strict rule of law that he cannot bring another action against the same party for the same cause.'[4] The effect can be draconian. Thus, in *Conquer v Boot*,[5] judgment for the claimant for damages for breach of warranty to build a house in a workmanlike manner was held to bar a claim for damages subsequently occurring in consequence of the breach of warranty.[6] Of course, this applies only to litigation arising out of the same facts.[7] If the facts change, then a judgment arising out of the earlier facts raises no estoppel.[8] There has nonetheless been a tendency to extend the idea underlying cause of action estoppel to claims which, though not the subject of formal adjudication, could have been brought forward as part of the cause of action in the proceedings which resulted in the judgment alleged to constitute an estoppel. In the frequently quoted words of Wigram VC:[9]

> where a given matter becomes the subject of litigation in, and of adjudication by, a court of competent jurisdiction, the court requires the parties to that litigation to bring forward their whole case, and will not (except under special circumstances) permit the same parties to open the same subject of litigation in

---

2   The expression is a rough equivalent for those claiming through the original party. Privies are said to be either 'in estate'—lessor and lessee or vendor and purchaser, for instance; 'in blood'—ancestor and heir; or 'in law'—testator and executor or intestate and administrator, for instance.

3   For a modern summary see Gordon (1998) NLJ, 25 September, 1394.

4   Per Lord Denning MR in *Fidelitas Shipping Co Ltd v V/O Exportchleb* [1966] 1 QB 630, at 640, [1965] 2 All ER 4, at 8. As explained by Lord Goff in *Indian Endurance* [1993] AC 410, [1993] 1 All ER 998, at 417, 1004 the doctrine of merger prevents further action when the claimant has succeeded, and it was to bolster that in cases involving foreign litigation that s 34 of the Civil Jurisdiction and Judgments Act 1982 was passed, whereas cause of action and issue estoppel operate where the claimant had failed in the earlier proceedings.

5   [1928] 2 KB 336. Applied in Australia in *Ebber v Isager* [1995] 1 Qd R 150.

6   This case was distinguished in *Purser & Co (Hillingdon) Ltd v Jackson* [1977] QB 166, [1976] 3 All ER 641 where there was a submission to arbitration and award was held to apply only to the matters covered by the submission.

7   But it does apply despite purely formal differences, eg where one action is in rem against a ship and the second is in personam against its owners, *Indian Endurance (No 2)* [1998] AC 878, [1997] 4 All ER 380.

8   *Thyssen-Bornemisza v Thyssen-Bornemisza* [1986] Fam 1, [1985] 1 All ER 328.

9   *Henderson v Henderson* (1843) 3 Hare 100, at 114.

respect of matter which might have been brought forward as part of the subject in contest, but which was not brought forward, only because they have, from negligence, inadvertence, or even accident, omitted part of their case. The plea of res judicata applies, except in special cases, not only to points upon which the court was actually required by the parties to form an opinion and pronounce a judgment, but to every point which properly belonged to the subject of litigation, and which the parties, exercising reasonable diligence, might have brought forward at the time.

This dictum has been applied in the Court of Appeal,[10] in the Privy Council,[11] and the House of Lords.[12] It has been extolled and applied in the field of personal injuries:[13]

It is a salutary rule. It avoids unnecessary proceedings involving expense to the parties, and waste of court time which could be available to others; it prevents stale claims being brought long after the event, which is the bane of this type of litigation; it enables the defendant to know the extent of his potential liability in respect of any one event; this is important for insurance companies who have to make provision for claims and it may also affect their conduct of negotiations, their defence and any question of appeal.

Obviously it is desirable to protect defendants from claimants who unnecessarily split up their claims against them;[14] but a rigid application of the words of Wigram VC could work great hardship on defendants who let judgment go against them by default, and the statement has been held to have no application to those judgments, the rules of cause of action estoppel being very narrowly applied in such cases.[15] Nor can the doctrine apply to bar subsequent litigation in respect of claims which had not been brought to maturity by the time of the original litigation,[16] even those pleaded without success as a defence, but subsequently relied upon as a counterclaim.[17] The rule has been said to be based upon public policy, and to be aimed at avoiding abuse of process,[18] so where there is no abuse of process there is no basis for applying the

---

10 *Greenhalgh v Mallard* [1947] 2 All ER 255. And applied by the Court of Appeal to industrial tribunals, *Divine-Bortey v Brent London Borough Council* [1998] ICR 886.

11 *Brisbane City Council v AG for Queensland* [1979] AC 411, [1978] 3 All ER 30.

12 *Arnold v National Westminster Bank Ltd* [1991] 2 AC 93, [1991] 3 All ER 41.

13 *Talbot v Berkshire County Council* [1994] QB 290, at 297, [1993] 4 All ER 9, at 15.

14 See *Chamberlain v Deputy Comr of Taxation* (1988) 164 CLR 502 where the High Court of Australia applied the doctrine of res judicatae rigidly to prevent recovery of the balance of tax outstanding after a claim had been understated by a factor of ten as a result of omitting a last digit of zero. The question of mistake was not raised.

15 *New Brunswick Rail Co v British and French Trust Corpn Ltd* [1939] AC 1, [1938] 4 All ER 747; *Kok Hoong v Leong Cheong Kweng Mines Ltd* [1964] AC 993, [1964] 1 All ER 300; there is no estoppel by record where an action is dismissed for want of prosecution (*Pople v Evans* [1969] 2 Ch 255, [1968] 2 All ER 743) or where proceedings are withdrawn (*Owens v Minoprio* [1942] 1 KB 193, [1942] 1 All ER 30), but there could be an estoppel by conduct in such a case. For bastardy proceedings see *Robinson v Williams* [1965] 1 QB 89, [1964] 3 All ER 12. Lord Devlin was critical of Wigram VC in *Connelly v DPP* [1964] AC 1254, at 1356 f.

16 *Duchess Theatre Co Ltd v Lord* [1993] NPC 163 where guaranties had not by then been called in; *Lordsvale Finance plc v Bank of Zambia* [1996] QB 752, [1996] 3 All ER 156 where no demand for payment had yet been made.

17 *Hoppe v Titman* [1996] 1 WLR 841 (see also NLJ (1996) 1 March p 279).

18 *Brisbane City Council v A-G for Queensland* [1979] AC 411, [1978] 3 All ER 30.

rule.[19] It has no application to causes of action available to different parties,[20] however closely connected in practice with the original litigating party.[1]

The rule has been extensively discussed in Australia where a distinction is drawn between different types of defence.[2]

2. Issue estoppel

The second kind of estoppel by record inter partes is often called 'issue estoppel'. It may be regarded as an extension of the first for, to quote Lord Denning MR: 'within one cause of action, there may be several issues raised which are necessary for the determination of the whole case. The rule then is that, once an issue has been raised and distinctly determined between the parties, then, as a general rule, neither party can be allowed to fight that issue all over again.'[3] Although Lord Denning went on to use words suggesting that the principle mentioned by Wigram VC in connection with cause of action estoppel might apply to issue estoppel, it may be better to regard the latter as restricted to issues actually determined in the former litigation for there may be many reasons why a litigant did not raise a particular issue, and it would be unjust to prevent him from raising it in later proceedings.[4] On the other hand when an issue has been determined, even by way of concession on an appeal, there is less reason to take a strict view, and every reason to uphold the estoppel.[5]

Issue estoppel is a branch of the law which has been developed recently and gradually. The basic principles were first clearly stated by Diplock LJ in *Mills v Cooper*,[6] and subsequently endorsed by the House of Lords in *Hunter v Chief Constable of*

---

19   For example where representative actions were brought for common forms of action in an effort to reduce the cost of litigation, it was thought inapplicable to prevent further litigation by those represented in respect of different forms of action arising from the same subject matter: *Barrow v Bankside Members Agency Ltd* [1996] 1 All ER 981, [1996] 1 WLR 257. It seems that a similar result would be achieved in Australia: see *Carnie v Esanda Finance Corpn* (1995) 183 CLR 398.

20   But see *Johnson v Gore Wood & Co* [1998] NPC 151, CA, discussed by Gordon (1999) NLJ, 5 March, 348, where the doctrine was applied to bar a personal claim by the principal shareholder and managing director of a company which had settled an action against the defendants.

1   *C (a minor) v Hackney London Borough Council* [1996] 1 All ER 973 (disabled and dependent child of one of the claimants in the earlier proceedings).

2   See the thorough discussion of the rule by the High Court of Australia in *Port of Melbourne Authority v Anshun Pty Ltd (No 2)* (1981) 147 CLR 589 where the defendant in negligence proceedings claimed contribution from a co-defendant, but failed to claim an indemnity, and was held to be estopped. In *Heid v Connell Investments Pty* (1987) 9 NSWLR 628 there was some suggestion that the rule applies more naturally to defendants than to claimants, not least in respect of a different cause of action; and in *Bryant v Commonwealth Bank of Australia* (1995) 130 ALR 129 it was applied in respect of counterclaims based on defences which had been withdrawn from the original action.

3   *Fidelitas Shipping Co Ltd v V/O Exportchleb* [1966] 1 QB 630, at 640, [1965] 2 All ER 4, at 8; see also the judgment of Diplock LJ in the same case and in *Thoday v Thoday* [1964] P 181, [1964] 1 All ER 341.

4   *Carl Zeiss Stiftung v Rayner and Keeler Ltd (No 2)* [1967] 1 AC 853, at 916 and 947, [1966] 2 All ER 536, at 555 and 573 per Lords Reid and Upjohn respectively. Lords Reid and Upjohn criticise the distinction taken by Diplock LJ in *Thoday v Thoday* [1964] P 181, at 198, [1964] 1 All ER 341, at 352, between issue estoppel and fact estoppel. Accordingly no reference is made to the latter in the text.

5   *Khan v Goleccha International Ltd* [1980] 2 All ER 259, at 267, [1980] 1 WLR 1482, at 1491, distinguishing *Jenkins v Robertson* (1867) LR 1 Sc & Div 117, and restricting it to cause of action estoppel proper.

6   [1967] 2 QB 459, at 468, [1967] 2 All ER 100, at 104.

West Midlands.[7] The House of Lords rejected an attempt by Lord Denning MR in the Court of Appeal to eliminate the requirements of privity and mutuality on the basis that it is unjust that a party against whom an issue has been determined after a full opportunity to contest it, should be permitted to raise precisely the same issue again in subsequent proceedings involving another. The House of Lords preferred to decide the case upon an issue upon which the Court of Appeal had been unanimous; that it amounted to an abuse of the process of the court to launch a collateral attack upon a decision of a court of competent jurisdiction, by raising an issue for a second time.[8] The House noted that this involved recognising a difference between the operation of the doctrine in England and in North America.[9] The conditions were subsequently and concisely reformulated by Lord Brandon in *DSV Silo—und Verwaltungsgesellschaft mbH v Owners of The Sennar:*[10]

> In order to create an estoppel of that kind, [issue estoppel per rem judicatam] three requirements have to be satisfied. The first requirement is that the judgment in the earlier action relied on as creating an estoppel must be (a) of a court of competent jurisdiction, (b) final and conclusive and (c) on the merits. The second requirement is that the parties (or privies) in the earlier action relied on as creating an estoppel and those in the later action in which that estoppel is raised as a bar must be the same. The third requirement is that the issue in the later action in which the estoppel is raised as a bar must be the same issue as that decided by the judgment in the earlier action.

In addition to these requirements it should be noted that in relation to issue estoppel an earlier judgment may not raise an estoppel if fresh matter has become available showing that the earlier decision was wrong.[11] It seems that for these purposes the fresh material showing the previous decision to have been wrong can consist either of new factual material conclusively showing it to be wrong, or even of a subsequent change in the interpretation of the law giving at least a very substantial chance that the earlier decision would be held to be wrong,[12] or an earlier remedy ineffective.[13]

Each of the requirements listed by Lord Brandon will be considered in turn.

(i) Previous judgment

This must first be one of a court of competent jurisdiction. This issue was analysed most clearly by Steyn J in *Speedlink Vanguard v European Gateway.*[14] In that case a

---

7   [1982] AC 529, at 541, [1981] 3 All ER 727, at 733.

8   It is likely that a court will be slow to recognise such an abuse since it cuts right across the reasoning in this area of the law. Some indication that it will be confined to blatant cases is provided by *Bragg v Oceanus Mutual* [1982] 2 Lloyd's Rep 132 where there were good reasons why the issue would be presented differently on the second occasion.

9   See eg in the United States *Bernhard v Bank of American National Trust and Savings Association* 122 P 2d 892 (1942); *Bruszewski v US* 181 F 2d 419 (1950); *Blonder-Tonque Laboratories Inc v University of Illinois* 402 US 313 (1971); and in Canada *Royal Bank of Canada v McArthur* (1985) 19 DLR (4th) 762.

10 [1985] 2 All ER 104, at 110, [1985] 1 WLR 490, at 499.

11 *Phosphate Sewage Co Ltd v Molleson* (1879) 4 App Cas 801, at 814 approved unanimously by the House of Lords in *Hunter v Chief Constable of West Midlands* [1982] AC 529, at 545.

12 *Arnold v National Westminster Bank* [1991] 2 AC 93, [1991] 3 All ER 41. See in Canada *Hockin v Bank of British Columbia* (1993) 123 DLR (4th) 538 where the earlier decision had been subsequently said to be wrong by the Supreme Court of Canada.

13 It is believed that an English court would take a similar view to that of the Scots in *Short's Trustee v Chung (No 2)* 1998 SC 105.

14 [1987] QB 206, [1986] 3 All ER 554.

collision at sea had been considered by a court of formal investigation, set up under the Merchant Shipping Act 1894. The court found negligence in the navigation of one of the ships, and it was argued that this finding estopped its being controverted in subsequent proceedings for damages in the Admiralty Court. It was held that as such a court of formal investigation acts primarily in an investigative role so far as the cause of the collision is concerned, and in an adjudicative capacity only so far as the certification of the relevant mariners is concerned, similarly it can be regarded as a court of competent jurisdiction only for its findings in the latter, and not in the former, respect. In similar vein it has been held that neither purely administrative decisions, whether of magistrates[15] or of administrative tribunals,[16] nor mere exercises of discretion.[17] can raise an estoppel. If however an inferior tribunal has an adjudicative function its decisions may ground an estoppel, provided that it is acting within such jurisdiction.[18] It should be noted further that partly inquisitorial procedure adopted in any such proceedings will not by itself prevent a court from being one of competent jurisdiction.[19]

A second condition is that the previous judgment must have been final. Matrimonial decisions apart,[20] a decision of an inferior court will operate as an estoppel in the High Court, but the decision must be one from which there could have been an appeal.[1] The mere fact that there was no appeal does not prevent a judgment from being final. A judgment can be final in this context even though made on an interlocutory application.[2] Where a decision is taken on a provisional basis it will not raise an issue estoppel if one of the parties failed to anticipate that it would be made on the basis of a full hearing. It seems that a decision about the admissibility of evidence made by the judge on a voir dire may also amount to a final decision, at least when the jury returns its verdict after considering the evidence so admitted.[3] If, on the other hand, the jury disagrees, and a re-trial is ordered, no rulings made at the first trial can raise an issue estoppel at the re-trial,[4] even on substantial issues.[5] Where a decision by a supranational body is subject to revocation by a national court it cannot raise an estoppel.[6] The third condition relating to the prior judgment is that it should have been made 'on the merits', a phrase

15   *Wiest v DPP* (1988) 81 ALR 129.
16   *R v Secretary of State for the Environment, ex p Hackney London Borough Council* [1983] 3 All ER 358, [1983] 1 WLR 524; but see in Australia *Secretary of Department of Aviation v Ansett Transport Industries Ltd* (1987) 72 ALR 188.
17   *Mullen v Conoco Ltd* [1998] QB 382.
18   *Crown Estate Comrs v Dorset County Council* [1990] Ch 297, [1990] 1 All ER 19. It is immaterial that the judgment is obtained by consent, and not yet entered into the Court's records, *Marks v National & General Insurance Co Ltd* (1993) 114 FLR 416.
19   In *DSV Silo-und Verwaltungsgesellschaft mbH v Owners of The Sennar,* above, the Dutch court's procedure in the decision creating the estoppel was partly inquisitorial.
20   And it seems matters determined on bankruptcy petitions which are liable to be set aside at a full hearing before a final order is made, *Eberhardt & Co Ltd v Mair* [1995] 3 All ER 963, [1995] 1 WLR 1180.
1   *Concha v Concha* (1886) 11 App Cas 541.
2   *Midland Bank Trust Co Ltd v Green* [1981] AC 513, [1981] 1 All ER 153. Cp in Australia *Re Martin* (1996) 141 ALR 117 where an interlocutory decision did raise an estoppel, and *Wilson v Union Insurance Co* (1992) 112 FLR 166 where it did not. See in New Zealand *Joseph Lynch Land Co Ltd v Lynch* [1995] 1 NZLR 37.
3   *Hunter v Chief Constable of West Midlands* [1982] AC 529, at 542, [1981] 3 All ER 727, at 734. But see in Canada *Duhamel v R* [1984] 2 SCR 555 where a ruling on the first voir dire in the accused's favour, crystallised by an acquittal, created no estoppel in respect of a second voir dire in respect of the same confession.
4   *Bobolas v Economist Newspaper Ltd* [1987] 3 All ER 121, [1987] 1 WLR 1101.
5   And certainly not rulings on the admissibility of evidence during a voir dire at the first aborted trial: *R v Blair* (1985) 1 NSWLR 584.
6   *Buehler AG v Chronos Richardson Ltd* [1998] 2 All ER 960 (decision of Opposition Division of the European Patent Office).

explained by Lord Diplock in *DSV Silo—und Verwaltungsgesellschaft mbH v Owners of The Sennar*:[7]

> What it means in the context of judgments delivered by courts of justice is that the court has held that it has jurisdiction to adjudicate on an issue raised in the course of action to which the particular set of facts give rise, and that its judgment on that cause of action is one that cannot be varied, re-opened or set aside by the court that delivered it or any other court of co-ordinate jurisdiction although it may be subject to appeal to a court of higher jurisdiction.

So expressed this condition seems to add little to the others,[8] though it may be the most appropriate explanation for disregarding matters pronounced upon by way of obiter dicta.[9]

(ii)   Same parties acting in the same capacity

In *Townsend v Bishop*,[10] the claimant was injured in a collision with the defendant's lorry when he was driving his father's car. The claimant's father sued for damages to the car, when the defendant's plea that it was caused by the contributory negligence of the claimant who was acting as his father's agent succeeded. It was held that the claimant was not estopped from denying his contributory negligence in an action in which he claimed damages for personal injuries. This was simply because the parties to the two actions were different. If allowance is made for the notion of privity under which one party may be estopped because the person through whom he derives his right would be estopped, the question of identity of parties is not usually likely to cause trouble;[11] but the unusual case of *Carl Zeiss Stiftung v Rayner and Keeler Ltd (No 2)*,[12] shows that the requirements of identity and privity are narrowly construed by the English courts. In a previous action brought in the West German courts it had been held that the claimants, a body known as the Council of Gera had no right to represent the Stiftung. The Stiftung then brought an action in the English courts by an English firm of solicitors, and it was held by a majority of the House of Lords that, although the solicitors were instructed by the Council of Gera, no estoppel precluded either the solicitors or the Stiftung from alleging that the action was duly authorised because the parties to the two proceedings were not identical and because there was no privity between the Council of Gera and the solicitors. Representation of a common principal does not lead of itself to privity.[13] Nor are directors, managers or employees bound by litigation against a company.[14]

---

7   [1985] 2 All ER 104, at 106, [1985] 1 WLR 490, at 494.
8   It does not, eg, exclude a consent judgment: *Palmer v Durnford Ford* [1992] QB 483, [1992] 2 All ER 122.
9   See *Penn-Texas Corpn v Murat Anstalt (No 2)* [1964] 2 QB 647, at 660, [1964] 2 All ER 594, at 597; *Green v Martin* (1986) 63 ALR 627.
10   [1939] 1 All ER 805. See also *Gleeson v J Wippel & Co Ltd* [1977] 3 All ER 54, [1977] 1 WLR 510; *Ramsay v Pigram* (1967) 118 CLR 271; *Reamsbottom v Raftery* [1991] 1 IR 531.
11   In *Bank of Montreal v Mitchell* (1997) 143 DLR (4th) 697 principals were estopped from contesting the result of claims being struck out in litigation involving their agents, which they had deliberately refused to join.
12   [1967] 1 AC 853, [1966] 2 All ER 536.
13   Lord Wilberforce, unlike the other members of the House, tended to think that the only ground on which it could be held that there was no estoppel was that the West German judgment was not final. From a realistic point of view he thought the parties were the same (the Council of Gera) and the issues raised in the causes of action were the same (passing off). There is American authority in favour of this more flexible approach.
14   *Shears v Chisholm* [1994] 2 VR 535.

In *Marginson v Blackburn Borough Council*,[15] the defendant's omnibus was involved in a collision with the claimant's car which was being driven by his wife as his agent. She was killed, the claimant sustained personal injuries and some houses were damaged as well as the omnibus. The owners of the houses recovered damages in an action brought against Mr Marginson and the borough council on the footing that each of them was vicariously liable for negligent driving. Both drivers were held to have been equally to blame, and the council failed in a claim against Mr Marginson for damages to the omnibus because Mrs Marginson and the council's driver were equally to blame. Mr Marginson subsequently claimed damages for his own injuries and also sued as his wife's personal representative under the Law Reform (Miscellaneous Provisions) Act 1934 and the Fatal Accident Acts. The Court of Appeal held that Mr Marginson's personal claim failed because he was estopped from denying the contributory negligence of his wife by the finding that she and the council's driver were equally to blame for the damage to the omnibus and, under the substantive law as it then stood, contributory negligence was a complete bar to recovery. On the other hand, it was held that Mr Marginson was not estopped from denying his wife's contributory negligence in relation to his claims as her personal representative because he made those claims in a different capacity.

(iii)   Same issues

A strict construction of the requirement concerning identity of parties and their capacity can be justified on the ground that no one ought to be wholly precluded from arguing a point by a decision taken in proceedings at which he was not represented. It is open to question whether the requirement with regard to identity of issues should be applied so strictly for it is undesirable that there should be conflicting decisions on what is in substance the same issue of fact even though there is a technical ground for treating it as different from that which was the subject of earlier litigation.

Some cases favour a narrow and some a broad approach to this question. In *Hoystead v Taxation Comr*[16] the Privy Council held that a taxing authority was estopped from making an assessment for the year 1920–21 by a previous judgment relating to the assessment for the year 1918–19. In *Society of Medical Officers of Health v Hope (Valuation Officer)*,[17] on the other hand, the House of Lords held that a local valuation officer was not estopped from assessing the Society's premises for rates by a decision on a previous year's assessment that the Society was exempt. The question in these cases was basically whether one year's assessment raises a different issue from another year's assessment although the same legal point is involved, and special rules may be applicable to tax cases.

In *Re Manley's Will Trusts (No 2)*[18] a narrow view was taken in the matter of will construction for, although the point of construction involved was the same, it was held that the issues were different as the second concerned the devolution of a different share of the testator's estate. The decision was also based on the fact that the parties to the two proceedings were different.

15   [1939] 2 KB 426, [1939] 1 All ER 273.
16   [1926] AC 155, not followed in *Mohamed Falil Abdul Carffoor (Trustees of the Abdul Caffoor Trust) v Income Tax Comr, Columbo* [1961] AC 584, [1961] 2 All ER 436.
17   [1960] AC 551, [1960] 1 All ER 317. Lord Keith of Avonholm also held (at 569) that an estoppel could not bind the rating officer as he was carrying out a statutory duty; this could hardly prevent a cause of action estoppel from arising. On the whole question of estoppel against statutes see Andrews (1966) 29 MLR 1.
18   [1976] 1 All ER 673.

The issue has arisen most often,[19] and proved most contentious, in 'running down' cases, where a collision occurs between two cars, injuring an innocent third party, most often a passenger in one of the cars. The question is whether a determination as between the responsibility of the two drivers arrived at in a first claim between two of the parties estops a contention for a different apportionment in a second claim involving the third of the parties.[20]

A narrow view of issue estoppel was taken in *Randolph v Tuck*.[1] The claimant was a passenger in a car driven by Tuck, the first defendant, and that car collided with a car driven by Steale, the third defendant, in the course of his employment with the second defendant. In an action brought by Tuck against Steale, Tuck was held solely to blame for the collision. Randolph was, however, held entitled to judgment against all three defendants and, on the claim for contribution by the second and third defendants, it was held that Tuck was not estopped from denying his sole responsibility for the damages due to the claimant. The decision proceeded primarily on the basis that Steal's breach of duty to Tuck and Tuck's contributory negligence, which were in issue in the first action were, in law, different issues from that of the responsibility of the first and third defendants as between themselves for the damages sustained by the claimant.

Since then the broad view has gained strength,[2] and has found recent expression in *Wall v Radford*.[3] This case involved a successful action by an innocent passenger against her driver as first defendant and the other culpable driver as second defendant,[4] with contribution held equal between the two defendants. The first defendant then sued the second defendant in respect of her own injuries, and the second defendant sought to estop her from claiming more than fifty per cent on the basis of the earlier finding. After examining the older, and Commonwealth, authority Popplewell J conceded that the duties to a passenger and to other road users were technically different as a matter of law, but thought them identical as a matter of fact. On the facts he found that there was no difference between the driver's negligence in respect of her own passenger, and her contributory negligence in respect of her own injuries. He encapsulated this view by remarking:[5]

> although a *separate* duty is owed to another driver from that owed to a passenger that does not mean in the instant case that the duty is in any way *different*.

Both a broad and a narrow approach is also adopted in the Australasian cases on negligence.[6] Although it must be admitted that the narrow view greatly preponderates, the attractions of the broader view are made manifest by the South Australian case of *Black v Mount and Hancock*.[7] Black and Hunt were passengers in a car driven by Hancock. That car collided with a car driven by Mount, and both Mount and Hancock

---

19 The cases down to 1957 are discussed by Street, 73 LQR 358.
20 Sometimes the issue is first litigated between the drivers directly, as in *Wood v Luscombe* [1966] 1 QB 169, [1964] 3 All ER 972; and sometimes between the innocent third party and one of the drivers, as a contribution point, as in *Bell v Holmes* [1956] 3 All ER 449, [1956] 1 WLR 1359.
1 [1962] 1 QB 175, [1961] 1 All ER 814, despite some examples of the broader view in this area such as *Marginson v Blackburn Borough Council* [1939] 2 KB 426, [1939] 1 All ER 273 and *Bell v Holmes*, above.
2 Eg *Wood v Luscombe* [1966] 1 QB 169, [1964] 3 All ER 972.
3 [1991] 2 All ER 741. See also *North West Water Ltd v Binnie & Partners* [1990] 3 All ER 547.
4 Not in fact the driver of the car collided with.
5 At 750. Original emphasis.
6 *Jackson v Goldsmith* (1950) 81 CLR 446; *Ramsay v Pigram* (1967) 118 CLR 271; *Murphy v Abi-Saab* (1995) 37 NSWLR 280; *Craddock's Transport Ltd v Stuart* [1970] NZLR 499; *Laughland v Stevenson* [1995] 2 NZLR 474; *X v Y* [1996] 2 NZLR 196.
7 [1965] SASR 167.

were held liable to Hunt for personal injuries sustained by him in consequence of the collision. As between Hancock and Mount, Hancock was held 85 per cent to blame for Hunt's injuries, Mount 15 per cent. Black then sued both drivers and was held entitled to judgment against each. It was also held that Hancock was estopped, as against Mount, from denying that he was 85 per cent to blame for the injuries sustained by Black. No doubt the duties owed by the drivers to each of the passengers were in law distinct, but the passengers were sitting in the same seat of Hancock's car, and it is difficult to dispute the force of the following remark of Chamberlain J in support of his view that there was an estoppel: 'The duties of care of each driver owed to the two passengers, the breach of those duties and the extent of their responsibility for the damage depended on precisely identical facts in each case'.[8]

Even when the issues are identical, differences in the onus of proof may sometimes prevent an estoppel from arising, so civil proceedings are not necessarily estopped by an acquittal in respect of the same matter.[9] A claimant might, however, be estopped from denying facts relied on by the defence as justification if he were to sue the Crown for damages for an assault by a police officer if those facts had been the subject of a criminal conviction for some such offence as drunkenness or using insulting words on the occasion in question.[10] In such a case the heavier burden borne by the prosecutor on a criminal charge could not possibly operate adversely to the claimant.

3. Pleading

In *Vooght v Winch*[11] it was held that the party alleging the existence of an estoppel by record must plead the former judgment and, if he fails to do so, it is merely an item of evidence in his favour which must be considered by the jury. If, notwithstanding the prior judgment or verdict, it is prepared to decide in favour of the opposite party, there is no reason why it should not do so, although it will no doubt be disposed to act as the tribunal did on the former occasion. The rules of procedure are, of course, less strict than they used to be, but it was still generally maintained under the old law that all estoppels should be specially pleaded.[12] The rule that, when a judgment was not pleaded, it might, nevertheless, be treated as evidence of the facts upon which it was based in later proceedings between the same parties is hard to reconcile on principle with the common law rule that the judgment is not admissible as evidence of these facts in proceedings between parties, or between one party to the earlier litigation and a stranger, but it will be shown in the next section that there is good reason for regarding the latter rule as the questionable one.

C. FAMILY PROCEEDINGS

The old law of divorce and separation used to lead to special problems for the law relating to estoppel.[13] The new regime instituted by the Family Law Act 1996 seems

---

8   At 170.
9   See *Halford v Brookes* [1991] 3 All ER 559, [1991] 1 WLR 428.
10   It would however be necessary for the normal conditions to be satisfied. *Hunter v Chief Constable of West Midlands* [1982] AC 529, [1981] 3 All ER 727.
11   (1819) 2 B & Ald 662. An estoppel may be pleaded in a second action although the claim form was issued before judgment in the first (*Morrison Rose & Partners v Hillman* [1961] 2 QB 266, [1961] 2 All ER 891).
12   Odgers *Principles of Pleading and Practice* (24th edn) 13.26. Estoppel does not figure among the examples of matters required by Practice Direction 16, para 10.2 to be included in the particulars of claim, but this is not, of course, decisive.
13   See previous editions of this work.

less likely to do so. However part of the difficulty with the old law lay in reconciling the inquisitorial nature of the proceedings, with the shutting out of evidence. The part now most obviously affected by such an inquisitorial approach is that relating to the care of and financial provision for children. This whole area was reviewed by Hale J in *Re B*[14] in the context of a dispute about the care of infants involving a father who had previously been adjudged guilty of sexual abuse of two other children, one of them his. The Court adopted a flexible policy towrds the reception of evidence relating to the earlier abuse. It was recognised that the old law had been reluctant to make conclusive determinations of status[15] on the basis of estoppel.[16] In family proceedings more generally important considerations militating against the application of the doctrine of estoppel include the inquisitorial nature of the proceedings, the overriding importance of the interests of the child, and the unlikelihood of the parties remaining identical and the situation static.[17] It is apparent that while the first two of these tend to suggest that the doctrine of issue estoppel should be inapplicable, the latter two suggest only that it not be applied, that is that a strict view should be taken of the conditions for its application. It should also be noted that there is in family cases, and especially those involving children, a strong argument in favour of preventing continual re-litigation and questioning of issues once decided. Resentment often smoulders, and it is very often regarded as important that a child should not be reminded of unpleasant experiences, and be forced back into contact with those who may have been responsible for them, and required to revive the memories of such incidents sufficiently graphically to be able to withstand cross-examination on points of minute detail in the course of such re-litigation.

The current attitude was anticipated by Diplock J soon after his authoritative exposition of the entire topic.[18] In *Thoday v Thoday*[19] he remarked that:

> If the court is required to exercise an inquisitorial function and may inquire into facts which the parties do not choose to prove, or would under the adversary system be prevented from proving, this is a function to which the common law concept of estoppel is alien. It may well be a rational rule to apply in the exercise of such an inquisitorial function to say that if a court having jurisdiction to do so has once inquired into the truth of a particular allegation of fact and reached a decision thereon, another court of co-ordinate jurisdiction in the exercise of its own discretion should not re-embark on the same inquiry but should accept the decision of the first court. But this is a different concept from estoppel as hitherto known in English law.

Similar views have prevailed in a number of more recent cases,[20] subject to an extension to decisions of courts of competent, but less than co-ordinate, jurisdiction.[1] The current view, as expressed by Hale J in *Re B*, is that the court has a discretion in relation to re-litigation of issues of fact which is broader than estoppel in that it applies even where parties at least are not identical, but weaker in that it can be overridden in the interests of justice. In exercising its discretion the court should consider the conflicting public policies involved in the circumstances of the case; that it should be

---

14 [1997] Fam 117, [1997] 2 All ER 29.
15 In this context a conviction for sexual abuse is akin to a status.
16 [1961] P 152, [1961] 1 All ER 236, for some qualification see Tolstoy (1968) 84 LQR 245.
17 This last factor was stressed in *B v Derbyshire County Council* [1992] 1 FLR 538.
18 In *Mills v Cooper* above p 82.
19 [1964] P 181, [1964] 1 All ER 341, at 197, 351.
20 *B v Derbyshire County Council* above, *Re L (minors) (care proceedings: issue estoppel)* [1996] 1 FCR 221, sub nom *Re S, S and A (care proceedings: issue estoppel)* [1995] 2 FLR 244.
1 *K v P (Children Act Proceedings: estoppel)* [1995] 1 FLR 248, at 253F.

more willing to allow a rehearing when the issues are central to the subsequent proceedings; and that it should consider carefully the strength of the ground for believing that a different result might be achieved by re-litigation.

D. CRIMINAL PROCEEDINGS

In criminal proceedings the rule against double jeopardy[2] plays a role roughly equivalent to that played by cause of action estoppel in civil proceedings. It accounts for some extensions of the plea of autrefois acquit resembling, but distinct from, issue estoppel which has been held by the House of Lords to be inapplicable in English criminal law.[3]

1.   Autrefois acquit[4] and autrefois convict

The most usual tests for determining the validity of the pleas in bar of autrefois acquit and autrefois convict are whether the accused had previously been acquitted or convicted of the same[5] offence; and whether he could have been convicted at the first trial of the offence with which he is charged at the second. The formulation and application of these tests has produced a great deal of case law which need not be considered here.[6]

Earlier editions of this work canvassed the questions of whether convictions adduced either to the credit of the accused under s 1(f) of the Criminal Evidence Act 1898, or on a handling charge under the provisions of s 27(3) of the Theft Act 1968, could be denied by the accused. The latter seems now to have been resolved by s 74(3) of the Police and Criminal Evidence Act 1984.[7] Under that section it is clear that no estoppel operates against the accused. He does however bear the burden of proving his innocence.

Doubt still persists as to the former question which is unaffected by s 74(3) since such a conviction might do no more than impugn the accused's credit as a witness,[8] and thus would not be relevant to 'an issue in the proceedings' as the section requires.[9] It is thus possible that the Act has created a situation in which the accused is estopped as against the Crown from asserting that his previous convictions are wrong if they are

---

2   Friedland *Double Jeopardy* (1969) Clarendon Press.
3   *DPP v Humphrys* [1977] AC 1, [1976] 2 All ER 497, but it can apply to habeas corpus proceedings despite their 'criminal' character, *R v Governor of Brixton Prison, ex p Osman* [1992] 1 All ER 108, [1991] 1 WLR 281. It is however conceivable that issue estoppel could apply in criminal proceedings in respect of attacks upon a witness's credit, for example based upon a suggestion of guilt of a crime in respect of which the accused had been acquitted, see *R v Neville* [1985] 2 Qd R 398.
4   This subject is currently under review by the Law Commission in the wake of the McPherson report into the matter of Stephen Lawrence.
5   *R v Beedie* [1997] 2 Cr App Rep 167.
6   See *Connelly v DPP* [1964] AC 1254, [1964] 2 All ER 401; and the judgments of Bray CJ and Wells J in *R v O'Loughlin, ex p Ralphs* [1971] 1 SASR 219.
7   Cmnd 4991 proposed the same result, but by different means.
8   *R v France* [1979] Crim LR 48; *R v Shepherd* (1980) 71 Cr App Rep 120; but see *R v Duncalf* [1979] 2 All ER 1116 and compare [1979] 1 WLR 918; for analysis see Pattenden [1982] Crim LR 707, and see below p 410.
9   That this phrase is designed to exclude questions going to credibility can be discerned from comparison of the terminology of cl 24 of the draft Bill annexed to the 11th Committee's Report from which this section derives and the terminology of cl 10 of that Bill which is not used in this Act.

put to him on the question of his credibility, but not if they are relevant to the issue. It can be argued in favour of this result that it is consistent with the general rule excluding rebuttal of collateral issues.[10] On the other hand it may be doubted whether in the case of the accused the distinction between credit and issue is readily separable by a jury, and if the accused can demonstrate his innocence of the crime for which he has been convicted it seems unjust to deny him the opportunity of doing so.

It should be noted that some flexibility has been introduced into this situation by the use of the concept of abuse of process to prevent the prosecution of the accused for a different and more serious offence based upon the same facts which led to an earlier conviction for a lesser.[11] This rule may be overridden but only in special circumstances related to the facts of the individual case.[12]

2.   Extensions of autrefois acquit

In *Sambasivam v Malaya Federation Public Prosecutor*[13] the appellant had been charged with two offences, carrying a firearm and being in possession of ammunition. He was acquitted of the second, but a new trial was ordered with regard to the first. At the second trial the prosecution relied upon a statement in which the appellant said that he was both carrying a firearm and in possession of ammunition. He was convicted of carrying a firearm but the Judicial Committee advised that his conviction should be quashed because the assessors had not been told that the prosecution had to accept that the part of the statement dealing with the ammunition must be regarded as untrue. Lord Macdermott said:[14]

> The effect of a verdict of acquittal pronounced by a competent court on a lawful charge and after a lawful trial is not completely stated by saying that the person acquitted cannot be tried again for the same offence. To that it must be added that the verdict is binding and conclusive in all subsequent proceedings between the parties to the adjudication, the maxim '*res judicata pro veritate accipitur*' is no less applicable to criminal than to civil proceedings. Here, the appellant having been acquitted at the first trial on the charge of having ammunition in his possession, the prosecution was bound to accept the correctness of that verdict and was precluded from taking any step to challenge it at the second trial. And the appellant was no less entitled to rely on his acquittal so far as it might be relevant in his defence.

The case fell outside the plea of autrefois acquit and there could have been no question of issue estoppel, but the knowledge that part of the accused's statement must be regarded as untrue might well have affected the assessors' attitude to the other parts. Any question that *Sambasivam* might not represent the current position in England has been resolved by the decision of the Court of Appeal in *R v Hay*.[15] There too the accused had confessed to two different crimes which were tried separately. It was held

10   Below p 297.
11   *R v Elrington* (1861) 1 B & S 688; *R v Forest of Dean Justices, ex p Farley* [1990] RTR 228.
12   *Connelly v DPP* [1964] AC 1254, [1964] 2 All ER 401; *R v Riebold* [1965] 1 All ER 653, [1965] 1 WLR 674; *R v Beedie* [1997] 2 Cr App Rep 167.
13   [1950] AC 458.
14   At 479.
15   (1983) 77 Cr App Rep 70. It has been repeatedly endorsed in New Zealand, *R v Olsen* [1982] 1 NZLR 578; *R v Davies* [1982] 1 NZLR 584; *R v Pene* [1982] 2 NZLR 652; see also *Bryant v Collector of Customs* [1984] 1 NZLR 280.

that after he had been acquitted of one of the crimes, having attacked the credibility of the confession, he was entitled to the benefit of that acquittal in his attack upon the same confession when he was subsequently tried for the other crime. It does not follow that because the accused was acquitted of earlier charges of a similar nature to that which he now faces, on the basis of evidence adduced by the same witness, that he may necessarily adduce evidence of his acquittal.[16] If the acquittal can be explained on some basis other than disbelief of the witness's evidence it is irrelevant,[17] or if it might result from an honest mistake as in a case of mis-identification.[18] In Canada the Supreme Court has applied[19] this view to a single confession to two crimes which was held inadmissible at the trial of the first which then resulted in an acquittal. The prosecution was nevertheless permitted to lead the same confession at the trial of the second, and the accused could rely on no issue estoppel, nor extension of autrefois acquit, to exclude it at the second, with the result that it was admitted, and his conviction was upheld. The only way of reconciling this result with that in *Hay*, must be that in *Duhamel* the question of the credibility of the confession was never reached at the first trial.[20]

In *G (an Infant) v Coltart*,[1] G, a domestic servant, was convicted of stealing goods from Mrs T, her mistress. Her defence was that she intended to return the goods to Mrs T. In order to rebut this the prosecution had adduced evidence that G had taken goods from Mrs Doig, a guest of Mrs T, and not returned them although told that she was going to South Africa. G had, however, been acquitted of stealing these goods at the instance of the prosecution on the mistaken assumption that the absence of Mrs Doig in South Africa was fatal to their case.[2] It was held that the conviction of stealing from Mrs T must be quashed because it was not open to the prosecution to invite the court to make an inference that G was guilty of an offence of which she had been acquitted. Like *Sambasivam v Malaya Federation Public Prosecutor, Coltart*'s case simply decided that the prosecution may not, in case B, rely on evidence which is relevant only on the assumption that the accused was guilty of the offence of which he was acquitted in case A.[3] What is alleged to have been wrongly challenged in the second case is the innocence of the accused in the first.[4] Nor is it a justification for casting such doubt that the law has changed since the earlier acquittal, and thus that it has less weight.[5]

16   See *R v Doosti* (1985) 82 Cr App Rep 181 where the evidence was of the finding of drugs in the same room by the same policeman.
17   *R v H* (1989) 90 Cr App Rep 440 where the question arose in relation to earlier proceedings for the same series of offences on some of which the accused had been acquitted and on some of which the jury had failed to agree. It is also irrelevant in the hands of the prosecution: see *R v Verney* (1993) 87 CCC (3d) 363.
18   *R v Hendrie; R v Paramasivan* (1994) Times, 27 July.
19   *Duhamel v R* [1984] 2 SCR 555.
20   In Australia in *Rogers v R* (1994) 181 CLR 251 the High Court relied upon abuse of process as a means of upholding the doctrine of *Sambasivam* rather than *Duhamel* (*Hay* was not discussed).
1   [1967] 1 QB 432, [1967] 1 All ER 271.
2   It is noteworthy that this was not a result arrived at after a trial on the merits, and in *R v M(RA)* (1994) 94 CCC (3d) 459 it was applied where the acquittal was part of a plea bargain.
3   See also *Re Mulligan, ex p Isidoro* [1979] WAR 198, where the acquittal occurred after a licence had been refused in respect of the facts constituting the offence, and the appeal against the refusal was bound to give credit for the acquittal.
4   Although the issue seems not to have been raised in these terms, in *Re H (minors) (sexual abuse: standard of proof)* [1996] AC 563, [1996] 1 All ER 1 the outcome there that the accused's previous acquittal of sexual abuse could not be relied upon to show the risk of his causing harm is consistent with the result of this rule; although the actual reasoning was not, since it seems that the facts of the crime for which the accused had been acquitted would have been admissible, if supported by other evidence, to support the contention of risk.
5   *R v N* [1998] Crim LR 886.

G (an Infant) v Coltart is to be contrasted with *R v Ollis*.[6] The accused had been charged and acquitted of obtaining a cheque by false pretences on 5 July, the alleged false pretence being that a cheque drawn by the accused and given to Ramsey would be honoured. Ollis was then charged with obtaining money by means of worthless cheques on 24 June, 26 June and 6 July respectively. He was convicted of these offences after Ramsey had given evidence concerning the incident of 5 July to the same effect as that given at the hearing which had resulted in an acquittal. The conviction was affirmed by a majority of the Court for Crown Cases Reserved. The court was unanimously of the opinion that the fact that he had been acquitted on the charge to which Ramsey deposed was immaterial, the judges differed over the question of the admissibility of the evidence under the similar fact rule. In *G v Coltart* Salmon LJ said:[7]

> But it seems to me that the distinction between that case and the present one is that in the present case the only relevance of the evidence tendered was to prove guilt in the Doig case, whereas in *R v Ollis* the prosecution were able to say; we are not alleging let alone relying on the defendant's guilt in respect of the first cheque; we are relying on the fact that the first cheque was not met only to show what the defendant's knowledge or state of mind was when he gave the other three cheques.

On the basis of the facts and judgments it is difficult to escape the conclusion that Ramsey's evidence was tendered in order to show that Ollis was acting dishonestly on 5 July in which case it went to show that he was at least guilty of an attempt to obtain by false pretences, an offence of which he was in danger of being convicted at his previous trial, but, whether or not it was applicable to the facts, the principle underlying the distinction drawn by Salmon LJ is clear enough. Evidence is no less admissible in the second case because it tends to show that the accused was guilty in the first provided that, in tendering it, the prosecution is not in effect denying the validity of the acquittal.

There could of course have been no question of a plea of autrefois acquit in *R v Ollis* because the accused was not in danger of a conviction on the Ramsey cheque. There was also no question of issue estoppel because it was impossible to say which particular issue, as distinct from the general one of his innocence had been decided in the accused's favour in the first case. Pleas of autrefois acquit and issue estoppel were likewise unavailable in *Connelly v DPP*[8] where the accused and others had previously been tried together and convicted of murder in the course of an armed robbery. Connelly had relied primarily on an alibi, but it was also submitted on his behalf that, even if he did participate in the robbery, he was not guilty of murder because he did not know that one of his co-accused was carrying a loaded gun. Connelly's conviction was quashed by the Court of Criminal Appeal on the ground of misdirection with regard to his alibi. Proceedings were then taken against him on the indictment concerning the robbery. He was convicted and his ultimate appeal to the House of Lords was unsuccessful.[9] Even if the quashing of the conviction of murder were treated as the

6   [1900] 2 QB 758; cf *R v Norton* (1910) 5 Cr App Rep 197.
7   [1967] 1 QB 432, at 440.
8   [1964] AC 1254, [1964] 2 All ER 401.
9   On the conviction for murder the robbery indictment had been marked 'not to be proceeded with without the leave of the court.' At the time there was a rule of practice against joining murder with other offences in one indictment. That rule was abolished by the House of Lords in *Connelly's* case. Today he would probably have been charged with both offences in the same indictment. Assuming that he was convicted of both, the quashing of the murder conviction for misdirection as to alibi would have entailed the quashing of the robbery conviction.

equivalent of a verdict of acquittal, there could have been no question of an extension of autrefois acquit to cover the robbery charge because there never was a question of double jeopardy. Issue estoppel was unavailable because there was no way of establishing that any separate issue had been decided in favour of Connelly either by analysing the verdict of the jury or by examining the judgment of the Court of Criminal Appeal by which that verdict was quashed.

3.   The rejection of issue estoppel in criminal cases[10]

Three of the Law Lords who heard *Connelly v DPP*[11] expressed the opinion that issue estoppel would be applicable on appropriate facts in an English criminal case. Lord Devlin thought that this would be undesirable if only because of the difficulty of ascertaining what precise issues are determined in criminal proceedings in which there are no pleadings, nothing but a general verdict of a jury and no reasoned judgments. There was the further problem of mutuality. If issue estoppel binds the Crown, it is hard to see why it should not also bind the accused. It was held that it did have this effect by Lawson J in *R v Hogan*,[12] a case in which it was possible to ascertain what issues had been determined by the jury at the first trial. Hogan had unsuccessfully relied on self-defence in answer to a charge of causing grievous bodily harm with intent to produce that result. He was then charged with murder after his victim had died. It was held that he was estopped from denying that he caused grievous bodily harm to the deceased without lawful excuse and with intent to do so. The result was that only such questions as whether the grievous bodily harm committed by Hogan had caused the deceased's death and the availability of a plea of provocation (inapplicable at the first trial) could be treated as live issues. Hogan was nonetheless acquitted.

This case was overruled by the House of Lords in *DPP v Humphrys*[13] when the House unanimously declared that issue estoppel does not apply in English criminal proceedings. Humphrys was acquitted on a charge of driving a motor vehicle on 18 July 1972 while disqualified from doing so. The only issue at the trial was whether a constable was correct in identifying him as the man he had stopped after seeing him drive a motorcycle on the day in question. Humphrys had given evidence in the course of which he denied having driven a motor vehicle at any time during 1972, and he was charged with perjury in having made this statement. Evidence tending to show that he had driven his motorcycle at various times during 1972 was tendered at the trial for perjury and, after the judge had overruled a submission that there was an issue estoppel, the same constable gave the same evidence as that which he had given on the former occasion, identifying Humphrys as the driver stopped by him on 18 July. Humphrys was convicted, his appeal to the Court of Appeal was allowed on the ground that the constable's evidence was precluded by issue estoppel, but the House of Lords restored the conviction. Differing views were expressed on the question whether a judge had power to stop proceedings for perjury based exclusively on evidence that had not been accepted at an earlier trial for another offence of which the accused was acquitted. It was also held that, even if issue estoppel does apply in English criminal law, it would

---

10   Issue estoppel remains part of the criminal law in Canada, *Gushue v R* [1980] 1 SCR 798; but not of Australia, *Rogers v R* (1994) 181 CLR 251. See also Lanham [1970] Crim LR 428, containing some criticisms of *Sambasivam v Malaya Federation Public Prosecutor* and *G (an Infant) v Coltart*; and compare Mirfield [1980] Crim LR 336 presenting a powerful case for the retention of issue estoppel in criminal proceedings.
11   [1964] AC 1254, [1964] 2 All ER 401.
12   [1974] QB 398, [1974] 2 All ER 142.
13   [1977] AC 1, [1976] 2 All ER 497.

have been inapplicable in *Humphrey*'s case because no estoppel is created by a judgment obtained by fraud (including wilfully false evidence).[14]

In view of the unanimous rejection of issue estoppel it is unlikely that much will be heard about it in relation to English criminal proceedings,[15] but the same cannot be said of the extensions of autrefois acquit which have been mentioned. They give rise to a number of problems which have, as yet, not been considered,[16] let alone solved, not the least of which is inconsistency between *Humphrys* and *Sambasivam*.[17]

SECTION 4.   JUDICIAL FINDINGS AS EVIDENCE OF THE FACTS UPON WHICH THEY WERE BASED[18]

In order to appreciate the problem with which the section is mainly concerned, it is necessary to refer to two distinctions mentioned in the previous section—the distinction between a judgment and the facts upon which it was founded and the distinction between evidence and estoppel. Every judgment is conclusive as to the state of things it actually effects. If the question whether A is a convicted criminal should be in issue, A's conviction for crime is conclusive, even if he is a stranger to the proceedings in which the issue arises. No judgment is conclusive against all the world as to the facts which must have been proved before it could be pronounced. If A has been convicted of stealing a motor car, he is not precluded from denying his guilt in an action for conversion brought against him by the owner of the car, and the insurer of the car would not be precluded from denying it was stolen should this fact be relevant in proceedings brought against him by the assured. Parties and their privies are, however, estopped from denying the facts on which a judgment was founded when the same question is raised in subsequent proceedings between them. The problem with which this section is primarily concerned is whether and to what extent a judgment can be treated as evidence of the facts upon which it was founded when the proceedings in which this question is raised are between a party and a stranger, or two strangers. If A is convicted of murder or robbery and he sues B for libel in describing him as a murderer or robber, would the conviction be admissible evidence in support of pleas of justification on B's part? If H obtains a divorce from W, involving a finding of her adultery with C, can Mrs C rely on this as evidence at the hearing of her petition for divorce alleging C's adultery with W? Before *Hollington v F Hewthorn & Co Ltd*[19] was decided there was authority for an affirmative answer to each of these questions, but the bulk of the earlier case law favoured a negative response.[20]

In *Hollington v F Hewthorn & Co Ltd*[1] the conviction of one of the defendants for careless driving was held to be inadmissible as evidence of his negligence in

14   In Canada where issue estoppel is part of the law it can be raised even in respect of a perjury charge unless the Crown produces new evidence that could not by reasonable diligence have been adduced at the first trial, *Grdic v R* [1985] 1 SCR 810. Different considerations apply if the first verdict is one of conviction despite the false statement, see *R v L(TW)* (1993) 87 CCC (3d) 143.
15   But see *R v Pervez and Khan* [1983] Crim LR 108 and the commentary thereon.
16   It is symptomatic that in *Customs and Excise Comrs v T* (1996) 162 JP 193 the Divisional Court applied *Humphrys* without any consideration of the law stemming from *Sambasivam.*
17   See Hirst [1991] Crim LR 510; and for an Australian view, Hunter (1995) 18 UNSWLR 151.
18   The common law is fully discussed in Cowen and Carter *Essays on the Law of Evidence* Essay 6 and V *Wigmore* para 1671(a).
19   [1943] KB 587, [1943] 2 All ER 35.
20   For an affirmative answer in the murder case see the judgment of Evans P in *Re Crippen's Estate* [1911] P 108, at 115; for an affirmative answer in the divorce case see *Partington v Partington and Atkinson* [1925] P 34.
1   [1943] KB 587, [1943] 2 All ER 35.

proceedings for damages on that ground against him and his employer. The main reason for the decision was that the conviction merely proved that another court, acting on evidence which was unknown to the tribunal trying the civil proceedings, was of opinion that the defendant was guilty of careless driving. The reception of the conviction as evidence of negligence would have infringed the hearsay as well as the opinion rule because it would have been treated as the equivalent of an assertion of negligence by a non-witness; but these points are indefensible technicalities.[2]

> Rationalise it how one will, the decision in this case offends one's sense of justice. The defendant driver had been found guilty of careless driving by a court of competent jurisdiction. The onus of proof of culpability in criminal cases is higher than in civil; the degree of carelessness required to sustain a conviction of careless driving is, if anything, greater than that required to sustain a civil action for negligence. Yet the fact that the defendant driver had been convicted of careless driving at the same time and place of the accident was held not to amount to even prima facie evidence of his negligent driving at that time and place.
>
> It is not easy to escape the implication in the rule in *Hollington v Hewthorn* that, in the estimation of lawyers, a conviction by a criminal court is as likely to be wrong as right.[3]

The rule in *Hollington v F Hewthorn & Co Ltd* has now been overruled so far as it governs proof of convictions and findings of adultery and paternity in civil proceedings, by the Civil Evidence Act 1968,[4] and so far as it governs proof of convictions in criminal proceedings, by the Police and Criminal Evidence Act 1984.[5] Some statutes also make specific provision for the use of convictions, or other judicial findings, as evidence of their underlying facts.[6] These provisions will be discussed in the first two parts of this section. The remaining parts will consider the status of evidence of acquittals, and of other findings.

A.   THE CIVIL EVIDENCE ACT 1968, SS 11–13[7]

1.   Previous convictions in subsequent civil proceedings

Section 11 (1) of the Civil Evidence Act 1968, provides that:

> In any civil proceedings the fact that a person has been convicted of an offence by or before any court in the United Kingdom or by a court martial there or elsewhere shall ... be admissible in evidence for the purpose of proving, where to do so is relevant to any issue in those proceedings, that he committed that offence ... but no conviction other than a subsisting one[8] shall be admissible in evidence by virtue of this section.

---

2   The *Hollington v F Hewthorn & Co Ltd* rule originated in the days when interested witnesses, parties and their spouses were incompetent in civil proceedings and may have been based on the possibility that the conviction would have been obtained by evidence which was inadmissible in the subsequent civil proceedings.

3   15th Report of the Law Reform Committee, para 3.

4   Sections 11, 13 (as amended). The rule has been retained in statutory form in Australia by s 91 Evidence Act 1995; for an example of the operation of the old rule, see *R v Burnett* (1994) 76 ACR 148.

5   Section 74.

6   See, for example, Company Directors Disqualification Act 1986, s 3.

7   The provisions with regard to previous convictions must be read subject to the Rehabilitation of Offenders Act 1974 (p 305 below).

Section 11(2) provides that:

In any civil proceedings in which by virtue of this section a person is proved to have been convicted of an offence by or before any court in the United Kingdom or by a court martial there or elsewhere (a) he shall be taken to have committed that offence unless the contrary is proved; and (b) without prejudice to the reception of any other admissible evidence for the purpose of identifying the facts upon which the conviction was based, the contents of any document which is admissible as evidence of the conviction and the contents of the information, complaint, indictment or charge sheet on which the person in question was convicted shall be admissible in evidence for that purpose.

Practice Direction 16, para 10.1 under the Civil Procedure Rules requires a party who intends to rely on s 11 to state that intention in his particulars of claim, to give details of the conviction and to indicate the issue to which it is relevant. On facts such as those of *Hollington v Hewthorn & Co Ltd* once the conviction has been proved, and the negligence in respect of which the driver was convicted identified, the court will be bound to find in favour of the claimant unless the driver or his employer disproves negligence on the balance of probabilities.[9]

Various observations have been made about the weight to be attached to the conviction in the subsequent civil proceedings in which it is proved. In *Wauchope v Mordecai*[10] the Court of Appeal did not suggest that the burden cast on the convicted defendant was a specially heavy one. In *Taylor v Taylor*,[11] on the other hand, it was said that the verdict of the jury finding the respondent to divorce proceedings guilty of incest was entitled to great weight, while Lord Denning MR and Buckley LJ took different views on this subject in *Stupple v Royal Insurance Co Ltd*.[12] In that case the claimant had been convicted of robbery from a bank which had been indemnified by the defendants. A sum of money found in the claimant's possession was paid over to the defendants under the Police (Property) Act 1897. The claimant sought this sum and the defendants counter-claimed for the balance of their indemnity. The Court of Appeal upheld the judgment for the defendants. Lord Denning said:[13]

I think that the conviction does not merely shift the burden of proof. It is a weighty piece of evidence of itself. For instance, if a man is convicted of careless driving on the evidence of a witness, but that witness dies before the civil action is heard (as in *Hollington v Hewthorn & Co Ltd*) then the conviction itself tells in the scale in the civil action. It speaks as clearly as the witness would have done, had he lived. It does not merely reverse the burden of proof. If that was all it did, the defendant might well give his own evidence, negativing want of care and say: 'I have discharged the burden. I have given my evidence and it has not been contradicted.' In answer to the defendant's evidence the plaintiff can say: 'But your evidence is contradicted by the convictions'.

---

8   See *Re Raphael, Raphael v D'Antin* [1973] 3 All ER 19, [1973] 1 WLR 998. A conviction subject to appeal is subsisting but the civil court has power to adjourn the case pending the appeal.
9   *Stupple v Royal Insurance Co Ltd* [1971] 1 QB 50, [1970] 3 All ER 230.
10   [1970] 1 All ER 417, [1970] 1 WLR 317.
11   [1970] 2 All ER 609, [1970] 1 WLR 1148.
12   [1971] 1 QB 50, [1970] 3 All ER 230. See the note by Zuckerman (1971) 87 LQR 21.
13   At 72. If available, the transcript or proof of evidence of the deceased witness in the criminal case would be admissible under the Civil Evidence Act 1968.

Buckley LJ said:[14]

> In my judgment, proof of conviction under this section gives rise to the statutory
> presumption laid down in s 11(2)(a) which, like any other presumption, will give
> way to evidence establishing the contrary on the balance of probability without
> itself affording any evidential weight to be taken into account in determining
> whether that onus has been discharged.

It is submitted that the approach of Buckley LJ is to be preferred. The assessment
of the weight of the conviction would be an impossibly difficult task. As Buckley LJ
pointed out, the propriety of the conviction is irrelevant in the civil action, the claimant
would not discharge the onus cast upon him by s 11(2)(a) by proving that every witness
who had given evidence against him at the criminal trial was guilty of perjury. He has
to adduce sufficient evidence to satisfy the civil court that he was not negligent and,
in spite of Lord Denning's suggestion to the contrary, his own testimony without more
will generally not suffice.[15] The House of Lords has affirmed that the burden is the
ordinary civil one, but nonetheless characterised as 'uphill' the task of a defendant[16]
to persuade the court of the contrary of a verdict beyond reasonable doubt.[17]

As the conviction constitutes the basic fact of a presumption, it should be capable
of supporting other evidence where support is required; it is stated by s 11(1) to be
'admissible in evidence for the purpose of proving that [the accused] committed the
offence'. In Mash v Darley[18] a Divisional Court treated the respondent's conviction of
unlawful intercourse with the applicant as corroboration of her evidence in affiliation
proceedings. The decision could hardly have stood with Hollington v Hewthorn &
Co Ltd but it may well have been resuscitated by the 1968 Act.

As long as convictions are not conclusive evidence of the guilt of the person
convicted, it is possible for him to obtain a retrial of the issues raised in the criminal
proceedings in a subsequent civil action by suing anyone implying that he was guilty
of the offence for defamation. Even if the civil action were decided in his favour, the
validity of the conviction would of course be unaffected. The Law Reform Committee
took the view that, as a matter of substantive law, no-one ought to be at risk of incurring
civil liability for stating that the claimant[19] was guilty of an offence of which he had

14   At 76. This view was followed in Wright v Wright (1971) 115 Sol Jo 173. For an argument in
      support of Lord Denning based on the statutory wording see Phipson Law of Evidence (14th
      edn).
15   Ludgate v Lovett [1969] 2 All ER 1275, [1969] 1 WLR 1016 (negligent bailee); see also 15th
      Report of the Law Reform Committee, para 25. Indeed Lord Denning's view might itself attach
      too much weight to an unsupported plea of guilty for the purposes of a substantial consequential
      civil claim: see eg Jacobsen v Suncorp Insurance & Finance (No 2) [1992] 1 Qd 385.
16   The House regarded it as difficult to conceive of a claimant seeking to rely upon his own
      conviction. It is not however impossible; for example, if a salesman is dismissed for not visiting
      his sales area, he might want to put in evidence his conviction for a motoring offence in the
      area at the relevant time in a claim for unfair dismissal. Any attempt by a claimant to do so by
      way of collateral attack upon the conviction will run the risk of being struck out as an abuse of
      the process of the court: Smith v Linskells [1996] 2 All ER 353, [1996] 1 WLR 763.
17   Hunter v Chief Constable of West Midlands [1982] AC 529, at 544, [1981] 3 All ER 727, at
      735, 736. In some cases where little or no new evidence is to be adduced leave to defend might
      be refused as an abuse of process, as in Brinks Ltd v Abu-Saleh [1995] 4 All ER 65, [1995] 1
      WLR 1478; but this is somewhat incompatible with the drafting of s 11, and the general rule
      would allow challenge by a defendant: J v Oyston [1998] 1 WLR 694; see also McCauley v
      Hope (8 December 1998, unreported) discussed by McLaren in (1999) 147 NLJ 228.
18   [1914] 1 KB 1 affirmed on other grounds [1914] 3 KB 1226.
19   The wording has been limited by s 12 of Defamation Act 1996 to actions brought by the person
      in question, so as not to impede unduly the investigation and reporting in the media of alleged
      improprieties by police or other third parties in the process of investigation and trial of a third
      party.

been convicted; and conversely, no-one ought to be entitled, without incurring civil liability, to state that the claimant was guilty of an offence of which he had been acquitted.[20] The Committee therefore recommended that, in defamation actions, where the statement complained of alleges that the claimant has been guilty of a criminal offence, proof that he has been convicted of that offence should be conclusive evidence of his guilt, and proof that he was acquitted should be conclusive evidence of his innocence. The first, but not the second, of these recommendations was accepted. Section 13(1) of the Civil Evidence Act 1968 now[1] provides that:[2]

> In an action for libel or slander in which the question whether the plaintiff did or did not commit a criminal offence is relevant to an issue arising in the action, proof that, at the time when the issue falls to be determined, he stands convicted of that offence shall be conclusive evidence that he committed that offence.

2.   Findings of adultery and paternity

Section 12(1) of the Civil Evidence Act 1968, as amended by s 29 of the Family Law Reform Act 1987, now provides that:

> In any civil proceedings—(a) the fact that a person has been found guilty of adultery in any matrimonial proceedings; and (b) the fact that a person has been found to be the father of a child in relevant proceedings before any court in England and Wales or has been adjudged to be the father of a child in affiliation proceedings before any court in the United Kingdom; shall ... be admissible in evidence for the purpose of proving, where to do so is relevant to any issue in those civil proceedings, that he committed the adultery to which the finding relates or, as the case may be, is (or was) the father of that child ... .

Section 12(2), as also so amended, now provides that:

> In any civil proceeding in which by virtue of this section a person is proved to have been found of adultery as mentioned in subsection (1)(a) above, or to have been found or adjudged to be the father of a child as mentioned in subsection 1(b) above—(a) he shall be taken to have committed the adultery to which the finding relates, or, as the case may be, to be (or have been) the father of that child, unless the contrary is proved[3] ... .

'Matrimonial proceedings' means, for the purposes of s 12(5)(a), 'Any matrimonial cause in the High Court or a county court in England or Wales, or in the High Court in Northern Ireland, any consistorial action in Scotland, or any appeal arising out of such cause or action', while 'relevant proceedings' for the purposes of s 12(2)(b) has been defined in an expanded form by s 29(4) of the Family Law Reform Act 1987 to include any public proceedings involving an adjudication of paternity.[4]

---

20   15th Report of the Law Reform Committee, paras 26–33.
1   As amended by s 12 of Defamation Act 1996.
2   On facts such as those of *Goody v Odhams Press Ltd* [1967] 1 QB 333, [1966] 3 All ER 369 in which one of those convicted of the great train robbery of 1963 claimed damages for a libel stating that he was guilty of the offence, the statement of claim, if it said no more, would be struck out.
3   On the balance of probabilities, *Sutton v Sutton* [1969] 3 All ER 1348, [1970] 1 WLR 183.
4   Section 12(5).

B.   PREVIOUS CONVICTIONS IN CRIMINAL CASES[5]

Although there was very little authority on the point, it seems that the principle of *Hollington v Hewthorn & Co Ltd* applied to criminal cases.[6] For example, the conviction of a principal was inadmissible as evidence of the commission of the main crime at the trial of an accessory,[7] and the conviction of the thief was inadmissible as evidence that the goods received were stolen at the trial of the handler.[8] One of the oldest justifications of the principle we have been considering applied in such cases for it would have been possible for the principal or thief to have been convicted on evidence which was inadmissible against the accessory or handler, such as evidence of their spouses. The matter was put beyond doubt by the enactment of s 74 of the Police and Criminal Evidence Act 1984 which largely followed the recommendation of the 11th report of the Criminal Law Revision Committee.[9] It provides that:

(1) In any proceedings the fact that a person other than the accused has been convicted[10] of an offence by or before any court in the United Kingdom or by a Service court outside the United Kingdom shall be admissible in evidence for the purpose of proving, where to do so is relevant to any issue in those proceedings, that that person committed that offence, whether or not any other evidence of his having committed that offence is given.

(2) In any proceedings in which by virtue of this section a person other than the accused is proved to have been convicted of an offence by or before any court in the United Kingdom or by a Service court outside the United Kingdom, he shall be taken to have committed that offence unless the contrary is proved.

(3) In any proceedings where evidence is admissible of the fact that the accused has committed an offence, in so far as that evidence is relevant to any matter in issue in the proceedings for a reason other than a tendency to show in the accused a disposition to commit the kind of offence with which he is charged, if the accused is proved to have been convicted of the offence:
(a) by or before any court in the United Kingdom; or
(b) by a Service court outside the United Kingdom,
he shall be taken to have committed that offence unless the contrary is proved.

The proceedings referred to are defined as criminal proceedings.[11] It was necessary to depart slightly from the form of the draft bill in the 11th Committee's report because its recommendation of statutory reform of the similar facts rule was not implemented. It was perhaps somewhat surprising to find this section enacted in its current form in view of the further failure to implement the Criminal Law Revision Committee's proposals for a radical revision of the hearsay rule in criminal cases, and especially in view of the withdrawal from the section dealing with confessions[12] of a provision making the out-of-court statements of one co-accused evidence against the other, and the disavowal

5   See Munday [1990] Crim LR 236.
6   *R v Shepherd* (1980) 71 Cr App Rep 120.
7   *R v Xaki* 1950 (4) SA 332.
8   *R v Turner* (1832) 1 Mood CC 347; *R v Lee* 1952 (2) SA 67; see also *Taylor v Wilson* (1911) 76 JP 69 and *R v Hassan* [1970] 1 QB 423, at 426.
9   Cmnd 4991.
10   It is immaterial that the conviction is based upon a plea of guilty, even one based upon hearsay, and perhaps double hearsay, *R v Pigram* [1995] Crim LR 808.
11   Section 82(1). But a similar result has been achieved in disciplinary tribunals by invocation of the rule forbidding collateral attacks upon convictions: *Re A Solicitor* (1996) Times, 18 March.
12   Section 76 of the Act as passed; the relevant provision was cl 69(5) of the Bill as introduced.

of any intention to change the law in that respect.[13] The result has been to create some judicial disquiet. It first surfaced in *R v O'Connor*[14] where the conviction of another for the very conspiracy charged against the accused was adduced in evidence. The other conspirator had first admitted conspiring with the accused, and had then pleaded guilty to that charge. No other person was alleged to have been involved. Since the other conspirator was not called to give evidence for either prosecution or defence the accused was put in the difficult position of having damning evidence against him, based upon the statements of a third party, without being able to cross-examine that third party. These are the very dangers which the hearsay rule is designed to avert. So uneasy was the court that it invoked its discretionary powers under s 78 of the Police and Criminal Evidence Act 1984 to exclude on the basis of the adverse effect of the evidence upon the fairness of the proceedings.[15] Exactly the same approach has been taken to a co-defendant's plea of guilty to a charge of gross indecency with the accused, in respect of a charge, not of conspiracy, but of gross indecency with the co-defendant.[16] If the conviction relates to a conspiracy to which there were alleged to have been other parties, the court has felt more ready to admit the evidence of the conviction.[17] There has however remained a residue of unease, and in *Robertson* itself the court urged that s 74 should be used sparingly.[18] Indeed in *R v Wardell*[19] the Court of Appeal apparently treated the admission of evidence under the provision as a matter of judicial discretion. Convictions may sometimes, on account of possible prejudice, be held in suspense pending challenge to the evidence in chief based upon them,[20] or if the nature of the defence justifies their use.[1] It has been said to be a factor in considering the application of discretion that a submission of no case is likely to succeed in relation to one of several co-accused, when the conviction is strictly relevant only to the case against that accused, but is likely to be prejudicial to those of the others.[2] The court seems most uneasy when the conviction follows a plea[3] rather than a contested trial, since there may be undisclosed reasons for pleading guilty beyond guilt itself.[4] The basic problem is that while a conviction following a contested trial may be more reliable than a simple out of court assertion to the same effect, a plea involving an assertion may easily be less reliable, just because of the possible ulterior motives. This has led in part to the development of a rather restricted view of what a conviction admitted under s 74

---

13   See the Lord Chancellor in 1262 H of L Official Report (5th series) col 705. The view that a confession is admissible *against* only the party who made it, though it may also be evidence *for* a third party, is still supported by the Law Commission in its proposals for reform of the hearsay rule in criminal cases, Law Com No 245 (Cm 3670, 1977) para 8.96.
14   (1986) 85 Cr App Rep 298.
15   *R v Mattison* [1989] NLJR 1417. In this case the court felt unable to apply the proviso so as to uphold the conviction.
16   *R v Mattison* [1989] NLJR 1417. In this case the court felt unable to apply the proviso.
17   *R v Robertson, R v Golder* [1987] QB 920, [1987] 3 All ER 231; *R v Lunnon* (1988) 88 Cr App Rep 71.
18   At 928, 237.
19   [1997] Crim LR 450. This cannot be explained as a reference to the s 78 discretion which is stated to be cumulative, and must be understood as an oblique reference to the judge's determination of relevance. Rather oddly a very similarly constituted court separated the two issues much more satisfactorily in another appeal decided on the same day: *R v Mahmood* [1997] 1 Cr App R 414.
20   *R v Rothwell* (1993) 99 Cr App R 388.
1   *R v Hillier and Farrar* (1993) 97 Cr App Rep 349.
2   *R v Skinner* [1995] Crim LR 805.
3   In *R v Marlow* [1997] Crim LR 457 the brief report even seems to go so far as to suggest that such evidence falls outside s 74 altogether, which in view of the wording of the section can only be shorthand for an indication of the way in which the judge's discretion will be most likely to be exercised.
4   *R v Lee* [1996] Crim LR 825.

can be used to prove,[5] a view which finds little support in the terminology of s 75. It has further been held that the trial judge must be meticulous in his direction to the jury of precisely what use it is permitted to make of a conviction proved under s 74.[6] Some technicality also seems to be creeping in so as to permit the use of convictions in cases other than conspiracy, provided only that the guilt of the accused does not follow as a logical necessity from the establishment of the facts underlying the admitted conviction.[7] This in turn opens a front for assault upon the relevance of a conviction showing so little.[8] Some other evidence supporting any inference of guilt which might be drawn is thus required.[9] Occasionally the relevant convictions may be of third parties, and used only to show the character of such third parties when relevant to the accused's guilt.[10]

Two more technical questions which have been resolved in these cases are that the 'matters in issue' to which reference is made extend beyond essential ingredients of the crime charged to more evidential issues,[11] and are by no means restricted to cases where the conviction relates to offences in which the accused played no part at all; and that reference to a 'conviction' applies to situations in which the third party has been found guilty, but has yet to be sentenced.[12] It is unsatisfactory to have a situation in which the instincts of the judiciary so conflict with the clear terminology of the relevant provision, that resort is made to restriction by way of technicality, and to amelioration by way of discretion. It is to be hoped that an opportunity may be taken to reconsider the anomaly between the generally restricted ambit of hearsay in criminal proceedings against the interests of the accused, and its implicit admission by way of proof of the convictions of third parties.

C. ACQUITTALS

So far as the previous acquittal of a party is concerned, it may, of course, be proved when it is a fact in issue as would be the case in an action for malicious prosecution, but there is a variety of reasons why it should not be admitted as evidence of innocence in subsequent civil proceedings. Chief amongst these is the fact that the standard of proof is different, so that an acquittal means only that the case against the accused has not been proved beyond reasonable doubt. It seems quite clear that acquittals are admissible as evidence of innocence in neither subsequent civil[13] nor criminal[14] proceedings.

---

5   See *R v Lunnon* above, and *R v Curry* [1988] Crim LR 527.
6   *R v Kempster* (1990) 90 Cr App Rep 14. In *R v Humphreys and Tully* [1993] Crim LR 288 an appeal was allowed even though the conviction did not expressly implicate the accused in the relevant conspiracy, just because the trial judge had not sufficiently balanced the possible prejudice to the accused against such relevance.
7   See *R v Bennett* (1989) 153 JP 317, [1998] Crim LR 686.
8   As in *R v Hall* [1993] Crim LR 527.
9   *R v Kempster*, above.
10   *R v Warner and Jones* (1993) 96 Cr App Rep 324.
11   *R v Robertson*, above, at 927, 236; *R v Grey* (1988) 88 Cr App Rep 375; *R v Castle* [1989] Crim LR 567; *R v Buckingham* (1994) 99 Cr App Rep 303.
12   *R v Golder*, above, at 931, 240.
13   *TD Radcliffe & Co v NFU Mutual Insurance Society* [1993] CLY 708. In Australia see *S & Y Investments (No 2) Pty Ltd v Commercial Union Assurance Co of Australia Ltd* (1986) 82 FLR 130; and in Canada, *Rizzo v Hanover Insurance Co* (1993) 103 DLR (4th) 577.
14   *Hui Chi-ming v R* [1992] 1 AC 34, [1991] 3 All ER 897. See also *R v Doosti* (1985) 82 Cr App Rep 181; *R v Henri* [1990] Crim LR 51.

D.   OTHER FINDINGS

I.   Judicial findings

Hollington v Hewthorn & Co Ltd could probably be cited as authority for the proposition that all judicial findings are inadmissible as evidence of the facts found in subsequent proceedings which are not between the same parties or their privies. From this it follows that judicial findings in cases falling outside ss 11–13 of the Civil Evidence Act 1968, are still, subject to other statutory provisions,[15] no evidence of the facts found. For example in an action for damages for negligence brought by a passenger injured in a bus accident, a finding of negligence in an earlier action brought by another passenger in respect of the same accident would be inadmissible. Nor is a finding in a civil case admissible in a subsequent criminal case.[16] It has also been held that a matter falling outside the explicit terms of s 75, even though as closely associated with a conviction as a confiscation order under the Drug Trafficking Act 1994, is not capable of proof under these provisions if tendered to show the amounts of the drug involved in the offence.[17] It was further argued in *McIlkenny v Chief Constable of West Midlands*[18] that an issue determined on the voir dire[19] remains governed by the rule in *Hollington v Hewthorn & Co*, since the relaxation in s 11 of the Civil Evidence Act 1968 is restricted to the use of convictions as evidence of the commission of the offences charged. A number of answers to this problem were propounded. Lord Denning MR was prepared to disregard *Hollington v Hewthorn & Co* as having been wrongly decided.[20] Goff LJ and the House of Lords were able to avoid a direct decision on this point. Goff LJ clearly thought the voir dire outside the provisions of the statute.[1] The view of the House of Lords is less clear. It seems to have regarded the decision on the voir dire as so vital on the facts to the ultimate decision of guilt[2] that evidence of the conviction amounted to evidence of the factual basis of that holding under the terms of s 11.[3] Sir George Baker, the only judge to have addressed the question in any detail, held that the rule in *Hollington v Hewthorn & Co* did not apply to such holdings because they were never expressly considered, and fell outside the policy of the rule, being readily identifiable issues, the subject of public reasoning by the judge, and determined according to the criminal standard of proof.[4] In a case where a confession is not the only basis upon which the accused could have been convicted, a court may have to choose between these views, and that choice will indirectly determine the question of whether findings in civil proceedings are admissible as evidence of the factual basis of the finding in subsequent civil proceedings between different parties, unless that question has by

15   See Phipson *Law of Evidence* (14th edn). S 33(2) of the Medical Act 1956 was repealed by the Medical Act 1978.
16   Or appeal, *R v D* [1996] QB 283, [1996] 1 All ER 881.
17   *R v Boam* [1998] Crim LR 205.
18   [1980] QB 283, [1980] 2 All ER 227, and on appeal as *Hunter v Chief Constable of West Midlands* [1982] AC 529, [1981] 3 All ER 727.
19   The same might apply to a factual issue decided only for the purposes of sentencing, see *Federal Police Comr v Hatfield* (1992) 59 ACR 392.
20   At 319, 237. A view shared in Western Australia, see *Mickelberg v Director of Perth Mint* [1986] WAR 365.
1   At 325, 241.
2   Cp *R v Vuckov and Romeo* (1986) 40 SASR 498 where an evidential issue arising on the voir dire was held to be sufficiently close to the issue of guilt to justify cross-examination under the local equivalent to s 1(f)(i) of the Criminal Evidence Act 1898.
3   At 542, 731, though it is also said at 543, 734 that *Hollington v Hewthorn & Co* is generally considered to have been wrongly decided which seems more consonant with Lord Denning's view.
4   At 342, 255. See also *R v Fatu* [1989] 3 NZLR 419.

then been decided directly. Evidence of findings in other jurisdictions remains subject to the rule in *Hollington v Hewthorn & Co*, and is, as such, inadmissible as evidence of the underlying facts.[5]

2. Inquisitions

As a result of Part 1 of the Civil Evidence Act 1968 hearsay can be admitted in civil proceedings only by virtue of that Act, by statute or by agreement of the parties. It has been stated that the rule in *Hollington v Hewthorn & Co* still applies to exclude from evidence the contents of reports of inspectors,[6] and of the findings of arbitrators,[7] though in appropriate cases s 9(2)(d) could be relied upon to support the evidence mentioned by Phipson's *Law of Evidence*:[8]

> Inquisitions, surveys, assessments, reports and returns are admissible, but not generally conclusive, in proof of their contents when made under public authority, and in relation to matters of public interest or concern.

This common law exception to the combined operation of the hearsay and opinion rules covers a heterogeneous mass of cases ranging from extracts from the Domesday Book to a return by a bishop to a writ from the Exchequer directing him to ascertain the vacancies and advowsons in his diocese.[9] It was once thought that the verdict of a coroner's jury could be received under this head as evidence of the cause of a death, but it is now settled that that is not the case owing partly to the essentially preliminary nature of the enquiry, and partly to the unlikelihood of the coroner's attention being drawn to some points that might be of interest in the proceedings in which it was sought to adduce his return.[10] It is, however, settled that the old inquisitions and former master's orders in lunacy are admissible, though not conclusive, evidence of the unsoundness of mind of the person to whom they refer.[11] In *Hill v Clifford*[12] the Court of Appeal adopted this analogy with regard to a finding of the General Medical Council that a dentist had been guilty of professional misconduct. The majority of the Court was prepared to treat it as evidence in subsequent proceedings for the dissolution of the dentist's partnership. *Hill v Clifford* was not cited in *Hollington v F Hewthorn & Co Ltd* but the cases can perhaps be distinguished because, being charged with the duty of inquiry, the General Medical Council fulfils a different function from that of a judge. The combined operation of the hearsay and opinion rules would appear to exclude the fact that someone got a first in law on the issue whether he was a competent academic lawyer in for example, a libel action. The absurdity of this result may lead some to doubt the soundness of the principles enunciated by Parke B in *Wright v Doe d Tatham*,[13] a

---

5   *Union Carbide Corpn v Naturin Ltd* [1987] FSR 538.
6   Peter Gibson J in *Savings and Investment Bank Ltd v Gasco Investments (Netherlands) BV* [1984] 1 All ER 296, at 303. And in New Zealand the report of a departmental inquiry, *R v Stephens* [1987] 1 NZLR 476.
7   *Land Securities plc v Westminster City Council* [1993] 4 All ER 124, [1993] 1 WLR 286.
8   Phipson (14th edn) para 31–30.
9   *Irish Society v Bishop of Derry* (1846) 12 Cl & Fin 641.
10   *Bird v Keep* [1918] 2 KB 692; *Calmenson v Merchants Warehousing Co Ltd* (1921) 90 LJPC 134; *Barnett v Cohen* [1921] 2 KB 461.
11   *Faulder v Silk* (1811) 3 Camp 126; *Harvey v R* [1901] AC 601.
12   [1907] 2 Ch 236.
13   See p 533 below.

subject to which it will be necessary to refer again in ch XIII. The occasional use of statute[14] to ensure the admissibility of certain types of finding suggests that in this area *Hollington v Hewthorn & Co Ltd* continues to hold sway.

14   See Companies Act 1985, s 441; Charities Act 1993, s 34. For a slightly different approach, in effect expanding the ambit of the Civil Evidence Act 1968, s 11, see Solicitors (Disciplinary Proceedings) Rules 1985, SI 1985/226, r 41 construed in *Re a Solicitor* [1993] QB 69, [1992] 2 All ER 335.

CHAPTER III

Burdens and proof

When an issue of fact has to be proved in a court of law it is first necessary to consider the burdens borne by the parties. The allocation of burden helps to determine which party should begin calling evidence, a procedural matter to be discussed further in ch VI, and by extension how to decide upon a submission that there is no case to answer.

The nature of a burden in the law of evidence is obscured by the use of the term in a number of different senses which are distinguished and discussed in the first section of this chapter. The two principal senses are the burden of adducing evidence and the burden of proving facts. In relation to both, questions arise as to the incidence of the burden, and the discharge of the burden. The second section considers the allocation of the burden in these two senses, at common law and under statutory provisions, and how it is affected by presumptions of the law or by agreement of the parties. The third section of the chapter, dealing with the discharge of the two burdens, is principally concerned with the extent of those burdens, and with the way in which the burden of proof has to be explained to the jury.

The key to clarity in this whole area lies in the precise definition and discrimination of the issues to be tried, and of the facts upon the determination of which they depend. Unfortunately this is hindered by the absence of formal particulars of claim or developed pre-trial proceedings in criminal cases, and more generally by the lack of an agreed terminology. These factors have contributed to some confusion in the authorities, for example on such issues of whether burdens of proof can shift, and as to the precise effect of presumptions.

SECTION I. NATURE OF THE BURDEN OF PROOF

Writing at the end of the nineteenth century, the American scholar Thayer claimed that the phrase 'burden of proof' is used in more than one sense. It is necessary to discuss only two of the three senses he mentioned because the third was said to be 'an indiscriminated use of the phrase, perhaps more common than either of the other two, in which it may mean either or both of the others.'[1]

---

1   *Preliminary Treatise on Evidence at the Common Law* 355.

Thayer's first sense of the term was:

> The peculiar duty of him who has the risk of any given proposition on which
> parties are at issue—who will lose the case if he does not make this proposition
> out, when all has been said and done.

This nearly corresponds to the persuasive burden, or burden of proof in the strict sense, which is discussed below. The correspondence is not complete because no allowance is made in the passage quoted for the fact that the burden in question is confined to particular issues.[2] Most cases involve more than one issue, and the burden of proof upon the different issues may be variously distributed between the parties—a fact which can be readily appreciated by considering a claim in contract in which the terms of the agreement are in dispute and infancy is relied upon as a defence, a claim for damages for negligence in which the defendant raises the issue of contributory negligence, or a criminal charge on which insanity is pleaded. Owing to the possible multiplicity of issues, a party may have 'the risk' of a given proposition and yet not lose the case if he fails to make the proposition out; an example would be a claim in contract in which the defendant relies upon both infancy and duress; the defendant bears the burden of proof on each of these issues, but failure on one of them does not entail the loss of the case.

Thayer's second sense of the phrase 'burden of proof' was:[3]

> The duty of going forward in argument or in producing evidence, whether at the
> beginning of a case, or at any later moment throughout the trial or discussion.

This corresponds in part to the evidential burden discussed below, but it is a much broader concept because, in addition to embracing argument as well as the adduction of evidence, it covers not merely the obligation placed on a party by the law to be able to point to the existence of sufficient evidence to raise an issue before the tribunal of fact, but also the tactical obligation to lead counter-evidence placed upon a party against whom evidence has been adduced. To anticipate, Thayer's second sense of the term 'burden of proof' conflates the evidential burden with what is sometimes called a 'provisional' or 'tactical' burden.

Just because Thayer failed to distinguish between the strict senses of the legal and evidential burden as described below, and the burdens which arise as between different issues, or as a matter of tactics in the course of a trial, his successors, both in extra-judicial writings,[4] and in judicial opinions,[5] have had to refine his terminology. These

---

2   Though surprisingly little attention is bestowed upon the critical matter of the precise discrimination of issues.

3   *Preliminary Treatise on Evidence at the Common Law* 355.

4   In addition to Thayer ch 9, reference may be made to IX *Wigmore* paras 2485–9; Stone (1944) 60 LQR 262, a commentary on *Joseph Constantine SS Line Ltd v Imperial Smelting Corpn Ltd* [1942] AC 154, [1941] 2 All ER 165; Denning (1945) 61 LQR 379; Bridge (1949) 12 MLR 273, a reply to Denning; Williams *Criminal Law, The General Part* (2nd edn 1961) ch 23; Adams in Clark (ed) *Essays on Criminal Law in New Zealand* (1971); Williams in Waller and Campbell (eds) *Well and Truly Tried* (1982).

5   Denning frequently used his own terminology, eg *Bratty v A-G for Northern Ireland* [1963] AC 386, at 413, [1961] 3 All ER 523, at 535. Williams's distinction between the persuasive and evidential burdens was adopted in the judgment of the Court of Criminal Appeal delivered by Edmund Davies J in *R v Gill* [1963] 2 All ER 688, [1963] 1 WLR 841, and in *Henderson v Jenkins & Sons and Evans* [1970] AC 282, at 301, [1969] 3 All ER 756, at 766, Lord Pearson distinguished the 'evidential burden of proof' from the 'formal, or legal or technical burden of proof'; but he spoke of the evidential burden in terms of Lord Denning's provisional burden and doubted the propriety of calling it a burden of proof. The terminology of probative and

refinements have not been uniform, and have contributed substantially to the confusion over the question of whether burdens can shift, exacerbated by parallel problems over the role and terminology of presumptions.

This section will first consider burdens in the strict sense, the other candidates for that terminology will then be considered in connection with the whole question of the shifting of burdens in the third part of this section.

A.   THE TWO PRINCIPAL SENSES OF BURDEN

I.   Persuasive burden

The persuasive burden is the obligation of a party to meet the requirement that a fact in issue be proved (or disproved) either by a preponderance of the evidence or beyond reasonable doubt as the case may be. The words in brackets are intended to cover the case in which a party has to negate a particular fact as the prosecutrix has to negate consent on a charge of rape. The words are also apt to cover a case in which a party has to negate a particular fact if his opponent adduces sufficient evidence of its existence. An example would be provided by a murder trial at which self-defence is pleaded; if there is sufficient evidence to raise a reasonable doubt in the minds of a reasonable jury, it is incumbent on the prosecution to prove beyond reasonable doubt that the accused was not acting in self-defence.

Wigmore spoke of the 'risk of non-persuasion'. Williams subsequently[6] sharpened this to the 'persuasive burden' by way of contrast to the 'the evidential burden'. This terminology is clear, and it is submitted, clearly preferable to such alternatives as the 'legal burden' employed by Lord Denning and is justified by the fact that its incidence is determined by the substantive law. Other English writers have referred to it as 'the burden of proof on the pleadings';[7] or 'the fixed burden of proof'.[8] Both burdens are 'legal' in the sense that they operate as a matter of legal rule; the particulars of claim do not always indicate which party bears the burden, and the 'evidential burden' also has claims to be described as 'fixed'. Nor is it satisfactory that some recent judgments in which the distinction between the principal burdens is mentioned simply refer to this one as the 'burden of proof'[9] or the 'probative burden',[10] even though such a course may be justified by the fact that the discharge of the other principal burden, the evidential burden, proves nothing.[11]

In a civil case where at the end of the day the evidence upon an issue is found to be too evenly balanced to determine the matter one way or the other, then the issue must be determined by the incidence of the persuasive burden, as the House of Lords has recognised:[12]

---

evidential burden, having been used in the Court of Appeal by Bridge J, was repeated without question by the House of Lords in *DPP v Morgan* [1976] AC 182, [1975] 2 All ER 347. The distinction between the two principal burdens is frequently mentioned by Australian, Canadian and American judges.

6   *Criminal Law (The General Part)* (1st edn 1953) ch 23.
7   Phipson *Law of Evidence* (14th ed, 1990).
8   Bridge (1949) 12 MLR 274.
9   Devlin J in *Hill v Baxter* [1958] 1 QB 277, at 284; *Bratty v A-G for Northern Ireland* [1963] AC 386, at 407, 414, [1961] 3 All ER 523, at 530.
10   *DPP v Morgan* [1976] AC 182, [1975] 2 All ER 347; *R v Bennett* (1978) 68 Cr App Rep 168.
11   *Jayasena v R* [1970] 1 All ER 219.
12   *Rhesa Shipping Co SA v Edmunds* [1985] 2 All ER 712, at 718, [1985] 1 WLR 948, at 955, 956; see also *Pickford v Imperial Chemical Industries plc* [1998] 3 All ER 462 at 472, [1998] 1 WLR 1189, 1200A.

No judge likes to decide cases on burden of proof if he can legitimately avoid having to do so. There are cases, however, on which owing to the unsatisfactory state of the evidence, or otherwise, deciding on the burden of proof is the only just cause for him to take.

In criminal cases also it can happen that where the evidence is equivocal between two co-accused, each of whom alleges that the crime was committed by the other, then both must be acquitted,[13] even though it is abundantly clear that the crime must have been committed by one or the other of them.[14]

2. Evidential burden

The evidential burden is the obligation to show, if called upon to do so, that there is sufficient evidence to raise an issue as to the existence or non-existence of a fact in issue, due regard being had to the standard of proof demanded of the party under such obligation. The concluding clause is designed to meet the point that the amount of evidence required to induce a judge to leave an issue to the jury varies according to whether the case is civil or criminal, and whether the party bearing the burden is claimant, prosecutor, defendant or accused.

The phrase 'evidential burden' is employed by Bridge and Williams (while Phipson spoke with equal accuracy of the 'burden of adducing evidence'[15]) a phrase which is coming to be increasingly used by the English judges.[16] Wigmore described it as the duty 'of passing the judge', and there is no doubt that the difference between the two principal burdens is best approached by considering the position of a claimant or prosecutor with regard to such issues which are about to be tried with a jury as defamation, or the doing of a criminal act by the accused. He has two hurdles to surmount. First, he must produce a sufficient quantity of evidence to prevent the judge from withdrawing the issue from the jury, and secondly he must convince that body. If he surmounts the first, he may yet fail at the second. This may be because the jury do not believe his witnesses,[17] or will not draw the necessary inferences, or else because of the doubt raised by the counter-evidence. To quote Wigmore:[18]

> The important practical distinction between these two senses of 'burden of proof' is this: the risk of non-persuasion operates when the case has come into the hands of the jury, while the duty of producing evidence implies a liability to a ruling by the judge disposing of the issue without leaving the issue open to the jury's deliberations.

Two further points must be stressed in connection with the definition of the evidential burden. In the first place, it caters for the abnormal situation where the party who bears the persuasive burden of proof does not also bear the evidential burden, as well as for the normal situation where they are each borne by the same person in the first instance. To vary an illustration which has already been given with reference to

---

13 In the absence of evidence of complicity between them.
14 *R v Aston; R v Mason* (1991) 94 Cr App Rep 180; see further below p 139.
15 Phipson *Law of Evidence* (14th edn).
16 LEXIS reveals that the phrase has been used in more than three hundred cases since 1945.
17 It is not necessarily sufficient to adduce uncontradicted evidence, if it is inherently implausible, and in such a case where the evidential burden is borne by the defence there is no further shifting of burden to the prosecution, *Godwin v DPP* (1993) 96 Cr App Rep 244.
18 IX *Wigmore* 284.

self-defence, on a prosecution for murder, for example, the Crown has the persuasive burden of negativing provocation, but questions of provocation do not have to be considered by the jury unless there is evidence on the subject, and it is up to the accused to produce this evidence, although he has to raise only a reasonable doubt in the minds of the jury as to whether his conduct was provoked or unprovoked.[19] Second, it must not be supposed that the production of evidence always involves the giving of testimony. This will be necessary in the vast majority of cases in which an evidential burden has to be discharged, but there are rare instances in which the evidence called on the other side is sufficiently equivocal to have this effect.[20] On a prosecution for murder, the Crown witnesses might say enough in-chief about the provocation to make the judge feel obliged to raise the question in his summing up, although the matter will usually be brought before the court in consequence of the cross-examination of the Crown witnesses, reinforced by the accused's evidence-in-chief. It is also possible that evidence may be sufficient to raise a defence which the accused does not wish to advance. In such a case it should not be left to the jury.[1]

3.   Illustrations of confusion

Two major sources of confusion in this part of the law are: first, failure to agree upon the discrimination of separate issues to which the rules are to apply; and second, failure to distinguish explicitly between the legal and evidential burden. One example will be given of each.

In *DPP v Morgan*[2] the accused were charged with rape. Their defence was that the victim consented, or at least that they believed her to be consenting. The trial judge directed the jury that it was for the prosecution to show that the act took place and to negative consent, but, in effect, that it was then for the accused to adduce some evidence to show that his belief in the victim's consent was reasonable. This view was upheld by the Court of Appeal where Bridge J distinguished between cases where the definition of the offence specified a particular mental state in which case the prosecution bore both legal and evidential burdens of showing it, and cases where there was no such definition in which case the issue of reasonable belief arose as a separate issue, the evidential burden of establishing which was on the accused. The House of Lords accepted Bridge J's analysis, but allowed the appeal because, by a majority, it took the view that in rape there was only one issue as to the accused's mental state, and as to that the prosecution bore both burdens. The whole difficulty arose simply because it was uncertain whether in relation to the accused's mens rea there was one issue, or two.

In *Woolmington v DPP*[3] the accused was charged with murdering his wife from whom he was separated, and he gave evidence to the effect that he had shot and killed her accidentally while endeavouring to induce her to return to live with him by threatening to shoot himself. Swift J's summing up to the jury contained the following passage:

---

19   *Mancini v DPP* [1942] AC 1, [1941] 3 All ER 272. See also *R v Lobell* [1957] 1 QB 547, [1957] 1 All ER 734 applying the same doctrine to self-defence; *Bullard v R* [1957] AC 635, at 642; *Rolle v R* [1965] 3 All ER 582, [1965] 1 WLR 1341.
20   See *Palmer v R* [1971] AC 814, at 823, [1971] 1 All ER 1077, at 1088.
1   *R v Campbell* (1986) 84 Cr App Rep 255.
2   [1976] AC 182, [1975] 2 All ER 347. For a similar confusion in relation to causing death see *R v Mellor* [1996] 2 Cr App Rep 245.
3   [1935] AC 462. For some amplification of the facts given in the official Report see (1992) 142 NLJ 330. See also in Australia *He Kaw Teh v R* (1985) 157 CLR 523.

If the Crown satisfy you that this woman died at the prisoner's hands, then he has to show that there are circumstances to be found in the evidence which has been given from the witness box in this case which alleviate the crime, so that it is only manslaughter, or which excuse the homicide altogether by showing that it was a pure accident.

Woolmington was convicted, but his appeal was allowed when it reached the House of Lords because the jury had been misdirected.

The actual decision turned on the point that Swift J's direction suggested that, the killing having been admitted, the persuasive burden of disproving malice aforethought shifted to the accused, but Lord Sankey's speech in the House of Lords also shows that, even in cases in which the defence consists of something other than a denial of an essential element of the prosecution's case, a plea of provocation or self-defence for instance, the accused does not, as was formerly believed, bear a legal as well as an evidential burden. The speech can be regarded either as marking a change in the law[4] or as an insistence on the distinction, ignored by the old authorities, between the persuasive and evidential burdens.[5] Whichever be the correct view, there is no doubt that many appeals have been decided on the point that the judge wrongly instructed the jury that the accused bore the burden of proof on a particular issue whereas all that was borne by him was an evidential burden, a matter with which the jury has no concern.[6]

B.   OTHER SENSES AND SHIFTING OF BURDEN

The definitions of the two principal senses of burden adopted above in this book render it difficult to speak meaningfully of the shifting of either of them. The evidential burden has been defined as the obligation to show, if called upon to do so, that there is sufficient evidence to raise an issue as to the existence or non-existence of a fact in issue. The persuasive, 'legal', or 'probative' burden has been defined as the obligation of a party to meet the requirement of a rule of law that a fact in issue must be proved or disproved. The question whether there is sufficient evidence to raise the issue of the existence of a particular fact can be answered only after both parties have called their evidence and, when there is a jury, the answer must be given by it after instruction from the judge. Writing about a criminal trial by jury Williams has said:[7]

[T]he evidential burden governs what the judge does in leaving the question to the jury or withdrawing it from them, the persuasive burden governs what he says in directing the jury how to reach their verdict.

The concept of the evidential burden is the product of trial by jury and the possibility of withdrawing an issue from that body. Unlike the concept of the persuasive burden it is not a logical necessity of litigation about questions of fact; 'If it were to be said of any issue, that it was not covered by an evidential burden, the only effect would be to remove the judge's filtering power in respect of that issue.'[8] It is accordingly difficult

---

4   *Jayasena v R* [1970] AC 618, at 625. See also *Vasquez v R* [1994] 3 All ER 674, at 679, [1994] 1 WLR 1304, at 1310.
5   Adams in Clark (ed) *Essays in New Zealand Criminal Law* 70–1.
6   *Chan Kau v R* [1955] AC 206, [1955] 1 All ER 266; *R v Lobell* [1957] 1 QB 547, [1957] 1 All ER 734; *R v Abraham* [1973] 3 All ER 694, [1973] 1 WLR 1270.
7   (1977) 127 NLJ 156.
8   (1977) 127 NLJ 156, at 158.

not to sympathise with Browne-Wilkinson V-C who preferred the expression not to be used in civil proceedings since it was so apt to be applied to the provisional burden as defined and described below.[9]

It is true that, when dissenting in *DPP v Morgan*,[10] Lord Simon of Glaisdale spoke of the shifting of the evidential burden 'backwards and forwards in the course of a trial', but he was attempting to justify the view of the Court of Appeal that, as a matter of law, someone charged with rape bears the evidential burden on the issue of his mistaken belief that the woman was consenting to intercourse.[11] The decision turned on the substantive law, but, so far as the evidential burden was concerned, the majority of the House of Lords appears to have accepted the argument of counsel for the appellant summarised as follows by Lord Cross of Chelsea:[12]

> If [the Crown] adduces evidence to show that intercourse took place and that the woman did not consent to it then in the absence of any evidence from the defendant the jury will certainly draw the inference that he was aware that she was not consenting. So as a practical matter he is bound—if he wishes to raise the point—to give evidence to the effect that he believed that she was consenting and as to his reason for that belief; and the weaker those reasons are the more likely the jury is to conclude that he had no such belief. But the issue as to the accused's belief in the woman's consent is before the jury from the beginning,[13] and is an issue in respect of which the evidential burden is on the Crown from the first to last. There is never any question of any evidential burden with regard to it being on the accused or of the judge withdrawing it from the jury.

It remains to be seen what judges, and others, really have in mind when they refer to the shifting of a burden.[14] Three possibilities are worthy of consideration. The first is that the concept of a burden has been attenuated to refer only to the provisional or tactical desirability of adducing evidence in order to avoid an adverse decision of the issue by the trier of fact. The second is that the concept of a burden has been expanded to apply outside the confines of a single issue, and to refer instead to the fluctuation of fortunes in a multiple issue case, considering the cumulative effect of the sequential resolution of each successive issue. The third uses burden in the sense so far discussed, but directs attention to cases where the allocation of one of the burdens is made conditional upon the proof of some other fact. The first two of these are considered in turn here, and the third in the next section in relation to the allocation of the burden of proof.

---

9   *Brady v Group Lotus Car Companies plc* [1987] 2 All ER 674, at 686, 687, approved by the Court of Appeal [1987] 3 All ER 1050, at 1056.

10 [1976] AC 182, at 217. See also *Dunlop Holding Ltd's Application* [1979] RPC 523, where Buckley and Bridge LJJ take a similar view, though Waller LJ analyses the situation entirely in terms of the distribution of persuasive and evidential burdens.

11 Even if that were law it would not have justified the trial judge's action in leaving to the jury the question whether the accused had reasonable grounds for their belief, although it might have justified the withdrawal of the issue of the accused's belief from the jury on the ground of insufficiency of supporting evidence.

12 [1976] AC 182, at 200. S 1(2) of the Sexual Offences (Amendment) Act 1976 declares that the presence or absence of reasonable grounds for an alleged belief in the victim's consent is a factor to be taken into account by the jury in conjunction with any other relevant evidence when considering whether the accused had such a belief.

13 The definition of rape then being unlawful sexual intercourse with a non-consenting woman knowing that she does not consent or being reckless as to whether she does so.

14 For a judge's own explanation see Mustill LJ in *Brady v Group Lotus Car Companies plc* [1987] 3 All ER 1050, at 1058.

I. The provisional burden

A provisional burden is one which is borne by the opponent of an issue after the proponent has discharged his evidential burden. The opponent must, in the words of Lord Denning, 'call evidence or take the consequences which may not necessarily be fatal'.[15] An example is provided by any criminal case in which the prosecution relies on the actus reus as evidence of mens rea. By not calling evidence on the subject the accused runs the risk of an adverse finding with regard to his mental state if the jury accepts the Crown's version of his external conduct. The degree of risk run by an opponent who does not adduce evidence on a particular issue varies from case to case. In civil proceedings the proponent's evidence may be so weighty that a verdict or decision in his favour will be demanded by common sense and a judge would be justified in directing a jury or himself accordingly.[16] In criminal cases tried with a jury[17] the situation is complicated by the rule that there cannot be a directed verdict of guilty, but judges sometimes allude to a shifting of the burden of proof on account of the strength of the evidence adduced by the accused on issues as to which he bears the evidential and persuasive burdens.[18]

Lord Denning even speaks of the provisional burden shifting to and fro in the course of a case.[19] No doubt judges often have something of this sort in mind when they refer to a shifting of the burden of proof, but the concept of a provisional burden (sometimes called a 'tactical burden') is devoid of legal significance because there is no means of telling when it has been brought into existence or when it has been discharged. It is evidential in the sense that it entails the calling of evidence but, by definition, it is non-existent at the beginning of a case when judicial ruling with regard to burdens may be obtained. Such a ruling may likewise be obtained at the end of a proponent's case if the judge is required to decide whether enough evidence to raise a particular issue has been adduced, but, in the first instance at any rate, a provisional burden is borne by the opponent. There can be no further ruling on burdens until the end of the case when the persuasive burden is the all important matter.

If a fact in issue may be inferred from the proof of another particular fact in a commonly recurring situation, the language of presumption is often employed. The fact which is proved can be referred to as the basic fact, and the fact inferred as the presumed fact. Thus Lord Denning refers to such a presumption as casting a provisional burden upon the opponent of the presumed fact. In other words the party proving the basic fact is likely to win on the issue to which the presumed fact relates in the absence of evidence to the contrary adduced by the other. According to older classifications, presumptions having this limited effect are described as 'presumptions of fact', such as the presumption of continuance,[20] the presumption of guilty knowledge arising from the possession of recently stolen goods[1] and the presumption of unseaworthiness in the case of a vessel which founders shortly after leaving port.[2] These are all inferences

15 (1945) 61 LQR 380.
16 *Ajum Goolam Hosen & Co v Union Marine Insurance Co* [1901] AC 362; cf *Pickup v Thames and Mersey Marine Insurance Co Ltd* (1878) 3 QBD 594.
17 The Queen's Bench Divisional Court frequently remits a case to magistrates on an appeal by the prosecutor on the ground that the weight of the evidence adduced by him was such that there was a case to answer.
18 *R v Matheson* [1958] 2 All ER 87, [1958] 1 WLR 474.
19 In *Amoco Oil Co v Parpada Shipping Co Ltd* [1989] 1 Lloyd's Rep 369 Lord Donaldson MR seems to have had such a burden in mind though he confusingly refers to it as an evidential burden.
20 See p 25, above.
1   See p 38, above.
2   *Ajum Goolam Hossen & Co v Union Marine Insurance Co* [1901] AC 362.

which may be drawn by the tribunal of fact. It is not obliged to draw them as a matter of law even if there is no further evidence, although there may be occasions on which a civil jury should be directed that they ought to draw the inference as reasonable men, and, in civil cases, a verdict, or even the decision of a judge sitting alone, might be set aside if the inference was not drawn.

A further example is the presumption of intention in its modern form. *DPP v Smith*[3] decided that, in certain circumstances, there was a conclusive presumption that normal people intend the natural consequences of their acts, and it is possible to point to many statements made before *Woolmington v DPP*[4] to the effect that the presumption applies until the contrary is proved. But s 8 of the Criminal Justice Act 1967 provides that:

A court or jury, in determining whether a person has committed an offence,–
(a) shall not be bound in law to infer that he intended or foresaw a result of his actions by reason only of its being a natural and probable consequence of those actions;
(b) shall decide whether he did intend or foresee that result by reference to all the evidence, drawing such inferences from the evidence as appear proper in the circumstances.

What used to be a presumption of law in criminal cases has thus become a presumption of fact. In the words of Lord Sankey in *Woolmington*'s case: '[I]f it is proved that the conscious act of the prisoner killed a man and nothing else appears in the case, there is evidence upon which the jury *may* not *must* find him guilty of murder.'[5] Although there are many statements in civil proceedings suggesting that the presumption of intention is one of law, it is best regarded as one of fact. As in the case of the presumption of seaworthiness, the tribunal of fact may be virtually obliged to find in favour of the presumption when there is nothing to suggest a contrary conclusion.

2.   The ultimate burden

The 'ultimate burden' as used by Lord Denning is a phrase appropriate only to a case involving more than one issue, but it is often used by other judges as a synonym for the legal or persuasive burden. To quote Lord Denning:[6]

Where the ultimate decision of a case depends on the determination of a number of separate issues, the burden on the ultimate issue needs to be distinguished from the burden on the separate issues.

The ultimate burden is thus the burden borne by the party against whom the persuasive burden on a particular issue has been discharged. Lord Denning illustrates his meaning by reference to a claim brought by the holder against the acceptor of a bill of exchange. The ultimate decision depends on whether the claimant is a holder in due course. He might begin by proving that he was the holder of a bill signed by the defendant as acceptor. He will succeed on his claim unless the defendant makes good some such defence as fraud in the negotiation of the bill. In his turn the defendant will

3   [1961] AC 290, [1960] 3 All ER 161.
4   [1935] AC 462.
5   [1935] AC 462, at 481, emphasis supplied. The same is true in the United States, see *Yates v Evatt* 500 US 391 (1991).
6   (1945) 61 LQR 380.

succeed unless the claimant makes good a reply such as value in good faith subsequent to the fraud: 'this shifting to and fro is often described as shifting of the burden of proof and so it is, but it is a shifting of the ultimate burden'.[7] No doubt such progression towards Lord Denning's ultimate burden (sometimes spoken of as 'the burden of proof on the whole case' or the 'general burden of proof') is what judges sometimes have in mind when they say that burdens have 'shifted',[8] but the concept is subject to the same objections as those which have been advanced against the provisional burden, and to the further objection that, in the context of the law of evidence, the expression 'burden of proof' is meaningless unless it is used with reference to a particular issue. The interaction of persuasive, evidential, provisional and ultimate burdens was conveniently illustrated in *Ratford v Northavon District Council.*[9] The authority levied a rate upon the receivers of a company occupying rateable property in their area. It was held that, provided there was some reasonable basis for supposing a person to be in occupation of such property, the authority was entitled to levy a rate upon them. In proceedings for non-payment the authority bore both evidential and legal burdens of showing that the rate had been duly made, demanded and not paid. The non-payer would then lose unless he satisfied the evidential and persuasive burden upon the next issue, that of showing a valid reason why he had not paid. In this case the receivers adduced evidence showing that, although empowered to do so, they had not in fact taken possession of the relevant premises. Once this had been done, and the evidential burden upon that issue satisfied, the only sense in which a burden could further shift was in the provisional sense, but its ultimate determination would decide the whole case. On this point the court endorsed the remarks of Donaldson LJ in *Forsythe v Rawlinson*[10] that it was like all burdens of proof in litigation a swinging burden in the sense that:[11]

> As the evidence of varying weight develops before the magistrates, the eventual burden of proof will, in accordance with ordinary principles of evidence, remain with or shift to the person who will fail without further evidence.

SECTION 2.   ALLOCATION OF THE BURDEN[12]

The burden of proof is, as noted above, capable of having a decisive effect upon the outcome of a case. It is generally allocated as a matter of common law, sometimes unconditionally, and sometimes conditionally upon the proof of certain facts, as in the case of true presumptions, though occasionally unconditional allocation borrows the language of presumption. The allocation may also be a matter of explicit provision, either by way of statutory allocation, itself either general or specific, or by agreement of the parties. These different modes of allocation will be considered in turn, and although all are capable of applying to burdens in either of the two principal senses of persuasive or evidential burden, it will be found that by far the greater attention has been paid to the allocation of the persuasive burden.

---

7   For a case in which the burden of proof was said to shift in this way see *Medawar v Grand Hotel Co* [1891] 2 QB 11; for a case of this type disposed of without any reference to the shifting of the burden of proof, see *Neal v Fior* [1968] 3 All ER 865, [1968] 1 WLR 1875.
8   See Mustill LJ in *Brady v Group Lotus Cars Companies Ltd* [1987] 3 All ER 1050, at 1058.
9   [1987] QB 357, [1986] 3 All ER 193.
10   [1981] RVR 97.
11   At 202.
12   See generally Williams in Waller and Campbell (eds) *Well and Truly Tried* (1982).

A.   UNCONDITIONAL ALLOCATION AT COMMON LAW

I.   Evidential burden

According to Taylor,[13] the right test for determining the incidence of the burden of proof is to consider first, which party would succeed if no evidence were given on either side, and secondly, what would be the effect of striking the allegation to be proved out of the record. The onus lies on whichever party would fail if either of these steps were taken. A moment's reflection should suffice to show that these tests are applicable only to the evidential burden; they cannot apply to the persuasive burden in all cases. Suppose, for example, that want of testamentary capacity is relied upon as a defence to a probate action. The defendant would fail on the issue if no evidence was given on either side, and the claimant would likewise succeed if the allegation was struck out of the record. Therefore, Taylor would have had to say that the burden of proof is on the defendant but the fact remains that the persuasive burden of establishing testamentary capacity is borne by the claimant.[14] Taylor's test is undoubtedly sound so far as the incidence of the evidential burden is concerned, although it has been said to be the statement of the effect of a rule, rather than the formulation of the principle underlying it.[15]

In other words resort must be had to the precedents. This is particularly true of criminal cases where the absence of formal statements of particulars of claim makes it unreal to speak of striking allegations out of the record. Even so general statements are attempted from time to time.[16] The general rule is that the party bearing the persuasive burden on an issue also bears the evidential burden. This means that, in a criminal case, the prosecution must normally adduce evidence fit to be left to a jury of the essential ingredients of the offence charged. It is not enough to adduce evidence which would be sufficient on one of two mutually exclusive hypotheses, and leave the jury to choose between them.[17] The general rule also means that the defence bears an evidential burden on the issue of insanity, by virtue of the common law, and on sundry other issues by virtue of statutory provisions, on which the persuasive burden is placed upon the defence by way of exception to the rule in *Woolmington v DPP*.[18] In these cases it must adduce evidence sufficient, if believed, to satisfy the jury of the existence of the defence on the balance of probabilities.[19] It seems that on issues arising out of special pleas the accused will bear an evidential burden, for example in relation to unfitness to plead[20] or autrefois convict[1] or acquit where the persuasive burden is on the accused; and perhaps even in cases where the persuasive burden is borne by the prosecution.[2]

---

13   *A Treatise on the Law of Evidence* (12th edn) para 365.
14   *Sutton v Sadler* (1857) 3 CBNS 87. Taylor's test was applied by Farwell LJ in *Talbot v Von Boris* [1911] 1 KB 854, at 863, but the court was there concerned with the evidential burden (see per Kennedy LJ, at 866). The test is based on *Amos v Hughes* (1835) 1 Mood & R 464, and is supported by Bowen LJ in *Abrath v North Eastern Rly Co* (1883) 11 QBD 440, at 457, where, however, the different burdens are not distinguished.
15   Wills *Law of Evidence* (3rd edn) 29.
16   See Williams (1978) 128 NLJ 182.
17   *Tsang Ping-Nam v R* [1981] 1 WLR 1462.
18   [1935] AC 462.
19   *R v Dix* (1982) 74 Cr App Rep 306, holding that some medical evidence must be adduced before the defence of diminished responsibility can be left to the jury.
20   *R v Podola* [1960] 1 QB 325. But see *R v Bradley (No 2)* (1986) 85 FLR 111 for some doubt in Australia.
1   *R v Coughlan and Young* (1976) 63 Cr App Rep 33.
2   See *R v Graham* (1983) 11 ACR 21 where this is true of a plea to the jurisdiction of the court.

With regard to a number of general common law defences it is settled that, although the prosecution bears the persuasive burden of disproving them, the accused bears the burden of adducing sufficient evidence to raise the issue of their existence.[3] Even when there are no words dealing expressly with the burden of proof, a statute will frequently be construed so as to place an evidential, if not a persuasive, burden on a particular issue on the accused.[4] Although there is little direct English authority on the point, it seems that where the accused bears an evidential, but not a persuasive, burden, he may discharge it by adducing evidence of a reasonable possibility of the existence of the defence.[5]

It is hardly surprising that there should be no direct authority because judicial generosity or, as the cynics would have it, the possibility of an appeal, leads to a disinclination to withdraw issues of which there is some defence evidence from the jury. This disinclination may also account for the dearth of authority on the question whether the accused bears an evidential burden in respect of all defences which are more than mere denials of an allegation necessary to the prosecution's case. Adams, a retired judge of the Supreme Court of New Zealand, answered the question in the affirmative[6] but Williams took the contrary view.[7] His contention was that it is logically impossible that both sides should carry an evidential burden on the same issue. This led him to conclude that the accused cannot bear an evidential burden with regard to alibi because his presence at or absence from the scene of the crime is put in issue by the prosecution. The prosecution also puts the accused's mens rea in issue at the outset of a criminal trial with the result, it is said, that he cannot bear an evidential burden with regard to the defence of accident. However weak the evidence on these matters may be, it must be left to the jury. The judge, Williams maintained, has no power to censor it as he has in the case of such general defences as self-defence and duress. There is force in these arguments, but there are counter-arguments. It could be said that, when the accused raises the defence of alibi,[8] or even accident, he is raising a fresh specific issue within the general issue. Such authority as there is leaves the point fairly open.[9]

---

3   *Mancini v DPP* [1942] AC 1, [1941] 3 All ER 272 (provocation); *Chan Kau v R* [1955] AC 206, [1955] 1 All ER 266 (provocation and self-defence); *R v Lobell* [1957] 1 QB 547, [1957] 1 All ER 734 (self-defence); *DPP v Walker* [1974] 1 WLR 1090 (no need to leave self-defence to the jury where no evidence that it was necessary); *R v Gill* [1963] 2 All ER 688, [1963] 1 WLR 841 (duress); *R v Bone* [1968] 2 All ER 644, [1968] 1 WLR 983 (duress).

4   See for example *R v John* [1974] 2 All ER 561, [1974] 1 WLR 624. In Canada, where the Charter invalidates the allocation of the persuasive burden to the accused, it has been held that any such attempt can be read down to allocate an evidential burden only to the accused: *R v Laba* [1994] 3 SCR 965.

5   See per Lord Devlin in *Jayasena v R* [1970] AC 618, at 624, and *R v Newcastle-upon-Tyne Justices, ex p Hindle* [1984] 1 All ER 770 (drink imbibed after accident but before breath-test); see also *R v Thornton* (1967) unreported, a Northern Irish case discussed by Comerton (1968) 19 NILQ 60.

6   *Criminal Onus and Exculpations* para 3.

7   (1977) 127 NLJ, at 157–8.

8   *R v Johnson* [1961] 3 All ER 969, [1961] 1 WLR 1478 cited by Adams and by Gooderson *Alibi* 23, does not turn on the evidential burden because the judge was held to have misdirected the jury by suggesting that the accused bore the persuasive burden, but the judgment of the Court of Criminal Appeal contains the suggestion that alibi should be treated in the same way as self-defence and provocation. (See Cross's Rede lecture *The Golden Thread of the English Criminal Law* (1976) CUP pp 12–13).

9   What appears to have been the view of the majority in *DPP v Morgan* [1976] AC 182, that the prosecution bears the evidential burden with regard to the accused's belief in consent might be cited in support of Williams, but the Court of Appeal had trailed a red herring by referring to the evidential burden when the point at issue was one of substantive law. The incidence of the evidential burden was irrelevant to the decision of the majority of the House of Lords. *Bratty v A-G for Northern Ireland* [1963] AC 386, [1961] 3 All ER 523 decides that the accused bears the evidential burden on the issue of non-insane automatism although the plea could be

So far as principle is concerned, there is surely something to be said for preventing the jury from considering the possibility of defences which lack any reasonable foundation: '[i]t is not every facile mouthing of some easy phrase of excuse that can amount to an explanation. It is for a judge to decide whether there is evidence fit to be left to a jury which could be the basis of some suggested verdict'.[10]

In civil cases the nature of the defence will usually be raised in the particulars of claim and case for the defence from which the allocation of the respective burdens can be deduced. Where this does not occur the principles which apply are similar to those in criminal cases. Even though the proponent of a proposition may bear the persuasive burden of proving an issue to the satisfaction of the court, he is not necessarily bound to anticipate every possible defeasing defence, especially when it could easily have been stated.[11] Thus in *Dunlop Holdings Limited's Application*[12] the opponents of a claim to patent a wheel had the burden of proving that the wheel had been in prior use. They were not however bound to anticipate a contention that such prior use had been secret. It was for the applicant to raise the issue by adducing some evidence, or at least by cross-examining the opponents' witnesses so as to show that the use had been in secret. Until this had been done proof of prior use without more was sufficient to entitle the opponents to succeed, though if the issue had been so raised they would have had to prove that the use was not secret upon the balance of probabilities.

2.   Persuasive burden[13]

So far as the persuasive burden is concerned, Wigmore has truly said 'There are merely specific rules for specific classes of case resting for their ultimate basis upon broad reasons of expedience and fairness',[14] but this does not often lead to difficulty in ascertaining the party upon whom the burden rests, for a fundamental requirement of any judicial system is that the person who desires the court to take action must prove his case to its satisfaction.[15] This means that, as a matter of common sense, the persuasive burden of proving all facts essential to their claims normally rests upon the claimant in a civil suit or the prosecutor in criminal proceedings.

The rule is sometimes expressed in terms of such maxims as *'omnia praesumuntur pro negante'*, and *'ei incumbit probatio qui dicit, non qui negat'* but this must not be taken to mean that the onus of proof cannot lie upon a party who makes a negative allegation. If this were so, the application of the rule could be made to depend upon the language in which a case happened to be stated. For instance, a claim for damages for breach of covenant to keep a house in repair may be expressed by saying, either that the defendant did not repair the house, or else that he allowed it to become dilapidated, but the persuasive burden is borne by the claimant, however the claim is expressed.[16] It is probably true to say that a positive averment can always be converted into a

said to be no more than a means of contradicting the prosecution's allegations, already before the jury, of actus reus and mens rea. Moreover Lord Kilmuir LC said (at 405) that the accused bears the evidential burden with regard to accident. See also *R v Bennett* (1978) 68 Cr App Rep 168, placing an evidential burden on the accused with regard to impossibility in a conspiracy case.

10   Lord Morris of Borth-y-Gest in *Bratty v A-G for Northern Ireland* [1963] AC 386, at 417.
11   Rule 16(5) of the Civil Procedure Rules both requires a statement of case by the defence, and specifies what it should include.
12   [1979] RPC 523.
13   See, in relation to the persuasive burden in criminal cases, Roberts [1995] Crim LR 783.
14   IX *Wigmore* 278.
15   *Dickinson v Minister of Pensions* [1953] 1 QB 228, at 232, [1952] 2 All ER 1031, at 1033.
16   *Soward v Leggatt* (1836) 7 C & P 613.

negative statement by appropriate linguistic manipulation. However this may be, there are numerous instances in which a claimant or prosecutor assumes the persuasive burden of proving a negative.[17] Absence of consent must be established by the Crown on a charge of rape or assault,[18] and where lack of consent[19] or want of due notice of a particular fact[20] is alleged in a civil action, these matters must be proved by the claimant. As Bowen LJ said in the leading case of *Abrath v North Eastern Rly Co*,[1] which decided that the persuasive burden of proving absence of reasonable and probable cause rests on the claimant in a claim for malicious prosecution, 'If the assertion of a negative is an essential part of the plaintiff's case, the proof of the assertion still rests upon the plaintiff.'

Difficulty may sometimes arise with regard to the question whether an assertion is essential to a party's case or that of his adversary. This is strikingly illustrated by *Joseph Constantine Steamship Line Ltd v Imperial Smelting Corpn Ltd*[2] where the charterers of a ship claimed damages from the owners for failure to load. The owners pleaded that the contract had been frustrated by the destruction of the ship owing to an explosion, and the only question of fact was whether this had been caused by their fault. As the evidence was scanty, it became necessary to determine which of the parties bore the persuasive burden with regard to this matter. If the rule were that charter parties cease to be binding when the vessel, without default of either party, is disabled by an overpowering disaster, the negation of fault would be an essential of the defendant's case; on the other hand, proof of fault would be an essential of the claimant's case, if the rule were that charter parties cease to be binding when the vessel is disabled by an overpowering disaster, provided that disaster is not brought about by the fault of either party. The House of Lords decided that the latter was the correct formulation, and accordingly held that the claimant has the persuasive burden of proving fault when frustration is stated as a defence to a claim on a contract. Their Lordships' speeches referred to principles, such as the difficulty of proving a negative and the presumption of innocence, but, as Stone has shown, general considerations of public policy probably constituted the decisive factor.[3] If such considerations are the guide where there is no governing precedent, it is obviously vain to seek for any set formula determining what facts are essential to a party's case and hence the incidence of the persuasive burden of proof can be ascertained only by consulting the precedents concerned with the various branches of the substantive law. In the case of bailment, for example, it is settled that the bailee has the onus of proving that the goods were lost without his fault,[4] and,

---

17   Although it is difficult to prove the negation of some facts, modern technology can sometimes make it as easy to prove a negative as a positive, see eg *US v Greenlee* 517 F 2d 889 (1975).

18   *R v Horn* (1912) 7 Cr App Rep 200; *R v Donovan* [1934] 2 KB 498.

19   *Toleman v Portbury* (1870) LR 5 QB 288.

20   *Williams v East India Co* (1802) 3 East 192.

1   (1883) 11 QBD 440, at 457. This decision was affirmed by the House of Lords (1886) 11 App Cas 247.

2   [1942] AC 154, [1941] 2 All ER 165.

3   It seems to be the case that frustration occurs more often than not without fault on anyone's part, and absence of fault is undoubtedly difficult to prove. Hence 'a rule requiring the defendant pleading frustration to negative fault will then ex hypothesi do injustice to the great majority of defendants. While, on the other hand, a rule requiring the plaintiff to prove fault will ex hypothesi do injustice to only a small minority of plaintiffs' ((1944) 60 LQR 278).

4   *Coldman v Hill* [1919] 1 KB 443; *Brook's Wharf and Bull Wharf Ltd v Goodman Bros* [1937] 1 KB 534, [1936] 3 All ER 696, and cases there cited; *Hunt and Winterbotham (West of England) Ltd v B R S (Parcels) Ltd* [1962] 1 QB 617, [1962] 1 All ER 111; *Houghland v R R Low (Luxury Coaches) Ltd* [1962] 1 QB 694, [1962] 2 All ER 159.

at a criminal trial, the accused has the persuasive burden on a plea of insanity.[5] No a priori tests could have produced these results; it is pointless to collect numerous isolated precedents.

3.   Use of terminology of presumption

As noted earlier, the burden of proof is sometimes allocated by way of the terminology of presumption. The terminology is properly applied to a situation in which the proof of one fact affects the burden relating to another, and consideration of this is postponed to the next part of this section. In some cases however there is no basic fact at all, and the presumption does no more than express the incidence of the relevant burden.[6] Typical examples are provided by the presumption of innocence, and the presumption of sanity in criminal cases.

(i)   Presumption of innocence[7]

When it is said that an accused person is presumed to be innocent, all that is meant is that the prosecution is obliged to prove the case against him beyond reasonable doubt. This is a fundamental rule of our criminal procedure,[8] and it is expressed in terms of a presumption of innocence so frequently as to render criticism somewhat pointless; but this practice can lead to serious confusion of thought, as is shown by the much discussed decision of the American Supreme Court in *Coffin v United States*.[9] The accused had been convicted of misappropriating the funds of a bank after the jury had been told that they should acquit him unless satisfied of his guilt beyond reasonable doubt, and a new trial was ordered because the judge did not enumerate the presumption of innocence among the items of evidence favourable to the accused. In other words, the Supreme Court considered that the presumption was something different from the rule concerning the onus of proof on a criminal charge, for they regarded it as an instrument of proof—an item of evidence which had been withheld from the jury. This decision has been universally condemned, it could hardly have been pronounced if the court had not been misled by the verbal dissimilarity between the rule that the prosecution bears the persuasive burden of proof, and the presumption of innocence.[10]

---

5   *McNaghten's Case* (1843) 10 Cl & Fin 200; *R v Smith* (1910) 6 Cr App Rep 19. For criticism, see Williams *Criminal Law (The General Part)* (2nd edn) 516; and for penetrating analysis see Jones (1995) 111 LQR 475. Under s 2(2) of the Homicide Act 1957, it is for the accused to prove diminished responsibility, see *R v Dunbar* [1958] 1 QB 1.

6   The language of presumption (deem) is occasionally used in a completely substantive way so as to define an offence with no possibility of rebuttal: see *International Bottling Co v Collector of Customs* [1995] 2 NZLR 579.

7   Allen *Legal Duties* 253. For a broader approach to this concept see Healy [1987] Crim LR 355, at 364, 365; for invaluable empirical research see Ashworth and Blake [1996] Crim LR 306.

8   Its strength is indicated in the construction by the Privy Council of the local constitution in *Vasquez v R* [1994] 3 All ER 674 so as to strike down statutory provisions clearly imposing a persuasive burden on the defence.

9   (1895) 156 US 432 discussed by Thayer *Preliminary Treatise on Evidence at the Common Law* App B.

10   The presumption that a child under the age of 14 is incapable of forming a criminal intent was formally abolished by s 34 of the Crime and Disorder Act 1998, but it is unclear whether the defence remains, subject to an evidential burden upon the accused.

The European Convention of Human Rights incorporates[11] the presumption of innocence, and it is possible that its implementation directly into English law will focus attention upon the operation of the presumption, and lead to changes in judicial attitudes.[12]

(ii) Presumption of sanity

In criminal cases, the presumption of sanity is no more than a conclusion which must be drawn until the contrary is proved for the McNaghten Rules have decreed:[13]

> that the jurors ought to be told in all cases that every man is presumed to be sane and to possess a sufficient degree of reason to be responsible for his crimes until the contrary be proved to their satisfaction.

The McNaghten Rules apply to criminal charges, and the presumption of sanity which they entail must be distinguished from the same presumption in some other branches of the law. If a rational will is produced, and shown to have been duly executed, the jury ought to be told to find in favour of the testator's competence.[14] The persuasive burden rests on the party who propounds the will, but the rule that he does not have to adduce evidence of capacity in the first instance is sometimes said to raise a presumption of sanity in testamentary cases. This presumption is dependent on the proof of a basic fact—the execution of a rational will, therefore it is an illustration of the proper use of the term.

(iii) Other examples

Allowance must be made for a number of presumptions without basic facts, for example Lord Kilmuir and Lord Denning spoke of 'the presumption of mental capacity' in *Bratty v A-G for Northern Ireland*[15] simply as a compendious way of expressing the fact that the accused bears the evidential burden on the issue of non-insane automatism. Although it is common enough to speak of a presumption that mechanical instruments were in working order as a means of indicating the fact that an evidential burden is borne by the party denying that this was the case,[16] it can hardly be said that any basic fact is involved.

Statutes occasionally employ exactly the same technique, thus s 79(2) of the Animal Health Act 1981 presumes that the owner of an animal knows of the existence of diseases from which it suffers unless and until he proves to the satisfaction of the court that he did not and could not with reasonable diligence have known of it.[17] Thus the effect of this section as against the accused is a precise counterpart of the operation of the presumption of sanity in criminal cases.

---

11 Article 6.2.
12 For a possible preview see the remarks of Lord Woolf construing a similar provision in Hong Kong in *A-G for Hong Kong v Lee Kwong-kut* [1993] AC 951.
13 See Jones (1995) 111 LQR 475.
14 See *Sutton v Sadler* (1857) 3 CBNS 87.
15 [1963] AC 386, at 407 and 413 respectively. In Australia see *R v Falconer* (1990) 171 CLR 30.
16 See p 54 above.
17 See also s 79(3).

B.   CONDITIONAL ALLOCATION AT COMMON LAW: PRESUMPTIONS

The structure of all true presumptions requires first the proof of a basic fact or facts. Once this has been done different consequences follow so far as the establishment of the presumed fact is concerned. In the weakest form of presumption the only effect of proving the basic fact is that the presumed fact may be found by the trier of fact. In other words the logical inference of the presumed fact from proof of the basic fact attracts a measure of formal endorsement.[18] Such presumptions have no effect upon the burden of proof in either of its two principal senses and need here be considered no further.[19] Two possibilities remain, one relating to the evidential, and one to the persuasive, burden.[20] If, after proof of the basic fact, the presumed fact must be taken to be established in the absence of evidence to the contrary, then an evidential burden has been cast upon the opponent of the presumed fact and the presumption can reasonably be described as an evidential presumption.[1] On the other hand, if, after proof of the basic fact, the presumed fact must be taken to be established unless the trier of fact is persuaded to the appropriate standard of the contrary, then a persuasive burden has been cast upon the opponent of the presumed fact, and the presumption can reasonably be described as a legal presumption. It is more accurate to speak of a shift in the burden of proof in the case of these stronger presumptions because they affect what the judge does in leaving an issue to the jury or withdrawing it from them, and they may determine the manner in which he must direct the jury at the end of the case.[2]

It would be unreasonable to expect anything approaching neat precision in this area of the law. Indeed it has been the subject of an extraordinary catalogue of complaints such as that:[3]

> Every writer of sufficient intelligence to appreciate the difficulties of the subject-matter has approached the topic of presumptions with a sense of hopelessness, and has left it with a feeling of despair.

There are a number of reasons for this. The precise delimitation and distinction of basic fact and presumed fact is assumed by the approach indicated above, but often not realised in practice.[4] This can mean that the same evidence rebuts both basic fact and presumed fact; for example, in the case of the presumption of death, evidence that the subject has been seen alive by one of his family may rebut both one of the basic facts of the presumption, that he has not been seen alive, and the presumed fact, that he is dead.[5] This could cause serious problems where the persuasive burden of proving the basic fact of the presumption is on the proponent of death, and the persuasive burden of rebutting the presumed fact of death upon his opponent.

Another example of overlapping between basic fact and presumed fact is provided by the presumption of legitimacy. The basic fact of that presumption is either the birth

18   A number of examples were given above, see p 113. The most plausible reason for such formal recognition is that it pre-empts legalistic arguments among the jury that the prosecution charged with proving one thing have failed to do so because they have proved only something different.
19   In traditional terminology these would be described as presumptions of fact.
20   In traditional terminology these would be described as rebuttable presumptions of law.
1   See Williams *Criminal Law (The General Part)* (2nd edn, 1961) 877ff.
2   When a statute speaks of a shifting of the burden of proof it is usually in relation to a rebuttable presumption of law created by the statute (see Bills of Exchange Act 1882, s 30 (2) below).
3   Morgan (1937) 12 Wash LR 255.
4   For a convincing demonstration of this, see Treitel (1954) 17 MLR 530. See also Stone (1981) 44 MLR 516 for the view that this presumption no longer has any practical effect.
5   See *Prudential Assurance Co v Edmonds* (1877) 2 App Cas 487.

of a child to a married woman during wedlock, or its conception during wedlock. In one case however the child was born slightly more than the normal period after the termination of a marriage by divorce.[6] In order to establish the basic fact of the presumption of legitimacy it was accordingly necessary to rely upon a different, and hitherto, unrecognised presumption the basic fact of which appeared to be the birth of a child within a possible period of gestation after the termination of a marriage, and the presumed fact that conception took place during the marriage.

Nowadays presumptions have much less importance than they did when the exclusionary rules were very much more restrictive. It is much less common for them to operate so as to determine the outcome in the absence of directly relevant evidence. Many of them reflect the evidential value of their basic facts. In the absence of further evidence, it would be highly unreasonable not to infer legitimacy from a child's birth in wedlock. On the other hand, a presumption may have the effect of increasing the probative value of the basic fact where there is no evidence contradicting such inferences as might be drawn from it. In the case of the presumption of death, for example, there is no special magic in seven years' absence so far as the ordinary tests of probative value are concerned. Someone who has been absent unheard of by those who would be likely to have heard from him for six and a half years is, for all practical purposes, just as likely to be dead as someone who has been absent in similar circumstances for seven years; but seven years' absence brings into play a rebuttable presumption of law, while absence for a shorter period merely gives rise to a more or less cogent presumption of fact that the person in question is dead. Reflections of this nature have led to the remark that: 'presumptions of law are nothing else than natural inferences or presumptions of fact which the law invests with an artificial or preternatural weight'.[7] While this may often be the case, it is by no means always the case. Some presumptions are clearly designed merely to resolve an impasse either of proof or procedure. Thus the statutory presumption contained in s 184(1) of the Law of Property Act 1925 provides that where two or more persons have died in circumstances rendering it uncertain which of them survived the other, such deaths shall (subject to any order of the court), for all purposes affecting the title to property, be presumed to have occurred in order of seniority, and accordingly the younger shall be deemed to have survived the elder. In such a case the evidential value of the basic fact is non-existent, and the whole effect of the presumption is expended on the allocation of the burden of proof.

It is however sometimes suggested that presumptions have an evidential effect in excess of the true probative worth of their basic fact, and quite independent of their effect in allocating the burden of proof.[8] It is submitted however that Lord Reid's words in *S v S* of the effect of the presumption of legitimacy are of more general application:[9]

> Once evidence has been led it must be weighed without using the presumption as a makeweight in the scale of legitimacy. So even weak evidence against legitimacy must prevail if there is no other evidence to counter-balance it. The presumption will only come in at that stage in the very rare case of the evidence being so evenly balanced that the court is unable to reach a decision on it.

6   *Knowles v Knowles* [1962] P 161, [1962] 1 All ER 659.
7   Gulson *Philosophy of Proof* (2nd edn) 371.
8   See per Lord Denning in *Stupple v Royal Insurance Co Ltd* [1971] 1 QB 50, at 72, [1970] 3 All ER 230, at 235–6, discussed in more detail above. It is however possible that the difference between Lord Denning and Buckley LJ in that case related only to the probative worth of the basic fact.
9   [1972] AC 24, at 41, [1970] 3 All ER 107, at 109.

If this is correct, and if the artificial force of presumptions is achieved by allocation of burden, it is hardly surprising to find that it is affected by other policies also directed to that end.[10] This is most obvious in criminal cases, especially in view of the decision of the House of Lords in *Woolmington v DPP*.[11] Although there is some older authority to the contrary[12] it is hard to believe, since the decision in *Woolmington*, that an English court[13] would be prepared to apply a common law presumption so as to cast a persuasive burden upon the accused in a criminal case.[14]

The stringent modern approach is illustrated in relation to the presumption of the lawfulness of official action, *praesumuntur rite esse acta* in *Dillon v R*.[15] The accused, a policeman, was charged with negligently permitting the escape of two prisoners who were lawfully within his custody. The prosecution failed to offer formal evidence of the lawfulness of the custody. The accused submitted that there was no case to answer, but both trial judge and appellate court held that the prosecution could rely upon the presumption. The Privy Council rejected this view, holding that the courts will not presume the existence of facts which are central to an offence, and that when the liberty of the subject is involved there is no room for presumptions in favour of the Crown. It also expressed the view that:[16]

> it would be contrary to fundamental principles of law that the onus should be on a prisoner to rebut a presumption that he was being lawfully detained, which he could only do by the (notoriously difficult) process of proving a negative.

It should be noted that when the issue is a central one, the prosecution will bear both an evidential and persuasive burden in relation to it, and the effect of the ruling is to deny even the provisional force of the presumption in such cases, that is to say, the presumption is insufficient to discharge the burden of adducing evidence to show the custody to have been lawful, and the accused is entitled to a directed verdict in his favour, in the absence of any other evidence on this issue.

Proof of the basic facts of a common law presumption can cast nothing more than an evidential burden on to the accused and nothing less than a persuasive burden on to the prosecution. If someone charged with incest with his daughter contends that, though conceived and born in wedlock, she is the child of another man, it is difficult to believe that any court would hold it incumbent upon him to do more than adduce such evidence as would suggest a reasonable possibility of illegitimacy. If, on the other hand, the prosecution were to contend that, though born during his wife's marriage to another man, the girl was in reality the accused's daughter, the judge should withdraw the case from the jury if the prosecution can do no more by way of rebuttal of the presumption of legitimacy than prove statements by the accused to the effect that the girl was his child.[17]

---

10   For an interesting suggestion that presumptions should be classified on the basis of the policies they are designed to promote, see Cohen (1981) 45 Albany LR 1079.

11   [1935] AC 462.

12   See *R v Curgerwen* (1865) LR 1 CCR 1; *R v Audley* [1907] 1 KB 383.

13   Though it has been done in Australia, see *R v Bonnor* [1957] VLR 227. In the United States this issue gives rise to constitutional problems, see *Re Winship* 397 US 358 (1970), at 364, for comment see Jeffries and Stephan (1979) 88 Yale LJ 1325.

14   See, for example, *R v Yacoob* (1981) 72 Cr App Rep 313, at 364, a strong case since the issue was merely collateral.

15   [1982] AC 484, [1982] 1 All ER 1017.

16   At 487, 1020.

17   *R v Hemmings* [1939] 1 All ER 417.

C.   ALLOCATION BY STATUTORY PROVISION

It is not uncommon for statutes to provide explicitly for the allocation of the burden of proof, though none seems so far ever to have distinguished explicitly between evidential and persuasive burdens. It has also been determined that it is possible for a statute to allocate the burden of proof implicitly.[18] Such an implicit allocation can be divined only by a process of statutory interpretation, and the common law developed certain principles which were subsequently encapsulated in a series of more general statutory provisions relating to summary proceedings.[19] It was at one time thought that these general statutory provisions for summary trials diverged in their effects from their counterparts at common law, perhaps because the accused could not before 1898 generally testify in his own defence, and perhaps because trial on indictment led to more serious consequences, thus justifying the imposition of a more onerous burden upon the prosecution. It is now clear that the rules are the same for both types of proceedings.[20] The accused has been a competent witness in his own defence since 1898, and it can be argued that since so many statutory offences are triable either upon indictment or summarily,[1] that it would be confusing, impractical, and undesirable to apply different burdens in respect of the same offence depending upon how it came to be tried, especially if this were to involve offering advantages in the more expensive and time-consuming proceedings upon indictment. The principal distinction is now between those statutes which make explicit, and those which leave implicit, allocation of the burden of proof, and they will be addressed in turn.

I.   Explicit allocation by statutory provision

It is not uncommon for statutes to provide that certain facts shall be deemed to exist until the contrary is proved. The precise words that are employed vary from statute to statute,[2] and they could have a decisive effect. It is possible to do no more here than provide a few representative examples. Examples are furnished by s 30(2) of the Bills of Exchange Act 1882, s 2 of the Prevention of Corruption Act 1916, and s 98(4)(b) of the Employment Rights Act 1996.[3] Where such provisions purport to cast a persuasive burden upon the accused they are likely in many, if not most, cases to be inconsistent with art 6 of the European Convention of Human Rights, and any conviction secured by their application is to be deemed unsafe. It was held in *R v DPP, ex p Kebilene*,[4] even before the Human Rights Act 1998 had been brought into force, that this consideration allows successful review of the exercise of the Director's discretion to permit prosecution under such a provision.[5]

18   *R v Hunt* [1987] AC 352, [1987] 1 All ER 1.
19   Culminating in the Magistrates' Courts Act 1980, s 101. In Scotland the comparable provisions apply both to summary trials and to trials on indictment, see Criminal Procedure (Scotland) Act 1975, ss 66 and 312(v). Similar provisions abound in Commonwealth jurisdictions.
20   Such assimilation may be thought inherent in the classic statement of Lord Sankey in *Woolmington v DPP* [1935] AC 462, at 482 that the rules are the same 'No matter what the charge or where the trial', see below, p 127.
1   With various permutations of options and consents by prosecution and defence.
2   And even within a given statute, see eg Criminal Law (Consolidation) (Scotland) Act 1995 which in relation to sexual offences alone uses four different formulations: s 1 (accused to prove); s 5 (defence if reasonable cause); s 8(4) (deemed); s 10(4) (proved to the satisfaction of the court).
3   Replacing a similar provision in earlier legislation.
4   [1999] 3 WLR 175.
5   Prevention of Terrorism (Temporary Provisions) Act 1989, ss 16A, 16B (as inserted by Criminal Justice and Public Order Act 1994, s 82.

(i)   Bills of Exchange Act 1882, s 30(2)

Section 30(2) of the Bills of Exchange Act 1882 provides that every holder of a bill is prima facie deemed to be a holder in due course; but if in a claim on a bill it is admitted or proved that the acceptance, issue, or subsequent negotiation of the bill is affected by fraud, duress, or force and fear, or illegality, the burden of proof is shifted, unless and until the holder proves that, subsequent to the alleged fraud or illegality, value has in good faith been given for the bill. In the light of cases decided before and after the Act came into force, when the subsection speaks of 'proof' it is clear that all that is meant is 'evidence upon which a jury would be entitled to base a verdict'.[6] The result is that the holder has the persuasive burden of proving that he gave value for the bill in good faith, but he does not bear the evidential burden on the point until the defendant has made out a prima facie case that the bill was tainted with fraud, duress or illegality. No doubt this is commercially fair even if, from the point of view of literal interpretation, there is something to be said for a construction less favourable to the defendant.[7]

(ii)   Prevention of Corruption Act 1916, s 2

By s 2 of the Prevention of Corruption Act 1916, on a charge under the Prevention of Corruption Act 1906, a consideration is to be deemed to be given corruptly unless the contrary is proved. In *R v Evans-Jones and Jenkins*,[8] this was held to mean that, if the jury is in doubt as to whether it should accept the accused's explanation of a gift to a public officer, it is its duty to convict, and this construction was also adopted by the Court of Criminal Appeal in *R v Carr-Briant*,[9] where however, the conviction was quashed because the jury had been misdirected with regard to the standard of proof. Humphreys J stated the judgment of the court in the following terms:[10]

> In any case where, either by statute or at common law, some matter is presumed 'unless the contrary is proved' the jury should be directed that it is for them to decide whether the contrary is proved, that the burden of proof required is less than that required at the hands of the prosecution in proving a case beyond reasonable doubt, and that the burden may be discharged by evidence satisfying the jury of the probability of that which the accused is called upon to establish.

These observations were plainly intended to apply to all cases in which a criminal statute casts the burden of proof on the accused, and it seems that they will be applied to all such cases by the courts.[11] subject only to the effects of the Human Rights Act 1998.

---

6   *Talbot v Von Boris* [1911] 1 KB 854, at 866 per Kennedy LJ; *Hall v Featherstone* (1858) 3 H & N 284.
7   For the commercial justification of the law on this subject see Alderson B in *Elkin v Janson* (1845) 13 M & W 655, at 664.
8   (1923) 87 JP 115.
9   [1943] KB 607, [1943] 2 All ER 156; followed in *Public Prosecutor v Yuvaraj* [1970] AC 913.
10   [1943] KB 607, at 612, [1943] 2 All ER 156, at 158.
11   *Jayasena v R* [1970] AC 618, [1970] 1 All ER 219; *Mizel v Warren* [1973] 2 All ER 1149, [1973] 1 WLR 899.

(iii) Employment Rights Act 1996, s 98(4)(b)

This provision, which replaces earlier legislation, is concerned with the determination of the question whether or not the dismissal of an employee was unfair. The employer must first show a proper reason, and then the question of fairness shall:

be determined in accordance with equity and the substantial merits of the case.

It seems that this form of words was intended to leave the persuasive burden neutral between the parties,[12] the evidential burden presumably being satisfied by adduction of a reason sufficient to satisfy the earlier parts of s 98. An interesting, and perhaps unintended, result of this technique is to effect a change in the standard of proof. As will be seen in the next section of this chapter, the normal standard of proof in civil proceedings is proof on the balance of probabilities. It is fundamental to that standard that it involves weighing the evidence to see if the required standard has been achieved. If it has not, the party bearing the persuasive burden loses, however little evidence his opponent has adduced. The effect of this change is that the only standard against which evidence can be weighed is that adduced by the opponent, in other words, if neither party bears the persuasive burden, then, if the case is to be decided at all, the party who adduces the greater amount wins, however little evidence he has adduced. In future in this area a party will win if he has adduced more evidence than his opponent, even though it may not, seen objectively, make his contention more probable than not. This is highly unsatisfactory, and the result may be that in an effort to avoid it cases will be fought out whenever possible on the question of the reason for dismissal, where the persuasive burden is borne by the employer,[13] though the nature of the issue may make that very difficult.[14]

2. Implicit allocation by statutory provision

A statute may allocate the burden of proof without explicit reference, and such statutes may concern civil,[15] or criminal liability. The most contentious issue relates to the imposition of a burden upon the accused in criminal proceedings. As noted above the general rule is that the prosecution bears both the evidential and persuasive burden in relation to issues necessary for the imposition of criminal liability. This general position was graphically expressed by the House of Lords in *Woolmington v DPP*:[16]

throughout the web of the English Criminal Law one golden thread is always to be seen, that it is the duty of the prosecution to prove the prisoner's guilt subject to what I have already said as to the defence of insanity and subject also to any statutory exception ... No matter what the charge or where the trial, the principle that the prosecution must prove the guilt of the prisoner is part of the common law of England and no attempt to whittle it down can be entertained.

It should be noted that Lord Sankey allowed for the defence of insanity, and for statutory exception. The question has arisen of how to construe the reference to

---

12   983 H of C Official Report (5th series) col 512.
13   Section 98(1) (show).
14   See Freedland (1972) 1 ILJ 20.
15   For example the Factories Act 1961, s 29(1) construed in *Nimmo v Alexander Cowan & Sons Ltd* [1968] AC 107, [1967] 3 All ER 187.
16   [1935] AC 462, at 481, 482.

statutory exception. It is quite clear that it applies to explicit statutory exceptions of the type exemplified above. Many statutes create offences without making any such explicit reference.[17] The question is whether they too are capable of being construed as casting a burden upon the accused, and if so, in what circumstances, and how it should be decided. Some guidance was provided at common law, these common law guides were encapsulated into general statutory provisions, and recent case law has clarified the situation. Various suggestions have been made for reform. Each of these matters will be considered in turn.

(i)   Common law

The common law used to attach importance to the distinction between exceptions and provisos and the effect of the defendant's peculiar knowledge of material facts. Something must be said about each of these matters before the effect of *R v Edwards*[18] is set out.

(a)   Exceptions and provisos

There was an old rule of pleading dating back to the seventeenth century according to which an indictment had to negative exceptions, but not provisos. In the words of Lord Mansfield: '[I]t is a known distinction that what comes by way of proviso in a statute must be insisted upon by way of defence by the party accused; but, where exceptions are in the enacting part of a law, it must appear in the charge that the defendant does not fall within any of them.'[19] But it did not follow from the fact that the prosecutor had to negative exceptions in the indictment that he bore any kind of burden with regard to them at the trial. This was the main point at issue in the leading case of *R v Turner*[20] in which the validity of an information under the game-laws was challenged on certiorari before the King's Bench. The accused was prosecuted for having pheasants and hares in his possession without the necessary qualifications or authorisation. Ten possible qualifications were mentioned in the relevant statute and the court held that, although the existence of any one of them was an exception, a fact which necessitated the reference to want of qualification in the information, it was unnecessary for the prosecution to adduce evidence on the subject. Lord Ellenborough made the point that proof of qualification was 'easy on the one side' whereas proof of total disqualification was 'almost impossible on the other'. It is arguable that *Turner*'s case decided no more than that, where a statute provides a plurality of excuses, the accused must raise the issue of the existence of those on which he relies.[1] The decision did not put an end to the distinction between exceptions and provisos if only because reliance was occasionally placed on the fact that an exempting clause was a proviso to justify the absence of any reference to it in the indictment and the imposition of some burden with regard to it on the accused.[2] There is however little doubt that *R v Turner* had a

17   Where a statute contains some provisions explicitly allocating persuasive burdens on the defence the juxtaposition of other provisions which do not do so may be taken as some indication that there is no implicit allocation of the persuasive burden in those cases: see eg *Polychronakis v Richards and Jerrom Ltd* [1998] Env LR 346.
18   [1975] QB 27, [1974] 2 All ER 1085.
19   *R v Jarvis* (1756) 1 East 643n.
20   (1816) 5 M & S 206.
1   See per Bowen LJ in *Abrath v North Eastern Rly Co* (1883) 11 QBD 440, at 457; and per Palles CB in *Graham v Belfast and Northern Counties Rly Co* [1901] 2 IR 13, at 26.
2   *R v James* [1902] 1 KB 540; *R v Audley* [1907] 1 KB 383.

great influence on the law concerning the incidence of the burden of proof because it showed that the mere fact that an allegation negativing an exception occurs in an indictment does not impose any burden on the Crown. Bayley J's justification of this result was treated as specially significant in a number of later cases.

(b) Facts peculiarly within the knowledge of the accused
Bayley J said that he had always regarded it as a general rule that:[3]

> If a negative averment be made by one party, which is peculiarly within the knowledge of the other, the party within whose knowledge it lies, and who asserts the affirmative, is to prove it and not he who asserts the negative.

It is important to grasp the limited extent of Bayley J's general rule. It is a rule of statutory interpretation confined to cases in which the affirmative of negative averments is peculiarly within the knowledge of the accused. There is nothing in the nature of a general rule that the burden of establishing any defence based on facts peculiarly within his knowledge is borne by him. Were there such a rule, someone charged with murder would bear the burden of proving many facts connected with provocation or self-defence, or even the burden of disproving an intention to kill, for few things can be more especially within a person's peculiar knowledge than his state of mind. The existence of such a rule was emphatically repudiated by the Court of Criminal Appeal in *R v Spurge*, a case in which a mechanical defect was the accused's answer to a charge of dangerous driving.[4] The most that can be said by way of generalisation is that a party's knowledge of essential facts may lessen the amount of evidence required to discharge an evidential burden borne by his adversary.[5] To quote Lord Mansfield:[6]

> It is certainly a maxim that all evidence is to be weighed according to the proof which it was in the power of one side to produce, and in the power of the other to have contradicted.

In consequence of Bayley J's rule of statutory interpretation the prosecution has been relieved of the necessity of showing that an apothecary charged with practising without a certificate did not possess one,[7] that a person charged with selling cocaine without a licence did not have a licence,[8] that a driver charged with infringing insurance regulations did not have a certificate,[9] that a sugar dealer charged with an offence against the Defence Regulations 1939 had not been granted a licence,[10] that a motorist had not

---

3   5 M & S 211. For a civil case in which the doctrine was applied see *General Accident, Fire and Life Assurance Corpn v Robertson* [1909] AC 404, at 413.

4   [1961] 2 QB 205, [1961] 2 All ER 688, (the appeal was dismissed because the accused was negligent); *R v Mandry, R v Wooster* [1973] 3 All ER 996, at 1000, [1973] 1 WLR 1232, at 1238. See also the striking decisions on ordinances based on s 106 of the Indian Evidence Act 1872: 'When any fact is essentially within the knowledge of any person the burden of proving that fact is upon him': *Attygalle v R* [1936] AC 338, [1936] 2 All ER 116; *Seneviratne v R* [1936] 3 All ER 36; *Ng v R* [1958] AC 173.

5   See *Dunlop Holding Ltd's Application* [1979] RPC 523, at 544 per Buckley LJ.

6   *Blatch v Archer* (1774) 1 Cowp 53, at 65. See also *R v Burdett* (1820) 4 B & Ald 95, at 140, cited in *Joyce v DPP* [1946] AC 347, at 380; Stephen *Digest of the Law of Evidence* (12th edn) art 104 applied in *R v Kakelo* [1923] 2 KB 793, at 795 and cited in *R v Cohen* [1951] 1 KB 505, [1951] 1 All ER 203.

7   *Apothecaries' Co v Bentley* (1824) 1 C & P 538.

8   *R v Scott* (1921) 86 JP 69.

9   Per Talbot J in *Williams v Russell* (1933) 149 LT 190, at 191.

10   *R v Oliver* [1944] KB 68, [1943] 2 All ER 800.

got a licence when he was charged with driving without one,[11] and that the accused was in the possession of drugs without a prescription.[12]

Some of these holdings have been criticised as unjustifiable extensions of the decision in *R v Turner* from statutes containing a number of qualifications under which the acts charged would be lawful to issues concerning a single negative which would be as easy to prove by prima facie evidence as the affirmative, and to those where the accused has no peculiar knowledge. Suppose, for example, that a motorist is charged with driving without a licence. In practice the only persons so charged are those who are unable to produce a licence on demand; the relevant register is accessible to the prosecution, and held in a form in which a negative is proved by the very same means as a positive.

(ii)   *General statutory provision*

Statutory guidance for the construction of statutes creating summary offences achieved its present form in s 101 of the Magistrates' Courts Act 1980 which provides:

> Where the defendant to an information or complaint relies for his defence on any exception, exemption, proviso, excuse or qualification, whether or not it accompanies the description of the offence or matter of complaint in the enactment creating the offence or on which the complaint is founded, the burden of proving the exception, exemption, proviso, excuse or qualification shall be on him; and this notwithstanding that the information or complaint contains an allegation negativing the exception, exemption, proviso, excuse or qualification.

There is comparatively little authority on the construction of this section. This is partly due to the fact that decisions which could have been reached by means of a direct application of this provision were based on the common law principles which govern trials on indictment,[13] but the matter has ceased to be of any importance since the Court of Appeal concluded in *R v Edwards*[14] that s 101 reproduces the common law. Before that decision it could be argued that there was a difference with regard to the burdens borne by the accused. The wording makes it difficult to escape the conclusion that s 101 is concerned with the persuasive burden and the authorities support this view,[15] but it was thought that the common law rules might cast nothing more than an evidential burden on an accused relying on an exception, exemption etc. Even in cases where as a matter of statutory construction the persuasive burden does not shift, it may nevertheless as a matter of tactics be desirable for the accused to adduce some evidence, for example, on a charge of supplying liquor to non-members of a club, that the persons in question were members.[16]

---

11   *John v Humphreys* [1955] 1 All ER 793, [1955] 1 WLR 325, not followed in *McGowan v Carville* [1960] IR 330 where the authorities are reviewed. See also *A-G (Comer) v Shorten* [1961] IR 304; cf *R v O'Brien* (1965) 50 DLR (2d) 92
12   *R v Ewens* [1967] 1 QB 322, [1966] 2 All ER 470.
13   The much discussed case of *John v Humphreys* [1955] 1 All ER 793, [1955] 1 WLR 325 is one such decision.
14   [1975] QB 27, [1974] 2 All ER 1085.
15   *Gatland v Metropolitan Police Comr* [1968] 2 QB 279, [1968] 2 All ER 100; *Taylor v Ellis* [1956] VLR 457, at 461–2; *Everard v Opperman* [1958] VLR 389, at 391; *Akehurst v Inspector of Quarries* [1964] NZLR 621.
16   *Oxford v Lincoln* (25 February 1982, unreported) QBD, (LEXIS), applying s 101 to construction of Licensing Act 1964, s 161.

Various tests have been suggested for determining when s 101 or one of its equivalents is applicable. One of the best known is the following:[17]

> Does the section [under which the accused is prosecuted] make the act described an offence subject to particular exceptions, qualifications, etc, which, where applicable, make a prima facie offence an innocent act, or does the statute make an act prima facie innocent an offence when done under certain conditions? In the former case the exception need not be negatived; in the latter words of exception may constitute the offence.

But this, like the other proposed tests, assumes that there is a logical distinction between the definition of an offence and an exception to it. In all cases turning on the applicability of s 101 the question is whether the words alleged to constitute an exception etc are an integral part of the definition of the offence or the equivalent of a defence which would operate by way of confession and avoidance. This is not a question which can be answered on principle. The form of the statute under consideration will often provide the answer. Words like 'unless',[18] 'other than'[19] or 'provided always' being fairly safe indications of the applicability of s 101, but there can be borderline cases.

Nimmo v Alexander Cowan & Sons Ltd,[20] a Scottish appeal to the House of Lords in civil proceedings, was concerned with the construction of s 29(1) of the Factories Act 1961, under which a place at which any person has to work 'shall, so far as is reasonably practicable, be made and kept safe for any person working therein'. Contraventions of the Act are made summary offences by s 155(1) and this accounts for the references which were made to the Scottish equivalent of s 101 of the Magistrates' Courts Act 1980. The issue was whether it was necessary for the claimant, a workman who had sustained injuries at his place of work, to plead and prove that it was reasonably practicable to keep the premises safe or whether it lay upon the defendant, his employer, to prove the contrary. By a majority of three to two the House held that the defendant had to plead and prove impracticability. The minority, Lords Reid and Wilberforce, took the view that the words 'so far as is reasonably practicable' are an integral part of the definition of the offence, but two members of the majority, Lords Guest and Pearson, considered that they were a qualification or excuse.[1] The status of the decision as a binding authority on the construction of s 101 of the Magistrates' Courts Act 1980, is debatable, but the importance of some observations of Lord Pearson is beyond dispute. He said that, while exceptions, exemptions and provisos would be easily recognisable from the use of such words as 'except' or 'provided always', the words 'excuse or qualification' showed an intention to direct attention to the substance rather than the form of the enactment. It therefore seemed that, at any rate when the form of words did 'not speak for itself', the courts could have regard to the object of the statute creating the offence charged when considering the applicability of s 101.[2]

---

17 Gibson J in *Shehan v Cork Justices* [1908] 2 IR 1, at 11.
18 *Buckman v Button* [1943] KB 405, [1943] 2 All ER 82.
19 *Baker v Sweet* [1966] Crim LR 51.
20 [1968] AC 107, [1967] 3 All ER 187. Applied in *Bilton v Fastnet Highlands Ltd* 1998 SLT 1323.
1   The third member of the majority, Lord Upjohn, did not base his opinion on the construction of the equivalent to s 101, but he was generally in agreement with Lord Pearson's speech. The assumption that the incidence of the burden of proof should be the same in civil proceedings and at a summary trial was questioned by Adams *Criminal Onus and Exculpations* (New Zealand 1968) para 125; and has been rejected both in Australia by the High Court in *Chugg v Pacific Dunlop Ltd* (1990) 170 CLR 249, and in New Zealand by the Court of Appeal in *R v Rangi* [1992] 1 NZLR 385.
2   See (1976) 92 LQR 402, at 418.

(iii)   Recent developments

The aspect of this area of the law has changed dramatically as a result of two recent cases, one in the Court of Appeal[3] and the other in the House of Lords.[4] The accused in *Edwards*[5] had been convicted of selling intoxicating liquor by retail without holding a Justices' licence authorising him to do so. He had not given evidence, the prosecution had adduced ample evidence from which sales might be inferred, but none with regard to the absence of a licence. The judgment of the Court of Appeal was delivered by Lawton LJ. He recognised the force, on the particular facts, of the point taken with regard to peculiar knowledge and raised some questions by way of general criticism of doctrines such as that enunciated by Bayley J in *R v Turner*. Who is to decide whether a fact is within the peculiar knowledge of the defendant? Is it a matter on which evidence is receivable? A review of the authorities culminated:[6]

> In our judgment this line of authority establishes that over the centuries the common law, as a result of experience and the need to ensure that justice is done both to the community and to defendants, has evolved an exception to the fundamental rule of our criminal law that the prosecution must prove every element of the offence charged. This exception, like so much else in the common law, was hammered out on the anvil of pleading. It is limited to offences arising under enactments which prohibit the doing of an act save in specified circumstances or by persons of specified classes or with specified qualifications or with the licence or permission of specified authorities. Whenever the prosecution seeks to rely on this exception, the court must construe the enactment under which the charge is laid. If the true construction is that the enactment prohibits the doing of acts, subject to provisos, exceptions and the like, then the prosecution can rely upon the exception.

This part of the judgment concludes with the clearly expressed opinion that the burden borne by the accused in cases covered by the statement was persuasive.

Lawton LJ's reformulation of the common law rules with regard to exceptions had the two great merits of avoiding problems with regard to the meaning of 'peculiar knowledge' and of equiparating the law governing trials on indictment with that applicable to summary trials.[7] Moreover the reference to the court's duty to construe the statute under which the charge is laid left room for a consideration of the object of the legislation before concluding that it prohibits the doing of acts subject to provisos, exceptions and the like.[8] Some guidance to the application of the principle was provided by *Guyll v Bright*[9] where the Divisional Court held the burden to be cast upon the defendant pursuant to these rules, despite the presence in the same statute of a

---

3   *R v Edwards* [1975] QB 27, [1974] 2 All ER 1085.
4   *R v Hunt* [1987] AC 352, [1987] 1 All ER 1. The speech of Lord Griffiths, in whose reasoning Lords Keith and Mackay explicitly concurred, is taken to express the decision of the House.
5   [1975] QB 27, [1974] 2 All ER 1085. For a criticism of some of the historical statements in the judgment and of the utility of the general principle stated in it see Zuckerman (1976) 92 LQR 401.
6   [1975] QB 27, at 39–40.
7   A cynic might suspect that elimination of any inducement for the choice of trial on indictment by way of the provision of a more favourable burden of proof was a significant motivation for the decision.
8   In accordance with the views of Lords Pearson and Guest in *Nimmo v Alexander Cowan & Sons Ltd* [1968] AC 107, [1967] 3 All ER 187.
9   (1986) 84 Cr App Rep 260.

provision explicitly casting upon the defendant the burden in relation to offences created by some other sections of the Act, but not by the one actually charged.

The whole matter was reviewed by the House of Lords in *R v Hunt*.[10] The accused was charged with unlawful possession of a controlled drug. The prosecution proved that the substance in question contained the relevant drug, but did not specify in what proportion it existed. Regulations made under the Act defined exempted substances to include those with a specified very small proportion of the otherwise illicit drug. It was argued that since the prosecution had not shown the proportion to exceed the low threshold, there was no case to answer. This view was rejected[11] both by the Crown Court and by the Court of Appeal. The House of Lords was invited to review the whole area, and to overrule *R v Edwards* on the basis that it was inconsistent with the decision of the House in *Woolmington*. The Misuse of Drugs Act 1971, s 5(2) under which the accused was charged does not in terms contain a proviso or exception, but is made subject to the relevant regulations. The regulations[12] did not themselves individually refer to exceptions or provisos, but were generally headed 'Exemptions from Certain Provisions for the Misuse of Drugs Act 1971', and were made pursuant to a power[13] granted to 'except' from the provisions of the Act by regulation. It should also be noted that the Act provides a number of defences capable of applying to an offence under s 5(2) whereby a persuasive burden is explicitly cast upon the accused.

The House of Lords took the opportunity to endorse the decision and reasoning in *R v Edwards*, subject only to widening its scope so that it applied not only to provisions which could be brought within the linguistic boundaries of exceptions and provisos,[14] but to provisions the import of which was to create exemptions from otherwise generally applicable provisions.[15] Its approach endorsed that taken in *Nimmo v Alexander Cowan & Sons Ltd*,[16] in suggesting that:[17]

> if the linguistic construction of the statute did not clearly indicate on whom the burden should lie the court should look to other considerations to determine the intention of Parliament, such as the mischief at which the Act was aimed and practical considerations affecting the burden of proof and, in particular, the ease or difficulty that the respective parties would encounter in discharging the burden.

Especial stress was laid upon the final consideration which was regarded as making it generally unlikely that Parliament would be taken to have imposed an onerous burden upon a defendant. It was by reference to this point that the House distinguished between the earlier decisions in *R v Oliver*[18] and *R v Putland and Sorrell*.[19] In the former the Court of Criminal Appeal upheld a conviction for selling sugar without a licence although the prosecution had offered no evidence of the absence of a licence, while in the latter it quashed a conviction for buying clothing without surrendering coupons because

---

10 [1987] AC 352, [1987] 1 All ER 1.
11 Though for different reasons.
12 Misuse of Drugs Regulations 1973, SI 1973/797.
13 Misuse of Drugs Act 1971, s 7.
14 No attention was paid to r 6(C) of the Indictment Rules 1971 excusing reference to exceptions etc in the statement of the offence in the indictment, presumably because of r 8 which provides that nothing in the rules affects the law of evidence.
15 This also seems to be the position in Australia, see *He Kaw Teh v R* (1985) 157 CLR 523; *DPP v United Telecasters Ltd* (1990) 168 CLR 594; and *Chugg v Pacific Dunlop Ltd* (1990) 170 CLR 249.
16 [1968] AC 107, [1967] 3 All ER 187.
17 At 374, 11.
18 [1944] KB 68, [1943] 2 All ER 800.
19 [1946] 1 All ER 85.

no evidence had been offered by the prosecution that no coupons had been surrendered. In the House's view a licensed trader could easily prove that he had a licence, but it would have been much more difficult for a purchaser of clothing to prove that he had surrendered coupons. It should also be noted that this was no mere incantation of high sounding theory, but was expressed in practical terms by reversing the Court of Appeal, and quashing the conviction upon the basis of a very strict construction of the relevant provision, which could be taken to reduce to a minimum the number of cases in which a persuasive burden[20] would be cast upon the defence.

Despite the result of its application in *Hunt* the reasoning of the House of Lords has been widely attacked by commentators.[1] The main burden of this criticism is that the argument gives insufficient weight to the principle of *Woolmington* by breaking down the strict limitation upon the exceptions to the general rule that the prosecution always bears the burden of proof in criminal cases, and substituting for it considerations of policy to be determined by the judges upon only the very vaguest of criteria. It has to be conceded that there has been inconsistency of interpretation of the position in summary proceedings.[2] It can further be argued that this may encourage much looser drafting of statutory offences by releasing the draftsman from the need to consider carefully each element of each new statutory offence with a view to deciding whether by explicit provision, or formulation as an exception or proviso, so as to cast a burden upon the accused.[3] On the other hand it can also be argued that by departing from the tyranny of verbal formulation the decision in *Hunt* permits reconsideration, even of those provisions which do contain the appropriate verbal formulae if policy argues against the imposition of a burden upon the defence.[4]

It is submitted that the effects of *Hunt* are unlikely to prove so deleterious as its critics assert,[5] nor so beneficial as its supporters may hope. Statutory provisions are likely to go on being drafted in the same careful way, and draftsmen will not willingly run the risk of an unwelcome construction if it can be pre-empted by use of an appropriate formula. It is doubtful whether judges will regard the reasoning in *Hunt* as a licence to re-write Acts of Parliament, or to subvert existing canons of construction. Its boundaries should also be noted. It was dealing only with statutory offences, and leaves unaffected the major common law defences[6] where the prosecution will continue to bear the legal, though often not the evidential, burden. It also seems that the court will be unlikely to extend its effects to those statutory offences which explicitly require mens rea by including some such term as 'knowingly',[7] or 'wilfully'.[8]

It was regarded as virtually axiomatic in *Hunt* that if a burden were to be cast upon the accused by a statutory provision it must be a persuasive burden, to be satisfied by proof upon the balance of probabilities. This was regarded as mandated by the need to provide congruence with the position in cases governed by s 101 of the Magistrates'

20   Though in some cases it has been very easily discharged by the prosecution: see eg *R v Jones* (1997) 161 JP 597.
1   See Healy [1987] Crim LR 355; Smith (1987) 38 NILQ 223; and Mirfield [1988] Crim LR 19 and [1988] Crim LR 233. It has also attracted some support: see Zuckerman (1987) 103 LQR 170; Birch [1988] Crim LR 221.
2   See Smith (1987) 38 NILQ 285, at 231–236.
3   For a more sceptical view of the draftsman's approach, see Bennion [1988] Crim LR 31.
4   This may account for its acceptance by the High Court of Australia: see *DPP v United Telecasters Ltd* (1990) 168 CLR 594.
5   Though the reasoning in *R v Alath Construction Ltd; R v Brightman* [1990] 1 WLR 1255 provides support for them: see Stein (1991) 54 MLR 570.
6   For the position in Code jurisdictions where such a clash may occur see *A-G's Reference (No 1 of 1989); R v Brown* [1990] Tas R 46.
7   See *Westminster City Council v Croyalgrange Ltd* [1986] 2 All ER 353, [1986] 1 WLR 674.
8   *Hirst and Agu v Chief Constable of West Yorkshire* (1986) 85 Cr App Rep 143.

Courts Act 1980 which, as noted above,[9] is worded so as to connote a persuasive burden by using the verb 'prove'. It is not obvious that this will always be the appropriate analogy. If there is nothing in the language of the statutory provision to be construed to indicate more than the need to distinguish the case from the general rule imposing both evidential and legal burdens upon the Crown, then general policy should be allowed to dictate whether the imposition should be of the one or of the other.

It remains to be seen how far these developments will impinge upon previously unsettled and unsatisfactory areas, such as the rules relating to the construction of s 57 of the Offences Against the Person Act 1861. The first proviso excludes foreigners from the definition of bigamy if the second marriage ceremony was celebrated elsewhere than in England or Ireland. It was held in *R v Audley*[10] that, in such a case, the accused must allege and prove that he was not a British subject at the material time. The decision is consistent with the rule laid down in *R v Edwards* provided the word 'prove' is taken to refer to the persuasive burden, but *R v Curgerwen*[11] is inconsistent with the rule. In that case the Court for Crown Cases Reserved held that the prosecution bears what must certainly be regarded as the persuasive burden of negativing part of the second proviso exempting persons marrying a second time whose husbands or wives shall have been continually absent for seven years 'and shall not have been known by such persons to be living within that time.' The decision was that the Crown bears the burden of proving the requisite knowledge. *R v Jones*[12] does no more than place an evidential burden on the accused on the issue of continuous absence; it is very difficult to see why, so long as *R v Curgerwen* stands, he should also bear a persuasive burden.[13]

(iv) Reform

We have seen that it was difficult to believe that what may be called the '*Carr-Briant*' construction would not have been applied by the courts to all criminal statutes which expressly place the burden of proof on the accused, state that 'proof' lies upon him or require him to 'prove' something. It was in accordance with the ordinary principles of literal statutory construction that the burden imposed on the accused should be the persuasive burden. The discharge of an evidential burden does not prove anything, and the construction of s 30 of the Bills of Exchange Act 1882, according to which 'proved' means 'sufficient evidence has been adduced', could be explained on the footing that the section was a statement of the pre-existing common law. The position seems to have changed with the enactment of the Human Rights Act 1998, and its incorporation into English law of art 6(2) of the European Convention of Human Rights.[14] As noted above the very prospect of the Act has already stultified prosecution based upon an express provision casting a persuasive burden on the accused.[15] In the light of s 3 of the Human Rights Act 1998 it has become much more unlikely that statutory

---

9   At p 130.
10   [1907] 1 KB 383.
11   (1865) LR 1 CCR 1.
12   (1883) 11 QBD 118.
13   *R v Broughton* [1953] VLR 572 decides that he does not, but the case was criticised in *R v Bonnor* [1957] VLR 227. See the discussions by Morris in (1955) 18 MLR 482 and by MacDougall (1958) 21 MLR 510.
14   For interpretation see *Salabiaku v France* (1988) 13 EHRR 379; see also International Covenant on Civil and Political Rights art. 14; for interpretation of its Hong Kong manifestation see *A-G of Hong Kong v Lee Kwong-Kut* [1993] AC 951.
15   *R v DPP, ex p Kebilene* [1999] 3 WLR 175.

provisions of a more ambiguous nature will be interpreted so as to cast a persuasive burden upon the accused, so by a different route achieving the result recommended in 1972 by the Criminal Law Revision Committee that no new statutory provisions should cast more than an evidential burden on the accused.[16]

It is interesting to note the range of interpretations of similar provisions in different jurisdictions, some of which were cited in *Kebilene*'s case. Sometimes they operate by way of judicial interpretation of a constitutional presumption of innocence. In Canada it is expressed in art 11(1)(d) of the Charter which is regarded as compatible with the reversal of onus in a statutory provision only if warranted by a pressing and substantial objective, and proportional in being rationally connected with that objective, impairs the protection as little as possible, and is not more deleterious than salutary.[17] In New Zealand, on the other hand, the Bill of Rights Act 1990, s 25(c) has the effect only of preventing a persuasive burden being imposed where the words are ambiguous: *R v Rangi*.[18] In Ireland the Constitution provides[19] for trial in due course of law, which seems to have been regarded in *Hardy v Ireland*[20] as incompatible with the imposition of a persuasive burden. It is perhaps surprising that no attempt has been made to outflank such provisions by retaining the persuasive burden on the prosecution, but reducing the standard of proof to the balance of probabilities, which would achieve effects very similar to those achieved by putting a persuasive burden of the same weight upon the accused.[1]

The truth of the matter is that most lawyers find it distasteful that a jury should ever have to be directed to convict when it thinks, after considering all of the evidence, that it as likely as not that the accused is innocent.[2]

D. THE INTERPRETATION OF AGREEMENTS AFFECTING THE BURDEN OF PROOF

The incidence of the burden of proof may be determined by the agreement of the parties in civil cases,[3] and, where there is such an agreement, there can be little doubt that the burden in question would generally be taken to be the legal one. This is also the burden which has been the subject of discussion in cases concerned with the construction of contracts for the carriage of goods by sea, and insurance against various types of loss.

---

16   *Evidence: General* Cmnd 4991, paras 137–142. These recommendations were rejected by the Law Commission in its review of codification of the English Criminal Law in Law Com 143 (1985), but subsequently reaffirmed by Smith, one of the prime movers in that debate, (1987) 38 NILQ 223, at 243.

17   As formulated in *R v Oakes* [1986] 1 SCR 103, modified in *Dagenais v Canadian Broadcasting Corpn* [1994] 3 SCR 835, and restated in *R v Laba* [1994] 3 SCR 965, at 1006, which also reads down an invalid attempt to impose a persuasive burden into the imposition of an evidential one. The Canadian approach has also been adopted in South Africa: *S v Zuma* 1995 (2) SA 642.

18   [1992] 1 NZLR 385.

19   Article 38 s 1.

20   [1994] 2 IR 550. Egan and Murphy JJ disagreed on this point.

1   Since the only case to be decided differently would be one where the trier of fact had not the slightest preference for one side rather than the other.

2   Although the danger of simply transforming regulatory provisions into offences of strict liability must always be considered. See the useful statistics in Ashworh and Blake [1996] Crim LR 306.

3   *Levy v Assicurazioni Generali* [1940] AC 791, [1940] 3 All ER 427. It seems also that in Scotland a concession as to the incidence of the burden of proof cannot be withdrawn, at least when it has been acted upon to the detriment of the other party, *John Thorburn & Sons v Border Harvesters Ltd* 1992 SLT 549.

I. Perils of the sea—The Glendarroch

If a claimant seekss damages from shipowners for breach of contract to carry goods safely, and the defendants rely on a clause exempting them from loss or damage occasioned to the goods by a peril of the sea, they must prove that the latter occurred, and alone[4] caused the damage in question; but, if the claimant relies upon a proviso to the exemption clause relating to negligence on the part of the defendants, the persuasive burden of proving negligence rests on him. These points were established in the leading case of *The Glendarroch*[5] where the ship on which the goods had been placed struck a rock, and Lord Esher said:[6]

The plaintiffs would have to prove the contract and the non-delivery. If they leave that in doubt, of course they fail. The defendants' answer is 'Yes; but the case was brought within the exception—within its ordinary meaning'. That lies upon them. Then the plaintiffs have a right to say there are exceptional circumstances, viz that the damage was brought about by the negligence of the defendants' servants, and it seems to me that it is for the plaintiffs to make out the second exception.

2. Insurance exceptions

This case was among those followed by Bailhache J in *Munro, Brice & Co v War Risks Association*,[7] which was concerned with an insurance policy covering the loss of a ship through the perils of the sea, subject to an exception in respect of enemy action. He held that the defendants bore the persuasive burden of proving that the ship was lost in consequence of the latter with the result that the claimants succeeded on their claim as the ship had not been heard of after she set sail, and there was no evidence of the cause of her disappearance. The law on this point cannot, however, be regarded as completely settled for, in the earlier case of *Hurst v Evans*,[8] Lush J had decided that, where an insurance policy against loss of jewellery contained an exception in respect of theft by the claimant's servants, it was incumbent on the claimant to negative loss from this cause. This is not the kind of problem that can be solved by logical argument, for there is no difference between a clause which is construed to read 'The insurers shall be liable for loss except that which occurs in specified circumstances' and a rule which says 'the insurers shall be liable for loss arising from all causes other than those specified',[9] but it is submitted that practical considerations as well as previous authority[10] are in favour of the view of Bailhache J. He said that if he had been asked to advise on evidence in *Hurst v Evans*, it would not have occurred to him to suggest that the claimant should call all his servants, one after the other to swear that they had

---

4   Such provisions are sometimes expressly controlled by statute, see Merchant Shipping Act 1995, Sch 6, Art 18.
5   [1894] P 226.
6   At 231; contrast *Slattery v Mance* [1962] 1 QB 676, [1962] 1 All ER 525. In the case of insurance of a ship against fire the insurer must establish scuttling on the balance of probabilities. See also *Doats v Weekes* (1986) 82 FLR 334.
7   [1918] 2 KB 78.
8   [1917] 1 KB 352.
9   Cf the arguments of Stone in (1944) 60 LQR 278.
10 *Gorman v Hand-in-Hand Insurance Co* (1877) IR 11 CL 224; his dictum was approved by Donaldson J in *M Golodetz & Co Inc v Czarnikow-Rionda Co* [1979] 2 All ER 726, at 743.

not stolen the jewels, 'The procession would be a long one if Messrs Whiteley were the claimants.'[11]

SECTION 3.   DISCHARGE OF THE BURDEN

Once the party who bears the evidential burden has discharged it by adducing evidence sufficient to justify consideration of a particular issue, it becomes necessary for the party bearing the persuasive burden on that issue, the proponent, to persuade the trier of fact that it should be decided in his favour. If his evidence is less persuasive than that of his opponent he must inevitably fail. If it is more persuasive, the question is whether he must equally inevitably succeed. The answer to that question demands consideration of the requisite standard of proof and how it should be explained to the jury. It is generally accepted that English law applies two main standards, though their precise connotation, formulation and application, the possibility of a third standard and their relationship to precisely quantifiable evidence, raise debatable issues which will be discussed in this section of the chapter. It is first necessary to consider the standard which must be achieved to discharge an evidential burden.

A.   DISCHARGE OF EVIDENTIAL BURDEN[12]

No precise formulae have been laid down with regard to the standard of proof required for the discharge of an evidential burden and, as this is not a matter upon which it can ever be necessary for a judge to direct a jury, there is no reason why it should ever become the subject of formulae. Some indication may be gleaned from appellate decisions on whether a verdict should be quashed as unsafe. When the evidential burden is borne by the Crown, it must be discharged, to quote Lord Devlin once more, by 'such evidence as, if believed, and if left uncontradicted and unexplained, could be accepted by the jury as proof'.[13] 'Proof' in this context must mean proof beyond reasonable doubt, and, in spite of occasional suggestions to the contrary,[14] the standard must, at least from the theoretical point of view, be higher than that required to discharge an evidential burden borne by a party to civil proceedings. In *R v Pacey*[15] it was held that the prosecution failed to discharge its evidential burden by inviting the jury to draw factual inferences contrary to the testimony of the sole prosecution witness, and in *Chappell v DPP*[16] that the failure of the defence to deny a possible inference was insufficient. Nor is it sufficient for the prosecution to rely alone upon evidence of a sort which experience shows to be unreliable, even if honestly tendered,[17] for example some forms of identification evidence.[18] Sometimes lay evidence will not be enough

---

11   [1918] 2 KB 78, at 86.
12   See Wood (1961) 77 LQR 491, and Glass (1981) 55 ALJ 842.
13   *Jayasena v R* [1970] AC 618, at 624.
14   *R v Smith* (1865) 34 LJMC 153: *Wilson v Buttery* [1926] SASR 150, at 154.
15   (1994) Times, 3 March. See also *R v Parkinson* [1990] 1 Qd R 382 where the prosecution's reliance upon a previous inconsistent statement rejected by the sole testifying witness was strongly deprecated.
16   (1989) 89 Cr App Rep 82.
17   This qualification is required to resolve any conflict with the decision in *R v Galbraith* [1981] 2 All ER 1060, [1981] 1 WLR 1039: see further below.
18   *R v Turnbull* [1977] QB 224, [1976] 3 All ER 549; *Reid v R* [1990] 1 AC 363, [1993] 4 All ER 95n; *Daley v R* [1994] AC 117, [1993] 4 All ER 86. See also below ch XVII.

without professional support.[19] A final consideration here is that the only evidence must not be equivocal between two co-accused, at least in the absence of some further showing of complicity between them.[20]

When the accused bears the evidential burden alone, it is necessary for there to be only such evidence as would, if believed and uncontradicted, induce a reasonable doubt in the mind of a reasonable jury as to whether his version might be true, for example as to whether he was provoked[1] or in a state of automatism.[2] To quote from the speech of Lord Morris of Borth-y-Gest in *Bratty v A-G for Northern Ireland*:[3]

> There was no sufficient evidence, fit to be left to a jury, on which a jury might conclude that the appellant had acted unconsciously and involuntarily or which *might leave a jury in reasonable doubt whether this might be so.*

In the words of Lord Devlin in the same case, the evidence must be enough to 'suggest a reasonable possibility'. There must be some evidence,[4] derived either from the prosecution[5] or adduced by the defence; it is not enough to rely upon an out of court self-serving statement,[6] and probably not enough to give equivocal evidence from which the jury is invited to draw a medical inference, itself contradicted by the evidence of a doctor.[7] Where the accused bears both the legal and evidential burdens, for example in relation to insanity and related defences such as diminished responsibility, it is necessary for him to go further and to adduce evidence such as might satisfy a jury on the balance of probabilities. Thus in *R v Dix*[8] it was held incumbent upon the accused to adduce some medical evidence before the defence of diminished responsibility could be left to the jury. It is incumbent upon the judge to leave to the jury all issues arising from the evidence, even when not explicitly relied upon by the defence for tactical reasons.[9] Such cases clearly raise complications so far as the analysis of evidential burden is concerned,[10] but it has been held that the

---

19   *R v Morris* (1997) 141 Sol Jo LB 231 (medical evidence needed to establish that non-physical assault could have physical result).
20   *R v Aston; R v Mason* (1992) 94 Cr App Rep 180; see further below p 148.
1   See *R v Cambridge* [1994] 2 All ER 760, [1994] 1 WLR 971 where it is submitted that the Court of Appeal went too far in apparently requiring the defence to go so far as to adduce sufficient evidence for a reasonable jury to conclude that there was provocation. But in that case the only issue was whether the defence should have been left at all, so since in the instant case it was held that the evidence was sufficient, this reference to the amount of evidence can be regarded as obiter dicta.
2   *A-G's Reference (No 2 of 1992)* [1994] QB 91, [1993] 4 All ER 683.
3   [1963] AC 386, at 419 (emphasis supplied). See also *R v St Pierre* [1995] 1 SCR 791.
4   In the context of a costs application, it was said that in order to surmount this threshold the evidence must not lack real substance: *R v Secretary of State for Environment, ex p Wakefield Metropolitan Borough Council* (1996) 75 P&CR 78. In Canada it has been said to require an air of reality about it: *R v Park* [1995] 2 SCR 836.
5   As in *R v McDonald* [1991] Crim LR 122 where the issue of provocation was held to have been raised solely by a self-serving letter from the accused put in as part of the prosecution case.
6   *R v Newcastle-upon-Tyne Justices, ex p Hindle* [1984] 1 All ER 770. But the exculpatory part of a mixed statement will be sufficient to raise an issue, even though likely to carry little weight at the end of the day: *R v Duncan* (1981) 73 Cr App Rep 359; *Western v DPP* [1997] 1 Cr App Rep 474.
7   *R v Bailey* (1983) 77 Cr App Rep 76.
8   (1982) 74 Cr App Rep 306.
9   See eg *R v Hopper* [1915] 2 KB 431, [1914–15] All ER Rep 914; *Mancini v DPP* [1942] AC 1, [1941] 3 All ER 272; *Bullard v R* [1957] AC 635, [1961] 3 All ER 470n.
10   See Doran [1991] Crim LR 878.

standard here is similarly that the evidence must be more than speculative[11] and such as a reasonable jury might accept.[12] Thus in a case of murder the House of Lords has held that there was no need for the judge to put an issue of provocation to the jury, when the accused consistently denied any suggestion of loss of self-control, and there was no evidence of any provoking words or conduct outside the general relationship of the parties.[13] In this situation it is incumbent on the judge to indicate to the jury which parts of the evidence support the issue he regards as raised by it.[14]

For the sake of theoretical completeness it may be added that when, in a civil case, the party with the persuasive burden on a particular issue also bears the evidential burden, it is discharged by the adduction of sufficient evidence to satisfy a reasonable trier of fact on the balance of probabilities.[15] If the party bearing the evidential burden does not bear the persuasive burden, the former is discharged by the adduction of sufficient evidence to leave the mind of a reasonable trier of fact in a state of equilibrium.

B.   DISCHARGE OF PERSUASIVE BURDEN[16]

I.   Degree of the burden

The cases show that there is a difference between the standards of proof in criminal and civil proceedings. The distinction was stated as clearly as it can be stated by Denning J in *Miller v Minister of Pensions*.[17] Speaking of the degree of cogency which the evidence on a criminal charge must reach before the accused can be convicted he said:[18]

> That degree is well settled. It need not reach certainty, but it must carry a high degree of probability. Proof beyond a reasonable doubt does not mean proof beyond the shadow of a doubt. The law would fail to protect the community if it admitted fanciful possibilities to deflect the course of justice. If the evidence is so strong against a man as to leave only a remote possibility in his favour, which can be dismissed with the sentence 'of course it is possible but not in the least probable' the case is proved beyond reasonable doubt, but nothing short of that will suffice.

11   There is certainly no obligation upon the judge to speculate in such a way himself when there is nothing in the evidence to raise the issue (*R v Walch* [1993] Crim LR 714), especially when the accused has deliberately abstained from testifying: *R v Hillier; R v Farrer* (1993) 97 Cr App Rep 349. It may indeed be a ground for appeal that magistrates have done so: *DPP v Ambrose* [1992] RTR 285.
12   *R v Cambridge* [1994] 2 All ER 760, [1994] 1 WLR 971.
13   *R v Acott* [1997] 1 All ER 706, [1997] 1 WLR 306 (unemployed middle aged man living with and dependent upon demanding aged mother).
14   *R v Stewart* [1995] 4 All ER 999, [1996] 1 Cr App Rep 229n.
15   It was not discharged by the exhibition of an anonymous letter from a third party to an affidavit sworn by the defendant: *Barclays Bank plc v Anderson* (1987) Times, 10 March; but see in Ireland, *Anheuser Busch Inc v Controller of Patents* [1996] 2 IR 242.
16   For an historical account see Shapiro *'Beyond Reasonable Doubt' and 'Probable Cause'* (1991). For the standard of proof at a trial within a trial, see p 169 below.
17   [1947] 2 All ER 372, at 373–374. For an earlier statement see *Cooper v Slade* (1858) 6 HL Cas 746, at 772.
18   The propriety of summing up in terms of probability and possibility was questioned in *R v McKenna* (1964) 81 (Pt 1) WN NSW 330; but the reference to probabilities can be regarded as a direction to use common-sense (*R v Coe* [1967] VR 712).

When speaking of the degree of cogency which evidence must reach in order that it may discharge the persuasive burden in a civil case, his Lordship said:

> That degree is well settled. It must carry a reasonable degree of probability, but not so high as is required in a criminal case. If the evidence is such that the tribunal can say: 'we think it more probable than not', the burden is discharged, but if the probabilities are equal it is not.

The validity of the distinction has not gone unquestioned. Lord Goddard once confessed that he had some difficulty in understanding how there are or can be two standards,[19] and Hilbery J is reported to have said: 'I personally have never seen the difference between the onus of proof in a civil and criminal case. If a thing is proved, it is proved, but I am not entitled to that view.'[20] Yet it can hardly be doubted that there are degrees of probability. If this much is conceded, the law can intelligibly require that a very high degree must be established by the prosecution at a criminal trial. So long as the proportions do not become excessive, it is better that people who are probably guilty should go free than that those whose innocence is reasonably possible should be convicted. The importance of the liberty of the subject contributes to the applicability of the criminal standard to cases of contempt of court in civil proceedings,[1] or to binding persons over to keep the peace.[2] It is not the complete explanation however since the application of the civil standard to a contempt by a corporate defendant[3] was subsequently disapproved by the Court of Appeal.[4] The criminal standard must be satisfied before summary judgment will be granted in civil proceedings,[5] and in such cases requires even more than enhancement under the flexible *Bater v Bater* standard, before an interim payment order will be ordered.[6] That standard may also be explicitly[7] required by statute or statutory instrument for other good reasons of policy.[8]

It will be submitted that there are no more than two standards of proof recognised by the law, though allowance must be made for the fact that some occurrences are antecedently more probable than others, and the consequences of some decisions are more serious than others. People are less likely to commit murder than to drive recklessly, and less likely to be fraudulent than to be negligent. It is more serious to be imprisoned for life for murder than to be conditionally discharged by a magistrate for assault, and it is more serious to determine the legitimacy of a child than whether or not a civil trespass has occurred. It may require less evidence to show that something discreditable occurred, than that it was perpetuated by a particular person.[9] For these reasons prosecutors on the more serious criminal charges or those carrying graver consequences, and claimants in some civil cases, have higher hurdles to surmount

---

19   *R v Hepworth and Fearnley* [1955] 2 QB 600, at 603.
20   In the course of argument in *R v Murtagh and Kennedy* (1955) 39 Cr App Rep 72.
1   *Re Bramblevale* [1970] Ch 128, [1969] 3 All ER 1062; *Nelson v Nelson* 1988 SCLR 663; *Re Kerrison* (1990) 101 ALR 525. It is not however required for proof of the conditions leading to an award of punitive damages in civil proceedings, where the enhanced civil standard suffices, *John v MGN Ltd* [1997] QB 586, [1996] 2 All ER 35, at 619B, 58b.
2   *Percy v DPP* [1995] 3 All ER 124, [1995] 1 WLR 1382.
3   In *West Oxfordshire District Council v Beratec Ltd* (1986) Times, 30 October (sequestration of company assets for breach of undertaking in action for nuisance).
4   In *Dean v Dean* [1987] FCR 96, [1987] 1 FLR 517.
5   But not before declaring a civil litigant vexatious: *A-G v Hayward* (1995) Times, 20 November.
6   See *Ricci Burns Ltd v Toole* [1989] 3 All ER 478, [1989] 1 WLR 993.
7   Or sometimes implicitly by the institution of separate proceedings for offences and civil penalties even in respect of the same dishonest behaviour, as in s 60 of the Value Added Tax Act 1994: see *1st Indian Cavalry Club Ltd v Commissioners of Customs and Excise* [1998] SCLR 47.
8   *Judd v Minister of Pensions and National Insurance* [1966] 2 QB 580, [1965] 3 All ER 642.
9   *H v H* [1990] Fam 86; *Re W (Minors)(Sexual abuse: standard of proof)* [1994] 1 FLR 419.

than when they are making less serious allegations or those with more trivial consequences. This led Denning LJ to speak of degrees of proof within the same standard:[10]

> It is of course true that by our law a higher standard of proof is required in criminal cases than in civil cases. But this is subject to the qualification that there is no absolute standard in either case. In criminal cases the charge must be proved beyond reasonable doubt, but there may be degrees of proof within that standard ... So also in civil cases the case must be proved by a preponderance of probability, but there may be degrees of probability within that standard. The degree depends on the subject-matter. A civil court, when considering a charge of fraud, will naturally require for itself a higher degree of probability than that which it would require when asking if negligence is established. It does not adopt so high a degree as a criminal court, even when it is considering a charge of a criminal nature; but still it does require a degree of probability which is commensurate with the occasion.

The point was put more succinctly by Morris LJ when he said:[11]

> Though no court and no jury would give less careful attention to issues lacking gravity than to those marked by it, the very elements of gravity become a part of the whole range of circumstances which have to be weighed in the scale when deciding as to the balance of probabilities.

This view cannot, of course, be taken to suggest the imposition of a stricter standard than that of proof beyond reasonable doubt in relation to the most serious criminal cases.[12] The application of a flexible standard has been endorsed and applied by the House of Lords to the judicial review of the decisions of immigration officers in illegal entry cases:[13]

> The reviewing court will therefore require to be satisfied that the facts which are required for the justification of the restraint put on liberty do exist. The flexibility of the civil standard of proof suffices to ensure that the court will require the high degree of probability which is appropriate to what is at stake.

It was generally agreed that the civil standard was more appropriate than the criminal, but Lord Scarman himself, echoing Lord Denning in *Bater v Bater* described this as largely a matter of words.[14] Even the difference in words is eroded however when the House speaks of requiring to be satisfied with nothing less than 'probability of a high degree' or 'convincing proof'.[15] It may be for such reasons that in the case of the most

---

10 *Bater v Bater* [1951] P 35, at 36–7. The passage has met with frequent judicial approval, for example that of Lord Pearce in *Blyth v Blyth* [1966] AC 643, at 673. See also *Thomas Bates & Son v Wyndhams (Lingerie) Ltd* [1981] 1 All ER 1077, [1981] 1 WLR 505.

11 *Hornal v Neuberger Products Ltd* [1957] 1 QB 247, at 266. This answers the observation of Allen (*Legal Duties* 288) that it would startle the legal world and the public if, when trying an action for damages, the judge were to say to the jury, 'You need not be as careful in arriving at your conclusion as if you were trying a criminal case.'

12 See *R v RLR* (1988) 65 CR (3d) 235.

13 *Khawaja v Secretary of State* [1984] AC 74, at 113–14, [1963] 1 All ER 765, at 784.

14 At 112, 783.

15 At 124, 792.

serious allegations of all,[16] or those with the most serious consequences,[17] the formal invocation of the criminal standard in its traditional form has been required.

This whole issue was reconsidered by the House of Lords in *Re H (Minors) (Sexual Abuse: Standard of Proof)*.[18] A man was charged with the rape of one of the daughters of the woman with whom he was living, and acquitted. The local authority sought to have interim care orders confirmed in respect of three other daughters of the woman, but the only evidence tendered to support the application related to facts adduced in the rape trial. Under s 31(2) of the Children Act 1989 such orders may be made only if the court is satisfied that the child has suffered, or is likely to suffer, harm. Only the second of these conditions was in issue. It was agreed that 'likely' connotated a real risk rather than a probability. The difficulty remained one of determining whether such a risk could be established, in other words what was required to discharge the persuasive burden upon the local authority to establish such a risk. It was agreed[19] that the enhanced criminal standard did not apply. The majority endorsed the application of the flexible approach to be seen in *Bater v Bater*,[20] explaining that although the result might be similar there is a conceptual difference between applying an enhanced standard of persuasion, and allowing for antecedent improbability in determining the amount of material required to achieve a given standard of persuasion. The minority was less inclined to elaborate in this way, and took the view that the standard was the simple one of the balance of probabilities, and that any embellishment in terms of the cogency of the evidence required to satisfy it was unnecessary.[1] In the result the majority took the view that it would be anomalous to find the apprehension of harm on the sole basis of the very evidence that had been rejected as showing the reality of harm. While suspicion may found a factual basis for an interlocutory application, final determinations require hard evidence.[2]

2. Description of the burden

It is possible that the law governing the different standards of proof is more settled and better understood than the preceding passages might suggest. There are nevertheless some specially difficult situations. It will be convenient first to consider the general problems involved in the choice of the language to describe the burden, and then to go on to consider the special problems presented by fragmented cases, and by the distinction between the civil and criminal standards, where there is an overlap.

16   Eg of murder in civil proceedings, *Halford v Brookes* [1992] PIQR P175. Though this seems inconsistent with earlier authority, and has been disapproved in Scotland (see below), and in *Francisco v Diedrick* (1998) Times, 3 April, the burden was discharged by no more than proof of a prima facie case to which the defendant failed to respond.

17   Eg loss of professional status: *Re A Solicitor* [1993] QB 69, [1992] 2 All ER 335, where the Court of Appeal was also influenced by the explicit requirement of the criminal standard in similar proceedings in relation to another branch of the legal profession.

18   [1996] AC 563, [1996] 1 All ER 1. Applied also to the welfare stage in *Re M and R (minors) (sexual abuse: expert evidence)* [1996] 4 All ER 239, [1996] 2 FLR 195.

19   Lord Nicholls in his majority speech at 586C, 17j; and despite their dissent on other points, Lord Browne-Wilkinson at 572E, 3f and Lord Lloyd at 577E, 8d. The trial judge came close to applying the criminal standard.

20   Above. Reference was made to its endorsement in a number of other cases, and formulations were quoted also from *Hornal v Neuberger Products Ltd* above, and *Re Dellow's Will Trusts* [1964] 1 All ER 771, [1964] 1 WLR 451, at 773E, 455.

1   Lord Lloyd at 578C, 9b. Lord Browne-Wilkinson agreed generally with Lord Lloyd, but did not considered this point explicitly.

2   Perhaps particularly those having devastating effects, and which fail to give full effect to a finding in favour of the liberty of the subject, following a full trial.

(i) General formulation

Some of the difficulty is created by the words in which the standard is formulated. In ordinary civil cases it is usually expressed as involving the 'preponderance of probability', the 'balance of probabilities', or the 'preponderance of evidence'. It might be argued that the last of these seems to involve no more than the preponderance of the evidence adduced by the proponent of an issue over that adduced by its opponent.[3] It is more common however to regard all of these terms as synonymous, and as connoting not merely relative preponderance over the evidence of the opponent but satisfaction of a prescribed level of probability.[4] The House of Lords has pronounced any other view as being contrary to common sense since a judge should not be forced to find proved an occurrence which he regards on the evidence as extremely improbable.[5]

> [The trial judge] adopted an erroneous approach to this case by regarding himself as compelled to choose between two theories, both of which he regarded as extremely improbable, or one of which he regarded as extremely improbable and the other of which he regarded as virtually impossible. He should have borne in mind, and considered carefully in his judgment, the third alternative which was open to him, namely that the evidence left him in doubt ..., and that, in these circumstances, the shipowners had failed to discharge the burden of proof which was upon them.

It has however been proposed that to avoid confusion a new formulation should be adopted which recognises the variability of amount required to satisfy the standard in different situations: the claimant (or the party on whom the burden rests) must satisfy the court that it is reasonably safe in all the circumstances of the case to act on the evidence before the court, bearing in mind the consequences which will follow.[6]

It is extremely rare to find a jury in a civil case, but even when one is present it is not necessary for the judge in every case to which it is relevant to give a direction about the flexibility of civil standards under the doctrine of *Bater v Bater* since this will often be no more than a matter of common sense.[7]

The problem of formulation is still more acute in criminal cases where a direction has to be given to the jury. In 1949 Lord Goddard CJ said:[8]

> Once a judge begins to use the words 'reasonable doubt' and to try to explain what is a reasonable doubt and what is not, he is much more likely to confuse the jury than if he tells them in plain language, 'It is the duty of the prosecution to satisfy you of the prisoner's guilt'.

3　Some support for this view can be gleaned from the speech of Viscount Simon in *Hickman v Peacey* [1945] AC 304, at 318, [1945] 2 All ER 215, at 220; and from that of Lord Reid in *S v S* [1972] AC 24, at 41, [1970] 3 All ER 107, at 109. It seems that even a very weak case may be pushed over the threshold by the failure of the opponent to adduce any relevant evidence: *Francisco v Diedrick* (1998) Times, 3 April; for a similar view in Ireland see *Anheuser-Busch Inc v Controller of Patents* [1996] 2 IR 242.

4　See *Ong Ah Chuan v Public Prosecutor* [1981] AC 648, at 669; *Larby v Armement L Hermans SA* [1956] 2 Lloyd's Rep 43, at 45. See also *Briginshaw v Briginshaw* (1938) 60 CLR 336. The same view prevails in the United States, see Devitt and Blackman *Federal Jury Practice and Instructions* (3rd edn, 1977) para 71.14. 'To establish by a preponderance of evidence means to prove that something is more likely so than not so.'

5　*Rhesa Shipping Co SA v Edmunds* [1985] 2 All ER 712, at 718, [1985] 1 WLR 948, at 956. Lord Brandon attributed the contrary view to an unjudicial dictum of Mr Sherlock Holmes.

6　*Re J S (a minor)* [1981] Fam 22, at 29, [1980] 1 All ER 1061, at 1066.

7　See *Lawrence v Chester Chronicle* (1986) Times, 8 February.

8　*R v Kritz* [1950] 1 KB 82, at 90, [1949] 2 All ER 406, at 410.

He returned to this theme in *R v Summers*,[9] but his words were much stronger as they amount to a prohibition on the use of the phrase 'reasonable doubt' by trial judges when summing up in criminal cases. He said:

> If the jury is told that it is their duty to regard the evidence and see that it satisfies them so that they can feel sure when they return a verdict of guilty, that is much better than using the expression 'reasonable doubt' and I hope in future that that will be done.

Lord Goddard subsequently indicated that his objection to the old formula was the difficulty of following explanations of what does, and does not, constitute a reasonable doubt. He thought that no real guidance is afforded by saying it must not be a fanciful doubt, and to say it must be such a doubt as would make jurymen hesitate in their own affairs does not suggest any particular standard because one juryman might hesitate where another would not do so.[10] In another case Lord Goddard said:[11]

> Let us leave out of account, if we can, any expression such as 'giving the prisoner the benefit of the doubt'. It is not a question of giving the benefit of a doubt; if the jury are left with any degree of doubt whether the prisoner is guilty, then the case has not been proved.

An appeal founded on the ground that the trial judge had not told the jury to give the accused the benefit of the doubt was dismissed in *R v Blackburn*[12] where a direction which did no more than stress the point that the jury must be satisfied of the accused's guilt was approved. In *R v Murtagh and Kennedy*,[13] on the other hand, an appeal was allowed because the summing up had not made it sufficiently clear that the jury must acquit if they were left in doubt concerning the accused's explanation of the facts. In *R v Hepworth and Fearnley*[14] an appeal was allowed on the ground that a direction to the effect that the jury must be satisfied of the accused's guilt was inadequate when the charge was one of receiving. The judgment of the Court of Criminal Appeal was delivered by Lord Goddard CJ:[15]

> One would be on safe ground if one said in a criminal case to a jury: 'you must be satisfied beyond reasonable doubt', and one could also say, 'you the jury, must be completely satisfied', or better still, 'you must feel sure of the prisoner's guilt'.

9   [1952] 1 All ER 1059.
10 *R v Hepworth and Fearnley* [1955] 2 QB 600, at 603, [1955] 2 All ER 918, at 919. For similar criticisms see *Brown v R* (1913) 17 CLR 570. The idea of a doubt which would cause jurymen to hesitate in their own affairs is traceable to the summing-up of Pollock CB in *R v Manning* (1849) 30 CCC Sess Pap 654: 'If the conclusion to which you are conducted be that there is that degree of certainty in the case which you would act upon in your own grave and important concerns, that is the degree of certainty which the law requires and which will justify you in returning a verdict of guilty.'
11 *R v Onufrejczyk* [1955] 1 QB 388, at 391, [1955] 1 All ER 247, at 249. The reference to giving the prisoner the benefit of the doubt has been traced back to the eighteenth century and appears to have the blessing of the House of Lords: *Woolmington v DPP* [1935] AC 462, at 481; *Mancini v DPP* [1942] AC 1, at 11, [1941] 3 All ER 272, at 279.
12 (1955) 39 Cr App Rep 84n. The Attorney-General refused his fiat for an appeal to the House of Lords in this case, but it is difficult to say what is left of the decision after *R v Murtagh and Kennedy* and *R v Hepworth and Fearnley* (above).
13 (1955) 39 Cr App Rep 72.
14 [1955] 2 QB 600, [1955] 2 All ER 918.
15 At pp 603, 920, respectively.

In spite of this approval of three different ways of saying the same thing, including the reference to the time-honoured standard of proof beyond reasonable doubt, the Court of Criminal Appeal and the Court of Appeal have had to express their disapproval of the trial judge's summing up concerning the standard of proof in a number of subsequent cases,[16] and similar difficulties have been experienced in other common law jurisdictions.[17] It is not enough to direct the jury simply to decide which of two conflicting witnesses for defence and prosecution they believe to be telling the truth.[18] It is hardly surprising that the English courts[19] and the Judicial Committee of the Privy Council[20] are against any set form of words:[1]

> If the jury are made to understand that they have to be satisfied and must not return a verdict against the defendant unless they feel sure, and that the onus is all the time on the prosecution and not on the defence, then whether the judge uses one form of language or another is neither here nor there.

It is the effect upon the jury of whichever words are used that matters, although the Court of Appeal has endorsed the specimen direction contained in guidance published by the Judicial Studies Board, and approved by the Lord Chief Justice, which recommends 'The burden of proof is upon the prosecution. It is for the prosecution to establish the defendant's guilt.' It is unwise[2] to go further.[3] The Court of Appeal has recommended that judges stop trying to define that which it is impossible to define,[4] and 'to keep the direction on this important matter short and clear.'[5]

Where there are 'cut-throat' mutually inconsistent defences the temptation to say that one of the accused cannot be acquitted unless the jury is satisfied of the guilt of the other should be resisted, since it would be wrong to suggest that the accused has to satisfy the jury of anything.[6]

It is vitally important for the judge to direct the jury both as to the allocation and standard of the burden of proof,[7] but in very exceptional cases the Court of Appeal may nevertheless apply the proviso despite failure to direct the jury on either the allocation,[8] or standard,[9] of proof. In both of these cases however the decision was

---

16   *R v Jones* [1961] Crim LR 322; *R v Johnson* [1961] 3 All ER 969, [1961] 1 WLR 1468; *R v Head and Warrener* (1961) 45 Cr App Rep 225; *R v Attfield* [1961] 3 All ER 243, [1961] 1 WLR 1135; *R v Stafford and R v Luvaglio* [1968] 3 All ER 752n; *R v Gray* (1973) 58 Cr App Rep 177; *R v Sweeney* (1983) Times, 22 October.
17   *Dunn v HM Advocate* 1986 JC 126; *People (A-G) v Byrne* [1974] IR 1; *Green v R* (1971) 126 CLR 28; *Victor v Nebraska* 114 S Ct R 1239 (1994); *R v Lifchus* [1997] 3 SCR 320.
18   *DW v R* [1991] 1 SCR 742; *R v E* (1995) 89 ACR 325.
19   *R v Allan* [1969] 1 All ER 91, [1969] 1 WLR 33.
20   *Walter v R* [1969] 2 AC 26; the direction upheld in this case is criticised in (1969) 32 MLR 217; but it was also upheld, with a preference for the time-honoured formula of 'beyond reasonable doubt' in *Ferguson v R* [1979] 1 All ER 877, [1979] 1 WLR 94.
1   Lord Diplock [1969] 2 AC 26, at 30.
2   Though not quite necessarily a misdirection, see *R v Pahuja* (1987) 30 ACR 118 (judge did misdirect); *R v Finlay and Grellette* (1985) 23 DLR (4th) 532 (judge did not misdirect).
3   But cp the definition proposed in the United States by the Federal Judicial Center, approved in *Victor v Nebraska,* above.
4   *R v Yap Chuan Ching* (1976) 63 Cr App Rep 7. See also further Commonwealth cases, *R v Flesch* (1986) 7 NSWLR 554; *R v Wilson* (1986) 42 SASR 203.
5   *R v Penny* (1992) 94 Cr App Rep 345, at 350.
6   *R v O'Rourke* (1993) 15 Cr App Rep (S) 650.
7   In *R v Gibson* (1983) 77 Cr App Rep 151 an appeal was allowed because the direction as to allocation and standard had been given only once.
8   *R v Donoghue* (1987) 86 Cr App Rep 267.
9   *R v Edwards* (1983) 77 Cr App Rep 5.

assisted by the fact that the failure to direct on the one question was compensated by a full and proper direction on the other. It is hard to conceive of circumstances in which the proviso would be applied if there were no proper direction on either.[10]

From time to time it has been suggested that further precautionary instructions are required in criminal cases but the House of Lords has refused to lay down a rule that, in addition to directing the jury that the prosecution bears the burden of proving the accused's guilt beyond reasonable doubt, the judge must, where the evidence is purely circumstantial, direct them to acquit unless the facts are not only consistent with the accused's guilt, but also inconsistent with any other rational conclusion.[11] Such a requirement was at one time assumed to exist by the Canadian courts on the authority of *Hodge*'s Case.[12] In that case great stress was properly placed on the destructive effect on the cumulative force of circumstantial evidence pointing to guilt, of one rational hypothesis of innocence; but the direction to the jury was, rightly it is submitted, treated by the House of Lords as no more than a formula suitable in some cases, for instructing the jury that they must be satisfied of the accused's guilt beyond reasonable doubt.[13]

A rule is very properly prescribed for the direction which must be given on issues on which the accused bears the persuasive burden. To repeat the words of Humphreys J:[14]

> In any case where, either by statute or at common law, some matter is presumed against an accused person 'unless the contrary is proved', the jury should be directed that it is for them to decide whether the contrary is proved, that the burden of proof required is less than that required at the hands of the prosecution in proving the case beyond a reasonable doubt, and that the burden may be discharged by evidence satisfying the jury of that which the accused is called upon to establish.

In this context the word 'satisfy' connotes satisfaction on the balance of probabilities. It is sometimes questioned whether, in a comparatively brief summing up, it is possible to make clear to a jury the distinction between the standard to be applied on issues on which the prosecution bears the persuasive burden and that to be applied when this burden is borne by the accused. If there is any difficulty in this regard, it is a further argument against placing the persuasive burden on the accused on any issue in a criminal case.

(ii)   Fragmented cases[15]

Litigation is often complex on account of fragmentation between different parties, different causes of action, different occurrences of such causes, different defences,

10   The Supreme Court of the United States regards the matter as so important as to exclude the doctrine of harmless error, *Sullivan v Louisiana* 113 S Ct R 2078 (1993). But see in Canada *R v Parnell* (1995) 98 CCC (3d) 83.
11   *McGreevy v DPP* [1973] 1 All ER 503, [1973] 1 WLR 276.
12   (1838) 2 Lew CC 227; for Australia see *Plomp v R* (1963) 110 CLR 234; *Barca v R* (1974) 133 CLR 82; *Stanton v R* [1981] WAR 185; for New Zealand see *Police v Pereira* [1977] 1 NZLR 547; for the current Canadian view see *Monteleone v R* (1987) 41 DLR (4th) 746.
13   As so stated by the High Court of Australia in *Knight v R* (1992) 66 ALJR 860.
14   *R v Carr-Briant* [1943] KB 607, at 612, p 104 above; see also *Public Prosecutor v Yuvaraj* [1970] AC 913; *Sodeman v R* [1936] 2 All ER 1138 (insanity); *R v Dunbar* [1958] 1 QB 1, [1957] 2 All ER 737 (diminished responsibility); *R v Podola* [1960] 1 QB 325, [1959] 3 All ER 418 (fitness to plead); *R v Milnes and Green* (1983) 33 SASR 211 (pardon).
15   For a helpful account of many of these situations see Smith [1988] Crim LR 335.

and different pieces of evidence. Criminal litigation is further complicated by the delegation of the determination of issues of fact to a jury, which is a collective body of lay people acting upon the direction of the judge. The issues which are required to be put are often complex in the ways mentioned above, and yet the judge has to direct the jury in its capacity as trier of fact, in the most simple and effective way. This tension is difficult to resolve. Its resolution in terms of direction as to the application of the rules as to burden of proof is best considered by separating out the different complicating factors.

(a)   Different defendants

If there are different defendants the evidence may implicate one or the other or both in the commission of the relevant crime. It may be quite conclusive so far as the commission of the crime is concerned, but quite inconclusive so far as the identity of the criminal is concerned, for example in a case where it is apparent that the deceased was killed by one of two accused, but the evidence is entirely neutral between them.[16] It is clear that in this situation it is immaterial that the evidence indicates that one or other of them must have committed the crime, and the jury must be directed that it may convict either of them only on the basis that all of the ingredients of the crime have been established to the appropriate criminal standard in relation to that particular one.

(b)   Different offences

It is necessary to distinguish between different situations. Sometimes the indictment will specify different crimes, but occasionally the law permits conviction of a different, and lesser offence, upon an indictment for another.[17] If the crimes arise out of the same incident but are quite distinct, say an assailant charged with theft and indecent assault, then the position is the same as with the co-defendants, and the jury should be directed to convict only in respect of an offence in respect of which a sufficient majority is convinced to the required standard. Where the crimes are not distinct, but are perhaps connected in having a similar actus reus, but different mens rea, as in the case of murder and manslaughter, the situation is different. Here it seems that if the evidence is capable of supporting a verdict for either offence, then the jury is entitled to return a verdict of the lesser,[18] so long as a sufficient majority is satisfied to the requisite high standard, that the accused was at least guilty of that, notwithstanding that a substantial[19] minority would find the accused guilty of the more serious offence, or that the jury may have different reasons for preferring the lesser offence.[20] This has led to disharmony between different Commonwealth courts. In *A-G for Hong Kong v Yip Kai-foon*[1] the Privy Council determined that it was wrong for the jury to be directed that once it had been convinced to the criminal standard that the accused was guilty of one or the other, then it could decide as a matter of probability which was the more likely. It should rather have been directed to try the more serious crime first, applying the ordinary criminal standard,

---

16   As in *R v Aston; R v Mason* (1991) 94 Cr App Rep 180 where there was no evidence of complicity.

17   See Criminal Appeal Act 1968, s 3, and the impact of the amendment to s 2 by the Criminal Appeal Act 1995, as explained in *R v Graham* [1997] 1 Cr App Rep 302. The situation in which this occurs because of the establishment of a mitigating defence is considered below.

18   See *R v Sinha* [1995] Crim LR 68 where the accused's intention was to pervert the course of justice in whatever tribunal might be seised of the matter.

19   Otherwise enough to acquit.

20   *R v Jones* (1999) Times, 17 February.

1   [1988] AC 642, [1988] 1 All ER 153. See also *R v Foreman* [1991] Crim LR 702.

and only if that were to result in acquittal should the lesser offence be considered. In relation to that the jury should again be directed to apply the ordinary criminal standard, and to convict only if persuaded to the appropriate standard in relation to all of the essential ingredients of that lesser offence.[2] Such a process of reasoning requires the jury to accept as true the state of facts consistent with acquittal, perhaps contrary to its actual opinion. It was rejected by the High Court of Australia in *R* v *Gilson*[3] on the basis that it did not erode the principle of *Woolmington* to permit the jury to determine between the two eligible crimes on a basis of reasonable probability.[4]

(c) Different defences

In much the same way as different offences may be spelled out of the evidence as to one count in an indictment, so they may be spelled out of different defences to that count. Thus a count of murder may be met by a defence of diminished responsibility or by one of provocation seeking to reduce the verdict to one of manslaughter.[5] The question arises as to the proper direction when the evidence is capable of proving one of a number of defences, or one of a number of components of a defence. In *R* v *More*[6] the question arose in relation to the defence of duress which has three elements, and it was held that as it was a matter of defence the jury should be directed that it was sufficient to defeat it that the requisite majority failed to accept all three elements, so it was immaterial that different members might reject different elements. Here it is submitted that it is necessary to distinguish between cases where the persuasive burden of establishing the defence is on the accused, as in diminished responsibility, and where the persuasive burden of disproving the defence is on the prosecution. In the former case if there is no sufficient agreement as to any essential element then the defence has not been proved, and the accused should be convicted; in the latter case the prosecution has not disproved the defence, and the accused should be acquitted.[7] The question is more complicated still if both diminished responsibility and provocation are raised in the same case, given the differential distribution of persuasive burden. In such a case there seems no alternative but to prescribe a sequential procedure.[8]

(d) Different counts

It is not at all uncommon for an indictment to contain a number of similar counts reflecting a succession of different incidents related by some common factors making joint trial appropriate.[9] In such a case there is no doubt at all that the jury must be

---

2   The Privy Council endorsed the decisions in *R* v *Griffiths* (1974) 60 Cr App Rep 14 and *R* v *Cash* [1985] QB 801, [1985] 2 All ER 128 that it was not necessary in relation to a charge of handling to show that it was committed 'otherwise than in the course of stealing'.
3   (1991) 172 CLR 353.
4   Here it need be no more than a matter of relative probability. The English view could lead to conviction by the jury for the offence which it believed it less likely that the accused had committed.
5   In relation to diminished responsibility the evidential and persuasive burdens are both borne by the accused, but as noted above the persuasive burden to disprove a defence may remain on the prosecution, for example in relation to provocation.
6   [1987] 3 All ER 825, [1987] 1 WLR 1578.
7   But see Smith [1988] Crim LR 335, at 340 where it is argued that in the latter case there is a disagreement, justifying a re-trial.
8   It is submitted that the accused should be permitted to elect which the jury should consider first, cp. the procedure adopted by Devlin J in *R* v *Roberts* (1953) unreported described in (1994) NLJ, 24 June.
9   See Indictment Rules 1971 r 9.

directed to consider each count separately[10] and to find the accused guilty only of those where all the ingredients have been proved to the appropriate criminal standard.

(e)   Different evidence

Sometimes even within a single count there may be evidence of more than one occurrence of one of the ingredients of the offence. For example in one of the earliest cases to consider this problem a number of false statements were alleged in support of a charge of procuring the execution of a valuable security by deception.[11] The Court of Appeal there took the view that it was wrong to prescribe too closely how the jury should reason, and that provided each juror was satisfied to the required standard that deception had been practised, it was immaterial that different jurors might have relied upon different statements. This does seem to contravene the *Woolmington* principle, and in a subsequent case where the jury explicitly asked whether it needed to agree on a particular ingredient, and was accordingly told that it need not, this was held to be a misdirection.[12] *Agbim* was distinguished on the basis that in that case there had been only one deception alleged in the indictment, though a number of different allegedly deceptive statements had been adduced as evidence of that one piece of deception. This appeared to make all turn upon the precise drafting of the particulars of the offence in the indictment. If more than one statement were specified then the jury must agree that one in particular was false, but if only one deceptive statement were specified, then the fact that its deceptive quality was to be derived from one of a number of allegedly false supporting statements was immaterial, and the jury need not agree upon the falsity of any one of them. This seems a very fine distinction now that it has been decided that the direction in *Brown* is appropriate despite the separate incidents relied upon to establish one count not being separately particularised.[13] Thus in *R v Smith*[14] it was held in a case of affray that while there was no need for the jury to agree on any separate incident in a course of continuing conduct, once it was established that there were two separate courses of conduct, then the jury did have to be instructed that it must be unanimous in relation to the same one of the two courses.

Even if a number of alternative allegations are made in the particulars it is not always necessary to direct the jury of the need for unanimity in respect of one,[15] as this may be accomplished implicitly by the prescription of a staged approach.[16] This may not be appropriate where the particulars specify two inconsistent methods of committing an offence, for example direct commission, and procuring commission by another.[17] The current position appears to be that if, but only if, there is a serious possibility of confusion then such a direction is necessary.[18]

---

10   Although evidence of one may be admissible in considering another, see further Ch VIII below.

11   *R v Agbim* [1979] Crim LR 171. See also *R v Ryder* [1995] 2 NZLR 271.

12   *R v Brown* (1983) 79 Cr App Rep 115. In *R v Keeton* [1995] 2 Cr App Rep 241 it was held that this form of direction was exceptional, and confined to cases where there was a real risk of confusion as a result of the prosecution's advancing alternative bases for liability.

13   *R v Houlden* (1994) 99 Cr App Rep 244.

14   [1997] 1 Cr App Rep 14.

15   *R v Price* [1991] Crim LR 465.

16   *R v More* [1987] 3 All ER 825, [1987] 1 WLR 1578; *R v Flynn* (1985) 82 Cr App Rep 319; *R v Rowe* [1990] Crim LR 344.

17   In *R v Gaughan* (1991) 155 JP 235 this was unexceptionable as the jury must have believed that if one of the methods had not been employed then the other must have been, though if this is not the case then it seems that the jury should be directed to acquit in the absence of agreement at to method, see obiter dicta of Lamer J differing from the majority in *Thatcher v R* [1987] 1 SCR 652.

18   *R v Mitchell* (1994) 26 HLR 394.

A still more esoteric question has been raised: can there be satisfaction beyond reasonable doubt of the guilt of the accused when there is no such satisfaction with regard to any of the evidentiary facts? On this the full court of South Australia has expressed itself as follows:[19]

> There is a clear distinction between drawing an inference of guilt from a combination of several proved facts, none of which by itself would support the inference, and drawing an inference of guilt from several facts whose existence is in doubt. In the first place [sic] the combination does what each fact taken in isolation could not do; in the second case the combination counts for nothing.

In the second case much would depend upon the degree of doubt entertained about the existence of the several facts whose existence was doubtful. An accumulation of evidentiary facts each of which is proved on a balance of probabilities may suffice to dispel all doubt about the existence of the fact to be proved. The South Australian court concluded that facts from which inferences are to be drawn must be 'clearly proved'.

These remarks were subsequently considered by the High Court of Australia in *R v Chamberlain (No 2)*[20] and by the Supreme Court of Canada in *R v Morin*.[1] The majority of the High Court in *Chamberlain* seemed to have taken the view that no inferences can be drawn from facts which are not themselves proved beyond reasonable doubt,[2] and that the jury should be so directed, but Deane J adopted a more discriminating approach, distinguishing between primary and intermediate facts.[3] The Supreme Court of Canada was divided on this question in *Morin*, but it was the minority[4] which took the view of the majority in the High Court of Australia, and even they qualified it by stressing that no fact was to be considered in isolation, but only in the light of all of the surrounding facts. Deane J and the majority[5] in *Morin* felt that this was to intrude too far into the jury's fact-finding process. They accepted that if guilt depends upon a chain of elements, each corresponding to a different piece of evidence, then the jury must be, and must be instructed to be, satisfied beyond reasonable doubt that the required elements have been established. This does not however imply that no inferences can be drawn from facts less well established, if they are not synonymous with essential elements of the offence.[6] Egglestone rightly points out that any other view would make nonsense of the rules relating to corroboration. As Deane J put it:[7]

> There is certainly no requirement of the law that the members of the jury must examine separately each item of evidence adduced by the prosecution and reject it unless they are satisfied beyond reasonable doubt that it is correct. Nor is it the law that a jury is in all circumstances precluded from drawing an inference from a primary fact unless that fact is proved beyond reasonable doubt.

These views have now prevailed.[8]

---

19   *R v Van Beelen* [1972] 4 SASR 353, at 374; criticised by Egglestone *Evidence, Proof and Probability* (3rd edn) p 122.
20   (1984) 153 CLR 521.
1   (1988) 66 CR (3d) 1.
2   See Gibbs CJ and Mason J at 538, 539; Murphy J at 570; and Brennan J at 599.
3   At 626, 627.
4   Wilson and Lamer JJ.
5   Sopinka J with whom Dickson CJC, McIntyre and La Forest JJ concurred.
6   Or at any stage constitute single links in a chain of reasoning to the inference of such an essential element.
7   At 626. See also *Thomas v R* [1972] NZLR 34.
8   *Shepherd v R* (1990) 170 CLR 573 where Dawson J ascribes the problem to the available nomenclature; *Edwards v R* (1993) 178 CLR 193. See also *Stratford v Ministry of Transport* [1992] 1 NZLR 486; *Mackenzie v R* (1993) 18 CR (4th) 133.

(iii)   Criminal issues in other proceedings

Special considerations apply when the question of whether a crime has been committed arises in other proceedings. The difficulty is that the court in those proceedings is placed in a dilemma in which it must abandon either consistency of standard of proof as between two different proceedings relating to the same issue, or abandon it as between two different issues arising in the same proceedings. Such a dilemma can arise in administrative proceedings for the recovery of compensation for criminal injuries,[9] or in an ordinary civil case. A claims damages for a libel in which B referred to him as a bigamist,[10] the insurer's defence to a claim on a policy of fire insurance is that the assured is guilty of arson[11] or the claimant simply seeks damages for a conspiracy to defraud. This is precisely what happened in *New York State v Heirs of Phillips*[12] where the advice of the Judicial Committee of the Privy Council delivered by Lord Atkin stated that the standard appropriate to criminal proceedings was the right one as 'the proposition has been laid down time and again by the courts of this country and appears to be just'.[13] If this remark was intended to apply to all civil cases in which criminal conduct is alleged, it must be admitted that observations which were capable of bearing a contrary meaning had previously been made in the House of Lords,[14] and in *Doe d Devine v Wilson*,[15] the Judicial Committee had favoured the contrary view when holding that a party relying on a deed could discharge the persuasive burden of negativing its forgery on a preponderance of probability. *Doe d Devine v Wilson* was preferred by the High Court of Australia in *Helton v Allen*,[16] and again in *Rejfek v McElroy*.[17] Similar views in favour of the civil standard have prevailed in Scotland,[18] New Zealand[19] and Canada.[20]

In *Hornal v Neuberger Products Ltd*[1] the Court of Appeal recognised that the earlier English cases conflicted, and concluded, in apparently general terms, that proof on a preponderance of probability will suffice when the commission of a crime is alleged in a civil action. The claimant claimed damages for breach of warranty and fraud on the ground that the defendant had falsely stated that a machine sold by him to the claimant had been reconditioned. So far as the alleged breach of warranty was concerned, the trial judge held that the words were spoken by the defendant, but the claim failed because he considered that the parties did not intend them to have contractual effect. The judge proceeded to award damages for fraud, although he said that he was merely satisfied on the balance of probability, and not beyond reasonable doubt, that the

9   *R v Criminal Injuries Compensation Board, ex p Crangle* (1981) Times, 14 November.
10   *Willmett v Harmer* (1839) 8 C & P 695 where the same strictness of proof was required in support of B's plea of justification as on a trial for bigamy. See also *Chalmers v Shackell* (1834) 6 C & P 475.
11   *Thurtell v Beaumont* (1823) 1 Bing 339 (jury should be as satisfied as in a criminal case); *Issaias v Marine Insurance Co Ltd* (1923) 15 Ll L Rep 186, where the same view is taken by Atkin LJ at 192. In *Slattery v Mance* [1962] 1 QB 676, [1962] 1 All ER 525 it was decided that the insurer has the burden of proving that the assured set fire to the insured ship on balance of probability only.
12   [1939] 3 All ER 952.
13   At 954.
14   *Lek v Mathews* (1927) 29 Ll L Rep 141, at 164 per Lord Sumner.
15   (1855) 10 Moo PCC 502.
16   (1940) 63 CLR 691.
17   (1965) 112 CLR 517. There seems to be no point in referring to other Australian authorities.
18   *Fisher and Donaldson Ltd v Steven* 1988 SCCR 337.
19   *Ellis v Frape* [1954] NZLR 341; *Cheape v New Zealand Law Society* [1955] NZLR 63; *MW Middleditch & Sons v Hinds* [1962] NZLR 570.
20   *Mutual Life Assurance Co of Canada v Aubin* [1979] 2 SCR 298.
1   [1957] 1 QB 247, [1956] 3 All ER 970.

statement was made. If the statement had in fact been made, the defendant would have been guilty of obtaining money by false pretences, for it was beyond dispute that he knew that the machine had not been reconditioned. The Court of Appeal dismissed the appeal mainly because:[2]

> it would bring the law into contempt if a judge were to say that on the issue of warranty he finds that the statement was made, and on the issue of fraud he finds it was not made.

Yet this would have been the result of holding that the claim for damages for fraud had to be established beyond reasonable doubt.

Although there were several previous decisions which were not discussed by the Court of Appeal, *Hornal*'s case may be taken to have settled the English law for the time being. An allegation of criminal conduct, even of murder,[3] need be established only on a preponderance of probability in a civil action. When the commission of a crime is alleged in civil proceedings, the stigma attaching to an affirmative finding might be thought to justify the imposition of a strict standard of proof; but the person against whom criminal conduct is alleged is adequately protected by the consideration that the antecedent improbability of his guilt is 'a part of the whole range of circumstances which have to be weighed in the scale when deciding as to the balance of probabilities'.[4] By applying the flexible civil standard the civil court may thus discriminate between the standard required to prove the commission of the same crime by different individuals.[5]

C.   THE QUESTION OF A THIRD STANDARD[6] AND THE POSSIBILITY OF ANOMALIES

Three standards of proof appear to be recognised in the United States, proof by 'clear, strong and cogent' evidence lying midway between proof on a preponderance of probability and proof beyond reasonable doubt.[7] It is certainly not difficult to find

---

2   At 258, 973, respectively, per Denning LJ. See also remarks of Sholl J in *McClelland v Symons* [1951] VLR 157, at 166. Lord Denning's remarks may be thought to conflict with his earlier observations in *Bater v Bater* (p 142 above) where he said the court will require a higher degree of probability for fraud than for negligence; but the ingredient of fraud which requires a high standard of probability is the defendant's knowledge of the falsity of his statement rather than the fact that he made it, and, if the statement was made, the defendant's knowledge of its falsity was beyond dispute in *Hornal*'s case. On the question whether the statement was made there is no reason why the degree of probability for fraud and warranty should differ.

3   *Re Dellow's Will Trusts, Lloyds Bank Ltd v Institute of Cancer Research* [1964] 1 All ER 771; *Nishina Trading Co Ltd v Chiyoda Fire and Marine Insurance Co Ltd* [1969] 2 QB 449, [1969] 2 All ER 776 (theft proved on balance). See also in England *Francisco v Diedrick* (1998) Times, 3 April and in Scotland *Mullan v Anderson* 1993 SLT 835 (murder in civil proceedings for assault), departing from and disapproving of any intimation to the contrary in *Halford v Brookes* [1992] PIQR P175; in Australia *G v M* (1995) 126 FLR 355 (sexual abuse in custody proceedings); and in New Zealand *Real Estate Institute of New Zealand Inc v Private Sale Co (Auckland Central) Ltd* [1996] 2 NZLR 371 (statutory crime relating to trading in civil proceedings for injunction).

4   Per Morris LJ (see p 142 above).

5   *G (a minor) Re* [1987] 1 WLR 1461 (more required to show father guilty of sexual abuse of child than would have been required for another).

6   See Pattenden (1989) 7 Civ JQ 220.

7   Morgan *Problems of Proof in the Anglo-American System of Trials* 82; Uniform Rules 1.04, see *Addington v Texas* 441 US 418 (1979), though there is still a presumption that the standard in a civil case will be on the balance of probabilities, *Grogan v Garner* 498 US 279 (1991). See

support for the view that English law recognises standards other than those of proof beyond reasonable doubt and on a balance of probabilities. A claim for rectification must, it has been said, be established by 'strong, irrefragable evidence',[8] and the Law Reform Committee, whilst conceding that the meaning, like the pronunciation of this expression is not beyond argument, considered it to be clear that a mere balance of probability is not enough.[9] A high standard has been called for in cases of alleged professional misconduct as the Judicial Committee[10] could not envisage professional men condemning each other on a mere balance of probabilities. The evidence in rebuttal of the presumption of the formal validity of a marriage must, it has been said, be 'strong, distinct and satisfactory';[11] while an intention to change domicile must be 'clearly and unequivocally proved'.[12] Observations of this sort will no doubt continue to be cited by the courts,[13] but they do not support the importation of a third standard, for as Nourse J remarked in connection with the proof of mutual wills:[14]

> that does not mean that there has to be a departure from the ordinary standard of proof required in civil proceedings. I have to be satisfied on the balance of probabilities that the alleged agreement was made, but before I can be satisfied of that I must find clear and satisfactory evidence to that effect.

In the same vein Lord Tucker was, it is believed, expressing the commonly held opinion when he said: 'I am quite unable to accede to the proposition that there is some intermediate onus between that which is required in criminal cases and the balance of probability which is sufficient in civil actions.'[15] There would be further difficulty in establishing a form of words, in determining exactly to which proceedings it should apply, and in explaining it to a jury. If, as the English cases allow, there is flexibility within the existing standards to accommodate different prior probabilities and outcomes, it seems totally unnecessary to add a further standard.[16]

D.   MATHEMATICS AND THE STANDARD OF PROOF

Since the standard of proof is concerned with the question of the amount of evidence which is required to persuade the trier of fact, there is an understandable tendency to

---

Cooper v Oklahoma 517 US 348 (1996) for unease in casting such a burden on the accused in a criminal case, even on a procedural issue (competence to stand trial). When the issue is what might happen in the future, eg whether an alleged offender might be prejudiced at his trial if returned to a designated country, something less than a preponderance of probability will suffice, Fernandez v Government of Singapore [1971] 2 All ER 691, [1971] 1 WLR 987. See also R v Askeland [1983] Tas NC 224 for an unequivocal view that the standard of proof of the voluntariness of a confession is in Australia intermediate between the usual two.

8   Countess Dowager Shelburne v Earl of Inchiquin (1784) 1 Bro CC 338, at 341; A Roberts & Co Ltd v Leicestershire County Council [1961] Ch 555, [1961] 2 All ER 545; cf Earl v Hector Whaling Ltd [1961] 1 Lloyd's Rep 459. See also Re Snowden, Smith v Spowage [1979] Ch 528, [1979] 2 All ER 172.

9   19th report para 26.

10   Bhandari v Advocates Committee [1956] 3 All ER 742, [1956] 1 WLR 1442. See also Willcox v Sing [1985] 2 Qd R 66.

11   Piers v Piers (1849) 2 HL Cas 331, at 389; Mahadervan v Mahadervan [1964] P 233, at 236.

12   Moorhouse v Lord (1863) 10 HL Cas 272, at 286.

13   See eg per Lord Simon of Glaisdale in Steadman v Steadman [1976] AC 536, at 563–4.

14   Re Cleaver, Cleaver v Insley [1981] 2 All ER 1018, at 1024, [1981] 1 WLR 939, at 947.

15   Dingwall v J Wharton (Shipping) Ltd [1961] 2 Lloyds Rep 213, at 216. See also the remarks of Brennan J in Neat Holdings Pty Ltd v Karajan Holdings Pty Ltd (1993) 67 ALJR 170.

16   As accepted in Re H [1996] AC 563, [1996] 1 All ER 1, at 587E, 17h.

attempt to apply the techniques of mathematics to its assessment. The temptation to count is an old one,[17] which still persists in some corroboration requirements as will be seen in ch V. It has appealed most to those of a theoretical disposition. Bentham was attracted to it, influenced by the observation that wagering and insurance both attach numerical values to probabilities.[18] As the number of ways in which modern technology can assist judicial enquiry grows, it has become increasingly necessary for courts to adopt methods of combining evidence of mathematical precision with less exact sources of information.[19] It is also common knowledge that many important decisions in fields such as business, national defence, and the formation of economic policy are increasingly taken upon the basis of the mathematical modelling of probabilities and decision theory. Whatever the reason, there has been a burgeoning of attention on the question of the possibility of applying mathematical techniques to law.[20] Much of this debate is, to say the least, remote from the practical concerns of trial lawyers. There has been a recent judicial reminder of this:[1]

> The concept of 'probability' in the legal sense is certainly different from the mathematical concept; indeed, it is rare to find a situation in which the two usages co-exist although, when they do, the mathematical probability has to be taken into the assessment of probability in the legal sense and given its appropriate weight.

In that case the Court of Appeal refused to 'transmute a mathematical probability into a forensic certainty' by determining the paternity of a child upon the basis of statistical blood grouping evidence, at least in the absence of a full investigation of all the surrounding circumstances. One of the problems is that the proper foundation for the application of the mathematical techniques is rarely present. A striking example of this, and one which sparked off much of the modern American interest, is provided by *People v Collins*.[2] In that case the trial judge admitted statistical evidence in an attempt to identify the accused with the perpetrators of the robbery in question. There was evidence that the guilty couple possessed six characteristics. A statistician was allowed to testify that the likelihood of their all being present in any couple was, upon certain assumptions, 12 million to one against. The accused couple possessed these six characteristics, and were found guilty. As was pointed out on appeal this procedure was quite inappropriate. There was no basis for the assumptions of the likelihood of

17 It appears in late Roman Law, Corpus Juris 4.20.9 (AD 334).
18 *Treatise on Judicial Evidence* (1825) ch 17.
19 DNA analysis presents particular problems, and has been used as a stalking horse in an attempt to encourage the use of Bayes theorem as a means of combination, but use of the theorem seems inappropriate for jury trial, and has been roundly condemned by the English courts: see *R v Adams* [1996] 2 Cr App Rep 467; *R v Adams (No 2)* (1997) Times, 3 November; and *R v Doheny and Adams* [1997] 1 Cr App Rep 369. For recent theory see 1 Int J of Evidence & Proof 253 et seq (1997).
20 Such techniques are canvassed in Cohen *The Probable and The Provable* (2nd edn, 1991); Eggleston *Evidence, Proof and Probability* (2nd edn, 1983); Finkelstein and Fairley, 1970) 83 Harv LR 489; Tribe (1971) 84 Harv LR 1329, see also pp 1801 and 1810 for continuation of debate; Glanville Williams [1979] Crim LR 297, 340; Cohen [1980] Crim LR 91, and see p 103 for a rejoinder by Glanville Williams; and Jackson (1980) 31 NILQ 223. The subject has generated massive theoretical attention in the United States, see the report of a symposium in (1986) 66 Boston ULR 377 running to more than 500 pages, and another in (1991) 13 Cardozo LR 253 running to more than 800.
1 *J S (a minor), Re* [1981] Fam 22, at 29, [1980] 1 All ER 1061 at 1066. See also *R v Shepherd* (1988) 85 ALR 387, at 392 by Roden J: 'Degrees of probability and degrees of proof with which juries are concerned are rarely capable of expression in mathematical terms.'
2 438 P 2d 33 (1968).

each of the characteristics occurring independently, and there was no ground for supposing that they were independent, indeed there was every ground for supposing that they were not. It will be extremely rare for the information required to make such estimates of probability to be available to a court. Nor should the court attempt to manufacture its own statistics where there is no evidence at all. A cautionary example here is provided by the opinion of Murphy J in *T N T Management Pty Ltd v Brooks*.[3] The claimant sought damages in respect of a road accident in which both drivers had been killed, and there was little evidence which was to blame. Murphy J took the view that it was too little. He was however prepared to uphold the claim on the basis that there were three possibilities, both to blame, claimant to blame or defendant to blame. Since two of these favoured the claimant's claim and only one opposed it, the balance of probabilities was satisfied. It is not clear why he excluded the possibility of neither to blame. Quite apart from that the procedure is obviously prone to cause injustice, for example in a case where only one of three injured employees caused the damage by his negligence in the course of his employment, but it is unknown which of them it was. In such a case the odds of any one being an innocent victim are also two to one on, with the startling consequence that all three can succeed although the whole calculation presupposes that one of them is not in fact entitled to do so.

If part of the difficulty is that there is usually an insufficient evidential basis for the mathematical exegesis, another is that the mathematical techniques are themselves controversial. Thus the statistical appendix to the judgment in *Collins* which purported to substitute an accurate statistical analysis for the faulty methods proposed by the trial judge has itself been attacked as being mathematically unsound,[4] and the inapplicability of classical Pascalian probability to law is the whole theme of Cohen's book.

There will, of course, be some statistical evidence which does have a satisfactory foundation, and some issues to which that evidence is relevant. Such evidence will not automatically be excluded on the basis that it falls short of absolute scientific certainty.[5] Blood group evidence may be of that character. If a question arises as to the paternity of a child it may be possible to establish that if the husband of the mother is not the father then it could be one in ten of the population. In such a case the court must be wary of the alluring precision of the figures, and must not be seduced from the path of weighing together all of the circumstances, for example the terms of the relationship between husband and wife, the opportunities and inclinations of the wife for extra-marital intercourse, and the motives of the parties in making any allegations.[6] It will be a rare case where mathematical techniques will make a decisive contribution to the resolution of forensic uncertainty.[7]

3   (1979) 53 ALJR 267, the rest of the court decided the case upon the quite different basis that the evidence adduced was just sufficient to prove negligence.
4   Fairley and Mosteller (1974) 41 U Chi LR 242.
5   *S v S* [1972] AC 24, [1970] 3 All ER 107; *R v Bracewell* (1978) 68 Cr App Rep 44.
6   In *R v Chedzey* (1987) 30 ACR 451 where there was little other evidence to show that the accused was the maker of a malicious telephone call the court refused to uphold a conviction based on evidence that the automatic trading procedure was 99.96% accurate.
7   But not unknown; fingerprint or other forensic matching is often decisive, see further above p 42.

CHAPTER IV

The functions of the judge and jury

Historically, the separation of the functions of the judge and jury has left so deep a mark upon English jurisprudence that the rules and habits of juristic thought, which it has engendered, are scarcely touched by the present day decline of jury trial in civil matters. If jury trial is ever abolished, many of these rules and conceptions will yet remain as long as the common law system is in being. The judge sitting alone must constantly be aware of the line which divides his two quite distinct functions. And the proper observation of the distinction is by no means a mere academic matter, but of the highest practical importance in its bearing on the exercise of appellate jurisdiction.[1]

A due appreciation of the respective functions of the judge and jury is therefore essential to a proper understanding of the law of evidence, and that is why a separate chapter has been allotted to them. The general rule is discussed in the first section, and some of the more direct methods of judicial control are considered in section 2. Empirical research is beyond the scope of this book. It must be admitted, however, that no discussion of the law of evidence in criminal cases will ever be completely satisfactory until we have some idea of the extent to which the average jury understands the directions which the law requires the judge to give, and whether jurors are as comprehending, uncomprehending or prejudiced as some of the rules of evidence suppose. Does the jury understand the direction that it is to use the victim's out of court complaint of rape, not as evidence of it, but only as confirming the victim's evidence in court? Does the jury assume that the accused who elects not to testify has previous convictions? And if he does testify, and has previous convictions put to him in cross-examination, does the jury understand that these do not prove his guilt directly, but only impair his credibility? These, and a number of similar questions could be answered satisfactorily only by controlled, and secret, monitoring of the deliberations of real juries in real cases. Unfortunately such monitoring would amount to contempt of court.[2] Recourse must, at present,[3] be had to simulations and generally less reliable

---

1   Bridge (1949) 12 MLR 275. Many of the matters considered in this chapter are discussed by Devlin in *Trial by Jury* (The Hamlyn Lectures for 1965, revd 1966). See also Cornish *The Jury* (1968); and Nokes (1956) 31 Tul LR 153.
2   Contempt of Court Act 1981, s 8.
3   Though the very first recommendation of the Royal Commission on Criminal Justice Cm 2263 (1993) was that section 8 be amended to permit proper scientific research into the working of juries.

methods of obtaining the information needed to provide a basis for understanding and improving the law of evidence.[4]

SECTION 1.   THE GENERAL RULE

The general rule is that questions of law must be determined by the judge and questions of fact must be determined by the jury, but there are some special cases as well as exceptions to the general rule.

A.   SOME SPECIAL CASES

1.   Construction

'The meaning of an ordinary word of the English language is not a question of law. The proper construction of a statute is a question of law'.[5] Lord Reid said this on the hearing of an appeal in a criminal case from a Divisional Court, but his remarks have since been held to apply to a criminal trial by jury.[6] The appeal was concerned with the meaning of the words 'insulting behaviour' in s 5 of the Public Order Act 1936. Lord Reid continued:

> If the context shows that a word is used in an unusual sense the court will determine in other words what that unusual sense is. But here there is in my opinion no question of the word 'insulting' being used in an unusual sense. It is for the tribunal which decides the case to consider, not as law but as fact, whether in the whole circumstances the words of the statute do or do not as a matter of ordinary usage of the English language cover or apply to the facts which have been proved.

Concern has been expressed lest this gives the jury too free a hand, but account must be taken of a number of limiting factors. The proper construction of a statute may require a judge to do more than decide whether words are used in an unusual sense and if so, what that sense is.[7] He may have to choose between a variety of possible meanings, including ordinary meanings of which there is sometimes more than one, and this will result in a direction on the law. Even when the sole question is the ordinary meaning of a word, the fact that it is a matter for the jury does not mean that they have an unfettered choice for Lord Reid recognised the possibility of an appeal on the ground that 'no tribunal acquainted with the ordinary use of the language could reasonably reach that decision'. The judge may therefore direct the jury that it is not open to them to give a particular meaning to ordinary words because that would be unreasonable, and, provided he makes it plain that the decision must be theirs, he can illustrate the

4   For examples, see Kalven and Zeisel *The American Jury* (1966); McCabe and Purves *Bypassing the Jury* (1972) and *The Jury at Work* (1972) ; Cornish [1973] Crim LR 208; Sealey and Cornish (1973) 36 MLR 496; Royal Commission on Criminal Justice Cm 2263; (1993) Res St No 19; (1993) *Crown Court Study* Ch 8.
5   *Brutus v Cozens* [1973] AC 854 at 861; see also *Sussex Investments Ltd v Secretary of State for Environment* [1997] NPC 190.
6   *R v Feeley* [1973] QB 530, [1973] 1 All ER 341.
7   Although in the case of ordinary words the judge is expected to employ his own knowledge, he may consider evidence to determine whether and what unusual sense is being employed, *Marquis Camden v IRC* [1914] 1 KB 641, at 650.

application of a word or phrase to various factual situations including that of the instant case.

Even so there is a danger of uncertainty when a jury is left to pronounce on such general matters as the question whether property was 'dishonestly' appropriated or obtained by the accused without anything more than a direction on what 'dishonestly' cannot reasonably mean and some illustrations of what it can mean. There could well be contradictory verdicts in different cases concerned with substantially the same facts. If this is undesirable it is the price we pay for the rule that, although a judge may direct an acquittal on appropriate facts, he has no power to direct a verdict of guilty even though he is satisfied that an acquittal would be perverse.[8]

The extent to which Lord Reid's words with which this section began can be generalised is an open question. It is tempting to say that the meaning of an ordinary word of the English language is always a matter of fact to be determined by the jury while construction is always a matter of law. There can be no doubt about the second of these propositions, but there is a good deal of eighteenth and nineteenth-century authority in support of the view that in a civil case tried with a jury the meaning of ordinary words comes within the sphere of construction.[9] The jury's role tended to be confined to the determination of specific facts such as the surrounding circumstances with reference to which a private document was executed and the intention of the parties. The rarity at the present time of jury trial in civil cases renders it impossible to predict, and pointless to speculate on, the extent to which the old authorities would be followed today.

2. Defamation

Endeavours to restrict the role of the jury in accordance with those authorities in cases of criminal libel were the precipitating cause of Fox's Libel Act 1792. It provides that, in criminal prosecutions for libel, the jury shall, after direction by the judge on the law, give a general verdict upon the whole matter. In consequence of this statute, it has come to be the practice for the judge to determine whether the document in question is capable of bearing the meaning alleged by the prosecution, while the jury decides whether it does in fact amount to a criminal libel. This has been said to be because the intention of the parties is always a question for the jury, and the meaning of the document is part of that intention;[10] but the same procedure is adopted in civil cases where the intention of the parties is, to say the least, not so important as on a criminal charge.[11] It is therefore best to regard the established practice as a compromise. Literal adherence to the rule that the construction of documents and the ordinary meaning of words is a matter of law for the judge would mean that the jury simply determines whether the alleged libel was published and whether the circumstances from which any suggested innuendo could be inferred exist. This was the usual practice before Fox's Libel Act, but it proved to be objectionable on political grounds, and because it contravened the jury's right to return a general verdict in criminal cases.[12]

8   See Williams [1976] Crim LR 472 and 532, and Elliott [1976] Crim LR 707.
9   See for example *Neilson v Harford* (1841) 8 M & W 806, at 823.
10 Per Lord Abinger CJ in *Morrell v Firth* (1838) 3 M & W 402, at 404–5.
11 *Nevill v Fine Arts and General Insurance Co* [1897] AC 68.
12 Holdsworth *History of English Law* (vol 10) 688.

3. Perjury

Under s 11(6) of the Perjury Act 1911, the question whether a statement on which perjury is assigned is material is one of law to be determined by the court of trial. In most cases the materiality of a statement would naturally be treated as a question of fact, and there are some express statutory provisions to this effect,[13] but, in the case of perjury, it is probably convenient that the matter should be treated as one of law in the interests of certainty and uniformity.[14]

B. EXCEPTIONS

I. Foreign law

So far as the courts of England and Wales are concerned, the law of other countries, including Scotland, Eire[15] since 1921, and the British Commonwealth, is a matter of fact to be determined on the evidence adduced in a particular case.[16] Thus, if the validity of a ceremony of marriage is among the facts in issue, proof of the ceremony will not be sufficient, for it must usually be shown to have constituted a formally valid marriage according to the law of the place of celebration.

Down to 1920, the evidence relating to the foreign law was submitted to the jury, but s 15 of the Administration of Justice Act of that year provided that, where for the purpose of disposing of any claim or any other matter which is being tried by a judge with a jury in any court in England or Wales it is necessary to ascertain the law of any other country which is applicable to the facts of the case, any question as to the effect of the evidence with respect to that law shall, instead of being submitted to the jury, be decided by the judge alone.[17] The difficulty of the points which may be involved is no doubt an ample justification for this provision which has been held to be wide enough to cover criminal proceedings.[18] A similar procedure applies to the determination of questions as to the meaning or effect of community treaties, or the validity, meaning or effect of community instruments.[19] They too are questions for the judge to decide, if necessary after hearing evidence, which in a criminal case would not be heard by the jury.[20]

---

13   Eg Marine Insurance Act 1906, s 20(7).

14   See *R v Traino* (1987) 27 ACR 271.

15   See Nokes (1960) 9 ICLQ 564. The Ireland Act 1949 under which Eire is for many purposes not a foreign country, has not affected the position (*Todd v Todd* [1961] 2 All ER 881, [1961] 1 WLR 951). So far as Northern Ireland is concerned the English courts would probably take judicial notice of the common law of Northern Ireland and of English statutes applying to Northern Ireland but not of statutes of the Northern Ireland Parliament. Under the Maintenance Orders Act 1950, s 22(2), judicial notice may be taken of the laws of all parts of the United Kingdom in maintenance proceedings.

16   Except that the House of Lords takes cognisance of the law of Scotland, and the Privy Council takes cognisance of the law of the British Commonwealth (*Elliot v Lord Joicey* [1935] AC 209, at 213 and 236). See also European Communities Act 1972, s 3(2), providing for the taking of judicial notice by the English courts of the community treaties and decisions of the European court.

17   Section 15 of the Administration of Justice Act 1920 has been repealed so far as the High Court is concerned by the Judicature Act 1925, but a similar provision is contained in s 69(5) of the Supreme Court Act 1981. See also s 68 of the County Courts Act 1984 as to county courts.

18   *R v Hammer* [1923] 2 KB 786. For proof of foreign law see ch XVII.

19   European Communities Act 1972, s 3(1).

20   *R v Goldstein* [1983] 1 All ER 434, [1983] 1 WLR 151.

2.   Reasonableness

The reasonableness of a particular belief or course of conduct is essentially a question of fact, and, as such, it normally has to be determined by the jury, but, in certain civil cases, it must be decided by the judge, although he may leave subsidiary issues upon which the question of reasonableness ultimately depends to the jury. In a claim for malicious prosecution, the question whether the defendant had a reasonable and probable cause for initiating the criminal proceedings must be answered by the judge.[1] It is also the duty of the judge to determine whether the terms of a covenant in restraint of trade are reasonably necessary for the protection of the covenantee;[2] but he may require the jury to find relevant facts concerning the information on which the defendant acted in the first case,[3] and the nature of the covenantee's business in the second.

3.   Facts affecting the admissibility of evidence[4]

There are conditions precedent which are required to be fulfilled before evidence is admissible for the jury. Thus, an oath, or its equivalent, and competency, are conditions precedent to admitting viva voce evidence; and the apprehension of immediate death to admitting evidence of dying declarations;[5] a search to secondary evidence of lost writings; and stamps to certain written instruments;[6] and so is consanguinity or affinity in the declarant to declarations of deceased relatives.[7] The judge alone has to decide whether the condition has been fulfilled. If the proof is by witnesses, he must decide on their credibility. If counter-evidence is offered, he must receive it before he decides; and he has no right to ask the opinion of the jury on the fact of a condition precedent.[8]

Other examples of the application of the rule are afforded by cases in which the accused objects to the reception of a confession on the ground that it does not satisfy the conditions of s 76 of the Police and Criminal Evidence Act 1984, or a witness claims to be privileged from answering a particular question.[9] In all such instances, the judge, and not the jury, must determine disputed facts, and the entirely separate nature of these preliminary or incidental issues was emphasised by the old practice under which witnesses who deposed to them were required to take a different oath, known as the 'voir dire' from that sworn by those giving evidence which was to be submitted to the jury. The trial of the incidental issues is often called 'a trial within a trial'.

It is often impossible to decide the question of admissibility without disclosing the evidence on which the dispute turns. If it is alleged that a confession was made under pressure, the question can often be settled only by considering the terms of the

---

1   *Herniman v Smith* [1938] AC 305, [1938] 1 All ER 1 (malicious prosecution); *Ward v Chief Constable of West Midlands* (1997) Times, 13 December (false imprisonment).
2   *Dowden and Pook Ltd v Pook* [1904] 1 KB 45.
3   Though not where those facts themselves involve issues of law: *Ward v Chief Constable of West Midlands Police* above.
4   See also ch I, section 2, part A (iii) above. For thorough, if, from the English point of view, rather elaborate, discussions of this subject see Maguire and Epstein (1926) 40 Harv LR 392, and Morgan (1929) 43 Harv LR 165. See also Morgan *Some Problems of Proof* ch 3.
5   Under an exception to the rule against hearsay as to the cause of death in prosecutions for homicide. For an early example of the exclusive control of the judge in such a case, see *R v Hucks* (1816) 1 Stark 521.
6   For an example see *Bartlett v Smith* (1843) 11 M & W 483.
7   Admissible under a common law exception to the rule against hearsay on genealogical issues (now applicable only in criminal cases).
8   *Doe d Jenkins v Davies* (1847) 10 QB 314, at 323 per Lord Denman CJ.
9   *Stace v Griffith* (1869) LR 2 PC 420, at 427–8.

accused's statements, and the jury could scarcely help being influenced by them even if they were to conclude that the surrounding circumstances rendered the confession inadmissible.[10] As Lord Mustill stated in *Wallace and Fuller v R* [11] the tasks of judge and jury in relation to disputed confessions, although theoretically distinct, are in practice very similar. The Privy Council thus felt no difficulty in rejecting a submission that reasons for the decision on admissibility should be canvassed, and in *Mitchell v R*[12] this was strengthened into a rule that no reference should be made in the presence of the jury to the substance of the matter determined on the voir dire, or even its result. It is however desirable for brief reasons to be given in the absence of the jury to facilitate a possible appeal.[13]

Although the validity of the reasons for the rule under consideration seems to be beyond dispute, its application has given rise to three practical difficulties—the question whether the evidence of facts constituting a condition precedent to admissibility should invariably be heard in the absence of the jury, the course which should be adopted when the facts are identical with the facts in issue and the distribution of the functions of judge and jury with regard to the admissibility of confessions.

(i)   Absence of the jury

Two settled rules in criminal cases are first, that the accused must be present throughout the entire trial of an indictable offence,[14] and secondly, that all the evidence should generally be given in the presence of the jury. Some qualifications are obviously necessary so far as the second of these rules is concerned, otherwise the accused might be prejudiced, and there is no doubt that the judge has power[15] to dismiss the jury while hearing arguments on the admissibility of evidence or while holding a trial within a trial.

The first of these rules requires the judge to hear all evidence in court, even though occasionally in the absence of the jury, when an exception to the second rule applies.[16] It has accordingly been held that the judge should neither retire to his private room in order to question a child so as to determine its competence to testify,[17] nor receive there the maker of a statement admitted as hearsay on the basis of being kept away by fear, in order to determine the true reason for the witness's non-attendance at the due time.[18]

The second rule gives rise to difficulty where there is a dispute as to the competency of a witness, or as to a condition of admissibility of evidence. The orthodox rule prescribes

---

10   See per Lord Goddard CJ in *R v Reynolds* [1950] 1 KB 606, at 608, [1950] 1 All ER 335, at 336.
11   [1997] 1 Cr App Rep 396, 407F.
12   [1998] AC 695, [1998] 2 Cr App Rep 35, at 704B, 43C.
13   *Thongjai v R* [1998] AC 54, at 59D.
14   *Lawrence v R* [1933] AC 699, at 708. There are exceptions; for example in cases in which the accused renders his continued presence in court impossible by his violence. See *R v Browne* (1906) 70 JP 472.
15   Even over the objection of the defence, see *R v Hendry* (1988) 88 Cr App Rep 187 overruling on this point *R v Anderson* (1929) 21 Cr App Rep 178. See also *R v Davis* [1990] Crim LR 860.
16   See *R v Preston* [1994] 2 AC 130, [1993] 4 All ER 638 where the House of Lords deprecated the course of a trial in which considerable periods were spent in argument before the judge from which both the accused and his solicitors were excluded.
17   *R v Dunne* (1929) 99 LJKB 117, under the old law.
18   *R v Setz-Dempsey* (1994) 98 Cr App Rep 23. The witness offered an innocent and wholly different explanation for his late arrival.

that in such a case the jury should remain present to hear the evidence which it will eventually have to consider in assessing the evidence. In the case of a child, the modern practice of inquisition[19] by the judge in the presence of the jury to determine competency was justified in *R v N*[20] as follows:

> One reason is that although the trial judge must decide whether the evidence of the child should be admitted in the first place, if it is admitted, it is in the end for the jury to decide whether to attach any weight to it. Therefore the jury should see and observe the basic enquiry into the child's competence as a potential witness: it is an important part of the relevant material which should be disclosed to them. Another reason is that the child is likely to be damaged by constant reiteration of the same material before different groups of people at court; first the judge and counsel and then, again, before the judge, counsel, and the assembled jury, as well, in each case, as other officials of the court and members of the public.

Sometimes the evidence to be heard relating to competence is that of a third party. The same principles should apply, and in a few cases where such evidence has been tendered on the preliminary issue in the absence of the jury, it has been repeated in open court at the trial proper.[1] The advantage of this procedure is that the jury is not then exposed to possibly prejudicial material in relation to a witness or evidence held incompetent or inadmissible. It was however held in *R v Robinson*[2] that such evidence could be admitted on a voir dire to determine the competence of a witness for the prosecution, but should not be called at the trial[3] as the effect of the evidence would be merely to bolster the testimony of the witness. It is however hard to reconcile this view with the preceding cases, none of which was cited to the court.

It is submitted that the best view is that such evidence should normally be tendered in the presence of the jury, but if it is likely to be especially prejudicial the judge should have a discretion to hear it on a voir dire, and the trial then continue according to the ordinary rules as to the admissibility of evidence impugning or supporting the credit of a witness or piece of evidence.[4]

(ii)   Identity of preliminary fact with fact in issue

In *Doe d Jenkins v Davies*,[5] the issue in an action of ejectment was whether one Elizabeth Stevens was legitimate. She was dead, and the defendant sought to call evidence of a declaration made by her to a solicitor when she handed him a certificate which apparently related to her parents' marriage. Statements by deceased persons as to pedigree are admissible at common law by way of exception to the rule against hearsay if they were made by legitimate members of the family in question. The claimant

19 That is a non-adversarial procedure in which counsel are not involved.
20 (1992) 95 Cr App Rep 256. See also *R v Reynolds* (1950) 34 Cr App Rep 60; *R v Khan* (1981) 73 Cr App Rep 190, under the old law.
1   *R v Mackenzie* (1993) 96 Cr App Rep 98; *R v Dunphy* (1993) 98 Cr App Rep 393. See also *R v Setz-Dempsey* (1994) 98 Cr App Rep 23.
2   (1994) 98 Cr App Rep 370.
3   At least in the absence of a specific attack on the witness.
4   This passage has been endorsed in Canada in *R v Ferguson* (1996) 112 CCC (3d) 342, at 357. In the Unites States r 104(c) of the United States Federal Rules reads: 'Hearings on the admissibility of confessions shall in all cases be conducted out of the hearing of the jury. Hearings on other preliminary matters shall be so conducted when the interests of justice require.'
5   (1847) 10 QB 314.

argued that the judge ought not to have received evidence on behalf of the defendant, tending to show that Elizabeth Stevens was legitimate, offered with a view to inducing him to admit her declaration. The answer given by Lord Denman CJ[6] was that:

neither the admissibility nor the effect of the evidence is altered by the accident that the fact which is for the judge as a condition precedent is the same fact which is for the jury in the issue.

The Court of Exchequer accordingly held that, after deciding that Elizabeth Stevens was legitimate (presumably without relying on her declaration), the judge had rightly allowed this declaration to form part of the evidence to go to the jury on the issue of legitimacy.

The judge had heard evidence on the voir dire from both sides before deciding the preliminary question of legitimacy. This course has two disadvantages when the preliminary question of fact to be determined by the judge as a condition precedent to the admissibility of an item of evidence is identical with the issue which has ultimately to be decided by the jury. In the first place it means that the judge has to sum up to the jury on an issue which he has already decided; secondly, it may mean that all the evidence given on the voir dire will have to be given over again, and this will certainly be so when the trial within a trial is held in the absence of the jury. Considerations of this nature led Lord Penzance, in *Hitchins v Eardley*,[7] a later case raising the same point as *Doe d Jenkins v Davies*, to reject evidence tendered on the voir dire by those denying legitimacy. He held that he ought to admit the declaration on being satisfied that those alleging legitimacy had adduced sufficient evidence of the fact to be left to the jury.

On practical grounds, the course taken by Lord Penzance may be preferable to that followed by *Doe d Jenkins v Davies*. However that may be there are certainly cases involving the reception of documentary evidence in which all that the judge can require, as a condition precedent to the admissibility of a copy, is prima facie evidence of the existence of a genuine original. In *Stowe v Querner*,[8] the claimant succeeded in a claim on an insurance policy which the defendant alleged had never been executed. The judge had allowed the claimant to give secondary evidence of the contents of the policy on the basis that the original had been lost and left the jury to decide the validity of the defendant's contention that the policy had never existed. It was held that the course followed by the judge was the right one for:[9]

Where the objection to the reading of a copy concedes that there was primary evidence of some sort in existence ... the judge must, before he admits the copy, hear and determine whether the objection is well founded. But where the objection goes to show that the very substratum and foundation of the cause of action is wanting, the judge must not decide upon the matter, but receive the copy and leave the main question to the jury.

A similar situation would arise in a case in which the defendant contends that the document on which the claimant is relying as giving him a basis for an action is forged.

Cases such as *Stowe v Querner* must be carefully distinguished from those in which the preliminary issue is whether a document has been lost, or which of two originals is

6   At 323–4.
7   (1871) LR 2 P & D 248.
8   (1870) LR 5 Exch 155.
9   At 158.

the proper one to place before the jury; in such cases the question of fact to be decided by the judge is not the same as that which has to be decided by the jury.[10] There is then no doubt that the judge must hear evidence on both sides on the voir dire and come to a definite decision on the preliminary issue instead of being content with prima facie evidence from the party arguing for admissibility.

The question whether the maker of a dying declaration was under a settled hopeless expectation of death, a condition precedent to its admissibility at a trial for homicide, should on principle be decided by the judge.[11] By way of contrast, the question whether a tape-recording was the original, being one which must ultimately be determined by the jury, the judge need do no more than decide whether there is sufficient evidence to leave the issue to it.[12]

(iii)   Confessions

If there is a dispute about it, it is for the judge to decide whether there is prima facie evidence that a confession was made, leaving the jury to determine whether it was in fact made.[13] In respect of many other issues relating to the admissibility of confessions the common law has been superseded by the provisions of s 76 of the Police and Criminal Evidence Act 1984, as will be explained in more detail in ch XVI below. Its effect on the division of responsibilities between judge and jury will alone be considered here. It is for the prosecution to prove beyond reasonable doubt that the confession has not been obtained by oppression,[14] or in consequence of anything likely to make it unreliable.[15] These issues must, as a result of the wording of the relevant provision[16] of the Police and Criminal Evidence Act 1984, be resolved by a trial within a trial before a confession can be admitted into evidence.[17] This represents a change in English[18] law,[19] and can lead to a 'pantomime',[20] if the accused prefers to withhold his attack upon the confession until the trial. It is nevertheless still possible for a judge to achieve much the same result as under the old law by exercising his discretion at common law[1] to direct the jury to disregard the confession, or to discharge it.[2] In most cases the accused will seek determination of the admissibility of a confession at a trial on the voir dire. If he does not do so there is now a statutory power for the court to initiate such

---

10   *Boyle v Wiseman* (1855) 11 Exch 360
11   But see *R v Christensen* [1923] 2 DLR 379; cf *R v Donohoe* [1963] SRNSW 38, where the question was decided by the judge in accordance with English authorities.
12   *R v Robson: R v Harris* [1972] 2 All ER 699, [1972] 1 WLR 651.
13   *R v Roberts* [1954] 2 QB 329, [1953] 2 All ER 340; *Ajodha v The State* [1982] AC 204, [1981] 2 All ER 193; *R v Mulligan* [1955] OR 240; *R v Gleeson* [1975] Qd R 399.
14   Section 76(2)(a).
15   Section 76(2)(b).
16   Section 76. The same applies to s 78 in relation to exclusion by discretion.
17   *R v Sat-Bhambra* (1988) 88 Cr App Rep 55, at 62. The same applies to summary trial before magistrates: *R v Liverpool Juvenile Court, ex p R* [1988] QB 1, [1987] 2 All ER 668; but not to a preliminary examination: *R v Oxford City Justices, ex p Berry* [1988] QB 507, [1987] 1 All ER 1244.
18   It was already the case at common law in South Africa: see *S v Nieuwoudt (No 3)* 1985 (4) SA 510.
19   For the previous position see *Ajodha v The State* [1982] AC 204, at 223, [1981] 2 All ER 193, at 202.
20   As it was judicially described in *R v Millard* [1987] Crim LR 196.
1   Expressly preserved by the Police and Criminal Evidence Act 1984, s 82(3).
2   *R v Sat-Bhambra*, above.

a trial of its own motion.[3] In *R v Brophy*[4] the House of Lords decided that if the accused should, on the voir dire, adduce evidence of the truth of a charge against him, such a confession would, nevertheless, be inadmissible at his trial if he should plead not guilty at that stage. Where such evidence is led by the prosecution there is an unedifying conflict between the decision of the Court of Criminal Appeal in *R v Hammond*[5] that such evidence could be elicited on the voir dire, and the decision of the majority of the Privy Council in *Wong Kam-ming v R* that it could not. Now that one of the conditions for excluding a confession is the existence of circumstances likely to render a confession unreliable the case for excluding the evidence has, if anything, become even stronger.[6] The statute does not however deal with any of the other matters which exercised the courts in these cases. One of these is the extent to which statements made by the accused on the voir dire could be used against him, either as an admission or as a previous inconsistent statement. The view which prevailed before the Act was that, if the confession were held to be inadmissible, then no later use could be made of admissions relevant to the issue of admissibility which had been made by the accused on the voir dire. In *R v Brophy* the House of Lords regarded this as fundamental:[7]

> If such evidence, being relevant, were admissible at the substantive trial, an
> accused person would not enjoy the complete freedom that he ought to have at
> the voire dire to contest the admissibility of his previous statements. It is of the
> first importance for the administration of justice that an accused person should
> feel completely free to give evidence at the voire dire of any improper methods
> by which a confession or admission has been extracted from him, for he can almost
> never make an effective challenge of its admissibility without giving evidence
> himself. He is thus virtually compelled to give evidence at the voire dire, and if
> his evidence were admissible at the substantive trial, the result might be a
> significant impairment of his so-called right to silence at the trial.

This ban on the use of a statement made on the voir dire applied both to use in chief by the prosecution as an admission, or use in cross-examination as a previous inconsistent statement to impeach the accused's credit, whether the trial was by judge alone or by judge and jury in the normal way.[8] The force of this reasoning seems undiminished by the passage of the 1984 Act. It is not quite so clear that it is equally unaffected by the statutory language. It should be noted that most of s 76 follows the recommendations and draft provisions proposed by the Criminal Law Revision Committee in its 11th Report.[9] The question of the use of admissions made by the accused on the voir dire had not by 1972 come into much prominence,[10] and was not

3   Police and Criminal Evidence Act 1984, s 76(3), following the recommendation of the Criminal
     Law Revision Committee, Cmnd 4991, para 54, and following the old rule, see *Ajodha v The
     State* [1982] AC 204, at 222, [1981] 2 All ER 193, at 202. It is the same in Australia, see
     McPherson v R (1981) 55 ALJR 594.
4   [1982] AC 476, [1981] 2 All ER 705, although it is not clear that in *Brophy* there was an
     extra-judicial confession confirmed on the voir dire, this ought, in principle, to be immaterial.
5   [1941] 3 All ER 318, 28 Cr App Rep 84, supported in this view by the Supreme Court of
     Canada in *De Clercq v R* [1968] SCR 902, and by Lord Hailsham in *Wong Kam-ming v R*
     [1980] AC 247, [1979] 1 All ER 939.
6   *Wong Kam-ming* was endorsed on this point by *R v Davis* [1990] Crim LR 860.
7   [1982] AC 476, at 481, [1981] 2 All ER 705, at 709.
8   At 482, 710. For criticism of this result see Pattenden (1983) 32 ICLQ 812.
9   Cmnd 4991, paras 53–69, and draft Bill, cl 2.
10   The question had been aired in Australia in an article by Neasey (1960) 34 ALJ 110 and see *R
     v Monks* (1955) an unreported Tasmanian case referred to in the article; *R v Gray* [1965] Qd
     R 373; *R v Wright* [1969] SASR 256; and *R v Banner* [1970] VR 240.

considered by the Committee, so its draft Bill contained no explicit provision on the matter. The problem is created by the impact of the new subsection. Subsection 76(1) in effect provides that a confession may not be given in evidence unless the prosecution is able to negate the circumstances mentioned in sub-s 76(2). An admission made by the accused on the voir dire would not appear either to have been obtained by oppression or in circumstances likely to render it unreliable. It would thus seem to be admissible under sub-s 76(1) as a matter of ordinary statutory interpretation. It is however submitted that there is nothing in the policy of the new Act which justifies such a departure from the existing position, and that a court will be tempted to exclude any such admissions in most ordinary cases as a matter of its discretionary control of a criminal trial.[11] It must however be accepted that this is an unsatisfactory solution, and one explicitly rejected by the House of Lords in *Brophy*.[12]

It should be noted that the drafting of s 76(2)(b) prevents[13] this problem from being eliminated by the simple expedient of admitting the disputed confession at the trial whenever the accused admits its truth at the voir dire.[14]

To the extent that prohibition of reference to statements made on the voir dire has been justified by reference to the impact of such reference upon the accused's right to silence at the trial,[15] it has been weakened by the abridgement of that right by the passage of s 35 of the Criminal Justice and Public Order Act 1994. It has been suggested[16] that the discretionary solution advanced above has been rendered less eligible by this change of policy, and that reliance can be rested only upon the idea that the accused must not be inhibited in any way from making a justified challenge to an alleged confession.

The resolution of this question must also determine the case where the admission is used as a previous inconsistent statement in order to discredit the accused's testimony. In *Brophy* the House of Lords felt that there was no difference between this situation and that where the evidence was led by the prosecution. It was settled in the old law that the terms of the excluded confession could not be used for this purpose,[17] and in *Wong Kam-ming*[18] the same reasoning was applied to admissions made on the voir dire. No explicit reference has been made to this situation in any subsequent official proposals for reform.[19]

It had also become quite settled in the old law that when the admissibility of the confession has been challenged unsuccessfully on the voir dire, counsel retained the right to cross-examine at the trial proper the witnesses who had previously given evidence at the voir dire.[20] It should be noted that the judge retains his control over the evidence ultimately to be submitted to the jury throughout the trial. Accordingly, if having admitted a confession on evidence given in the absence of the jury, the judge concludes, in the light of subsequent evidence, that the confession ought not to have

11 Expressly preserved by Police and Criminal Evidence Act 1984, s 82(3). It might alternatively choose to exercise the statutory discretion provided by s 78.
12 At 483, 710. But see *Burns v R* (1975) 132 CLR 258, at 263.
13 In its distinction between hypothetical and actual reliability.
14 *R v Cox* [1991] Crim LR 276.
15 See the last sentence of the extract from *Brophy* quoted above.
16 By Mirfield who first exposed the problem in [1995] Crim LR 612, at 617. See also his *Silence, Confessions and Illegally Obtained Evidence* (1997) pp. 71–75.
17 *R v Treacy* [1944] 2 All ER 229, 30 Cr App Rep 93.
18 [1980] AC 247, at 259, [1979] 1 All ER 939, at 945.
19 Neither in the 1984 legislation, nor in that proposed by the Law Commission in Law Com No 245 *Evidence in Criminal Proceedings: Hearsay and Related Topics* Cm 3670 (1997).
20 *R v Murray* [1951]1 KB 391, [1950] 2 All ER 925. See also *Jackson v R* (1962) 108 CLR 591; *People, The (A-G) v Ainscough* [1960] IR 136 (unrepresented accused, having cross-examined on the voir dire, must be told of his right to cross-examine again at the trial).

been admitted, he may either direct the jury to disregard it, or, where there is no other sufficient evidence against the accused, direct an acquittal, or, presumably, direct a new trial,[1] though the circumstances in which he will decide to take any of these courses are likely to be rare, especially now that this is no more than a matter of the judge's residual discretion.[2] After some uncertainty[3] it became accepted that the primary purpose of such re-examination at the trial was simply to ascertain the weight to be attached to the confession, and not to try again the issue of its admissibility.[4] This position was accepted by the Criminal Law Revision Committee in the 11th Report,[5] and the terminology of ss 76 and 78, by referring to the position only before the admission of the confession, strengthens this view, so it may be taken as representing the current law. When this issue has been ventilated again in this way the court will often be well-advised to direct the jury specifically on the credibility of the confession.[6]

It was also established in *Wong Kam-ming v R* that even when a confession was admitted after a voir dire, other admissions made at it by the accused could not be led against him. The problem is similar to that discussed above in relation to cases where the confession was excluded after a voir dire, except that even under the old law the argument for exclusion was recognised to be weaker when the confession was admitted.[7] The statutory interpretation argument also applies more strongly in favour of admissibility. If, as submitted above, exclusion can now, after the statute, only be by way of discretion, then that discretion may be more rarely exercised in favour of the accused when the confession has been admitted after a voir dire. If so, this will be consistent with the general admission of such statements to impeach the credit of the accused by putting them to him in cross-examination. This use of statements made by the accused at the voir dire, and inconsistent with his testimony at the trial, was allowed by the Privy Council in *Wong Kam-ming* in cases where the confession was admitted.[8] Under the new provisions, and still more in the light of the effect of the Criminal Justice and Public Order Act 1994 mentioned above, this reasoning will be stronger still.

It will have been noted that a distinction has been drawn between cases where the accused denies that any confession was made, and those where he asserts that it was made only as a result of improper pressure. In the latter case alone is there an issue to be tried on the voir dire. In real life the situation will be less clear-cut. The accused may both deny some material parts of the confession, and assert that the whole was obtained by improper pressure, or he may admit having signed a statement but complain that he was induced to do so by threats, or misrepresentation of the contents. These more complicated situations were considered in *Ajodha v The State*.[9] The Privy Council held that there was no difference between a case where the accused claimed that the confession had been obtained by improper means, and those in which he claimed that he had been induced to sign or acknowledge one obtained by such means. In both cases it was appropriate to hold a trial on the voir dire. The only situation where there

1   Only the first two possibilities were mentioned by Lord MacDermott in *R v Murphy* [1965] NI 138, at 144. See also *Cornelius v R* (1936) 55 CLR 235.
2   See above p 166.
3   Engendered by dicta in *R v Bass* [1953] 1 QB 680, at 684, [1953] 1 All ER 1064, at 1066.
4   *Chan Wei-Keung v R* [1967] 2 AC 160, [1967] 1 All ER 948; *Hunter v Chief Constable of West Midlands* [1982] AC 529, [1981] 3 All ER 727. See also *Basto v R* (1954) 91 CLR 628; *R v McAloon* [1959] OR 441.
5   Cmnd 4991, para 67.
6   *R v McCarthy* [1980] 70 Cr App Rep 270, as explained in *Prasad v R* [1981] 1 All ER 319, [1981] 1 WLR 469.
7   [1980] AC 247, at 258, [1979] 1 All ER 939 at 944.
8   At 260, 946, subject only to the provisions of the Criminal Procedure Act 1865, s 4, discussed in ch VI below.
9   [1982] AC 204, [1981] 2 All ER 193.

is no issue to be tried on the voir dire is that in which the accused simply denies having made or acknowledged the statement.[10] If the accused denies having made a statement, and there is[11] also an issue of mistreatment by the police to force him to confess, he is entitled to have the latter issue determined first on a voir dire.[12]

It may occasionally happen that the voir dire is conducted only after the prosecution has opened its case at the trial proper. In such a case it seems that the trial judge may evaluate the evidence given on the voir dire in the light of the evidence thus far tendered or elicited at the trial proper.[13]

(iv)   The burden and standard of proof at a trial within a trial

We have seen in ch III that decisions on the question of which party bears the burden of establishing a particular issue are generally decisions on the substantive law. Decisions as to which party bears the burden of establishing a fact constituting a condition precedent to the admissibility of an item of evidence belong to the law of evidence. However, there is very little authority on the subject, no doubt because, as a matter of common sense, the conditions of admissibility have to be established by those alleging that they exist.

It is settled that the burden of proving the facts constituting the condition precedent to the admissibility of confessions[14] and dying declarations[15] is borne by the person seeking to tender them in evidence. These items of evidence are admissible as exceptions to the rule against hearsay, and it is reasonable to suppose that the burden of establishing the facts rendering hearsay admissible is always borne by the party tendering the evidence.

It was held in *R v Yacoob*[16] that the persuasive burden of establishing the competence of its witnesses beyond reasonable doubt is borne by the prosecution, though the evidential burden of raising the issue is naturally upon the accused. In the case of a claim to privilege by a witness, the burden of establishing the privilege would presumably be borne by the witness. It is much less clear who bears the burden on disputed issues of fact when the question of the exclusion of evidence by discretion is being tried on a voir dire.[17]

We have seen in ch III that there are two standards of proof according to which facts may have to be established, proof on a balance of probabilities, the standard appropriate to civil cases, and proof beyond reasonable doubt, the standard demanded of the prosecution in criminal cases. Where the issue is one which must be decided once and for all by the judge, it would seem proper to hold that, in criminal cases when the evidence is tendered by the prosecution, such fact must be proved beyond

10   See also *MacPherson v R* (1981) 147 CLR 512.
11   Which need not be raised by evidence adduced by the accused, but may arise from the prosecution's own evidence, or be put in cross-examination to prosecution witnesses.
12   *Thongjai v R* [1998] AC 54.
13   *R v Tyrer* (1989) 90 Cr App Rep 446.
14   Police and Criminal Evidence Act 1984, s 76(2). A statute putting the persuasive burden in respect of one aspect of this matter onto the accused has been condemned as unconstitutional in South Africa: *S v Zuma* 1995 (2) SA 642.
15   *R v Jenkins* (1869) LR 1 CCR 187, at 192.
16   (1981) 72 Cr App Rep 313.
17   Cp *Vel v Owen* (1987) 151 JP 510 apparently putting it upon the defence and *R v Keenan* [1990] 2 QB 54, at 64, [1989] 3 All ER 598 at 605 apparently asserting this not necessarily to be the case. In Australia it is borne by the defence: *MacPherson v R* (1981) 147 CLR 512, at 519 (threats); *R v Gudgeon* (1995) 133 ALR 379, at 390 (deception).

reasonable doubt, but when tendered by the defence[18] or in civil cases when tendered by either party, the preliminary fact must be proved to the satisfaction of the judge on a preponderance of probability. The English rules on confessions[19] and the authorities on dying declarations[20] and proof of handwriting tendered for comparative purposes[1] bear out the above views, at least so far as the standard of proof demanded of the prosecution on the voir dire is concerned.

It has, however, been held in Australia with regard to both confessions[2] and dying declarations,[3] that the prosecution need only establish facts justifying admissibility on the balance of probabilities. The English rule at least has the merit of ensuring that the utmost care is taken before a confession is placed before the jury, and this is particularly important because, in many cases, to admit a confession is virtually to ensure the conviction of the accused. Where the judge merely has to be satisfied that there is prima facie evidence, for example, that a confession was made, that a previous consistent statement amounted to a complaint, or that a tape-recording was the original, he need hear evidence only from the party tendering the confession, previous consistent statement or tape-recording. In *R v Robson*[4] the Court of Appeal regarded this as equivalent to a requirement that such evidence need reach only the standard of the balance of probabilities for fear of usurping the function of the jury. It is submitted that the better view is that the requirement is no different from that applying to the satisfaction of an evidential burden, namely whether the evidence, if believed by the jury, would be sufficient to prove the matter asserted to the standard required to satisfy the legal burden, namely beyond reasonable doubt, when borne by the prosecution in a criminal case. This involves no usurpation of the function of the jury since the jury is free not to believe the evidence, and may well not do so after taking into account its contravention by the other side. Such a view is in complete harmony with the ordinary rules on the discharge of an evidential burden, the determination of whether or not there is a case to answer, and the proper distribution of functions between judge and jury.[5]

SECTION 2.   JUDICIAL CONTROL OF THE JURY

The exceptions to the general rule that questions of fact must be determined by the jury are one facet of the subject of judicial control of that body. Another facet of the same subject is illustrated by the rules governing rebuttable presumptions of law which restrict to some extent the jury's power of finding facts but this section is concerned with more direct methods of control by means of withdrawing an issue from the consideration of the jury, by exercising discretion to exclude otherwise admissible evidence, by summing up and by setting aside verdicts on appeal.

18   This view was approved in *R v Mattey and Queelay* [1995] 2 Cr App Rep 409.
19   Police and Criminal Evidence Act 1984, s 76. See also *R v Pickett* (1975) 31 CRNS 239.
20   *R v Jenkins* (1869) LR 1 CCR 187; in *R v Booker* (1924) 88 JP 75 the words used were 'If it appears to the satisfaction of the judge.'
1   *R v Ewing* [1983] QB 1039, [1983] 2 All ER 645, overruling *R v Angeli* [1978] 3 All ER 950, [1979] 1 WLR 26. See also *R v Mazzone* (1985) 43 SASR 330; *R v Sim* [1987] 1 NZLR 356.
2   *Wendo v R* (1963) 109 CLR 559; *R v Clark* (1984) 11 ACR 257. The Federal position in the United States is the same for all preliminary matters, *Bourjaily v United States* 483 US 171, at 175 (1987).
3   *R v Donohoe* [1963] SRNSW 38.
4   [1972] 2 All ER 699, [1972] 1 WLR 651.
5   See *Timm v R* [1981] 2 SCR 315, applying this principle to the question of whether a complaint was made by the victim of a rape (but distinguishing the questions of whether it was spontaneous or recent).

A.   WITHDRAWAL OF AN ISSUE FROM THE JURY

Before an issue can be submitted to the jury the judge must be satisfied that there is sufficient evidence in support of the proponent's contention for its consideration, and, if he is of opinion that the evidence is insufficient, he must decide the issue in favour of the opponent.[6]

> It has always been considered a question of law to be determined by the judge,[[7]] subject, of course, to review, whether there is evidence which, if it is believed, and the counter-evidence if any, not believed, would establish the facts in controversy. It is for the jury to say whether and how far the evidence is to be believed. And if the facts, as to which evidence is given, are such that from them a further inference of fact may legitimately be drawn, it is for the jury to say whether that inference is to be drawn or not. But it is for the judge to determine, subject to review, as a matter of law, whether from those facts that further inference may legitimately be drawn.

These remarks were made in the case of *Metropolitan Rly Co v Jackson*,[8] in which a passenger's thumb had been crushed by the slamming of the door of a railway carriage. There was evidence that the defendants had been guilty of negligence in allowing the carriage to become overcrowded, but there was no evidence that the overcrowding had caused the claimant's thumb to be where it was when the door was slammed, and the House of Lords held that the judge should have withdrawn the case from the jury for this reason.

When a judge comes to the conclusion that evidence in support of the contention of the proponent of an issue is insufficient, the course which he should adopt will vary from case to case. Sometimes he should discharge the jury and enter judgment for the opponent of the issue, as in a civil suit in which there is insufficient evidence in support of the claimant's allegation of negligence,[9] on other occasions, he will direct the jury to return a verdict in favour of the opponent, as in a criminal case where the prosecution's evidence is insufficient; while there may be other issues to be left to the jury, as on a criminal charge when the judge rules that there is insufficient evidence of insanity (an issue of which the accused is the proponent), and it is none the less necessary for the jury to decide whether the prosecution has established the accused's guilt in other respects. Whichever of these courses is adopted, the judge is obviously exercising considerable control over the jury, for he is either totally withdrawing facts from its consideration, or else directing it to come to a certain conclusion, whatever its own view may be.

The extent of this method of control increased during the nineteenth century, for as Willes J said in *Ryder v Wombwell*:[10]

---

6   The proponent is the party by whom the issue must be raised in the first instance. He is usually the claimant in a civil case, and the prosecutor on a criminal charge, but this is not necessarily so. The proponent bears the evidential burden in the first instance. He usually bears the legal burden also, but this is not always the case. Wigmore uses the term to describe the party bearing the legal burden of proof.

7   In the absence of the jury: *Crosland v R* [1995] Crim LR 958.

8   (1877) 3 App Cas 193, at 207 per Lord Blackburn.

9   Even in this kind of case it may be desirable to have the damages assessed by the jury.

10   (1868) LR 4 Exch 32 at 39. In *Jones v Great Western Rly Co* (1930) 144 LT 194, the trial judge referred to the scintilla rule in deciding to leave the case to the jury.

It was formerly considered necessary in all cases to leave the question to the jury if there was any evidence, even a scintilla, in support of the case; but it is now settled that the question for the judge (subject of course to review) is, ... not whether there is literally no evidence but whether there is none that ought reasonably to satisfy the jury that the fact sought to be proved is established.

The test to be applied by the judge in order to determine whether there is sufficient evidence in favour of the proponent of an issue, is for him to inquire whether there is evidence which, if uncontradicted, would justify men of ordinary reason and fairness in affirming the proposition which the proponent is bound to maintain, having regard to the degree of proof demanded by the law with regard to the particular issue.[11] This test is easy to apply when the evidence is direct, for, unless their cross-examination was utterly shattering, the question whether witnesses are to be believed must be left to the jury, but it is necessarily somewhat vague when circumstantial evidence has to be considered. In that case, little more can be done than inquire whether the proponent's evidence warrants an inference of the facts in issue, or whether it merely leads to conjecture concerning them.[12] At this stage the submission should succeed only if the circumstantial evidence raises no hypothesis consistent with guilt.[13]

Although it is sometimes the judge's duty to withdraw an issue from the jury of his own motion,[14] questions of the sufficiency of evidence are usually raised on a submission that there is no case to answer made by the opponent of the issue.[15] The judge must rule in favour of the submission if there is insufficient evidence to prove an essential element in the proponent's case, or if the evidence which has been adduced is so tenuous that no jury properly directed could convict upon it. It is not enough when any weakness in the proponent's case depends upon matters within the exclusive jurisdiction of the jury, such as the reliability of witnesses,[16] or the resolution of equivocal evidence.[17] Any apparent contradiction between these rules was resolved by Lord Mustill in *Daley v R*[18] on the basis that while the honesty of a witness should properly remain to be decided by the jury, there were situations,[19] such as

11   *Bridges v North London Rly Co* (1874) LR 7 HL 213, at 233 per Brett J. The last seventeen words which appeared in the first edition have been reinstated out of deference to Edwards, see (1970) 9 Western Australian Law Review 169.

12   Mere improbability is not enough, *Rafidain Bank v Agom Universal Sugar Trading Co Ltd* [1987] 3 All ER 859, [1987] 1 WLR 1606. See also *Kerr v Ayr Steam Shipping Co* [1915] AC 217 at 233; *Jones v Great Western Rly Co* (1930) above, at 202; *Caswell v Powell Duffryn Associated Collieries Ltd* [1940] AC 152, at 169, [1939] 3 All ER 722, at 733.

13   See *Torrance v Cornish* (1985) 79 FLR 87; *R v Haas* (1986) 22 ACR 299. Certainly not the converse that it should succeed unless all inferences inconsistent with guilt have been negated, *R v Morgan* [1993] Crim LR 870.

14   *R v Brown* (1997) Times, 13 December, CA.

15   On the whole subject see articles by Williams in [1965] Crim LR 343 and 410, and Pattenden [1982] Crim LR 558.

16   *R v Galbraith* [1981] 2 All ER 1060, [1981] 1 WLR 1039; *Haw Tua Tau v Public Prosecutor* [1982] AC 136, at 151, [1981] 3 All ER 14 at 19; *R v Fulcher* [1995] 2 Cr App Rep 251. But see *R v Boakes* [1996] CL 1393 where the witness should have been determined by the judge to be too incredible for her evidence to be left to the jury at all. Similar principles apply to committal for extradition: *R v Governor of Pentonville Prison, ex p Osman* [1989] 3 All ER 701, at 721,[1990] 1 WLR 277, at 299; *R v Governor of Pentonville Prison, ex p Alves* [1993] AC 284, sub nom *Alves v DPP* [1992] 4 All ER 787. The High Court of Australia has held that the same should apply to questions of inconsistency: *Doney v R* (1990) 171 CLR 207, at 214.

17   *R v Sanders* [1997] Crim LR 751.

18   [1994] AC 117, at 129, [1993] 4 All ER 86, at 94.

19   The Law Commission in Law Com 245 *Evidence in Criminal Proceedings: Hearsay and Related Topics* Cm 3670 (1997) paras 11.26–11.32, rec 47, draft bill, cl 14 has suggested that the admission of hearsay by the prosecution should be another.

identification,[20] where the evidence even of an honest witness might be regarded as tenuous. Similar considerations may also apply where the maker of a confession suffers from a serious mental defect.[1] The Royal Commission on Criminal Justice recommended[2] that the rule in *Galbraith* be reversed, and that the trial judge have the general power to withdraw an issue from the jury when he considers the evidence demonstrably unsafe or unsatisfactory, or too weak. If he rules against the submission, the issue must be determined by the jury, but, even when the opponent calls no evidence, its decision will not necessarily be in favour of the proponent. The jury may disbelieve the testimony given on his behalf, or, if it does accept it, it may not be prepared to draw the requisite inference.

There are certain practical differences in the procedure which ought to be followed by the judge according to the class of case which he is trying.

1. Civil cases tried by a judge alone

A submission that there is no case to answer may be made by one of the parties to proceedings before a judge alone, but, if this is done in a civil case, the judge must decline to rule on the submission unless the party making it elects not to call evidence,[3] even in a case of civil contempt.[4] At least two considerations justify this requirement. In the first place, the judge has to determine the facts as well as the law, and he ought not to be asked to express an opinion on the evidence until it is complete. No one would ask a jury at the end of a claimant's case to say what verdict they would be prepared to give if the defendant called no evidence.[5] Secondly, the parties might be put to extra expense if the judge ruled in favour of the submission before the evidence was complete, for, if the Court of Appeal were to decide against his ruling, a new trial would be necessary so that the party who made the submission could call his evidence.

2. Civil cases tried with a jury

Neither of these considerations apply to civil cases tried with a jury. Accordingly, it has been held that the judge has a discretion in such cases, and he may rule on the submission without putting the party who makes it to his election whether to call

---

20   As in *R v Turnbull* [1977] QB 224, [1976] 3 All ER 549, and in *Daley* itself. See also *Mezzo v R* (1986) 30 DLR (4th) 161.
1   As in *R v MacKenzie* (1993) 96 Cr App Rep 98; *R v Wood* [1994] Crim LR 222. The defect must have the effect of making the confession unconvincing on a submission of no case although the party making the submission will normally be put to his or her election (*Yuill v Yuill* [1945] P 262. See also *R v Heaton* [1993] Crim LR 593 where expert evidence of mental handicap was itself not sufficiently cogent to be admitted on the voir dire. In Australia the Court may also consider whether the mental defect contributed to the decision to make any statement at all, *R v Pfitzner* (1996) 85 ACR 120.
2   Cm 2263 (1993) para 4.42, rec 86.
3   *Alexander v Rayson* [1936] 1 KB 169. In matrimonial causes, the cases establish that the judge has a discretion whether to put a party to his election on a submission of no case although the party making the submission will normally be put to his or her election (*Yuill v Yuill* [1945] P 15, [1945] 1 All ER 183; *Inglis v Inglis and Baxter* [1968] P 639, [1967] 2 All ER 71). It is only in the most exceptional circumstances that a new trial will be ordered by the Court of Appeal after an election (*Portland Manufacturers Ltd v Harte* [1977] QB 306, [1976] 1 All ER 225). In Australia it has become discretionary whether to allow a submission without an election: *J-Corp Pty Ltd v ABLFUW* (1992) 110 ALR 510.
4   *Barclays De Zoete Wedd Securities Ltd v Nadir* (1992) Times, 25 March.
5   Per Romer LJ [1936] 1 KB 169, at 178.

evidence.[6] If the judge decides in favour of the submission, there would have to be a new trial if his ruling is reversed on appeal, but this would also be the case if he deferred his ruling until the evidence was completed, for the verdict of the jury would have to be obtained in either event.

Whether a civil case is tried with a jury or not, it seems that, if a judge rules that there is a case to answer and the defendant gives evidence, the defendant's liability must be judged on the whole of the evidence and an appeal may be dismissed although the Court of Appeal is of opinion that the judge should have ruled in favour of the submission when it was made.[7]

3.   Criminal cases tried with a jury

In criminal cases tried with a jury, the accused is never put to his election whether to call evidence or not before a ruling is made on his submission that there is no case to answer. Even where the accused bears the evidential burden in respect of a special defence he may rely upon its having been raised by evidence adduced by the prosecution as part of its case.[8] If the ruling is in favour of the submission the jury is directed to acquit. If the submission fails, the accused calls his evidence in the ordinary way. Contrary to what was once decided by the Court of Criminal Appeal,[9] it has been said that on an appeal against conviction, the Court of Criminal Appeal considers the evidence as a whole, and can therefore dismiss the appeal although it may be of opinion that the judge ought to have ruled that there was no case to answer at the close of the prosecution's evidence if, as sometimes happens, the accused is incriminated by his own evidence.[10] But this does not apply to a case in which the Court of Appeal is of opinion that there is no case to answer and the trial judge allows the case to go to the jury only in fairness to a co-accused, who incriminates the accused.[11]

4.   Magistrates

A submission of no case may be made in proceedings before magistrates, but in the case of an exhibit should be made as soon as the exhibit is produced, and should normally be justified by cross-examination or producing evidence.[12] If the proceedings are criminal, there is no question of the accused being put to his election.[13] If the proceedings are civil, the party making the submission may be put to his election. If the magistrates rule against the submission, they should give the party making it a further opportunity to address them on the facts.[14] This is because a finding that there is a

6   *Young v Rank* [1950] 2 KB 510, [1950] 2 All ER 166 where the authorities are reviewed by Devlin J.
7   *Payne v Harrison* [1961] 2 QB 403, [1961] 2 All ER 873.
8   Even when only by the exculpatory part of a mixed statement, *R v Duncan* (1981) 73 Cr App Rep 359; *R v Hamand* (1985) 82 Cr App Rep 65.
9   *R v Joiner* (1910) 4 Cr App Rep 64.
10   *R v Power* [1919] 1 KB 572; but see *R v Berry* [1998] Crim LR 487 where evidence subsequently emerging in relation to co-accused were to be disregarded.
11   *R v Abbott* [1955] 2 QB 497, [1955] 2 All ER 899; applied in *R v Lane* (1985) 82 Cr App Rep 5. See the discussion of the earlier authorities in Wood (1961) 77 LQR 491.
12   *R v Pydar Justices, ex p Foster* (1995) 160 JP 87.
13   An unsuccessful submission that there was no sufficient case to answer does not deprive the accused of his right to give evidence at committal proceedings (*R v Horseferry Road Magistrates' Court, ex p Adams* [1978] 1 All ER 373, [1977] 1 WLR 1197).
14   *Mayes v Mayes* [1971] 2 All ER 397, [1971] 1 WLR 679. The same applies to a special immigration adjudicator, *Kriba v Secretary of State for Home Department* 1998 SLT 1113.

case to answer is not a decision of the whole case against the party making the submission. It is perfectly proper for magistrates to hold that there is a case to answer and decide the issue in favour of the party making the submission. They may come to the conclusion that the evidence of the opposite party is not to be believed.[15] They should however not normally exercise any exclusionary discretion in an attempt to determine whether they should commit, certainly in an extradition case.[16]

B.   DISCRETION TO EXCLUDE EVIDENCE[17]

If the judge has not altogether dictated the decision on an issue by withdrawing it from the trial or by directing a verdict, the next most powerful way in which he can affect its decision is by overriding the rules governing the admission of evidence relevant to that issue. The general question is how far the judge has a discretion to do so. In 1790, Grose J dreaded 'that rules of evidence should ever depend upon the discretion of the judges', he wished to find the rule laid down and to abide by it.[18] Channell J also believed it to be 'better to apply the rules strictly than to allow it to be supposed that a judge has a discretion to relax them if he thinks they will work an injustice.'[19] Lord Halsbury expressed himself in similar vein in 1914,[20] but he was in a minority and since then there have been many dicta concerning the judge's power to exclude admissible evidence because its reception would create undue prejudice or be unfair in some other respect.[1] In *R v Sang*[2] the House of Lords affirmed the existence of a discretion to control the use of evidence so as to ensure a fair trial, and the matter has been put upon a statutory footing by s 78 of the Police and Criminal Evidence Act 1984. The implications of that affirmation and the impact of the statutory provision must both be explored. It will also be necessary to distinguish between the different situation in criminal and civil cases, but first the very nature of discretionary control must be examined.

1.   Nature of the discretion

Not for the first, or last, time in the exposition of the law of evidence, it is necessary to beware of the danger inherent in the loose use of terminology, in this case the use of

15   *De Filippo v De Filippo* (1963) 108 Sol Jo 56.
16   *R v King's Lynn Magistrates' Court, ex p Holland* (1993) 96 Cr App Rep 74. In *R v Governor of Pentonville Prison, ex p Alves* [1993] AC 284, sub nom *Alves v DPP* [1992] 4 All ER 787 it seems to have been accepted that the same principles determine committal and a submission of no case.
17   This has become a much more prominent issue in recent times and reflects a fundamental shift away from rigid exclusionary rules. For fuller examination see Pattenden *Judicial Discretion and Criminal Litigation* (1990); Livesey [1968] CLJ 291; Weinberg (1975) 21 McGill LJ 1; Cross (1979) 30 NILQ 289.
18   *R v Inhabitants of Eriswell* (1790) 3 Term Rep 707, at 711. Exactly the same sentiments prevented the adoption of the United States Model Code. See Wigmore (1942) 28 ABA Jo 23.
19   *R v Cargill* (1913) 8 Cr App Rep 224, at 229. This passage was criticised in *R v Funderburk* [1990] 2 All ER 482, at 492, [1990] 1 WLR 587, at 599 so far as it suggested countenancing injustice.
20   *R v Christie* (1914) 10 Cr App Rep 141, at 149.
1   In *Rozens v Beljajev* (1994) 126 ALR 481 a residual discretion to ensure a fair trial was recognised, but outside the area of confessions it was thought likely to be overshadowed by the discretion to reject evidence on the basis of being more prejudicial than probative. In most circumstances potential unreliability should not be a ground for discretionary exclusion.
2   [1980] AC 402, [1979] 2 All ER 1222.

the word 'discretion' in a number of different senses.[3] It is particularly important to distinguish between the idea that the judge has the responsibility of deciding upon the application to the facts before him of an inherently vague term, and the idea that he is free to act in any way he chooses upon the facts which he finds to exist.[4] The difference is that in the former case the judge must act in a particular way once he has found the facts, and in the latter he is still free to choose which action to take after finding them. In many practical situations the dichotomy may not appear so clear, the distinction has not always been present in the mind of judges, and the terminology of discretion has been used indiscriminatingly to apply to both. Nevertheless there are signs that the distinction is now being taken. Thus in considering Lord Edmund Davies' speech in *D v National Society for the Prevention of Cruelty to Children*[5] Cross deplored 'the use of the word "discretion" to describe the judge's duty to perform the contemplated balancing act.'[6] Nor is such criticism limited to academic commentators. In *R v Viola* the Court of Appeal said of the court's earlier judgment in *R v Mills*[7] on the issue of allowing questions to be asked in cross-examination about the complainant's sexual history that: [8]

> it is wrong to speak of a judge's 'discretion' in this context. The judge has to make a judgment whether he is satisfied or not in the terms of s 2 [of the Sexual Offences (Amendment) Act 1976]. But once having reached that judgment on the particular facts, he has no discretion. If he comes to the conclusion that he is satisfied it would be unfair to exclude the evidence, then the evidence has to be admitted and the questions have to be allowed.

Exactly the same approach was taken to the operation of s 78 of the Police and Criminal Evidence Act 1984 in *R v Chalkley* where the court was quite explicit in stating[9] that 'the task of determining admissibility under s 78 does not strictly involve an exercise of discretion.' This view was then reinforced by comparison with what the Court regarded as a genuine discretion to prevent abuse of process.

One practical consequence of making this distinction is simply that the grounds upon which an appellate court will review a discretion, although now much more extensive than was once the case,[10] are still not so extensive as those in which it will reverse the incorrect application of a rule.[11] Nor will it even consider exercising an exclusionary discretion for the first time on appeal when the matter has not been put to

---

3   Pattenden (n 17 above) distinguishes a number of senses. Three different exclusionary discretions were urged upon an Australian court in *R v Rowley* (1986) 23 ACR 371; see also *R v Duke* (1989) 38 ACR 305.

4   Dworkin in *Taking Rights Seriously* (1977) pp 31–33 describes these as weak and strong senses of discretion.

5   [1978] AC 171, at 246, [1977] 1 All ER 589, at 618.

6   (1979) 30 NILQ 289, at 294.

7   (1978) 68 Cr App Rep 327.

8   [1982] 3 All ER 73, at 77, [1982] 1 WLR 1138, at 1142. See also *R v Murukami* [1951] SCR 801, at 803.

9   [1998] QB 848, [1998] 2 All ER 155, at 874D, 178d.

10   *Evans v Bartlam* [1937] AC 473, [1937] 2 All ER 646, is often seen as the turning point. See also *House v R* (1936) 55 CLR 499.

11   *Charles Osenton & Co v Johnston* [1942] AC 130, [1941] 2 All ER 245, where it was said that there is a presumption that the discretion has been exercised correctly. In *Cookson v Knowles* [1979] AC 556, at 566, [1978] 2 All ER 604, at 607, Lord Diplock explicitly distinguished between the role of an appellate court in relation to rule and discretion. For a similar view in the context of criminal proceedings see *R v Chung* (1991) 92 Cr App Rep 314, at 323.

the trial judge.[12] In general terms the exercise of a discretion will stand so long as the judge 'does not err in law, takes into account all relevant matters and excludes consideration of irrelevant matters'.[13] In criminal cases it has been held that the appellate court will not intervene unless no reasonable trial judge could have so exercised his discretion,[14] although there is also evidence of the possibly less stringent standard of its having been 'incumbent' on the trial judge to exercise his discretion to exclude.[15] Where a list of factors has been enumerated for consideration by the trial judge in the exercise of a broad discretion, the prospects of a successful appeal may be still more thin.[16] There may, however, be less reluctance to intervene when the trial judge's view was clearly obiter, and designed merely to bolster exclusion by rule,[17] or perhaps where the appeal made by the prosecution against the exercise of the discretion *to exclude* by a magistrate.[18] The appellate court may also be more inclined to overturn the exercise of an inclusionary discretion, such as that conferred by s 26 of the Criminal Justice Act 1988.[19] A further consequence is that it becomes much more difficult for even consistent practice to mature into a rule. Thus in *Selvey v DPP*[20] the House of Lords rejected an attempt to claim that this had happened, and been recognised to have happened,[1] in relation to disallowance of cross-examination of the accused as to his bad character under the provisions of s 1(f)(ii) of the Criminal Evidence Act 1898. Thus Lord Pearce said:[2]

> The courts have been right, however, in thinking that the question is whether this attack on the prosecution, ought to let in *these* convictions on the particular facts of the case, and on such a point rules are no substitute for a discretion in producing a fair trial. I appreciate that in the result an accused cannot be certain exactly how far he can go without letting in his convictions.

In some situations the nature of the rule of evidence which is in question is defined in such terms that it is difficult to discern any possible role for the application of an exclusionary discretion.[3] Sometimes the rule is drafted in much more rigid terms, and in

---

12　*R v Goldenberg* (1988) 88 Cr App Rep 285, at 289, though it seems immaterial that the first reference to the discretion at the trial was too late for its valid exercise, *R v Kempster* [1989] 1 WLR 1125, 90 Cr App Rep 14. The same view prevails in relation to appeals from the magistrates by way of case stated, and it is immaterial there that the clerk wrongly advised that no discretion was available: *Braham v DPP* (1995) 159 JP 527.

13　*R v Scarrott* [1978] QB 1016, at 1028, [1978] 1 All ER 672, at 681; applied to the statutory s 78 discretion in *R v Rankin* (1995) Times, 5 September. Thus in New Zealand where the old categorisation criticised in *Viola* still prevailed, the court refused to reverse the trial court's decision to disallow cross-examination of the victim of rape as to sexual history because it was an exercise of discretion, *R v Bills* [1981] 1 NZLR 760.

14　*R v Quinn* [1995] 1 Cr App Rep 480, at 489C; *R v Dures* [1997] 2 Cr App Rep 247, at 262A. For a rare case where this rigorous standard was reached, see *R v Miller* [1998] Crim LR 209 (trial judge considered the wrong Code of Practice).

15　*R v Duffy* [1998] Crim LR 650.

16　*Yates v Thakeham Tiles Ltd* [1995] PIQR P135.

17　As in *R v Samuel* [1988] QB 615, at 630, [1988] 2 All ER 135, at 147.

18　As in *DPP v Clarkson* [1996] CLY 1124.

19　As it did in *R v Radak* [1999] 1 Cr App Rep 187.

20　[1970] AC 304, [1968] 2 All ER 497.

1　In *R v Flynn* [1963] 1 QB 729, [1961] 3 All ER 58; *Coca-Cola v Gilbey* [1995] 4 All ER 711, [1996] FSR 23.

2　At 360, 528, emphasis in original.

3　It is arguable that this is the situation with regard to the admissibility of similar fact evidence, see p 372 , below. The High Court of Australia has expressed a similar view in relation to the exclusion in that jurisdiction by discretion of confessions which have passed the local test for exclusion by rule, see Brennan J in *Collins v R* (1980) 31 ALR 257, at 315.

such cases it is feasible to construct guidelines for the exercise of a discretion designed to avoid injustice.[4]

If the distinction mentioned above is accepted it is tolerably clear that the exercise of a discretion can only be to exclude otherwise admissible evidence. It cannot be used to admit otherwise inadmissible evidence as remarked by Lord Reid in *Myers v DPP*:[5]

> It is true that a judge has discretion to exclude legally admissible evidence if justice so requires, but it is a very different thing to say that he has a discretion to admit legally inadmissible evidence.

It is true that some exclusionary rules are phrased in such vague terms that some judges occasionally appear to suppose that they are exercising an inclusionary discretion, but such cases are best explained as ones in which the vague question is resolved in such a way that the exclusionary rule does not apply.[6] This is becoming increasingly true of the discretion to exclude evidence leading to unfairness of the proceedings enacted as s 78 of the Police and Criminal Evidence Act 1984.[7] It may be that in that context some influence is exerted on account of the possibility that the burden of adducing some evidence of a factual basis for triggering the discretion rests upon the accused.[8] The influence of the burden of proof which will normally rest upon the person seeking to persuade the court to exercise a discretion also explains the insistence of the courts, especially in Australia,[9] that the weighing of proof and prejudice in relation to similar fact evidence should remain a matter of law, rather than discretion.

A true inclusionary discretion is sometimes conferred by statute, as where s 6(2)(a) of the Civil Evidence Act 1995 empowers the court to admit previous consistent statements of witnesses even though the conditions for their admissibility prescribed by the Act have not been fulfilled,[10] and where s 26 of the Criminal Justice Act 1988 permits the discretionary acceptance of documentary hearsay even though made in contemplation of criminal proceedings. It is noteworthy that the Law Commission regards the introduction of an inclusionary discretion as an essential feature of its proposals for the reform of the hearsay rule in criminal cases.[11] It further proposes to complement existing discretion to exclude prosecution evidence with a new discretion to exclude even defence evidence where its probative value is substantially outweighed by the danger that it would result in an undue waste of time.[12]

It is interesting to note that in proceedings where the general exclusionary rules of evidence do not apply, for example in some tribunals,[13] there is no room for an

---

4   *R v Britzman* [1983] 1 All ER 369, at 373, [1983] 1 WLR 350, at 355. This course is favoured by Pattenden.

5   [1965] AC 1001, at 1024, [1964] 2 All ER 881, at 887. But see *R v Greasby* [1984] Crim LR 488.

6   Eg *R v Dodd* (1982) 74 Cr App Rep 50; *R v Miller* [1997] 2 Cr App Rep 178 . See also *R v Wilson* (1987) 32 ACR 286, at 293.

7   See eg *R v Gillard and Barrett* (1990) 92 Cr App Rep 61, at 65 where the Court warns of fettering the operation of the discretion by too readily excluding confessions under s 76, a sentiment which makes sense only if the discretion is regarded as inclusionary.

8   See further below p 623.

9   See the powerful arguments of McHugh J in *Pfennig v R* (1995) 182 CLR 461, at 515.

10   On the court's discretion with regard to affidavits see *Rossage v Rossage* [1960] 1 All ER 600, [1960] 1 WLR 249, and *Re J (an infant)* [1960] 1 All ER 603, [1960] 1 WLR 253; *Savings and Investment Bank Ltd v Gasco Investments (Netherlands) BV (No 2)* [1988] Ch 422, [1988] 1 All ER 975.

11   *Evidence in Criminal Proceedings: Hearsay and Related Topics* Law Com No 245 Cm 3670 (1997) paras 8.133–8.149; recs 28–30; draft bill, cl 9.

12   Paras 11.16–11.18; rec 43; draft bill, cl 15(1).

13   See ch 1 section 2 above.

exclusionary discretion. Where statute has sought to extend the range of material available to the tribunal, it is not for the tribunal to cut it down as it chooses by the exercise of any such discretion.[14] It was also held that in cases where the function of the tribunal was merely to establish the existence of a case to answer, as in the case of magistrates on committal proceedings, there was no room for an exclusionary discretion. That discretion came into play only at the trial.[15]

2. Discretion to exclude relevant evidence in criminal proceedings

The existence of some such discretion at common law[16] has been recognised in criminal cases in the highest appellate tribunals since *R v Christie*.[17] In *Selvey v DPP* when the prosecution mounted a general attack on the existence of such a discretion in the context of the Criminal Evidence Act 1898, 1(f)(ii), Viscount Dilhorne said:[18]

> it is far too late in the day even to consider the argument that a judge has no such discretion. Let it suffice for me to say that in my opinion the existence of such a discretion is now clearly established.

Lord Hodson made it clear that in his opinion the discretion applied in all criminal cases.[19] The general question was certified once again in *R v Sang*:[20]

> Does a trial judge have a discretion to refuse to allow evidence, being evidence other than evidence of admission, to be given in any circumstances in which such evidence is relevant and of more than minimal probative value.

Their Lordships were unanimous in agreeing to an answer which distinguished two situations:[1]
(1) A trial judge in a criminal trial has always a discretion to refuse to admit evidence if in his opinion its prejudicial effect outweighs its probative value.
(2) Save with regard to admissions and confessions and generally with regard to evidence obtained from the accused after commission of the offence, he has no discretion to refuse to admit relevant admissible evidence on the ground that it was obtained by improper or unfair means. The court is not concerned with how it was obtained. It is no ground for the exercise of discretion to exclude that the evidence was obtained as the result of the activities of an agent provocateur.
　Strictly speaking, the ratio decidendi is expressed by the last sentence of this answer.[2] Nevertheless the rest of it might have been expected to have a very powerfully

14　*Rosedale Mouldings Ltd v Sibley* [1980] ICR 816, at 822.
15　*R v Horsham Justices, ex p Bukhari* (1982) 74 Cr App Rep 291; *R v Governor of Pentonville Prison, ex p Voets* [1986] 2 All ER 630, [1986] 1 WLR 470. For criticism of the former see commentary in [1982] Crim LR 180, and for a different approach in Australia see *Seymour v A-G for Commonwealth* (1984) 53 ALR 513, at 540. Despite the introduction of a statutory discretion by the terms of s 78 of the Police and Criminal Evidence Act 1984 it seems that its exercise will be inhibited by similar considerations: *R v King's Lynn Justices, ex p Holland* (1993) 96 Cr App Rep 74.
16　Fuller discussion of the statutory discretion superimposed upon the existing law by s 78 of the Police and Criminal Evidence Act 1984 is deferred until the end of this section.
17　[1914] AC 545, [1914–15] All ER Rep 63.
18　[1970] AC 304, at 341, [1968] 2 All ER 497, at 510.
19　At 346, 515.
20　[1980] AC 402, at 431, [1979] 2 All ER 1222, at 1225.
1　At 437, 1231.
2　See Lord Diplock at 431, 1226 and Lord Scarman at 456, 1246.

persuasive effect. In a subsequent case Lord Roskill asserted not only that *Sang* settled existing doubts, but that it would be a retrograde step to 'enlarge the now narrow limits of that discretion or to engraft an exception'.[3] It is useful first to examine these limits.

Two situations seem to be distinguished, those in which the court is concerned to afford the accused a fair trial, and those in which it is concerned to afford him fair treatment. In the former case the accused is to be protected by the exclusion from his trial of evidence which might have an unreliable effect upon the result; in the latter case he is to be protected by the exclusion from his trial of evidence which has been obtained by improper methods, however reliable the effect might be. There is a wide variety of discretions operating in relation to evidence in a criminal trial.[4] Of those which have mainly occupied the courts, any discretion relating to the exclusion of evidence of extrinsic discreditable conduct upon the basis that it is more prejudicial than probative,[5] and the exclusion of cross-examination about broadly similar matters under s 1(f) of the Criminal Evidence Act 1898, comes into the former category. Conversely any discretion to exclude real evidence obtained from the accused by improper means, or in breach of the principle underlying the privilege against self-incrimination, comes into the latter category. Confessional material straddles the two categories,[6] especially in view of s 76(2) of the Police and Criminal Evidence Act 1984 which excludes confessions obtained:

> in consequence of anything said or done which was likely, in the circumstances existing at the time, to render unreliable any confession which might be made by him [the accused] in consequence thereof.

The section itself recognises that a confession obtained in such circumstances might in fact be reliable, or even true. It is also obvious that a confession can be unreliable for many other reasons, for example that the person who confesses is mentally handicapped,[7] or confesses to something of which he has no knowledge.[8]

It will be convenient to consider the application of the common law discretion to exclude separately in relation to each such category, then to consider the statutory discretion conferred by s 78 of the Police and Criminal Evidence Act 1984, and finally discretion as applied to confessional statements.

(i)   Fair Trial

Two major sub-categories in relation to which the discretion operates, if at all, in pursuance of a fair trial, are evidence of the accused's[9] discreditable extrinsic conduct,

3   *Morris v Beardmore* [1981] AC 446, at 469, [1980] 2 All ER 753, at 767.

4   For a very comprehensive list, see Pattenden *Judicial Discretion and Criminal Litigation* (1990).

5   For Australian analysis of these terms in this content, see *R v Hasler, ex p A-G* [1987] 1 Qd R 239.

6   For an unusual example see *R v Gudgeon* (1995) 133 ALR 379 where the accused sought to have a confession in earlier proceedings, induced only by the admission of inadmissible prosecution evidence, excluded by discretion from a re-trial.

7   See *R v Miller* [1986] 3 All ER 119, [1986] 1 WLR 1191; and the statutory recognition of such a possibility by the prescription of a special direction in s 77 of the Police and Criminal Evidence Act 1984; both were considered in *R v Bailey* [1995] 2 Cr App Rep 262.

8   See *Comptroller of Customs v Western Electric Co* [1966] AC 367, at 371, [1965] 3 All ER 599, at 601.

9   There is no discretion to exclude relevant evidence of discreditable disposition or conduct adduced by the defence, for example in relation to the conduct of a victim to support a claim of self-defence: see *R v Masters* [1987] 2 Qd R 272. In *R v Foreman* [1991] Crim LR 702 the Court appears to have entertained the possibility of excluding evidence of the discreditable behaviour

and cross-examination of the accused as to the otherwise excluded matters under s 1(f) of the Criminal Evidence Act 1898. As will be seen in ch VIII below, evidence of discreditable extrinsic conduct is generally inadmissible in chief at common law. It will be argued that this results from a rule that such evidence is inadmissible when its prejudicial effect exceeds its probative value. If this is the rule it is clear that evidence which is admitted after applying it cannot be excluded by the exercise of a discretion cast in the same terms.[10] It must be conceded however that the language of discretion is still used in this context.[11] This can be explained as no more than the wider use of the word 'discretion' to apply to a situation in which the operation of the exclusionary rule depends upon the comparative weight of indeterminate concepts such as probative force and prejudicial effect which can be accomplished only by the most delicate exercise of judgement. Even if this is the case there is still scope for discretion in the true sense in cases where the admissibility of such evidence is governed not by the common law, but by statute. Clear instances are provided by prosecutions for receiving stolen goods in which reliance is placed on s 27(3) of the Theft Act 1968.[12] Evidence of the accused's previous convictions of offences involving fraud or dishonesty is admissible in chief on the issue of guilty knowledge, but it has been held that the judge has an exclusionary discretion when there is a danger that the jury may consider such evidence also on the question of possession.[13] The convictions that may be proved on a handling charge are restricted to those of handling and theft. The reason for applying a discretion in these cases is simply that the statute gives a blanket power to the judge to admit the evidence for the stated purpose without expressing any restriction at all. In some circumstances this can lead to prejudice, and so the court exercises a discretion to prevent it. Exactly the same rationale applies to cross-examination about convictions, commission of offences, charges and bad character under s 1(f) of the Criminal Evidence Act 1898, the substance of which will be discussed fully in ch IX below. There too the statute gives a blanket permission without any explicit qualification once the conditions have been satisfied. The whole question was ventilated in the House of Lords in *Selvey v DPP*[14] where the prosecution launched a full-scale argument against the existence of any discretion to prevent cross-examination once the conditions prescribed by s 1(f)(ii) of the statute had been satisfied. The question of the existence of any discretion is intimately connected with the construction of the conditions permitting cross-examination. It was just because the conditions were unqualified[15] in s 1(f)(ii) that the discretion was developed.[16] The subsequent history of the interpretation of the section confirmed this with each fresh re-affirmation of the rigour of the statutory wording closely followed by a new re-avowal of the existence of the discretion to soften its effect. Thus in *Selvey* itself Lord Guest said:[17]

---

of third parties if it could have been shown to be unduly prejudicial to the accused, which there it could not.

10　See Tapper in Campbell and Waller (eds) *Well and Truly Tried* (1982).

11　Even in *DPP v Boardman* [1975] AC 421, [1974] 3 All ER 887; and such reference persists, see *R v Lunt* (1986) 85 Cr App Rep 241 proposition 5, at 244, and repeated in *R v Shore* (1988) 89 Cr App Rep 32, at 41. See further at p 371 below.

12　Repealing, and re-enacting with some modifications, Larceny Act 1916, s 43(1). The Law Commission has proposed the abolition of this provision: *Evidence in Criminal Proceedings: Previous Misconduct of a Defendant* Consultation Paper 141 (1996) para 14.13, rec 44.

13　*R v Perry* [1984] Crim LR 680; *R v Wilkins* [1975] 2 All ER 734, 60 Cr App Rep 300. Under the old provisions, *R v List* [1965] 3 All ER 710, [1966] 1 WLR 9; *R v Herron* [1967] 1 QB 107, [1966] 2 All ER 26.

14　[1970] AC 304, [1968] 2 All ER 497.

15　*R v Hudson* [1912] 2 KB 464, at 470.

16　*R v Watson* (1913) 8 Cr App Rep 249, at 254.

17　[1970] AC 304, at 351, [1968] 2 All ER 497, at 519.

If I had thought that there was no discretion in English Law for a judge to disallow admissible evidence, as counsel for the Crown argued, I should have striven hard and long to give a benevolent construction to s 1, proviso (f)(ii).

The problem here is one common to all attempts to replace, or even to supplement, rules with discretion, namely the unpredictability of its exercise. This is vitally important in this context since it is necessary to make important decisions as to whether or not to call the accused to give evidence, and whether or not to run a particular line of defence, the validity of which are likely to depend entirely upon the accuracy of such a prediction. Awareness of such problems has fostered attempts to improve predictability by the creation of guidelines for the exercise of the discretion.[18] It has been settled since *R v Turner*[19] that a defence of consent to a charge of rape does not justify cross-examination under the section, though it is less clear that such a result reflects consistent exercise of this discretion.[20] A more general guideline was promoted in *R v Flynn*[1] that where the very nature of the defence necessarily involves an imputation upon the prosecution then the discretion should, as a general rule, be exercised in favour of the accused. The court then acted upon this view by holding that the trial judge had there exercised his discretion wrongly in principle. The notion of any such general rule was emphatically rejected in *Selvey*. Lord Guest went so far as to assert that:[2]

> If it is suggested that the exercise of this discretion may be whimsical and depend on the individual idiosyncracies of the judge, this is inevitable where it is a question of discretion, but I am satisfied that this is a lesser risk than attempting to shackle the judge's power within a straight jacket.

Other members of the House saw the contrast in less vivid hues. Lord Pearce was prepared to accept that the conditions mentioned in *Flynn* were valid factors to be weighed in exercising the discretion, but not that they could constitute even presumptive rules subject to exceptions in individual cases.[3] It is hard to reconcile these dicta with the apparent accession of the whole House to the view expressed in *R v Cook*[4] that an appellate court could interfere with the exercise of a discretion by a trial judge on the basis that he had erred in principle. Such a view clearly demands the existence of some principle upon which the discretion should be exercised. It was explicitly recognised by the House in *Selvey*[5] that the decision provided no guidance to the accused. It is hard to understand how the guiding star of a fair trial avowed in *Selvey* can lead to a situation in which the accused is left completely in the dark as to the best way in which to conduct his defence. Practice has continued to diverge,[6] and once again the Court of Appeal has attempted to propound guidelines for the exercise of the discretion.[7] It is noteworthy that a number of the considerations mentioned in those guidelines cannot

18   This solution is favoured in this context by the Law Commission: see *Evidence in Criminal Proceedings: Previous Misconduct of a Defendant* Consultation Paper 141 (1996) para 9.57, rec 9.
19   [1944] KB 463, [1944] 1 All ER 599.
20   Although the question was left open in *Selvey* it must militate against any such view that the same result was reached in *R v Sheean* (1908) 21 Cox CC 561, without reference to any discretion and some years before any was recognised in the context of the Criminal Evidence Act.
1   [1963] 1 QB 729, [1961] 3 All ER 58.
2   [1970] AC 304, at 352, [1968] 2 All ER 497, at 520.
3   At 360, 527.
4   [1959] 2 QB 340, at 348, [1959] 2 All ER 97, at 101.
5   [1970] AC 304, at 361, [1968] 2 All ER 497, at 528; see above p 177.
6   See *R v Britzman* [1983] 1 All ER 369, at 372, [1983] 1 WLR 350, at 353.
7   At 355, 373.

easily be subsumed under the need to balance probative force and prejudicial effect. It will be interesting to discover whether or not the court's abstinence from the terminology of rules will protect the decision. Similar abstinence is to be found in *R v Nye*[8] where the court first referred to a principle of exercising the discretion so as to prevent cross-examination upon the basis of convictions 'spent' under the Rehabilitation of Offenders Act 1974, and then acted upon it by allowing an appeal against the trial judge's failure to do so.

It has subsequently become clear that *Selvey* still represents English law in this area. Its guidance has, in a series of decisions,[9] been re-affirmed by the Court of Appeal. In *Burke* the relevant convictions were for drug-related offences; in *Powell* for controlling prostitutes; in *Owen* for theft from the person; and in *McLeod* for robbery. These decisions have resulted in the enumeration[10] of a number of points for the judge to bear in mind in this area: first, that the primary purpose of such cross-examination is to show that the accused is unworthy of belief, and not that he has a disposition to the commission of crimes of the relevant type; second, that any such cross-examination should not be unduly prolonged for fear of diverting the jury; third that similarities of defence thereby revealed may be relevant; fourth, the fact that the underlying facts indicate particularly prejudicial matters should be balanced against the gravity of the attack on the prosecution witness; fifth, that any objection to revelation of the underlying facts of the relevant convictions should be taken as early as possible; sixth, that unless objection is taken at the time it will be difficult to contend later that the discretion was wrongly exercised, and in any case an appellate court will interfere with its exercise only upon established principles; and seventh, that the judge must stress in summing up that the convictions go only to credit and not to issue. It will be argued below[11] that to the extent that the range of such questioning in cross-examination exceeds that which would be permitted by the application of the rules relating to the admissibility of such evidence in chief, it demonstrates the disadvantages of reliance upon discretion rather than rule to protect the interests of the accused.

It should be noted that a similar direction has been approved by majorities in the High Court of Australia,[12] the Supreme Court of Canada,[13] and the Court of Session in Scotland.[14] In *Phillips v R* the majority[15] was concerned that the discretion should be unfettered by rules,[16] and attached weight to the fact that since in the case before them the convictions were for offences of dishonesty they would not be particularly prejudicial on a charge of rape.[17] In his dissenting judgment Deane J raised the interesting point that the nature of the imputation, namely that the victim and the accused had been associated in the misuse of drugs, reflected equally badly on both of them, so there was no upset balance to redress.[18] In Canada, as in the United States, once the accused chooses to testify he enjoys no such special regime of protection as that conferred by the Criminal Evidence Act 1898, s 1(f). In such circumstances a majority[19] of the Supreme Court of Canada regarded such discretionary protection as nevertheless

8   (1982) 75 Cr App Rep 247.
9   *R v Burke* (1985) 82 Cr App Rep 156; *R v Powell* [1986] 1 All ER 193, [1985] 1 WLR 1364; *R v Owen* (1985) 83 Cr App Rep 100; *R v McLeod* [1994] 3 All ER 254, [1994] 1 WLR 1500.
10   In *McLeod*.
11   At p 408.
12   *Phillips v R* (1985) 159 CLR 45.
13   *Corbett v R* [1988] 1 SCR 670.
14   *Leggate v HM Advocate* 1988 JC 127, at 144.
15   Mason CJ, Wilson, Brennan and Dawson JJ.
16   Deane J also agreed on this point.
17   Even though it had been accomplished by breaking into a dwelling house.
18   For an analysis stressing this factor see Seabrooke [1987] Crim LR 231.
19   Dickson CJC, Beetz, Lamer and La Forest JJ (agreeing on this point).

available. In Scotland the legislation is in the English form, but used to be interpreted differently,[20] and the situation is complicated by statutory restriction on the use of previous convictions in court.[1] In *Leggate* however the rule, and apparently[2] its discretionary gloss, was assimilated to that applied in England.

It must be emphasised that this discretion is based upon the need for a fair trial to be conducted. That this may differ from the rationale of fair treatment of the individual concerned is illustrated by cases in which there is more than one accused. In such a case the court has no discretion to intervene so as to prevent one of several co-accused from adducing evidence which is more prejudicial than probative, nor to prevent cross-examination by the co-accused under the provisions of the Criminal Evidence Act.[3]

If, as suggested earlier, the former question really turns on judgment about the application of a vague rule rather than discretion, authority for that view in this context is to be found in the judgment of Devlin J in *R v Miller*:[4]

> In the case of the prosecution, a question of this sort may be relevant and at the same time prejudicial, and, if the court is of the opinion that the prejudicial effect outweighs its relevance, then it has the power, and, indeed, *the duty,* to exclude the question ... No such limitation applies to a question asked by counsel for the defence. His duty is to adduce any evidence which is relevant to his own case, and assists his client, whether or not it prejudices anyone else.

The same point is nevertheless sometimes expressed more loosely in the terminology of discretion as in *R v Neale* where Scarman LJ speaking for a particularly strong court[5] said:[6]

> The discretionary control the judge has in a joint trial or indeed in any trial, that is to say the discretion to refuse to allow the Crown to adduce, or elicit, evidence which though probative is so prejudicial that it should not be accepted, does not exist or arise when application is being made by a co-defendant.

The existence of a discretion to disallow cross-examination by one co-accused as to the other co-accused's record when the conditions specified under sub-s 1(f)(ii) of the Criminal Evidence Act 1898 apply, although recognised in the earlier practice, divided the House of Lords in *Murdoch v Taylor*.[7] The majority took the view that there was no discretion in such a case: it is not explicit in the statute, and the co-accused is entitled to insist on his strict rights. Lord Pearce dissented on the ground that such an unrestricted right could lead to unfairness to the co-accused, either because one co-accused had been trapped into giving evidence against the other, or where the conflict

---

20   *O'Hara v HM Advocate* 1948 JC 90.
1   Criminal Procedure (Scotland) Act 1975, s 161.
2   Though no reference was made to the most recent English authority, and the tenor of the decision, which applied the discretion to exclude such cross-examination, might suggest that practice will continue to diverge.
3   Though evidence adduced by the prosecution and probative of the case against one co-accused may be excluded because it is unduly prejudicial against others: *R v Rogers* and *R v Tarran* [1971] Crim LR 413; *R v Skinner* [1995] Crim LR 805. I am grateful to Dr Pattenden for bringing this situation to my attention.
4   [1952] 2 All ER 667, at 669, 36 Cr App Rep 169, at 171, emphasis supplied. It should be noted that relevance here includes relevance to credit as well as directly to issue, *R v Thompson* [1995] 2 Cr App Rep 589.
5   The other members were Lane LJ and Donaldson J.
6   (1977) 65 Cr App Rep 304, at 306.
7   [1965] AC 574, [1965] 1 All ER 406.

between the stories was trivial and far out-weighed by the prejudice created by the revelation of the record. It is interesting to note that the Criminal Law Revision Committee in endorsing the majority view opined that since there was a conflict of evils, to grant a discretion would lead to inconsistency of application.[8] In some cases the injustice of not disallowing cross-examination in these circumstances can be alleviated by the operation of a different discretion, to permit separate trials; but not in all.[9]

The existence of such residual discretion at common law to exclude any otherwise admissible evidence, if its admission would be prejudicial to a fair trial, was reaffirmed by the Privy Council in *Scott v R; Barnes v R*[10] in relation to depositions of deceased persons identifying the accused.[11] Another example of the operation of this branch of the discretion is to be seen in relation to the exclusion of excessively inflammatory evidence, such as gruesome pictures[12] or unduly vivid terminology.[13] It seems not however to be regarded as inimical to a fair trial that the prosecution comes innocently into the possession of material which would be privileged in the hands of the accused.[14]

(ii)   Fair treatment

Two apparent examples of a discretion to exclude evidence pursuant to a desire to achieve the fair treatment of the accused seemed to be those designed to protect him from compulsory self-incrimination, and from the use of improper methods to procure evidence against him.[15] This whole area was reviewed by the House of Lords in *R v Sang*.[16] The accused was charged with conspiracy to utter forged banknotes. He argued that he had been entrapped by the activities of an agent provocateur, and that evidence obtained as the result of such activities could be excluded by the trial judge at his discretion on the basis that it had been obtained by unfair methods. If this argument were correct it would in effect have endowed the judge with the discretion to allow a defence of entrapment in the circumstances of that case, since there was too little other evidence to secure a conviction. The House of Lords had no doubt that whatever the extent of this discretion it did not go so far as that.

There was less unanimity on the precise ambit of the discretion, though all of their Lordships subscribed to the answer to the certified question quoted above.[17] The difficulty resides in the precise delineation between the general denial of a discretion to exclude evidence obtained by improper means, and the exclusion from that denial of evidence obtained from the accused after the commission of the offence. It seems that Lord Fraser understood the exclusion to extend to evidence obtained from the premises

---

8   Cmnd 4991 (1972) para 132
9   *R v Varley* [1982] 2 All ER 519, at 522, 75 Cr App Rep 242, at 246. For discussion of this discretion elsewhere: see in Australia, *R v Darby* (1982) 148 CLR 668; and in Canada, *Guimond v R* [1979] 1 SCR 960.
10   [1989] AC 1242, [1989] 2 All ER 305.
11   In England such matters would now be governed by the statutory discretion embodied in s 78 of the Police and Criminal Evidence Act 1984, see *R v O'Loughlin and McLaughlin* [1988] 3 All ER 431, 85 Cr App Rep 157 (depositions, see also Criminal Justice Act 1988, s 26, below), for the position in Australia see *R v Collins* [1986] VR 37; and *R v O'Leary* (1988) 87 Cr App Rep 387 (identification).
12   See *R v Murphy* (1987) 37 ACR 118; *R v Baker* [1989] 3 NZLR 635.
13   See *R v Millar* (1989) 71 CR (3d) 78.
14   See *R v Tompkins* (1977) 67 Cr App Rep 181; *R v Cottrill* [1997] Crim LR 56.
15   Including improper methods of bringing the accused into the jurisdiction, *R v Horseferry Road Magistrates Court, ex p Bennett* [1994] AC 42, [1993] 3 All ER 138.
16   [1980] AC 402, [1979] 2 All ER 1222.
17   See above, p 179.

of the accused.[18] He also expressed the view that the decision left judges with a discretion to exclude in accordance with their individual views of what is unfair, oppressive or morally reprehensible. It is hard to reconcile that view of the discretion with Lord Diplock's view that there is no discretion to exclude evidence discovered as a result of an illegal search.[19] It is also difficult to be sure exactly what relation there is between the discretion as applied to confessions and that applying to improperly obtained evidence. Lord Diplock explained the cases of *R v Barker*[20] and *R v Payne*[1] on the basis of an analogy between the two situations.[2] In the former, incriminating books of account of impeccable reliability were obtained by deception; while in the latter, the accused was persuaded by similar means to submit to a medical examination, once again yielding perfectly reliable evidence. It seems then that the analogy is achieved by explaining the confession rule not on considerations of unreliability, but on those restricting self-incrimination.[3] In this way it is possible to by-pass the argument that evidence obtained by these means may be quite reliable. That is secured however only at the cost of blurring the line between the role of the discretion in ensuring a fair trial which is legitimate, and that of ensuring fair treatment of the accused independent of his trial which is not. It is thus not at all surprising to find that Viscount Dilhorne who drew this distinction most strongly of all their Lordships refused to extend the exclusionary discretion to improperly obtained evidence outside the special case of confessions, and pointedly made no reference to self-incrimination.[4] It is however baffling to find that Lord Fraser and Lord Scarman still insisted that the discretion was exercisable solely as a by-product of a fair trial.[5]

Inconsistencies in the reasoning immediately attracted the attention of academic commentators.[6] The lack of guidance was also recognised by the Court of Appeal which remarked that the limited exception to the general denial of exclusionary discretion in respect of improperly obtained evidence had not been fully considered, though it was clear that where it existed one of its purposes was to control the police:[7]

> As there was no deliberate misconduct by the officer, this hardly seems to be a case in which the Court should seek to discipline the police, even though there may be cases where the exclusion of the evidence for disciplinary purposes may be justified.

Subsequent English case law failed to take matters very much further before the advent of the statutory discretion in s 78 of the Police and Criminal Evidence Act 1984.[8] In other jurisdictions very different approaches are adopted.[9] They will be discussed more fully in ch XI. It is sufficient to note here that the Canadian approach was, before

---

18   At 450, 1241.
19   At 436, 1230.
20   [1941] 2 KB 381, [1941] 3 All ER 33.
1   [1963] 1 All ER 848, [1963] 1 WLR 637.
2   At 436, 1229.
3   Lord Diplock at 436, 1230, Lord Fraser at 449, 1241, and Lord Scarman at 456, 1247.
4   Though he was apparently prepared to equate a case like *Barker* with the confession cases.
5   Lord Fraser at 450, 1241; Lord Scarman at 456, 1247.
6   See commentary in [1979] Crim LR 656; Cross [1979] 30 NILQ 289; Polyviou in Tapper (ed) *Crime, Proof and Punishment* (1981), and Pattenden *Judicial Discretion and Criminal Litigation* (1990).
7   *R v Trump* (1979) 70 Cr App Rep 300, at 303. A similarly disciplinary discretion was mentioned in *R v Heston-Francois* [1984] QB 278, [1984] 1 All ER 785.
8   Many of the cases have concerned breath-testing, compare *Trump* where there was discretion to exclude the evidence (although it was held right not to exercise it) and *Winter v Barlow* [1980] RTR 209, where there was held to be no discretion.
9   See Pattenden (1980) 29 ICLQ 664; (1981) 13 MULR 31.

the enactment of the new Charter, arguably more restrictive than that illustrated in *Sang*,[10] and the Irish,[11] Scottish[12] and Australian more expansive. In the leading Australian case it was denied that the discretion:[13]

> takes as its central point the question of unfairness to the accused. It is, on the contrary, concerned with the broader question of high public policy, unfairness to the accused being only one factor which, if present, will play its part in the whole process of consideration.

The High Court also explained that the reason for this was that:[14]

> it is not fair play that is called in question in such cases but rather society's right to insist that those who enforce the law themselves respect it, so that a citizen's precious right to immunity from arbitrary and unlawful intrusion into the daily affairs of private life may remain unimpaired.

In one recent decision the High Court has taken the view that in the case of entrapment involving the commission of crime by the authorities the discretion passes beyond that of merely excluding particular pieces of evidence, and extends to the exclusion of any evidence of a crime so committed:[15]

> a trial judge possesses a discretion to exclude, on public policy grounds, evidence of an offence or of an element of an offence in circumstances where its commission has been brought about by unlawful conduct on the part of law enforcement officers.

(iii)   The Police and Criminal Evidence Act 1984, s 78[16]

In England the position has been overtaken by the passage of s 78 of the Police and Criminal Evidence Act 1984 which provides:[17]

> (1) In any proceedings the court may refuse to allow evidence on which the prosecution proposes to rely to be given if it appears to the court that, having regard to all the circumstances in which the evidence was obtained, the admission of the evidence would have such an adverse effect on the fairness of the proceedings that the court ought not to admit it.
>
> (2) Nothing in this section shall prejudice any rule of law requiring a court to exclude evidence.
>
> (3) This section shall not apply in the case of proceedings before a magistrates' court inquiring into an offence as examining justices.

---

10   *R v Wray* [1971] SCR 272.
11   *The People (A-G) v O'Brien* [1965] IR 142.
12   *Lawrie v Muir* 1950 JC 19.
13   *Bunning v Cross* (1978) 141 CLR 54, at 74; affirmed as being of quite general application in *Cleland v R* (1982) 151 CLR 1. See also *R v Ireland* (1970) 126 CLR 321; *Pollard v R* (1992) 176 CLR 177; *Foster v R* (1993) 113 ALR 1; *Ridgeway v R* (1995) 184 CLR 19.
14   (1978) 141 CLR 54, at 75.
15   *Ridgeway* above at 35, 36.
16   For a full account of the operation of this discretion see Grevling (1997) 113 LQR 667.
17   Section 78(3) was added by the Criminal Procedure and Investigations Act 1996, Sch 1, cl 26.

This section was introduced at a very late stage, and replaced a clause introduced in the House of Lords on the motion of Lord Scarman which would have spelled out a reverse onus exclusionary rule, linked explicitly to the codes of practice issued under the Act. An important difference between that approach and this, is that under s 78 exclusion is by discretion, and, unlike Lord Scarman's clause, not by rule. It is interesting that the section uses the phrase 'evidence on which the prosecution proposes to rely'. This may be construed more widely than Lord Scarman's phrase which was 'evidence (other than a confession) proposed to be given by the prosecution'.[18] The new section is wider in abstaining from any explicit exclusion of confessions,[19] and in perhaps extending to evidence assisting the prosecution, but tendered by, say, a co-accused. The section appears to follow the reasoning of those of their Lordships in *Sang* who sought to blur the distinction between fair trial and fair treatment in its explicit linkage of the circumstances of obtaining the evidence with the fairness of the proceedings, so it has tended to pre-empt both aspects of the discretion at common law.[20] It still remains uncertain what sorts of impropriety will be regarded as having such an effect. The provenance of the section made it doubtful whether mere breach of one of the Codes of Practice would necessarily suffice, since this was explicitly and separately mentioned in Lord Scarman's provision, but was omitted here. It is noteworthy also that while Lord Scarman's version referred to 'the fair administration of the criminal law', the section as enacted refers to 'the fairness of the proceedings'. The former phrase would more easily have been capable of being construed in the spirit of *Bunning v Cross*.

It should be noted that s 78 applies only to criminal proceedings,[1] from which committal proceedings have now been excluded.[2] Since its enactment s 78 has become the focus of attempts to secure the exclusion by discretion of evidence, both real and confessional, which has been unfairly obtained.[3] It is used both in conjunction with other discretions, and as a discretionary backstop to the exclusionary rules.[4] Its advent[5] seems to have transformed judicial practice. Whereas in *Sang* the House of Lords was referred to only one appellate case in which the discretion to exclude operated on the basis of the evidence having been obtained unfairly, it has now been exercised to such effect in hundreds of cases.[6] Some general points have become clear. First, the discretion is at least as broad as the discretion at common law;[7] second, as part of a codifying

18   In *R v Cottrill* [1997] Crim LR 56 it was applied in a case where the prosecution's reliance was conditional upon the accused's disavowal of the statement, which did not materialise.
19   Although its interpretation in relation to confessions may be different: see *R v McCarthy* [1996] Crim LR 818.
20   But see *R v Chalkley* [1998] QB 848, [1998] 2 All ER 155, at 875C, 179b where the Court of Appeal takes great pains to stress the need to show that the conduct in question is linked to the quality of the evidence obtained for the purposes of s 78, leaving all other aspects of fair treatment to the Court's admittedly discretionary power to restrain abuse of process.
1   This will also have the consequential effect of exempting extradition proceedings as a result of the operation of the Extradition Act 1989, s 9(2): see *R v Governor of Brixton Prison, ex p Levin* [1997] AC 741, [1997] 3 All ER 289, per Lord Hoffmann at 748H, 295a.
2   Section 78(3), inserted by the Criminal Procedure and Investigation Act 1996, Sch 1, para 26.
3   For some empirical evidence of its use, see Hunter [1994] Crim LR 558.
4   For attacks upon the breadth of its interpretation in this context see Robertson (1989) 139 NLJ 1223; Gelowitz (1990) 106 LQR 327.
5   As in Canada and New Zealand have the enactment of the new constitutional provisions of the Charter and Bill of Rights, see in Canada, *R v Collins* [1987] 1 SCR 265, at 286, 287; and in New Zealand, *Ministry of Transport v Noort* [1992] 3 NZLR 260, at 271.
6   See Hunter above at 558 n 2.
7   *R v Khan* [1997] AC 558, [1996] 3 All ER 289, at 578E, 298f. Though this is immaterial since the common law discretion is preserved by s 82(3) of the Police and Criminal Evidence Act 1984. In *R v Caldwell and Dixon* (1993) 99 Cr App Rep 73 that provision was invoked by the defence in relation to questionable procedures relating to identification.

provision, it will not be construed as subject to any common law restrictions expressed in *Sang*;[8] third, the circumstances to be taken into account in assessing its exercise are not limited to those which would be admissible, or likely to be admitted, in evidence;[9] fourth, impropriety is not a necessary condition to its exercise;[10] fifth, oppression is not a sufficient condition for its exercise;[11] sixth, it is the reality of unfairness rather than its appearance which is decisive;[12] seventh, and more controversial, fairness to other accused,[13] the prosecution[14] or public[15] should be taken into account as well as fairness to the defence;[16] eighth, not all unfairness in the proceedings will suffice to trigger the discretion, since the section refers to the exclusion only of matters having *such* an adverse effect, implying that some adverse effects are tolerable.[17] It seems that the exclusion of real evidence by reference to this discretion will still be exercised relatively rarely in serious[18] cases. Purely technical,[19] or even numerous and culpable,[20] breaches of the Codes of Practice seem unlikely alone to suffice. Indeed the use of physical force,[1] or its threat,[2] has been insufficient.

It should be noted that there was some doubt how far s 78 affected the principle, expressed in *Sang,* that the substantive rule that entrapment[3] is no defence could not be undermined by the use of an evidential discretion.[4] In *R v Smurthwaite and Gill*[5] it was accepted that s 78 had introduced some discretion to exclude evidence in this situation, and indicated that its exercise should take into account how far the officer was acting as an agent provocateur, how active or passive his role, the nature of the

---

8   *R v Fulling* [1987] QB 426, at 432, [1987] 2 All ER 65, at 69.
9   *R v Bailey* [1995] 2 Cr App Rep 262, at 271F.
10 *Fulling*, above; *R v O'Leary* (1988) 87 Cr App Rep 387.
11 *R v Chalkley* [1998] QB 848, [1998] 2 All ER 155, at 874A, 178a.
12 *R v Ryan* [1992] Crim LR 187; but cp *R v Gall* (1989) 90 Cr App Rep 64. In this respect the concept of unfairness coheres both with that at common law (*R v Christou* [1992] QB 979, [1992] 4 All ER 559) and with that under the European Convention of Human Rights (*R v Khan* [1997] AC 558, [1996] 3 All ER 289) since it has been held that its meaning cannot change according to its context.
13 (1990) 91 Cr App Rep 371, at 376.
14 See *R v Walsh* (1989) 91 Cr App Rep 161, at 163, where fairness under s 78 seems to subsume fairness required under s 58.
15 *R v Smurthwaite and Gill* [1994] 1 All ER 898, at 903.
16 *R v Warner, R v Jones* (1992) 96 Cr App Rep 324, at 330. This may be intended to act as a counterweight to the availability of reliance upon the discretion only to the defence, and may induce a more expansive approach to initial admissibility of prosecution evidence.
17 *R v Walsh* (1989) 91 Cr App Rep 161, at 163.
18 But perhaps more readily in less serious ones: see *Matto v Wolverhampton Crown Court* [1987] RTR 337 (illegally secured breath test).
19 *R v McCarthy* [1996] Crim LR 818, disapproving of *R v Fennelley* [1989] Crim LR 142 in relation to deficiencies in the information provided prior to a search.
20 *R v Stewart* [1995] Crim LR 500 (unauthorised entry to premises by electricity officials).
1   *R v Hughes* (1994) 99 Cr App Rep 160 (pinching his nose to compel the accused to disgorge the contents of his mouth).
2   *R v Cooke* [1995] 1 Cr App Rep 318 (three policemen in full riot gear to overcome the accused's initial refusal to provide a hair sample).
3   In *R v Edwards* [1991] Crim LR 45 a somewhat restrictive view of the concept of entrapment was adopted.
4   Compare *DPP v Marshall* [1988] 3 All ER 683; *R v Harwood* [1989] Crim LR 285 and *London Borough of Ealing v Woolworths plc* [1995] Crim LR 58 with *R v Gill and Ranuana* [1989] Crim LR 358. For a useful survey of the law in a number of common law jurisdictions see Roser (1993) 67 ALJ 722.
5   (1994) 98 Cr App Rep 437, which asserts an indicative rather than definitive intent. See also *R v Governor of Pentonville Prison, ex p Chinoy* [1992] 1 All ER 317.

entrapment,[6] how reliable its recording, and whether or not the officer, being undercover, had attempted to circumvent the restrictions on questioning imposed by the Code of Practice.[7]

These situations extend to those in which the accused are deceived into producing evidence against themselves, either by the interception of communications, or by some form of trick,[8] or both. They do not extend to those where use is made of some extrinsic form of compulsory process, so long as it is not abused.[9] Nor do they extend to the situation where the accused is tricked into coming within the jurisdiction of the court.[10] It seems that undercover police operations which provide an opportunity for the commission of crime,[11] or the disposal of its fruits,[12] will not necessarily attract the operation of the discretion. It is important though that such an operation be reliably recorded, and that the situation not be treated as an expedient to evade the conditions for police questioning set out in the Codes of Practice.[13] Sometimes illegal or deceptive conduct is undertaken to obtain a recording which may itself be incriminating, or even amount to a full confession. In *R v Khan*[14] the police illegally[15] installed a listening device on private premises, yet the House of Lords approved the trial judge's refusal to exclude the incriminating material so obtained in his discretion under s 78.[16] In the sphere of trickery, while it has been thought appropriate to apply the discretion to a full confession secured only after deception addressed, after the accused's arrest, to his legal adviser,[17] a different view has been taken of a surreptitious recording of a

6   See in Australia, *R v Venn-Brown* [1991] 1 Qd R 458; in Canada, *Mack v R* [1988] 2 SCR 903; and in New Zealand, *R v O'Shannesy* [1973] 1 CRNZ 1 where the preceding considerations are also applied.

7   This falls far short of excluding all statements made to undercover policemen: *R v Lin* [1995] Crim LR 817. But see *R v Smith* (1994) 75 ACR 327 for a decision in Australia which approaches such a view.

8   This seems the most acceptable explanation of *R v Nathaniel* [1995] 2 Cr App Rep 565 where compelling DNA evidence crucial to a very serious charge was excluded, apparently because of an assurance to the accused that a sample was required only for one particular charge, and that it would be destroyed if he were acquitted, even though the retention of the sample had been the result of an innocent mistake.

9   *R v Saunders* [1996] 1 Cr App Rep 463 (examination by compulsory process under ss 432(2) and 442 of the Companies Act 1985). An indication of permissible limits is seen in the the trial judge's discretionary exclusion of answers obtained *after* the accused had been charged, and in the holding in *R v Smith* [1994] 1 WLR 1396, 99 Cr App Rep 233 that the discretion should have been exercised when the accused was under the mistaken belief that his interrogation related only to a non-criminal issue. See also *R v Crown Court at Southwark, ex p Bowles* [1998] AC 641, [1998] 2 All ER 193 (investigation into whether a person had benefitted from criminal conduct under Criminal Justice Act 1988, s 93H).

10   *R v Latif* [1996] 1 All ER 353, [1996] 1 WLR 104. This was treated as a by-product of holding that this conduct did not amount to an abuse of process, for comparison with *Ridgeway* see Grevling, (1996) 112 LQR 401. In *Sammak v R* (1993) 2 Tas SR 339 breach of a temporal condition to jurisdiction was not sufficient to trigger exclusion.

11   *Williams v DPP* [1993] 3 All ER 365 (a van full of cigarettes apparently left unattended).

12   *R v Christou* [1992] QB 979, [1992] 4 All ER 559 (a shop apparently prepared to deal in stolen goods). Cp *R v Stead* (1992) 62 ACR 40 (apparently willing participant in stripping down stolen cars).

13   *R v Bryce* [1992] 4 All ER 567, 95 Cr App Rep 320 (an apparently genuine purchaser of a stolen car). See also *R v Okafor* [1994] 3 All ER 741, 94 Cr App Rep 97 (plain clothes customs officer apparently ignorant of illicit contents of package).

14   [1997] AC 558, [1996] 3 All ER 289. For a similar result in Australia in relation to the illegal installation of a video camera, see *R v McNamara* (1994) 73 ACR 539.

15   Probably in breach of both civil and criminal law, but in conformity with Home Office guidelines!

16   And also failed to stay the proceedings as an abuse of process: see further Tapper (1997) 1 Int J of Ev & Proof 162.

17   *R v Mason* [1987] 3 All ER 481, [1988] 1 WLR 139. See also *R v H* [1987] Crim LR 47.

conversation in a police station, even though suspicion was lulled[18] by an elaborate charade enacted by the investigating and custody officers,[19] and of a recording of an incriminating telephone call obtained by an elaborate trick involving co-operation between an accomplice and customs officers.[20] Nor is it appropriate to apply the discretion to earlier acts of third parties which led to the interception being arranged.[1] These results seem to accord with those arrived at in England under the common law discretion,[2] though a different view is taken in some overseas jurisdictions.[3]

It should also be noted that the new statutory discretion to preserve the fairness of the proceedings in s 78 has, perhaps surprisingly, been held even to permit the exclusion of evidence of convictions obtained in other proceedings, despite their clearly satisfying the relevant statutory conditions.[4]

(iv) Confessions

The final area in which the discretion must be considered is that relating to confessional statements which was at first carefully distinguished from those cases mentioned above concerned with real evidence, but to which it was explicitly applied by the High Court of Australia in *Cleland v R*,[5] and to which the operation of the statutory discretion in s 78 of the Police and Criminal Evidence Act 1984 has been held to apply.[6] As noted earlier it has hitherto been possible to explain the exclusion of some confessional

---

18 Amazingly successfully, despite a warning from the accused's solicitor of the exact stratagem likely to be employed.

19 *R v Bailey* [1993] 3 All ER 513, 97 Cr App Rep 365. This may be regarded as going further than *R v Jelen and Katz* (1989) 90 Cr App Rep 456 (where the deception was practised by a third party), *R v Ali (Shaukat)* (1991) Times, 19 February (where the recording was surreptitiously made in the police station but without any specific deception or charade), or *R v Roberts* [1997] 1 Cr App Rep 217 (where the recording was made in a cell bugged without the knowledge of either the accused or the co-accused who the police knew would be likely to try to provoke a confession). Where the interception is made under the provisions of the Interception of Communications Act 1985 a still more complicated situation arises, but it has been held that it does not enlarge the scope of discretionary exclusion under s 78, *R v Preston* [1994] 2 AC 130, at 169, [1993] 4 All ER 638, at 669. See also *R v Effik: Mitchell* [1995] 1 AC 309, [1994] 3 All ER 458.

20 *R v Maclean: R v Kosten* [1993] Crim LR 687.

1 *R v Dixon: R v Mann* [1995] Crim LR 647.

2 . Such as those in *R v Mills: R v Rose* [1962] 3 All ER 298, [1962] 1 WLR 1152 (conversation in police cell overheard without any deception beyond setting up a tape recorder without prior warning); *R v Buchan* [1964] 1 All ER 502, [1964] 1 WLR 365 (accused believed, and police knew he believed, that confession was not being recorded); *R v Maqsud Ali* [1966] 1 QB 688, [1965] 2 All ER 464 (presence in secretly bugged room in police station); *R v Stewart* [1970] 1 All ER 689n, [1970] 1 WLR 907 (conversation in cell overheard by officer posing as prisoner); *R v Keeton* (1970) 54 Cr App Rep 267 (accused's telephone call to wife overheard by police switchboard operator).

3 See in Australia, *Pavic v R ; R v Swaffield* (1998) 192 CLR 159 (statements recorded by co-accused fitted out by police, but acting on his own initiative; statements recorded by undercover police officer in course of investigations into another suspected offence) in which earlier authority is extensively reviewed; in Canada, *R v Hebert* [1990] 2 SCR 151 (policeman posing as fellow prisoner and asking questions) and *R v Broyles* [1991] 3 SCR 595 (friend acting under instructions of police, and functional equivalent of interrogation), where the evidence was excluded; but in the United States, *Illinois v Perkins* 496 US 292 (1990) (undercover policeman and friend of prisoner eliciting statement in prison)k where the evidence was admitted. Cp *Pfennig* as to another incident (fellow prisoners not acting under police instructions and not clear whether questioning took place), where the evidence was not excluded.

4 Police and Criminal Evidence Act 1984, s 74, see further, above, p 100.

5 (1983) 151 CLR 1, subject only to the unlikelihood of being able to make out a case for the application of the discretion if the rules for admissibility had been satisfied. See also *Seymour v A-G for Commonwealth* (1984) 53 ALR 513, for a full discussion.

6 *R v Mason* [1987] 3 All ER 481, [1988] 1 WLR 139, at 144.

statements either on the basis of the need for a fair trial, in which case the unreliability of such statements, and perhaps the question of self-incrimination, will be emphasised, or on the basis of the need for fair treatment, in which case the protection of the accused, and perhaps[7] of the community's self-respect, will become more prominent.

The Police and Criminal Evidence Act 1984, s 76 changed the basis of rules relating to the admissibility of confessions. Quite apart from the application to confessions of s 78, it has also retained the court's general discretion to exclude in s 82(3):

> Nothing in this Part of this Act shall prejudice any power of a court to exclude evidence (whether by preventing questions from being put or otherwise) at its discretion.

Following the pronouncement as to the limitations of s 78 in *R v Chalkley* it is possible that there will be a revival in the use of this provision in relation to cases where the link to the fairness of the proceedings is harder to discern. It is thus necessary to see what discretion existed before 1984. It was recognised when the rule excluding involuntary statements was put into its traditional form in *Ibrahim v R*.[8] In *R v Voisin*[9] the exclusionary discretion was considered in relation to the Judges' Rules which had been devised to govern questioning by the police. The court was unwilling to concede the force of law to the Rules, but recognised the discretion of the judge to exclude statements 'obtained from prisoners, contrary to the spirit' of the Rules. Some stress was laid upon the use of the discretion to exclude statements which had not been made voluntarily, or which were unreliable, but a residual category of unfairness was also mentioned. By 1964 when a new set of Judges' Rules were produced,[10] oppression had been added as a second ground of mandatory exclusion. Perhaps the most common argument advanced for the exercise of the exclusionary discretion in relation to confessions was that they had been obtained after breaches of the Judges' Rules. After a few early successes such arguments began to fall on stonier ground. The nadir of this aspect of the exclusionary discretion was reached in *R v Prager*. In that case the Court of Appeal seemed to submerge any breach of the Judges' Rules within the ordinary voluntariness test for exclusion by rule:[11]

> Their non-observance may, and at times does, lead to the exclusion of an alleged confession; but ultimately all turns on the judge's decision whether, breach or no breach, it has been shown to have been made voluntarily.

This proved to be an ephemeral stage in the development of this discretion which was re-affirmed by the Court of Appeal.[12] It should be noted that it was immaterial whether a breach of the Judges' Rules themselves was alleged, or breach of the principles accompanying the Rules,[13] or of the administrative guidelines published by the Home Office for the use of the police.[14] The essence of this discretion was concern for the fair treatment of the accused,[15] and governed by the principles which

---

7   Especially in Australia; it seems following the decision in *R v Chalkley* [1998] QB 848, [1998] 2 All ER 155 that this is now still less likely to be recited as a justification in England. Even in Australia there is authority to restrict the concept of prejudice, to prejudice to a fair trial: see *R v Morris* (1995) 78 ACR 465, at 469.

8   [1914] AC 599, at 609.

9   [1918] 1 KB 531.

10   *Practice Note* [1964] 1 All ER 237, [1964] 1 WLR 152.

11   [1972] 1 All ER 1114, at 1118, [1972] 1 WLR 260, at 266.

12   *R v MacIntosh* (1982) 76 Cr App Rep 177.

13   *R v Gowan* [1982] Crim LR 821.

14   *R v Westlake* [1979] Crim LR 652; but see *R v King* [1980] Crim LR 40.

15   Though it was implausibly ascribed to the balance of probative force and prejudicial effect in *R v Ovenell* [1969] 1 QB 17, at 26, [1968] 1 All ER 933, at 939.

inspired the exclusionary rule itself as Lord Hailsham expressed them in *Wong Kamming v R*:[16]

> This is not only because of the potential unreliability of such statements, but also, and perhaps mainly, because in a civilised society it is vital that persons in custody or charged with offences should not be subjected to ill-treatment or improper pressure in order to extract confessions.

The exercise of the discretion before 1984 was accordingly not limited to breaches of the rules and their direct accompaniments, but was equally inspired by other similar factors such as the detention of the accused in excess of the period permitted by statute,[17] or in breach of other statutory requirements.[18] It was also unsurprising to find that discretion remained a second string for the exclusion of statements obtained after oppressive behaviour. Before 1984 voluntariness had often been treated as a rather rigid and technical concept thus permitting some scope for the exercise of an exclusionary discretion in cases falling outside its confines. In *R v Hudson* the existence of such a discretion was accepted quite unequivocally.[19]

The statutory discretion in s 78 has been exercised in relation to confessional statements in two main areas, first in respect of conduct clearly falling outside the exclusionary provisions of s 76 of the Police and Criminal Evidence Act 1984,[20] and second as a buttress to those provisions.[1]

Statutory exclusion of confessions on the basis of potential unreliability is limited to those made 'in consequence of anything said or done' by an interlocutor.[2] It is clear that this cannot apply to one who spontaneously blurts out a confession,[3] and has been held not to apply where the effective cause[4] of confessing is some defect inherent in the speaker,[5] rather than proper questioning by the police. Even in cases where the police act improperly, for example by interviewing a juvenile in the absence of an appropriate adult,[6] it seems that a confession will be excluded under the s 78 discretion only when deliberate advantage has been taken of the juvenile.[7] In the case of a deranged person,[8] or one suffering from some other disability,[9] a court may also

---

16 [1980] AC 247, at 261, [1979] 1 All ER 939, at 946.
17 *R v Hudson* (1980) 72 Cr App Rep 163.
18 *R v Platt* [1981] Crim LR 622 (breach of s 62 of Criminal Law Act 1977 in not informing parent of accused child's arrest).
19 At 170. See also *R v Wilson* [1981] 1 NZLR 316.
20 See *R v Howden-Simpson* [1991] Crim LR 49 where the Court of Appeal quite explicitly stated that although a threat was not enough to make a confession potentially unreliable it was enough to trigger the discretion, see further ch XV, below.
1   Both in New Zealand and in the state of Victoria, where broadly similar provisions have been in force for many years, it has been held that there is still scope for an exclusionary discretion alongside, see *R v Phillips* [1949] NZLR 316, at 345; *R v Lee* (1950) 82 CLR 133, at 150.
2   In most Commonwealth jurisdictions a 'voluntariness' test applies, but it tends to be interpreted less technically than was the case in England, so, eg in Australia, in extreme cases of impairment a confession may be excluded by rule, while in some cases it is a matter for discretion, see *Sinclair v R* (1947) 73 CLR 316; *McDermott v R* (1948) 76 CLR 501, at 507; *Murphy v R* (1989) 167 CLR 94; *R v Parker* (1990) 47 ACR 281; and in New Zealand, see *R v Cooney* [1994] 1 NZLR 38.
3   Or to a case in which a confession is made to a solicitor, and passed to the prosecution in error without any suggestion of impropriety on the part of prosecution or police: *R v Cottrill* [1997] Crim LR 56.
4   Though this again will not be allowed to degenerate into technicality, *R v Barry* (1991) 95 Cr App Rep 384, at 389.
5   *R v Goldenberg* (1988) 88 Cr App Rep 285.
6   Contrary to Code of Practice, C.13.1.
7   Compare *R v Fogah* [1989] Crim LR 141 with *R v Maguire* (1989) 90 Cr App Rep 115.
8   *R v Miller* [1986] 3 All ER 119, [1986] 1 WLR 1191; *R v Moss* (1990) 91 Cr App Rep 371.
9   *R v Clarke* [1989] Crim LR 892 (deafness); *R v Li* [1993] 2 VLR 80 (foreigner unable to understand without interpreter).

consider excluding a confession under s 78.[10] It should be noted that a direction warning of a special need for caution in cases substantially relying upon confessions by the mentally handicapped made otherwise than in the presence of independent persons has now been prescribed for such cases by s 77 of the Police and Criminal Evidence Act 1984.[11] Such a provision clearly contemplates that some such confessions will be admitted. A different aspect of unfairness may arise if the accused is induced to confess by being led to believe that what he says will be 'off the record', but is then confronted with his statement at the last minute.[12] A number of cases are concerned with access to legal advice during an interview. There is some presumption that its denial[13] will trigger the discretion to exclude,[14] but it is rebutted where such access is unlikely to have made any difference.[15] Conversely access to legal advice[16] may serve to neutralise breaches of the Code,[17] and a court is likely to be highly sceptical of any suggestion that such access actually induced a false confession.[18]

The second area of application of s 78 to confessional statements is when it is used as a secondary argument in favour of discretionary exclusion if a principal argument based upon exclusion by rule should fail.[19] In many cases such a claim is linked to a breach of the Codes of Practice issued pursuant to s 66 of the Police and Criminal Evidence Act 1984. It is now clear that breach of the Code is neither a necessary, nor a sufficient,[20] condition for discretionary exclusion of a confession under this provision. It has indeed been held that the wording of s 78 itself indicates that some breaches may not lead to exclusion.[1] On the other hand although police impropriety is not a necessary condition for the application of s 78 it seems that it is a powerful factor inclining the court to infer from such unfair treatment that the fairness of the proceedings has also been sufficiently adversely affected.[2]

It must be stressed that the discretion to exclude operates only in respect of confessional statements. It is not available to exclude statements made by witnesses, however oppressively they may have been induced by the police. That is a matter going only to weight.[3]

---

10   Since a plea of guilty was disregarded in *R v Swain* [1986] Crim LR 480 and the conviction quashed, it would be odd if the court had no power to exclude evidence of the overturned plea as a confession at a retrial, should one have been ordered.

11   Omission of which may be fatal to conviction: see *R v Bailey* [1995] 2 Cr App Rep 262.

12   As in *R v Woodall* [1989] Crim LR 288.

13   Especially in respect of an interview at which such access is denied after a less productive one at which it was granted, see *R v Marshall* (1992) Times, 28 December.

14   *R v Walsh* (1989) 91 Cr App Rep 161, at 163. In Trinidad, despite a constitutional right to be informed of a right to such access, breach does not automatically lead to exclusion, though there the discretion was itself, somewhat mysteriously, said to be neither presumptively exclusionary nor inclusionary: *Mohammed (Allie) v State* [1999] 2 WLR 552.

15   *R v Dunford* (1990) 91 Cr App Rep 150.

16   Despite some well-founded doubts as to its competence in many cases: see Royal Commission on Criminal Justice Res St Nos 2 and 16 (1992); *R v Paris* (1992) 97 Cr App Rep 99, at 110; *R v Glaves* [1993] Crim LR 685.

17   *R v Dunn* (1990) 91 Cr App Rep 237; *R v Hoyte* [1994] Crim LR 215.

18   See *R v Francis* [1992] Crim LR 372.

19   See eg *R v Alladice* (1988) 87 Cr App Rep 380; *R v Delaney* (1988) 88 Cr App Rep 338; ; *R v McGovern* (1990) 92 Cr App Rep 228 (where both parts of s 76 were also invoked); *R v Barry* (1991) 95 Cr App Rep 384.

20   *R v Parris* (1988) 89 Cr App Rep 68, at 72 where the trial judge seems to have regarded it as the former, and the Court of Appeal negated, in addition, the latter. For the situation in Australia, see *Pollard v R* (1992) 176 CLR 177.

1   *R v Walsh* (1989) 91 Cr App Rep 161, at 165.

2   *R v Alladice* (1988) 87 Cr App Rep 380, at 386. For the converse view that punctilious observation of the Code of Practice militates against a finding of unfairness, see *Re Walters* [1987] Crim LR 577.

3   *R v Austin* (1982) Lexis Transcript, 18 June.

The Royal Commission on Criminal Justice[4] was generally well-disposed towards the use of the discretionary exclusion of evidence in criminal proceedings, and recommended[5] the adoption in England of a rule corresponding to rule 403 of the Federal Rules of Evidence in the United States.[6] It is arguable that many of the considerations taken into account in that rule are already present in the assessment of the relevance of evidence in England,[7] and that the intervention of the judge to exclude unnecessarily cumulative evidence may intrude upon the function of the jury since it cannot be known which pieces of admissible evidence a jury will accept, nor how much weight it will attach to them. It seems in any event that the judge may already have a discretion to achieve these ends by the operation of time limits upon the processes of examination, cross-examination and re-examination of witnesses.[8]

3. Discretion to exclude relevant evidence in civil proceedings[9]

This topic may now have been transformed by r 32.2 of the Civil Procedure Rules which starkly provides that 'The court may use its power under this rule to exclude evidence that would otherwise be admissible'. This is supplemented by the conferment of far-reaching powers to determine relevance. All will depend upon how this new discretion is exercised. For the time being all that can be done is to explain what has hitherto been the practice.

It remains to consider whether the fair trial or fair treatment rationales for the exercise of an exclusionary discretion applied in civil proceedings. In England consideration was given to the existence of such a discretion in cases where evidence had been unlawfully obtained, and in cases where information was being withheld from the court.[10] There seem to be no English cases asserting a discretion to exclude, pursuant to the fair trial categorisation, on the basis that the evidence will be more prejudicial than probative in revealing evidence of extrinsic discreditable acts.[11] It was explicitly rejected in *Bradford City Metropolitan Council v K*.[12] In some cases while accepting this view

4 Cm 2263 (1993).
5 Para 8.13, rec 181.
6 'Although relevant, evidence may be excluded if its probative value is substantially outweighed by the danger of unfair prejudice, confusion of the issues, or misleading the jury, or by considerations of undue delay, waste of time, or needless presentation of cumulative evidence.'
7 See above p 56.
8 *Vernon v Bosley* [1995] 2 FCR 78, on the assumption that it applies in criminal proceedings as well as in civil.
9 See Pattenden (1997) 1 Int J Ev & Proof 361; and from an Australian perspective Forbes (1988) 62 ALJ 211.
10 In Scotland there is no common law discretion to exclude otherwise admissible evidence in civil proceedings, *McVinnie v McVinnie* 1995 SLT 81, a decision of Sheriff MacPhail, endorsed by the Outer House in *Glaser v Glaser* 1997 SLT 456; but see also *Lobban v Phillip* 1995 SCLR 1104.
11 Such a discretion was denied in Australia: see *Polycarpou v Australian Wire Industries Pty Ltd* (1995) 36 NSWLR 49, where all of the authorities were reviewed by Kirby P. Statutory exclusionary discretions are now provided for civil proceedings by the Evidence Act 1995 (Cwth) ss 135 and 138, and a discretion to limit the use of evidence by s 136. It may be noted that the corresponding r 403 of the US Federal Rules does apply to civil proceedings. Although the terminology of discretion was employed in this context in *Berger v Raymond & Son Ltd* [1984] 1 WLR 625, it seems likely that it was used no more than loosely to characterise those elements of the exclusionary rule of an essentially indeterminate nature or perhaps to prevent prejudice in the case of surprise or unduly lengthening the proceedings by adducing evidence of dubious relevance. See further below at p 381.
12 [1990] Fam 140. Although in terms applying only to the civil jurisdiction of magistrates the language is general, and contains no hint of restriction to lower courts.

as technically correct the court has softened its impact, either by suggesting the possibility of discounting weight,[13] or by subsuming such matters into the initial determination of relevance.[14]

It was denied in *Ibrahim v R*[15] that there was any discretion to exclude improperly obtained statements in civil proceedings. In *Helliwell v Piggott-Sims* where the Court of Appeal assumed the evidence to have been obtained by improper means the same view was repeated:[16]

> in criminal cases the judge may have a discretion. That is shown by *Kuruma v R*.[17] But so far as civil cases are concerned, it seems to me that the judge has no discretion. The evidence is relevant and admissible. The judge cannot refuse it on the ground that it may have been unlawfully obtained in the beginning.

The other context in which the question has been raised is in relation to claims of privilege which will be dealt with in detail in chs X and XI below. If an established privilege already exists no question of discretion arises because in the words of Lord Wilberforce: 'to substitute for the privilege a dependence on the courts' discretion would substantially be to the defendant's detriment'.[18] It arises only when a witness makes an unsuccessful claim to be privileged from answering a question. Does the judge then have a residual discretion not to allow the question to be put? In *D v National Society for the Prevention of Cruelty to Children* Lord Simon was quite clear that in such a case 'it must be law, not discretion, which is in command'.[19] Unfortunately Lord Hailsham took the opposite view, accepting the views expressed in the sixteenth report of the Law Reform Committee on privilege in civil proceedings:[20]

> Privilege in the main is the creation of the common law whose policy, pragmatic as ever, has been to limit to a minimum the categories of privileges which a person has an absolute right to claim, but to accord to the judge a wide discretion to permit the witness, whether a party to the proceedings or not, to refuse to disclose information where disclosure would be a breach of some ethical or social value and non-disclosure would be unlikely to result in serious injustice in the particular case in which it is claimed.

The position has been reconsidered in subsequent authority though the issue has, at best, arisen on the periphery of a claim based on a resistance to discovery. Since

13   *Re C (Minors)* [1993] 4 All ER 690, at 694.
14   *Vernon v Bosley* [1994] PIQR P337 where Hoffmann LJ explicitly equates considerations relating to such an assessment with the operation of the discretion.
15   [1914] AC 599, at 610, [1914–15] All ER Rep 874, at 878.
16   *Helliwell v Piggott-Sims* [1980] FSR 356, at 357, echoing similar sentiments expressed in *R v Christie* [1914] AC 545, [1914–15] All ER Rep 63, by Lord Moulton at 559, 69 and by Lord Reading at 564, 71. See also *ITC Film Distributors v Video Exchange Ltd* [1982] Ch 431, [1982] 2 All ER 241.
17   [1955] AC 197.
18   *Rank Film Distributors Ltd v Video Information Centre* [1982] AC 380, at 442, [1981] 2 All ER 76, at 81.
19   [1978] AC 171, at 239, [1977] 1 All ER 589, at 613. The House was numerically equally divided on this point. Lord Edmund Davies delivered a speech to the same effect as Lord Simon, Lord Diplock did not mention the matter, and Lord Kilbrandon contented himself with agreeing with Lord Hailsham. In *British Steel Corpn v Granada Television Ltd* [1981] AC 1096 at 1113, [1981] 1 All ER 417, at 431, Megarry VC thought the balance favoured Lord Hailsham's view.
20   Para 1, citing *A-G v Clough* [1963] 1 QB 773, [1963] 1 All ER 420 and *A-G v Mulholland* [1963] 2 QB 477, [1963] 1 All ER 767, which, however do not entirely justify the statement. See also para 51.

discovery is an equitable remedy it always has a discretionary element.[1] It is far from clear that the same principles apply to prevent evidence from being adduced. Thus in *McGuiness v A-G of Victoria* Sir Owen Dixon in refuting a claim that the rules limiting discovery applied to evidence said: 'The answer is that it is not a rule of evidence but a practice of refusing in an action for libel ... to compel discovery of the name of ... informants.'[2] It might be argued that this passage relates only to the question of total immunity as a matter of law, and does not touch the question of discretionary exclusion. When the issue arose during a trial a judge always had control over the propriety of the proceedings before him, and could certainly disallow vexatious or irrelevant questions. It is possible that the dicta in the authorities cited to justify the Law Reform Committee's view in its report, relied upon that power.[3] At first instance in *Granada* Megarry VC urged separate consideration of the position first in interlocutory proceedings, second at the trial, and third in deciding upon a remedy.[4] In the Court of Appeal Lord Denning rejected this view and asserted that the same principles applied at each stage.[5] In the House of Lords it is less clear how far the decision that the court has a discretion extends beyond the precise question of pre-trial disclosure. The better view is that it did extend to evidence at the trial. Lord Wilberforce referred to the duty as one to disclose to a court,[6] not as one to disclose to an opponent. Then in his final summary of his reasons, after asserting that the court undoubtedly had a discretion, he went on to consider those parts of Megarry VC's reasons which explicitly related to a discretion in relation to evidence, and not to the discretion in relation to a remedy which he had carefully segregated.[7] It seems that the principle upon which the discretion was to be exercised was that stated by the House of Lords in *Science Research Council v Nassé*, namely:[8]

> to consider fairly the strength and value of the interest in preserving confidentiality and the damage which may be caused by breaking it; then to consider whether the objective, to dispose fairly of the case, can be achieved without doing so.

It is probably now too late to argue that this process related only to the determination of the initial obligation to answer, rather than to that of determining whether the obligation should be overridden in the circumstances of a particular case at the discretion of the judge.[9] In the particular case of the disclosure of the source of information contained in a publication, the matter came to be regulated, not by judicial discretion, but by a statutory rule that disclosure may be compelled only in the interests of justice or national security or for the prevention of disorder or crime.[10] It was faintly suggested that an inclusionary discretion might exist in some cases, but this was rejected in relation to the discretionary admission of hearsay in proceedings involving children, both in

---

1   In *British Steel Corpn v Granada Television Ltd* [1981] AC 1096, at 1174, [1981] 1 All ER 417, at 459, Lord Wilberforce said 'the remedy (*being equitable*) is discretionary' (emphasis supplied).
2   (1940) 63 CLR 73, at 104, a passage quoted with approval by Viscount Dilhorne in *Granada*.
3   As decided in *Re Buchanan* (1964) 65 SRNSW 9.
4   [1981] AC 1096, at 1111, [1981] 1 All ER 417, at 427.
5   At 1129, 441.
6   At 1168, 455.
7   At 1175, 460.
8   [1980] AC 1028, at 1067, [1979] 3 All ER 673, at 681. Although in terms limited to questions arising in relation to discovery, it should be noted that this passage is justified by reference to cases like *Mulholland* and *Clough* where no question of discovery arose.
9   As argued by Cross (1979) 30 NILQ 289.
10   Contempt of Court Act 1981, s 10.

the higher,[11] and lower,[12] courts. It is also significant that in *Savings and Investment Bank Ltd v Gasco Investments (Netherlands) BV (No 2)*[13] where the Court of Appeal held contempt proceedings to be civil for the purposes of the admission of hearsay, it asserted, not that such hearsay could be excluded at the court's discretion, but rather that it would be unlikely to be accorded sufficient weight to satisfy the heavy burden of proof.

It seems that the judge has a discretion to impose strict time limits upon the examination, cross-examination and re-examination of witness which in effect amounts to a discretion to exclude at least some unnecessarily cumulative evidence.[14] It was however suggested by Butler Sloss LJ in *Re M and R (minors)*[15] that further review should take place with a view to instituting an exclusionary discretion at least in non-adversarial proceedings.[16] The new Civil Procedure Rules seem to have been designed specifically to respond more generally to this problem.

C.   THE SUMMING UP

It is difficult to estimate the amount of control which a judge exercises over a jury by means of his summing up, for, quite apart from the legal rules that govern the matter, juries expect and receive considerable guidance with regard to the evidence submitted to them, and this guidance may be expressed in emphatic terms.[17] The legal rules on the subject have never been precisely formulated, but it seems that a judge must always put defences raised by the evidence to the jury,[18] must not interrupt his rehearsal of the evidence with one-sided and unfair comment,[19] and can never be justified in directing a jury that they must accept his view of disputed facts,[20] although he may, in a civil case, and sometimes should, tell them they ought to do so as reasonable men.[1] If a party tenders no evidence on a contested issue the judge may instruct the jury to draw the most favourable inference possible from the evidence tendered by the other.[2] In *DPP v Stonehouse*[3] Lord Salmon referred to the judge's duty to direct an acquittal in a criminal case if satisfied that there is no evidence before the jury to justify them in convicting and said:

> This rule which has long been established, is to protect the accused against being wrongly convicted. But there is no converse rule—although there may be some

11   *H v H* [1990] Fam 86, at 107, [1989] 3 All ER 740, at 754.
12   *Bradford City Metropolitan Council v K* [1990] Fam 140.
13   [1988] Ch 422, [1988] 1 All ER 975.
14   *Vernon v Bosley* [1994] PIQR P337, at 340.
15   [1996] 4 All ER 239, at 255.
16   A view rejected by Pattenden and Forbes above p 195 fn 9 on the basis that relevance is a sufficiently flexible concept to achieve anything not achievable by the residuary powers of the judge to regulate proceedings before him.
17   For general statements see *Clouston & Co Ltd v Corry* [1906] AC 122, at 130 per Lord James of Hereford and *R v Lawrence* [1982] AC 510, [1981] 1 All ER 974, at 519F, 977e per Lord Hailsham LC.
18   *R v Keith Keba Badjan* (1966) 50 Cr App Rep 141.
19   *R v Spencer* [1995] Crim LR 235.
20   *Dublin Wicklow and Wexford Rly Co v Slattery* (1878) 3 App Cas 1155, at 1186.
1   See eg *Pickup v Thames and Mersey Marine Insurance Co* (1878) 3 QBD 594, at 600.
2   *Ross v Associated Portland Cement Manufacturers Ltd* [1964] 2 All ER 452, [1964] 1 WLR 768.
3   [1978] AC 55, at 80.

who think that there should be.[4] If the judge is satisfied that, on the evidence, the jury would not be justified in acquitting the accused and indeed that it would be perverse of them to do so, he has no power to pre-empt the jury's verdict by directing them to convict. The jury alone have the right to decide that the accused is guilty.

The trial judge had directed the jury to find the accused guilty of an attempt to obtain money for his wife by deception if they were satisfied that he staged his death with the dishonest intention of causing an insurance company to pay over the amount due on his life policies. The question whether the accused's conduct was sufficiently proximate to the crime attempted, a question of fact for the jury,[5] was thus withdrawn from that body. By a majority of three to two the House of Lords held that the direction was wrong, although the House was unanimous in applying the proviso to s 2 of the Criminal Appeal Act 1968 and affirming the conviction.

   In a criminal case the overriding duty of the judge is to put the defence fairly and adequately to the jury,[6] which in almost every case will involve a summing up explaining the constituents of the offences charged,[7] and the relevance to them of the evidence which has been adduced.[8] The judge must not direct the jury to convict,[9] and must leave to the jury any defence which is raised, unless in an exceptional case there is no evidence at all to support it.[10] It is even enough if the only evidence in support is the exculpatory part of a pre-trial mixed statement.[11] Where potentially prejudicial evidence has been admitted the judge must direct the jury on its potentially probative value, which is then for the jury to determine.[12] The judge may comment quite robustly on the evidence, but must not direct he jury to accept it,[13] even in the case of uncontradicted medical evidence.[14] He must direct the jury in a balanced way, and cannot content himself by simply reiterating the incantation that it is for the jury to decide the facts.[15] This is especially important if the jury has sought further guidance.[16]

   It is clearly the duty of the judge to instruct the jury on all matters of law, including the effect of any relevant presumption of law and the incidence of the onus of proof.[17] This may oblige him to direct the jury that they must find one of the facts in issue to be proved if they are satisfied as to the existence of some other fact, for, when a rebuttable presumption of law applies to a case, proof of one fact is legally equivalent to proof of some other fact in the absence of further evidence. Thus, if the legitimacy of a child is among the facts in issue in civil proceedings, and the proponent adduces evidence to

---

4   See Lord Diplock at 69 and Lord Dilhorne at 72. They both dissented on this point although they concurred in affirming the conviction.
5   See Criminal Attempts Act 1981, s 4(3).
6   *R v Spencer* [1987] AC 128, [1986] 2 All ER 928, at 142G, 938c.
7   *R v Brower* [1995] Crim LR 746.
8   *R v Martins; R v Katthoeffer* [1996] CLY 1419.
9   *DPP v Stonehouse* above; the same is true in Ireland, see *People v Danis* [1993] 3 IR 1. For academic commentary see Williams [1976] Crim LR 472, 532.
10   As in *R v Briley* [1991] Crim LR 444.
11   *R v Silverman* (1987) 86 Cr App Rep 213; *R v Bass* [1992] Crim LR 647.
12   *R v Bethelmie* (1995) Times, 27 November.
13   The Royal Commission on Criminal Justice Cmnd 2263 (1993) para 8.23 suggests that the judge should not express any view as to the credibility of a witness.
14   *R v Lanfear* [1968] 2 QB 77, [1968] 1 All ER 683.
15   *R v Gilbey* (1990) (26 January 1990, unreported) cited in *Mears v R* (1993) 97 Cr App Rep 239. See also *R v Gibbons* (1993) Times, 19 July.
16   *Mears*, above. Though even then he need not remind the jury of cross-examination as well as evidence in chief, unless it has also been requested *R v Morgan* [1996] Crim LR 600.
17   *R v Zarrabi* (1985) Times, 23 February where a conviction was quashed because the judge directed only upon the standard, and not upon the incidence of the burden, of proof.

show that the child was born in wedlock, the judge must direct the jury to find in favour of the proponent if they accept this evidence, unless the opponent satisfies them on a balance of probabilities that there was no intercourse between the child's mother and her husband by which it could have been begotten. Similarly, if it becomes necessary to establish that a particular person is dead, the judge may have to tell a civil jury that they must find in favour of the proponent on being satisfied that the person in question had been absent for more than seven years, without having been heard of by those with whom he would most probably have communicated if he were alive. In criminal cases, where the accused is the opponent, it is probably necessary for him only to adduce or elicit or point to evidence adduced or elicited by his adversary which is sufficient to raise a reasonable doubt.

When the judge directs the jury on the effect of a presumption of law, he is not telling them that they must accept his view of the facts. As a matter of ordinary reasoning, many people, including the judge, might not be prepared to infer legitimacy from birth in wedlock if there was evidence of prolonged intimacy between the child's mother and her lover, any more than they would be prepared to infer her death from seven years' absence if the person in question was young and healthy when she was last heard of. For a number of different reasons, the law attaches what may be an artificial probative value to certain facts, and the judge's direction in such a case informs the jury of the legal consequences which follow upon their finding these facts to exist.

D.   APPEALS

1.   Criminal cases tried with a jury[18]

Statement of the law in this area has been much simplified by the Criminal Appeal Act 1995 which now provides that:[19]

> (1)   Subject to the provisions of this Act, the Court of Appeal—
> (a)   shall allow an appeal against conviction if they [sic] think that the conviction is unsafe; and
> (b)   shall dismiss such an appeal in any other case.

The term 'unsafe' is not defined, and as the Act is intended to codify the law, it is permissible to refer to the pre-existing law in relation to any doubtful term.[20] It can hardly be denied in the light of serious controversy in relation to the use of this word in the previous legislation that its meaning was doubtful, and reference to that law would accord with the government's expressed intention of restating the existing practice of the Court of Appeal.[1] On the other hand such an interpretation would defeat the hopes of the Royal Commission on Criminal Justice, upon whose report the reform was based, that the Court of Appeal had been too heavily influenced by the role of the jury, reluctant to consider whether it had reached a wrong decision, and accordingly 'should

---

18   See Smith [1995] Crim LR 920 for discussion of the impact of the new legislation in an article described as 'penetrating' by Lord Bingham CJ in *R v Graham* [1997] 1 Cr App Rep 302, at 308B.

19   By substituting the new provision into s 2 of the Criminal Appeal Act 1968, replacing the old sub-s (1), and the proviso to it.

20   *Bank of England v Vagliano Bros* [1891] AC 107, at 144.

1   See Hansard Vol 256, para 24 (6 March 1995) (Home Secretary on Second Reading); Standing Committee B (21 March 1995) (Minister of State at col 26).

be *readier* to overturn jury verdicts than it had shown itself to be in the past.'[2] Yet in one of the earlier cases[3] to consider the impact of the new provision, the Court of Appeal appears to have felt that the new formula had neither retained existing practice, nor made it readier to allow an appeal, but had resulted in its being less ready to allow an appeal from a conviction which it believed to be safe, despite some irregularity in the course of the trial.[4] It seems however that at least some forms of pre-trial misbehaviour remain capable of rendering a conviction unsafe if they have resulted in an abuse of process.[5]

It should be noted that the 1995 legislation[6] also makes provision, even after an appeal has been disposed of, for a further appeal to be considered on the basis of fresh evidence or new arguments, upon a reference back to the Court of Appeal by a Criminal Cases Review Commission, provided only that the Commission takes the view that there is a realistic possibility of the conviction or verdict not being upheld. It seems that such a reference may be made at any time, and the appeal considered on the basis of the state of the law at the time of the further review, not at that of the original trial; so, in theory, it is now possible for changes in the law of evidence to be given retrospective effect.

No formal amendment[7] has been made to s 7 of the Criminal Appeal Act 1968 relating to the power to order a retrial, which remains open-endedly to depend upon the Court's perception of the requirements of the 'interests of justice'. Section 4 of the Criminal Appeal Act 1995 does however accept the recommendation[8] of the Royal Commission in changing the definition of the fresh evidence which the Court is empowered to receive from 'likely to be credible' to 'capable of belief'. This appears to have been an attempt to ameliorate the test and, despite the logical and linguistic difficulty in doing so,[9] this seems likely to be how it will be interpreted.[10] Although the Royal Commission disapproved[11] of the decision in *Stafford v DPP*[12] that the appellate court should be guided by its own view of fresh evidence rather than its assessment of the view that a jury might take, no recommendation was made to that effect, and no action has been taken to change the law.

2.   Civil cases tried with a jury

After a civil case has been tried with a jury, the party against whom their verdict has been given may apply to the Court of Appeal for an order for a new trial and, if such an

---

2   Royal Commission on Criminal Justice Cm 2263 (1993) ch 10, para 3.
3   *R v Chalkley* [1998] QB 848, [1998] 2 All ER 155, at 868E, 173a. This runs flatly contrary to the view, and expectation, of Smith in [1995] Crim LR 920, at 924. See Clarke [1999] Crim LR 108.
4   Indeed it suggests that there might be some other way of marking the Court's disapproval of the irregularity than by allowing the appeal, and that this is reflected in the jurisprudence of the European Court of Human Rights.
5   *R v Mullen* (1999) Times, 15 February. But not if the result of an erroneous ruling on the admissibility of evidence has precipitated a plea of guilty: *R v Callaghan* (5 March 1999, unreported), CA.
6   Criminal Appeal Act 1995, Part II.
7   Despite the view of the Royal Commission on Criminal Justice that there should be greater readiness to order re-trials: Cm 2263, ch 10, para 65.
8   Ch 10, para 60, rec 322.
9   As explained by Smith [1995] Crim LR 920, at 928.
10 In the older test 'likely to be credible' was often construed as if it read 'likely to be credited', and it is submitted that the new test is likely to be read as 'likely to be capable of belief'.
11 Ch 10, para 62.
12 [1974] AC 878, [1973] 3 All ER 762. See also *R v McMahon* (1978) 68 Cr App Rep 18.

order is made, the verdict of the jury is set aside. A new trial may be sought on the ground that there was no evidence which ought properly to have been left to the jury in favour of the proponent of the issue in question, or because the verdict of the jury was against the weight of the evidence.[13] In order that a new trial should be granted on the latter ground: it is not enough that the judge who tried the case might have come to a different conclusion on the evidence than the jury, or that the judges in the Court where the new trial is moved for might have come to a different conclusion, but there must be such a preponderance of evidence, assuming there is evidence on both sides to go to the jury, as to make it unreasonable, and almost perverse, that the jury when instructed and assisted properly by the judge should return such a verdict.[14]

If the Court of Appeal concludes that the judge ought not to have left an issue to the jury because there was insufficient evidence in support of the proponent's case, it will enter judgment for the opponent forthwith. It may also adopt this course where the evidence in support of the opponent's case was very strong, although there was some evidence favourable to the proponent, provided it is clear that no further material would be available at a second trial.[15] This is the result of the construction which has been placed on Ord 59, r 10(3) of the Rules of the Supreme Court under which the Court of Appeal has power to draw inferences of fact and make any order which ought to have been made, but serious doubts have been expressed on the question whether it entitles the Court of Appeal to enter judgment for the proponent of an issue after setting aside a verdict for the opponent.[16]

3. Civil cases tried by a judge alone

The appeal is a rehearing when a civil case has been tried by a judge alone, so the result is usually judgment for one of the parties rather than an order for a new trial. The Court of Appeal may hear fresh evidence, but only on special grounds, except on matters which have occurred after the decision from which the appeal is brought, and the case is usually dealt with on the basis of a transcript or note of the proceedings in the court below.[17] Appeals on matters of law may involve questions of the wrongful admission or rejection of evidence, and these are disposed of in the same way as appeals involving any other legal issue. The Court of Appeal will naturally be loath to disturb a finding of fact by the trial judge who has had the advantage of observing the demeanour of the witnesses, 'their candour or their partisanship, and all the incidental elements so difficult to describe which make up the atmosphere of an actual trial'.[18] Although the court occasionally takes the view that the judge was wrong to give credence to a particular

---

13 A new trial may be ordered on a number of other grounds conveniently discussed in Odgers *Civil Court Actions* (24th edn, 1996) 435–439.

14 Per Lord Selborne in *Metropolitan Rly Co v Wright* (1886) 11 App Cas 152, at 153.

15 See the judgment of Lord Atkin in *Mechanical and General Inventions Co Ltd and Lehwess v Austin and the Austin Motor Co* [1935] AC 346.

16 [1935] AC 346 at 369 and 379 per Lord Wright reiterating doubts of Lord Halsbury in *Toulmin v Millar* (1887) 12 App Cas 746; but see *Croker v Croker* [1932] P 173 and *Winterbotham Gurney & Co v Sibthorp and Cox* [1918] 1 KB 625, at 634. This Order remains in force under Civil Procedure Rules 1999, Sch 1.

17 The Civil Procedure Rules, Sch 1 preserves RSC Ord 59, r 10(2). There is no distinction between cases tried with and without a jury so far as the hearing of fresh evidence is concerned (*Leeder v Ellis* [1953] AC 52, [1952] 2 All ER 814). On the refusal to hear fresh evidence see *Ladd v Marshall* [1954] 3 All ER 745, [1954] 1 WLR 1489, and see further above p 14.

18 Per Lord Macmillan in *Watt v Thomas* [1947] AC 484, at 490–1, [1947] 1 All ER 582, at 590.

witness,[19] it will be far more ready to reverse his decision in a case which depends on inferences from admitted or undisputed facts.[20]

Appeals lie from decisions of judges who have sat without a jury in civil cases tried in the county court, and there may be appeals in matrimonial causes as well as criminal cases tried by the magistrates, but they do not call for separate discussion in a work of this nature.

---

19 Eg *Coghlan v Cumberland* [1898] 1 Ch 704; *Yuill v Yuill* [1945] P 15, [1945] 1 All ER 183; and *M v M (Custody Application)* [1988] 1 FLR 225, at 233. In Australia it has been said that the same applies to total rejection of a witness by the trial judge, *In the Marriage of Prpic* (1994) 119 FLR 434.
20 Cf *Powell v Streatham Manor Nursing Home* [1935] AC 243 with *Flower v Ebbw Vale Steel Co* [1936] AC 206.

Chapter V

Witnesses

The most common vehicle for proof is the evidence of witnesses, and this chapter considers some special considerations relating to them. It will first give a brief description of the development of this branch of the law, and set out the standard incidents of testimony; it will then go on to discuss factors peculiar to particular categories of witness, such as children, spouses, and offenders; and the final section will deal with the nature of supporting evidence.

SECTION I.   STANDARD CASE

This section first sets out to sketch the way in which this aspect of the subject has changed over time, and will then deal with the procedures for taking testimony in the standard case.

A.   HISTORICAL OVERVIEW

It is not much of an exaggeration to say that the old common law in this area was predominantly a law of witnesses, mainly concerned with their qualification to testify. Witnesses were largely divided into two classes; those who were not permitted to testify, and those who could be compelled to do so. The obligation was to testify generally, but might be mitigated by a privilege of not answering certain types of question.[1] The death knell of that old system was sounded by Bentham, and its execution mainly accomplished by the passage of the Evidence Act 1843 which abolished the largest and most technical of the categories of those who were disqualified from testifying, namely those with an interest in the outcome of the proceedings. This general abolition still left a few categories of witness subject to the old rules of disqualification, such as parties, including the accused in a criminal case, and spouses. These exclusions

---

1   What remains of this mitigation is discussed in chapter X below.

were mitigated by legislative enactment in the nineteenth century,[2] often by introducing a distinction between the competence of witnesses to testify and their compulsion to do so,[3] or by requiring corroboration in some relevant respect.[4] The common law similarly reflected the older system of disqualification by developing mandatory rules as to corroboration for certain categories of witness and situation.[5] To these were added further analogous categories, but often on a less mandatory basis. It was hardly surprising that the technicality of the distinctions between the various components of this patchwork grated upon the judges, and that moves toward rationalisation and reform were undertaken in most common law jurisdictions, sometimes by legislation[6] and sometimes by judicial innovation.[7] This movement has owed something to the decline in jury trial in civil cases, and much to a desire for greater flexibility in the form of direction to the jury. A further contributing factor has been a changed perception of the capabilities of witnesses, especially of children, and a feeling that some of the distinctions were demeaning.[8]

The current situation in the general case then is that all of those who can give relevant testimony may be compelled by witness summons to attend at the court to testify, and in the case of trial by jury, the jury will be instructed as to the approach they should adopt to such testimony, tailored to the facts of the particular trial, and untrammelled by technical rules. In recent times this fabric has been overlaid by the development of special procedures for special situations, and types of witness.[9]

B. OATHS[10]

The old law developed from the notion that only those who were prepared to testify on oath on the Gospel were competent witnesses, but other forms of oath and affirmation were gradually permitted. The present law is contained in the Oaths Act 1978, which consolidates earlier enactments. Section 1 of the Act prescribes the form in which an oath shall be administered to Christians and Jews. It also allows for the administration of an oath to those with other religious beliefs in other forms.[11] In such cases the Act is merely directive, and requires only that the form of the oath should be regarded by both court and witness as binding.[12] The fact that a person taking an oath has no

2   Principally the Evidence Act 1851 (parties in civil cases), the Evidence Amendment Act 1853 (spouses in civil cases), the Evidence Further Amendment Act 1869 (parties and spouses in breach of promise and on issues of adultery), and the Criminal Evidence Act 1898 (accused and spouse in criminal cases).

3   Eg Evidence Amendment Act 1853, s 3.

4   Eg Evidence Further Amendment Act 1869, s 2.

5   Such as complainants in sexual cases.

6   Eg the abolition of corroboration requirements in Scotland by the Civil Evidence (Scotland) Act 1988, s 1.

7   Eg the abolition of corroboration requirements in the cases of accomplices in Canada by the Supreme Court of Canada in *Vetrovec v R* [1982] 1 SCR 811.

8   Especially that which treated complainants in sexual cases, overwhelmingly female, as being peculiarly unreliable.

9   These special procedures will be augmented if, as seems likely, the Youth Justice and Criminal Evidence Bill 1999 is enacted in something like its current form.

10   See Eleventh Report of the Criminal Law Revision Committee 1972 (Cmnd 4991) paras 279–81 which, so far unavailingly, recommended abolition of an oath in favour of a declaration, and more generally Australian Law Reform Commission Research Paper No 6 'Sworn and Unsworn Evidence'.

11   But they are not available as a matter of right, and a witness who refuses to swear in the normal form, or to affirm, is not entitled to give unsworn evidence: *Vitalis v CPS* [1995] CLY 1186.

12   *R v Chapman* [1980] Crim LR 42 (witness not holding the book when swearing); *R v Kemble* [1990] 3 All ER 116, [1990] 1 WLR 1111 (Muslim swearing on New Testament).

religious belief does not prevent it from being binding.[13] Under s 5 anyone objecting to being sworn is permitted to make a solemn affirmation, and such an affirmation may be required of any person in relation to whom it is not reasonably practicable to administer an oath in the manner appropriate to his religious belief. An affirmation has the same force and effect as an oath which means that a false affirmer may be punished as a perjurer.

In a few of the special categories to be mentioned in the next section there is no need for a witness to be sworn. Other cases in which a witness need not be sworn depend, at present,[14] on the common law. Someone who simply produces a document pursuant to a witness summons does not have to be sworn if there is another witness who can identify the document.[15] This means that the person producing it cannot be cross-examined. Another person who need not be sworn is the advocate giving evidence of the terms of a compromise reached between the parties to litigation in which he acted for one of them. It is customary for his statement to be made from the well of the court[16] but the matter is dependent on convention and there is really no authority on the question whether he can insist on his right not to take the oath.[17]

The right of the accused to make an unsworn statement at his trial which existed at common law was abolished by s 72 of the Criminal Justice Act 1982, in accordance with the recommendations of the Criminal Law Revision Committee.[18]

C. PROCEDURE[19]

The procedure for determining whether or not a witness is competent, and if so whether or not the evidence should be given sworn or unsworn, may occasion certain problems. Questions may also arise as to the role of the court in advising the witness upon matters of competence and compellability, in commenting upon the decision not to call a witness, and as to the precise extent to which a witness is compellable. In *R v Yacoob*,[20] where a question arose whether or not a witness in criminal proceedings was married to the accused, it was decided that the proper procedure was for the judge to resolve the matter on the voir dire in the absence of the jury. The witness could be heard on that issue, even though it related to the witness's own competency. In the case of a young child being sworn in civil proceedings,[1] the judge will normally conduct a voir dire in which the child will be examined.[2] Indeed if the child is of tender years such an inquiry

13   Section 4(2).
14   The Youth Justice and Criminal Evidence Bill 1999 proposes to extend the entitlement to give recorded testimony unsworn (cll 26, 27) to children (cl 16) and to new categories of witnesses eligible for special measures on the basis that the quality of their evidence is likely to be diminished by fear or distress (cl 17).
15   *Perry v Gibson* (1834) 1 Ad & El 48.
16   *Hickman v Berens* [1895] 2 Ch 638. But see *Pioneer Concrete Gold Coast Pty Ltd v Cassidy (No 2)* [1969] Qd R 290.
17   There are obvious objections to an advocate acting as a witness in a case in which he is professionally engaged (*R v Secretary of State for India in Council, ex p Ezekiel* [1941] 2 KB 169, [1941] 2 All ER 546); but it would probably be going too far to say that he is not a competent witness in such circumstances.
18   Cmnd 4991, paras 102–6.
19   In criminal proceedings the Youth Justice and Criminal Evidence Bill 1999 proposes to regulate the procedures for determining competency (cl 53), and whether a witness is to be permitted to give unsworn testimony (cll 54, 55).
20   (1981) 72 Cr App Rep 313.
1   This was the old procedure in criminal proceedings, so now that the rules which formerly obtained in criminal proceedings have been imported, it seems likely that the procedure for implementing them will be imported also.
2   *R v Hayes* [1977] 2 All ER 288, [1977] 1 WLR 234.

becomes mandatory.[3] It seems that the party suggesting incompetence bears an evidential burden on that issue, but that the legal burden resides upon the party calling the witness. If the witness is called by the prosecution, the standard is proof beyond reasonable doubt;[4] if called by the defence it is presumably proof on the balance of probabilities. Judges have a wide general power over the procedure to be adopted before them, and may alter the arrangement of their court in the interests of doing justice. To this end they may permit vulnerable witnesses and especially children, to be screened from sight of the accused.[5] If such a course be adopted the jury should be directed not to allow the adoption of such an arrangement to create prejudice against the accused.[6]

The court takes an active part in matters affecting the competence and compellability of witnesses. In the case of spouses it has been said to be desirable[7] that the court should take the initiative and explain to a competent, but non-compellable, spouse the precise nature of that situation, so as to inform the witness's choice whether or not to testify.[8] The choice is particularly important because it is exhausted once a witness has decided to testify. There is then no further chance of refusing, and if a witness attempts to resile from his proof he is liable to be treated as hostile, and to be cross-examined on any previous statement he may have made, a procedure explained more fully in the following chapter. In several reported cases the accused has been found guilty despite, or perhaps because, a spouse witness for the prosecution has attempted to shield him, and then been treated as hostile.[9] It is noteworthy that notwithstanding the recommendation of the Criminal Law Revision Committee[10] that the prohibition[11] on comment upon the accused's spouse's failure to testify should be lifted, it was instead re-enacted.[12] It is still more surprising that this provision has[13] remained in force despite the ban on comment upon the accused's similar failure having been lifted by the Criminal Justice and Public Order Act 1994.[14]

Witnesses appear to have become increasingly reluctant to testify, especially in criminal cases, either through disinclination, or from fear.[15] Attendance can be compelled by means of the Criminal Procedure (Attendance of Witnesses) Act 1965. Testimony can then be required, its refusal sanctioned by summary proceedings for contempt of court, and in some cases compensated for by admission of previous statements in

---

3 *R v Khan* (1981) 73 Cr App Rep 190.
4 *Yacoob* at 317. The Youth Justice and Criminal Evidence Bill 1999 proposes to reduce the onus in the case of prosecution witnesses to the balance of probabilities (cl 53(2)).
5 *R v Smellie* (1919) 14 Cr App Rep 128. See also the Youth Justice and Criminal Evidence Bill 1999 (cl 22).
6 *R v X,Y and Z* (1989) 91 Cr App Rep 36. See also the Youth Justice and Criminal Evidence Bill 1999 (cl 31).
7 Though failure to do so is not by itself sufficient to quash a conviction, *R v Nelson* [1992] Crim LR 653.
8 *R v Acaster* (1912) 7 Cr App Rep 187; *R v Pitt* [1983] QB 25, [1982] 3 All ER 63. See also *Bates v HM Advocate* 1989 SLT 701.
9 *Hoskyn v Metropolitan Police Comr* [1979] AC 474, [1978] 2 All ER 136; *R v Pitt* above; *R v Nelson* above.
10 Eleventh Report 1972 (Cmnd 4991) para 154.
11 Then Criminal Evidence Act 1898, s 1(b).
12 Police and Criminal Evidence Act 1984, s 80(8).
13 It is now proposed to be repealed by the Youth Justice and Criminal Evidence Bill 1999 (Sch 4, para 13(2)),
14 Section 35(3); see also Sch 11 which repeals Criminal Evidence Act 1898, s 1(b) but omits all reference to Police and Criminal Evidence Act 1984, s 80(8).
15 Concern about this phenomenon inspired the enactment of the special offence of intimidation of witnesses in s 51 of the Criminal Justice and Public Order Act 1994, and many of the provisions of the Youth Justice and Criminal Evidence Bill 1999, which was more directly foreshadowed by the Home Office Report of Interdepartmental Working Group *Speaking Up For Justice* (1998).

derogation of the hearsay rule. Since the adversarial system, with its underpinning of orality, is still fundamental to the system of criminal trial, it is important to encourage witnesses to testify, both by the provision of support and information before trial, and by the amelioration of stress and fear at trial.[16] Pressure may also be relieved by taking a limited view of the evidence required of witnesses. Thus not only must evidence be relevant, but it is permissible for the judge to accept the assessment of counsel, instructed by the witness, of such relevance.[17] Similarly in relation to oral evidence required by a foreign court, witnesses should be protected by a narrow specification of the issues to which the evidence is alleged to be relevant.[18] Nor does such relevance extend to documents which can be used only in cross-examination.[19] Where evidence may be material however the police must allow access by the defence to potential witnesses.[20]

Refusal to testify can be visited by summary proceedings for contempt, the normal punishment for which is a custodial sentence,[1] even where the refuser is the victim of the relevant crime.[2] Although the accused will not be liable for contempt for refusal to testify at his own trial,[3] if he chooses to testify he must answer all questions,[4] presumably upon pain of being in contempt, and certainly upon pain of having adverse inferences drawn from his refusal.[5]

Section 23(3) of the Police and Criminal Evidence Act 1984 was designed to permit the use of hearsay in cases where witnesses failed to testify through fear, and the Law Commission has now recommended further improvement.[6]

SECTION 2.   SPECIAL CATEGORIES

As indicated above in a number of cases special rules have been devised to cater for suspect categories of witness, sometimes special rules of competence and compulsion, sometimes rules requiring supporting evidence, and sometimes rules of practice dictating the form of direction to be given to the jury when considering such evidence.

---

16   In some situations anonymity is allowed: see *R v Saville of Newdigate (Lord)* (1999) Times, 15 April. For more general consideration see Royal Commission on Criminal Justice Cm 2263 Ch 8 paras 36–47, recs 196–207, some of these proposals are provided for by special measures under the Youth Justice and Criminal Evidence Bill 1999 (cll 22–29), and by restrictions on reporting (cll 43–50). A similar approach has been suggested by the New Zealand Law Commission in its Prel Pap 29 (1997), but pending its enactment there is in that jurisdiction some reluctance to permit anonymous testimony from those in fear: see *R v Hines* [1997] 3 NZLR 529.

17   *R v W(G) and W(E)* [1997] 1 Cr App Rep 166.
18   *First America Corpn v Sheik Zayed Al-Nahyan* [1998] 4 All ER 939.
19   *R v H(L)* [1997] 1 Cr App Rep 176; *R v Azmy* [1996] 7 Med LR 415.
20   *Connolly v Dale* [1996] 1 Cr App Rep 200.
1   *R v Montgomery* [1995] 2 Cr App Rep 23.
2   *R v Holt* (1997) 161 JP 96. Where the production of real evidence would require an intrusive physical examination of a complainant, it is extremely unlikely that refusal would be visited by such a sanction: see *R v B* [1995] 2 NZLR 172.
3   Criminal Justice and Public Order Act 1994, s 35(4).
4   Other than those he is excused from answering on the basis of privilege: see further ch X below.
5   Criminal Justice and Public Order Act 1994, s 35(5); *R v Ackinclose* [1996] Crim LR 747.
6   *Evidence in Criminal Proceedings: Hearsay and Related Topics* Law Com 245, paras 8.48–8.70, rec 14. See further below p 598.

A. CHILDREN[7]

It is not long since the evidence of children was regarded as so suspect as to justify strict tests of competence, to require corroboration in some cases, and a particularly emphatic warning of the dangers of convicting on the basis of such evidence. The child was required to testify in much the same way as any other witness in open court, and exposed to the ordinary rigour of cross-examination. This situation aroused serious concern, both for the well-being of children required to undergo such ordeals, and for the administration of justice, if, as a result of failures so induced, the guilty should not be convicted. That situation has changed dramatically.[8] It is useful to examine the rules relating to the compellability and competence of children; special pre-trial procedures for securing their evidence; the manner in which their evidence may be given; some special considerations relating to the support it may be given; and the way in which the jury should be directed in assessing its weight.

1. Compellability

One focus of concern has been the possibility of harm being caused to a child witness. The evidence is necessarily inconclusive since much of the work has been done in sexual abuse cases where it is extremely difficult to distinguish between the trauma of the crime and of the trial.[9] If a child is a ward of court leave is required before the child can be interviewed.[10] However it has been held that leave is not required to call the child as a witness in criminal proceedings, whether application is made before or after the wardship order, and whether for prosecution or defence.[11] Competent children are, in principle, compellable witnesses, even when they are parties to care proceedings, but it will rarely be appropriate to compel them to give evidence, and the court will be anxious to exercise its residual discretion as to the conduct of its own proceedings to prevent oppression,[12] especially in view of the alternative possibility of using hearsay evidence more extensively than in the case of adults.[13] Compellability has also been

---

7   See generally Spencer and Flin *The Evidence of Children* (2nd ed, 1993); and for an international perspective Spencer, Nicholson, Flin and Bull (eds) *Children's Evidence in Legal Proceedings: An International Perspective* (1989).
8   For explicit affirmation see *R v McKenzie* (1996) 106 CCC (3d) 1. There has been substantial concern, and pressure for further reform, see eg *The Evidence of Children* (1996) a report by a highly qualified working party of the Royal College of Psychiatrists; Brown P (1998) 148 NLJ 510. Further extensive modification to the law relating to the position in criminal proceedings is proposed in Part II of the Youth Justice and Criminal Evidence Bill 1999. In some jurisdictions, such as Australia, evidential rules (see *In the marriage of N and E* (1994) FLR 99) and discretions (see *In the marriage of Parker and Williams* (1993) 117 FLR 1) can be disregarded in favour of children.
9   See Spencer and Flin above, ch 13, where the evidence is examined.
10 *Practice Direction* [1988] 1 All ER 223, [1987] 1 WLR 1739; as modified by *Practice Direction* [1988] 2 All ER 1015, [1988] 1 WLR 989. Prior application may be waived for interview by the police in an emergency, so long as proper procedures for all juveniles are observed, *Re R, Re G* [1990] 2 All ER 633, [1990] 2 FLR 347.
11 *Re K* [1988] Fam 1, [1988] 1 All ER 214 (before and for prosecution); *Re R* [1991] Fam 56, [1991] 2 All ER 193, (after and for defence). A fortiori if the child is not a ward, *R v Highbury Corner Magistrates' Court, ex p Dearing* [1997] 1 FLR 683.
12 *Ex p P* [1997] 2 FLR 447, which is likely to be found, especially with younger children.
13 *R v B County Council, ex p P* [1991] 2 All ER 65, [1991] 1 WLR 221. This general position is not proposed to be changed by the Youth Justice and Criminal Evidence Bill 1999, but it should be noted that the bill does contain provisions permitting further special measures to be introduced by Parliament under the affirmative resolution procedure (cl 18(4)).

mitigated by statute in relation to committal proceedings, at least where the defence raises no objection.[14]

2. Competence[15]

Here the concern is not so much with the welfare of the child as with the proper administration of justice. It was decided in *R v Brasier*[16] that at common law no evidence could be given otherwise than on oath.[17] The judges to whom this question had been referred in the case of a child tendered to give evidence of an assault nevertheless took a flexible approach:[18]

> [t]here is no precise or fixed rule as to the time within which infants are excluded from giving evidence, but their admissibility depends upon the sense and reason they entertain of the danger and impiety of falsehood, which is to be collected from their answers to questions propounded by the court.

In criminal cases the current position is that all children under the age of fourteen must give their evidence unsworn,[19] their competence to do so assessed according to the criteria specified by a new s 2A inserted into s 33A:[20]

> A child's evidence shall be received unless it appears to the court that the child is incapable of intelligible testimony.

This makes it absolutely clear that it is if doubts arise only *after* the child begins to testify that the court will be called upon to decide whether it is competent.[1] The law takes the view that that is a matter for the jury for which expert testimony is usually unnecessary in the case of 'normal' witnesses,[2] and the current trend is to regard children as 'normal' for such purposes.[3] While it is obvious that there must be a lower

---

14   Magistrates' Courts Act 1980, s 103, as amended by Criminal Justice Act 1988, s 33, and subject to some other qualifications: see *R v H* (1990) 155 JP 561.

15   The general competence of children will be subsumed under the new general rule of competence proposed in the Youth Justice and Criminal Evidence Bill 1999, cl 52(1): 'At every stage in criminal proceedings all persons are (*whatever their age*) competent to give evidence' [emphasis supplied].

16   (1779) 1 Leach 199.

17   Despite the contrary suggestion of Hale in relation to the evidence of young children, 1 *Pleas of the Crown* 634.

18   At 238.

19   Criminal Justice Act 1988, s 33a, inserted by Criminal Justice Act 1991, s 52(1). Although it is possible for a child over fourteen to give evidence on oath ratifying statements made elsewhere, this must not be done without explanation to the jury, and not as a simple means of correcting a mistake in taking evidence unsworn, when it should have been sworn: *R v Sharman* [1998] 1 Cr App Rep 406.

20   By Criminal Justice and Public Order Act, Sch 9, cl 33. The Youth Justice and Criminal Evidence Bill 1999 proposes a test based upon the ability to understand questions and to give answers which can be understood (cl 52(3)).

1   Removing forebodings expressed by Spencer (1991) 141 NLJ 787. See Memorandum of Good Practice on Video Recorded Interviews with Child Witnesses for Criminal Proceedings (1992) para 2.13.

2   *Re M and R (minors)* [1996] 4 All ER 239, at 253j; *G v DPP* [1998] QB 919, [1997] 2 Cr App Rep 78 (rejecting psychiatric testimony).

3   See eg *R v Z* [1990] 2 QB 355, [1990] 2 All ER 971; *R v N* (1992) 95 Cr App Rep 256. In *R v Robinson* [1994] 3 All ER 346 the Court of Appeal was content for this category to embrace 'an illiterate, mentally defective [who]...had the mental capacity of a seven or eight year old. [Who] was mentally within the bottom 1% of 15 year olds.' Expert evidence will be generally allowed under the provisions of the Youth Justice and Criminal Evidence Bill 1999 (cl 53(5)).

age at which a child cannot be regarded as competent, there is now no accepted rule of thumb according to which this will be assessed.[4] In many cases the child's testimony will take the form of a video-recording, and the judge will look at and listen to the tape in private in order to determine the child's intelligibility. If he does not do so, or wishes to investigate further, he may question the child in the presence of the accused, but not of the jury.[5] It is desirable that at an early stage the child be reminded of the importance of telling the truth.

In civil proceedings the situation is different. Civil proceedings were in 1989 brought into line with the then current state of criminal proceedings by allowing some young children to testify unsworn.[6] Under that provision the old test of competency in criminal proceedings of the child having sufficient understanding of the duty to tell the truth and to justify the reception of his evidence was explicitly enacted. The practice was for the judge to question the child in the presence of the jury[7] to establish those matters.[8] Those authorities were disapproved in *R v Hampshire* for the purposes of criminal proceedings, and it seems more likely now that in the unlikely event of a civil jury trial in which a child testifies that any questioning of either child, or third party witness, will take place in the absence of the jury.

3. Pre-trial procedure[9]

As part of the concern to reduce the stress on child witnesses of proceedings in court, the need for their presence has been reduced, by a number of special measures. These include provision for the elimination of the need for a child witness to testify at certain[10] committal proceedings,[11] and substitution of pre-recorded video tapes of interviews to be used instead of the child's evidence in chief.[12] The core[13] provisions of s 32A relating to the latter are as follows:

(2) In any such proceedings a video recording of an interview which–

---

4   *DPP v M* [1998] QB 913, [1997] 2 All ER 749 (child of four not to be presumed unintelligible unheard).
5   *R v Hampshire* [1995] 2 Cr App Rep 319.
6   Children Act 1989, s 96.
7   Third party evidence would not however be heard in the presence of the jury.
8   *R v Reynolds* [1950] 1 KB 606, [1950] 1 All ER 335.
9   This will be subject to a completely new regime under the proposed provisions of the Youth Justice and Criminal Evidence Bill 1999 which will repeal and replace the enactments set out below. The position in Scotland is different: see Law Reform (Miscellaneous Provisions) Scotland Act 1990, ss 56–60. For interpretation, see *Brotherston v HM Advocate* 1996 SLT 1154, and for commentary, Murray (1995) 40 JLSS 314.
10 In outline, serious offences against the child, or to which he was an eye-witness.
11 Criminal Justice Act 1991, s 53.
12 Criminal Justice Act 1991, s 55 (committal proceedings); Criminal Justice Act 1988, s 32(A) inserted by Criminal Justice Act 1991, s 54, 32(C) inserted by Criminal Procedure and Investigation Act 1996, s 62. See also Crown Court Rules 1982, SI 1982/1109, r 23C as inserted by Crown Court (Amendment) Rules 1992, SI 1992/1847; *Practice Note* [1992] 3 All ER 909. In New Zealand the Court of Appeal has authorised the use of these statutory provisions to extend its own statutory provisions by analogy as an exercise in judicial creativity: *R v Moke* [1996] 1 NZLR 263.
13 Other provisions define the proceedings in which such tapes may be used (which include those in which children are not victims but third party witnesses: see *R v Lee* [1996] 2 Cr App Rep 266), and the ages of the children by whom they are permitted. It creates confusion that the age limits for video recording, which need not be on oath but is still capable of amounting to evidence in chief, are different from those for giving oral testimony on oath, given that the witness must be available for cross-examination: see *R v Day* [1997] 1 Cr App Rep 181.

(a) is conducted between an adult and a child who is not the accused or one of the accused ('the child witness'); and

(b) relates to any matter in issue in the proceedings, may, with the leave of the court, be given in evidence in so far as it is not excluded by the court under subsection (3) below.

(3) Where a video recording is tendered in evidence under this section, the court shall (subject to the exercise of any power of the court to exclude evidence which is otherwise admissible) give leave under subsection (2) above unless–

(a) it appears that the child witness will not be available for cross-examination;

(b) any rules of court requiring disclosure of the circumstances in which the video was made have not been complied with to the satisfaction of the court; or

(c) the court is of the opinion, having regard to all the circumstances of the case, that in the interests of justice the recording ought not to be admitted; and where the court gives such leave it may, if it is of the opinion that in the interests of justice any part of the recording ought not to be admitted, direct that that part shall be excluded.

(4) In considering whether any part of a recording ought to be excluded under subsection (3) above, the court shall consider whether any prejudice to the accused, or one of the accused, which might result from the admission of that part is outweighed by the desirability of showing the whole or substantially the whole of the recorded interview.

(5) Where a video recording is admitted under this section–

(a) the child witness shall be called by the party who tendered it in evidence;

(b) that witness shall not be examined in chief on any matter which, in the opinion of the court, has been dealt with adequately[14] in his recorded testimony.

(6) Where a video recording is given in evidence under this section, any statement made by a child witness which is disclosed by the recording shall be treated as if given by that witness in direct oral testimony; and accordingly–

(a) any such statement shall be admissible evidence of any fact of which such testimony by him would be admissible;

(b) no such statement shall be capable of corroborating any other evidence given by him; and in estimating the weight, if any, to be attached to such a statement, regard shall be had to all the circumstances from which any inference can be drawn as to its accuracy or otherwise).

Procedures for interviewing children and creating such a tape were examined by the Butler Sloss Report[15] and recommendations were included in a government memorandum.[16] Although now required in criminal cases, adherence to them is also desirable in civil cases,[17] though the tension between therapeutic and forensic considerations should always be borne in mind.[18] It was however held in *R v Dunphy*[19]

---

14 This word was inserted by Criminal Justice and Public Order Act 1994, s 50.

15 (1988) Cmnd 412.

16 (1992); see above p 210.

17 Recordings taken for the purpose of criminal proceedings are discoverable in subsequent civil proceedings, *Re M (minors) (care proceedings: police videos)* (1995) Times, 7 July.

18 *Re D (minors) (child abuse: interviews)* [1998] 2 FLR 11. See also (1994) 144 NLJ 1451. For extended consideration of the implementation of the guidelines, see Department of Health/ Social Services Inspectorate *The Child, The Court and the video* (1994).

19 (1994) 98 Cr App Rep 393. In Canada, inconsistency, allegations of leading questions and inability to remember by the time of trial are all factors going to the weight of video recordings rather than to their admissibility, unless they are truly extreme: *R v CCF* [1997] 3 SCR 1182; see also in Australia *R v Morris* (1995) 78 ACR 465.

that such guidelines had deliberately not been given the same force as a Code of Practice, and a fortiori that departure from them would not automatically amount to a ground for quashing a conviction. It is, of course, vital that, in accordance with the normal procedures for the reception of evidence adduced in chief, the child be not led in any way.[20] There is however a number of reported cases which illustrate the pressures sometimes exerted on children to testify on tape in a particular way when the guidelines are not observed.[1] A pre-recorded video should not be tendered if it has subsequently been retracted.[2] It is desirable that the filming be done in such a way as not to deprive the court of a full opportunity of observing the demeanour of the child.[3]

It seems that where such recording has been made and played to the jury in court, a transcript may be supplied to the jury to assist them to follow the tape,[4] but while it is very exceptionally permissible for the transcript to be allowed to be taken into the jury room,[5] this should normally be at the request of the jury itself, not against the wishes of the defence in a criminal case,[6] and the judge should warn the jury not to attach more weight to the transcript than to the rest of the evidence given in the ordinary way.[7] A possible way of ameliorating the situation might be to tape the cross-examination,[8] and to allow the jury to see that in the jury room, as well as the pre-recorded evidence in chief.

4. Trial

Two aspects of the position at trial should be mentioned, both of them concerned to minimise the stress upon child witnesses. First there are special relaxations of the hearsay rule, and second there are provisions for evidence in chief to be given in a less stressful manner.

(i) Hearsay

In criminal proceedings the ordinary law of hearsay applies to children, just as it does to any other witnesses,[9] subject only to the provisions discussed above for the reception of videotaped pre-trial interviews to stand for evidence in chief.[10]

---

20 See further below p 262.
1   For critical comments see *Re A and B (Minors) (investigation of alleged abuse)* [1995] 3 FCR 389; *Re N (a minor)* [1996] 4 All ER 225, [1996] 1 WLR 153 is another egregious example. See also in the United States *Idaho v Wright* 497 US 805 (1990).
2   *R v Parker* [1996] Crim LR 511. But cp *R v D* [1996] QB 283 where testimony which was subsequently recanted by a child was not regarded as thereby removed from possible acceptance by the jury, although in such a case a particularly careful warning is required *R v Walker* [1996] Crim LR 742.
3   *R v P (indecent assault)* [1998] CLY 882 (not filmed full face).
4   *R v Welstead* [1996] 1 Cr App Rep 59.
5   *R v Rawlings; R v Broadbent* [1995] 1 All ER 580; *R v M* [1996] 2 Cr App Rep 56.
6   *R v Coshall* [1995] 12 LS Gaz R 34.
7   *R v Morris* [1998] Crim LR 416.
8   Which will often have been accomplished by video link, so reducing technical problems.
9   See further below chs XIV and XV.
10 Though strictly this is in derogation not of the hearsay rule but of the rule against narrative. The child witness remains available for cross-examination. Under the Youth Justice and Criminal Evidence Bill 1999 provision for video recording may be extended to cross-examination and re-examination (cl 27). In New Zealand cross-examination is regarded as so important that even when there is a sufficient reason for the child not to be present to be cross-examined, a conviction obtained upon the basis of a pre-trial statement has been quashed: *R v J* [1998] 1 NZLR 20.

In some civil proceedings,[11] special provision[12] is made for the reception of hearsay, which will often emanate from witnesses less than 18 years of age. In general the court attaches less weight to hearsay than to direct evidence, and some emphasis has been put upon the need to look at the evidence 'anxiously and consider carefully the extent to which it can properly be relied upon.'[13] On the other hand some judges have been reluctant to receive direct evidence from children, even when tendered, if they think it unnecessary.[14]

(ii)   Reduction of stress[15]

Courts have always had some discretion to conduct their own proceedings in the manner most conducive to the administration of justice, and have used such discretion in favour of reducing the stress of child witnesses, for example by permitting them to give their evidence screened from the accused.[16] These powers have been augmented by statutory provision, for example by prohibiting the reporting of proceedings in such a way as to reveal the identity of a child concerned in them.[17] One of the most notable innovations has been a power to give leave for a child to testify in a remote location by videolink[18] in certain types of criminal proceedings.[19] Opinions vary as to whether this is more conducive to convictions on the basis that the witnesses are more willing to testify under such conditions, or less conducive on the basis that the emotional impact of such testimony is diluted. These links are available for the conduct of cross-examination,[20] to which similar considerations apply. A further measure designed to reduce stress has been the prohibition of cross-examination in person of a child by the unrepresented accused.[1] It should also be remembered that in sexual cases there is some restriction upon the ambit of cross-examination imposed by the provisions of the Sexual Offences (Amendment) Act 1976.[2]

---

11   Any proceedings in connection with the upbringing, maintenance or welfare of a child.
12   Children (Admissibility of Hearsay) Order 1993 (SI 1993/621), made under Children Act 1989, s 96(3).
13   Butler Sloss LJ in *R v B County Council, ex p P* [1991] 2 All ER 65, at 72, [1991] 1 WLR 221, at 230, endorsing Neill LJ in *Re W (minors) (wardship evidence)* [1990] 1 FLR 203, at 227.
14   *Nottinghamshire County Council v P* [1993] 1 FCR 180, at 188.
15   Many of the special measures to be provided in the Youth Justice and Criminal Evidence Bill 1999 have been designed with this aim.
16   See also Home Office Circular 61/1990 encouraging this practice in magistrates' courts. In *R v Levogianmis* [1993] 4 SCR 475 this practice was held to be compatible with the Canadian Charter of Rights and Freedoms.
17   Children and Young Persons Act 1933, s 49 (as amended by Criminal Justice and Public Order Act 1994, s 49).
18   For commentary on the practical working of this system see Davies and Noon noted at (1992) 142 NLJ 115. In *White v Ireland* [1995] 2 IR 268 this practice was held compatible with the Irish Constitution; in *R v L (DO)* [1993] 4 SCR 419 with the Canadian Charter of Rights and Freedoms; and in *Maryland v Craig* 497 US 836 (1990) with the confrontation clause in the Sixth Amendment to the Constitution of the United States.
19   Criminal Justice Act 1988, s 32, as amended by Criminal Justice Act 1991, s 55. These provisions regulate the type of proceedings, type of court and ages of child for which such links may be used. CPR 32.1 has endowed the judge in civil proceedings with a wide discretion over the form of evidence, and CPR 32.3 explicitly permits the use of video links.
20   Not only in cases where evidence has been tendered in chief by this method, but also in those where a videotaped interview has been used as evidence in chief.
1   Criminal Justice Act 1988, s 34A, inserted by Criminal Justice Act 1991, s 55(7). These provisions are to be vastly extended and strengthened under the provisions of the Youth Justice and Criminal Evidence Bill 1999 (cl 34).
2   See further below p 315. These are also extended and strengthened under the provisions of the Youth Justice and Criminal Evidence Bill 1999 (cl 33).

It should further be noted in this connection that in *R v Smith*[3] the court endorsed a procedure whereby a social worker was permitted to sit near enough to a child witness while the child was testifying as to be able to speak to the child in a way inaudible to the jury. It is not clear whether the social worker had been previously concerned with the case.[4] The court expressed the view that any accompanist should say as little as possible to the witness, and preferably nothing at all.[5]

5. Supporting evidence

It used to be the case that special provisions applied to the support, or corroboration, of the evidence of children. None of the few provisions which require more than one witness now seems particularly likely to involve child witnesses.[6] In criminal proceedings the current position is currently[7] as stated above[8] that the evidence of children under 14 is to be given unsworn. Such evidence may corroborate other evidence of the same sort.[9] No special requirements for the support or the corroboration of the evidence of children have ever existed in English civil law.

It should be noted however that the general rule in English law remains that the evaluation of the evidence of normal witnesses is the exclusive function of the jury, and that expert evidence as to the credibility of witnesses, including 'normal' children is unlikely to be helpful.[10] It is certainly rarely uncontentious.[11]

6. Direction

Even when corroboration was not strictly required in the old law, there was sometimes either a mandatory requirement or a rule of practice requiring that the jury be warned of the danger of convicting on the basis of the uncorroborated evidence of a child. Such requirement was abrogated by s 34(2) of the Criminal Justice Act 1988, and any lingering vestige eliminated by the extension of such abolition in cases of children to all remaining such requirements[12] in s 32 of the Criminal Justice and Public Order Act 1994.[13] These

---

3   [1994] Crim LR 458. See also in Canada *R v Peterson* (1996) 106 CCC (3d) 64 where the child's father was permitted to sit near a six-year-old child in the room from which video-linked testimony was being transmitted.

4   If this was the case it runs counter to the guidance given by Watkins LJ as to the identity of the suitable adult allowed to be present with the child witness who is testifying by live video link, as reported in Spencer and Flin *The Evidence of Children* (2nd ed) at p 106.

5   The Youth Justice and Criminal Evidence Bill 1999 proposes the provision of intermediaries (cl 28) among other special measures.

6   Especially after the repeal by s 33 of the Criminal Justice and Public Order Act 1994 of a number of such requirements which previously existed under the Sexual Offences Act 1956.

7   But will change if the Youth Justice and Criminal Evidence Bill 1999 is enacted in its present form.

8   At p 210.

9   Criminal Justice Act 1988, s 34(3) as amended by the Criminal Justice and Public Order Act 1994.

10 *R v Robinson* [1994] 3 All ER 346; *Re M and R (minors) (sexual abuse: expert evidence)* [1996] 4 All ER 239. But see the changes proposed by the Youth Justice and Criminal Evidence Bill 1999 (cll 53(5), 54(6)). See, in Canada, *R v Olscamp* (1994) 95 CCC (3d) 466 for a robust critique of the value of psychological testimony to this effect in the current state of scientific knowledge: cp *R v C(G)* (1996) 110 CCC (3d) 233, at 262.

11 For stark disagreement see *Re A and B (minors) (investigation of alleged abuse)* [1995] 3 FCR 389.

12 Principally for accomplices and victims of sexual offences.

13 Embodying the recommendations of Law Commission No 202 (Cm 1620, 1991) *Corroboration of Evidence in Criminal Trials*.

provisions apply to proceedings before magistrates as much as to those in the higher courts.

It should still be noted that the reasons for the rule advanced in *R v Dossi*,[14] namely that children are more susceptible to the influence of third persons, and may allow their imagination to run away with them, could still persuade the judge to exercise his discretion so as to give an appropriate warning. Although not absolutely mandatory, some warning of the difficulties faced by the defence when charged with the sexual abuse of those who were then children, when the trial took place many years later, is desirable.[15] As noted above,[16] it may also be necessary to instruct the jury very carefully as to the permissible use of transcripts,[17] or replays, of pre-recorded video interviews.

The Youth Justice and Criminal Evidence Bill 1999 provides both that evidence given under any of the special measures which may be ordered is entitled to the weight appropriate to the circumstances,[18] and that the jury must be warned against drawing any prejudicial inference adverse to the accused from the fact that the special measures have been ordered.[19]

B.   THE MENTALLY INCAPABLE[20]

This category is not one which has attracted so much attention as that of some of the other categories, and it is proposed here to deal with only three aspects of the law, the competence of such witnesses; the extent to which their hearsay might be admitted; and the nature of any warning which might need to be included in the judge's direction to the jury.

I.   Competence

At one time it appears to have been thought that lunatics so found were absolutely excluded from testifying, but *R v Hill*[1] decided that, in all cases where it is contended that the witness is of too weak an intellect to admit of his giving evidence, it is for the judge to decide whether he understands the nature of an oath and, if the judge answers this question in the affirmative, it is for the jury to say what degree of credit is to be given to the testimony. The inmate of an asylum whose only delusion was that spirits talked to him was accordingly allowed to give evidence at a prosecution for manslaughter. In *R v Bellamy*[2] where the mental ages of the adult witnesses were equivalent to those of children, the common law rules for children were regarded as

---

14   (1918) 13 Cr App Rep 158, at 161.
15   *R v E (sexual abuse: delay)* [1996] 1 Cr App Rep 88.
16   At 213.
17   In *R v McQuiston* [1998] 1 Cr App Rep 139 recommended for transcripts read out, even in the absence of a replay of the video. See also *R v Springer* [1996] Crim LR 903
18   Cl 30(4).
19   Cl 31. The judge has the duty to decide what warning, if any, is necessary.
20   This topic will also undergo major change under the provisions of the Youth Justice and Criminal Evidence Bill 1999 (cl 16(2)(a)). Its provisions extend also to the physically disabled (cl 16(2)(b)).
1   (1851) 2 Den 254. See also *R v Dunning* [1965] Crim LR 372.
2   (1985) 82 Cr App Rep 222. See also in Canada *R v Farley* (1995) 99 CCC (3d) 76. In *R v Hall* (1987) 86 Cr App Rep 159 it appears that a woman with an IQ in the bottom 1% of the population, and held to be severely mentally impaired, was allowed to testify, though without conspicuous benefit.

appropriate to determine competence. If it appears that, though duly sworn before the jury, the witness is in fact too weak-minded to testify or that, for some other reason, such as deafness or dumbness, the evidence cannot be taken, the judge may declare the witness to be incompetent.[3] If expert evidence is admitted as to the witness's mental state it should not be taken in the presence of the jury over the objection of the accused.[4] Temporary incapacity occasioned by illness or intoxication would presumably lead to an adjournment in an appropriate case.

Under the proposals of the Youth Justice and Criminal Evidence Bill 1999 both the mentally incapable and physically disabled will be presumptively competent,[5] but eligible for the provision of special measures.

2. Hearsay

Under the provisions of Part II of the Criminal Justice Act 1988[6] permitting the use of documentary hearsay one of the conditions specified by s 23(2)(a) is that the witness be unfit to attend as a witness. It was held in *R v Setz-Dempsey*[7] that in this context a mentally ill witness who was physically able to attend, and had indeed testified to a certain extent, was nevertheless unfit to attend for the purpose of admitting his earlier statements.[8]

3. Direction

Section 77 of the Police and Criminal Evidence Act 1984 imposes an obligation upon the court to warn the jury of special need for care in convicting upon the confession of a mentally handicapped person, obtained by the police otherwise than in the presence of an independent person.[9] The section further provides that the reason for such need should also be explained. Apart from this provision no special rule applied to the evidence of those with a mental handicap, even though in one case the witnesses were patients in a special hospital for the criminally insane, and the allegations were made against nurses in the hospital.[10] It is noteworthy however that the judge still thought it appropriate to direct the jury that one such witness could not corroborate another, and specified the reasons for the evidence of such witnesses being suspect. This direction was commended by the House of Lords. It does not justify the uncritical

---

3   *R v Whitehead* (1866) LR 1 CCR 33; cf *Jacobs v Layborn* (1843) 11 M & W 685. It was held in *The People (A-G) v Keating* [1953] IR 200 that the judge must examine the witness although he has examined the same witness in a previous case.

4   *R v Deakin* [1994] 4 All ER 769. In this case the expert evidence was directed exclusively to the competence of the witness, leaving credibility to the jury alone.

5   For the test see above p 210.

6   See generally below p 581.

7   (1994) 98 Cr App Rep 23.

8   Subject to the statutory discretions in ss 25 and 26. See also in Canada, *R v Pearson* (1994) 95 CCC (3d) 365 where a hearsay statement was admitted to supplement the evidence of a mentally handicapped witness.

9   The Code of Practice for Police Questioning provides that a mentally handicapped person shall be interviewed in the absence of an independent person only in cases of urgency under Annex C to the Code. A family member has been held not sufficiently independent: *R v Bailey* [1995] 2 Cr App Rep 262.

10   *R v Spencer* [1987] AC 128, [1986] 2 All ER 928. For similar approaches elsewhere see in Australia, *Bromley v R* (1986) 161 CLR 315; and in New Zealand, *R v Harawira* [1989] 2 NZLR 714.

acceptance of the evidence of a psychotic,[11] or leaving the evidence of a witness suffering from psychiatric disorder to the jury without any warning at all.[12]

C.   SPOUSES AND OTHERS[13]

When interest was the principal ground for disqualification there was no need for special rules relating to the evidence of spouses, ex-spouses or close relations. After 1843 when interest ceased to be a principal ground for disqualification special rules of spouse competence and compellability were created. It is here necessary to consider the rules relating to competence, to compellability, to their specific application to spouses of a co-accused and to ex-spouses, and very briefly to mention the claims to special consideration of other close relatives.

I.   Competence

Subject to comparatively unimportant exceptions which were confined to criminal cases, a party's spouse was incompetent as a witness for or against him at common law.[14] The incompetence extended to spouses of either sex and to testimony concerning events occurring before as well as during the marriage.[15] It was immaterial that the marriage was contracted after the occurrence of the relevant events,[16] or even after the commencement of proceedings,[17] and whatever the motive for marrying.[18]

The one clear exception to the common law rule related to criminal charges involving personal violence by the accused against his or her spouse, and was established in *Lord Audley's Case*[19] in which a wife was held competent to testify against her husband who was charged as accessory to her rape. The decision was based on necessity. Were the law otherwise the injured spouse would frequently have had no remedy. In *R v Sergeant*[20] it was said that a wife was in all cases a competent witness for her husband when admissible against him, and there was no reason to doubt that this doctrine applied to all the exceptions to the common law rule of the incompetency of spouses, and to husbands as well as to wives.

After a long, complicated and thoroughly unsatisfactory process of development, the modern law on this topic was greatly simplified by the Police and Criminal Evidence Act 1984, s 80.[1] Most difficulty has been experienced in criminal proceedings. Spouses have been competent and compellable witnesses in civil proceedings since 1853.[2]

---

11   *Re A and B (Minors) (Investigation of Alleged Abuse)* [1995] 3 FCR 389.
12   *R v Cooper* [1995] CLY 1095.
13   See Creighton [1990] Crim LR 34.
14   *Bentley v Cooke* (1784) 3 Doug KB 422; *Davis v Dinwoody* (1792) 4 Term Rep 678.
15   *Pedley v Wellesley* (1829) 3 C & P 558.
16   *Hoskyn v Metropolitan Police Comr* [1979] AC 474, [1978] 2 All ER 136.
17   See *S v Leepile (No 3)* 1986 (2) SA 352.
18   For an unsuccessful attempt to introduce an exception to the common law rule which still applies in Canada, for the complicated means of remedying the position, and for discussion of the principles underlying this area, see *Hawkins and Morin v R* [1997] 3 SCR 1043.
19   (1631) 3 State Tr 401 followed in *R v Azire* (1725) 1 Stra 633.
20   (1826) Ry & M 352.
1   Similar reform has been undertaken in other jurisdictions, see eg Criminal Procedure (Scotland) Act 1975, s 143; Evidence Act (Cwth) 1995, ss 18, 19.
2   As a result of the Evidence Further Amendment Act 1853, as further amended.

Section 80 of the Police and Criminal Evidence Act 1984 states the current[3] law in its principal provisions as follows:[4]

(1) In any proceedings[5] the wife or husband of the accused shall be competent to give evidence–
(a) subject to subsection (4) below, for the prosecution; and
(b) on behalf of the accused or any person jointly charged with the accused.

(2) In any proceedings the wife or husband of the accused shall, subject to sub-section (4) below, be compellable to give evidence on behalf of the accused.

(3) In any proceedings the wife or husband of the accused shall, subject to sub-section (4) below, be compellable to give evidence for the prosecution or on behalf of any person jointly charged with the accused if and only if–
(a) the offence charged involves an assault on, or injury or a threat of injury to, the wife or husband of the accused or a person who was at the material time under the age of sixteen; or
(b) the offence charged is a sexual offence[6] alleged to have been committed in respect of the person who was at the material time under that age; or
(c) the offence charged consists of attempting or conspiring to commit, or of aiding, abetting, counselling, procuring or inciting the commission of, an offence falling within paragraph (a) or (b) above.

(4) Where an information or indictment charges a husband and his wife jointly with an offence neither spouse shall at the trial of the information or indictment be competent or compellable by virtue of subsection (1)(a), (2) or (3) above to give evidence in respect of that offence unless that spouse is not, or is no longer, liable to be convicted of that offence at the trial as a result of pleading guilty or for any other reason.

These provisions were modelled upon those proposed by the Criminal Law Revision Committee in its 11th Report, and set out in the draft bill annexed to the report.[7] A major change from the position at common law was that the spouse became a competent witness for the prosecution in all cases subject only to the minor exception of proceedings in which the spouses were being tried jointly. Incompetence extended to matters occurring before, as well as during, the marriage,[8] and to those occurring after a judicial separation.[9] The Criminal Law Revision Committee felt that the preservation of marital harmony could not justify the retention of such incompetence,[10] and that the only argument of any substance at all was the dilemma that would be created for spouses in cases where there was no compellability. Since the Act did not make the spouse

3   Further reform is proposed in the general proposals for competency contained in the Youth Justice and Criminal Evidence Bill 1999 (cl 52), which proposes to make spouses generally competent, but to amend s 80 by repealing s 80(1) and (8), and by substituting amended sub-ss (2)–(4) which will retain some rules restricting compellability.
4   For convenience of arrangement the whole section is set out here, those parts dealing with compellability as well as those dealing only with competence.
5   Defined as criminal proceedings by s 82(1). In Australia proceedings for a penalty have not been regarded as criminal for these purposes: *Australian Federal Police Comr v McMillan and Hordes* (1987) 70 ALR 203.
6   Defined by s 80(7) as an offence under the Sexual Offences Act 1956, the Indecency with Children Act 1960, the Sexual Offences Act 1967, s 54 of the Criminal Law Act 1977 or the Protection of Children Act 1978.
7   Evidence (General) Cmnd 4991, paras 143–57 and Annex 1, draft Bill, para 9.
8   *Hoskyn v Metropolitan Police Comr* [1979] AC 474, [1978] 2 All ER 136.
9   *Moss v Moss* [1963] 2 QB 799, [1963] 2 All ER 829.
10   But see Lempert (1981) 66 Iowa LR 725 criticising the similar situation arrived at by judicial interpretation in the United States in *Trammel v US* 405 US 40 (1980).

compellable for the prosecution in all cases this dilemma still exists, but the committee's recommendation that it should not stand in the way of change was accepted.

2.   Compellability[11]

Since it was not thought universally desirable to apply to spouse witnesses the general rule of the common law that competence implies compellability,[12] many of the old problems which formerly related to spouse competence reappeared in relation to spouse compellability for the prosecution.[13] The Act deals with three situations; offences involving assault or injury to the spouse, offences of a similar character against children, and sexual offences against children. Each requires separate consideration.

(i)   Assault on spouse

At the time of the Criminal Law Revision Committee's report it was thought that in cases of violence against them, spouses were compellable at common law.[14] The policy underlying such a rule was accepted by the Criminal Law Revision Committee.[15] This position was overturned by the decision of the House of Lords in *Hoskyn v Metropolitan Police Comr*.[16] In that case the accused was charged with wounding a woman. They were married two days before the trial, and the wife was compelled to testify over her objection. Her evidence was unhelpful to the prosecution, but it secured leave to treat her as a hostile witness and the accused was convicted. His appeal to the Court of Appeal was rejected on the authority of *Lapworth*. The House of Lords allowed the appeal overruling *Lapworth* on the ground that it was inconsistent both with the common law,[17] and also with the analogy of the position in statutory offences scheduled to the Criminal Evidence Act 1898.[18] Neither ground was very plausible. As Lord Edmund Davies pointed out in his dissent[19] *R v Inhabitants of All Saints, Worcester* was decided on the basis not of non-compellability, but of privilege. *Leach v R* can be criticised on many grounds.[20] The House of Lords also doubted the policy underlying the law as understood in *Lapworth* and as accepted by the Criminal Law Revision Committee. That policy was simply that to allow the spouse a choice would often, in effect, be to subvert the rule of criminal law that the consent of a spouse is no defence to a charge of assault upon that spouse. It may also be argued that where one spouse has used such violence against the other as to be charged with it, there can be little confidence that the victim's choice not to testify has been inspired by marital affection rather than by fear. The argument on the other side is that it is generally unsatisfactory to compel

---

11   This topic will be simplified by the provisions of the Youth Justice and Criminal Evidence Bill 1999 amending s 80 of the Police and Criminal Evidence Act 1984 (Sch 4 para 12).

12   *Ex p Fernandez* (1861) 10 CBNS 3.

13   It has been held to be desirable, but not necessary, to inform a spouse witness that she is not compellable: *R v Nelson* [1992] Crim LR 653 (where the prosecution went on to have her treated as a hostile witness).

14   As decided in *R v Lapworth* [1931] 1 KB 117.

15   Cmnd 4991, para 149.

16   [1979] AC 474, [1978] 2 All ER 136.

17   As expounded in *R v Inhabitants of All Saints, Worcester* (1817) 6 M & S 194, at 200 by Bayley J, and as interpreted by Taylor *On Evidence* (9th edn, 1895) p 892.

18   As decided in *Leach v R* [1912] AC 305.

19   It may be noted that Lord Edmund Davies had been chairman of the Criminal Law Revision Committee at the time of the 11th report.

20   For some of them, see Zuckerman (1979) 94 LQR 321.

witnesses to testify against their will, and repugnant to compel a wife to testify unwillingly against her husband. The Act reflects the policy applied in *Lapworth* and recommended by the Criminal Law Revision Committee. There are however differences in the drafting. The Bill annexed to the committee's report referred to cases where 'the act or any of the acts constituting the offence charged consists of an assault, etc'. The Act refers to cases 'where the offence charged involves an assault etc'. The effect of this change is obscure. Its construction is not assisted by the use of the verb 'consists' in sub-s 80(3)(c). It is arguable that the difference in wording suggests that 'involves' must be given a different meaning from 'consists' and a possible interpretation would be that it makes it sufficient for s 80(3)(a) that an assault or injury to the spouse occurs even though it is not reflected in the formal charge. The use of the present tense for 'involves' and the contrast with the past 'was' in relation to age makes this a somewhat forced interpretation however. Another possibility is that the wording is simply an attempt to achieve the same result a little more elegantly. Such a view is however weakened by observation that the Bill's original terminology for the substance of the matter covered by s 80(3)(a), although abandoned for that purpose, was taken over in s 80(3)(c), which did not appear at all in the Criminal Law Revision Committee's draft Bill. A further difference between the draft Bill and the Act is that the former referred only to assault or threat of violence, while the latter refers to assault, injury or threat of injury. It is perhaps clearer from the terminology of the Act that a case like *R v Verolla*,[1] where the accused was charged with attempting to murder his wife by poisoning her, would still be covered, though in view of the inclusion of s 80(3)(c) which covers that situation exactly there would be no need to rely upon 80(3)(a). The explicit reference to threat of violence also removed the difficulty found at common law in relation to competence in *R v Yeo*[2] where a wife was held not competent to testify against her husband who was charged with sending a letter threatening to murder her. On the other hand it seems clear that a wife would still not be compellable if her husband should be prosecuted for living on her immoral earnings.[3] It remains unclear whether a spouse would be compellable upon a charge like arson which had in the circumstances put the other in fear.[4] On balance the wording seems not apt to go quite so far. 'Injury' is less redolent of intent than 'violence', so it is possible that a spouse will be compellable for the prosecution in respect of offences where injury is caused recklessly or negligently. Retention of the concept of assault means that a wife is compellable in the prosecution of her husband for buggering her, presumably irrespective of her consent at the time, though it is hard to imagine any circumstances in which such a charge would be brought to trial if the wife were unwilling to testify.[5] Indeed empirical evidence suggests that in practice it is extremely rare for a prosecution to be brought for a violent assault if the spouse is reluctant to co-operate, thus rendering compellability something of a dead letter.[6]

1   [1963] 1 QB 285, [1962] 2 All ER 426.
2   [1951] 1 All ER 864n.
3   Assuming the absence of assault, injury or threat of injury. Under the old law she was not even competent (*DPP v Blady* [1912] 2 KB 89) though in the United States compellability has been achieved at common law: *Wyatt v US* 362 US 525 (1960).
4   See *R v Sillars* [1979] 1 WWR 743; *R v Czipps* (1979) 101 DLR (3d) 323.
5   *R v Blanchard* [1952] 1 All ER 114, 35 Cr App Rep 183.
6   Cretney and Davis (1997) 37 Brit Jo of Criminology 75.

(ii)   Assaults on children

The next category, offences involving assault, injury or threat of injury to children under sixteen, had no predecessor at common law. It too was foreshadowed in the Criminal Law Revision Committee's Report. There is however one important difference. The committee's recommendation was that the scope of the offences should be limited to those against children who were also members of the same household as the accused.[7] It was felt that the basic reason for enacting compellability in such cases was to try to secure the availability of some evidence where otherwise there might be none, and some cases, for example of cruelty to children too young to testify, might otherwise have to go unpunished. This would be most likely to occur in cases where the child was a member of the same household as the accused. The Act has, it is submitted rightly, adopted the more expansive policy of protecting children generally.

(iii)   Sexual offences[8] against children

The Act also implemented the committee's recommendation[9] that no distinction be drawn between offences involving injury to children and those of sexual offences. Here too consent is irrelevant. This means that the accused's wife is compellable against him if he kissed a 15-year-old, however much encouragement was offered, but not if he raped and murdered a 16-year-old. If the potential availability of evidence is an important consideration, cases of homicide might seem eligible for addition to the category where the spouse is compellable.

3.   Application to spouse of co-accused[10]

It should be noted that both the general provision as to competence, and these exceptional cases of compellability, apply to the spouse of a co-accused exactly as to the spouse of a sole accused. The Act also simplified the law in relation to the competence and compellability of a spouse witness for the defence. The position before the Act appeared to be that a spouse was a competent,[11] but not a compellable, witness for the accused.[12] The Act provides explicitly that one spouse is a competent,[13] and a compellable,[14] witness for the other, subject only to the minor exception that where both spouses are being tried jointly, they are still not compellable.[15]

The old law provided that the accused's spouse was sometimes competent for a co-accused only with the consent of the accused,[16] and sometimes without the necessity for any such consent.[17] The Act provides that a spouse is always a competent witness

---

7   Para 151, draft Bill, cl 9(3)(a).
8   As defined in s 80(7).
9   Para 150, draft Bill, cl 9(3)(b).
10   This section will become obsolete upon the enactment of the Youth Justice and Criminal Evidence Bill 1999. It should be noted that this means *currently* co-accused, and it is submitted that the law in England is the same as in New Zealand, in that at a retrial of one accused after the acquittal of a co-accused, the wife of that acquitted co-accused would be treated as an ordinary witness: see *R v Bradley* [1996] 1 NZLR 441.
11   Criminal Evidence Act 1898, s 1.
12   *R v Boal* [1965] 1 QB 402, at 416, [1964] 3 All ER 269, at 275.
13   Section 80(1)(b).
14   Section 80(2).
15   Section 80(4).
16   Criminal Evidence Act 1898, s 1(c).
17   Eg Theft Act 1968, s 30(3).

for the other's co-accused,[18] but compellable for such a person only in the circumstances in which the spouse would have been compellable for the prosecution against the other spouse.[19] The result of these provisions upon spouse compellability can be expressed in the form of a table, first supposing A and B to be jointly tried for a non-sexual offence against neither a spouse nor a child, and then supposing them to be jointly tried for an assault on Mrs A.

	FOR PROSECUTION		FOR DEFENCE	
	Against A	Against B	For A	For B
GENERAL CASE				
Mrs A	No	No	Yes	No
	80(3)	80(3)	80(2)	80(3)
Mrs B	No	No	No	Yes
	80(3)	80(3)	80(3)	80(2)
ASSAULT ON MRS A				
Mrs A	Yes	Yes	Yes	Yes
	80(3)(a)	80(3)(a)	80(2)	80(3)(a)
Mrs B	No	No	No	Yes
	80(3)	80(3)	80(3)	80(2)

These provisions are in line with the recommendations of the Criminal Law Revision Committee.[20]

4. Ex-spouses

In the case of criminal proceedings the Act followed the recommendation of the Criminal Law Revision Committee[1] in providing that:[2]

> In any proceedings a person who has been but is no longer married to the accused shall be competent and compellable to give evidence as if that person and the accused had never been married.

This changed the position at common law as exemplified in *R v Algar*,[3] whereby the position of an ex-spouse, whether as a result of divorce or the annulment of a voidable marriage, was assimilated to that of a current spouse, following *Monroe v Twisleton*.[4] Parties to a void marriage are regarded as strangers to each other for these purposes.[5] As a result of this provision, competence and compellability was bestowed upon all of these categories of ex-spouses. The existing law whereby a marriage is treated as subsisting for these purposes notwithstanding that the parties are living apart, even

18 Section 80(1)(b).
19 Section 80(3). The wife is compellable in respect of a co-accused charged on the same indictment, but not for the same offence: *R v Woolgar* [1991] Crim LR 545.
20 Cmnd 4991, para 155, draft Bill, cll 9(2) and 9(3).
1 Cmnd 4991, para 156, draft Bill, cl 9(4).
2 Section 80(5).
3 [1954] 1 QB 279, [1953] 2 All ER 1381.
4 (1802) Peake Add Cas 219.
5 So a party to a polygamous marriage, bigamous in England, is competent and compellable, *R v Khan* (1986) 84 Cr App Rep 44.

pursuant to a judicial order for separation or non-cohabitation,[6] was retained. Nor does there seem likely to be much basis for excluding the evidence of such a witness upon the basis of its making the proceedings unfair, though an unsuccessful attempt to do so has been made.[7]

5. Other relationships

Little consideration seems to have been given in this country to claims in respect of other relationships. In Victoria[8] and in Israel[9] the rules relating to compellability have been relaxed as between parents and children. The Australian Evidence Act 1995, s 18 has relaxed the rules in criminal with regard to 'de facto' spouses, as well as to parents and children.

D. OFFENDERS

This generic term comprehends those who have been convicted of crime in the past, those who are now charged with committing crimes, and those who have been concerned in the commission of the crime with which the accused is charged. Since the abolition of the disqualification of witnesses who had been convicted of serious crimes, and given the absence of any formal[10] compulsion for the accused[11] to testify, the principal concern is with issues relating to the competence of the accused and co-accused to testify. The second special issue relating to this generic class of witness is that of support. It is now possible to present this in a vastly simplified form on account of the abolition of formal corroboration rules in relation to the evidence of accomplices by s 32(1) of the Criminal Justice and Public Order Act 1994:[12]

> Any requirement whereby at a trial on indictment it is obligatory for the court to give the jury a warning about convicting the accused on the uncorroborated evidence of person merely because that person is–
> (a)   an alleged accomplice of the accused,...
> is hereby abrogated.

It was possible to make so radical a change in part because in the old law alongside the formal corroboration requirements for accomplices *stricto sensu* were informal requirements for analogous cases, which appeared to work more satisfactorily, and which perhaps[13] remain. They will constitute the second section of this part of the chapter.

6   *Moss v Moss* [1963] 2 QB 799, [1963] 2 All ER 829.
7   *R v Mathias* [1989] Crim LR 64, unaffected on this point by the appellate proceedings (1989) 137 NLJ 1417.
8   Crimes Act 1958, s 400 (as amended).
9   Evidence Ordinance 1971, cl 4.
10   Though under the Criminal Justice and Public Order Act 1994, s 35 adverse inferences may be drawn against the accused who fails to testify without good cause, thus providing some informal incentive to testify.
11   Extended in Canada to a party in civil contempt proceedings: *Vidéotron Ltée v Industries Microlec Produits Electroniques* [1992] 2 SCR 1065.
12   Following the recommendation of the Law Commission, (Cm 1620, 1991) Law Com No 202.
13   The question is whether they have been completely overtaken by the width of the interpretation of the new law in *R v Makanjuola and Easton* [1995] 3 All ER 730, [1995] 1 WLR 1348. For detailed consideration of this issue see Hartshorne (1998) 2 Int J of Ev & Pr 1, and for an indication that they have been so overtaken see *R v Warwick Muncaster* [1999] Crim LR 409.

I. Competence of the accused[14]

It is helpful to consider separately the competence of the accused as a witness for the prosecution, for himself and for a co-accused.

(i) As a witness for the prosecution

The general rule is[15] that the accused is not a competent witness for the prosecution in any criminal case. The rule is the result of the common law which, so far as this point is concerned, was not modified by the Criminal Evidence Act 1898, because that statute conferred competence on the accused only as a witness for the defence. In *R v Grant*[16] and *R v Sharrock*[17] committals were quashed because one co-prisoner had been called on behalf of the prosecution at the preliminary examination. In so far as these cases decided that an indictment based on inadmissible evidence is necessarily bad, they have been overruled,[18] but they still serve as a warning to over-zealous prosecutors.

Where several people are charged in the same indictment there are various devices by which the prosecution can render one of them competent and compellable against the others. A *nolle prosequi* may be filed with reference to his case; it may be stated that no evidence will be offered against him when he will be acquitted; an order for separate trials may be obtained or he may plead guilty. In this last event it is a matter for the discretion of the court whether or not the witness should be sentenced before being called on behalf of the prosecution.[19] In such a case the increased flexibility of any direction to the jury in the modern law may militate in favour of sentencing after the testimony has been given.

It was said in *R v Pipe*[20] that an accomplice[1] against whom proceedings are pending must not, as a matter of practice, be called on behalf of the prosecution unless it is made plain that the proceedings will be discontinued. No doubt the ban would apply to a case in which proceedings, though not actually pending, were likely, but the judgment of Lawton LJ in *R v Turner*[2] suggests that the matter is basically one of judicial discretion. An accomplice who had turned 'King's evidence' was, together with his family, accorded police protection, an advantage which he might have lost if he had not testified in accordance with statements previously made by him. Lawton LJ said that it could not always be irregular to call an interested witness on behalf of the

14 Likely to be construed strictly so as to permit even a policy-making director to be compelled to testify for the prosecution against the firm whose policy he makes, see *Penn-Texas Corpn v Murat Anstalt* [1964] 1 QB 40, [1963] 1 All ER 258, distinguishing between officer and corporation in the context of compulsory process. See also *R v N M Peterson & Sons* [1980] 2 SCR 679, to the same effect in Canada. See also the definition of a person charged in criminal proceedings in the Youth Justice and Criminal Evidence Bill 1999 (cl 52(5)).
15 It is not proposed to alter this rule which will be retained as the one exception to the provision of general competence proposed in the Youth Justice and Criminal Evidence Bill 1999 (cl 52(4)).
16 [1944] 2 All ER 311.
17 [1948] 1 All ER 145.
18 *R v Norfolk Quarter Sessions, ex p Brunson* [1953] 1 QB 503, [1953] 1 All ER 346.
19 *R v Palmer* (1993) 99 Cr App Rep 83, re-considering *R v Payne* [1950] 1 All ER 102. See also Gooderson (1953) 11 CLJ 279.
20 (1966) 51 Cr App Rep 17.
1 Presumably including an accessory after the fact: see *R v Bleich* (1983) 150 DLR (3d) 600.
2 (1975) 61 Cr App Rep 67, applied *R v Governor of Pentonville Prison, ex p Schneider* (1981) 73 Cr App Rep 200; but see *R v Treadaway* [1997] CLY 1134 where the evidence of two 'supergrasses' was held insufficient to sustain a conviction because it was manifestly tainted. See also *R v Weightman* [1978] 1 NZLR 79; *R v Brown* (1983) 74 FLR 97.

prosecution. He instanced a case in which a reward would be due to an informant on the conviction of the person against whom he testified.

(ii)   As a witness for himself

The effect of s 1 of the Criminal Evidence Act 1898 is that the accused is a competent witness on his own behalf at every stage of a criminal trial.[3] Doubts have been raised whether that which an accused person says when testifying on his own behalf may be used against a co-accused, whether the statement was made in-chief or in cross-examination.

(a)   Evidence in-chief

In *R v Rudd*,[4] the leading case on the availability of the testimony of one of several accused given on his own behalf as evidence for the prosecution, the Court of Criminal Appeal held that the trial judge had rightly refrained from telling the jury to disregard the evidence implicating the appellant given by his co-accused. Humphreys J said:

> While a statement made in the absence of the accused person by one of his co-defendants cannot be evidence against him,[5] if the co-defendant goes into the witness box and gives evidence in the course of a joint trial, then what he says becomes evidence for all the purposes of the case including the purpose of being evidence against his co-defendant.

These remarks were well supported by authority, if not entirely to the extent suggested by Humphreys J,[6] and it is submitted that they are sound in principle because it is the common lot of a party to litigation to have adverse as well as favourable testimony given by his own witnesses and, not infrequently, by himself. But, even in modern times language is sometimes used which suggests that nothing said by one or two accused in the witness box is evidence against the other.[7] There was some authority in support of this view before the Act of 1898 when doubts were expressed whether the evidence of a prisoner who had been acquitted and testified for one of the two remaining co-accused was admissible against the other,[8] but it is submitted that this, and similar hesitancy, sprang from a failure to distinguish between one co-accused's out-of-court testimonial assertions or unsworn statements in court which were certainly not evidence against the other,[9] and his sworn evidence in court which is analogous to that of any other witness.

3   Even after a plea of guilty he may give evidence in mitigation of sentence (*R v Wheeler* [1917] 1 KB 283). The accused may also give evidence on the voir dire (*R v Cowell* [1940] 2 KB 49, [1940] 2 All ER 599).

4   (1948) 32 Cr App Rep 138. To the same effect are *R v Hunting and Ward* (1908) 1 Cr App Rep 177; *R v Paul* [1920] 2 KB 183; and *R v Garland* (1941) 29 Cr App Rep 46n. See also *Young v H M Advocate* 1932 JC 63 where the earlier English and Scottish authorities are reviewed.

5   Because of the hearsay rule, but see *Mawaz Khan v R* [1967] 1 AC 454, [1967] 1 All ER 80 where such a statement was regarded as original evidence.

6   His Lordship said it had been the invariable rule to state the law in the same way (32 Cr App Rep 138, at 140).

7   For a ruling that comes near to telling the jury to disregard the evidence of one accused when considering the case against the other see *R v Meredith* (1943) 29 Cr App Rep 40. It was assumed that one accused's testimony was evidence against the other in *Rigby v Woodward* [1957] 1 All ER 391, [1957] 1 WLR 250.

8   *R v Burdett* (1855) Dears CC 431.

9   As noted at p 206 above, the right to make such an unsworn statement has now been abolished.

(b) Evidence elicited in cross-examination

In principle there can be no doubt that what a witness says in cross-examination may be relied on by the person responsible for the cross-examination as evidence in his favour. This would mean that anything that one accused says when he is being cross-examined by the prosecution may be treated as evidence against the other; but principle sometimes has to give way to considerations of policy, and, if it is sound policy to prohibit the prosecution from calling accused persons to testify against each other, it is pertinent to remember that the policy is liable to be circumvented whenever the prosecution is allowed to rely on the statements of an accused elicited in cross-examination as evidence against his co-accused. To some extent it is only proper that this permission should be accorded, but it is arguable that the court went too far in *R v Paul*.[10] Paul, Goldberg and others were jointly charged with an offence. Goldberg was told that he need not give evidence, but nonetheless went into the witness-box, and declared that he was guilty. This was all he said in-chief, but the Court of Criminal Appeal held that the judge had rightly allowed the prosecution to cross-examine him on Paul's alibi—a subject on which his evidence assisted the Crown. This case was criticised by Lord Justice General Clyde in *Young v H M Advocate*.[11] The court has a discretion with regard to the cross-examination it will permit, and Lord Clyde considered that this discretion should have been exercised in favour of Paul. It is, however, possible to exaggerate the criticisms of *R v Paul* because, had the accused pleaded guilty in the first instance, he would have been compellable for the prosecution, although it is true that his evidence could not then have been obtained by means of leading questions and other forms of pressure permissible in cross-examination.

(iii) As a witness for the co-accused

The general rule is that the accused is a competent but not a compellable witness for anyone being tried jointly with him. This is the effect of s 1 of the Criminal Evidence Act 1898.[12] It means that, if A and B are being tried together, B may call upon A to testify for him provided A is willing to do so. Within the meaning of the Criminal Evidence Act 1898, a prisoner who has pleaded guilty is not a 'person charged' because he is not concerned in any issue before the jury; he is therefore both competent and compellable for a co-accused.[13] For the same reason someone who was originally jointly indicted with the accused but has been acquitted or directed to be tried separately is both competent and compellable for the accused.[14] It is not a sufficient ground to sever a trial that one co-accused will be deprived of the evidence of the other, if the other chooses not to give evidence.[15] An accused who gives evidence is liable to be cross-examined by his co-accused as well as by the prosecution even if his evidence was in no way adverse to the accused,[16] although he will enjoy the protection of s 1(f) of the

10 [1920] 2 KB 183.
11 1932 JC 63, though some of the views there expressed were regarded as outmoded in *Todd v HM Advocate* 1984 JC 13.
12 See *R v Payne* (1872) LR 1 CCR 349 as to incompetence before the Act. The rule was expressly left unaffected in its application to a co-accused spouse, Police and Criminal Evidence Act 1984, s 80(4). It will however be changed by the amendments to s 80 proposed by the Youth Justice and Criminal Evidence Bill 1999 (Sch 4 para 12).
13 *R v Boal* [1965] 1 QB 402, at 414, [1964] All ER 269, at 275.
14 *R v Conti* (1973) 58 Cr App Rep 387 (directed acquittal); *R v Richardson* (1967) 51 Cr App Rep 381 (separate trials).
15 *R v Kerry and Staveley* [1995] Crim LR 899, because to allow this would offer an opportunity for tactical manipulation.
16 *R v Hilton* [1972] 1 QB 421, [1971] 3 All ER 541.

Criminal Evidence Act 1898 against certain types of cross-examination if he does not give evidence against someone charged in the same proceedings.

2. Supporting evidence

As stated above the law in this respect has been greatly simplified by the abolition of the formal rules relating the corroboration of the evidence of accomplices. These rules had been successfully abolished by judicial decision in Canada,[17] and by-passed here in relation to those not strictly accomplices,[18] or to accomplices when called by the defence.[19] It seems likely that the approach taken in those English cases will now be extended to the evidence of all witnesses involved in some way in the commission of the crime with which the accused is charged. In England the judge has always had considerable power to comment upon the evidence when summing up to the jury.[20] This power must be exercised so as to present the case fairly. It is particularly important to bring out matters which might not be obvious to the jury. In these cases it usually will be obvious that a co-accused testifying on his own behalf is quite likely to be trying to minimise his own involvement, in some cases at the expense of his co-accused.[1] What might be less obvious to the jury is that a witness testifying for the prosecution might still have reason to minimise his involvement,[2] and might because of that involvement be able to lie more convincingly on account of being able to conceal a small, but effective, amount of falsity in a substantial quantity of demonstrable truth.[3]

It seems that there is now an obligation to warn the jury to proceed on the basis of such a witness with caution. In *R v Beck* Ackner LJ said:[4]

> we in no way wish to detract from the *obligation* on a judge to advise a jury to proceed with caution where there is material to suggest that a witness's evidence may be tainted by an improper motive, and the strength of that advice must vary according to the facts of the case....

This approach was approved by the House of Lords in *R v Spencer*,[5] where it was again stressed that no particular form of words is required, so long as the direction is fair and the reasons for proceeding with caution explained, so far as the facts of the case require. It is interesting that in *Spencer* the jury required such a direction, not only because the witnesses were mentally incapacitated, but also because they were convicted criminals, perhaps with scores to settle, and so for that reason within this broad generic class, despite being victims rather than accomplices. It seems highly

---

17   *Vetrovec v R* [1982] 1 SCR 811.
18   *R v Beck* [1982] 1 All ER 807, [1982] 1 WLR 461.
19   *R v Loveridge* (1983) 76 Cr App Rep 125.
20   See eg *R v Sparrow* [1973] 2 All ER 129, at 135, [1973] 1 WLR 488, at 495.
1   See eg *R v Knowlden and Knowlden* (1983) 77 Cr App Rep 94 (decided in 1981); *R v Lovell* [1990] Crim LR 111.
2   Eg if not yet sentenced. For that reason it is essential that the facts be brought to the attention of the jury, but if they are, the question becomes one simply of weight: *Chan Wai-Keung v R* [1995] 2 All ER 438, [1995] 1 WLR 251.
3   It was for that reason above all that the old law distinguished between accomplices called for the prosecution and for the defence.
4   [1982] 1 All ER 807, at 813, [1982] 1 WLR 461, at 469. Emphasis supplied. See also *R v Mills* [1993] Crim LR 210 (where an appeal was allowed in respect of failure to warn in respect of the evidence of a co-accused).
5   [1987] AC 128, at 140, [1986] 2 All ER 928, at 938.

unlikely that any of the technicality of the old law[6] relating to the definition of accomplices, the use of the word 'dangerous', the question of whether one suspect witness could corroborate another, or the need to list all of the matters which might or might not, corroborate, remains as a matter of law, but it is not inconceivable that parts of it will be applied if the judge should, in his discretion, think it appropriate.[7]

E. VICTIMS OF SEXUAL OFFENCES

There were two respects in which such victims were treated as falling into a special category. First some such victims were treated differently in some respects when testifying, and second a rule of practice required a special corroboration warning to be given to the jury.

I. Testimony[8]

One mainly procedural point is that in the more limited sub-class of 'rape offences'[9] publication of the name and address of a complainant will normally be suppressed, as an incentive to the reporting and prosecution of such offences.[10] The accused may apply to the Judge to exercise his discretion to lift the ban, on the basis of seeking witnesses or other prejudice to his trial, but it is rare for the Judge to do so.

It is also the case that the Judge may in his discretion permit the use of screens to reduce the stress felt by adult complainants of sexual offences just as in the case of children, and even to allow the witness to be accompanied in the witness box by the court usher and a representative of a victim support group.[11] The Court has a discretion to limit unnecessary cross-examination,[12] but it is likely to exercise it with restraint in the case of unrepresented persons,[13] which has caused concern in relation to such cross-examination of complainants in sexual cases.[14]

2. Supporting evidence

Here too the law has undergone considerable simplification as a result of the abolition of the requirement of corroboration of evidence of victims of sexual offences.[15] It has

---

6   See earlier editions of this work.
7   This also seems to be the position in Australia: see *Webb v R* (1994) 181 CLR 41.
8   The Youth Justice and Criminal Evidence Bill 1999 proposes to treat complainants in sexual cases as eligible for a special measures order unless the court is satisfied that the conditions for making such an order do not apply (cl 17(4)). It will also bar cross-examination of complainants in sexual offences (as defined in cl 61(1)) by the accused in person (cl 33).
9   As defined in the Sexual Offences (Amendment) Act 1976, s 7(2).
10   Sexual Offences (Amendment) Act 1976, s 4, following the recommendation of the Advisory Group on the Law of Rape (1975) Cmnd 6352. See also Adler *Rape on Trial* (1987) pp 56–64.
11   *R v Lynch* [1993] Crim LR 868; *R v Foster* [1995] Crim LR 333, less reluctantly than in *R v Cooper and Schaub* [1994] Crim LR 531.
12   *R v Kalia* (1974) 60 Cr App Rep 200.
13   Cp *R v Morley* [1988] QB 601, [1988] 2 All ER 396.
14   Such cross-examination in a particularly notorious, and widely-publicised, case led to the review of this whole area of the law by the interdepartmental working group which published its report *Speaking Up for Justice* in 1998, and which itself inspired the proposals in the Youth Justice and Criminal Evidence Bill 1999.
15   By s 32(1)(b) of the Criminal Justice and Public Order Act 1994 upon the recommendation of the Law Commission in Law Com No 202 (Cm 1620, 1991). Corroboration requirements have also been abolished in Australia: see Evidence Act (Cwth) 1955, s 164.

since been made clear that:[16] while the legislation does not prohibit a cautionary direction, it will be strongly discouraged in all but the most extreme cases;[17] some evidential basis[18] will be required to justify such a direction; its permissible terms are quite fluid, need to be adapted to the circumstances of the case, and should be discussed in advance between judge and counsel; and no appeal against the form of the direction will succeed unless it is *Wednesbury* unreasonable. The change in the law has made no difference to the admissibility of a recent complaint to support the consistency of the complainant, so long as that limited purpose is properly explained to the jury.[19]

F.   OTHER WITNESSES AND SPECIAL SITUATIONS

While the preceding parts of this section cover the majority of the cases where rules of competence, compellability and corroboration were invoked, there remains a miscellaneous rag-bag of further situations where some of them arose. It may also be noted that, at least in the non-technical sense, there has been some demand for greater support in particularly contentious situations, such as that relating to the evidence of eye-witnesses and of policemen reporting an oral confession, especially when it was subsequently denied to have been made. The most significant sub-group is the class where some such requirement has been made by direct statutory provision. Some of the latter will be described very briefly in the first part, and then a few other situations which have been mooted will be mentioned.

I.   Statutory provision

The Law Commission largely confined its investigation to corroboration at common law.[20] Most statutory provisions have been cast in terms of requiring some corroborative evidence, rather than a warning against convicting in its absence.

(i)   Statutes requiring two or more witnesses[1]

Some statutes have provided that the accused can be convicted[2] only on the oath of two or more credible witnesses. These included s 1 of the Treason Act 1795, penalising the compassing of the death or restraint of the Queen, and s 168(5) of the Representation

---

16   *R v Makanjuola; R v Easton* [1995] 3 All ER 730, [1995] 1 WLR 1348.

17   Although in such an extreme case an appeal may be allowed if no sufficient direction is given: *R v Walker* [1996] Crim LR 742.

18   It is as yet uncertain what will be required: see Lewis (1997) 7 King's College LJ 140. In *R v Walker* the only evidence appears to have been a previous inconsistent statement of the testifying witness.

19   *R v Makanjuola and Easton* at 736g, 1355F. In Australia, the High Court has held it permissible to refer to the victim's failure to complain under the rather different form of local statutory abolition of a compulsory direction: *Crofts v R* (1996) 88 ACR 232.

20   Except where there was significant overlap, as in relation to a requirement of corroboration or a warning in some provisions in the Sexual Offences Act 1956 which have now been removed: Criminal Justice and Public Order Act 1994, s 33.

1   The same rule applies to an attempt to commit such an offence: Criminal Attempts Act 1981, s 2(1)(g).

2   The Criminal Procedure (Insanity and Unfitness to Plead) Act 1991, s 1 is unusual in requiring two witnesses before a jury may *acquit.*

of the People Act 1983 (now repealed) dealing with impersonation at elections. These provisions are of no practical importance from the point of view of the general law of evidence, and their repeal was recommended in the 11th Report of the Criminal Law Revision Committee.

(ii)   Section 89 of the Road Traffic Regulation Act 1984

Under s 89 of the Road Traffic Regulation Act 1984,[3] a person charged with the offence of driving a motor vehicle at a speed greater than the maximum allowed shall not be liable to be convicted solely on the evidence of one witness to the effect that in the opinion of the witness the person charged was driving the vehicle at such greater speed. The effect of this provision is that where the evidence is that of the opinion of witnesses concerning the speed at which the accused was travelling, there must be two or more of them, and it has been held that their opinion must concern the accused's speed over the same stretch of road at the same time. A's opinion that the accused was travelling at a particular speed in one place, and B's opinion that he was travelling at that speed a little further on will not suffice.[4] There may, however, be a conviction on the evidence of one witness if it amounts to something more than his opinion. In *Nicholas v Penny*,[5] a police officer's evidence that he followed the accused in a police car and consulted its speedometer which showed an excessive speed was held to be sufficient. The speedometer reading is prima facie evidence of the speed recorded, although it is of course always open to the accused to raise a doubt whether the instrument was working properly.[6] The reading is evidence of a fact, and not a statement of opinion. As a general rule the opinion of witnesses who are not experts is excluded, but we shall see in ch XII that it is admissible in a number of cases in which its exclusion would be absurd. Estimates of the speed at which a vehicle was travelling are among these cases, but the fact that such estimates are more liable to be inaccurate than testimony concerning direct perception amply justifies the provisions of s 89 of the Road Traffic Regulation Act 1984. Where the opinion is not based upon an estimation from observation of the vehicle in motion, but upon calculation from real evidence, such as skid marks and the effects of impact, there is not the same danger, and a generous view has been taken allowing such evidence to supplement the testimony of the expert deriving the appropriate inference from it.[7]

(iii)   Perjury

Section 13 of the Perjury Act 1911 provides:

> A person shall not be liable to be convicted of any offence against this Act, or of any offence declared by any other Act to be perjury or subornation of perjury, or to be punishable as perjury or subornation of perjury solely upon the evidence of one witness as to the falsity of any statement alleged to be false.

---

3   Re-enacting earlier legislation.
4   *Brighty v Pearson* [1938] 4 All ER 127.
5   [1950] 2 KB 466, [1950] 2 All ER 89, where earlier decisions are reviewed.
6   If no reason is adduced for doubting such a reading the trier of fact must accept it as corroboration: *Burton v Gilbert* (1983) 147 JP 441.
7   *Crossland v DPP* [1988] 3 All ER 712.

This confirmed the common law as settled in *R v Muscot*,[8] but the reason for the rule given in that case, 'else there is only oath against oath', is open to question because it would justify a requirement of corroboration in any number of situations in which it is not necessary as matter of law or practice. There is an historical basis for the rule in the fact that perjury was originally punished in the Star Chamber, a court whose procedure was to some extent influenced by the civil law which usually applied the principle that the testimony of one witness was insufficient. The requirement of corroboration in the case of perjury and kindred offences may also be justified on the ground that nothing must be allowed to discourage witnesses from testifying, and the fact that a conviction for perjury might be secured on the oath of one witness could have this effect. A second witness to the falsity of the impugned statement is not, however, essential. A letter, the authenticity of which is duly proved or admitted, and which might be construed as a subornation to someone else to commit perjury in relation to the same matter will suffice.[9] If all that is proved is that the accused contradicted the impugned statement, there is not enough evidence to support a conviction, for nothing more is established than that one of two allegations made by the accused is untrue. Additional evidence, such as the repetition of the contradiction of the impugned statement on a number of occasions to different people, will, however, be sufficient.[10]

Although it is necessary for the judge to give an appropriate direction to the jury,[11] it is noted that only the falsity of the statement need be corroborated.[12] It is however sufficient for this purpose that two different witnesses heard the same admission of falsity by the accused.[13]

The Criminal Law Revision Committee recommended, as did the Law Commission, that the requirement of corroboration should be confined to perjury in judicial proceedings and should not, like the present law, apply to such other offences under the Act of 1911 as the making of false statutory declarations.[14] This is because the encouragement of people to testify without fear of too easy a prosecution is regarded as the justification of the requirement of corroboration. This recommendation has not yet been implemented.

2.   Claims against the estates of deceased persons

A claim against the estate of a deceased person will not generally be allowed on the unsupported evidence of the claimant, but there is no rule of law against allowing it[15] in England. The absence through death of one of the parties to the transaction calls for caution in such a case, but claims have been allowed where there was no corroboration.[16]

---

8   (1713) 10 Mod Rep 192, and extended it to a wider range of offences; see *R v Barker* [1986] 1 NZLR 252.
9   *R v Threlfall* (1914) 10 Cr App Rep 112.
10   *R v Hook* (1858) Dears & B 606. See also *R v Atkinson* (1934) 24 Cr App Rep 123 and *R v Stokes* [1988] Crim LR 110.
11   *R v Hamid* (1979) 69 Cr App Rep 324; *R v Carroll* (1993) 99 Cr App Rep 381.
12   *R v O'Connor* [1980] Crim LR 43. If the falsity of the statement is not an issue, or is formally admitted by the accused, no reference need be made to s 13, see *R v Rider* (1986) 83 Cr App Rep 207. See also *R v Willmot* [1987] 1 Qd R 53 where the falsity of the statement was admitted under oath in the earlier proceedings.
13   *R v Peach* [1990] 2 All ER 966, [1990] 1 WLR 976, contrary to the view expressed in para 192 of the 11th Report of the Criminal Law Revision Committee (1972) Cmnd 4991.
14   Ibid, para 191.
15   *Re Hodgson, Beckett v Ramsdale* (1885) 31 Ch D 177; *Rawlinson v Scholes* (1898) 15 TLR 8; *Vavasseur v Vavasseur* (1909) 25 TLR 250; *Re Cummins, Cummins v Thompson* [1972] Ch 62, [1971] 3 All ER 782; see note in 87 LQR 268.
16   It is required by statute in some Canadian jurisdictions: see *Ken Ertel Ltd v Johnson* (1986) 25 DLR (4th) 233.

3. The sovereign and diplomats

It goes without saying that the sovereign is not a compellable witness. The same applies to heads of other sovereign states, because they are not subject to legal process. Under various statutes diplomatic and consular officials, and officials of, and other persons connected with, certain international organisations, enjoy total or partial immunity from compellability to give evidence.[17]

4. Experts

While in most cases parties have no choice of witnesses, this is not usually the case with expert opinion witnesses, and it is appropriate to modify the rules relating to compellability where it is the case that there is a range of witnesses competent to provide the evidence required, and there are good reasons[18] for the proposed expert to decline.[19] If this were not so, the burden upon the most popular experts could easily become intolerable.

5. Bankers

Reference must finally be made to the limited immunity enjoyed by bankers under the Bankers' Books Evidence Act 1879. Section 6 provides that:[20]

A banker or officer of a bank shall not, in any legal proceeding to which the bank is not a party, be compellable to produce any banker's book the contents of which can be proved under this Act, or to appear as a witness to prove the matters, transactions and accounts therein recorded, unless by order of a judge made for special cause.

The object of this statute is to save the time of bankers and protect them and their customers from the inconvenience of producing the originals of their books. We shall see in ch XVI that, although it is sufficient to produce a copy of a public document to the court, the original of a private document has to be produced as a general rule. Bankers' books, apart from those of the Bank of England, rank as private documents, but the Act of 1879 provides for their proof by means of a copy. There are various safeguards which it is not necessary to mention, beyond saying that the authenticity of the copy can usually be established by affidavit, thus sparing any bank official the necessity of attending court.

---

17 See in particular Diplomatic Privileges Act 1964 (c 81), s 2(1), Sch 1, arts 1, 31(2), 37(1), (2); Consular Relations Act 1968 (c 18), s 1(1), Sch 1, arts 1(1), 44, 58(2); International Organisations Act 1968 (c 48); Diplomatic and Other Privileges Act 1971 (c 64), s 4; International Organisations Act 1981 (c 9); Arms Control and Disarmament (Privileges and Conventions) Act 1988 (c 2). The assistance of G V Hart, late secretary of the Criminal Law Revision Committee, on this subject is acknowledged.
18 Such as the disruption of other work.
19 *Society of Lloyd's v Clementson (No 2)* [1996] CLC 1205.
20 See also Companies Act 1985, s 452(3); Companies Act 1989, s 69.

6. Other possible cases

In *The People (A-G) v Casey (No 2)*,[1] Kingsmill-Moore J speaking for the Supreme Court of Eire said:

> The category of circumstances and special types of case which call for special directions and warnings from the trial judge cannot be considered as closed. Increased judicial experience and, indeed, further psychological research, may extend it.

The case before the court concerned the reliability of evidence of visual identification and it was said that, in all such cases, whether or not there was a plurality of witnesses, the jury's attention should be drawn to the necessity of caution because there have been cases in the past in which responsible witnesses to identification have been subsequently proved to have been mistaken.

The words of Kingsmill-Moore J were repeated with approval by the Lord Chancellor in *DPP v Kilbourne*;[2] but, as we shall see,[3] the problem of identification has been dealt with by the English courts in a different way. The precautions mentioned in *R v Turnbull*[4] must be observed, but they do not prescribe an invariable requirement of corroborative evidence or a warning to the jury of the danger of convicting in its absence. Indeed the Report of the Devlin Committee on Evidence of Identification in Criminal Cases which preceded the decision in *R v Turnbull* spoke of the declining belief in the value of a requirement of corroboration and said that the law on the subject had become too technical.[5]

The tide of judicial feeling seems to be running strongly against the ritualistic observation of rigid rules in this area, and for this reason new categories of witnesses[6] or further areas for the application of rules or practices of requiring an inflexible warning are highly unlikely to open up.[7] The question was considered by the Royal Commission on Criminal Justice in relation in particular to the corroboration of confessions made to the police.[8] The majority view was that such confessions should continue to be admissible despite the absence of supporting evidence,[9] but that a warning should be given, tailored to the facts of the particular case and referring to the reasons which sometimes account for false confessions being made, and to any particular reasons raised by the defence in the particular case. It was felt that the jury should be directed to look for supporting evidence, but that it should be supporting evidence in the looser *Turnbull* sense rather than that which passed the old stricter tests.[10] The Law

---

1   [1963] IR 33, at 38.
2   [1973] AC 729, at 740.
3   See p 673 below.
4   [1977] QB 224, [1976] 3 All ER 549.
5   Paras 4.36 and 4.53. See ch XVII section 2, below for an account of the report and evidence of identification generally.
6   The House of Lords has refused to erect patients in a secure mental hospital into such a category, *R v Spencer* [1987] AC 128, [1986] 2 All ER 928.
7   In *Nembhard v R* [1982] 1 All ER 183, 74 Cr App Rep 144, extension of the old corroboration requirement to dying declaration cases was denied.
8   Cm 2263 (1993) paras 4.56–4.87, recs 89, 90. See also Res St No 13.
9   Though Res St No 13 showed that this would be likely to occur in no more than 5% of cases.
1 0   In Australia warnings in relation to the *making* of disputed and uncorroborated confessions to the police were required at common law, *R v McKinney and Judge* (1991) 171 CLR 468, and may now be required under the provisions of the Evidence Act (Cwth) 1995, s 165. For the interaction of the two see *R v Beattie* (1996) 40 NSWLR 155. See generally Pattenden (1991) 107 LQR 317. For the position in Ireland see *People v Quilligan (No 3)* [1993] 2 IR 305.

Commission has also resiled[11] from its provisional view that unsupported hearsay alone should be insufficient to sustain a conviction.[12] In Australia it has also been suggested that an informal warning will normally be required in relation to the evidence of prison informers.[13]

SECTION 3. THE NATURE OF SUPPORTING EVIDENCE

Even under the old law it was said that 'corroboration' was not a technical term, but simply meant 'confirmation' or 'support'.[14] Nevertheless much of the momentum for reform was sustained by the technicality with which the old law of corroboration was engulfed, principally in the definition of what amounted to corroboration, and in the obligation upon the judge to direct the jury in detail as to what could and could not amount to corroboration. This was seen as a tricky and time-consuming exercise which made the task of the jury difficult, and occasionally led to unmeritorious acquittals. As cases involving multiple counts and many defendants tended to increase, reflecting the need for economy in the trial process, and the increasing complexity of offences, especially of commercial fraud, so the problem became more acute.

As noted above the response of the Law Commission was to recommend wholesale abolition of the warning requirement in criminal cases. It had no doubt that the consequence of this should be that the technical rules of definition and direction should fall with that obligation:[15]

> With the abolition of the obligation to give a corroboration warning, the rules as to what is capable of being corroboration in law will simply have no standing, no grounding and no purpose, because those rules have been developed for the precise and only purpose, and solely and only in the context of deciding what counts as 'corroboration' in order to fulfil the requirements of that warning, and the obligations that the form of that warning places on the jury. With the abolition of the obligation to give the corroboration warning, the rules as to the content of that warning simply fall away.

In the nature of things the provisions of the Criminal Justice and Public Order Act 1994 which implement the recommendations of the Law Commission, contain no explicit reference to these rules.[16] It seems that in accordance with that general approach there is likely to be less inclination in England to retain elements of the old rules than has sometimes been apparent in Australia.[17] In Scotland too the robust judical view has been expressed that 'when Parliament has removed the rules which once existed, I should be most reluctant to see the courts developing any supposed new rules.'[18]

---

11 *Evidence in Criminal Proceedings: Hearsay and Related Topics* Law Com 245 Cm 3670 (1997) para 5.41.
12 *Evidence in Criminal Proceedings: Hearsay and Related Topics* Law Com Consultation Paper 138 (1995) para 9.5 rec 14.
13 *Pollitt v R* (1992) 174 CLR 558.
14 *DPP v Hester* [1973] AC 296, at 325, [1972] 3 All ER 1056, at 1073.
15 Para 4.12 (footnote omitted).
16 In that, as in all other significant respects, adopting the Law Commission's draft bill.
17 Compare the approach of the Court of Appeal in *R v Makanjuola and Easton* [1995] 3 All ER 730, [1995] 1 WLR 1348 with that of the High Court of Australia in *Longman v R* (1989) 168 CLR 79 and *Crofts v R* (1996) 88 ACR 232. See also in Canada *B(G) v R* [1990] 2 SCR 3; *Bevan v R* [1993] 2 SCR 599.
18 *L v L* 1997 SCLR 866, at 871E.

While the old law developed a number of technical rules relating to the definition of 'corroboration' over the years, some at least of the learning represented no more than the encapsulation of common sense, and it may well be the case that certain elements of the old considerations will remain relevant to the practice of the courts in directing juries, albeit within the flexibility of the new law.[19]

It may be accepted that the rigidity of the old demarcation of the limits of rules will be replaced by more rational and relevant construction, but in some instances the core of common sense will remain. At least until a new set of indicators has been developed, it is worth a brief glance at the old categories to see what if anything can be expected to be adopted on a discretionary basis to guide the form of direction which the judge may choose to give. This account can now be much abbreviated, but it is worth distinguishing in the old way between support provided from the source requiring support, and support in some fashion from the accused against whom it is required. A final part of this section will deal with procedural considerations.

A.   SUPPORT FROM THE SOURCE REQUIRING IT

One of the most fundamental tenets of the old law was that in order to amount to corroboration the evidence had to emanate from a source independent of the witness to be corroborated,[20] or in still more extreme a form from a different type of source from the witness to be corroborated.[1] This led to difficult distinctions depending upon whether the evidence did, or did not, emanate from an independent source, regardless of the strength of the evidence.[2] It may now be expected that any direction will deal only with the strength of the support offered by the evidence.

Even under the old law it was accepted that a fact relating to the witness requiring support might amount to corroboration, for example the distress of the victim of a sexual offence discerned by an observer of whom the victim was unaware.[3] On the other hand it was well established that while in certain cases complaints of victims of sexual offences could be admitted to show consistency, they were not allowed to corroborate, or indeed to amount to evidence of the facts which they alleged.[4] In *R v Makanjuola*[5] in the course of its general explanation of the impact of the abolition of the old corroboration requirement the Court of Appeal explicitly upheld the continued admissibility of recent complaints, but it is still incumbent upon the judge to explain, perhaps now more flexibly, the limited purpose for which they are admitted.[6] It should also be emphasised that the mere absence of a motive to lie does not support the truth of whatever is asserted.[7] It

19   See Mirfield [1995] Crim LR 448; Birch [1995] Crim LR 424; Hartshorne (1998) 2 Int Jo Ev & Pr 1.
20   *R v Baskerville* [1916] 2 KB 658.
1   See the discussion of the position relating to children in *DPP v Hester* [1973] AC 296, [1972] 3 All ER 1056; and that relating to accomplices in *DPP v Kilbourne* [1973] AC 729, [1973] 1 All ER 440.
2   Contrast *R v Willoughby* (1988) 88 Cr App Rep 91 (allegation that assailant had spots *was not* corroborated by accused having spots) with *R v McInnes* (1989) 90 Cr App Rep 99 (allegation that assailant had sweet papers in his car *was* corroborated by accused having car littered with sweet papers).
3   *R v Redpath* (1962) 46 Cr App Rep 319.
4   See below p 273.
5   [1995] 3 All ER 730, [1995] 1 WLR 1348. See in Australia *Crofts v R* (1996) 88 ACR 232.
6   *R v Islam* [1999] 1 Cr App Rep 22.
7   *R v Jovanovic* (1997) 42 NSWLR 520, where it was held the judge should have intervened to prevent this line of cross-examination.

has however been held that evidence of the demeanour of the complainant, and the effect upon it of having made the complaint is inadmissible.[8]

A different source of difficulty under the old law was that it was necessary for the evidence to implicate the accused in a material particular, and doubts arose in cases where individual pieces of evidence needed to be added together to achieve such implication,[9] or where it was unclear which of a number of accused persons were implicated.[10] It is to be hoped that complications like these may now be disregarded,[11] and the jury instructed in such cases in a more flexible manner.

B. SUPPORT FROM THE OBJECT AGAINST WHOM REQUIRED

The question of how far the conduct of the accused constituted corroboration of the evidence against him was a matter of some debate under the old law. It was considered in previous editions of this work under the heads of the admission of the party against whom corroboration is required, lies told by him, his failure to give evidence, his silence when charged out of court, his failure to provide a sample of real evidence and his conduct on an occasion previous to that with which the trial is concerned. It is worth retaining that division of topics, although their substance has, in some of these situations, been much affected by specific provision in the Criminal Justice and Public Order Act 1994.[12]

I. Admission of defendant or accused

Statements intended as mitigation or exculpation in court may be held to support the case against their maker. In *R v Dossi*[13] for instance, it was held that the accused's admission in evidence that he had platonically fondled the child who gave sworn testimony to the effect that he had indecently assaulted her could be treated as some corroboration of her statement. As Atkin LJ said: 'The question of corroboration often assumes an entirely different aspect after the accused person has gone into the witness box and has been cross-examined.'[14] Whether anything that emerges in the course of the evidence of the defendant or accused does support his opponent's witnesses is of course a question of fact dependent on the circumstances of the particular case. Much may depend upon the issues which remain contested, and the extent of any admission.[15]

8   *R v Keast* [1998] Crim LR 748.
9   See *R v Hills* (1987) 86 Cr App Rep 26 construing some especially cryptic remarks in *Thomas v Jones* [1921] 1 KB 22.
10 See *R v Franklin* [1989] Crim LR 499.
11 Though first indications are not encouraging: see *R v Mullen and Mullen* [1996] CLY 1354.
12 Quite different from that specifically withdrawing an obligation to give a corroboration warning.
13 (1918) 13 Cr App Rep 158; *Goguen and Goguen v Bourgeois and Bourgeois* (1957) 6 DLR (2d) 19. See also *R v Simpson* [1994] Crim LR 436 where minor sexual activity was admitted during interview about a range of offences, some much more serious, which were then charged.
14 At 162.
15 See Munday [1985] Crim LR 190, pointing out that in *R v Tragen* [1956] Crim LR 332 Lord Goddard CJ seems to have taken a different view of facts superficially similar to those in *Dossi*.

2.   Lies of defendant or accused[16]

As a matter of common-sense, to tell a lie may indicate consciousness of guilt and so support suspect testimony. In *Tumahole Bereng v R*[17], however, Lord MacDermott said that a prisoner does not corroborate an accomplice merely by giving evidence which is not accepted and must therefore be regarded as false:

> Corroboration may well be found in the evidence of an accused person, but that is a different matter, for there confirmation comes, if at all, from what is said, and not from the falsity of what is said.

There is nothing in the context which suggests that this dictum is applicable only to the testimony of an accomplice. To quote from a South Australian judgment in affiliation proceedings: [18]

> The court cannot, as is sometimes suggested, prefer the evidence of the mother to that of the defendant and then use its disbelief of his evidence as the basis of an inference to be used in corroboration of the mother's testimony.

This is the type of error into which the trial judge seems to have fallen in *R v Chapman and Baldwin*,[19] a case in which the judgment of the Court of Appeal could be construed as meaning that the accused's lies in court can never corroborate evidence given against him. This view has been rejected both in the Commonwealth,[20] and in England, where it has been said that: [1]

> To be capable of amounting to corroboration the lie told out of court must first of all be deliberate. Secondly, it must relate to a material issue. Thirdly the motive for the lie must be a realisation of guilt and a fear of the truth. The jury should in appropriate cases be reminded that people sometimes lie, for example, in an attempt to bolster up a just cause, or out of shame or out of a wish to conceal disgraceful behaviour from their family. Fourthly the statement must be clearly shown to be a lie by evidence other than that of the accomplice who is to be corroborated, that is to say by admission or by evidence from an independent witness.

It was regarded as sensible to apply exactly the same principles to lies told in court, and provided that the conditions can be satisfied there seems no reason to suppose that they cannot also be applied to the adoption of lies told by others.[2] If the lie is being used only as part of the background of the case, for example to discredit the witness, there is no need for such a direction.[3]

Such a direction is however complex, and might confuse the jury if it were given when it is unnecessary as in the ordinary case where little more than a conflict of

---

16   See Heydon (1973) 89 LQR 552.
17   [1949] AC 253, at 280.
18   Napier J in *Pitman v Byrne* [1926] SASR 207, at 211.
19   [1973] QB 774, [1973] 2 All ER 624.
20   *R v Collings* [1976] 2 NZLR 104, *R v Perera* [1982] VR 901.
1   *R v Lucas* [1981] QB 720, [1981] 2 All ER 1008, rejecting the construction of *Chapman* mentioned above. See *Edwards v R* (1993) 178 CLR 193 for careful analysis of this direction by the High Court of Australia.
2   See *R v Perera*, above.
3   *R v Smith* [1995] Crim LR 305.

testimony occurs between the testimony of the accused and of other evidence.[4] In *R v Burge and Pegg*[5] the Court of Appeal suggested four possible occasions for the direction: first, where the defence relies on alibi;[6] second, where the judge suggests that the jury should look for support for a piece of evidence and refers it to lies told by the accused; third, where the prosecution relies on the lies as an independent part of its case;[7] and fourth, where the judge thinks it possible that the jury will do so.[8]

Here, as elsewhere, it is submitted that the best solution is to mould the direction closely to the facts of the case, and to resist the temptation to resort to rules of thumb which will do no more than replace old technicalities with new.

3.   Failure to give evidence

Under the old law the failure of the accused to testify could not amount to corroboration of the evidence against him.[9] The Criminal Law Revision Committee in its Eleventh Report recommended that the accused's failure to give evidence should, if the fact were such that an inference of guilt might properly be drawn therefrom, be treated as capable of amounting to corroboration of any evidence given by the prosecution.[10] Its recommendations were largely[11] implemented here[12] by s 35 of the Criminal Justice and Public Order Act 1994.[13] Since s 38(3) prevents conviction solely upon an inference from failure to testify, its effect was affirmed in *R v Cowan*[14] as being:

> that the court or jury may regard the inference from failure to testify as, in effect, a further evidential factor in support of the prosecution case.

The court was quite clear that the inference was in no way exceptional, and that the trial judge had considerable flexibility in tailoring his direction to the facts of the case,[15] although it recommended starting from the Judicial Studies Board's specimen direction.[16] Although it has been claimed[17] that this is different from inviting the jury

---

4   This may become more common if the Criminal Justice and Public Order Act 1994 has its desired effect of promoting statements by the accused both before and at the trial.
5   [1996] 1 Cr App Rep 163, at 173D.
6   Though even here there is no invariable requirement: *R v Harron* [1996] 2 Cr App Rep 457. It is immaterial that the lie relates to the reason for a former admittedly false alibi: *R v Peacock* [1998] Crim LR 681.
7   See *R v Goodway* [1993] 4 All ER 894, 98 Cr App Rep 11 which in its reference to *R v Dehar* [1969] NZLR 763 recognised that even in this situation it might not be necessary to give a full *Lucas* direction. In Australia a distinction is drawn between lies which go to credit only, and do not require a special direction, and those which are in effect implied admissions, and do: see *Edwards v R* (1993) 178 CLR 193. The same distinction is made in New Zealand; see *R v Oakes* [1995] 2 NZLR 673, at 684.
8   See *R v Richens* [1993] 4 All ER 877, at 886. This aspect of *Goodway* has been rejected in Australia: *R v Renzella* (1996) 88 ACR 65.
9   *R v Jackson* [1953] 1 All ER 872, [1953] 1 WLR 591. See in Australia *R v Kanaveilomani* (1994) 72 ACR 492 re-assessing the position in the light of *Weissensteiner v R* (1993) 178 CLR 217.
10   11th Report, para 111. The same reasoning would apply a fortiori to failure to call a spouse.
11   The accused is not however formally called upon to testify as the Committee had recommended.
12   Its precursor in Northern Ireland was the Criminal Evidence (Northern Ireland) Order 1988. See *Murray v DPP* (1993) 97 Cr App Rep 151, criticised by Jackson in (1993) 44 NILQ 103.
13   See further below ch IX sect 1 part A.
14   [1996] QB 373, [1995] 4 All ER 939, at 379C, 943c.
15   Especially in its endorsement of the opinions expressed by Kelly LJ in relation to its Northern Ireland predecessor in *R v McLernon* [1990] 10 NIJB 91, at 102.
16   Set out in *Cowan* at 380G, 944f.
17   By Lord Slynn in *Murray* at p 160.

to infer that the accused who fails to testify is guilty, the difference is barely discernible once a prima facie case has been established.

It is scarcely necessary to add that failure to cross-examine a witness does not amount to support of the witness's evidence.[18]

4.   Silence when charged

There is a broad principle of common sense which was stated by Cave J in the course of his judgment in *R v Mitchell*:[19]

> Undoubtedly, when persons are speaking on even terms, and a charge is made, and the person charged says nothing, and expresses no indignation, and does nothing to repel the charge, that is some evidence to show that he admits the charge to be true.

This principle was acted on in *R v Cramp*[20] in which the accused's failure to answer the observation of the girl's father about some pills was held to be capable of corroborating her evidence that the accused had attempted to procure her miscarriage. But what if the persons in question are not speaking on even terms? Silence in the face of police questioning[1] is governed by the Criminal Justice and Public Order Act 1994.[2] In the case of failure to mention facts subsequently relied upon, the accused need mention only those which it is reasonable to expect that he would mention. Given the failure to require more disclosure of the case against the accused than emerges from the arrest or charge,[3] it is unclear quite what will be regarded as a reasonable excuse. The Court of Appeal seems to be opposed to laying down any fixed rules,[4] and to prefer to leave it all to the judgment of the trial court in the light of particular facts. In Northern Ireland it was held that the failure to provide access to a legal adviser was insufficient to prevent inference from silence prior to his arrival,[5] but such failure may itself be in breach of art 6 of the European Convention of Human Rights,[6] more especially because of the inference from silence permitted by the relevant legislation.[7] It is possible that it was the incorporation of the Convention which has now led to the introduction of legislation to exclude such an inference when no opportunity of access to a solicitor has been allowed.[8]

---

18   *Dingwall v J Wharton (Shipping) Ltd* [1961] 2 Lloyd's Rep 213, at 219. Not even under the Criminal Justice and Public Order Act 1994.
19   (1892) 17 Cox CC 503. In Scotland this extends to failure to contradict an allegation made in the accused's presence to a third party, *McDonnell v HM Advocate* 1997 SCCR 760.
20   (1880) 14 Cox CC 390. See also *Bessela v Stern* (1877) 2 CPD 265, and contrast the position where the charge is made by letter when it would often, though not invariably, be wrong to draw an adverse inference from failure to reply (*Wiedmann v Walpole* [1891] 2 QB 534).
1   Or others charged with the duty of investigating offences, for further exegesis see below p 631.
2   S 34 (failure to mention facts later relied on in defence); s 36 (failure to account for objects, marks and substances believed by the police to be incriminating); and s 37 (failure to account for presence in a particular place believed by the police to be incriminating).
3   The primary duty of prosecution disclosure under the Criminal Procedure and Investigations Act 1996 arises at a later stage in the process.
4   *R v Condron and Condron* [1997] 1 WLR 827, [1997] 1 Cr App Rep 185; *R v Argent* [1997] 2 Cr App Rep 27; and *R v Roble* [1997] Crim LR 449.
5   *R v Quinn* (LEXIS) 17 September 1993.
6   Right to fair trial.
7   *Murray v United Kingdom* (1996) 22 EHRR 29.
8   The Youth Justice and Criminal Evidence Bill 1999 (cl 57). The explanatory notes explicitly refer to *Murray*, and the bill is prefaced by an annotation that in the view of the Lord Chancellor

It is further provided that this ground for adverse inference is additional to any existing power, so those cases where it has been established that the parties are on even terms, despite one of them being a member of the police force will continue to have the same effect.[9]

It should also be noted that any adverse inference must be proper. Given that it is expressly provided that such an inference may contribute to the establishment of a prima facie case, it seems that it is capable of supporting the elements of the prosecution case in general, and is not limited to weakening the defence evidence of the matter relied upon at the trial.[10]

In the cases of failure to explain objects, substances and marks or presence in a particular place it is incumbent upon the police officer to make his belief in the incriminating nature of the relevant thing apparent to the accused, and explain in clear terms what the consequences of failure will be. Here the adverse inference even more clearly goes directly to guilt since it is the prosecution evidence[11] which is strengthened by the accused's failure to explain.

5. Failure to provide a sample of real evidence

Since no one is obliged to provide a sample of real evidence[12] it might be thought that refusal to do so should not be regarded as supportive of other evidence. This seemed not to be the case. It was held in *R v Smith*[13] that the accused's arbitrary refusal to provide a sample of his hair, after being told that the hair to which it was to be matched had been found at the scene of a robbery, could corroborate the testimony of a witness treated as an accomplice. In affiliation proceedings similar reasoning was applied in *McVeigh v Beattie*[14] to the refusal by a putative father to take a blood test[15] at the direction of the court. It should perhaps be noted that in both of these cases the person who refused to provide the sample was at the time in receipt of legal advice. The matter has also been altered by more general statutory provision. Section 62(10) of the Police and Criminal Evidence Act 1984 expressly permitted inferences from failure to provide an intimate sample to be used to corroborate relevant evidence. In the case of fingerprints and non-intimate samples no such provision is made, but there is power to require the provision of such evidence in the absence of consent, upon satisfaction of the relevant conditions.[16]

---

its provisions are compatible with rights under the Convention. The provision qualifies ss 34, 36, 37 and 38 of the Criminal Justice and Public Order Act 1994.

9   As in *R v Chandler* [1976] 3 All ER 105, [1976] 1 WLR 585 where the accused was accompanied by a solicitor.

10   For more extensive, and persuasive, discussion see Mirfield *Silence, Confessions and Improperly Obtained Evidence* (1997) ch 9.

11   Although it is not a formal condition that the matter be put in evidence by the prosecution, it would be most exceptional if this did not occur.

12   Apart from special situations governed by statute, such as alcohol samples from drivers, and powers of the police and prison authorities mentioned below.

13   (1985) 81 Cr App Rep 286.

14   [1988] 2 All ER 500.

15   In New Zealand refusal of a blood sample for DNA analysis has been held to be a basic human right such that no adverse inference may be drawn from it: *R v Martin* [1992] 1 NZLR 313.

16   Police and Criminal Evidence Act 1984, ss 61 (fingerprints) and 63 (non-intimate samples); the distinction between intimate and non-intimate samples was amended by the Criminal Justice and Public Order Act 1994, s 58 (principally to transfer dental impressions and mouth swabs to the non-intimate category). See also further amendment by Criminal Evidence (Amendment) Act 1997, principally to extend the powers to create DNA databases to those convicted before 1995, and those detained after acquittal or being found unfit to plead on account of mental impairment.

6. Conduct on other occasions

We shall see in ch VIII that facts tending to show that someone committed a crime or civil wrong, or conducted himself improperly on other[17] occasions, may not normally be proved in order to establish his commission of the crime or civil wrong into which the court is inquiring, if they are relevant only as showing a disposition to commit crimes or civil wrongs generally, or the kind of crime or civil wrong with which the court is concerned. This may sometimes exclude evidence of the previous conduct of the party against whom support is required, but evidence is admissible if regarded by the judge as prima facie more probative than prejudicial. It may be relevant, either directly by showing it to be more likely that the accused committed the offence in issue on account of his propensity to do so; or indirectly by showing the accused either to have made a true confession, or a false denial, of having committed another offence.

(i)   Previous conduct to show specific propensity

As will be elaborated later[18] there are some inhibitions in adducing evidence of previous misconduct, especially of the accused in criminal proceedings. The rules for its admission have however become more relaxed, and it is no longer necessary either to show that the misconduct is strikingly similar to that now charged,[19] nor to show in advance that there was no collusion between the witnesses to the relevant misconduct.[20] In the previous state of the law there was no doubt that once evidence of the previous misconduct was admissible, it was also corroborative of the evidence of the misconduct under consideration.[1] Despite the relaxation of the requirement of absence of collusion as a prior test the law in relation to support remains the same, namely that admissible evidence of other misconduct of the accused is capable of supporting evidence directly relating to the current charge, subject only to the direction of the judge.[2] It is further remarked that with the abolition of formal corroboration requirements, this has become much less important a consideration.[3] It is perhaps surprising that the House of Lords has first felt free to extend the admissibility of similar fact evidence by reference to corroboration, where looser requirements of relevance were balanced by some guarantee of probative force by virtue of the independence of the evidence, and then to apply back so extended a category to supply support when there is no guarantee of such independence.

(ii)   Previous conduct to corroborate statement to witness

Evidence which tends to show that the accused incited a course of conduct resulting in the commission of the crime charged certainly supports the evidence against him. Accordingly anything which confirms a witness's story with regard to such incitement will be held to constitute support when this is required, and it sometimes happens that the alleged incitement takes the form of a reference to previous misconduct. In *R v*

17   It may be subsequent conduct, see *Masolini v Siebel* [1979] 1 WAR 115 (continued association after knowledge of pregnancy to corroborate on issue of paternity).
18   Ch VIII below.
19   *DPP v P* [1991] 2 AC 447, sub nom *R v P* [1991] 3 All ER 337.
20   *R v H* [1995] 2 AC 596, [1995] 2 All ER 865.
1   *Kilbourne, Boardman.*
2   *R v H* at 612E, 877f.
3   Ibid.

Mitchell,[4] for instance, a clergyman was charged with indecently assaulting a girl named Sheila, who gave sworn evidence against him. In addition to deposing to the assault upon her, Sheila said that he told her about his behaviour with a girl named Judy and it was held that this girl's testimony with regard to the accused's conduct corroborated the evidence of Sheila who could hardly have heard of Judy from any other source as the two girls lived in different parts of the country.

C. FUNCTIONS OF JUDGE AND JURY[5]

The aim of reforming this part of the law was largely to rid it of its cumbersome and counter-productive technicality. Two of the most unpopular parts of the old law were the constraints on the form of words[6] used in directing the jury, and insistence on a review of the evidence applying the old rigid categorisation to it.

It was accepted under the old law to be desirable for the judge to discuss with counsel, in the absence of the jury, and before closing speeches, the form in which he should direct the jury.[7] This view was endorsed by the Law Commission in its Report, for application to the new law:[8]

it would be beneficial if it were provided that, in any case that involved issues of fact or the credibility of evidence that needed or might need special treatment in the summing-up, the judge should before final speeches discuss those issues with counsel in the absence of the jury. The purpose of that discussion would be if possible to agree on the terms of the summing-up, and if not so possible at least to clarify, and to assist the judge on, the points of disagreement. The discussion would not be intended to be elaborate and should not in any event be used as an excuse for the introduction by counsel of arguments or submissions that are not warranted by the present law.

The Law Commission recommended the issue of a Practice Direction to this effect,[9] and further reinforcement has been provided by the Court of Appeal.[10] It is to be hoped that directions will now be more often tailored to the circumstances of the case, subject only to the requirement that they be fair. This will prevent the practice of ritual incantation which was deplored under the old law, and which sometimes led to the direction being undermined by expression of judicial disapproval of it.[11] It need hardly be added that in a case of a warning being given to himself in the case of trial by judge alone, he must not then disregard it.[12]

---

4   (1952) 36 Cr App Rep 79.
5   For full discussion see Hartshorne (1998) 2 Int J of Ev & Pr 1.
6   See *R v Chambers* (1993) Times, 7 May; *R v Fullerton* [1994] Crim LR 63 (in both descending even to the order in which points were to be put in the direction).
7   *R v Ensor* [1989] 2 All ER 586, at 593, [1989] 1 WLR 497, at 505; *R v Nagy* [1990] Crim LR 187; *R v Royle, R v Hall* [1993] Crim LR 57.
8   (Cm 1620, 1991) Law Com No 202, para 4.29. In Canada, where a similar change to that proposed by the Law Commission was accomplished by judicial decision, this consequence has also been accepted: *Bevan v R* [1993] 2 SCR 599.
9   Para 4.30.
10   *R v Makanjuola and Easton* [1995] 3 All ER 730, [1995] 1 WLR 1348; *R v Walker* [1996] Crim LR 742.
11   *R v Chambers* (1993) Times, 7 May.
12   *Miles v Cain* (1989) Times, 15 December (an unusual civil trial for rape).

CHAPTER VI

The course of evidence[1]

In this chapter an account is given of the principal rules[2] governing the examination-in-chief, cross-examination and re-examination of witnesses. Such an account can hardly hope to be entirely satisfactory because it is concerned with regulations that are either matters of common knowledge or else can be thoroughly mastered only by experience, but the rules with which it deals are among the most characteristic of the English law of evidence. The elucidation of facts by means of questions put by parties or their representatives to witnesses summoned, for the most part, by them, called mainly in the order of their choice, before a judge, acting as umpire rather than inquisitor,[3] is the essential feature of the English 'adversary' or 'accusatorial' system of justice. Not only is an appreciation of this procedure desirable for its own sake, but it is necessary for a proper understanding of such matters as the law concerning the admissibility of the convictions, character and credibility of parties and witnesses, or the structure of s 1(f) of the Criminal Evidence Act 1898, considered in the three following chapters. It must be recognised however that there is an increasing call, to some extent driven by the soaring cost of litigation, for greater intervention by the judge by way of management of the progress of a case, both at the pre-trial and trial stages.[4]

Section 1, below, deals with some procedural matters which appear to be essential to the exposition of the subject covered in this and subsequent chapters.

---

1 See generally Australian Law Reform Commission Research Paper No 8 'Manner of Giving Evidence'.
2 The Civil Procedure Rules came into force as this edition was going to press, and have transformed the background into which the law of evidence in civil proceedings is set. This chapter will be more affected by those changes than many of the others, but it is, at this stage, uncertain quite how profound those changes will turn out to be, since such wide and indeterminate power has deliberately been delegated to the judges, and all will depend upon how they choose to exercise it.
3 *R v Whybrow and Saunders* (1994) 144 NLJ 124.
4 See in relation to civil proceedings Report by Lord Woolf *Access to Justice* (1996) Sect II where the Civil Procedure Act 1997 paved the way for the implementation of its main recommendations in the Civil Procedure Rules; and to criminal proceedings, Royal Commission on Criminal Justice (1993) Cm 2263, para 8.2.

SECTION I. MISCELLANEOUS PROCEDURAL MATTERS

A. EVIDENCE BEFORE TRIAL

It is here that enormous changes have occurred, and are still occurring, in both civil and criminal proceedings. In both areas the situation has been transformed over the last two decades, with important repercussions for the law of evidence in its traditional sense. In part these have been exacerbated by an increasing overlap between civil and criminal proceedings, especially in the area of commercial fraud. It has become increasingly difficult to isolate pre-trial proceedings from those at the trial, and civil proceedings from criminal.[5]

1. Civil cases

There are two main areas of pre-trial activity in civil litigation, the first broadly concerned with the identification and preservation of relevant material,[6] and the second with its provision in the form in which it is to be used at the trial. It is first necessary to mention these two important and burgeoning areas, however briefly. In addition evidence may be taken before trial and read at the trial when it is given by affidavit, on commission, under letters of request, in answer to interrogatories or by way of perpetuation of testimony.

(i) Disclosure and inspection[7]

The principal means of identifying relevant material used to be by the system of compulsory revelation known as discovery, originally developed by the Court of Chancery, and available in the Supreme Court as a whole since the Judicature Act.[8] This spawned a whole panoply of parasitic procedures, largely as a result of judicial innovation as described by Hoffmann J in *Arab Monetary Fund v Hashim (No 5)*:[9]

> The last 20 years have seen a judge-made revolution in English civil procedure. Under pressure from the increase in cases of commercial fraud, the courts have provided plaintiffs with remedies and investigative powers which previously, if they existed at all, were available only to the police. In many large cases involving allegations of fraud and embezzlement, the greater part of the early interlocutory stages of the action is concerned with endeavours to trace assets against which claims can be made. The function of the judge at this stage is not so much to decide or even define the issues between the parties as to supervise an investigation by the plaintiff. On the plaintiff's application, usually in the first instance ex parte, the judge issues orders freezing assets, appointing receivers of companies, requiring defendants to permit searches for evidence, demanding documents and information from third parties.

---

5   For consideration of the procedural implications of this overlap in the United States see *Degen v US* 517 US 820 (1996).
6   Including the identity of parties, their assets, and the subject matter of the dispute as well as testimonial material. Increased powers in these respects have been conferred by Civil Procedure Act 1997, s 7.
7   See generally the Civil Procedure Rules Part 31, formerly called Discovery and regulated by RSC Order 24.
8   On an automatic basis since 1964.
9   [1992] 2 All ER 911, at 913

It is at these early stages[10] that the setting for the operation of many evidential rules is fixed, and an increasing part of the subject is concerned with the environment they establish. The traditional rule in English law was that parties must reveal relevant[11] materials in their possession or power for the purposes of disposing fairly of the matter or of saving costs, but that mere witnesses could not be so compelled.[12]

This rule was gradually extended. In *Norwich Pharmacal Co v Customs and Excise Comrs*[13] it was held that third parties 'mixed up' in the fraudulent activities of others were compellable to reveal the identities of the fraudsters so as to permit proceedings to be initiated against them, and this was then extended to cases where without the disclosure it could not be known whether any tort had been committed.[14] In *Mackinnon v Donaldson Lufkin and Jenrette Securities Corp*[15] the effect of this change was said to be to impose a duty on such persons to produce evidence and documents before trial comparable with that imposed upon third parties to produce them at trial[16] pursuant to a subpoena duces tecum.[17]

This exercise of judicial innovation has been supplemented by statutory provision. Under s 236 of the Insolvency Act 1985[18] anyone[19] thought capable of providing information relating to an insolvent company may be required either to submit documents, or even to attend for oral examination.[20] This provision may not however be used to the prejudice of third parties by being invoked against intermediate institutions which had themselves come into the possession of the evidence only by the exercise of statutory compulsion, at least not without notice to the affected party.[1] Nor should liquidators voluntarily disclose evidence coming to them under these compulsory powers to third parties for the purpose of legal proceedings.[2] The fact that information

---

10   Increased powers to make orders before the commencement of proceedings were conferred by the Civil Procedure Act 1997, s 8.

11   In *Cie Financiere et Commerciale de Pacifique v Peruvian Guano Co* (1982) 11 QBD 55 this was given a broad meaning, but in *Electrolux Northern Ltd v Black & Decker* [1996] FSR 595 it was, disapproving earlier authority, surprisingly held not to extend to providing evidence of unsuccessful experiments despite the tender of the results of those which were successful.

12   In principle the judge should not have exercised his discretion not to order discovery without first inspecting the documents, once a prima facie showing of relevance had been made: *Wallace Smith Trust Co v Deloitte, Haskins & Sells* [1996] 4 All ER 403, [1997] 1 WLR 257.

13   [1974] AC 133, [1973] 2 All ER 943.

14   *P v T Ltd* [1997] 4 All ER 200, [1997] 1 WLR 1309; but this was not to be used as a disguised means of discovery from known third parties: *Axa Equity & Law Life Assurance Society v National Westminster Bank* [1998] PNLR 433.

15   [1986] Ch 482, at 498, [1986] 1 All ER 653, at 661.

16   Though it seemed that such an obligation might itself operate before the trial: see *Khanna v Lovell White Durrant* [1994] 4 All ER 267, [1995] 1 WLR 121.

17   The limits of this obligation were explored by Hoffmann J in the *Arab Monetary Fund* case above. For application to video recordings of police interviews with children in cases of sexual abuse, see *Re M* [1995] 2 FLR 571.

18   See also Insolvency Rules 1986, SI 1986/1925, r 9.5.

19   Including foreign nationals holding documents overseas: *Re Mid-East Trading Ltd* (1997) Times, 20 December.

20   Though this is a drastic power and will not be sanctioned except within strict limits, especially in relation to attendance for oral examination, *Cloverbay Ltd v Bank of Credit and Commerce International* [1991] Ch 90, [1991] 1 All ER 894. These limits seem to be stricter in England than in Australia: see *England v Purves* (1998) Times, 29 January.

1   *Morris v Director of the Serious Fraud Office* [1993] Ch 372, [1993] 1 All ER 788 (evidence acquired by the application of Criminal Justice Act 1987, s 2); *Marcel v Metropolitan Police Comr* [1992] Ch 225, [1992] 1 All ER 72 (evidence acquired under Police and Criminal Evidence Act 1984, s 18); *Soden v Burns* [1996] 3 All ER 967 (evidence acquired by Board of Trade inspectors under Companies Act 1985, s 432).

2   Not even to defendants in criminal proceedings: *Re Barlow Clowes Gilt Managers Ltd* [1992] Ch 208, [1991] 4 All ER 385.

was obtained by the exercise of compulsory powers is not however enough in itself to bar compulsory disclosure under the provisions of the Civil Procedure Rules.[3]

It should be noted that the obligation applied only to documents within the power and possession of the person obliged,[4] and did not extend to an obligation upon him to secure documents from third parties,[5] or to documents in the possession of his employees in their private capacity.[6]

It should be noted in general that the obligation to disclose was a continuing one, which remained in force until judgment, so affecting evidence acquired after initial discovery and production,[7] and that there was an obligation not to use materials obtained in this way otherwise than in the litigation for which they were disclosed.[8]

Lord Woolf identified[9] excessive disclosure as one of the two principal defects of the old system of procedure, and proposed radical change in this area. In very broad outline he recommended more general pre-trial and non-party disclosure,[10] but a reduced obligation to disclose in the course of litigation.[11]

(ii) Exchange of witness statements[12]

In civil cases at common law[13] the traditional position was that all the evidence was normally given viva voce at the hearing, but here too the position underwent a revolution in recent times. As Lord Donaldson MR said in *Mercer v Chief Constable of Lancashire*:[14]

> Over the last quarter of a century there has been a sea change in legislative and judicial attitudes towards the conduct of litigation, taking the form of increased positive case management by the judiciary and the adoption of procedures designed (a) to identify the real issues in dispute and (b) to enable each party to assess the relative strengths and weaknesses of his own and his opponent's case at the earliest possible moment and well before any trial. Not only does this

3   Part 31. See under the old rules *Wallace Smith Trust Co Ltd v Deloitte Haskins and Sells* [1996] 4 All ER 403, [1997] 1 WLR 257; *British and Commonwealth Holdings plc v Barclays De Zoete Wedd Ltd* [1999] 1 BCLC 86.
4   Which does not include those which he is under a statutory obligation not to disclose: *Re Galileo Group Ltd* [1999] Ch 100, [1998] 1 All ER 545.
5   *Dubai Bank v Galadari (No 6)* (1992) Times, 14 October. It should be noted that in the case of litigation involving a department of government, other departments are not regarded as third parties: *R v Blackledge* [1996] 1 Cr App Rep 326.
6   *Macmillan Inc v Bishopsgate Investment Trust plc* [1993] 4 All ER 998, [1993] 1 WLR 1372.
7   *Vernon v Bosley (No2)* [1999] QB 18, [1997] 1 All ER 614. The rule in Ireland is less stringent: *Bula Ltd v Tara Mines (No 5)* [1994] IR 487.
8   *Riddick v Thames Board Mills Ltd* [1977] QB 881, [1977] 3 All ER 677, strictly applied in *Miller v Scorey* [1996] 1 WLR 1122, [1996] 3 All ER 18.
9   *Access to Justice* para 13.1.
10 Implemented by Civil Procedure (Modification of Enactments) Order 1998, SI 1998/2940 coming into force at the same time as the Civil Procedure Rules. See also Civil Procedure Rule 31.18.
11 Standard disclosure is limited by Civil Procedure Rules 31.6, 31.7 to those documents upon which a party relies or which after reasonable search (i) adversely affect his own case; (ii) adversely affect another party's case; (iii) support another party's case; or which he is required to disclose by a practice direction. It is envisaged that the process will be a continuing one actively supervised by the judge. See further ch XVI below.
12 See generally the Civil Procedure Rules Pt 32; cp the old system under RSC Ord 38, r 2A, as amended by SI 1992/1907.
13 But not in Chancery where it was more often prepared before the hearing and sealed up in the form of an affidavit to be revealed only at the trial.
14 [1991] 2 All ER 504, at 508,509, [1991] 1 WLR 367, at 373.

make for shorter trials and save costs, even more important it facilitates and encourages settlements. The most important change has been the requirement that, save in exceptional cases, witness statements be exchanged prior to the trial.

This system of advance provision of evidence began in limited areas, but was gradually extended to embrace the whole range of legal proceedings.[15] Although such statements could stand as evidence in the case,[16] they did not become evidence until the trial. It was for this reason that no objection on the ground of privilege could be raised in relation to them, since they could be used only with the consent of the party adducing the evidence, and by so doing he waived his privilege in the statements,[17] and to the extent that he intended to adduce them, privilege in associated documents referred to.[18] In this way the aim of the change, to encourage full exchange in advance of the trial was promoted, without trenching on fundamental rights.[19] It should be stressed that such exchange always was within the discretion of the court which might sometimes be exercised against exchange so as to prevent injustice, or even extraneous harm.[20]

Similar provision for the advance production of other evidential material was made by the old Ord 38, r 5, and there was no exemption from this in the case of a video recording of a party, even though it might suggest that a claim were fraudulent.[1] Even in the case of sensitive matters involving children the presumption favoured disclosure.[2]

This broad system has been built upon and clarified by Part 32 of the Civil Procedure Rules. The main feature of this part is the extensive power of the judge to control the process, but it is envisaged that witness statements[3] will normally be exchanged in advance for use in pre-trial proceedings, and will stand as evidence in chief at the trial, although the maker will normally be required to be present for cross-examination, or, with the leave of the court, to amplify the witness statement.

(iii)   Affidavits[4]

In a number of cases, specially provided for by Rules of Court, evidence may be by affidavit.[5] This was allowed in matters coming before the Chancery Division on

---

15   The terms of the rule were unlimited, and accorded a literal construction in *Richard Saunders & Partners v Eastglen Ltd* [1990] 3 All ER 946. It applied also to proceedings in the county court: CCR Ord 20, r 12A. A similar approach was taken to proceedings for committal for contempt: *Re B* [1996] 1 WLR 627.
16   Though they need not necessarily have done so, and in case of conflict the judge could order the witness to attend to give oral evidence: *Cole v Kivells* (1997) Times, 2 May.
17   The extent of any such waiver was however determined by the law of privilege: see *Abigroup Ltd v Akins* (1997) 42 NSWLR 623.
18   *Vista Maritime Inc v Sesa Goa* [1997] CLC 1600. In *Clough v Tameside and Glossop Health Authority* [1998] 2 All ER 971 this was extended to include otherwise privileged background material relied on and referred to in the otherwise privileged material disclosed.
19   An approach explained by Hoffmann J in *Comfort Hotels Ltd v Wembley Stadium Ltd* [1988] 3 All ER 53, [1988] 1 WLR 872, and endorsed in Courts and Legal Services Act 1990, s 5(2).
20   See *B v B (Child Abuse Evidence)* [1991] 2 FLR 487 refusing to order the advance provision of a video recording a child's allegations of abuse to the allegedly abusing party.
1   *Khan v Armaguard Ltd* [1994] 3 All ER 545, [1994] 1 WLR 1204. Cp in Canada *Chmara v Nguyen* (1993) 104 DLR (3d) 244.
2   *Re D (minors) (adoption reports: confidentiality)* [1996] AC 593, [1995] 4 All ER 385; *Re M (minors) (disclosure of evidence)* [1994] 1 FLR 760.
3   If a witness statement cannot be obtained, then a witness summary may be used: see Civil Procedure Rule 32.9.
4   See generally Civil Procedure Rule 32.15, formerly RSC Ord 41.
5   And is now required to be in those cases specified in para 1.4 of Practice Direction 32 under the Civil Procedure Rules.

originating summons or motion, and orders could be made for the proof of particular facts by affidavit on an interlocutory summons in any division of the High Court. The statements in the affidavit were, of course, not subject to cross-examination, and were sometimes based on the knowledge, information or belief of the deponent, but, in appropriate cases, he could be obliged to attend for cross-examination.[6]

One of the changes made here by the Civil Procedure Rules is that interim orders can be supported not only by affidavits, but by witness statements, or the facts stated in the application for the order or in the statement of case filed in the proceedings, provided that there is a statement of truth.[7]

(iv) Commissions

Under the old Ord 39, r 1, of the Rules of the Supreme Court, the court or a judge could, in any cause or matter where it appeared necessary for the purposes of justice, make any order for the examination upon oath before the court or judge or any officer of the court, or any other person, and at any place, of any witness or person, and empower any party to any such cause or matter to give such deposition in evidence therein, on such terms, if any, as the court or a judge directed. The order was usually made when the witness was ill or abroad, or likely to be abroad at the time of the hearing. A practising lawyer, rather than an officer of the court, was usually named as examiner. The witnesses, parties and advocates attended before him, and the witnesses were examined, cross-examined and re-examined. The examiner took a note of any objection to the admissibility of evidence that was raised. The judge could allow the deposition to be read at the hearing, without the consent of the party against whom it was given only if the maker was still unable to attend court.[8]

These rules are now subsumed within Part 34 of the Civil Procedure Rules which deals with the whole question of depositions and the court attendance of witnesses.

(v) Letters of request[9]

Letters of request may be issued to a foreign, dominion or colonial court asking one of their judges to take the evidence of a specific person within the jurisdiction of the court.[10] The depositions are remitted to the High Court, and may be read at the trial.[11] Documents may be requested under the inherent jurisdiction of the court, provided that they are

---

6   But not normally before the trial: *Lonrho plc v Fayed (No 3)* (1993) Times, 24 June, although this has been allowed in relation to an affidavit of assets in relation to a Mareva injunction: *Yukong Line Ltd of Korea v Rendsburg Investment Corpn of Liberia* [1996] 2 Lloyd's Rep 604.

7   Practice Direction 32, para 1.3.

8   The governing statute remains the Supreme Court Act 1981, s 36, which applies to securing evidence for both civil and criminal cases, and from both within the United Kingdom and abroad. The taking of evidence in England for the use of a foreign court is governed by the Evidence (Proceedings in Other Jurisdictions) Act 1975: see *State of Norway's Application* [1990] 1 AC 723, [1989] 1 All ER 745; *First American Corpn v Sheikh Zayed Al-Nahayan* [1998] 4 All ER 439; and is also subject to the Protection of Trading Interests Act 1980. See also RSC Ord 70 which is an interlocking order preserved by Sch 1 to the Civil Procedure Rules. Any restrictions cannot be evaded by starting parallel domestic proceedings, *Dailey Petroleum Services Corpn v Pioneer Oil Tools Ltd* (1993) Times, 3 December. Such evidence may be ordered to be supplied on videotape: *J Barber & Sons v Lloyd's Underwriters* [1987] QB 103, [1986] 2 All ER 845. For the position in Scotland see *Stewart v Callaghan* 1996 SLT 12.

9   See the Civil Procedure Rules Part 34, esp 34.13, PD 34, para 5.

10   It is for the recipient court to determine whether to reply, for example if the request has become stale: *R v Central Criminal Court, ex p Hunt* (1995) Times, 21 February.

11   Civil Procedure Rule 34.11.

specified with particularity similar to that required in relation to a subpoena duces tecum, and that the request is not camouflage for extended discovery.[12] It should be noted that now that the Civil Procedure Rules[13] have clarified and confirmed the practice of securing evidence from abroad by video link or other means the use of letters of request may become rather rare.

(vi)   Further information[14]

The old system of interrogatories has been replaced with a simplified procedure for securing further information by way of request and response, the latter of which must be supported by a statement of truth.

2.   Criminal cases

Here, as in the case of civil proceedings, there has been radical change in relation to pre-trial procedural provision. Particular attention has been directed to the situations in which disclosure must be made by one side to the other before the trial. This will be mentioned first, and then the section will go on to consider the various provisions permitting evidence recorded before the trial to be used at it. Agreed statements of fact may be received under the s 9 of the Criminal Justice Act 1967. Statements secured at the instance of liquidators of a company under the provisions of s 236 of the Insolvency Act 1986, or by officers of the Serious Fraud Office under the provisions of s 2 of the Criminal Justice Act 1987 may be required for use in evidence, as may evidence secured under various other statutory provisions.

(i)   Disclosure[15]

This part of the law has been transformed by the passage of the Criminal Procedure and Investigation Act 1996.[16] That legislation has replaced the common law[17] with a new statutory scheme,[18] the full practical effects of which are still being established. It was designed to alleviate the burdens of disclosure perceived to lie upon the police and prosecution under the old law, which it was felt were being exploited by those accused of crime.[19] It is proposed here first to outline the new procedure, then to consider the nature of the material to which it applies, its effects, and its evaluation,

---

12   *Panayiotou v Sony Music Entertainment (UK) Ltd* [1994] Ch 142, [1994] 1 All ER 755.
13   Rule 32.3. For the previous practice see *Garcin v Amerindo Investment Advisors Ltd* [1991] 4 All ER 655, [1991] 1 WLR 1140. See in New Zealand *B v Dentists' Disciplinary Tribunal* [1994] 1 NZLR 95 reviewing the position in the whole common law world.
14   See generally the Civil Procedure Rules Part 18.
15   See the extensive and learned discussion of the history of this topic in *R v Sobh* [1994] 1 VR 41. For discussion of the impact of the Human Rights Act 1998 see Sharpe [1999] Crim LR 273.
16   Parts I and II, and its accompanying regulations, and Code of Practice.
17   With the sole exception of the rules relating to material subject to restriction on grounds of public policy, s 21(2). See further ch XI below. Although it does not explicitly concern itself with the period between arrest and committal it has effectively supplanted the common law there also: *R v DPP, ex p Lee* [1999] 2 All ER 737.
18   Universally and compulsorily for trials on indictment, and voluntarily (s 6) for summary trials.
19   Home Office Consultation Paper *Disclosure* (Cm 2864, 1995) ch 1. See Ley (1995) 145 NLJ 1124 for suggestions of manipulation of the common law rules by the prosecution.

especially in the light of the impending incorporation of the European Convention of Human Rights. The section will finally consider other possible means of securing pre-trial disclosure.

(a)   Outline of provisions
The broad scheme[20] of the legislation imposes a staged process, shifting between the parties: first upon the investigator of crime a duty to record[1] and retain[2] relevant material; then for the prosecutor[3] to make primary disclosure to the defence of material which it is not proposed to use, but which in his judgment might undermine the case for the prosecution,[4] and a schedule listing other unused non-sensitive material;[5] then for the accused to disclose the nature of the defence;[6] then for the prosecutor to make secondary disclosure of any material, not so far disclosed by him, which in the light of its disclosure might reasonably be expected to assist the defence;[7] and finally in the event of a dispute for the defence to raise it, and the court to dispose of it.[8] The situation must be kept under review, and the prosecutor must continue to disclose further material which comes to his attention, and would have had to be disclosed either on the primary or secondary basis.[9]

(b)   Nature of material to be disclosed
Since there is as yet a dearth of authority on the interpretation of the provisions of the new Act, it is perhaps helpful to consider the most recent high authority on the construction of the old law, at least to the extent that it employs the same terminology, especially where the litigation was conducted in awareness of the imminence of the new provisions coming into force. Under the old criteria for prosecution disclosure as set out in *R v Keane*[10] three categories are required to be disclosed: relevant evidence; evidence raising a new issue; and evidence which might realistically lead to either of the preceding categories. It seems that the use of the phrase 'might undermine' the prosecution case was designed to be narrower than the notion of relevance.[11] Its width can also be assessed by reference to the definition of material to be disclosed at the secondary stage, which includes anything which might reasonably be expected to assist the accused's defence as disclosed. It is left unclear whether the prosecution can at the primary stage disregard defences which might be raised, but which appear to it unlikely, or whether the secondary stage is expected to cater only for defences which could not have been anticipated at all.

Shortly before the Criminal Procedure and Investigation Act 1996 was brought into force the House of Lords considered the obligation to disclose material going to the

---

20   For full discussion see Leng and Taylor *Criminal Procedure and Investigation Act 1996* (1996).
1   Section 23(1)(b).
2   Section 23(1)(c).
3   But only after committal papers have been served. S 47 and Sch I make substantial and significant alterations to committal procedures, and the use of material employed in them.
4   Section 3. For criticism of the uncertain criterion of 'undermining' see Sharpe (1999) 63 J Cr L 67.
5   Section 4.
6   Section 5.
7   Section 7.
8   Section 8.
9   Section 9.
10   (1994) 99 Cr App Rep 1.
11   *Disclosure* para 26; 567 HL Official Report cols 1437–1438.

credibility of its own, or the defence's probable witnesses. In *R v Brown*[12] it was held that there was no obligation to disclose in advance evidence which damaged the credibility of a defence witness. This seems entirely in accordance with the policy underlying the new legislation. This is less obviously true of the House's decision in *R v Mills and Poole*[13] that the prosecution should disclose statements made by its witnesses which are inconsistent with the evidence they are expected to give in court.[14] The obligation to disclose previous convictions and disciplinary offences of prosecution witnesses was upheld in *R v Guney*,[15] and indeed amplified to include specific material of a discreditable nature explicitly requested by the defence,[16] and evidence of any previous cases where the prosecutions had failed on account of the lack of veracity of such witnesses. It was regarded as immaterial that such material might not have been capable of being deployed at trial by the defence.

At no stage is the prosecution bound to disclose material which it is held not to be in the public interest to disclose,[17] or which is barred under the Interception of Communications Act 1985.[18]

It should be noted that the new legislation relates only to disclosure of information in the possession of the prosecutor, or inspected by him.[19] It leaves unaffected the common law in relation to third party disclosure,[20] and the procedure for determining its materiality.[1]

So far as defence disclosure is concerned s 5 requires reasoned disclosure of the general nature of the defence and of disputed parts of the prosecution case,[2] and in addition in the case of an alibi, names and addresses of, or information which might help the prosecution to locate, witnesses to the alibi.

(c) Effect

It is necessary to consider both the effect of non-disclosure,[3] and of disclosure. If the prosecution fails in its obligation to make primary disclosure it runs the risk of any

---

12 [1998] AC 367, [1997] 3 All ER 769. This also accords with the decision in *R v Imran and Hussain* [1997] Crim LR 754 that there is no obligation to disclose evidence to a suspect at an early stage which might indicate what parts of a potential statement could be demonstrated to be lies.

13 [1998] AC 382, [1997] 3 All ER 780, overruling *R v Bryant and Dickson* (1946) 31 Cr App Rep 146. Some reliance was placed upon the decision of the Supreme Court of Canada in *R v Stinchcombe* [1991] 3 SCR 326.

14 Although this very situation is used to exemplify the obligation to give primary disclosure in *Disclosure* para 46.

15 [1998] 2 Cr App Rep 242, also decided under the old law.

16 One of the reasons for the reform was to seek to prevent purely speculative, or fishing, enquiries: *Disclosure* para 19.

17 It may be expected that under the new law, as much as under the old, the court will be astute to detect cases where the defence has been specially manufactured to justify disclosure, or more accurately abandonment of the prosecution in lieu of non-disclosure: see *R v Turner* [1995] 3 All ER 432, [1995] 1 WLR 264.

18 Sections 3(6), (7); 7(5), (6); 8(4), (5).

19 Section 3(2).

20 See *R v Maguire* [1992] QB 936, [1992] 2 All ER 433. For the obligation of a complainant to submit to a medical examination in advance of trial, see in New Zealand *R v B (No 2)* [1995] 2 NZLR 752.

1   See *R v Whittle* [1997] 1 Cr App Rep 166.

2   This represents a softening of the recommendation in *Disclosure* para 51 of extension of the requirement to provide names and addresses in respect of all defence witnesses. For a common law approach to advance disclosure of alibi evidence, see in Canada *R v Cleghorn* [1995] 3 SCR 175.

3   Widely construed here to include defective disclosure.

conviction being overturned as unsafe, as at common law; and if it fails even to purport to comply, no obligation upon the defence to disclose arises. Delay in compliance will amount to abuse of process, only if as a result the accused is denied a fair trial.[4] In the case of the defence, disclosure under s 5 is required as a condition precedent to an application under s 8 for further or better disclosure by the prosecution. Section 11(3) also permits comment upon non-disclosure by the defence where disclosure is required, and allows adverse inferences to be drawn.[5] These are not to amount to the sole evidence to justify conviction,[6] but may apparently help to constitute a case to answer. It seems that they will justify a direct conclusion of guilt, and that their effect will not simply be to negate the defences which were not raised or sufficiently supported.[7]

Where information has been disclosed in criminal proceedings the question has arisen of the extent to which it can be used for collateral purposes outside those proceedings, for example to found a civil claim for defamation. To the extent that the disclosure is of material not intended to be used by the prosecution pursuant to the Criminal Procedure and Investigation Act 1996, such collateral use is regulated by s 17. The effect of that section is broadly to ban the collateral use of such material,[8] unless it has been read out in open court.

(d) Evaluation[9]

The motivation for the Criminal Procedure and Investigation Act 1996 was to withhold some relevant material from disclosure in advance to the defence, yet in *Edwards v United Kingdom*[10] the European Court of Human Rights had pronounced disclosure of all material evidence to the accused to be a requirement of a fair trial pursuant to art 6 of the Convention. Conversely it was intended to put pressure upon the defence to provide more detail of its intended defence in advance, and to employ failure satisfactorily to comply to help construct a prima facie case, yet in *Saunders v United Kingdom*[11] the use of compulsorily acquired material was also regarded as derogating from a fair trial. While it is not impossible to reconcile the current state of the law with those decisions, the incorporation of the European Convention of Human Rights seems likely to lead, at the very least, to a restrictive interpretation of these provisions.

(e) Other means

The courts are astute to prevent the prosecution from obtaining the effect of compulsory disclosure of evidence in advance by other means, except where expressly contemplated by a statutory provision. Thus in *R v Crown Court at Southwark, ex p Bowles*[12] the

---

4　Section 10.
5　In terminology very similar to that in comparable parts of the Criminal Justice and Public Order Act 1994.
6　Section 11(5).
7　By analogy with the construction of the similar phraseology of s 35 of the Criminal Justice and Public Order Act 1994 in *R v Cowan* [1996] QB 373, [1995] 4 All ER 939.
8　Except after application to, and with the leave of, the court, s 17(4), even in civil proceedings: *Taylor v Serious Fraud Office* [1998] 4 All ER 801.
9　For discussion of disclosure in the United States see *Brady v Maryland* 373 US 83 (1963); *Kyles v Whitley* 514 US 419 (1995). For the impact of Charter considerations on disclosure obligations in Canada see *R v Chaplin* [1995] 1 SCR 727 (onus in relation to suspected wiretapping); *R v O'Connor* [1995] 4 SCR 411 (medical records of complainants); *R v Carosella* [1997] 1 SCR 80 (destruction of records to pre-empt disclosure); *R v La* [1997] 2 SCR 680 (lost records).
10　(1992) 15 EHRR 417.
11　(1997) 23 EHRR 313. As seems now to have been recognised by the interpolation of cl 58 into the Youth Justice and Criminal Evidence Bill 1999.
12　[1998] AC 641, [1998] 2 All ER 193.

House of Lords condemned an attempt to secure disclosure of material from a third party with a view to its use in subsequent criminal proceedings, by use of an application[13] for the information to determine whether a person had benefited from criminal conduct. It should also be noted that a witness summons under s 2 of the Criminal Procedure (Attendance of Witnesses) Act 1965 can be addressed only to documents which are likely to be material evidence, and thus not to those which may lead to the discovery of such evidence, or which could be used only in cross-examination.[14]

(ii)   Committal proceedings

Committal proceedings have been modified by Sch I to the Criminal Procedure and Investigation Act 1996. Under the new provisions committal is to be made on the basis of documents and exhibits only. One drastic, and rather surprising, change is to permit statements and depositions of witnesses at such proceedings to stand as evidence in the trial,[15] thus creating another huge exception to the hearsay rule,[16] subject only to discretionary exclusion.[17] It is, as yet, quite unclear how this discretion will be exercised.

(iii)   Coroners

When depositions are taken by a coroner, there does not appear to be any similar statutory provision for their being read at any trial that takes place on the coroner's inquisition; but in *R v Cowle*[18] it was held that the deposition of a dead deponent might be read if it was signed by him and the coroner, and the accused had had an opportunity of cross-examination.

(iv)   Letters of request

Given that hearsay has been made more widely admissible in criminal cases under the provisions of the Criminal Justice Act 1988, and following the recommendations of the Roskill Committee,[19] provision has been made for evidence to be secured for the purposes of criminal proceedings by the issue of letters of request.[1] Such evidence may be secured even before proceedings have been instituted, if they are likely to be so instituted if the evidence is obtained, and the procedure may also be invoked by the accused, though in his case only if proceedings have been instituted. Such evidence

---

13   Under Criminal Justice Act 1988, s 93H.
14   *R v Reading Justices, ex p Reading County Council* [1996] 1 Cr App Rep 239.
15   Section 68, and Sch II.
16   Exacerbated by the width of the power of the magistrates to order depositions under s 97A of the Magistrates' Courts Act 1980, and associated rules.
17   Deplored for this reason, and repeal recommended, by the Law Commission in Law Com No 245 *Evidence in Criminal Proceedings: Hearsay and Related Topics* (Cm 3670, 1997) paras 8.108–8.113, rec 21.
18   (1907) 71 JP 152, contra *R v Butcher* (1900) 64 JP 808; see also *R v Black* (1909) 74 JP 71 and *R v Marriott* (1911) 75 JP 288. In Australia there is discretion to reject such a deposition, *R v Collins* [1986] VR 37.
19   Report of the Departmental Inquiry on Fraud Trials 1986, para 5.43.
1   Criminal Justice (International Co-operation) Act 1990, s 3. This legislation also provides in s 4 for the converse situation where evidence is required for a criminal court overseas, and even for the mutual international transportation of prisoners to testify, ss 5–6. See *R v Secretary of State for the Home Department, ex p Fininvest SPA* [1997] 1 Cr App Rep 257.

must satisfy the provisions of ss 23 or 24,[2] and is further subject to the discretionary control of s 25, though it is excluded from the requirements of s 26.[3] Evidence may also be secured from abroad by videolink, even in the absence of extradition from the jurisdiction concerned.[4]

(v)   Statements under s 9 of the Criminal Justice Act 1967[5]

Agreed statements may be admitted under these provisions, but it is arguable that there is such a discrepancy between the detail of the rules that govern the recording of statements made by the accused and the informality which obtains in this context that reform is required.[6]

(vi)   Statements under s 236 of Insolvency Act 1986

Section 236 allows the liquidators of a company to invoke the assistance of the court to conduct a compulsory investigation so as to assist with the recovery of assets. The threat of such an investigation may be sufficient to induce witnesses to provide evidence on a voluntary basis to the liquidators. This was the situation in *R v Clowes*[7] where the question arose of whether the transcripts of such interviews could be secured for use by the defendants in subsequent criminal proceedings. Since the transcripts were not merely relevant but also admissible[8] it was held that their production could be compelled.[9] Although it was recognised that this would to some extent impinge upon the confidentiality of such statements it was nevertheless held that on balance the interests of justice in enabling the accused to present a defence to a serious charge should prevail.

(vii)   Statements under s 2 of the Criminal Justice Act 1987

This provision permits compulsory interrogation by officials of the Serious Fraud Office of those believed to be in possession of information relevant to the investigation of serious fraud. The legislation further provides that evidence so obtained shall not be generally admissible in evidence in subsequent criminal proceedings,[10] but may be used as a previous inconsistent statement.[11] Such statements may be obtained even

---

2   Section 23(2)(b) will probably be invoked most often.
3   It has been suggested the courts adopt a more inclusionary approach to the exercise of discretion over evidence obtained abroad, see Gane and Mackerel [1997] Crim LR 720.
4   *R v Forsyth* [1997] 2 Cr App Rep 299.
5   See further below p 593.
6   Heaton-Armstrong and Wolchover [1992] Crim LR 160.
7   [1992] 3 All ER 440; see also *Re Barlow Clowes Gilt Managers Ltd* [1992] Ch 208, [1991] 4 All ER 385.
8   As a result of s 24 of the Criminal Justice Act 1988, see further below p 585, thus enabling the contrary decision in *R v Cheltenham Justices, ex p Secretary of State for Trade* [1977] 1 All ER 460, [1977] 1 WLR 95 to be distinguished.
9   So long at least as they were at least conditionally required with a view to being adduced as evidence of their contents, and not simply to being used for purposes of contradiction in cross-examination.
10   It is admissible on charges ancillary to the power itself under s 2(14) of the Act. Nor need material obtained under these powers be disclosed to the defence while the investigation is continuing: *R v Serious Fraud Office, ex p Maxwell* (1992) Times, 9 October.
11   Section 2(8)(b).

after criminal proceedings have been commenced,[12] and the trial judge has no power to regulate the process of securing them.[13]

(viii)   Miscellaneous statutory provisions

Under s 42 and s 43 of the Children and Young Persons Act 1933, the deposition of a child or young person may be taken out of court, and used at the preliminary examination or trial of a person for an offence under the Act.[14] The conditions are that the child's attendance in court would cause serious danger to his life or health, and that the accused should have had an opportunity of cross-examining him.[15] These provisions were not regarded as affording sufficient protection for young children, and have now been supplemented by permitting young children[16] to testify by live television link in certain proceedings by leave of the court.[17] The aim of providing for a live link was to preserve the possibility of cross-examination, but a strong body of opinion felt that this still failed to provide sufficient protection, and that video recordings of interviews before the trial were preferable.[18] The matter was highly controversial, since there is a clear danger of prejudice to the accused if he is unable to make an effective challenge to any possible leading of perhaps suggestible witnesses.[19] Accordingly a compromise has been adopted whereby a child's evidence in chief may in certain circumstances take the form of a video recording, but only when the child is available for cross-examination[20] by the accused.[1] It has been held that in such circumstances the judge has a discretion to permit the jury to witness[2] a replay of the tape after retiring.

It should be noted that the Family Proceedings Rules[3] require application to the court to disclose for the purposes of criminal, or disciplinary,[4] proceedings any documents adduced in care proceedings under the Children Act 1989.

12   *R v Director of Serious Fraud Office, ex p Smith* [1993] AC 1, [1992] 3 All ER 456. The position has now been reconsidered in the light of the decision of the European Court of Human Rights in *Saunders v United Kingdom* (1996) 23 EHRR 313, and amendment has been proposed in the Youth Justice and Criminal Evidence Bill 1999.
13   *R v Nadir* [1993] 4 All ER 513, [1993] 1 WLR 1322.
14   See Spencer and Tucker (1987) NLJ 816.
15   See also Children and Young Persons Act 1963, as to committal proceedings in the case of sexual offences.
16   And witnesses who are outside the United Kingdom, in their case without limitation as to the class of proceeding.
17   Criminal Justice Act 1988, s 32, as amended. See generally above p 214.
18   See Spencer [1987] Crim LR 76; Temkin 140 NLJ 352, 410.
19   Such fears find some justification in judicial criticism of commonly used interviewing techniques in cases of alleged sexual abuse of children where such recordings have been tendered in civil proceedings, see, eg *C v C* [1987] 1 FLR 321. In the United States it has been held contrary to the confrontation clause in the constitution even to screen a child witness from the accused: *Coy v Iowa* 487 US 1012 (1988), but see also *Maryland v Craig* 497 US 836 (1990).
20   Criminal Justice Act 1991, s 54 inserting a new s 32A in the Criminal Justice Act 1988 adopting parts of the recommendations of the Report of the Advisory Committee on Video Evidence (1989); see in New Zealand *R v Accused (32/91)* [1992] 1 NZLR 257.
1   Though not in person.
2   But only in open court, subject to being reminded of any criticism in cross-examination, and upon direction that it should not attach increased importance to evidence which it would then hear twice: *R v Rawlings; R v Broadbent* [1995] 1 All ER 580, [1995] 1 WLR 178.
3   Rule 4.23: see *Re G (A Minor) (Social Worker: Disclosure)* [1996] 2 All ER 65, [1996] 1 WLR 1407; *Re C (A Minor) (Care Proceedings:Disclosure)* [1997] Fam 76, [1996] 2 FLR 725.
4   *Re A (A minor) (Disclosure of medical records to GMC)* [1999] 1 FCR 30.

B.   THE RIGHT TO BEGIN

The claimant, prosecutor or their respective advocates open every case in the sense that they explain the issues to the court, but questions sometimes arise concerning the right to begin calling evidence.

The Crown will almost always have the right to begin in criminal cases where there is a plea of not guilty,[5] because there will be some issue upon which the evidential, if not the legal, burden will be borne by the prosecution; but, now that there can be formal admissions and agreed statements of fact under s 10 and s 9 of the Criminal Justice Act 1967, respectively, there can be exceptional cases in which the accused has the right to begin.

In civil cases, the judge now has wide powers to regulate the way in which evidence is presented.[6] Under the old law the claimant had the right to begin unless the defendant had the burden of proof on every issue[7] and, in this context, 'burden of proof' was taken to mean 'evidential burden'.[8] This was established in *Mercer v Whall*,[9] a claim for wrongful dismissal in which the defendant admitted that he determined the claimant's contract of service prematurely, but alleged that he was justified in doing so. It was held that the claimant ought to begin calling evidence because the damages claimed by him were not agreed. If damages had not been in issue, the defendant would have had the right to begin, because there would have been no fact with regard to which the claimant bore the evidential burden.

C.   THE ADVOCATES' SPEECHES

The judge's decision on who is to begin the case may affect the order in which the advocates' speeches are made to the court. If the old procedure is followed in civil cases, if the claimant begins, he will open the case to the court,[10] call his witnesses and sum up if the defendant does not call witnesses. The defendant will then reply and thus secure the last word. If the defendant calls witnesses, the claimant will not sum up at the conclusion of his case, but the defendant will open his case, call his witnesses and sum up, leaving the claimant with the right of reply. The foregoing procedure will be reversed if the defendant begins.

In criminal cases tried on indictment, the prosecutor opens and calls his evidence. If the accused does not call evidence, the prosecutor sums up leaving the accused with the right of reply. If the accused calls evidence, the prosecutor's closing speech is made after the close of the evidence for the defence with the result that the accused

---

5   Where a special plea is raised, such as autrefois convict, and there is a dispute of fact, the accused would begin. A plea of guilty does not admit everything on the depositions (*R v Riley* [1896] 1 QB 309, at 318; *R v Maitland* [1964] SASR 332 according to which an accused pleading guilty should call evidence as to disputed facts).

6   Civil Procedure Rule 32.1.

7   Ord 35, r 7(6).

8   *Re Parry's Estate, Parry v Fraser* [1977] 1 All ER 309, [1977] 1 WLR 93n; *Pontifex v Jolly* (1839) 9 C & P 202, showing that an amendment will not be allowed for the sole purpose of altering the right to begin. See *W Lusty & Sons Ltd v Morris Wilkinson & Co (Nottingham) Ltd* [1954] 2 All ER 347, [1954] 1 WLR 911 showing that, where a claim is admitted in court, the defendant may begin calling evidence on his counterclaim. See also *Seldon v Davidson* [1968] 2 All ER 755, [1968] 1 WLR 1083.

9   (1845) 5 QB 447.

10   He must not allude to facts with regard to which he cannot call evidence (*Faith v M'Intyre* (1835) 7 C & P 44; *R v O'Neill* (1950) 34 Cr App Rep 108).

has the right of reply.[11] In both civil and criminal cases, the above procedure may be interspersed with a submission that there is no case to answer, arguments about the admissibility of evidence,[12] or arguments on points of law.

D.   THE CALLING OF WITNESSES AND THE ROLE OF THE JUDGE

It was said in the first paragraph of this chapter that the essential feature of the English adversary or accusatorial system of justice is the questioning of witnesses by the parties or their representatives, summoned for the most part by them, and called mainly in the order of their choice before a judge acting as umpire rather than as inquisitor.[13] A few words may now be added by way of enlargement on and qualification of these remarks. All the matters discussed belong rather to the realm of procedure than to that of evidence.

Most of the qualifications relate to criminal proceedings. In civil cases the parties may call as many or as few witnesses able to give admissible evidence as they choose, in the order which commends itself to them,[14] and the judge can call a witness only with their consent.[15] In criminal cases the prosecution is obliged to call certain witnesses and to have others available to be called by the defence, there is a restriction on the order in which defence witnesses may be called and the judge may[16] call a witness without the consent of the parties.

The advent of the Criminal Procedure and Investigation Act 1996 has changed the situation relating to the tendering of witnesses and statements to the defence completely. It is now settled that the prosecution discharges its obligation to the defence by reading a committal statement.[17] If a witness is, in the opinion of the prosecutor, incapable of belief there is no need to use the statement for committal purposes, or to call the witness at trial. Whether it should be disclosed will depend: at the primary stage, upon the prosecutor's opinion as to whether of not it might undermine the prosecution case, and at the secondary stage, upon whether it might assist the defence. It seems that the prosecutor will not reasonably consider a statement unworthy of belief simply because it is inconsistent with the majority of the evidence supporting the prosecution

11   Criminal Procedure (Right of Reply) Act 1964. For further details see Archbold (1998 edn) ch 4–XV. For summary trial see Magistrates' Courts Rules 1981, rr 13 and 14.

12   If, as will usually be the case, counsel knows that objection will be taken to an item of evidence, he should not refer to it in opening, and the objection should be raised when the evidence is about to be given (*R v Cole* (1941) 28 Cr App Rep 43; *R v Zielinski* (1950) 34 Cr App Rep 193). This procedure can be applied to civil cases tried with a jury. The point is not so important when there is no jury.

13   Re-emphasised in *R v Grafton* [1993] QB 101, at 104, [1992] 4 All ER 609, at 610, 611.

14   *Briscoe v Briscoe* [1968] P 501, [1966] 1 All ER 465. Cp *Vernon v Bosley* [1995] 2 FCR 78; and risks as to costs. In the Commercial Court the judge can direct that factual evidence from both parties be heard before evidence from experts if that appears to him to be desirable, *Bayer v Clarkson Puckle Overseas Ltd* [1989] NLJR 256.

15   *Re Enoch and Zaretsky, Bock & Co's Arbitration* [1910] 1 KB 327: but such consent is unnecessary on motions to commit for contempt (*Yianni v Yianni* [1966] 1 All ER 231n, [1966] 1 WLR 120). Opinions differ as to whether the limitation still applies in Australia, cp *Obacelo Pty Ltd v Taveraft Pty Ltd* (1986) 66 ALR 371 and *Clark Equipment Credit Pty Ltd v Como Factors Pty Ltd* (1988) 14 NSWLR 552.

16   And should do so, rather than stay the proceedings, where the witness is material, and there are good reasons for neither side wishing to call him: *R v Haringey Justices, ex p DPP* [1996] QB 351, [1996] 1 All ER 828. In New Zealand a full Court of Appeal has said this to be justified in only the most exceptional circumstances: *R v Bishop* [1996] 3 NZLR 399. In Canada the judge is required to enquire why such a witness is not being called by the prosecution: *R v Cook* (1996) 107 CCC (3d) 334.

17   *R v Armstrong* [1995] Crim LR 831.

case.[18] Nor will it be enough that the statement might help the accused to manufacture a false defence.[19] In neither case is the prosecution under an obligation to call the witness itself.[20] On the other hand if witnesses are worthy of belief, named in the indictment, assist the prosecution case and are present in court, then the prosecution is not at liberty simply to close its case, and to refuse to call or tender them.[1] Nevertheless if the prosecution case is sufficiently established by other witnesses, it is not absolutely essential that the victim of a crime testify.[2]

The restriction upon the order in which defence witnesses may be called relates to the accused himself. In *R v Morrison*[3] Lord Alverstone CJ said:

> In all cases I consider it most important for the prisoner to be called before any of his witnesses. He ought to give his evidence before he has heard the evidence and cross-examination of any witnesses he is going to call.

It has since been said that there are rare exceptions to this rule under which a formal witness, or one about whose evidence there is no controversy, might, with the leave of the court, give evidence before the accused.[4] A majority of the Criminal Law Revision Committee thought the rule a good one, but the committee unanimously recommended that the discretion to allow for exceptions should be unlimited.[5] This general rule, and the unfettered discretion to depart from it, has achieved statutory form in the Police and Criminal Evidence Act 1984, s 79.

In civil and criminal proceedings the parties must, as a general rule, call all their evidence before the close of their cases.[6] The authorities are mainly concerned with the question when the Crown may call evidence in rebuttal in criminal proceedings. It was once said that leave to call such evidence should be given only : 'if any matter arises ex improviso which no human ingenuity can foresee',[7] but this formulation of what is universally considered to be a rule of practice rather than law has since been said to be too wide.[8] In *R v Francis*[9] the court's discretion was said to extend beyond merely technical matters or those arising ex improviso, but the court declined to particularise further, except to re-affirm that such extension would be most exceptional.[10]

---

18   *R v Russell-Jones* [1995] 3 All ER 239. [1995] 1 Cr App Rep 538.
19   *R v Brown* [1998] AC 367, [1997] 3 All ER 769.
20   *R v Nugent* [1977] 3 All ER 662, [1977] 1 WLR 789. See also in Australia, *R v Kizon* (1985) 18 ACR 59; and in New Zealand *R v Wilson* [1997] 2 NZLR 500.
1   *R v Wellingborough Magistrates' Court, ex p Francois* (1994) 158 JP 813.
2   *Swanston v DPP* (1997) 161 JP 203.
3   (1911) 6 Cr App Rep 159, at 165.
4   *R v Smith* [1968] 2 All ER 115, [1968] 1 WLR 636.
5   11th Report, para 107.
6   Though in civil cases the court has a general discretion in the interests of justice to allow evidence to be led at a later stage, *Neigut v Hanania* (1983) Times, 6 January; compare *R v Gainsborough Justices, ex p Green* (1984) 78 Cr App Rep 9, illustrating the much more constrained situation in criminal cases, especially after a submission of no case to answer.
7   Per Tindal CJ in *R v Frost* (1839) 4 State Tr NS 85, at 376.
8   *R v Crippen* [1911] 1 KB 149, at 156 per Darling J; *R v Owen* [1952] 2 QB 362, at 366 per Lord Goddard CJ.
9   [1991] 1 All ER 225, 91 Cr App Rep 271. In some circumstances it is acceptable for such further material to be presented by the judge: see *R v Bowles* [1992] Crim LR 726 (reading out an incontrovertible piece of technical evidence apparently inspired by a juror's question).
10   Especially after the case for the defence has been opened (*R v Munnery* (1992) 94 Cr App Rep 164) though it is not barred completely even then: see *R v Doran* (1972) 56 Cr App Rep 429; *R v Patel* [1992] Crim LR 739. The same general rule applies in Australia in civil proceedings: see *Urban Transport Authority of New South Wales v Nweiser* (1992) 28 NSWLR 471. In Canada the prosecution has been prevented from holding back similar fact evidence to rebut a defence of alibi: *R v Biddle* [1995] 1 SCR 761; and adopts a restrictive attitude in general: *R v G(SC)* [1997] 2 SCR 716.

A possible illustration is the admission of a tape recording, as the original evidence, which may be required to resolve a problem with the transcripts upon the basis of which the trial was conducted.[11] In *R v Day*[12] a conviction of forgery was quashed because the judge allowed the prosecution to call a handwriting expert after the close of its case, and the Court of Criminal Appeal considered that the necessity of such evidence should have been foreseen at the outset. The prosecution is not, however, required to react to any suggestion emanating from the accused, especially if it comes outside the evidence given at the trial and appears insubstantial and unlikely to be repeated.[13] It seems that the rule has now become relaxed to the extent of investing the judge with a discretion to permit prosecution evidence in rebuttal of any line of defence which could not reasonably have been anticipated,[14] and the absence of any evidence, or cross-examination, to support a suggestion of fact in counsel's closing argument may be enough.[15] This seems more practicable and more just. The court will normally allow evidence in rebuttal to be called in order to make good a purely formal omission such as the prosecutor's failure to prove that the leave of the Director of Public Prosecutions to bring proceedings had been obtained,[16] especially if earlier objection had deliberately been eschewed for tactical reasons.[17] It would, however, be wrong to allow the Crown to split its case as it wished, especially if in so doing the accused might be compelled to testify in reply, and be exposed to cross-examination.[18]

An even stronger rule prevents further evidence from being adduced after the jury has retired.[19] The jury should be discharged if further evidence emerges after its retirement, unless the defence is prepared for the evidence to be disregarded, and the jury to continue upon that basis.[20] In Ireland however the Supreme Court has held that the judge has a discretion to allow a witness to be called up to the time when the jury returns its verdict.[1] The English rule nevertheless makes for tidiness because the witness who was called would have to be cross-examined, and the process might lead to suggestions that further witnesses should be called.

At a trial on indictment the rule prevents the judge from calling a witness after the jury has retired. Up to that point he has a discretion to do so, although it has been stressed that there must be good reason for such an interference with the adversarial process and reference has even been made to the ex improviso rule in this context.[2]

---

11   *R v Riaz and Burke* (1992) 94 Cr App Rep 339, *R v Tonge* (1993) 157 JP 1137; see above p 53 for discussion of restrictions and conditions.

12   [1940] 1 All ER 402. See also *R v McCarthy* (1984) 14 ACR 73.

13   *R v Hutchinson* (1985) 82 Cr App Rep 51.

14   *R v Scott* (1984) 79 Cr App Rep 49. See also *R v Harrington* [1984] Crim LR 487.

15   *R v O'Hadhmaill* [1996] Crim LR 509.

16   *Price v Humphries* [1958] 2 QB 353, [1958] 2 All ER 725.

17   *Yearly v Crown Prosecution Service* [1997] CLY 1101.

18   See *John v R* [1985] 2 SCR 476; *R v Chin* (1985) 157 CLR 671 where the principle was extended to matters introduced for the first time in cross-examination.

19   *R v Davis* (1975) 62 Cr App Rep 194; as to proceedings before justices, see *Pheland v Back* [1972] 1 All ER 901, [1972] 1 WLR 273. The rule is not so rigid in Australia: see *R v Delon* (1992) 29 NSWLR 29 where a view was taken after the jury had retired.

20   *R v Kaul and Collin* [1998] Crim LR 135.

1   *The People (A-G) v O'Brien* [1963] IR 65. This rule was also recommended in England by the Criminal Law Revision Committee in its 11th Report *Evidence (General)* (Cmnd 4991, 1972) para 216.

2   *R v Cleghorn* [1967] 2 QB 584, [1967] 1 All ER 996 where the conviction was quashed and stress was placed on the fact that, in *R v Tregear* [1967] 2 QB 574, [1967] 1 All ER 989, the judge was in effect requested by the defence to call the witness in question. An examining magistrate probably has no such power in committal proceedings where the only issue is whether the prosecution has presented a prima facie case, *R v Epping and Harlow Justices, ex p Massaro* [1973] QB 433, [1973] 1 All ER 1011. For the position in Australia see *R v Apostilides* (1984) 154 CLR 563; and for that in Canada see *R v Finta* [1994] 1 SCR 701, at 855.

The Court of Appeal will be extremely reluctant to interfere with the discretion of the trial judge, and in *R v Roberts*[3] remarked that it knew of no case where an appeal had been allowed because the trial judge had refused to exercise it to call a witness.

The power to call a witness in criminal cases serves as a reminder that the English judge is more than an umpire in the strict sense of the word. It is true that he must not descend into the dust of the arena,[4] for example by cross-examining a defence witness, and creating the impression of having made up his own mind that the accused is guilty before verdict.[5] Even after re-examination his power to ask questions must be restricted to clarification, and not amount to cross-examination.[6] He may nevertheless intervene to exclude clearly inadmissible evidence despite the absence of any objection by counsel.[7] We have seen that he may exert a very considerable influence over the jury,[8] he has a discretion to exclude certain types of evidence[9] and he can question witnesses in the cause of clarification. His position was well summed up in the following passage from a judgment of Denning LJ:[10]

> In the system of trial which we have evolved in this country, the judge sits to hear and determine the issues raised by the parties, not to conduct an investigation or examination on behalf of society at large as happens, we believe, in some foreign countries. Even in England, however, a judge is not a mere umpire to answer the question 'How's that?' His object, above all, is to find out the truth, and to do justice according to law ...

SECTION 2. EXAMINATION-IN-CHIEF

The object of examination-in-chief is to obtain testimony in support of the version of the facts in issue or relevant to the issue for which the party calling the witness contends. The facts in issue and the concept of relevancy have already been discussed, while the various exclusionary rules which prohibit the proof of certain facts are considered elsewhere in this book. The concern here is with the way in which witnesses who can, ex hypothesi, give relevant and admissible evidence must be treated. Generally speaking they may not be asked leading questions, and, although a witness may refresh his memory by referring to documents previously prepared by him, he cannot usually be asked about his former statements with a view to their becoming evidence of the facts stated, or in order to demonstrate his consistency. A party may call someone else to contradict his witness who has given unfavourable evidence with regard to a fact in issue or relevant to the issue, but he may discredit his witness only if the judge considers that witness to be hostile. This section is accordingly concerned with leading questions, refreshing memory, previous statements of witnesses consistent with their present testimony, and unfavourable or hostile witnesses.

---

3   (1984) 80 Cr App Rep 89, at 96.
4   *R v Grafton* [1993] QB 101, [1992] 4 All ER 609.
5   As in *R v Roncoli* [1998] Crim LR 584.
6   *R v Wiggan* (1999) Times, 22 March.
7   *R v Hook* (1994) 158 JP 1129.
8   Ch IV above.
9   Ch IV, section 2 above.
10 *Jones v National Coal Board* [1957] 2 QB 55, at 63.

A.　LEADING QUESTIONS

I.　Definition and illustration[11]

A leading question is one which either (a) suggests the answer desired, or (b) assumes the existence of disputed facts as to which the witness is to testify.[12] An example of the first type would be the following question put to one of the claimant's witnesses in a running-down case—'Did you see another car coming very fast from the opposite direction?' It should be split up into something like the following—'Did you notice any other traffic? Which direction was it coming from? Was it going fast or slow?' A typical example of the second type of leading question would be, 'What did you do after Smith hit you?' put to the claimant in a claim for assault before he had deposed to being hit by Smith.

Lord Ellenborough once said that if questions are asked to which the answer 'yes' or 'no' would be conclusive, they would certainly be objectionable;[13] but this is untenable as a test for determining whether a question is leading. The answer 'yes' or 'no' would be conclusive to such a question as 'Did you notice any traffic?' but it would not be leading if put to a witness who had just said that he was standing on the side of the road. Again, such a question as 'Did you hear what A said?' would be a leading question of the second type if the presence of A in the witness's company, or the fact that A said anything were in dispute, and as yet unproved by the witness, otherwise it would fall outside the definition of a leading question. As Best said, 'It should never be forgotten that "leading" is a relative, not an absolute term';[14] everything depends on the context.

The answers to leading questions are not inadmissible in evidence although the method by which they were obtained may rob them of all or most of their significance.[15] Leading questions are objectionable because of the danger of collusion between the person asking them and the witness, or the impropriety of suggesting the existence of facts which are not in evidence. Account must also be taken of human laziness—it is easy to say 'yes' or 'no' on demand, and most leading questions can be answered in this way, even if the same is true of some questions that are not leading. There is, however, no doubt that leading questions save time, they are often an indispensable prelude to further interrogation and a travesty could be made of any examination-in-chief by an over-emphatic insistence on the prohibition. There are, therefore, numerous recurring situations to which it does not apply. If no objection is taken to a leading question any answer amounts to evidence in the case, but may be regarded as being of diminished weight.[16]

2.　Exceptions to the prohibition

A witness may always be led on the formal introductory part of his testimony. The following is the beginning of almost any examination-in-chief—'Is your name John Smith?' 'Are you a baker?' 'Do you live at 1 Any Street, Anywhere?' Undisputed matters

11　This discussion was approved in *R v Saunders* (1985) 15 ACR 115.
12　This is in effect the definition in Stephen *Digest of the Law of Evidence* (12th edn) art 140, and in Australia in the Dictionary to the Evidence (Cwth) Act 1995. The alternative is to describe questions of type (b) as improper rather than leading.
13　*Nicholls v Dowding and Kemp* (1815) 1 Stark 81.
14　*Law of Evidence* (12th edn) 562.
15　*Moor v Moor* [1954] 2 All ER 458, [1954] 1 WLR 927.
16　Ibid; *Gabrielsen v Farmer* [1960] NZLR 832, at 834.

belong to the same category. In a divorce case in which the marriage was not denied by the respondent, the examination might well continue 'Were you married at St John's Church, Tooting?' 'Did you live happily with the respondent until last June?'

It would often be impossible to persuade a witness to identify a person or thing in court without the aid of leading questions. Accordingly such questions as 'Was he the man you saw?' or 'Was that the book he lent you?' have to be allowed every day.[17] Questions with regard to the identification of persons or things are, in fact, an example of a broader class of question rendered necessary in order to focus the witness's mind on a particular point. Someone is called to prove a partnership; in order to stimulate his memory, he may be asked whether named persons did, or did not, participate in the business.[18]

Lists are sometimes drawn up of the matters with regard to which leading questions are permissible. Introductory or undisputed matters, questions of identity and questions designed to bring the witness's mind to the point are among the items that commonly appear on such lists, but the subject does not lend itself to exhaustive treatment of this nature. There are bound to be cases which do not fall within any list. A witness is in court while a previous witness is giving evidence about the contents of a letter; when the time comes for the second witness to give his evidence-in-chief, he says that he read the letter; he can be asked whether it contained a particular passage.[19] A magistrate dies in the course of a case in which many witnesses have given evidence; provided there is an opportunity of cross-examination, each witness can be recalled before a new magistrate. After the witness has considered his disposition, he can be asked whether the document represents his evidence because long leading questions may be allowed, even in-chief, at the discretion of the judge.[20] No one would have dreamed of including these cases in any list before they were decided.

It is said on good authority[1] that leading questions may always be put in cross-examination. No doubt this is true so far as questions suggesting the desired answer are concerned; but those which suggest the existence of unproved facts might well be disallowed, even in cross-examination, and in *R v MacDonnell*,[2] it was said that questions put to a prisoner in cross-examination ought to be put in an interrogative form; they should commence 'did you?' and not 'you did'. The judge has a wide discretion in these matters, and it is difficult to say more than that leading questions will usually be disallowed in-chief, or in re-examination, although they will generally be permitted in cross-examination.[3]

B. REFRESHING MEMORY[4]

Perhaps the most important feature of an English trial, civil or criminal, has been its 'orality'. Much greater weight is still attached to the answers given by witnesses in court on oath or affirmation than to written statements previously made by them. All

---

17 *R v Watson* (1817) 2 Stark 116, at 128.
18 *Acerro v Petroni* (1815) 1 Stark 100; *Nicholls v Dowding and Kemp* (1815) 1 Stark 81.
19 *Courteen v Touse* (1807) 1 Camp 43.
20 *Ex p Bottomley* [1909] 2 KB 14, at 21.
1   *Parkin v Moon* (1836) 7 C & P 408.
2   (1909) 2 Cr App Rep 322.
3   In a case where there are multiple parties, the effective role of witnesses may vary according to the function their evidence is serving as between the parties, and the right to ask leading questions will vary accordingly; see for example *Peabody Donation Fund (Governors) v Sir Lindsay Parkinson* [1983] CLY 1660 (unaffected on this point by subsequent proceedings).
4   Newark and Samuels [1978] Crim LR 408.

previous statements of witnesses, whether made orally or in writing, are now admissible, with the leave of the court, as evidence of the facts stated in civil cases under the Civil Evidence Act 1995;[5] but the persistence of faith in orality is shown by the fact that the Act still requires the leave of the court[6] to put in a previous statement[7] made by a witness who is called to testify. Preference for orality is even stronger in criminal cases,[8] and was invoked to water down the originally radical proposals to admit documentary hearsay proposed by the Roskill Committee.[9] As a result the Criminal Justice Act 1988 requires oral evidence whenever it is available rather than documentary hearsay except in the case of expert reports, and accepts it there only with the leave of the court.[10] Similar considerations motivated the Law Commission to reject the general admissibility of previous statements in criminal proceedings as in civil.[11] It does however seek to clarify situations in which this is to be permitted, and to expand the categories in which such statements are admitted as evidence of their truth.

1. Out of court

Yet, for all its apparent orality, an examination-in-chief is rarely conducted 'out of the blue'. The witness has usually given a statement (commonly called his 'proof of evidence') to the solicitor for the party calling him or, if he is a prosecution witness in a criminal case, he will have made a signed statement to the police. It is on the basis of these documents that the questions put to the witness in-chief will be framed. The statement will frequently have been made a considerable time before the trial, and the witness may or may not have retained a copy of it. In these circumstances, it is inevitable and desirable that the witness should read his proof shortly before the hearing or even be taken through it by the person to whom it was made. If it were to transpire that there had been anything in the nature of 'coaching' by such person, or some kind of pre-trial confabulation between the witnesses,[12] the judge should inform the jury, and condemn the practice, even though in exceptional circumstances, despite being weakened, it might remain admissible.[13] It was, however, once suggested that it is objectionable for prosecution witnesses to be provided with copies of their statements to the police to be read or gone through shortly before the trial;[14] but it would have been difficult to justify or enforce a special rule for this particular case, and, if the statement were an elaborate one, as even statements to the police sometimes are, the rule would have been absurd. The practice has since been held to be perfectly proper,[15] although it is desirable, but not essential as a matter of law, for the defence to be notified of what has

---

5   Subject only to the notice and competence requirements of ss 1 and 5. See further below p 564.
6   Section 6(2)(a), or to rebut a suggestion of fabrication, s 6(2)(b).
7   See also Civil Procedure Rule 32.5.
8   The reasons for this were eloquently elaborated by the High Court of Australia in *Butera v DPP* (1987) 164 CLR 180, at 189.
9   Report of the Departmental Inquiry on Fraud Trials (1986).
10   Criminal Justice Act 1988, s 30(2).
11   Law Com 245. *Evidence in Criminal Proceedings: Hearsay and Related Topics* (Cm 3670, 1997) para 10.34.
12   See Stephenson [1990] Crim LR 302.
13   *R v Arif* (1993) Times, 17 June; *R v Skinner* (1993) 99 Cr App Rep 212.
14   *R v Yellow and Thay* (1932) 96 JP 826.
15   *R v Richardson* [1971] 2 QB 484, [1971] 2 All ER 773. Nor need the judge give any special direction to the jury, *Rooke v Auckland City Council* [1980] 1 NZLR 680. For criticism see Howard [1972] Crim LR 351.

taken place.[16] The defence is free to cross-examine on a document[17] used in this way, just as if refreshment had taken place in court.[18] No other conditions concerning the documents which may be used to refresh memory out of court have been laid down.

2. In court

It will be convenient to enumerate the conditions on which a witness is allowed to refer to a document in order to refresh his memory while giving evidence, before distinguishing between the two types of case in which memory is said to be 'refreshed' in court. The document must have been made or read over and accepted as accurate by the witness while the facts were still fresh in his memory.[19] It must be produced to the court or opposite party on demand, and, in one class of case, the document must be the original.

(i) Freshness

At one time it was thought that the document should have been made contemporaneously with the events it recorded, but a laxer approach has now prevailed. The judge has a discretion to permit the witness to refresh his memory from a document made when the events were sufficiently recent, and whether or not this was the case will naturally depend upon the nature of the evidence. The conditions were stated in the leading case of *R v Da Silva*[20] as follows:

> (1) ... the witness indicates that he cannot now recall the details of events because of the lapse of time since they took place, (2) that he made a statement much nearer the time of the events and that the contents of the statement represented his recollection at the time he made it, (3) that he had not read the statement before coming into the witness box and (4) that he wished to have an opportunity to read the statement before he continued to give evidence.

The third of these conditions has now been abandoned, since it makes no sense that under a discretionary rule everything should depend upon whether the witness had properly taken in what he had read out of court.[1]

---

16 *Worley v Bentley* [1976] 2 All ER 449; *R v Westwell* [1976] 2 All ER 812. It is even more desirable for such refreshment to take place in court wherever feasible, *R v Tyagi* (1986) Times, 21 July.

17 Even those otherwise subject to legal professional privilege, *Mancorp Pty Ltd v Baulderstone Pty Ltd* (1991) 57 SASR 87 (where many English authorities are considered).

18 *Owen v Edwards* (1983) 77 Cr App Rep 191. But not in Scotland, *Hinshelwood v Auld* 1926 JC 4, *Deb v Normand* 1996 SCCR 766. See also *Mather v Morgan* [1971] Tas SR 192; *R v Pachonick* [1973] 2 NSWLR 86; *R v Kingston* [1986] 2 Qd R 114.

19 It is sufficient if the documents are read to and accepted by the witness (*R v Kelsey* (1982) 74 Cr App Rep 213) but it is doubtful whether the English courts would follow *R v O'Linn* 1960 (1) SA 545, and allow refreshment of memory from a document dictated by the witness but not checked by him. See also *R v Berniquez* (1996) 112 CCC (3d) 380 where a number of intermediate versions had been unchecked by the primary witness.

20 [1990] 1 All ER 29, at 33, [1990] 1 WLR 31, at 36. Accepted, despite fierce attack, in New Zealand in *Equiticorp Industries Group Ltd v R* [1995] 3 NZLR 243.

1 *R v South Ribble Magistrates' Court, ex p Cochrane* [1996] 2 Cr App Rep 544.

(ii)   Document read over or accepted as accurate by the witness

It is unnecessary for the document to have been made by the witness.[2] A striking example is provided by *Dyer v Best*[3] where a witness was allowed to refresh his memory concerning the day on which certain proceedings were brought by referring to an article in a newspaper which he had read at the time and then believed to be true. Pollock CB said:[4]

> If a man at the time he has a recollection of certain facts reads a document containing a statement, which he knows to be true, of the facts, he may again refer to it to refresh his memory although, at the time when he first read it, he made no memorandum.

A witness may refresh his memory from a copy of a document provided the accuracy of the transcription is properly verified. In *Burton v Plummer*[5] a clerk was allowed to refresh his memory from a ledger which contained copies, made under his supervision, from a waste-book kept by him. In *Topham v McGregor*[6] the state of the weather at a particular period fourteen years earlier was a relevant fact. The author of an article which appeared at the time was allowed to refresh his memory from a copy of the newspaper containing it, the editor having deposed to the destruction of the manuscript and the accuracy of the copy. After reading the article the author swore that he had no doubt that the facts were as therein stated.

The courts are not over-insistent on the exactitude of the copy provided they are satisfied that the document by which memory is to be refreshed substantially reproduces what was said in the original. It has been held proper for a surveyor to refresh his memory from a printed report based on his original notes[7] and for a police officer to do likewise from the statement prepared by him for use in committal proceedings from his notebook which was not available at the trial.[8] In *R v Mills*[9] it was held that a police officer might refresh his memory by referring to a note which he had checked from a tape recording of a conversation between the two appellants. The officer had overheard the conversation but had used the recording, which was not put in evidence, to confirm and improve his note.

(iii)   Production of the document

The document must be handed to the opposite party or his advocate to enable him to inspect it and, if he so desires, to cross-examine the witness with regard to its contents.[10]

2   But if made by someone else it must have been verified by the witness while the matter is sufficiently fresh in his mind: *R v Eleftheriou and Eleftheriou* [1993] Crim LR 947.

3   (1866) 4 H & C 189. See also Indian Evidence Act 1872, s 159.

4   At 192.

5   (1834) 2 Ad & El 341. In *Jones v Stroud* (1825) 2 C & P 196, a witness was not allowed to refresh his memory from a copy made six months after the date of the original, but the original was covered in figures when the copy was made and the judge's suspicions appear to have been justifiably aroused concerning the accuracy of the copy. In *R v Chisnell* [1992] Crim LR 507 the police witness was allowed to refresh from a copy made from a lost original nine months later.

6   (1844) 1 Car & Kir 320.

7   *Horne v Mackenzie* (1839) 6 Cl & Fin 628.

8   *R v Cheng* (1976) 63 Cr App Rep 20; *A-G's Reference (No 3 of 1979)* (1979) 69 Cr App Rep 411.

9   [1962] 3 All ER 298, [1962] 1 WLR 1152.

10   *Beech v Jones* (1848) 5 CB 696. See below as to the effect of cross-examination.

The jury may also see the document as it could assist them in estimating the witness's credibility.[11]

(iv)   The original

It was held in *Doe d Church and Phillips v Perkins*[12] that a witness may refresh his memory by any book or paper if he can afterwards swear to the fact from his own recollection, but, if he cannot swear to the fact from recollection any farther than saying that he will do so because he finds it in some book or paper, the original must be produced.[13] Allowance must of course be made for cases in which the original is lost or destroyed in which event a witness will, if he is prepared to do so, be allowed to swear to a fact that he does not recollect, because he finds it in a copy.[14]

3.   Distinction between cases in which memory is refreshed and those in which it is not refreshed

The distinction between cases in which a witness's memory is refreshed by the sight of a document and those in which it is not, although he is prepared to swear to the accuracy of his former statement, appears to be of importance in English law solely in connection with the question whether the original should be produced. Wigmore systematised the distinction under the headings of 'present recollection revived' and 'past recollection recorded'. His main contentions were that there should be no conditions concerning the document by which the former might be achieved while in the latter case the document should be received in evidence under what is probably best regarded as an exception to the rule against hearsay.[15] These contentions have been influential in the United States and, although neither of them represents English law, a few words about each may not be out of place here.

(i)   Present recollection revived

As long ago as 1835 Lewin made the suggestion that a witness should be allowed to refresh his memory by any means because:[16]

> Common experience tells every man that a very slight circumstance, and one not in point to the existing inquiry, will sometimes revive the history of a transaction made up of many circumstances.

---

11   *R v Bass* [1953] 1 QB 680, [1953] 1 All ER 1064; *R v Fenlon* (1980) 71 Cr App Rep 307, at 312.
12   (1790) 3 Term Rep 749; *Howard v Canfield* (1836) 1 Jur 71; *R v Harvey* (1869) 11 Cox CC 546; *Ames v Nicholson* [1921] SASR 224; *Collaton v Correl* [1926] SASR 87; *King v Bryant (No 2)* [1956] Qd R 570.
13   Some latitude in this respect appears to have been allowed in *McLeod v Fraser* [1986] SCR 271.
14   As in *Topham v McGregor* (above).
15   III *Wigmore* ch 28. See in particular Chadbourn revision, paras 754 and 754A.
16   Note on *Lawes v Reed* (1835) 2 Lew CC 152, at 153. There is no English case-law on the refreshment of memory by the production of an object, but see *Smith v British Aerospace* [1982] ICR 98, where memory was refreshed from a photograph.

The desirability of carrying out the suggestion has been enhanced by the acceptance of the practice, recognised by Lewin, of allowing a witness to refresh his memory out of court. If that is not subject to restrictions concerning the type of document which may be used, it is difficult to justify the retention of such restrictions when it is sought to refresh memory in court.[17] The document which 'triggered off' the train of memory is available for inspection should any question of credibility arise, but the witness's oral testimony is the evidence on which the tribunal of fact is invited to act.

(ii)   Past recollection recorded

According to English law this is also the case when present recollection is not in the least revived by the sight of the document, although there are theoretical difficulties which do not appear to have been considered by our courts. The ineptitude of the term 'refreshing memory' in such circumstances has been the subject of judicial comment:[18]

> That is a very inaccurate expression; because in nine cases out of ten the witness's memory is not at all refreshed: he looks at it [the document] again and again; and he recollects nothing of the transaction; but, seeing that it is in his own handwriting, he gives credit to the truth and accuracy of his habits and, though his memory is a perfect blank, he nevertheless undertakes to swear to the accuracy of his notes.

The number of cases in which the witness's memory remains a 'perfect blank' may not be as high as that suggested, but allowance must be made for numerous situations in which memory is only partly revived. When police officers are allowed to read their notes of interviews in the course of their testimony, it is unlikely that their minds are in a state of complete oblivion with regard to the subject matter, but it is even more unlikely that they could give a coherent account of what was said by any means other than that of reciting their notes. Whether the case be one of total or partial oblivion, English legal theory maintains that the matters mentioned in the document are not proved by the statements contained in it under an exception to the hearsay rule but by the witness's oral testimony.[19] In many of the cases the document to the accuracy of which the witness deposes, though remembering nothing about the matters to which it refers, would have been inadmissible in evidence and the courts have been at pains to emphasise the fact that the evidence is oral, not documentary. Thus, in *Maugham v Hubbard*,[20] a witness was called to prove the receipt of money. Being unable to remember that the payment was made to him, he was shown an unstamped acknowledgement signed by himself whereupon he said that he had no doubt that he had received the sum specified in it, although he did not recall having done so. It was held that this was sufficient evidence of the payment in spite of the prohibition on the use of unstamped receipts in litigation:[1]

17   See per Lawton LJ in *R v Cheng* (1976) 63 Cr App Rep 20, at 23,4.
18   Hayes J in *Lord Talbot de Malahide v Cussack* (1864) 17 CLR 213, at 220. See also *R v Bryant* (1946) 31 Cr App Rep 146, at 150.
19   *Jacob v Lindsay* (1801) 1 East 460; *Kensington v Inglis* (1807) 8 East 273; *Maugham v Hubbard* (1828) 8 B & C 14; *R v St Martin's, Leicester* (1834) 2 Ad & El 210; *Birchall v Bullough* [1896] 1 QB 325; the rule against hearsay was not mentioned in any of these cases.
20   Above.
1   Lord Tenterden CJ at 16.

The paper was not used as evidence of the receipt of the money, but only to enable the witness to refresh his memory; and when he said that he had no doubt that he had received the money there was sufficient parole evidence to prove the payment.

Exactly the same reasoning applies in cases of the refreshment of memory of the number of a motor car by reference to a contemporaneous note. If the number has been dictated to a third party who has not himself seen it, his note is inadmissible as evidence of the number since it is hearsay,[2] but it can be used by the dictator, who cannot remember the number, to 'refresh' his memory.[3] It is not surprising that this result has been judicially castigated as being absurd.[4]

Are these instances, of which others are mentioned in ch XIII, of the unwitting reception of evidence infringing the rule against hearsay? According to that rule as formulated in this book an assertion other than one made by a person while giving oral evidence in the proceedings is inadmissible as evidence of any fact asserted. The question can best be approached by distinguishing between the different circumstances in which someone who does not recollect an event might yet have no doubt that it occurred. A man who regularly shaves every morning might well have no doubt that he did so on a named day a little while back, and accordingly be prepared to testify to that effect, although he does not remember shaving on the day in question. He vouches for the regularity of his habits and the absence of anything to lead him to suppose that they might have been broken on the day in question. The further back in time the question goes the less likely is he to be prepared to swear to having shaved on account of the greater chance of some forgotten reason for not having done so. The case may be described as one of 'reconstruction' and it is of a kind which counts as personal knowledge for the purpose of the rule that witnesses must have such knowledge of the facts to which they testify. Now let us suppose that someone who recollects having dined in his college hall on a particular day is asked what he was offered for dinner. His mind may well be a complete blank on the subject and his memory may be in no way refreshed by the sight of the menu prepared by the chef and used on the occasion in question; yet he might well be prepared to swear that he was offered the items of food mentioned on the menu. His reasoning might be: 'I have never known a college menu to err; therefore I have no doubt that I was offered the dishes mentioned on the menu for that day.' He is thus prepared to vouch for the accuracy of the chef. This too is a case of reconstruction, but the witness lacks personal knowledge of the matters to which he is testifying, for the knowledge is derived from the menu, not from the regularity of his habits. *Maugham v Hubbard* resembles this last example more than that of the regular shaver. The witness was vouching for the accuracy of what he had said in a document concerning a long forgotten event.[5]

As long as the rule against hearsay is formulated in such a way as to embrace previous statements of the witness who is testifying, it is difficult to escape the conclusion that it was infringed in such cases. A hearsay statement[6] is none the less a hearsay statement because someone who has no recollection of the matters to which it refers swears that it is accurate. To meet this point r 803(5) of the Federal Rules of

2   *Jones v Metcalfe* [1967] 3 All ER 205, [1967] 1 WLR 1286.
3   *R v Kelsey* (1982) 74 Cr App Rep 213.
4   By Diplock LJ in *Jones v Metcalfe*, above, at 208, 1291.
5   In some circumstances the fact that a statement was made may be in issue rather than whether or not it is true, and in such cases no question of hearsay arises and the recorder of that statement may refresh his memory from his record of what was said, see *Wentworth v Rogers (No 9)* (1987) 8 NSWLR 388, at 406.
6   For definition, see p 46 above.

Evidence of the United States provides for an exception to the rule against hearsay in the following terms:

> A memorandum or record concerning a matter about which a witness once had knowledge but now has insufficient recollection to enable him to testify fully and accurately, shown to have been made or adopted by the witness when the matter was fresh in his memory and to reflect that knowledge correctly.

In civil cases the previous statement of a witness, whether or not used to refresh memory, is admissible evidence of its contents under the Civil Evidence Act 1995, but in criminal cases this is currently the case only if the person making or taking down the statement were acting in the course of a business at the time.[7]

The Law Commission has however recommended that in all cases where a document is admitted to refresh memory it should become evidence of the truth of its contents, irrespective of whether or not the witness's memory really was revived by it.[8]

4.   Cross-examination on documents used to refresh memory

There is an old general rule,[9] inadequately explored in the modern authorities, that, if a party calls for and inspects a document held by the other party, he is bound to put it in evidence if required to do so.[10] But:[11]

> Where a document is used to refresh a witness's memory, cross-examining counsel may inspect that document in order to check it without making it evidence. Moreover he may cross-examine upon it without making it evidence provided that his cross-examination does not go further than the parts which are used for refreshing the memory of the witness.

If, therefore, a witness refreshes his memory concerning a date or an address by referring to a diary, he may be cross-examined about the terms or form of the entries used to refresh his memory without there being any question of the right of the party calling him to insist that the diary should become evidence in the case.[12] On the other

---

7   Criminal Justice Act 1988, s 24.

8   Law Com No 245 *Evidence in Criminal Proceedings: Hearsay and Related Topics* (Cm 3670, 1997) paras 10.73–10.80, rec 38.

9   It has been held to apply just as much to documents used to refresh memory out of court, *Owen v Edwards* (1984) 77 Cr App Rep 191. See also *R v Kingston* [1986] 2 Qd R 114.

10   *Wharam v Routledge* (1805) 5 Esp 235; *Calvert v Flower* (1836) 7 C & P 386; *Palmer v Maclear and M'Grath* (1858) 1 Sw & Tr 149; *Stroud v Stroud* [1963] 3 All ER 539, [1963] 1 WLR 1080. In Australia subject to the discretionary control of the judge, *R v Moore* (1995) 77 ACR 577.

11   *Senat v Senat* [1965] P 172, at 177. This case probably does not, as the headnote suggests, conflict with *Stroud v Stroud* (above) where the documents called for and inspected were not used to refresh memory. See also *Gregory v Tavernor* (1833) 6 C & P 280; *Payne v Ibbotson* (1858) 27 LJ Ex 341; *R v Newall* (1983) 5 DLR (4th) 352.

12   *Lloyd v Freshfield* (1826) 2 C & P 325 (cross-examination on other half of entry used to refresh memory did not make entry evidence); *R v Ramsden* (1827) 2 C & P 603 (witness could be asked whether entry written on a particular day without making it evidence); *R v Fenlon* (1980) 71 Cr App Rep 307, at 312 (prosecution could not insist on notes used by policemen to refresh memory of interview, upon which they had been cross-examined, being put before the jury). See also *R v McGregor* [1984] 1 Qd R 256 (where two people wrote different things on the same piece of paper and only one was cross-examined about his entry, only that part could strictly become evidence).

hand, if the witness is cross-examined about other parts of the diary, the party calling him may insist on its being treated as evidence in the case.[13]

In civil proceedings such a statement, when so treated becomes evidence of the truth of its contents:[14]

> (4) Nothing in this Act affects any of the rules of law as to the circumstances in which, where a person called as a witness in civil proceedings is cross-examined on a document used by him to refresh his memory, that document may be made evidence in the proceedings.
>
> (5) Nothing in this section shall be construed as preventing a statement of any description referred to above from being admissible by virtue of section 1 as evidence of the matters stated.

In criminal proceedings such a statement is, at present, evidence only of the consistency of its maker.[15] Such a rule would however be inconsistent with the Law Commission's more general proposal for the admission of hearsay in criminal proceedings, and it has accordingly made a special recommendation that such documents should also become, when so admitted, evidence of the truth of their contents.[16]

C.   PREVIOUS CONSISTENT STATEMENTS

The general rule at common law is that a witness may not be asked in-chief[17] whether he has formerly made a statement consistent with his present testimony. He cannot narrate such statement if it was oral or refer to it if it was in writing (save for the purpose of refreshing his memory), and other witnesses may not be called to prove it.[18] The rule against hearsay as defined in this book[19] prohibits the reception of the statement as evidence of the facts stated, but there is an independent common law ban on proof of the previous oral or written statements of the witness as evidence of his consistency.[20] Thus, in *R v Roberts*,[1] the accused was charged with murdering a girl by shooting her as she was letting him into her house. His defence, supported by his evidence at the trial was that the gun went off accidentally while he was trying to make up a quarrel with the girl. Two days after the event he told his father that the defence would be accident. The trial judge would not allow this conversation to be proved, and the Court of Criminal Appeal held that he had been right.

In this case, the reason given for the ban (sometimes loosely described as 'the rule against narrative' or 'the rule against self-corroboration') was the ease with which

---

13   *R v Britton* [1987] 2 All ER 412, [1987] 1 WLR 539, expressly approving the statement of law in this paragraph.
14   Civil Evidence Act 1995, ss 6(4), 6(5).
15   *R v Virgo* (1978) 67 Cr App Rep 323.
16   Law Com No 245 *Evidence in Criminal Proceedings: Hearsay and Related Topics* (Cm 3670, 1997) paras 10.81–10.82, rec 39.
17   Nor in cross-examination where the witness is not adverse to the cross-examiner: *R v Wood* (1989) 51 CCC (3d) 201, at 231.
18   The two preceding statements were adopted as an accurate statement of the law by the Privy Council in *White v R* (1998) Times, 25 September.
19   See p 46 above.
20   For this reason the Civil Evidence Act 1995 not only abolishes the hearsay rule in s 1, but also makes separate provision for the admission of previous statements in s 6; for a similar strategy in Scotland, see Civil Evidence (Scotland) Act 1988, ss 2, 3.
1   [1942] 1 All ER 187.

evidence of this nature can be manufactured.[2] But, generally speaking, this can only be apposite when the witness is a party and, in any event, the ease with which evidence can be fabricated is a matter which should affect its weight rather than its admissibility. A more convincing reason was given by Evans in his notes to Pothier[3] when he said that in an ordinary case the evidence would be at least superfluous, for the assertions of a witness are to be regarded in general as true, until there is some particular reason for impeaching them as false. The necessity of saving time by avoiding superfluous testimony and sparing the court a protracted inquiry into a multitude of collateral issues which might be raised about such matters as the precise terms of the previous statement is undoubtedly a sound basis for the general rule.[4]

The distinction between receiving a witness's previous statement as evidence of the facts stated and as evidence of consistency is often of no practical importance because the statement is no more than an earlier version of the testimony. In some situations[5] the time at which, or circumstances in which, the statement was made may sometimes be an additional guarantee of the trustworthiness of the testimony.

In the case of the common law exceptions to the ban on the reception of previous statements as evidence of consistency there is some reason, other than the mere fact that it preceded the testimony, why the statement should have enhanced the witness's credibility. When a witness's previous statement is admissible as evidence of the facts stated by way of exception to the hearsay rule, it is also received as evidence of consistency on the principle that the greater includes the lesser.

Previous consistent statements of witnesses are now admissible in civil cases as evidence of the facts stated in them, as a result of the Civil Evidence Act 1995, but they are not yet so admissible in criminal proceedings, because there was no comparable provision in the Criminal Justice Act 1988.[6] The reception of statements under the Acts of 1995 and 1988 will be considered in chapters XIV and XV below. At this stage it is proposed to consider three well-recognised exceptions to the general common law prohibition of the proof of a witness's prior statements as evidence of consistency—complaints in sexual cases, statements forming part of the same transaction as that to which they refer (admitted as part of the res gestae) and previous statements admitted to rebut the suggestion that the witness's testimony was a later fabrication. The first may almost certainly be taken to be confined to criminal cases, but the second and third are still relevant to civil as well as criminal proceedings, the second because the leave of the court is required for the reception of statements to which they apply, and

2   At 191 per Humphreys J. See too per Swinfen-Eady LJ in *Jones v South Eastern and Chatham Rly Co's Managing Committee* (1918) 87 LJKB 775, at 778.
3   *Pothier on Obligations* (1806 edn) vol 2, p 289.
4   This reason was explicitly approved by the Law Commission in Law Com No 245 *Evidence in Criminal Proceedings: Hearsay and Related Topics* (Cm 3670, 1997) para 10.12. See also 'Generally speaking, as is well known, such confirmatory evidence is not admissible, the reason presumably being that all trials, civil and criminal, must be conducted with an effort to concentrate evidence on what is capable of being cogent' per Lord Radcliffe in *Fox v General Medical Council* [1960] 3 All ER 225, at 230.
5   See eg the facts of *Gillie v Posho Ltd* [1939] 2 All ER 196 (timing of previous letter to same effect as testimony significant); and *Corke v Corke and Cooke* [1958] P 93, [1958] 1 All ER 224 (circumstantial inference of making telephone call to same effect as testimony significant) though the legal results would no longer be the same.
6   Though, as will be seen, some change is recommended in Law Com No 245 *Evidence in Criminal Proceedings: Hearsay and Related Topics* (Cm 3670, 1997) ch X. It has also been suggested that an unintended by-product of the silence provisions in the Criminal Justice and Public Order Act 1994 is that it will now be easier to secure the admission of a statement prepared in advance by the accused (or his legal adviser) whenever the accused chooses to exercise his right of silence on account of having prepared and presented such a statement: see Wright [1998] Crim LR 44.

the third by special provision.[7] There are in addition some further ill-defined exceptions to the common law rule which probably apply only to criminal cases, and a word must be said in conclusion about the possibility of the reception of the statements made by a witness out of court under the influence of a truth drug.

1. Complaints in sexual cases

In the Middle Ages it was essential that the victim should have raised the hue and cry if an appeal of rape were to succeed. By the beginning of the eighteenth century, when the modern law of evidence was beginning to take shape, the absence of complaint was no longer an absolute bar to success, but Hawkins still referred to the strong presumption against a prosecutrix in a case of rape if she made no complaint within a reasonable time of the alleged offence.[8] If the absence of such complaint could tell against a prosecutrix it seemed to follow that the fact of having made a complaint ought to tell in her favour, and if failure to complain could be proved by the defence then the fact of making a complaint should be capable of proof by the prosecution. Such proof does however raise problems since it grates against the rule excluding previous consistent statements, the hearsay rule and the rule against self-corroboration. It is necessary to consider, first, the range of cases in which such a complaint is admissible, second, the definition of such a complaint and the conditions to which its admissibility is subject, third, the use which may be made of it, fourth, other rules which permit evidence of complaints to be led, and in conclusion whether it is worth retaining the rule.

(i)   Range of application

As noted above the original point of admitting evidence of a complaint was to rebut the adverse inference that might otherwise be drawn from the victim's failure to complain of the attack upon her. It is sufficient to rebut any such inference to prove merely that a complaint was made. To have admitted the terms of the complaint would have courted the risk of the jury's using them as evidence of the facts which they asserted, contrary to the hearsay rule. Originally therefore no more than the fact of a complaint having been made was admitted, though this limitation was neither fully understood,[9] nor fully accepted,[10] by the judges. Nor was it clear how far the rule extended.[11] These matters were subsequently clarified.

In *R v Lillyman*[12] the Court for Crown Cases Reserved, without conspicuous understanding of the reason for the limitation to the admission of evidence of the complaint having been made, extended admissibility to its terms, influenced in part by the effect of persistent attempts to undermine it, like those countenanced in *Wink*. A further consideration was that the exclusion of evidence of the terms effectively left the decision of whether a statement amounted to a complaint to the complainant or her auditor. The problem of hearsay was proposed to be resolved by specific instruction to the jury that the complaint was to be used only as 'evidence of the consistency of

---

7   Section 6(2)(b).
8   1 PC ch 41, s 9.
9   See Parke B in *R v Walker* (1839) 2 Mood & R 212.
10   See *R v Wink* (1834) 6 C & P 397 where Patteson J was perfectly prepared to permit the limitation to be undermined.
11   In *Wink* it was applied to a complaint of robbery.
12   [1896] 2 QB 167.

the conduct of the prosecutrix with the story told by her in the witness box, and as being inconsistent with her consent to that of which she complains'.[13] In *Lillyman* consent was not formally in issue on the relevant count, but had, in fact, been denied.[14] In *R v Osborne*[15] the court took the matter a step further by holding that consent need not be in issue, neither in form nor in fact, in order to admit evidence of the terms of a complaint. The ambit of the rule was, however, restricted to 'cases of this kind'. It seems that this ambiguous phrase was intended, somewhat unhistorically[16] and illogically,[17] merely to exclude non-sexual charges. Any further ambiguity as to whether or not it extended to complaints by young male victims was resolved in favour of such a view by the decision of the Court of Criminal Appeal in *R v Camelleri* to extend it to a complaint made by a young boy.[18] Lord Hewart CJ intimated that in the case of adult males little weight might be ascribed to such a complaint, but the reason for this is obscure. The point is, however, virtually moot in the United Kingdom since the absence of consent is[19] now required in relation to offences against adult males, and the question of consistency seems not to be dependent upon age.[20] From time to time attempts have been made to extend the exception beyond sexual criminal offences, now that the principal purpose is to support the consistency of the witness's story. This view was espoused by Chapman J in *R v McNamara*[1] very soon after *Osborne* had made such rationale explicit. In Canada it was also applied to cases involving illegal confinement, even in the absence of any overt sexual purpose.[2] In England there are dicta in *Jones v South Eastern and Chatham Rly Co's Management Committee*[3] suggesting extension to any complaint of violence whether in criminal or civil proceedings. There are also isolated examples of complaints not being unreservedly rejected,[4] and even admitted,[5] in other cases. It is, however, submitted that the rule does not in England extend beyond sexual offences, whatever the sex of the victim.[6] The best justification for singling out such offences is that more hinges on questions of the credibility of the participants than in most other areas, just because sexual activity tends to take place in private and is usually kept secret, thus restricting the amount of other evidence which is likely to be available. It was upon that basis that the rule of practice requiring corroboration warnings, again in relation to both sexes, was maintained, and it may

13   At 170.
14   It seems that Hawkins J, who had delivered the judgment in *Lillyman*, himself regarded this as a necessary condition, see *R v Rowland* (1898) 62 JP 459.
15   [1905] 1 KB 551.
16   The original requirement of 'hue and cry' applied to all appeals of felony, and, as noted above, as late as 1834 the rule was being applied to non-sexual offences.
17   If consent is not in issue the only recognised purpose is to demonstrate credibility by reference to consistency of complaint and testimony, and the credibility of witnesses is relevant whatever the issue to which they testify.
18   [1922] 2 KB 122. This step had already been taken by the Court of Appeal in New Zealand, see *R v McNamara* [1917] NZLR 382, and by a lower court in England, see *Chesney v Newsholme* [1908] P 301.
19   In the vast majority of cases.
20   See, for example, *R v Hurst and Miller* (1966) 55 WWR 358, at 365.
1   Above, at 402.
2   *R v Frame* (1976) 31 CCC (2d) 332 (a girl): *R v MacHay* (1979) 48 CCC (2d) 468 (boys).
3   (1918) 87 LJKB 775, at 778. See Gooderson (1968) CLJ 64.
4   *Fromhold v Fromhold* [1952] 1 TLR 1522 (complaint of cruelty rejected only because not sufficiently contemporaneous).
5   *O'H v O'H* (1916) 33 TLR 51 (complaint of marital difficulty); *McIlkenny v Chief Constable of West Midlands* [1980] QB 283, at 313, [1980] 2 All ER 227, at 232 where Lord Denning MR considered evidence of complaints of ill-treatment at the hands of the police made by prisoners.
6   This view was explicitly approved in *R v Jarvis and Jarvis* [1991] Crim LR 374. See also *R v Greenwood* [1993] Crim LR 770.

have seemed right to admit any other evidence which could perhaps help the jury to resolve the customary direct conflict of testimony. The Law Commission has however taken the view that the admission of complaints could profitably be applied as a general rule, and used as evidence of the truth of the matters asserted, subject only to considerations as to the weight of the evidence.[7]

(ii) Conditions of admissibility

In *R v Osborne*[8] Ridley J summarised the conditions governing this exception to the rule otherwise prohibiting proof of previous consistent statements:

> It applies only when there is a complaint not elicited by questions of a leading and inducing or intimidating character and only when it is made at the first opportunity after the offence which reasonably offers itself.

There are thus three conditions, although each is interpreted liberally: that the statement be spontaneous; that it be contemporaneous; and that it amount to a complaint. All are matters for the judge, though it has been suggested that the third may be further reconsidered by the jury.[9] These will be considered in turn.

(a) Spontaneous

In *R v Merry*[10] it had been held that a statement elicited by the questioning of the victim's mother could not be adduced because it was a conversation rather than a complaint. No details were given of the form of questioning, so in *Osborne*, where the complaint was made only after the girl had been asked by a friend why she had not waited in the chip shop as arranged, Ridley J attempted to discriminate between different forms of questioning:

> the mere fact that the statement is made in answer to a question in such cases is not of itself sufficient to make it admissible as a complaint. Questions of a suggestive or leading character will, indeed, have that effect, and will render it inadmissible; but a question such as this, put by the mother or other person, 'What is the matter?' or 'Why are you crying?' will not do so.

Even this was thought to be too dogmatic in relation to leading questions, and in *R v Norcott*, where the auditor refused to let the complainant go until she had spoken, the Court of Criminal Appeal explained *Osborne*:[11]

> The court is concerned to see that in the present case the statement made by the girl was spontaneous in the sense that it was her unassisted and unvarnished statement of what happened. That she may have been persuaded to tell her unassisted and unvarnished story is no reason why the evidence of her having made the statement should be rejected.

---

7   Law Com No 245 *Evidence in Criminal Proceedings: Hearsay and Related Topics* (Cm 3670, 1997) paras 10.53–10.61, rec 36.
8   [1905] 1 KB 551, at 561.
9   See *Lillyman* at 178.
10 (1900) 19 Cox CC 442.
11 [1917] 1 KB 347, at 350.

The whole matter was said in *Osborne* to be a matter for the discretion of the trial judge, and to depend upon all of the relevant circumstances. Thus in one case[12] a complaint elicited by the question 'have you been raped or something?' was admitted because the victim had already indicated sufficient distress for this to be regarded as merely accelerating, rather than suggesting, the complaint. On the other hand complaints elicited by threat of force,[13] or by cross-examination after disbelief of a different statement,[14] have been rejected on this basis. The ultimate consideration should be simply whether the purpose of enhancing the witness's credibility by showing consistency between complaint and testimony will be achieved by admitting the earlier statement.

(b)   Contemporaneous
The general principle underlying this exception is that the nature of the offence is such that some complaint might be expected.[15] It might well be expected to be made soon after the event, but not necessarily to the first person to be encountered. It seems quite reasonable for the victim to choose to wait until she can complain to a congenial person.[16] On the other hand if a person is obviously appropriate, and a complaint is eventually made to her, a court will be less prepared to excuse the spurning of an earlier opportunity.[17] In general the condition will be interpreted generously in view of the subjective condition of the victim who might easily be too upset to talk about the offence at all for some time.[18] If the victim testifies to having made a complaint, but the auditor either denies that it was made,[19] or it cannot be used because it is regarded as not having been sufficiently spontaneous,[20] then a subsequent complaint may be proved if made reasonably soon afterwards. In *Breen v R*[1] the High Court of Australia was prepared to admit several complaints made soon after the event, despite the victim not having referred to many of them in her testimony. This seems questionable, and there is force in the view[2] that if the only point is to demonstrate consistency then one is enough, and that more may be prejudicial, making it even more likely that the jury will be inclined to regard them as evidence of the truth of what they assert.

(c)   Complaint
The third requirement is that the statement should amount to a complaint. This will rarely cause difficulty though some statements have been rejected as 'conversation'[3]

---

12   *R v Freeman* [1980] VR 1. See also *R v Gallagher* (1986) 41 SASR 73.
13   *S v T* 1963 (1) SA 484 (A).
14   *R v Adams and Ross* [1965] Qd R 255.
15   Though modern research suggests that very often complaint is not made, see Temkin *Rape and the Legal Process* (1987) pp 145, 146.
16   Thus in *R v Valentine* [1996] 2 Cr App Rep 213 it was held that a young woman could reasonably delay her complaint of rape until she was alone with her boyfriend the next day, and need not complain earlier to her parents or brother; see also *R v Cummings* [1948] 1 All ER 551.
17   Dicta in *R v Peake* (1974) 9 SASR 458 (though on the facts such a complaint was admitted).
18   See *R v Freeman* [1980] VR 1; *R v N* [1994] 3 NZLR 641.
19   As in *R v Lee* (1911) 7 Cr App Rep 31 (where the complaint admitted was actually the third alleged to have been made, the first being denied in crucial details by the accused's mother to whom it had been made, and the second, to the victim's father, relating only to a physical injury). See also *R v McDonald* (1985) 17 ACR 297.
20   As seems to have been the case in *R v Wilbourne* (1917) 12 Cr App Rep 280.
1   (1974) 50 ALJR 536. See also *R v Roisetter* [1984] 1 Qd R 477.
2   *R v Wilson* (1986) 42 SASR 203, at 226; *R v Tanda* (1986) 43 SASR 161. See also *R v Wilson* [1996] 2 NZLR 79 (second complaint two weeks later excluded, even though the first opportunity of complaining to *that* person).
3   *R v Merry* (1900) 19 Cox CC 442.

or 'narrative'.[4] It has been held in Australia that the complaint must relate to the sexual element of the offence.[5] Here too a generally relaxed view is taken, perhaps because this condition is regarded as being capable of being reconsidered by the jury,[6] though it is hard to believe that any jury would really engage in so arcane an exercise.

(iii)   Permissible use

Both in *Lillyman*[7] and in *Osborne*[8] reference was made to the complaint being used to show consistency with the victim's testimony, and being inconsistent with consent. In *Kilby v R*,[9] it is submitted rightly, the High Court of Australia emphasised that this could not be taken to mean that it amounted to evidence of the absence of consent, nor its absence to evidence of consent. That would be to make the very hearsay use of the complaint warned against by Hawkins J, in *Lillyman*. The correct view is that the victim's testimony is evidence of lack of consent, and the complaint does no more than support the credibility of the victim in so testifying.[10]

It sometimes happens that the testimony of the victim is inconsistent with the complaint. In such a case there is no reason why it should not be used as such by the opponent in cross-examination, and there is some authority for permitting its use for this purpose as a complaint, apparently on the basis that if consonance of complaint and testimony enhances credibility, dissonance should be allowed to diminish it.[11]

Since the purpose of admitting evidence of the complaint is simply to enhance the credibility of the victim's testimony it follows that evidence of the complaint is admissible only if the victim testifies,[12] though not necessarily to having made a complaint.[13] It seems, however, that if the victim can testify, it is immaterial that such testimony differs in some details from the terms of the original complaint.[14] When the victim does testify a complaint could not under the old law amount to corroboration of her testimony, whether it was exceptionally proved by the victim herself,[15] or, as was more usual, by the auditor.[16] It follows that the rule is unaffected by the abolition of the corroboration rule for complainants in sexual cases. It has been emphasised however that a direction as to the permissible use of such a complaint is still required, and the Judicial Studies Board's recommended form of words is rehearsed in *R v Islam*.[17] If the only evidence

---

4   *De B v De B* [1950] VLR 242; but see *R v Robertson* [1991] 1 Qd R 262, at 276.
5   *R v Saunders* [1965] Qd R 409 (where the victim was believed by her auditors to be male).
6   *R v Manwaring* [1983] 2 NSWLR 82, at 91, so interpreting dicta in *Lillyman; Daniels v R* (1989) 1 WAR 435..
7   [1896] 2 QB 167, at 170.
8   [1905] 1 KB 551, at 557, 558.
9   (1973) 129 CLR 460.
10   Reaffirmed in *R v Islam* [1999] 1 Cr App Rep 22.
11   *R v Askew* [1981] Crim LR 398.
12   *Sparks v R* [1964] AC 964, [1964] 1 All ER 727 (complainant too young); *Ugle v R* (1989) 167 CLR 647 (complainant abroad).
13   *R v Nazif* [1987] 2 NZLR 122.
14   *R v Braye-Jones* [1966] Qd R 295; *R v Askew* [1981] Crim LR 398.
15   As in *R v Lee* (1911) 7 Cr App Rep 31 where the auditor refused to testify to the complaint, and in *R v Duell* [1964] Qd R 451 where she was unable to remember it. But see *White v R* [1999] 1 Cr App Rep 153; *R v Kincaid* [1991] 2 NZLR 1.
16   *R v Lovell* (1923) 17 Cr App Rep 163. See also *Eade v R* (1924) 34 CLR 154; *Thomas v R* [1952] 4 DLR 306.
17   [1998] Crim LR 575. In Australia, under the Evidence (Cwth) Act 1995, such statements are now admitted as evidence of the truth of their contents, so such a direction is there no longer necessary: *R v H* (1997) 92 ACR 168.

of the complaint is provided by its maker, and the normal situation rendering such evidence immaterial applies, it is essential that the jury be warned against attaching evidential significance to it.[18]

If evidence of the absence of a recent complaint is to be used to weaken the credibility of the victim it seems only fair that evidence explaining why such a complaint was not forthcoming should be admissible. It clearly is admissible before the judge when he is deciding whether the conditions for admitting the statement as a complaint have been established. As a matter of fairness judges will normally direct juries not only as to the use they are permitted to make of the terms of an admissible complaint but also what inference they may draw from a failure to make such a complaint. While *Kilby v R*[19] proscribes any direction that this is evidence of consent, it approves a direction that it weakens the credibility of the victim, though in New South Wales, even before it became mandatory by statutory amendment,[20] it was customary for juries to be warned of the reasons which might inhibit such complaint.[1] Since this second direction sanctioned by *Kilby* has survived the statutory reform,[2] it is submitted[3] that it is only fair that evidence relevant to the reasons for not complaining sooner, or at all, should be admissible at the trial.

(iv)   Other rules

As indicated above a complaint inconsistent with the eventual testimony of the victim may be put in cross-examination as a previous inconsistent statement, in which case also it will affect only credibility, and will not amount to evidence of the facts it states. It is, however, possible to imagine situations in which a recent complaint might become evidence of its assertions by way of exception to the hearsay rule. It is possible that the complaint might be made in the presence of the accused, and accepted by him.[4] If a complaint is made as a dying declaration it will be admissible as evidence of its truth in the limited circumstances in which such declarations are admissible.[5] Attempts have also been made to secure the admission of such complaints as part of the res gestae,[6] but this is usually unsuccessful, because the complaint is made only after the stress of the crime has somewhat subsided.[7] It is, however, possible to conceive of cases where the line is not so clear, and the protest is made, and heard, while the offence is taking place or in its immediate aftermath.[8]

---

18   *White v R*, above.
19   (1973) 129 CLR 460, at 465.
20   Crimes Act 1900, new s 405B.
1   *R v Zorad* [1979] 2 NSWLR 764, at 772; the rule is the same in Canada: *R v M(TE)* (1996) 110 CCC (3d) 179.
2   See *R v Davies* (1985) 3 NSWLR 276.
3   This has been disputed in Canada: cp *R v Kistendey* (1975) 29 CCC (2d) 382; *R v Walters* (1980) 53 CCC (2d) 119, at 130.
4   As it was argued had occurred in *R v Christie* [1914] AC 545.
5   See further, below, ch XV.
6   See further, below, ch XV.
7   See for example, *Sparks v R* [1964] AC 964, at 979.
8   See *R v Kooyman* (1979) 22 SASR 376, at 380, 381.

(v)   Reform

The rule has been heavily criticised in the United States,[9] and in New Zealand,[10] and abrogated in Canada.[11] It has also been abolished or severely restricted in a number of other Commonwealth jurisdictions,[12] though in South Australia after being abolished it was subsequently restored. The argument for abolition is its inconsistency with other rules, its illogicality, its capacity to prejudice the accused, its arbitrary scope, and the resentment created by allowing the credibility of one of the parties to the dispute to be bolstered, but not that of the other.[13] The argument for retention is that in a contest of credibility technical rules should not stand in the way of anything which assists the jury to resolve it satisfactorily, and that the legal rules still operate in sexual cases to the disadvantage of complainants to such an extent that it would be unfair to remove a rule which does a little to redress the balance. Technicality creates its own injustice however, not least in unmeritorious acquittals, and it is submitted that it is better to reform what is still shown to be wrong in the law of procedure as it applies to sexual offences directly, rather than to seek to counterbalance one injustice by a different anomaly. Most of the legitimate work to be done by the recent complaints rule could be better accomplished by use of the rule permitting the use of previous consistent statements to rebut any suggestion of afterthought.[14] There seems no reason why sexual offences should not be proved and tried in just the same way as any others.[15]

2.   Previous consistent statements admitted as part of the res gestae

As indicated above there is no longer any reason to rely upon this rule in civil proceedings since the Civil Evidence Act 1995 provides for the admission of such statements by witness either with the leave of the court, or to rebut any suggestion of fabrication.[16]

The rule may still have some small room for application in criminal proceedings.[1]

3.   Previous consistent statements admitted to rebut suggestion of fabrication

When giving judgment in *R v Coll*,[2] Holmes J said:

---

9   In *Commonwealth v Cleary* (1898) 172 Mass 175 Justice Holmes described it as 'a perverted survival', see also *Wigmore* para 1140.
10   *R v H* [1997] 1 NZLR 673, at 697 ('indefensible and its continued application unconscionable').
11   Canadian Criminal Code, s 275. See *R v N(L)* (1989) 52 CCC (3d) 1; *R v F(JE)* (1993) 85 CCC (3d) 457; Dawson (1984) 27 Crim LQ 57.
12   See, for example, Evidence (Amendment) Ordinance (No 2) 1985, s 76C(1) (ACT); Crimes Act, s 405B (NSW); Acts Amendment (Sexual Assaults) Act 1985, s 15 enacting new s 36BD (WA); Evidence Amendment Act 1985, s 3 (New Zealand).
13   See *R v Newsome* (1980) 71 Cr App Rep 325.
14   See, below.
15   Under Law Com No 245 *Evidence in Criminal Proceedings: Hearsay and Related Topics* (Cm 3670, 1997), rec 36 this result would be achieved not by abolishing the rule, but by retaining it, extending it to all other types of complaint, and making all admissible previous statements evidence of the truth of their contents.
16   Section 6(2).
1   The definition of hearsay in Law Com No 245 *Evidence in Criminal Proceedings: Hearsay and Related Topics* (Cm 3670, 1997) reduces the scope of the exception even though its retention is recommended in paras 8.114–8.129, recs 22–24, see further below p 594.
2   (1889) 25 LR Ir 522, at 541.

It is I think clear that the evidence of a witness cannot be corroborated by proving statements to the same effect previously made by him; nor will the fact that his testimony is impeached in cross-examination render such evidence admissible. Even if the impeachment takes the form of showing a contradiction or inconsistency between the evidence given at the trial and something said by the witness on a former occasion it does not follow that the way is open for proof of other statements made by him for the purpose of sustaining his credit. There must be something either in the nature of the inconsistent statement, or in the use made of it by the cross-examiner to enable such evidence to be given.

The fact that the whole of the witness's testimony is attacked will not bring the exception into play.[3] Nor is it enough that an inconsistent statement has been used to discredit the witness.[4] It has been said that the nature of the cross-examination must be such that it can be interpreted[5] as containing the direct question 'when did you first invent this story?'[6] It should be noted that even when this is the question it is not rebutted by showing the concurrence of a similar statement at that time, even though it allege a preceding incident.[7]

If it is alleged that a prisoner's story is a recent concoction, a previous statement concerning the nature of his defence becomes admissible,[8] so too does a statement made by an accused's wife to a solicitor before she had seen her husband after his arrest if it is suggested in cross-examination that her evidence was the result of collusion with him;[9] and an allegation that a policeman is fabricating his testimony allows his notebook to be put in evidence.[10] The rationale of the exception requires that there be independent evidence of the statement's having been made.[11] Generally speaking the previous statement will be put to the witness in re-examination, but circumstances are conceivable in which he would be asked about it in-chief. This might be done when the cross-examination of a previous witness had contained a suggestion of fabrication by himself and the succeeding witness, or at a criminal trial when something of the sort had been suggested at the proceedings before the magistrates.

The question whether a situation has arisen in which a previous statement may be proved under this head is, both in civil and criminal cases, largely a matter for the judge's

---

3   *Fox v General Medical Council* [1960] 3 All ER 225, [1960] 1 WLR 1017; *R v Burrows* (1988) 36 ACR 408.

4   *R v Beattie* (1989) 89 Cr App Rep 302 explicitly, endorsing these remarks in *Coll*; cp dicta in *Ahmed v Brumfitt* (1967) 112 Sol Jo 32. See also *R v P(GR)* [1998] Crim LR 663. In Scotland however consistent parts of the allegedly inconsistent statement can be adduced, *Coyle v HM Advocate* 1994 JC 239. In Canada the rule appears to be still less strict: see *R v Simpson* (1988) 46 DLR (4th) 466, at 482; *R v Evans* [1993] 2 SCR 629.

5   It need not be explicit: *R v Martin* (1996) 86 ACR 198.

6   *Flanagan v Fahy* [1918] 2 IR 361. In the United States in *Tome v US* 513 US 150 (1995) the Supreme Court decided by a bare majority that the equivalent rule in that jurisdiction operated only where the previous statement antedated the alleged motive to lie. See also in Australia *R v Fraser* (1995) 85 ACR 385.

7   *R v Y* [1995] Crim LR 155.

8   *R v Roberts* [1942] 1 All ER 187, at 191 per Humphreys J.

9   *R v Oyesiku* (1971) 56 Cr App Rep 240. See also *R v Okai* [1987] Crim LR 259. It is immaterial where the statement amounts to a complaint of a sexual offence that it was not made early enough to be admitted as a complaint, if it nevertheless precedes the time at which fabrication is alleged to have begun: *R v Tyndale* [1999] Crim LR 320.

10   *R v Benjamin* (1913) 8 Cr App Rep 146.

11   *Pearse v Sommers* (1992) 28 NSWLR 492.

decision. It is difficult to improve on the following observations of a former Chief Justice of Australia:[12]

> In as much as the rule forms a definite exception to the general principle excluding statements made out of Court and admits a possibly self-serving statement made by the witness, great care is called for in applying it. The judge at the trial must determine for himself, upon the conduct of the trial before him, whether a case for applying the rule of evidence has arisen—and must exercise care in assuring himself not only that the account given by the witness in his testimony is attacked on the ground of recent invention or reconstruction or that a foundation for such an attack has been laid—but also that the contents of the statement are in fact to the like effect as his account given in his evidence and that having regard to the time and circumstances in which it was made it rationally tends to answer the attack.

Section 6(2)(b) of the Civil Evidence Act 1995 provides that:

> A party who has called or intends to call a person as a witness in civil proceedings may not in those proceedings adduce evidence of a previous statement made by that person, except -
> (a) with the leave of the court, or
> (b) for the purpose of rebutting a suggestion that his evidence had been fabricated.

Such a statement thus does not require special leave, but it is subject to notice requirements, and when admitted is accepted as evidence of the truth of its contents. At common law, and therefore at present in criminal cases, the statement is simply admissible as circumstantial evidence negativing the suggestion of afterthought or fabrication; but, in view of the requirement of close correspondence between the statement and the witness's testimony, the distinction is unimportant, if not non-existent.[13]

4. Other exceptions

It was not until 1968 that a thorough account was given of other common law exceptions to the general prohibition of proof of a witness's prior consistent statements.[14] Mention must be made of three further exceptions described in that article, statements by the accused when arrested, statements by the accused when incriminating articles are recovered from his possession, and statements by witnesses when identifying the accused out of court.[15] Finally a new category seems to have emerged resembling, but not identical to, some of those discussed above.

12 Dixon CJ in *Nominal Defendant v Clements* (1961) 104 CLR 476, at 479. This statement was cited in the Court of Appeal (Criminal Division) in *R v Oyesiku*, above. See also *Damon v Snyder* [1970] VR 81. (Cross-examination on answers to interrogatories inconsistent with testimony held not to be within the recent invention rule.)
13 The Law Commission has recommended adoption of the civil law provision in Law Com No 245 *Evidence in Criminal Proceedings: Hearsay and Related Topics* (Cm 3670, 1997) paras 10.41–10.45, rec 34. For discussion of the application of statutory reform in Australia, see *R v Singh-Bal* (1997) 92 ACR 397.
14 By Gooderson (1968) CLJ 64.
15 A further exception is the previous statement contained in a writing used to refresh memory made evidence in the case by cross-examination on other parts of the document (p 270 above).

(i) Statements on arrest

Perhaps this exception would be better described as 'statements made by the accused to the police when taxed with incriminating facts', for such statements are admissible whether or not there is an arrest. If they are partly or wholly adverse to the accused they are admissible for or against him as confessions,[16] provided that they satisfy the conditions established by the Police and Criminal Evidence Act 1984.[17] If they[18] are partly inculpatory and partly exculpatory, then both parts are admissible as evidence of their truth.[19] This is allowed partly because it would be unfair to admit the inculpatory part, but not a qualification or explanation in the exculpatory part; and partly because any direction discriminating between them would be hard for the judge to formulate and for the jury to understand. There are considerable difficulties both of definition and of principle in this position.[20] It may be difficult to determine exactly which assertions by the accused are to be regarded as the same and which are discrete in a period of continuing but interrupted questioning. It may also be difficult to distinguish between inculpatory elements in the offence which can be established independently but have simply been repeated in the accused's statement, and those which depend for their force significantly upon having been made by him.[1]

If no part of them is adverse to the accused they have been held to be admissible because:[2]

> A statement made voluntarily by an accused person to the police is evidence in the trial because of its vital relevance as showing the reaction of the accused when first taxed with incriminating facts.

If an exculpatory statement has no such relevance, perhaps because made only after careful consideration and upon legal advice, it need not be admitted.[3] If admitted, it is still, unlike a confession, not evidence of the facts stated in it, and the judge need neither take it into account in deciding whether or not there is a case to answer,[4] nor draw it to the jury's attention, if the accused fails to testify at his trial.[5] It is not clear that the slight relevance of such a statement either on grounds of consistency of story or as showing reaction is worth the risk of attempting to explain so illogical and anomalous a rule to the jury.[6] It should be noted that the Law Commission has nevertheless proposed no change in this respect.[7]

16   They may not be adduced by the accused making such a mixed statement since this would open the door to the admission of statements overwhelmingly exculpatory coupled with some minimal admission as evidence of their truth, thus creating a massive exception to the hearsay rule in favour of the accused.

17   Section 76.

18   This point applies to all 'mixed statements' whether made on arrest, or at any other time before trial.

19   *R v Aziz* [1996] AC 41, [1995] 3 All ER 149 robustly endorsing *R v Sharp* [1988] 1 All ER 65, [1988] 1 WLR 7 and *R v Duncan* (1981) 73 Cr App Rep 359. Approved in Ireland, *People v Clark* [1994] 3 IR 289; and in Australia, *M v R* (1994) 62 SASR 364.

20   For cogent consideration see Birch [1997] Crim LR 416.

1   *R v Garrod* [1997] Crim LR 445.

2   *R v Storey* (1968) 52 Cr App Rep 334, at 337.

3   *R v Newsome* (1980) 71 Cr App Rep 325, explaining *R v Pearce* (1979) 69 Cr App Rep 365. See also *R v Steel* (1981) 73 Cr App Rep 173, at 185, where the statement was made, not to the police, but to the accused's solicitor. See also *R v Squire* [1990] Crim LR 341.

4   *R v Storey* above.

5   *R v Barbery* (1975) 62 Cr App Rep 248.

6   It leads to the accused sometimes being better off if his statement is to some extent inculpatory with the odd result that the defence argues that it inculpates the accused, and the prosecution that it wholly exculpates him: see *R v Garrod* [1997] Crim LR 445.

7   Law Com No 245 *Evidence in Criminal Proceedings: Hearsay and Related Topics* (Cm 3670, 1997) paras 8.90–8.92, rec 18.

(ii) Statements made on recovery of incriminating articles

We saw in ch I that, if someone is found in possession of recently stolen goods, there is a presumption of fact that he was either the thief or a guilty handler of them. What he says by way of explanation is therefore admissible on principles similar to those discussed in the last paragraph and, if he is subsequently charged, it may be valuable proof of consistency if he tells the same story in court.[8]

(iii) Previous identification of the accused

To quote Ferguson J, a judge of the Supreme Court of New South Wales, '... evidence has been admitted in criminal trials from time immemorial of the identification of the accused (by witnesses) out of court'.[9] There can be no doubt that identification at the time of or soon after the offence will often strengthen the value of the witness's identification of the accused in court, and nothing more need be said in order to justify the reception of statements forming part of his act of identification.[10] The Law Commission has not only accepted this situation as an exception to the hearsay rule, but has widened it also to cover statements identifying things and places.[11]

(iv) Previous statements alleged to have been concocted

It has been held[12] that where it is alleged in cross-examination that a document, amounting to a previous consistent statement and used by the witness to refresh his memory, has been concocted, then, if the form of the document might be taken by the jury to indicate that the allegation is false,[13] it is admissible in evidence at the instance of the party calling the witness. This differs from the rule relating to cross-examination on parts of the document not used to refresh memory as discussed above, in that here the cross-examination need not extend to any such part. It differs from the rule relating to rebutting a suggestion of subsequent fabrication by reference to a previous consistent statement, since here it is the previous consistent statement itself which is alleged to have been concocted. When such a document has been admitted it is not evidence of the truth of its contents, except to the extent that they relate to its own authenticity.

5. Statements validated by scientific means

Wigmore once said that 'if ever there is devised a psychological test for the valuation of witnesses, the law will run to meet it'. Three possibilities which have been considered involve the use of lie-detectors, truth drugs and hypnosis. None has been received

8   Among the English authorities cited by Gooderson were *R v Abraham* (1848) 3 Cox CC 430; *R v Exall* (1866) 4 F & F 922; *R v Muller* (1865) 4 F & F 383 n, and 388, 389 n (a murder case); *R v Manzano* (1860) 2 F & F 64, 65 n. The Law Commission has also proposed the retention of this rule in its rec 18 above. See also *R v Graham* (1972) 7 CCC (2d) 93.

9   *R v Fannon* (1922) 22 SRNSW 427, at 430.

10   For the position where the maker of the statement gives no evidence of identification or gives hesitant evidence, see pp 49 above and 680 below.

11   Law Com 245, paras 10.46–10.52, rec 34, draft bill, cl 8(5).

12   *R v Sekhon* (1987) 85 Cr App Rep 19.

13   This is vital: cp *R v Fenlon* (1980) 71 Cr App Rep 307; *R v Dillon* (1983) 85 Cr App Rep 29n.

with any enthusiasm. Evidence of the use of a lie-detector has been rejected by the Supreme Court of Canada, whether the relevant subject testifies,[14] or chooses not to do so.[15] In the latter case the accused had been given a truth-drug, and the evidence of the psychiatrist who administered it was admitted at the trial. The admissibility of that evidence was not in issue before the Supreme Court, and in any event did not consist of statements of fact relevant to the issues made under the influence of the drug. That situation did however arise in New Zealand in *R v McKay*.[16] The evidence was rejected because it infringed the rules excluding previous consistent statements and hearsay, because it would distort the process of trial, and because it was unreliable.[17] In Scotland facilities for taking such a statement have been refused, once again because it would involve distortion of the trial process.[18] The evidence of statements made during, and indeed after, a hypnotic trance which had been induced, apparently inadvertently, by a police interrogator, was rejected by the Supreme Court of Canada in *Horvath v R*, largely on grounds of unreliability.[19] Despite arguments[20] in favour of the admission of such statements, it is submitted that the unproven reliability of these techniques, together with the danger of the jury's attributing more weight to such unfamiliar scientific evidence than it deserves, justify the English courts in following the example of their counterparts in the rest of the common law world in excluding such statements unless a convincing case can be made for their reliability, as by following Home Office guidelines.[1] Similar considerations would presumably apply to any other memory enhancing therapy.[2]

D.   UNFAVOURABLE AND HOSTILE WITNESSES[3]

A party calling a witness to prove certain facts may be disappointed by his failure to do so, and his difficulties may be increased by the witness's manifest antipathy to his cause. This lies at the root of the distinction between unfavourable and hostile witnesses. An unfavourable witness is one called by a party to prove a particular fact in issue or relevant to the issue who fails to prove such fact, or proves an opposite fact. A hostile witness is one who is not desirous of telling the truth at the instance of

14   *R v Béland* [1987] 2 SCR 398.
15   *Phillion v R* [1978] 1 SCR 18, not accepting the contrary decision in *R v Wong* [1977] 1 WWR 1, but following the then majority view in the United States, stemming from *Frye v United States* 293 F 1013 (1923). Failure may affect the admissibility of a subsequent confession: *R v Amyof* (1990) 58 CCC (3d) 312; *R v Wheelton* (1992) 71 CCC (3d) 477.
16   [1967] NZLR 139.
17   See Mathieson [1967] Crim LR 645.
18   *Meehan (petitioner)* 1970 JC 11.
19   [1979] 2 SCR 376. See also in Canada, *R v Taillefer* (1995) 100 CCC (3d) 1, *R v Robinson* (1996) 107 CCC (3d) 159; and in Australia, *R v Geering* (1984) 39 SASR 111, and cp *Van Vliet v Griffiths* (1978) 19 SASR 195.
20   See for example, Haward and Ashworth [1980] Crim LR 469, and Harnon [1982] Crim LR 340. For an excellent exposition of the problems see Elliott in Campbell and Waller (eds) *Well and Truly Tried* (1982) and, from a psychological standpoint, Gudjonsson *The Psychology of Interrogations, Confessions and Testimony* (1993).
1   *R v Mayes and McIntosh* [1995] CLY 930, although disclosure of a defective session arriving at inconsistent conclusions from the testimony of the witness was regarded as a material irregularity in *R v Browning* [1995] Crim LR 227 (where the Home Office guidelines are conveniently summarised). See *R v McFelin* [1985] 2 NZLR 750; *R v Jenkyns* (1993) 32 NSWLR 712 for safeguards elsewhere.
2   See *R v Tillott* (1995) 38 NSWLR 1 (EMDR therapy) where many different codes and guidelines for the forensic use of hypnosis are discussed.
3   See Pattenden (1992) 56 J Cr L 414.

the party calling him.[4] It will be convenient to state the common law with regard to unfavourable and hostile witnesses separately, and then to mention the relevant statutory provisions—s 3 of the Criminal Procedure Act 1865, and the Civil Evidence Act 1995; but something must first be said of the prohibition against a party impeaching his own witness.

1. The prohibition against impeaching a party's own witness[5]

A party against whom a witness is called may impeach him in various ways.[6] He may cross-examine him by means of leading questions, ask him about his previous inconsistent statements and prove them if they are denied—a matter which is now covered by statute; he may cross-examine him with regard to his discreditable conduct in the past with a view to showing bad character, or he may ask the witness about his previous convictions or the existence of bias, and prove these two matters by other evidence if they are denied. Finally a party may call evidence to show that the opponent's witness is not to be believed on oath. The prohibition against a party impeaching his own witness means that there is a general rule preventing a litigant from taking any of the above steps with regard to witnesses called by him.[7] It is for the judge to determine whether and to what extent a witness is unfavourable to the party calling him, and no such determination should be made before the witness has been sworn and given a chance to come up to his proof.[8] Such procedure renders a voir dire generally unnecessary[9] on this issue, though where a previous inconsistent statement is relevant to such a determination it should not be revealed to the jury before the witness has been adjudged hostile.[10] It seems that a party may nevertheless invite the Court to disregard his witness's evidence, even though it is consistent with the initial presentation of the case, and in accord with the witness's proof, if the course of the trial has indicated that the party's case would by that stage be better served by so disregarding the evidence.[11]

Various reasons have been given for the general rule. It is said that a party ought not to have the means of discrediting his witness, or that he guarantees the trustworthiness of the evidence he adduces, or that it would be unfair to subject the witness to two cross-examinations. None of these is very convincing, and even though the rule seems to work well enough in ordinary circumstances as applied to unfavourable witnesses, it would be ludicrous to apply it to a hostile witness in its full rigour.[12]

4   Stephen *Digest of the Law of Evidence* (12th edn) art 147; endorsed in *R v Prefas* (1988) 86 Cr App Rep 111. See Pattenden above, where a broader definition is suggested allowing both for animus against the party calling the witness and absence of desire to tell the truth as alternatives.

5   III Wigmore para 896 f. See also Bryant (1982) 32 Univ of Tor LJ 412, (1983) 33 Univ of Tor LJ 108.

6   See further below ch VII sect 2.

7   Even when done for devious reasons under the guise of examination in chief: *R v C(JR)* (1996) 110 CCC (3d) 373.

8   *R v Darby* [1989] Crim LR 817; though this is a matter within the discretion of the court, see *R v Birkby* [1994] 2 NZLR 38.

9   Though permissible: see *R v Jones* [1998] Crim LR 579 (where in contrast to the situation in relation to those apparently hostile, a potentially unfavourable witness may be asked whether the previous statement is true).

10   *R v Darby,* above. See also *Price v Bevan* (1978) 8 SASR 81; *R v Hadlow* [1992] 2 Qd R 440.

11   *Anonima Petroli Italiana SpA v Marlucidez Armadora SA (The Filiatra Legacy)* [1991] 2 Lloyd's Rep 337, at 362.

12   The rule was abrogated by r 607 of the United States Federal Rules (following the Model Code and Uniform Rules), but the Criminal Law Revision Committee was in favour of its retention (11th Report, para 162).

2.   Unfavourable witnesses[13]

At common law a party was allowed to contradict his own witness by calling other evidence[14] if he was unfavourable, but this did not amount to a modification of the prohibition against discrediting his witness because it did not involve resort to any of the methods mentioned at the beginning of the last section. In *Ewer v Ambrose*[15] someone whom the defendant called to prove a partnership proved the contrary, and it was held that the defendant could rely on the testimony of other witnesses in support of the existence of the partnership. In the words of Holroyd J:

> If a witness proves a case against the party calling him, the latter may show the truth by other witnesses. But it is undoubtedly true, that if a party calls a witness to prove a fact, he cannot, when he finds the witness proves the contrary, give general evidence to show that the witness was not to be believed on his oath, but he may show by other evidence that he is mistaken as to the fact which he is called to prove.

This last kind of evidence would necessarily concern the issue more directly than evidence with regard to the witness's credibility, and, in order to appreciate the enormity of the injustice which might be occasioned by rejecting it, a case may be supposed in which a party has four witnesses to support his version of the facts. If he happened to begin by calling a witness who disproved his case, he would be deprived of the testimony of the other three. If he called these before the one who disproved his case, it would have been a question for the jury upon the evidence whether they gave credit to the three or the one. The order in which the witnesses happen to be called ought not to make any difference.[16] Of course, there is a sense in which a man is being discredited if someone asks the court to believe what another man says in preference to his testimony concerning a fact in issue or relevant to the issue, but, although the question is one of degree, the discrediting is a great deal more obvious if one of the methods mentioned at the beginning of the last section is adopted. When this is done, the whole of his testimony is impugned, but this is not necessarily the case when he is contradicted with regard to a particular fact. If a party contradicts part of the testimony of an unfavourable witness, he is not precluded from relying on the rest of that testimony.

3.   Hostile witnesses[17]

The judge may allow the examination-in-chief of a hostile witness to be conducted in the manner of a cross-examination to the extent to which he considers it necessary for

13   'Unfavourable' is used in this sense also in s 38 of the Evidence Act (Cwth) 1995: *R v Souleyman* (1996) 40 NSWLR 712.

14   If the original evidence takes the form of an interrogatory the conflicting testimony may even come from the very same witness: see *Mundy v Bridge Motors Pty Ltd* (1987) 45 SASR 125.

15   (1825) 3 B & C 746. If the prosecution calls a witness to identify the accused and he fails to do so, he is not contradicted by evidence that he did identify the accused given by a police officer who saw him do so at a parade (*R v Osborne and Virtue* [1973] QB 678, [1973] 1 All ER 649), although the officer's evidence gives rise to hearsay problems not as yet fully considered in the English cases.

16   This is the basis of the judgment of Littledale J in *Ewer v Ambrose*. See also *Bradley v Ricardo* (1831) 8 Bing 57.

17   See Newark [1986] Crim LR 441.

the purpose of doing justice.[18] If the witness is not compellable, the possibility of being cross-examined as a hostile witness should be explained before the witness is sworn.[19] The witness may be asked leading questions, challenged with regard to his means of knowledge of the facts to which he is deposing or tested on such matters as the accuracy of his memory and perception; but the party by whom he is called cannot ask about his previous bad conduct and convictions, nor can he adduce evidence of the witness's doubtful veracity. This is the result of the common law, but it used not to be clear whether a statement inconsistent with his present testimony could be proved against a hostile witness—a matter that became increasingly important with the growth of the practice among attorneys of taking a proof of the evidence which a person was prepared to give.[20] As Erle CJ observed:[1]

> There are treacherous witnesses who will hold out that they can prove facts on one side in a cause and then, for a bribe or for some other motive, make statements in support of the opposite interest. In such cases the law undoubtedly ought to permit the party calling the witness to question him as to the former statement, and ascertain, if possible, what induces him to change it.

In *R v Fraser and Warren*,[2] Lord Goddard CJ said that if, in a criminal case, counsel for the prosecution has a statement contradicting a Crown witness who says, at the trial, that he is unable to identify the accused, he should at once show the statement to the judge and ask for leave to cross-examine the witness, but it is doubtful whether the mere existence of an inconsistency between a witness's previous statement and his testimony at the trial will necessarily lead the judge to allow the witness to be treated as hostile. In a civil case, the mere fact that the witness is the other litigant does not mean that he may be treated as hostile.[3] Although the matter has been much more fully discussed in the Commonwealth than in this country, there seems to be no doubt that, in deciding whether to allow the witness to be treated as hostile, the judge may have regard to the witness's demeanour, the terms of any inconsistent statement and the circumstances in which it was made.[4] As the matter is dependent on judicial discretion, the judge's decision will seldom be reversed by an appellate tribunal[5] It is uncertain how an English court will react to the idea of calling a witness known to be hostile for the sole purposes of cross-examining by reference to a previous inconsistent

18   *Bastin v Carew* (1824) Ry & M 127.
19   *R v Pitt* [1983] QB 25, [1983] 3 All ER 63, though failure to do so is not necessarily fatal, *R v Nelson* [1992] Crim LR 653.
20   See, for example, the difference of opinion in *Wright v Beckett* (1834) 1 Mood & R 414.
1   *Melhuish v Collier* (1850) 15 QB 878, at 890.
2   (1956) 40 Cr App Rep 160. See also *R v Pitt* [1983] QB 25, [1982] 3 All ER 63; *R v Mann* (1972) 56 Cr App Rep 750.
3   *Price v Manning* (1889) 42 Ch D 372.
4   *The People v Hannigan* [1941] IR 252; *R v Hunter* [1956] VLR 31 (citing *R v Harris* (1927) 20 Cr App Rep 144, at 146 and doubting whether *Coles v Coles and Brown* (1866) LR 1 P & D 70 supports the view that demeanour alone can be considered); *R v Hayden and Slattery* [1959] VLR 102; *McLellan v Bowyer* (1962) 106 CLR 94; *Wawanesa Mutual Insurance Co v Hanes* (1961) 28 DLR (2d) 386.
5   *Rice v Howard* (1886) 16 QBD 681. In a sufficiently strong case a new trial could be ordered by an appellate tribunal (see the review of the authorities by the High Court of Australia in *McLellan v Bowyer* above).

statement.[6] Although there are cases where it seems to have been allowed,[7] it seems inconsistent with the spirit of the adversarial system.[8]

Although there does not appear to be a fully reported case on the point,[9] it is believed that judges take different views on the question whether a party who has obtained leave to treat his witness as hostile has a right to re-examine him. If the hostility is made manifest only at the stage of re-examination, then cross-examination is naturally permitted.[10]

4. Statutory provisions

(i)   Criminal Procedure Act 1865, s 3

Section 22 of the Common Law Procedure Act 1854 was passed in order to settle the law in civil cases with regard to proof of inconsistent statements by a party's own witness. As was pointed out five years later in *Greenough v Eccles*,[11] the terms of the section were confusing so far as unfavourable witnesses were concerned, but they were re-enacted in s 3 of the Criminal Procedure Act 1865.

This governs a party's right to impeach a hostile witness in civil and criminal cases alike at the present day.[12] It reads as follows:

A party producing a witness shall not be allowed to impeach his credit by general evidence of bad character, but he may, in case the witness shall, in the opinion of the judge, prove adverse, contradict him by other evidence, or, by leave of the judge, prove that he has made at other times a statement inconsistent with his present testimony; but before such last-mentioned proof can be given the circumstances of the supposed statement, sufficient to designate the particular occasion, must be mentioned to the witness, and he must be asked whether or not he has made such statement.

The prohibition on general evidence of bad character applies to hostile and unfavourable witnesses alike. This part of the section is declaratory of the common law and means that the witness cannot be asked about his bad conduct on former occasions or his previous convictions, in order that he may be discredited, while the party calling him cannot adduce evidence of his mendacious disposition.[13] In *Greenough v Eccles* it was decided that 'adverse' means hostile, so the concluding portions of the section are unambiguous so far as the proof of such a witness's previous statements is concerned. The section gives rise to two remaining questions—its effect

---

6   See Munday [1989] Crim LR 866. See also in Australia, *Blewitt v R* (1988) 80 ALR 353; in New Zealand, *R v Schriek* [1997] 2 NZLR 139; and in Canada, *R v Soobrian* (1994) 96 CCC (3d) 208.

7   *R v Honeyghon and Sayles* [1999] Crim LR 221. See also *R v Vibert* (21 October 1973, unreported), CA; *R v Dat* [1998] Crim LR 488.

8   See eg the rule in *Spenceley v De Willott* (1806) 7 East 108 forbidding questioning on irrelevant matters designed to secure false denials so as to discredit the witness.

9   See *R v Wong* [1986] Crim LR 683.

10   As in *R v Powell* [1985] Crim LR 592; *R v Norton and Driver* [1987] Crim LR 687. See also *Willis v Magistrates' Court of Victoria* (1996) 89 ACR 273.

11   (1859) 5 CBNS 786.

12   See *R v Booth* (1981) 74 Cr App Rep 123 (leave required before accused could put inconsistent statement to his own hostile witness).

13   See eg *R v Hutchison* (1990) 53 SASR 94, at 95, 96; cp Pattenden, above.

on the old law concerning unfavourable and hostile witnesses and the evidential value of the inconsistent statements that are proved or admitted under the Act.

(a)   Unfavourable witnesses
The words 'he may, in case the witness shall, in the opinion of the judge, prove adverse, contradict him by other evidence' suggest that a party cannot do this when his witness is merely unfavourable and not, in the opinion of the judge, hostile. If this is so, the section has altered the common law as illustrated by cases such as *Ewer v Ambrose*.[14] It appears to be universally agreed that this is not the effect of the section, and, as long ago as 1859, Cockburn CJ said of the identical provision in the Common Law Procedure Act 1854:[15]

> There has been a great blunder in the drawing of it, and on the part of those who adopted it ... Perhaps the better course is to consider the second part of the section as altogether superfluous and useless.

The alternative, and probably the sounder method, of ignoring the implications of the section is that adopted by Williams and Willes JJ:[16]

> We think the preferable construction is, that in case the witness shall, in the opinion of the judge, prove 'hostile', the party producing him may not only contradict him by other witnesses, as he might heretofore have done, and may still do, if the witness is unfavourable, but may also, by leave of the judge, prove that he has made inconsistent statements.

Whatever means may be adopted in order to reach it, the conclusion is that an unfavourable witness can be contradicted with regard to facts in issue or relevant to the issue, he cannot be cross-examined or discredited in any other way.

(b)   Hostile witnesses
Section 3 of the 1865 Act has not affected the common law according to which the judge has a discretion to allow a hostile witness to be examined by means of leading questions or with reference to a previous statement[17] for this does not amount to impeachment of credit 'by general evidence of bad character'. In *R v Thompson*[18] the accused was convicted of incest with his daughter who was called as a witness by the prosecution. After answering some formal questions she said that she did not wish to give evidence. The judge allowed her to be treated as hostile with the result that she was examined on a statement she had made to the police and by means of leading questions. The Court of Appeal held that the judge had acted properly and affirmed the conviction. The witness did not deny making the statement to the police but, even if she had done so, it is doubtful whether s 3 would have applied to the case for the girl's statement was not 'inconsistent with her present testimony'. If the section does not apply in such circumstances, it is questionable whether the statement can be proved.[19]

14   (1825) 3 B & C 746, p 286 above.
15   *Greenough v Eccles* (1859) 5 CBNS 786, at 806.
16   The quotation is from 28 LJCP 160, at 163.
17   *Clarke v Saffery* (1824) Ry & M 126; *Bastin v Carew* (1824) Ry & M 127.
18   (1976) 64 Cr App Rep 96. See also *R v Lawrie* [1986] Qd R 502; *R v Hadlow* [1992] 2 Qd R 440.
19   See *R v Booth* above.

(c)   Evidential value of previous inconsistent statements

A question naturally arises concerning the use that may be made of inconsistent statements when they are admitted by, or proved against, the witness. Are they evidence of the facts stated, or do they merely constitute a ground for disbelieving the witness's testimony? As s 3 of the Act of 1865 deals only with procedure, the answer depended on the common law which still governs criminal cases on this point. Although judicial expression of the first view was not wanting,[20] the English judges' view of the common law was that statements of witnesses who are not parties put in evidence under s 3 of the Criminal Procedure Act 1865 (and the same is true of those proved or admitted under s 4 and s 5, set out in the next section of this chapter), could not be treated as proof of the facts stated,[1] and the jury should be so warned.[2] When the witness was a party, his previous statement might be admissible as evidence of the facts stated because it was an admission.[3]

An illustration of the common law is provided by *R v White*. Several witnesses called by the prosecution had previously made statements to the police indicating that the accused had participated in a riot. At the trial these witnesses gave evidence in which they said that the accused did not participate in the riot. The previous statements were admitted, and the judge told the jury that they could choose between the witnesses' evidence at the trial and their statements to the police. The jury must have acted on the latter for they returned a verdict of guilty; but the conviction was quashed because:[4]

> quite obviously it is one thing to say that, in view of an earlier statement, the witness is not to be trusted: it is another thing to say that his present testimony is to be disbelieved and his earlier statement, which he now repudiates, is to be substituted for it.

The Court of Criminal Appeal has said:[5]

> when a witness is shown to have made previous statements inconsistent with the evidence given by that witness at the trial the jury should not merely be directed that the evidence given at the trial should be regarded as unreliable; they should also be directed that the previous statements whether sworn or unsworn do not constitute evidence upon which they can act.

In that case the jury had been warned that the testimony was unreliable, so the apparent suggestion that a direction to disregard the testimony is mandatory, was obiter.[6] It has

---

20   See the judgment of Pollock CB in *A-G v Hitchcock* (1847) 16 LJ Ex 259, where he spoke of the jury being at liberty to believe either the one account or the other. The same view was taken by the Supreme Court of Canada in *R v B(KG)* [1993] 1 SCR 740, subject in the majority's view to adequate criteria of reliability.

1   *R v Golder, Jones and Porritt* [1960] 3 All ER 457, [1960] 1 WLR 1169; *R v Oliva* [1965] 3 All ER 116, [1965] 1 WLR 1028.

2   *R v Nelson* [1992] Crim LR 653.

3   The witness is not likely to be a party in the case of statements admitted under s 3 (see *Vocisano v Vocisano* (1974) 130 CLR 267 for a highly unusual case where he was), but might be in the case of those admitted under s 4 and s 5. A non-party witness may of course render his previous statement evidence of the facts stated by admitting its truth in cross-examination (*Birkett v A J Little Ltd* [1962] NSWR 492).

4   Per Lord Hewart CJ (1922) 17 Cr App Rep 60, at 64.

5   *R v Golder, Jones and Porritt* [1960] 3 All ER 457, at 459. See also *R v Oliva* [1965] 3 All ER 116, [1965] 1 WLR 1028; *R v Pearson* [1964] Qd R 471; *R v Schmahl* [1965] VR 745.

6   See *Driscoll v R* (1977) 137 CLR 517, at 537.

not always been acted upon in England,[7] and despite similar remarks in earlier,[8] and blanket endorsement in later,[9] cases, any such necessity has been convincingly criticised by courts of high authority elsewhere in the Commonwealth,[10] and even in England.[11] Circumstances are quite conceivable in which so completely satisfactory an explanation is given that it would be perverse to require the jury to regard the testimony as unreliable. It also seems that where for some reason an earlier inconsistent statement is evidence in the case, then it is a matter for the decision of the court whether it might outweigh subsequent inconsistent testimony.[12] It was accepted in *R v Goodway*[13] that there is now no absolute obligation to disregard such testimony in England, and that the judge has discretion in directing the jury how much may be accepted. It should perhaps be added that if the prior inconsistent statement should be unequivocally accepted as accurate by the witness when put to him, it is then, in effect, incorporated into his testimony, and as such capable of being accepted as evidence of the truth of its contents.[14] The Law Commission has drawn attention to the anomaly whereby a witness too terrified to testify at all may have a previous consistent statement used as evidence, but one terrified only enough to become hostile cannot, and has accordingly recommended that when admitted such statements should become evidence of the truth of what they assert.[15]

(ii) Civil Evidence Act 1995

Section 10(3) of the Civil Evidence Act 1995 leaves intact the provisions of ss 3, 4 and 5 of the Criminal Procedure Act 1865 so far as they relate to the admissibility of previous consistent statements of witnesses, but by s 10(5) does make such statements, when so admissible, evidence of the truth of what they assert.

SECTION 3. CROSS-EXAMINATION AND RE-EXAMINATION

The object of cross-examination is twofold, first, to elicit information concerning the facts in issue or relevant to the issue that is favourable to the party on whose behalf the cross-examination is conducted, and, secondly, to cast doubt upon the accuracy

---

7   See *R v Williams* (1913) 8 Cr App Rep 133.
8   *R v Harris* (1927) 20 Cr App Rep 144, at 147, 148.
9   Eg *R v Oliva* [1965] 3 All ER 116, [1965] 1 WLR 1028.
10 In Australia in *Driscoll*, above; in New Zealand in *R v Morgan* [1981] 2 NZLR 164. In Canada such statements may now be admissible as evidence of their contents: *R v B(KG)* [1993]1 SCR 740; for the older view see *R v Bevan* [1993] 2 SCR 599 (trial held before decision in *R v B(KG)*).
11 *R v Pestano* [1981] Crim LR 397.
12 See *R v Governor of Pentonville Prison, ex p Alves* [1993] AC 284, at 292, sub nom *Alves v DPP* [1992] 4 All ER 787, at 793 (where the statutory procedures for extradition made the earlier foreign statement evidence); *R v Donat* (1985) 82 Cr App Rep 173 (where the earlier statements made in chief were retracted under cross-examination).
13 [1993] 4 All ER 894, at 899.
14 *R v Carrington* [1969] NZLR 790. Though its weight would normally be impaired by the initially inconsistent testimony.
15 Law Com No 245 *Evidence in Criminal Proceedings: Hearsay and Related Topics* (Cm 3670, 1997) paras 10.99–10.101, rec 40. This is quite different from the approach of the Criminal Law Revision Committee in its Eleventh Report *Evidence (General)* (Cmnd 4991, 1972) draft bill, cl 11.

of the evidence-in-chief given against such party.[16] So far as cross-examination to the issue is concerned, the ordinary rules with regard to the admissibility of evidence apply so that the prosecution cannot cross-examine the accused on the contents of an inadmissible confession,[17] and, in criminal cases, the rule against hearsay applies with as much force to the answers given by a witness in cross-examination as it does to those given by him in-chief. Thus, in *R v Thomson*,[18] it was held that a doctor charged with aborting a woman since deceased had been rightly refused permission to ask a prosecution witness in cross-examination whether the deceased had not told her that she intended to operate on herself and later that she had in fact done so. If the accused had called a witness to prove these statements, they would have been inadmissible hearsay and they would not have lost that character by being elicited in cross-examination. There are decisions to the same effect in civil cases,[19] but it seems that, in civil proceedings, the court would now have a discretion to admit statements of deceased persons elicited from a witness under cross-examination as evidence of any fact of which the deceased could have given direct oral evidence.[20]

Any matter upon which it is proposed to contradict the evidence-in-chief given by the witness must normally be put to him[1] so that he may have an opportunity of explaining the contradiction,[2] and failure to do this may be held to imply acceptance of the evidence-in-chief, but is not an inflexible rule[3] and has been held to be unsuitable to proceedings before lay justices,[4] and less applicable to parties, including the complainant in a sexual case.[5] Failure to put the evidence to the witness does not make it inadmissible, but does make it desirable for the witness to be recalled, so as to have an opportunity to comment on it.[6] In criminal proceedings material proposed to be put to the accused in cross-examination should normally have been led by the prosecution as part of its case-in-chief.[7] Leading questions may be employed in cross-examination,[8] but, whether this is directed to the issue or the credit of the witness, the judge has a

16   It was held in Australia in *R v Maslen and Shaw* (1995) 79 ACR 199 that this could be accomplished by showing the accused to have been lying in respect of an irrelevant matter to which he had mistakenly been permitted to testify.

17   *R v Treacey* [1944] 2 All ER 229, 30 Cr App Rep 93; endorsed in *Wong Kam-Ming v R* [1980] AC 247, at 259, [1979] 1 All ER 939, at 945; see also *R v Brophy* [1982] AC 476, [1981] 2 All ER 705, where it was apparently regarded as too obvious to need separate explanation. In Canada it was said in *R v C(G)* (1996) 110 CCC (3d) 233 to be beyond dispute that cross-examination as to tactics at the voir dire was forbidden. See also *R v Neville* [1985] 2 Qd R 398 where cross-examination was forbidden on a previous inconsistent statement which had formed the foundation of a charge of which the witness had been acquitted.

18   [1912] 3 KB 19.

19   *Beare v Garrod* (1915) 85 LJKB 717; *Sharp v Loddington Ironstone Co Ltd* (1924) 132 LT 229.

20   Civil Evidence Act 1995, s 1; it is assumed that a statement is 'given in evidence' within the meaning of this rule if the statement is elicited in cross-examination.

1   Although this may in some circumstances be implicit, or accomplished by raising an eyebrow, see *R v Lovelock* [1997] Crim LR 821.

2   *Browne v Dunn* (1893) 6 R 67; *R v Fenlon and Neal* (1980) 71 Cr App Rep 307. See also *Allied Pastoral Holdings Pty Ltd v Comr of Taxation* [1983] 1 NSWLR 1; *Machado v Berlet* (1986) 32 DLR (4th) 634 applying the rule to a video recording of the claimant.

3   Even in Australia where it is taken very seriously: see *R v Popescu* (1989) 39 ACR 137; *R v Martin* (1990) 48 ACR 208.

4   *O'Connell v Adams* [1973] RTR 150.

5   *R v Grant* (1989) 49 CCC (3d) 410.

6   *R v Cannan* [1998] Crim LR 284.

7   *R v Dartey* (1987) 84 Cr App Rep 352. In most common law jurisdictions outside North America cross-examination of the accused is restricted by statutory provision (see ch IX below for the English rules). In those jurisdictions which pursue a more open policy some restriction is imposed at common law: see eg in Canada *R v Stewart* (1991) 62 CCC (3d) 289

8   *Parkin v Moon* (1836) 7 C & P 408.

discretion under which he may disallow questions which he considers to be improper or oppressive, and this would include leading questions of the second kind mentioned above,[9] or questions requiring the accused to speculate about matters of which he has no first-hand knowledge.[10] Cross-examination by the accused in person of some child witnesses has been restricted by statutory provision.[11] The judge has a residual discretion to regulate the proceedings before him and this may be used to curb excessive cross-examination.[12] Such a power should however be exercised sparingly, and only as a last resort if counsel abuse the restraint expected of them.[13] The judge may also curb cross-examination if the witness becomes too ill,[14] or distressed,[15] for it to continue, and may leave the case to the jury subject to an appropriate warning after such truncation.

All witnesses are liable to be cross-examined except one who is called for the sole purpose of producing a document and one who is not examined-in-chief because he has been called by mistake.[16] A witness who does not come within these excepted categories is liable to be cross-examined, not merely by the opponent of the party calling him, but also by all other parties.[17] All parties have the right to cross-examine witnesses not called by them, whether or not the witness is himself a party, whether or not the witness has given evidence against the party seeking to cross-examine him, and even though the witness is a co-accused.[18] Of course it would be wrong to allow a party to endeavour to discredit a witness who had not given evidence against him, but, so far as cross-examination to the issue is concerned, it is difficult to disagree with the following statement of a South African judge: 'An accused ought, if a fair trial is what

9   At 262. See also the statement of the Bar Council set out in Phipson *Law of Evidence* (14th edn) para 12–16. In New Zealand the use of hypothetical questions has been regulated, see Practice Note [1985] 1 NZLR 386.

10   For example why the prosecution witnesses should be telling lies: *Palmer v R* (1997) 186 CLR 499.

11   Criminal Justice Act 1988, s 34A, inserted by Criminal Justice Act 1991, s 55(7); see *R v De Oliveira* [1997] Crim LR 600 for the judge's role in this situation. This is in addition to the residual power of the judge to control cross-examination of a complainant by the accused in person at common law: *R v Brown* [1998] 2 Cr App Rep 364.

12   See under the old law *Vernon v Bosley (No 2)* [1995] 2 FCR 78; cp *Vernon v Bosley* [1994] PIQR P337. This power has been fortified by Civil Procedure Rule 32.(3) 'The court may limit cross-examination', especially when coupled with the stress on a more 'hands-on' approach, and greater latitude in determining relevance.

13   *Wakeley v R* (1990) 64 ALJR 321, where the High Court refers to *R v Kalia* (1974) 60 Cr App Rep 200 and *R v Maynard* (1979) 69 Cr App Rep 309. In Canada an appeal has been allowed despite there being an overwhelming case against the accused because of the prejudice caused by abusive cross-examination: *R v R(AJ)* (1994) 94 CCC (3d) 168.

14   *R v Stretton and McCallion* (1988) 86 Cr App Rep 7.

15   *R v Wyatt* [1990] Crim LR 343. See in Canada *R v Wyatt* (1997) 115 CCC (3d) 288 where the witness became distressed very early in the cross-examination, and the conviction was quashed.

16   *Wood v Mackinson* (1840) 2 Mood & R 273. The position of a witness called by the judge is not altogether clear. In *R v Tregear* [1967] 2 QB 574, at 580, the judge said that counsel for the prosecution and defence should both have an opportunity of examining and cross-examining the witness he was calling. It has been held in South Australia that there is no absolute right to cross-examine a witness on a voir dire: *R v Henderson and Panagaris* (1984) 14 ACR 274.

17   *Allen v Allen* [1894] P 248, at 254; *Dryden v Surrey County Council and Stewart* [1936] 2 All ER 535, at 537–8 (adversity of interest enough); *Re Baden's Deed Trusts, Baden v Smith* [1967] 3 All ER 159; unless his having been called by a formal opponent has merely pre-empted his being called by the party seeking to cross-examine: *Governors of Peabody Donation Fund v Sir Lindsay Parkinson & Co Ltd* [1983] CLY 1660 (not reported on this point in subsequent proceedings).

18   *R v Fenlon and Neal* (1980) 71 Cr App Rep 307; *R v Hilton* [1972] 1 QB 421, [1971] 3 All ER 541; *Murdoch v Taylor* [1965] AC 574, especially per Lord Morris at 584. *R v Hadwen* [1902] 1 KB 882; *State v Langa* 1963 (4) SA 941; *Nyense v R* [1962] R & N 271; but see *Gemmel and McFadyen v MacNiven* 1928 JC 5.

is aimed at, to be at liberty to cross-examine a co-accused or any witness not called by him who may not have inculpated him in any way in order to establish facts which might tend to support an alibi.'[19] The absence of a right to discredit in such a situation led the other member of the court to prefer to speak of the accused having a right to put questions to rather than cross-examine his co-accused.

The matters that call for further treatment at this stage are the previous contradictory statements of witnesses under cross-examination (a subject which may conveniently be followed by some general remarks concerning cross-examination on documents), and the outline of the rule that a witness's answers to questions that are collateral to the issue must be treated as final. More detail upon these matters, and in relation to impugning the credit of a witness is postponed until the next chapter. A final brief part mentions re-examination.

A.   PREVIOUS INCONSISTENT[20] STATEMENTS[1]

The proof of previous statements[2] of a witness under cross-examination that are inconsistent with his evidence-in-chief is governed by ss 4 and 5 of the Criminal Procedure Act 1865,[3] but their evidential effect is dependent on the common law and the Civil Evidence Act 1995. Under the Civil Procedure Rules a testifying witness may always be cross-examined on his witness statement, whether he referred to it in chief or not.[4] It seems that they are not to be regarded as being used *against* the witness for the purposes of being excluded under provisions abrogating the privilege against self-incrimination.[5]

I.   Criminal Procedure Act 1865, s 4

Under s 4 of the Criminal Procedure Act 1865:

> If a witness, upon cross-examination as to a former statement made by him relative to the subject-matter of the indictment or proceeding, and inconsistent with his present testimony, does not distinctly admit that he has made such statement, proof may be given that he did in fact make it; but before such proof can be given, the circumstances of the supposed statement, sufficient to designate the particular occasion, must be mentioned to the witness, and he must be asked whether or not he has made such statement.

---

19   Harcourt J in *State v Langa* 1963 (4) SA 941, at 945. On the whole subject see Carvell [1965] Crim LR 419.

20   There is no English authority on what constitutes an inconsistency for this purpose (see *Carbury v Measures* (1904) 4 SRNSW 569 and V *Wigmore* para 1040). There is Victorian authority for the sound view that, if the statement is both consistent and inconsistent, the whole must go in (*R v Titijewski* [1970] VR 371 citing *R v Riley* (1866) 4 F & F 964).

1   See generally Bryant (1984) 62 Crim BR 43.

2   The statement may be proved in the form of an audio-visual tape, see *R v Andrews* [1987] 1 Qd R 21; but cp *R v Parks* (1993) 84 CCC (3d) 353 requiring a transcript. Special rules apply however when video-recordings made by a child under s 32A of the Criminal Justice Act 1988, one of which has been adduced as evidence in chief, are inconsistent: *R v Eldridge and Salmon* [1999] Crim LR 166.

3   These sections apply to civil as well as criminal cases (s 1), and they re-enact ss 23 and 24 of the Common Law Procedure Act 1854.

4   Rule 32.11.

5   *Re K* [1994] 3 All ER 230, sub nom *Kent County Council v K* [1994] 1 WLR 912.

This is, almost, if not entirely, declaratory of the common law.[6] If a statement is admitted or proved under the section, it merely impugns the testimony of the witness under cross-examination (unless he happens to be a party when the statement may amount to an admission); it does not constitute evidence of the facts stated at common law,[7] and in a criminal case it is a matter for the discretion of the judge how much of the inconsistent statement should be revealed to the jury.[8] Under s 6 of the Civil Evidence Act 1968 the statement is, however, also admissible in civil proceedings as evidence of any fact of which the maker could have given oral evidence.[9]

2. Criminal Procedure Act 1865, s 5

Section 5 of the Act of 1865 applies to cases in which the previous statement is in writing:

> A witness may be cross-examined as to previous statements made by him in writing or reduced into writing relative to the subject-matter of the indictment or proceeding, without such writing being shown to him; but if it is intended to contradict such witness by the writing, his attention must, before such contradictory proof can be given, be called to those parts of the writing which are to be used for the purpose of so contradicting him; provided always, that it shall be competent for the judge, at any time during the trial, to require the production of the writing for his inspection, and he may thereupon make such use of it for the purposes of the trial as he may think fit.

The witness can be asked whether he made a statement[10] and be cross-examined on the general nature of its contents without being shown the document.[11] The cross-examiner is not obliged to put it in evidence, even if he shows it to the witness, but he must do so if he wishes to use the document as a contradictory statement[12] and the witness must be given an opportunity of explaining the contradiction.[13] It seems appropriate that the section apply only to documents made, or approved, by the

---

6 See the judgment of Parke B in *Crowley v Page* (1837) 7 C & P 789. The only doubtful point seems to have concerned the position when the witness did not clearly deny or admit the statement. See *R v Hart* (1957) 42 Cr App Rep 47, at 50. This case confirms that the section is in no way confined to previous statements on oath.

7 See *R v Askew* [1981] Crim LR 398. Though it may now do so in Canada, *R v B(KG)* [1993] 1 SCR 740.

8 *R v Longden* (1995) Times, 31 May. For doubts as to the merits of this procedure, see *R v Hawes* (1994) 35 NSWLR 294.

9 For this conflict between civil and criminal proceedings, see p 291 above. The Law Commission in Law Com No 245 *Evidence in Criminal Proceedings: Hearsay and Related Topics* (Cm 3670, 1997) paras 10.87–10.101, rec 40 proposes its elimination.

10 In contrast to s 4 it need not be an *inconsistent* statement: see *R v Manapouri* [1995] 2 NZLR 407.

11 Wrottesley *The Examination of Witnesses* (2nd edn) 61 f. Cross-examining counsel must have the document with him even if he does not intend to contradict the witness with it (*R v Yousry* (1914) 11 Cr App Rep 13; *R v Anderson* (1929) 21 Cr App Rep 178).

12 *R v Riley* (1866) 4 F & F 964; *R v Wright* (1866) 4 F & F 967.

13 Even if this means recalling a witness before the Court of Appeal if the statement has been made after the trial, *R v Conway* (1979) 70 Cr App Rep 4.

witness.[14] In civil proceedings the document is evidence of the facts stated in it by virtue of s 6 of the Civil Evidence Act 1995, but not yet[15] in criminal proceedings because the proviso to s 5 of the 1865 Act with regard to the judge making such use of it as he may think fit[16] does not extend to his directing the jury to choose between it and the testimony of the witness.

A cross-examiner cannot make the contents of a document evidence in a case simply by requiring the person under cross-examination to read it aloud. Thus, in *R v Gillespie and Simpson*,[17] the manageress and cashier of a store were charged with theft and false accounting, the case against them being that they had accounted for sums less than those shown to have been received by documents prepared by salesgirls. Some of the girls gave evidence, but documents prepared by others were handed to the accused in cross-examination with a request, notwithstanding their dissent from what was said in the documents, to read them aloud. This was duly done and the judge referred to the documents in his summing-up. The procedure was held to have been improper by the Court of Appeal which quashed the convictions:[18]

> As it seems to this court, if a document is produced to a witness and the witness is asked; 'Do you see what that document purports to record?' the witness may say 'I see it, I accept it as true' in which case the contents of the document become evidence: or he may say: 'I see what is there written, I do not accept it as true', whereupon that which is purported to be recorded in the document is not evidence against that person who has rejected the contents; it becomes what one might call non-evidence, the document itself being nothing but hearsay.

B.   CROSS-EXAMINATION ON DOCUMENTS GENERALLY[19]

But there are situations in which a document may become evidence of the facts stated in it by virtue of the common law rules concerning cross-examination. If, at the trial, a party calls for and inspects a document held by his adversary, he is bound to put it in evidence if required to do so, provided the document was not being used to refresh the memory of one of the adversary's witnesses. If the document was being used for this purpose, neither the inspection, nor cross-examination on such parts of the document as were used to refresh memory, makes it evidence in the case, though cross-examination on other parts will have this effect.

In *Stroud v Stroud*,[20] a divorce case in which a doctor was giving evidence on behalf of the wife, the husband's counsel called for and inspected medical reports from other doctors which were in the hands of the doctor who was testifying although he was not referring to them for any purpose. Wrangham J held that the reports were thus made evidence in the case at the option of the wife. Unfortunately Wrangham J did not say,

---

14   *R v Walker* (1993) 61 SASR 260.
15   The Law Commission in Law Com No 245 *Evidence in Criminal Proceedings: Hearsay and Related Topics* (Cm 3670, 1997) paras 10.87–10.101, rec 40 proposes the elimination of this distinction.
16   For antipodean discussion of the extent of the discretion of the judge see McHugh [1986] NZLR 309; *R v Thompson* [1995] 3 NZLR 423.
17   (1967) 51 Cr App Rep 172, applied in *R v Cooper* (1985) 82 Cr App Rep 74; *R v Cross* (1990) 91 Cr App Rep 115.
18   Winn LJ.
19   For a helpful set of notes see Glass (ed) *Evidence Seminars* p 136.
20   [1963] 3 All ER 539, [1963] 1 WLR 1080. The headnote to *Senat v Senat* [1965] P 172, [1965] 2 All ER 505 suggests that that case conflicts with *Stroud v Stroud*, but this is doubtful because the diaries with which *Senat*'s case were concerned were used to refresh memory.

any more than do any of the older authorities on cross-examination on documents, whether or not they were used to refresh memory,[1] or for what purpose the reports could have been made evidence in the case. They might have contained matter consistent with the doctor's testimony or inconsistent with the evidence of one of the husband's witnesses or their contents might have been received as hearsay statements in support of the wife's case.

In Australia, it has been held that a document called for in cross-examination may become evidence of the facts stated in it at the option[2] of the party thus obliged to produce it, although the rule against hearsay would have prevented him from relying on the document for this purpose in the first instance. Thus, in *Walker v Walker*[3] a wife was applying for a maintenance order against her husband. She made a statement in-chief with regard to his income, and was cross-examined concerning her means of knowledge of this matter. She mentioned a letter received by her father from an accountant who had been making enquiries. Counsel for the husband called for the letter, and it was held that he had rightly been obliged to put it in evidence at the request of the wife's counsel. A majority of the High Court was also of the opinion that the trial judge had been correct in treating the letter as some evidence of the husband's means.

C.   FINALITY OF ANSWERS TO COLLATERAL QUESTIONS

I.   The general rule

There is a sound general rule, based on the desirability of avoiding a multiplicity of issues,[4] that the answers given by a witness to questions put to him in cross-examination concerning collateral facts must be treated as final. They may or may not be accepted by the jury, but the cross-examiner must take them for better or worse and cannot contradict them by other evidence.[5]

As relevance is a matter of degree, it is impossible to devise an exhaustive means of determining when a question is collateral for the purpose of the rule under consideration; Pollock CB said in the leading case of *A-G v Hitchcock*:[6]

> The test whether a matter is collateral or not is this: if the answer of a witness is a matter which you would be allowed on your own part to prove in evidence— if it have such a connection with the issues, that you would be allowed to give it in evidence—then it is a matter on which you may contradict him.

---

1   *Wharam v Routledge* (1805) 5 Esp 235; *Wilson v Bowie* (1823) 1 C & P 8; *Calvert v Flower* (1836) 7 C & P 386; *Palmer v Maclear and M'Grath* (1858) 1 Sw & Tr 149.

2   Opinions have differed on whether the option persists or expires after the end of the cross-examination; cp *R v Foggo, ex p A-G* [1989] 2 Qd R 49 (persists) and *Hatziparadissis v GFC (Manufacturing) Pty Ltd* [1978] VR 181 (expires).

3   (1937) 57 CLR 630. The rule was not applied to criminal proceedings in *R v Weatherstone* (1968) 12 FLR 14, and has been recommended for abolition by the Australian Law Reform Commission, Interim Report No 26 (1985) para 617. For a consideration of the limits of the decision in *Walker v Walker*, see *O'Brien v Clegg* [1951] Qd R 1.

4   And secondarily upon considerations of fairness to the witness, *Natta v Canham* (1991) 104 ALR 143.

5   Nor should he suggest to the witness that he can, *S v Damalis* 1984 (2) SA 105.

6   (1847) 1 Exch 91, at 99. Pollock CB was really saying no more than that a witness may be contradicted on matters relevant to the issue (see per Ogilvy-Thompson JA in *S v Sinkankanka* 1963 2 SA 531, at 539). See also *Palmer v Trower* (1852) 8 Exch 247.

The defendant was charged with using a cistern for making malt without complying with various statutory requirements. One Spooner gave evidence of the use of the cistern and was asked in cross-examination on behalf of the defendant whether he had not told Cook that the excise officers had offered him twenty pounds to say that the cistern had been used. Spooner denied that he had ever made such a statement, and it was held that the defendant could not ask Cook to narrate the alleged conversation. If Cook had been able to prove that Spooner had actually received a bribe from the excise officers, his testimony would have been admissible because it would have tended to show bias under an exception to the rule prohibiting contradictory evidence on collateral issues.[7]

The effect of the judgments in *Hitchcock*'s case is aptly stated in the following passage from an American author:[8]

> Independent evidence may be given to prove a self-contradictory statement by a primary witness only if (a) the statement contradicts testimony by the primary witness about a matter directly in issue in the litigation, or (b) the statement contradicts testimony by the primary witness as to 'those matters which affect the motives, temper and character of the witness, ... with reference to his feelings toward one party or the other'.

It seems however that the general rule is necessarily circular, and would be just as well expressed in terms of sufficient relevance to justify rebuttal, especially in relation to cases where the witness is a participant in the events in issue.[9]

The Australian case of *Piddington v Bennett and Wood Pty Ltd*[10] prompts speculation on the merits of the finality rule. One of the claimant's witnesses in a running-down claim was asked in cross-examination how he accounted for his presence at the scene of the accident, and he said that he had been to the bank on behalf of the named person. A new trial was ordered on the ground that the judge had wrongly allowed the bank manager to give evidence to the effect that no business was done on that day on behalf of the man named by the witness. Similar speculations are prompted by the Irish case of *R v Burke*[11] in which a witness was giving evidence through an interpreter. He was cross-examined about his knowledge of English, and it was held that evidence could not be given to contradict his statement that he was ignorant of the language. No doubt the questions of how a witness came to be where he was and whether an interpreter was really necessary were collateral, but the first could have been a step towards challenging the witness's presence at the accident,[12] and the second casts doubt on the honesty of the whole of his testimony. The indubitable value of the finality rule should not blind us to the undesirability of a closed list of exceptions to it.

---

7   For a clear, recent restatement by the Supreme Court of Canada of the effect of this rule prohibiting rebuttal of other types of attack on credibility, see *Krause v R* [1986] 2 SCR 466, softened to some extent in *R v Aalders* [1993] 2 SCR 482.

8   Maguire *Evidence, Common Sense and Common Law* 67. The sub-quotation is from the judgment of Pollock CB.

9   See the extensive discussion of the authorities in *Natta v Canham* above where it is also suggested that the rule might be applied more flexibly where trial is by judge alone. This view was also adopted in New Zealand in *R v M* [1996] 3 NZLR 502. See also Seabrooke [1999] Crim LR 387.

10   (1940) 63 CLR 533.

11   (1858) 8 Cox CC 44.

12   This has been held to go to the issue in Nova Scotia (*Tzagarakis v Stevens* (1968) 69 DLR (2d) 466, a decision which seems to follow from *Toohey v Metropolitan Police Comr* [1965] AC 595, [1965] 1 All ER 506).

2.   Exceptions to the general rule

The nature of the cross-examination will sometimes entitle the party calling the witness to call another one to testify to matters which could not have been deposed to in the absence of the cross-examination. For example, if the claimant in a running-down case is cross-examined in such a way as to suggest that he has suppressed information about a later accident in which he sustained injuries, his solicitor may be called to prove the prompt disclosure of those injuries. The point is directly relevant to the amount of damages claimed,[13] but cases of this sort do not constitute a real exception to the rule that a witness's answers to collateral questions or questions concerning credit only are final.

There are three well-recognised exceptions—the fact that a witness has been convicted of a crime, the fact that he is biased in favour of the party calling him and the fact that he has previously made a statement inconsistent with his present testimony.[14] Nothing more need be said about the third exception, and both of the other two will be discussed in the following chapter.

D.   RE-EXAMINATION[15]

The subject of re-examination can be disposed of briefly. Leading questions may not be put, any more than they may be put in-chief; previous consistent statements can be put to the witness only if rendered admissible by the terms of the cross-examination, or under the Civil Evidence Act 1995, s 6, or to refresh memory.[16] The most important rule is that the re-examination must be confined to matters arising out of the cross-examination, and new matter may be introduced only by leave of the judge. Thus, in *Prince v Samo*,[17] a claim for malicious arrest arising out of the non-payment of a loan alleged by the claimant to be a gift, the claimant had given evidence at the trial of one of the defendant's witnesses for perjury. The claimant's attorney was present at the trial, and he was called as a witness on behalf of his client in the present proceedings. The attorney could not be asked in-chief about statements made by the claimant at the earlier trial on account of the rule against hearsay, and the prohibition on evidence of a witness's prior consistent statements; but he was asked in cross-examination whether the claimant had not said, in the course of his evidence in the previous proceedings, that he had repeatedly been insolvent. It was held that he could not be asked in re-examination about other portions of the claimant's earlier evidence which had no connection with the statement concerning his insolvency. The rule is sound in principle because it prevents the reception of inadmissible evidence in re-examination,[18] under the guise of dealing with points emerging from the cross-examination, and any hardship that the rule may occasion can be mitigated at the discretion of the judge. It is nowadays

---

13   *Drakos v Smith* [1958] VLR 536; the solicitor's evidence was also admissible on the ground that it rebutted the cross-examiner's allegation of recent invention. Had the defendant been in a position to rebut the claimant's denials of his failure to disclose the later accident, no doubt he would have been allowed to call a witness to do so.

14   See *R v Aldridge* (1990) 51 ACR 281 for a neat exploitation of this exception to evade the result in *Hitchcock* in a somewhat similar situation.

15   Yet another stage of re-cross-examination about a matter raised in re-examination was permitted in Australia in *R v Cheshire* (1994) 76 ACR 261.

16   *R v Harman* (1984) 148 JP 289.

17   (1838) 7 Ad & El 627.

18   See eg *Petty and Maiden v R* (1991) 173 CLR 95 where it was employed to prevent cross-examination on the accused's failure in committal proceedings to raise a defence advanced only in the course of presenting the defence case at trial.

likely to be exercised to promote 'the best chances of learning the truth',[19] and in *R v Sutton*[20] refreshment of memory was permitted on re-examination in relation to matters omitted from evidence in chief more it seemed because of their intrinsic relevance than as a response to cross-examination.

The terms of the cross-examination may, however, let significant and prejudicial evidence in through the re-examination although such evidence would not be admissible in-chief. Perhaps the most striking example is provided by a case in which it was held that a suggestion to a child witness in cross-examination that her testimony was activated by hatred for the accused, would permit re-examination to show that such hatred was derived from the witness's belief that the accused had attempted to murder someone.[1]

19   *R v Richardson* [1971] 2 QB 484, [1971] 2 All ER 773.
20   (1991) 94 Cr App Rep 70.
1   *R v Phair* [1986] 1 Qd R 136. See also *R v Nation* [1954] SASR 189; *Wojcic v Incorporated Nominal Defendant* [1969] VR 323; *R v Singleton* [1986] 2 Qd R 535.

CHAPTER VII

Character and credibility

This chapter, and the two which follow, deal with the important and complicated topic of how far evidence may be adduced bearing upon the record and disposition of a person when either directly or indirectly relevant to matters before the court.[1] Like much of the law of evidence the topic is complicated by confusion of terminology, by the disparity of contexts to which the terminology is applied, by the vicissitudes of history, and by the impact of piecemeal statutory change. The topic is at its most important when it is concerned with the character of the accused person in a criminal case. Special rules have been developed at common law to deal with the extent to which the prosecution can lead in chief evidence showing the accused in a discreditable light, in England generally described as similar fact evidence. Cross-examination of the accused about such matters is governed by the Criminal Evidence Act 1898. Those two topics will be dealt with in the chapters which follow. This chapter will deal with the rules which govern the use of evidence relating to the character of witnesses, and other cases where character is for some reason or another relevant. In relation to non-party witnesses such questions normally go only to the credibility of the witness; in the other cases they may more readily go directly to the issues before the court. It is convenient to divide the chapter into three principal sections dealing with the character of a party's own witness, the character of an opponent's witness, and other cases where character is in issue. A final short section deals with the rebuttal of character when it has been impugned. It is always necessary to consider the distinctions between evidence of good character and of bad; evidence of disposition, of reputation, of record, and of discreditable conduct; evidence going to the issue and evidence going only to credit; and whether the evidence is to be led in chief, to be the subject of cross-examination, or to be adduced in rebuttal.

---

1   Many of these matters are currently under review by the Law Commission, and were discussed in its consultation paper No 141 *Evidence in Criminal Proceedings: Previous Misconduct of a Defendant* (1996).

SECTION I.   CHARACTER OF PARTY'S OWN WITNESS

Evidence explicitly commending the good character of the party's own witness[2] is rarely led, even though as going to the credibility of the witness, a matter which is automatically in issue, it might logically be thought material and relevant. Thus in *R v Turner*, where the dispute related to the intention of the accused, Lawton LJ said: 'in general evidence can be called to impugn the credibility of witnesses but not led in chief to bolster it up.'[3] The rule applies equally to cases where there is a conflict of testimony on a question of fact. In *R v Robinson*[4] it was said in general terms that 'the Crown cannot call a witness of fact and then, without more, call a psychologist or psychiatrist to give reasons why the jury should regard that witness as reliable.' Such a procedure is regarded as usurping the function of the jury.

It is nevertheless common for a party to present his witnesses with as respectable an appearance as possible,[5] and introductory questions are commonly asked about the employment and marital status of the witness so as to enhance such an impression.[6] Very occasionally reference is made to the good character of a witness as justifying reliance upon his evidence, both in criminal[7] and in civil proceedings.[8] If the impression conveyed in this way is totally false, it may be sufficiently serious to provide grounds for a successful appeal,[9] or even, if it emerges after an appeal, for the conviction of a lower court to be quashed by certiorari.[10] The court accepts that in general a party tenders a witness as capable of being believed. If a party, and especially the prosecution in a criminal case, tenders a witness whose character may be impugned, for example by proof of previous convictions, the court expects candour. If a prosecution witness has such convictions, thus tending to undermine the case for the prosecution, there is now[11] a primary statutory obligation to disclose them in advance, and to inform the jury of them at the outset.[12] In such cases the party asks the court to accept the testimony of the witness despite his bad character. It very occasionally happens that a party seeks to prove the bad character of his own witness in order to enhance his credibility on a particular matter, and there appears to be no reason to object to this.[13] In general a

2   Except in cases to be considered later in this chapter where the witness is a party to the events in issue, such as the accused or a complainant.

3   [1975] QB 834, at 842, [1975] 1 All ER 70, at 75; see also Lord Ellenborough CJ in *Bamfield v Massey* (1808) 1 Camp 460, at 460, 461. See further, above, p 284 on the use of scientific means to accomplish this.

4   [1994] 3 All ER 346, at 352. See also *R v Nelson* [1982] Qd R 636 where the evidence was adduced by the defence.

5   See Cmnd 4991, para 135.

6   Such introductory questioning of the accused in a criminal case should be very carefully confined so as to avoid any suggestion that it amounts to giving evidence of good character under the Criminal Evidence Act 1898, s 1(f)(ii); see *R v Coulman* (1927) 20 Cr App Rep 106 (regular employment); *R v Baldwin* (1925) 18 Cr App Rep 175 (marital status). See further, ch IX below.

7   See eg *R v Kemp* [1995] 1 Cr App Rep 151, at 152.

8   See eg *Orchard v South Eastern Electricity Board* [1987] QB 565, [1987] 1 All ER 95, at 578, 104.

9   *Meek v Fleming* [1961] 2 QB 366, [1961] 3 All ER 148, where the court was deliberately left with the impression that a police witness, sued for assault, had retained the rank of chief inspector, when he had in fact been demoted to sergeant for being concerned with the presentation of false evidence to a court.

10   *R v Knightsbridge Crown Court, ex p Goonatilleke* [1986] QB 1, [1985] 2 All ER 498.

11   Criminal Procedure and Investigations Act 1996, s 3. For the earlier position, see *R v Guney* [1998] 2 Cr App Rep 242. For a comparative survey see *Wilson v Police* [1992] 2 NZLR 533.

12   *R v Taylor: R v Goodman* [1999] Crim LR 407, unless requested not to do so by the defence.

13   It occurred in *R v Brophy* [1982] AC 476, [1981] 2 All ER 705 (membership of IRA to support allegation of police misconduct); and in Australia on a similar basis in *R v von Rijssen* (1995) 77 ACR 566.

party is neither inclined, nor permitted, to impeach the credibility of his own witness,[14] not even when the witness is the opposing party.[15] This rule is enshrined by the Criminal Procedure Act 1865 to the extent that it prohibits a party from impeaching his own witness 'by general evidence of bad character',[16] and was defended by the Criminal Law Revision Committee,[17] largely on the basis that a party should not be in a position to intimidate a witness into testifying, perhaps falsely, in his favour. This argument fails to address the situation where a party might discover only after a witness has testified adversely just why he should have chosen to do so.[18] For this reason the rule has been condemned as unconstitutional in the United States, at least as concerns the accused in a criminal trial,[19] and has been widely abrogated by statute.[20] It clearly cannot be applied to a hostile witness in its full rigour. Apart from the statutory provision for inconsistent statements dealt with in the previous chapter, the rules relating to the impeachment of hostile witnesses are still governed by the common law in other respects. It seems clear that the witness cannot be impeached by evidence of convictions or discreditable acts unconnected with his testimony, so far as those matters are not governed by the statutory prohibition against general evidence of bad character, which must be understood in its common law sense of reputation.[1] Nor may he be cross-examined about his general veracity. It is however equally clear that he can be cross-examined about his means of knowledge, and general capacity. It is slightly less certain whether or not he can be cross-examined about possible bias against the party calling him, but the better view is that he may be so cross-examined.[2]

SECTION 2.   CHARACTER OF OPPONENT'S WITNESS

An opponent's witness may be discredited in a wider variety of ways than one's own. In addition to demonstrating lack of knowledge or capacity and inconsistent statements, it is possible to raise his previous convictions, discreditable conduct, bias, corruption or lack of veracity. There are however two general restrictions. The first is that the matter must be relevant, at least to the witness's credibility,[3] though this sometimes seems rather notional. If it is relevant only to credit, the general rule is that evidence may not be adduced to rebut the witness's denial. Thus in *R v Cargill*[4] where the accused was charged with a sexual offence against a child he was not permitted to adduce evidence to rebut her denial of being a prostitute, despite the fact that she had, in error, been allowed to assert in chief that she was a virgin. Since she was a child, consent was not in issue, and her prostitution, even if it could be proved, was relevant

---

14   As noted above at p 286. See also III *Wigmore* para 896.
15   See *Scott v Sampson* (1881) 8 QBD 491, at 498; *Skender v Barker* (1987) 44 DLR (4th) 106, at 125.
16   Section 3, above p 288.
17   Cmnd 4991, paras 162–4. These arguments were rejected by the Australian Law Reform Commission, Research Paper No 8 'Manner of Giving Evidence' ch 9.
18   See Lord Denman CJ in *Dunn v Aslett* (1838) 2 Mood & R 122.
19   *Chambers v Mississippi* 410 US 285, at 294 (1973), though this view has been rejected in Canada: see *R v Williams* (1985) 44 CR (3d) 351.
20   See, for example, r 607 of Federal Rules (following the Model Code and Uniform Rules).
1   *R v Rowton* (1865) Le & Ca 520, discussed further below at p 325.
2   Despite dicta to the contrary in *Fenton v Hughes* (1802) 7 Ves 287, at 290, and in *R v Ball* (1839) 8 C & P 745, at 746, the point seems settled by *R v Chapman* (1838) 8 C & P 558, at 559, *Dunn v Aslett* (1838) 2 Mood & R 122, at 123, and *Melhuish v Collier* (1850) 15 QB 878, at 890.
3   In *R v Humphreys and Tully* [1993] Crim LR 288 questions simply showing association with criminals were rejected on this basis.
4   (1913) 8 Cr App Rep 224.

only to credit. The second general restriction is that the judge has the duty to prevent questioning of an unduly offensive, vexatious or embarrassing character,[5] and to prevent the process of the court from being abused to torture witnesses by oppressive cross-examination.[6] It is now convenient to consider the different ways of attacking the character of an opponent's witness. Convictions, which are the subject of an explicit statutory rule, will be considered first. They can be regarded as affecting credit only on the basis that they show the witness in a generally unfavourable light. Since the same light is shed by equally discreditable conduct which does not happen to have become the subject of a conviction, it is necessary to consider also evidence of that character. Traditionally, bias in the sense of underlying and undue sympathy or hostility felt by the witness towards a party has been regarded as relevant to credit, and has been distinguished from corruption, in the sense of more specific interference with testimony, typically by way of bribery. Finally there is a special technique of the common law permitting an attack upon the general veracity of a witness. For convenience of exposition these will be considered separately, but similar principles underpin them all.

A.   CONVICTIONS[7]

It was relatively rare for witnesses who had convictions to be regarded as competent to give evidence at common law.[8] The question became important only after the passage of the Evidence Act 1843. It was considered by the Common Law Commissioners who recommended in 1853 that cross-examination be confined to 'offences which imply turpitude and want of probity, and more especially absence of veracity—as for instance, perjury, forgery, obtaining money or goods under false pretences and the like.'[9] For some reason this limitation was not included in the ensuing statutory provision which now reads: [10]

> A witness may be questioned as to whether he has been convicted of any ... misdemeanour and upon being so questioned, if he either denies or does not

---

5   *Vassiliades v Vassiliades* (1941) 18 Cyprus LR 10, at 22 per Lord Wright; *Wong Kam-Ming v R* [1980] AC 247, at 260, [1979] 1 All ER 939, at 946 per Lord Edmund-Davies. See also *Fanjoy v R* (1985) 21 DLR (4th) 321.

6   *Re Mundell* (1883) 48 LT 776, at 778; *R v Brown* [1998] 2 Cr App Rep 364. See also in Canada, *R v Walker* (1994) 90 CCC (3d) 144 where the cross-examination was of the accused who there attracts no special protection when testifying.

7   In some situations adjudications of disciplinary tribunals seem to be assimilated to convictions: see eg *R v Edwards* [1991] 2 All ER 266, at 275, [1991] 1 WLR 207, at 216; but this may lead to difficulty since such adjudications are unaffected by the provisions of either s 6 of the Criminal Procedure Act 1865, of s 11 of the Civil Evidence Act 1968 or s 74 of the Police and Criminal Evidence Act 1984 which apply in the relevant respects only to convictions. Cp *R v Dick* [1982] Tas R 282. In Canada convictions have been held to comprehend those in which an appeal is still pending: *R v Watson* (1996) 108 CCC (3d) 310 (though there the conviction had relevance both to issue, and to credit in other ways as well). The convictions must be those of the accused himself for the purpose of this rule: *R v Dupuis* (1995) 98 CCC (3d) 496 (not his father's); *R v Kino and Mete* [1997] 3 NZLR 24 (not those of a non-testifying co-accused).

8   In *Bugg v Day* (1949) 79 CLR 442, at 467, Dixon J, dissenting on this point, took the view that at common law questions had to be restricted to convictions for offences involving the veracity of the witness.

9   Second Report of Her Majesty's Commissioners for Inquiry into the Process, Practice and Pleading in the Superior Courts of Law (1853) at 21.

10   Criminal Procedure Act 1865, s 6. Canada Evidence Act 1985, s 12 is in similarly wide terms: see *R v Watkins* (1992) 70 CCC (3d) 341. For historical background see Ladd (1936) 4 U Chi LR 69.

admit the fact, or refuses to answer, it shall be lawful for the cross-examining party to prove such conviction.

Whatever the reason for enacting the statute in this form it was generally taken to authorise cross-examination about any previous conviction.[11] The Criminal Law Revision Committee recommended the requirement of an explicit link between the conviction and the credibility of the witness, leaving the interpretation of such provision to the courts without further guidance. It is to be regretted that no such provision has yet been included in any subsequent legislation[12] in England.[13] It should be noted however that where convictions are of a minor character, the accused is entitled, nevertheless, to a direction, if he is otherwise qualified to have one, as to his good character.[14] It should be noted that although convictions which are 'spent' under the provisions of the Rehabilitation of Offenders Act 1974 are technically admissible in criminal proceedings,[15] the court, as a matter of practice, requires leave to be sought before permitting cross-examination on such convictions.[16] Cross-examination is subject to the discretion of the judge to disallow such questioning, a discretion recommended to be exercised as benevolently to the accused as possible,[17] only as a last resort if justice can be done in no other way,[18] and less generously than in cases of live convictions.[19] This has been applied where cases of assault depended upon a conflict of testimony[20] as to which party was the aggressor, when one had spent convictions for dishonesty and violence.[1] In civil proceedings a spent conviction can be put to a witness in the discretion of the court when it is relevant to an issue, including relevance to credit, when justice cannot otherwise be done, though such a conclusion should not be reached without consideration also of the prejudice it may cause.[2]

11 In *Clifford v Clifford* [1961] 3 All ER 231, at 232, [1961] 1 WLR 1274, at 1276, per Cairns J, 'It has never, I think, been doubted that a conviction for any offence could be put to a witness by way of cross-examination as to credit, even though the offence was not one of dishonesty'. In *R v Latimer* [1988] 11 NIJB 1 a witness's credibility was attacked by cross-examination about the theft of a pound of butter nineteen years before. But see *R v Sweet-Escott* (1971) 55 Cr App Rep 316, at 320.

12 Cmnd 4991, paras 159–61, draft Bill, cl 10(1). In Canada it has been held that the dishonesty of the basis for the conviction trumps the triviality of the sum involved: *R v Turlon* (1989) 70 CR (3d) 376.

13 In the United States rule 609 of the Federal Rules of Evidence was amended in 1990 so as to subject convictions used under it to impeach witnesses other than the accused to the general balancing test in rule 403. In New South Wales s 56 of the Evidence Act confers a discretion to exclude reference to convictions which 'do not materially affect the credibility of the witness': see *R v Aldridge* (1990) 20 NSWLR 737.

14 *R v Durbin* [1995] 2 Cr App Rep 84, see further below p 321.

15 Section 7(2)(a), and 25-year-old convictions have been permitted to be put to an accused person aged under 50: *R v Bailey* [1989] Crim LR 723.

16 *Practice Note* [1975] 2 All ER 1072, [1975] 1 WLR 1065. Non-compliance with the direction is however not necessarily fatal to a conviction, *R v Smallman* [1982] Crim LR 175.

17 *R v Nye* (1982) 75 Cr App Rep 247. See also *R v O'Shea* [1993] Crim LR 951.

18 See broad dicta in *R v Hastings Justices, ex p McSpirit* (1994) Times, 23 June, 162 JP 44.

19 *R v Lawrence* [1995] Crim LR 815.

20 And even in its absence when the accused's account was otherwise before the court: *R v Whelan* [1996] Crim LR 423.

1   *R v Paraskeva* (1982) 76 Cr App Rep 162; *R v Evans* (1992) 156 JP 539.

2   *Thomas v Metropolitan Police Comr* [1997] QB 813, [1997] 1 All ER 747, which comes dangerously close to emasculating the Practice Direction. In *R v Isleworth Crown Court, ex p Marland* (1998) 162 JP 251 a decision so admitting a spent conviction was upheld even though, or because, no transcript of reasons justifying such a decision at trial was available.

The statute itself provides for proof of the conviction if the witness should deny it,[3] thus constituting an explicit statutory exception to the general rule that denial of a collateral matter cannot be rebutted.[4]

B.   DISCREDITABLE ACTS

If the character of a testifying[5] witness is relevant to the issue, then he may be cross-examined about it, and any denial rebutted, and in such a case the judge should be particularly careful to ensure that the jury understands that the evidence may be regarded as going both to credit and to issue.[6]

The traditional rule of the scope of cross-examination and rebuttal was laid down by Lawrence J in *Harris v Tippett*:[7]

> I will permit questions to be put to a witness as to any improper conduct of which he may have been guilty for the purpose of trying his credit; but, when the questions are irrelevant to the issue on the record, you cannot call witnesses to contradict the answers he gives.

There are thus two issues: first, whether cross-examination about the discreditable matter is to be allowed at all; and, second, if it is, whether a denial can be rebutted. These will be considered in turn.

If the question imputes a crime of which the witness has not been convicted[8] he may claim the benefit of the privilege against self-incrimination so as to refuse to answer.[9] Subject to that, and to the judge's discretion to disallow improper questions, cross-examination about discreditable acts was widely permitted.[10] The width and tone[11] of such cross-examination caused some disquiet which was not wholly stilled by a new rule of court made in 1883.[12] Principles governing the discretion to disallow cross-examination to credit were propounded by Stephen, incorporated into the Indian Evidence Act, and endorsed by Sankey LJ in *Hobbs v Tinling & Co Ltd*[13] to the effect that (i) questions are proper only when answers would seriously impair the credibility of the witness; (ii) questions are improper if they relate to matters so remote in time or of such a character that if true they could not seriously impair the credibility of the

---

3   The marginal note to the section suggests that it was principally designed to facilitate such proof.
4   Under the old law a false denial could always provide the basis for a charge of perjury, *R v Baker* [1895] 1 QB 797. See now *R v Sweet-Escott* (1971) 55 Cr App Rep 316. See also *R v Livingstone* [1987] 1 Qd R 38.
5   See below p 326 for discussion of evidence of the character of the co-accused, and p 331 for that of a non-testifying third party.
6   *R v Arcangioli* [1994] 1 SCR 129.
7   (1811) 2 Camp 637, at 638.
8   If the witness has been charged, but not yet convicted, Canadian authority distinguishes between witnesses for the defence where the question may not be asked because there is nothing to discredit the witness, and witnesses for the prosecution whose credibility may be affected by the desire to curry favour with the prosecuting authorities: *Titus v R* [1983] 1 SCR 259.
9   In the early nineteenth century he could invoke an analogous privilege in respect of questions the answers to which would disgrace him.
10   Although it must be the matter put in cross-examination itself, and not a false denial alone which impugns the credibility of the witness: *Spenceley v De Willott* (1806) 7 East 108.
11   See in Australia for modern concern about the tone of cross-examination on such matters, *R v Power and Power* (1996) 87 ACR 407, at 416.
12   Order 36, r 38, not carried over into the new rules in 1965. The rules of the bar do however set out appropriate principles, see *R v Guney* [1998] 2 Cr App Rep 242, at 259D.
13   [1929] 2 KB 1, at 51.

witness; and (iii) questions are improper if there is a substantial disproportion between the importance of the imputation against the witness's character and the importance of his evidence to the issue to be decided.[14]

In *R v Edwards*[15] the Court of Appeal considered how far it was proper to cross-examine a police witness about previous improprieties to the effect that there was systematic perversion of justice, that some officers had been the subject of criminal or disciplinary processes in relation to the falsification of evidence, and that acquittals had been secured in cases where the witnesses had testified. The Court rejected the first line of attack as too remote,[16] accepted the second only to the extent that the proceedings had culminated in adverse findings,[17] and the third only where there was no other reasonable explanation for the acquittal than a determination that the witness must have been lying.[18] It is dubious how far a witness may be asked about criticisms of his testimony made by a judge in earlier proceedings, whether or not an acquittal resulted.[19]

Attention has been focused on this problem by high profile investigations into improper practices in particular units of the police force,[20] and in the view of the Lord Chief Justice an inclination to construct defences especially to take advantage of such suspicion.[1] The first conclusion in *Edwards* that the court will not entertain cross-examination based on generalised allegations against the officers of a unit has largely been endorsed,[2] and explained in *R v Guney* on the basis that it is unfair to cross-examine about the misconduct of another, and that there is a danger of a bandwagon effect when a multiplicity of unproved allegations is put to a police officer. This raises the issue of the extent to which unproved allegations can be put to a police officer, or reliance placed upon the failure of a prosecution in which he has been heavily involved. In *R v Edwards* the court looked carefully at the circumstances of each allegation and each unsuccessful case. It must be recognised that acquittal does not necessarily lead to the conclusion that any particular prosecution witness[3] was lying, still less success of an appeal against conviction,[4] and perhaps least of all a decision not to proceed with a prosecution at all. It has nevertheless been accepted that if, on analysis of the earlier case, it appears that doubt as to the credibility of the police officer in a relevant respect accounted for the failure to prosecute successfully, then that may be put in

---

14 These principles still allow considerable latitude to a cross-examiner, see *R v Longman and Richardson* [1969] 1 QB 299, [1968] 2 All ER 761, where it was put to a witness not only that she was generally unreliable but that she was a drunkard, suffered from hallucinations, entertained groundless fears, was a prostitute and a deliberate perjurer, and in the words of the court her whole history and background were brought out.

15 [1991] 2 All ER 266, [1991] 1 WLR 207.

16 See also *R v Irish* [1995] Crim LR 145. It is not obvious why this reverse similar fact argument is rejected so perfunctorily.

17 Though this seems more restrictive than the statutory view in the Criminal Evidence Act 1898, s 1(f) where it seems to be assumed that charges may impugn credit.

18 See the discussion of *R v Thorne* (1977) 66 Cr App Rep 6; *R v Cooke* (1986) 84 Cr App Rep 286. The earlier cases of *R v Hay* (1983) 77 Cr App Rep 70 and *R v Doosti* (1985) 82 Cr App Rep 181, and the later cases of *R v Lewis* (1992) Guardian, 9 April, *R v Lucas* [1993] Crim LR 599 and *R v Gale* [1994] Crim LR 208 should also be considered.

19 See *Humphries v R* (1987) 75 ALR 31.

20 Reported cases have referred to the investigations of the West Midlands Serious Crime Squad, and the Stoke Newington drugs squad. The principles apply generally to professional misconduct, see *R v Guney* above at 260A.

1 Lord Taylor CJ in the 1994 Tom Sargent lecture (1994) NLJ, 28 January, at 127.

2 See *R v Meads* [1996] Crim LR 519; *R v Clancy* [1997] Crim LR 290; *R v Guney*; but see *R v Maxine Edwards* [1996] 2 Cr App Rep 345; *R v Whelan* [1997] Crim LR 353.

3 The same applies to key lay prosecution witnesses: *R v H* (1990) 90 Cr App Rep 440.

4 *R v Guney* above at 262C.

cross-examination.[5] Given the recognition[6] in *R v Guney* of a culture of discreditable behaviour, solidarity and misplaced loyalty in some police units, this seems remarkably limited.

If a question is allowed, then as stated above, the rule used to be that the witness's denial could not be rebutted on a purely collateral matter, but here as elsewhere there are now signs of a more liberal approach to rebuttal,[7] certainly in criminal cases.[8] A modern example is *R v Busby*[9] where it was suggested that a police witness for the prosecution had fabricated an oral confession and threatened a potential witness for the defence so as to prevent him from testifying. Both allegations were denied by the police officer, and the defence proposed to call the man who had been threatened to rebut the denial of a threat. The judge refused to permit rebuttal applying the traditional collateral matter rule, but the Court of Appeal quashed the conviction on the basis that the defence should have been allowed to rebut the denial because it went to a fact in issue. This seems quite contrary to the decision in *Harris v Tippett*,[10] and to most tests for the distinction between credit and issue,[11] in whether to allow the original question to be put. It should be noted that in this case the argument seems simply to have been that a man who would tamper with potential witnesses in the way alleged was a man whose testimony was likely to be unreliable, and one who ought not to be believed when there was a conflict with the testimony of the accused who alleged that the witness's evidence of an oral confession was a fabrication. It was not suggested that there was any special animus against the accused,[12] or that the witness's testimony had been secured by corruption. A similar approach is also apparent in the Divisional Court's agreement[13] that 'a matter going to the credit of a witness in a criminal case cannot be said to be collateral to the vital issue; ... especially where ... the witness in question provides the only evidence upon that issue.' This is especially likely to be the case where the issue arises in a sexual case where there is a clear conflict of evidence

---

5   See *R v Beattie* (1996) 89 ACR 393 for a similar decision in Australia under the provisions of the Evidence Act (NSW) 1995.

6   At 261A.

7   This passage was cited with apparent approval, and applied in *R v Nagrecha* [1997] 2 Cr App Rep 401. See also in Canada, *Aalders v R* [1993] 2 SCR 482, *R v R(D)* [1996] 2 SCR 291, at 313; and in Australia, *Natta v Canham* (1991) 104 ALR 143; *Urban Transport Authority of New South Wales v Nweiser* (1991) 28 NSWLR 471.

8   Though the suggestion in *R v Funderburk* [1990] 2 All ER 482, at 486, [1990] 1 WLR 587, at 591 that there is a separate category permitting rebuttal in cases where the police have gone to improper lengths to secure a conviction was explicitly rejected by Lord Lane CJ in *R v Edwards* at 274, 215. The stringent approach of *Harris v Tippett* has been maintained in civil litigation in Australia: see *Kurgiel v Mitsubishi Motors Australia Ltd* (1990) 54 SASR 125.

9   (1981) 75 Cr App Rep 79. See also *R v Mendy* (1976) 64 Cr App Rep 4, where a witness's denial that he had received an improper communication to assist his testimony for the accused was permitted to be rebutted.

10   (1811) 2 Camp 637. Though Pattenden has questioned the degree of inconsistency: see [1992] Crim LR 549, at 551.

11   Various formulations were advanced in *A-G v Hitchcock* (1847) 1 Exch 91, at 99. For further discussion see *R v Funderburk* [1990] 2 All ER 482, [1990] 1 WLR 587.

12   *Busby* was nevertheless characterised as a case of bias in *Edwards*; but if so, it is bias in an extended sense overlapping this category, a view endorsed by Wolchover in [1992] Crim LR 863, at 865.

13   In *R v Knightsbridge Crown Court, ex p Goonatilleke* [1986] QB 1, at 11. For further examples of liberality see also *R v Marsh* (1985) 83 Cr App Rep 165; *R v Barton* (1986) 85 Cr App Rep 5, at 13. For an Australian application to the credibility of a sexual complainant by reference to other sexual relations between the parties, see *Bannister v R* (1993) 10 WAR 484; but see also *Hickman v R* (1993) 60 SASR 415 where the issue upon which credibility depended was too remote from the facts in issue.

as to the truth of an allegation about sexual contact in private.[14] It remains the case however that in cases where rebuttal may be time-consuming, confusing and inconclusive, rebuttal is less likely to be allowed.[15] So too the more remote the issue from the central issues of the trial, the less the court will be inclined to allow rebuttal.[16]

C. BIAS[17]

Bias was more important under the old law when incompetence on account of interest was widespread. If a wife was totally incompetent to testify for a spouse, it was not unnatural for a court to allow a witness to be asked whether she was the mistress of the party for whom she was testifying, and even for her denial to be rebutted.[18] In the modern law it is quite clear that many witnesses, such as parties and their close relatives, are likely to be biased, and there is no special need to bring this out. In some cases it may not be obvious, and it is then perhaps desirable to make the true position clear by permitting rebuttal of a denial,[19] but not if the evidence is peripheral.[20] It seems similarly reasonable in a case where some special factor is present in addition to foreseeable bias, such as the information passed to the accused's husband while he was waiting outside the court before giving his evidence in his wife's favour in *R v Mendy*,[1] to allow it to be brought out, once again by rebuttal of a denial. The English courts have not had reason to consider the question whether an admission of bias for one reason lets in evidence of bias for another reason; the Supreme Court of Victoria has held that it does not.[2]

D. CORRUPTION

Corruption requires separate treatment, if only because the bias cases have been expressly distinguished on the ground of constituting a separate area.[3] The scope for an allegation of corruption is limited because if the corruption were attempted by a party to the proceedings, it could in any event be proved as a form of admission by

---

14   *R v Nagrecha* above, in such a case denial of a previous disputed complaint of sexual contact is especially likely to be permitted to be rebutted.

15   In *R v S* [1992] Crim LR 307 the Court of Appeal distinguished between an attempt to rebut the denial that an allegation of rape was false by readily controvertible evidence such as consent, and by effectively incontrovertible evidence such as proof of absence abroad.

16   In *R v Neale* [1998] Crim LR 737 this was taken to the extent of excluding rebuttal of lies alleged to have been made by the complainant in other parts of the same complaint on which the accused was charged, but against his wife who had not been charged, even though these complaints were of the same general character as those made against the accused, and had a sexual context.

17   It seems that in the United States generic bias is included: see Park (1996) 67 U of Col LR 747 (analysis of cross-examination about racial bias of police witness in the OJ Simpson case).

18   See *Thomas v David* (1836) 7 C & P 350. In *R v Richardson and Longman* [1969] 1 QB 299, [1968] 2 All ER 761, a witness was even permitted to be called to rebut the testimony of a mistress that she was afraid of her paramour.

19   As in *R v Phillips* (1936) 26 Cr App Rep 17, where relations between the accused and his wife and children had become poisoned.

20   *R v Young* [1995] Crim LR 653.

1   *R v Mendy* (1976) 64 Cr App Rep 4.

2   *Bakopoulos v General Motors Holdens Pty Ltd* [1973] VR 190 (although it allowed evidence of more extreme bias than had been admitted).

3   In *A-G v Hitchcock* (1847) 1 Exch 91, at 100. The connection remains close since the offer of a bribe is some evidence of the bias of the offeror.

conduct.[4] The whole area was reviewed in *A-G v Hitchcock*[5] where a witness for the prosecution in an excise case was cross-examined as to whether he had said that he had been offered a bribe to testify, impliedly falsely, for the prosecution. The prosecution argued that his denial of so saying could not be rebutted because it was a collateral matter, and more collateral than his denial of the actual receipt of a bribe would have been, which, they argued, could not have been rebutted either. The defence argued that the matter was not completely extrinsic. The court held that the denial could not be rebutted because the question was collateral in the sense that even if it could be shown that the witness had said that he had been offered a bribe it would constitute no disparagement of him. This however would seem to make the question not merely collateral, but wholly irrelevant. His denial of having said he had been offered a bribe might indeed disparage him if false, but it was already well-established by 1847 that it was impermissible to make an irrelevant allegation, merely in the hope of securing a false denial which could be rebutted so as to discredit the witness.[6] It seems hard to contend that saying that a bribe has been offered in any way reveals that one has been accepted. In such a situation the man who has accepted a bribe will either keep quiet if he is speaking to a stranger, or confide that he has accepted it if speaking to a close friend. The only man who will openly admit that he has been offered a bribe is one who implies that he has rejected it. It seems that if the issue relates to the solicitation of a bribe by the witness rebuttal is permitted.[7] In *A-G v Hitchcock* the court had been careful not to accede to the full width of the argument advanced by the prosecution, though it is hard to fit the case of an actual bribe into the formulations of the various tests for the distinction between collateral and crucial issues propounded by the different judges. It may however be the case that here too the only test is the importance of the allegation in the context of the case. This certainly seems to have been the view of Lord Hewart CJ in *R v Phillips*,[8] where the question was whether the denial of the child victims of alleged incest by their father that they had been schooled by their mother could be rebutted.[9] It is conceivable that some witnesses may become so tainted as to become impervious to cross-examination, even when denials can be rebutted, and in such a case there may be no alternative but to preclude their testimony altogether.[10]

E.   LACK OF VERACITY

From the very beginning of the modern law of evidence it has been possible to call a witness to swear that the opponent's witness cannot be believed upon his oath.[11] It was established that the impugning witness must speak from his personal knowledge,[12]

---

4   *Moriarty v London, Chatham and Dover Rly Co* (1870) LR 5 QB 314.
5   See above.
6   *Spenceley v De Willott* (1806) 7 East 108.
7   *Jackson v Thomason* (1861) 8 Jur NS 134; *R v Denley* [1970] Crim LR 583; *R v Aldridge* (1990) 20 NSWLR 737. Cp *R v Umanski* [1961] VLR 242. Any solicitation of a bribe by a witness for the prosecution must be disclosed to the defence, *R v Rasheed* (1994) 158 JP 941.
8   (1936) 26 Cr App Rep 17.
9   The rebuttal was to have been by two women to whom they had admitted that this was so, but it is not clear why this would not have been inadmissible as hearsay. In *R v S* (1988) 39 ACR 288 where a denial of an allegation of corruption was rebutted, surrebuttal of that rebuttal was permitted.
10   The Ontario Court of Appeal divided on this issue in *R v Buric and Parsniak* (1996) 106 CCC (3d) 97.
11   Wigmore traces the rule back to 1664.
12   *Trial of O'Connor* (1798) 26 How St Tr 1192, 27 How St Tr 32.

but that he could not refer to particular events to justify his belief.[13] The pattern of the question moved from the general to the more particular, by asking first 'Have you the means of knowing what the general character of the witness is?', and then 'From such knowledge of his general character would you believe him on oath?'[14] It was not necessary that the witness have personal knowledge of false testimony by the witness,[15] and even if he did, he would not be allowed to refer to it under the ban on collateral matters.[16] The rule was reconsidered in *R v Brown and Hedley*[17] in the light of the decision in *R v Rowton*[18] that a witness could not express his personal opinion of the accused's character in rebuttal of a character witness called by the accused. The reasoning of the court was not wholly satisfactory, but the outcome was to endorse the existing practice, and to condense the questioning to elicit a simple asseveration that the impugning witness would not believe the opponent's witness on his oath.[19] It became very rare in practice for this cumbersome, anomalous and unconvincing exercise to be conducted.[20] Its continued availability was however endorsed by a unanimous House of Lords in *Toohey v Metropolitan Police Comr.*[1] In *R v Richardson and Longman*[2] strenuous efforts were made to impugn the credibility of a key witness for the prosecution. The defence called a witness in the hope that he would testify that this witness could not be believed on her oath if she were frightened, and her own evidence was that she was frightened of the accused. The trial judge allowed the witness to be asked if he were aware of her reputation for veracity, and whether he would believe her on oath. After a caution from the trial judge the witness replied that in certain particulars she could be believed, whereupon the judge intervened to prevent any qualification of that statement, though the witness had got so far as to indicate that he wished to make some qualification. Nor, despite counsel's persistence, would the trial judge allow the witness to be asked to give an opinion of her credibility on oath on the basis of his personal knowledge of her. It was held that the further question should have been permitted, and that a witness is allowed to express his opinion of the veracity of another on the basis both of the general reputation for veracity, and of his personal knowledge, of the impugned witness. No final view was expressed about the intervention to prevent qualification, though the court seemed to incline to the view that qualification is impermissible if it is adduced only as a means of introducing in chief particular reasons for the qualification, though cross-examination about such reasons is permissible. It should also be noted that the party tendering the witness is not entitled to anticipate attack in court on this basis, and gets its rebuttal in first, as that is indistinguishable from inadmissible 'oath-helping'.[3]

This long-standing rule is to be distinguished from the situation in which the witness's lack of veracity is imputed to some specific medical or mental condition.[4] In

13   *R v Rudge* (1805) Peake Add Cas 232, a decision of Lawrence J who also presided in *Harris v Tippett* (1811) 2 Camp 637.
14   See *Mawson v Hartsink* (1802) 4 Esp 102.
15   *R v Bispham* (1830) 4 C & P 392.
16   *R v Hemp* (1833) 5 C & P 468.
17   (1867) 10 Cox CC 453 (a better report than (1867) 1 CCR 70).
18   (1865) Le & Ca 520.
19   See also *R v Watson* (1817) 2 Stark 116, at 152 for this form of question.
20   None of the Lords of Appeal, nor any of the counsel, in *Toohey*, below, could recall its ever having happened.
1   [1965] AC 595, [1965] 1 All ER 506.
2   [1969] 1 QB 299, [1968] 2 All ER 761.
3   *R v Beard* [1998] Crim LR 585.
4   See Pattenden [1986] Crim LR 92; *Murphy v R* (1989) 86 ALR 35; *R v Kliman* (1996) 107 CCC (3d) 549, at 564 correcting just such confusion by the trial judge.

Toohey v Metropolitan Police Comr[5] the accused was charged with assault, and wished to call medical evidence that the victim, who had testified for the prosecution, was suffering from hysteria. The courts below refused to permit such evidence.[6] In the House of Lords counsel did not seek to support that decision, and it was overruled, the rule being held to be that:[7]

> Medical evidence is admissible to show that a witness suffers from some disease or defect or abnormality of mind that affects the reliability of his evidence. Such evidence is not confined to a general opinion of the unreliability of the witness, but may give all the matters necessary to show not only the foundation of and the reasons for the diagnosis but also the extent to which the credibility of the witness is affected.

It seems clearly right that such evidence should be before the jury, and the possibility in these circumstances of prolonging the trial unduly is remote. There is some danger of attempts to influence the jury's assessment of the credibility of a witness by calling medical evidence to prove matters within the jury's normal competence, such as the propensity of some witnesses, who could perfectly well tell the truth, to tell lies.[8] Such cases are best dealt with on the basis of the relevance of the evidence, and the proper function of expert witnesses.[9] The rule in *Toohey* applies just as much to evidence adduced by the prosecution as by the defence.[10] Expert testimony as to the effect of a marginal mental condition upon a witness's veracity is more likely to be received when it is offered to rebut testimony that the witness should not be believed on oath,[11] than where it is offered in advance of any attack.[12]

Although not strictly relevant to impugning the testimony of an opponent's witness by medical evidence, it is convenient to consider here the question of how far a statement tendered by the prosecution can be discredited by medical evidence of the condition of the maker at the time that the statement was made. It has been argued above[13] that the court has, at least, a discretion to reject a confession made by an accused person suffering at that time from mental instability. Under s 76 of the Police and Criminal Evidence Act 1984 a confession may be excluded if it were obtained in consequence of anything done which was likely in the circumstances existing at the time to render a confession unreliable. It might well be argued that to question a mentally disturbed person was so likely.[14] In such cases it would seem right that the defence should be able to adduce medical evidence of the accused's condition at such a time.[15] Such

5   [1965] AC 595, [1965] 1 All ER 506.
6   In reliance upon *R v Gunewardene* [1951] 2 KB 600, [1951] 2 All ER 290.
7   At 609, 512.
8   See *R v Ashcroft* [1954] Qd R 81, at 85; *R v MacKenney* (1980) 72 Cr App Rep 78.
9   See below ch XII. The attempt in *R v MacKenney* to limit the decision in *Toohey* to total incapacity to tell the truth appears to be inconsistent with the last sentence of Lord Pearce's speech quoted above.
10   *R v Eades* [1972] Crim LR 99.
11   As in *R v Taylor* (1986) 31 CCC (3d) 1 (allegation of sexual abuse by borderline schizophrenic).
12   As in *R v B* [1987] 1 NZLR 362 (allegation of sexual abuse by slightly retarded twelve year old).
13   See above, p 194.
14   As recognised by the prescription of a mandatory direction to the jury of the need for caution in convicting upon such a basis: Police and Criminal Evidence Act 1984, s 77.
15   Expert medical evidence of the accused's condition at the time of confessing adduced to impugn its reliability was admitted in *R v Powell* [1980] Crim LR 39, and held admissible in *R v Ward* [1993] 2 All ER 577. It was rejected in *R v Weightman* (1990) 92 Cr App Rep 291 where the relevant condition was held not sufficiently beyond the comprehension of normal people.

evidence has been admitted in Commonwealth jurisdictions.[16] To the extent that *Toohey* is relied upon to justify these decisions it is somewhat questionable whether it goes so far.[17] In these cases the accused himself often testifies inconsistently with his confession, and it would appear that the expert evidence could be regarded as simply bolstering the testimony of the accused in the way criticised by the Court of Appeal in *R v Turner*.[18]

SECTION 3. CHARACTER OF PARTY

There are a number of rather miscellaneous situations to be considered in this section. Strictly not all of the subjects are parties, for example, prosecutions for rape are normally undertaken by the police, and not by the complainant, whose character may be put in issue. The first part of this section deals with the admissibility of evidence of character in relation to such cases, loosely categorised, as the character of the prosecutor. The second part is concerned with the rules of common law governing the character of the accused in those cases where it is not adduced in chief by the prosecution, for example where the character of the accused is put in issue by a character witness called on his behalf. The third part deals with the admissibility of evidence of the character of a third party who was, or is alleged to have been, closely concerned with the events in issue, often as the true perpetrator of the crime.

A. PROSECUTOR

By far the greatest accumulation of authority has accreted around the question of the admissibility of evidence and questioning as to the character of the complainant on an allegation of rape or allied crimes. There are a number of reasons for this. One is that rape is rare in being a crime where the state of mind of the complainant is important; in evidential terms, her disposition may be relevant to the question of whether or not she consented. It is also a defence to rape that the accused believed the complainant to be consenting, so her reputation for unchastity may become relevant. It has also been remarked that sexual intercourse, whether or not consensual, most often takes place in private, and leaves few visible traces of having occurred. Evidence is often effectively limited to that of the parties, and much is likely to depend upon the balance of credibility between them.[19] This has important effects for the law of evidence since it is capable of reducing the difference between questions going to credit and questions going to the issue to vanishing point.[20] If the only issue is consent and the only evidence is the testimony of the complainant, the conclusion that she is unworthy of credit must be decisive of the issue. The difficulties caused by these factors are also present in relation to much of the evidence used to resolve them. If it is sought to prove consent by evidence that the complainant is sexually promiscuous, it is likely to be just as difficult for the

16 See *Sinclair v R* (1947) 73 CLR 316; *Jackson v R* (1962) 108 CLR 591; *Phillion v R* [1978] 1 SCR 18 (though this aspect of the case was not the subject of the appeal); *Murphy v R* (1989) 86 ALR 35.
17 See *R v McKay* [1967] NZLR 139, at 153.
18 [1975] QB 834, at 842, [1975] 1 All ER 70, at 75. See also *R v Moore* [1982] 1 NZLR 242.
19 Although it has been upheld in Canada to be wrong to present the issue to the jury in that way: *R v NM* [1995] 2 SCR 415; and in Australia, it has been held to be wrong to cross-examine the accused as to his knowledge of any reason why the complainant should lie: *Palmer v R* (1997) 186 CLR 499.
20 See *R v Viola* [1982] 3 All ER 73, at 77, [1982] 1 WLR 1138, at 1143. See Seabrooke [1999] Crim LR 387 where he suggests that it is the *significance* of the distinction which diminishes.

defence to rebut her denials of such promiscuity as it is for the prosecution to prove that she did not consent on the occasion in issue. If it is alleged that she has made a previous false allegation of rape it is unclear how its falsity could satisfactorily be established.[1] In other words the collateral issues in such cases are likely to prove particularly time-consuming, difficult to resolve and confusing to the jury.

It is also likely to be more than usually unfair without warning to confront the complainant at the trial with isolated examples of her extrinsic sexual behaviour, since sexual activity tends to occur frequently, and it really would be tantamount to forcing her to defend her whole life in a way clearly less true than in relation to, say, allegations of crime. It has already been noted that the law has, in other respects, been influenced by the supposition that the testimony of complainants of sexual crimes may be tainted by considerations not obvious to juries. It should now be noted that juries in sexual cases may be influenced by considerations not intended by the law.[2] It must finally be remembered that the common law has developed during a period of rapidly changing sexual manners. Is it then at all surprising that the law should be confused and confusing, and latterly the subject of investigation and legislative reform?

The position broadly established at common law at the beginning of the nineteenth century was that the complainant could be cross-examined about her promiscuity in general,[3] but not about particular acts of intercourse with named men.[4] This position crystallised into rules prohibiting rebuttal of her denials by adducing evidence of particular acts of sexual intercourse,[5] subject to three exceptions. According to these her denials could be rebutted by evidence of her prostitution,[6] of other acts of intercourse with the accused,[7] or of other sexual acts constituting part of the surrounding circumstances.[8] It seems that such rebuttal was usually justified on the basis that it went to consent, though this argument was not available in *R v Barker*, where it was regarded as going to credibility.[9] The concept of prostitution was itself somewhat vague, and became interpreted in such a wide manner that it defeated one of the professed objects of the general ban on rebuttal of denials, namely, that it exposed the complainant to cross-examination upon the whole of her sexual life without notice.[10] It was also possible to adduce extrinsic evidence, cross-examine and rebut if denied on all the surrounding circumstances of the incident in question, including the sexual behaviour of the complainant.[11]

---

1   In *R v Nagrecha* [1997] 2 Cr App Rep 401 this problem was side-stepped because the making of any complaint of a sexual nature was denied, so it was unnecessary to explore its falsity. This seems questionable since the cross-examination was relevant only upon the premise that the complaint was false.

2   See Kalven and Zeisel *The American Jury* (1966) 249–54.

3   *R v Clarke* (1817) 2 Stark 241.

4   *R v Hodgson* (1812) Russ & Ry 211.

5   *R v Holmes* (1871) 12 Cox CC 137.

6   *R v Barker* (1829) 3 C & P 589.

7   *R v Martin* (1834) 6 C & P 562; *R v Riley* (1887) 16 Cox CC 191.

8   *R v Turner* [1944] KB 463, [1944] 1 All ER 599.

9   (1829) 3 C & P 589. It should be noted that in *Thomas v David* (1836) 7 C & P 350, *R v Cargill* (1913) 8 Cr App Rep 224, and *R v Richardson and Longman* [1969] 1 QB 299, [1968] 2 All ER 761, it was accepted that an allegation of prostitution impugned the credit of a witness.

10   See *R v Krausz* (1973) 57 Cr App Rep 466, at 474, 'Evidence which proves that a woman is in the habit of submitting her body to different men without discrimination, whether for pay or not, would seem to be admissible.'

11   However much it might show the complainant to be 'a filthy, nasty woman, utterly filthy' per Charles J in *R v Turner* [1944] KB 463, [1944] 1 All ER 599.

This state of the law was widely regarded as unsatisfactory, and has become the subject of investigation and reform in many parts of the common law world.[12] In England the Advisory Group on the Law of Rape reported that the present law was widely criticised, and itself expressed the view that:[13]

> In contemporary society sexual relationships outside marriage, both steady and of a more casual character, are fairly widespread, and it seems now to be agreed that a woman's sexual experiences with partners of her own choice, are neither indicative of untruthfulness nor of a general willingness to consent.

Notwithstanding this general view the committee was not prepared to bar all cross-examination, or evidence in rebuttal, as to the complainant's sexual history. It was generally prepared to countenance it when the evidence was relevant to an issue in the case, and seems to have taken the view that it would always be so relevant if it related to other acts involving the accused himself, or when the acts involving other men bore a striking resemblance to that with which the accused was charged. These precepts were embodied in a complicated clause in a Bill presented to Parliament implementing the committee's recommendations.[14] It was regarded as much too complicated by some of the Law Lords,[15] and a less elaborate provision was adopted as s 2 of the Sexual Offences (Amendment) Act 1976:[16]

> (1) If at a trial any person is charged with a rape offence to which he pleads not guilty, then, except with the leave of the judge, no evidence and no question in cross-examination shall be adduced or asked at the trial, by or on behalf of any defendant at the trial, about any sexual experience of a complainant with a person other than that defendant.
>
> (2) The judge shall not give leave in pursuance of the preceding subsection for any evidence or question except on an application made to him in the absence of the jury by or on behalf of a defendant; and on such an application the judge shall give leave if and only if he is satisfied that it would be unfair to that defendant to refuse to allow the evidence to be adduced or the question to be asked.

The section goes on to provide that it does not authorise the asking of any questions which could not otherwise be asked.[17] This is a very limited provision. It applies only to 'rape offences',[18] and more importantly it makes no attempt to regulate evidence

---

12　There is specific legislation in Scotland, in Canada, in many of the Australian jurisdictions and in New Zealand. In the United States 'rape shield' statutes are in force in almost all of the states, and Federal law appears in r 412 of the Federal Rules. The truly bewildering variety of approaches is analysed and summarised in the Australian Law Reform Commission's Research Paper No 11 'Character and Conduct'. In some jurisdictions where the accused is accorded formal constitutional protection doubts have arisen as to the constitutional validity of such legislation: see in Canada *Seaboyer v R* [1991] 2 SCR 577, and in the United States *Michigan v Lucas* 500 US 145 (1991).

13　Cmnd 6352, para 131.

14　The group's report did not itself contain a draft Bill.

15　See 376 HL Official Report (5th series) cols 1518–20.

16　For criticism of this general scheme see Temkin (1984) 47 MLR 625; *Rape and the Legal Process* (1987) chs 3, 5. For consideration of the comparable provision in Canada, see *R v Crosby* [1995] 2 SCR 912; Paciocco (1993) 21 CR 4th 223.

17　Section 2(4).

18　Defined in s 7(2) to exclude indecent assault and forcible buggery of a woman, though the common law appears to have applied to the former: see *R v Holmes* (1871) LR 1 CCR 334, at 336; but see also *R v Ahmed and Khan* [1994] Crim LR 669 for an ingenious solution to this difficulty in the latter. The tendency nevertheless will be to interpret common law rules in

relating to the complainant's sexual activities with the accused himself, nor does it apply at all to evidence of anything other than 'sexual experience'. Acceptance of the common law in relation to activities with the accused himself was recommended by the advisory group, apparently on the basis that it was relevant to consent. The rationale for this wholesale exemption is quite unclear. It seems to suggest that once a woman has consented to have intercourse with a man she will never again refuse. This is hardly a self-evident proposition, and it looks very odd beside the rule that no special defence is available to husbands.[19] It is hard to see why special rules should apply to this situation, different from those that apply in relation to third parties.[20] In both, the critical consideration should be the precise contribution which admission of the evidence will make to the just resolution of the issues between the parties in the circumstances of the case. The advisory group was concerned to exclude evidence of a vague and general character, but the Act appears not to affect such evidence which is still left to the operation of the rules of common law. The advisory group took the view that evidence of sexual behaviour with third parties should be admitted only where it was relevant to an issue in the case, normally consent, and admitted then only when it showed a striking similarity to the acts alleged by the accused. The Act seeks to accomplish this result by its reference to the new and undefined term 'sexual experience',[1] and by imposing the overriding condition that the judge shall allow the question or evidence only where it would be unfair to the defendant to refuse. While it is clear that acts of intercourse with other men constitute 'sexual experience', it is surprising to find that conversations about such acts also constitute 'sexual experience' even in the absence of any suggestion that the conversations had any basis in fact.[2] How much further it might go, or how specifically it should be related to particular incidents with particular men is a matter for speculation. It is restricted to sexual behaviour 'with a person', and thus does not exclude cross-examination about self-abuse.[3] It would presumably not include having undergone sexual education at school,[4] or having merely associated with prostitutes.[5] It is less clear that evidence of solicitation as a prostitute does not amount to being about 'sexual experience'. The whole basis both of the common law and of the

---

adjacent areas sympathetically, see *R v Funderburk* [1990] 2 All ER 482, [1990] 1 WLR 587. The Home Office Interdepartmental Working Group advocated formal extension of revised provisions in *Speaking Up for Justice* (1998) para 9.71, rec 63, and draft provisons have been inserted into the Youth Justice and Criminal Evidence Bill 1999 cll 40–42, though these have themselves aroused controversy, and have been amended during the passage of the bill. It has been held in Australia that where other counts are being tried jointly that the restrictions applying to rape do affect cross-examination on the other counts, *R v Luckowski* (1990) 54 SASR 169.

19   *R v R* [1992] 1 AC 599, [1991] 4 All ER 481.

20   Such a change has now been recommended by the Criminal Law Revision Committee, 15th Report on Sexual Offences (Cmnd 9213) para 2.90.

1   The Youth Justice and Criminal Evidence Bill 1999 uses the term *sexual behaviour*, and defines it in cl 41(1)(c) apparently more widely than *sexual experience*.

2   *R v Hinds and Butler* [1979] Crim LR 111. In *R v Viola* [1982] 3 All ER 73, [1982] 1 WLR 1138, no regard was paid to these words at all and the court appears to have accepted that evidence of the complainant's having made unaccepted, and less than explicit, sexual advances to particular men, and having a naked man in her flat, amounted to evidence of her sexual experience. Compare *Beck v R* [1984] WAR 127 (evidence that woman had previously cut man's pubic hair not within statute unless followed by sexual intercourse).

3   *R v Barnes* [1994] Crim LR 691, the Youth Justice and Criminal Evidence Bill 1999, cl 41(1)(c) would remedy this. In Australia where the same term is used in the Crimes Act (NSW), s 409B controversy has arisen over whether it is implicitly limited to consensual sexual activity: *R v G* (1997) 42 NSWLR 439, at 457.

4   See *R v Byczko* (1977) 16 SASR 506.

5   One of the allegations in *R v Barker* (1829) 3 C & P 589.

advisory group's recommendations on this matter is obscure. Both the judges[6] and the group[7] recognise that prostitutes can be raped. It is much less clear why an allegation of prostitution is regarded as being relevant to consent. Prostitutes customarily demand payment in advance for their services. It is rare for the accused to allege such payment in cases where he seeks to raise the complainant's prostitution in evidence. In the absence of such payment it seems more, rather than less, likely that the complainant will have refused consent. Here too a better rule would be to allow the question to be raised when it is shown by the special circumstances to be relevant. Thus in a case like *R v Krausz*[8] where the allegation was that the complainant habitually, and unusually, demanded payment only after the consummation of the act, there is a real issue as to consent to which the disputed evidence is relevant. It is easy to understand why the advisory group approved of the common law's allowing rebuttal in those circumstances; it is incomprehensible in the light of their general approach why they approved of the decision in *R v Clay*,[9] where the only evidence was of isolated acts of prostitution some twenty years before the incident in question. It is hard to avoid the conclusion that trials for rape are, in fact, conducted upon the basis of a contest more about the character of the complainant than anything else.[10] The prosecution frequently seeks to assert the prior virginity of the complainant in support of its contention that she didn't say yes,[11] and the defence seeks to assert her prior sexual experience in support of its contention that she didn't say no.[12] Such inferences are so patently irrational that it would surely be better to go further in guiding the courts towards concentration upon the issues to which the character of the complainant, in its widest sense, is truly relevant.[13] The Act does not purport to offer more by way of guidance than that the evidence or questioning should be allowed if refusal would be unfair to the defendant. In most cases where leave is sought the defence appears to suggest that the evidence or questioning is relevant to consent,[14] and it certainly seems to have been the intention both of the advisory group[15] and of Parliament[16] that it should go to an issue in the case. Although this was emphasised in *R v Viola*[17] to be the general effect, it is understandable that in *R v Cox*,[18] where the complainant could be shown to have made an admittedly false complaint of rape in very similar circumstances in the past, it was

6   See Byles J in *R v Holmes* (1871) LR 1 CCR 334, at 337.

7   Para 136.

8   (1973) 57 Cr App Rep 466. See also *R v Starkey* (1987) 26 ACR 113 (previous acts of consensual sexual activity involving bondage); *R v Mohamed* (1993) 85 CCC (3d) 182 (previous acts of consensual sexual activity when preceded by physical violence).

9   (1851) 5 Cox CC 146.

10   See *R v Gun* (1977) 17 SASR 379; Kalven and Zeisel *The American Jury* (1966) pp 249–54; Adler (1982) 45 Mod LR 664; *Rape on Trial* (1987) ch 6. Thus in *R v Hickmet* [1996] Crim LR 588 the trial judge declined to give an unqualified good character direction in relation to the accused without also giving one in relation to the complainant.

11   Though particular circumstances may occasionally make prior virginity relevant: *R v SMS* [1992] Crim LR 310; *R v Allingham* [1991] Qd R 429. In *R v Crane* (1991) 69 CCC (3d) 300 the prosecution was not allowed to prove virginity in rebuttal because it had *not* called it in chief.

12   It was even suggested in *R v C* [1996] Crim LR 37 that in this situation as a matter of logic allegations of sexual intercourse with third parties would always be relevant, thus depriving the judge of any exclusionary discretion.

13   But see Elliott [1984] Crim LR 4.

14   Eighty per cent of Adler's sample.

15   Paragraphs 134–8.

16   See 376 HL Official Report (5th series) col 1518 and 911 HC Official Report (5th series) col 1989.

17   [1982] 3 All ER 73, at 77, [1982] 1 WLR 1138, at 1143.

18   (1986) 84 Cr App Rep 132, where it was felt that the force of the point would be lost without reference to the sexual intercourse which had then taken place.

held to have been unfair to the accused not have allowed the complainant to be questioned about the incident. It is, if anything, even more surprising to find that despite the statutory wording which appears to exclude it as a consideration, in *R v Hinds and Butler*,[19] the judge took the probable effect of the questioning of the complainant into account in determining whether to give leave. In *R v Viola*[20] the Court of Appeal has, it is submitted quite correctly, stressed the importance of determining the relevancy of the evidence or questioning, that it should normally relate to an issue, and perhaps most important of all that it should be related to the way in which the trial is being run. It is made quite clear that s 2(2) invests the trial judge with a duty to be exercised in the light of his judgment, and not with a discretion, and that the Court of Appeal may properly substitute its own judgment for his. It should be emphasised that the difference between a defence of lack of consent and of belief in lack of consent is far from decisive. In the latter case the issue relates to belief at the time of the act that the victim is consenting then, not to belief at some earlier time that she is likely to consent.[1] In either case the evidence of previous sexual experience must relate strictly and strongly to proof of the relevant issue, and a simple allegation of belief in consent conveys no general warrant for such cross-examination.[2] It nevertheless remains the case that a generous view has been taken of the circumstances in which cross-examination is permitted.[3] It is also wider in its effect than cross-examination of the accused about his previous convictions.[4] A general rule seems to be developing that where the prosecution seeks[5] to bolster its case with detail[6] which can be rebutted by reference to other sexual experience, or when reference to it is made in a statement to the police by the accused put in as part of the prosecution case,[7] reference is allowed.[8] It has however been established that counsel must have reasonable grounds for his belief in the truth of the allegation that he is putting to the complainant, and if he has no

19   [1979] Crim LR 111, though despite the fact that the complainant was only 14 years old and had already made an attempt to commit suicide, leave was granted.

20   [1982] 3 All ER 73, [1982] 1 WLR 1138. In *Viola* the issue was consent, see also *R v Fenlon and Neal* (1980) 71 Cr App Rep 307, where the court was prepared to allow questions only to account for the presence of semen at the relevant time, and *Gregory v R, Sharwood v R* (1983) 151 CLR 566, where the evidence refuted the complainant's denial of other sexual acts at the same time and place.

1   *R v Barton* (1987) 85 Cr App Rep 5.

2   *R v Brown* (1989) 89 Cr App Rep 97.

3   Criticised by Temkin in [1993] Crim LR 3. A more structured approach, perhaps based on ss 274, 275 of the Criminal Procedure (Scotland) Act 1995 was recommended by the Home Office Interdepartmental Working Group in *Speaking Up for Justice* (1998) paras 9.66–9.72, rec 63, now introduced as the Youth Justice and Criminal Evidence Bill 1999, cll 40–43; it is not worth setting these clauses out in full, and analysing them in detail since they seem still to be in a state of transition, and have already been amended during the stages of the bill in the House of Lords.

4   In *R v Taylor* (1993) 157 JP 1147 an appeal was allowed when the trial judge used the model direction for that situation in this.

5   This may sometimes be implicit as in *R v SMS* [1992] Crim LR 310.

6   *R v Ellis* [1990] Crim LR 717 (bathing after rape); *R v Riley* [1991] Crim LR 460 (abstention in presence of child).

7   *R v Barnes* [1994] Crim LR 691.

8   Though failure to make it is not in itself a ground of appeal on the basis of incompetent representation: *R v Jackson* [1994] Crim LR 216. Sometimes, perhaps because of distaste, the court fails to distinguish between allegations which do go to the heart of the case, and those which do not: see *R v Cleland* [1995] Crim LR 742, where the pre-incident abortion, which was of tenuous relevance, appears to have been treated in the same way as the post-incident abortion, which clearly was crucial.

admissible evidence to support it, that the discretion will be exercised against allowing the question.[9]

There are a number of other situations in which the character of the prosecutor or victim of a crime may be regarded as relevant.[10] Thus in *Toohey v Metropolitan Police Comr*[11] the defence hinged completely on the personality of the alleged victim, namely, that he was subject to hysteria and quite capable of misunderstanding, exaggerating and over-reacting to the most solicitous of treatment. The House of Lords had no doubt that such evidence was admissible irrespective of whether the victim had testified or not. Similarly, if self-defence is pleaded in defence of a charge of murder the accused may show that the deceased was of violent disposition,[12] or where there are special features of the defence dependent upon facets of the victim's character, for example, that the killing occurred in the course of resisting a violent homosexual advance, then those relevant aspects may be proved also.[13] In all such cases it is however essential that the evidence shall be relevant,[14] and relevant at the stage of the proceedings at which it is raised.[15]

B. ACCUSED

The most common situations involving evidence of the bad character of the accused are those in which it is adduced in chief by the prosecution, and in which the accused is cross-examined about it. These are dealt with in the two following chapters. This section is concerned with those cases where the accused adduces evidence of his own good character, and the extent to which that opens the way to cross-examination, or rebutting evidence, and cases where the accused seeks to adduce evidence, or cross-examine, as to the bad character of his co-accused.

I. Good character

The accused has been permitted to adduce evidence of his own good character from very early times.[16] Questions arise as to the interconnected issues of the precise purpose for admitting such evidence, the type of evidence to be permitted, and the effect of such evidence when admitted. Evidence of the good character of the accused could be admitted because it goes to the issue of guilt or innocence, because it supports the credibility of the accused, or simply so as to predispose the jury in the accused's favour. Since such evidence was admitted long before the accused became a competent witness it is clear that, in origin at least, it was not admitted to support his credibility as a witness. In the leading case of *R v Rowton*[17] only Baron Martin was at all inclined to accept that

9   *R v Howes* [1996] 2 Cr App Rep 490, disapproving *R v C* [1996] Crim LR 37 to the extent that it suggested anything else.
10 It has been convincingly argued by Ellison [1998] Crim LR 605 that rape trials are in practice no different from others, and that the faults lie with the breadth of cross-examination to credit allowed in general, and the adversarial tradition.
11 [1965] AC 595, [1965] 1 All ER 506.
12 But not, it seems, in Scotland, see *Brady v HM Advocate* 1986 SCCR 191.
13 As in *R v Biggin* [1920] 1 KB 213.
14 See *R v Harmer* (1985) 28 ACR 35.
15 In *Gleaves v Deakin* [1980] AC 477, [1979] 2 All ER 497, it was held that the reputation of the prosecutor for criminal libel was not relevant at the stage of the committal proceedings, but could be raised at the trial.
16 See *R v Turner* (1664) 6 State Tr 565, at 613; *R v Harris* (1680) 7 State Tr 926, at 929.
17 (1865) 34 LJMC 57, at 65.

it was admitted simply so as to predispose the jury in favour of the accused. So far as relevance to an issue is concerned the process of reasoning was explained in *R v Stannard*:[18]

> the object of laying it before the jury is to induce them to believe, from the improbability that a person of good character should have conducted himself as alleged, that there is some mistake or misrepresentation in the evidence of the prosecution, and it is strictly evidence in the case.

Attempts are sometimes made to distinguish between relevance to innocence simpliciter, and relevance via disbelief of the prosecution's witness.[19] This seems both confusing and pointless though the judgments in *R v Rowton* show some difference of emphasis. Thus Cockburn CJ said:[20]

> It has been put that evidence in favour of the character of a person on his trial raises a collateral issue. I can hardly think that it is a collateral issue in the proper sense of the term. It becomes one of the points on which the jury are to found their verdict.

While Willes J said:[1]

> it is a mistake to suppose because only the prisoner can raise the question of character, that therefore it is evidence on a collateral issue. It is not. It is evidence which is admissible, because it makes it less probable that that which the prosecution has averred ... should be true. It is evidence strictly relevant to the issue.

Both of these purposes, excluding only simple prejudice in favour of the accused, re-appear in recent cases. It has been held that elementary fairness requires that the jury be directed, not as a matter of discretion, but as one of practice, of the significance of the accused's good character.[2] Both a propensity and a credibility direction are required if the issue of the accused's good character has been raised, unless to do so would, in the circumstances, amount to an insult to common sense.

The issue may be raised by calling evidence of good character, by putting questions asserting it, or at the request of the defence; the judge is not bound to raise the issue of his own motion,[3] nor to solicit evidence to enable him to give a direction.[4] The judge may also refrain from responding to an extra-curial assertion of good character traits which is before the jury, when he knows that the accused in fact has previous convictions which would prevent a good character direction from being given,[5] and presumably a similar discretion would apply, if the accused were entitled only to a qualified direction, but might then be exercised differently. Conversely the judge may wish to give such a direction upon a corrective basis, when the prosecution adduces evidence which might be taken to indicate the accused's bad character.[6]

---

18   (1837) 7 C & P 673, at 674.
19   See *R v Trimboli* (1979) 21 SASR 577.
20   (1865) 34 LJMC 57, at 60.
1   At 66.
2   *R v Aziz* [1996] AC 41, [1995] 3 All ER 149.
3   *Thompson v R* (16 February 1998, unreported); *Barrow v R* (1998) Times, 31 March.
4   *R v Prayag* (1991) Times, 31 July.
5   *R v Thorpe* [1996] 1 Cr App Rep 269.
6   *Guevara v R* [1996] CLY 1386 (identification from batch of photographs produced by police).

The accused may now testify, and in *R v Bellis* Lord Widgery CJ said that 'possession of a good character is primarily a matter which goes to credibility.'[7] In cases where the accused does not exercise his option to testify he is still entitled to have evidence of his good character considered as relevant to the issue,[8] a view which has recently been re-emphasised.[9] If an extra-curial mixed statement has been admitted, the accused is entitled a direction as to his good character in relation to the exculpatory part.[10] In *R v Fulcher*[11] this was held also to be true of wholly exculpatory extra-curial statements which were reflected by the defence at a trial, but Lord Steyn's remarks in *R v Aziz* appear deliberately to have been cast so as not to go so far, and it is submitted that it would be a dangerous step to extend the rules applicable to testimony to such statements, which are not themselves evidence in the case. In *R v Vye* the Court of Appeal clarified the law by stating it in three propositions:[12]

'(1) A direction as to the relevance of his good character to a defendant's credibility is to be given where he has testified or made pre-trial answers or statements.

(2) A direction as to the relevance of his good character to the likelihood of his having committed the offence charged is to be given whether or not he has testified, or made pre-trial answers or statements.

(3) Where defendant A of good character is jointly tried with defendant B of bad character (1) and (2) still apply.'

Such a direction is to be given[13] even though the accused admits having told lies to the police,[14] pleads guilty to a lesser crime arising from the same facts,[15] or to a second count arising from the same facts, and even when he has a previous convictions for old,[16] different and trivial offences.[17] It is immaterial that the co-accused in question has attempted to cast the blame on another co-accused buy running a cut-throat defence.[18] If the accused admitted significant dishonesty,[19] or serious criminal conduct of a gravity similar to that charged,[20] then no direction would be appropriate,[1] unless it occurred as part and parcel of the course of conduct within which the crime charged

---

7   [1966] 1 All ER 552n, at 552, [1966] 1 WLR 234, at 236; see also *Berry v R* [1992] 2 AC 364, [1992] 3 All ER 881.

8   *R v Bryant, R v Oxley* [1979] QB 108, [1978] 2 All ER 689. In Australia it now seems clear that the accused is entitled to a direction which does not explicitly exclude either ground, see *R v Murphy* (1985) 63 ALR 53, at 64; *R v Palazoff* (1986) 23 ACR 86, especially at 96.

9   *R v Berrada* (1989) 91 Cr App Rep 131n.

10   *R v Aziz* above.

11   [1995] 2 Cr App Rep 251.

12   [1993] 3 All ER 241, at 248, [1993] 1 WLR 471, at 479. Approved, explained and applied in *R v Aziz* above.

13   A conviction may be quashed if it is not, even if by inadvertence no application has been made: *R v Kamar* (14 May 1999, unreported).

14   As in *R v Kabariti* (1990) 92 Cr App Rep 362.

15   As in *R v Teasdale* [1993] 4 All ER 290; but see the limitation placed upon this decision in *R v Challenger* [1994] Crim LR 202.

16   Especially if spent: *R v Heath* [1994] 13 LS Gaz R 34.

17   *R v Durbin* [1995] 2 Cr App Rep 84, even ones involving dishonesty.

18   *R v Aziz* above at 53H, 158j.

19   *R v Buzalek and Schiffer* [1991] Crim LR 115.

20   *R v Zoppola-Barraza* [1994] Crim LR 833.

1   Although it still might be given in the judge's discretion: *R v Burnham* [1995] Crim LR 491. And if one is given the court is likely to be more generous towards it: *R v Akram* [1995] Crim LR 50.

occurred.[2] It was construed in *R v Cain*[3] not to prevent a direction on the good character of one co-accused when the convictions of another were already before the trier of fact, and a third co-defendant had not adverted at all to his character. The form of the direction is naturally left largely within the discretion of the judge in the light of the circumstances of the trial,[4] who is bound to direct the jury straightforwardly without sarcasm,[5] but may qualify the direction in cases where the good character is somewhat blemished, but not to the extent of depriving the accused of entitlement to such a direction completely.[6] If the accused does testify, he is presumably entitled to have his good character considered on both grounds.

When the only possible purpose was relevance to the issue it made good sense to restrict the evidence of character to those aspects relevant to the nature of the charge. Thus when the accused was charged with treason it was held that evidence of his good character should not be general, but limited to his character for loyalty and as being peaceable.[7] The rule seems however to have been disregarded both before 1898,[8] and after.[9] It was accepted by all of the judges in *R v Rowton* that such evidence could not consist of particular examples of good acts, since it did not follow that the accused never acted otherwise.[10] It was impossible to maintain such a rule consistently in practice once it was accepted that answers to questions in cross-examination could constitute evidence of good character, since such questions invariably condescend to particularity.[11] Nevertheless the rule still retains sufficient vitality in this respect to have prevented a man accused of homosexual offences from adducing evidence of particular heterosexual acts as evidence of his proclivities.[12]

The matter for decision in *R v Rowton*, as will be seen below, related to the type of evidence which could be adduced in rebuttal of good character, but by parity of reasoning the majority held that a witness to the good character of the accused could speak only to the accused's reputation, and not to his personal opinion of the accused's disposition. The court confessed its unfamiliarity with any practice in this area and even admitted the rule to be anomalous and illogical. It is also arguable that it confused general evidence of character, with which it was concerned, with evidence of general character, with which the principal authorities cited to it were concerned. Nevertheless the limitation, in this context at least, of evidence of character to signify reputation has

2   *R v Durbin*, above.
3   [1994] 2 All ER 398; see also *R v Shepherd* [1995] Crim LR 153. If the accused does testify, he is presumably entitled to have his good character considered on both grounds.
4   The Judicial Studies Board's specimen direction is set out in Munday [1997] Crim LR 247, at 251. It seems that an English court would be no more inclined than the Australian in *R v Jackson and Hakim* (1988) 33 ACR 413 to discriminate between a direction that good character made guilt 'less likely' or 'unlikely'.
5   *R v Berrada* above.
6   *R v Durbin* above.
7   *R v Turner* (1817) 32 State Tr 957, at 1007.
8   See *R v Burt* (1851) 5 Cox CC 284 (evidence of general good character on a charge of receiving); for judicial recognition of widespread abuse in the older law, see *R v Jones* (1809) 31 State Tr 251 at 310.
9   See *R v Savory* (1942) 29 Cr App Rep 1 (good character as railway porter on a charge of indecent assault); for judicial recognition of widespread abuse in the newer law, see *R v Butterwasser* [1948] 1 KB 4, at 6, [1947] 2 All ER 415, at 416.
10   (1865) 34 LJMC 57, at 67; though in *R v Williamson* (1807) 3 C & P 635, Lord Ellenborough CJ permitted a male midwife charged with manslaughter to adduce evidence of his kind and skilful attention to other women.
11   See *R v West* (1890) 112 CC Ct Cas 724 for a particularly harsh example in which the negative answer given by a police witness when asked by counsel for the defence whether anything was known against the accused was held to amount to evidence of good character sufficient to permit rebuttal.
12   *R v Redgrave* (1981) 74 Cr App Rep 10. See also in Australia *R v Zaidi* (1991) 57 ACR 189; but cp in Canada *R v Aylward* (1992) 71 CCC (3d) 71. In *R v Mohan* [1994] 2 SCR 9 the Court refused to accept evidence of a novel distinction of bad character profiles adduced by the accused.

not, so far, been overruled. No detailed analysis of such reputation evidence has been attempted in England, but it was suggested by Wigmore[13] that it should extend to reputation in any relevant field,[14] and need not be confined to reputation in the local community. Given the tendency to apply the rule to issue, as well as credibility, this seems good sense.[15] Though if it is taken to imply a narrowing of possible sources of information then there must be an increased danger of conflict with the rule against hearsay.[16] Nor has much attention been devoted here to the question of how much need be done to constitute evidence of good character.[17] As noted above it was in one case held to apply where a question was asked in cross-examination of a prosecution witness about the absence of convictions.[18] This has stimulated distinctions in South Australia between negative good character,[19] good character, and positive good character.[20] This seems needlessly elaborate.

The final question here relates to the effect of the evidence when adduced. It was long considered that its effect was for the jury to take it into account only when otherwise left in doubt.[1] It was then claimed in *R v Bliss Hill*[2] that this reduced its effect to nil, since if the jury was in doubt the accused was in any event entitled to be acquitted. This is unconvincing because there must be a point at which the jury requires only the slightest extra evidence to feel the reasonable doubt sufficient to acquit the accused, and that surely must have been the situation contemplated.[3]

2. Rebuttal

It was settled[4] in *R v Butterwasser* that the bad character of the accused can be brought out at common law only when the accused has put his character in issue. It is not enough for him to attack the character of the witnesses for the prosecution:[5]

13 Paragraph 245 et seq, a view accepted in many American jurisdictions; see also Federal Rules of Evidence, r 803(21).
14 For example among business associates.
15 It has been adopted in Canada: see *R v Levasseur* (1987) 35 CCC (3d) 136.
16 The borderline could not have been very far away in *Levasseur* where the witness testified on the basis of his own limited knowledge and that of fifteen business acquaintances with whom he had discussed the accused's reputation in business matters.
17 See further below p 400.
18 See also *R v Lopatta* (1983) 35 SASR 101 where a question was asked of a prosecution witness as to whether the accused was a good person. In New Zealand absence of convictions has not been unequivocally accepted as evidence of good character: *R v Falealili* [1996] 3 NZLR 664, and was roundly condemned by Thomas J.
19 Absence of convictions, suggested distinction in *R v Mandica* (1980) 24 SASR 394, at 406. In *R v W* [1994] 2 All ER 872 it was however agreed that in order to avoid a possible inference of commission of similar crimes to that charged two minor offences of a different character could be admitted, but the accused not presented to the jury as a man of good character. In that case he was held not to be entitled to a direction distinguishing between effects on credibility and propensity.
20 Doing good works in the community, canvassed by the trial judge as reported in *R v Palazoff* (1986) 43 SASR 99, at 111.
1 See *R v M* (1994) 72 ACR 269 for a modern direction to this effect.
2 (1918) 13 Cr App Rep 125. Re-affirmed in *R v Brittle* (1965) 109 Sol Jo 1028. See also *R v Falconer-Atlee* (1973) 58 Cr App Rep 348, at 358; *R v Tarrant* (1981) 34 OR (2d) 747; *R v Lawrence* [1984] 3 NSWLR 674.
3 This may account for the persistence of the older form of direction: see *R v Islam* (1969) 113 Sol Jo 185.
4 It was challenged by the Royal Commission on Criminal Justice (1993) Cm 2263, para 8.34 and rec 193, but the Law Commission in its consultation paper No 141 *Evidence in Criminal Proceedings: Previous Misconduct of a Defendant* (1996) paras 12.81 -12.119 is equivocal. It has been approved in Canada, *R v A(WA)* (1996) 112 CCC (3d) 83; and in New Zealand, *R v Kino* [1997] 3 NZLR 24.
5 [1948] 1 KB 4, [1947] 2 All ER 415.

I do not see on what principle it can be said, that if a man does not go into the box and put his character in issue, he can have evidence against him of previous bad character when all that he has done is to attack the witnesses for the prosecution. The reason is that by attacking the witnesses for the prosecution and suggesting that they are unreliable, he is not putting his character in issue; he is putting their character in issue.

The problem then is to determine when the accused does put his character into issue at common law. The most obvious way is to call witnesses to testify as to his good character, indeed if character means reputation, it is not clear that the accused can testify to his own good character. It seems that if the witness testifies to the accused's good character without premeditation, for example, in response to a question in cross-examination, not requiring an answer relating to the accused's character, such character will not normally be put in issue. In *R v Gadbury*[6] the question was asked by the accused's counsel, but was not intended to elicit evidence of good character even though the answer to the matter in issue could incidentally be construed as showing the accused's good character; while in *R v Redd*[7] a witness who had been called by an unrepresented defendant to do no more than prove a document, blurted out his encomium of the accused without external stimulation. On the other hand it has been held that rebuttal cannot be shut out or restricted by confining the evidence of the accused's good character to a particular period,[8] or trait.[9]

It is possible to rebut evidence of the accused's good character either by eliciting evidence of his bad character in cross-examination, or by leading extrinsic evidence of it. Despite some uncertainty[10] and confusion[11] in the earlier law, it now seems settled that a witness may be asked about the accused's previous convictions.[12] It is equally possible to ask about the accused's previous bad acts, notwithstanding the *Rowton* rule as to the inadmissibility of evidence of good acts for the accused in chief.[13] This seems to have been put beyond doubt by the decision of the Court of Appeal in *R v Bracewell*[14] where such cross-examination was justified by the accused's having put his good character in issue, when it would not be countenanced on the basis of simple relevance to facts in issue. There have been suggestions that the witness can be cross-examined as to rumours about the accused,[15] but this seems to have been an unfortunate attempt to restrict cross-examination to reputation, and to be inconsistent with subsequent authority.[16] No final decision was reached in *R v Waldman*[17] as to whether the witness could be cross-examined about a previous acquittal. The court seemed prepared to accept that the same principles apply at common law as apply under the

6   (1838) 8 C & P 676.
7   [1923] 1 KB 104.
8   *R v Shrimpton* (1851) 2 Den 319.
9   *R v Winfield* (1939) 27 Cr App Rep 139.
10   It was doubted in *R v Wood and Parker* (1841) 5 Jur 225.
11   Although accepted as a general rule in *R v Redd* [1923] 1 KB 104, both the authorities which were relied upon (*R v Gadbury* (1838) 8 C & P 676 and *R v Shrimpton* (1851) 2 Den 319) depended upon particular statutory provisions.
12   *R v Waldman* (1934) 24 Cr App Rep 204, a strong case because the undoubted admissibility of a previous conviction was held to outweigh the dubious admissibility of a previous acquittal; *R v Winfield* (1939) 27 Cr App Rep 139; *R v B, R v A* [1979] 3 All ER 460, [1979] 1 WLR 1185.
13   *R v Hodgkiss* (1836) 7 C & P 298; *R v Rogan and Elliott* (1846) 1 Cox CC 291.
14   (1978) 68 Cr App Rep 44.
15   *R v Wood and Parker* (1841) 5 Jur 225.
16   *R v Savory* (1942) 29 Cr App Rep 1, where the prosecution was not permitted to cross-examine the character witness about complaints made of the accused in the relevant respect which had not become the subject of formal proceedings against him.
17   (1934) 24 Cr App Rep 204.

Criminal Evidence Act 1898. In *Maxwell v DPP*[18] the House of Lords had held that an acquittal could not be used in cross-examination to the extent that it was relied upon to suggest that the accused had really been guilty despite his acquittal. It could however be put if relevant as a genuine acquittal, as for example by providing a reason for the accused to act carefully so as to avoid the danger of a further false accusation. It has already been noted that extrinsic evidence may be led to rebut a denial on a material issue. Thus since the accused's good character is relevant to issue as well as to credibility it would seem that a denial by a character witness of the accused's previous convictions or of his bad acts could be rebutted by leading evidence. This seems to be the case. Adduction of the accused's previous convictions was upheld in *R v B, R v A*,[19] and in *R v Bracewell*[20] the court was prepared to allow evidence of specific bad acts. The prosecution may also adduce evidence to rebut evidence of his good character given by a witness on his behalf. In *R v Rowton*[1] only Baron Martin had any doubt that in such a case the prosecution had such a right, the problem which caused most difficulty related to the nature of that evidence. The accused, who was charged with an offence of indecency, called witnesses to testify that he was a moral and well-conducted man, and the prosecution called a witness in rebuttal to swear that while he knew nothing of the opinion of the neighbourhood, the opinion of the witness and of his brothers who had attended the accused's school, was that he was a man 'capable of the grossest indecency and the most flagrant immorality'. It was not suggested that these three brothers constituted a community within which the accused's reputation was bad. The dispute centred around the question of whether it was permissible for the witness to express his personal opinion of the accused's disposition, or whether he was limited to reporting the reputation of the accused. The dissentient minority argued that the whole purpose of the evidence was to determine whether or not the accused had a disposition to acts of indecency upon which he had acted. It was more direct to derive it from the witness's personal knowledge of that disposition than to try to infer it from the general consensus of opinion in the neighbourhood which constituted the accused's reputation. The majority argued rather narrowly that precedent supported the view that as neither particular acts nor personal opinions could be given in support of the accused's good character, so it would be wrong to allow its refutation by different means. This defence is somewhat ironic since the authorities were by no means so opposed either to evidence of particular acts[2] or of personal opinion[3] as the court supposed, but arguments of general principle were available. If the evidence is restricted to that of reputation the trial can be insulated from the confusion, surprise and prejudice likely to be engendered by collateral attack in the form of counter-examples of particular discreditable acts.[4] The fatal flaw in such argument however is in the nature of the evidence being defended. Evidence of reputation, general or specific, is thoroughly unconvincing.[5] It necessarily rests upon hearsay, gossip and rumour, and permits a witness without perjury to state something which he believes to be unjustified, and which he knows will be used as the foundation for an inference which he believes to be

18   [1935] AC 309.
19   In *R v Forbes* (1999) Times, 5 May this was threatened if after giving evidence of good character the accused had in fact, as he proposed, discontinued his testimony once a ruling that he could be cross-examined about his previous convictions had been made.
20   [1979] 3 All ER 460, [1979] 1 WLR 1185.
1   (1978) 68 Cr App Rep 44.
2   (1865) Le & Ca 520; 34 LJMC 57.
3   See for example *R v Turner* (1817) 32 State Tr 957.
4   For the modern operation of the rule in this way in Canada see *R v Manahan* (1990) 61 CCC (3d) 139; *R v F(JE)* (1993) 85 CCC (3d) 457.
5   Reputation, whether good or bad, is especially unconvincing in relation to sexual disposition: see *R v Profit* [1993] 3 SCR 637. But cp *R v Marr* (1989) 90 Cr App Rep 154.

false. It is uncomfortable to have to rely upon a rule defended by the Supreme Court of the United States only on the ground that 'to pull one misshapen stone out of the grotesque structure is more likely simply to upset its present balance between adverse interests than to establish a rational edifice'.[6] It is hardly surprising to find that the rule was roundly condemned by commentators,[7] ignored in practice,[8] and rejected as a model for the construction of the now much more important provisions of the Criminal Evidence Act 1898.[9]

3. Co-accused

Another area largely governed by common law rules is that dealing with evidence of the bad character of a co-accused. It is not wholly governed by the common law since cross-examination of a co-accused is subject to the provisions of the Criminal Evidence Act 1898, and will be dealt with in ch IX. This part is concerned with the question of how far other witnesses can be cross-examined about the co-accused's character, and how far evidence of the bad character of a co-accused can be led either to rebut any denial, or simply to inculpate the co-accused. The case of *R v Miller*[10] provides a convenient starting point. The co-accused were charged with offences in connection with the evasion of customs duties. The defence of one of them was that he had not been concerned, and that the offences were all committed by another of the co-accused. In developing that defence he asked a witness for the prosecution whether or not it was true that the offences stopped when that co-accused was sent to prison, and re-started only after he was released. Devlin J held that such a question was perfectly proper, and that if necessary it could be justified by calling evidence in support. In his judgment a co-accused was bound only by considerations of relevance, though such relevance would require careful consideration, and the decision:[11]

> does not open the field to any question of this kind by counsel for an accused person against the character of another accused. In the ordinary way the character of the accused is no more relevant at the hands of the defence than it is at the hands of the prosecution.

The authority of that decision has been accepted by the Privy Council[12] and by the Court of Appeal.[13] In both the question arose out of a similarly 'cut throat' defence. In *Lowery* the two co-accused were alone present when a young girl was viciously murdered. The crime must have been committed by one or the other, or by both acting in concert. Each accused adduced evidence of the unlikelihood of his having committed the murder. In the case of Lowery such evidence took the form of evidence of his reputation, his aversion to the sadism involved in the murder, and his generally favourable prospects and happy family circumstances motivating him towards good

---

6   *Michelson v United States* 335 US 469, at 486 (1948).
7   See Stephen *History of Criminal Law* (1882) vol 1 p 450, 'The decision [in *Rowton*] settled the law, but in practice it is impossible to act upon it, and it may be doubted whether it is desirable to try to do so.'
8   See for example *R v West* (1890) 112 CCC Sess Pap 724, where the rebuttal consisted in part of evidence of the accused's known association with criminals.
9   See *R v Dunkley* [1927] 1 KB 323, at 329. It was also subjected to penetrating and convincing criticism in New Zealand in *R v Ravindra* [1997] 3 NZLR 242.
10   [1952] 2 All ER 667, 36 Cr App Rep 169. See also *R v Gibb and McKenzie* [1983] 2 VR 155.
11   At 669, 172.
12   *Lowery v R* [1974] AC 85, [1973] 3 All ER 662.
13   *R v Neale* (1977) 65 Cr App Rep 304, where *Miller* is referred to as 'famous'.

behaviour. King, Lowery's co-accused, sought to adduce expert psychiatric testimony indicating that of the two, Lowery had the personality more disposed towards the commission of acts of the type in question. Each supplemented his evidence with direct testimony of the other's dominant role at the time of the incident. The expert evidence called by King was admitted at the trial over Lowery's protests, and the decision was upheld both by an appellate court in Victoria, and by the Privy Council. The Privy Council took pains to deny that the psychiatric evidence was related either to crime or to criminal tendencies,[14] or even amounted to evidence of the character of the two men.[15] It is hard to square this approach to the nature of character evidence with the Privy Council's earlier statement that an accused person puts his character in issue when he asks the jury 'to take the view that he is not one who would be disposed to have committed or would be likely to have committed the crime in question.'[16] It is also instructive to note that the Privy Council endorsed the view of the court below that the evidence could not have been led by the prosecution. It may be best to regard *Lowery* as a case very much influenced by its special facts,[17] and the way in which the case was run. The psychiatric evidence might well have been regarded as inappropriate for use by the prosecution, either because its prejudicial effect, which may have been vast, would then have exceeded its true probative value, which may have been small, or because it was simply irrelevant to the contention of the prosecution that the two men were acting in concert.

In *R v Bracewell*,[18] just as in *Lowery*, two men were charged with a brutal murder, this time of a very old man in the course of a burglary. Here too each claimed that the killing was done by the other when alone with the victim. Bracewell wished to cross-examine his co-accused's mistress, his own sister, who was a witness for the prosecution, about violent, and uncontrolled, attacks which his co-accused had made upon her. The Court of Appeal upheld the trial court's refusal to permit such cross-examination at that stage on the basis that it was insufficiently relevant, and because it was, unlike the evidence in *Miller* and *Lowery*, factually controversial and so capable of raising a confusing collateral issue. However Lockwood, the co-accused, had himself tried to cast the blame upon Bracewell by contrasting his own professional coolness as an experienced burglar with Bracewell's panicky inexperience. The Court of Appeal took the view that this put his character in issue, and that Bracewell could, for that reason alone, cross-examine him about his uncontrollable episodes of violence towards his mistress, and if they were denied, adduce evidence of them. It is immaterial that the co-accused are acting not as part of a joint enterprise, but individually, if their acts so overlap as to engender a defence drawing a comparison between them.[19] If one co-accused wishes to cross-examine another about his criminal acts committed with a third party, in order to show that they were committed with that party on this occasion, there is no doubt but that the other co-accused would, if he were denying the third party's involvement, be entitled to cross-examine the co-accused about their joint criminal activity with a view to showing that it was repeated on this occasion. If however the other admits the third party's involvement on this occasion, and that the co-accused was not involved, then a question arises of how far the prosecution can cross-examine that other co-accused about joint commision of crimes by both co-accused in order to show that they committed the crime charged together. It is clearly arguable that the initial question should be excluded as irrelevant in the circumstances; but if it is not, it

---

14   At 101, 671.
15   At 102, 672.
16   At 102, 671.
17   It was so treated in *R v Turner* [1975] QB 834, at 842, [1975] 1 All ER 70, at 75.
18   (1978) 68 Cr App Rep 44.
19   *R v Douglass* (1989) 89 Cr App Rep 264.

has been held in *R v Fletcher*[20] that the prosecution will be entitled to cross-examine about the previous convictions for offences committed jointly by both co-accused, only if the detail satisfies the requirement of enhanced value required of evidence of bad character adduced by the prosecution in chief under the similar facts rule.[1]

In *R v Knutton*[2] the co-accused were charged with an assault. Each advanced a defence of alibi, but neither testified. Knutton sought to cross-examine a police witness about the motivation and involvement of his co-accused. The trial judge then permitted cross-examination of the witness as to Knutton's lengthy criminal record. It was sought to justify such cross-examination upon analogy with section 1(f)(ii) of the Criminal Evidence Act 1898 either on the basis that Knutton by making the implicit comparison had put his own character in issue, or that he was attacking his co-accused's character, and that his own character should be exposed on a tit for tat basis. Neither contention was accepted by the Court of Appeal. It was argued that Knutton's character was irrelevant in the light of his defence of alibi and of the fact that the offence easily could have been, and was alleged to have been, committed by both in concert rather than by one or the other, and that the cross-examination did nothing to diminish Knutton's bad character, merely suggesting that his co-accused was no better. On the second point the analogy to attacks under section 1(f)(ii) was rejected on the basis that this part of the statute will not sustain one, and that on analysis the cross-examination did not amount to an attack on the character of the co-accused since it consisted merely of imputations which were denied. This part of the reasoning seems unconvincing since that is very often the case when cross-examination under the statutory provision is permitted on this ground.[3]

The importance of the nature of the defence in determining the relevance of the evidence was further stressed in *R v Neale*.[4] In that case Neale's defence to charges of arson and manslaughter arising out of a fire in an institution was that he was not present at the relevant time. He wished to adduce evidence that his co-accused, Burr, had on two previous and on two subsequent occasions set fires while acting alone. It was held that the only question to be considered was whether or not the evidence was relevant to his defence. It was decided that it was not, because even if accepted it could not logically found an inference that on this occasion Burr was acting alone, rather than in concert with Neale. The logic of that argument would seem to be equally applicable whether Neale's argument were that he was not present at all, or that although present he did not participate.

It is possible to derive from these cases a reasonably coherent pattern of admissibility.

At one end of the scale there will be cases, though none of these are among them, where the evidence of the accused's evil disposition will be so strong, and so relevant to the case of both the prosecution and co-accused, that it will be admissible at the instance of either. It is possible to imagine a situation in which a girl and two men are alone together taking drugs. The girl complains of having been given a highly unusual incapacitating drug, and of then being raped by both men. One co-accused may have a long history of having used this drug to secure sexual intercourse, but put forward the defence that the whole episode is a drug-induced fantasy on the part of the girl and his co-accused. His co-accused may defend himself on the basis that the drug was

20   [1995] Crim LR 727.
1   This is an unfortunately rare example of what is submitted to be the salutary practice of applying similar standards of admissibility to adducing evidence of bad character in chief and to putting it in cross-examination.
2   (1992) 97 Cr App Rep 115.
3   See below pp 404–412.
4   (1977) 65 Cr App Rep 304.

also used to incapacitate him, and that his participation was imagined by the girl who was the victim only of his co-accused. In these circumstances it is submitted that both prosecution and the second co-accused could cross-examine, and lead evidence, of the first co-accused's previous use of this highly unusual drug.

The next position on the spectrum of relevance is occupied by the situation, of which *Miller*, and perhaps *Lowery*,[5] provide examples, where the bad character of the co-accused is necessarily brought out by evidence which is clearly relevant to the defence of the co-accused, though not at all to the case for the prosecution. There too the co-accused is entitled to cross-examine a witness,[6] and lead evidence, without waiting for character to be put in issue, and without the need to balance probative effect against possible prejudice, as required in the case where such evidence is to be led by the prosecution, and without any danger of the exercise of judicial discretion to prevent him.[7]

The next gradation, illustrated by *Bracewell*, is that in which the evidence is not sufficiently relevant to the issues either for the prosecution, or for the co-accused. It seems to be the case that the accused may however introduce general evidence of his good character, even though it would not meet the standard of relevance required for evidence of his bad character tendered initially by either prosecution or co-accused. It seems reasonable that when good character has been claimed by such evidence that a co-accused should be permitted to attempt to rebut it by evidence coming up to the same standard of relevance. If the co-accused contents himself with an attack on the character of his co-accused without making any comparison with his own, then *Knutton* excludes cross-examination of the co-accused on the analogy of the tit for tat principle of section 1(f)(ii) of the Criminal Evidence Act 1898. The final position on the spectrum is illustrated by the facts of *Neale*.[8] Here the evidence is insufficiently relevant either at the instance of prosecution or of co-accused, and so in the absence either of good character being claimed by the co-accused, or of any attack being made upon the character of the other, there is no ground for its admission. A further complication[9] here relates to whether the bad character evidence tendered by a co-accused need meet the enhanced standard of probative force demanded of disposition evidence when adduced by the prosecution in chief.[10] It is submitted that it need not on the basis that the enhanced standard is itself apparently diminishing; upon the analogy of the absence of a protective exclusionary discretion in relation to cross-examination of a co-accused;[11] and upon the general desirability of decisions being made upon the basis of as much relevant evidence as possible.

---

5   It is uncertain how crucial it was that the co-accused had put his character in issue. In Canada it appears not to be necessary, *R v Kendall and McKay* (1987) 35 CCC (3d) 105.

6   The Criminal Evidence Act 1898, s 1(f), might sometimes prevent cross-examination of the co-accused himself.

7   The discretion cannot be exercised at common law to prevent prejudice to a co-accused: see *R v Dellapatrona* (1993) 31 NSWLR 123, at 131.

8   See also *R v Mason, Lidgard and Herrington* [1996] Crim LR 325; and in Australia, *R v Priestley and Mason* (1985) 19 ACR 388.

9   See *R v Kracher* [1995] Crim LR 819; *R v Thompson, Sinclair and Maver* [1995] Crim LR 821; and the useful commentaries by Birch.

10 See further below ch VIII. For consideration of this issue in the light of the provisions of the Evidence Act (NSW) 1995, see *R v Lockyer* (1996) 89 ACR 457.

11 *Murdoch v Taylor* [1965] AC 574, [1965] 1 All ER 406, see further below p 412.

4. Parties to civil proceedings

Evidence of character may be relevant in civil proceedings in a number of different ways. Quite apart from its possible relevance as 'similar fact' evidence it may itself be in issue, as in defamation cases, or it may be used to impugn the credibility of a party witness. It seems that the general good character of a party may not be adduced, unlike that of the accused in criminal proceedings. This was clearly stated by Eyre CB in *A-G v Bowman*,[12] a suit for a penalty, and elaborated by Baron Martin in *A-G v Radloff*:[13]

> In criminal cases evidence of the good character of the accused is most properly and with good reason admissible in evidence, because there is a fair and just presumption that a person of good character would not commit a crime; but in civil cases such evidence is with equal good reason not admitted, because no presumption would fairly arise, in the very great proportion of cases, from the good character of the defendant, that he did not commit the breach of contract or of civil duty alleged against him.

As one would expect exactly the same rule applies to evidence of good character of the claimant.[14]

A complainant's character may be directly in issue on the question of liability in a claim for defamation when justification is pleaded, and the question whether specific acts, rumours or reputation can be received will depend upon the pleadings in the particular case.[15] The claimant's character is also relevant to the amount of damages recoverable by him in proceedings for defamation. In *Scott v Sampson*[16] it was decided that the evidence which might be adduced in mitigation of damages for defamation must be confined to the complainant's reputation, and might not consist of rumours or testimony concerning specific acts. This case was subsequently approved by the House of Lords.[17] It is clear that the evidence of reputation must relate to the segment of the complainant's life to which the defamation relates, and some of their Lordships pointed to the difficulty of drawing up a sharp distinction between evidence of specific acts and evidence of reputation. Although evidence of specific acts is not admissible to show that they were performed, it may be admissible to show that the complainant has the reputation of being a man who is in the habit of performing such acts.[18] Such matters as rumours and specific acts may be put to the complainant in cross-examination as to credit, his answers are final in accordance with the general rule, and the judge must endeavour to separate the issue of credibility from that concerning the quantum of damages when he sums up to the jury.[19]

12 (1971) 2 Bos & P 532n.
13 (1854) 10 Exch 84, at 97.
14 *Cornwell v Richardson* (1825) 1 Ry & M 305. See also *Deep v Wood* (1983) 143 DLR (3d) 246.
15 *Maisel v Financial Times Ltd* (1915) 84 LJKB 2145.
16 (1882) 8 QBD 491.
17 *Plato Films Ltd v Speidel* [1961] AC 1090, [1961] 1 All ER 876. In that case there was a plea of justification and the decision turned on the propriety of the particulars in the defendant's defence.
18 *Waters v Sunday Pictorial Newspaper Ltd* [1961] 2 All ER 758, [1961] 1 WLR 967.
19 *Hobbs v CT Tinling & Co Ltd* [1929] 2 KB 1.

In a claim for defamation, the complainant's previous convictions for offences relevant to the alleged defamation may be proved in mitigation of damages[20] as well as in cross-examination to credit:[1]

> They are the raw material upon which bad reputation is built up. They have taken place in open court. They are matters of public knowledge. They are acted on by people generally as the best guide to his reputation and standing.

They are also in defamation cases conclusive evidence of the accused having committed the offence of which he has been convicted.[2]

The exclusionary rules of the law of evidence play a very limited role in modern civil law, and it is certain that there are very many more examples of evidence of the character of a party being adduced without the slightest advertence to this branch of law.

C. THIRD PARTIES

Sometimes a key figure in a case, or even the alleged alternative perpetrator of a crime is not the co-accused, but a third party. If such third party is not called as a witness questions arise as to the extent to which the character of such a person may be explored. In *R v Murray*[3] relevance alone appeared to be the key, with evidence[4] of the bad character of a third party[5] whose conduct was alleged to have frightened the accused into reckless driving being held to be admissible on that count, but not on a count relating to unlawful wounding of a passenger in the third party's car after the vehicles had stopped, here alleged as self-defence. Perhaps the driver's record was regarded as too remote from the accused's fear of the driver's passenger. It has been suggested in Canada that the degree of probative force of such evidence need not be so great when adduced by the defence because of the lower onus upon the accused, merely to raise a reasonable doubt, and because there is no prejudice to balance against such reduced probative force.[6]

Similar issues may arise in civil proceedings, where a generous view tends to taken of the possible scope for attacking the character of third parties.[7]

SECTION 4. REHABILITATION

As noted above[8] it is generally impermissible to support the credibility of a witness in advance of an attack, even when one is reasonably anticipated.[9] The witness may of

---

20 Similarly the character of a complainant of sexual harassment may be relevant to the detriment suffered, see *Snowball v Gardner Merchant Ltd* [1987] ICR 719.
1 *Goody v Odhams Press Ltd* [1967] 1 QB 333, at 340, [1966] 3 All ER 369, at 372.
2 Civil Evidence Act 1968, s 13. Acquittals are however no evidence of innocence.
3 [1995] RTR 239.
4 To be elicited by cross-examination of a police prosecution witness.
5 Though the convictions were mainly for offences of dishonesty with offences of violence or in respect of driving offences in a very minor key.
6 *R v A(GJ)* (1989) 70 CR (3d) 298 (where expert defence evidence was admitted to show the phenomenon of 'transference' by which a child might accuse an innocent person of a perpetrated crime rather than her own father, supported by evidence of the perpetration of acts very similar to those in question, perpetrated by the father in the past on other daughters).
7 *Hurst v Evans* [1917] 1 KB 352, at 355.
8 See above, p 302.
9 *Bamfield v Massey* (1808) 1 Camp 460.

course deny any allegation made against him, and if the allegation is made in cross-examination not of him but of a subsequent witness, the impugned witness may even be recalled for re-examination in order to have an opportunity to make such a denial.[10] If a witness were impeached by calling evidence as to his lack of veracity, it was always open to a party to call a witness in rebuttal to affirm his veracity.[11] There seems to have been some confusion as to the permissibility of adducing evidence to rebut a specific allegation of misconduct falling short of the commission of a crime, when such an allegation was permitted.[12] It can certainly be argued that the same need to conduct a trial expeditiously which dictates the general rule that denials should not be rebutted by extrinsic evidence should be applied to evidence in support of them. On the other hand some have felt that a simple denial in response to cross-examination may be too unconvincing a response, at least when the allegation can be answered conclusively.[13] Despite some confusion in the earlier authorities,[14] it has now been authoritatively stated that when an attack is made upon the veracity of a witness by reference to particular facts, the matter is collateral, and a denial cannot be rebutted.[15]

10   *R v Noel* (1834) 6 C & P 336.
11   *R v Murphy* (1753) 19 State Tr 693, at 723, 724.
12   Compare *Bamfield v Massey* above; *Dodd v Norris* (1814) 3 Camp 519; *Bate v Hill* (1823) 1 C & P 100; *Provis v Reed* (1829) 5 Bing 435; and *Doe d Reed v Harris* (1836) 7 C & P 330.
13   See for example IV *Wigmore* para 1104.
14   Compare *Bamfield v Massey* (1808) 1 Camp 460 (where it was denied) with *R v Clarke* (1817) 2 Stark 241 (where it was allowed).
15   *R v Hamilton* (1998) Times, 25 July, reaffirming *R v Wood* [1951] 2 All ER 112n, 35 Cr App Rep 61, *R v Redgrave* (1981) 74 Cr App Rep 10.

CHAPTER VIII

Similar fact evidence[1]

This chapter complements the discussion of character and credibility in ch VII, and together with it lays the foundations for the discussion of cross-examination of the accused in ch IX. These three chapters cover topics which lie at the very heart of the law of evidence as it applies in criminal cases. The subject matter of this chapter is the exclusionary rule which in Commonwealth jurisdictions is commonly known as the 'similar facts' rule, terminology which is less common in the United States, and is certainly misleading.[2] It is indeed doubly misleading because it describes the exclusionary rule in a phrase more apt to describe one of the principal exceptions to it,[3] and because it suggests a unifying factor between the situations in this area which they do not necessarily possess.[4] The terminology is nevertheless too deeply engrained to be abandoned.[5] If it cannot be abandoned, it must be explained. It is used here to connote that part of the law of evidence concerned with the rule which prevents a party, usually the prosecutor,[6] from leading evidence showing the discreditable

---

1 For recent Law Commission consideration: see in England, Law Com Con Pap No 141 *Evidence in Criminal Proceedings: Previous Misconduct of a Defendant* (1996) especially Pts 2, 3, 6–10; and in New Zealand, Prel Pap No 27 *Evidence Law: Character & Credibility* (1997) especially Pts 1–4. For recent academic discussion in the United States see 49 Hastings LJ 717 et seq (1998).

2 See in Canada, *R v Green* (1988) 40 CCC (3d) 333, at 353; and in Australia *Pfennig v R* (1995) 182 CLR 461, at 465. For deprecation of its use in civil cases see *Sheldon v Sun Alliance Australia Ltd* (1989) 53 SASR 97, at 137.

3 This seems to be the best explanation of the terminological distinction made in *R v Lewis* (1982) 76 Cr App Rep 33, at 35; *R v Wright* (1989) 90 Cr App Rep 325, at 329; and *R v Fulcher* [1995] 2 Cr App Rep 251, at 257.

4 See Elliott [1983] Crim LR 284, at 288. In *Pfennig* above the majority regarded 'similar fact' evidence as a sub-set of propensity evidence, and distinguished it from 'relationship' and 'identity' evidence.

5 This may be too pessimistic a view. In *R v Wright* (1990) 90 Cr App Rep 325, at 329 Mustill LJ referred to the '*so-called* similar facts rule'; and in *R v Ananthanarayanan* [1994] 2 All ER 847, [1994] 1 WLR 788, at 849a, 793F Laws J said that it was what the area *used to be called* (emphasis supplied).

6 For cases where similar fact evidence is sought to be adduced by the defence, see in Canada, *R v Arcangioli* [1994] 1 SCR 129; and in Australia, *Duff v R* (1979) 39 FLR 315, at 347; *Cheney v R* (1991) 99 ALR 360.

disposition[7] of the other,[8] usually the accused, as derived from his discreditable acts, record, possessions, or reputation. The chapter is not concerned with evidence of these matters when they are themselves in issue, as they would be if justification were pleaded in a claim for libel based upon allegations that the claimant had taken things which did not belong to him, been convicted of theft, been found in possession of housebreaking implements, and had the reputation of being dishonest.

As noted above this subject is at its most important in criminal proceedings. The reason is simply that such evidence is believed to be very influential in its effect upon a jury.[9] It is likely both to help prove the guilt of the accused, and to prejudice the jury against him. The prosecution justifiably seeks its inclusion for the former purpose, and the defence equally justifiably seeks it exclusion for the latter reason.[10] Similarly the strength of public revulsion against those believed to be sexual offenders, to whom the rules are often applicable, cuts both ways: exacerbating public disapprobation of strict exclusion perceived to lead to wrongful acquittals; and, especially through the reflection of such revulsion in the prison system, magnifying the effects of wrongful convictions caused by relaxed admission.

Although it seems incumbent upon the judge to give a direction as to any limited use that might be made of such evidence,[11] the task of the judge is extremely difficult, since any further reference to so prejudicial a matter is liable to exacerbate the effect of admitting it at all.[12] The need for a direction is paramount in cases where there is no exclusionary discretion because the defence has introduced the evidence for a limited purpose as in *B v R* above; may occasionally be necessary if both inculpatory and exculpatory inferences can be drawn from the same events;[13] and is unhelpfully exaggerated in cases where a distinction is drawn between 'background' and 'disposition' evidence: see further below p 343. The current tendency to admit evidence which may be of extremely low cogency on account of collaboration also complicates the task of directing the jury.[14]

The dilemma created by these competing aims generates the problems discussed in the first section of this chapter which deals with the rules at common law excluding 'similar fact' evidence when tendered in chief by the prosecution in a criminal case.

---

7   Throughout this chapter the term 'disposition' is used to denote a propensity to act, think or feel in a particular way. It must however be the disposition of the *accused*, and in cases of rape where consent is alleged as a defence, the evidence of other non-consensual acts cannot be used to show, or to corroborate evidence, that the acts in question were non-consensual: *R v Movis* (1994) 75 ACR 416.

8   For cases where the accused adduced evidence of his own discreditable conduct, see *R v Kenny* [1992] Crim LR 800 (to show that his record excluded the type of crime alleged); *B v R* (1992) 175 CLR 599 (to show that his past conduct had caused the complainant to react vindictively).

9   This commonly held belief is largely confirmed by the results of empirical investigation, see Law Com No 141 App D. In *R v Bills* [1995] 2 Cr App Rep 643 a conviction was quashed because the jury attempted to change its verdict after hearing for the first time of the accused's record at the sentencing stage; in *R v Johnson* [1995] 2 Cr App Rep 1 the Court of Appeal thought that there was no case to answer without the disputed evidence, but that with it a conviction was inevitable.

10   It is accordingly extremely rare, but not quite unknown (see eg *R v McKenzie* [1991] Crim LR 767), for a conviction to be upheld despite the wrongful admission of such evidence; or in the face of a misdirection as to its relevance (but for an exception see *R v B(CR)* [1990] 1 SCR 717).

11   *R v Wright* (1989) 90 Cr App Rep 325, at 335; *BRS v R* (1997) 148 ALR 101, HCA.

12   *Crofts v R* (1996) 186 CLR 427, at 440. A retrial was ordered because the jury had not been discharged after the inadmissible evidence of other acts had been adduced (there at the late stage of re-examination).

13   *R v Winner* (1995) 79 ACR 528.

14   See *R v Davies* [1996] CLY 1351.

The remaining, and much less important, sections deal with those few statutory rules which affect the position in criminal cases, and the position in civil proceedings.

SECTION I.   EXCLUSION AT COMMON LAW IN CRIMINAL PROCEEDINGS

This aspect of the law of evidence was said by the Criminal Law Revision Committee to constitute 'far the most difficult of all the topics which we have discussed'.[15] It is also one of the most keenly litigated, and has been described by Lord Hailsham as a 'pitted battlefield'.[16] Its legendary difficulty is largely a reflection of the dilemma created by the clash of probative force and prejudicial effect which is at its most strident in this area. Significant confusion of terminology, long historical development and the absence of statutory intervention so throwing more weight upon the precise formulation of appellate opinions than they can reasonably bear have, no doubt, all contributed to the problem. They are less significant than the basic dilemma which is fundamentally insoluble, and inescapable. The first part of this section will set out the three most significant landmarks in the development of the exclusionary rule. Its scope, constituent elements and application will then be examined in turn. An attempt to cut the Gordian knot by invocation of judicial discretion will be considered, and the final part will examine some suggestions for reform of the rule. A preliminary formulation of the rule is that evidence of the character or of the misconduct of the accused on other occasions (including his possession of discreditable material), tendered to show his bad disposition, is inadmissible unless it is so highly probative of the issues in the case as to outweigh the prejudice it may cause.[17]

A.   DEVELOPMENT OF THE RULE[18]

An exclusionary rule seems to have been established by the beginning of the nineteenth century, and is stated in recognisably modern terms in *R v Cole*: 'in a prosecution for an infamous crime, an admission by the prisoner that he had committed such an offence at another time and with another person, and that he had a tendency to such practices, ought not to be admitted'.[19] The application of the rule was uncertain throughout the nineteenth century.[20] It was first considered by a final appellate court in *Makin v A-G for New South Wales*.[1] This was an important case not only because of the eminence of the court which decided it, but also because on its facts it represented a construction of the rule admitting similar fact evidence more readily than in any previous example. Makin and his wife were tried for the murder of a baby which it was alleged they had

15   Cmnd 4991, para 70.
16   *DPP v Boardman* [1975] AC 421, at 445, [1974] 3 All ER 887, at 898.
17   This formulation has twice been explicitly approved by the Supreme Court of Canada, *R v Robertson* [1987] 1 SCR 918, at 941; *R v D (LE)* [1989] 2 SCR 111, at 120.
18   The history of the rule is traced by Stone (1933) 46 Harv LR 954.
19   As reported in Phillips *Evidence* (1814), at 69. The trial judge's original note is appended to the judgment in *R v Sims* as reported in [1946] KB 531, at 544.
20   Compare the reasoning in the poisoning cases of *R v Geering* (1849) 18 LJMC 215, *R v Winslow* (1860) 8 Cox CC 397, and *R v Hall* (1887) 5 NZLR 93, for example. Nor did these varieties exhaust the possibilities, in the infamous case of Neill Cream the evidence of other poisonings was admitted by Hawkins J 'as corroboration', Shore *Trial of Neill Cream* (1923), at 154.
1   [1894] AC 57. For additional facts and social background see Palmer (1993) 67 Law Inst J 1171.

taken in for informal adoption upon the payment of a small premium by the infant's mother. As asserted by the Supreme Court of New South Wales,[2] and accepted by the Privy Council,[3] there was ample evidence that the accused were guilty as charged. The mother was able to give evidence of the transaction handing the child over, of deceit and evasion by the accused when she tried to see it again, including an attempt to pass off a different child as hers, and of the identity of clothing found on the child's dead body. There was evidence of damaging admissions made by the accused both by word and action. The premium was plainly inadequate to support the child for very long. There was evidence that the accused received the baby in good health one day in one set of premises, removed surreptitiously to another two days later without the child, and that a corpse found wearing the baby's clothes was found secretly buried on the premises from which the accused had so departed. Such circumstantial evidence would surely have been sufficient for a verdict of guilty, even on so serious a charge. The prosecution was not content however and wished to adduce evidence of a number of other mothers who had placed babies with the accused on the payment of similarly inadequate premiums. The accused had flatly denied having received any of these children. The prosecution also tendered evidence of thirteen bodies of babies having been found on three different sets of premises occupied at different times by the accused. It was argued that this evidence tended to rebut any possible defence of accidental death, and showed a systematic course of conduct by the accused, vulgarly known as 'baby farming'. The defence attempted to counter this argument by asserting that the evidence of the other bodies was admissible only to show the mens rea of the accused once it had been shown that it was a result of their acts that the baby had met its death, but that there was no clear evidence of that. The evidence was in fact admitted to rebut the accused's presumed[4] defence that they had not engaged in a systematic practice of 'baby farming'. This was shown by the direct evidence of the five mothers who testified to having handed over their babies, and by the finding of so many dead bodies of babies in so many different premises occupied by the accused which rendered quite incredible any suggestion that there was no connection between the bodies found on the premises, and the acts of the accused while they lived there. The majority of the Supreme Court denied that it was necessary to show even a prima facie connection between the acts of the accused and the deaths of any of the babies before evidence of the latter became admissible, though the denial was obiter since the court, as noted above, held that there was plenty of evidence of such a connection in the case before them. In more analytical and less descriptive terms the evidence tending to show other discreditable acts, and through them the disposition of the accused to commit the discreditable act in issue, was admissible to corroborate circumstantial evidence both of the commission of the actus reus of the crime and of the mens rea required for it. It should be noted that at no stage did the accused raise a defence of accidental death,[5] they simply disclaimed all connection with either mother or baby, and all knowledge of any of the bodies. It was against this background that the Privy Council delivered the passage[6] characterised so appreciatively by the House of Lords in *DPP v Boardman*:[7]

2   (1893) 14 LR NSW 1, at 19.
3   At 64.
4   Derived from statements made to the police during interrogation, and at an inquest into the deaths of the children. At the trial the accused seem merely to have put the prosecution to their proof.
5   But see Palmer above n 1.
6   [1894] AC 57, at 65.
7   [1975] AC 421, [1974] 3 All ER 887, 'always been accepted as expressing cardinal principles' (Lord Morris at 438, 892); 'can [not] be better stated' (Lord Hailsham at 435, 905); 'stated with crystal clarity' (Lord Salmon at 461, 912). And as a result still frequently cited, see eg *DPP v P* [1991] 2 AC 447, [1991] 3 All ER 337; *Pfennig v R* (1995) 182 CLR 461, at 465.

It is undoubtedly not competent for the prosecution to adduce evidence tending to show that the accused had been guilty of criminal acts other than those covered by the indictment, for the purpose of leading to the conclusion that the accused is a person likely from his criminal conduct or character to have committed the offence for which he is being tried. On the other hand, the mere fact that the evidence adduced tends to show the commission of other crimes does not render it inadmissible if it be relevant to an issue before the jury, and it may be so relevant if it bears upon the question whether the acts alleged to constitute the crime charged in the indictment were designed or accidental, or to rebut a defence which would otherwise be open to the accused.

It is also significant that this passage was both preceded and succeeded by a warning that its application might prove extremely difficult. The source of such difficulties was identified by Lord Hailsham as residing in the fact that while the rule depends heavily on questions of weight and degree best left to a jury, the function of the rule, because it combines considerations of relevance and prejudice, properly falls to be decided in advance,[8] by the judge. There was for a long time a tendency to construe Lord Herschell's words as if they were part of a criminal statute, and in particular to treat the examples given in the second sentence as if they constituted a closed list of rigid categories. These words are more naturally read as stressing the importance of, and illustrating by examples, the relevance of the evidence to the issues in the case.[9]

It was certainly in such a sense that they were read in *DPP v Boardman*, an authoritative modern restatement of this principle.[10] In that case the accused, a middle-aged headmaster, was charged with one count of buggery, and two of incitement to buggery with pupils at his school. Each count related to a different youth, and in his evidence each youth recounted other incidents involving himself which, if true, amounted to criminal offences. No application was made for separate trials, nor does any objection seem to have been taken to the admission of evidence of the other incidents involving a particular youth on the count relating to that youth. The count of buggery and evidence on one of the counts of incitement related to an incident in which the accused had sought to play the passive role. Because neither the second incitement itself, nor the other incident related by that victim, possessed that peculiarity, the trial judge instructed the jury that the evidence on that count neither corroborated, nor was itself corroborated by, evidence on the other counts.[11] The trial judge held that all of the evidence on the remaining counts was mutually corroborative, though it should be noted that a number of the incidents adduced in relation to the count of buggery did

---

For criticism of such survival see Carter (1985) 48 MLR 29; Mirfield (1987) 46 CLJ 83. Zuckerman (1987) 103 LQR 187 regards *Boardman* as representing little, if any, advance on *Makin*.

8   The various stages at which such questions arise were helpfully dissected in *R v Scarrott* [1978] QB 1016, [1978] 1 All ER 672. For the serious difficulties which this causes in relation to the standard of proof of preliminary issues see Mahoney [1993] Crim LR 185. The desire to limit such incursion into the jury's role has been influential in a number of recent cases, such as *R v H* [1995] 2 AC 596, [1995] 2 All ER 865.

9   That this represented the view of the profession in England even before the decision in *Makin* is shown by the terms of a letter, appended to the relevant volume of the law reports, (1893) 14 LR (NSW) 1, written to Windeyer J by Hawkins J, an English judge with very extensive experience of presiding over criminal trials, and who when asked to comment on the judgment of the Supreme Court of New South Wales wrote, 'Relevancy to the issue is ... all that is required to make evidence (not otherwise objectionable) admissible.'

10 [1975] AC 421, [1974] 3 All ER 887, see also commentaries by Hoffmann (1975) 91 LQR 193; Cross [1975] Crim LR 62; Tapper (1975) 38 MLR 206.

11 Evidence had to be both admissible and credible before it could amount to corroboration, *DPP v Kilbourne* [1973] AC 729, [1973] 1 All ER 440.

not explicitly suggest a passive role on the part of the accused. It was argued that the evidence on one count should have been held irrelevant to the determination of the other.[12] Their Lordships all held the evidence to have been rightly considered relevant and admissible to guilt on the other count. The speeches are inconsistent in some aspects of their reasoning, but unanimous in requiring the 'similar fact' evidence to be more than barely relevant to guilt.[13] This decision was accepted elsewhere by the highest courts in the Commonwealth.[14]

It was reconsidered by the House of Lords in *DPP v P*.[15] In this case the accused was charged with offences of rape and incest in respect of two daughters. His application to have the trial severed as between the charges relating to each daughter was refused, and he was convicted[16] of a number of offences in respect of each daughter. His appeal against conviction was allowed by the Court of Appeal on the basis that there were no striking similarities between the offences relating to the daughters, the detail of the offences constituting no more than the 'stock-in-trade' of the incestuously inclined parent. The House of Lords, in a judgment longer on quotation than analysis, allowed an appeal by the prosecution. It was emphasised that the test for admissibility is:[17]

> that its probative force in support of the allegation that an accused person committed a crime is sufficiently great to make it just to admit the evidence, notwithstanding that it is prejudicial to the accused in tending to show that he was guilty of another crime.

The House of Lords took the view that probative force could be supplied in a number of different ways depending upon the circumstances of each case. It held that while 'striking similarity' is required in some cases, it is not a necessary requirement. In particular it is required less when the commission of the offence is in issue, than when the identity of the offender is in issue:

> Where the identity of the perpetrator is in issue, and evidence of this kind[[18]] is important in that connection, obviously something in the nature of what has been called in the course of the argument a signature or other special feature will be necessary. To transpose this requirement to other situations where the question is whether a crime has been committed, rather than who did commit it is to impose an unnecessary and improper restriction upon the application of the principle.

Nowhere is it suggested that the evidence should achieve a particularly high degree of probative value. Indeed it was even suggested that the link between the situations need be no stronger than that required in Scotland for one piece of evidence to

---

12 The verdict on the second incitement count had been quashed by the Court of Appeal.
13 It should be 'of close or striking similarity' (Lord Morris at 441, 895); 'striking similarity' (Lord Wilberforce at 444, 897); 'striking resemblance' (Lord Hailsham at 455, 907); 'exhibit very striking peculiarities' (Lord Cross at 460, 911); and 'be uniquely or strikingly similar' (Lord Salmon at 462, 913). The phrase 'striking similarity' is derived from *R v Sims* [1946] KB 531, at 540, [1946] 1 All ER 697, at 701.
14 See *Sutton v R* (1984) 152 CLR 528 (Australia); *R v Hsi En Fong* [1985] 1 NZLR 222 (New Zealand); *R v Robertson* [1987] 1 SCR 918 (Canada).
15 [1991] 2 AC 447, [1991] 3 All ER 337; see Tapper (1992) 108 LQR 26. It was to some extent anticipated by the decision of the Privy Council in *Reza v General Medical Council* [1991] 2 AC 182, [1991] 2 All ER 796.
16 He was also acquitted of some.
17 At 460, 346.
18 Ie establishing 'striking similarity'.

corroborate another.[19] It is submitted that the combination of these inroads into the standard required for the admission of propensity evidence constitutes the least satisfactory part of the reasoning,[20] and has led to a number of questionable subsequent decisions. It has however been claimed by the majority of the High Court of Australia in *Pfennig v R*[1] now to represent the law in the principal jurisdictions of the Commonwealth.[2]

B. SCOPE OF THE RULE[3]

The first point to note is that the rule excludes only evidence that is otherwise relevant. It is an exclusionary exception to the general and fundamental principle that all relevant evidence is prima facie admissible. It has been perceptively noted that many of the difficulties experienced by the courts in their attempts to apply Lord Herschell's remarks in *Makin* might have been eliminated if his two famous sentences had been delivered in the converse order, making it clear that the second was not so much an exception to the first, as the first to the second.[4] The operation of this limitation upon the scope of the rule is not always easy to recognise. In the first place the baneful tendency to use 'relevant' and 'admissible' interchangeably clouds the issue. A second problem is that the rule demands exclusion when prejudicial effect exceeds probative force. Relevance, as will be seen, is merely one element constituting probative force, and if the evidence is to be excluded in any event there is no point in the court's agonising over the distinction between excluding the evidence because it is insufficiently relevant, and excluding it because its prejudicial effect exceeds its probative force, all elements considered. This difficulty is illustrated by two cases of high authority.

In *Noor Mohamed v R*[5] the accused was charged with the murder of his mistress. She had undoubtedly died from cyanide poisoning, and the accused, who was a goldsmith and who was on bad terms with her, had access to cyanide. There was however no evidence that the accused had administered poison to her. The prosecution wished to adduce evidence of the death from cyanide poisoning of the accused's former wife, with whom he had also been on bad terms. The accused had never been charged with causing her death, but there was some evidence that he might have tricked her into taking the cyanide. The court reasoned that even assuming it to be established that he had tricked her, it still did not follow that, in the absence of the slightest evidence of such a trick in the instant case, he had tricked his mistress. This sounds like the language of irrelevance, but the court was so adamant in rejecting dicta in *R v Sims*[6] that similar fact evidence was prima facie admissible so long only as it was logically probative, that it may be that the Privy Council thought the evidence was of too much prejudice rather than of too little relevance.

19 Relying upon *Moorov v HM Advocate* 1930 JC 68; the leniency of which is indicated by its interpretation in *Reynolds v HM Advocate* [1995] SCCR 504 as excluding similar fact evidence only if on *no possible* view could there be *any* connection to the instant offence.
20 Now exacerbated by the decision of the House of Lords in *R v H* [1995] 2 AC 596, [1995] 2 All ER 865.
1 (1995) 182 CLR 461.
2 Citing in Australia, *Hoch v R* (1988) 165 CLR 292; in Canada, *R v B(CR)* [1990] 1 SCR 717; in New Zealand, *R v McIntosh* (1991) 8 CRNZ 514.
3 Palmer (1994) 16 Adel LR 161.
4 Schiff *Evidence in the Litigation Process* (3rd edn, 1988) p 821; McNamara (1984) 57 ALJ 143.
5 [1949] AC 182, [1949] 1 All ER 365, one of very few cases of murder reported this century in which the similar fact evidence has been excluded.
6 [1946] KB 531, [1946] 1 All ER 697.

Much the same analysis may be made of a case decided soon afterwards in the House of Lords. In *Harris v DPP*[7] the accused, a policeman, was charged on eight counts of breaking into shops in a market he was patrolling, and of stealing part of the cash on the premises. The evidence on the first seven was exiguous, amounting to little more than that all the thefts were committed by a similar technique, that all had occurred when the accused was on duty and could have been in the area, and that none had occurred when he was not on duty. The evidence on the eighth count implicated the accused more directly since a trap had been set, and the accused had been identified in the area, had been seen to disappear briefly before going to the assistance of the policemen whom he knew and who had set the trap, and marked money was found in a place which he could have reached in the time he was absent. He was acquitted by the jury on the first seven counts, but found guilty on the eighth. The House of Lords quashed his conviction on the ground that the jury should have been warned that 'the evidence called in support of the earlier counts did not in itself provide confirmation of the last charge.'[8] Once again this suggests that it was irrelevant, but it is probably more accurate to attribute the failure of probative force to lack of cogency rather than to irrelevance.[9] Perhaps the clearest example of lack of relevance is a case where the accused has been acquitted on a charge involving the conduct relied upon as constituting the similar fact evidence. In *G (an infant) v Coltart*[10] the accused was charged on two counts of stealing, to both of which the defence was that there was no intention permanently to deprive. There was good evidence of such an intention on the first count, but as the principal witness was abroad, no evidence was offered and the accused acquitted. It was held that the prosecution was not able to rely upon an alleged intent to deprive in the first case since it was negated by the acquittal. This may perhaps be regarded as irrelevance of rather technical a character. In*R v Rodley*[11] it was straightforward. The accused was charged with housebreaking with intent to commit rape. His conviction was quashed because of the admission of evidence of his subsequently entering a nearby house by climbing down a chimney and having consensual intercourse with the occupant. However bizarre, such evidence was simply irrelevant, and excluded as such without any need to rely upon the rule excluding evidence of similar facts.[12] Because of the key importance of relevance in this context it has been urged that the judge should be meticulous in spelling out the purpose for which the evidence is adduced.[13]

---

7   [1952] AC 694, [1952] 1 All ER 1044. See also *Sweitzer v R* [1982] 1 SCR 949.
8   At 711, 1050.
9   In *R v Miller* [1952] 2 All ER 667, 36 Cr App Rep 169, it was regarded as relevant that the commission of crimes did not occur when one of the accused was in prison, though the cases are not exactly comparable.
10   [1967] 1 QB 432, [1967] 1 All ER 271. See also *R v Holloway* [1980] 1 NZLR 315.
11   [1913] 3 KB 468.
12   This also seems to be the best explanation of *R v Tricoglus* (1976) 65 Cr App Rep 16 (accused charged with rape committed after victim picked up by 'kerb crawler' in city centre, evidence of 'kerb crawling' by accused in city centre on other occasions held inadmissible); and of *R v Mills* [1992] Crim LR 802 (antique dealer charged with burglary after taking picture, evidence of persistently seeking to buy other pictures from other people held inadmissible). See also *R v Horry* [1949] NZLR 791 (accused charged with indecent assault of woman tricked into meeting him, evidence of similar tricks upon other women not accompanied by any indecency held to be irrelevant).
13   Notably by both majority and dissenters in *R v B(CR)* [1990] 1 SCR 717, at 738, 750 (where the trial judge took it to go to identity rather than commission). Cp *B v R* (1992) 175 CLR 599 where the accused adduced the evidence as relating to the complainant's credibility but it was held proper when once admitted for it also to be considered on the issue of his commission of the offence.

The second condition which must be satisfied before the rule may be invoked is that the evidence should be relevant by way of an argument relying at some stage upon an inference drawn from the disposition of the accused.[14] The distinction is drawn most clearly by Lord Hailsham in *Boardman*:[15]

> what is not to be admitted is a chain of reasoning and not necessarily a state of facts. If the inadmissible chain of reasoning be the *only* purpose for which the evidence is adduced as a matter of law, the evidence itself is not admissible. If there is some other relevant, probative purpose than the forbidden type of reasoning, the evidence is admitted, but should be made subject to a warning from the judge that the jury must eschew the forbidden reasoning.

This is a most important requirement, and understood correctly, helps make the similar facts rule much more comprehensible. It is worth examining some of the ways in which evidence of the relevant discreditable conduct of the accused may be relevant otherwise than by way of an argument involving a step relying upon his disposition so suggested. In these cases the evidence, if sufficiently relevant according to ordinary standards of relevance, is admissible without reference to the similar facts rule, though the evidence may, in appropriate cases, be excluded by the exercise of the judge's discretion if he believes that to admit it will be unduly prejudicial to the accused.

In some cases the revelation that the accused has committed a crime is inherent in the background to the facts of the case, and no one even considers making an objection. Thus in *R v Neale*[16] the accused was a resident in an institution for ex-Borstal boys where the crime had been committed, so it could be inferred that he had at some time in the past committed a crime. Similarly in *R v Straffen*[17] the accused's presence in the area at the relevant time could be fixed only by reference to the time at which he had escaped from Broadmoor.[18] So too in *R v Malik*[19] where the accused was charged with stirring up racial hatred by reference to his experience in prison it was inevitable that the jury should become aware that he had been convicted of other crimes. Sometimes the commission of an extrinsic crime is part and parcel of the crime with which the accused is charged. A good example of this is furnished by the old case of *R v Salisbury*[20] where the accused was a letter carrier, and the substance of the crime charged against him was the taking of notes from one letter to replace notes taken by him from another. Clearly evidence of both takings had to be given. In *R v Ellis*[1] the accused was charged with embezzling six marked coins from a till in the shop where he was employed. It was not possible to monitor the exact extent of his depredations from the till without alerting

---

14 The contrary view, which has much to recommend it, that the rule applies in all cases where the accused's disposition is revealed, whether as an essential part of the argument or not, was adopted by McHugh J in *Pfennig v R* (1995) 182 CLR 461, at 513. For support of the view in the text see Palmer, above n 3.
15 [1975] AC 421, at 453, [1974] 3 All ER 887, at 907, emphasis in original. It will however be argued that the consequences of drawing the distinction are over-stated in this passage, and that such a chain of reasoning is acceptable in a few exceptional cases.
16 (1977) 65 Cr App Rep 304.
17 [1952] 2 QB 911, [1952] 2 All ER 657.
18 One of the most spectacular examples of this genre where the similar fact point was argued is provided by *R v Sims and Anderson* [1967] Qd R 432, where the accused who had escaped from prison were charged with breaking into a nearby house and stealing clothes, and sought, rightly without success, to suppress evidence that their discarded prison clothing had been found on the premises.
19 [1968] 1 All ER 582n, [1968] 1 WLR 353.
20 (1831) 5 C & P 155. See also a case referred to in *R v Whiley* (1804) 2 Leach 983, at 985 (shirt stolen from one house found in another burgled on the same night).
1 (1826) 6 B & C 145.

him, and the prosecution was allowed to prove the total deficiency from the till, which corresponded to the total in the accused's possession at the end of the day, although he was charged only in respect of the marked coins. In *R v Cobden*[2] the matter was a stage further removed as three men were charged with breaking into a railway booking office and stealing property from it. None of that property was found in the possession of one of the three accused, but it was held permissible to prove similar break-ins in other booking offices on the same night, since the third accused might have received his share of the night's takings exclusively from those. Bramwell B opined that 'the events of that night relating to these burglaries are so intermixed that it is impossible to separate them.' Sometimes the other crime relates to the means for committing the principal crime with which the accused is charged, for example the theft of a car,[3] or an attempt to conceal its commission, for example by destroying evidence.[4]

In all of these cases the fact that the impermissible line of reasoning is not involved can be tested by supposing the extrinsic matter to be in no way discreditable to the accused and so not indicative of an evil disposition, and then seeing if that would make any difference. It can easily be seen that it would make no difference to the reasoning in cases like *Neale, Straffen* and *Malik* that the relevant institution had been, say a boarding school, rather than some sort of penal institution. Similarly in cases like *Salisbury, Ellis* or *Cobden* it would be immaterial that the accused had interchanged or mixed something to which he was perfectly entitled with the stolen property, nor would it have made the slightest difference in cases like *Mortimer* and *Thomas* that the car in question had been innocently lent to the accused. It follows that the forbidden line of reasoning has no necessary place in such cases, and that the evidence is, in principle, admissible. This is not to say however that the judge should not be alert to warn the jury against the forbidden line of reasoning as suggested by Lord Hailsham,[5] and to prevent attention being drawn to associated, but logically unconnected, criminality, by severing the indictment as suggested by Lord Goddard.[6]

Two cases involving young children may be considered in this context. A particularly difficult situation arose in *R v Chambers*[7] where the accused was charged with the rape of his ten year old grand-daughter. No similar fact evidence was adduced in chief, but when the witness admitted under cross-examination that the act had occasioned her no pain, it was held that she could be asked in re-examination whether the accused had done the same thing before on other occasions. Once again it was strictly immaterial that what occurred was discreditable to the accused. Any occurrence, however innocent and however unconnected with the accused, which might have had the same result would have been equally relevant. It is however clear that this explanation was extremely prejudicial, and in the modern law every sinew would be strained to prevent such a question being asked, whether by some form of

---

2   (1862) 3 F & F 833.

3   As in *R v Mortimer* (1936) 25 Cr App Rep 150 (theft of cars used to run down female cyclists). In *R v Thomas* (1949) 33 Cr App Rep 74, Lord Goddard CJ deplored the joinder of charges for such ancillary offences, in that case offences under the Road Traffic Act in relation to the taking and reckless driving of a car in which a rape, which constituted the principal charge, was alleged to have been committed.

4   As in *Nelson v HM Advocate* 1994 JC 94 (accused charged with supplying drugs was shown to have swallowed them on spotting the police, and unsuccessfully sought to have the evidence of having done so excluded on the basis that it showed the offence of obstructing the police).

5   See also *R v Ducsharm* [1956] 1 DLR 732.

6   See also Lord Cross, with whom Lord Wilberforce expressly agreed on this point, in Boardman at 459, 911. The problem becomes more and more acute as the evidence nears the point of admissibility because of its high probative force, see generally Weinberg in Campbell and Waller (eds) *Well and Truly Tried* (1982).

7   (1848) 3 Cox CC 92.

bowdlerisation, or exclusion at the discretion of the judge.[8] Another case best considered in this connection is *R v Mackie*[9] where the accused was convicted of the manslaughter of a child. The prosecution tendered evidence of previous assaults upon the child by the accused in order to explain the child's fear of the accused, which was relevant to explain the circumstances of his death. It was held that the evidence was admissible to show the disposition of the child, not that of the accused. It is arguable that it was immaterial how the child came to have that disposition, and that it could just as easily have been caused by previous assaults by another.[10] It is submitted that it was because the case was not strictly covered by the similar facts rule that the evidence was held to be admissible, even though its prejudicial effect was conceded by the Court of Appeal to exceed by far its probative force.[11]

It is possible to categorise these various cases as being those in which the evidence from which the inference of the accused's disposition is drawn is so closely entwined and involved with the evidence directly relating to the facts in issue that it would amount to distortion to attempt to edit it out. Such an approach is potentially dangerous because the notion of involvement is rather vague, and could easily be used to smuggle in otherwise inadmissible similar fact evidence by an extended view of what is to count as a single event.[12] English courts have so far insisted on very close involvement, and in *R v Devins*[13] were reluctant to accept that where a theft took place in connection with an affray that it could be assumed that there was sufficiently close involvement for a confession of commission of the theft to be admitted on the charge of affray. This should be contrasted with the decision of the Court of Appeal in New Zealand that evidence relating to a murder which immediately preceded a rape was admissible after the murder count had been severed, and tried first.[14] It would be quite wrong to adduce evidence of the commission of other uncharged crimes[15] simply as background information without satisfying the normal conditions of admissibility for evidence of discreditable conduct or disposition.[16]

Similar reasoning has also been applied in the rather different situation where the whole history of the relationship between the victim and accused is opened up.

---

8   See in Canada, *R v Biddle* [1995] 1 SCR 761 where the accused's alibi to the rape of a woman was refuted by evidence of following another woman in suspiciously similar circumstances.

9   (1973) 57 Cr App Rep 453. For an equally disturbing decision in the same context in the United States see *Estelle v McGuire* 502 US 62 (1991).

10   There are some parallels with *Toohey v Metropolitan Police Comr* [1965] AC 595, [1965] 1 All ER 506.

11   Identification from police photographs is another situation in which the accused's discreditable past is incidentally revealed to the jury, and where admissibility is not governed by the similar facts rules, but the discretion to exclude on the balance between probative force and prejudicial effect comes into play: see *Alexander v R* (1981) 145 CLR 395; *R v Aziz* [1982] 2 NSWLR 322.

12   The dangers are illustrated by *R v Litchfield* [1993] 4 SCR 333 (where the evidence held to be contextual would normally be regarded as straightforward, and extremely prejudicial, disposition evidence).

13   [1985] LS Gaz 3082. The doctrine has been further developed in Australia, see *O'Leary v R* (1946) 73 CLR 566; though strictness of interpretation varies: cp *Bell v R* (1985) 63 ALR 433 and *R v Hocking* [1988] 1 Qd R 582. It was extensively elaborated by McHugh J in *Harriman v R* (1989) 167 CLR 590.

14   *R v Shortland* [1991] 1 NZLR 428 (though the fact of trial and conviction was suppressed).

15   Even though those charged were merely representative samples.

16   *Anderson v DPP* [1978] AC 964, [1978] 2 All ER 512; *R v Marshall* [1989] Crim LR 819. See also *R v Accused* (CA 247/91) [1992] 2 NZLR 187 where Cooke P said that it was immaterial whether such evidence was described as similar fact or res gestae, and required the same test to be satisfied in either case (though admittedly a rather weak one). But for a contrary view see McHugh J in *Harriman v R* above at 633, arguing that such evidence is automatically admissible, and not even susceptible to discretionary exclusion.

Although in *R v Berry*[17] the Court of Appeal attempted to limit such an approach in a case where prior acts of violence were tendered to prove the nature of the relationship by excluding the evidence, this view was subsequently repudiated[18] on the basis that prior events might be proved as part of an ongoing relationship when that was relevant. It is accepted that in such a case the evidence is not automatically inadmissible provided it is sufficiently probative. It is submitted though that it still falls within the ambit of the exclusionary rule, and that the question of its inadmissibility should be determined by the application of the ordinary process of balancing probative force against prejudicial effect.[19] It is wrong to regard it as falling outside the rule on the same basis as those cases where the evidence showing evil disposition is merely incidental, as in the prison location or intermingling type of case. In them argument from disposition plays no part in the argument; here it plays a prominent part, and so the ordinary rule assessing the balance of probative force and prejudicial effect should be applied.[20] This reasoning applies also to cases where the evidence shows a disposition not so much related to the particular victim as to a special class of which the victim is a member.[1] In such cases there clearly is reasoning from disposition, though it is sometimes simply, indeed vacuously, said that the instances possess an underlying unity.

Similar reasoning seems also to be present in cases where the courts have admitted previous[2] offences or possession to show the purposes for which items are currently possessed; here too reliance is placed upon disposition, so it is submitted that the more stringent criteria required for admissibility should be required.[3]

Another possible situation which has been mooted as falling outside the range of cases where the similar fact evidence is relevant because it shows the accused's bad disposition is that where it is used to rebut a suggestion of coincidence.[4] This has some plausibility, but it is submitted that it is best regarded as falling within the scope of the rule.

The argument was developed and elegantly deployed by Hoffmann in relation to the facts of *Makin*.[5] He asserted that the evidence of finding all of the bodies operated on a statistical basis. It was inherently improbable that all thirteen of the children should have died by accident. The only plausible explanation was that Makin had killed them. Makin's disposition plays no part in this argument. It is only after the argument has been made, and because it succeeds, that Makin's bad disposition is established. This is an interesting approach. It should perhaps be noted that in fact the prosecution case was that Makin was engaged in a system of taking in children at inadequate premiums

17   (1986) 83 Cr App Rep 7.
18   In *R v Williams* (1986) 84 Cr App Rep 299 by reference to *R v Ball* [1911] AC 47. See also *R v Bond* [1906] 2 KB 389, at 400; and more recently *R v Fulcher* [1995] 2 Cr App Rep 251 and *R v Stevens* [1995] Crim LR 649, both citing *R v Pettman* LEXIS 2 May 1985.
19   See *R v Underwood* [1999] Crim LR 227 for an egregious example of the dangers of not doing so.
20   See *R v Cleall* [1996] CLY 1322. This point was very clearly made in Australia in *R v AH* (1997) 42 NSWLR 702, see also *Charlie v R* (1998) 115 NTR 1, and *R v G* (1996) 88 ACR 489; in *R v Wackerow* (1996) 90 ACR 297 it was said to be a consequence of the reasoning of the High Court in *Pfennig v R* (1995) 182 CLR 461.
1   See *R v Sidhu* (1992) 98 Cr App Rep 59 where the evidence of terrorist disposition was directed against a particular political and religious faction; in *Thompson v R* (1989) 169 CLR 1 the class was the much smaller one of a group of very close relatives.
2   Sometimes it is extremely difficult to establish whether the possession relates to past or present transactions: *R v Wilkinson* [1997] CLY 1104; *R v Lovelock* [1997] Crim LR 821.
3   As in *R v Gordon* [1995] 2 Cr App Rep 61. For an unconvincing attempt to isolate such evidence from the exclusionary rule in Canada, see *R v Lepage* [1995] 1 SCR 654. See further below p 378.
4   Especially in recent Australian authority, such as *Pfennig v R* (1995) 182 CLR 461.
5   Hoffmann (1975) 91 LQR 193, at 198.

and killing them. It was integral to this case that Makin took in a large number of children, that his disposition was murderous, and that this supported their case that he murdered the child in respect of which he was charged. It may also be noted that the defence never raised any question of accident at the trial.[6] Nevertheless the case could have been run differently, and the argument should be considered on its merits. It is conceded that the statistical argument does not rely upon Makin's disposition. It is however submitted that the best that the statistical argument can establish is that Makin must have murdered most of the children. If there had been only one death the possibility of accident was not rebutted. It was only when there were so many that it became incredible all could be accidental. This is not however enough for the prosecution. They must establish not that most of the deaths were deliberately caused, but that one in particular was deliberate.[7] It has however already been established that one death might be accidental. It is only because of the association of the one charged with all of the others that any inference can be drawn that it too was deliberate. In other words the last and essential link in the chain of reasoning still depends upon the accused's disposition.[8] The real justification for this view is that it is only when there is a large number of incidents that the argument will succeed in the absence of close similarity of detail. One other death in *Makin* would, it is submitted not have been enough unless the detail were very similar indeed.[9] But in that case it is obvious that the coincidence is based upon the propensity of the accused to act in a very peculiar way. The larger the number of deaths the less detail required in each to establish a propensity. If propensity played no part in a case like *Makin* one would have to concede that a point would come at which the number of deaths had grown so large that the chance of one occurring by accident would become extremely likely,[10] and that in the absence of further specification the accused would be entitled to be acquitted.[11]

The third condition which evidence must satisfy in addition to being relevant, and relevant by way of an argument from the accused's disposition, before the similar fact rule can be applied to it, is that the evidence must be discreditable to the accused in some way. It is noticeable that in the famous passage quoted above from *Makin* Lord Herschell refers only to 'criminal acts' and 'criminal conduct or character'.[12] In *Harriman v R*[13] Brennan J restricted the exclusion still further to crimes of a similar character. It is quite clear that discredit extends further than evidence of the commission of crimes. In some cases the evidence in question suggests no more than immorality,[14] in others it

---

6   But see Palmer (1993) 67 Law Inst J 1171.
7   As Lord Herschell himself once said in a civil case in this context 'Cases of this description are not determined upon probabilities, but upon evidence of what happened upon the particular occasion': *Kennedy v Dodson* [1895] 1 Ch 334 at 338.
8   But see Ligertwood *Australian Evidence* (2nd ed, 1993) at p 98 for a contrary view arguing that, if a disposition at all, this is not the prior disposition with which the rule is concerned. Dawson J adopted a view similar to that in the text in *Harriman v R* (1989) 167 CLR 590, at 600; but it was roundly rejected by McHugh J in *Pfennig v R* (1995) 182 CLR 461, at 531.
9   As it was in *Pfennig*.
10 See Acorn (1991) 11 OJLS 63.
11 Unless one were to accept a purely probabilistic basis for a decision, as to which see Lord Herschell's remark quoted above, and more generally see p 154.
12 It was held in *R v Ananthanarayanan* [1994] 2 All ER 847, at 853 that there is no de minimis rule, and even minor crimes are sufficient.
13 (1989) 167 CLR 590 at 593, and took the view that using heroin and selling it were sufficiently dissimilar from importing it.
14 As in *R v Butler* (1986) 84 Cr App Rep 12 where it consisted of the details of consensual heterosexual acts, and of the places where they occurred. See also in Canada, *R v Robertson* [1987] 1 SCR 918; cp in Australia *R v Von Einem* (1985) 38 SASR 207, at 211 where it was suggested, it is submitted wrongly, that allegations of homosexuality fell outside the rule to the extent that it had been legalised in South Australia.

is of some, in itself non-criminal, aspect of the criminal act. One of the clearest examples of the first sort is provided by *R v Ball*.[15] In that case a brother and sister were charged with incest contrary to the Punishment of Incest Act 1908. In order to show that sexual intercourse had occurred between them at a time after the passage of the Act when they were sharing a bed the prosecution wished to prove that the brother had fathered his sister's child, conceived before incest became a crime under the Act. In that case the act while not criminal when committed subsequently became criminal; in *R v Shellaker*[16] the act, although criminal at the time of commission, had ceased to be subject to criminal proceedings at the time it was adduced in evidence owing to lapse of time; in both the evidence was nevertheless held admissible. The question was also mooted in *R v Barrington*.[17] In that case the prosecution sought to bolster the evidence of three young complainants of various acts of indecency by the accused with evidence from three other girls. The evidence of those girls indicated that the accused had gone through much the same preliminary technique of recruiting them ostensibly for baby-sitting, by the same false pretences, and had attempted to induce them into a compliant attitude and compromising situation by the use of similar inducements, including the provision of pornographic magazines and photographs. It was not however alleged that any acts of indecency or criminal conduct had occurred. The court admitted the evidence notwithstanding. *Ball* was not cited to the court, which was wrongly informed that there were no reported cases in which similar fact evidence had been admitted even though no crime had occurred. Instead, the court relied upon cases where the non-criminal circumstances of other crimes had been stressed. It should also be noted that in a number of cases the accused's propensity had been proved by the possession of articles of an indecent character even though such possession was in itself no offence and there was no suggestion that they had ever been used in connection with the commission of the offence.[18] In the case of other articles it has been held that evidence of possession of implements only of the sort actually used for the housebreaking in question are admissible.[19] In these cases the possession of certain articles may not be unequivocally discreditable in itself, though they may be capable of being used for discreditable purposes. It seems that if there is a suggestion that otherwise innocent articles, such as walkie-talkie radios and imitation police uniforms, may be used for criminal purposes it is not necessary that any such occasion on which they have been so used need be identified, provided that there is some issue to which their possession is sufficiently relevant.[20] It has even been held that the possession of money may in certain circumstances both indicate a discreditable disposition and be liable to be prejudicial so as to attract some form of balancing, and to require a clear direction to the jury of the use it may make of such possession.[1]

15   [1911] AC 47, 6 Cr App Rep 31.
16   [1914] 1 KB 414, 9 Cr App Rep 240.
17   [1981] 1 All ER 1132, [1981] 1 WLR 419. See also *R v Seaman* (1978) 67 Cr App Rep 234, where the evidence was also of acts probably preliminary to commission of a crime, though not there of an inherently discreditable character.
18   See *Thompson v R* [1918] AC 221, 13 Cr App Rep 61 (photographs); *R v Twiss* [1918] 2 KB 853 (photographs). But see *R v Gillingham* [1939] 4 All ER 122, 27 Cr App Rep 143, where the court seemed to require at least possible use in a crime of the sort in question, but took a broad view of the possible uses of indecent photographs (heterosexual photographs to stimulate homosexual activity). In *R v Gordon and Gordon* (1991) 57 ACR 413 possession of such items was used to rebut a suggestion that a child had been coached.
19   *R v Manning* (1923) 17 Cr App Rep 85; *R v Taylor* (1923) 17 Cr App Rep 109. See also, in Canada, *Guay v R* [1979] 1 SCR 18 (indecent book used in commission of crime); and in Australia, *R v Hofer* (1991) 55 ACR 225 (book on similar method of cultivating marijuana) .
20   *R v Reading* [1966] 1 All ER 521n, [1966] 1 WLR 836.
1   *R v Wright* [1994] Crim LR 55; *R v Batt* [1994] Crim LR 592; *R v Morris* [1995] 2 Cr App Rep 69, 159 JP 1. See in Australia *R v Lewis* (1989) 46 ACR 365.

As has already been noted, and as will be seen later, the similar fact rule depends upon the relevance of the evidence under consideration to the issues in the case. This usually requires detailed comparison of the facts in issue and the evidence showing the accused in a discreditable light. It is thus necessary to examine that other conduct in some detail. Many of the details, often the most important, are not essential features of the criminality or discreditability of the other conduct, but incidental to it. It was suggested in *R v Novac*[2] that evidence of surrounding circumstances, not in themselves criminal, could not be adduced if they were not sufficiently proximate to the commission of the crime charged. In that case the evidence related to the place at which young boys were solicited for indecent purposes. The suggestion has however been rejected in subsequent cases.[3] This seems to reflect no more than a difference between the opinion of the different courts as to the relevance of the evidence in question. It is highly unlikely that the Court of Appeal was in *Novac* seeking to cast any doubt upon one of the most famous of all similar fact cases, *R v Smith*,[4] where a number of undoubtedly innocent features of the conduct in question were stressed, such as the celebration of marriage with a lady,[5] taking out insurance on her life, exhibiting solicitude about her health, and purchasing a bath for her use. These features were rightly admitted, and emphasised, since they were vitally relevant to establish the circumstantial basis for the inference that all of these ladies had been murdered by the accused.

It can now be seen that evidence revealing the accused's discreditable disposition is excluded under the similar facts rule only when such disposition is an essential step in the argument.[6] If the evidence of disposition is irrelevant, it is excluded for that reason. If it is relevant, but upon a line of argument unconnected with the accused's discreditable disposition, it is, in principle, admissible, but remains subject to exclusion by way of judicial discretion if its prejudicial effect is regarded as sufficiently outweighing its probative value.

It has been noted that in a number of modern Australian cases the use of evidence of the accused's past discreditable conduct has been regarded as being admitted on a basis otherwise than that of propensity or 'similar facts'. There has been a tendency in such cases to argue that such admissibility is circumstantial, and that the stringent test favoured in Australia for the admission of such evidence, that it have no other rational explanation other than the guilt of the accused be applied to it.[7] As pointed out by McHugh J in *Pfennig v R*[8] such an approach is so demanding as to eliminate any need for balancing probative force against prejudicial effect, either by way of rule or discretion, since the balance would always, and inevitably, come down on the side of admission. It is suggested that to adopt the approach to circumstantial evidence indicated above is both too restrictive, in eliminating less strong evidence; and too inflexible, in supposing that such evidence has no disposition element requiring consideration of the factors normally taken into account in this area.[9]

2   (1977) 65 Cr App Rep 107, at 112.
3   *R v Scarrott* [1978] QB 1016, at 1025, [1978] 1 All ER 672, at 679; *R v Barrington* [1981] 1 All ER 1132, at 1141, [1981] 1 WLR 419, at 430.
4   (1915) 11 Cr App Rep 229. See also *Lanford v General Medical Council* [1990] 1 AC 13, [1989] 2 All ER 921.
5   In fact the marriage was bigamous, but clearly the proof of it still falls into the class of case where the evidence of the discreditable nature is relevant otherwise than as showing the accused's disposition.
6   The importance of distinguishing between the admissibility of evidence of discreditable matters which does and does not proceed by way of an argument relying upon disposition has received statutory recognition in Police and Criminal Evidence Act 1984, s 74(3).
7   See eg *Hoch v R* (1988) 165 CLR 292, at 296 (Mason CJ, Wilson and Gaudron JJ); *Harriman v R* (1989) 167 CLR 590, at 602 (Dawson J), 607 (Toohey J) and 613 (Gaudron J).
8   (1995) 127 ALR 99, at 138.
9   See Palmer (1994) 16 Adel LR 161.

C.   ELEMENTS OF THE RULE[10]

The rule comprises two elements conveniently set out by Lord Wilberforce in *Boardman*:[11]

> Whether in the field of sexual conduct or otherwise, there is no general or automatic answer to be given to the question whether evidence of facts similar to those the subject of a particular charge ought to be admitted. In each case it is necessary to estimate (i) whether, and if so how strongly, the evidence as to other facts tends to support, ie to make more credible, the evidence given as to the fact in question; (ii) whether such evidence, if given, is likely to be prejudicial to the accused. Both these elements involve questions of degree.

The two elements to which reference is made have been called above 'probative force' and 'prejudicial effect'. Both are composite notions, and will be considered in turn.

I.   Probative force

The probative force of similar fact evidence depends upon three principal factors: (a) the cogency of the evidence showing the accused's bad disposition; (b) the extent to which proof of such disposition supports the inference sought to be drawn from it; and (c) the degree of relevance of that inference to some fact in issue in the proceedings. These three variable factors interact with each other, and strength in one can mitigate weakness in another.[12] The skeleton of this analysis is sketched out here, many of the examples are discussed in more detail in the next part of this section.

(i)   Cogency of evidence showing bad disposition

There is a wide range of possibilities, from the accused's plea of guilty[13] or his confession of extrinsic discreditable conduct[14] or disposition,[15] or his conviction for the conduct after a trial,[16] to such weak possibilities as charges for which the evidence is scanty,[17] or even, of which he has already been acquitted.[18] In some cases the

---

10   For a helpful discussion see Williams (1979) 5 Dal LJ 281.

11   [1975] AC 421, at 442, [1974] 3 All ER 887, at 896.

12   Thus in *R v Wilmot* (1988) 89 Cr App Rep 341 the number of incidents outweighed minor dissimilarities, and it should be noted that an initial ruling of inadmissibility was reversed when evidence of further similar incidents became available. See also *R v Bedford* (1990) 93 Cr App Rep 113, at 117.

13   Eg *Pfennig v R* (1995) 182 CLR 461.

14   Eg *R v Straffen* [1952] 2 QB 911, [1952] 2 All ER 657.

15   Eg *R v King* [1967] 2 QB 338, [1967] 1 All ER 379.

16   Eg *R v Harrison-Owen* [1951] 2 All ER 726, 35 Cr App Rep 108. But see *R v Shepherd* (1980) 71 Cr App Rep 120, suggesting that the fact of conviction will rarely be relevant, and this case is expressly excluded from the generally curative effect of s 74 of the Police and Criminal Evidence Act 1984. The same difficulty exists in Australia, see *Tedge v R (No 2)* [1979] WAR 89.

17   Eg *Harris v DPP* [1952] AC 694, [1952] 1 All ER 1044, where the evidence was so scanty that the accused was acquitted on the relevant counts.

18   Eg *R v Ollis* [1900] 2 QB 758, 19 Cox CC 554; *R v Adams* (1993) Times, 8 April (an acquittal because of a statutory time limit); *R v Caceres-Mureira* [1995] Crim LR 489. Difficulty may be experienced in reconciling some of these cases with the rule that full credit must be accorded

probative force consists solely of an inference sought to be drawn from equivocal conduct,[19] from statements made by the accused,[20] from the possession of articles,[1] or even of letters written by a third party.[2] It is immaterial that the supporting evidence is derived from conduct after the commission of the alleged offence,[3] or even after having been charged with it.[4] In some cases the evidence was too weak to be accepted. It is interesting that in some cases less cogently established evidence is tendered when stronger is available. This tends to occur where the accused has previously been convicted of similar offences, so the evidence is clearly cogent, but is charged with a large number of incidents of the same character in different counts in the current indictment, all of which are denied. This is not at all uncommon in cases of homosexuality.[5] It appears to reflect a sentiment not very different from that inspiring the plea of autrefois convict, namely a desire not to make the accused suffer twice for the same act.

In some cases evidence of a number of incidents is adduced on the basis that the accused committed all of them. It seems now to be asserted that this situation comprises two different scenarios, to which the rules apply in different ways.[6] In the first there may be very strong evidence that the accused committed one of the crimes,[7] and then evidence from that one can be adduced to show that he committed the others, provided that there is sufficient strength to overcome any prejudice. In the second, if there is very strong evidence to show that the same man committed all of them, then weaker evidence connecting the accused with each incident may be adduced to show that he was the common criminal. In such cases it is necessary first to adduce persuasive evidence that the same man did commit all of them.[8] In order to do so, it is submitted that the discriminatory power of the evidence needs to reach a very high standard, either from peculiarity of aim or method,[9] or from aggregation and repetition of more commonplace matters, especially time and place,[10] so as to reduce the danger of circular argument.[11] If the strength of the evidence rests on peculiarity, it is particularly susceptible to failure in any one instance.[12] If it is supplied by accumulation of commonplace detail, a conviction may be sustained even though the evidence would not have been sufficient to dispel reasonable doubt in one instance if it stood alone.[13]

---

to an acquittal: see above p 91. If the acquittal arose from an earlier trial this may be accomplished more easily than in relation to other counts in the current indictment: cp *R v Wilson* [1997] 2 NZLR 161 and *R v Patton* (1996) 88 ACR 365. Compare in Canada *R v Cullen* (1989) 52 CCC (3d) 459 ; *R v Singh* (1996) 108 CCC (3d) 244.

19   Eg *R v Hall* [1952] 1 KB 302, [1952] 1 All ER 66, the first two counts.

20   Eg *R v Horwood* [1970] 1 QB 133, [1969] 3 All ER 1156.

1   Eg *R v Mustafa* (1976) 65 Cr App Rep 26

2   Eg *R v Cole* (1941) 28 Cr App Rep 43.

3   Eg *Pfennig v R* (1995) 182 CLR 461.

4   Eg *R v Simpson* (1994) 99 Cr App Rep 48.

5   *Boardman* and *Kilborne* both fell into this category.

6   *R v Downey* [1995] 1 Cr App Rep 547; *R v Barnes* [1995] 2 Cr App Rep 272; *R v Grant* [1996] 2 Cr App Rep 272.

7   For example, by a plea of guilty one of the incidents: see in England *R v Black* (1995) Times, 1 March; in Australia *Pfennig v R* (1995) 182 CLR 461; and in Canada *R v Brisbin* (1996) 101 CCC (3d) 334.

8   For a particularly clear exposition, see in Australia *R v Familic* (1994) 75 ACR 229.

9   As in *R v Straffen* [1952] 2 QB 911.

10   As in *R v Downey, R v Barnes* and *R v Grant*, above.

11   For a case in which it failed to have sufficient strength, see *R v Trew* [1996] 2 Cr App Rep 138; and for a particularly vivid example in Canada, see *R v Khan* (1996) 108 CCC (3d) 108.

12   As in *R v McGranaghan* [1995] 1 Cr App Rep 559n (where the forensic evidence showed that the accused could not have committed one of the crimes). See also in Australia *Sutton v R* (1984) 152 CLR 528; and in Canada *Sweitzer v R* [1982] 1 SCR 949.

13   As explicitly accepted in *R v Grant.*

A further dimension of the cogency of evidence of bad disposition relates to the danger of collaboration between the witnesses to the evidence extrinsic to the charge and those to the conduct in respect of which the accused is being tried. It assumes particular importance where the principal justification for the admission of the evidence of bad disposition lies in the support it affords a primary witness. This has been much controverted in England. In *R v H*,[14] the House of Lords dismissed this factor as one to be taken into account in determining admissibility,[15] except in a case where the contamination were so blatant as to render the evidence totally unworthy of belief. In all other cases the House of Lords took the view that the admissibility of the evidence should be determined on the supposition that there were no contamination at all, and the evidence considered on the basis that it were true. This would then leave this aspect of probative force entirely to the determination of the jury. This view was justified on the basis that in many, if not most, such cases there is some *danger* of contamination, and that it would be too stringent to exclude evidence simply on that basis. It was felt that to preserve this aspect of probative force as a relevant factor relating to admissibility would dilute the effect of *DPP v P*.[16] It remains to be seen how workable this will leave a test requiring comparison of prejudicial effect with so enhanced an assessment of probative force.

(ii)   Strength of the inference from evidence of bad disposition

It is obvious that the cogency of the evidence counts for nothing unless it tends to prove what it is tendered to prove, and unless that matter is itself relevant to a fact in issue.[17] The former of these two questions has to be resolved in the light of the other evidence in the case and the form of reasoning to be adopted. The greatest difficulty is experienced in cases where it is necessary to show by the extrinsic evidence, because of the absence of direct oral testimony of the matter, both that a criminal act occurred, and if it did, that it was the accused who committed it.[18] In some cases identity may be conceded, indeed be undeniable, but the commission of a criminal act hotly disputed.[19] *Straffen* fell into the converse category where the commission of the crime by someone was undeniable, but dispute centred upon the identity of the accused as the criminal in the absence of direct testimony of identification. It is in such cases that the courts require the very strongest evidence of similarity, indeed peculiarity, of technique because the evidence must by itself be so compelling as to be the equivalent of a signature, or the discovery of the accused's fingerprints in each separate connection.[20]

14   [1995] 2 AC 596, [1995] 2 All ER 865.
15   See further below p 363.
16   [1991] 2 AC 447, [1991] 3 All ER 337.
17   For a clear exposition see in Canada *R v Pascoe* (1997) 113 CCC (3d) 126 (no attempt to show the likely acts of one with the propensity weakly established by expert psychiatric testimony).
18   Though as a matter of tactical necessity usually only one of these issues will be fought seriously. *Makin v A-G for New South Wales* [1894] AC 57, *R v Smith* (1915) 11 Cr App Rep 229, and *Noor Mohamed v R* [1949] AC 182 all fall into this category in theory, but in none of them was it seriously argued that if the victim was deliberately killed, it was done by someone other than the accused, so effectively putting such cases into the following category.
19   As in *R v Ball* [1911] AC 47, 6 Cr App Rep 31.
20   See *R v Carroll* (1985) 19 ACR 410 where it was held inadmissible to identify the accused, who lied about an alibi, as the man who had abducted a female infant, dressed her in adult underwear, sexually assaulted her, bitten her on the thigh, damaged her right eye, and strangled her, by evidence that he had been subsequently divorced having on a number of occasions apparently bitten the thigh of his own female infant and once damaged her eye, though she had not been strangled, and it could not be proved whether or not she had been sexually assaulted or dressed in adult underwear.

It is suggested that the connection must be so compelling that the accused would be entitled to be acquitted if he could prove his innocence of a further crime involving exactly the same characteristics.[1] In other cases where there is direct evidence of the commission of the crime, and it is merely sought to support such evidence, as in *Boardman v DPP, DPP v P* and *R v H*, a lower standard of peculiarity may be tolerated, and in cases where there is still more compelling further evidence, such as keeping an appointment to meet at a pre-arranged place at a pre-arranged time, even less similarity is required, as in *Thompson* where evidence of no more than homosexual disposition sufficed. Similarly if the issue is solely as to the intent, motive or knowledge of the accused, the commission of the act and the identity of the actor being conceded,[2] this requirement sinks lower still, as stated most clearly in a Canadian case:[3]

> The degree of similarity required will depend upon the issues in the particular case, the purpose for which the evidence is sought to be introduced and the other evidence ... That test [striking similarity] has been applied when the Crown seeks to prove identity, but the test is less stringent where the evidence is adduced to show knowledge, intent or state of mind or ... to refute the defence of accident.

There may however be a lower limit when the evidence is of conduct[4] or propensity[5] so commonplace as to deprive it of any real probative value in any situation.

(iii) Degree of relevance to facts in issue

This is the second of the two questions mentioned at the beginning of the last section. Even if, say, the act of the accused can be established by reference to evidence of bad disposition, its establishment is no more than prejudicial if the act, or intent,[6] of the accused, so established, is not in dispute. In a sense a plea of not guilty puts every element of the crime into issue, as Lord Goddard said in *Sims*:[7]

> the accused should not be able, by confining himself at the trial on one issue, to exclude evidence that should be admissible and fatal if he ran two defences; for that would make the astuteness of the accused or his advisors prevail over the interests of justice.

However the stringency of such a view has now been recognised, and in the light of adverse comments in *Noor Mohamed* Lord Goddard himself expressed the more traditional and generous view in *R v Hall*:[8]

> in criminal cases ... the prisoner does not plead in writing; he pleads orally and a plea of not guilty is a plea of the general issue, and when the general issue is

---

1   See *R v Downey* [1995] 1 Cr App Rep 547, at 552.
2   As in *R v Ollis* [1900] 2 QB 758, 19 Cox CC 554, the first two counts in *R v Hall* [1952] 1 KB 302, [1952] 1 All ER 66, or *R v Rance and Herron* (1975) 62 Cr App Rep 118.
3   *R v Carpenter (No 2)* (1982) 142 DLR (3d) 237. See also *Sutton v R* (1984) 51 ALR 435, at 451 per Brennan J.
4   See *R v Wilson* (1973) 58 Cr App Rep 169 (to make sexual advances after a dance). For a rare Scottish example see *O'Neill v HM Advocate* 1995 SCCR 816 (armed robbery in Glasgow, by masked robbers using a sawn-off shotgun).
5   See *R v Turney* (1990) 52 SASR 438 (to indulge in consensual anal and oral intercourse).
6   *R v Sandhu* [1997] Crim LR 288 (offence of strict liability, so intent relevant only to sentence).
7   [1952] 1 KB 302, at 307, [1952] 1 All ER 66, at 68.
8   [1946] KB 531, at 539, [1946] 1 All ER 697, at 701.

pleaded all defences are open to a prisoner, but it would not, on that account, be right at once in all cases to assume that a prisoner is going to set up a defence which is theoretically open to him.

The question is clearly complicated by the paucity of pre-trial proceedings in criminal cases, and by the frequent desire of the defence to show its hand at as late a stage as possible. It is nevertheless clear that the line of defence taken[9] by the accused may either contract or expand the ambit of relevance of evidence of bad disposition. Thus a charge of rape might be defended on the grounds of alibi, impotence or consent of the victim. If the alibi line is chosen the prosecution could adduce evidence of any relevant conduct of the accused, including criminal conduct, which took place in circumstances inconsistent with his alibi. If the impotence line is taken the prosecution could adduce evidence of any acts of sexual intercourse, including criminal acts, to rebut the defence.[10] But other acts of criminality which might be proved on the first hypothesis would not now be relevant because of the different line taken by the accused. If the defence were consent of the victim, then neither evidence of general criminality, nor of intercourse with others would be admissible.[11] Indeed in such a case it has been held[12] that evidence of other rapes by the accused would be inadmissible, since the fact that one woman did not consent to intercourse with him does not logically show that others may not have done so. Sometimes when the nature of the defence lets in a new range of extrinsic material it becomes relevant in a much wider way than would otherwise have been the case. Thus in *R v Mitchell*[13] the accused denied not only the commission of the acts in question, but also the conversation leading up to them. For this reason the prosecution was able to corroborate the evidence of its principal witness with evidence of further discreditable conduct of the accused which could have come to the knowledge of the victim only by way of such a conversation. It then became a matter of little consequence how different the details of the two incidents were.

Sometimes the defence may attack the credibility of a prosecution witness by showing bias against the accused, but if in order to do so it adduces evidence of discreditable conduct by the accused towards the victim it exposes itself to the danger of having the evidence used against it on the substance of the matter to prove guilt.[14]

It is sometimes possible by unwavering concentration upon the matters actually put in issue by the nature of the defence to protect the accused by insisting upon a similarly restricted scope of the evidence admitted to rebut them. In the United States the prosecution is not bound to accept an admission[15] designed to limit the scope of

---

9   It may occasionally occur that the accused initially develops a line of defence perhaps on the voir dire, making similar fact evidence admissible, but subsequently resiles from it. It has been held in South Australia that in such a case it would be wrong to quash a conviction simply because the evidence had been admitted at a time when it seemed likely to be relevant, see *R v Wright* (1986) 19 ACR 17.

10   See for example *R v Solomons* 1959 (2) SA 352, where the accused's denial of possession of a knife let in evidence of other stabbings, and *R v Ward* [1963] Qd R 56, where the accused's denial of knowing how to drive let in evidence of driving offences.

11   See *R v Rodley* [1913] 3 KB 468. See also *R v Clermont* (1986) 32 DLR (4th) 306.

12   *R v Movis* (1994) 75 ACR 416.

13   (1952) 36 Cr App Rep 79. This is a better example than the more usual *R v Chitson* [1909] 2 KB 945 because, as noted above, it is not there completely clear why the prosecution witness was permitted to testify to a conversation which occurred a day after the events in question. See also *R v Hasler, ex p A-G* [1987] 1 Qd R 239.

14   *B v R* (1992) 175 CLR 599.

15   Cp *R v Edwards* [1998] Crim LR 207.

similar fact evidence, but the matter remains one of balancing relative[16] probative force against prejudicial effect.[17]

This raises the closely related question of cumulative testimony. In the United States the same Federal Rule[18] which bestows a discretion to exclude unduly prejudicial evidence also bestows one to exclude needlessly cumulative evidence. Suppose the accused raises alibi as a defence, and that the prosecution has plenty of convincing evidence to rebut it quite apart from evidence of his commission of a crime which also tends to rebut it. Should the prosecution be allowed to adduce evidence of the crime in addition to its other evidence to rebut the alibi? The answer is not straightforward. On the one hand if there is plenty of other evidence the issue might plausibly be regarded as being as little in real contention as one in respect of which the accused has made an explicit concession, and thus the evidence of the extrinsic crime might seem simply prejudicial. On the other hand the issue is still open, and there is no predicting what view the jury might take of any particular piece or pieces of evidence. Nor is it manifestly just that the weaker the case for the prosecution the worse off the accused should become so far as the admission of evidence of discreditable extrinsic matters is concerned. It is submitted that the least unsatisfactory procedure depends upon the delicate art of balancing proof and prejudice.[19]

2.   Prejudicial effect

It is clear from the discussion above that evidence of discreditable extrinsic conduct or disposition can be relevant in a large number of different ways, for example by showing a system of discreditable conduct and so tending to prove criminal intent; by showing a particular modus operandi and so tending to identify the accused as the criminal; by showing something discreditable about the accused which only the accused could have communicated to the witness and which was communicated as part of the technique of committing the crime and so tending to corroborate the witness; or by showing some unusual and discreditable attribute of the accused and so tending to corroborate identification of the accused by a witness. There is nothing inherently prejudicial in these processes of reasoning. If the accused's system were in no way discreditable, say a particular and highly unusual system of arranging a client's affairs so as to reduce tax before a change in the law made it illegal, if after the change such an arrangement were found to have been made, there could be no objection to proving that system as tending to show the unlikelihood of a coincidence, and thus that the accused was involved in the, now illegal, arrangement. If the accused could be shown to be in the habit of wearing outlandish clothes, such as an Indian head-dress, in perfectly innocent pursuits, there could be no objection to proving such an unusual habit as tending to show that the accused was the criminal who was also so attired.[20] If the accused could be shown to be in the relevant location at the relevant time his alibi would equally be disproved whether his activities there and then were innocent or discreditable. If the

16   The gap between the probative force of the admission, and the probative force of the evidence if unbowdlerised.

17   *Old Chief v US* 117 S Ct R 644 (1997).

18   Rule 403.

19   In the analogous context of cross-examination to the accused's record discussed below at p 408 it will be seen that cumulation is one of the considerations recommended to be taken into account: *R v Britzman* [1983] 1 All ER 369, at 374.

20   See *R v Baird* [1993] Crim LR 778 where the fact that the accused admitted dressing up in an unusual costume when with the alleged victims, despite the clothing having no intrinsically discreditable character and misconduct being denied, was nevertheless regarded as a relevant factor in considering whether or not to sever.

accused told the victim something perfectly innocent, say the number of his bank account, as part of his technique of committing a fraud, the witness's knowledge of that number would corroborate his testimony just as much as if his knowledge related to some discreditable act of the accused. If the accused has some innocent attribute, say being a bird-watcher, and the criminal also has this attribute, then the fact that the person identified as the criminal by the witness also happens to be a bird-watcher strengthens the inference that the identification is accurate, just as much as if it related to some discreditable characteristic.

It is thus apparent that it is not the line of reasoning as such which prejudices the accused, nor even the fact that as a result of its application he is more likely to be convicted.[1] It is rather the tendency of the evidence indicating a bad disposition to persuade the jury to convict the accused for reasons other than its logical force which constitutes the justification for excluding such evidence.[2] Its admission is undesirable at two levels. The first relates to the trial process itself, and constitutes what is usually understood by prejudice in this context. Beyond it there lie further ranges of institutional perils which will accrue whenever prejudice of the former type occurs.

(i)   Trial level[3]

In the absence of any satisfactory psychological studies of the reasoning processes of actual juries, or even of a sufficient corpus of reliable scientific evidence derived from carefully controlled experiments, it is not possible to do more than speculate upon the lines of argument which may occur.[4] Common sense suggests a number of possibilities. The first, and the most obvious, is that the jury might simply take the view that the evidence shows the accused to be bad, that crimes are more often committed by the bad than by the good, and hence the evidence tends to show the accused likely to be guilty. It has already been suggested that there is statistical support for this reasoning process, and it is strengthened the greater the similarities and peculiarities of the evidence are, and the stronger the probative force in the ways outlined above.[5] In short, the principal danger is that the jury may concentrate too much upon the moral infirmities of the accused, and too little upon other factors in the case leading to the opposite conclusion. It may be swayed more by revulsion for the

---

1   Thus the distress of a witness which might well prejudice the accused in the ordinary sense of the word is not properly to be taken into account here: *R v Simpson* (1994) 99 Cr App Rep 48, at 54.

2   See *R v Wilmot* (1988) 89 Cr App Rep 341, at 348 where 'proper' and 'improper' prejudice are distinguished. See also *R v Da Silva* [1990] 1 All ER 29, [1990] 1 WLR 31 where, it is submitted the Court went too far in reducing this concept. As Street CJ said in *R v Stalder* [1981] 2 NSWLR 9, at 20, 'It is not *mere* prejudice, no matter how inevitable or grave that may be, which is the touchstone; it is *undue* or *disproportionate* prejudice having regard to the probative significance of the evidence upon an issue falling for determination by the jury' (emphasis in original). See also Brennan J in *Sutton v R* (1984) 51 ALR 435, at 450, 451.

3   See *R v D (LE)* [1989] 2 SCR 111 where the Supreme Court of Canada held that the direction to the jury had not sufficiently guarded them against these very dangers.

4   For some North American evidence see Doob and Kirshenbaum (1972) 15 Crim LQ 88; Note (1961) 70 Yale LJ 763, quoting Broeder's reflections on the evidence obtained from the Chicago jury study; Schaefer and Hansen (1990) 14 Crim LR 157.

5   It has been argued that this statistical evidence may not be so strong as it seems at first sight unless the statistics are related only to cases in which the accused has chosen to stand trial, the plausible thesis being that many of those with previous convictions who are in fact guilty, plead guilty; while many of those with previous convictions who are in fact innocent, plead not guilty; see Lempert and Saltzburg *A Modern Approach to Evidence* (2nd edn, 1982) p 217.

accused than persuasion by the rest of the evidence.[6] It is for very similar reasons that the court is required to be sparing in the admission of gruesome photographs or particularly revolting details of the crime committed so as not to permit the accused to be made a scapegoat for the jury's abhorrence of the crime which has been committed, and for its determination that the wrong not go unpunished.

A different danger is that the jury, after hearing the evidence of the accused's discreditable extrinsic conduct or disposition may not try sufficiently conscientiously to determine whether or not the accused really is guilty of the crime with which he is charged. In the former case the danger is that the jury may too readily infer from the evidence that the accused is guilty, here the danger is that the jury may simply infer from the evidence that the accused is the sort of man who ought to be punished whether he has been proved guilty of the crime with which he has been charged, or not. They may feel that once it has been proved that the accused has committed crimes in the past, or that he has a disposition which makes it likely that he will commit crimes in the future, then he ought to be punished for what he has already done or be prevented from doing what he might go on to do, and that for these reasons he should be convicted and sentenced. If the evidence consists of crimes for which the accused has already been convicted he may suffer from a tendency for the jury not to give him the same benefit of any doubt which might have been given to one with no previous convictions. A jury may well wish to be much more sure before inflicting upon a man for the first time all the opprobrium which attaches to those found guilty of crimes. If such opprobrium already attaches to him the jury may not regard a mistake as quite so serious a matter.

A slight variant on this line of reasoning is that the jury may feel that the accused has probably committed many other crimes beyond those for which he has previously been convicted, but in some cases has gone undetected, in others has not been charged because of insufficient evidence, and in others has been acquitted upon a technicality of some sort. It might then seem eminently fair to convict him on the current charge, guilty or innocent. A similar line of reasoning may be applied in the class of case where the evidence in dispute relates to a large number of incidents in respect of which the accused has not so far been convicted, including some where the incidents are charged in other counts in the indictment,[7] and others where the evidence does not constitute a separate count in the indictment, but is merely used to support it.[8] In these cases the remarks made by Lord Hewart CJ in *R v Bailey* are most pertinent:[9]

> the risk, the danger, the logical fallacy is indeed quite manifest to those who are accustomed to thinking about such matters. It is so easy to derive from a series of unsatisfactory allegations, if there are enough of them, an accusation which at least appears satisfactory. It is so easy to collect from a mass of ingredients, not one of which is sufficient, a totality which will appear to contain what is missing. That of course is only another way of saying that when a person is dealing with a considerable mass of facts, in particular if those facts are of such

6 In *R v Wright* (1990) 90 Cr App Rep 325, at 328 Mustill LJ remarked that 'it was rightly agreed on all hands that the appellant could have no prospect of dispassionate consideration by the jury if the disgusting video had been shown to them'; see also *R v Orgles* [1993] 4 All ER 533, [1993] 1 WLR 108 where the trial judge failed to direct the jury how it should use evidence of subsequent dissimilar, if equally unpleasant, conduct.

7 As in *Scarrott*.

8 As in *Makin*.

9 [1924] 2 KB 300, at 305, 18 Cr App Rep 42, at 44. It should be noted that in this case the prejudice appears to have been so profound as to have induced the jury to convict upon one count upon which prosecuting counsel conceded that there was not even a case to answer, see [1924] 2 KB 300, at 303, 18 Cr App Rep 42, at 42.

a nature as to invite reprobation, nothing is easier than confusion of mind; and, therefore, if such charges are to be brought in a mass, it becomes essential that the method upon which guilt is to be ascertained should be stated with a punctilious exactness.

A rather different danger operating at this level is that the jury may become genuinely confused, and concentrate so much upon resolving the question of whether the accused really did commit the extrinsic discreditable acts urged against him, that once having done so, the verdict upon them is simply substituted for that upon the issue which the jury is really trying. Even where there is no danger of simple substitution of one bad act for another, the intrusion of an issue of extrinsic discreditable conduct may deflect attention from the real issue of intrinsic discreditable conduct. This possibility was canvassed in *R v Mackie*: [10]

> the jury might have considered that the evidence admitted was evidence of excessive chastisement on the part of the appellant which made it unnecessary for them to consider whether the conduct on April 4 was itself so excessive or unreasonable as to be unlawful, and they might have been misled into thinking that they need not trouble whether it was lawful or unlawful in the light of what has been proved about the appellant's earlier conduct; in either case he was morally responsible for the boy's death.

(ii)   Secondary prejudice[11]

If prejudice of this sort is tolerated at the trial, and if evidence of bad disposition is admitted whenever it is barely relevant to the issues of the accused's guilt, an undesirable ripple effect is likely to occur. It may be expected that prosecutors will rely upon such evidence more and more, and in the absence of any explicit restriction will sometimes seek to use it even to establish a prima facie case. At an earlier stage the police may be inclined to base their enquiries still more strongly upon the personalities and propensities of criminals known to be living in their areas. This danger is likely to be at its most acute in relation to identification evidence, since eye witnesses are very likely to be shown photographs of those with criminal records in an attempt to detect the criminal. It is well known how unreliable such identification can be,[12] and how much danger it already creates. If criminal records are themselves to be more readily adduced in evidence these dangers will be seriously enlarged. Not only will the police be more likely rely upon such matters to find people to charge, they will also be in a much stronger position to exert pressure to plead guilty or to confess by persuading the accused that a man with such a record stands little chance of acquittal in a contested case. Some people will have records so damning and will be so vulnerable to successful prosecution as to become easily manipulated by the police. No doubt most prosecutors and most policemen are both honourable, and energetic and are unlikely to change their current practices, but it is not unduly cynical to suppose that there could be some who might be tempted into an easier and more certain path to secure convictions to clear up crimes, especially when convinced of the accused's guilt.

Greater admissibility of evidence of extrinsic discreditable conduct or disposition would also lead to the complication and prolongation of the process of trial. Some such

---

10   (1973) 57 Cr App Rep 453, at 464.
11   For judicial recognition see in Australia McHugh J in *R v Pfennig* (1995) 182 CLR 461, at 513.
12   See below p 676.

conduct might have occurred long before the trial, and the means of proving it might be most unsatisfactory. Since the accused can be expected to deny the truth of such allegations as vigorously as possible, the chances of a scrupulous jury remaining unconvinced beyond reasonable doubt might be unduly high, and the administration of justice easily be brought into disrepute by the spectacle of continual re-litigation of past events, perhaps with differing results, or in relation to conduct for which the perpetrator was never charged at the time. The proliferation of such issues will inevitably slow litigation down still more. It will complicate trials by requiring very careful direction of juries on the weight and point of previous judicial findings, and will lead to special difficulty where indictments contain multiple counts and involve several co-accused. All this will generate more and more appeals.

The matter can also be viewed from the perspective of rehabilitation. The modern tendency is to encourage rehabilitation of offenders so far as possible by making it possible to live down a criminal past, and not have it brought up against one over and over again.[13] If having a criminal record becomes a passport to police scrutiny, harassment and unjustified reconviction, all of these aims will be frustrated. Indeed to the extent that such a system did lead to unjustified conviction, it would rapidly poison the atmosphere in prisons still further, and generate still greater contempt for the forces of law. It should also be noted that the effects would be exponential. More convictions would mean longer records, and so increase the chances of reconviction still further.

D.   APPLICATION OF THE RULE

In *Makin v A-G for New South Wales* Lord Herschell introduced his celebrated passage by saying: 'the principles which must govern the decision of the case are clear, though the application of them is by no means free from difficulty'.[14] He concluded it by saying: 'The statement of these general principles is easy, but it is obvious that it may often be very difficult to draw the line and to decide whether a particular piece of evidence is on the one side or the other.'[15]

These passages were re-echoed and approved in *DPP v Boardman*.[16] One of the problems relates to the nature of the rule, which was recognised in *Boardman* to depend upon questions of degree and weight, but ones which have to be decided by the judge rather than by the jury. The various stages at which the rule may have to be considered were summarised by Scarman LJ in *R v Scarrott*.[17] He distinguished the pre-arraignment stage from the trial stage.

At the former this matter is governed by Indictment Rules 1971, r 9[18] which provides that:

Charges for any offences may be joined in the same indictment if those charges are founded on the same facts, or form or are part of a series of offences of the same or similar character.

13   Rehabilitation of Offenders Act 1974; see s 7(2)(a), which exempts references in evidence in criminal proceedings.
14   [1894] AC 57, at 65.
15   At 65.
16   [1975] AC 421, [1974] 3 All ER 887; see Lord Morris at 438, 892, and Lord Hailsham at 450, 903.
17   [1978] QB 1016, [1978] 1 All ER 672.
18   See *Ludlow v Metropolitan Police Comr* [1971] AC 29, [1970] 1 All ER 567, and commentary from an Australian perspective by Weinberg in (eds) Campbell and Waller *Well and Truly Tried* (1982). For the view in the United States see *Zafiro v US* 113 S Ct R 933 (1993).

It will be noted that this provision applies only to joinder of charges, and can thus extend only to part of the field of similar fact evidence, since often there is no more than one formal charge.[19] Nor can it be regarded simply as a sub-set of similar fact cases since it can apply to a series of offences even though evidence of some is inadmissible on others on such a basis.[20] The general provision is however qualified by a discretionary power to sever an indictment conferred by s 5(3) of the Indictments Act 1915:

> Where before trial, or at any stage of a trial, the court is of opinion that a person charged may be prejudiced or embarrassed in his defence by reason of being charged with more than one offence in the same indictment, or that for any other reason it is desirable to direct that the person should be tried separately for any one or more offences charged in the indictment, the court may order a separate trial on any count or counts of such indictment.

Despite earlier dicta to the contrary[1] it was authoritatively reaffirmed in *R v Christou*[2] that this discretion of the trial judge is unconstrained, and in particular that there is no rule[3] or presumption in favour of severance in sexual cases where the evidence on one count is inadmissible on the other. Factors mentioned[4] as relevant for consideration were how discrete were the facts, the impact of ordering separate trials on the accused and on the victim and, most importantly, whether the judge believed that fair joint trial could be achieved by suitable direction of the jury. It remains unclear whether or not in cases where the prosecution case is that one man must have committed all of the offences, incidents where the evidence does not sufficiently support the common features or method, may be joined.[5]

At the trial stage the question of admissibility ought to be decided in the absence of the jury at the outset of the trial.[6] The judge is not however rendered functus officio by the judgments he makes at so early a stage without having had the opportunity to take into account the way the trial develops. He may still permit evidence which would have been relevant to a severed count to be tendered if he becomes convinced, contrary to his provisional view, of its admissibility. He may also instruct the jury to disregard evidence which he now believes himself wrong to have allowed,[7] or in a really serious case, where such a course is likely to be ineffective to prevent prejudice, he may discharge the jury and order a fresh trial.

These considerations make the application of the rule a difficult one for the judge to perform.[8] It was perhaps for such a reason that in the years between *Makin* and

---

19   It was pointed out in *R v Williams* [1993] Crim LR 533 that it is not necessary to include an incident as a charge in an indictment in order to secure the admission in evidence of the details relating to it, if they are relevant and otherwise admissible.

20   See eg *R v Cannan* (1991) 92 Cr App Rep 16.

1   See *DPP v Boardman* [1975] AC 421, [1974] 3 All ER 887 at 459, 910; *DPP v P* [1991] 2 AC 447, [1991] 3 All ER 337, at 462, 348. See also in Australia *Hoch v R* (1988) 165 CLR 292, at 298.

2   [1997] AC 117, [1996] 2 All ER 927. Lord Hope at 130, 937 made it clear that the rule is the same in Scotland.

3   In New Zealand there appears to be a rule that cases where there is little nexus beyond the identity of the victims, separate sexual offences by different offenders should be severed: *R v D and S* [1996] 2 NZLR 513.

4   At 129D, 937b.

5   See *R v Trew* [1996] 2 Cr App Rep 138 (not cited in *R v Christou*); *R v Naylor* [1998] Crim LR 662 (although a decision on admissibility, it also seems appropriate to severance considerations).

6   See Lord Cross in *Boardman* at 459, 910

7   As occurred in *R v Flack* [1969] 2 All ER 784, [1969] 1 WLR 937.

8   It should be noted that the rule applies to criminal proceedings at all levels including summary proceedings, see, for example, *R v Rochford Justices, ex p Buck* (1978) 68 Cr App Rep 114.

Boardman a tendency grew up to consider the application of the rule in terms of rigid categories which dictated either admission or exclusion. An early example is provided by the judgment of Bray J in *R v Bond*: 'A careful examination of the cases where evidence of this kind has been admitted shows that they may be grouped under three heads ... '.[9] This practice was roundly condemned in *Boardman* because 'where what is important is the application of principle, the use of labels or definitive descriptions cannot be either comprehensive or restrictive'.[10] Some of the labels so applied in the past such as 'innocent association', and 'system', were explicitly condemned.[11] All of their Lordships seem to have agreed that the matters to be considered involved the interpretation of principle by the application of logic and common-sense which 'are not susceptible of exact codification when applied to the actual facts of life in its infinite variety'.[12] *DPP v P* added further flexibility in its insistence that:[13]

> Once the principle is recognised, that what has to be assessed is the probative force of the evidence in question, the infinite variety of circumstances in which the question arises demonstrates that there is no single manner in which this can be achieved. Whether the evidence has sufficient probative value to outweigh its prejudicial force must in each case be a question of degree.

Such a view opens rather than closes the door to exemplification of, and to the provision of guidelines for, the application of the rules, so long as such examples and guides are not regarded as automatic shackles or escape hatches.

As decided in *Boardman*, confirmed by *DPP v P*, and as formulated here, the application of the rule depends upon the precise balance between probative force and prejudicial effect. It is perhaps difficult to understand by what common criterion such balancing can be achieved.[14] It is submitted that the most serious deficiencies of the decision in *DPP v P* lay in its reluctance to emphasise the high standard which such evidence needs to achieve to overcome its inevitably prejudicial effect,[15] or to explore very far the ways in which this could be achieved. Probative force depends upon relevance and cogency. Relevance is heavily influenced by the line of defence adopted by the accused,[16] and cogency by the other evidence in the case. These two practical considerations, rather than time-worn clichés of presentation, govern the form of exemplification here. Issues are considered simply in terms of the elements which arise in any criminal case, such as the occurrence of an actus reus, its commission by the accused, and his intention, motive and state of knowledge in so committing it.

They are affected, not only by the formal definition of the crime, but also by the defences actually advanced by the accused, or reasonably open to him. These constitute the primary vehicle for the exemplification which follows, but within them there operate considerations of cogency, and predominantly the question of whether or not there is direct testimony of the commission of the crime. If there is, the similar

9   [1906] 2 KB 389, at 414, 21 Cox CC 252. *R v Flack* [1969] 2 All ER 784, [1969] 1 WLR 937, illustrates the persistence of the tendency up to the period of *Boardman*. There is even some evidence of its continued survival: see *R v Lewis* (1982) 76 Cr App Rep 33.
10   Lord Morris at 439, 893.
11   By Lord Wilberforce at 443, 896.
12   Lord Hailsham at 452, 904.
13   At 460, 346.
14   It is, at least superficially, a matter of balancing considerations of logic against those of emotion.
15   Its difficulty in this respect appears to have been acknowledged by prosecuting counsel in *R v Simpson* (1993) 99 Cr App Rep 48, at 53. It has been further exacerbated by the subsequent decision in *R v H* [1995] 2 AC 596, [1995] 2 All ER 865.
16   See eg *R v Sokialiois* [1993] Crim LR 872 (possession of large quantity of cocaine to rebut defence that 'set-up').

fact evidence operates to corroborate it; if there is not, the similar fact evidence operates simply as circumstantial evidence of guilt.

1. Commission of crime

In many cases the commission of a crime cannot be denied, and the only question to be decided is the identity of the criminal.[17] In others although it would be possible to deny that any crime were committed, the line of defence operates to convert the case into one of identity or participation.[18] This leaves cases where the evidence is sufficiently equivocal for the commission of any crime at all to remain open to doubt. The most common cases are those of 'victimless' offences, the commission of which may leave no physical trace, and of murder where there may either remain insufficient evidence of the cause of death to exclude the possibility of a natural cause,[19] or where it may be possible for the accused to allege accident,[20] or suicide.[1] In the case of many sexual offences there is direct testimony from the victim for the similar fact evidence to corroborate. In murder and in the case of 'victimless' offences it is less likely that there will be such direct testimony. It is useful to consider the two situations separately.

At one time it was thought that evidence of the accused's bad disposition could not be relied upon to establish the existence of an actus reus. This view was firmly rejected in *Makin* where the evidence of finding the other bodies was admitted solely to show that the Makins had developed a system of taking babies in at low sums, insufficient to support them, and then murdering them, thus helping to prove it more likely that the child in respect of which they were charged had been murdered by them than that it had died from natural causes. So too in *Smith* the evidence of the other deaths tended to rebut a possible defence of accident. It was inherently implausible that so many accidents would happen. The main authority on the 'victimless' crime situation is *R v Ball*.[2] A brother and sister were accused of incest. There was evidence that they had been living in the same household, sleeping in the same bed, and passing themselves off as man and wife. In addition there was evidence that the sister had borne her brother's child, conceived before incest became a criminal offence. The House of Lords received the evidence of the conception of the child to show the disposition of the accused to have sexual relations with each other, and hence that such relations took place when they were sharing a bed. The case is particularly significant in this context as the Court of Criminal Appeal had refused to uphold the trial judge's admission of the similar fact evidence just because it was being used to show the commission of the actus reus which it held an impermissible purpose.

In all of these cases where the evidence is used to show the commission of a criminal act in the absence of direct testimony to that effect, the evidence of disposition needs to be particularly strong. In the traditional terminology these often tend to be the cases where 'system' is alleged. *Makin* and *Smith* might well have been decided differently if there had been no more than one other example, just as happened in *Noor Mohamed*.

---

17   Many cases of murder and robbery fall into this category, *R v Straffen* [1952] 2 QB 911, [1952] 2 All ER 657, and *R v Robinson* [1953] 2 All ER 334, sub nom *Practice Note* [1953] 1 WLR 872, are typical examples.

18   *Thompson v R* [1918] AC 221, 13 Cr App Rep 61, and *R v Neale* (1977) 65 Cr App Rep 304, are clear examples.

19   As in *Makin*.

20   As in *R v Smith* (1915) 11 Cr App Rep 229.

1   As in *Noor Mohamed v R* [1949] AC 182, [1949] 1 All ER 365.

2   [1911] AC 47, 6 Cr App Rep 31. A leading Australian example is *Martin v Osborne* (1936) 55 CLR 367 (evidence of regular trips to establish operation of unlicensed bus service).

The disposition was however made out in the one case because there were so many other examples, plus a good deal of circumstantial evidence; and in the other because the situations were so remarkably similar to each other in all of their details.[3] In *Ball* much depended upon the circumstantial evidence, and the way in which Scrutton J, the trial judge, wisely widened the period within which the commission of the crime was alleged.

Where there is direct testimony of the commission of the crime, usually from the victim in sexual cases, the evidence need not be so strong. These are the cases sometimes categorised as ones of 'innocent association'. The accused admits an opportunity for the commission of the crime, but denies that advantage was taken of it. The more compromising and contrived the opportunity the more readily the evidence will be admitted. Thus in *R v King*[4] the accused not only made the acquaintance of the victims, who were total strangers to him, in a public lavatory frequented by homosexuals, but then invited the boys back to his flat where he shared a bed with one of them. Here the supporting evidence was so strong that evidence of a general disposition to homosexuality was of sufficient probative force to be admitted. Where the supporting evidence is not so strong, as in *R v Horwood*,[5] where the initial meeting was less questionable, and where no such close contact as sharing a bed was admitted, evidence of the accused's homosexuality was excluded. In some of the recent cases involving allegations of the sexual abuse of children the requirement of relevance seems to have sunk very low indeed.[6] Thus in *R v Simpson*[7] evidence of kissing a different girl five years after the alleged rape for which the accused was being tried was held admissible. It is disconcerting that this allegation was not reflected in a separate count in the indictment, when a number of stronger allegations against other girls were so reflected, and the accused was acquitted of all of those. It has become very difficult to imagine how any conceivably credible evidence of the accused's disposition is ever to be held inadmissible in cases involving allegations of sexual abuse of children in the same household[8] after *DPP v P* and *R v H*.[9] Despite, or indeed on account of, the vagueness of the reasoning in those cases as to precisely how the evidence acquires logical force, it is submitted, as mentioned above,[10] that it should be explained in detail to the jury in the light of the circumstances of the particular case.[11] It seems unfortunate also that it

3   It is interesting to note that suspicion was cast upon Smith by a letter written to the police by the husband of the landlady of the premises in which the second victim had been murdered categorised as commenting upon the 'striking similarity' between that death and the third, a report of the inquest upon which he had read in his newspaper: see Watson *Trial of Joseph Smith* Notable British Trials (1922), at 28.

4   [1967] 2 QB 338, [1967] 1 All ER 379, the case was treated as if the evidence had been led in chief rather than elicited in cross-examination with the result that the Criminal Evidence Act 1898, s 1(f), which should have governed it, was ignored.

5   [1970] 1 QB 133, [1969] 3 All ER 1156. See also *R v Bedford* (1990) 93 Cr App Rep 113 where the boys were strangers, and the supporting evidence was of incidents to which the accused had pleaded guilty, so less similarity was required, and indeed described as being near the borderline.

6   See *R v Channing* [1994] Crim LR 924 (mundane similarities and some dissimilarities; it is interesting that the accused was acquitted on the one count which was severed).

7   (1994) 99 Cr App Rep 48.

8   It is notable that in *R v C* [1994] Crim LR 590 there appears to be some suggestion that a new category of 'same household' evidence is growing up separate from 'similar fact' evidence.

9   In *R v Burrage* [1997] Crim LR 440 in an effort to do so the court seems to have been forced back into a form of the old automatic reasoning by category.

10 At p 351.

11 As urged in *R v Carrington* [1990] Crim LR 330 where the evidence related to a different threat to the same victim, so there was no element of mutually supporting credibility. See also *R v Williams* [1990] Crim LR 409 where the evidence did not go to the only live issue which was consent.

has been held unnecessary for the judge to give an explicit warning of the danger of prejudice.[12] A similar situation arises when the accused denies commission of a sexual crime on the basis that the victim consented. Here too, if the probative force of the evidence exceeds its prejudicial effect, which may well be great, it may be admitted.[13]

In a number of reported cases[14] since *Boardman* the commission of a criminal act was in issue, in all of which there was some direct testimony of the commission of the act in question. They provided no clear guidance to the amount of probative force required. In some the evidence relied upon as being strikingly similar had been regarded as relating to no more than the stock-in-trade of the perpetrator of the crime in question, and the evidence accordingly rejected.[15] That approach was overturned in *DPP v P.*[16] It was there held that in cases where there was direct evidence of the commission of the crime in question and of the other incidents relied upon, it was immaterial that they were not strikingly similar, since probative force could be provided in other ways.[17] It seems that the House had in mind the unlikelihood of several witnesses independently,[18] and falsely, attributing even vaguely similar conduct to the same person. Where a number of different witnesses, without any suggestion of collaboration, all testify that the same thing has happened, it is indeed significant, particularly where the detail is either unusual,[19] or tallies in some very minute particulars over a large number of cases.[20] As Lord Cross indicated in *Boardman* the essence of the argument is the unlikelihood of a coincidence of testimony, and that unlikelihood increases the more peculiar the circumstances and the greater the number of instances. It does however then become absolutely vital that the testimony should be truly independent, and free from any danger of collaboration, or any other cause common to the witnesses.[1] Indeed in *Boardman* Lord Wilberforce emphasised that this:[2]

---

12   Such a failure was not fatal in *R v Roy* [1992] Crim LR 185, though the judge had there given
a direction relating to the previous good character of the accused. See also *R v Sokialiois* [1993]
Crim LR 872, though there the judge did indicate the relevance of the evidence very clearly.

13   *R v Wilmot* (1988) 89 Cr App Rep 341.

14   They include *R v Novac* (1976) 65 Cr App Rep 107; *R v Johannsen* (1977) 65 Cr App Rep
101; *R v Scarrott* [1978] QB 1016, [1978] 1 All ER 672; *R v Inder* (1977) 67 Cr App Rep 143;
R v Clarke (1977) 67 Cr App Rep 398; *R v Downes* [1981] Crim LR 174; *R v Barrington*
[1981] 1 All ER 1132, [1981] 1 WLR 419; *R v Lewis* (1982) 76 Cr App Rep 33 (as to one
incident); *R v Lunt* (1987) 85 Cr App Rep 241; *R v Shore* (1988) 89 Cr App Rep 32; *R v Brooks*
(1991) 92 Cr App Rep 36.

15   *R v Inder* above; *R v Brooks* above; *R v P* [1991] Crim LR 291.

16   [1991] 2 AC 447, [1991] 3 All ER 337.

17   These are not clearly specified.

18   It was explicitly assumed in the question posed to the House of Lords that there had been no
collusion between the witnesses: see at 452, 339.

19   This was an important factor in *Boardman* (two separate suggestions that the middle-aged
party played the passive role in homosexual conduct with youths), and in *Barrington* (two
separate reports of the impersonation of the same minor celebrity).

20   *R v Sims* [1946] KB 531, [1946] 1 All ER 697, is a very good example where four victims all
alleged that they had been induced to sit with the accused in order to play cards, and the court
stressed that 'whereas the jury might think one man might be telling an untruth, three or four
are hardly likely to tell the same untruth unless they were conspiring together'.

1   In *R v Ananthanarayanan* [1994] 2 All ER 847 complaints against the accused had been solicited
by an employing authority.

2   [1975] AC 421, at 444, [1974] 3 All ER 887, at 897. Original emphasis.

may be a real possibility; something much more than mere similarity and absence of proved conspiracy is needed if this evidence is to be allowed. This is well illustrated by *Kilbourne's* case where the judge excluded 'intra group' evidence because of the possibility *as it appeared to him*, of collaboration between boys who knew each other well. This is ... the right course rather than to admit the evidence unless a case of collaboration or concoction is made out.

It might have been thought that this referred to the admissibility of the evidence as similar fact evidence, but it was, in *R v H*,[3] interpreted by the House of Lords to refer to its use as corroboration, and to relate to the *use* of the evidence rather than to its admissibility. The contrary view expressed in previous editions of this work, echoed by the High Court of Australia in *Hoch v R*, and endorsed in a number of cases in the Court of Appeal,[4] was disapproved, and the cases overruled. It was argued that if the possibility of contamination were to be regarded as a condition of admissibility, it would undermine the operation of the rule in *DPP v P* by removing too many cases from the jury altogether. In *R v H* the evidence consisted of allegations of sexual impropriety by the accused perpetrated upon two children of his former household, one an adopted daughter and the other a step-daughter. No striking similarity was suggested, and there was some evidence of motivation[5] for the manufacture of false allegations, and of collaboration[6] between the girls which was accepted by the House as creating at least a risk of contamination. It was felt that in such a situation the evidence should all go to the jury, directed that it should convict only if convinced beyond reasonable doubt that the girls had not concocted the allegations. The House felt that it would be impracticable, and wrong, in most cases for a voir dire to be conducted. The analogy to the case of confessions was rejected, in part because it would be too difficult to keep the basis of admissibility separate from the issue to be decided by the jury.

While there is undeniable force in these arguments it is submitted that they fail to convince,[7] largely because they attach little more than lip service to the prejudice likely to be caused to the accused by the admission of such evidence if it is contaminated, and because so little explanation is even attempted of the role which such evidence serves.

It is true that the House of Lords envisaged that in the very occasional extreme case the evidence of contamination might be so strong that the evidence could in no circumstances at all be capable of belief, but the chance of this being apparent on the papers, without any recourse to a voir dire, must be highly remote. In this very case the prime witness had made no immediate complaint but had waited for several years to elapse, had first made the allegation when a clear motive for concocting a story had emerged, had admitted approaching the other alleged victim and to persisting despite the other's initial denial of any impropriety, and had admitted her own considerable sexual impropriety and the commission of criminal offences.[8] It is difficult to imagine

---

3   [1995] 2 AC 596, [1995] 2 All ER 865. This view was anticipated in New Zealand in *R v W* [1995] 1 NZLR 548, at 555.

4   *R v Ananthanarayanan* [1994] 2 All ER 847; *R v Ryder* [1994] 2 All ER 859; *R v W* [1994] 2 All ER 872.

5   The allegations were first made some years after the incidents were said to have occurred, and resulted in the introduction to the household of the prime witness's then current sexual partner, despite her still being below the age of consent.

6   The second girl denied any impropriety when first questioned by the prime mover.

7   The Supreme Court of Canada in *R v Burke* [1996] 1 SCR 474, seems to have been unconvinced by them.

8   Both normally regarded as impugning a witness's credibility: see below ch IX.

that many cases would be much stronger. The Lord Chancellor was nevertheless so dismissive of such danger as to remark only that:[9]

> in *some circumstances* the probative force required for evidence to be similar fact evidence *might be affected* by circumstances such as collusion between the witnesses or other contamination of their evidence.

It is also significant that despite his own clear asseveration in *DPP v P*[10] that the question of admissibility is one of rule rather than discretion, the Lord Chancellor nevertheless in *R v H* foresaw a role for the discretion conferred by s 78 of the Police and Criminal Evidence Act 1984. This seems to contemplate that the reduction in the test for admissibility might lead to a situation where evidence satisfies it which would nevertheless have such an adverse effect on the fairness of the proceedings that the court ought not to admit it.

It was because of the consistent underplaying of the danger of admitting the evidence that the House seemed to be prepared to lower the threshold for admission below that formerly required even for one piece of admissible evidence to corroborate another. It seemed also to be for this reason that the House of Lords removed the requirement that evidence of mere allegations needed to be bolstered by the unlikelihood of similar false stories being manufactured independently. Clearly if the allegations are the fruits of collaboration they have no such added weight. This raises the question of what particular contribution to the reasoning process is made by the admission of such allegations. The most that seems to have been suggested is that the evidence completed the picture, and that it facilitated the balancing of probative force against prejudicial effect as a matter of common sense. In view of the vast potential effect of such evidence[11] this hardly seems enough. One is left with the uneasy feeling that the evidence does indeed do little more than show the accused to be the sort of man who would do that sort of thing, and thus one who did it on the occasion in question. It should be noted however that this dilution of the conditions for admissibility may be restricted to the situation where the similar fact evidence consists of allegations contained in other counts of the indictment, and to cases where no question of the identity of the offender or his opportunity of committing it are in question.[12]

If the evidence emanates from one witness, it will also be less cogent for similar reasons however many incidents are recounted and however similar their details, since it is little more difficult to concoct[13] accounts of many incidents than to concoct an account of one.[14]

2.   Commission by accused[15]

Quite often the commission of an act constituting the crime cannot be denied. This applies to many cases of murder, rape, robbery, burglary and theft. In this situation the

---

9   Emphasis supplied.
10   [1991] 2 AC 447, at 461, [1991] 3 All ER 337, at 346.
11   As eloquently expressed in the passage cited above on p 355 from *R v Bailey* [1924] 2 KB 300, at 305, 18 Cr App Rep 42, at 44.
12   And perhaps not to extend to those where the defence is anything other than a simple denial of the conduct in question.
13   But see *R v Carrington* [1990] Crim LR 330 where although the threats were made to the same victim they were contemporaneously reported, thus reducing the danger.
14   This consideration may have influenced the Court in *R v Tetlow* (1986) 27 ACR 198 to reject evidence of a course of previous injections of the same drug by the same accused upon the same victim over a continuing period culminating in the occasion charged.
15   See Pattenden (1996) 112 LQR 446.

accused must usually seek to deny that he was the perpetrator. Although the cases are sometimes categorised as being ones of identity, it is helpful[16] to distinguish between those where the identity of the accused is established by circumstantial evidence of peculiarity of disposition, and those where there is direct evidence of identification which it is sought to support by the dispositional evidence.[17] It is submitted that much stronger evidence of disposition is required in the former situation, than in the latter. The strength may come from the peculiarity of aim or technique,[18] or from the accumulation of less unusual detail,[19] or from the strength of the evidence identifying the accused as the perpetrator of one, or more, of the incidents.[20]

A very straightforward example of a situation in which there was no direct evidence of identification is provided by *R v Straffen*.[1] The accused had been immured in Broadmoor after being found unfit to plead to two charges of having killed two small girls without having molested them sexually, and then having left their bodies unconcealed where they could readily be discovered. He escaped, and soon afterwards while he was still in the vicinity of the hospital, a small girl was killed not having been molested sexually, and her body was left unconcealed in a place where it could readily be discovered. Straffen admitted having seen the girl, but denied he had killed her. The evidence was held to have been rightly admitted for the purpose of showing that Straffen was the murderer. It should be noted that it was agreed on all sides that the similarities between all of the crimes were very strong, and that the accused's involvement in the earlier crimes was established as a virtual certainty. The court argued that the evidence was admitted because it showed the identity of the murderer. This is somewhat specious. In all criminal cases it is necessary to show that the man charged is the man who committed the relevant crime, and *Thompson* which the court relied upon differed in that there was there evidence of identification to be corroborated. It is the existence of cases like *Straffen*, where as Lord Cross put it in *Boardman* 'the evidence of the other murders ... was simply evidence to show that Straffen was a man likely to commit a murder of that particular kind', that prevents unqualified acceptance of Lord Hailsham's view quoted above that the 'inadmissible chain of reasoning' inevitably leads to exclusion. If the chain is strong enough, and relevant enough to a live issue, evidence of bad disposition alone may, exceptionally, be admitted. It is however vital in this situation to be sure that the evidence is strong enough. It must identify the accused in the same sort of way as the discovery of his fingerprints at the scene of the crime. In *R v Mansfield*[2] the strength of the evidence could have been no more than barely sufficient. The accused was charged with offences arising out of three fires which occurred on his employer's premises. There was evidence that he was present at the scene of the fire on all three occasions, there was some weak evidence of suspicious behaviour by him, and there was similarly weak evidence that all of the fires had been

16 The situation is complex, and variables also include the sort of evidence relied upon to show disposition, its strength, and whether it consists of other counts in the indictment.

17 Although there is a continuum between cases where the direct evidence of identification is very strong, such as *Thompson v R* where not only were there two direct witnesses, but they testified to the criminal having made an appointment to meet them again; and those where it is very weak, such as *Pfennig* where it consisted of no more than the sound of the accused's van.

18 Classically referred to as striking similarity. Because peculiarity relates to modus operandi it requires virtual identity and is thus easily destroyed by any dissimilarity.

19 Often referred to as underlying unity. Here because it often relies upon contiguity of time and place, and no two events can coincide there is inevitably some dissimilarity, and an exercise of judgment is necessary to draw the line.

20 In *R v Black* (1995) Times, 1 March the accused had pleaded guilty in respect of some of the incidents relied upon; in *R v Ruiz* [1995] Crim LR 151 he had admitted the highly unusual feature of administering a soporific drug in one of the cases of which this was a unifying feature.

1 [1952] 2 QB 911, [1952] 2 All ER 657. For further factual detail see McConnell (1993) NLJ, 10 September.

2 [1978] 1 All ER 134, [1977] 1 WLR 1102.

started by the use of a similar, though in itself by no means peculiar, technique. It should be noted that here the accused's involvement in the other fires was denied, and the technique was not particularly unusual. So in those respects the evidence was much less strong than that in *Straffen*. The factor which must have tilted the balance was that the fires occurred in three different locations, and once it was accepted that an employee had started all three, it became clear that only two employees had been in all three locations, and there was no suggestion whatever that the other had been involved. *Mansfield* is a good illustration of the need to consider the similar fact evidence in the context of all of the other evidence in the case, which there strengthened its probative force considerably.[3]

An intermediate situation is illustrated by *R v McGranaghan*[4] where there was some direct evidence from the victims, but it was rather weak identification evidence. In that situation it is suggested that the scale slides down from its requirement of so striking a similarity as to amount to a signature. A further feature determining the outcome in *McGranaghan* itself was that there was strong negative evidence suggesting that it could not have been the accused who committed one of the crimes which the prosecution claimed all to have been committed by the same man.[5] It has already been noted that there are two different scenarios. The first starts from the proposition that the same man committed all of the offences, proved either by their striking similarity, or[6] their underlying unity;[7] the second from the strength of the evidence[8] that the accused committed one of the offences.[9]

It is common for evidence of the accused's involvement to be the direct testimony of a victim. That was the situation in one of the pre-*Boardman* cases to reach the House of Lords. In *Thompson v R*[10] the accused was charged with offences of gross indecency involving two boys. According to their account he committed the offences with them in a public lavatory, and made an appointment to meet them there again. A trap was set. Thompson arrived at the arranged time and place. He spoke to the boys, gave them money, and then the trap was sprung. He was found to be carrying powder puffs,[11] and to have indecent photographs of boys in his lodgings. His defence was that he was not the man who had committed the offences, and that the boys had mis-identified him. The evidence of his disposition to homosexuality as shown by his possessions was admitted to corroborate the evidence of identification: 'That the boys should pick out as the guilty person someone who, unknown to them, possessed these objects,

---

3   See also *R v Mullen* [1992] Crim LR 735 where the evidence was that there were no more than six burglars in the area who used the relevant technique, which would have been insufficient without further supporting forensic evidence; and in Australia, *R v Mills* [1986] 1 Qd R 77 where there were only two possible assailants, and there was evidence of previous injury inflicted upon the same child by the accused on earlier occasions.

4   [1995] 1 Cr App Rep 559n.

5   *R v Johnson* [1995] Crim LR 53 was a similar situation in which there was weak identification evidence, there of the sound of the criminal's voice, and a number of dissimilarities between the circumstances of the incidents alleged to have a common perpetrator.

6   Lord Mackay's remarks in *DPP v P* apparently requiring striking similarity have been construed to apply only to the situation where there is virtually no other evidence of identity, and at most very weak evidence of identification: *R v John W* [1998] 2 Cr App Rep 289.

7   Sometimes categorised as the cumulative approach.

8   For example by admission: see in England, *R v Straffen* above; *R v Black* (1995) Times, 1 March; in Australia, *Pfennig v R* (1995) 182 CLR 461, 127 ALR 99; and in Canada, *R v Brisbin* (1996) 101 CCC (3d) 334.

9   Sometimes categorised as the sequential approach.

10   [1918] AC 221, [1918–19] All ER Rep 521.

11   Assumed by the court to indicate a disposition to homosexual practices.

confirms their accuracy.'[12] In that case the evidence of disposition was weak, but the evidence of identification strong. In other cases the evidence of identification may be much weaker, but compensated for by much stronger evidence of disposition, typically in cases where there has been a series of crimes of a similar character at about the same time and in about the same area.[13]

It should be noted that in this sort of case, just because the similar fact evidence is not the sole means of identifying the accused it need not be uniquely denominative of him. In *Thompson* the evidence showed the accused to have a disposition to homosexuality, or perhaps to paedophilia, but it went no further, and without the element of direct supporting testimony would certainly be decided differently today.[14] The importance of this factor was stressed in a number of other cases. One of the more influential was *R v Robinson* where the accused was charged in respect of two separate robberies. He was identified practising for one, and committing the other. The importance of these acts of identification was stressed: 'if Robinson is not a guilty man, he is a singularly unfortunate man. He is identified by different people, or said to be identified by entirely different people, in respect of two entirely different raids.'[15]

The strength of the inference depends, as in all such cases, upon the cogency of the evidence. Two important factors here are the certainty of the implication of the accused in both events, and the independence of the witnesses who testify to it.[16] Thus in *R v Tricoglus*,[17] although two of the acts were sufficiently similar and peculiar, the direct testimony of the accused's involvement in them was unsatisfactory. An example of a case in this category where the evidence was probably sufficiently strong only because it confirmed direct identification of the accused, is provided by *R v Mustafa*. The accused was charged with four offences involving the use of a stolen credit card to buy large quantities of frozen meat from specialist freezer stores. Apart from the identification testimony, there was evidence of finding a stolen credit card, of a different brand, and a paper containing attempts to forge its signature in the accused's dwelling. Despite the fact that it was a different card, a different signature, and that the attempted forgeries were not of consistently high quality, the evidence was admitted because: 'in the particular circumstances ... the Access card evidence does bear a similarity to the Barclaycard frauds sufficiently striking to make it admissible *in corroboration of identification.*'[18]

A more difficult situation occurs if the various offences are committed by members of a group, since it may be easier to prove by these means that the same group was involved on each occasion than that the same member of the group perpetrated any

---

12   Lord Sumner at 233, 527. See also Viscount Finlay at 226, 523 'to show the probability of the truth of the boys' story as to identity', and Lord Atkinson at 224, 522 'to prove ... that the boys were not making any mistake whatever in their identification of him'.

13   As in *R v Downey* [1995] 1 Cr App Rep 547; *R v Barnes* [1995] 2 Cr App Rep 491; *R v Grant* [1996] 2 Cr App Rep 272; *R v John W* [1998] 2 Cr App Rep 289.

14   Although at the time some of their Lordships seemed to have regarded these traits as very much more unusual and peculiar than would be generally thought today. In *Boardman* Lord Cross said that the expression of such views in *Thompson* 'sounds nowadays like a voice from another world'. Evidence of things found in the accused's possession, used to support direct testimony, is often very weak: see also *Morris v R* [1983] 2 SCR 190.

15   Direction of trial judge, quoted only in (1953) 37 Cr App Rep 95, at 106.

16   This makes it very difficult to understand the reasoning in *Perkins v Jeffery* [1915] 2 KB 702, 25 Cox CC 59 where, on a charge of indecent exposure, the court was more ready to accept evidence by the complainant of previous exposure to her, than evidence by other female witnesses of exposure to them.

17   (1976) 65 Cr App Rep 16.

18   (1976) 65 Cr App Rep 16, at 31 (emphasis supplied).

particular crime,[19] though the same problem does not arise when the whole of the group commits the crime.[20]

3.   Voluntary act of accused

The prosecution must always establish that the commission of the actus reus was voluntary. In the absence of some special line of defence this can usually be inferred from the nature of the act in question. Sometimes physical contact, capable of amounting to an indecent assault is claimed to have occurred involuntarily, and similar fact evidence can be adduced to show other cases of similar contact.[1] Sometimes an apparent drug courier will testify to ignorance of the presence of the drugs.[2] Occasionally, and usually in the last straits of desperation, the accused does not deny the commission of the relevant act, but denies all recollection of having done it. In some such cases similar fact evidence has been admitted to rebut this defence. This was the accused's line of defence in *R v Mortimer*[3] when charged with the murder of a female cyclist by driving a car at her. The court admitted evidence of his having driven at three other women cyclists at around the same time. This case seems to have been overlooked in *R v Harrison-Owen*[4] where the accused who had been found in a house at night after taking keys from a car outside, and who first gave a false explanation for being there and then attempted to run away, raised as a defence that he had no recollection of having entered the house. The trial judge took the initiative in having his long record of previous convictions for housebreaking and burglary put in. In the Court of Appeal Lord Goddard CJ took the view that this was to confuse accident and intent, apparently confining accident to the situation, like that in *Makin* or *Smith*, in which any actus reus was denied, and held that the evidence should have been excluded.[5] In the nature of things there can be no direct testimony from any other witness of the accused's mental processes, so no possibility of corroboration arises here.

4.   Intention of the accused

Sometimes the criminality of an act[6] depends upon the purpose for doing it. An early example of this sort of case is provided by *R v Bond* where the accused, a doctor, was charged in respect of the abortion of a girl whom he had impregnated. His defence was that the girl had spontaneously miscarried when he was engaged in a routine procedure, not designed to accomplish such a result. The prosecution was permitted to call another girl whom he had also impregnated, to testify to an unsuccessful attempt to abort her, to which she had been induced to submit by his claim that he had 'put dozens of other

---

19   *R v Lee* [1996] Crim LR 825; but see *R v Gourde and Garland* [1997] CLY 1128 where a more relaxed approach seems to have been applied to a group of two.
20   As in *R v Brown, Wilson, McMillan and McClean* [1997] Crim LR 502.
1   As in *R v Huijser* [1988] 1 NZLR 577.
2   As in *R v Morgan* [1993] Crim LR 56; *R v Peters* [1995] 2 Cr App Rep 77. In such cases it is enough that the supporting evidence show only the most general connection with drug dealing.
3   (1936) 25 Cr App Rep 150, although the court said that the evidence showed his intent, his defence was simply that his mind went blank and he did not know what he had done.
4   [1951] 2 All ER 726, 35 Cr App Rep 108.
5   It is interesting that both in this case, and in *R v Coombes* (1960) 45 Cr App Rep 36 where a similar point arose, the similar fact evidence comprised previous convictions, the facts of which were not elaborated.
6   Or its degree of criminality, see *R v Blackwell* (1996) 87 ACR 289 (presence of things used by dealers, and absence of things used by addicts, to show possession with intent to supply).

girls right'. Although there was some division of opinion among the judges, the reasoning was succinctly expressed by Lawrence J:[7]

> That the same accident should repeatedly occur to the same person is unusual, especially so when it confers a benefit on him. The degree of improbability will depend upon the number of times it is shown to have occurred and the similarity of the circumstances on each occasion.

A steady trickle of similar cases has subsequently approved the admissibility of similar fact evidence for this purpose,[8] although the intent must relate strictly to the actus reus alleged, and a careful direction may be required.[9] It is less common to permit the prosecution to use similar fact evidence to rebut a defence of self-defence, though it equally relates to the motivation of an admitted voluntary act. It has been said that such evidence will only rarely be admissible, and a high requirement of similarity insisted upon.[10]

It is sometimes appropriate to show the state of knowledge of the accused as a step on the way to showing his intent. This line of reasoning is well illustrated by one of the oldest cases, *R v Francis*,[11] which involved a charge of attempting to obtain money from a pawnbroker by the false pretence that a diamond ring was genuine. Blackburn J admitted the evidence at first instance, and his decision was upheld by the Court for Crown Cases Reserved,[12] on the basis that the evidence of other attempts to pass false articles as genuine, including the same ring, showed that the accused was not mistaken about the falsity of the ring. In these cases it may not be necessary to show quite the same high degree of similarity as is required in cases where the establishment of an actus reus is in question.[13] In *R v Ollis*[14] it was immaterial that the accused had been acquitted in respect of the conduct which was relied upon to establish knowledge of the state of his bank account.[15] Such a consideration may have motivated the court in *R v Rance and Herron*[16] to re-phrase the test so as to require 'positive probative value'.

---

7   [1906] 2 KB 389, at 420, 21 Cox CC 252, at 273.

8   For example, *Perkins v Jeffery* [1915] 2 KB 702, 25 Cox CC 59 (to show that exposure was with indecent intent); *R v Hall* [1952] 1 KB 302, [1952] 1 All ER 66 (on first two counts to show that handling of victim was with indecent intent); *R v Williams* (1986) 84 Cr App Rep 299 (to show that threats were intended to be taken seriously). See also *Thompson v R* (1989) 86 ALR 1 (to show that deaths apparently caused by a car accident were really murder by shooting); *R v Seaman* (1978) 67 Cr App Rep 234 (to show that removal of goods from self-service shop without paying was deliberate); *R v Lewis* (1982) 76 Cr App Rep 33 (on three counts to show that handling of victims was with indecent intent). In *R v Rodley* [1913] 3 KB 468 there was no suggestion that it was inappropriate to show the intent with which the breaking had been accomplished by similar fact evidence, the evidence was simply insufficiently probative of that intent; *R v Gurney* [1994] Crim LR 116 (to show that forced entry was with intent to rape); *R v Wright* [1994] Crim LR 55 (to show possession of drugs was with intent to supply).

9   *R v Gordon* [1995] 2 Cr App Rep 61 (possession of various items and large quantities of cash to show intent to deal in drugs); see also *R v Smith* [1995] Crim LR 940, et seq.

10   *R v Beggs* (1989) 90 Cr App Rep 430.

11   (1874) 43 LJMC 97.

12   This case was apparently overlooked when it was asserted in *Makin* that only one case had previously been decided in the Court for Crown Cases Reserved.

13   But there is no absolute rule forbidding it: *R v Guney* [1998] 2 Cr App Rep 242 ('lifestyle' evidence permitted to show fact of possession, and not merely intent to deal with admittedly possessed items); see also *R v Yalman* [1998] 2 Cr App Rep 269; *R v Nadiri* [1995] Crim LR 889.

14   [1900] 2 QB 758, 19 Cox CC 554.

15   Though on the facts it is extremely difficult to disagree with the dissenting opinion of Bruce J with whom Ridley J concurred.

16   (1975) 62 Cr App Rep 118.

In that case the accused director of a building company was charged with making a corrupt payment to a local councillor in respect of securing a contract from the local authority. His defence was that he signed both the false authorisation and the cheque without knowing the true state of affairs. The prosecution was allowed to adduce evidence of two other transactions in which the accused had signed false papers for a similar purpose, though in one of them he had handed the money over in a parcel. It should perhaps be noted that there was direct testimony that he really did know the true state of affairs, and the similar fact evidence simply corroborated that testimony. Because it was immaterial to establishing such knowledge that the situations exhibiting it should be identical the use of the new form of words is unexceptionable. It is however important that it should not be allowed to weaken the rigour of the exclusionary rule when the evidence is relied upon for a different purpose, and where the probative force of the evidence is quite different.

In the case of a child accused of crime it is necessary to show that he is capable of forming a criminal intention, and it has been held that this may be done by reference to a previous allegation of similar acts.[17] Although the court denied that this rule was involved, it seems that the evidence did involve the use of the accused's disposition as shown by the evidence adduced, and that the normal approach assessing the probable prejudicial effect should have been applied.[18]

E.   ROLE OF DISCRETION[19]

As noted above, the rule excluding evidence of the accused's bad disposition extends back at least to the early years of the nineteenth century. There appears to be no English case in which any judicial discretion to exclude such evidence was mentioned before the beginning of the twentieth century.[20] Its appearance seems to derive from the judge's general control over the proceedings before him, and was for many years expressed in terms of judicial persuasion of counsel not to press for the admission of similar fact evidence even though strictly admissible.[1] Its development so soon after the decision in *Makin*, and the analogy of the cognate discretion in relation to cross-examination under the Criminal Evidence Act 1898, s 1(f), suggest that it was used to soften the rigidity with which the words of Lord Herschell so rapidly came to be interpreted. Under pressure from counsel the discretion metamorphosed from being one of persuasion to becoming one of exclusion.[2] This function was recognised by the Privy Council in *Noor Mohamed v R*.[3] Although no pronouncement on this aspect of the judge's discretion could form part of the ratio decidendi of the House of Lords

---

17   *G (a minor) v DPP* (1997) Times, 27 November.
18   It is possible that the fact that this was not a trial by jury may have induced the court to believe that the limited purpose of the admission of the evidence would be acted upon, and that the magistrates would have been able to avoid being prejudiced.
19   See above ch VI section 2 part B. For fuller discussion, to which the editor is much indebted, see Pattenden *Judicial Discretion and Criminal Litigation* (1990) 235–243.
20   Such a discretion was referred to, but not exercised, by Darling J in *R v Ollis* [1900] 2 QB 758, at 780, 19 Cox CC 554, at 566. The earliest reported case in which the discretion seems to have been exercised is *R v Miller* (1901) 65 JP 313.
1   It was put in this way by Lords Moulton and Reading in *R v Christie* [1914] AC 545, at 559, 564, [1914–15] All ER Rep 63, at 69, 71. Although *Christie* was not itself a similar fact case, this view seems to have been anticipated in *R v Shellaker* [1914] 1 KB 414, at 418, 9 Cr App Rep 240, at 244. It was repeated in the House of Lords in this form by Viscount Simon in *Harris v DPP* [1952] AC 694, at 707, [1952] 1 All ER 1044, at 1048.
2   It was so treated by Humphreys J in *R v Cole* (1941) 28 Cr App Rep 43, at 51.
3   [1949] AC 182, at 192, [1949] 1 All ER 365, at 370.

in *R v Sang* it was recognised to exist, and to have an exclusionary function. Lord Scarman may even have intended to allude to the change in function in his remark that 'the discretion now extends further than was contemplated by Lord Halsbury LC and Lord Moulton in *R v Christie*, or even by Lord Simon in *Harris*'s case'.[4]

In the same way as there existed two different versions of the function of any such discretion there also existed two different formulations of the circumstances in which it could be exercised. In *Noor Mohamed*, the first really authoritative asseveration of its exclusionary function, Lord Du Parq considered that it should be applied only to cases 'in which it would be unjust to admit evidence of a character gravely prejudicial to the accused even though there may be some tenuous ground for holding it technically admissible'.[5] This approach stresses the trifling probative value of the evidence to be excluded. The alternative formulation stresses the disproportion between probative force and prejudicial effect. In *R v Sang* Lord Fraser adverted to the discrepancy, and supported the latter formulation:[6]

> The judge in these circumstances has a discretion to exclude the evidence not only if its probative weight is 'trifling' (see *Noor Mohamed v R*), but whenever its prejudicial effect would be 'out of proportion to [its] true evidential value': see *Harris v DPP*, Viscount Simon quoting Lord Moulton in *R v Christie*. I read the latter expression as meaning that the discretion can be exercised where the prejudicial value of the evidence would greatly exceed its probative value.

It is interesting that only one member of the House of Lords in *Sang* had been party to the decision in *Boardman*, which, for perfectly good reasons, was not cited. It will be apparent from Lord Fraser's formulation of the discretion quoted above that there is a problem in reconciling it with Lord Wilberforce's formulation of the exclusionary rule in *Boardman* quoted earlier.[7] If the exclusionary rule is designed to balance probative force and prejudicial effect it is hard to see how there will ever be any evidence to which the discretion can, as formulated by Lord Fraser, ever apply.

It is submitted that *Boardman* is good authority for the proposition that the balancing of probative force and prejudicial effect is required by the exclusionary rule. Thus Lord Cross said:[8]

> the reason for this general rule is not that the law regards such evidence as inherently irrelevant, but because it is believed that if it were generally admitted jurors would in many cases think that it was more relevant than it was—so that ... its prejudicial effect would outweigh its probative value ... In the end—although the admissibility of such evidence is a question of law not of discretion—the question ... must be one of degree.

The problem arises because most of their Lordships also recognise the continued existence of a discretion to exclude, formulated in virtually identical terms.[9] Thus Lord Salmon said that the trial judge: 'still, of course, has a discretion to exclude [relevant

---

4   [1980] AC 402, at 452, [1979] 2 All ER 1222, at 1243.
5   At 192, 370.
6   At 446, 1238.
7   Part C.
8   This was clearly the line taken by Lord Wilberforce, and Lord Hailsham also said, at 451, 904, 'the evidence is to be excluded under the first rule in *Makin* because its prejudicial effect may be more powerful than its probative effect.' The terminology was echoed by Lord Mackay LC in *DPP v P* [1991] 2 AC 447, at 461, [1991] 3 All ER 337, at 346.
9   As noted on p 364 above the discretion is also invoked by the Lord Chancellor in *R v H* [1995] 2 AC 596, at 612G, [1995] 2 All ER 865, at 877h despite his view in *DPP v P*.

and admissible similar fact evidence] on the ground that its probative value is minimal and altogether outweighed by its likely prejudicial effect.'[10] A third view expressed by Lord Morris seems to have been that the two processes should take place simultaneously: 'at whatever stage a judge gives a ruling he must exercise his judgment and his discretion having in mind both the requirements of fairness and also the requirements of justice'.[11]

It has nowadays become increasingly realised that the notion of 'discretion' may be used in a number of different senses.[12] It may be used either in a 'strong' sense to recognise that its possessor has a choice of alternatives free of binding criteria, or in a weak sense to recognise that its possessor is bound by criteria, but criteria formulated in such a way that he has to exercise his personal judgment in determining whether or not they have been satisfied. In another context within the law of evidence it has been decided that the judge's task is of the latter type, and that the terminology of discretion is best eschewed to avoid possible confusion.[13] In this context the difference is between taking the view that the judge can properly decide that the prejudicial effect of evidence outweighs its probative value, and still admit it; and taking the view that once the judge has decided that the prejudicial effect outweighs its probative value he is bound to exclude it.[14] It is submitted that the latter is clearly the better view. It also accords better with the authorities both before and after *Boardman*. Thus in *R v Doughty* Lord Parker CJ had said:[15]

> Where the evidence of indecency is tenuous to a degree and where, even if held to be indecent, it is a different form of indecency, then the court can only exercise its discretion in one way, by excluding that evidence, the reason being that its prejudicial value is quite overwhelming. The court feels ... that ... this discretion could properly be exercised in only one way, by excluding the evidence.

It has been noted above that the House of Lords has rejected the notion that a proposition permitting exercise only in one way can properly be regarded as a discretion.[16] It seems therefore that as stated by Lord Cross in the passage quoted above from *Boardman*, and as stated by Lord Scarman in *Sang*, 'The law, not the judge's discretion, determines what is admissible evidence'.[17] Although perhaps less plangent, the same approach can be seen to inform the practical guidance for trial judges offered by the Court of Appeal in *R v Scarrott*.[18] The phraseology of that advice has clearly

---

10   At 463, 913. Lord Hailsham also said at 453, 906 'The judge also has a discretion, not as a matter of law, but of good practice, to exclude evidence, whose prejudicial effect, though the evidence be technically admissible on the decided cases, may be so great in the particular circumstances as to outweigh its probative value to the extent that a verdict of guilty might be considered unsafe or unsatisfactory.'

11   At 439, 893.

12   For a theoretical examination of the use of the concept see Dworkin in *Taking Rights Seriously* (1977) at 27, 31.

13   *R v Viola* [1982] 3 All ER 73, at 77, [1982] 1 WLR 1138, at 1142, in the not wholly dissimilar context of making a judgment about the fairness of cross-examination of a complainant in a case of rape about her sexual experience.

14   The argument becomes even stronger if the proposition is framed in the terms quoted above from Lord Salmon in *Boardman* and from Lord Fraser in *Sang*.

15   [1965] 1 All ER 560, at 562, [1965] 1 WLR 331, at 334. In *R v Novac* (1976) 65 Cr App Rep 107, at 111, Bridge LJ also suggests the discretion as being capable of exercise only one way.

16   See above ch IV section 2 part B noting the treatment of similar view advanced in *R v Flynn* [1963] 1 QB 729, [1961] 3 All ER 58, by the House of Lords in *Selvey v DPP* [1970] AC 304, at 331, [1968] 2 All ER 497, at 510.

17   At 454, 1245.

18   [1978] QB 1016, [1978] 1 All ER 672.

been chosen with great care, and it is significant to note the shift of emphasis between the description of the judge's role at the pre-arraignment stage where the judge has a real discretion,[19] and that of his role at the trial stage. In describing the former, Scarman LJ said:

> It is important to appreciate that *at this stage*, the pre-arraignment stage, the ultimate decision of the judge is *an exercise of judicial discretion ... at this stage* the judge is taking no final decision as to the admissibility of evidence.

But in describing the latter, he said: 'it will then be for the judge to rule, in accordance with *the laws of evidence*, whether the evidence is admissible or not.'[20] It is significant that there is no further use of the word 'discretion' once the trial stage has been reached.[1] This is quite consistent with the view expressed by Devlin J in the influential case of *R v Miller*, though there in the context of cross-examination, that: 'if the court is of the opinion that the prejudicial effect outweighs its relevance, then it has the power, and, indeed, the *duty* to exclude the question.'[2] It has also been held that the court has a duty to consider the question, and an appeal allowed where the trial judge failed to do so.[3]

It is worth considering the results of the contrary view that a discretion exists in the usual sense. Such a view would contradict the general restrictive policy of the law by casting upon the accused the initiative of activating the discretion. As noted above, such a view might also justify a judge's decision to admit evidence even though he found that its prejudicial effect exceeded, or perhaps even greatly exceeded, its probative value. This may be regarded as fanciful,[4] though even that tells significantly against any such view. It is not so fanciful to suppose that an appellate court might, despite disagreeing with the trial judge's assessment, nevertheless feel obliged to uphold his decision if he had taken the right considerations into account.[5] Indeed this very situation occurred in *R v Mackie* where the Court of Appeal said: 'we agree that the prejudicial effect of the evidence admitted was enormous and far outweighed its value in proving that the child was frightened of the appellant', but then went on to decide that: 'the judge was entitled to exercise his discretion as he did and to admit this evidence'.[6] It is much easier to avoid such injustice elsewhere if exclusion is recognised to be by application of a rule, subject to the ordinary processes of appellate review. Another

---

19   Partly because the decision has to be made upon an inadequate basis, and can be revised in the light of later developments.

20   At 1028, 681, emphasis supplied.

1   The Court of Appeal also avoided use of the word in its decision on this point in *R v Barrington* [1981] 1 All ER 1132, [1981] 1 WLR 419.

2   [1952] 2 All ER 667, at 669, 36 Cr App Rep 169, at 171, emphasis supplied.

3   *Cottle v R* [1977] AC 323, at 328. Although the term 'discretion' was employed, it seems clear that it was used in the loose sense to mean 'judgment'. No question of applying both rule and discretion arose, principally because no question of the admissibility of the evidence relating to one count or another was considered at all.

4   But see *R v Da Silva* [1990] 1 All ER 29, [1990] 1 WLR 31 where the trial judge's decision to admit the evidence was upheld on appeal despite his own characterisation of the relevance of the evidence as no more than 'marginal' and his expressed view that if admitted 'the defendant's chances of acquittal have gone.'

5   In *R v Straffen* [1952] 2 QB 911, at 913 it is revealed that counsel declined even to address the appellate court on the question of exclusion on account of prejudice because that was a matter within the trial judge's discretion. Cp the reversal of the trial judge's exercise of discretion in *R v Fletcher* [1995] Crim LR 727 (in an admittedly unusual situation); and in Canada *R v Litchfield* [1993] 4 SCR 333 where the trial judge's alternative ground of decision on the basis of discretion was simply said to be wrong by the appellate court.

6   (1973) 57 Cr App Rep 453, at 464, 465.

possible consequence of regarding the discretion in the usual way relates to the effect of such a view upon the operation of the basic exclusionary rule. The only possible way of reconciling such a discretion with the rule, is to divorce the question of prejudicial effect from that of probative force. The rule then excludes only those cases where there is insufficient probative force, and the discretion excludes even those where it is sufficient, if that force is greatly outweighed by its prejudicial effect. It can then be argued that the existence of a discretion cast in such terms shows that some evidence of, to use Lord Salmon's formulation quoted above, 'minimal probative value', passes the test. It may next be possible to attempt to utilise the change of terminology in *R v Rance and Herron*[7] to 'positive probative value' to suggest that similar fact evidence is always, prima facie, admissible so long as it is barely relevant, and subsequent exclusion wholly reliant upon the operation of the trial judge's discretion, itself minimally subject to appellate control. Such an argument would seem very far-fetched had it not been adopted by the Full Court of the Supreme Court of Victoria in *R v Chee.*[8] It was however subsequently disavowed in Victoria,[9] and still more authoritatively by the High Court of Australia.[10]

It may thus be accepted that the similar facts rule operates, as Lord Wilberforce explained in *Boardman*, to exclude evidence the prejudicial effect of which exceeds its probative force. Does this leave any role for the operation of an exclusionary discretion? Many commentators have argued that it does not.[11] This view appears not to be shared by very many judges.[12] In a sense this is unimportant. It does not matter very much that a discretion should be regarded as existing despite having been rendered redundant by the reformulation of the exclusionary rule, so long at least as reasoning like that in *Chee* can be avoided. It remains to be considered whether a more useful role can be ascribed to such a discretion in this context. Two possibilities suggest themselves. The first is that there may still, as will be seen in the next section, be a role for such a discretion when the evidence showing the accused's bad disposition has been admitted under a statutory rule. The second is consequential upon the restriction of the common law rule as formulated here to the exclusion of evidence showing the accused's bad disposition when that disposition constitutes an essential step in the process of reasoning. This formulation then leaves simple relevance to govern admissibility when disposition forms no part of the chain of reasoning. It will nevertheless often be desirable to exclude such evidence to avoid the possibility of causing prejudice. If the accused's presence at the scene of a theft with which he is charged is supported by evidence of, say, his promiscuous homosexuality with others in the area at the time, it might well be thought right to exclude the evidence. Such an interpretation of the use of the discretion

---

7   (1975) 62 Cr App Rep 118.

8   [1980] VR 303. Criticised by Tapper in Campbell and Waller (eds) *Well and Truly Tried* (1982). A similar argument can be discerned in *R v Burns* [1996] Crim LR 322. The principal danger of the dilution of the test for admissibility in *DPP v P* [1991] 2 AC 447, [1991] 3 All ER 337 is that it may revive this argument in England; and the decision in *R v H* [1995] 2 AC 596, [1995] 2 All ER 865 seems to justify this gloomy prophecy, at least in the cases to which it applies. Similar results seem apparent in Canada: see *R v B(CR)* [1990] 1 SCR 717 where the majority was reluctant to overrule the trial judge's approach in what it regarded as a borderline case of admissibility.

9   *R v Vaitos* (1982) 4 ACR 238, at 297.

10   *Perry v R* (1982) 44 ALR 449, at 453, 454, and a further attempt to resurrect it was quelled in no uncertain terms by the High Court of Australia in *Sutton v R* (1984) 51 ALR 435.

11   See for example, Cowen and Carter *Essays on the Law of Evidence* (1956), at 155; Hoffmann (1975) 91 LQR 193, at 204; Eggleston *Evidence, Proof and Probability* (2nd edn, 1983), at 97; Pattenden *Judicial Discretion and Criminal Litigation* (1990), at 240.

12   But see *Perry v R* (1982) 44 ALR 449, at 469 per Wilson J; and *Sutton v R* (1984) 51 ALR 435, at 439 per Gibbs CJ, and at 464 per Dawson J.

is also quite consistent with the decision of the Court of Appeal in *R v Mackie*[13] where the evidence was not admitted to show the accused's propensity, and where it was made quite clear that a discretion, and not a rule, was being applied, since the Court of Appeal refused to intervene once it was satisfied that the trial judge had taken the correct considerations into account, even though it disagreed with his judgment of them. Another case illustrating the usefulness of the discretion in this context is *R v Fitzpatrick*.[14] The accused was charged with two offences of indecency which occurred very soon after each other, perhaps within a three minute period. The Court of Criminal Appeal took the view that the only possible basis for the admission of evidence of the one on the other was that they occurred during one continuous period of sexual excitement. Such an argument may be regarded as falling outside the scope of the similar fact rule as defined here, but the court held that the trial judge should at least have considered the possible application of the discretion to exclude on the basis of the preponderance of possible prejudicial effect over probative value.

This view accordingly preserves a useful role for the discretion, and helps to explain the judicial reaffirmation of its continued existence. Its role has nevertheless diminished since *Boardman* established, and *DPP v P* confirmed, the balance of probative force and prejudicial effect as the basis of the modern rule of admissibility.

F.   REFORM OF THE RULE

As noted earlier in this chapter the English rule is a product of the common law, and has in its most recent manifestation in *Boardman* and *DPP v P* been adopted and approved throughout the Commonwealth. Apart from one small area[15] and one major jurisdiction[16] there has been little statutory intervention. It is thus necessary to consider the various suggestions made by law reform bodies.

The first to suggest really radical change was the English Criminal Law Revision Committee in its 11th Report,[17] but its proposals seem most unlikely ever to be enacted.[18] The Royal Commission on Criminal Justice took the view that the law on this topic was 'difficult to comprehend', and that the decisions upon it were 'not always easily reconcilable'.[19] This hardly seems an over-statement. The topic was accordingly referred to the Law Commission to be considered as part of its general review of the law of evidence in criminal proceedings.[20] Its consultation paper[1] was published in 1996, and its final report is now imminent.

It is somewhat difficult to isolate its recommendations[2] on this topic since the report covered the whole field of discrediting evidence, whether tendered in chief or put in cross-examination. It canvassed different definitions of the sort of evidence with which it was concerned, rejecting those concentrating on the nature of the matters proved,[3]

---

13   (1973) 57 Cr App Rep 453.
14   [1962] 3 All ER 840, [1963] 1 WLR 7
15   Proof of mens rea on handling charges under Theft Act 1968, s 27(3).
16   Australia, Evidence (Cwth) Act 1995 especially Pt 3.6.
17   Cmnd 4991. Criticised by Tapper (1973) 36 MLR 56.
18   As anticipated at the time by Professor Cross, a signatory: see [1973] Crim LR 400.
19   Cm 2263, para 8.30.
20   Rec 191.
1   No 141. *Evidence in Criminal Proceedings: Previous Misconduct of a Defendant* (1996).
2   Since it is a *consultation* paper any recommendations or rejections can be no more than provisional.
3   Because of the difficulty of isolating the matters in dispute from background evidence.

or the nature of the reasoning process involved,[4] in favour of those concentrating on the prejudicial[5] effect engendered.[6] It found the present situation profoundly unsatisfactory, being both needlessly complex and incoherent. It nevertheless rejected the view that the same rules should govern admissibility in chief and in cross-examination, which it envisaged as necessitating a discretionary approach.[7] It rejected a number of other approaches extending admissibility, some of them proposed in earlier reports, and others enacted elsewhere. Thus it rejected[8] an option canvassed by the Criminal Law Revision Committee in its Eleventh Report that the accused's record should be adduced as a matter of course at the beginning of the trial.[9] It rejected[10] two further recommendations of the Report, namely that similar fact evidence should be admitted in a number of situations set out in cl 3 of its draft bill,[11] and that it should be admitted wherever the accused admitted the actus reus of the offence charged.[12] It rejected[13] a proposal that the record of those charged with sexual offences should be made more freely admissible as a separate category.[14] On the other hand it also rejected a, rather smaller, number of proposals aimed at restricting admissibility, such as one that evidence of previous misconduct should be admitted only when part of the definition of the offence charged,[15] a version of the common law test in Australia that the evidence should be admitted only if there is no rational view of the evidence inconsistent with the guilt of the accused,[16] and the new statutory rule in Australia.[17]

The Report rejects both a general inclusionary rule tempered by an exclusionary discretion,[18] and a general exclusionary rule tempered by an inclusionary discretion,[19] in favour of a single exclusionary rule, subject to separate exceptions both for the admission of discreditable evidence in chief, and for its subsequent use.[20]

The Report recommends the admission of prejudicial dispositional evidence only if it is relevant to a specific issue, and its probative value outweighs its prejudicial effect and any other factors militating against admission. The aim of this proposal is to concentrate attention on the specific issue to which the evidence is relevant, and an interesting feature is that it is envisaged that relevance should be judged only in relation to live issues in the case. The Report then endorses a balancing exercise in which such probative value is required to outweigh both prejudice[1] and other factors such as distraction of the jury or waste of time. A number of factors to be considered is then

---

4   This was taken to disqualify not only the approach of Lord Hailsham LC in *Boardman v DPP*, but also that of the prohibition of tendency or coincidence evidence in the manner of Pt 3.6 of the Evidence (Cwth) Act 1995 in Australia.

5   Resulting from either reasoning or moral prejudice.

6   Paras 9.74–9.92.

7   Paras 9.58–9.73.

8   Para 9.23.

9   A procedure available in some jurisdictions on the continent of Europe.

10   Paras 10.46, 10.36.

11   Claimed to represent the existing law in 1972, but in the view of most commentators allowing the evidence in more generously.

12   A proposal never yet implemented in any major jurisdiction.

13   Para 9.38.

14   As enacted in the United States in 1994 as rr 413–415 of the Federal Rules of Evidence.

15   Para 9.44.

16   Para 10.59.

17   Para 10.70, largely on broad grounds of complexity and vagueness.

18   Para 9.69.

19   Para 9.71.

20   Principally in cross-examination, as considered more fully in the next chapter.

1   Reasoning and moral.

mentioned.[2] It is somewhat surprising that although this is regarded as an exception to the rule of exclusion its nature is still apparently thought to be discretionary. This feature is exacerbated by a steadfast refusal to set an enhanced probative value for the admission of such evidence. The reason for this is said to be the difficulty of quantifying such an enhanced standard, though once a weighing approach has been adopted, implying comparison at multiple levels, it is hard to understand quite why this should be thought so difficult. Given that the decision is discretionary, that no enhanced value is required, and that the structured nature of the discretion indicates the factors to be taken into account, there must be some danger of creating a system of unappealable admissibility of prejudicial dispositional evidence if these proposals are implemented.

SECTION 2.   STATUTORY PROVISIONS

Two[3] statutes abrogate the rule discussed in this section in the particular circumstances to which they apply, namely s 1(2) of the Official Secrets Act 1911, and s 27(3) of the Theft Act 1968.

Section 1(1) of the Official Secrets Act 1911 (as amended by the Official Secrets Act 1920), punishes various forms of spying if the accused's purpose was prejudicial to the state. Section 1(2) provides that it shall not be necessary to show that the accused person was guilty of any particular act tending to show a purpose prejudicial to the safety or interests of the state and, notwithstanding that no such act is proved against him, he may be convicted if, from the circumstances of the case, or his conduct, or his known character as proved, it appears that his purpose was a purpose prejudicial to the safety or interests of the state. The wording of this subsection shows that evidence of the accused's misconduct may be given although it is relevant only because it shows that he is the kind of man whose purpose in doing certain acts might be of the type proscribed by the statute.

Section 27(3) of the Theft Act 1968, reads as follows:

Where a person is being proceeded against for handling stolen goods (but not for any offence other than handling stolen goods), then at any stage of the proceedings, if evidence has been given of his having or arranging to have in his possession the goods the subject of the charge, or of his undertaking or assisting in, or arranging to undertake or assist in, their retention, removal, disposal or realisation, the following evidence shall be admissible for the purpose of proving that he knew or believed the goods to be stolen goods:
(a)   evidence that he has had in his possession, or has undertaken or assisted in the retention, removal, disposal or realisation of, stolen goods from any theft taking place not earlier than twelve months before the offence charged; and
(b)   (provided that seven day's notice in writing has been given to him of the intention to prove the conviction) evidence that he has within the five years preceding the date of the offence charged been convicted of theft or handling stolen goods.

---

2   Paras 10.79–10.80. See also the more detailed list in draft s 19 of the Code proposed by the New Zealand Law Commission in its Prel Pap 27 *Evidence Law: Character and Credibility* (1997).

3   There are other statutes which exceptionally allow proof of other convictions for limited purposes; see eg Social Security Administration Act 1992, s 120.

The subsection re-enacts with some significant differences,[4] s 43(1) of the Larceny Act 1916, which, in its turn, re-enacted s 19 of the Prevention of Crimes Act 1871. Section 19 abrogated the effect of the decision in *R v Oddy*.[5] In that case, the third count of the indictment charged the accused with knowingly receiving stolen cloth which was found in his possession shortly after the theft, and the trial judge admitted evidence of the fact that other cloth which had been stolen three months previously was also found in the accused's house. The Court for Crown Cases Reserved held that he ought not to have done so, as the evidence merely went to show that the accused was in the habit of receiving stolen cloth. It would have been different if there had been some further connecting link between the two items of evidence. For example, if the cloth had been stolen by the same person the fact of the discovery of both pieces in the accused's house would have been relevant as suggesting the existence of some arrangement for its disposal between the thief and the receiver.[6] Proof of guilty knowledge is, however, a notoriously difficult matter, in a receiving case, and the statutory provisions may be regarded as supplementary to the case-law concerning the provisional presumption arising from the accused's possession, shortly after the theft, of the property mentioned in the indictment.[7]

This provision has proved so unpopular with English judges as to be given a highly restricted interpretation.[8] In particular there has been anxiety that it be restricted to proof of guilty knowledge,[9] and, despite the apparently mandatory language, the court has invested itself with, and applied, discretion to exclude evidence should there be any danger of this restriction being undermined.[10] Similar motives have led to the application of a strictly literal construction being placed upon the ambit of the evidence admitted under the provision. Thus in the case of s 27(3)(a) it has been determined that no surrounding detail of the previous possession can be adduced beyond the barest description of the relevant goods.[11] Similarly in relation to s 27(3)(b) no more than the formal details of the relevant conviction may be adduced, corresponding to those certified under the provisions of s 73(2) of the Police and Criminal Evidence Act 1984. This permits little more than a brief description of the goods,[12] and the result of the case. Here too there is a discretion to exclude the evidence if it seems likely to be unfairly prejudicial. It has been argued[13] that this effort has been counter-productive since the elimination of detail makes it very difficult for the jury to evaluate the true significance of the evidence, and gives rise to the possibility of exacerbating the very prejudice

4   On which see the 8th Report of the Criminal Law Revision Committee (Cmnd 2977, 1966), paras 157–9.

5   (1851) 2 Den 264. If the facts were to recur the decision would still be the same because there were also counts for theft.

6   *R v Dunn* (1826) 1 Mood CC 146; *R v Mansfield* (1841) Car & M 140; *R v Powell* (1909) 3 Cr App Rep 1. Admissibility at common law has been unaffected by the statutes.

7   See p 38, above.

8   It is no more popular in its local form in Australia, see *R v Cresswell* (1987) 8 NSWLR 56 where faint ambiguity in the drafting of the starting point for time beginning to run was resolved in favour of inadmissibility.

9   *R v Wilkins* (1975) 60 Cr App Rep 300; *R v Bradley* (1979) 70 Cr App Rep 200. It cannot be used to undermine the accused's general credibility for example, see *R v Duffas* (1993) Times, 19 October.

10   *R v Herron* [1966] 2 All ER 26; see above p 181.

11   *R v Wood* (1987) 85 Cr App Rep 287, preferring *R v Bradley* (1979) 70 Cr App Rep 200 to *R v Smith* [1918] 2 KB 415.

12   Until the decision of the House of Lords in *R v Hacker* [1995] 1 All ER 45, [1994] 1 WLR 1659, no detail at all of the stolen goods had been permitted. See in New Zealand *R v Brosnan* [1951] NZLR 1030, at 1039.

13   By Smith in his note in the Criminal Law Review to the case of *R v Bradley* [1980] Crim LR 173, and Munday [1988] Crim LR 345.

which it is designed to eliminate. The prosecution is in no way hampered since it can adduce any detail which is sufficiently relevant under the ordinary similar facts rules which the provision supplements, while the accused has no ready means to avoid the prejudice since it would hardly help his cause to draw attention to the variety and versatility of his previous criminal conduct.[14]

SECTION 3.   CIVIL CASES

Although some early civil cases[15] rejected similar fact evidence as res inter alios acta, it was soon accepted that the rule of exclusion was certainly no stricter than that in criminal cases.[16] The real question was whether there was a special rule of exclusion at all, or whether it were not rather a question of simple relevance in each case.[17] In some cases the nature of the issue determined the question in favour of admissibility, as Stephen J remarked in *Brown v Eastern and Midlands Rly Co*: 'when the question is whether a particular act is a public nuisance, it is difficult to see how it can be proved to be so except by shewing cases in which it has interfered with a public right'.[18] Similarly evidence of previous complaints about accidents was admitted to show that the proprietors of a dock knew of its dangerous condition,[19] and previous outbreaks of skin complaints among the defendant barber's customers to show his negligent practice.[20]

The enactment of enforceable rights against discrimination has extended the admissibility of similar fact evidence in civil proceedings. Thus in *West Midlands Passenger Executive v Singh*[1] the Court of Appeal accepted that statistical evidence of consistent employment practice in relation to particular ethnic groups was both necessary and relevant to prove discrimination, and an order for discovery was upheld. In other cases where a claim does not depend upon showing consistent practice, but where previous malpractice might be sought to be used in cross-examination such discovery may be regarded as oppressive.[2] It should be noted however that in the criminal sphere there is no requirement that systematic conduct need be alleged as part of the definition of the offence in order for similar fact evidence to be admitted.[3] The

---

14   The Law Commission in its Consultation paper No 141 *Evidence in Criminal Proceedings: Previous Misconduct of a Defendant* (1996) para 14.13 recommends its repeal, as did the Criminal Law Revision Committee, and as occurred in 1973 in the State of Victoria. Such a course would leave this situation to the operation of the ordinary rules.

15   *Spencely v De Willott* (1806) 7 East 108 (usurious contracts); *Holcombe v Hewson* (1810) 2 Camp 391 (bad beer).

16   *Blake v Albion Life Assurance Society* (1878) 4 CPD 94 (fraudulent trading). See also *Thorpe v Greater Manchester Chief Constable* [1989] 2 All ER 827, [1989] 1 WLR 665 (certificate of the results of disciplinary proceedings involving acts of similar misconduct by the relevant policemen). In Australia this attitude was in *Sheldon v Sun Alliance Australia Ltd* (1989) 53 SASR 97, at 144, 155 ascribed to *Martin v Osborne* (1936) 55 CLR 367 (described as 'quasi-criminal').

17   In *DF Lyons Pty Ltd v Commonwealth Bank of Australia* (1990) 100 ALR 468 Gummow J pointed out that such evidence might be relevant either to establish the facts directly, or to support the credibility of a direct witness. In either case similarity in the facts was significant only if it related to a legally significant factor.

18   (1889) 22 QBD 391, at 393, 58 LJQB 212, at 214.

19   *Moore v Ransome's Dock* (1898) 14 TLR 539. See also *McKenna v Greco* (1981) 125 DLR (3d) 268 (previous violence in defendant's hotel to show knowledge of likelihood of violence).

20   *Hales v Kerr* [1908] 2 KB 601, 77 LJKB 870.

1   [1988] 2 All ER 873.

2   See *Thorpe v Greater Manchester Chief Constable* above. See also *Kennedy v Dodson* [1895] 1 Ch 334.

3   See especially *R v Bond* [1906] 2 KB 389.

general tendency has indeed been for further relaxation. Lord Reid doubted whether the same considerations which justified the rule in criminal cases applied in the civil law.[4] The most authoritative statement of the position was made by Lord Denning MR in *Mood Music Publishing Co Ltd v de Wolfe Publishing Ltd.* The claimants in a claim for infringement of copyright wished to tender evidence of previous infringements of copyright by the defendant. The trial judge decided the question of admissibility on considerations of ordinary relevance without reference to any special exclusionary rule. In this he was upheld by the Court of Appeal, on the basis that no more than such relevance was required in civil cases by contrast with criminal:[5]

> The criminal courts have been very careful not to admit such evidence unless its probative value is so strong that it should be received in the interests of justice; and its admission will not operate unfairly to the accused. In civil cases the courts will admit evidence of similar facts if it is logically probative, that is if it is logically relevant in determining the matter which is in issue; provided that it is not oppressive or unfair to the other side; and also that the other side has fair notice of it and is able to deal with it.

This passage may be interpreted as applying in civil cases a similar sort of balancing approach to the rules for admissibility of similar fact evidence as applies in criminal cases. The factor favouring admissibility is the probative force of the evidence. Lord Denning's remarks seem to suggest that simple relevance is sufficient, but some cases seem to take a strict view of the circumstances in which other discreditable conduct is relevant, denying such categorisation to other acts of similar police misconduct,[6] fraudulent overcharging for similar services on other occasions,[7] other cases of cattle suffering disease after consuming the defendant's feed,[8] other dubious, factually different, insurance claims,[9] and other fraudulent misrepresentations made to different tenants in respect of the same building development.[10] However, in other cases fraudulent representations to the purchasers of shares,[11] and forgeries of the signatures of some other members of the same family, have been regarded as sufficiently relevant.[12] In *Designers Guild Ltd v Russell Williams (Textiles) Ltd*[13] the nature of the balancing was well illustrated by disallowance of cross-examination of previous copying which had not been alleged to infringe and which had been the subject of an unsuccessful attempt to amend the pleadings; but allowance of cross-examination as to a proved instance of infringement of the copyright of a third party which had come to the knowledge of the claimant only shortly before the trial. As in criminal cases the estimation of probative force is a complex one depending upon the precise circumstances of the case and the issues being contested. The factors to be weighed against such probative effect are however different on account of the peculiar position of the accused in criminal cases. There is very high authority accounting for the existence

4   *Cummings (McWilliams) v Sir William Arrol & Co* [1962] 1 All ER 623, at 630, [1962] 1 WLR 295, at 305.
5   [1976] Ch 119, at 127, [1976] 1 All ER 763, at 766.
6   *Thorpe v Greater Manchester Chief Constable*, above.
7   *British Coal Corpn v Dennis Rye Ltd (No 2)* [1988] 3 All ER 816, [1988] 1 WLR 1113.
8   *Laubscher v National Foods Ltd* 1986 (1) SA 553.
9   *Kurgiel v Mitsubishi Motors Australia Ltd* (1990) 54 SASR 125.
10   *HW Thompson Investments Pty Ltd v Allen Property Services Ltd* (1984) 77 FLR 254 refusing to follow earlier decisions admitting such evidence; *Peet & Co Ltd v Rocci* [1985] WAR 164; *DF Lyons Pty Ltd v Commonwealth Bank of Australia* (1991) 100 ALR 468.
11   *MacDonald v Canada Kelp Co Ltd* (1973) 39 DLR (3d) 617.
12   *Berger v Raymond & Son Ltd* [1984] 1 WLR 625.
13   [1998] FSR 275.

of an exclusionary discretion in criminal cases solely by reference to the accused's vulnerability to prejudice.[14] It has accordingly been held in Australia that in civil cases there is no comparable exclusionary discretion in respect of similar fact evidence on the basis of an excess of prejudice over probative force. It is significant that Lord Denning refers not to prejudice, but to oppression and unfairness.[15] This approach was elaborated by Warner J in *Berger v Raymond & Sun Ltd* where a question of forgery by a defendant of some share transfers was in issue. Evidence of other transfers alleged to have been forged by the defendant was adduced. Warner J took the view that *Mood Music* had equated the test for the admissibility of similar fact evidence in criminal and civil cases, but that the discretion to exclude operated upon a different basis. He adverted to such factors as the burden imposed upon the defendant in adducing evidence, the lengthening of the trial, and the undesirability of re-litigating issues disposed of in previous proceedings. Given the weight of authority opposed to the existence of an exclusionary discretion in civil proceedings it seems that Warner J was employing the term to indicate factors relevant to the exercise of the rule as to admissibility which were incapable of precise determination, and hence ultimately depended upon the assessment of the judge. Indeed the affirmation by Warner J of the essential similarity of the approach in both criminal and civil cases lends weight to the view that exclusion is by rule, albeit one involving the assessment of imprecise elements, and not by discretion.

The issue may arise however not at the stage of admissibility at trial, but at the stage of amendment of pleadings to allow allegations of similar conduct in the past,[16] where the judge clearly has a discretion to weigh factors such as the difficulty of proof which such an amendment might create against the probative force of the allegations in the context of the case, or in relation to discovery where the inclusion of the allegations in the statements of claim is likely to be of critical importance.[17]

14   *R v Christie* [1914] AC 545, at 559, 564, [1914–15] All ER Rep 63, at 69, 71; *Ibrahim v R* [1914] AC 599, at 609, [1914–15] All ER Rep 874, at 878. See further p 179, above.

15   See also *R v Isleworth Crown Court, ex p Marland* (1998) 162 JP 251 where it is stressed that in civil cases fairness to both parties is to be considered, and where the admission of spent convictions was upheld in a forfeiture application.

16   See *Perrin v Drennan* [1991] FSR 81.

17   *EG Music v SF (Film) Distributors Ltd* [1978] FSR 121.

Chapter IX

Criminal Evidence Act 1898

Section 2 of this chapter is mainly a gloss on the last one, for s 1(f) of the Criminal Evidence Act 1898 defines the extent to which the accused may be cross-examined on the subject of his disposition and character; some points of a more general nature are discussed in section 1.

SECTION I. THE GENERAL EFFECT OF THE ACT

It has already been shown how s 1 of the Act made the accused and his spouse competent witnesses for the defence in all criminal cases,[1] and the limited extent to which the accused's spouse is compellable as a witness on his behalf, or competent or compellable as a witness for the prosecution or a co-accused has likewise been considered.[2] Two matters will be examined here, first, the position of an accused who does not give evidence, and second, the position of one who does.

Section 1(a) of the Act provides that the person charged can be called as a witness only on his own application. It is doubtful whether many people in 1898 would have favoured a provision under which the accused would have become a compellable witness in the sense that he would be liable to imprisonment for contempt if he refused to answer questions, and it is difficult to believe that their numbers have greatly increased in the meantime.[3] Nevertheless, in any system under which the accused is neither incompetent to give evidence on his own behalf nor compellable to answer questions put to him by

---

1   Chapter V.

2   Chapter V. See Police and Criminal Evidence Act 1984, s 80.

3   This possibility seems neither to have been considered by the Royal Commission on Criminal Justice Cm 2263 (1993), nor by the Law Commission in its consultation paper No 141 *Evidence in Criminal Proceedings: Previous Misconduct of a Defendant* (1996). Clause 28(2)(a) of the original version of the Criminal Justice and Public Order Bill did provide for the court to call upon the accused to testify, refusal to be inhibited by the prospect of adverse comment. For the final version see s 35(4) of the Act. It may be noted that a similar clause was first proposed by the Criminal Law Revision Committee in its Eleventh Report 'Evidence (General)' Cmnd 4991, para 110, cl 5(2) of the annexed draft bill. This recommendation was enacted in Singapore as s 188(2) of the Criminal Procedure Code 1982. For judicial interpretation see *Haw Tua Tau v Public Prosecutor* [1982] AC 136, at 154.

the prosecution or the judge, adverse inferences are liable to be drawn from his failure to go into the witness box. The Act of 1898 can thus be said to have confronted the accused with the choice of opting not to give evidence with the consequential risk that adverse inferences would be drawn, or going into the witness box and thus exposing himself to cross-examination which might cause him to incriminate himself. Reflections of this nature even led some lawyers to regard the Act as a retrograde step.[4]

The problem raised by the Act with regard to an accused who does choose to testify concerns the position of an accused with a bad character. Is he to be liable to cross-examination to credit on his previous convictions and bad character like any other witness; or is he to be protected against such cross-examination and, if so, to what extent? It should be noted that despite reference in s 1 of the Criminal Evidence Act 1898 to a 'person charged with an offence' it seems that it applies not so much to an 'offence', as to an indictment,[5] so that an accused charged on an indictment containing more than one count cannot elect to testify upon some counts, but not upon others. Once he has elected to testify as to one, he is exposed to cross-examination as to all, unprotected as to the others by the privilege against self incrimination.[6]

A. THE ACCUSED WHO DOES NOT GIVE EVIDENCE[7]

Bentham expressed a commonly held view in observing that 'Innocence claims the right of speaking as guilt invokes the privilege of silence.'[8] There may however be legitimate reasons for an accused person to wish to refrain from[9] testifying, and so as to allow for this situation the Criminal Evidence Act 1898 prohibited[10] comment by the prosecution upon such failure. This prohibition was construed not to apply to adverse comment either by the judge,[11] or by counsel for a co-accused.[12] On the other hand it prevented even favourable or ostensibly neutral comment by the prosecution.[13] In some jurisdictions under the influence of a heightened sense of the relevance and importance in this context of the privilege against self-incrimination, a more stringent prohibition on comment was established, extending to judge as well as prosecuting counsel.[14] Given the likelihood of the jury's drawing an adverse inference from the accused's failure[15]

4   See Williams (1914) 30 LQR 297.
5   In which several counts may validly be joined.
6   *R v Phillips* (1987) 86 Cr App Rep 18.
7   For general discussion see Greer (1990) 53 Mod LR 709; Williams (1994) 110 LQR 629.
8   *Treatise on Evidence* p 241.
9   In New Zealand it has been said that since the accused is under no obligation to testify, this verb more appropriate than 'to fail', *R v Accused (CA 78/88)* [1988] 2 NZLR 385, at 391.
10   Section 1(b).
11   *R v Rhodes* [1899] 1 QB 77.
12   *R v Wickham, R v Ferrara and R v Bean* (1971) 55 Cr App Rep 199; and for a very full discussion of the English antecedents of the American rule in the latter context see *De Luna v US* 308 F 2d 140 (1962). In Canada while such comment is permitted, *R v Creighton* (1993) 80 CCC (3d) 421, it must not be excessive *R v Unger* (1993) 83 CCC (3d) 228.
13   *R v Everitt and R v Riley* (1989) 91 Cr App Rep 208, disapproving any suggestion to the contrary in *R v Brown and R v Routh* [1983] Crim LR 38.
14   In Australia, see Evidence Act (Cwth) 1995, s 20, and for comment see Palmer 18 UNSWLR 130. The judge is released from restriction if any such comment is made by a co-accused. In the United States the fifth amendment to the Constitution has been so interpreted: see *Griffin v California* 380 US 606 (1965). But see *US v Robinson* 485 US 25 (1988) permitting prosecutional comment in response to an explicit claim that the accused had not been given an opportunity to answer the charge against him. In New Zealand no comment was allowed until 1966 when an amendment was made to permit judicial comment alone.
15   So likely was this effect that it was recommended that where the accused decided not to testify in England under the old regime counsel should make a note to that effect and have the accused sign it: *R v Bevan* (1993) 98 Cr App Rep 354.

to testify whether so instructed or not,[16] it is sometimes questioned whether the accused necessarily benefits from a blanket ban on comment:[17]

> How can it be said that the inferences drawn by a jury will be more detrimental to a defendant under the limiting and carefully controlling language of the instruction here involved than would result if the jury were left to roam at large with only its untutored instinct to guide it, to draw from the defendant's silence broad inferences of guilt.

The answer of the majority was: 'What the jury may infer, given no help from the court, is one thing. What it may infer when the court solemnises the silence of the accused into evidence against him is quite another.'[18]

I.   Right to Comment

Whatever the theoretical argument, the position in England is now governed by s 35 of the Criminal Justice and Public Order Act 1994:

(1) At the trial of any person[19] for an offence, subsections (2) and (3) below apply unless–
(a) the accused's guilt is not in issue; or
(b) it appears to the court that the physical or mental condition of the accused makes it undesirable for him to give evidence;
   but subsection (2) below does not apply if, at the conclusion of the evidence for the prosecution, his legal representative informs the court that he will give evidence or, where he is unrepresented, the court ascertains from him that he will give evidence.
   (2) Where this subsection applies, the court shall, at the conclusion of the evidence for the prosecution, satisfy itself (in the case of proceedings on indictment, in the presence of the prosecution, satisfy itself (in the case of proceedings on indictment, in the presence of the jury) that the accused is aware that the stage has been reached at which evidence can be given for the defence and that he can, if he wishes, give evidence, and that, if he chooses not to give evidence, or having been sworn, without good cause refuses to answer any question, it will be permissible for the court or jury to draw such inferences as appear proper from his failure to give evidence or his refusal, without good cause to answer any question.
   (3) Where this subsection applies, the court or jury, in determining whether the accused is guilty of the offence charged, may draw such inferences as appear proper from the failure of the accused to give evidence or his refusal, without good cause, to answer any question.
   (4) This section does not render the accused compellable to give evidence on his own behalf, and he shall accordingly not be guilty of contempt of court by reason of failure to do so.

16 Possibly even in defiance of a contrary instruction.
17 Dissent in *Griffin,* at 621; see also *Weissensteiner v R* (1993) 178 CLR 217, at 225, 234. In Canada it has been held that it is not contrary to the Charter to prevent all comment, even though the effect may be to deprive the accused of the benefit of a direction to the jury that no adverse inference should be drawn from his failure to testify: *R v Bass* (1988) 68 CR (3d) 123.
18 At 614.
19 The original restriction to persons over 14 was removed by s 35 of the Crime and Disorder Act 1998.

(5) For the purposes of this section a person who, having been sworn, refuses to answer any question shall be taken to do so without good cause unless–

(a) he is entitled to refuse to answer the question by virtue of any enactment, whenever passed or made, or on the ground of privilege; or

(b) the court in the exercise of its general discretion excuses him from answering it.

The Court of Appeal set out to provide authoritative guidance on the general approach to the interpretation of this provision in *R v Cowan*.[20] It took a broad view of its application, and declined the invitation to apply its provisions only in exceptional cases. In particular it rejected argument that such a course should be adopted because the provisions effectively forced the accused to testify; reversed the onus of proof; and encroached upon legal professional privilege by requiring reasons for failure to testify,[1] which might involve the revelation of legal advice. It pointed out that the Act explicitly preserves the accused's right not to testify;[2] that s 38(3) provides that failure to testify is not alone to constitute a basis for conviction, but requires supplementation by other evidence, to which any adverse inference drawn under these provisions merely adds weight; and that nothing asked of counsel is a matter of confidence. These arguments seem somewhat formal since it is accepted by the court that the whole aim of the Act is to bring pressure upon the accused to testify; that it is designed to ease proof of guilt when the accused fails to do so; and that apart from the provisions of the Act, legal advice as to the tactics to be employed by the defence is at the very centre of the protection provided by legal professional privilege. The court apparently thought that some protection would be provided as a result of its view that not only the judge, but also the jury would have to be satisfied that there was a case to answer, before any inference could be drawn from the accused's failure to testify; but since that question can be answered by the jury only in the course of its final consideration of its verdict, this seems artificial, and unlikely to occur.[3] It has nevertheless been held to be fatal not to give such a direction.[4]

The only substantial exception now[5] recognised by the Act relates to those whose physical and mental condition appear to be such as to make it undesirable for them to testify. This provision too has been given a restrictive interpretation, and in *R v Friend*[6] a person aged only 15, but with a mental age of nine was held not to come within it. The court appeared to have been influenced by the protective measures nowadays employed to ease the ordeal of testifying, evidence of the accused's above average performance on a suggestibility test, and his apparently cunning behaviour after the commission of the crime in an attempt to conceal or withhold incriminating evidence. The court seemed to come close to equating the operation of this exclusion with cases where the accused

---

20   [1996] QB 373, [1995] 4 All ER 939.

1   The Practice Note [1995] 2 All ER 499, [1995] 1 WLR 657, para 3 requires the judge to enquire whether or not the client has been advised of his position under the Act.

2   Section 35(4), as noted above, by way of departure from the draft bill. In Northern Ireland where the original form was enacted the House of Lords has held that a witness called by the judge under the relevant provision and is thereby made available for cross-examination did not 'fail to give evidence' for the purposes of drawing adverse inferences: *R v Bingham and Cooke* (1999) Times, 15 March.

3   It would, in effect, require the jury to reason that with the inference from failure there was proof beyond reasonable doubt that the accused was guilty, but that without it there would not have been; and that it must thus pronounce a verdict of not guilty upon a person it believes beyond reasonable doubt to be guilty.

4   In *R v El-Hannachi* [1998] 2 Cr App Rep 226; *R v Birchall,* [1999] Crim LR 311.

5   Since the exception for those under 14 was removed by s 35 of the Crime and Disorder Act 1998.

6   [1997] 2 All ER 1011, [1997] 1 WLR 1433.

was unfit to plead. It was nevertheless prepared to concede a very wide discretion to the judge, upon the basis that:[7]

> It cannot be said that he applied the wrong test if only because there is no right test. Indeed we do not consider it appropriate to spell out a test to be applied in such a situation.

The court took refuge from the obvious implication of unreviewable palm-tree justice in its observation that only *proper* inferences could be drawn, and that any medical evidence adduced in support of the contention[8] that it was undesirable for any inference to be drawn, could be relied upon for the purpose of determining what inference was proper.

It should be noted that even where so strict a view determines that an adverse inference is possible, the judge still retains a discretion to decline to direct the jury to draw it if the accused has a good cause not to testify.[9] Here too in *R v Cowan* the court rejected any attempt to develop the notion of a good cause[10] in such a way as to cramp the exercise of the discretion. It was particularly scathing of the suggestion that an accused person with a long record would have good cause not to testify, arguing that to accept it would be to prefer those with records over those who had none. This does not seem to meet the point that the latter would have no incentive not to testify on this account. Of the other contentions raised, it did not dismiss out of hand suggestions that a weak prosecution case,[11] other evidence contradicting the prosecution case, a particularly likelihood of the accused being an unimpressive witness,[12] an abnormal medical condition,[13] or fear, duress or desire to protect others, could be taken into account, though it was not inclined to consider them expansively,[14] and in general[15] required an evidential basis[16] for considering them at all.

Since nothing appears to the contrary,[17] and s 1(b) of the Criminal Evidence Act 1898 has been repealed,[18] it may be assumed that comment, now including either a

---

7   At 1020f, 1442H. Its only gloss, is that 'A physical condition might include the risk of an epileptic attack; a mental condition, a latent schizophrenia where the experience of giving evidence might trigger a florid state.' In *R v Lee* [1998] 6 CL 102 it was suggested that the fact that giving evidence might itself further impair the accused's mental state, or that he might be prone to embarrassing outbursts might be relevant factors to consider.

8   The judge need not raise the issue of his own motion and may decide it on a voir dire, but it does require a proper evidential basis: *R v A* [1997] Crim LR 883.

9   Section 35(3).

10   Note that s 35(5) otherwise limits the exception to statutory rule and privilege.

11   This does however seem to have been so dismissed by the Court of Appeal in *R v Byrne* (1995) LEXIS, 21 November.

12   As being nervous, inarticulate or generally unlikely to perform well.

13   Falling short of the requirement of s 35(1)(b).

14   Reiterated in *R v Napper* [1996] Crim LR 591 in rejecting an argument that because the accused had been interviewed by the police soon after the events in relation to only one of eight incidents it was a good reason not to testify that the accused's memory might not have been refreshed.

15   At 380E, 944d the judgment does seem to recognise the possibility of exceptional cases without an evidential basis.

16   Counsel's argument is not to be regarded as sufficient to raise them.

17   It is interesting, but probably not significant, that no explicit reference is made to direction or comment, but only to permissible inference by court or jury.

18   See Sch XI. But not s 80(8) of the Police and Criminal Evidence Act 1984 which prohibits comment by the prosecution upon the failure of the accused's spouse to testify. It is unclear how this provision will now apply if husband and wife are co-defendants. A lenient view seems now to be taken of such failure: see *R v Whitton* [1998] Crim LR 492; cp *R v Naudeer* [1984] 3 All ER 1036.

direction or an invocation to draw an adverse inference, will continue to be allowed to the judge and to counsel for a co-accused, and now permitted also by counsel for the prosecution.

2. Form of comment

It should be noted that it is incumbent upon the judge to ensure that the accused understands the danger of adverse inference upon failure to testify.[19] In *R v Cowan* the Court of Appeal rehearsed,[20] and recommended, the specimen direction recommended by the Judicial Studies Board.[1] In particular it required the judge to tell the jury that the accused was entitled not to testify, that any adverse inference was not alone sufficient,[2] that the jury must itself determine that the prosecution had established a case to answer irrespective of failure to testify and, perhaps most importantly, that the jury must draw an adverse inference only if after hearing all of the evidence it concluded that 'the silence can only sensibly be attributed to the defendant's having no answer or none that would stand up to cross-examination'.[3] It is significant that in two of the three cases dealt with under *R v Cowan* the appeal was allowed on account of failure to remind the jury of this last factor.[4] This formulation makes it quite clear that the adverse inference is as to the accused's guilt at large, and is in no way limited to disbelief of any particular defence. It was however held in *Murray v DPP* that because of the complexity of issues in a criminal trial, it is necessary to consider the precise impact of the inference separately in respect of each of them in the light of the surrounding evidence.[5] Failure to testify has thus had an adverse effect on a challenge to evidence of identification,[6] an attempt to bolster the credibility of extra-testimonial statements,[7] and a defence based on lack of intent.[8]

It is not yet clear whether the position at common law that adverse comment could be made more than once without necessary impropriety[9] still applies.

3. Impact of human rights legislation[10]

It is worth considering how far the current position is likely to be affected by the incorporation into English law of the provisions of the European Convention of Human

19   Section 35(2). Failure to do so is irrecoverable, *R v Price* [1996] Crim LR 738.
20   At 380G, 944f.
1   No self-direction is required by justices who refrain from drawing an adverse inference: *Radford v Kent County Council* (1998) 162 JP 697.
2   Though the wording of the provision appears not to preclude a conviction based on a combination of pre-trial silence, and refusal to testify.
3   This reflects Lord Mustill's words in *Murray v DPP* [1994] 1 WLR 1, 99 Cr App Rep 396.
4   Though in each of them accompanied by another failure, different in each case.
5   In *R v Cowan* this view is supported by reference to the judgment of Kelly LJ in *R v McLernon* (1990) 10 NIJB 91, at 102 in relation to the comparable provision in Northern Ireland. For general appraisal of the law in Northern Ireland, see Jackson [1995] Crim LR 587.
6   *Elliott v DPP* [1996] CLY 1387.
7   *R v Burnham* [1995] Crim LR 491.
8   *R v Callender* [1998] Crim LR 337.
9   *R v Sparrow* [1973] 2 All ER 129, [1973] 1 WLR 488. But a sense of proportion is required, and appeals have been allowed where the judge commented in *Waugh v R* [1950] AC 203 on the accused's failure to testify on nine separate occasions, and in *R v Berry* [1993] Crim LR 973 on no fewer than twelve.
10   See Munday [1996] Crim LR 370 upon which the editor has relied in this section.

Rights. Although these do not in terms endorse the right to silence, or a privilege against self-incrimination, it has nevertheless been proclaimed in *Murray v United Kingdom*:[11]

> that there can be no doubt that the right to remain silent under police questioning and the privilege against self-incrimination are internationally recognised standards which lie at the heart of the notion of a fair procedure under Article 6.

and that:

> it is self-evident that it is incompatible with the immunities under consideration to base a conviction solely or mainly on the accused's silence or on a refusal to to answer questions or to give evidence himself.

In that case the court refused to condemn the Northern Ireland version of this legislation, largely upon the basis that the accused retained the right to refuse to testify, that the prosecution had to make out a prima facie case otherwise than upon silence, and that the justification for drawing the inferences was made in a reasoned opinion by an experienced judge, itself subject to review. It should also be noted that there was a very strong case against the accused, fully supported by direct oral testimony and convincing real evidence, of the commission of brutal terrorist offences.

It is far from obvious that in a case where silence played a more prominent role,[12] or where a jury trial took place in which the jury's use of adverse inferences was as little susceptible of appeal as the judge's discretion to permit such inference under the abdication from control indicated by the dicta in *R v Friend*[13] that the decision would remain unscathed. It may well prove to be the case that the incorporation of the European Convention of Human Rights will necessitate some reshaping of this area of the law of evidence.

B.   THE ACCUSED WHO DOES GIVE EVIDENCE[14]

In the words of Lord Sankey:[15]

> When Parliament by the Act of 1898 effected a change in the general law and made the prisoner in every case a competent witness, it was in evident difficulty and it pursued the familiar English system of compromise.

If the ordinary rules governing the examination and cross-examination of witnesses were to be applied to the accused without restriction or modification, he would have been unduly favoured in one respect and unduly prejudiced in another. He would have been unduly favoured because he could have claimed the privilege against self-incrimination on the ground that his answer to a question might show that he had committed the crime under investigation. This danger was met by proviso (e) to s 1 of

---

11 (1996) 22 EHRR 29, at 60, citing *Funke v France* (1993) 16 EHRR 297.
12 For example by operating in addition to more than one form of pre-trial silence, perhaps cumulatively constituting a case to answer.
13 See above p 385.
14 The accused cannot insulate his testimony from the intended sanction by refusing to continue to testify after a ruling has been made that the conditions justifying cross-examination about the otherwise prohibited matters have been satisfied. If necessary those matters can then be put in by way of rebuttal: *R v Forbes* (1999) Times, 5 May.
15 *Maxwell v DPP* [1935] AC 309, at 317.

the Act under which he may be asked any question in cross-examination notwithstanding that it would tend to incriminate him as to the offence charged, and it has been held that the proviso applies when one prisoner confines his evidence to statements exculpating his co-accused.

It was thought that the accused would have been unduly prejudiced if he had anything in the nature of a criminal record because he would have been exposed to cross-examination concerning his past misdeeds as a matter affecting his credibility. This danger was met by s 1(f) which is itself a compromise because cross-examination as to credit is neither wholly prohibited nor invariably permitted. Its principal effect is to provide the accused with a shield which is thrown away only if he gives evidence of his good character or casts imputations on the prosecutor or the witnesses for the prosecution. When the shield is thrown away, the accused is liable to be cross-examined on his criminal record and past misdeeds.

Although the accused who gives evidence is technically in the same position as any other witness, subject to the important exceptions made by s 1(e) and s 1(f) of the Act of 1898, it is unrealistic to regard the two positions as substantially similar from the practical point of view. We have already seen that it is difficult, in practice, to discriminate between the use to be made of the answers given by the accused in cross-examination to credit and cross-examination to the issue. The sanctions of the law of perjury may operate quite differently in the case of the accused from the way in which they apply to an ordinary witness. The latter is confronted with the choice of telling the truth or taking the risk of a prosecution for perjury. This risk is bound to appear in a somewhat different light if the choice is to take it or run the risk of conviction for the perhaps more serious offence for which he is on trial.[16] The Court should certainly abstain from stressing the peril of the accused as a reason for disbelieving his testimony.[17] Considerations of this nature have led the judges to be a great deal more solicitous about the propriety of the cross-examination of the accused than that of any other witness.[18] No doubt they have a discretion to disallow questions in each case, but it is most often stressed in relation to the questioning of the prisoner under the Act of 1898.[19] Counsel for the prosecution is repeatedly admonished not to drive the accused into throwing his shield away.[20] Even if this was not, in any sense, the purpose of the cross-examination, it may be held to have been improper because the crucial question is its effect upon the minds of the jury, not the purpose with which it was administered.[1] A further safeguard is provided by the requirement that Crown counsel should obtain the approval of the judge before embarking on cross-examination under s 1(f).[2] So too

16   See (1956) 19 MLR 704.
17   See in Canada, *R v Murray* (1997) 115 CCC (3d) 225; and in Australia, *Robinson v R* (1991) 180 CLR 531; *R v Ellem* (1994) 75 ACR 370 (comment by prosecutor).
18   For a graphic example of unfairness in cross-examination of the accused, see *R v R(AJ)* (1994) 94 CCC (3d) 168.
19   See especially *R v Baldwin* (1925) 18 Cr App Rep 175.
20   *R v Eidinow* (1932) 23 Cr App Rep 145.
1   *R v Ellis* [1910] 2 KB 746; *R v Sugarman* (1935) 25 Cr App Rep 109. Contrast the position in Canada where there is no equivalent of the Criminal Evidence Act 1898, s 1(f), and cross-examination revealing bad character is permitted when its primary relevance goes directly to issue, and shows bad disposition only incidentally, *R v Jackson* (1991) 68 CCC (3d) 385, at 433.
2   *R v McLean* (1926) 19 Cr App Rep 104. Appeals have been allowed on account of improper questioning by the judge (*R v Ratcliffe* (1919) 14 Cr App Rep 95) and counsel for a co-accused (*R v Roberts* [1936] 1 All ER 23) as well as counsel for the prosecution. Under s 399 of the Crimes Act (Victoria), the judge's leave to cross-examine under the equivalent of s 1(f)(ii) must be obtained in the absence of the jury. See also in Canada, *R v Underwood* [1998] 1 SCR 77; in New Zealand, *R v Kino* [1997] 3 NZLR 24.

should counsel for a co-accused,[3] especially if there is any doubt as to the status of the matters to be put to the witness.[4]

Section 1(f) has, however, led to numerous difficulties so far as its construction is concerned, and it is now necessary to consider them.

SECTION 2.   THE INTERPRETATION OF s 1(f)[5]

Section 1 (f) reads as follows:

A person charged and called as a witness in pursuance of this Act shall not be asked, and if asked shall not be required to answer, any question tending to show that he has committed or been convicted of or been charged with any offence other than that wherewith he is then charged, or is of bad character, unless–

(i)   the proof that he has committed or been convicted of such other offence is admissible evidence to show that he is guilty of the offence wherewith he is then charged; or

(ii)   he has personally or by his advocate asked questions of the witnesses for the prosecution with a view to establish his own good character, or has given evidence of his good character, or the nature or conduct of the defence is such as to involve imputations on the character of the prosecutor or the witnesses for the prosecution; or the deceased victim of the alleged crime;[6] or

(iii)   he has given evidence against any other person charged in the same proceedings.[7]

It will be observed that the section begins with a prohibition on four types of question—those tending to show previous charges, those tending to show previous offences,[8] those tending to show previous convictions and those tending to show bad character.[9] Reference is then made to the situations in which such questions are permitted.[10] So far as sub-paras (f)(ii) and (iii) are concerned, the situations must be brought into existence by the accused himself; he must either put his character in issue, or cast imputations on the witnesses for the prosecution or give evidence against someone charged in the same proceedings.[11] No action on the part of the accused is

---

3   *Murdoch v Taylor* [1965] AC 574, at 585, [1965] 1 All ER 406, at 410.

4   *R v McGregor* (1992) 95 Cr App Rep 240 (where a plea of *nolo contendere* had been entered to relevant charges in the United States, and was treated as if it were an admission of guilt).

5   Section 1(f) must be read subject to s 16(2) of the Children and Young Persons Act 1963. Someone aged 21 or more cannot be asked about convictions before he was 14. The proviso must also be read subject to the practice direction of 30 June 1975, made in consequence of the Rehabilitation of Offenders Act 1974: see ch VI, section 2, part A above.

6   The words 'the deceased victim of the alleged crime; or' were added by the Criminal Justice and Public Order Act 1994, s 31.

7   The words 'in the same proceedings' were substituted for 'with the same offence' by the Criminal Evidence Act 1979.

8   In Scotland this has been held not to exclude cross-examination about a previous conviction which is the foundation of the charge, for example in relation to the offence in issue at the trial when perjury is alleged: *Milne v HM Advocate* 1996 SLT 775.

9   Which may extend beyond criminality: *R v Carter* [1997] Crim LR 505.

10   In *R v Kennedy* [1992] Crim LR 37 cross-examination of a co-accused about a previous conviction seems to have been permitted without any reference to the Act

11   So strictly has this been taken in Australia that a conviction has been quashed, and application of the proviso refused, where at the time of cross-examining the requisite conditions had not been met, even though the accused intended to, and then did, conduct his defence in such a way as to satisfy them later: *R v Hayler and Henry* (1988) 39 ACR 374.

necessary to render questions admissible under s 1(f)(i), but the omission from this part of the proviso of any reference to the fact that the accused has been charged with another offence or is of bad character renders it difficult to reconcile some of the decisions with the strict words of the statute.

It will be convenient to begin by considering the construction of the prohibition and then to discuss the situations in which cross-examination is permitted under s 1(f).

A.   THE PROHIBITION

Although the prohibition is absolute in its terms, it does not prevent questions concerning his record being put to the accused in-chief on the comparatively rare occasions when he wishes to testify on that subject. Such words as 'shall not be asked' and 'shall not be required to answer' are considered to be inapplicable to evidence which is tendered voluntarily in-chief.[12] If the accused raises no objection to cross-examination violating the Act at the time he will, in England,[13] not necessarily be assumed to have waived his right.

Problems have been raised with regard to the relation between the prohibition and proviso (e), the meaning of the words 'tending to show', the meaning of the word 'charged' and the relation of the prohibition to the permissions conferred by the rest of s 1(f). These problems were considered by the House of Lords in the leading cases of *Jones v DPP*,[14] *Stirland v DPP*[15] and *Maxwell v DPP*.[16]

I.   The relation of proviso (e) to proviso (f)[17]

According to proviso (e) the accused may be asked any question in cross-examination notwithstanding that it would tend to criminate him as to the offence charged. Its relation to proviso (f) was not discussed before *Jones*'s case, but the two main views on the subject expressed in *Jones*'s case were discernible in the earlier authorities. They may be described as the 'literal' and 'broad' views respectively. According to the literal view, proviso (e) permits questions tending directly to criminate the accused as to the offence charged, while proviso (f) prohibits, subject to exceptions which must be construed literally, questions tending to incriminate the accused indirectly as well as those which simply go to his credit as a witness. This view is supported by *R v Cokar*[18] where cross-examination about a previous charge was held to have infringed the statute although it related to an issue concerning liability, as distinct from credibility. At his trial for breaking and entering with intent to steal, Cokar's defence was that he had entered the house in question for the sake of warmth and in order to sleep. In the course of his cross-examination, he denied that he knew it was no offence to enter a house in order to sleep, and the trial judge allowed counsel for the prosecution to put questions concerning a previous charge of breaking and entering which had resulted in an acquittal. It was probable that the accused had learned, in connection with that charge

12   *Jones v DPP* [1962] AC 635, at 663, [1962] 1 All ER 569, at 575 per Lord Reid.
13   *R v Khan* [1991] Crim LR 51. Cp the position in Scotland *Cordiner v HM Advocate* 1993 SLT 2.
14   [1962] AC 635, [1962] 1 All ER 569.
15   [1944] AC 315, [1944] 2 All ER 13.
16   [1935] AC 309.
17   See McNamara (1983) 9 Adel LR 290.
18   [1960] 2 QB 207, [1960] 2 All ER 175. The literal view is also supported by the tenor of Lord Sankey's speech in *Maxwell*'s case.

that it is not an offence to enter a house in order to go to sleep. He was convicted, and his conviction was quashed by the Court of Criminal Appeal on the ground that the question concerning the previous charge had been wrongly admitted. Section 1(f)(ii) and (iii) did not apply to the case because Cokar had neither put his character in issue, nor cast imputations nor given evidence against a co-accused, while questions concerning charges resulting in anything other than a conviction were held to be outside the purview of s 1(f)(i) from which the word 'charged' is omitted.[19]

According to the broad view, proviso (e) permits questions which tend to criminate the accused as to the offence charged directly or indirectly, and, in cases to which none of the exceptions apply, the prohibition in proviso (f) relates solely to cross-examination to credit. This view is supported by *R v Chitson*[20] and *R v Kurasch*.[1] Chitson was charged with unlawful intercourse with a girl of fourteen. In the course of her evidence in-chief, the prosecutrix stated that he had told her that he had done the same thing to another girl. There was no evidence whether this other girl was beneath or above the age of sixteen at the material time, but it was held by the Court of Criminal Appeal that the prisoner had been properly examined with regard to his relations with her because, although the questions tended to show that he was of bad character, they also tended to incriminate him as to the offence charged; if he had had intercourse with the other girl, that fact would confirm the prosecutrix's statement with regard to what he told her. If the other girl had been under 16 at the material time, the case would have come within s 1(f)(i) because evidence that Chitson had committed another offence would have been admissible in-chief[2] but, if the other girl was over sixteen at the material time, no offence would have been committed against her; nevertheless despite the omission of the words 'bad character' from s (1)(f)(i) the cross-examination was held to be permissible because it was relevant to an issue in the case. In *R v Kurasch*, the appellant was charged with a conspiracy to defraud by means of a mock auction. His defence was that he was merely the servant of the proprietress of the auction room, and a question suggesting that she was his mistress was held by the Court of Criminal Appeal to have been properly put to him in cross-examination simply because it was relevant to the issue. The accused had done nothing to throw his shield away under s 1(f)(ii) or (iii), and, as the question merely tended to show immorality as opposed to the commission or conviction of another offence, the case fell outside the literal words of s 1(f)(i).

2.   The meaning of 'tending to show'—Jones v Director of Public Prosecutions

In *Jones v DPP*[3] a majority of the House of Lords sanctioned a construction of s 1(f) which does much to reduce the practical effect of the difference between the two views concerning the relationship of provisos (e) and (f). Jones was charged with the murder of a Girl Guide. His evidence was an uncorroborated alibi that he had been with a

---

19   This reasoning leads to the perverse result that the cross-examination would have been permissible if the accused had acquired his knowledge in the course of a case in which he had been convicted rather than acquitted.

20   [1909] 2 KB 945. See also *R v Kennaway* [1917] 1 KB 25.

1   [1915] 2 KB 749.

2   Even then a sufficient foundation for the cross-examination should have been laid by the evidence in-chief; cf the treatment of *R v Kennaway* by the majority of the House of Lords in *Jones v DPP*.

3   [1962] AC 635, [1962] 1 All ER 569. The text represents part of an article by Cross in (1962) 78 LQR 407.

prostitute, and he deposed to the details of a conversation he had had with his wife on his return home. It was necessary for him to explain why, before setting up his alibi, he had endeavoured to establish another one which would have been corroborated. He did so by raising in cross-examination of a prosecution witness the question of some previous trouble of his to support the inference that he was afraid that the police would not pay much attention to an uncorroborated alibi. The alibi which Jones ultimately set up bore a striking resemblance to that which he had set up at an earlier trial resulting in his conviction for the rape of another Girl Guide. He was cross-examined with regard to the resemblances between the two alibis and between the conversations with his wife to which he deposed at each trial. Although the terms of the cross-examination did not actually show that he had committed another offence, it was common ground among the members of the House of Lords who heard the appeal that the questions suggested that he was a person of bad character who had previously been suspected of, if not charged with, a serious crime. Jones was convicted, and the propriety of the cross-examination was challenged in the Court of Criminal Appeal. That court held that proviso (f) had not been infringed because the words 'tending to show' mean 'make known to the jury', and the jury had already been made aware of the fact that the accused had previously been in trouble by means of his evidence in-chief.[4] Jones appealed to the House of Lords, and the House was unanimously in favour of dismissing the appeal. Lords Simonds, Reid and Morris did so for the reason given by the Court of Criminal Appeal, but Lords Denning and Devlin expressly disagreed with it. They were in favour of dismissing the appeal on the broader ground that the cross-examination was relevant to the issue of the prisoner's liability because it tended to disprove his alibi; a considerable strain was put on the credulity of the jury when they were asked to believe that identical alibis were true, and that identical conversations took place between Jones and his wife. Lords Simonds, Reid and Morris were of course also of the opinion that the cross-examination was relevant for this reason, but, in their view, that did not of itself suffice to render the questions admissible under the statute. Had Jones not alluded in-chief to his previous trouble, the majority would have allowed the appeal.[5]

The view that 'tending to show' means 'make known' or 'reveal' to the jury for the first time goes a long way towards reducing the practical effect of the difference between the literal and broad views concerning the relation between provisos (e) and (f) of the Criminal Evidence Act 1898, if it applies to cases in which the evidence tending to show bad character has been given by the prosecution.

There is now further authority on the interpretation of these words. In *R v Anderson*[6] the accused was charged, together with a number of others, with various terrorist offences, having been found in possession of apparently incriminating articles such as a gun, false documents, and a large amount of cash. Her explanation, advanced for the first time at her trial, was that she had come from Northern Ireland to escort escaped prisoners on their route to the continent of Europe, and that most of the materials found in her possession were there for that purpose. The prosecution were permitted to ask her in cross-examination whether she was a 'wanted' person in Northern Ireland, their aim being to show that, as such, she would be most unlikely to have been chosen to play the role she professed. They had not adduced the evidence in-chief, because at that time they had had no inkling of the line of defence which made such evidence relevant. The defence argued that s 1(f) prohibited such cross-examination.[7] The trial judge allowed the cross-examination, and the appeal was dismissed upon the basis

---

4   *R v Jones* [1962] AC 635, [1961] 3 All ER 668.
5   Unless they would have been prepared to apply the proviso as it then was.
6   [1988] QB 678, [1988] 2 All ER 549; see (1988) 51 MLR 785.
7   And that it was not permitted by s 1(e) either.

that the nature of the accused's defence had itself revealed the commission of crimes,[8] and that no further prejudice would be occasioned to her by the cross-examination. This was regarded as equivalent to the situation in *Jones* as not tending to show any of the prohibited matters, in the sense of revealing them to the jury for the first time.

It should however be noted that in *Anderson*, in critical distinction from *Jones*, not even the most imperceptive juror could have supposed the accused to be 'wanted' at the relevant time in respect of crimes which had then been undiscovered, or even uncommitted. The decision thus seems to erode the natural meaning of the words of the prohibition still further. Lord Lane CJ consoled himself with the reflection that little damage had been done since the prosecution, having been taken by surprise by the defence, would have been successful in an application to re-open its case so as to call in-chief evidence of the matters in fact put to the accused in cross-examination, and that the course adopted in *Anderson* had done no more than short-circuit the process. It is submitted that this ignores the grave disadvantage to the accused[9] of having such material sprung upon her in cross-examination, without prior argument in the absence of the jury, without the production of a suitable prosecution witness,[10] and by means of leading questions. It was to prevent just such a situation that s 1(f) was enacted in the first place.

In fact it seems that the same result could have been better achieved in *Anderson*, without undue distortion of the wording of the section, by the simple application of s 1(f)(i)'s permission of questions relating to the commission of a crime as showing the accused's guilt.[11]

It has been held elsewhere that nothing further is shown when details of the relevant offences have already been adduced by the accused in attempting to have confessional material excluded at a voir dire,[12] or where they have already been brought before the jury in relation to other charges,[13] or by a special form of pleading.[14] Neither of these situations seems very satisfactory either. In the former it is submitted that the accused should no more be inhibited in the conduct of his defence by fear of the use of such material than of that of confessional material.[15] In the latter the party prejudiced was in no way himself responsible for the prior revelation to the jury.

It cannot be denied that the majority view in *Jones* does diminish the protection apparently bestowed by the natural meaning of the words of the prohibition in s 1(f). Nor, however, can it reasonably be denied that such a reading bestows an anomalous and unjustifiable degree of protection. In particular there seems no reason why the accused should not be exposed to cross-examination on any evidence admitted in chief, whether it consists of evidence of convictions for or commission of crimes,[16] or whether it consists of evidence of charges or of bad character.[17] It would be better for evidence

---

8   Such as illegal possession of firearms, forgery and conspiracy. It should also be noted that here the prosecution justified its cross-examination by 'revelations' of matters different from those charged, not shown to be true, and which the prosecution itself necessarily maintained to be false. I am grateful to Mr David Kell for pointing this out to me.

9   Which had been recognised in *Jones*.

10   Who would then be available for cross-examination by the defence.

11   By rebutting a defence raised by the accused. The court adverted to this justification but while expressing its inclination to accept it, for some reason preferred the justification criticised above.

12   *R v Vuckov and Romeo* (1986) 40 SASR 498.

13   Although the evidence of them had been held insufficient even to raise a case to answer.

14   *Dodds v HM Advocate* 1987 SCCR 678.

15   See above p 167.

16   As permitted by s 1(f)(i) when relevant to guilt

17   Apparently, on the natural interpretation of s 1(f)(i), incapable of being so used.

admitted in chief, and for that available for use in cross-examination to cohere.[18] If similar fact evidence has been admitted in chief, then the accused, if he choose to testify, should be exposed to cross-examination about such matters. If such evidence has not been so adduced, though admissible, then the prosecution should be permitted to re-open its case to adduce it in chief, subject to satisfying the requirements for so re-opening its case. This would give the accused the choice of whether to expose himself to further cross-examination by testifying in denial of such further evidence. If the evidence is inadmissible in chief as similar fact evidence, or if the prosecution is unable to satisfy the conditions for re-opening its case, then the accused should not be exposed to cross-examination in relation to such evidence.

3. The meaning of 'charged'—Stirland v Director of Public Prosecutions

In *Stirland v DPP*[19] the House of Lords decided that the word 'charged' as used in s 1(f) means 'charged in court'. Accordingly, when a prisoner accused of forgery put his character in issue and said that he had never been charged before, it was reasonable to suppose that he was using the word in this sense, and the trial judge should have disallowed questions concerning the suspicions that had been entertained against the accused by one of his employers. Lord Simon LC concluded his speech with six propositions to some of which it will be necessary to refer later. The first summarises the effect of s 1(f). According to the second, the accused may be cross-examined as to any of the evidence he has given in-chief, including statements concerning his good record, with a view to testing his veracity or accuracy or to showing that he is not to be believed on oath.[20] The accused had been questioned before leaving his previous employment and was presumably well aware of the suspicions. Accordingly, he could presumably have been cross-examined on the subject if he had said in-chief that he had never previously been suspected of an offence. Lord Simon's fifth proposition was that it is no disproof of good character that a man has been suspected or accused of a previous crime. Such questions as 'Were you suspected' or 'Were you accused' are inadmissible because they are irrelevant to the issue of character and can be asked only if the accused has sworn expressly to the contrary. When he does this, he may be said to have adopted a particular method of putting his character in issue. According to the sixth proposition, the fact that a question put to the accused is irrelevant is no reason for quashing his conviction, though it should have been disallowed by the judge. If the question is not only irrelevant but is unfair to the accused as being likely to distract the jury from considering the real issues and so lead to a miscarriage of justice, it should be disallowed, and if not disallowed, is a ground on which an appeal against conviction may be based. As there had been no miscarriage of justice, *Stirland*'s appeal was in fact dismissed.

In *R v Smith*[1] on a charge of assault the accused was asked in-chief whether she had ever been convicted of such an offence, and gave a negative response. She was then cross-examined about a pending[2] charge for such an offence. The court held this

---

18   As has been achieved by amendment of the relevant provisions in other jurisdictions.
19   [1944] AC 315, [1944] 2 All ER 13. See also *R v Wadey* (1935) 25 Cr App Rep 104; and *R v Nicoloudis* (1954) 38 Cr App Rep 118.
20   See p 399 below.
1   [1989] Crim LR 900.
2   The Act leaves it unclear whether 'charge' in s 1(f) is limited to adjudicated charges.

to be improper, apparently on the ground of unfairness,[3] and because the question went to the issue rather than to credibility.

4.   The relation of the prohibition to the permission conferred by the rest of s 1(f): Maxwell v Director of Public Prosecutions

When the accused has thrown away the shield provided by the first part of s 1(f), it would be wrong to suppose that he can always be asked questions tending to show that he has committed, been convicted of or charged with other offences or is of bad character, because such questions must be relevant either to his liability[4] or else to his credit.[5] Accordingly, it was decided by the House of Lords in *Maxwell v DPP*[6] that, although a doctor charged with manslaughter by means of an illegal operation gave evidence of his good character, he ought not to have been asked whether a similar charge of which he was acquitted had been made against him in the past. In the instant case, it was impossible to say that the fact that the accused had been acquitted on a previous charge was relevant, or that it tended to destroy his credibility as a witness, and the appeal was allowed. Lord Sankey LC recognised the possibility of circumstances in which the fact of a charge resulting in an acquittal might be elicited. Among the instances he mentioned was that of a man charged with an offence against the person who might be asked whether he had uttered threats against his victim because he was angry with him for having brought an unfounded charge. A further instance is suggested by the later case of *R v Waldman*[7] in which the Court of Criminal Appeal upheld a conviction for receiving stolen goods although the accused, who had put his character in issue, had been asked about a previous acquittal on an earlier charge of receiving. The court appears to have considered that *Maxwell*'s case could be distinguished because the question was addressed to a character witness as well as to *Waldman*, and because the question was linked with one concerning a possibility that a previous acquittal of receiving might be relevant to the accused's guilty knowledge on a subsequent occasion because the previous investigation ought to have stimulated the most careful inquiries in the later transaction, and thus militated against the credibility of statements to the effect that the accused acquired goods cheaply without asking questions about their origin.

It should be emphasised that both *Maxwell v DPP* and *R v Waldman* were concerned with situations in which the shield had been thrown away. When this is not the case, it is extremely doubtful whether the accused could be asked about a previous charge resulting in an acquittal owing to the restricted phraseology of s 1(f)(i).[8]

---

3   The short report makes no reference to s 1(e).
4   Although relevance is required, it is not necessary to show the same preponderance of probative force over prejudicial effect as must be shown to justify admission in chief: see *R v Bracewell* (1978) 68 Cr App Rep 44; the same is true in Canada: *R v Farrant* (1983) 147 DLR (3d) 511.
5   In *R v Cooper* (1985) 18 ACR 1 a new trial had to be ordered for this reason, despite the manifest guilt of the accused.
6   [1935] AC 309.
7   (1934) 24 Cr App Rep 204. *Maxwell*'s case was in fact decided earlier in 1934 although it was not reported in the Appeal Cases.
8   Such cross-examination appears to have been permitted in Tasmania: see *R v Unsworth* [1986] Tas R 173, at 174.

B. THE INTERPRETATION OF s 1(f)(i)[9]

Section 1(f)(i) allows the accused to be questioned about other offences when proof that he has committed or been convicted of them is admissible to show that he is guilty of the offence charged. The subsection makes no reference to questions about charges or about bad character. There is surprisingly little direct authority on its interpretation.[10] The effect of the reasoning of the majority of the House of Lords in *Jones* is to make it clear that when evidence of a previous offence has been adduced in chief, cross-examination of the accused about such offence is permitted, at least to the extent that it reveals no more of the prohibited matters.[11] In that situation the prohibition is inoperative, so there is no need to rely upon this subsection. This reduces its practical effect considerably, and may help to explain the dearth of authority. It does not however deprive it of all effect because the subsection requires the justifying evidence to be 'admissible', not 'to have been admitted', thus leaving open the possibility of cases where no revelation of the otherwise prohibited matter has been made. It was nevertheless said in *Jones* that where cross-examination about such matter is intended, some foundation should normally be laid for it by adducing evidence of the otherwise prohibited matter in chief.[12] The Court of Criminal Appeal regarded such a course as desirable because unless it were taken, if:[13]

> the accused desired to dispute or explain the alleged similarity of circumstances or pattern of the two offences he would thereby be deprived of any opportunity to cross-examine prosecution witnesses and be exposed to the gravely prejudicial effect of suggestive questions to which his negative answer might be of no avail.

This still leaves a residual class of case where the prosecution has a good reason for choosing not to adduce the prohibited matter in chief, perhaps from a desire not to prejudice the accused unnecessarily, or to spare a possible witness,[14] or because the relevance of such evidence becomes apparent only after an unanticipated defence has been raised.

The last of these possibilities was the one which had occurred in *R v Cokar*.[15] It will be recalled that the prosecution were not there permitted to cross-examine the accused about a previous charge of which he had been acquitted in order to show that it was the source of his knowledge of the efficacy of a particular line of defence to a charge of burglary. The reason for this was apparently the omission from s 1(f)(i) of any reference to charges or to bad character. This confirms that natural reading of the subsection as an exception to the prohibition in the enacting part, and not as a condition for lifting the prohibition in its entirety.[16] It also illustrates the absurdity of the result so achieved. It is surely much less likely that a defence will be raised a second time after it has failed,[17]

---

9   See Cross (1960) 76 LQR 537; Tapper in Tapper (ed) *Crime, Proof and Punishment* (1981).
10   Although Wigmore regarded it as the most important part of the section, I Wigmore p 662.
11   This was how the majority in *Jones* justified the decisions in *R v Chitson* [1909] 2 KB 945, 79 LJKB 10 and *R v Kennaway* [1917] 1 KB 25, 12 Cr App Rep 147.
12   [1962] AC 635, [1962] 1 All ER 569, at 668, 578 (Lord Denning), at 685, 589 (Lord Morris).
13   [1962] AC 635, at 646, [1961] 3 All ER 668, at 675.
14   As in *Jones*.
15   [1960] 2 QB 207, [1960] 2 All ER 175, above p 391.
16   The appearance of 'such' in s 1(f)(i) can be justified only upon this basis, though the consequence is that its effect is quite different from that of s 1(f)(ii) and s 1(f)(iii) which must be construed as defining conditions for a total relaxation of the prohibition in the enacting part.
17   Though this did occur in *Jones*.

than after it has succeeded,[18] yet it is only in the former case that the subsection permits cross-examination. The subsection is so badly drafted[19] that the High Court of Australia refused to adopt a literal construction of it.[20]

The provision refers to proof of commissions and of convictions. It will generally be the circumstances of the commission of the crime that are relevant to prove guilt.[1] The reference to convictions may have been included to cater for cross-examination in those cases where proof of a conviction is expressly permitted by statute.[2] As noted by Lord Devlin in *Jones*[3] the inclusion in s 1(f)(i) of 'such' appears to confine its ambit to specified criminality. As he further noted, this reading has nothing whatever to recommend it as a matter of policy. If it is relevant to the issue to show that the accused was in prison on a particular occasion in the past, but unnecessary, and perhaps prejudicial to show what his precise offence was on that occasion, it is hard to see why the prosecution should be forced to be specific.[4]

The purpose of cross-examination of the accused under this subsection is expressed as being 'to show that he is guilty of the offence wherewith he is then charged'. This seems to exclude any suggestion that it could be used simply to discredit the accused, either generally or with regard to some particular part of his testimony. In *Jones* Lord Reid refused to accept a wide reading of 'to show that he is guilty' as including anything tending to convince the jury that he is guilty, however indirect the route.[5] It has, however, been submitted[6] that the suggestion advanced, and not rejected, in *R v Anderson*[7] that it comprehend rebuttal of a defence actually advanced should be accepted. The majority in *Jones* was also explicit in rejecting any general application of the second proposition advanced by Viscount Simon in *Stirland v DPP*[8] permitting cross-examination of the accused as to any statement made by him in chief with a view to 'testing his veracity'. The application of that proposition was confined to cases in which, as in *Stirland*, the accused came within one of the other parts of s 1(f).[9]

C.   THE INTERPRETATION OF s 1(f)(ii)

It will be convenient to divide the discussion of s 1(f)(ii) into two main parts—cases in which the accused puts his character in issue, and those in which the nature or conduct

---

18   As in *Cokar*. See also *R v Cohen* [1938] 3 All ER 380, 26 Cr App Rep 190, where cross-examination showing bad character was held impermissible in accordance with this construction, but where the court appeared to believe cross-examination about previous convictions still more impermissible. Such a view accords much better with common sense than with the drafting of the subsection.

19   See *R v Anderson* [1988] QB 678, at 686, [1988] 2 All ER 549, at 554. A private member's amendment to the original draft of the prohibition in s 1(f) was accepted during the passage of this subsection, see 60 Official Report (4th series) col 712 (30 June 1898), and no consequential amendment to s 1(f)(i) appears to have been proposed.

20   *Attwood v R* (1960) 102 CLR 353. See now Evidence Act (Cwth) 1995, s 104.

1   See Lord Morris in Jones at 687, 590. See also *R v Shepherd* (1980) 71 Cr App Rep 120.

2   See ch VIII section 2 above.

3   At 700, 598.

4   Cf *R v Miller* [1952] 2 All ER 667, 36 Cr App Rep 169.

5   At 663, 575.

6   Above p 394.

7   [1988] QB 678, at 688, [1988] 2 All ER 549, at 556.

8   [1944] AC 315, [1944] 2 All ER 13.

9   Nor may such evidence be admitted to support the credibility of prosecution witnesses unless it is brought under one of the other exceptions: *R v Weekes* [1983] Crim LR 801. For a most helpful discussion, and for some unreported authority allowing cross-examination to credit under s 1(f)(i), see Pattenden [1982] Crim LR 707.

of the defence involves imputations on the character of the prosecutor or one of his witnesses.

1. Character in issue

In order that the first part of the second exception to the prohibition may be brought into play, the court must be satisfied that the accused: 'has personally or by his advocate asked questions of the witnesses for the prosecution with a view to establish his own good character, or has given evidence of his good character'.[10] This clearly excludes cases where the reference to good character is elicited from defence witnesses only as a result of cross-examination by the prosecution.[11] The latter phrase is apt to cover a case in which the prisoner calls a witness to character but does not cross-examine on the subject or allude to it in his own evidence in-chief. It is not sufficient that counsel raises the accused's good character in his opening if nothing falling explicitly under this provision should be elicited or adduced.[12] The exception is not brought into play when a defence witness volunteers a statement concerning the character of the accused which he had not been asked to make;[13] nor is the exception brought into play by the accused's reference to one of his many previous convictions as a ground for fearing the police because it would be wrong to infer that he meant that the occasion of the conviction was the only occasion on which he had previously been in trouble.[14] It may be noted that the exception makes no reference to the consequence of eliciting the accused's good character by cross-examination of a co-accused, or a witness called by him. It is uncertain how far the accused puts his own character in issue by suggesting a favourable contrast with the bad character of others who might have committed the crime. If those others are called as witnesses for the prosecution the matter is governed by the second limb of s 1(f)(ii). If they are not so called it seems to depend upon exactly how pointedly the contrast is made. Thus in *R v Lee*[15] where the accused was charged with theft from a house in which he was lodging it was held not sufficient that he had pointed out that others with criminal records had access to the house. In *R v Bracewell*[16] by contrast it was regarded as sufficient that one of two men accused of murder in the course of a burglary had contrasted his own cool professionalism with the panic-prone inexperience of his companion. A general examination by the accused in the course of his evidence into the circumstances surrounding the alleged crime with a view to establishing innocence does not expose him to cross-examination under s 1(f)(ii).[17] Thus, in *R v Ellis*,[18] a dealer was charged with obtaining cheques from a customer by false pretences concerning the cost price of antiques and he answered questions about his conduct towards the alleged victim with a view to negativing any

10 An attempt to distinguish on a purposive line derived from the difference in the terminology of these two phrases was resisted in *R v Fuller* (1994) 34 NSWLR 233.
11 See *R v Stronach* [1988] Crim LR 48.
12 *R v Ellis* [1910] 2 KB 746. It is also unclear how far the mere repetition in court of words claiming a good character uttered upon arrest (*R v Solomon* (1909) 2 Cr App Rep 80); or a claim made in a letter probably intended to read only in mitigation of sentence (*R v Parker* (1924) 18 Cr App Rep 14) will suffice. See also *Malindi v R* [1967] 1 AC 439, [1966] 3 All ER 285.
13 *R v Redd* [1923] 1 KB 104.
14 *R v Thompson* [1966] 1 All ER 505, [1966] 1 WLR 405 following dicta of Oliver J in *R v Wattam* (1952) 36 Cr App Rep 72, at 78.
15 [1976] 1 All ER 570, [1976] 1 WLR 71.
16 (1978) 68 Cr App Rep 44.
17 Expressed in terms of res gestae in *R v Holman* (1992) Times, 9 September.
18 [1910] 2 KB 746.

intent to defraud. The Court of Criminal Appeal held that he ought not to have been asked questions under s 1(f)(ii) as the evidence had not been given with a view to establishing good character. No doubt it had that tendency, but an assertion of innocence might equally well be said to be tantamount to giving evidence of character. The position is the same if the accused calls witnesses to his business transactions which are in question.[19]

Generally speaking the accused's own evidence of his character takes the form of allusions to his innocent or praiseworthy past, and the decisions certainly do not indicate any great reluctance on the part of the courts to hold that he has put his character in issue by such a reference. A man's allegations concerning his regular attendance at mass,[20] his assertion that he had been earning an honest living for a considerable time,[1] and his affirmative answer to the question whether he is a married man with a family in regular work[2] have been treated as instances in which the shield provided by s 1(f) would be thrown away. There seems to be some doubt whether a reference to honourable discharge from the army would have this effect,[3] and similar uncertainty prevails with regard to the statement by a man charged with traffic offences that he disapproved of speeding.[4] In R v Samuel,[5] the Court of Criminal Appeal did not experience much difficulty in arriving at the conclusion that someone who was charged with larceny by finding put his character in issue when he gave evidence with regard to previous occasions on which he had returned lost property to its owner.

It is necessary to consider the meaning of 'character' as used in s 1(f) in general and the first part of s 1(f)(ii) in particular, the purpose of cross-examination under the exception, the question of the divisibility of the accused's character, and the availability of judicial discretion to disallow cross-examination otherwise allowed by this part.

(i)   The meaning of character

We have seen that, in ordinary language, 'character' may mean either the reputation or the disposition of the person about whom the inquiry is being made, and that, at common law, a character witness might only be asked about the reputation of the accused.[6] The word is used no less than four times in proviso (f) and, in R v Dunkley,[7] a case concerned with imputations against a witness for the prosecution, Lord Hewart CJ said:

> It is not difficult to suppose that a formidable argument might have been raised on the phrasing of this statute, that the character which is spoken of is the character which is so well known in the vocabulary of the criminal law—namely, the general reputation of the person referred to; in other words that 'character' in that context and in every part of it, in the last part no less than in the first, in the third part no less than in the second, bears the meaning which the term 'character' was held to bear, for example, in the case of R v Rowton.[8]

19   R v Stronach [1988] Crim LR 48.
20   R v Ferguson (1909) 2 Cr App Rep 250.
1   R v Baker (1912) 7 Cr App Rep 252.
2   R v Coulman (1927) 20 Cr App Rep 106 per Swift J in the course of the argument.
3   R v Parker (1924) 18 Cr App Rep 14.
4   R v Beecham [1921] 3 KB 464.
5   (1956) 40 Cr App Rep 8. Cp Holman above where it was not enough that the accused explained his possession of the goods in respect of which he was on trial in a similarly innocent way.
6   See p 322 above.
7   [1927] 1 KB 323, at 329. See also Malindi v R [1967] 1 AC 439, [1966] 3 All ER 285.
8   (1865) Le & Ca 520.

Lord Hewart concluded that it was much too late in the day to consider such an argument because it could not prevail without the revision, and, to a great extent, the overthrow of a very long series of decisions. When speaking of the first part of s 1(f)(ii) in *Stirland v DPP*,[9] Lord Simon LC said:

> There is perhaps some vagueness in the use of the term 'good character' in this connection. Does it refer to the good reputation which a man may bear in his own circle, or does it refer to the man's real disposition as distinct from what his friends and neighbours may think of him?

Lord Simon was inclined to think that both conceptions were combined in s 1(f). In *Jones v DPP*,[10] Lord Denning took Lord Hewart's view that it is too late to argue that 'character' as used in the Act of 1898 means 'reputation' and nothing else, but Lord Devlin expressed the opinion that this was the meaning intended by the draftsman of the statute.[11] He also thought that the point was still open at the level of the House of Lords. The effect of such a construction would be revolutionary and difficult to apply. When the accused testifies to his own good character, he must almost inevitably speak of his own good past acts[12] and it would certainly upset past decisions if it were to be held that a man who swore that he had led a good clean life and gone to mass every Sunday had not 'given evidence of his own good character'. If, throughout the entirety of s 1(f) 'character' were to mean 'reputation', it would be difficult to construe that part of s 1(f)(ii) under which the accused loses his shield if the nature or conduct of his defence involves imputations on the 'character of the prosecutor or the witnesses for the prosecution'. It would then become possible to argue that someone who swore that a policeman had extracted a confession from him by violence was not casting imputations on the character of a witness for the prosecution.

It was just such an argument that was rejected by the House of Lords in *Selvey v DPP*,[13] a case turning on the construction of the second part of s 1(f)(ii), in which someone accused of buggery alleged that the prosecutor had offered to go on the bed with him for a pound, told him that he had already gone on the bed for that sum with another man, and, because his offer was rejected, dumped indecent photographs in the accused's room out of pique. It may therefore now be taken to be settled law that 'character' when used in the Act of 1898 means both disposition and reputation.

(ii)   The purpose of cross-examination under the first half of s 1(f)(ii)[14]

There are three possible purposes for such cross-examination. It could be used simply to rebut the good character claimed by the accused; it could be used to discredit the accused so that his testimony should not be believed; or it could be used to go directly to the issue and to show that the accused is guilty as charged.

---

9   [1944] AC 315, at 324, [1944] 2 All ER 13, at 17.
10   [1962] AC 635, at 671, [1962] 1 All ER 569, at 580.
11   [1962] AC 635, at 699, [1962] 1 All ER 569, at 604.
12   See per Lord Denning in *Plato Films Ltd v Speidel* [1961] AC 1090, at 1143: 'The plaintiff cannot speak as to his own character and reputation because he does not know what other people think of him, or at any rate he cannot give evidence as to what they think of him.' Lord Devlin considered the word 'character' to mean 'reputation' throughout the law of evidence (see *Dingle v Associated Newspapers Ltd* [1961] 2 QB 162, at 195 and 198; see also Fridman in (1962) 1 Sol Q 211).
13   [1970] AC 304, [1968] 2 All ER 497.
14   See Pattenden [1982] Crim LR 707.

The first of these interpretations was rejected in *R v Richardson* and *R v Longman* where Edmund Davies LJ both summarised the argument, and gave the answer of the Court of Appeal:[15]

> it is contended ... that evidence of bad character can do no more than rebut or cancel out the evidence of good character and the jury must be instructed not to be influenced by the evidence of bad character in general assessment of the accused's credibility. We do not think that this is the general practice, and we have the gravest doubts whether a jury could be expected to understand such a direction, which verges on the metaphysical ... In our view, evidence of character, when properly admitted, goes to the credibility of the witness concerned, whether the evidence discloses good character or bad character. If the accused calls evidence of good character and is shown by cross-examination to have a bad character, the jury may give this fact such weight as they think fit when assessing the *general* credibility of the accused. They cannot be expected to execute the metaphysical feat of treating the evidence as relevant to credibility on one issue, but irrelevant on another, and they are not required to do so.

This passage shows that such evidence goes to the credibility of the accused. In some cases it is incapable of doing more. Thus in *R v Wood*[16] the evidence was of conviction for a subsequent offence, and was accepted as showing the bad character of the accused, not at the time of the commission of the offence with which he was charged, but at the time of his trial for it. Similarly in *R v Winfield*[17] the evidence was of convictions for offences totally dissimilar from those with which the accused was charged. In most cases however the evidence is also capable of showing the accused's guilt of the offence charged. It has already been seen that rebuttal of the accused's good character before 1898 must necessarily have gone to show his guilt.[18] It is also well-established that after 1898 possession of a good character is not relevant only to credibility, but also goes directly to the issue of guilt or innocence.[19] It might thus be supposed that refutation of it by cross-examination to bad character would also go to the same issue, and it is possible so to construe some remarks of Lord Sankey in *Maxwell v DPP*:[20]

> if the prisoner by himself or his witness seeks to give evidence of his own good character, for the purpose of showing that it is unlikely that he committed the offence charged, he raises by way of defence an issue as to his good character so that he may fairly be cross-examined on that issue just as any witness called by him as to his good character may be cross-examined to show the contrary.

There appear to be no reported cases in which cross-examination under this part of s 1(f)(ii) has been accepted as unequivocally going to the issue of guilt or innocence. The nearest approach to such acceptance is exhibited by the judgment of Lord Goddard CJ in *R v Samuel*[1] where it was explained that in the case of the accused the distinction between cross-examination to credit and issue is rather illusory, but even then it was accepted that technically the cross-examination ought to be regarded as going to credit.

---

15   [1969] 1 QB 299, at 311, [1968] 2 All ER 761, at 767, emphasis in original.
16   [1920] 2 KB 179, 14 Cr App Rep 149.
17   [1939] 4 All ER 164, 27 Cr App Rep 139.
18   See above ch VII, section 3, part B(1).
19   *R v Bellis* [1966] 1 All ER 552 n, [1966] 1 WLR 234; *R v Bryant, R v Oxley* [1979] QB 108, at 119, [1978] 2 All ER 689, at 696.
20   [1935] AC 309, at 319, 24 Cr App Rep 152, at 171.
1   (1956) 40 Cr App Rep 8, at 12. But see in Australia *R v Chinmaya* (1994) 73 ACR 316.

Another case which is very close to the line, if not over it, is *R v Marsh*[2] where the evidence of good character was simply the absence of convictions for violence,[3] but when the judge proposed to allow cross-examination on the accused's disciplinary record for violence so as not to mislead the jury about the accused's true disposition, reliance upon the absence of convictions was withdrawn by the defence, so the issue remained moot. The view that cross-examination under this part cannot go directly to the issue of guilt or innocence is supported by another part of Lord Sankey's speech in *Maxwell* where he said:[4]

> the question whether a man has been convicted, charged or acquitted, even if it goes to credibility, ought not to be admitted if there is any risk of the jury being misled into thinking that it goes not to credibility but to the probability of his having committed the offence with which he is charged.

This view has also been taken by the High Court of Australia,[5] is in accordance with the best recent view of the purpose of cross-examination under the second limb of s 1(f)(ii),[6] and accords with the general principle that the prosecution should not be allowed to reveal the bad character of the accused to the jury unless they can demonstrate that its probative force is likely to exceed its prejudicial effect, and that this should normally be done by seeking to lead such evidence in chief, rather than to elicit it in cross-examination without first having laid a foundation.

(iii)   The divisibility of the character of the accused

When the prisoner urges that he ought to be believed when he swears that he was innocent of a sexual crime because he has a good character for sexual morality, it certainly does tend to refute his contention to show that he was convicted of an indecent assault; but it is open to question whether a conviction for theft has the same effect. This raises the issue of the propriety of a dictum in *R v Winfield* on the assumption that the accused was cross-examined about his character. According to this dictum: 'there is no such thing known to our procedure as putting half a prisoner's character in issue and leaving out the other half'.[7] It will be recollected that Winfield was convicted of indecent assault upon a woman and that he called a witness to speak of his good behaviour with ladies. He had previously been convicted of larceny, and it is not clear whether this conviction was put to his character witness, in which case the matter fell to be determined by the common law principles that have already been discussed, or whether the cross-examination concerning the conviction was of Winfield himself under s 1(f)(ii) of the Act of 1898. In either event, the Court of Criminal Appeal appears to have approved of the cross-examination, although their observations on the subject were obiter dicta because the conviction was quashed on account of the inadequacy of the direction to the jury on the subject of corroboration. So far as the cross-examination of the prisoner

2   [1994] Crim LR 52.
3   In *R v Buzalek and Schiffer* [1991] Crim LR 116 some doubt was expressed whether this was sufficient evidence of good character to trigger the normal two part direction: see above p 321.
4   [1935] AC 309, at 321, 24 Cr App Rep 152, at 173. See also *R v Smith* [1989] Crim LR 900.
5   *Donnini v R* (1972) 128 CLR 114, at 123; *Matusevich v R* (1977) 137 CLR 633, at 659; see also *R v Beech* (1978) 20 SASR 410, at 420; *Maiden and Petty v R* (1991) 173 CLR 95.
6   See *R v Watts* [1983] 3 All ER 101, 77 Cr App Rep 126, and below p 412.
7   (1939) 27 Cr App Rep 139. *Winfield's* case is discussed from the point of view of the Criminal Evidence Act 1898, by Gooderson in 11 CLJ 386. The case is considered above, p 324, from the point of view of the cross-examination of a character witness at common law.

was concerned, it ought not to have been used by the jury as a direct means of establishing his guilt, because it was relevant only on the very doubtful footing that a thief is more likely to commit an indecent assault than an honest man. Its relevance to the credibility of the prisoner's testimony is not much greater, although there is a little more force in the argument that a convicted thief is more likely to lie than others.

Viewed as a matter affecting credibility, however, Winfield's cross-examination can be justified on the footing that having put his character in issue, he forfeited his right to be treated, as regards cross-examination, otherwise than as an ordinary witness, and an ordinary witness may be cross-examined about a conviction for any offence. The law on this subject may not be beyond reproach, but it is the outcome of the view that cross-examination about a conviction for any offence is permissible under s 6 of the Criminal Procedure Act 1865,[8] and has nothing to do with the Criminal Evidence Act 1898. Lord Simon's third proposition in *Stirland*'s case[9] was:

> An accused who 'puts his character in issue' must be regarded as putting the whole of his past record in issue. He cannot assert his good conduct in certain respects without exposing himself to inquiry about the rest of his record so far as this tends to disprove a claim to good character.

R v Winfield was cited, and it remains to be seen whether this will be held tantamount to House of Lords' approval of the course that was adopted in that case.

(iv)   Discretion to disallow questioning

Most of the learning about the judicial discretion to prevent cross-examination under s 1(f)(ii) relates to the second limb as will be seen below. The need to avoid prejudice also arises in this connection, often to an even more acute extent[10] when the evidence of good character is of the vaguest character, and the cross-examination will go to the detail of offences, sometimes very similar in character to those with which the accused has been charged.[11] The application of the discretion should be considered when a particular piece of evidence, capable of being construed as a claim to a better character than is wholly justified, is adduced to explain a special feature of the prosecution case.

2.   Imputations on the character of the prosecutor or the witnesses for the prosecution[12]

It is clear that a strictly literal construction of s 1(f)(ii) would be unfavourable to the accused because it would mean that, in many cases, a plea of not guilty coupled with an assertion of innocence in the witness box would render the accused liable to cross-examination on his criminal record, on account of the tacit suggestion that the prosecutor or one of his witnesses had been guilty of perjury. First the ways in which the application

---

8   See p 304 above. See also *R v Morris* (1959) 43 Cr App Rep 206 (cross-examination on conviction for dishonesty permitted by imputation of immorality against prosecution witnesses on charge of incest).

9   [1944] AC 315, at 324, [1944] 2 All ER 13, at 18.

10   Although it was suggested in *R v Marsh* [1994] Crim LR 52 that the discretion would be exercised more readily under the second limb.

11   As in *R v Davison-Jenkins* [1997] Crim LR 816.

12   See articles in (1961) Crim LR 142 and 213, and 29 MLR 492. See also Munday (1985) CLJ 62.

of the limb has been defined by the interpretation of the concepts of prosecutor and witness for the prosecution, and of imputation will be considered. It will be shown how attempts to resolve a somewhat uneasy conflict of authority have involved invocation of the court's exclusionary discretion before going on to discuss the rationale of the later part of s 1(f)(ii), and the purpose of the cross-examination which it permits.

(i)   Scope

Questions have arisen both as to the identity of the prosecutor, and what amounts to a witness for the Crown. It seems that an attack upon the conduct of a magistrate, or police officer not called as a witness for the Crown, does not relate to the prosecutor for these purposes.[13] At common law it was held that an attack upon the character of a deceased victim of the crime charged[14] was also insufficient.[15] This latter situation was however reversed by s 31 of the Criminal Justice and Public Order Act 1994.[16]

It is becoming increasingly common for the prosecution to adduce hearsay, especially under the provisions of the Criminal Justice Act 1988. It was held in *R v Miller*[17] that the term 'witness' is for this purpose to be given an expansive meaning, including the authors of hearsay statements, makers of depositions, and makers of statements under s 9 of the Criminal Justice Act 1967. In effect the word is used in its lay sense of one who has information to provide about an event, often one of which he has first hand knowledge, rather than in its more technical sense of one who testifies to it, and is available for cross-examination. In part this reflects a policy of reducing the incentive to dissuade witnesses from testifying, by removing a possible advantage of so doing.

(ii)   Imputations

It is not possible to lay down any clear definition of what amounts to an imputation since so much necessarily depends upon the detailed facts of particular cases.[18] Some general guidance may be furnished by the following examples. A mere denial of guilt, even one couched in emphatic language, is not necessarily an imputation upon the prosecutor;[19] nor is an allegation of relatively venial misconduct, such as drunkeness or swearing.[20] It is not however necessary that the allegation be of the commission of a criminal offence, immorality may be sufficient.[1] It may be enough that the allegation

---

13   *R v Westfall* (1912) 7 Cr App Rep 176.
14   Any crime where the victim has died before trial; it is not limited to charges of his homicide.
15   *R v Biggin* [1920] 1 KB 213. See also in Scotland, *HM Advocate v Grudins* 1976 SLT (Notes) 10.
16   See Munday (1995) 145 NLJ 855, 895.
17   [1997] 2 Cr App Rep 178. See Munday (1997) 161 JP 379. The Law Commission recommended this solution in Law Com No 141, para 12.80, rec 34.
18   In *R v Stanton* [1994] Crim LR 834 on a charge of robbery the court was careful to distinguish between an allegation that the victim might have miscalculated the amount of money in his possession before the attack, and an allegation that the victim was the initiator of the violence.
19   *Selvey v DPP* [1970] AC 304, [1968] 2 All ER 497, Viscount Dilhorne's fourth proposition; *R v Lasseur* [1991] Crim LR 53.
20   *R v McLean* [1978] Crim LR 430, the court was quite explicit that the decision had nothing to do with discretion.
1   *R v Jenkins* (1945) 31 Cr App Rep 1 (woman's heterosexual immorality); *R v Bishop* [1975] QB 274, [1974] 2 All ER 1206, (man's homosexual immorality).

is elicited only as a result of cross-examination by the prosecution,[2] or that it goes beyond a limited admission of bad character by the prosecution witness in question,[3] or that it raises no issue extrinsic to the evidence which has been given by the witness in question.[4] It is immaterial whether the matter alleged is accepted to be true, as it normally will be when previous convictions are alleged; or is denied, as it usually will be when improper conduct is alleged. In *R v Wainwright*[5] the relevant bad character of the deceased victim was put before the court as part of a statement agreed between prosecution and defence. In that case also the incremental effect of the cross-examination objected to was small since the fact that the killing was of one prisoner by another revealed the accused's criminality, and no objection was made to cross-examination about offences of dishonesty, as opposed to the one for violence. A common situation is one in which the accused challenges the circumstances surrounding a purported confession put in evidence by a police witness for the prosecution. The problem is here most acute. The accused with a long criminal record has a double dilemma. He is likely to be at risk if he chooses to challenge the confession without himself giving evidence.[6] If he does choose to testify, he is then confronted with a choice between failing to contest an alleged confession which might well prove fatal to any chance of an acquittal,[7] and contesting it, with the result of letting in evidence of his previous record, which is likely to prove equally fatal.[8] It is clear that any allegation of gross misconduct by a police witness in securing a confession,[9] or of concocting one,[10] or in alleging failure to mention facts subsequently relied upon in the defence,[11] will amount to an imputation. Attempts have been made to alleviate the harshness of this result by suggesting that this conclusion can be avoided if there is no more than a conflict of testimony between the accused and a single police witness about the making of a confession,[12] or if the suggestion is not made explicitly, but merely left as a matter of inference.[13] The most recent decisions reject both lines of argument.[14] The simple truth of the matter is that, in the absence of any plausible explanation by way of mistake or misunderstanding,[15] it is an imputation upon the character of a witness for the

2   *R v Rappolt* (1911) 6 Cr App Rep 156; *R v Courtney* [1995] Crim LR 63 (where the imputation was also among the more venial to have allowed attack). But see *R v Jones* (1909) 3 Cr App Rep 67; *R v Stratton* (1909) 3 Cr App Rep 255; *R v Eidinow* (1932) 23 Cr App Rep 145.
3   *R v Cohen* (1914) 10 Cr App Rep 91. But see *R v Watson* (1913) 8 Cr App Rep 249.
4   *R v Marshall* (1899) 63 JP 36.
5   [1998] Crim LR 665.
6   Such a practice attracts strong judicial disapproval, see *R v O'Neill, R v Ackers* (1950) 34 Cr App Rep 108, at 111; *R v Callaghan* (1979) 69 Cr App Rep 88, at 91.
7   Research conducted on behalf of the Royal Commission on Criminal Procedure by Baldwin and McConville revealed that, overall, fewer than five per cent of those alleged to have made a written confession, and fewer than 10 per cent of those alleged to have made an oral confession, were acquitted after a trial in the Crown Court 'Confessions in Crown Court Trials' (1980) Research Study No 5, Table 3.2; similar results were found by Vennard in relation to summary trials, 'Contested Trials in Magistrates' Courts' (1980) Research Study No 6, Table 3.1.
8   [1973] Crim LR 208; McCabe and Purves *The Jury at Work* (1972) Table 4; Doob and Kirshenbaum (1972) 15 Crim LQ 88. Doubts were, however, expressed by the Supreme Court of Canada about the conclusiveness of these studies in *Corbett v R* [1988] 1 SCR 670.
9   *R v Cook* [1959] 2 QB 340, [1959] 2 All ER 97.
10   *R v Clark* [1955] 2 QB 469, [1955] 3 All ER 29.
11   *R v Showers* [1996] Crim LR 739.
12   Wolchover [1981] Crim LR 312, attempting to reconcile the decisions in *R v Tanner* (1977) 66 Cr App Rep 56 and *R v Nelson* (1978) 68 Cr App Rep 12.
13   Cohen [1981] Crim LR 523. In *Tanner* the judge intervened to make the suggestion explicit, as he did in his ruling in *R v Britzman, R v Hall* [1983] 1 All ER 369, [1983] 1 WLR 350.
14   *Britzman* above; *R v Owen* (1985) 83 Cr App Rep 100, at 104.
15   Though a court is likely to construe these concepts fairly broadly in order to prevent every conflict of evidence from entitling the prosecution to cross-examine so as to reveal the accused's record: see *R v St Louis and Fitzroy Case* (1984) 79 Cr App Rep 53; *R v Goodwin* (1993) Times, 26 November (denial of knowledge of presence of item found on premises by police).

prosecution to allege that he has either coerced or concocted the confession to which he has testified. Courts will nevertheless seek to allow some leeway to counsel in cross-examining even where there is no real possibility of mistake or misunderstanding, especially when the accused's record is particularly damaging.[16]

(iii) Reading words into s 1(f)(ii)

It is often said that s 1(f) is to be construed literally. If so, it should be noted that the second limb of 1(f)(ii) requires that the questions be 'such as to' involve imputations, and by contrast with the formulation of the first limb not necessarily 'with a view to' doing so. This suggests that an unintended imputation should be enough to forfeit protection. Such a view was not accepted before the development of discretion as a form of longstop protection.[17] It now seems that this limb is to be read literally, and that discretion should be used to mitigate its effects.[18] It may also be noted that this limb mentions both the nature and the conduct of the defence, though it is rare for any explanation of the difference between them to be advanced.[19] Closely akin to the questions of what does or does not amount to an 'imputation' is the question whether it can be said that the accused is exposed to cross-examination concerning his record only when the nature or conduct of the defence is such as to involve 'unnecessary' or 'unjustifiable' imputations upon the character of the prosecutor or the witnesses for the prosecution. If the answer is in the negative, the prisoner who alleges that it was not he, but a Crown witness, who committed the crime charged, that the prosecutrix who asserts his guilt of rape was a consenting party to acts of immorality or that the man he assaulted was the aggressor will be unable to develop his defence without throwing his shield away. After an early tendency to answer the question in the affirmative,[20] an emphatic negative was the reply of a full Court of Criminal Appeal in *R v Hudson*,[1] a prosecution for larceny to which the defence was that the crime had been committed by a Crown witness. Soon after *Hudson*'s case, however, it came to be recognised that the court has a discretion to prohibit cross-examination under s 1(f)(ii) although it is permissible as a matter of law.[2]

In *R v Turner*[3] the Court of Criminal Appeal decided, on the strength of the preponderance of earlier authority, that allegations by someone accused of rape that the prosecutrix had not merely consented to intercourse but had also been guilty of gross indecency as a preliminary, did not, as a matter of law, deprive him of his shield, the case being one in which: 'some limitation must be placed on the words of the section since to decide otherwise would be to do grave injustice never intended by Parliament.' With this exception, the difficulties mentioned in the last paragraph have been met, in so far as they have been met at all,[4] by the exercise of the court's discretion. In *Selvey*

---

16 *R v Wignall* [1993] Crim LR 62 (though there the allegation that the witness had embroidered her evidence did seem clearly to fall into the imputation category); *R v Desmond* [1999] Crim LR 313.

17 *R v Preston* [1909] 1 KB 568, 2 Cr App Rep 24.

18 *R v Watts* [1983] 3 All ER 101, 77 Cr App Rep 126.

19 Some attempt was made in *O'Hara v HM Advocate* 1948 JC 90.

20 *R v Bridgwater* [1905] 1 KB 131; *R v Preston* [1909] 1 KB 568.

1 [1912] 2 KB 464. Decisions to the same effect are *R v Cohen* (1914) 10 Cr App Rep 91; *R v Jenkins* (1945) 31 Cr App Rep 1; *R v Sargvon* (1967) 51 Cr App Rep 394; and *R v Bishop* (above). See also *Kerwood v R* (1944) 69 CLR 561; *Dawson v R* (1961) 106 CLR 1.

2 *R v Watson* (1913) 8 Cr App Rep 249; *R v Cook* [1959] 2 QB 340, [1959] 2 All ER 97.

3 [1944] KB 463, [1944] 1 All ER 599.

4 See *R v Brown* (1960) 44 Cr App Rep 181, for a case of self-defence in which they were hardly met.

v DPP[5] the House of Lords reviewed the authorities on the second half of s 1(f)(ii). According to Lord Dilhorne they establish the following propositions:[6]

(a)   the words of the statute must be given their ordinary natural meaning;

(b)   the section permits cross-examination of the accused as to character both when imputations on the character of the prosecutor and his witnesses are cast to show their unreliability as witnesses independently of the evidence given by them and also when the casting of imputations is necessary to enable the accused to establish his defence;

(c)   in rape cases the accused can allege consent without placing himself in peril of cross-examination;

(d)   if what is said amounts in reality to no more than a denial of the charge, expressed, it may be, in emphatic language, it should not be regarded as coming within the section.

The rape cases may be treated either as sui generis[7] or else explained on the ground that the defence of consent is nothing more than a denial by the accused that the prosecution has established one of the essential ingredients of the charge.[8] There is certainly no disposition on the part of the courts to extend the scope of these decisions. In *R v Lasseur*[9] an attempt to use them to extend to any case where the imputation arose in denial of an essential element of the prosecution case was rejected.

(iv)   The discretion of the court and the duty to warn

In *Selvey*'s case the House of Lords confirmed, after full argument, the existence of a judicial discretion to prohibit cross-examination despite its justification as a matter of law by the terms of s 1(f)(ii);[10] but the House denied the existence of a general rule that the discretion should be exercised in favour of the accused when the proper development of his defence necessitates the casting of imputations on the prosecutor or his witnesses.[11] In *R v Britzman, R v Hall*[12] the Court of Appeal suggested guidelines for the application of this discretion. These were that it should be exercised in favour of the defence if the imputation amounted to no more than a denial of a single act or short series of acts relating to a single incident or interview, though not where the denial was of everything occurring over an extended period; that allowance should be made for the strain imposed by cross-examination of the accused, and too much weight should not be placed upon the phraseology of particular answers; and that the discretion should normally be exercised in favour of the defence when the evidence against him was overwhelming. If the accused's record is particularly bad, the court will be likely to exercise its discretion against allowing cross-examination unless a particularly serious attack has been made.[13] It cannot be pretended that such guidelines offer very

---

5   [1970] AC 304.
6   At 339. See *R v Nelson* (1978) 68 Cr App Rep 12, applying propositions 2 and 4 (b and d).
7   *R v Cook* [1959] 2 QB 340, at 347.
8   *R v Turner* [1944] KB 463, at 469.
9   [1991] Crim LR 53.
10   In New Zealand where the discretion is formally open ended it is construed as if it were appended to the English statute: see *R v Potter* [1984] 2 NZLR 374; *R v Kalo* [1985] 1 NZLR 219. A similar discretion is applied in Canada where the statute is of much broader scope: see *Corbett v R* [1988] 1 SCR 670.
11   As had been suggested in *R v Flynn* [1963] 1 QB 729, [1961] 3 All ER 58.
12   [1983] 1 All ER 369, at 374, [1983] 1 WLR 350, at 355.
13   *R v Taylor: R v Goodman* [1999] Crim LR 407.

substantial protection.[14] The fact that the existence of the discretion was not recognised in the early days of the Criminal Evidence Act is a matter to be borne in mind when the early decisions are under consideration; it is possible that some of them should now be treated as cases in which there was an imputation although the judge would have been justified in prohibiting cross-examination in the exercise of his discretion, had he known that he possessed such a thing. Even now, in cases in which the judge does not apply his mind to the question of discretion, the Court of Appeal may exercise its own discretion.[15] It may also uphold the judge's decision to allow cross-examination on a different ground from that upon which he relied.[16]

In *R v Cook*,[17] the Court of Criminal Appeal stressed the importance of giving some sort of warning to the defence that it was going too far. It was said that it has always been the practice for prosecuting counsel to indicate in advance that he is going to claim his rights, or for the judge to give the defence a caution. This is especially needful when the prisoner is unrepresented,[18] but can be regarded as giving the accused the best of both worlds when he is represented by counsel,[19] and is ultimately within the discretion of the trial judge.[20]

(v)   The rationale of the second half of s 1(f)(ii)

The rationale of this part of s 1(f)(ii) was stated in the following passage in a judgment of Channell J:[1]

> If the defence is so conducted, or the nature of the defence is such, as to involve the proposition that the jury ought not to believe the prosecutor or one of the witnesses for the prosecution upon the ground that his conduct—not his evidence in the case, but his conduct outside the evidence given by him—makes him an unreliable witness, then the jury ought also to know the character of the prisoner who either gives that evidence or makes that charge, and it then becomes admissible to cross-examine the prisoner about his antecedents and character with the view of showing that he has such a bad character that the jury ought not to rely upon his evidence.

In other words, it was seen as a case of tit for tat.[2] This view appears to ignore the significant disparity of effect between making prejudical imputations upon a mere witness and upon the accused, and to overlook the disparity created between the position of the prosecution which can cast imputations upon the defence witnesses as much as it likes, while the defence is severely inhibited in casting exactly the same

---

14   *R v Showers* [1996] Crim LR 739 is a rare recent case in which failure to exercise the discretion so as to exclude was overturned, there on the basis that extrinsic speculation upon the cost implications of the decision were taken into account, when they should not have been.
15   *R v Miller* [1997] 2 Cr App Rep 178.
16   *R v Clark* [1955] 2 QB 469, at 473.
17   Above.
18   For the appropriate procedure at a summary trial see *R v Weston-Super-Mare Justices, ex p Townsend* [1968] 3 All ER 225n.
19   See *R v Brown* (1960) 44 Cr App Rep 181; *R v McGee and Cassidy* (1979) 70 Cr App Rep 247.
20   *R v Stanton* [1994] Crim LR 834.
1   *R v Preston* [1909] 1 KB 568, at 575. See also per Singleton J in *R v Jenkins* (1945) 31 Cr App Rep 1, at 14–15: 'It is only fair that the jury should have material to enable them to determine whether to believe the accused or the prosecution'.
2   This policy has been held in Canada not to infringe the Canadian Charter of Rights and Freedoms, *Corbett v R* [1988] 1 SCR 670.

imputations upon prosecution witnesses, for fear of prejudice to the more highly vulnerable position of the accused. This rationale seems popular among trial judges, and there are numerous examples of the judge himself taking the initiative and requiring the accused's record to be put to him over the objections of prosecuting counsel.[3]

(vi)   Purpose of the cross-examination allowed by the second half of s 1(f)(ii)[4]

Such a rationale means that cross-examination under this limb of s 1(f)(ii) is directed to the credibility of the accused. There is room for difference of opinion as to whether it merely goes to the credibility of his imputation upon the prosecutor,[5] or more generally to the credibility of the whole of his testimony.[6] In some cases the sequence of events determines that the cross-examination is capable of going only to credibility.[7] More often it is logically capable of going also to the issue of guilt or innocence.

The extent to which questions indicating commission of similar offences may be put, the extent to which the underlying facts may be brought out, and the operation of the judge's discretion to exclude such lines of questioning have been considered in a number of recent cases, culminating in R v McLeod.[8] That case explicitly concerned the first two of the considerations mentioned above, and endorsed dicta in R v Burke[9] on the third.[10]

Heavy reliance has been placed upon the practice of the trial judge[11] in Selvey v DPP,[12] and on its effective acceptance by the House of Lords in its concentration on the issue of discretion. In Selvey the trial judge had directed cross-examination to be restricted to previous convictions for similar offences, and allowed sufficient exploration of the underlying facts as to reveal the ages of the victims of the accused's sexual attentions. Some subsequent cases[13] which disallowed cross-examination about incidents closely similar to the subject matter of the trial were discounted largely because Selvey was not cited. It is not easy to square this approach with Lord Sankey's remarks in Maxwell v DPP:[14]

> the question whether a man has been convicted, charged or acquitted, even if it goes to credibility, ought not to be admitted if there is any risk of the jury being misled into thinking that it goes not to credibility but to the probability of his having committed the offence with which he is charged.

3   The House of Lords in Selvey v DPP [1970] AC 304, [1968] 2 All ER 497 expressed no disapproval of such a course by the trial judge there; recently approved in R v Chinn [1996] Crim LR 729.
4   See Pattenden [1982] Crim LR 707.
5   As suggested by the formulation in R v Cook [1959] 2 QB 340, at 348, [1959] 2 All ER 97, at 101.
6   As suggested by the formulation in Preston quoted in the text
7   As in R v Coltress (1978) 68 Cr App Rep 193.
8   [1994] 3 All ER 254, [1994] 1 WLR 1500.
9   (1986) 82 Cr App Rep 156, at 161, as supplemented by R v Owen (1986) 83 Cr App Rep 100, at 105.
10   Though the numbered propositions in McLeod appear to range wider than the nature of the questions which may properly be put, and overlap with the considerations which should influence the judge's discretion.
11   Who was the instigator of the cross-examination as to record.
12   [1970] AC 304, [1968] 2 All ER 497.
13   R v Vickers [1972] Crim LR 101; R v France and France [1979] Crim LR 48; R v Duncalf [1979] 2 All ER 1116, [1979] 1 WLR 918; R v Watts [1983] 3 All ER 101; R v John and Braithwaite (24 November 1983, unreported).
14   [1935] AC 309, at 321, 24 Cr App Rep 152, at 173. No serious consideration was given to this aspect of Maxwell in Selvey.

The justification advanced both in *Selvey* and *McLeod* was that the jury should know the character of the person making the imputations. The dilemma is that such a formulation leaves it unclear whether the imputation is to be rejected because in this particular sort of situation the accused has a record of lying, or perhaps special reasons for lying; or that he is in general dishonest, and likely to lie in any difficult situation. It is sharpened by the qualification stressed in *McLeod* that the primary purpose of the cross-examination must relate to the credibility of the accused, and thus go only indirectly to his guilt, rather than to his disposition to commit the sort of crime in question, and go to his guilt more directly.[15] This pulls the horns of the dilemma apart. If the first sort of credibility is in question then the closer the facts of the earlier case, the more likely the accused's credit is to be affected, and the more readily the cross-examination should be allowed; while if the second sort of credibility is in question, then the more distant the facts the less likely that the jury will be to be distracted into a prejudicial consideration of the accused's disposition. Thus in *McLeod* itself the accused was charged with a violent robbery one of the features of which was the movement of a stolen van for use as 'the attack vehicle', and raised a defence of alibi alleging concoction of a confession by the police. It was accepted that this line of defence would trigger this limb of s 1(f)(ii), and to minimise its impact the accused's own counsel asked briefly about his previous convictions. Prosecuting counsel cross-examined about eight offences of dishonesty, some involving motor vehicles, without any objection.[16] The case focussed on cross-examination about the detail of a further four offences, one of which involved a false alibi to a charge of robbery, another to the use of violence of a rather different character in the course of a different sort of robbery, and the remaining two of which related to offences involving the stealing and movement of motor vehicles. The Court upheld the cross-examination in all respects. It can be seen however that different lines of justification are necessary. Thus in respect of the first offence the justification relied upon *similarity*:[17]

> there was nothing wrong in asking the appellant about his plea and defence of alibi that was rejected, *particularly where, as here,* the appellant giving evidence in chief persisted in his denial of guilt.

The justification in respect of the second offence relied on *dissimilarity*:

> it merely showed that this offence was somewhat more ruthless than may normally be the case in a robbery where, by definition, violence or the threat of violence, is used. The circumstances were in any event *quite different* from the instant case.

In the case of the remaining offences the justification was that the offences were old and not particularly distinctive, thus falling within the second line of justification. It is a sad commentary on the rigour of the analysis in *McLeod* that opposed considerations apparently lead to the same conclusion.

There is some suggestion in the formulation of the first numbered proposition in *McLeod*[18] that one factor relates to the purpose of the cross-examination, and if it is

---

15 Though in the case of the accused it has been repeatedly recognised that this distinction is highly tenuous.

16 Presumably on the basis of the second sort of attack on the accused's credibility.

17 At 267, 1512. Emphasis supplied.

18 At 267, 1512.

overtly to canvass disposition, then it should be rejected.[19] Much the same consideration appears to inspire the third numbered proposition which justifies detail about rejected defences on the basis that it shows disposition only indirectly. It is far from clear how this purpose is to be divined, given that it is unlikely to be avowed by counsel.

The second numbered proposition in *McLeod* is most directly concerned with the second principal issue, namely the linked question of how much detail should be allowed to be brought out in the cross-examination. It is stressed that this should be limited so as not to undermine the similar facts rule[20] too far. To some extent that consideration is reinforced by the seventh numbered proposition which is that the jury must be instructed to consider the matter only in relation to credit, and not to disposition.[1] Failure to make this clear, particularly in a situation where the matter put in cross-examination is of a particularly prejudicial nature, may well be fatal.[2]

The final matter relating to the application of the discretion has been considered above.[3] Particular stress is placed in the fourth numbered proposition in *McLeod* on the prejudice likely to be caused by the sort of character incidentally revealed, such as that indicating the sexual abuse of children.[4]

The unfortunate result of this line of authority is that material which could not be used in chief on account of its being more prejudicial than probative, may nevertheless be used in cross-examination where its prejudicial effect is likely to be enhanced and its probative force minimised.

D.   THE INTERPRETATION OF s 1(f)(iii)[5]

The rationale underlying s 1(f)(iii) according to which the accused may be cross-examined about his past misconduct if he has 'given evidence against any other person charged in the same proceedings' is, presumably, that he is in the same position as a witness for the prosecution so far as the co-accused is concerned, and nothing must be done to impair the right of a person charged to discredit his accusers.[6] Accordingly it has been held that the court has no discretion to refuse leave for a co-accused to cross-examine under s 1(f)(iii) if it considers that the subsection applies to the case,[7] although it would have such a discretion if the application under the subsection were made by the prosecution.[8] It should also be remembered that the judge has a separate discretion to order separate trials which may be used to prevent prejudice which might otherwise be caused by the absence of a discretion to prevent cross-examination by a

---

19   The decisions in *R v Vickers* [1972] Crim LR 101; *R v Khan* [1991] Crim LR 51; and *R v Barsoum* [1994] Crim LR 194 appear to be explained away on this basis.

20   See further ch VIII above.

1   Though it should be noted that most commentators, and some judges, have regarded such an exercise as futile. It is difficult to improve upon the stinging words of Lord Lane CJ in *R v Watts* [1983] 3 All ER 101, at 104, 77 Cr App Rep 126, at 129 that categorised it as a 'feat of intellectual acrobatics' and one 'practically impossible' of accomplishment.

2   See *R v Lawrence* [1995] Crim LR 815.

3   Above p 183.

4   The decision in *R v Watts* [1983] 3 All ER 101, 77 Cr App Rep 126 is explained on this basis.

5   See generally Elliott [1991] Crim LR 5.

6   An alternative explanation is that this is like the second limb of s 1(f)(ii) another case of tit for tat.

7   *Murdoch v Taylor* [1965] AC 574, [1965] 1 All ER 406, but note Lord Pearce's dissent on this point and see *Sandlon v H M Advocate* 1983 JC 22.

8   See *Matusevich v R* (1977) 137 CLR 633.

co-accused under s 1(f)(iii).[9] It is not enough to trigger that discretion automatically that cut-throat defences are being run between co-accused even if only one has a bad record, and even though that one might suffer injustice, if there are countervailing considerations.[10] If cross-examination is conducted on the basis of evidence having been given against a co-accused, but as a result of a change of tactics it ceases to be 'against' him, the judge may terminate proceedings, and order a re-trial.[11] The construction, scope and purpose of cross-examination under this proviso will now be considered.

1. Construction

(i) 'Given evidence against'

Much more weight has been cast upon the construction of these words in the proviso as a result of the decision that there is no discretion to disallow cross-examination under it by a co-accused, that as a result of s 35 of the Criminal Justice and Public Order Act 1994 adverse inferences may now be drawn against a co-accused who fails to testify, and that courts seem increasingly set against ordering separate trials. In *Varley* the Court of Appeal attempted to clarify matters. The accused, and one Dibble, were accused of participating in a robbery. Dibble's defence was that although he did participate, he was acting under the coercion of Varley. Varley's defence was that he had not been involved at all. He argued that such a defence ought not to be construed as amounting to giving evidence 'against' Dibble. The Court of Appeal reviewed a number of decisions,[12] and distilled from them the following propositions: [13]

> (1) If it is established that a person jointly charged has given evidence against the co-defendant that defendant has the right to cross-examine the other as to previous convictions and the trial judge has no discretion to refuse an application. (2) Such evidence may be given either in chief or during cross-examination. (3) It has to be objectively decided whether the evidence either supports the prosecution case in a material respect or undermines the defence of the co-accused. A hostile intent is irrelevant. (4) If consideration has to be given to the undermining of the other's defence care must be taken to see that the evidence clearly undermines the defence. Inconvenience to or inconsistency with the other's defence is not of itself sufficient. (5) Mere denial of participation in a joint venture is not of itself sufficient to rank as evidence against the co-defendant. For the proviso to apply, such denial must lead to the conclusion that if the witness did not participate then it must have been the other who did. (6) Where the one defendant asserts or in due course would assert one view of the joint venture which is directly contradicted by the other such contradiction may be evidence against the co-defendant.

---

9   *R v Varley* [1982] 2 All ER 519, 75 Cr App Rep 242. If, at an earlier stage, the prosecution has promised one of two co-accused that he would not be prosecuted, the substituted prospect of a joint trial has been regarded as enhancing an allegation of abuse of process, *R v Townsend, Dearsley and Bretcher* [1998] Crim LR 126.

10 *R v Edwards and Lake* [1998] Crim LR 756 (where it would have been undesirable to expose the child victim of a sexual assault to the greater ordeal of having to testify at separate trials).

11 *R v Tyrer* (1988) Times, 13 October. See Munday [1990] Crim LR 92.

12 *Murdoch v Taylor* [1965] AC 574, [1965] 1 All ER 406; *R v Stannard* [1965] 2 QB 1, [1964] 1 All ER 34; *R v Davis* [1975] 1 All ER 233, [1975] 1 WLR 345; *R v Bruce* [1975] 3 All ER 277, [1975] 1 WLR 1252; *R v Hatton* (1976) 64 Cr App Rep 88.

13 At 522, 246.

Such elaboration has been deplored by the Court of Appeal.[14] It must be accepted that the second of these propositions is not easily reconciled with the literal wording of the proviso, and in particular with the absence from (iii) of the reference to 'asking questions' which is present in proviso (ii). It is also difficult to disentangle the last three propositions as shown by the factual situation in *R v Crawford* where three women were alleged to have participated in a robbery, with which only two were charged, and those two gave inconsistent accounts of what occurred, but without the inconsistency being such as inevitably to lead to the conclusion that the attacked co-accused must, if the inconsistency were corrected, have been guilty.[15] In that situation the court substituted 'may' for 'must' in (v), though it stressed that the passage was to be regarded as a summary of the effect of previous decisions, and not as a set of formal rules to be construed as if it were part of a statutory provision.

It should be noted that a co-defendant retains an interest capable of being undermined so long as he persists in his plea of not guilty, however much his case may have been damaged by the time the question arises.[16] It is irrelevant that the impaired co-accused chooses not to testify himself.[17] It seems certain that the application of these principles will do little to avert the result regretted by Lord Reid in *Murdoch v Taylor* that:[18]

> an accused person with previous convictions, whose story contradicts in any material respect the story of the co-accused who has not yet been convicted, will find it almost impossible to defend himself, and if he elects not to give evidence his plight will be as bad.

(ii)   'Any other person charged in the same proceedings'

The Act of 1898 originally referred to cases in which evidence was given against any other person 'charged with the same offence'. These words were unduly restrictive because there are many joint trials in which the accused cannot by any stretch of the imagination be said to be charged with the same offence. The phraseology was criticised in the House of Lords when they held, in *Metropolitan Police Comr v Hills*,[19] that two motorists who had collided with the result that a pedestrian was killed were not charged with the same offence when tried together on successive counts of the same indictment for causing death by dangerous driving. The Criminal Evidence Act 1979 substituted the words 'charged in the same proceedings' for 'charged with the same offence'. The wording is wide enough to cover all the old cases in which cross-examination was held to have been impermissible, and it has caused no difficulty.

---

14   *R v Crawford* [1998] 1 Cr App Rep 338, at 345A.
15   This can lead to a very fine line between situations in which inconsistency does and does not undermine the co-accused's defence in a material respect: cp *R v Kirkpatrick* [1998] Crim LR 63.
16   *R v Mir, Ahmed and Dalil* [1989] Crim LR 894.
17   *R v Adair* [1990] Crim LR 571, which also confirms that the third proposition is disjunctive.
18   [1965] AC 574, at 582, [1965] 1 All ER 406, at 408.
19   [1980] AC 26, [1978] 2 All ER 1105. The solution which has been adopted was suggested by Mirfield: see [1978] Crim LR 725.

2. Scope

In *R v Lovett*[20] Lovett was charged with stealing a television set and G, his co-accused, was charged with handling it. Lovett cast serious imputations on a witness for the prosecution and gave evidence against G. G's counsel immediately cross-examined him on his previous convictions; he was convicted and G was acquitted. On Lovett's appeal the Court of Appeal held that cross-examination under s 1(f)(iii) as it was then worded was improper because the two accused were not charged with the same offence but, as counsel for the prosecution had intended to seek leave to cross-examine under s 1(f)(ii), the Court of Appeal exercised the discretion which the judge would have had and dismissed the appeal. On the authority of *R v Seigley*,[1] the court expressed the view that the prosecution may, subject to the discretion of the judge to prohibit such a course, cross-examine under s 1(f)(iii). As the law then stood the prosecution could not have been allowed to cross-examine under that proviso in *R v Lovett*, and it is only in very exceptional circumstances that an application for leave to do so would be likely to succeed. A possible instance would be a case in which two persons charged in the same proceedings each gave evidence against the other, but, because they both had criminal records, neither cross-examined the other under s 1(f)(iii). There is, however, something to be said for the conclusion of the High Court of Australia that the Crown has no power to cross-examine under an identically worded proviso.[2]

The High Court of Australia held in the same case, contrary to what was said in *R v Lovett*, that the accused has no right, where imputations have been cast by a co-accused on a witness for the prosecution, to cross-examine under s 1(f)(ii). Such a right is difficult to justify on principle, although it is not excluded by the wording of the statute. It might occasionally have been useful before the wording of s 1(f)(iii) was changed. For example the Court of Appeal recognised that G might have sought leave to cross-examine Lovett under s 1(f)(ii), but it is not easy to think of situations in which it would now be called for.

There appears to be no authority on the extent to which one co-accused may invoke s 1(f)(i) in order to cross-examine another about the commission of crimes or previous convictions. A literal construction presents no impediment to such a course, and it might be useful in cases where the cross-examination was intended to go to more than the co-accused's credit. It should be noted though that in such a case the wording of the first proviso would exclude cross-examination about charges or bad character falling short of the commission of crimes, and that it would have to show the co-accused's guilt of the crime with which he was charged.

3. Purpose of cross-examination under s 1(f)(iii)[3]

There seems little doubt that the only proper purpose of such cross-examination is to attack the credibility of the accused. It was so stated in *Murdoch v Taylor*.[4] In many cases credibility and issue are so intertwined that a court is likely, even without reference to s 1(f)(i), to permit cross-examination so long as some issue of credibility can be

---

20   [1973] 1 All ER 744, [1973] 1 WLR 241.

1   (1911) 6 Cr App Rep 106.

2   *Matusevich v R* (1977) 137 CLR 633. The decision turned in part on the absence of a statutory requirement of an application for leave to cross-examine such as was required in the equivalent to s 1(f)(ii) in s 399 of the Crimes Act of Victoria.

3   See Pattenden [1982] Crim LR 707.

4   [1965] AC 574, at 584 (Lord Morris), at 593 (Lord Donovan), [1965] 1 All ER 406, at 409 and at 416.

discerned.[5] Nor is it necessarily fatal to a conviction that the trial judge fails to explain this limited purpose to the jury, again no doubt because of the difficulty of distinguishing between the various purposes in the case of a defendant.[6]

E.   PROPOSALS FOR REFORM

This is one of the least satisfactory parts of the law of evidence, characterised by indeterminacy of aim, and inept intervention by the legislature. The problem is acute and difficult to resolve. Very many different approaches have been proposed to the solution of the problem of cross-examination of the accused who gives evidence. There are two basic traditions, one current in North America and another obtaining elsewhere in the common law world. The North American tradition has tended to favour treatment of the accused as an ordinary, but not compellable, witness.[7] As such he is free to choose whether or not to testify, but if he chooses to do so, he enjoys little special protection. There is small room for doubt that this tends to inhibits many accused persons with criminal records from testifying.[8] Within this tradition, where the same rules have to apply to the accused as apply to other witnesses, the only means of amelioration would seem to be either to make the accused a compellable witness, or to reform the techniques for the cross-examination of all witnesses to such an extent that the accused would be no longer so inhibited. It should be noted that no more than the fact of a conviction can be put, that the judge has a discretion to disallow even this,[9] and that the Canadian courts are endowed with a discretion to disallow any other oppressive cross-examination of the accused.[10]

In the English tradition deriving from the Criminal Evidence Act 1898 the accused is treated differently from other witnesses, and accorded special protection in cross-examination. Here the difficulty lies in deciding upon the precise nature and detail of that protection. There is widespread dissatisfaction with the current state of the law in virtually every jurisdiction within the tradition, and it is hardly surprising to discover that there is no unanimity in the various proposals for reform.[11]

In England the Law Commission considered this topic under three headings: assertions of good character;[12] cross-examination of the impugning accused;[13] and

5   *R v Reid* [1989] Crim LR 719.
6   *R v Hoggins* [1967] 3 All ER 334, [1967] 1 WLR 1223.
7   Although in Canada the Uniform Law Conference proposed a measure within the alternative tradition, see Report of Canadian Task Force, App 3; and in the United States the Commonwealth of Pennsylvania has operated within that tradition since 1911, see Tapper in Tapper (ed) *Crime, Proof and Punishment* (1981) pp 307–10.
8   Royal Commission on Criminal Justice Cm 2263 (1993) Research Study No 19 *Crown Court Study*, paras 4.5.1, 4.6.8. Under s 35 of the Criminal Justice and Public Order Act 1994 fewer defendants may now express their inhibition by refraining altogether from testifying. See also Report of Canadian Task Force p 411.
9   *Corbett v R* [1988] 1 SCR 670; such a decision must be made, if necessary on a voir dire, *before* the accused is required to choose whether or not to testify: *R v Underwood* [1998] 1 SCR 77.
10   See *Fanjoy v R* [1985] 2 SCR 232; *Brown and Murphy v R* [1985] 2 SCR 273.
11   The Criminal Law Revision Committee rehearsed very sharp disagreements on many points. Various suggestions were well analysed by the Australian Law Reform Commission in its Research Paper No 11 'Character and Conduct' ch 8. Two more recent contributions are the Law Commission's Consultation Paper No 141 *Evidence in Criminal Proceedings: Previous Misconduct of a Defendant* (1996), and the New Zealand Law Commission's Preliminary Paper No 27 *Evidence Law: Character & Credibility* (1997), to both of which are appended accounts of approaches elsewhere.
12   Part XI.
13   Part XII.

cross-examination of the co-accused.[14] It is worth considering these separately, and then to consider some more general matters.

1.   Assertions of good character

Apart from minor exercises of clarification,[15] the principal recommendation here is that character should no longer be regarded as indivisible, but that the accused should be permitted to limit evidence of good character, and its rebuttal, to good character in a particular respect.[16] This view was partly inspired by the general view of the effect of evidence of good character in operating both in relation to issue and to credibility. It was more coherent therefore, both as a matter of policy and of practicability, explicitly to permit rebuttal evidence also to be considered both in relation to issue and credibility.[17] The Commission perceived little problem in relation to the good character of a non-testifying accused, since there would normally be an opportunity to cross-examine the relevant witness.[18]

2.   Imputations

Imputation is by far the most common way in which the accused's previous convictions become known to the jury.[19] The Law Commission was unconvinced by the rationale for this part of the rule, and regarded the current extensive reliance upon amelioration by discretion as indicative of the rule's unsatisfactory state. Here too it was exercised by the elusiveness of the boundary between credibility and issue in the case of the accused. If a man is charged with theft and has a conviction for indecent assault few would disagree that the relevance of the conviction to issue is remote, and that to credibility little more. If on the other hand the charge is of indecent assault, even though the conviction were for a different form of indecent assault, it would be perceived to have more relevance to issue, but this might easily be subsumed under credit on the basis that the truth was to be discovered by comparison of the testimony of the complainant with that of the accused, and that the conviction of the one for the very offence was relevant to determining which of them was more likely to be telling the truth.[20] For some reason the Law Commission considered only two possible options for change,[1] rejecting the solution proposed by the Royal Commission that the shield

---

14   Part XIII.
15   Relating to the circumstances in which such an assertion is to be taken as having been made.
16   Para 11.42, rec 29. This is in accordance with the position in Australia under s 104(a) of the Evidence Act (Cwth) 1994.
17   Para 11.45, rec 30.
18   It nevertheless left open the possibility of adducing evidence of bad character in this situation, largely on account of parity of reasoning with the case of a non-testifying witness who made imputations, where it also left the matter open.
19   Royal Commission on Criminal Justice Cm 2263 (1993) Research Study No 19 *Crown Court Study*, Table 4.14. This applies only to convictions, and the contrast might not be so pronounced in relation to the other matters mentioned in s 1(f).
20   The reasoning in *Selvey v DPP* [1970] AC 304, [1968] 2 All ER 497 follows just such a pattern. Its application by jurors was supported by experiments at Oxford University: see Law Commission No 141 App D.
1   Cp the range of options considered by the New Zealand Law Commission in Prel Pap 27 above, paras 207–218.

should be lost only if the imputation were not central to the defence case,[2] but recommending the Australian solution[3] that the shield be lost only if the imputation were as to the conduct of the witness outside his conduct in the case. A serious disadvantage of this is that it may prove extremely difficult to distinguish conduct outside and inside the confines of the case, and it does nothing to eliminate the prejudice likely to be caused to the innocent accused by allowing the jury to be made aware of material which may be undeniably more prejudicial than probative.[4] Given the evidence that juries in practice use such evidence to go directly to guilt, rather than to credibility,[5] there seems little justification for admitting it on a more[6] relaxed basis than evidence in chief. The Law Commission, despite its view that the issue had become less important, devoted considerable attention to the desirability of departing from the principle of *R v Butterwasser*[7] and allowing evidence of the accused's bad character to be adduced, even when he had not testified to support an imputation on the prosecutor or his witnesses. In the end it made no recommendation, and left three[8] totally opposed options open for consultation.[9]

3. Co-accused

The Law Commission was driven by its views on the matters mentioned above to conclude that this part of the subject was still more flawed, since the defects stemming from the difficulty of distinguishing issue from credibility are if anything still stronger, and not here ameliorated by the exercise of an exclusionary discretion. No fewer than seven options for reform were considered but the final recommendation was for a solution similar to that proposed for the problem of imputations, that is one based on distinguishing between evidence within and outside the confines of the case, but qualified, and here by way of innovation, by the application of an exclusionary discretion.[10] It is envisaged that the presumption would favour acceptance when the application was made by the attacked co-accused, but would favour refusal when made by the prosecution, or a third, and unattacked, co-accused.[11] One of the reasons for doubt in the *R v Butterwasser* situation was the disparity between the effect of attacks on prosecution witnesses and on the accused. This disparity does not exist as between two co-accused, and the Law Commission proposes that in that situation it should be possible to adduce evidence of a non-testifying co-accused's bad character when he attacks the other in respect of matters outside the confines of the case.[12]

---

2   Royal Commission on Criminal Justice Cm 2263 (1993) para. 8.33, rec 193. This is similar to the approach of the Criminal Law Revision Committee in its 11th Report *Evidence: General* Cmnd 4991 (1972) Draft Bill, cl 6(4).
3   Evidence Act (Cwth) 1995, s 104(5)(b).
4   As the Law Commission accepts, para 13.17.
5   As the Law Commission also accepts, para 6.84.
6   It is arguable that because of the more prejudicial way in which material emerges in cross-examination there is a case for its being allowed only on a more stringent basis.
7   Above p 323.
8   It rejected two as going beyond its scope.
9   Para 12.118.
10   Para 13.46, rec 38.
11   Para 13.55, rec 39.
12   Para 13.50, rec 40.

4.   General

It is submitted that the Law Commission is correct in its assessment of the impossibility both as a matter of logic and practice of separating those aspects of the accused's character going to guilt from those going to credibility. Its general policy of encouraging the accused to testify on matters in issue, by restricting the loss of a shield to matters within the confines of the case, is also commendable. It is thus all the more disappointing to find so many of its recommendations in this area still content to operate an overtly retributive, and comparative, policy of tit-for-tat, acquiescing in the use of material more prejudicial than probative. It is submitted that it would have been better to have made more strenuous attempts to establish one common standard for the admissibility of evidence of the accused's bad character, and to apply it universally, both to the admissibility of evidence in chief, in cross-examination and rebuttal.[13]

---

13   To the extent that such an approach would create anomaly with the rules for the cross-examination to credit of other witnesses, then it is accepted that radical restriction should apply there also.

CHAPTER X

Privilege[1]

A witness is said to be privileged when he may validly[2] claim not to answer a question or to supply information which would be relevant to the determination of an issue in judicial proceedings. Because the effect of such rules is to deprive the tribunal of relevant evidence powerful arguments are required to justify their existence, and the tendency of the modern law of evidence has been to reduce both their number and their scope,[3] although this has in some cases been balanced by an increase in status.[4] Only four heads of privilege are sufficiently important to require discussion here, the privilege against self-incrimination, legal professional privilege, privilege for statements made without prejudice as part of an attempt to settle a dispute, and a privilege derived from the former for statements made to a conciliator. A few preliminary observations are also necessary.

In the first place, as the privilege is that of a particular person or class, matters covered by it may always be proved by the evidence of other witnesses.[5] Parke B once said:[6]

---

1 See generally, with an Australian emphasis, McNichol *Law of Privilege* (1992).
2 Some evidential basis for refusal to answer is required, it is not enough for example that the witness might be put in personal jeopardy by doing so: *The Coca Cola Company v Gilbey* [1996] FSR 23; see also *S v Sithole* 1991 (4) SA 94.
3 Recommendations to this effect in the 16th Report of the Law Reform Committee (Cmnd 3472, 1967) and in the 11th Report of the Criminal Law Revision Committee (Cmnd 4991, 1972) have been largely implemented in Civil Evidence Act 1968, s 16, and Police and Criminal Evidence Act 1984, s 80 (9). Even in the United States there is strong resistance to the creation of new heads of privilege: see *University of Pennsylvania v Equal Employment Opportunity Commission* 493 US 182, at 188 (1990).
4 See eg *Brannigan v Davison* [1997] AC 235, at 249D (against self-incrimination); *R v Derby Magistrates, ex p B* [1996] AC 487, [1995] 4 All ER 526, at 507D, 541a (legal professional privilege). This tendency may be further enhanced when the European Convention on Human Rights is enacted as part of English law since art 6.1 guaranteeing a fair trial has been interpreted as extending to the privilege against self-incrimination: *Saunders v United Kingdom* [1997] BCC 872; such enactment will not however be anticipated by staying proceedings in the meantime: *R v Morrisey and Staines* [1997] 2 Cr App R 426, see also *R v Secretary of State for Trade and Industry, ex p McCormick* [1998] BCC 379.
5 See also in Australia, *Bond v Tuohy* (1995) 128 ALR 595; cp in Canada, *Del Zotto v The Queen* (1997) 147 DLR (4th) 457.
6 *Lloyd v Mostyn* (1842) 10 M & W 478, at 481–2 in the course of argument.

Where an attorney entrusted confidentially with a document communicates the contents, or suffers another to take a copy, surely the secondary evidence so obtained may be produced. Suppose the instrument were even stolen, and a correct copy taken, would it not be reasonable to admit it.

It was on the authority of Parke B's remark that the Court of Appeal allowed copies of proofs of witnesses with notes on the evidence in a former claim brought by the claimant's predecessor in title to be put in by the defendant in *Calcraft v Guest*,[7] the originals having been handed over by the defendant's solicitor to the claimant to whom they belonged. Such secondary evidence cannot however be used if it consists of, or is derived from, a document brought into court by an opponent, or his legal representative, and then improperly obtained.[8] The Law Reform Committee felt that such a rule should apply generally in cases where secondary evidence had been obtained by the commission of a crime or tort, but refrained from making any recommendation pending the 11th Report of the Criminal Law Revision Committee.[9] No recommendation was made upon this matter, nor was it dealt with in the Police and Criminal Evidence Act 1984. The matter is thus left to the general common law rules relating to the admissibility of improperly obtained evidence, where as will be explained more fully in the next chapter the rules in England generally favour admissibility more than those in some other common law jurisdictions, and very much more than the rules in the United States.[10]

Second, the personal nature of the privilege means that a party will not necessarily be entitled to succeed on an appeal, or obtain an order for a new trial, when the claim to privilege of his own, or his opponent's witness has been wrongly rejected or accepted in the court below. There is express authority for this view in a case in which the witness had unsuccessfully invoked the privilege against self-incrimination,[11] and practically all the decisions of appellate courts in which the judge's ruling on a question of privilege has been varied or reversed relate to issues in which the person claiming the privilege was a party to, and not merely a witness in, the proceedings. Many of them are concerned with the disclosure of documents, or requests for further information since the issue of privilege is often raised in interim proceedings before the actual trial of a civil action.

Third, according to English law, no adverse inference should normally[12] be made from the fact that the privilege is claimed,[13] though it is hard to believe that in practice

7   [1898] 1 QB 759.

8   *ITC Film Distributors v Video Exchange Ltd* [1982] Ch 431, [1982] 2 All ER 241. If there has been no impropriety in obtaining such a document, it may apparently be used, see *R v Tompkins* (1977) 67 Cr App Rep 181; for a more restrictive view in New Zealand see *R v Uljee* [1982] 1 NZLR 561.

9   Cmnd 3472, para 32. The committee assumed that secondary evidence of a privileged document could be given however it had been obtained; see also Lord Simon's view in *Waugh v British Railways Board* [1980] AC 521, at 536, [1979] 2 All ER 1169, at 1177.

10   The Report of the Law Reform Committee referred to r 26 of the Uniform Rules which conferred very wide protection on the privilege holder; there is no equivalent in the Federal Rules under which privilege is governed by the common law.

11   *R v Kinglake* (1870) 22 LT 335. In *Doe d Egremont v Date* (1842) 3 QB 609, a decision on title deeds, a distinction was suggested between cases in which the witness's claim to privilege was successful in which event a party could contend that he had been deprived of a possible means of proving a fact, and those in which it failed, in which event the aggrieved party cannot complain because the privilege might have been waived, but the distinction does not seem to have been taken in other cases.

12   But see *R v Wilmot* (1988) 89 Cr App Rep 341; *Ridehaulgh v Horsefield* [1994] Ch 205, at 237, [1994] 3 All ER 848, at 866.

13   *Wentworth v Lloyd* (1864) 10 HL Cas 589, at 590–592; for commentary see Young (1991) 65 ALJ 412. The contrast with r 233 of the Model Code is striking: 'if a privilege to refuse to

none is ever drawn. It is interesting to note that refusal to answer on the basis of privilege is one of the circumstances excepted[14] from the authorisation of comment and the drawing of adverse inferences from failure to answer a question conferred by the Criminal Justice and Public Order Act 1994.

The last general observation concerns the effect of upholding a claim to privilege. This involves withholding important information from the court at the expense of what may be abstract justice to one of the parties.[15] It follows that there should be good cause, plainly shown, for the existence of any privilege,[16] and it remains to consider whether this is the case for all of the privileges discussed here. The crucial question is whether there is some interest protected by the privilege which is at least as significant as the proper administration of justice. It is also important not to exclude the possibility that the law is defective by failing to recognise legitimate claims to privilege, and not merely by protecting interests which do not deserve it. The influence of public opinion should not be ignored. The proper administration of justice mentioned above includes the notion of the rejection of relevant evidence because its reception would be unduly offensive to contemporary public opinion. It follows that that which was the subject of privilege in one generation should not necessarily be privileged in the next, and vice versa.

SECTION I.   THE PRIVILEGE AGAINST SELF-INCRIMINATION[17]

The privilege against self-incrimination originated in the unpopularity of the procedure in the Star Chamber under which those who were charged with an offence were interrogated on oath. This contributed to the rule that the accused could not testify in a criminal case, and the idea that no one could be obliged to jeopardise his life or liberty by answering questions on oath came to be applied to all witnesses in all proceedings in the course of the seventeenth century. In the narrowest sense the privilege operates to permit a witness in legal proceedings to refuse to answer questions the answers to which may tend to incriminate him by exposing him to subsequent criminal proceedings. The common law was said by Lord Diplock[18] to have been stated so far as offences and penalties provided by the law of England are concerned in s 14 of the Civil Evidence Act 1968 as:

(1)   The right of a person in any legal proceedings other than criminal proceedings to refuse to answer any question or produce any document or thing if to do so would tend to expose that person to proceedings for an offence or for the recovery of a penalty.

---

disclose, or a privilege to prevent another from disclosing, matter is claimed and allowed, the judge and counsel may comment thereon, and the trier of fact may draw all reasonable inferences therefrom'; but this rule was not adopted by the Uniform Law Commissioners (see Uniform Rules, r 39).

14   Section 35(5)(a).

15   This may be exceptionally important in separate criminal proceedings against co-accused: see *R v Swick* (1997) 150 DLR (4th) 566.

16   VIII *Wigmore* p 67.

17   VIII *Wigmore* (McNaughton revision), paras 2250–51 contains a classic statement of the history and rationale of the rule. See also Morgan (1949) 34 Minn LR 1; Levy *Origins of the Fifth Amendment* (1968); for a modern Australian perspective, see McNicol *Law of Privilege* (1992); for a different view see McNair (1990) 10 OJLS 66. For analysis and suggestions for general reform, see New Zealand Law Commission Prel Paper 25 *The Privilege Against Self-Incrimination* (1996).

18   *Rio Tinto Zinc Corpn v Westinghouse Electric Corpn* [1978] AC 547, at 636, [1978] 1 All ER 434, at 464.

This narrow sense has however come under conflicting pressures on the one hand from those who think the privilege a bastion of human freedom from oppression by the state, to be construed expansively:[19]

> The privilege against compulsory self-incrimination is part of the common law of human rights. It is based on the desire to protect personal freedom and human dignity. These social values justify the impediment the privilege presents to judicial or other investigation. It protects the innocent as well as the guilty from the indignity and invasion of privacy which occurs in compulsory self-incrimination; it is society's acceptance of the inviolability of human personality.

And on the other from those who think it an impediment upon the administration of justice, to be construed restrictively:[20]

> It is difficult to see any reason why in civil proceedings the privilege against self-incrimination should be exercisable so as to enable a litigant to refuse relevant and even vital documents which are in his possession or power and which speak for themselves....I regard the privilege against self-incrimination exercisable in civil proceedings as an archaic and unjustifiable survival from the past when the court directs the production of relevant documents and requires the defendant to specify his dealings with the plaintiff's property or money.

Given such conflicting pressures, and the intervention of the legislature in support of the increasing role of the state in social affairs, it is hardly surprising that the contours of the privilege should be somewhat uncertain.[1] It is desirable first to consider the scope of the privilege, then the procedure by which it is invoked, and finally the inroads into it made by statute. It will finally be appropriate to consider proposals for the reform of the privilege

A. SCOPE OF THE RULE

A number of different matters require consideration here. It is clear that the privilege extends beyond mere permission not to answer while testifying to entitlement not to comply with pre-trial process to compel production by way of discovery, but there are serious questions as to exactly which pre-trial processes qualify for protection by the privilege. This merges with a second question as to how far, if at all, the privilege extends to different forms of self-incrimination. A final matter here relates to the range of deleterious consequences beyond personal exposure to criminal prosecution which the privilege applies to protect. These will be considered separately for the purposes of exposition, despite some measure of overlapping.

I. Range of application

One area of pressure has been to extend the privilege further and further before the occasion of testifying. It is useful to distinguish here between pre-trial civil and criminal proceedings.

---

19   Per Murphy J in *Pyneboard Pty Ltd v Trade Practices Commission* (1983) 152 CLR 328, at 346.
20   Per Lord Templeman in *Istel Ltd v Tully* [1993] AC 45, at 53, [1992] 3 All ER 523, at 530.
1   Nor that the limits should be differently drawn in different jurisdictions.

(i)   Civil proceedings

As noted above there is no doubt but that the privilege can be claimed at the stage of disclosure and inspection,[2] indeed it is at that stage in civil proceedings that it most commonly would be claimed. It has become necessary for speedy interim action to be taken in civil cases, often ex parte, especially by way of search orders and freezing injunctions. The question arises of whether, and how, the privilege should be invoked in relation to that type of pre-trial proceeding. It seems now to be agreed that the privilege does apply at such a stage,[3] and in relation to 'all aspects of discovery in a fraud action'.[4] It has indeed been suggested that this is so serious a matter that the application of the privilege should be abrogated in such cases by legislative intervention as a matter of urgency.[5] It seems that proceedings to inquire into the means to pay taxes preliminary to a committal order for that failure may attract the privilege.[6] In some jurisdictions the privilege has been held to apply to various pre-trial procedures to gather evidence for civil proceedings.[7] In England the privilege has been held not to apply in proceedings to disqualify a company director,[8] although in Australia the High Court has affirmed more generally that it cannot be contended that the privilege is inherently incapable of application in non-judicial proceedings.[9] In Canada it has been held that pre-trial investigation of a formally criminal, but essentially administrative, nature falls outside the protection offered by the privilege.[10]

(ii)   Criminal proceedings

It is useful to emphasise at the outset that this privilege, like all others, operates simply as a shield against an obligation of compulsory disclosure. It is unhelpful to conflate those rules which limit the situations in which compulsory powers exist, with those of privilege which, given the existence of such compulsory powers confer a limited immunity from their exercise in certain situations.

---

2   *Istel Ltd v Tully* above is a recent and convenient example.
3   *Rank Film Distributors Ltd v Video Information Centre* [1982] AC 380, [1981] 2 All ER 76 (necessitating statutory intervention, see below p 434). And even when not strictly available because the incrimination was under foreign law it seems that it might still be relevant to the exercise of discretion, *A-G for Gibraltar v May* (1998) Times, 20 November.
4   *Tate Access Floors Inc v Boswell* [1991] Ch 512, at 527, [1990] 3 All ER 303, at 312.
5   By Browne-Wilkinson VC in *Sociedad Nacional de Combustiveis de Angola UEE v Lundqvist* [1991] 2 QB 310, at 338, [1990] 3 All ER 283, at 302 (disclosure in aid of a freezing injunction); *Tate Access Floors Inc v Boswell*, above at 532, 315, 6 (search orders).
6   *R v Highbury Corner Magistrates, ex p Watkins* [1992] RA 300 (though there no privilege arose because the question involved no risk of incrimination, leading only to such committal). The freedom of questioning about affairs relevant to tax assessment from the constitutional protection of the privilege was affirmed in Canada in *Re 462657 Ontario Ltd* (1989) 62 DLR (4th) 666.
7   In Australia, to questioning with a view to instituting disciplinary proceedings against a police constable, *Police Comr v Justin* (1991) 55 SASR 547; or a customs officer, *Re Comptroller-General of Customs* (1992) 107 ALR 480. In Canada, to compulsory statements to insurers after a motor accident, *R v Spyker* (1990) 63 CCC (3d) 125.
8   *R v Secretary of State for Trade and Industry, ex p McCormick* [1998] BCC 379.
9   *Pyneboard Pty Ltd v Trade Practices Commission*, above at p 341.
10   *Thomson Newspapers Ltd v Director of Investigation and Research* [1990] 1 SCR 425. The position in Canada has been highly influenced by the impact and drafting of the *Canadian Charter of Rights and Freedoms*. Purely disciplinary proceedings have still been held to fall outside the range of those in which the privilege operates, *R v Wigglesworth* [1987] 2 SCR 577; *Knutson v Saskatchewan Registered Nurses' Association* (1990) 75 DLR (4th) 723.

In criminal proceedings elaborate rules define the extent of such compulsory powers so far as the accused is concerned, many of them incorporated into the Codes of Practice promulgated pursuant to s 67(9) of the Police and Criminal Evidence Act 1984. Occasionally persons, having compulsory powers of investigation,[11] fall outside the ambit of this provision not being 'charged with the duty of investigating offences or charging offenders'. In such cases the privilege may not be invoked to prevent such construction when it would frustrate the whole purpose of the investigation.[12] Where an aspect of evidence falls outside the ambit of the Code the general law applies, and in principle the gathering of evidence for the purpose of a criminal prosecution is not subject to the privilege.[13] This has been held to permit the gathering of real evidence, such as the sound of a person's voice,[14] or samples from a person's body,[15] subject only to obedience to the normal rules relating to trespass and assault,[16] and not to be controllable by reference to the privilege against self-incrimination. Indeed in such cases it seems that adverse comment could be made upon, and adverse inferences drawn from, the accused's exercise of his rights of refusal.[17] Section 36 of the Criminal Justice and Public Order Act 1994 makes more general provision to this effect :

(1) Where—
(a) a person is arrested by a constable, and there is–
    (i) on his person; or
    (ii) in or on his clothing or footwear; or
    (iii) otherwise in his possession; or
    (iv) in any place in which he is at the time of his arrest,
    any object, substance or mark, or there is any mark on any such object; and
(b) that or another constable investigating the case reasonably believes that presence of the object, substance or mark may be attributable to the person arrested in the commission of an offence specified by the constable; and
(c) the constable informs the subject that he so believes, and requests him to account for the presence of the object, substance or mark; and
(d) the person fails or refuses to do so,
then [the court may draw such inferences from the failure or refusal as appear proper].

---

11 Almost invariably conferred by statute, and discussed further in Part C below.
12 *R v Seelig* [1991] 4 All ER 429, [1992] 1 WLR 149 inspectors appointed to investigate the affairs of a company under s 432 of the Companies Act 1985).
13 In Canada however, under the Charter, if the primary purpose for exercising a collateral compulsory power is to secure an evidential basis for a prosecution, the privilege applies: see *British Columbia Securities Commission v Branch* [1995] 2 SCR 3; *Phillips v Nova Scotia (Westray Mine Inquiry)* [1995] 2 SCR 98; but much depends upon the detail of the entitlement to compel.
14 *R v Deenik* [1992] Crim LR 578.
15 *R v Apicella* (1985) 82 Cr App Rep 295, and see Easton [1991] Crim LR 18 with particular reference to DNA testing. The rule is similar in the United States *Schmerber v California* 384 US 757 (1966) confines the privilege, even in the case of an accused, to evidence of a testimonial or communicative nature, but this is, of course, subject to the rights accorded to an accused by the constitutional provision against unreasonable searches. It has however been suggested that in some circumstances the privilege could be invoked in relation to an order to produce a child addressed to its mother: *Baltimore Department of Social Service v Bouknight* 493 US 549 (1989).
16 Or any more specific rules and regulations, such as the Code of Practice, or the Family Law Reform Act 1969 in relation to blood samples: see above p 43.
17 At common law, see *R v Smith* [1985] Crim LR 590; or by specific statutory provision, see Family Law Reform Act 1969, s 23 (blood tests).

The privilege applies to proceedings in the Coroner's Court.[18] It also applies at all curial stages of the criminal process.[19] It is further available in relation to ancillary orders sometimes made to secure enforcement of other orders in criminal proceedings, such as a disclosure order to assist with a restraint order made pursuant to s 77 of the Criminal Justice Act 1988.[20]

2.   Range of incrimination

So far the focus has been on the type of proceedings in which the privilege might be claimed. It here shifts to the range of issues in respect of which questioning might be regarded as triggering the privilege. Those which have principally occupied the courts have been; first, the extent to which the question must go towards establishing the relevant criminality; second, the extent to which a question criminating another can be objected to, in particular a spouse or those between whom some form of vicarious responsibility might exist; and third whether there are any special rules applicable to fiduciaries.

(i)   Indirect incrimination

The rule extends beyond answers[1] that would directly criminate the witness to those which might be used as a step towards obtaining evidence against him.[2] In *R v Slaney*,[3] for instance, a witness who was giving evidence at a prosecution for a criminal libel contained in an advertisement in a newspaper was asked whether he knew who wrote to the proprietors with the advertisement, and, after he had answered in the affirmative, Lord Tenterden CJ upheld his objection to stating the name of the writer of the letter:

> You cannot only not compel a witness to answer that which will criminate him, but that which tends to criminate him: and the reason is this, that the party would go from one question to another, and though no question might be asked, the answer of which would directly criminate the witness, yet they would get enough from him whereon to found a charge against him.

(ii)   Incrimination of another

In civil cases s 14(1)(b) of the Civil Evidence Act 1968 has extended the privilege to questions tending to criminate a spouse. The Criminal Law Revision Committee

---

18   Coroners' Rules 1984 (SI 1984/552), r 22(1). *R v Coroner, ex p Alexander* [1982] VR 731; see also *R v Zurlo* (1990) 57 CCC (3d) 407 considering the impact of the Canadian Charter of Rights and Freedoms on this situation.

19   At committal, on the voir dire, and at the post-verdict sentencing stage; on the last see in the United States, *Powell v Texas* 492 US 680 (1989).

20   *Re O (Restraint Order)* [1991] 2 QB 520, [1991] 1 All ER 330. It should be noted that the now customary condition restraining further use of the material in evidence, recommended in *Re O* as a means of circumventing the problem, does not prevent its use in cross-examination to credit: *R v Martin and White* [1998] 2 Cr App Rep 385.

1   It does not extend to an order for the subsequent disclosure of an incriminating statement obtained voluntarily, and filed in the court without objection, *Re L* (1995) Times, 25 April.

2   In *Sociedad Nacionale de Combusiveis Angola UEE v Lundqvist* [1991] 2 QB 310, at 325, [1990] 3 All ER 283, at 292 Staughton LJ was inclined to limit it to matter capable of constituting evidence in the case, even though not alone conclusive.

3   (1832) 5 C & P 213. See also *Short v Mercier* (1851) 3 Mac & G 205, at 217 per Lord Truro.

recommended a similar rule for witnesses in criminal proceedings, excepting only the accused and his spouse,[4] though no such rule has as yet been enacted. It was unwilling to recommend such a general rule in respect of the accused or the spouse of the accused, nor has any such rule been included in the Police and Criminal Evidence Act 1984. Despite some old dicta to the contrary it seems that the privilege did not extend so far at common law.[5] Thus in *R v Pitt*[6] it was held that a spouse should be advised that if she chose to testify for the prosecution she would be treated like any other witness. In such circumstances she can be treated as hostile. All of this would be quite futile if she could nevertheless claim a privilege against incriminating her spouse. It need hardly be added that there is no privilege against incriminating strangers.[7]

As noted above, the common law rule was that the privilege against self-incrimination applied only to the crimination of the claimant. In England there seems to be no doubt that the privilege can be claimed by any entity having legal personality,[8] but this is not the case in North America,[9] nor now in Australia.[10]

In *Rio Tinto Zinc Corpn v Westinghouse Electric Corpn* the question of the extent to which an individual director could claim the privilege in relation to material which might incriminate his company was raised. It was not necessary for their Lordships to express a final view on this question, which they felt required further consideration, since if some such privilege were not recognised that of the company might be rendered nugatory.[11]

(iii) Fiduciaries

In some old cases it was suggested that as a party could validly contract not to exercise the privilege against another, it followed that by simply choosing to act as a fiduciary he impliedly put himself in the same position.[12] Attempts to invoke this doctrine in

---

4   Cmnd 4991, para 169.
5   Dicta of Bayley J in *R v All Saints, Worcester Inhabitants* (1817) 6 M & S 194, at 201; compare Lord Diplock in *Rio Tinto Zinc Corpn v Westinghouse Electric Corpn* [1978] AC 547, at 637, [1978] 1 All ER 434, at 465, 'At common law ... the privilege against self-incrimination was restricted to the person claiming it and not anyone else.'
6   [1983] QB 25, [1982] 3 All ER 63.
7   *R v Minihane* (1921) 16 Cr App Rep 38.
8   *Triplex Safety Glass Co Ltd v Lancegaye Safety Glass (1934) Ltd* [1939] 2 KB 395, [1939] 2 All ER 613; *Rio Tinto Zinc Corpn v Westinghouse Electric Corpn* [1978] AC 547, [1978] 1 All ER 434.
9   *US v White* 322 US 694 (1944); *Braswell v US* 108 S Ct 2284 (1988); *R v Judge of General Sessions of the Peace for the County of York, ex p Corning Glassworks of Canada Ltd* (1970) 16 DLR (3d) 609; *R v N M Paterson & Sons Ltd* [1980] 2 SCR 679; *R v Amway Corpn* [1989] 1 SCR 21.
10 *Environment Protection Authority v Caltex Refining Co Pty Ltd* (1993) 178 CLR 477: Evidence Act 1995, s 187(2). Neither can the privilege against exposure to a penalty be so claimed in respect of documents, either in response to a notice to produce: *Trade Practices Commission v Abbco Iceworks Pty Ltd* (1994) 123 ALR 503; or on discovery: *Trade Practices Commission v CC (New South Wales) Pty (No 4)* (1995) 131 ALR 581.
11 It is clear that an individual not authorised to speak on behalf of the corporation cannot invoke the privilege on behalf of the corporation, *Walkers Snack Foods Ltd v Coventry County Council* [1998] 3 All ER 163. Before the change in *Environment Protection Authority v Caltex Refining Co Pty Ltd* above, the privilege was denied in Australia to a company director in respect of documents which might incriminate his company in *Burden v NSW Crime Commission* (1993) 68 ACR 410 and to the executive secretary of an unincorporated association in respect of documents which might incriminate the association in *Rochfort v Trade Practices Comrs* (1982) 153 CLR 134. Cf *Upjohn & Co v US* 449 US 383 (1981) for the position in the United States; and *R v Nova Scotia Pharmaceutical Society* (1990) 73 DLR (4th) 184 for that in Canada.
12 *Green v Weaver* (1827) 1 Sim 404; *Chadwick v Chadwick* (1852) 22 LJ Ch 329; *Robinson v Kitchin* (1856) 21 Beav 365. See generally Grevling in Rose (ed) *Consensus ad Idem* (1996) at 38.

modern cases have been uniformly unsuccessful,[13] and affirmation of the basic premise has been conspicuously withheld.

3.   Range of effects

There is a number of possible unpleasant effects to which an answer might expose a witness. The central case is conviction of a crime under the law of the forum.[14] On the other hand a witness cannot claim to be privileged from answering questions on the ground that the answers will expose him to civil liability either at the suit of the Crown or of any other person.[15] Nor will exposure to other unpleasant consequences be enough, such as rendering the witness liable to bankruptcy,[16] or to professional disciplinary proceedings,[17] but there are a number of other possibilities which need to be mentioned.

(i)   Liability to conviction in a different jurisdiction

The few authorities dealing with this question at common law tended to conflict with each other, both here[18] and elsewhere.[19] In the light of such uncertainty the Privy Council in *Brannigan v Davison*[20] relied upon principle[1] in stressing that no sovereign[2] state could contemplate its domestic law being frustrated by the law of another expressed through the operation of the privilege. This applied whether or not the privilege related to evidence of a crime already committed, or where the foreign

13   See *Rank Film Distributors Ltd v Video Information Centre* [1982] AC 380, [1980] 2 All ER 273, where the point was defeated by a majority in the Court of Appeal, and not even argued in the House of Lords; *Tate Access Floors v Boswell* [1991] Ch 512, [1990] 3 All ER 303; *Mirror Group Newspapers plc v Maxwell* [1993] Ch 1, [1992] 2 All ER 856. In the latter two the proposition was held to be inconsistent with the reasoning in the earlier cases of *Parkhurst v Lowten* (1819) 2 Swan 194n and *Paxton v Douglas* (1809) 16 Ves 239, and with the result in the later one of *Sociedade Nacional de Combustiveis de Angola UEE v Lundqvist* [1991] 2 QB 310, [1990] 3 All ER 283. See also in Australia *Reid v Howard* (1995) 184 CLR 1.

14   For a recent straightforward example unalloyed by statutory intervention see *United Norwest Co-operatives Ltd v Johnstone* (1994) Times, 24 February.

15   Witnesses Act 1806. Liability to a penalty for civil contempt will suffice, see below p 429.

16   *Re XY, ex p Haes* [1902] 1 KB 98.

17   See *Re Fang and College of Physicians and Surgeons of Alberta* (1985) 25 DLR (4th) 632; *Re Johnstone and Law Society of British Columbia* (1987) 40 DLR (4th) 550; *Re Prousky and the Law Society of Upper Canada* (1987) 41 DLR (4th) 565, though in Canada the position has been much affected by the Canadian Charter of Rights and Freedoms which these decisions construe. In the United States the privilege has been held not to extend to protect a foreign bank account from compulsory disclosure: *Doe v US* 487 US 201 (1988); nor to prevent the accused from being shown to be 'a sexually dangerous person': *Allen v Illinois* 478 US 364 (1986).

18   Cp *King of the Two Sicilies v Willcox* (1851) 1 Sim NS 301 and *Re Atherton* [1912] 2 KB 251, at 255 with *United States of America v McRae* (1868) 3 Ch App 79.

19   Cp in Australia *Adstream Building Industries Pty Ltd v The Queensland Lime and Cement Co Ltd (No 4)* [1985] 1 Qd R 127 with *FF Seeley Nominees v El Ar Initiations (UK) Ltd* (1990) 96 ALR 468, at 472, 473; and in the United States *US v (Under Seal)* (1986) 794 F 2d 920 (1986) (4th Cir) with *Mishima v US* (1981) 507 F Supp 131, now resolved by the Supreme Court against the privilege, see *US v Balsys* 524 US 666 (1998).

20   [1997] AC 238; for commentary see Pattenden (1997) 2 Int J Ev & Pr 44.

1   It approved the statement of it in *Murphy v Waterfront Commission of New York Harbour* 378 US 52 (1964), at 55.

2   It recognised that modification might be necessary to accommodate internal operation within federal jurisdictions.

legislation made the tendering of such evidence itself a crime.[3] By statute in the United Kingdom s 14(1)(a) of the Civil Evidence Act 1968, expressly confines the privilege to 'criminal offences under the law of any part of the United Kingdom and penalties provided for by such law'.[4] Even then the court retains a discretion, at least in respect of discovery,[5] and its exercise of such discretion may be influenced by the prospect of incrimination under foreign law.[6] The precise delimitation of the discretionary powers of the court at common law was left unresolved[7] in *Brannigan v Davision*.

(ii) Liability to the imposition of a penalty

The rule that a witness cannot be obliged to answer a question if the answer would expose him to the risk of a penalty seems to have originated in the doctrine that equity would not assist a common informer by making an order for discovery in his favour. This rule survived the Judicature Acts.[8] Proceedings for penalties, as opposed to compensation,[9] were virtually obsolete, but the Law Reform Committee considered that the privilege should continue so long as penalties are recoverable in some civil proceedings.[10] The category of penalties in respect of which the privilege may be claimed has been augmented by accession to the European Union, since penalties imposed for breach of the terms of the EEC Treaty, and of Council Regulations, have been held to qualify.[11] It has further been held that penalties for civil contempt come within the category of those in respect of which the privilege can be claimed, and that there is nothing in the wording of s 14 of the Civil Evidence Act 1968 to the contrary.[12] This is however subject to the qualification that where the order could have been made in one set of contempt proceedings, a second set cannot be frustrated by the privilege on the basis that they might expose the party to a penalty in the first set,[13] at least where it is no more than a technicality that there are formally two sets of proceedings.[14]

3   A similar result was achieved in this respect in Canada in *Spencer v R* [1985] 2 SCR 278, and in the United States in *US v Field* 532 F 2d 404 (1976).
4   There was a corresponding provision in cl 15(1)(a) of the draft Bill attached to the 11th Report of the Criminal Law Revision Committee, but no such clause appeared in the Police and Criminal Evidence Act 1984.
5   And in relation to revelation pursuant to a freezing injunction, *A-G for Gibraltar v May* [1999] 1 WLR 998.
6   *Arab Monetary Fund v Hashim* [1989] 3 All ER 466, [1989] 1 WLR 565. It should be noted however that in *Levi Strauss & Co v Barclays Trading Corpn Inc* [1993] FSR 179 it was not regarded as a sufficient answer for failure to discover that to do so would effectively deprive the party of his privilege against self-incrimination elsewhere.
7   At 251D.
8   *Hunnings v Williamson* (1883) 10 QBD 459; *Martin v Treacher* (1886) 16 QBD 507.
9   *Adams v Batley* (1887) 18 QBD 625.
10 16th Report, para 13.
11 *Rio Tinto Zinc Corpn v Westinghouse Electric Corpn* [1978] AC 547, [1978] 1 All ER 434. It is also of importance in other common law jurisdictions where regulations are enforced by the imposition of penalties, often by a commission or tribunal: see *Pyneboard Pty Ltd v Trade Practices Commission* (1983) 45 ALR 609; though in Australia this has been mitigated by extension of the exclusion of corporate persons from the benefit of this aspect of the privilege in exactly the same way as with regard to exposure to ordinary criminal prosecution: *Trade Practices Commission v Abbco Ice Works Pty Ltd* (1994) 123 ALR 503.
12 *Bhimmji v Chatwani (No 3)* [1992] 4 All ER 912, [1992] 1 WLR 1158, preferring the dicta of Lord Denning MR in *Comet Products UK Ltd v Hawkex Plastics Ltd* [1971] 2 QB 67, at 74, [1971] 1 All ER 1141, at 1144 to the decision of Walton J in *Garvin v Domus Publishing Ltd* [1989] Ch 335, [1989] 2 All ER 344.
13 *Crest Homes plc v Marks* [1987] AC 829, at 859, [1987] 2 All ER 1074, at 1082.
14 So not in *Cobra Golf Ltd v Rata* [1998] Ch 109, [1997] 2 All ER 150, where the two sets of proceedings were separate, and the search order in the second used to secure evidence for committal in the first.

(iii)   Liability to forfeiture

The inclusion of answers tending to establish liability to a forfeiture within this privilege was attributable to the rule that equity would not grant discovery or order interrogatories in aid of a forfeiture of property which also survived the Judicature Acts. The Law Reform Committee could see no reason for the continued existence of this branch of the privilege against self-incrimination now that the courts possess wide powers of relief against forfeiture, and it was accordingly abolished, so far as civil cases are concerned, by s 16(1)(a) of the Civil Evidence Act 1968.[15]

(iv)   Liability to a finding of adultery

There can be little doubt that answers which might be used to establish the witness's adultery were once thought to be included in the common law privilege against self-incrimination, but this view was rendered obsolete by the decision of the Court of Appeal in *Blunt v Park Lane Hotel Ltd*.[16]

B.   PROCEDURE

The privilege strictly applies only to answering; it does not prevent the relevant question being asked.[17] The judge will often warn a witness that he is not obliged to answer criminating questions, but there is no rule of law to this effect,[18] and the fact that the witness was ignorant of his rights does not prevent the court from utilising his evidence in the case in which it was given, or in subsequent criminal proceedings brought against him.[19]

The practice to be followed when someone objects to answering a question because he might be incriminated if he were to do so was laid down in *R v Boyes*.[20] The witness's mere statement that his answer might have this effect is not sufficient, although it is on oath and even if there is no doubt concerning his bona fides. The court must see, from the circumstances of the case and the nature of the evidence which the witness is called to give, that there is reasonable ground to apprehend danger to him from his answer.[1]

---

15   There was a corresponding provision in cl 16(1)(a) of the draft Bill annexed to the 11th Report of the Criminal Law Revision Committee.

16   [1942] 2 KB 253, [1942] 2 All ER 187. See also *Evans v Evans and Blyth* [1904] P 378, and *Elliot v Albert* [1934] 1 KB 650.

17   *Allhusen v Labouchere* (1878) 3 QBD 654, at 660. Contrast the introductory words of the Criminal Evidence Act 1898, s 1(f).

18   Though it has been said that a judge should warn a witness of the absence of the privilege: *R v Pitt* [1983] QB 25, [1982] 3 All ER 63; and in Canada once the accused has indicated his possible commission of a further crime he must be readvised of his right to counsel: *R v Sawatsky* (1997) 150 DLR (4th) 750.

19   *R v Coote* (1873) LR 4 PC 599. Cf *S v Lwane* 1966 (2) SA 433. For the stage in the proceedings at which the objection should be taken, see *Spokes v Grosvenor Hotel Co* [1897] 2 QB 124; *A J Bekhor v Bilton* [1981] QB 923, [1981] 2 All ER 565. It seems that a warning is not mandatory in relation to incrimination under foreign law: *R v Bateman and Cooper* [1989] Crim LR 590.

20   (1861) 1 B & S 311; *Re Reynolds, ex p Reynolds* (1882) 20 Ch D 294

1   *Triplex Safety Glass Co Ltd v Lancegaye Safety Glass (1934) Ltd* [1939] 2 KB 395, [1939] 2 All ER 613, approved in *Rio Tinto Zinc Corpn v Westinghouse Electric Corpn* [1978] AC 547, [1978] 1 All ER 434. The claimant bears the evidential burden of showing this: *Sociedad Nacional de Combustiveis de Angola UEE v Lundqvist* [1991] 2 QB 310, [1990] 3 All ER 283; and is unlikely to discharge it when the claim is inconsistent with his own affidavit which remains unretracted: *Downie v Coe* (1997) Times, 28 November.

There must be no nice balancing of odds;[2] the judge must come to the conclusion that such danger is real and appreciable with reference to the ordinary operation of law in the ordinary course of things, not a danger of an imaginary and insubstantial character, having reference to some extraordinary and barely possible contingency so improbable that no reasonable man would suffer it to influence his conduct.

In *Boyes*'s case, a witness who had been handed a pardon under the Great Seal was obliged to answer a question with reference to its subject matter although he might still have been impeached for the offence according to strict legal theory because a pardon cannot be pleaded in answer to an impeachment. If a witness has already made himself liable to a criminal prosecution by an admission, his refusal to answer may be held not to be bona fide,[3] or a form of waiver.[4] If the offence was of a trifling nature, or committed many years ago, a court might be inclined to regard the danger as too insubstantial to allow the plea to succeed. It will also be responsive to diminution of particular dangers in the light of changes of practice, and alert to the risk of defendants seeking to avoid civil liability by exaggerating dangers of prosecution,[5] especially where the offence to which the privilege is claimed to apply is overshadowed by others to which it does not.[6] Perhaps surprisingly the House of Lords has held an informal assurance by the prosecuting authorities of the absence of any intention to rely upon materials discovered in any subsequent criminal proceedings enough to dispel danger, and to avert the operation of the privilege.[7]

The burden of showing that the danger is real is borne by the witness asserting the privilege. If that burden has been discharged, the court will not be deterred by commercial inconvenience from upholding the privilege. Thus in *Rank Film Distributors Ltd v Video Information Centre*, where the defendant raised the privilege to defeat the application of a search order summarily requiring him to furnish certain information about his infringement of copyright in certain video films, the danger of a criminal charge of conspiracy to defraud was very real. The House of Lords upheld the claim for privilege even though it accepted that the result of so doing would be the practical destruction of the usefulness of search orders.[8]

Anything that a person was wrongly compelled to say after he had claimed his privilege was treated as having been said involuntarily, with the result that it was inadmissible in subsequent proceedings brought against him,[9] but the provisions and,

---

2   *Re Westinghouse Electric Corpn Uranium Contract Litigation N D L Dock 235* [1977] 3 All ER 703, at 726.
3   *Brebner v Perry* [1961] SASR 177, where various English authorities are mentioned.
4   *Registrar Court of Appeal v Craven* (1994) 120 FLR 427.
5   *Rank Film Distributors Ltd v Video Information Centre* [1982] AC 380, at 441, [1981] 2 All ER 76, at 80.
6   *Khan v Khan* [1982] 2 All ER 60, [1982] 1 WLR 513; *Renworth Ltd v Stephansen* [1996] 3 All ER 244.
7   *AT & T Istel Ltd v Tully* [1993] AC 45, [1992] 3 All ER 523: see (1993) 109 LQR 48. For a similar result in Australia see *Saffron v Federal Commr of Taxation* (1992) 109 ALR 695 relying in part upon some dicta of Lord Diplock in *R v McDonald* [1983] NZLR 252, at 255.
8   See Lord Fraser at 445, 83. It was thought necessary to enact s 72 of the Supreme Court Act 1981 to restore the position, though in New Zealand a similar result was achieved at common law: see *Thorn EMI Ltd v Kitching and Busby* [1984] FSR 342. For a similarly stringent approach in the context of freezing injunctions, see *Sociedad Nacional de Combustiveis de Angola UEE v Lundqvist* [1991] 2 QB 310, at 338, [1990] 3 All ER 283.
9   *R v Garbett* (1847) 1 Den 236; it is not clear that this result can be reconciled with the new test provided by s 76(2) of the Police and Criminal Evidence Act 1984. Obiter dicta to the same effect in *R v Coote* (1873) LR 4 PC 599, have however been used in New Zealand to assist the court to resist a claim to the privilege on an application for a search order because it made the chance of criminal proceedings being brought more remote, *Thorn EMI Video Ltd v Kitching and Busby* [1984] FSR 342.

to some extent, the construction of statutes have prevented this result from being reached in a number of cases.

C. STATUTORY PROVISION

It is not unknown for some statutes to endorse the operation of this privilege quite explicitly.[10] It is, however, much more common to find some degree of statutory abridgement usually designed to facilitate effective extra-curial investigation.[11] Some such statutes have a draconian effect. Their effect is that the privilege is abolished for all purposes in the cases to which they apply. The net result is that, if information has been lawfully obtained pursuant to those statutory provisions[12] and there is no restriction on the use which can be made of the information, the person giving it cannot object to its being used in evidence against him either on the ground that such use would infringe his privilege against self-incrimination or because the information would not have been given voluntarily.[13]

To a large extent this is the result of the decision of the majority of the Court for Crown Cases Reserved in *R v Scott*.[14] It turned on the construction of s 117 of the Bankruptcy Law Consolidation Act 1849 under which it was lawful for the official receiver to examine the debtor 'touching all matters relating to his trade dealings or estates'. A subsequent section provided for the punishment of false answers as perjury, but there was no provision explicitly permitting subsequent use of the answers in any legal proceedings. Under some pressure the debtor answered questions of the relevant kind, and it was held that his answers were admissible against him at his subsequent trial for mutilating his books.

The continued strength of such provisions was illustrated in *R v Kansal*[15] where it was held not only that s 433 of the Insolvency Act 1986 had such an effect, but that it prevailed despite the relevant acts arguably falling under the more emollient régime of s 31 of the Theft Act 1968. A similarly stringent approach is adopted in relation to corporate insolvency. In *Bishopsgate Investment Management Ltd v Maxwell*[16] after a lengthy review of the previous statutory provisions in relation to both personal and corporate insolvency it was held[17] that the privilege did not apply in investigations under s 236 of the Insolvency Act 1986, subject only to a discretion to relieve the respondent from any oppression, though it is obvious from the result that exposure to criminal proceedings alone cannot be regarded as oppressive.[18] The Court was

10   See, for example, the Consumer Protection Act 1987, s 47(2); Social Security Administration Act 1992, s 110(7) ; Social Security Act 1998, s 16(5) (all of which extend to the incrimination of a spouse).

11   Bankruptcy legislation goes back to the earliest times, and as early as 1820 Lord Eldon held that it prevailed over the privilege against self-incrimination: *Ex p Cossens* (1820) Buck 531, at 540.

12   In Australia it has been held that where a statute also provides reasonable excuse as a defence this should be brought to the attention of the subject of the questioning (*Workcover Authority of New South Wales v Seccombe* (1998) 43 NSWLR 390) as a condition of overriding the privilege.

13   *R v Scott* (1856) Dears & B 47; *R v Coote* (1873) LR 4 PC 599; *Customs and Excise Comrs v Harz* [1967] 1 AC 760, [1967] 1 All ER 177; *George v Coombe* [1978] Crim LR 47.

14   Above. Cf *R v Sloggett* (1856) Dears CC 656 where the point was left open.

15   [1993] QB 244, [1992] 3 All ER 844.

16   [1993] Ch 1, [1992] 2 All ER 856.

17   Approving *Re Jeffrey S Levitt* [1992] Ch 457, [1992] 2 All ER 509.

18   It may become necessary to reconsider this position in the light of the determination of the European Court of Human Rights that the exercise of such powers contravenes the European Convention on Human Rights; see *Saunders v United Kingdom* [1997] BCC 872.

disinclined to adopt a technical approach seeking to differentiate between different forms of provision requiring an answer. It explicitly rejected[19] the view that qualification of the questioning as 'reasonable' necessarily incorporated an implied importation of the privilege. Some protection is provided by restriction of public access to the records of such investigations.[20] This protection must itself yield however to a requisition under different statutory provisions, for example by the Serious Fraud Office in its investigations.[1] Similar provisions govern investigation by inspectors[2] into the affairs of a company,[3] and again the privilege is implicitly excluded.[4] It should also be noted that no protection can be derived in these cases from the provisions of the Police and Criminal Evidence Act 1984 relating to proper procedures to be observed by those charged with the duty of investigating offences, since here the primary focus is on tracing assets, and regulating trading rather than upon prosecution.

In *R v Scott* the court declined to imply a proviso that the answers could not be used in subsequent criminal proceedings against the debtor. Among the grounds for this conclusion was that:[5]

> When the legislature compels parties to give evidence accusing themselves, and means to protect them from the consequences of giving such evidence, the course of legislation has been to do so by express enactment.

The existence of statutes providing that information obtained in a particular inquiry may be used in evidence against the person questioned could be invoked in favour of a converse argument that the absence of such words implies the continued availability of the privilege against self-incrimination.[6] It must be admitted, however, that in England most cases statutory provisions are construed in the manner suggested in *R v Scott.*

This scenario is well-illustrated by development in the law relating to intellectual property. In order to secure the elimination of 'piracy' in respect of copyright in such things as recordings and computer programs, the courts developed a special summary procedure, the search order, requiring a defendant to provide materials and to answer enquiries. Given the operation of criminal sanctions in the area, compliance with such orders could lead to self-incrimination and, as noted above, in *Rank Film Distributors*

---

19 At 40, 884.
20 In this case under r 9.5 of the Insolvency Rules 1986. It should also be noted that there is a general, but not absolute, duty of confidence in relation to material secured under compulsory powers: *Marcel v Metropolitan Police Comr* [1992] Ch 225, [1992] 1 All ER 72; see also *Re Barlow Clowes Gilt Managers Ltd* [1992] Ch 208, [1991] 4 All ER 385, as modified in *Re Arrows Ltd (No 4)* [1995] 2 AC 75, [1994] 3 All ER 814. Nor is there any obligation to disclose on the same basis to defence and prosecution: *Re Arrows (No 4)* [1995] 2 AC 75, [1994] 3 All ER 814.
1   *Re Arrows (No 4),* where it was said by Lord Nolan at 110D, 834g that the only remedy against abuse of the compulsory power was that of discretionary exclusion under s 78 of the Police and Criminal Evidence Act 1984. Its ambit nevertheless remains limited in this context pending the embodiment of the European Convention of Human Rights into English law: see *R v Saunders* [1996] 1 Cr App R 463.
2   Eg under the Companies Act 1985, ss 431, 432, 442 and 446 as amended.
3   Or by the Bank of England into the affairs of a bank under the Banking Act 1987, s 42.
4   *R v Seelig* [1991] 4 All ER 429, [1992] 1 WLR 148; *Re London United Investments plc* [1992] Ch 578, [1992] 2 All ER 842; *Bank of England v Riley* [1992] Ch 475, [1992] 1 All ER 769.
5   Lord Campbell at 60.
6   *R v Savundranayagan and Walker* (1968) 52 Cr App Rep 637, at 644; but see *R v Harris* [1970] 3 All ER 746, [1970] 1 WLR 1252. See also in Australia *X v McDermott* (1994) 123 ALR 226 where express abridgement in relation to a more formal enquiry was held to lead to the conclusion that the privilege was retained for a less formal enquiry which the relevant statute also provided but as to which it was silent on the question of abridgement.

Ltd v Video Information Centre[7] the House of Lords upheld the privilege at common law. Almost immediately legislation was enacted as s 72(1) of the Supreme Court Act 1981 to abrogate the privilege, but in compensation also provided instead that:

> (3) ... no statement or admission made by a person—
> (a) in answering a question put to him in any proceeding to which subsection (1) applies; or
> (b) in complying with any order made in such proceedings, shall, in proceedings for any related offence or for the recovery of any related penalty, be admissible in evidence against that person or (unless they married after making of the statement or admission) against the spouse of that person.
>
>   (4) Nothing in subsection (3) shall render any statement or admission made by a person as there mentioned inadmissible in evidence against that person in proceedings for perjury or contempt of court.

This technique of abrogating the privilege in return for abstention from use of the material so obtained has been employed for many years. It can lead to difficulty in establishing the range of proceedings in respect of which the material so obtained cannot be used.[8] It should be noted also that here the abrogation of the privilege is wider than its restoration in such proceedings.[9]

Investigation into serious fraud which has been present in many of the cases mentioned above is now largely governed by the provisions of the Criminal Justice Act 1987. Section 2(2) of the Act provides for the compulsory questioning of a person under investigation, and s 2(3) for the compulsory production of documents. It is interesting to note that s 2(8) provides that statements provided under compulsion may be used against their provider only for defective compliance with the Act, or to rebut an inconsistent statement in subsequent proceedings,[10] but gives no protection in relation to the compulsory production of documents. This has been held to justify compulsory provision of evidence provided under the previously mentioned compulsory investigative proceedings, notwithstanding that if such questioning had been undertaken under the provisions of the Criminal Justice Act itself, it would have had to be conducted pursuant to s 2(2) where protection *is* provided against subsequent use. This strong view applies also to permit investigation under the provisions of s 2(2) even after a criminal charge has been laid.[11] Any residual protection for such an accused person must reside in the more general powers of the trial judge to prevent oppression of the accused, and abuse of process. Where the privilege has been abrogated it may nevertheless be just, and within the discretion of the court, to stay contemporaneous civil proceedings, so that the criminal proceedings can be completed without such

---

7   [1982] AC 380, [1981] 2 All ER 76.
8   Section 72(5) of the Supreme Court Act 1981 contains a definition of a 'related offence' and a 'related penalty' in terms which the House of Lords found it difficult to construe in *Crest Homes plc v Marks* [1987] AC 829, [1987] 2 All ER 1074; see also *Universal City Studios Inc v Hubbard* [1984] Ch 225, [1984] 1 All ER 661.
9   The abrogation extends to materials discovered while the restoration is limited to admissions and statements.
10   Even this use was condemned by the European Court of Human Rights in *Saunders v United Kingdom* [1997] BCC 872.
11   *R v Director of Serious Fraud Office, ex p Smith* [1993] AC 1, [1992] 3 All ER 456. Although it now seems that it is not the general policy to do so: see *R v Secretary of State for Trade and Industry, ex p McCormick* [1998] BCC 379.

encroachment upon the accused's position.[12] It will often be still better wherever possible to defer any civil proceedings until after the termination of related criminal trials.[13]

There is a number of important provisions of this character in the Children Act 1989,[14] designed to secure statements from parents and carers in order to facilitate the best treatment of the child. The protection offered there is extensive in that it limits subsequent use in evidence to proceedings for perjury. Perhaps for that reason it has been interpreted restrictively so as not to protect statements made in advance of proceedings in court,[15] nor where there is no more than a remote chance of the maker being charged with an ancillary offence,[16] and that such statements can be disclosed,[17] and used, to discredit their maker, at least if the maker is not the alleged principal offender.

Section 1(e) of the Criminal Evidence Act 1898 provides that the accused may be asked any question in cross-examination notwithstanding that it would tend to incriminate him as to the offence charged. This was thought an essential corollary to the main provision of the Act enabling the accused to give evidence on his own behalf. His position with regard to questions tending to show that he had committed other offences is governed by special provisions in s 1(f) already considered in ch IX above.

The number and effect[18] of these abrogations of the privilege should give pause for thought on the part of anyone who regards the privilege as a fundamental principle of English law. These statutes relate not only to the investigation of serious offences such as infringements of s 1 of the Official Secrets Act 1911,[19] but also to such matters as taxation, gambling and road traffic.[20]

It seems now to have been accepted[1] that the Canadian Charter of Rights and Freedoms has colonised the privilege against self-incrimination in that jurisdiction by enacting in s 11(c) that a person accused of crime may not be compelled to testify, and in s 13 that a witness may not have incriminating evidence used against[2] him in subsequent proceedings.[3] Contrary to some early indication[4] it seems unlikely that the ambit of the privilege will be extended by reference to s 7 of the Charter, since so expanded a concept is not regarded as a 'principle of fundamental justice' in Canada.[5]

---

12   *Jefferson Ltd v Bhetcha* [1979] 2 All ER 1108, [1979] 1 WLR 898. See for a similar approach in Australia, *Kirk v Australian Federal Police Comr* (1988) 81 ALR 321; and in Canada, *Saccamanno v Swanson*, above.

13   As urged by Lord Diplock in *R v IRC, ex p Rossminster* [1980] AC 952, at 1012, [1980] 1 All ER 80, at 94.

14   Sections 48, 50 and 98.

15   *Re C (a minor) (care proceedings: disclosure)* [1997] Fam 76.

16   *K (minors), Re* [1994] 3 All ER 330, sub nom *Kent County Council v K* [1994] 1 WLR 912. The same view was taken by the Supreme Court of Canada in *R v Kuldip* [1990] 3 SCR 618.

17   Restrictions on disclosure are imposed by the Families Proceedings Rules 1991, r 4.23.

18   In the United States since the decision of the Supreme Court in *Counselman v Hitchcock* 142 US 547 (1892) it has become more common for abrogation of the privilege to lead to complete immunity from prosecution for the relevant offence rather than merely to the inadmissibility in it of evidence so obtained.

19   See s 6 of the Act of 1920 under which it is an offence to withhold information from a duly authorised officer of police.

20   On the whole subject see Heydon (1971) 87 LQR 214; and as it relates to corporations, McCormack (1993) JBL 425.

1   *Thomson Newspapers v Director of Investigation and Research* [1990] 1 SCR 425.

2   This has been held not to prevent use to impugn credit, *R v B (WD)* (1987) 45 DLR (4th) 429.

3   The exegesis of this concept has proved problematical, see eg *R v Dubois* [1985] 2 SCR 350; *R v Mannion* [1986] 2 SCR 272.

4   *R L Crain v Couture and Restrictive Trade Practices Commission* (1983) 6 DLR (4th) 478.

5   *Thomson Newspapers* above, see also *R v McKinlay Transport Ltd* (1987) 48 DLR (4th) 765. This reflects long experience of s 5 of the Canada Evidence Act which merely provided use immunity.

In civil proceedings a witness can rely only upon the protection offered by the Charter against use of his testimony in any subsequent proceedings.[6]

D.   REFORM

The idea that a man should be compelled to give answers exposing himself to the risk of criminal punishment is probably still repellent to public opinion, although it is no longer based on the unpopularity of the Star Chamber. There is the additional consideration that people must be encouraged to testify freely, and they might not be prepared to come forward as witnesses in the absence of some kind of privilege against incrimination. Although reliance on the privilege will sometimes obstruct the course of justice in the case in which it is claimed, and may militate against the discovery of crimes which ought to be traced in the public interest, there is probably sufficient justification for protecting a witness from exposing himself to the peril of criminal proceedings. When it is invoked as a justification of the accused's right not to testify and the suspect's right not to answer the questions of investigating officials, additional bases of the privilege which are frequently mentioned are the need to keep the officials up to scratch and the desirability of requiring them, as representatives of the state, to shoulder the entire burden of establishing the accused's guilt.

Considerations of this character have in some jurisdictions led to the extension of the doctrine of protection against self-incrimination beyond the confines of an evidential privilege into the status of a constitutional right. Thus in Canada the Supreme Court has remarked:[7]

> Recent case law has taken the traditional doctrine of privilege and placed it on a new plane. Privilege is no longer regarded merely as a rule of evidence which acts as a shield to prevent privileged materials from being tendered in evidence in a courtroom. The courts, unwilling to restrict the concept, have extended its application well beyond those limits.

In Australasia, where a similar view has developed, its implications are in the process of being worked out,[8] although it has been held that no new exceptions can be created by judicial action.[9] It is submitted that such an approach conflates a number of quite separate rules having different rationales, different histories and different incidents,[10]

6   *Caisse Populaire Laurier d'Ottawa Ltee v Guertin (No 2)* (1983) 150 DLR (3d) 541;
    Saccomanno v Swanson (1987) 34 DLR (4th) 462.
7   *Solosky v R* [1980] 1 SCR 821, at 836 (the generality of these remarks occurred within the
    context of a claim for solicitor and client privilege). For similar sentiments in relation to the
    principle against self-incrimination see especially Lamer CJ in *R v P(MB)* [1994] 1 SCR 555,
    at 579, and distinguishing the *principle* against self-incrimination from its emanation in the
    privilege, in *R v Jones* [1994] 2 SCR 229, at 249. For a more qualified view see Iacobucci J in
    R v S (RJ) [1995] 1 SCR 449, at 486.
8   *Sorby v Commonwealth* (1983) 152 CLR 281 is the leading case: developed in *Trade Practices
    Commission v TNT Management Pty Ltd* (1984) 53 ALR 214; *Scanlon v Swan, ex p Swan*
    [1984] 1 Qd R 21; *Re Packer v Deputy Comr of Taxation* [1985] 1 Qd R 275; *Controlled
    Consultants Pty Ltd v Comr for Corporate Affairs* (1985) 156 CLR 185; *Police Service Board
    v Morris* (1985) 156 CLR 397; *Environment Protection Authority v Caltex Refining Co Pty Ltd*
    (1993) 178 CLR 477; *Reid v Howard* (1995) 184 CLR 1. See McNicol *Law of Privilege* (1992).
    See also in *New Zealand Apple and Pear Marketing Board v Master and Sons Ltd* [1986] 1
    NZLR 191.
9   *Reid v Howard* supra at 12.
10 See especially the masterful analysis accomplished by Lord Mustill in *R v Director of Serious
    Fraud Office, ex p Smith* [1993] AC 1, [1992] 3 All ER 456.

with the consequential dangers of confusion and anomaly explained in the seminal dissenting opinions of Brennan J in the High Court of Australia.[11]

In England there was less indigenous pressure to adopt such a view, but as result of the censure of abrogation of this privilege in *Saunders v United Kingdom*,[12] and it seems as a direct result of the enactment of the Human Rights Act 1998, an amendment to confer use immunity has been proposed by amendment to the original draft of the Youth Justice and Criminal Evidence Bill 1999.[13]

The more immediate current pressure is to reduce the impact of the privilege in the early stages of civil proceedings. As a result of some judicial concern[14] the Lord Chancellor's Department undertook to consider possible means of reforming the operation of the privilege in civil proceedings, and a Consultation paper was published in July 1992.[15] This paper recommended a switch from the current operation of the privilege which it regarded as leading to injustice and uncertainty to a system based on what it described as 'secondary privilege'.[16] This would simply amount to the withdrawal of the privilege in civil proceedings, but then to provide that information so divulged could not be used in subsequent criminal proceedings. This secondary privilege would in principle exclude documents on the basis that the privilege is least justifiable in relation to the production of material which existed before the commencement of the civil proceedings.[17] It would however remain available to be used in a prosecution for perjury,[18] and to discredit the witness if he testified inconsistently with it[19] in any subsequent criminal proceedings.[20] The mechanism would not require the claim to privilege to be made before the attempted use of the information in the subsequent criminal proceedings,[1] and would be determined by the judge at the criminal trial.

The paper recognises that to bestow a secondary privilege in this way could lead to abuse, for example by a collusive civil claim designed to insulate information from use in an apprehended prosecution. It was partly to meet this danger that the paper suggested that the privilege should exclude pre-existing documents, and it is proposed also that the secondary privilege should not apply to statements or admissions relied upon by the claimant in the precedent civil proceedings.

Although, as its title suggests, the paper is principally concerned with the operation of the privilege in civil proceedings it suggests that there is no reason for its proposals not to apply to witnesses, apart from the accused, in criminal proceedings.[2]

11 Notably in *Pyneboard Pty Ltd v Trade Practices Commission* (1983) 152 CLR 328, at 354; and *Sorby* above at 316; Brennan J held a similar view in relation to the closely related topic of legal professional privilege: see *Baker v Campbell* (1983) 153 CLR 52, at 105.
12 [1997] BCC 872.
13 Cl 58, Sch 3. The Criminal Justice Act 1987 is one of the scheduled pieces of legislation to be affected by the change.
14 Above p 424.
15 Consultation Paper *The Privilege Against Self-Incrimination in Civil Proceedings* (Lord Chancellor's Department, 1992).
16 Para 30. The less radical alternative proposal is that existing secondary privilege provisions be consolidated and applied to all proceedings involving an allegation of dishonesty.
17 Para 11, though the recommendation goes further in proposing the exclusion from the secondary privilege of all documents, except those recording the civil proceedings since to exclude those would subvert the secondary privilege altogether.
18 Or in contempt proceedings: para 19.
19 This appears to be the situation at common law where an order has been made forbidding direct use of compulsorily disclosed material: *R v Martin: R v White* [1998] 2 Cr App Rep 385.
20 The paper devoted little attention to the privilege relating to the imposition of a penalty.
1   Paras 20–22.
2   Para 24. The application of similar immunities to the accused has been extensively discussed in Canada, see eg *BC Securities Commission v Branch* [1995] 2 SCR 3. The proposed relaxation in cl 58 of the Youth Justice and Criminal Evidence Bill 1999 is confined to the accused.

So far the result of this consultation has not been published in the form of a final paper, and no action has been taken. Any inroad into the traditional privilege may be felt unacceptable for political reasons, or perhaps the anomalies to which partial reform would give rise are preventing further progress. It is even possible that the bold step of abolishing the privilege without substituting any form of secondary privilege is being considered.

SECTION 2.   LEGAL PROFESSIONAL PRIVILEGE[3]

The central case of this privilege is a communication passing between lawyer and client conveying legal advice relating to the conduct of on-going litigation which need not be given in evidence or disclosed by the client and, without the client's consent, may not be given in evidence or disclosed by the legal adviser. Its scope is however broader than that in that it extends as between lawyer and to client to legal advice outside the context of on-going litigation, and within the context of litigation, when it is sometimes described as 'litigation privilege',[4] to communications by lawyer or client with third parties, or to documents compiled in connection with the litigation, and not communicated to anyone. Some influential recent authority suggests the distinction to be less clear cut,[5] and less dispositive,[6] than often supposed.[7] It is nevertheless convenient first to describe the privilege as it applies between lawyer and client for the purpose of furnishing legal advice, bearing in mind that many of the characteristics of this branch are shared by the litigation branch; then to consider some special features of the litigation branch of the privilege; to go on to describe some general exceptions from the privilege; and finally to examine claims made for similar rules to be extended to relationships other than that between lawyer and client.

A statutory formulation[8] of the privilege stated by the Police and Criminal Evidence Act 1984, s 10(1) provides that:

3   Lord Wilberforce has criticised this label as inaccurate because the privilege is that of the client: *Waugh v British Railways Board* [1980] AC 521, at 531, [1979] 2 All ER 1169, at 1172; see also *AM & S Europe v EC Commission* [1983] QB 878, at 894, 910, [1983] 1 All ER 705, at 718, 730. The expression however retained statutory endorsement: see e g Courts and Legal Services Act 1990, s 63. It was last used in 1996, and subsists in some 31 provisions. In some other statutes one of the two adjectives is omitted: 'professional privilege' appears in four provisions, the most recent in 1993; 'legal privilege' in 19, the most recent in 1997 (as indicated by a search on LEXIS conducted in July 1998).

4   *Re Highgrade Traders Ltd* [1984] BCLC 151 (in a search in July 1998 LEXIS indicated 31 cases in which this phrase had been used). There is no statutory use of this phrase.

5   *Re Barings plc* [1998] Ch 356, [1998] 1 All ER 673 where despite authority to the contra Scott VC was inclined to limit litigation privilege to such communications revelation of which would reveal the nature of legal advice passing from lawyer to client, though he safeguarded his decision by distinguishing contrary authority from the case before him on the basis that he was dealing with a case where there was a statutory duty to submit the relevant report.

6   Lord Nicholls, with whom Lord Mustill agreed, in *Re L (a minor)(police investigation: privilege)* [1997] AC 16, [1996] 2 All ER 78, where he dissented from the majority view that the distinction could justify differential overriding of legal professional privilege in the best interests of a child. In Australia the Evidence Act 1995 distinguishes explicitly between 'client legal privilege' (s 118) and 'litigation' privilege (s 119).

7   See Passmore 147 NLJ 1655 (14 November 1997) suggesting that the former view justified reconsideration of the nature of the litigation branch.

8   For a slightly different formulation see Criminal Justice Act 1993, s 18 inserting a new s 26B(9) into the Drug Trafficking Offences Act 1986. See also the statutory formulation in Australia in Part 3.10 Division 1 of the Evidence Act 1995; although this deals in terms with the operation of the privilege only at the trial stage, it seems that similar rules will be applied at other stages: see *Towney v Minister for Land and Water Conservation for NSW* (1997) 147 ALR 402 , approving earlier cases to the same effect.

(1) Subject to subsection (2) below[9] in this Act 'items subject to legal privilege' means-
   (a) communications between a professional legal adviser and his client or any person representing his client made in connection with the giving of legal advice to the client;
   (b) communications between a professional legal adviser and his client or any person representing his client or between such an adviser or his client or any such representative and any other person made in connection with or in contemplation of legal proceedings and for the purposes of such proceedings; and
   (c)   items enclosed with or referred to in such communications and made—
      (i) in connection with the giving of legal advice; or
      (ii) in connection with or in contemplation of legal proceedings and for the purposes of such proceedings; when they are in the possession of a person who is entitled to possession of them.

and has been authoritatively stated[10] to reproduce the common law.[11] It should be noted that in s 10(1)(c) it seems that 'made' refers to items enclosed or referred to, and not to the communication itself.[12]

A. LEGAL ADVICE PRIVILEGE

This part of the privilege will be taken to focus upon the rule of evidence that confidential communications passing between legal adviser and client with a view to giving or securing legal advice are privileged so far as the client is concerned, but may be frustrated by the admissibility of secondary evidence. Each of these components requires some discussion below, though not necessarily in that order.[13]

I.   Rule of evidence

In England the rule was traditionally regarded as a rule of evidence, and applied only to prevent compulsory disclosure either by way of pre-trial disclosure, or in the actual course of judicial[14] or quasi-judicial proceedings.[15] In many other parts of the Commonwealth the extension of the rule to proceedings not falling within so strict a category, or in respect of earlier and more peripheral activities relevant to such

9   This refers to communications for a criminal purpose, see further below p 457.
10   By Lord Goff in *R v Central Criminal Court, ex p Francis & Francis* [1989] AC 346, at 392, [1988] 3 All ER 775, at 797.
11   Cp the formulation in para 17 of the 16th Report of the Law Reform Committee 'Privilege in Civil Proceedings' Cmnd 3472 (1967).
12   It has even been applied to a sample of blood prepared for submission to a prospective expert witness: *R v R* [1995] 1 Cr App Rep 183.
13   Much of what is said applies to both branches of the privilege.
14   Even then the privilege will not operate to prevent disclosure of communications relating to legal advice on other unrelated proceedings, for example when the personal liability to tax of a solicitor is in question: *R v IRC, ex p Taylor (No 2)* [1990] 2 All ER 409.
15   See Diplock LJ in *Parry-Jones v Law Society* [1969] 1 Ch 1, at 9, [1968] 1 All ER 177, at 180. It does not protect the identity of the client (or presumably of the lawyer) *Bursill v Tanner* (1885) 16 QBD 1. But in *AM & S Europe v EC Commission* [1983] QB 878, at 895, 896, [1983] 1 All ER 705, at 719, 720, Advocate-General Warner seemed to suggest that there was no reason not to apply the Commonwealth approach, as exhibited in the *West-Walker* and *Shell Canada* cases (below), to the construction of English statutes.

proceedings was the subject of intense judicial debate. The privilege was elevated into something more nearly resembling a basic constitutional principle, expressed in the rhetoric of rights.[16] In Australasia[17] after some uncertainty,[18] and despite some dissent,[19] the doctrine was extended beyond the strict field of the law of evidence. Its capacity to apply in derogation of valid search warrants, by the application of very strict principles of construction to the relevant empowering legislation, led to some encroachment.[20] In Canada similar steps have been taken, and some of the Canadian cases were influential in Australia. In one[1] a search warrant was quashed because it was directed to the seizure of documents subject to privilege, and in another the principle underlying the privilege was applied to regulate the opening of mail passing between a solicitor and his client, who was in prison.[2] It now seems well-established there also that the legal effects of the relationship between solicitor and client extend beyond the protection from disclosure in legal proceedings of relevant communications which pass between them.[3] So far however the doctrine appears not to have been extended so far as to protect communications which implicate third parties.[4] The position is nevertheless far from being fully worked out in Canada, and further development seems inevitable.

This view of the status of the privilege has now been resoundingly echoed here in Lord Taylor's speech in *R v Derby Magistrates' Court, ex p B*:[5]

> Legal professional privilege is thus much more than an ordinary rule of evidence, limited in its application to the facts of a particular case. It is a fundamental condition on which the administration of justice as a whole rests.

He went on to describe it as a fundamental human right, protected by the European Convention for the Protection of Human Rights and Fundamental Freedoms, though admitting that no argument had been heard to that effect.[6]

---

16   See *Sorby v Commonwealth* (1983) 152 CLR 281, at 314 per Brennan J.
17   See eg Deane J in *A-G for The Northern Territory v Maurice* (1986) 161 CLR 475, at 490.
18   See *Crowley v Murphy* (1981) 34 ALR 496; *O'Reilly v Comr of State Bank of Victoria* (1982) 153 CLR 1; *Baker v Campbell* (1983) 153 CLR 52; and in New Zealand, *IRC v West-Walker* [1954] NZLR 191; *Rosenberg v Jaine* [1983] NZLR 1.
19   Most notably from Brennan J.
20   See especially *Baker v Campbell* and *Rosenberg v Jaine*, above; *Arno v Forsyth* (1986) 65 ALR 125; *Federal Comr of Taxation v Citibank Ltd* (1989) 85 ALR 588. Now magnified by extension of the range of litigation privilege as the result of s 119 of the Evidence Act 1995 substituting 'dominant' for 'sole' purpose as the test.
1   *Re Borden and Elliot v R* (1975) 70 DLR (3d) 579; in England this seems to have been achieved by statutory intervention, *R v Southampton Crown Court, ex p J and P* [1993] Crim LR 962; in Australia see *Horowitz, Bilinsky & Spinak v Condie, Woods, Jones & Corby* (1989) 41 ACR 285.
2   *Solosky v R* [1980] 1 SCR 821, without however going so far as to sever all evidentiary connection, with the result that the claim was disallowed.
3   *Descoteaux v Mierzwinski* (1982) 141 DLR (3d) 590 (here too the discussion was strictly obiter and did not govern the actual result); *Re Ontario Securities Commission and Greymac Credit Corpn* (1983) 146 DLR (3d) 73; *Re Director of Investigation and Research and Shell Canada Ltd* (1975) 55 DLR (3d) 713. See also Kasting (1978) 24 McGill LJ 115; Chasse (1977) 36 CRNS 349.
4   *Re Gowling and Henderson and R* (1982) 136 DLR (3d) 292, where some doubt was expressed upon the general policy of expansion of the privilege at the expense of the public interest in the detection and successful prosecution of criminal activities.
5   [1996] AC 487, [1995] 4 All ER 526, at 507D, 540,541.
6   At 507G, 541d. For criticism of so exalted a view of the status of the privilege, see Tapper (1997) 1 Int J of Evidence and Proof 5.

2. Legal adviser[7]

In England, at common law, the term 'legal adviser' simply includes a solicitor and a barrister. Counsel's opinion taken by a solicitor is privileged either because counsel counts as the client's legal adviser, or else because he is the alter ego of the solicitor.[8] The privilege extends to communications to salaried legal advisers in that capacity.[9] This has been explained on the basis that they are professionally qualified, members of professional bodies with disciplinary powers to enforce their rules, and owe a duty to the court.[10] Legal professional privilege has also been extended by statute to patent,[11] and to trademark,[12] agents in respect of civil proceedings, to licensed conveyancers,[13] and to authorised advocates and litigators.[14] It is not otherwise enough that someone without formal legal professional qualification is performing the functions of a legal adviser, such as a legal aid officer in a prison,[15] a probation officer,[16] or a personnel consultant in an industrial dispute.[17]

It should be noted however that there may sometimes be an alternative route to the suppression of the evidence on the basis of public policy.[18]

---

7   The rule stated below applies to communications with a foreign legal adviser and to cases in which the litigation contemplated is foreign (*Re Duncan, Garfield v Fay* [1968] P 306, [1968] 2 All ER 395). It also extends to proceedings under the rules of the European Union Community: see *AM & S Europe v EC Commission* [1983] QB 878, [1983] 1 All ER 705.

8   *Bristol Corpn v Cox* (1884) 26 Ch D 678. See also *Koowarta v Bjelke-Petersen* (1988) 92 FLR 104, where claims for public policy immunity in respect of cabinet documents failed, but a claim in respect of counsel's opinion succeeded.

9   *Alfred Crompton Amusement Machines Ltd v Customs and Excise Comrs (No 2)* [1972] 2 QB 102, at 129, [1972] 2 All ER 353, at 376 (this point was neither raised nor questioned in the subsequent proceedings in the House of Lords); see also in Canada *Campbell and Shirose v R* (1998) SCC, 22 April.

10   *New Victoria Hospital v Ryan* [1993] ICR 201, at 203.

11   Copyright, Designs and Patents Act 1988, s 280, enlarging the privilege previously bestowed by Patents Act 1977 to include non-litigious communications. For the situation in Australia see *Sepa Waste Water Treatment Pty Ltd v JMT Welding Pty Ltd* (1986) 6 NSWLR 41.

12   Trade Marks Act 1994, s 87, reversing the position at common law: see *Dormeuil Frères SA v Dormière Menswear Ltd* [1983] RPC 131.

13   Administration of Justice Act 1985, s 33.

14   Courts and Legal Services Act 1990, s 63.

15   *R v Umoh* (1986) 84 Cr App Rep 138, although in some circumstances immunity may be available on grounds of public policy, or the evidence may be excluded in criminal proceedings by way of discretion under s 78 of the Police and Criminal Evidence Act 1984 if the fairness of the proceedings might be jeopardised by its admission.

16   *R v Secord* [1992] 3 NZLR 570; see also *R v Walker* (1992) 74 CCC (3d) 97.

17   *New Victoria Hospital v Ryan* [1993] ICR 201, distinguishing *M & W Grazebrook Ltd v Wallens* [1973] 2 All ER 868.

18   *Evans v Chief Constable of Surrey* [1988] QB 588, [1989] 2 All ER 594, see further below p 481. This dealt with communications from the police to the Director of Public Prosecutions and the policies applied were highly reminiscent of those applied to the privilege for legal advice. In *Goodridge v Chief Constable of Hampshire* [1999] 1 All ER 896 it was held that whether such communications do fall within the privilege is a matter determined by strength of the analogy to a private legal adviser in the circumstances of each case. Elsewhere they have been held to fall within it: see in Australia *A-G (NT) v Kearney* (1985) 158 CLR 500; *Waterford v Commonwealth of Australia* (1987) 163 CLR 54. It has further been held in Australia that communications conveying legal advice by the Director of Public Prosecutions to an official department are privileged even though perhaps ultra vires, if reasonably believed to be within the powers of the Director: *Grofam Pty Ltd v Australia and New Zealand Banking Group Ltd* (1993) 117 ALR 669.

3. Communication

The privilege applies only to communications; a solicitor can be obliged to disclose the identity of his client[19] and the privilege does not prevent the disclosure of facts observed by either party in the course of their relationship as client and legal adviser.[20] In *Brown v Foster*,[1] for instance, it was held that a barrister who saw a book produced at the trial of his client could testify without the client's consent, in subsequent proceedings, on the question whether it contained a particular entry when he previously saw it at the preliminary examination. Similarly, in *Dwyer v Collins*,[2] it was held that the claimant's attorney must say whether he had a particular document in court with him although he could not be obliged to produce it. In *Conlon v Conlons Ltd*[3] the defence to a claim for damages for personal injury alleged that the claimant had agreed to accept a sum in full settlement. In his reply, the claimant denied that his solicitor had been authorised to settle the claim and it was held that he could be obliged to answer an interrogatory as to whether he had authorised his solicitor to negotiate a settlement. If settlements made before the issue of a claim form are to be binding the client's instruction to his solicitor in this regard ought to be held to be outside the rule relating to legal professional privilege, for a solicitor has no implied authority to conclude negotiations at that stage, although he may bind his client by doing so later.

If a third party is consulted by a legal adviser for the purposes of litigation, perhaps as a potential witness, a question may arise as to the extent to which privilege can be claimed in respect of communications to him.[4] Since there is no property in a witness,[5] the third party is compellable. He is then free to testify, subject only to the ordinary operation of legal professional privilege, which will not protect documents submitted to him for expert advice, not otherwise protected.[6] It is dubious how far the old privilege in respect of witness statements can survive the modern practice of requiring disclosure[7] in advance of trial.[8]

4. Confidentiality and waiver

Confidence lies at the very heart of legal professional privilege.[9] In order to attract privilege the communications passing between legal adviser and client must be intended

---

19   *Bursill v Tanner* (1885) 16 QBD 1; or potential client, *Police v Mills* [1993] 2 NZLR 592. See Morrick (1980) 124 Sol Jo 303 for possible qualification to allow for the operation of the privilege against self-incrimination.

20   *R v Jack* (1992) 70 CCC (3d) 67 (client's attitude towards husband as manifested during interview for advice on separation, when husband subsequently tried for wife's murder).

1   (1857) 1 H & N 736; *Re Cathcart, ex p Campbell* (1870) 5 Ch App 703.

2   (1852) 7 Exch 639.

3   [1952] 2 All ER 462.

4   It has been held that legal professional privilege will not itself provide a basis for restraining disclosure of such communications by the supplier: *W v Egdell* [1990] Ch 359, [1990] 1 All ER 835.

5   *Harmony Shipping Co SA v Davis* [1979] 3 All ER 177, [1979] 1 WLR 1380. See also *Trade Practices Commission v Ampol Petroleum (Victoria) Pty Ltd* (1994) 126 ALR 111 (transcripts provided to witnesses at preceding statutory examination).

6   *R v King* [1983] 1 All ER 929, [1983] 1 WLR 411, although it seems that it will protect his expression of opinion derived from an object provided to him for the purposes of legal advice: *R v R* [1995] 1 Cr App Rep 183. See also *R v Ward* (1980) 3 ACR 171.

7   See above p 247.

8   See *Trade Practices Commission v Ampol Petroleum (Victoria) Pty Ltd*, above commenting on *Re Strachan* [1895] 1 Ch 439. Cp *Carbone v National Crime Authority* (1994) 126 ALR 79.

9   Bingham LJ in *Ventouris v Mountain* [1991] 3 All ER 472, at 475, [1991] 1 WLR 607, at 611.

to pass in confidence.[10] That confidential character may be lost by waiver,[10a] express or implied; or by accident.

Legal professional privilege may always be waived by the client. While making the advice public would certainly amount to waiver, it seems that more limited disclosure, seeking to exclude the claimant will not do so.[11] The fact that a conversation between a client and his solicitor takes place in the presence of a third party does not necessarily amount to a waiver,[12] although it will no doubt usually be held to have this effect. If a presumptively privileged document is offered to an opponent to read, the privilege is waived whether or not he reads it.[13] An agreement to waive the privilege attaching to a medical report will not, however, be implied from the acceptance of the opposite party's unconditional production of his medical report.[14]

It is here necessary to distinguish between the situation at different stages. The extent of pre-trial waiver may be determined by the party making it,[15] except that it is always necessary to reveal enough of the material so as not to mislead. So long as the material disclosed is fairly severable from that which is suppressed, its disclosure will not waive privilege in that which has been suppressed.[16] At the stage of discovery under the old law, subject to this qualification, it was made clear that privilege could attach to, and validly be claimed for, part of a document only.[17] It may also have been possible to waive the privilege for legal advice, without waiving it for that in respect of litigation.[18]

Difficult questions may arise as to the extent of any implied waiver by reliance upon a document in the preparation and presentation of a case. Waiver does not necessarily extend to all otherwise privileged documents dealing with any matter merely mentioned in such a document.[19] Simple reference to a privileged document in an affidavit will

---

10   *Gardner v Irvin* (1879) 4 Ex D 49, at 53; *Webster v James Chapman & Co* [1989] 3 All ER 939, at 944. See also *A-G for The Northern Territory v Maurice* (1986) 161 CLR 475, at 490.

10a In Canada it has been held that privilege may be waived by reference to legal advice in the statement of a party's defence, even though no explicit revelation of the advice has been made: *Campbell and Shirose v R* (1998) SCC, 22 April.

11   *Gotha City v Sothebys* [1998] 1 WLR 114. See also in New Zealand, *C-C Bottlers Ltd v Lion Nathan Ltd* [1993] 2 NZLR 445. In Australia however if the party making such disclosure does so in order to secure an advantage in the litigation he may still be taken to waive the privilege by making it: *Goldberg v Ng* (1995) 185 CLR 83.

12   *R v Braham and Mason* [1976] VR 547. In *R v Atkinson* [1990] 2 NZLR 513 a conversation between two men at a solicitor's home when he was absent, but in the presence of his secretary, was held not to qualify on this basis.

13   *Argyle Brewery Pty Ltd v Darling Harbourside* (1994) 120 ALR 537.

14   *Causton v Mann Egerton (Johnsons) Ltd*, above. For special rules relating to the discovery of privileged medical reports see RSC Ord 38, rr 36–38.

15   *Lyell v Kennedy (No 3)* (1884) 27 Ch D 1, at 24.

16   *R v Secretary of State for Transport and Factortame Ltd* (1997) 9 Admin LR 591.

17   *GE Capital Corporate Finance Group v Bankers Trust Co* [1995] 2 All ER 993 per Hoffmann LJ in highly persuasive obiter dicta; endorsing the approach of Saville J in *The Good Luck* [1992] 2 Lloyd's Rep 540, eulogising that of McPherson J in *Curlex Manufacturing Pty Ltd v Carlingford Australia General Insurance Ltd* [1987] 2 Qd R 335, and distinguishing *Great Atlantic Insurance Co v Home Insurance Co* [1981] 2 All ER 485, [1981] 1 WLR 529; *The Sagheera* [1997] 1 Lloyd's Rep 160. It seems that the same is true under the Civil Procedure Rules: see CPR 31.19(3), Practice Direction 31, para 6.1.

18   *George Doland Ltd v Blackburn Robson Coates & Co* [1972] 3 All ER 959, [1972] 1 WLR 1338; but see *General Accident Fire and Life Assurance Corpn Ltd v Tanter* [1984] 1 All ER 35, [1984] 1 WLR 100.

19   *General Accident Fire and Life Assurance Corpn Ltd v Tanter*, above. See also *A-G for The Northern Territory v Maurice* (1986) 69 ALR 31 where the High Court of Australia insisted that the test was whether use of part only of the material, or even oblique reference to it, would be unfair or misleading.

thus not necessarily amount to waiver,[20] but more extensive reliance may well do so.[1] The fact that the final version of a document will become public does not prevent earlier drafts from remaining privileged.[2]

Privilege may be waived by the legal adviser, even though acting under a mistake, and against the client's interests and wishes.[3] Such waiver may be implied from failure by the adviser to assert privilege.[4] It may be waived by the supply of otherwise privileged material to an expert who testifies upon its basis,[5] or to the prosecution who may then use it for the purposes of cross-examination of the accused.[6] Waiver may be implied from the use of a privileged document in court,[7] for example by its use for the purposes of cross-examination,[8] or to refresh a witness's memory whether in court or out.[9] In *R v Wilmot*[10] the accused sought to rebut a suggestion of recent fabrication of a particular claim, and it was held that it in no way trenched upon the privilege that the judge remarked upon the accused's failure to waive his privilege and call his solicitor to prove an earlier manifestation of the claim. Privilege may however be lost if the accused in a criminal case, in an attempt to avoid any adverse inference under the provisions of the Criminal Justice and Public Order Act 1994, expatiates upon the nature of the legal advice which induced him to remain silent.[11]

A client impliedly waives privilege in respect of any matter in which he commences a claim against his legal adviser, but such waiver does not extend to unrelated matters in respect of which the adviser acted,[12] nor to cases where the client sues not his legal adviser, but other advisers, even though part of the same team,[13] nor to communications with other legal advisers, even in respect of the same matter.[14]

Attempts are sometimes made to infer waiver from accidental disclosure by one side to the other. In modern litigation with voluminous documentation, severe pressure of time, and the extensive use of unqualified staff,[15] such accidents are highly prone to

20   *Tate and Lyle International Ltd v Government Trading Corpn* [1984] 81 LS Gaz R 3341.
1   *Equiticorp Industries Group Ltd v Hawkins* [1990] 2 NZLR 175.
2   *Highland Fisheries Ltd v Lynk Electric Ltd* (1989) 63 DLR (4th) 493 (earlier drafts of expert report).
3   *Great Atlantic Insurance Co v Home Insurance Co* above at 494, 539. The same may apply to any waiver made under the ostensible authority of the client's legal adviser: see *Causton v Mann Egerton (Johnsons) Ltd* [1974] 1 All ER 453, [1974] 1 WLR 162; but see *Frank Truman Export Ltd v Metropolitan Police Comr* [1977] QB 952, at 957, [1977] 3 All ER 431, at 436. See also *R v CKC* (1987) 62 CR (3d) 131 where privilege was held not to have been waived in Canada when a report was disclosed by counsel as part of an unauthorised plea bargain.
4   *Spedley Securities Ltd (in liq) v Bank of New Zealand* (1991) 26 NSWLR 711, at 729.
5   As in *Clough v Tameside and Glossop Health Authority* [1998] 2 All ER 971.
6   *R v Cottrill* [1997] Crim LR 56.
7   But not from disclosure in advance under the provisions of RSC Ord 38, r 2A, if any intention to adduce the document in evidence is subsequently disavowed, *Vista Maritime Inc v Sesa Goa* [1997] CLC 1600. See Passmore (1998) NLJ 1366 for comparison with *Clough v Tameside*, above.
8   *Nea Karteria Maritime Co v Atlantic and Great Lakes SS Co (No 2)* [1981] Com LR 138. See also *Buttes Gas and Oil Co v Hammer (No 3)* [1981] QB 223, at 268, [1980] 3 All ER 475, at 502 (unaffected on this point by subsequent proceedings).
9   *Mancorp Pty Ltd v Baulderstone Pty Ltd* (1991) 57 SASR 87 (though the court has more discretion in relation to the production of a privileged document so used than in the case of an unprivileged one, see further above p 263).
10   (1988) 89 Cr App Rep 341.
11   *R v Bowden* [1999] 1 WLR 823; see also *R v Condron and Condron* [1997] 1 WLR 827, [1997] 1 Cr App Rep 185; *R v Roble* [1997] Crim LR 449.
12   *Lillicrap v Nalder & Son* [1993] 1 All ER 724.
13   *Nederlandse Reassurantie Groep Holding NV v Bacon & Woodrow* [1995] 1 All ER 976.
14   *Paragon Finance plc v Freshfields* [1999] 1 WLR 1183.
15   In *Transamerica Computer Co v IBM Corpn* 573 F 2d 646 (9th Cir, 1978) no fewer than 1,138 privileged documents were inadvertently disclosed when 17 million pages had had to be vetted in three months.

occur. It seems that where it is obvious to the party seeking to use a document that it must have been disclosed in error, then no question of waiver can arise,[16] and the question becomes one of practicality and the ability of the court to override the normal incidents of privilege by a protective injunction.[17] If however a reasonable recipient could believe that privilege was being waived, then the fact that a mistake had indeed been made is irrelevant, and the privilege is lost.[18] Under the Civil Procedure Rules the consequences of inadvertent disclosure and inspection are specifically placed under the control of the judge.[19]

Privilege may be claimed at an interim stage of the proceedings, but waived at trial.[20] Nor is the privilege waived by reference in interim proceedings to only so much of the document as demonstrates that it is indeed subject to privilege, since this would defeat the purpose of a motion to prevent the use of such material by the opponent at trial.[1]

It should also be noted that waiver applies only for the purposes of the proceedings, or part of the proceedings,[2] in which the privilege was waived. Thus documents handed over to the police by the claimant in a civil suit, for the purpose of prosecuting the defendant in that suit, remained privileged in the civil suit.[3] The same applies to civil proceedings, even to the extent of different actions between the same parties.[4]

Where a communication passing between potential joint-defendants is privileged on account of anticipation of proceedings by one of them, the privilege is not waived automatically, and may not be waived by one, without the authority of the other.

5. Legal advice

The first head of legal professional privilege was the last to gain full recognition by the courts for it was not until *Greenough v Gaskell* was decided in 1833[5] that it was clear that the privilege attaches to communications between client and legal adviser, even though no litigation was contemplated by the client. In that case Lord Brougham said:[6]

> If the privilege was confined to communications connected with suits begun, or intended or expected or apprehended, no-one could safely adopt such precautions as might eventually render any proceedings successful, or all proceedings superfluous.

16 *Guinness Peat Properties Ltd v Fitzroy Robinson Partnership* [1987] 2 All ER 716, [1987] 1 WLR 1027; *Derby & Co Ltd v Weldon (No 8)* [1990] 3 All ER 762, [1991] 1 WLR 73. See also *Kenning v Eve Construction Ltd* [1989] 1 WLR 1189 where the relevant document had to be disclosed for a different reason. The position in New Zealand is the same: *National Insurance Co Ltd v Whirlybird Holdings Ltd* [1994] 2 NZLR 513.
17 See further below p 449.
18 *Pizzey v Ford Motor Co* [1994] PIQR P15.
19 CPR 31.20.
20 Though at peril as to costs: *Buttes Gas and Oil Co v Hammer (No 3)* [1981] QB 223, [1980] 3 All ER 475; *Somerville v Australian Securities Commission* (1993) 118 ALR 149.
1 *Def American Inc v Phonogram Ltd* (1994) Times, 16 August.
2 *Goldman v Hesper* [1988] 3 All ER 97, [1988] 1 WLR 1238 where legal professional privilege attaching to documents put forward on taxation of costs under Ord 62, r 29(7) was waived, to the extent that disclosure was voluntary, for that purpose only. See also *R v Harper-Taylor and Bakker* [1991] RTR 76.
3 *British Coal Corpn v Dennis Rye Ltd (No 2)* [1988] 3 All ER 816, [1988] 1 WLR 1113.
4 *Bourns Inc v Raychem Corpn* [1999] 1 All ER 908. See also CPR 31.20.
5 (1833) 1 My & K 98; some would say not until the judgment of Lord Selbourne in *Minet v Morgan* (1873) 8 Ch App 361.
6 At 103.

Although the privilege under consideration applies to communications made with the object of retaining a solicitor's services even if they are not in fact retained, the relationship of solicitor and client must at least be contemplated and the communications must be fairly referable to that relationship: 'The mere fact that the person speaking is a solicitor and the person to whom he speaks is his client affords no protection.'[7] It has been held to cover information communicated by the solicitor to the client for the purpose of tendering advice, despite the information emanating from a third party, being passed on as received, and there being no litigation in prospect.[8] It does not, however, include communications to a client from his opponent's solicitor, since such a communication is hardly likely to convey legal advice,[9] though if such a communication contemplates settlement of a dispute it may be within the protection conferred by the privilege to be described in the next section of this chapter. Nor does it extend to communications to a third party informing him of a claim to be made against him.[10]

The ambit of communications passing between solicitor and client covered by this privilege is not to be construed too narrowly, and extends to all communications relating to the normal legal business of a solicitor, thus extending to routine communications between them in relation, for example, to a conveyancing transaction.[11] It also extends in cases where some legal advice is involved to all of the peripheral aspects of the matter, even though some might not in isolation be concerned with the communication of strictly legal advice.[12] The difficulty of separating strictly legal and more general advice is especially acute in the case of institutional lawyers.[13]

While it is possible in a few cases for the content of advice to be inferred from the form of a communications between lawyer and client not ostensibly conveying legal advice,[14] or for the advice to be inextricably intertwined with the extrinsic material,[15] this is likely to be rare, and such documents as records of attendance will not normally attract the privilege,[16] nor will their disclosure waive privilege in any underlying associated privileged material.[17]

---

7   *Minter v Priest* [1930] AC 558, at 568 per Lord Buckmaster. The mere fact that a solicitor advising trustees is himself a trustee does not exclude the privilege (*O'Rourke v Darbishire* [1920] AC 581). In Australia in *Global Funds Management (NSW) Ltd v Rooney* (1994) 36 NSWLR 122 it was held, after consideration of the older English cases, that a bona fide and reasonable belief in the existence of the relationship will suffice so long as the belief persists.

8   *Re Getty (Sarah C) Trust* [1985] QB 956, [1985] 2 All ER 809.

9   *Hadley v Baddock* [1987] WAR 98.

10 *CHC Software Care Ltd v Hopkins & Wood* [1993] FSR 241.

11 *Balabel v Air-India* [1988] Ch 317, [1988] 2 All ER 246; but see *R v Crown Court at Inner London Sessions, ex p Baines & Baines* [1988] QB 579, [1987] 3 All ER 1025 which appears not to have been cited in *Balabel*.

12 *Nederlandse Reassurantie Groep Holding NV v Bacon & Woodrow* [1995] 1 All ER 976. It seems that the dominant purpose test applies in relation to the object of the retainer as a whole: see *The Sagheera* [1997] 1 Lloyd's Rep 160.

13 As in *Waterford v Commonwealth of Australia* (1987) 163 CLR 54 (advice to Treasury by Attorney-General partly on policy and partly on law).

14 See *Rosenberg v Jaine* [1983] NZLR 1.

15 As in *Churton v Frewen* (1865) 2 Drew & Sm 390.

16 *R v Manchester Crown Court, ex p R* (1999) Times, 15 February; see also *Packer v Deputy Comr of Taxation* [1985] 1 Qd R 275 (bill of costs); *Re Merit Finance and Investment* [1993] 1 NZLR 152. In Canada a lawyer has been permitted to testify to transfer of moneys between client accounts, though the rule excepting transactions in pursuance of crime may have played a part there: *R v Joubert* (1992) 69 CCC (3d) 553.

17 *Lake Cumbeline Pty Ltd v Effem Foods Pty Ltd* (1994) 126 ALR 58.

6.   Privilege of client

At common law[18] legal professional privilege in both of its aspects is that of the client,[19] though it also extends to communications by the client's agent[20] to the clerk or other subordinate of the adviser and vice versa.[1] It enures for the benefit of his successors in title[2] with regard, for instance, to documents handed over by him,[3] and the Court of Appeal accordingly held that the original of the proofs and notes on evidence with which the case of *Calcraft v Guest*[4] were concerned were privileged from production. The fact that they had been brought into existence for the purposes of a particular claim which had been concluded was treated as immaterial. Lindley MR stated this conclusion in terms of a general rule – 'once privileged, always privileged'; but it is important to remember that this simply means that, once a particular client's privilege has attached to a document, it remains for his benefit and that of his successors in title. It is not necessary that subject matter or parties be identical.[5] A time may come when the party denying the continued existence of the privilege can prove that the party relying on it no longer has any interest to protect, as where a solicitor takes a statement from a witness who has been party to the proceedings, and the prosecution wish to use the communication against the witness.[6] In *Schneider v Leigh*[7] the claimant had sought damages for personal injuries against a company, whose solicitor obtained the usual medical report – a document in relation to which the company enjoyed the ordinary litigant's privilege. The report was made by the defendant and the claimant contended that it libelled him. It was held that the defendant could claim no privilege with regard to his report. This case illustrates what Lord Atkin once described as the 'double nature'

18   But a number of statutes, such as the Banking Act 1987, s 39(13) extend privilege to legal advisers which is not available to their clients.
19   *Wilson v Rastall* (1792) 4 Term Rep 753; *CHC Software Care v Hopkin* [1993] FSR 241; *Nationwide Building Society v Various Solicitors (No 2)* (1998) Times, 1 May.
20   See *Mudgway v New Zealand Insurance Co Ltd* [1988] 2 NZLR 283 where the agent was not an employee but a third party acting as *agent*, and so distinguished from a true third party. In Canada the police are not regarded as clients, employees or agents of the Crown in relation to the protection of advice from government lawyers: *R v Gray* (1992) 74 CCC (3d) 267; the position appears to be different in Australia: *Dunesky and Bay Wool Pty Ltd v Elder* (1992) 60 ACR 459.
1   But in Canada it has been held that the Crown does not act as agent or trustee for native Indians within its care for the purpose of denying privilege to communications between the Crown and its legal advisers in relation to native title litigation: *Samson Indian Band v Canada* (1995) 125 DLR (4th) 294.
2   And so may be waived by his personal representative: *Chant v Brown* (1849) 7 Hare 79; *Re Molloy* [1997] 2 Cr App Rep 283; or by his trustee in bankruptcy: *Re Konigsberg (a bankrupt)* [1989] 3 All ER 289. Special rules apply in the case of wills, where the evidence of what transpired between solicitor and client may be decisive in determining who the successor is, with the result that privilege will not normally apply to prevent the solicitor from testifying as to his instructions, and the circumstances in which they were conveyed: *Russell v Jackson* (1851) 9 Hare 387, at 392. See also in the United States *Swidler & Berlin v US* (25 June 1998, unreported); and for a similar view in Canada in relation to wills see *Geffen v Goodman Estate* [1991] 2 SCR 353; but for a different view in relation to a receiver, see *Re Ontario Securities Commission and Greymac Credit Corpn* (1983) 146 DLR (3d) 73. In Australia it has been held that the privilege of a corporate body which is not claimed by the body in which it vests persists and is not waived by a failure by such body to claim it: *Lake Cumbeline Pty Ltd v Effem Foods Pty Ltd* (1994) 126 ALR 58. It may there be waived by a liquidator acting in the interests of the creditors or the company: *Re Dallhold Investments Pty Ltd* (1995) 130 ALR 287.
3   *Minet v Morgan* (1873) 8 Ch App 361; followed in *Crescent Farm (Sidcup) Sports Ltd v Sterling Offices Ltd* [1972] Ch 553, [1971] 3 All ER 1192.
4   [1898] 1 QB 759, above.
5   *The Aegis Blaze* [1986] 1 Lloyd's Rep 203.
6   *R v Ataou* [1988] QB 798, [1988] 2 All ER 321. See also *R v Craig* [1975] 1 NZLR 597.
7   [1955] 2 QB 195, [1955] 2 All ER 173.

which problems relating to professional privilege may assume. First, there is the question whether the document or statement need be put in evidence—a general question of adjectival law; and, secondly, there is the question whether the occasion on which the statement (ex hypothesi before the court) was published is an occasion of absolute or qualified privilege—a question with which the substantive law of defamation is concerned.[8] On facts such as those of *Schneider v Leigh*, a claim for qualified privilege might ultimately succeed although the claims of professional privilege failed. It seems that the result would be different if the claim against the witness were in respect of the very same subject matter in the original litigation.[9]

If a lawyer swears that a question cannot be answered without disclosing communications made to him professionally by his client his oath is conclusive unless it appears from the nature of the question that the privilege cannot be applicable.[10] There is little case law on this subject due no doubt to the fact that the issue of legal professional privilege is most frequently raised in connection with pre-trial disclosure of documents which the judge has power to inspect.[11]

Privilege may however be claimed by one not strictly a client of the legal adviser, if he has an interest in common with such a client, for example as a joint tenant or as one of several victims of a common calamity.[12] Such privilege cannot be claimed against such other party,[13] and only in respect of communications made while the common interest exists, not after it has ended,[14] or is in abeyance.[15]

At common law the rule was clear that legal professional privilege did not attach to documents or things which had come into existence before the relationship of solicitor and client had become established, even though submitted to a legal adviser for his advice,[16] or sent by him to a third party in connection with litigation.[17] The privilege was regarded as that of the client, and if the document or thing were not protected in the hands of the client it could not attract protection merely by being submitted to a legal adviser. The rule is now stated by the Police and Criminal Evidence Act 1984.

Other confidential material passing between solicitor and client, although not protected by this privilege,[18] is nevertheless subject to a special procedure to secure access under the Police and Criminal Evidence Act 1984.[19]

---

8   *Minter v Priest* [1930] AC 558, at 579.

9   *Lee v South West Thames Regional Health Authority* [1985] 2 All ER 385, [1985] 1 WLR 845.

10   *Morgan v Shaw* (1819) 4 Madd 54.

11   A power which the majority of the High Court of Australia in *Grant v Downs* (1976) 135 CLR 674 felt should be exercised more readily. See CPR 31.19(6)(a).

12   *Buttes Gas and Oil Co v Hammer (No 3)* [1981] QB 223, [1980] 3 All ER 475 (unaffected on this point by subsequent proceedings).

13   *Cia Barca de Panama SA v George Wimpey & Co* [1980] 1 Lloyd's Rep 598, at 614.

14   *Talbot v Marshfield* (1865) 2 Drew & Sm 549.

15   *Leif Hoegh & Co A/S v Petrolsea Inc* [1993] 1 Lloyd's Rep 363.

16   *R v Peterborough Justices, ex p Hicks* [1978] 1 All ER 225, [1977] 1 WLR 1371 (forged power of attorney deposited for legal advice in relation to impending prosecution).

17   *R v King* [1983] 1 All ER 929, [1983] 1 WLR 411 (document sent by defence to handwriting expert to use for comparison with prosecution documents in connection with impending prosecution). This case disapproved comments in *Frank Truman Export Ltd v Metropolitan Police Comr* [1977] QB 952, [1977] 3 All ER 431, and endorsed the criticism of them made in the 5th edn (1979) of this work.

18   Police and Criminal Evidence Act 1984, s 14(2).

19   See *R v Central Criminal Court, ex p Francis & Francis* above, *R v Inner London Crown Court, ex p Baines & Baines* [1988] QB 579, [1987] 3 All ER 1025. See also *Intrusive Surveillance Code of Practice* paras 2.4, 2.6.

7.   Secondary evidence

A legal adviser owes a twofold duty to his client with regard to confidential communications. In the first place he must claim privilege for them in legal proceedings and second he must not disclose their contents to anyone without the client's consent. A problem may occur when those contents have become known to a third party who wishes to prove them in litigation against the client. The disclosure may have been due to the adviser's wilful or negligent breach of duty, to accident, or to the wrongful act of a third party. The information sought to be proved in the litigation may be the outcome of oral communication or the previous reading of a document, but more often than not it will be contained in a copy of a privileged document. In *Calcraft v Guest*[20] the Court of Appeal allowed copies of proofs of witnesses with notes on the evidence in a former claim brought by the claimant's predecessor in title to be put in by the defendant. In that case the originals had accidentally fallen into the defendant's hands, but the principle of the decision applies to all methods of obtaining. It overlaps with the rule which has already been mentioned in section 2 of ch IV and to which further reference is made in ch XI section 3, that illegally and improperly obtained evidence is admissible provided that it is relevant. A recent example of the operation of this principle is provided by *Re Briamore Manufacturing*[1] where inadvertent disclosure of privileged documents was made. The party to whom such disclosure was permitted made notes and copies of some, but the mistake had been discovered before receipt of a request for copies of all, which was refused. It was held to be futile to maintain such refusal since as a result of *Calcraft v Guest*[2] the party to whom such disclosure had been mistakenly made could use all of his secondary evidence at the trial,[3] and it was clearly preferable to have the trial conducted on the basis of the best evidence, namely the original documents.

One exception to the principle of *Calcraft v Guest* occurs when a document subject to legal professional privilege is brought into court by one party, is improperly obtained by his opponent, and is then sought to be put into evidence by the wrongdoer. In *ITC Film Distributors v Video Exchange Ltd*[4] Warner J restrained the use of documents obtained in such a way on the basis that the interests of the proper administration of justice required him to do so. This restriction does not however apply when the party seeking to use the document has obtained it without impropriety. Thus in *R v Tompkins*[5] a note which the accused had written to his counsel was found on the floor of the courtroom during an adjournment and handed to prosecuting counsel who was thus enabled to secure devastating effect in cross-examination.

---

20   [1898] 1 QB 759.
1   [1986] 3 All ER 132, [1986] 1 WLR 1429. *R v Cottrill* [1997] Crim LR 56 is another (prosecution allowed to adduce in cross-examination of the accused as a previous inconsistent statement one supplied to them by his former solicitors).
2   Above, which was conceded to apply.
3   It is not futile if the secondary evidence is incomplete, and the fact that an application is made strongly suggests that the party making it has not got all that he wishes: see *Hooker Corpn Ltd v Darling Harbour Authority* (1987) 9 NSWLR 538.
4   [1982] Ch 431, [1982] 2 All ER 241. No such rule appears to exist in Canada, see *R v Dunbar and Logan* (1982) 138 DLR (3d) 221.
5   (1977) 67 Cr App Rep 181. See also *Re Girouard and the Queen* (1982) 138 DLR (3d) 730; but in New Zealand it has been held that a policeman could not testify to a conversation between a solicitor and his client which he had, without any impropriety, overheard, *R v Uljee* [1982] 1 NZLR 561, a decision preferred to *Tompkins* in obiter dicta by Nourse LJ in *Goddard v Nationwide Building Society* [1987] QB 670, at 686, [1986] 3 All ER 264, at 272.

By far the most common occurrence is that in which there is no impropriety[6] but under the pressure of litigation a privileged document is disclosed in error. If *Calcraft v Guest* stood alone there would be little question but that privilege would be lost, and secondary evidence of the privileged material admissible. But it does not stand alone. In *Lord Ashburton v Pape*[7] the defendant, a bankrupt, obtained possession of correspondence passing between Lord Ashburton and his solicitor, taking copies before he returned it. Lord Ashburton sought, and eventually secured, an unqualified injunction against any use being made of those copies on the general ground that equity will act to restrain a breach of confidence. It was unclear exactly how these two rules related to each other.[8] The matter has now been clarified by recent decisions of the Court of Appeal, as explained in *Webster v James Chapman & Co.* The matter is governed by the principle of *Ashburton v Pape* so long as any relief is practicable, that is until the documents have been used, or otherwise relied upon, in the relevant litigation.[9] It is not necessary to commence separate proceedings; an application can be made at any time. It seems that this relief depends upon purely equitable considerations, and is largely unaffected by the potential application of the privilege. The judge should take into account both any degree of impropriety in obtaining or using the material, and on the other hand the importance to the administration of justice of securing and using as much relevant evidence as possible. Familiar equitable principles, such as the effect of delay, may apply. The main influence of the privilege may reside in the undesirability of subverting the rule limiting professional privilege for confidential communications to those made in connection with legal advice or litigation. It is necessary also to consider the question of any implied waiver when any carelessness leading to disclosure is that of a party in conducting the very litigation in which the document is to be used. In some situations extrinsic duties may compel disclosure to the party seeking to use the information, and in such cases neither privilege nor the equity to restrain use can be invoked. Nor may the equitable duty prevail against the interest of the Crown in conducting a public prosecution.

The resultant law can be criticised on two grounds: (1) the contrast between *Calcraft v Guest* and *Lord Ashburton v Pape* makes the client's success in getting evidence excluded depend on the date at which he found out that he was the victim of a wrongdoer; (2) the distinction between public prosecutions and other legal proceedings is unjustified. If they can be answered, the answer to the first criticism seems to be that trials at which it was claimed that the contents of a confidential document ought not to be put in evidence, although no previous injunction had been obtained, would be unduly protracted by the collateral inquiry into the circumstances in which the document was obtained; while the answer to the second criticism may be that, in criminal proceedings, the accused receives as much protection as he should receive from the law of privilege in the strict sense and it would be going too far to afford him the protection afforded by the law of confidentiality.

6   Though in *English and American Insurance Co Ltd v Herbert Smith & Co* [1988] FSR 232 the Vice-Chancellor intimated that to peruse plainly confidential material, known at the time to be privileged was not entirely innocent, even though received in error. Such material should be returned to the sender without further scrutiny, and if scrutinised the adviser should no longer continue to act: *Ablitt v Mills & Reeve* (1996) Times, 25 October.
7   [1913] 2 Ch 469.
8   See Tapper (1972) 35 MLR 83; Heydon (1974) 37 MLR 601.
9   In *Shaw v Harris (No 1)* (1992) 3 Tas R 153 this principle was applied to documents secured without impropriety from the courtroom. Even that is no longer decisive under CPR 31.22 which deals with this very situation, and invests the judge with a wide discretion.

B.   LITIGATION PRIVILEGE[10]

This second head of legal professional privilege has only recently become distinguished from that for legal advice. Its contours are obscure, partly because it has been so recently recognised; partly because the two overlap, since the central case of legal advice is indeed advice rendered in connection with on-going litigation;[11] and partly because the culture of litigation is currently changing.[12] The traditional position at common law was that litigation was conducted in a wholly adversary fashion, with nothing revealed to an opponent except the statement of claim and pleadings. Thereafter, little further[13] disclosure of a party's case took place until witnesses were called to testify to prove the allegations upon which the pleadings were premised. It was axiomatic that law and not evidence was to be pleaded. Inroads were made upon this procedure in the nineteenth century when some incidents[14] of the very different form of trial in Chancery were engrafted on to the old common law system.[15]

It remained the case however that a party's 'brief' remained immune from discovery since its revelation would have been completely contrary to the adversarial system of litigation then employed.[16] The strength of this view is encapsulated in the words of James LJ in *Anderson v Bank of British Columbia*[17] that:

> as you have no right to see your adversary's brief, you have no right to see that which comes into existence merely as the materials for the brief.

Thus communications with potential witnesses by lawyer[18] or by client for onward communication to his lawyer, and the lawyer's own documentary preparation for the litigation in prospect remained immune from discovery. Matters have now changed very radically, and litigation is conducted to a much greater extent with cards on the

---

10   While by no means identical, this head of privilege resembles that isolated in the United States as 'lawyers' work product': see *Hickman v Taylor* 329 US 495 (1946). Its differentiation from legal advice privilege by Lord Denning MR in *Buttes Gas and Oil Co v Hammer (No 3)* [1981] QB 223, [1980] 3 All ER 745, at 243, 474 was described as orthodox by Bingham LJ in *Ventouris v Mountain* [1991] 3 All ER 472, [1991] 1 WLR 607, at 482a, 617D.

11   Indeed in *Re Barings plc* [1998] Ch 356, [1998] 1 All ER 673 Scott VC was inclined to favour the view that litigation privilege is effectively a sub-set of legal advice privilege, although he recognised that there was binding authority to the contrary; for an explicit rejection of this limiting view see in Canada *Samson Indian Band v Canada* (1995) 125 DLR (4th) 294, especially at 300c.

12   See Lord Donaldson MR in *Mercer v Chief Constable of Lancashire* [1991] 2 All ER 504, at 508, [1991] 1 WLR 367, at 373. This change largely dictated the tenor of the Civil Procedure Rules.

13   Though clarification was permitted by way of requests for particulars.

14   Especially pre-trial discovery. Scepticism was sometimes expressed in Chancery as to the competence of the common lawyers to handle these doctrines, see Jessel MR in *Anderson v Bank of British Columbia* (1876) 2 Ch D 644, at 654.

15   See Williams (1990) 9 Civ JQ 139 to which the editor is greatly indebted in this section.

16   In *Re Strachan* [1895] 1 Ch 439 Lindley LJ said 'our rules of evidence and of discovery are not based upon the theory that it is advantageous to let each side know what the other can prove, but rather the reverse.' It is significant that this view was explicitly rejected on account of the new practice of litigation in *Trade Practices Commission v Ampol Petroleum (Victoria) Pty Ltd* (1994) 126 ALR 111.

17   Above, at 656. The statement was obiter dictum, but strong for that very reason since it was made without any impulsion from the exigency of the litigation in question.

18   *Curling v Perring* (1835) 2 My & K 380.

table.[19] Three aspects of litigation privilege will be considered here: the extent to which a lawyer's own work in preparation for litigation can be shielded from his client's opponent; the protection afforded to communications with third parties within the context of litigation; and the question of communication with an opponent.

I.   The legal adviser's own work

There is no doubt that this has to be protected to some extent to make adversarial litigation a feasible proposition. The question is really only one of how far it extends. It seems that the essential criterion is whether or not the particular disclosure is likely to reveal the structure of the resister's case. It has been held that disclosure of a selection of pieces of evidence may be protected upon such a basis.[20] This may necessitate the drawing of highly technical distinctions.[1] It may also lead to some unpalatable results if all of the incidents of legal advice privilege are to be applied to it.[2] The impact of the compulsory disclosure of witness statements remains contentious, and some consider that a new category of privilege is required to regulate just what can and cannot be done with such disclosed statements in advance of their adduction in evidence.[3]

2.   Communications with third parties[4]

There is an important distinction between the legal advice and litigation heads arising from the fact that, when litigation is not contemplated, communications between the adviser and third parties to enable him to obtain information before giving his opinion are not always privileged. This was decided in the leading case of *Wheeler v Le Marchant*,[5] where the defendant was obliged to produce reports made to his solicitor by a surveyor with regard to property that became the subject of litigation, the litigation not having been contemplated when the reports were made. Cotton LJ observed that documents such as those with which the case was concerned had hitherto been protected only when made in contemplation of some litigation, and he did not consider that all communications between a solicitor and a third person in the course of advising

---

19   Contrasted by the district judge in *Khan v Armaguard Ltd* [1994] 3 All ER 545 with the older 'adversarial cat-and-mouse' approach, and said by Woolf LJ in *B v John Wyeth & Brother Ltd* [1992] 1 All ER 443, at 447 to be one where the cards are placed on the table *face up*.

20   *Lyell v Kennedy (No 3)* (1884) 27 Ch D 1; *Dubai Bank Ltd v Galadari (No 7)* [1992] 1 All ER 658. The continued validity of this line of authority has been doubted in Australia: see *Bond v JN Taylor Holdings Ltd* (1992) 57 SASR 21, at 46.

1   As in *Lyell v Kennedy (No 3)* above where it was recognised that a reference in a report to 'the tomb of George Duncan' might have to be treated differently from a reference to 'the tomb of *the said* George Duncan'.

2   See *Dingle v Commonwealth Development Bank of Australia* (1989) 91 ACR 239 where Pincus J remarked that on the 'once-privileged always privileged basis' it would mean that witness statements taken by a legal adviser for A in litigation between A and B, never shown to A or used in the litigation, could be insulated from use in litigation between total strangers entirely at A's whim.

3   See Grainger (1995) 145 NLJ 961, 1062. The obligation is expressed in CPR 32.4(2) unqualified by any new privilege, although the judge is invested with a considerable measure of control over how it may subsequently be used: see CPR 32.12.

4   The privilege extends to communications passing between the members of a business organisation or government department and its salaried permanent legal advisers (*Alfred Crompton Amusement Machines Ltd v Customs and Excise Comrs (No 2)* [1972] 2 QB 102, [1972] 2 All ER 353, the point was not argued before the House of Lords), and there can be little doubt that this would be true of confidential communications in order to obtain legal advice simpliciter.

5   (1881) 17 Ch D 675.

clients ought to be protected. It should be noted that both client and legal adviser can act through an agent, and it is often a difficult question whether the communication was between client and legal adviser through an agent in which case legal advice privilege is apposite and litigation need not be contemplated, or whether the intermediary is not to be regarded as the alter ego of client or legal adviser, in which case the availability of the privilege depends upon the contemplation of litigation.[6]

In order that communications between the client or his legal adviser and third parties should be privileged, there must be a definite prospect of litigation in contemplation by the client, and not a mere vague anticipation of it;[7] but it is not necessary that a basis for a claim should have arisen;[8] nor is it essential that the third party should anticipate litigation.[9] The communication must have been made, or the document brought into existence,[10] for the purpose of enabling the legal adviser to advise or act with regard to the litigation. In the ordinary case this requirement gives rise to no particular difficulty. A mere request for information, unaccompanied by any suggestion that it is required for legal advice, is clearly not privileged, however probable the litigation may have been at the time the request was made.[11] There have been, however, a number of troublesome borderline cases in which the communication was made for more than one purpose, and it was difficult to say much more with regard to the decisions in these cases than that they showed that the utilisation of the communication in litigation must have been one of its main purposes, even though the client may have intended to settle the claim without litigation if he could.[12]

Examples of material which had been held not to be privileged include reports made to the directors of a railway company simply for the purpose of conveying information even if litigation were contemplated;[13] information supplied by a member of a trade union to officials of the union to enable them to decide whether to refer his claim for wrongful dismissal to the union's solicitor for legal action;[14] and the report of a private inquiry into an accident aimed primarily at preventing the recurrence of such an event.[15] Examples falling on the other side of the line include reports of an accident made to the director of a company to be placed before the company's solicitors;[16] and correspondence by the Transport Commission with its servants concerning the cause of an accident intended to be placed before the Commission's solicitors.[17]

In *Alfred Crompton Amusement Machines Ltd v Customs and Excise Comrs (No 2)*[18] the company notified the Commissioners in 1967 that it was dissatisfied with the

6   See *C-C Bottlers Ltd v Lion Nathan Ltd* [1993] 2 NZLR 445.
7   Bray on *Discovery*, cited by Lord Denning MR in *Alfred Crompton Amusement Machines Ltd v Customs and Excise Comrs (No 2)* above at 130, 377.
8   *Bristol Corpn v Cox* (1884) 26 Ch D 678.
9   *Di Pietrantonio v Austin Hospital (Heidelberg)* [1958] VR 325.
10   In *R v R* [1994] 4 All ER 260 the ambit of the privilege was extended to an expert opinion based upon a sample of blood provided by the client through his legal advisers to the expert for the purpose of supplying an expert opinion (which was not in fact used).
11   *Anderson v Bank of British Columbia* (1876) 2 Ch D 644 (though this seems an odd decision on the facts).
12   *Ogden v London Electric Rly Co* (1933) 149 LT 476.
13   *Woolley v North London Rly Co* (1869) LR 4 CP 602.
14   *Jones v Great Central Rly Co* [1910] AC 4.
15   *Longthorn v British Transport Commission* [1959] 2 All ER 32, [1959] 1 WLR 530; *Warner v Women's Hospital* [1954] VLR 410.
16   *Southwark Water Co v Quick* (1878) 3 QBD 315; *Ankin v London and North Eastern Rly Co* [1930] 1 KB 527.
17   *Seabrook v British Transport Commission* [1959] 2 All ER 15, [1959] 1 WLR 509; *Britten v FH Pilcher & Sons* [1969] 1 All ER 491.
18   [1974] AC 405, [1973] 2 All ER 1169. See also *Silver Hill Duckling Ltd v Minister of Agriculture* [1987] IR 289.

agreed formula under which it had been paying purchase tax. The prescribed procedure in the event of disagreement was that the Commissioners should state their opinion concerning the basis on which purchase tax was payable and, if this was not accepted, the taxpayer could proceed to arbitration. The Commissioners expressed their opinion in 1968 and the parties proceeded to arbitration. Both the Court of Appeal and House of Lords took the view that the Commissioners had reasonably anticipated arbitration after receipt of the company's notification of dissatisfaction with the agreement in 1967. The Commissioners claimed legal professional privilege in respect of (1) communications with their salaried legal advisers in order to obtain advice, (2) communications with their legal advisers in order to obtain evidence for the anticipated arbitration, (3) internal communications with their officers and agents concerning the proper assessment of the purchase tax payable by the company, and (4) documents received in confidence from third parties concerning the market value of machines sold by the company. There was no argument in the House of Lords with regard to the first set of communications, so the decision of the Court of Appeal that they were privileged stands; the House held that privilege attached to the second set, even if it were assumed that litigation had to be anticipated to found it; but the majority held that the third and fourth sets were not subject to legal professional privilege because they came into existence for one single purpose—to assist the Commissioners to form an opinion about the basis on which purchase tax should be paid by the company, and not for the dual purpose of enabling an opinion to be formed and resisting the company's contentions in the arbitration. It was held that the third and fourth sets of communications ought not to be disclosed in the public interest, a matter which is considered in the next chapter.

Having regard to the decision under heads (3) and (4) everything said in the House about dual or multiple purpose communications was obiter, but the majority favoured a restrictive view with regard to the recognition of privilege in such cases. Two major vehicles existed for the expression of such a view. The privilege could be restricted to communications made solely for use in litigation, or to those made for the dominant purpose of such use.[19] The former position was adopted by the majority of the High Court of Australia.[20] Barwick CJ was unwilling to be quite so restrictive, and was prepared to allow the privilege not only when such use was the sole purpose, but also when it was merely the dominant one.[1]

In England the House of Lords rejected the approach of the majority in *Grant v Downs* in favour of that proposed by Barwick CJ. In *Waugh v British Railways Board*[2] the House of Lords was unanimous in approving of the 'dominant' purpose test, and overruling previous decisions of the lower courts to the extent of any inconsistency with it. Their Lordships felt that a 'sole purpose' test would go too far in denying privilege for communications whose overwhelming purpose was for litigation, but for which some other minor purpose could be discovered. Lord Russell who initially favoured the more restrictive approach, was eventually persuaded that it would mean that it would be virtually impossible ever to raise a claim for privilege on this basis. None of their Lordships anticipated any difficulty in applying a test of dominance, which is familiar in other branches of the law.[3]

---

19   Because litigation involves the provision of legal advice the purpose of securing the latter does not diminish the dominance of the former: *The Sagheera* [1997] 1 Lloyd's Rep 160, at 166,167.
20   *Grant v Downs* (1976) 135 CLR 674 (Stephen, Mason and Murphy JJ).
1   Jacobs J adopted a third formulation in requiring this purpose to account for the existence of material.
2   [1980] AC 521, [1971] 2 All ER 1169 (an accident report case).
3   It was subsequently applied to documents made in the course of an inquiry into the conduct of the police under s 49 of Police Act 1964 following a complaint and threat of legal action,

A problem may arise in relation to original documents which are not subject to the privilege because themselves not made in contemplation of litigation, but which are then copied for the purpose of litigation.

In cases where copies of documents held by third parties have been made specifically for the litigation in respect of which disclosure is sought the privilege has been upheld.[4] If, however, the originals would have been unprivileged in the hands of the opponent, then merely copying them for the purposes of the litigation should not shield them from discovery.[5] It now seems that in England privilege is not available for copies of unprivileged documents, whether the original is in the hands of the client,[6] or third party,[7] and even though the copy has been made for the purpose of securing legal advice in the litigation.[8] This position acknowledges the inconvenience of distinguishing for these purposes between original and copy in the age of the photocopier, fax and computer.[9] It has also been suggested[10] that it ignores the importance of *communication with a lawyer* in the definition of the privilege, and concentrates unduly on the status of the document. It is submitted that this criticism is misplaced, since it promotes the anomaly of distinguishing between the communication of an unprivileged original to a lawyer for advice, which must on any view be produced, and the communication of a copy for that purpose which is not to be produced, and all of this made in a context where the distinction has become impractical in the light of modern copying technology. Legal effect depends upon the content of the original document, and the provenance of the means of proof seems strictly secondary. If production of the original by the lawyer cannot be refused, it is hard to understand why his production of a copy should be treated differently.

3.   Communications with opponent

It looks like a truism to say that privilege cannot be claimed for communications passing between one party and another or his agent, but the cases show that problems can

---

Neilson v Laugharne [1981] QB 736, [1981] 1 All ER 829 (compare *Konia v Morley* [1976] 1 NZLR 455 where the same result was reached even on the basis of the older test), and to reports on the cause of a suspicious fire commissioned by the solicitors to the insurers of the relevant premises, *Re Highgrade Traders Ltd* [1984] BCLC 151. *Waugh* has been approved in Canada, see *Levin v Boyce* (1985) 19 DLR (4th) 128 citing cases from various Canadian jurisdictions; for New Zealand see *Guardian Royal Exchange Assurance of New Zealand Ltd v Stuart* [1985] 1 NZLR 596; and for South Africa see *A Sweidan and King (Pty) Ltd v Zim Israel Navigation Co Ltd* 1986 (1) SA 515. Even in Australia it now applies under s 119 of the evidence Act 1995, and as a matter of judicial construction at interim stages as well as at trial: *Adelaide Steamship Co Ltd v Spalvins* (1998) 152 ALR 418.

4   *The Palermo* (1883) 9 PD 6; *Watson v Cammell Laird & Co (Shipbuilders and Engineers) Ltd* [1959] 2 All ER 757, [1959] 1 WLR 702. See also *Hodgkinson v Simms* (1988) 55 DLR (4th) 577 where the court applied the principle to a single document. It is unclear that the reasoning of these cases can survive the more general endorsement of disclosure by third parties in CPR 31.17.

5   *Chadwick v Bowman* (1886) 16 QBD 561.

6   *R v Board of Inland Revenue, ex p Goldberg* [1989] QB 267, [1988] 3 All ER 248 where the privilege was, in fact, allowed, but the case was held in *Dubai Bank Ltd v Galadari* [1990] Ch 98, at 108, [1989] 3 All ER 769, at 775 to have been wrongly decided.

7   *Dubai Bank* above.

8   *Lubrizol Corpn v Esso Petroleum Ltd* [1992] 1 WLR 957. Different views prevail elsewhere; see in Australia, *Federal Police Comr v Propend Finance Ltd* (1997) 188 CLR 501; and in Canada, *Regional Municipality of Ottawa-Carleton v Consumers' Gas Co Ltd* (1990) 74 DLR (4th) 742.

9   *Lubrizol Corpn v Esso Petroleum Ltd* [1992] 1 WLR 957, at 961.

10   By McHugh J in *Propend* at 552.

arise under this head. In *Grant v South Western and County Properties Ltd*[11] the claimant caused a tape-recording to be made of a conversation between himself and one of the defendants and it was held that he could not claim privilege from the obligation to disclose the recording. So far as the defendant was concerned there was no intention that it should be placed before the claimant's solicitor; so far as the claimant himself was concerned, what he said to the defendant could not be privileged. From the point of view of the privilege the recording was the equivalent of a letter and copy letter exchanged between the parties. Conversely the mere intention to place into the hands of an opponent a document received from an expert in the course of preparing for litigation is not sufficient to displace the privilege if the legal adviser changes his mind and never does despatch the document.[12]

In *Baker v London and South Western Rly Co*,[13] a case in which executors were claiming damages for personal injuries to the deceased, the defendants alleged that their medical officer had visited him and negotiated a settlement. It was held that the officer's report was not privileged from disclosure. The decision seems to have been correct on its particular facts because, subject to the without prejudice rule, there is no reason why privilege should attach to discussions aimed at achieving a settlement.[14] The judgment contains a suggestion that privilege could never attach to an agent's report of what took place at an interview with the opposite party, but there is subsequent authority for the proposition that statements taken from the victim on behalf of a potential defendant for the purpose of laying them before his solicitor are privileged in accident cases.

In *Feuerheerd v London General Omnibus Co*[15] the claimant mistakenly believed that she was making a statement to her solicitor about the accident in which she had sustained her injuries, when she was in fact being interrogated by the company's claims manager. It was held that the defendants could claim privilege for the statement as a documentary record made for the purpose of laying it before their solicitors. The Court of Appeal laid stress on the fact that the manager acted in good faith. Had he not done so the claim to privilege would presumably have failed on the ground that the defendants could not take advantage of their agent's wrong.[16] There was no discussion of the effect of the claimant's mistake as to the person to whom she was speaking. Subject to this point there is no obvious reason why the victim's statement should be differentiated in this context from those of other witnesses taken on behalf of a potential defendant shortly after the occurrence of an accident. A cynic is entitled to ask why, if the victim does not take the precaution of getting a copy of his statement at the time it was made, he should have a right to its production at a later stage in order to trim his evidence accordingly.[17]

---

11   [1975] Ch 185, at 199. See also *Telebooth Pty Ltd v Telstra Corpn Ltd* [1994] 1 VR 337.
12   *Derby & Co Ltd v Weldon (No 9)* [1991] 2 All ER 901, [1991] 1 WLR 652.
13   (1868) LR 3 QB 91.
14   Neither litigation privilege nor that for without prejudice negotiations is waived by disclosure of a mere attendance note recording the fact of a conversation with an opponent's legal adviser, *Parry v News Group Newspapers Ltd* [1990] NLJR 1719.
15   [1918] 2 KB 565.
16   Although it might have been argued that, if a person may steal a document and put it in evidence, there is no reason why evidence should not be given of what occurred at any interview obtained by deception.
17   See the judgment of Thesiger J in *Britten v F H Pilcher and Sons Ltd* [1969] 1 All ER 491. See also per Cotton LJ in *Kennedy v Lyell* (1883) 23 Ch D 387, at 404. In Australia see *Aydin v Australian Iron and Steel Pty Ltd* [1984] 3 NSWLR 684; *Hadley v Baddock* [1987] WAR 98.

C. EXCEPTIONS[18]

There are a number of exceptional situations where material which would otherwise be privileged must be disclosed for reasons of policy. There are similarities in the policies which determine the exclusion at common law[19] of communications to facilitate the commission, or evasion from detection, of crime and fraud; to establish the innocence of the accused; or to those which are claimed in the course of a dispute between client and legal adviser. These will be considered first, and then a residual category of cases where there has been some statutory intervention.

I. Communications to facilitate crime or fraud[20]

In the leading case of *R v Cox and Railton*,[1] the Court for Crown Cases Reserved decided that, if a client applies to a lawyer for advice intended to guide him in the commission of a crime or fraud, the legal adviser being ignorant of the purpose for which his advice is wanted, the communication between the two is not privileged. Accordingly a solicitor was compelled to disclose what passed between the prisoners and himself when they consulted him with reference to drawing up a bill of sale that was alleged to be fraudulent. As Stephen J pointed out when delivering the judgment to the court, if the law were otherwise, a man intending to commit treason or murder might safely take legal advice for the purpose of enabling himself to do so with impunity, and the solicitor to whom the application was made would not be at liberty to give information against his client in order to frustrate his criminal purpose.[2] If the lawyer participates in the criminal purpose he ceases to act as a lawyer. Stephen J concluded that the court must judge whether the evidence is admissible on the special facts of each particular case, and every precaution should be taken against compelling unnecessary disclosures. It has been held not enough in Canada that a party consults a lawyer as to his course of action, and then on the basis of the advice commits what turns out to be a crime.[2a]

The doctrine of *R v Cox and Railton* has been applied to civil cases[3] in which fraud[4] was alleged and it has since been stressed that there should be prima facie evidence[5]

---

18 Some authorities would deny that there are any real exceptions to the privilege, and that the situations described below, to the extent that they are allowed, merely fall outside the ambit of the privilege: see Lord Taylor CJ in *R v Derby Magistrates' Court, ex p B* [1996] AC 487, [1995] 4 All ER 526, at 508, 509, 542d: 'no exception should be allowed to the absolute nature of legal professional privilege, once established.' See also McHugh J in *Carter v Managing Partner of Northmore Hale Davy & Leake* (1995) 183 CLR 121, at 163 'the so-called exceptions to the doctrine are in truth not exceptions at all'. This may be no more than a matter of semantics, since it is quite clear that the ambit of communication with a legal adviser which may be disclosed, notwithstanding the privilege, cannot be foretold, in advance of any such consultation, with any accuracy or certainty.
19 Though the first now also finds statutory expression in the Police and Criminal Evidence Act 1984, s 10(2).
20 See generally Newbould (1990) 53 MLR 472.
1 (1884) 14 QBD 153.
2 Cf *R v Smith* (1915) 11 Cr App Rep 229.
2a *Campbell and Shirose v R* (1998) SCC, 22 April.
3 *Williams v Quebrada Railway, Land and Copper Co* [1895] 2 Ch 751; *Gamlen Chemical Co (UK) Ltd v Rochem Ltd (No 2)* (1979) 124 Sol Jo 276.
4 Or abuse of statutory power, see in England, *Dubai Aluminium Co Ltd v Al Alawi* [1999] 1 All ER 703; and in Australia, *Freeman v Health Insurance Commission* (1997) 157 ALR 339. Trespass and conversion would not however be enough: see *Dubai Aluminium* above at 707h.
5 The strength of the evidence required may vary with the circumstances and the nature of the proceedings: *Derby & Co Ltd v Weldon (No 7)* [1990] 3 All ER 161, [1990] 1 WLR 1156. It

that it was the client's intention to obtain advice substantially[6] in furtherance of his criminal or fraudulent purpose before the court will consider whether the situation comes within the exception to the rule relating to professional privilege.[7] It seems that in the case of conveyancing transactions it is enough that the object is to deprive a creditor of his security,[8] and opinions have differed as to whether a mere mis-statement of the purpose for seeking a loan will suffice.[9] It is not necessary that the claim be based upon the fraud, if the otherwise privileged material is relevant to it.[10] The judge retains a discretion to exclude evidence if he believes that the public interest in supporting a party in the preparation of his case outweighs that of disclosure, and this is particularly likely to be exercised against disclosure at proceedings to secure interim orders,[11] especially when the fraud amounts to an allegation that the legal proceedings have themselves been brought fraudulently. It has been remarked[12] that if this were not so a party need only allege fraud in bringing any proceedings to secure sight of the whole of his opponent's brief. The same consideration applies to an allegation of fraud in securing legal aid in respect of launching proceedings.[13] Still less is the privilege likely to be lost in respect of communications with their legal advisers by innocent assignees of goods obtained by the fraud of third parties.[14]

In its codification of the law relating to police powers of search the Police and Criminal Evidence Act 1984, s 10(2) provides a statutory version of this limitation upon the privilege: 'Items held with the intention of furthering a criminal purpose are not items subject to legal privilege.' In *R v Central Criminal Court, ex p Francis & Francis*[15] the majority of the House of Lords took the view that this provision had left the rule unaffected, and in particular that its reference to the intention with which documents were held was capable of referring to the intention, not of the adviser but of the client, with the result that documents[16] held innocently by a solicitor remain outside the protection of the privilege if the client's intention is fraudulent. It seems that the restriction to 'furthering a criminal purpose' is probably no more restrictive than the position at common law in its reliance upon the concept of 'fraud', which in this context had been held not to extend to every act or scheme which was unlawful such, for example, as an inducement of breach of contract;[17] or an unsolicited letter to a client advising him that certain conduct could lead to his being prosecuted;[18] or a conveyance

---

seems that it need not come dehors the allegedly fraudulent document, which the court may inspect to determine its purpose: *R v Governor of Pentonville Prison ex p Osman* [1989] 3 All ER 701, [1990] 1 WLR 277, *Seamar Holdings Ltd v Kupe Group Ltd* [1995] 2 NZLR 274. On the other hand it has been held in Australia that it must be raised by admissible evidence: *Australian Federal Police Comr v Propend Finance Pty Ltd* (1997) 188 CLR 501.

6   *Royscott Spa Leasing Ltd v Lovett* [1995] BCC 502.
7   *O'Rourke v Darbishire* [1920] AC 581; *Bullivant v A-G for Victoria* [1901] AC 196.
8   *Barclay's Bank plc v Eustice* [1995] 4 All ER 511, [1995] 1 WLR 1238.
9   See *Nationwide Building Society v Various Solicitors* [1998] NLJR 241 disapproving *Birmingham Midshires Mortgage Services Ltd v Phillips* [1998] PNLR 468.
10   *Dubai Bank v Galadari (No 6)* (1991) Times, 22 April (unaffected on this point by the reversal in the Court of Appeal). There is some suggestion that the criteria are more rigorous in relation to litigation privilege.
11   But not apparently if the preparation of a case has involved deliberate breach of statutory provisions, such as those relating to data protection: *Dubai Aluminium Co Ltd v Al Alawi* [1999] 1 All ER 703.
12   By Hoffmann J in *Chandler v Church* [1987] NLJ Rep 451.
13   *R v Snaresbrook Crown Court, ex p DPP* [1988] QB 532, [1988] 1 All ER 315.
14   *Banque Keyser Ullmann SA v Skandia (UK) Insurance Co Ltd* [1986] 1 Lloyd's Rep 336.
15   [1989] AC 346, [1988] 3 All ER 775
16   Especially if forged: *R v Leeds Magistrates' Court, ex p Dumbleton* [1993] Crim LR 866.
17   *Crescent Farm (Sidcup) Sports Ltd v Sterling Offices Ltd* [1972] Ch 553, [1971] 3 All ER 1192.
18   *Butler v Board of Trade* [1971] Ch 680, [1970] 3 All ER 593.

without consideration designed to defeat creditors.[19] It seems that in order to determine whether documents fall within this exception the judge himself is entitled to inspect them.[20]

Since fraud unravels all confidence the legal adviser need not await a claim by a third party, but may himself initiate proceedings.[1]

2. Information tending to establish innocence

In *R v Barton* an exception to the privilege was suggested in favour of the accused in criminal proceedings who required access to otherwise privileged materials to establish his defence,[2] analogous to a similar exception to public interest immunity.[3] Such an exception has however now been rejected by the highest courts both here, in *R v Derby Magistrates ex p B,*[4] and in Australia, in *Carter v Managing Partner of Northmore Hale Davy & Leake.*[5] The English case involved a prosecution for murder in which two men were involved, one of them then tried and acquitted. The second was then charged with the murder, and sought access to the first's communications with his lawyer in advance of the first trial.[6] It was a strong case for the exception since the first party whose communications were sought was no longer in jeopardy, having been acquitted of the very crime. The House of Lords nevertheless rejected the suggested exception,[7] largely on the ground that to allow an exception, which it felt would lead to a balancing exercise in every case, would run counter to the general policy of legal professional privilege which it saw as encouraging private citizens to consult lawyers, secure in the knowledge that their communications would remain forever inviolate. It is arguable that this reasoning confuses the balancing necessary to establish a *general* rule of exception with the balancing necessary to derogate from an established rule in a *particular* case, and underplays the number of situations in which what transpires in the course of communication with a lawyer, either to seek legal advice or to prepare for litigation, may be revealed contrary to the expectations, and against the wishes and interests, of the client.

Although there is no reason to doubt that privilege may be successfully pleaded on behalf of the client of a solicitor called by the prosecution in a criminal case,[8] we shall see that the client's right to confidentiality as against third parties in respect of the contents of a letter written to him by his solicitor may have to yield to the Crown's right to prove them in a public prosecution.[9]

---

19 See *Re Konigsberg (a bankrupt)* [1989] 3 All ER 289, [1989] 1 WLR 1257.
20 *R v Governor of Pentonville Prison, ex p Osman* [1989] 3 All ER 701, [1990] 1 WLR 277.
1   *Finers v Miro* [1991] 1 All ER 182, [1991] 1 WLR 35.
2   [1972] 2 All ER 1192, [1973] 1 WLR 115; accepted here in *R v Ataou* [1988] QB 798, [1988] 2 All ER 321, in Canada in *R v Dunbar and Logan* (1982) 138 DLR (3d) 221, and in New Zealand in *R v Craig* [1975] 1 NZLR 597; but rejected in Australia in *R v Connell (No 2)* (1992) 8 WAR 148, and effectively in South Africa in *S v Safatsa* 1988 (1) SA 868.
3   See below p 489.
4   [1996] AC 487, [1995] 4 All ER 526; for criticism see Tapper (1996) 1 Int J of Ev & Proof 5.
5   (1995) 183 CLR 121, though largely resurrected there by s 123 of the Evidence Act 1995.
6   Which there were good reasons to suspect might have indicated his commission of the crime for which he had been acquitted.
7   And overruled both *Barton* and *Ataou*.
8   As it was in *R v Ataou*, above.
9   *Butler v Board of Trade* [1971] Ch 680, [1970] 3 All ER 593.

3.   Disputes between clients and legal advisers

Since the whole point of legal professional privilege is to encourage the fullest possible disclosure between legal adviser and client it follows that no privilege can arise between them, but only with respect to disclosure to a third party. The client may not therefore make a claim against his legal adviser, and at the same time take advantage of legal professional privilege to the adviser's disadvantage. It seems that even here however the privilege is recognised to exist and to inhere in the client, but if he fails to waive it, then he exposes himself to adverse inference.[10] If the privilege is waived, for example by suing a former solicitor, privileged material in the hands of subsequent legal advisers is unaffected.[11] This constraint applies not only to litigation formally between client and legal adviser, but may extend to other cases where the interests of solicitor and client are clearly opposed.[12] This constraint is, in England, firmly rooted in fairness between lawyer and client, and if the client is suing a third party, then the privilege remains intact.[13] If the interests of different clients with a joint interest in litigation themselves become temporarily opposed, then legal advice tendered during such estrangement loses its privilege as against a third party in the main dispute so long as such estrangement and separate advice persists.[14] Similar considerations may also apply to cases where a third party in conflict with the client is entitled to disclosure from the legal adviser.[15] For similar reasons privilege cannot be claimed between those already under a mutual duty of disclosure to each other.[16]

4.   Statutory exclusion

There are few if any statutes abrogating legal professional privilege by express reference[17] and the subject has not attracted much case law so far as implied abrogation is concerned.[18] In this respect there is a striking contrast with the privilege against self-incrimination.[19] One area in which it has arisen, and caused difficulty, relates to the provision of s 1 of the Children Act 1989 that: 'the child's welfare shall be the court's paramount consideration'. This matter was considered at length by the House of Lords in *Re L (a minor)(police investigation: privilege)*[20] in the context of a claim to privilege

10   *Ridehaulgh v Horsefield* [1994] Ch 205, [1994] 3 All ER 848.
11   *Paragon Finance plc v Freshfields* [1999] 1 WLR 1183, overruling *Hayes v Dowding* [1996] PNLI 578, and doubting *Kershaw v Whelan* [1996] 2 All ER 404, [1996] 1 WLR 358. See also *Goldberg v Ng* (1995) 185 CLR 83.
12   As in *R v Charbonneau* (1992) 74 CCC (3d) 49 (where the legal adviser was charged with an alleged attempt to pervert the course of justice by persuading the client to commit perjury in separate proceedings. The client was a willing witness for the prosecution in the attempt proceedings against his erstwhile adviser, but sought to invoke the privilege to avoid cross-examination).
13   *Nederlandse Reassurantie Groep Holding NV v Bacon & Woodrow* [1995] 1 All ER 976.
14   *Leif Hoegh & Co A/S v Petrolsea Inc* [1993] 1 Lloyd's Rep 363.
15   *Brown v Guardian Royal Exchange Assurance plc* [1994] 2 Lloyd's Rep 325 (the entitlement arose under a contract of which the client was fully aware and to which he raised no objection).
16   *Dockrill v Coopers & Lybrand* (1994) 111 DLR (4th) 62 (partners); *French v Fish* (1997) 143 DLR (4th) 626 (subrogated parties).
17   See *R v IRC, ex p Taylor (No 2)* [1990] 2 All ER 409 for consideration of Taxes Management Act 1970, s 20 where it is preserved for legal advisers, but only when so acting, and not in relation to their position as taxpayers.
18   Implied abrogation by Banking Act 1987, s 39 was upheld in *Price Waterhouse v BCCI Holdings (Luxembourg) SA* [1992] BCLC 583. In Australia express provision is required: *Yuill v Corporate Affairs Commission* (1990) 20 NSWLR 386.
19   See *Re Compass Airlines Pty Ltd* (1992) 109 ALR 119.
20   [1997] AC 16, [1996] 2 All ER 78.

to prevent revelation to the police of a doctor's report on the death of a child,[1] prepared for the purpose of care proceedings. The majority took the view that however absolute the privilege might be in relation to legal advice, its litigation branch could not operate to suppress the disclosure of evidence,[2] which would in other circumstances be privileged, when in care proceedings the best interests of the child would be promoted by disclosure. The minority view would have prevented disclosure on the basis of the privilege, which it regarded as applicable in both of its branches as an 'absolute' rule. The majority took the view that litigation privilege operated differently in non-adversarial proceedings, assimilating care proceedings to wardship proceedings[3] for this purpose. The minority rejected the sharpness of the distinction between legal advice and litigation privilege, arguing that proceedings involving children are often extremely contentious,[4] and resting ultimately on the absolute nature of legal professional privilege in both of its principal branches as a bulwark of a fair trial. The rejection of this proposition by the majority must cast some doubt upon the validity of some of the more extreme remarks in the *Derby Justices* case.

Jones v G D Searle & Co Ltd[5] shows that s 33 of the Limitation Act 1980 is a clear instance of a statutory exception to the rule of legal professional privilege for the claimant was required to answer an interrogatory inquiring whether the legal advice he had received was favourable or unfavourable. The section empowers the court to give leave to bring a claim out of time having regard to a number of factors affecting the delay, including the nature of the advice received. It has however become increasingly common to preserve the privilege by express provision,[6] and in criminal cases the Police and Criminal Evidence Act 1984 has not only insulated material covered by the privilege from the issue of search warrants, but has also invalidated all previous legislation to the extent of any inconsistency.[7]

A further exception has now been added by CPR 48.7(3) under which privileged material may be ordered to be divulged to the court, or to the other party, by either lawyer or client, in the course of considering a wasted costs order.

D. THE CLAIMS OF OTHER RELATIONSHIPS

The distinction between professional privilege and the protection of confidentiality lies at the root of the present law concerning the disclosure by doctors and priests of statements made by a patient or penitent. There is no doubt that the voluntary disclosure of such matters would be restrained by injunction. There is equally no doubt that in England[8] such statements are not privileged from compulsory disclosure in court by the person to whom they are made. For this reason it may be doubted whether an

1   Commissioned by the child's mother, who authorised the disclosure to the doctor of the materials in the case upon which the report had been based.
2   The majority was careful to avoid describing this as an exception to, or as overriding, legal professional privilege.
3   See *Re A (minors) (disclosure of material)* [1991] 2 FLR 473.
4   Although such an argument seems to invest the word 'adversarial' with its popular rather than with its technical meaning, as the minority itself recognised.
5   [1978] 3 All ER 654, [1979] 1 WLR 101.
6   See for example Data Protection Act 1984, s 31(2); Banking Act 1987, ss 39(13), 41(11) and 42(6) (there limited to documents); Criminal Justice Act 1993, ss 18, 26.
7   Section 9(2).
8   It is interesting that in New Zealand in *R v Rapana* [1995] 2 NZLR 381 the court was prepared to use the broad provision of s 35 of the Evidence (Amendment) Act No 2 1980 in favour of confidential communications to supplement the more narrowly phrased medical privilege in s 33 in the case of a communication to a psychotherapist.

injunction would ever extend to compulsory disclosure in court, but this has not been the subject of case law to date.[9] The problem is simply whether the equivalent of legal professional privilege which covers confidential communications between client and legal adviser in the course of obtaining advice, should be extended to other relationships. Does the fact that legal advice inevitably takes the form of a statement like 'If you do so and so it could lead to litigation', coupled with the fact that full and free disclosure is essential to the obtaining of good advice about litigation, justify the peculiar treatment by English law of the lawyer-client relationship?

It is hardly surprising that privilege should, at different times, have been claimed for confidential communication between friends,[10] documents in the possession of an accountant,[11] auditor,[12] or banker[13] relating to his client's affairs and even for information supplied to a pursuivant of the Royal College of Heralds.[14] All of these claims have been unsuccessful.

It is necessary only to add a few remarks on the subject of the non-recognition by the law of privilege of the relationship between priest and penitent, and physician and patient. There are, however, two points that should be stressed before this is done. In the first place, although law rather than discretion may be in control 'if it comes to the forensic crunch', the court always has had a discretion to disallow questions unless they are relevant and necessary, or such as to serve a useful purpose in relation to the proceedings in hand,[15] second it is a mistake to suppose that the choice lies between a privilege of complete secrecy on the one hand, and on the other hand, compulsory disclosure without restriction. It is possible, and sometimes desirable, that the claimant to the privilege should decline to produce documents or give evidence until he is ordered to do so by the court. Such a course is contemplated by statute and approved by the cases. Thus, s 7 of the Bankers' Books Evidence Act 1879, assumes that an application will be made to the court for an order for inspection of a banker's books, and in *R v St Lawrence's Hospital*[16] Lord Goddard CJ approved the refusal of medical officers to disclose their communications with the visitors to a hospital under the Mental Deficiency Acts without an order of the court. When such an order is made, it can be on such terms as, for example, that no use will be made of the information disclosed outside the particular proceedings before the court.[17] Non-compliance with the order

9   An injunction may however be granted to prevent such disclosure to a foreign court: *XAG v A bank* [1983] 2 All ER 464, [1983] 2 Lloyd's Rep 535.
10   *Duchess of Kingston's Case* (1776) 20 State Tr 355.
11   *Chantrey Martin & Co v Martin* [1953] 2 QB 286, [1953] 2 All ER 691. There would be no obligation to disclose if the documents were the client's property but that is not the result of the law of privilege.
12   *Price Waterhouse v BCCI Holdings (Luxembourg) SA* [1992] BCLC 583.
13   *Robertson v Canadian Imperial Bank of Commerce* [1995] 1 All ER 824, PC.
14   *Slade v Tucker* (1880) 14 Ch D 824. See also *Jones v Great Central Rly Co* [1910] AC 4 (trade union official). So far as bankers are concerned, their contractual duty is not to disclose the state of their customer's account without his consent except under order of the court or pursuant to a public duty (*Tournier v National Provincial and Union Bank of England* [1924] 1 KB 461). See also *R v Daye* [1908] 2 KB 333. In the case of a company's bankers support is to be found in s 452 of the Companies Act 1985.
15   *A-G v Mulholland* [1963] 2 QB 477, at 489 and 492 per Lord Denning MR and Donovan LJ respectively. Any such discretion is enlarged by the broad and indeterminate powers conferred by CPR 32.1.
16   *R v St Lawrence's Hospital, Caterham Statutory Visitors, ex p Pritchard* [1953] 2 All ER 766, at 772. A statute may affect the terms upon which an order for discovery may be made (see *McIvor v Southern Health and Social Services Board* [1978] 2 All ER 625). See also *Church of Scientology of California v Department of Health and Social Security* [1979] 3 All ER 97.
17   See the order in *Chantrey Martin & Co v Martin* (above). In wardship and custody proceedings there may be disclosure to the court leaving it to the discretion of the judge to decide whether there should be any disclosure to the parties; see for example *Official Solicitor of the Supreme*

would constitute a contempt of court,[18] but it must be admitted that there are circumstances in which disclosure, even on the most stringent terms as to dissemination of the information, is abhorrent to the witness. He may not consider himself to be adequately protected by the discretion of the court simply because there are cases in which the question is both relevant and, from the point of view of the party putting it, necessary. Some general factors mentioned by Wigmore as apposite to consideration of any proposal to extend this head of privilege will then be considered, and finally a rather differently framed privilege mooted for the media of communication will be touched upon.

I. Priest and penitent

A possible case for the creation of a new privilege is that of the Roman Catholic priest called upon to testify with regard to that which took place in the confessional.[19] There is very little judicial authority on the subject, but such as there is, like the opinion of all the text-writers, is against the existence of any privilege according to English law.

Were the problem to arise in an acute form in practice, most judges would probably sympathise with Best CJ when he said 'I, for one, will never compel a clergyman to disclose communications made to him by a prisoner; but if he chooses to disclose them I shall receive them in evidence'.[20]

A privilege is conferred on penitential communications by statute in various parts of the Commonwealth,[1] and in most American states[2] but both the Law Reform Committee and the Criminal Law Revision Committee were opposed to any change in the English law.[3]

Court v K [1965] AC 201, [1963] 3 All ER 191; *Re M* [1973] QB 108, [1972] 3 All ER 321. The number of such cases may be increasing, see *Science Research Council v Nassé* [1980] AC 1028, [1979] 3 All ER 673 (anti-discrimination legislation); and *Campbell v Tameside Metropolitan Borough Council* [1982] QB 1065, [1982] 2 All ER 791 (psychologists' reports on children).

18   Even in the absence of a special order it amounts to contempt to use a document obtained by discovery for any purpose ulterior to the purposes of the litigation in which it was obtained, *Harman v Secretary of State for the Home Department* [1983] 1 AC 280, sub nom *Home Office v Harman* [1982] 1 All ER 532.

19   The usual claim is that the privilege is that of the penitent, but it is sometimes said that it should belong to the priest alone as distinct from being exercisable by him on behalf of an absent person.

20   *Broad v Pitt* (1828) 3 C & P 518 (obiter). A clergyman was obliged to disclose an admission of adultery made in conversation by a friend in *Normanshaw v Normanshaw and Measham* (1893) 69 LT 468.

1   In Australia such a privilege has a statutory basis as s 127 of the Evidence Act 1995; in Canada the situation has been affected by s 2 of the Canadian Charter of Rights and Freedoms; for fuller discussion see *Gruenke v R* [1991] 3 SCR 263; in New Zealand see *R v Howse* (1983) 1 CRNZ 32, *R v L* [1998] 2 NZLR 141 (construing such a confession strictly).

2   It has also been accepted in the Federal courts without the benefit of statute: *Mullen v US* 263 F 2d 275 (1958).

3   16th Report of the Law Reform Committee, paras 46–7; 11th Report of the Criminal Law Revision Committee, paras 272–5. Even so the police have given an informal undertaking not to conduct intrusive surveillance in such a way as to infringe the secrecy of the confessional, *Intrusive Surveillance Code of Practice* para 2.3.

2.   Physician and patient[4]

There is more judicial authority on the subject of communications between doctors and their patients than there is on statements made to clergymen. It is uniformly against the existence of any privilege,[5] although Buller J once said it was much to be regretted that legal professional privilege had not been extended to medical persons.[6] The problem is much more likely to arise in practice than that which relates to statements made to clergymen, for these are likely to be relevant to litigation only when they constitute admissions, and in many cases, no one will know whether they were made, whereas questions concerning medical treatment are both more likely to arise in a law suit, and more likely to be the subject of such knowledge as could warrant the calling of a doctor as a witness.

In the United States the Federal Rules of Evidence leave the creation of new privileges to the common law, and the Supreme Court in *Jaffee v Redmond*[7] so acted for those engaged in psychotherapy. This matter is also dealt with by statute in various parts of the Commonwealth,[8] but both the Law Reform Committee and the Criminal Law Revision Committee were against any change in the English law.[9]

In the legislation which has been enacted to date it has been found necessary to provide for exceptions. Not only is there a tendency to confine medical privilege to civil proceedings, a restriction which some would advocate in the case of the priest and penitent, it has also been found desirable to impose special limitations in civil cases. Examples are actions for medical negligence brought by a patient against his doctor, cases in which the patient's sanity is in issue and claims by the patient in respect of personal injuries the nature, duration, extent or effect of which is in issue. In the case of medical, and especially psychiatric, evidence there are obvious dangers in according to the patient complete control over the disclosure of information relating to his medical condition, and it has been held that the doctor cannot be inhibited by considerations of confidentiality from discharging his duty to the community.[10]

A doctor, like a clergyman, may be able to rely on some other head of privilege or exemption, such as that which relates to negotiations between estranged spouses or the possible protection from disclosure on the ground of public interest of communications with the Minister relating to the National Health Service.[11] It is also possible that in some situations it would be unfair within s 78 of the Police and Criminal Evidence Act 1984 to use statements made to a doctor, but it would be unwise to prescribe conditions under which this might be the case.[12]

---

4   When the claim to privilege is made it is always treated as that of the patient.
5   *Duchess of Kingston's Case* (1776) 20 State Tr 355; *R v Gibbons* (1823) 1 C & P 97; *Wheeler v Le Merchant* (1881) 17 Ch D 675, at 681; *Garner v Garner* (1920) 36 TLR 196; *Hunter v Mann* [1974] QB 767, [1974] 2 All ER 414; *R v Smith* [1979] 3 All ER 605, [1979] 1 WLR 1445; *Campbell v Tameside Metropolitan Borough Council* [1982] QB 1065, [1982] 2 All ER 791.
6   *Wilson v Rastall* (1792) 4 Term Rep 753, at 760. See also per Lord Edmund Davies in *D v National Society for the Prevention of Cruelty to Children* [1978] AC 171, at 245, [1977] 1 All ER 589, at 618a; he long thought that the law should be altered.
7   518 US 1 (1996). Legislation enacting such privileges exists in many states.
8   For the position in Canada see *Metropolitan Life Insurance Co v Frenette* [1992] 1 SCR 647; *M v Ryan* (1997) 143 DLR 4th 1; in Australia the Evidence Act 1995 makes no provision for a medical privilege though a few states have one.
9   16th Report of the Law Reform Committee, paras 48–52; 11th Report of the Criminal Law Revision Committee, para 276.
10   *W v Egdell* [1990] Ch 359, [1990] 1 All ER 835; *R v Crozier* [1991] Crim LR 138.
11   66 LQR 92.
12   See *R v McDonald* [1991] Crim LR 122.

It should be noted that while special restrictions are put upon access to some confidential material falling short of being the subject of legal professional privilege by the Police and Criminal Justice Act 1984, these apply for the protection of the adviser, not of the subject, and thus voluntary disclosure by the medical adviser is not liable to the subject's control by a claim in the nature of privilege.[13]

3. Conclusions

In a much quoted paragraph[14] Wigmore mentioned four preconditions of a privilege of the lawyer-client type.[15] They are that:

(1) the communications must originate in a confidence that they will not be disclosed;
(2) the element of confidentiality must be essential to the full and satisfactory maintenance of the relationship between the parties;
(3) the relationship must be one that in the opinion of the community ought to be sedulously fostered;
(4) the injury that would inure to the relationship by the disclosure of the communication must be greater than the benefit gained through the correct disposal of the litigation.

Wigmore had no doubt about the compliance of the lawyer-client privilege with these conditions. He was unsympathetic to medical privilege and suggested that, in its case, preconditions 2 and 4 are not fulfilled, while he thought that there might be some uncertainty with regard to precondition 3 in the case of the priest-penitent privilege, with which he was sympathetic. Some people would no doubt disagree with him on both points. It is difficult to assess the merits of the present English law until it is known whether, 'when it comes to the forensic crunch', the judge has a discretion to exclude even relevant and necessary questions in civil proceedings. The House of Lords was equally divided on this point in *D v National Society for the Prevention of Cruelty to Children.*[16]

4. Identity of informant

As will be seen in the following chapter, it has been recognised as being contrary to public policy to require the names of informants to the police, or to some other bodies conducting similar functions, to be revealed in civil proceedings. An allied privilege has occasionally been claimed by journalists.[17] The privilege differs from the professional privileges considered above in that the claim is not normally made in

---

13   *R v Singleton* [1995] 1 Cr App Rep 431 (here the adviser was a dentist).
14   Para 2285.
15   In *Slavotych v Baker* [1976] 1 SCR 254, at 260 Spence J expressed approval of this approach, but his remarks were obiter, and subsequently criticised by McLachlin (now a Justice of the Supreme Court of Canada) (1977) 11 UBCLR 266.
16   [1978] AC 171, [1976] 2 All ER 993. See below p 486.
17   *A-G v Clough* [1963] 1 QB 773, [1963] 1 All ER 420; *A-G v Mulholland* [1963] 2 QB 477, [1963] 1 All ER 767. See also *McGuiness v A-G of Victoria* (1940) 63 CLR 73; *Wran v Australian Broadcasting Commission* [1984] 3 NSWLR 241; *Independent Commission against Corruption v Cornwall* (1993) 116 ALR 97.

respect of the content of the communication, which has usually been revealed already;[18] and in the absence of any clear recognition that the privilege belongs to the informant and not to the journalist himself. Such a privilege is recognised in some other jurisdictions,[19] but at least in an absolute form, was rejected here.

The question was considered by the House of Lords in *British Steel Corpn v Granada Television Ltd.*[20] A confidential document belonging to the claimants came into the hands of the defendants, and was knowingly used as part of a television programme. The claimants secured an order for the return of the documents, but the defendants mutilated them so as to try to conceal any indication of the identity of their supplier. The claimants then sought an order for the revelation of his identity. It transpired that an undertaking to respect the anonymity of the source had been given. The majority of their Lordships was quite clear that journalists had no privilege akin either to that of lawyer and client, or in respect of the non-disclosure of their sources of information akin to that of the police. It was said that such a privilege would:[1]

> place journalists (how defined?) in a favoured and unique position as compared with priest-confessors, doctors, bankers, and other recipients of confidential information and would assimilate them to the police in relation to informers.

This decision caused some disquiet in the media of communication, and a new statutory privilege was created in an attempt to assuage it:

> No court may require a person to disclose, nor is any person guilty of contempt of court for refusing to disclose, the source of information contained in a publication for which he is responsible, unless it be established to the satisfaction of the court that disclosure is necessary in the interests of justice or national security or for the prevention of disorder or crime.[2]

It was not clear that this section would have a very radical effect upon the law as established in *Granada*. It was recognised there that even though there was no absolute immunity, the judge still had some discretion in relation to questioning about the source.[3] The vague formula in the statute appeared to impose little more constraint upon, or to offer very much more guidance for, the action of the court. It was however clearer that the burden of satisfying the court that the conditions existed was upon the party desirous of disclosure, and that within the relevant area disclosure was governed by the statutory rule, and not by discretion.[4]

The judge nevertheless retains discretion after the Act to refuse to order disclosure in an extreme case even when the conditions for disclosure have been satisfied.[5] There

---

18   In *Moysa v Alberta (Labour Relations Board)* (1989) 60 DLR (4th) 1 the unsuccessful claim related to information conveyed by the journalist to a known party.

19   It is recognised in many United States jurisdictions; for an extensive discussion see *Branzburg v Hayes* 408 US 665 (1972).

20   [1981] AC 1096, [1981] 1 All ER 417.

1   Lord Wilberforce at 1171, 457. See also Viscount Dilhorne at 1181, 465; Lord Fraser at 1196, 476; Lord Russell concurred.

2   Contempt of Court Act 1981, s 10, partly in an attempt to implement art 10 of the European Convention of Human Rights. Much the same result seems to have been reached in Canada as a matter of the construction of s 2 of the Canadian Charter of Rights and Freedoms, see *The Citizen v Coates* (1986) 29 DLR (4th) 523.

3   See ch XI, section 1 below.

4   *Secretary of State for Defence v Guardian Newspapers Ltd* [1985] AC 339, [1984] 3 All ER 601.

5   *Re Insider Dealing Inquiry* [1988] AC 660, at 703, [1988] 1 All ER 203, at 208. See also in Ireland *Burke v Central Independent Television* [1994] 2 IR 61 where disclosure might have endangered the lives of the sources.

has now been a certain amount of interpretation of this provision. In particular the concept of disclosure being necessary has been clarified. In *Secretary of State for Defence v Guardian Newspapers Ltd*[6] Lord Diplock pointed out that this requirement was mandatory, and it has been further explained that administrative convenience is insufficient.[7] It seems that where an end, such as the assessment of damages, can be achieved without disclosure, but by other means, such as a firm jury direction, the availability of such means removes any necessity for disclosure.[8] It is not however enough to prevent disclosure automatically that the issue arises during proceedings to secure interim orders.[9] In the case of prosecution of crime it has been held that the reference is to crime in general, and not to a specific crime, so there is no need to demonstrate that some particular crime will be prevented by disclosure,[10] nor that disclosure would necessarily prevent the commission of further crime,[11] if it would have that tendency. In the case of the interest of the administration of justice, the concept is to be construed narrowly,[12] typically referring to proceedings in a court of law,[13] including proceedings to secure interim orders,[14] or proceedings to identify a tortfeasor,[15] though there must be evidence of some intention to initiate such proceedings.[16] The privilege in respect of police informants,[17] cannot be claimed to the prejudice of the defence in criminal case. There is no such expressed limitation here, and as noted above the accused would bear the burden of establishing grounds for disclosure.

SECTION 3.   STATEMENTS MADE WITHOUT PREJUDICE[18]

As part of an attempt to settle a dispute,[19] the parties frequently make statements 'without prejudice'. When this is done, the contents of the statement cannot be put in

6 Above at 350, 607.
7 In the *Insider Dealing* case, above, at 704, 208, the meaning was said by Lord Griffiths to lie between being 'indispensable' and 'useful or convenient', and capable of being paraphrased as 'really needed'.
8 *Maxwell v Pressdram Ltd* [1987] 1 All ER 656, [1987] 1 WLR 298.
9 *Michael O'Mara Books Ltd v Express Newspapers plc* [1998] EMLR 383.
10 *Insider Dealing*, above, at 705, 209.
11 See also *X v Y* [1988] 2 All ER 648.
12 See *Saunders v Punch Ltd* [1998] 1 All ER 234 where the court was neither prepared to add to the heads justifying disclosure, nor to construe the interests of justice expansively so as to allow disclosure in furtherance of the protection of legal professional privilege by disclosure of a source who might have been in breach of the confidence protecting it.
13 *Guardian Newspapers Ltd*, above, at 350, 607.
14 *Guardian Newspapers Ltd*, above.
15 *X Ltd v Morgan-Grampian (Publishers) Ltd* [1991] 1 AC 1, [1990] 2 All ER 1. In the very same situation the European Court of Human Rights came to the opposite conclusion in *Goodwin v United Kingdom* (1996) 22 EHRR 123 in its construction of art 10 of the European Convention which s 10 was intended to implement, though in *Camelot Group plc v Centaur Communications Ltd* [1999] QB 124, [1998] 1 All ER 251 this was explained upon the basis of the two courts taking a different view of the factual basis of the dispute. It remains to be seen whether the view that the two provisions have an identical effect will survive the formal incorporation of the Convention into English law.
16 *Handmade Films (Productions) Ltd v Express Newspapers plc* [1986] FSR 463.
17 See below ch XI, section 1, part G.
18 For the history of this privilege see Vaver (1974) 9 UBCLR 85. It appears in statutory form in Australia in the Evidence Act 1995, s 131, and for exegesis see *GPI Leisure Corpn Ltd (In Liquidation) v Yuill* (1997) 42 NSWLR 225.
19 One of the principal concerns of the Woolf Report, reflected in the Civil Procedure Rules Part 36 was the creation of an environment more conducive to settlement of litigation, and CPR 36.19 explicitly applied the concept of without prejudice offers to the new regime.

evidence without the consent of both parties, the case being one of joint privilege. The statements often relate to the offer of a compromise, and, were it not for the privilege, they would constitute significant items of evidence on the ground that they were admissions. Obviously it is in the public interest that disputes should be settled and litigation reduced to a minimum,[20] so the policy of the law is in favour of enlarging the cloak under which negotiations may be conducted without prejudice.[1] This policy is carried out by means of a rigorous insistence on the absence of any magic in the form of words used by the parties, everything being made to depend upon their intention and the objective circumstances of the case, but difficulty occasionally arises as to the scope and effect of the privilege.

A.   SCOPE

This privilege has been authoritatively stated to be 'founded on the public policy of encouraging litigants to settle their differences rather than litigate them to a finish'.[2] The detail represents no more than a number of illustrations of this guiding principle. It follows that literal use of the phrase 'without prejudice' is no more than indicative that evidence[3] prefaced by it may be intended to lead to the settlement of a dispute, and so be protected.[4] It is certainly immaterial that a different formulation is adopted, or the words used elsewhere than at the beginning of a document.[5] It is unnecessary to use the words, or any equivalent, if it is clear from the surrounding circumstances that the evidence is part of a continuing negotiation,[6] or obtained pursuant to one.[7] If negotiations for a settlement during which without prejudice documents pass between the parties fail, either party is then free to open subsequent correspondence between them over the objection of the other, and despite the fact that such subsequent correspondence itself seeks to negotiate a settlement.[8] Any such change in status must be intimated clearly, and if it is, then it becomes immaterial that the recipient fails to understand its significance or is unwilling to accept it.[9]

Use of the phrase 'without prejudice' is inefficacious if the statement is not made as part of a genuine attempt to negotiate a settlement. Thus evidence of letters written by a debtor to his creditors declaring his inability to pay was admissible in bankruptcy

---

20   Difficult questions may arise as to the extent to which litigation can be severed in the course of negotiation, and how far without prejudice correspondence in arriving at a partial settlement can be protected: see *Tomlin v Standard Telephones & Cables Ltd* [1969] 3 All ER 201, [1969] 1 WLR 1378 (holding that a without prejudice statement on contribution could be adduced even though the attempted full settlement failed on the issue of quantum). See also *Lukies v Ripley (No 2)* (1994) 35 NSWLR 283 for a full discussion of policy in this context.

1   Such an aim lies at the core of the new regime of civil procedure, and can be expected to influence the interpretation of this branch of the law: see *Unilever plc v Procter & Gamble Co* [1999] 2 All ER 691.

2   By Lord Griffiths in *Rush & Tompkins Ltd v Greater London Council* [1989] AC 1280, at 1299, [1988] 3 All ER 737, at 739.

3   The rule applies to oral as well as to documentary statements.

4   *South Shropshire District Council v Amos* [1987] 1 All ER 340, at 344, [1986] 1 WLR 1271, at 1277.

5   *Cory v Bretton* (1830) 4 C & P 462.

6   *Paddock v Forrester* (1842) 3 Man & G 903, where the heading of the first of a series of letters invested later ones with the privilege, and *Oliver v Nautilus SS Co* [1903] 2 KB 639, where so labelling a later document invested an earlier one with the privilege.

7   *Rabin v Mendoza & Co* [1954] 1 All ER 247, [1954] 1 WLR 271.

8   *Dixons Stores Group Ltd v Thames Television plc* [1993] 1 All ER 349.

9   *Cheddar Valley Engineering Ltd v Chaddlewood Homes Ltd* [1992] 4 All ER 942, [1992] 1 WLR 820.

proceedings as an act of bankruptcy, despite having been headed 'without prejudice'.[10] If, for example, a threat to pursue an admittedly false claim is made under the rubric it will not be privileged, even though designed to force a settlement of a related dispute.[11] Similarly an unequivocal admission of the matters in issue may be received, even though made under the rubric in the context of negotiation, though an English court may be more alert than some others[12] to find such equivocation.[13] Another difficult situation arises in relation to a simple statement of a legal claim so headed. If the document contains no other hint of any intention to negotiate it will be insufficient,[14] but the court will be astute to detect such an intention, and it is certainly not the case that a letter first intimating a dispute can never be made without prejudice.[15] The privilege protects all relevant statements made in a genuine attempt to negotiate a settlement, and is not confined to admissions.[16]

B. EFFECT

If the privilege can be established it is sometimes uncertain exactly what it prohibits. It seems clear that it can prevent use, not only by parties to the relevant negotiation, but also by third parties.[17] A party to negotiations to settle a dispute might well be inhibited from making damaging admissions if he knew that they could be used by a different adversary. Similarly, solicitors for the parties may claim privilege for statements made in letters written on their clients' behalf in proceedings in which they are sued personally;[18] but the statement in respect of which privilege is claimed must have some bearing on negotiations for a settlement.[19]

For some purposes reference can be made to without prejudice statements. Even when genuinely made in the context of a negotiation it seems that a statement can be put in evidence for some purpose not directly linked to the truth of the statement, such as to identify the handwriting of a party,[20] to prove the severance of a joint tenancy,[1] to show notice of the exercise of an option,[2] or to show, in the context of a subsequently disputed settlement that it was false.[3] Thus if the negotiations succeed, and constitute a binding contract, this may be proved by the use of without prejudice material.[4] It has also been said that it is permissible to refer to such statements, and the dates upon

---

10 *Re Daintrey, ex p Holt* [1893] 2 QB 116. Similarly an illegal threat as in *Kurtz & Co v Spence & Sons* (1887) 58 LT 438, or a libel is not protected simply because headed 'without prejudice'.
11 *Hawick Jersey International Ltd v Caplan* (1988) Times, 11 March. See also *Greenwood v Fitt* (1961) 29 DLR (2d) 260; *Cedenko Foods Ltd v State Insurance Ltd* [1996] 3 NZLR 205.
12 See in Australia in *Davies v Nyland* (1974) 10 SASR 76, at 91, adopting the view of Wigmore; *J A McBeath Nominees Pty Ltd v Jenkins Development Corpn Pty Ltd* [1992] 2 Qd 121.
13 *Forster v Friedland* (1992) LEXIS, 10 November per Hoffmann LJ; *Alizadeh v Nikbin* (1993) Times, 19 March.
14 *Buckinghamshire County Council v Moran* [1990] Ch 623, [1989] 2 All ER 225.
15 *South Shropshire District Council v Amos,* above.
16 *Unilever plc v Procter and Gamble Co* [1999] 2 All ER 691.
17 *Rush & Tompkins v Greater London Council* above. In Canada see *I Waxman and Sons Ltd v Texaco Canada Ltd* (1968) 67 DLR (2d) 295; in Australia it seems that reference may be made in certain statutory proceedings: *Hong Kong Bank of Australia Ltd v Murphy* (1992) 28 NSWLR 512.
18 *La Roche v Armstrong* [1922] 1 KB 485.
19 *Field v Comrs of Railways for New South Wales* (1957) 99 CLR 285, where the authorities are reviewed.
20 *Waldridge v Kennison* (1794) 1 Esp 143.
1 *McDowell v Hirschfield Lipson & Rumney and Smith* [1992] 2 FLR 126.
2 *Tenstat Pty Ltd v Permanent Trustee Australia Ltd* (1992) 28 NSWLR 625.
3 *Muller v Linsley* (1995) 139 Sol Jo LB 43.
4 *Tomlin v Standard Telephones and Cables Ltd* [1969] 3 All ER 201, [1969] 1 WLR 1378.

which they were made, in order to establish laches.[5] On the other hand no such reference can be made upon an application to secure costs.[6] These decisions may be reconciled upon the basis that in the former it was not necessary to do more than establish the context within which the letters were written, whereas in the latter reliance had to be placed upon the contents of the documents as admissions. Similar considerations have caused difficulty in relation to disputes about the taxation of costs. The general rule is that negotiations made without prejudice cannot be taken into account when considering questions of costs.[7] This principle has, however, been eroded to the extent that the court will permit a sort of hybrid 'without prejudice' statement to be made, which reserves the right to refer to it,[8] but only on questions of costs.[9] The reason for this is simply that such an erosion is more likely to promote speedy settlement.[10]

It has further been held[11] that there is no exception to this privilege by close analogy with the rule in *R v Cox and Railton*[12] since here the question relates not to the propriety of an underlying transaction, but to the procedure for vindicating it, and different principles apply.[13] Nor is it possible to import the notion of waiver from legal professional privilege, since where 'without prejudice' privilege exists it is essentially joint. Even though discovery is not limited to documents which are admissible in evidence, it does not extend to those covered by this branch of privilege.[14]

SECTION 4.   WITHOUT-PREJUDICE NEGOTIATIONS BETWEEN ESTRANGED SPOUSES

This emerged from the womb of the privilege for 'without prejudice' statements as an independent privilege.[15] If a solicitor were consulted by both husband and wife, professional privilege might attach to statements made to him by either of them so that he might not disclose them in subsequent matrimonial proceedings without the consent of the maker.[16] The ordinary law concerning without-prejudice statements applies to negotiations between the parties personally, or between their solicitors, which take place with a view to compromising a matrimonial cause. With the greater emphasis in

---

5   By Lindley LJ in *Walker v Wilsher* (1889) 23 QBD 335, at 338. See also *McFadden v Snow* (1951) 69 WN NSW 8 where it was decided in Australia that such a statement could be referred to in order to rebut an inference of an admission by otherwise apparent silence.

6   *Simaan General Contracting Co v Pilkington Glass Ltd* [1987] 1 All ER 345, [1987] 1 WLR 516.

7   *Walker v Wilsher* above, applied to arbitrations in *Stotesbury v Turner* [1943] KB 370.

8   This is indeed the model adopted by Civil Procedure Rule 36.19 for part 36 offers. It seems that the reservation must be made explicitly, see in Australia *In the marriage of Steel* (1992) 107 FLR 143.

9   *Calderbank v Calderbank* [1976] Fam 93, [1975] 3 All ER 333; *Cutts v Head* [1984] Ch 290, [1984] 1 All ER 597.

10   See generally Civil Procedure Rules, Pt 36.

11   *Forster v Friedland* (1992) LEXIS, 10 November.

12   (1884) 14 QBD 153, above p 457.

13   As explained in *Chandler v Church* [1987] NLJ Rep 451; *Derby & Co Ltd v Weldon (No 7)* [1990] 3 All ER 161, at 170, [1990] 1 WLR 1156, at 1174,5.

14   *Rabin v Mendoza & Co* [1954] 1 All ER 247, [1954] 1 WLR 271; see also in *Australia Trade Practices Commission v Arnotts Ltd* (1989) 88 ALR 69, at 74,5. Nor for the reasons given above does disclosure imply waiver.

15   *D v National Society for the Prevention of Cruelty to Children* [1978] AC 171, at 226, 236, [1977] 1 All ER 589, at 601, 610; *Re D (Minors)* [1993] Fam 231, [1993] 2 All ER 693.

16   *Harris v Harris* [1931] P 10.

the modern law relating to the family and children upon the concept of conciliation[17] it was necessary to protect also statements made to a conciliator, and the law was developed in a series of cases.[18] It has been held[19] that the effect of this privilege is different from that described in the previous section of this chapter, partly on account of the greater concern of the law to prevent the breakdown of marriage than the onset of litigation; and partly because of the paramount consideration of the well-being of children.

In particular these have operated so far as the former is concerned for the protection not only for statements made in a sincere effort to achieve reconciliation, but for all statements made in the course of such meetings designed to accomplish that end. Thus threats, which would not be protected as 'without prejudice' statements,[20] might be shielded under this head. On the other hand the paramount need to secure the well-being of children dictates a narrow exception from the general rule in relation to statements which 'clearly indicate that the maker has in the past caused or is likely in the future to cause serious harm to the well-being of a child'.[1]

The precise limits of this new privilege have still to be determined, and it is not clear whether older limitations to the scope of the privilege survive. It has been suggested that the privilege should be that of the mediator, at any rate when he is a marriage guidance officer, but the Law Reform Committee was against the creation of a statutory privilege for court welfare officers and marriage guidance counsellors.[2] No privilege attached in affiliation proceedings to a statement made by the respondent to a case worker acting for an adoption society,[3] nor to a report prepared by a court welfare officer.[4]

---

17 Expansively defined to include reconciliation and mediation in addition to conciliation stricto sensu.

18 Including *McTaggart v McTaggart* [1949] P 94, [1948] 2 All ER 754; *Mole v Mole* [1951] P 21, [1950] 2 All ER 328; *Pool v Pool* [1951] P 470n, [1951] 2 All ER 563; *Henley v Henley* [1955] P 202, [1955] 1 All ER 590n; *Theodoropoulas v Theodoropoulas*, [1964] P 311, [1963] 2 All ER 722; and *Pais v Pais* [1971] P 119, [1970] 2 All ER 491. See also in New Zealand *G v R* [1981] 2 NZLR 91.

19 In *Re D* above.

20 *Kitcat v Sharp* (1882) 48 LT 64.

1 *Re D (Minors)* above at 241, 699. For a similar exception in Australia see *Hutchings v Clarke* (1993) 113 ALR 709, and for its limits see *Re Marriage of Day* (1994) 115 FLR 450.

2 16th Report, paras 39, 40.

3 *R v Nottingham Justices, ex p Bostock* [1970] 2 All ER 641, [1970] 1 WLR 1117.

4 *Re H (conciliation: welfare reports)* [1986] 1 FLR 476. See in Australia *In the marriage of Wardle* (1990) 100 FLR 107 and in Canada, *Re Child Welfare Act, Brysh v Davidson* (1963) 42 DLR (2d) 673; but in New Zealand, see *G v R* above, where a new head of privilege was recognised in this situation.

Chapter XI

Public policy

Relevant evidence must be excluded on the ground of public policy when it concerns certain matters of public interest considered to be more important than the full disclosure of facts to the court, and when it relates to miscellaneous matters connected with litigation. These subjects are discussed in the first two sections of this chapter. Evidence which has been illegally obtained—considered in section 3—is not usually discussed under the head of public policy. There is nothing in the nature of a general exclusionary rule but, if such a rule were ever to be developed, its basis might well be the desirability of discouraging a resort to illegality by the police.[1] The public interest in the conviction of guilty criminals would have to be weighed against the public interest in the preservation of basic civil liberties.

This topic is made more difficult by the very wide variety of situations to which it can be considered to apply. An important distinction is between its application at the stage of disclosure, and its application during the course of the trial. In the former context it is sometimes difficult to differentiate between rules which apply generally to disclosure, and those which are peculiar to a claim for immunity on the basis of public interest. It is also necessary to distinguish between those considerations which relate to a claim for inspection by the court, and those which relate to actual production. As will be seen, a wide spectrum of public interests may be urged in favour of immunity, some of them apparent upon the face of the documents in question, and others apparent only to those possessing intimate acquaintance with the operation of the public service, and with the psychology of those who work in it, or supply information to it. A final complicating factor is that while in many cases a party may share the public interest concerned, and be instrumental in ensuring that it is brought to the attention of the court, this will not necessarily be so. The court must itself always be alert to the possibility of such an interest being involved. Such a possibility may be very hard to detect in cases where the claim does depend upon knowledge of esoteric, and perhaps secret, aspects of the conduct of affairs of state.

Before considering some of the major varieties of claim, it is worth mentioning the impact of the factors set out above upon the terminology of this branch of the law,

---

1   Just such a justification for just such a rule has been propounded by the High Court of Australia, see *R v Ireland* (1970) 126 CLR 321, at 355; *Bunning v Cross* (1978) 141 CLR 54, at 74.

upon the question of waiver and upon the admissibility of secondary evidence of excluded matter.

At one time this branch of the law of evidence was subsumed under the rubric of 'Crown Privilege'. The reasons for abandoning such a categorisation were stated by Lord Simon so long ago as 1942:

> The withholding of documents on the ground that their publication would be contrary to the public interest is not properly to be regarded as a branch of the law of privilege connected with disclosure. 'Crown privilege' is for this reason not a happy expression. Privilege, in relation to disclosure, is for the protection of the litigant and could be waived by him, but the rule that the interest of the state must not be put in jeopardy by producing documents which would injure it is a principle to be observed in administering justice, quite unconnected with the interests or claims of the particular parties in litigation, and, indeed, is a rule on which the judge should, if necessary, insist even though no objection is taken at all.[2]

In *Rogers* Lord Simon expressed the view that the term privilege was properly applicable only to a claim which could be waived. This view was reasserted by Lord Fraser in *Air Canada v Secretary of State for Trade (No 2)*: 'Public interest immunity is not a privilege which may be waived by the Crown or by any party.'[3] At first sight this view might seem inconsistent with some dicta of Lord Cross in *Alfred Crompton Amusement Machines Ltd v Customs and Excise Comrs (No 2)*[4] to the effect that where the claim is made in order to protect the interests of third parties in the confidentiality of information supplied to public authorities the privilege can be waived. There is no real inconsistency however. Before waiver can take place there must be some claim based upon public interest to be waived. It is material to the determination of that question whether or not the suppliers of information are willing for it to be revealed. It may well in many cases be hard to demonstrate a public interest in keeping information secret on behalf of those quite willing for it to be revealed, if that is the only basis for the claim.[5] In such a case the correct analysis is not that a valid public interest claim is waived, but that no public interest is ever established.[6] It should also be remembered that as the immunity is claimed in the public interest, any waiver can be made only by someone representing that public interest, and not by a stranger.[7]

In similar fashion where the archive of an international organisation was accorded inviolability on the same basis as that of a diplomatic mission, the House of Lords held that no objection could be taken to the use in litigation of documents which had been voluntarily communicated to third parties.[8] The act of communication prevented such documents from any longer attracting immunity, and the situation should be

---

2　*Duncan v Camell Laird & Co Ltd* [1942] AC 624, at 641. See also *Rogers v Secretary of State for the Home Department* [1973] AC 388, [1972] 2 All ER 1057.

3　[1983] 2 AC 394, at 436, [1983] 1 All ER 910, at 917; *Carey v The Queen in right of Canada* [1986] 2 SCR 637, at 653; *Fletcher Timber Ltd v A-G* [1984] 1 NZLR 290, at 291.

4　[1974] AC 405, at 434, [1973] 2 All ER 1169, at 1185. See also *Peach v Metropolitan Police Comr* [1986] QB 1064, at 1071, [1986] 2 All ER 129, at 131 (applying the same view to statements made to the police in the course of an internal inquiry).

5　Indeed it might sometimes even be regarded as contrary to the public interest that information should be withheld when its suppliers wished it to be revealed.

6　Such an analysis was suggested by Brightman LJ in *Hehir v Metropolitan Police Comr* [1982] 2 All ER 335, at 341, [1982] 1 WLR 715, at 723, and approved by Lord Woolf in *R v Chief Constable of West Midlands, ex p Wiley* [1995] 1 AC 274, [1994] 3 All ER 420, at 299A, 440d.

7　See Lord Woolf in *Wiley* at 298G, 440b.

8　*Shearson Lehman Bros Inc v Maclaine Watson Co Ltd (No 2)* [1988] 1 All ER 116.

distinguished from deliberate waiver for the purposes of litigation. In these circumstances it is sometimes said where consent has been given to the release of the relevant information, and a fortiori where it has in fact been released, that the claim for immunity is not waived, but rather evaporates.[9]

Nor is the question of the admissibility of secondary evidence free from confusion. The general rule in this case was stated many years ago by Bayley J: 'If the document cannot, on principles of public policy be read in evidence, the effect will be the same as if it was not in evidence, and you may not prove the contents of the instrument.'[10] It is important to understand that this prohibition is limited to secondary evidence of the documents, and does not necessarily, or even often,[11] extend to secondary evidence of the matters dealt with in the documents. Indeed it is often a reason for upholding public interest immunity that the information contained in the relevant documents adds nothing to information in the hands of the parties which they may adduce in evidence without constraint.[12] This is not however to deny where the claim is based upon the vital importance of the contents of some documents, a national defence secret for example, that any oral evidence of the matter in question might be prohibited.

It may thus be appreciated that while there are clear analogies between claims for private privilege which were considered in the previous chapter and those under consideration here, there are nevertheless important points of distinction emphasised by the use of the currently fashionable terminology of 'public interest immunity'. In some cases other private privileges[13] have been asserted in addition to public interest immunity. Any tendency to exploit the overlap in an attempt to resuscitate arguments based on candour, following the government's acceptance[14] of the recommendations of the Scott report,[15] was deprecated by Scott VC in Re Barings plc.[16]

Far and away the most important ground of exclusion on account of public interest is that of state interest discussed in the early part of section 1. Before referring to matters of detail, it would be well to emphasise the devastating effect which the exclusion of evidence at the instance of the head of a government department can have on the substantive rights of litigants. It may render it totally impossible for them to rely on matters which would otherwise have constituted an unanswerable claim or a complete defence. It is particularly unacceptable when the entity seeking to suppress is party to the litigation, and most unacceptable of all when that party is the Crown, and the litigation a criminal prosecution in which the information, or document, is vital to the defence.[17]

---

9   *Multi-Guarantee Co Ltd v Cavalier Insurance Co* (1986) Times, 24 June.
10   *Cooke v Maxwell* (1817) 2 Stark 183, at 186. See also Lynskey J in *Moss v Chesham UDC* (17 January 1945, unreported) cited by Simon (1955) CLJ 62, 'if it is contrary to public interest to produce the original documents, it must be equally contrary to public interest to produce copies which the maker of the document has kept for his own information.'
11   Per Lord Woolf in *R v Chief Constable of West Midlands, ex p Wiley* [1995] 1 AC 274, [1994] 3 All ER 420, at 306G, 447d.
12   See *Air Canada v Secretary of State for Trade (No 2)* [1983] 2 AC 394, at 442, [1983] 1 All ER 910, at 920, where Lord Wilberforce emphasised this point by describing the available documents as 'primary' evidence of the contentions advanced, and those for which immunity was claimed as 'secondary'.
13   Most often legal professional privilege.
14   See the Attorney-General's paper *Public Interest Immunity* laid before the Houses of Parliament in December 1996.
15   *Report of the Inquiry into the Export of Defence Equipment and Dual-Use Goods to Iraq and Related Prosecutions* (1996) Vol IV Pt 5 Sect K ch 6.
16   [1998] 1 All ER 673, at 689.
17   As in the Matrix Churchill prosecution which precipitated the Scott inquiry.

SECTION I. MATTERS OF PUBLIC INTEREST

This category of evidence is now recognised to be wider than it once was, and to be capable of modification by the courts, as Lord Hailsham remarked in *D v National Society for Prevention of Cruelty to Children*: 'The categories of public interest are not closed and must alter from time to time whether by restriction or extension as social conditions and social legislation develop.'[18] On the other hand the court will not lightly create a new class-based public interest since as Lord Woolf remarked in *R v Chief Constable of West Midlands, ex p Wiley* 'the recognition of a new class-based public interest immunity requires clear and compelling evidence that it is necessary.'[19] The tide of opinion seems also to be running towards increasingly open government.[20] Although the initiative has come from central government, its resonance is likely to be felt in surrounding areas.[1] Lord Hailsham's remark was made in the context of an extension of public interest outside the confines of central government. It was also based upon a claim for the preservation of the anonymity of a supplier of information. That consideration raises the question of the basis for making such a claim. On occasion it is raised because the public interest demands that a particular piece of information not be revealed, and sometimes because it demands that a particular source of information remain inviolate. Such demands are not, of course, mutually exclusive. The basis of the claim may also affect the procedure for determining it, and in particular the desirability of the court's inspecting the relevant document in order to assist its decision. It is best to examine first the considerations and procedure which govern the clearest cases, those where vital interests of state are affected, and then to go on to consider how far the principles that apply there extend to less vital interests, such as material relating to parliamentary proceedings, to the police, to local government and to matters of a confidential nature. It is finally necessary to consider how far the rules extend to criminal cases.

No distinction is drawn between cases in which the Crown or a government department is a party to the proceedings, and those in which the parties are private citizens or corporations. The former class of case has, however, increased since the Crown Proceedings Act 1947 came into force, and although an order for disclosure may be made against the Crown under s 28 of that statute, it is expressly made subject to this doctrine of public policy.

It should be noted that while the only basis for immunity from disclosure in the English courts is the public interest of the United Kingdom, and the interests of a foreign state are thus not, in principle, alone sufficient,[2] two possible qualifications might be made. The first is that now that this country is a member of the European Union similar considerations apply to confer immunity in respect of the interests of organs of the Community, including the European Commission.[3] The second is that a government may regard its own interests as being affected, and so certify, by the disregard of its own courts for the public interests of a foreign state. This is particularly likely where the foreign state is a confidential source of vital information which is likely to dry up if

---

18 [1978] AC 171, at 230, [1977] 1 All ER 589, at 605.
19 [1995] 1 AC 274, at 305, [1994] 3 All ER 420, at 446.
20 See the Citizen's Charter, and the Code of Practice on Access to Government Information. Further legislation was promised by the 1997 White paper *Your Right to Know: Freedom of Information* (Cm 3818).
1 As envisaged in the Attorney-General's 1996 paper *Public Interest Immunity* s 4.6.
2 *Buttes Gas and Oil Co v Hammer (No 3)* [1981] QB 223, [1980] 3 All ER 475.
3 *Hasselblad (GB) Ltd v Orbinson* [1985] QB 475, [1985] 1 All ER 173. But see *Silver Hill Duckling Ltd v Steele* [1987] IR 289 (Standing Veterinary Committee of the European Community); *Duff v Minister of Agriculture and Food* [1992] 1 IR 198 Council of European Community).

revealed. It should also be noted that the discretionary power of the court extends to refusing to issue letters of request in relation to evidence seeking to impugn the motives of a foreign legislature.

A.   VITAL INTERESTS OF STATE

The importance of particular pieces of information or classes of source to the interests of the state must obviously vary, not only from subject to subject but also from time to time. There can be no clearly defined line between cases where such vital interests are at stake and those where they are not. It is now recognised that many factors enter into any such estimation, and such recognition has contributed to the current practice of assessing the relative importance of the policies suggesting suppression, and those favouring disclosure. Some particular pieces of information are of so important a nature at some times that it is hard to see how any contravening policy in favour of the administration of justice could outweigh them. Thus in *Asiatic Petroleum Co Ltd v Anglo-Persian Oil Co Ltd*,[4] the defendants, acting under the direction of the Board of Admiralty, refused to produce a letter to their agent on the ground that it contained information concerning the government's plans with regard to one of the Middle Eastern campaigns of the First World War. The information had, of course, been given to the defendants by the Board of Admiralty under the seal of the strictest security, but as Swinfen-Eady LJ observed:[5]

> The foundation of the rule is that the information cannot be disclosed without injury to the public interests, and not that the documents are confidential or official, which alone is no reason for their non-production: the general public interest is paramount to the interests of the suitor.

The defendant's objection was upheld, and a similar principle was successfully invoked in *Duncan v Camell Laird & Co Ltd*,[6] where the defendants to a claim for damages for negligence in relation to the construction of a submarine were directed by the Board of Admiralty to object to the production of numerous documents in their possession in their capacity as government contractors. The structure of submarines is clearly a matter that affects national security, and ought to be kept secret while the country is at war, as in that case.[7]

In both cases the interest of the state would have been threatened by disclosure of the particular information contained in the relevant documents. All claims in this category are based on the damage to a vital public interest which disclosure will cause. It was formerly accepted that documents falling within certain, rather ill-defined, classes were automatically exempt from disclosure upon this basis.[8] It became impossible to sustain such a view once courts began to adopt a balancing approach towards, and to inspect for themselves, documents falling into such prime examples of such classes as

---

4   [1916] 1 KB 822.
5   At 830.
6   [1942] AC 624, [1942] 1 All ER 587.
7   It should be noted that the public interest in the security even of such pieces of information is ephemeral and could hardly prevail once the campaign had been fought, or the design of the submarine become common knowledge.
8   See eg per Lord Reid in *Conway v Rimmer* [1968] AC 910, at 952, [1968] 1 All ER 874, at 888; per Lord Salmon in *Rogers v Secretary of State for the Home Department* [1973] AC 388, at 412, [1972] 2 All ER 1057, at 1071.

cabinet documents,[9] and those relating to the secret security services.[10] In *Commonwealth v Northern Land Council*[11] the High Court of Australia distinguished between documents prepared for consideration by the cabinet, and notes of the actual discussions and decisions of the cabinet. The latter were regarded as particularly sensitive, and liable to be disclosed only in the most exceptional situations, highly unlikely ever to arise outside the context of criminal proceedings where they might, just conceivably, be essential to establish the truth about a very serious offence.[12] This matter is occasionally the subject of direct statutory intervention.[13] The United Kingdom government has now declared[14] in the Attorney-General's important paper *Public Policy Immunity*[15] that as a matter of practice it will no longer claim suppression solely upon a document's membership of a given class. Instead it will in all cases seek to show in detail in the certificate or affidavit the nature of the damage which disclosure will be likely to cause.[16] It should nevertheless be noted that in some cases the damage to the public interest may be incremental, and that it does not necessarily follow that a document innocuous on its face can never qualify for suppression.

The operation of the new system is illustrated[17] in the paper in the three areas of national security, internal governmental discussion and advice, and international relations. The paper also sets out the way in which it is envisaged that the new regime will operate in practice. This builds upon the procedure set out most clearly by Bingham J in *Air Canada v Secretary of State for Trade (No 2)* at first instance,[18] and upon the approach adopted by Lord Woolf in *R v Chief Constable of West Midlands, ex p Wiley*.[19]

9   See eg in England *Air Canada v Secretary of State for Trade (No 2)* [1983] 2 AC 394, at 432, [1983] 1 All ER 910, at 915; in Australia *Sankey v Whitlam* (1978) 142 CLR 1; in New Zealand *Environmental Defence Society Inc v South Pacific Aluminium Ltd. (No 2)* [1981] 1 NZLR 153; in Canada *Carey v The Queen in right of Canada* (1986) 35 DLR (4th) 161; and in the United States *Nixon v US* 418 US 683 (1974). In Canada the same approach has been utilised in relation to the oral evidence of a cabinet minister, *Smallwood v Sparling* (1982) 141 DLR (3d) 395, but see *Re Mulroney and Coates* (1986) 27 DLR (4th) 118. In Ireland however it has been held that the only remedy in respect of refused cabinet papers is political: *A-G v Hamilton* [1993] 2 IR 259.

10 See eg in Australia *Alister v R* (1983) 154 CLR 404; and in Canada, *Re Henrie and Security Intelligence Review Committee* (1988) 53 DLR (4th) 568. In England the courts showed more reluctance in relation to this category: see *Balfour v Foreign and Commonwealth Office* [1994] 2 All ER 588, [1994] 1 WLR 681 (where documents relating to the security services were unsuccessfully required for the prosecution of a claim for unfair dismissal). The Security Services themselves seem to have adopted a more robust approach: see Scott Report Vol III para G18.40.

11 (1993) 176 CLR 604.

12 Normally required by the defence to establish innocence; but still more exceptionally to support an allegation against a member of the cabinet.

13 Eg Parliamentary Commissioner Act 1967, s 8(4); Health Service Commissioners Act 1993, s 12(5). In these circumstances the only sanction for refusal becomes political: see *Minister of Energy v Auditor General of Canada* [1989] 2 SCR 49. See also Canada Evidence Act, ss 37 – 39; *Gold v The Queen in right of Canada* (1986) 25 DLR (4th) 285; *Re A-G of Canada and Central Cartage Co* (1990) 71 DLR (4th) 253; *Re Canadian Association of Regulated Importers and A-G of Canada* (1991) 87 DLR (4th) 730.

14 It accepted the recommendation of the Scott Report vol IV ch 6 para K.1 that legislation was undesirable in this area.

15 Section 4.1.

16 Ibid, s 4.5.

17 These categories are not intended to be exhaustive.

18 [1983] 1 All ER 161, at 164. Although his judgment was reversed on one point, his general approach was endorsed both by the House of Lords and by the Court of Appeal, where he was described as an acknowledged authority upon the subject.

19 [1995] 1 AC 274, [1994] 3 All ER 440.

When the question first arises, usually at the stage of disclosure,[20] it will be for the minister to consider whether a claim to immunity arises at all. It is envisaged that this will occur much less often under the new regime, partly because of the elimination of class claims; partly because of the use of editing so as to eliminate material damaging to the relevant aspect of the public interest while releasing those parts of the document necessary for the aspect of public interest concerned with the administration of justice;[1] and partly because the disclosure provisions of the Criminal Procedure and Investigation Act 1996[2] will enable a sharper focus to be made of which issues are relevant in criminal proceedings. The burden of this decision will also be reduced by the use of sampling techniques in relation to repetitive documents, provided that the techniques for such sampling are stated in the relevant certificate. The decision must however normally be made at ministerial level, although the minister need not be the most senior in line,[3] and where the decision relates to a previous administration the permanent secretary to the ministry may act.[4] It is also envisaged in the Attorney-General's paper[5] that exceptionally a minister will not be involved because a department is not headed by a minister, or where the court is content for the matter to be raised by an affidavit from an official, or even simply raised by counsel. It is to be hoped that little use will be made of these exceptions since the best guarantee that claims will be made only in the most serious cases is to insist upon direct ministerial involvement. Officials might well be inclined to make claims on behalf of their departments which they would not wish to take to a minister. It is expected that the minister will in future be given adequate time to make this decision, and will have access to legal advice.[6] It has been made clear by the decision in *R v Chief Constable of West Midlands, ex p Wiley*[7] that the minister should claim only if he is satisfied that there will be substantial danger in disclosure, or if he is uncertain. In either case the certificate or affidavit must explain the nature of the apprehended danger as fully as possible, consistent with not precipitating it, and may also claim immunity in respect of oral evidence of the documents. If the government is not a party, nor closely involved, it is open for one of the parties to seek a certificate from the government.[8] The question may in any event always be raised by a party, or by a witness, and should be taken by the court on its own initiative whenever it appears to arise.[9]

20　See CPR 31.19, and Practice Direction 31, for detail of the current procedure. Similar principles applied to interrogatories, and will presumably extend to requests for further information under Part 18 of the Civil Procedure Rules. See also *Whitlam v ACP Ltd* (1985) 73 FLR 414, at 417.

1　As recommended in by Lord Woolf in *Wiley* at 307A, 447f, where he also canvasses other possibilities such as the provision of information rather than a particular document, or a summary, or restricted disclosure (despite his reluctance to disclose to counsel but not client), or by assurances or other forms of co-operation between counsel.

2　See further above at 250.

3　In *Burmah Oil Co Ltd v Bank of England* [1980] AC 1090, [1979] 3 All ER 700 the claimant was the Chief Secretary of the Treasury, who although of cabinet rank was subordinate to the Chancellor of the Exchequer; and also in that case it was regarded as appropriate for the Attorney-General to present the argument for immunity, even to the extent of arguing before the House of Lords without being made a party. In *Continental Reinsurance Corpn (UK) Ltd v Pine Top Insurance Ltd* [1986] 1 Lloyd's Rep 8, at 12 a junior and non cabinet minister was accepted as appropriate.

4　As in *Air Canada*.

5　Section 2.4.

6　Section 2.3.

7　[1995] 1 AC 274, [1994] 3 All ER 440.

8　In *Buttes Gas and Oil Co v Hammer (No 3)* [1981] QB 223, [1980] 3 All ER 475, such an application was made, but was unsuccessful.

9　*Rogers v Secretary of State for the Home Department* [1973] AC 388, at 400, [1972] 2 All ER 1057, at 1065. It is permissible for the question to be raised on appeal without notice as it was in the *Buttes Gas* case. The failure of a party to challenge the certificate is no admission of the truth of its contents: *Sethia v Stern* (1987) Independent, 30 October.

If a claim is made it must then be subject to review by the court. Its first task is to establish that the information or document for which the claim is made is indeed relevant, and in this context it has been held that this means that it must be shown by the claimant that the document sought was not only relevant to the dispute between the parties, but also that it would assist his own case.[10] In *Air Canada* the documents in question related to fixing landing fees at Heathrow Airport. The plaintiffs contended that the Secretary of State had acted upon criteria different from those specified by the relevant statutory provision, and sought disclosure of relevant documents which included some cabinet papers, and documents relating to meetings held between the Secretary of State and his advisers, and between the advisers. The plaintiff was not in a position to demonstrate that these documents would support his case, and even if they did, it was felt that they could add nothing to other evidence of the matters in question which was already available to the plaintiffs. This point, one of the law of disclosure[11] rather than that of evidence, decided the appeal.

The problem for the party seeking disclosure was that because of the requirements of English law[12] as reiterated in *Air Canada* he had to show that the documents were very likely to assist his case before he has had any opportunity to see them. Under the Civil Procedure Rules[13] a party who believes that disclosure has been defective may apply for specific disclosure, but he must adduce evidence to justify his claim.[14] While it is perfectly reasonable to prevent anything in the nature of 'fishing', it would not seem unreasonable to put the burden of showing that the documents need not be disclosed upon the party who usually has them in his possession, and is refusing to do so.

Once a claim has been made upon such a basis, or if the judge discerns such an interest for himself, for example in a case to which the Crown is not a party,[15] the judge's task is to compare the public interest in the administration of justice secured by disclosure with that set out in the certificate, or discerned by the court, in favour of suppression.[16] In striking a balance the court will take into account factors such as the seriousness of the claim for which disclosure is sought,[17] whether or not the government is itself a party or alleged to have acted unconscionably,[18] the relevance of the particular evidence to the dispute,[19] taking into account other possible sources of evidence[20] and, on the other side, the nature of the state's interest,[1] and the length of time which has elapsed since the relevant discussion took place.[2] In one Canadian case the fact

10   It would usually now have to fulfil the criteria set out in CPR 31.6.
11   Discovery as it was then called.
12   It is significant that in jurisdictions where the rules of discovery are different there has been much less inclination to refuse inspection upon any such basis, even in the case of higher state documents: see in New Zealand *Fletcher Timber Ltd v A-G* [1984] 1 NZLR 290, at 293; and in Canada *Carey v The Queen in right of Canada* (1986) 35 DLR (4th) 161, at 194.
13   CPR 31.12
14   Practice Direction 31, para 5.2.
15   CPR 31.19(1) is careful to refer to a 'person' rather than to a 'party', see; also CPR 31.19(6)(b).
16   The existing law on public interest immunity is preserved by CPR 31.19(8). The Rules affect only procedure.
17   Thus in *Henrie*, above, the fact that it related to security clearance so as to permit promotion within the government service was thought insufficiently compelling.
18   See *Burmah Oil*, above, at 1128, 720. See also *Sankey v Whitlam*, above, at 56; *Carey*, above, at 673; *Koowarta v Bjelke-Petersen* (1988) 92 FLR 104 . In these circumstances there is a danger that justice will not be done because the interest of the government has been assimilated to that of the state, and a certainty that it will not have been seen to be done.
19   See *Hospitals Consolidated Fund of Australia v Hunt* (1983) 76 FLR 408.
20   An important consideration in *Air Canada*, above.
1   Preferring disclosure of discussion even at the highest level if the subject was of commercial rather than security matters: see *Hospitals Fund of Australia*, above.
2   *A-G v Jonathan Cape Ltd* [1976] QB 752, at 770, [1975] 3 All ER 484, at 496. See also *Sankey v Whitlam*, above, at 41, 42.

that the government had set up the relevant Royal Commission before which the evidence was sought to be tendered was regarded as favouring admissibility.[3] Only if the court is in doubt about the balance, or provisionally in favour of disclosure will it seek to inspect the documents in question.[4] In the latter case it would normally always inspect to confirm its provisional view before ordering disclosure, and in the case of a lower court would postpone disclosure pending any appeal.[5] It is important to distinguish the separate questions of whether the document should be inspected by the court, and that of whether it should be disclosed to the other party. These questions arise at different stages of the reasoning process, and must not be run together.[6]

The court's power to inspect applied even under the old law to documents of vital state interest, such as cabinet papers.[7] This became clearer when it was recognised that the power to inspect was not limited to cases where the court was in doubt as to whether the documents really fell within the public interest claimed in the certificate, but also extended to cases where the doubt was whether or not that claim overbalanced the countervening public interest in the administration of justice. A further advantage of inspection is that it may enable the court to secure partial disclosure of documents. In some cases it may be possible, without distortion, to sever the parts most relevant to the litigation from those disclosure of which would be overly inimical to vital interests of state.[8] It is also possible in some cases for the courts to restrict disclosure to the legal advisers of the parties,[9] to order proceedings to be held in camera,[10] and to impose orders restricting the reporting of proceedings.[11] It is always the case that documents compulsorily disclosed under Part 31 of the Civil Procedure Rules should be used only for the purposes of the litigation in question, and not for any ulterior purpose,[12] even

---

3   *Re The Queen and the Royal Commission into the Donald Marshall Junior Prosecution* (1988) 51 DLR (4th) 705.

4   Inspection by the court is sometimes allowed by a party despite his claim for immunity, see Lord Wilberforce in *Burmah Oil* at 1116, 711 citing *Tito v Waddell* [1975] 3 All ER 997, [1975] 1 WLR 1303 and *Barty-King v Ministry of Defence* [1979] 2 All ER 80, [1979] STC 218.

5   In *Burmah Oil* Lord Keith said at 1136, 727 that a judge should not even undertake inspection without allowing time for an appeal, but he invoked Lord Reid in *Conway v Rimmer* as authority for this, and it seems clear that Lord Reid was referring only to production. In *Air Canada* Bingham J accordingly proposed the procedure stated in the text on this question, and was said by Lord Fraser to have adopted the proper practice.

6   See under the old law *Continental Reinsurance Corpn (UK) Ltd v Pine Top Insurance Ltd* [1986] 1 Lloyd's Rep 8; see now the Civil Procedure Rules Part 31 which clearly distinguishes disclosure and inspection.

7   See under the old law eg Lord Fraser in *Air Canada* at 432, 915; but see *Balfour v Foreign and Colonial Office* [1994] 2 All ER 588, [1994] 1 WLR 681; see now CPR 31.19(6)(a)

8   See eg Lord Keith in *Burmah Oil* at 1135, 726.

9   *Church of Scientology of California v Department of Health and Social Security* [1979] 3 All ER 97, [1979] 1 WLR 723, though it seems that the court should not discriminate between counsel and solicitors; *WEA Records Ltd v Visions Channel 4 Ltd* [1983] 2 All ER 589, [1983] 1 WLR 721. In *Baker v Paper Sacks* [1995] 12 CL 451 the restriction was to a party's medical advisers.

10   In the very case which enunciated the general obligation for courts to sit in public it was recognised that they could sit in camera if the administration of justice so required: *Scott v Scott* [1913] AC 417. This inherent power has been supplemented in certain cases by explicit statutory provision; for example Official Secrets Act 1920, s 8(4).

11   Contempt of Court Act 1981, s 11, stilling doubts vented in *A-G v Leveller Magazines Ltd* [1979] AC 440, [1979] 1 All ER 745

12   CPR 31.22(1). For the practice under the old law see *Riddick v Thames Board Mills Ltd* [1977] QB 881, [1977] 3 All ER 677. The ban even extended to closely related proceedings against the same defendants: *Miller v Scorey* [1996] 3 All ER 18, [1996] 1 WLR 1122.

after being put in evidence in open court.[13] There is no general public policy to prevent disclosure of documents acquired by compulsory process, for example by liquidators, to prosecutors or regulatory authorities,[14] or conversely from prosecutors or regulatory authorities to liquidators,[15] although no disclosure will be ordered without giving the party affected a chance to be heard.[16]

B. REPORTS OF PROCEEDINGS IN PARLIAMENT

Questions have arisen as to the immunity from use in evidence of reports of proceedings in Parliament. It has been settled since 1688[17] that proceedings in Parliament ought not to be questioned[18] in any court. In *Church of Scientology v Johnson-Smith*[19] this was interpreted broadly to exclude the use of such reports in evidence to impugn the motives and intentions of members in any proceedings. It seems to be the case that the judge has the duty, as in other public policy situations, to intervene on his own initiative if the point is not taken by the parties.[20] In an extreme case where it would be impossible to adjudicate on a claim without access to such excluded material the court may stay an action, but it is normally immaterial that the claim is brought by a member of the body concerned, and the material required by way of defence.[1]

C. POLICE MATTERS[2]

Information may come into the hands of the police either in the course of an internal inquiry, or from outside the police force in the ordinary course of the business of the police.[3] Other documents may be generated by the police themselves in either pursuit,

13 *Home Office v Harman* [1983] 1 AC 280, [1982] 1 All ER 532. This case is particularly significant since the material revealed had been the subject of a claim to public interest immunity, and the documents had been ordered to be produced only after inspection by the judge: *Williams v Home Office* [1981] 1 All ER 1151. The extent of this obligation was accorded a most conservative construction under the old law, see *Apple Corpn Ltd v Apple Computer Inc* [1992] 1 CMLR 969; *Singh v Christie* (1993) Times, 11 November; *SmithKline Beecham Biologics SA v Connaught Laboratories Inc* [1998] CLY 342, and now made subject to explicit judicial control: CPR 31.22(3).
14 *Re Headington Investments* [1993] Ch 452, [1993] 3 All ER 861.
15 *Wallace Smith Trust Co Ltd v Deloitte, Haskins & Sells* [1996] 4 All ER 403.
16 *Soden v Burns* [1996] 3 All ER 967, [1996] 1 WLR 1612.
17 Bill of Rights 1688, art 9.
18 It has been held not to amount to such questioning to admit reports of parliamentary proceedings to assist with questions of construction: *Pepper v Hart* [1993] AC 593, [1993] 1 All ER 42; or of judicial review: *R v Secretary of State for the Home Department, ex p Brind* [1991] 1 AC 696, [1991] 1 All ER 720; or more generally when the court was otherwise required to determine the purpose with which a statute had been passed: *Three Rivers District Council v Bank of England (No 2)* [1996] 2 All ER 363, especially if there were a European dimension to the issue.
19 [1972] 1 QB 522, [1972] 1 All ER 378.
20 See *R v Murphy* (1986) 64 ALR 498.
1 *Prebble v Television New Zealand Ltd* [1995] 1 AC 321, [1994] 3 All ER 407, but in that situation where the evidence was required by a member for the purpose of defending a defamation claim the position has been amended by statute both in England by the Defamation Act 1996, s 13, and in Australia by the Parliamentary Privileges Act 1987.
2 It was explicitly denied in Australia in *R v Robertson, ex p McAuley* (1983) 71 FLR 429, at 438 that police documents are sufficiently homogenous to constitute a class of documents to which immunity can attach.
3 In *Spigelman v Hocken* (1933) 50 TLR 87 a claim was made for completely routine witness statements made to the police after a road accident.

or indeed independently. Despite the fact that the police are not strictly to be regarded as an emanation of the state, it has been common[4] to accord public policy immunity to some, at least, of such documents. *Conway v Rimmer*,[5] the genesis of much of the modern law on the whole topic of public interest immunity, itself fell into the former inquiry category. In that case the appellant had been a probationary police constable. He was accused by a fellow probationer of stealing a cheap torch, and was ultimately prosecuted by the respondent, a superintendent in that police force. The prosecution was unsuccessful, but the appellant was dismissed from the police force. He brought a claim for malicious prosecution and sought disclosure of probationary reports upon him, made both before and after the allegations of theft, and of a report to the Director of Public Prosecutions about the circumstances of the alleged theft. The Home Secretary claimed Crown privilege for these reports upon the basis that their disclosure would be injurious to the public interest. The House of Lords was unwilling to be bound by such a claim in respect of ostensibly routine documents such as the probation reports, or in the case of the report to the Director of Public Prosecutions after the occasion of the prosecution had passed. It was clearly regarded as relevant that the documents were of crucial importance to the outcome of the case.[6]

More often the issue is raised in relation to information which comes to the police from external sources. The facts of *Rogers v Secretary of State for the Home Department*[7] provide a neat transition to that situation. An applicant to the Gaming Board for a gaming licence was unsuccessful. Subsequently he came into possession of a copy of a letter written to the board by a police officer in relation to his application which, he alleged, contained defamatory statements about him. He sought to prosecute the officer for criminal libel, and served witness summonses upon the secretary of the Gaming Board and the relevant chief constable to give evidence, and to produce relevant documents including the original letter. The summonses were set aside by the Divisional Court. The House of Lords upheld this decision, not on the basis that the letter was a policy document, but because its production might jeopardise the working of the public service. The House was impressed by the fact that the police in responding to inquiries from the Gaming Board, and the board itself, depended upon the provision of information from members of the public, and that such sources might be threatened if protection from disclosure could not be guaranteed.

A good example of documents generated by the police otherwise than in the course of an inquiry or investigation occurred in *Goodwin v Chief Constable of Greater Manchester*[8] where the plaintiffs sought discovery of a police operations manual in support of their claim for personal injuries suffered in the course of operations of the sort included in the manual. There the claim failed because of insufficient demonstration of the need for disclosure of the manual.

It must be stressed that most often discovery is sought in the course of civil proceedings, and in such cases the first hurdle to overcome is to demonstrate that the documents sought relate to the cause of action, and their inspection necessary to dispose fairly of it. Some of the cases seeking information from the police have fallen at this stage, rendering any consideration of public interest immunity strictly irrelevant.

In a number of cases claims were made by complainants for documentation arising in the course of the police complaints procedure[9] to assist with civil litigation arising

4   *Conway v Rimmer* [1968] AC 910, [1968] 1 All ER 874, per Lord Reid at 953G, 889D said never to have been doubted.
5   See also *Konia v Morley* [1976] 1 NZLR 455.
6   They were requested by both parties.
7   [1973] AC 388, [1972] 2 All ER 1057.
8   [1993] PIQR P187.
9   The earlier cases were concerned with the procedure established by Police Act 1964, s 49, and the later with that under Pt IX of the Police and Criminal Evidence Act 1984.

from the subject matter of the complaints. Such a claim was denied in *Neilson v Laugherne*[10] on the basis that unless immunity were provided lay persons would be disinclined to co-operate with the tribunals. The result was unpopular both with the police who were unable to use such documentation in their defence,[11] and with complainants who increasingly refused to co-operate just because they could not secure access to the documentation.[12] Courts criticised it,[13] found reasons not to apply it,[14] and practice diverged from precept.[15] It still caused difficulty however, and in *Makanjuola v Metropolitan Police Comr*[16] the whole area was reconsidered by a strong Court of Appeal. In the course of his judgment Bingham LJ appeared to seek to correct any suggestion of an imbalance between the use of such material as between prosecution and defence, and said:

> Public interest immunity is not a trump card vouchsafed to certain privileged players to play when and as they wish. It is an exclusionary rule, imposed on parties in certain circumstances even where it is to their disadvantage in the litigation. This does not mean that in any case where a party holds a document in a class prima facie immune he is bound to persist in an assertion of immunity even where it is held that, on any weighing of the public interest, in withholding the document against the public interest in disclosure for the purpose of furthering the administration of justice, there is a clear balance in favour of the latter.

The decision was however interpreted, especially in government circles, to require public interest immunity to be claimed wherever it might conceivably arise, so as to pass the relevant decision on to the court. This view was criticised by the Scott Report,[17] and overruled in *R v Chief Constable of the West Midlands Police, ex p Wiley*.[18] Judicial review[19] was sought of the refusal of the chief constables[20] to give an undertaking that complaints material[1] would not be used in the preparation of defences to civil claims alleging police misconduct. In the House of Lords[2] both applicants and the chief

10   [1981] QB 736, [1981] 1 All ER 829. See also *Hehir v Metropolitan Police Comr* [1982] 2 All ER 335, [1982] 1 WLR 715; *Halford v Sharples* [1992] 3 All ER 624, [1992] 1 WLR 736; *Makanjuola v Metropolitan Police Comr* [1992] 3 All ER 617 (decided in 1989).

11   Or in bringing a claim for defamation against the complainant as attempted in *Ex p Coventry Newspapers Ltd* [1993] QB 278, [1993] 1 All ER 86.

12   Triennial Review of Police Complaints Authority 1988–1991 HC 1990 No 352, para 4.5.

13   Lawton LJ in *Hehir v Metropolitan Police Comr* [1982] 2 All ER 335, at 338, [1982] 1 WLR 715, at 719; and his attempt to apply it was criticised by Lord Denning MR in *Campbell v Tameside Metropolitan Borough Council* [1982] QB 1065, at 1072, [1982] 2 All ER 791, at 795.

14   In *Conerney v Jacklin* [1985] Crim LR 234 it was held that the complainant could receive a copy of the original complaint since the regulations in force then allowed the policeman to be supplied with a copy, so it was reasoned that no public interest immunity arose; in *Peach v Metropolitan Police Comr* [1986] QB 1064, [1986] 2 All ER 129 it was held that the complaint was not made predominantly for the purposes of the complaints procedure, but in relation to the investigation of the death to which the complaint related; in *Ex p Coventry Newspapers Ltd* [1993] QB 278, [1993] 1 All ER 86 simply because it would be unjust to do so, and suppression would not promote the objects of the rule.

15   See letter in (1986) 136 NLJ 14.

16   [1992] 3 All ER 617 (decided in 1989).

17   Vol III para G18.52 et seq.

18   [1995] 1 AC 274, [1994] 3 All ER 420.

19   And injunctions against its use.

20   Two appeals were consolidated.

1   It should be noted that in *Halford v Sharples* [1992] 3 All ER 624, [1992] 1 WLR 736 this category had been extended to internal complaints as well as to complaints from the general public under s 49 of the Police Act 1964.

2   But not before, since *Neilson v Laugherne* was binding up to the level of the Court of Appeal.

constables agreed that complaints material was not as a class entitled to public policy immunity,[3] and eventually even the Police Complaints Authority agreed.[4] Although perhaps to some extent weakened by the absence of argument to the contrary the House of Lords expressed its unanimous adherence to the view that no class immunity extended to police complaints procedure material, and overruled the cases[5] asserting the contrary. It was conceded that in some cases a 'contents' claim might be made for particular pieces of complaints material, and the possibility of a 'class' claim for a sub-category, such as the report of the officer investigating a complaint, was not totally excluded.[6] It has indeed since been accepted.[7] That acceptance has itself since been confirmed, opining rather ominously that in the case of routine reports the claim can be made at a low level within the police force.[8] Indeed despite the Attorney-General's paper disavowing class claims in relation to government documents, this was subsequently said to correspond to the government's thinking.[9] It does however seem, even in such cases, that the threshold test to secure inspection by the judge is no higher than that for discovery in general.[10] This should serve to prevent suppression of such reports as a matter of routine.

The House of Lords offers support for the views expressed in earlier cases that a 'class' claim in this area can be no more than provisional, both as to inspection by the court,[11] and to liability to disclose to the applicant when the administration of justice so dictates in relation to a particular document.[12] It was also remarked that the balance between different aspects of the public interest may change as the factual basis of the case develops.[13] It also seems that this aspect of public policy may be overridden by the administration of justice, not only where that operates in favour of the accused, but occasionally against his interests, for example in the best interests of a child.[14]

As noted above the matter was raised in *R v Chief Constable of the West Midlands, ex p Wiley* by way of an application for judicial review of the decisions of the Chief Constables, and for an injunction to prevent use of immune material. The House of Lords thought it better than the matter normally be raised in the civil proceedings for which the material was required. In *Bennett v Metropolitan Police Comr*[15] the procedural context was the still more unusual one of a claim against the relevant minister for impropriety in the consideration of whether to make a claim for immunity. It is significant that although the point was not finally determined, it was held arguable that the minister is under a duty to weigh the aspect of the administration of justice against that of suppression of a class[16] of police documents before making a claim. The facts of that case reveal the vital importance of continuing judicial control over the actions of the executive in this matter, since it was evident that no damage would be done to

3   The Attorney-General declined to intervene.
4   Though it still wished to assert public policy immunity in a number of different narrower respects.
5   *Neilson, Hehir* and *Makanjuola.*
6   Lord Woolf, with whom all of the other judges agreed, was inclined against such a claim, but on this Lord Slynn and Lord Lloyd expressly reserved their view.
7   *Taylor v Anderton* [1995] 2 All ER 420, [1995] 1 WLR 447.
8   *O'Sullivan v Metropolitan Police Comr* (1995) Times, 3 July.
9   *Kelly v Metropolitan Police Comr* [1997] 33 LS Gaz R 28.
10   *Goodridge v Chief Constable of Hampshire* [1999] 1 All ER 896.
11   *R v Backhouse* [1993] Crim LR 69.
12   See eg *Makanjuola v Metropolitan Police Comr* [1992] 3 All ER 617, at 623; *Ex p Coventry Newspapers Ltd* [1993] QB 278, at 289, [1993] 1 All ER 86, at 93; *Taylor v Anderton* above.
13   A point also stressed in *R v Bower* [1994] Crim LR 281.
14   See *Re M (care proceedings: police videos)* [1995] 2 FLR 571 where police videos which would normally have been subject to public interest immunity were made available for use in care proceedings involving a different child.
15   [1995] 2 All ER 1, [1995] 1 WLR 488.
16   There communications with overseas police forces.

any wider interest than the preservation of an agency of government[17] from an embarrassing disclosure.

D. LOCAL GOVERNMENT MATTERS[18]

Immunity is granted, and granted only, in the public interest. If no public interest is asserted, but only an interest of a local authority it will not be accepted as alone constituting a valid ground for immunity.[19] It often happens however that a matter of national concern raising a clear public interest is entrusted to a local authority. In such a case it is not conclusive against the recognition of immunity from disclosure that the claim is made by the local authority, even though it may be unsupported by an affidavit from a Minister.[20] Still less is it conclusive in favour of immunity that the question arises in wardship proceedings.[1] Thus in *D v National Society for the Prevention of Cruelty to Children* the House of Lords recognised, obiter, such a claim in relation to information given to the local authority to enable it to discharge its statutory duties in relation to the care of children.[2] It is however likely to be rare that a claim for public interest immunity, raised only by a local authority, and supported by affidavits not from Ministers, but local professional advisers, will prevail against the public interest in the administration of justice, especially in a case where the documents are of the utmost significance to the outcome of the litigation for which they are required,[3] or where different official bodies take opposing views in relation to disclosure.[4] In this area, as in others involving public policy immunity, the principles laid down in *Air Canada* regarding balancing for both inspection and disclosure are appropriate,[5] and more than mere relevance is required before disclosure of social service files will be ordered.[6] It should be noted that the decision remains one for the judge even though a local official may have given assurances of confidentiality to the supplier of the relevant information.[7]

---

17   The Crown Prosecution Service's employment of a stratagem to evade the unwelcome absence of an extradition treaty with the relevant jurisdiction.
18   See Tapper 9 Ch and Fam LQ 1 (1997).
19   *Blackpool Corpn v Locker* [1948] 1 KB 349, [1948] 1 All ER 85, as interpreted by Lord Edmund-Davies in *D v National Society for the Prevention of Cruelty to Children* [1978] AC 171, at 245, [1977] 1 All ER 589, at 618.
20   The procedure is set out in *Re C (child cases: evidence and disclosure)* [1995] 1 FLR 204.
1   *Re M (a minor)* [1990] 2 FLR 36, disapproving *Re S* [1987] Fam 199.
2   *Re D (infants)* [1970] 1 All ER 1088, [1970] 1 WLR 599, is similar, but *Campbell v Tameside Metropolitan Borough Council* [1982] QB 1065, at 1077, [1982] 2 All ER 791, at 798, shows its strictly confined ambit.
3   Most especially if required by a party against whom sexual abuse of a child is alleged: see *R v Hampshire County Council, ex p K* [1990] 2 QB 71, [1990] 2 All ER 129, though even in criminal proceedings for such an offence the judge must perform a balancing exercise: *R v Higgins* [1996] 1 FLR 137n. See also *R v K(DT) (Evidence)* (1993) 97 Cr App Rep 342. For North American attitudes see in Canada *R v O'Connor* [1995] 4 SCR 411; and in the United States *Pennsylvania v Ritchie* 480 US 62 (1993).
4   As in *Re G (a minor)(social worker: disclosure)* [1996] 2 All ER 65, [1996] 1 WLR 1407.
5   *Re M,* above.
6   *R v Reading Justices, ex p Berkshire County Council* [1996] 1 Cr App Rep 239.
7   *Re G (welfare report: disclosure)* [1993] 2 FLR 293.

E.   CONFIDENTIAL MATTERS

It was stated quite clearly by Lord Cross in *Alfred Crompton Amusement Machines Ltd v Customs and Excise Comrs (No 2)* that: ' "Confidentiality" is not a separate head of privilege, but it may be a very material consideration to bear in mind when privilege is claimed on the ground of public interest.'[8] This proposition has impeccable historical credentials,[9] and has subsequently been reaffirmed by the House of Lords.[10] It is necessary to restate it on account of the modern approach to public interest immunity exhibited in the quotation from Lord Hailsham's speech in *D v National Society for the Prevention of Cruelty to Children* with which this section of the chapter began. The judgments in the Court of Appeal in that case exhibit the conflicting views current at the time. There was on the one hand Lord Denning's view that breach of confidence was a sufficient basis for making a claim for immunity from disclosure on the basis of public interest, and would prevail unless over-balanced by the public interest in the administration of justice. On the other there was the view of the majority that the categories of public interest immunity were strictly limited to the sorts of claim on behalf of central government which had been recognised in the past. The House of Lords attempted to steer a middle course between these views. The case arose out of the visit without any prior warning of an inspector of the NSPCC to the home of the mother of a young child. It transpired that the visit was to investigate an allegation that the child had been ill-treated. There was no evidence of such ill-treatment, and no subsequent proceedings were set in train. The mother was most upset by the incident, and eventually brought a claim for negligence against the NSPCC in respect of its conduct in the matter, pursuant to which she sought discovery of all relevant documents in its possession, some of which would be very likely to reveal the identity of the society's informant. The society sought an order that no such documents should be discovered. This application was dismissed by the master, upheld by the judge, and dismissed by the majority of the Court of Appeal, but only over the dissent of Lord Denning. It may be noted that there could be no reasonable doubt that such documents existed, and that they would assist the plaintiff's case. It is also the case that the plaintiff was interested only in the identity of the informant, and that the society relied upon no certificate or affidavit from any official in support of its claim that it would be contrary to the public interest to make such a revelation to the plaintiff. Nor was the issue capable of being disposed of simply as a matter for the discretion of the judge at the stage of discovery. The case was accepted, and discussed, by the House of Lords on the basis that it affected the law of evidence,[11] in the sense that the decision involved also the range of questions which could be put at the trial of the action. The unanimous view of the House was that it could not be regarded as fatal that no arm of central government was involved, so long as the defendant's claim was capable of subsumption under a head of public policy, at least analogous to one previously recognised. In the particular case it was felt that there was a clear analogy to the public policy of preserving from disclosure in a civil case the identity of informants to the police. This option may not however be available to all of those giving a guarantee of confidentiality.[12] Even where witnesses were encouraged to testify by reference to the use immunity qualifying the statutory abrogation of the privilege against self-incrimination in s 98(2) of the Childen

8   [1974] AC 405, at 433, [1973] 2 All ER 1169, at 1184
9   See VIII *Wigmore* para 2286.
10   Eg *D v National Society for the Prevention of Cruelty to Children* [1978] AC 171, at 238, [1977] 1 All ER 589, at 612; *Science Research Council v Nassé* [1980] AC 1028, at 1080, [1979] 3 All ER 673, at 691.
11   See Lord Diplock at 219, 595, Lord Hailsham at 221, 600, and Lord Simon at 241, 615.
12   *Re G (a minor)(social worker: disclosure)* [1996] 2 All ER 65, [1996] 1 WLR 1407.

Act 1989 it was held that details of their evidence could be supplied to the police.[13] Such an analogical approach opens up the field of public interest immunity just because the closeness of the necessary analogy is left for subsequent development. The facts of the case demonstrate that the analogy may be close enough even though no organ of central government is involved, and notwithstanding the absence of official certification of any public interest.[14]

The House regarded the role of confidence as being essentially confirmatory, in the sense that it is unlikely that the argument for refusing disclosure of any statement made otherwise than in confidence would ever be supported by a public policy so strong as to override the public interest in the proper administration of justice.

The ambit of this extension of public interest immunity was soon afterwards explored in two discrimination cases, eventually heard together by the House of Lords.[15] In both cases discrimination was alleged in relation to employment; in both the claimant sought disclosure of confidential reports upon the successful applicants; and in both disclosure was ordered at a lower level, but denied by the Court of Appeal. One of the respondents rested its case upon a claim for public interest immunity. This was rejected by the whole House. Most of their Lordships were concerned to point out that there was no such analogy to a recognised form of public interest immunity as there had been in *D v National Society for the Prevention of Cruelty to Children.* It was pointed out that the interest of the employers, even though one was a public body, was of a private and not a public nature. Nor was Parliament's expression of public policy in setting up the relevant commissions compatible with a public interest immunity which would effectively prevent them from discharging their statutory functions. It is perhaps least likely of all that the courts will recognise public interest immunity in an area which has been excluded from the limited scope of private privilege, such as banking documentation.[16] It seems that sometimes however the courts have themselves developed practices of automatically refusing disclosure to particular types of document, such as records of case conferences in relation to wards of court.[17] It has been held in the light of *D v National Society for the Prevention of Cruelty to Children* that such a decision should never be automatic, but taken only after a balancing exercise has been conducted,[18] and one, even in adoption proceedings, undertaken subject to a strong presumption in favour of disclosure.[19] A similar view has been taken in relation to the disclosure of social welfare documents sought by the police with a view to bringing criminal proceedings.[20] One relevant factor is whether the ward himself is seeking disclosure, especially after attaining his majority.[1] It is here as elsewhere for the seeker

13   *Re C (a minor) (care proceedings: disclosure)* [1997] Fam 76, [1996] 2 FLR 725; the factors to be taken into account in striking the balance are helpfully summarised.

14   This may however be relevant to the burden of proof which Lord Edmund-Davies at 246, 619 here regarded as being borne by the party resisting disclosure, apparently at the standard of the balance of probabilities, by contrast to his view in *Burmah Oil* at 1127, 719 and repeated in *Air Canada* at 442, 922 that the burden in those cases, where there was such a certificate, was borne by the party seeking disclosure, and at an apparently high standard ('the scales must come down decisively').

15   *Science Research Council v Nassé, Leyland Cars (BL Cars Ltd) v Vyas* [1980] AC 1028, [1979] 3 All ER 673.

16   See eg *Kaufman v Crédit Lyonnais Bank* (1995) 7 Admin LR 669; *Price Waterhouse v BCCI Holdings (Luxembourg) SA* [1992] BCLC 583.

17   In this case the confidentiality is that of the court administering the ward's affairs, rather than that of the ward personally.

18   *Re M (a minor) (disclosure of material)* [1990] 2 FLR 36.

19   *Re D (adoption reports: confidentiality)* [1996] AC 593, [1995] 4 All ER 385, per Lord Mustill at 609A, 393a.

20   *Re W (minors) (social worker: disclosure)* [1998] 2 All ER 801, where the seriousness of the allegation against the parent was regarded as a reason for rather than against disclosure.

1   *Re Manda* [1993] Fam 183, [1993] 1 All ER 733.

of the information to be sufficiently specific in identifying the relevant documents to avoid any suggestion of a fishing expedition.[2] Medical records are often regarded as particularly confidential,[3] though to refuse disclosure automatically would, in much the same way as mentioned above in relation to banking records undermine the limitation of private professional privilege to legal matters.[4] Nor is there much point in refusing advance disclosure if they are likely to be the subject of a subpoena duces tecum at the trial.[5] In exceptional circumstances there may even be a compelling reason to disclose medical,[6] or police,[7] records held in confidence on account of a greater public interest,[8] such as the safety of others.[9]

Despite some dicta in *D v National Society for the Prevention of Cruelty to Children* tending to elide the distinction between private privilege and public interest immunity in some respects, the House clearly reaffirmed its acceptance of the doctrine that any immunity based upon public interest cannot be waived by the parties, and must be taken up by the court even if not explicitly claimed by one of them.[10] On the other hand a court may be more prepared to protect the confidentiality of documents secured by compulsory process,[11] such as pre-trial discovery[12] or disclosure,[13] than those divulged voluntarily,[14] for example, in an arbitration,[15] at least when disclosure is sought from the body holding the documents as a result of that process.[16] It has also been held that there is no general principle of allowing a claim in respect of all documents divulged in confidence to a regulatory body.[17] In principle, as in the case of private privilege, the right to claim or waive resides in the person to whom the confidence is owed, and not the person who owes it.[18] It should also be noted that the privilege persists only so long as the document or information remains confidential, and is lost when it is made

2   *Re X* [1992] Fam 124, [1992] 2 All ER 595. For a useful procedural device to avoid difficulty in this context see Rodwell [1998] Crim LR 332.
3   And have for the purposes of the Police and Criminal Evidence Act 1984, s 12 been construed as extending beyond records of medical treatment to those of dates of attendance at a hospital: see *R v Cardiff Crown Court, ex p Kellam* (1993) 16 BMLR 76.
4   See the discussion of this issue by the Supreme Court of Canada in *M(A) v Ryan* [1997] 1 SCR 157.
5   *Dunn v British Coal Corpn* [1993] ICR 591.
6   *W v Egdell* [1990] Ch 359, [1990] 1 All ER 835; *R v Kennedy* [1998] Crim LR 739.
7   *Hellewell v Chief Constable of Derbyshire* [1995] 4 All ER 473, [1995] 1 WLR 804.
8   In Australia there has been some reluctance to override statutory requirements of confidentiality by reference to considerations such as the paramount interest of a child in care proceedings: see *Mallia v Collins* (1993) 115 FLR 35; *Piras v Thaisawat* (1993) 115 FLR 79.
9   *Re M (care proceedings: police videos)* [1995] 2 FLR 571.
10 See Lord Wilberforce at 1067, 681; Lord Edmund-Davies at 1074, 686; Lord Fraser at 1082, 693.
11 Though it will be reluctant to impede foreign proceedings where there is an obligation of disclosure: *Bank of Crete SA v Koskotas (No 2)* [1993] 1 All ER 748, [1992] 1 WLR 919; especially if there is an allegation of fraud: *Pharaon v Bank of Credit and Commerce International* [1998] 4 All ER 455.
12 *Riddick v Thames Board Mills* [1977] QB 881, [1977] 3 All ER 677.
13 *Taylor v Serious Fraud Office* [1998] 4 All ER 801.
14 Though contrary arguments can be based upon the need to encourage candid voluntary disclosure as intimated by Lord Browne-Wilkinson in *Re Arrows (No 4)* [1995] 2 AC 75, [1994] 3 All ER 814, at 101F, 826f.
15 *Shearson Lehman Hutton Inc v Maclaine Watson Co Ltd* [1989] 1 All ER 1056, [1989] 2 Lloyd's Rep 570.
16 Thus in *Lonrho plc v Fayed (No 4)* [1994] QB 775, [1994] 1 All ER 870 copies of tax returns were not immune in the hands of the taxpayer; see also in Australia, *Pooraka Holdings Pty Ltd v Participation Nominees Pty Ltd* (1989) 52 SASR 148.
17 *Kaufmann v Credit Lyonnais Bank* (1995) 7 Admin LR 669 disagreeing with *MGN Pensions Trustees v Invesco Asset Management Ltd* (14 October 1993, unreported).
18 *Price Waterhouse v BCCI Holdings (Luxembourg) SA* [1992] BCLC 583.

public, for example when a statement made under caution to the police is read out in open court.[19]

F.   CRIMINAL PROCEEDINGS[20]

It seems clear that rules both of privilege and of public policy immunity apply differently in criminal proceedings.[1] It has already been noted that a claim to legal professional privilege may be overridden when the evidence may enable the accused to resist an allegation made by the Crown or to establish his innocence.[2] In relation to public policy immunity it was stated by a Lord Chancellor that:[3]

> if medical documents, or indeed other documents, are relevant to the defence in criminal proceedings, Crown privilege should not be claimed.

It was made clear that the rule was far-reaching and applied even to prosecutions for minor offences. It should however be noted that the reference is to the practice of claiming Crown privilege, and not to its non-existence as a matter of law. Indeed such existence is rather presumed by the form of the statement, and may well be necessary since it can hardly be supposed that there are no means of preventing disclosure of the most vital national secrets just because they are relevant to the defence of one accused of some most trivial offence.[4] On the other hand it also seems clear that in cases where the liberty of the claimant is at stake[5] the public interest in the administration of justice will weigh very heavily in the balance,[6] though it may be outweighed if the relevance of the material is at best peripheral.[7] It is officially expected that the occasion for claiming public interest immunity in criminal cases will be much diminished by Part 1 of the Criminal Procedure and Investigation Act 1996.[8]

One of the more sensitive aspects of public policy immunity in this connection is that relating to police matters, and especially to evidence tending to reveal the identity

---

19   *Bunn v BBC* [1998] 3 All ER 552.

20   For a full account of the position immediately before the passage of Part 1 of the Criminal Procedure and Investigation Act 1996 see the Scott Report (above p 474) Vol IV Part 5 Sect K.6.

1   Said in *R v Brown, R v Daley* (1987) 87 Cr App Rep 52, at 57 'always to have been accepted'. But see *R v Robertson* (1983) 21 NTR 11. It has also been recognised by statute, see Iron and Steel Act 1982, s 33(1). Some statutory provisions of a like character, such as the Interception of Communications Act 1985, s 9 which prohibits any evidence or cross-examination on certain sensitive matters, apply indifferently to both civil and criminal proceedings alike.

2   Page 459 above, *R v Barton* [1972] 2 All ER 1192, [1973] 1 WLR 115. The rules apply in the ordinary way to evidence required by the prosecution: see *R v King* [1983] 1 All ER 929, at 931, [1983] 1 WLR 411, at 414.

3   197 HL Official Report (5th series) col 745 quoted by Lord Reid in *Conway v Rimmer* [1968] AC 910, at 942, [1968] 1 All ER 874, at 881.

4   See the converse in *R v Clowes* [1992] 3 All ER 440, 95 Cr App Rep 440 where the seriousness of the charge militated against suppression.

5   Though not once liberty has been lost, as in the case of someone already a prisoner: *R v Secretary of State for Home Department, ex p Mulkerrins* (1998) Times, 3 February.

6   *R v Governor of Brixton Prison, ex p Osman* [1992] 1 All ER 108, at 116, [1991] 1 WLR 281, at 288.

7   *Re Manda* [1993] Fam 183, [1993] 1 All ER 733; *Morrow, Geach and Thomas v DPP* [1994] Crim LR 58.

8   See Attorney-General's paper *Public Interest Immunity* (1996) s 2.5 et seq.

of informers.[9] Here too the general rule is relaxed in favour of the defence, as Lord Simon of Glaisdale recognised in *Rogers v Home Secretary*:[10]

> Sources of police information are a judicially recognised class of evidence excluded on the grounds of public policy *unless their production is required to establish innocence in a criminal trial.*

Since the rule exists for the protection of informers[11] it cannot, without further justification, be applied to prevent the informer himself from adducing evidence of his having performed such a role,[12] though this may lead to difficulty in the case of co-accused where different attitudes are adopted.[13]

The earliest cases[14] involved vital state interests and were resolved in favour of the application of the privilege. In less important situations the cases diverged,[15] and in the leading case of *Marks v Beyfus*[16] it was regarded as a matter for discretion[17] by the judge at the trial. It is for the defence to show[18] that disclosure is necessary for the proper presentation of the defence case.[19] The judge should take into account the nature of the information to be revealed and its importance to the accused's defence.[20] For example if the defence is that the accused was inveigled into a compromising situation by a particular third person, the fact that the third person was an informer with a motive for so behaving ought not to be suppressed.[1] Once the court has ruled in favour of disclosure, a consequential decision by the prosecution to abandon the case is not a ground for the court to reverse its decision.[2] The court is not however prepared to countenance 'fishing' expeditions, and has refused to lift the immunity when the

9   The concept and definition of an informer was examined by Mustill LJ in *R v Agar* [1990] 2 All ER 442, 90 Cr App Rep 318, at 444g, 320.

10   [1973] AC 388, at 407, [1972] 2 All ER 1057, at 1067 (emphasis supplied) citing *R v Hardy* (1794) 24 State Tr 199; *Hennessy v Wright* (1888) 21 QBD 509; and *Marks v Beyfus* (1890) 25 QBD 494. See also *Roviaro v US* 353 US 53 (1957) for a similar approach in the United States.

11   The strength of this interest is indicated in *Swinney v Chief Constable of Northumbria* [1997] QB 464, [1996] 3 All ER 449 where the Court of Appeal decided that the police are under a duty of care to keep an informer's identity confidential.

12   *Savage v Chief Constable of Hampshire* [1997] 2 All ER 631.

13   As in *R v Adams* [1997] Crim LR 292.

14   *R v Hardy*, above, *R v Watson* (1817) 32 State Tr 1, *R v Cobbett* (1831) 2 State Tr NS 789, and *R v O'Connor* (1846) 4 State Tr NS 935.

15   In *A-G v Briant* (1846) 15 LJ Ex 265, disclosure was not compelled, while in *R v Richardson* (1863) 3 F & F 693, and *Webb v Catchlove* (1886) 3 TLR 159, the contrary view prevailed. See also *Thomson v Neilson* 1900 8 SLT 147.

16   At 498. The position seems not to be materially different in Ireland where a number of cases have allowed privilege not to disclose the names of informers in criminal cases: see eg *A-G v Simpson* [1959] IR 105, discussed by O'Connor (1980) 15 IJ (NS) 111.

17   In *R v Hallett* [1986] Crim LR 462 it was emphasised that it was not truly a matter of discretion since once the judge found the relevant condition to be established he was bound to allow the evidence to be given or questions to be asked.

18   *R v Hennessey* (1978) 68 Cr App Rep 419, at 426. Preliminary negotiations between counsel may be called for, and these must be conducted with delicacy and accuracy: see *R v Smith* [1998] 2 Cr App Rep 1.

19   This formulation of the test seems to have been adopted in *R v Williams* [1988] Crim LR 113.

20   In a number of jurisdictions a distinction is made between relaxation of the immunity where it helps the defence directly, but reluctance to do so when it might merely show that a warrant was unlawfully obtained: see *Hilton v Wells* (1985) 59 ALR 281; *R v Hunter* (1987) 57 CR (3d) 1; *McCray v Illinois* 386 US 300 (1967).

1   *R v Williams*, above; *R v Agar* [1990] 2 All ER 442, 90 Cr App Rep 318; *R v Reilly* [1994] Crim LR 279; cp *R v Menga and Marshalleck* [1998] Crim LR 58.

2   *R v Vaillencourt* [1993] Crim LR 311. In that case the prosecution's decision was made even though the initial order for discovery was limited to counsel.

accused did not know the identity of certain persons who might have been informers[3] and in a position to 'plant' incriminating material,[4] or where the identity of the informer is on a correct analysis irrelevant to the defence.[5] Editing so as to conceal the identity of the informer is a hazardous undertaking since it may be far from clear just which details will operate to reveal it.[6]

The law relating to pre-trial disclosure by the prosecution to the defence has now been put on a statutory footing by Part 1 of the Criminal Procedure and Investigation Act 1996,[7] but specific provision is made for material to be withheld on the basis of public policy.[8] In general it is for the court to decide this matter, so notice must be given to the defence, indicating at least the category of the material, and allowing scope for representations by the defence. Some situations are so sensitive that they would be compromised even by informing the accused that information was not being disclosed on the basis of the public interest, in which case an ex parte application is inevitable.[9] Where the material emanates not from the prosecution but from a third party, it has been held that public policy will be still less likely to be overridden by the need to protect the accused.[10]

A more controversial step has been the extension of immunity to protect the identity, not of informers, but of those who make premises available to the police as observation posts. In *R v Rankine* it was said that:[11]

> the reasons which give rise to the rule that an informer is not to be identified apply with equal force to the identification of the owner or occupier of premises used for surveillance *and to the identification of the premises themselves*. The cases are indistinguishable, and the same rule must apply to each.

It is vital to note that the words emphasised above do not constitute a separate basis for protection, but are subordinate to the consideration of protecting the identity of the owner or occupier. If taken as an independent basis the reasoning could easily be extended to the protection of methods of surveillance. Such a further extension was attempted in *R v Brown and Daley*[12] where the police refused to describe cars used for surveillance purposes. As the court pointed out such an extension would distort the reason for the rule, and destroy the analogy with the case of informers. The critical difference is that in the case of an informer the prosecution must elect either to take the direct benefit of the informer's information by calling him to testify, in which case his identity is revealed and he is available for cross-examination, or to secure only indirect benefit from his information by using it to lead them to evidence which they can then adduce without revealing his identity. If the extension to the identity of observation

---

3   But see *R v Baker* [1996] Crim LR 55 where disclosure was ordered although the defence believed that there had been no informer, and the application was designed to expose that situation.

4   *R v Hardy* [1988] Crim LR 687.

5   *R v Slowcombe* [1991] Crim LR 198.

6   *R v Leipert* [1997] 1 SCR 281.

7   Adopting the recommendations made in the government's consultation paper *Disclosure* Cm 2864 (1995). See above p 250.

8   Sections 3(6), 7(5), 8(4) and 21(2). Some amendment has been made to the procedure in magistrates' courts: see s 14 and *R v South Worcestershire Magistrates, ex p Lilley* [1995] 4 All ER 186, [1995] 1 WLR 1595.

9   *R v Davis* [1993] 2 All ER 643, [1993] 1 WLR 613. The court disapproved of disclosure to counsel on the basis that no further disclosure would take place to solicitor or client.

10   *Re Barlow Clowes* [1992] Ch 208, [1991] 4 All ER 385.

11   [1986] QB 861, at 867, [1986] 2 All ER 566, at 570, emphasis supplied.

12   (1987) 87 Cr App Rep 52.

posts were to be accepted the prosecution would be able to secure the direct benefit of evidence observed from the post while at the same time insulating that evidence from any effective cross-examination by suppressing any indication of its location. Since this information will normally be necessary for such cross-examination it is to be expected that the occasions for applying the analogy to informers, and suppressing the information, will be rare. In particular it was said to be necessary for the prosecution to satisfy the court that there was a particular need for the observation post, and for anonymity, before any such suppression would even be considered.[13] It seems however that some erosion of these conditions has taken place, with the rules relating to identification posts being equated with those relating to informers, without consideration of more than the similar motives for reluctance to be identified.[14] It now seems that more restrictions will be placed on the evidence that can be given,[15] less basis required for reluctance to be located,[16] and more trivial crimes in which the application is made.[17] In neither the case of an informer nor of an owner of an observation point should the defence be permitted to exploit the exception as a substitute for discovery.[18] Nor should an order ever be made ex parte.[19]

SECTION 2.   MISCELLANEOUS MATTERS CONNECTED WITH PREVIOUS LITIGATION

Judges cannot be compelled to give evidence concerning cases tried by them, and more or less closely analogous rules exist concerning the evidence of arbitrators, jurors or barristers.

A.   EVIDENCE OF JUDGES

This subject was authoritatively re-examined by Lord Woolf MR in *Warren v Warren*.[20] He cited the dicta of Cleasby B in *Duke of Buccleuch v Metropolitan Board of Works*[1] who said:

> With respect to those who fill the office of judge it has been felt that there are grave objections to their conduct being made the subject of cross-examination and comment (to which hardly any limit could be put) in relation to proceedings before them; and, as everything which they can properly prove can be proved by others, the courts of law discountenance and I think I may say prevent them being examined.

---

13   *R v Johnson* [1989] 1 All ER 121, [1988] 1 WLR 1377.
14   See *R v Hewitt, R v Davis* (1991) 95 Cr App Rep 81.
15   *Blake v DPP; Austin v DPP* (1992) 97 Cr App Rep 169 (refusal even to identify where the crime was observed to have been committed); *R v Grimes* [1994] Crim LR 213 (bearing of crime from post suppressed).
16   *Blake v DPP; Austin v DPP* above (no special reason for apprehension); *R v Grimes* above (ascertained by telephone call rather than personal visit).
17   *Blake v DPP; Austin v DPP* above (indecency in churchyard).
18   *R v Robertson* (1983) 21 NTR 11.
19   *R v Guildhall Justices, ex p DPP* (1983) 78 Cr App Rep 269.
20   [1997] QB 488, [1996] 4 All ER 664.
1   (1872) LR 5 HL 418, at 433. A subpoena may be issued against a magistrate's clerk to bring and produce notes of proceedings before the magistrates.

Although this makes no distinction of rank between judges,[2] Lord Woolf explicitly recognised that magistrates are treated differently.[3] Despite the last sentence of the quoted passage, he held judges to be competent, but not compellable,[4] witnesses to all matters relating to and resulting from the performance of their judicial functions.[5]

B. EVIDENCE OF ARBITRATORS

So far as arbitrators are concerned, it is settled that they can be compelled to give evidence with regard to occurrences at the arbitration, and to state what matters were included in the submission, but they must not be asked questions about the reasons for their award.[6] Such a limitation may be justified on the ground that the evidence would be irrelevant as the reasons for an award could only be material at the hearing of an application to have it set aside, but there is also the point that the award must be treated as final in the absence of any proceedings of this nature.[7]

C. EVIDENCE OF JURORS

There is a settled rule that jurors may not give evidence[8] of discussions that took place in the jury box or jury room concerning the cases in which they were[9] acting. Even if they are all prepared to swear that they intended to return a verdict for a greater sum of damages than that which appeared on the record, no alteration can be made.[10] Hard as it is, the point made in the judgment that it is better for the plaintiff to suffer an inconvenience than that his application should be allowed is probably a sound one. If the statement of all the jurors concerning their intentions would justify a variation of the verdict, what would happen if some, or a majority of them, made such a statement? The exclusionary rule is confined to evidence of discussions concerning their verdict

---

2   Masters of the Supreme Court are judges for this purpose.
3   For the position of magistrates' clerks, see *McKinley v McKinley* [1960] 1 All ER 476, [1960] 1 WLR 120. Quasi-judicial offices such as that of an inspector presiding over a planning appeal seem likely to be assimilated to the position of magistrates: *Jones and Jones v Sexcretary of State for Wales* (1995) 70 P & CR 211.
4   Nor can disclosure be claimed of in camera discussion, even between members of a professional disciplinary tribunal: *Roylance v General Medical Council* (1999) 47 BMLR 63.
5   The Supreme Court of Canada has held the exemption from compellability to extend beyond strictly judicial to administrative matters, such as the reasons for the composition of a particular court: *MacKeigan v Hickman* [1989] 2 SCR 796; for a different approach in New Zealand see *Tau v Durie* [1996] 2 NZLR 190.
6   *Buccleuch's* case (above), applied to a member of a medical board under the National Insurance (Industrial Injuries) Act 1946, in *Ward v Shell Mex and BP Ltd* [1951] 2 All ER 904, and to the PIA Ombudsman and his staff in *Brooks v Reliance Mutual Ltd* (1997) Independent, 3 November.
7   It was noted by Hoffmann LJ in *Land Securities plc v Westminster City Council* [1993] 4 All ER 124, [1993] 1 WLR 286 that where an award is relevant in *other* proceedings then the rule in *Hollington v Hewthorn & Co Ltd* [1943] KB 587, [1943] 2 All ER 35 applies: see further above p 103.
8   And in Canada cannot be compelled to testify before a public inquiry set up to consider wrongful convictions: *Re Morin* (1997) 154 DLR (4th) 146.
9   It seems however that they may be questioned as a body in open court about cases in which they *are* acting so as to determine whether or not they should be discharged: *R v Orgles* [1993] 4 All ER 533, [1994] 1 WLR 108.
10 *Jackson v Williamson* (1788) 2 Term Rep 281. See also *Nesbitt v Parrett* (1902) 18 TLR 510; and *R v Thompson* [1962] 1 All ER 65; and in Canada *R v Wilson* (1993) 78 CCC (3d) 568.

that took place between the jurors,[11] but may extend beyond matters disclosure of which would contravene s 8(1) of the Contempt of Court Act 1981.[12] Accordingly in *Ellis v Deheer*,[13] a new trial was ordered on the ground that some jurymen had not been present in court when their verdict was announced, and it is probable that the fact that one of the jurors did not understand English would be a good ground for setting aside their verdict. As Lord Atkin observed, finality is a good thing, but justice is better.[14]

D.   EVIDENCE OF ADVOCATES

There are obvious reasons why an advocate should not give evidence in a case in which he is acting, and it is not customary to compel him to testify in later litigation concerning such matters as the terms of a compromise of a previous suit, but the whole question is more dependent on professional etiquette than anything in the nature of an exclusionary rule of evidence,[15] and nothing more need be said about it in a work of this nature.

SECTION 3.   IMPROPERLY OBTAINED EVIDENCE

The problem is whether relevant evidence is inadmissible because it was obtained improperly, for example by a crime, tort, breach of contract or an infringement or evasion of official regulations, typically one of the Codes of Practice. At present in English law the short answer is that confessions may not be admitted if they were obtained by oppression, or made in consequence of anything said or done likely in the circumstances to render them unreliable;[16] but, subject to that important qualification, there is no other such exclusionary rule. The cases which lead to this conclusion are few, and there has been no full examination of the principles at stake by an English court. Yet these principles are of the highest significance. On the one hand, there is the general rule that all relevant evidence is admissible, and the fact that it was obtained improperly is immaterial so far as the case before the court is concerned; in particular, the method by which incriminating evidence was obtained may be thought not to justify the release of a guilty man, although it may warrant punitive or remedial proceedings against those responsible for the impropriety. On the other hand, there is the argument that the slightest encouragement of delinquent methods of obtaining evidence, and in particular, the barest toleration of improper police practice is a worse evil than the escape of an occasional criminal. To quote from an important Scottish judgment:[17]

---

11   In *R v Hood* [1968] 2 All ER 56, 52 Cr App Rep 265, the Court of Appeal admitted an affidavit sworn by a juror relating to his knowledge of the accused's previous convictions, but ostensibly only on the basis that it dealt exclusively with extrinsic matters and did not relate to discussions between jurors or to the reasons for verdict, though it is hard to understand how such a limitation applied in the circumstances there present.

12   *R v Miah; R v Akhbar* [1997] 2 Cr App Rep 12.

13   [1922] 2 KB 113.

14   *Ras Behari Lal v The King-Emperor* (1933) 102 LJPC 144, disapproving in the Privy Council the decision of the Court of Criminal Appeal in *R v Thomas* [1933] 2 KB 489. For evidence of statements by jurors to third parties see *R v Syme* (1914) 10 Cr App Rep 284; *R v Armstrong* [1922] 2 KB 555; *R v Box* [1964] 1 QB 430, [1963] 3 All ER 240.

15   See *R v Jacquith and Emode* [1989] Crim LR 508 where the Court of Appeal suggested reconsideration of such etiquette after a barrister had testified in a case in which he was acting.

16   Police and Criminal Evidence Act 1984, s 76.

17   Lord Cooper in *Lawrie v Muir* 1950 JC 19, at 26.

The law must strive to reconcile two highly important interests which are liable to come into conflict—(a) the interest of the citizen to be protected from illegal or irregular invasions of his liberties by the authorities, and (b) the interest of the state to secure that evidence bearing upon the commission of a crime and necessary to enable justice to be done shall not be withheld from courts of law on any mere formal or technical ground. Neither of these objects can be insisted upon to the uttermost. The protection for the citizen is primarily protection for the innocent citizen against unwarranted, wrongful and perhaps high-handed interference, and the common sanction is an action for damages. The protection is not intended as a protection for the guilty citizen against the efforts of the public prosecutor to vindicate the law. On the other hand the interest of the state cannot be magnified to the point of causing all the safeguards for the protection of the citizen to vanish, and of offering a positive inducement to the authorities to proceed by irregular methods.

We shall see that the most recent Scots decisions have gone far towards providing for a compromise between the two competing interests by according a large measure of discretion to the trial judge. These interests have produced conflicting views in the United States. The impropriety of acquitting A, who is guilty, on account of the illegal conduct of B, was forcefully put by Cardozo J when he said:

A room is searched against the law, and the body of a murdered man is found. If the place of discovery may not be proved, the other circumstances may be insufficient to connect the defendant with the crime. The privacy of the home has been infringed, and the murderer goes free.[18]

The contrary view was forcefully put by Holmes J when he said:

We must consider the two objects of desire both of which we cannot have and make up our minds which to choose. It is desirable that crimes should be detected, and to that end too all available evidence should be used. It is desirable that the government should not itself foster and pay for other crimes, when they are the means by which the evidence is to be obtained. If it pays its officers for having got evidence by crime I do not see why it may not as well pay them for getting it in the same way, and I can attach no importance to protestations of disapproval if it knowingly accepts and pays and announces that in future it will pay for the fruits. We have to choose, and for my part I think it a less evil that some criminals should escape than that the government should play an ignoble part.[19]

The American authorities are mainly concerned with the provisions of the Constitution of the United States,[20] and anything in the nature of a detailed discussion is beyond the scope of this book; but it is relevant to point out that the American courts have hitherto adhered fairly rigidly to the doctrine of the exclusion of the 'fruits of the poisoned tree', and, by way of contrast with the English courts, have stressed the disciplining of the police as the motivation of the exclusionary rule. To quote from the

18 *The People v Defoe* 242 NY 413 (1926).
19 *Olmstead v United States* 277 US 438 (1928).
20 Similar approaches can be detected in those Commonwealth jurisdictions to have adopted a more constitutional basis for the protection of human rights: see eg in Canada, *R v Collins* [1987] 1 SCR 265; and in New Zealand, *R v H* [1994] 2 NZLR 143. The position in Australia has moved in the same direction without the benefit of formal constitutional support.

majority judgment in the leading case of *Mapp v Ohio*:[1] '... the purpose of the exclusionary rule is to deter—to compel respect for the constitutional guarantees [against illegal searches] in the only effective available way—by removing the incentive to disregard it.' The cost to the public due to acquittals caused by the exclusion of reliable real evidence is, however, a matter of some judicial concern in the United States, and has now led to a change of approach.[2]

The English cases that will now briefly be considered concern first the admissibility of facts discovered in consequence of inadmissible confessions, and second the admissibility of evidence procured by some other improper means. The distinction reflects the now almost entirely statutory regime relating to all aspects of the admissibility of confessions, while much more of the law relating to other forms of impropriety is less rigidly regulated. In each category both inadmissibility by rule and exclusion by discretion will be considered.

A. FACTS DISCOVERED IN CONSEQUENCE OF INADMISSIBLE CONFESSIONS

Section 76 of the Police and Criminal Evidence Act 1984 now provides:

(4) The fact that a confession is wholly or partly excluded in pursuance of this section shall not affect the admissibility in evidence–
(a) of any facts discovered as a result of the confession; or
(b) where the confession is relevant as showing that the accused speaks, writes or expresses himself in a particular way, of so much of the confession as is necessary to show that he does so.

(5) Evidence that a fact to which this subsection applies was discovered as a result of a statement made by an accused person shall not be admissible unless evidence of how it was discovered is given by him or on his behalf.

(6) Subsection (5) above applies–
(a) to any fact discovered as a result of a confession which is wholly excluded in pursuance of this section; and
(b) to any fact discovered as a result of a confession which is partly so excluded, if the fact is discovered as a result of the excluded part of the confession.

These provisions were intended to clarify what had become a particularly unsatisfactory and unsettled area of the common law. Subsection (4) followed the recommendations of the 11th Report of the Criminal Law Revision Committee,[3] and was consistent with the reasoning of the Royal Commission on Criminal Procedure.[4]

---

1   367 US 656 (1961); the judgment was quoting from that in *Elkins v US* 364 US 206 (1960), at 217. The underlying psychology is highly questionable. The 'bent' police officer thinks that no point will be taken on his illegal methods of obtaining evidence or that, if it is, he will be able to lie himself out of trouble.

2   See *United States v Leon* 104 S Ct 3405 (1984) (no exclusion if constable acts in good faith upon basis of apparently valid warrant); *Segura v United States* 104 S Ct 3380 (1984) (no exclusion where link between illegality and discovery so attenuated as to dissipate any taint); *Immigration and Naturalisation Service v Lopez-Mendoza* 486 US 1032 (1984) (no application to deportation proceedings). For an accessible, concise and relatively recent statement of the position in the United States, see Stuntz [1989] Crim LR 117.

3   Cmnd 4991, para 68, draft Bill, cl 2(5)(a) and (c).

4   Cmnd 8092, para 4.123f.

Subsection (5) however adopted the minority view of the Criminal Law Revision Committee.[5]

The effect of sub-s (4) was intended to preserve the position established in the old case of *R v Warickshall*[6] where a woman who was charged as an accessory after the fact to theft and as a receiver of stolen goods was improperly induced to make a confession in the course of which she said that the property in question was in her lodgings where it was in fact found. The court held that the exclusion of a confession 'forced from the mind by the flattery of hope, or by the pressure of fear' was not based on any breach of public faith that might be involved in its reception, but was due to the fact that the confession comes in so questionable a shape, when it is to be considered as evidence of guilt, that no credit ought to be given to it. But:[7]

> this principle respecting confessions has no application whatever as to the admission or rejection of facts, whether the knowledge of them be obtained in consequence of an extorted confession or whether it arises from any other source; for a fact, if it exist at all, must exist invariably in the same manner whether the confession from which it derives be in other respects true or false. Facts thus obtained, however must be fully and satisfactorily proved without calling in the aid of any part of the confession from which they may have been derived.

It was immaterial that the 'fact' which was discovered was a document.[8] The Criminal Law Revision Committee also took the view that other forms of evidence derived indirectly from an inadmissible confession should be permitted. A confession may be of evidential value because it shows that its maker writes, speaks or expresses himself in a particular way and thus helps to identify him as the culprit. For example, in *R v Voisin*[9] the accused was convicted of the murder of a woman, part of whose body was found in a parcel in which there was also a piece of paper with the words 'blady belgiam'. The accused had been asked by a police officer if he had any objection to writing down the two words 'bloody Belgian' and had said 'Not at all' and had written down 'Bladie Belgiam'. The accused appealed unsuccessfully against his conviction on the ground, among others, that this writing ought to have been rejected as he had not been cautioned before being asked to write the words down. There was no question of an inadmissible confession, but it seemed to the Criminal Law Revision Committee that, if the words had been written in an inadmissible confession, it would be right that they should be admissible for the purpose of showing that the accused writes, speaks or expresses himself in a particular way; and sub-s (4) so enacted.

It can be argued that in exactly the same way it ought to be possible to rely upon an otherwise inadmissible confession to show that it was the accused who provided the information leading to the discovery of the relevant facts, or to show his knowledge of some independently verifiable circumstance.[10] The latter possibility seems to have aroused little, if any, judicial discussion, was specifically rejected by the Criminal Law Revision Committee, and is not provided for in the Act. The former situation has aroused

5   Para 69. The Royal Commission did not descend to this level of detail.
6   (1783) 1 Leach 263, reaffirmed in *R v Berriman* (1854) 6 Cox CC 388.
7   At 264.
8   *R v Leathem* (1861) 8 Cox CC 498. The extremely unsatisfactory case of *R v Barker* [1941] 2 KB 381, [1941] 3 All ER 33 which appeared to assimilate false accounts with a confession of false accounting, and which was overturned on its facts by Finance Act 1942, s 34 (see now Taxes Management Act 1970, s 105), appears to be inconsistent with s 76(4)(a) as a matter of law, and can be supported only upon the basis of the judge's discretion: see Lord Diplock in *R v Sang* [1980] AC 402, at 435, [1979] 2 All ER 1222, at 1229.
9   [1918] 1 KB 531, [1918–19] All ER Rep 491.
10 See Andrews [1963] Crim LR 15, 77.

more concern. In some cases where the location of the facts found in consequence of the otherwise inadmissible confession was less indicative of the accused's guilt than in *Warickshall*, the court permitted the prosecution to testify that it was the accused whose statement revealed the location of the goods.[11] This practice was endorsed by a majority of the Criminal Law Revision Committee, and a provision included in its draft Bill.[12] No such provision was however made in the Police and Criminal Evidence Act 1984, presumably upon the ground that to admit such evidence would tend to subvert the exclusion of the confession itself.[13]

A question might be raised as to whether facts permitted to be proved under s 76(4) might nevertheless be excluded under the discretion in s 78. While there is no indication in s 78 that it does not apply to such facts, and s 78 has, in other contexts, been used to secure the discretionary exclusion of evidence made admissible by other specific provisions of the Police and Criminal Evidence Act 1984,[14] the issue has not yet been tested, and it seems likely that it would have been so tested were it believed to be a realistic possibility.

B.   EVIDENCE PROCURED BY IMPROPER MEANS

The modern law stems from the decision of the Privy Council in *Kuruma, Son of Kaniu v R*,[15] an appeal from Kenya whose law on this subject may be taken to have been the same as that of England. The accused had been convicted of being in unlawful possession of ammunition which had been discovered in consequence of a search of his person by a police officer below the rank of those who were permitted to make such searches. Although it referred the case to the Colonial Secretary on other grounds, the board was of opinion that the evidence had been rightly admitted. Its view was that, if evidence is relevant, it matters not how it was obtained. Their Lordships made it plain that they were not qualifying the law with regard to the admissibility of confessions in any way whatsoever. This strict view was qualified by an accumulating body of authority suggesting that as a matter of discretion the trial judge could exclude evidence from a criminal trial if the strict rules of admissibility would operate unfairly against the accused, illustrated by the example of a document obtained by a trick.[16] The House of

---

11   *R v Grant* (1801) and *R v Hodge* (1794) cited in East 2 Pleas of the Crown 658. Practice was far from consistent, for different approaches see *R v Griffin* (1809) Russ & Ry 151; *R v Gould* (1840) 9 C & P 364; *R v Garbett* (1847) 2 Car & Kir 474, at 490; *R v Berriman* (1854) 6 Cox CC 388.

12   Para 69, cl 2(5)(b).

13   It seems clear that in Scotland, no part of an inadmissible confession can be received however much of it is confirmed (*Chalmers v HM Advocate* 1954 JC 66). In Canada the same result has been achieved since 1982 by interpretation of the relevant provisions of the Canadian Charter of Rights and Freedoms, and especially by s 24(2) under which evidence obtained in breach of the provisions of the Charter which would be likely to bring the administration of justice into disrepute must be excluded: *R v Black* [1989] 2 SCR 138. In Australia it was held in *R v Scott, ex p A-G* [1993] 1 Qd R 537 that the discretion to exclude such parts of a confession is governed solely by considerations of fairness to the accused, and is unaffected by considerations relevant to the exclusion of real evidence as enunciated in *Bunning v Cross* (1978) 141 CLR 54. Subsequently discovered facts are admissible under the Indian Evidence Act 1872, s 27.

14   See *R v O'Connor* (1986) 85 Cr App Rep 298 applying it to evidence of a conviction admissible under s 74. See further above p 101.

15   [1955] AC 197, [1955] 1 All ER 236.

16   Formulated in those terms by Lord Goddard CJ in *Kuruma, Son of Kaniu v R* [1955] AC 197, at 204, [1955] 1 All ER 236, at 239. Further dicta are to be found in *R v Payne* [1963] 1 All ER 848, [1963] 1 WLR 637; *Callis v Gunn* [1964] 1 QB 495, at 501, [1963] 3 All ER 677, at 680; *King v R* [1969] 1 AC 304, at 319, [1968] 2 All ER 610, at 617; and *Jeffery v Black* [1978] QB 490, at 498, [1978] 1 All ER 555, at 559.

Lords subsequently decided[17] in *R v Sang*[18] that any such discretion was much more circumscribed than such dicta suggested, and applied only in respect of evidence obtained from the accused[19] after the commission of an offence. The reference to trickery was taken to refer to situations where the accused was so induced to deliver up a document, or a piece of real evidence contrary to the principle underlying the privilege against self-incrimination, and thought also to underlie the exclusion of involuntary confessions.[20] So narrow a view of the discretion proved to be unpalatable, and a late amendment to the Police and Criminal Evidence Act 1984[1] introduced a new statutory formulation in s 78 that:

> In any proceedings the court may refuse to allow evidence on which the prosecution proposes to rely to be given if it appears to the court that, having regard to all the circumstances, including the circumstances in which the evidence was obtained, the admission of the evidence would have such an adverse effect on the fairness of the proceedings that the court ought not to admit it.

Despite the vagueness of its terms, and the lack of logical progression from the unfairness of the means of obtaining the evidence to the unfairness of the proceedings in which it is adduced,[2] it became widely accepted that the discretion provided by s 78 was at least as wide as the common law discretion mentioned in *R v Sang*,[3] and in practice it hitherto dominated the area.[4] There have even been signs of its transformation into an inclusionary discretion,[5] perhaps influenced by increasing stress on account being taken of fairness to the prosecution as well as to the defence.

Impropriety can take many forms, but a number of different clusters can be discerned, and used as a focus for discussion, although it is recognised that the divisions adopted here are neither exclusive nor exhaustive. Statutory procedures apply[6] in a number of areas, generally with a more prescriptive effect.

---

1 7   Although technically obiter outside the area of entrapment, it has been highly persuasive, see Lord Roskill in *Morris v Beardmore* [1981] AC 446, at 469, [1980] 2 All ER 753, at 767; *R v Adams* [1980] QB 575, [1980] 1 All ER 473, and *Cameron v Charles Simpson Motors* [1980] CLY 2630.

18   [1980] AC 402, [1979] 2 All ER 1222.

19   It was unclear how far it applied to evidence obtained from the accused's premises, see p 186 above.

20   It is not clear how this doctrine could be reconciled with the decision in *R v Derrington* (1826) 2 C & P 418, where a letter obtained from the prisoner by the turnkey under a false promise that he would post it was admitted in evidence for the prosecution. Cf *R v Pamenter* (1872) 12 Cox CC 177.

1   For a fuller account of its genesis and operation see Grevling (1997) 113 LQR 667.

2   For recognition of this difficulty see *DPP v Marshall* [1988] 3 All ER 683, and the temptation mentioned by Staughton LJ in the Court of Appeal in *R v Latif* [1995] 1 Cr App R 270, at 278D. Nor is it completely obvious how it can render a conviction on its basis unsafe, but the Court of Appeal has now decided otherwise: *R v Mullen* (1999) Times, 15 February.

3   Preserved by s 82(3) of the Police and Criminal Evidence Act 1984, despite which the majority of the High Court of Australia remarked in *Ridgeway v R* (1995) 184 CLR 19, at 35, that s 78 amounted to the legislative reversal of the reasoning in *R v Sang*.

4   See Lord Nolan in *R v Khan* [1997] AC 558, [1996] 3 All ER 289, at 578E, 298f endorsing the view of Lord Taylor CJ below. In *Horseferry Road Magistrates' Court, ex p Bennett* [1994] 1 AC 42, [1993] 3 All ER 138 it was said by Lord Griffiths, at 61A, 149g, to have enlarged the exclusionary discretion. But see now *R v Chalkley* [1998] QB 848, [1998] 2 All ER 155: see further p 188 above.

5   See its formulation by Simon Brown LJ in *R v Bailey* [1993] 3 All ER 513, 97 Cr App Rep 365, at 520j, 372; by Lord Taylor CJ in *R v Smurthwaite; R v Gill* [1994] 1 All ER 898, 98 Cr App R 437, at 903a, 440; and by Lord Bingham CJ in *R v Morrisey and Staines* [1997] 2 Cr App Rep 426, at 443B (referring to the decision in *R v Khan*).

6   Sometimes indirectly as where statutory provision is made for the operation of a Code of Practice.

1. Improper searches

Here the general view of English law was laconically expressed by Crompton J in *R v Leatham*,[7] when he said: 'It matters not how you get it if you steal it even, it would be admissible in evidence.' Thus in *Jones v Owen*[8] a constable searched the appellant illegally and found a quantity of young salmon in his pocket. This evidence was held to be admissible on a charge of unlawful fishing, Mellor J expressing the view that:

> It would be a dangerous obstacle to the administration of justice if we were to hold, because evidence was obtained by illegal means, it could not be used against a party charged with an offence.

These views have continued to prevail. Crompton J's dictum was cited in *Kuruma's* case, and it will be recollected that *Calcraft v Guest*,[9] the leading authority on the admissibility of secondary evidence of privileged documents was decided on a similar principle. In *R v Khan*[10] the House of Lords took into account in relation to the placing of listening devices on private premises,[11] trespass to and slight damage of private premises, the possibility that this might have amounted to criminal damage, and breach of privacy; but nevertheless concluded[12] that 'as a matter of English law, evidence which is obtained improperly or even unlawfully remains admissible.' It is sometimes the case that breach of the precise formulation of the rules relating to breath, urine or alcohol levels leads to the exclusion of reliable real evidence discovered as a result.[13] This will normally involve a special test,[14] and may thus necessitate an arrest in order to accomplish it. It now seems that even if the test is conducted only after, and in consequence of, an illegal arrest, the evidence is nevertheless admissible in subsequent proceedings for driving with excess alcohol in the body.[15] A sample is admissible notwithstanding that the device used to obtain it had not been duly approved.[16] Nor is it relevant that the substance found is used in relation to a different offence from that for which its use was originally envisaged.[17] However in *ITC Film Distributor v Video Exchange Ltd*[18] where the material in question was found to have been obtained by

---

7   (1861) 8 Cox CC 498, at 501. See the same judge in *Phelps v Prew* (1854) 3 E & B 430, at 441. See also *Stockfleth v De Tastet* (1814) 4 Camp 10. To the same effect is *Lord Ashburton v Pape* [1913] 2 Ch 469, at 473.
8   (1870) 34 JP 759.
9   [1898] 1 QB 759, and see p 450 above.
10   [1997] AC 558, [1996] 3 All ER 289. This result is in accord with that arrived at in the different constitutional and legislative context in the United States: *Dalia v US* 441 US 238 (1979); and in Canada: *Lyons v R* (1984) 14 DLR (4th) 482; but not in Australia: *Coco v R* (1994) 120 ALR 415.
11   Though the police were conceded to have been acting in general in accordance with procedures approved by Parliament.
12   At 578A, 298a. Subject only to discretionary power to exclude.
13   But even here there is a developing tendency to eschew technicality see *DPP v Kay* (1998) Times, 13 April. See also in Australia *Police v Astley* (1997) 69 SASR 319.
14   The precise specification of which may lead to inability to use reliable real evidence: see *Evans v DPP* (1996) Times, 30 May.
15   *R v Fox* [1986] AC 281, sub nom *Fox v Chief Constable of Gwent* [1985] 3 All ER 392. This situation is to be distinguished from that where an offence of refusing a test is charged, since the conditions may there require that the arrest be lawful, *Morris v Beardmore* [1981] AC 446, [1980] 2 All ER 753.
16   *Criminal Proceedings Against Lemmings* [1998] All ER (EC) 604.
17   *R v Kelt* [1994] 2 All ER 780, [1994] 1 WLR 765.
18   [1982] Ch 431, [1982] 2 All ER 241.

means of a contempt of court it was held that it should not be admitted.[19] The combination of these approaches leads to the conclusion that in England, illegally obtained evidence is admissible as a matter of law, provided that it involves neither a reference to an inadmissible confession of guilt, nor the commission of an act of contempt of court.[20]

It remains to be considered how far this result is mitigated by the exercise of discretion under s 78. In the case of real evidence obtained by an illegal search the position seems to be that while the discretion may be taken into account, it is exceedingly difficult to persuade a court to exercise it. In *Fox v Chief Constable of Gwent*[1] the House of Lords regarded it as justifying the refusal of the magistrates to exercise their discretion to exclude the evidence that the police had acted 'in good faith, and that the specimen itself had been obtained without inducement, threat ..., trick or other impropriety'. Similarly it has not been exercised to exclude an intimate sample taken from a prisoner wrongly informed that he was bound to submit,[2] nor a non-intimate sample obtained after police in riot gear had entered the suspect's police cell and made it clear that force would be used if he resisted,[3] nor the observation of illicit electricity connections within a dwelling house secured by the threat of forcible entry,[4] and not even the forcible interference with a suspect's breathing so as to force him to disgorge the contents of his mouth.[5] It is then hardly surprising to find that the breach of an international convention[6] relating to the treatment of those with diplomatic immunity failed to suffice.[7] The possibility that this might occur was not however rejected completely if there were sufficient bad faith and flagrant enough breaches of the Code on the part of the searchers. *R v Nathaniel,*[8] where the police not only failed to follow the statutory instruction to destroy the DNA profile but in failing to do so broke the assurance under which they had secured the accused's agreement to provide it, is one of the few cases where such an argument has succeeded.

Many other common law jurisdictions seem readier to exclude evidence obtained by improper searches. In Scotland the discretion is inclusionary. Illegally obtained evidence is excluded in the absence of an excuse for its reception.[9] There are even signs that the discretion may exist under Scots law in civil cases, while there was no

---

19 It seems that the same will apply where although the document may have been obtained perfectly lawfully, for example on discovery, its use in different proceedings would amount to contempt: per Waller LJ in *Riddick v Thames Board Mills Ltd* [1977] QB 881, at 911, [1977] 3 All ER 677, at 702.

20 This statement of the law was explicitly approved by the Court of Appeal in *R v Khan* [1995] QB 27, [1994] 4 All ER 426, at 37B, 434c.

1 Above at 290, 395. Section 78 had been enacted, but not brought into force, at the relevant time.

2 *R v Apicella* (1985) 82 Cr App Rep 295.

3 *R v Cooke* [1995] 1 Cr App Rep 318.

4 *R v Stewart* [1995] Crim LR 500.

5 *R v Hughes* [1994] 1 WLR 876, 99 Cr App Rep 160. For the same result in New Zealand see *R v Roulston* [1998] 2 NZLR 468.

6 Even though given statutory force in the United Kingdom by the Diplomatic Privileges Act 1964.

7 *R v Khan, Sakkarevej and Pamarapa* [1997] Crim LR 508 where *R v Fennelley* [1989] Crim LR 142, one of the few cases to have excluded real evidence obtained by breach of the Code of Practice, was disavowed.

8 [1995] 2 Cr App R 565. Although the result seems to have been inspired by incompetence rather than dishonesty, and was achieved despite the decisive nature of the evidence in relation to the serious crime of rape.

9 *Lawrie v Muir* 1950 JC 19; *McGovern v HM Advocate* 1950 JC 33. In *HM Advocate v Turnbull* 1951 JC 96 the evidence was excluded by the judge. For a case in which the Scottish courts would have been prepared to receive illegally obtained evidence because of the danger that the accused would destroy the evidence against him, see *Hay v HM Advocate* 1968 JC 40.

parallel development in English procedure.[10] In the Scots divorce case of *Rattray v Rattray*,[11] it was held that a letter from the wife of the co-defendant must be received although it had been stolen from the post office by the husband who had suffered criminal punishment on account of his conduct. Lord Young dissented because he thought that the court was bound to take notice of the statute law enacting that the pursuer's conduct was a crime, and to reject as evidence anything obtained by a violation of the law. This case was followed in *Maccoll v Maccoll*,[12] but the judge said that, had he been a member of the court in *Rattray v Rattray* he would have dissented with Lord Young and on the same grounds.

In Canada, as noted above, the whole position is now governed by the Charter of Rights and Freedoms. This has adopted a position intermediate between the English[13] rule that evidence is in principle admissible however it has been obtained subject only to an exclusionary discretion, and the American rule that illegally obtained evidence must, in principle, be excluded. The Canadian compromise is to exclude evidence obtained in breach of the Charter, but only if its admission is likely to bring the administration of justice into disrepute. It is obvious that such a position requires detailed elaboration, and the Supreme Court of Canada has been deluged with appeals to this end. The leading case is still *R v Collins*,[14] which seems broadly to regard the administration of justice as brought into disrepute more by evidence secured by conscripting the accused against himself[15] than by other forms of illegality. The test also recognises that the administration of justice may sometimes also be brought into disrepute by the exclusion of reliable evidence, and that the good faith of the police,[16] or even the obnoxious reaction of the suspect,[17] may cure any technical illegality from this point of view.[18] The test does not however apply in its full rigour to administrative, as opposed to investigative acts, and thus not to the actions of a coroner in determining the cause of death.[19]

By contrast, in Australia, the position is determined by the common law and the following statement of Barwick CJ is applied:[20]

> On the one hand there is the public need to bring to conviction those who commit criminal offences. On the other hand there is the public interest in the protection of the individual from unlawful and unfair treatment. Convictions obtained with the aid of unlawful and unfair acts may be obtained at too high a price. Hence the judicial discretion.

10   At common law. Such a discretion is now provided under CPR 32.2.
11   (1897) 25 R (Ct of Sess) 315.
12   1946 SLT 312.
13   It also represented the previous position in Canada: see *R v Wray* (1970) 11 DLR (3d) 673.
14   [1987] 1 SCR 265, where Lamer J set out the principles according to which s 24(2) of the Charter was to be construed, although these have been under a process of continuing and considerable development, see eg *R v Burlingham* [1995] 2 SCR 206; *R v Stillman* [1997] 1 SCR 607. In *R v Silveira* [1995] 2 SCR 297 the court went so far as to institute prospective development by refusing to exclude evidence obtained by an illegal search while at the same time intimating that it would probably take a different view in similar circumstances in the future.
15   A concept extended to include the illegal obtention of constituent parts of the human body and its contents: see *R v Therens* [1985] 1 SCR 613 (breath); *R v Dersch* [1993] 3 SCR 768 (blood); *R v Stillman* (hair, saliva, mucous samples, and dental impressions); *R v Greffe* [1990] 1 SCR 755 (contents of rectum). It also applies to fingerprints obtained after an illegal arrest: *R v Feeney* [1997] 2 SCR 13.
16   Or other infringer of Charter priciples: see *R v Lerke* (1986) 25 DLR (4th) 403.
17   See *Tremblay v R* [1987] 2 SCR 435.
18   *Sieben v R* [1987] 1 SCR 295.
19   *R v Colarusso* [1994] 1 SCR 20.
20   *R v Ireland* (1970) 126 CLR 321, at 335.

The notions of public policy and fairness are combined in this statement. The former is predominant in the following remark made by Kingsmill Moore J in the Supreme Court of Eire:[1] 'I am disposed to lay emphasis not so much on alleged unfairness to the accused as on the public interest that the law should be observed in the investigation of crime.' It is interesting that in *King v R*[2] a similar policy was found by the Privy Council to underlie the common law discretion.

2. Perpetration of illegal acts[3]

Sometimes the impropriety occurs not in searching for evidence, but in inducing, or even participating in, the commission of the crime charged. Since entrapment is not of itself a substantive defence to a criminal prosecution in England,[4] or in most other common law jurisdictions,[5] it was held in *R v Sang* that such a rule would be undermined by the automatic exclusion of evidence obtained of a crime committed in such circumstances.[6]

The most controversial aspect of *R v Sang* related to the application of the court's discretion to exclude such evidence, and eventually led in England to the passage of s 78 of the Police and Criminal Evidence Act 1984. It is thus necessary to consider the impact of discretion. It should be noted that this will involve consideration, not only of the discretion to exclude unfairly obtained evidence, but also the court's inherent discretion to stay proceedings for abuse of process. In *R v Horseferry Road Magistrates' Court, ex p Bennett*[7] this power was justified as based upon refusal to countenance behaviour that threatened the rule of law, and as amounting to violations of international law, and the law of another state. In that case the accused had been brought into this country by a stratagem designed to overcome the absence of an extradition treaty with the relevant foreign jurisdiction. In *R v Latif; R v Shahzad*[8] this reasoning was applied in a case where the accused were tried for being concerned in the fraudulent importation of a controlled drug, when the gang had been infiltrated by the authorities, and the actual illegal importation accomplished by an informer and a customs agent. Lord Steyn accepted that in those circumstances the judge was obliged to maintain the integrity of the criminal justice system, and:[9]

> must weigh in the balance the public interest in ensuring that those that are charged with grave crimes should be tried and the competing public interest in not

1   *People (A-G) v O'Brien* [1965] IR 142, at 160.
2   [1969] 1 AC 304, at 319F. The search must not have constituted 'conduct of which the Crown ought not to take advantage.'
3   For a fuller discussion see Birch [1994] CLP 73.
4   *R v McEvilly* (1973) 60 Cr App Rep 150; *R v Mealey* (1974) 60 Cr App Rep 59, approved in *R v Sang* [1980] AC 402, [1979] 2 All ER 1222, at 432A, 1226e.
5   See in Australia, *Ridgeway v R* (1995) 184 CLR 19, at 30; in Canada, *R v Mack* [1988] 2 SCR 903, at 947; and in New Zealand, *R v Katipa* [1986] 2 NZLR 121, at 125. Though sometimes it may be in the United States, see *US v Russell* 411 US 423 (1973), at 435.
6   At 433D, 1227f. This view was affirmed in *R v Smurthwaite; R v Gill* [1994] 1 All ER 898, 98 Cr App Rep 437, at 902f, 440. In the United States much turns on the extent to which the suspect is predisposed to commission of the crime: see *Jacobson v US* (1992) 503 US 540 where the evidence of a minor crime was excluded after an over two-year campaign by government agents to secure its commission by the accused. Predisposition seems also important in the jurisdiction of the European Court of Human Rights: see *Texeira de Castro v Portugal* [1998] Crim LR 751.
7   [1994] AC 42; see eg 62A, 67G.
8   [1996] 1 All ER 353, [1996] 1 WLR 104.
9   At 361d, 113B.

conveying the impression that the court will adopt the approach that the end justifies any means.

Although on the facts he found there to be no case for a stay[10] he recognised that where the conduct was still more unworthy or shameful the result might not be the same. It is enlightening to compare this approach with that adopted by the High Court of Australia on rather similar facts in *Ridgeway v R*[11] where it was also said[12] that 'the basis in principle of this discretion lies in the inherent or implied powers of our courts to protect the integrity of their processes'. There too the case embodied a classical 'sting' operation, whereby the police acting through undercover agents infiltrated a drug smuggling operation, and co-operated in the illegal importation of drugs into Australia in order to secure an arrest within the jurisdiction. The accused was charged with possession of the illegally imported drugs.[13] The element of illegal importation caused the problem. It had to be proved[14] because it was an essential element of the offence, yet it had been committed by the police themselves. This stuck in the craw of the majority. It held that where commission of an offence has been procured by agents of the state it would be in only a rare case[15] that prosecution would be appropriate. The remedy involved a stay of the proceedings for abuse of the process of the courts. Much of the discussion in the case considers the relationship of such a remedy to that of the discretionary exclusion of evidence. There is a clear overlap since the exclusion of the illegally obtained evidence might leave so little that a prosecution would inevitably fail, and to bring a prosecution that will inevitably fail is clearly an abuse of process. It is surprising that so little attention has hitherto[16] been devoted by the courts[17] in this jurisdiction to the relationship between that remedy and the exclusion of evidence under s 78.[18]

In those cases the participation of the authorities in the crime was active, and the identities of at least some of the potential law-breakers known. In *Williams v DPP*[19] neither was the case. The police simply left an apparently vulnerable vehicle in an area where thefts from vehicles were common. It was held that the evidence of the accused's actions in attempting to steal the contents of the vehicle was admissible, and that its admission was not so unfair as to trigger the operation of s 78. The court refused to

10   Or to exercise the s 78 discretion to exclude the evidence of the illegal importation.

11   (1995) 184 CLR 19. See also in Canada *Campbell and Shirose v R* (1998) SCC, 22 April. See further Grevling (1996) 112 LQR 401.

12   At 31, the reference is to the *Bunning v Cross* discretion.

13   Contrary to s 233B(1) Customs Act 1901 (Cwth).

14   It would not have had to be proved under state offences of possession of illegal substances, and the majority, rather surprisingly in view of their apparent outrage at the procedure in the Commonwealth prosecution, regarded prosecution for such offences as not merely tolerable, but even to justify quashing the convictions for the Commonwealth offences.

15   For example where there was no high level involvement, and the officers actually involved have been punished.

16   It has now been addressed in *R v Chalkley* [1998] QB 848, [1998] 2 All ER 155 in the context of a stratagem to install a listening device: see below 507.

17   But see Choo *Abuse of Process and Judicial Stays of Criminal Proceedings* (1993) especially ch 4 for extended academic consideration.

18   In *R v Latif* [1996] 1 All ER 353, [1996] 1 WLR 104 where the issues were similar to those in *Ridgeway v R* and both issues were raised, the House of Lords simply regarded the s 78 question as concluded by its refusal of a stay for abuse of process; while in *R v Khan* no question of abuse of process was raised at all, despite the prosecution's evidence having been derived from a deliberate decision at a high level within the police to indulge in illegality to attempt to secure it.

19   [1993] 3 All ER 365, 98 Cr App Rep 209. For a similar decision in Canada see *R v Barnes* [1991] 1 SCR 449 where the character of the area was crucial (despite more active involvement by the police).

distinguish this situation from one in which the offence had already been committed,[20] or from those discussed above where the role of the police had been more active.

In all of these cases it was an inherent part of the plan that the relevant crime should be committed. Sometimes it is not intended to go so far, and to stop short at the point at which evidence of an intention to commit the crime has been gathered with a view to prosecution for an inchoate offence. Here again there has been reluctance to employ the discretion in s 78 to exclude the evidence. Thus in *R v Smurthwaite; R v Gill*[1] the court refused to exclude evidence secured by an undercover police officer posing as a contract killer. The court did however accept that the role of the police as agents provocateurs was a relevant consideration to weigh in the balance, although it was felt that no precise guidance could or should be given on the operation of s 78 in this area.[2]

3.   Improper interception or recording of communications[3]

Evidence of communications encouraged by the police and then intercepted were not automatically inadmissible as such at common law.[4] It has also been held irrelevant that the accused would not have spoken had he not been misled into believing that his words were not being recorded.[5] In *R v Maqsud Ali; R v Ashiq Hussain*[6] the use of a hidden tape recorder in a public building to record the conversation of two suspects was regarded as acceptable. Even the performance of an elaborate charade to encourage the suspects to believe that the police had not installed such a device has been allowed. Nor was it held sufficient to exclude that there had probably been a breach of the Code of Practice for Police Questioning, and arguably breach of the spirit of the Code, in that the accused had been charged, and chosen to exercise a right of silence, but then manipulated into a situation in which it was likely[7] that they would speak, and that the police would be able to record what they said.[8] Only in the case of telephone calls made from police premises is there provision in the Code of Practice for warning the suspect that the call may be overheard.[9]

The interception of telephone calls, having been declared by the European Court of Human Rights to require guarantees against abuse,[10] was subjected to statutory control in the Interception of Communications Act 1985, perhaps designed[11] to prevent the

---

20   *R v Christou* [1992] QB 979, [1992] 4 All ER 559.

1   [1994] 1 All ER 898, 98 Cr App Rep 437; see also *R v Dixon; R v Mann* [1995] Crim LR 647 where the result was the same in very similar circumstances.

2   See also *R v Governor of Pentonville Prison, ex p Chinoy* [1992] 1 All ER 317 where the entrapment related to crimes under foreign law for which extradition was sought.

3   See further Carter (1997) 113 LQR 468, Uglow [1999] Crim LR 287.

4   *R v Derrington* (1826) 2 C & P 418, where a letter obtained from the prisoner by the turnkey under a false promise that he would post it was admitted in evidence for the prosecution. Similarly in *R v Keeton* (1970) 54 Cr App Rep 267 it was irrelevant that the accused assumed that a telephone call to his wife from the police station would not be intercepted and put in evidence.

5   *R v Buchan* [1964] 1 All ER 502, [1964] 1 WLR 365.

6   [1966] 1 QB 688, [1965] 2 All ER 464. See also *R v Mills; R v Rose* [1962] 3 All ER 298, [1962] 1 WLR 1152; *R v Stewart* [1970] 1 All ER 689n, [1970] 1 WLR 907.

7   Despite having been warned by their own lawyers that just such a stratagem was likely to be tried by the police.

8   *R v Bailey* [1993] 3 All ER 513, 97 Cr App Rep 365 where many of the earlier cases are reviewed.

9   Code C para 5.7 reversing the previous position as determined in *R v Keeton* (1970) 54 Cr App Rep 267.

10   *Malone v United Kingdom* (1984) 7 EHRR 14.

11   Section 2(2) as interpreted in *R v Preston* [1994] 2 AC 130, at 169, [1993] 4 All ER 638, at 669.

use of intercepted material from being used in evidence.[12] This is however interpreted strictly, and does not apply to interception where one of the parties consents,[13] or where the device is not in fact part of the public telecommunications service,[14] or even to cases where no warrant has issued.[15] It has understandably been held not to be conclusive, although fit to be taken into consideration in the exercise of the s 78 discretion, that the interception took place overseas, and in breach of foreign or international law, since breach of such a law should not be more weighty in the English courts than breach of English law.[16] The lack of territorial effect seems also to prevent acts which would be illegal in England from leading to discretionary exclusion when in conformity with the law in the jurisdiction in which they were done.[17] It seems that where a telephone call is recorded by one of the parties to it in an attempt to secure evidence, that one of the considerations relating to the operation of s 78 is the extent to which this method has been employed to evade the restrictions of the Code of Practice on Police Questioning.[18]

Sometimes the recording is made on a free-standing device rather than through interception or recording of a telephone conversation.[19] This situation was considered

12   A different approach was however taken in the Intelligence Services Act 1994, s 2(2)(a)(iv). Both the Security Services Act 1996, s 1(1) and the Police Act 1997, s 93(2)(a) use the terminology of the Interception of Communications Act 1985, s 2(2), though they lack any close equivalent to s 9 of that Act positively forbidding reference to intercepted communications. There is however in the terminology of s 103(3) of the Police Act 1997 some indication of an assumption that the evidence can be used in the prosecution of crime as well as in its detection and investigation, and this is emphasised in the Code of Practice issued to implement the Act. *Intrusive Surveillance*: see Guidance Note 1A, para 2.28. The government has announced its intention to review the operation of the Interception of Communications Act 1985: see statement of Home Secretary to House of Commons on 2 September 1998, 1799 Official Report col 749.
13   See *R v Cadette* [1995] Crim LR 229; *R v Rasool* [1997] 4 All ER 439, [1997] 1 WLR 1092 where more controversially it was also held that no cross-examination could be conducted to show that the interception was not consensual: see also *R v Owen: R v Stephen* [1999] Crim LR 406. Recording of a call by one party without the knowledge of the other has also been upheld elsewhere: see eg in New Zealand *Talbot v Air New Zealand Ltd* [1996] 1 NZLR 414.
14   As the transmission between a base unit and a cordless telephone receiver was held not to be in *R v Effik* [1995] 1 AC 309, [1994] 3 All ER 458; and it is immaterial that it emanates from abroad: *R v Taylor-Sabori* [1999] 1 All ER 160. Such an interception may however infringe the European Convention of Human Rights if conducted without positive statutory authorisation, *Halford v United Kingdom* [1998] Crim LR 753.
15   *Morgans v DPP* [1998] 1 WLR 968 where it was held in reliance upon dicta of Buxton LJ in *R v Owen and Stephen* that the House of Lords in *R v Preston* had left the reasoning in the Court of Appeal in *R v Effick* unaffected in that situation.
16   *R v Governor of Pentonville Prison, ex p Chinoy* [1992] 1 All ER 317; see also *R v Aujla* [1998] 2 Cr App Rep 16.
17   *R v Konscol* [1993] Crim LR 950. In Canada, a distinction is drawn between the acts of Canadians outside the jurisdiction which is governed by the Charter and the acts of foreigners which are not: *Harrer v R* [1995] 3 SCR 562; in the United States the evidence will be admissible even though the acts are performed in the foreign jurisdiction by US citizens: *US v Verdugo-Urquidez* 494 US 259 (1990). See Mackarel and Gane [1997] Crim LR 720.
18   Thus in *R v H* [1987] Crim LR 47 where the accused had already been arrested and questioned a further telephone call from the alleged victim seeking to elicit incriminating remarks was held to be inadmissible, whereas in *R v Jelen and Katz* (1990) 90 Cr App Rep 456 where matters were at a much earlier stage evidence of a call was not excluded, although had an interview been conducted the accused would have had to be cautioned.
19   The situations are closely connected since a free-standing device might pick up a telephone call, and in some cases where both techniques have been used the Court has not thought it necessary to distinguish between them. See also *Code of Practice Intrusive Surveillance* Note for Guidance 1A which adverts to this very problem in relation to the new procedures under the Police Act 1997 which were designed to regularise the situation revealed in *R v Khan*.

by the House of Lords in *R v Khan*. A listening device had been installed in the house of a third party, and while the accused was there as a visitor he was heard to confess to the crime with which he was subsequently charged. The installation of the listening device had no statutory authorisation, involved civil trespass, probably constituted a criminal offence, and perhaps infringed art 8 of the European Convention of Human Rights.[20] The House of Lords held that in view of the veniality of these matters, and the seriousness of the offence with which the accused was charged, the trial judge's refusal to exclude the evidence under s 78 was justified. Where there is less illegality and more deception in the conduct of the police as in *R v Chalkley; R v Jeffries*[1] the result is the same. It was however stressed in that case that the criteria for exercising the discretion to stay for abuse of process were quite distinct from those which apply to that to exclude evidence under s 78:[2]

> The exercise for the judge under s 78 is not the marking of his disapproval of the prosecution's breach, if any, of the law in the conduct of the investigation or the proceedings, by a discretionary decision to stay them, but an examination of the question whether it would be unfair to the defendant to admit the evidence.

4. Deception[3]

Many of the situations considered above include elements of deception, and this final residual category is intended to encompass principally those where the deception is primarily designed to generate evidence of offences which have already been committed, otherwise than by improper searches or the use of electronic interception of communications. The clearest example in modern English law is provided by *R v Christou*[4] where the police engaged in an elaborate and long-running operation to secure evidence of theft, by operating a shop which bought and sold jewellery.[5] The Court of Appeal took the view that the evidence obtained from this operation in the form of video and aural recordings, including evidence of incriminating conversations with the undercover operators, and real evidence in the shape of fingerprints, was admissible. It was regarded as important that the operation had no precise targets,[6] and that there was no attempt to subvert the operation of the Codes of Practice by the simple expedient of pretending not to be police officers.[7] This aspect of the decision was underlined soon afterwards by the decision in *R v Bryce*[8] where evidence of an

---

20 Although it was conceded by counsel that his argument would have been the same had only the last of these been the case.

1 [1998] 2 All ER 155, the police wished to secure access to the accused's home to service a recording device, and arranged to secure a warrant for their arrest on quite separate charges so as to secure their absence from home during the relevant period.

2 At 180b.

3 See further Ashworth 114 LQR 108 (1998).

4 [1992] QB 979, [1992] 4 All ER 559.

5 The shop offered market rates, and the trial judge's view that the offences had already been committed seems to have been accepted, so as to rebut allegations of entrapment. This is however dubious in view of the charges of handling, and the court's own later treatment, at 991G, 567b of allegations of facilitation of crime.

6 See at 989A, 564h 'the trick was not applied to the appellants; they voluntarily applied themselves to the trick.' See also *R v Lin, Hung and Tsui* [1995] Crim LR 817 where the accused were targeted by the undercover officers, but in respect of a different crime.

7 At 991C, 566h. Although breach alone will not necessarily be enough to trigger the discretion, even when it results in there not being an objective record of what had been said: see *R v Edwards* [1997] Crim LR 348.

8 [1992] 4 All ER 567, 95 Cr App R 320.

incriminating conversation between an undercover police officer and the accused was excluded under the s 78 discretion because it was felt that the operation did subvert the Codes. In particular the police already had reason to suspect the accused, they asked questions going critically to guilt, and they failed to secure any adequate recording of the alleged statements.[9] Similarly if the undercover agent plays too active a part in eliciting the evidence it is more likely to be excluded.[10]

It is extremely common for the police to seek evidence of a crime by attempting to deceive the suspect into believing that an undercover police officer, or a member of the public, is a secure confidant for the suspect, and then to record any incriminating statements or admissions that he might make. In England, although it has repeatedly been denied that any general principles operate, it seems that evidence obtained in this way is more likely to be admitted than in many other Commonwealth jurisdictions. In *R v Roberts*[11] the police had good reason to believe that one of two suspects would attempt to persuade the other to exculpate him, and in so doing inculpate himself. They accordingly, and covertly, fitted recording devices in the suspects' cells. The resulting admissions were held to be admissible, and the trial judge's decision not to exclude them under the s 78 discretion was upheld, despite the fact that both had been charged with the relevant offences, and the accused had asserted his right to remain silent. On the other hand the court went out of its way to stress several factors in the situation with the implication that if they had been different they would have militated in favour of exclusion. In particular the court emphasised its belief that the second suspect was not in active collusion with the police, that they still harboured hopes of convicting him, that they were concerned to recover a firearm which had been used, that proper authority had been obtained for the installation of recording apparatus into the cells, and that neither of the suspects knew that the cells were so fitted out. This decision may be contrasted with decisions,[12] and even legislation,[13] elsewhere, although it must be stressed that in some jurisdictions there are relevant constitutional differences, and in none is there anything approaching the detailed guidance provided here by the Codes of Practice for interviews known to be by or on behalf of the police.

C. CONCLUSION

In conclusion it is submitted that the remarks of Cardozo J and Holmes J which were cited at the outset of this discussion are both tendentious. So far as those of Cardozo J

---

9   Which the accused denied (even if unconvincingly).
10   As in *R v Hall* (unreported, Leeds Crown Court, 2 March 1994) and *R v Stagg* (unreported, Central Criminal Court, 14 September 1994) in both of which undercover female police officers exploited the sexual predilections of the male suspects as a means of eliciting the evidence. Compare *R v Kennedy* [1998] Crim LR 739 where an element of enticement of a prisoner to speak by psychiatrists and a probation officer was held insufficient.
11   [1997] 1 Cr App Rep 217.
12   It is possible to do no more than indicate the trend of the most important recent decisions. In Australia, discretion has been exercised to exclude evidence elicited by an undercover police officer from a suspect who had been charged, and under the Judges' Rules was entitled no longer to be questioned in the absence of a caution; but not in another case where the evidence was secured by an associate of the accused whom the police expected to attempt to persuade the accused to exculpate him: *R v Swaffield; Pavic v R* (1998) 151 ALR 98; in Canada, evidence secured both by an undercover policeman sharing the suspect's cell: *R v Hebert* [1990] 2 SCR 151; or by the use of a member of the public acting on the instructions of the police: *R v Broyles* [1991] 3 SCR 595; has been excluded by discretion under the Charter; in the United States, no caution was required in the case of an undercover police officer posing as a fellow criminal in respect of a conversation recorded in a cell: *Illinois v Perkins* 496 US 292 (1990).
13   Eg Criminal Law (Undercover Operations) Act 1995 in South Australia.

are concerned, if a room is searched and a dead body is found in it, it would certainly be a terrible thing if the guilty occupant were allowed to go free on a charge of murder because the search was technically illegal, but there must be some limit to this doctrine. What if admission were gained to the room in consequence of a violent assault, or what if the whereabouts of the corpse were ascertained by means of prolonged torture of the accused? On the other hand, in spite of the contrary opinion of Holmes J, the government does not foster and pay for other crimes whenever illegally obtained evidence is admitted. It is a mistake to suppose that the choice lies between admitting the evidence and leaving the aggrieved party to pursue such civil or criminal remedies against the wrongdoer as may be available, or rejecting the evidence as a warning to officialdom that convictions cannot be obtained by illegal action. Such an approach assumes that the conduct of the police is exclusively influenced by the number of convictions obtained. It leaves out of account the all-important sanctions provided by the opinion of those who pursue the same occupation as the person by whom the evidence was illegally obtained. Is it to be supposed that when the Lord Chief Justice said, 'The sooner the Bristol police study, learn and abide by the Judges' Rules, the better',[14] the conduct of the police of Bristol was unaffected because his Lordship admitted a confession obtained in consequence of a breach of those rules? What was deplorable was the total absence of criticism of the behaviour in cases such as *Jeffrey v Black*[15] where there was no element of emergency and the suspected offence was comparatively venial. Since the enactment of the Police and Criminal Evidence Act 1984 and the implementation of the Codes of Practice under s 66 a more healthily critical attitude has become apparent.[16] In spite of the great weight of opinion to the contrary, too much importance may be attached to the rejection of illegally obtained evidence as an incentive to good behaviour on the part of the police.[17] Delinquent behaviour, it is felt, is prompted more by the hope that it will not be brought to the notice of the court,[18] than by the belief that evidence discovered in consequence of it will be received in any event.

14 *R v Mills and Lemon* [1947] KB 297, at 299, [1946] 2 All ER 776, at 777. The effect is likely to be stronger still if the Canadian approach in *R v Silveira* [1995] 2 SCR 297 of complementing such disapproval with a threat to exclude in the future if the practice should persist.
15 [1978] QB 490, [1978] 1 All ER 555.
16 It may become still more apparent when the Human Rights Act 1998 comes to be implemented. For a foretaste of the arguments see JUSTICE *Under Surveillance* (1998) esp ch 3.
17 It is noteworthy that substantial exemplary damages may be awarded against the police in respect of assaults upon accused persons even though the evidence thereby secured resulted in a conviction, *Treadaway v Chief Constable of West Midlands* (1994) Times, 25 October.
18 By precipitating a plea of guilty it may often achieve its purpose behind the scenes.

CHAPTER XII

Opinion[1]

The law relating to evidence of opinion is much less developed in the United Kingdom than it is in North America where as long ago as 1898, Thayer said, 'the quantity of decisions on the subject is most unreasonably swollen'.[2] In 1940, Wigmore felt able to assert that, so far as the United States was concerned, the rule 'had done more than any other rule of procedure to reduce our litigation towards a state of legalised gambling'.[3] In England, the reported decisions on the subject are comparatively few, and it is difficult to believe that the exclusionary rule gives rise to very much trouble in practice. There are however some theoretical difficulties, and some residual problems in criminal cases.[4] In the area of procedure however Lord Woolf concluded that the development and cost of a system of expert witnesses was one of the principal blemishes upon the process of litigation, and recommended radical procedural reform, which has now been implemented in Part 35 of the Civil Procedure Rules.

This chapter will first consider the rationale of the rule, and especially the nature of its relationship to the rules excluding hearsay to be examined in greater detail in the chapters which follow. The operation of the rule will then be illustrated, together with the two areas of expert and non-expert opinion where there are exceptions, and the final section will deal with reform of the rule.

SECTION I.   RATIONALE OF THE RULE

A.   STATEMENT OF THE RULE

A witness may not give his opinion on matters which the court considers call for the special skill or knowledge of an expert unless he is an expert in such matters, and he

---

1   See generally, Hodgkinson *Expert Evidence: Law and Practice* (1990); Law Commission of New Zealand Preliminary paper No 18 'Evidence Law: Expert Evidence and Opinion Evidence' (1991); Woolf Report: *Access to Justice* (1996) ch. 13; the Civil Procedure Rules Part 35.
2   *Preliminary Treatise on Evidence at the Common Law* 525. By 1990, 86% of trials in California heard expert testimony, and on average there were 3.3 experts per trial, Gross (1991) Wisc LR 1113, at 1119.
3   VII Wigmore p 27.
4   Which was left unaffected by the passage of the Civil Evidence Act 1972 which enacted the principal recommendations of the Law Reform Committee's 17th Report.

may not give his opinion on other matters if the facts upon which it is based can be stated without reference to it in a manner equally conducive to the ascertainment of the truth.[5]

There are thus two broad spheres of evidence of opinion. The first concerns matters calling for specialised skill or knowledge. In this sphere the only questions are whether the subject of inquiry does raise issues calling for expertise and whether the witness is a qualified expert. This part of the rule is exclusionary only in the sense that the testimony of non-experts is excluded on matters calling for a specialist. In the residuary non-expert sphere, evidence of opinion will be excluded if the subject is one with regard to which fact and inference can conveniently be kept separate. In *R v Robb*[6] these two spheres overlapped in relation to the identification of the voice of the accused on the telephone, with expert opinion admitted from an auditory specialist, and evidence of composite fact admitted from police officers who had become familiar with the voice of the accused.[7]

B. NATURE OF OPINION

In the law of evidence 'opinion' means any inference from observed facts, and the law on the subject derives from the general rule that witnesses must speak only to that which was directly observed by them. The treatment of evidence of opinion by English law is based on the assumption that it is possible to draw a sharp distinction between inferences and the facts on which they are based.[8] The drawing of inferences is said to be the function of the judge or jury, while it is the business of a witness to state facts. But the law recognises that, so far as matters calling for special knowledge or skill are concerned, judges and jurors are not necessarily equipped to draw the right inferences from facts stated by witnesses. A witness is therefore allowed to state his opinion with regard to such matters provided he is expert in them.

Although the distinction between fact and inference is clear enough up to a point, there are borderline cases. The statement that a car was being driven on the left side of the road is essentially one of fact[9], while the assertion that a particular piece of driving was negligent is equally a matter of inference from observed facts. Statements concerning speed, temperature, or the identity of persons,[10] things[11] and handwriting

5   See *Sherrard v Jacob* [1965] NI 151, at 157,8 per Lord MacDermott.
6   (1991) 93 Cr App Rep 161.
7   The accused did not testify so the jury did not have sufficient opportunity to hear his voice live in Court; whereas in *R v Hersey* [1998] Crim LR 281, where there was no auditory record but a witness testified to recognising the accused's voice at the time of the crime, and confirmed it on a staged voice comparison, expert evidence was not admitted.
8   For an alternative view based upon the disputability of an assertion, see Cox J in *R v Perry (No 4)* (1982) 28 SASR 119, at 123.
9   Though even there the statement may verge on opinion if the witness did not have a clear view, or if the car were near the centre of the road, or if the relevant point of time were not precisely that of the observation.
10 In *R v Stockwell* (1993) 97 Cr App Rep 260 the court distinguished between a clear case of identification from a photograph where the jury could decide for itself as a matter of fact, and the case where the accused had been disguised and expert evidence of opinion was appropriate. See also *R v Clare; R v Peach* [1995] 2 Cr App Rep 333 where a security video film was short and confused and a police offficer acquired expertise by studying it, and was permitted to testify as an expert in the interpretation of that film. This is not unlike the expertise of the audio typist in *Hopes and Lavery v HM Advocate* 1960 JC 104. Knowledge of the appearance of the accused at the time of the crime was not however in Australia sufficient to qualify the police to give expert evidence of the identification of the accused when disguised by wearing a stocking mask: *R v Griffith* (1995) 79 ACR 125.
11 See eg *R v Barker* (1988) 34 ACR 141 where it was denied that a police officer's evidence that pipes were of the type used for smoking marijuana was opinion rather than fact.

are, however, indissolubly composed of fact and inference. Similarly a witness's view of what another would do in certain circumstances is a matter of opinion, but his view of what he himself would do is a matter of fact.[12] The law makes allowances for these borderline cases by permitting witnesses to state their opinions with regard to matters not calling for special knowledge whenever it would be virtually impossible for them to separate their inferences from the facts on which those inferences are based.

In so far as is possible for them to do so, the courts set themselves against receiving evidence from any witness as to the very matter which the judge or jury has to decide. This is because litigants are entitled to have their disputes settled by a judge, with or without a jury, and not by the statements of witnesses. If witnesses are too readily allowed to give their opinion concerning an ultimate issue, there is a serious danger that the jury will be unduly influenced, yet it must always be free to reject even unanimous expert evidence, for example if it rejects the facts upon which it is based.[13] Even when they are receiving expert evidence, it has generally been the practice of the judges to prevent a witness from stating his opinion on an ultimate issue, such as the reasonableness of a covenant in restraint of trade,[14] the validity of a patent, or the construction of a document: 'The admission of the opinion of eminent experts upon the issues leads to the balance of opinions and tends to shift responsibility from the bench or the jury to the witness box.'[15] The exclusion of opinion evidence on the ultimate issue can easily become something of a fetish, and we shall see that the law has been explicitly relaxed for civil proceedings by s 3 of the Civil Evidence Act 1972.[16]

C.   REASONS FOR EXCLUDING EVIDENCE OF OPINION

There have been two main and two subsidiary reasons for the exclusion of those kinds of evidence of opinion that fall within the rule stated at the beginning of this chapter. The two main reasons are founded on the principle that evidence of opinion is excluded when its reception would not assist, and might even mislead, the court. In the first place it is said that opinion evidence is irrelevant,[17] and this is largely true of non-expert opinion on a subject requiring expertise as well as opinion evidence concerning matters which do not call for expertise, although some writers prefer to say that the evidence is insufficiently relevant to be admissible.[18] Secondly, it is said that the reception of opinion evidence would usurp the functions of the jury. To the extent that this suggests that the witness might undesirably indicate what factual evidence he accepted or rejected, the danger can be avoided by stressing the hypothetical basis for any opinion;[19] to the extent that it suggests an opinion might be unduly influential, it will be discussed below.

The two subsidiary reasons for the rejection of certain kinds of evidence of opinion are the fact that a witness who merely speaks to his opinion cannot be prosecuted for

---

12   *Allstate Life Ins Co v ANZ Banking Pty Ltd* (1996) 136 ALR 627.
13   *R v Ratti* [1991] 1 SCR 68.
14   *Haynes v Doman* [1899] 2 Ch 13.
15   *Joseph Crosfield & Sons Ltd v Techno-Chemical Laboratories Ltd* (1913) 29 TLR 378, at 379.
16   But no similar statutory relaxation has been made for criminal proceedings, contrary to the recommendation of the Criminal Law Revision Committee, see Cmnd 4991, para 270, and draft Bill, cl 43. See further below p 519
17   Goddard LJ in *Hollington v Hewthorn & Co Ltd* [1943] KB 587, at 595, [1943] 2 All ER 35, at 40.
18   Cowen and Carter *Essays on the Law of Evidence* 169.
19   Though a long hypothetical tracking all of the alleged facts may itself be prejudicial, see *R v Ryan* (1993) 80 CCC (3d) 514.

perjury,[20] and the danger that the reception of such evidence might indirectly evade other exclusionary rules. The first reason is of some antiquity,[1] but, although Lord Mansfield had it in mind when he said, in *Folkes v Chadd*,[2] that Mr Smeaton could have been prosecuted if he had wilfully given false testimony, no great stress is placed upon it at the present day. As a matter of substantive law, the precise extent of the proposition is debatable. There is more force in the second reason, but it has not been much mooted by the judges. The exclusionary rules most likely to be indirectly infringed by the reception of opinion evidence are those according to which irrelevant matter and hearsay are inadmissible, and those limiting the reception of the findings of other tribunals. A witness can always be cross-examined on the grounds for his opinion, and, if these appear to be irrelevant the evidence can be ignored. The relationship of the opinion rule to the rule against hearsay calls for separate consideration.

D. RELATION TO THE HEARSAY RULE

The rule with regard to evidence of opinion originated in the same doctrine as that to which the rule against hearsay can be traced—every witness must be able to say that he had seen or heard that to which he deposes. He must have been 'oyant' and 'voyant',[3] but the two rules are now quite distinct although the same item of evidence may occasionally call for a consideration of both of them. For example, A is prepared to swear that he heard B, who witnessed a collision between two cars driven by C and D, say, some time after the event, that it was due to the negligence of D. A's evidence would clearly infringe the rule against hearsay if tendered to prove D's negligence on his prosecution for careless driving, because an assertion other than one made by a person while giving oral evidence would be tendered as evidence of the truth of that which was asserted. The evidence would also be inadmissible because B's assertion was an assertion of opinion of a kind that could not have been received if proffered by B himself from the witness box. If A had been at hand at the time of the collision, and he had heard B make some exclamation concerning the negligent manner in which D was driving, it is possible that he would be allowed to relate the assertion as evidence of D's negligence, although B was not called as a witness.[4] This is because there may be an exception to the rule against hearsay covering exclamations concerning an event made contemporaneously with its occurrence. So far as the opinion rule is concerned, B's opinion was spontaneous, or impulsive, as it was not the result of deliberation on his part; accordingly A's evidence as to what B said would probably be admissible.

The leading case on evidence calling for consideration of both the hearsay and the opinion rules is *Wright v Doe d Tatham*[5] which was elaborately argued on three occasions between 1830 and 1838. The sanity of a deceased testator named Marsden was in issue, and those who contended that he was sane when he executed his will tendered three letters written to him by acquaintances at the time. The writers of these letters had since died, and it was contended that the documents ought to be received (a) because they concerned business matters and showed that their authors regarded the addressee as sane, and (b) because Marsden displayed his sanity in the manner in

---

20   And is not liable for negligence in respect of expert evidence tendered in court or contained in a witness statement, *Stanton v Callaghan* [1998] 4 All ER 961.
1   *Adams v Canon* (1621) 1 Dyer 53b.
2   (1782) 3 Doug KB 157; see p 521 below.
3   Thayer *Preliminary Treatise on Evidence at the Common Law* 523,4.
4   See per Pollock CB in *Milne v Leisler* (1862) 7 H & N 786, at 796.
5   (1838) 4 Bing NC 489. An analogous case is *Backhouse v Jones* (1839) 9 LJCP 99 where the statements were oral.

which he acted on the letters. They were rejected in the Court of King's Bench, the judges in Exchequer Chamber were evenly divided and a majority of the judges advised the House of Lords that the letters were inadmissible. The judgment of the King's Bench was accordingly affirmed. The second ground upon which it was contended that the letters should be received was of no particular moment as it raised a question of fact. Evidence of the conduct of the testator is always admissible in such a case provided it is relevant, but the majority view was that there was no sufficient proof that Marsden had acted on the letters so as to indicate a rational appreciation of their contents. The first ground upon which it was contended that the evidence was admissible raised problems in connection with the rule against hearsay and the reception of opinion which have never since been so fully examined in England.[6] The letters indicated that the writers treated Marsden as sane, therefore they were equivalent to an assertion of that fact, therefore they infringed the rule against hearsay, and the majority of the judgments proceeded on this footing. If the writers of the letters had been called as witnesses they could have been asked for their views concerning the testator's sanity. However, it does not follow that a layman's opinion on such an issue is admissible because the question is, as we have seen, merely 'a compendious mode of ascertaining the result of the actual observation of the witness, from acts done, as to the habits and demeanour of the deceased'. Accordingly it is arguable that the letters had to be rejected both because their reception would have infringed the rule against hearsay and also because they were mere statements of opinion on a matter with regard to which an ordinary witness's opinion, unsupported by details concerning his observations, would have been inadmissible. This seems to have been the view of the majority of the judges, although it was only Parke B who gave much consideration to this aspect of the case.

An opinion is generally admissible only if it is based upon facts which have been, or are to be, proved by admissible evidence,[7] or have been admitted.[8] It follows that it may not be based upon hearsay, unless it can be admitted notwithstanding the rule excluding hearsay. It may be useful to summarise these situations.[9] In some cases the opinion may be based upon statements which fall within an exception to the hearsay rule. In civil cases the matter is now governed entirely by statute as will be explained in ch XIV below. Thus if an expert relies for his opinion upon facts related to him by a third party who had observed them, this would provide a sufficient foundation for the admissibility of his opinion. Spontaneous statements made in the circumstances examined more fully in ch XV below may also provide such a foundation. A more usual situation is one in which the opinion is based upon expertise in part derived from hearsay material, which may indeed be incorporated into the expert's evidence, notwithstanding that he has no personal knowledge of its factual basis, and which may either be in the form of general works of reference,[10] particular studies,[11] or information gleaned from

6   Though they were re-examined by the House of Lords in *R v Kearley* [1992] 2 AC 228, [1992] 2 All ER 345; and for a very thorough examination in Canada, see *R v Zundel* (1987) 35 DLR (4th) 338, at 384.

7   See eg *Blagojevic v HM Advocate* 1995 SLT 1189 where the accused had not testified to the pressure alleged against the police, and upon which the expert opinion was premised.

8   See *R v Jackson* [1996] 2 Cr App Rep 420, where this is strongly suggested as a means of saving expense, and see the suggestions of the Law Commission, below p 527. It is important that any admission be not only of the fact that the evidence involves expertise, but also of the facts upon which it is based: *Lenaghan v Ayrshire and Arran Health Board* 1994 SC 365.

9   See, further, Pattenden [1982] Crim LR 85. The situation was generally approved by the Law Commission in Law Com No 245 *Evidence in Criminal Proceedings: Hearsay and Related Topics* (Cm 3670, 1997) para 9.8, rec 32.

10   *Rowley v London and North Western Rly Co* (1873) LR 8 Exch 221 (mortality tables). See also *Borowski v Quayle* [1966] VR 382 (standard pharmaceutical guide).

11   *H v Schering Chemicals Ltd* [1983] 1 All ER 849, at 853, [1983] 1 WLR 143, at 148 (research studies into drug). See also *R v Abadom* [1983] 1 All ER 364, 76 Cr App Rep 48 (statistics of refractive index of samples of glass).

others in the course of professional life.[12] In *R v Zundel*,[13] it was necessary to prove the basic facts of The Holocaust. The court took the view that while judicial notice[14] might be taken of such a notorious matter based upon historical treatises, it was better[15] to prove it by calling expert witnesses who could themselves rely upon historical treatises,[16] and also contemporaneous documents of the sort relied upon by historians in preparing such treatises. An opinion will not be admissible if it is based upon more specific hearsay not falling under any such exception,[17] though the dividing line between generic and specific hearsay may occasionally prove difficult to draw with any precision. If the opinion is not solely based upon inadmissible hearsay, then the statements may be proved not as evidence of their truth, but as an additional basis for the opinion.[18]

SECTION 2.   OPERATION OF THE RULE

In so far as it is exclusionary, two classes of case are contemplated in the formulation of the rule in the previous section, and it is hardly surprising that there should be but few reported decisions falling within the first class. Where the rule does operate to exclude opinion, it does so both for the prosecution and the defence, and there is no discretion to permit the use of otherwise inadmissible opinion, merely because it would assist a co-accused in the presentation of a 'cut-throat' defence.[19]

A.   LACK OF EXPERTISE

A litigant would normally have to be in desperate straits before he thought of calling a witness who was not an expert on the matter in question to give his opinions on a subject involving special skill or knowledge.[20] This may have been the position of counsel for the defence in *R v Loake*[1] when he applied to the Court of Criminal Appeal for leave to call fresh evidence in support of the accused's plea of insanity. Among the witnesses he wished to call were a friend of the accused who saw him three days before the crime was committed and formed the opinion that he was insane, together with a magistrate who had come to a similar conclusion after visiting the prisoner in his cell. The court disposed of the application so far as these witnesses were concerned by saying that the friend's evidence was clearly inadmissible, and the magistrate was not

---

1 2   *English Exporters (London) Ltd v Eldonwall Ltd* [1973] Ch 415, at 420, [1973] 1 All ER 726, at 730 (general knowledge of property values derived from reports of transactions conducted by others). See also *Wilson v H M Advocate* 1988 SCCR 384 (briefings of police, as to methods of importing drugs).

1 3   (1987) 35 DLR (4th) 338.

1 4   See further above p 68.

1 5   Because an expert witness could be cross-examined, and because of the undesirability of establishing by judicial notice a major part of the prosecution case.

1 6   Such use of treatises constitutes an acknowledged exception to the hearsay rule.

1 7   See *Eldonwall* and *Borowski* above, in each of which some bases for the opinion were excluded for this reason; *Mobil Oil Corpn v Registrar of Trademarks* (1983) 51 ALR 735 (excludes opinion survey evidence in trademark case).

1 8   *R v Abbey* (1982) 138 DLR (3d) 202.

1 9   *R v Theodosi* [1993] RTR 179.

2 0   Though it may be hard to separate such cases from those where a witness tendered as an expert is held to have inappropriate or insufficient expertise, see *Seyfert v Burnaby Hospital Society* (1986) 27 DLR (4th) 96 (emergency physician inappropriate to testify to qualities required of emergency physician); *Gaudiuso v Walker* (1989) 56 DLR (4th) 355 (doctor competent to testify to medical examination but not to theory of scientific tests used).

1   (1911) 7 Cr App Rep 71.

an expert. Non-experts may be asked to state whether they consider a person with whom they are well acquainted to be sane, but this has been said to be no more than a 'compendious mode of ascertaining the result of the actual observation of the witness, from acts done, as to the habits and demeanour' of such person.[2] There was no suggestion that either of the proposed witnesses in *Loake's* case were at all intimately acquainted with the accused. It has also been held[3] that where psychiatric harm is alleged, it is not enough to rely upon the evidence of the subject, but it is necessary to call appropriately qualified expert evidence.

B.   UNNECESSARY EXPERTISE

An expert's opinion is admissible to furnish the court with scientific information which is likely to be outside the experience and knowledge of a judge or jury. If on the proven facts a judge or jury can form their own conclusions without help, then the opinion of an expert is unnecessary. In such a case if it is given dressed up in scientific jargon it may make judgment more difficult. The fact that an expert witness has impressive scientific qualifications does not by that fact alone make his opinion on matters of human nature and behaviour within the limits of normality any more helpful than that of the jurors themselves; but there is a danger that they may think it does.

These words[4] provide us with as clear an explanation as can be asked for of the basis of the second limb of the exclusionary rule. Evidence of opinion on matters not calling for expertise is generally excluded because, like the evidence of non-experts on matters calling for expertise, it does not help the court. At best it is superfluous,[5] and it could be a cause of confusion. Its rejection is sometimes tied to an interpretation of the substantive law which removes the matter to which the evidence relates from those which are in issue.[6]

In *R v Chard*[7] the Court of Appeal held that the judge had rightly excluded medical evidence concerning the intention at the material time of someone charged with murder where there was no question of his being insane or suffering from diminished responsibility. A judge and jury are as competent as a psychiatrist to form an opinion about the past intention of a normal man. On similar grounds it has been held that expert evidence is inadmissible to explain the ordinary meaning of words such as 'obscene or indecent'[8] or 'calculated to deprave or corrupt',[9] or perhaps 'severe impairment',[10]

---

2   Per Parke B in *Wright v Doe d Tatham* (1838) 4 Bing NC 489, at 543,4. Cf *R v Davies* [1962] 3 All ER 97, [1962] 1 WLR 1111.

3   *R v Morris* [1998] 1 Cr App Rep 386 (where the support of a general medical practitioner was not enough to raise the issue).

4   Per Lawton LJ in *R v Turner* [1975] QB 834, at 841, cited with approval by Lord Wilberforce in *DPP v Jordan* [1977] AC 699, at 718, [1976] 3 All ER 775, at 779b.

5   Thus in *R v Land* [1999] QB 65, [1998] 1 All ER 403 it was held that the jury did not require expert assistance to determine the age of a child depicted in a photograph.

6   As in *R v Coles* [1995] 1 Cr App Rep 157 where the evidence of a psychiatrist was admissible only on the basis, which was rejected, that subjective foresight of risk was necessary in a prosecution for manslaughter.

7   (1971) 56 Cr App Rep 268.

8   *R v Stamford* [1972] 2 QB 391, [1972] 2 All ER 427.

9   *R v Anderson* [1972] 1 QB 304, [1971] 3 All ER 1152. For possible exception see *DPP v A B and C Chewing Gum Ltd* [1968] 1 QB 159, [1967] 2 All ER 504 pp 501, 502.

10   *R v Hall* (1987) 86 Cr App Rep 159.

when used in a modern general Act of Parliament, or the phrase 'following the settlement' in a contract of insurance.[11] Expert opinion may never be received on a question of domestic law.[12]

R v Turner, the case from which the passage quoted above is taken, is more controversial on account of the problem of reconciling it with the decision of the Privy Council in *Lowery v R*.[13] The accused unsuccessfully pleaded provocation in answer to a charge of murder of his girlfriend whom he alleged that he had killed in a fit of rage caused by her sudden confession of infidelity. He appealed on the ground that the judge had wrongly refused to allow him to call a psychiatrist. This witness would have sworn that the accused was not mentally ill; that he had a deep relationship with the girl which was likely to cause an explosive outburst of rage at her confession; and that his subsequent behaviour showed profound regret at what he had done. The Court of Appeal held that no evidence was called for with regard to the first of these matters which was undisputed, and that jurors do not need a psychiatrist to tell them how ordinary people who are not suffering from mental illness are likely to react to the stresses and strains of life. This would appear to provide a basis for reconciling their decisions with *Lowery v R* in which case, it will be recollected, Lowery and King were charged with a murder which must have been committed by either or both of them and the Privy Council held that the judge had acted properly in allowing King to call a psychiatrist to swear that he was less likely to have committed the crime than Lowery. Juries do not need to be told that normal men are liable to lose control of themselves when their women admit to infidelity, but they require all the expert assistance they can get to help them determine which of two accused has the more aggressive personality. Another way of reconciling the cases would be to treat the fact that Lowery had put his character in issue as crucial to the decision of the Privy Council, the psychiatric evidence then being admissible to impugn the credibility of his testimony. Unfortunately we are left without any guidance on the subject from the Court of Appeal who contented themselves with saying that *Lowery's* case was decided on its special facts.[14]

In England there has been little inclination to extend the category of those in respect of whom expert psychiatric testimony may be received. Thus in *R v Masih*[15] such evidence was held inadmissible[16] in relation to a borderline mental defective, in *R v Weightman*[17] to an abnormal and histrionic, but not mentally ill or handicapped individual[18] and in *R v Loughran*[19] to a young man with female characteristics, on the basis that it could show no organic or psychiatric link to his claimed impotence. Such evidence may however be admitted in the case of an otherwise normal person who is

---

11   *Royal Insurance Australia Ltd v Government Insurance Office of New South Wales* [1994] 1 VR 123.

12   See *R v Century 21 Ramos Realty Inc* (1987) 37 DLR (4th) 649.

13   [1974] AC 85, [1973] 3 All ER 662 (p 326 above). See Pattenden [1986] Crim LR 92.

14   It would probably be a mistake to regard *R v Turner* as closing the door to the admissibility of psychiatric evidence on behalf of the accused in all cases of provocation, especially having regard to changes in the substantive law on the subject effected by *R v Camplin* [1978] AC 705, sub nom *DPP v Camplin* [1978] 2 All ER 168, indeed some encouragement to the tendering of such evidence appears to have been offered in *R v Ahluwalia* [1992] 4 All ER 889, at 898, 96 Cr App Rep 133, at 141. For a similar approach to self-defence in Canada, see *R v Lavallee* [1990] 1 SCR 852.

15   [1986] Crim LR 395. See also; in Australia, *R v Hoogwerf* (1992) 63 ACR 302; in Canada, *Roy v R* (1988) 62 CR (3d) 127; and in New Zealand, *R v B* [1987] 1 NZLR 362.

16   Rejecting the more liberal view affirmed by the majority of the High Court of Australia in *Murphy v R* (1989) 167 CLR 94.

17   (1990) 92 Cr App Rep 291.

18   The general rule was stated to be that an intelligence quotient of less than 70 was required to justify the admissibility of expert psychiatric evidence of credibility.

19   [1999] Crim LR 404.

temporarily suffering from an abnormal condition having an impact upon his mental state.[20] Some slight flexibility in this formulation has however been exploited to admit such evidence outside these strict limits in the case of the young. A distinction has been drawn[1] between evidence which attacks the credibility of an out of court statement tendered by the prosecution,[2] and that which supports the credibility of the oral testimony of a witness.[3] This is largely attributable to the procedural prohibition on bolstering a witness.[4] Where the credibility of a witness is in issue, expert evidence is not automatically excluded, but its use needs to be restrained by a strict doctrine of necessity.[5] In most cases the court will not require outside assistance to enable it determine whether or not a witness is credible. In Canada there seems to have been wider extension still to permit expert opinion on such evidential issues as the likelihood of pre-trial recantation,[6] of pre-trial lapse of memory,[7] of the difference between visual and verbal memory,[8] or even of the unlikelihood of the witness having been coached,[9] at least in relation to child complainants of sexual abuse by an adult.

In some Australian cases emphasis has been placed upon the difference between expert psychiatric evidence in relation to testimony for the purpose of testing its credibility, and in relation to out of court statements for the same purpose, or as going to an issue in the case.[10] In a somewhat similar fashion a distinction has also been made between the rejection of expert evidence as to the sincerity of views expressed by individual members of the public in response to a survey, and its acceptance as the expert's opinion of the public's view, even though derived from perusal of the results of the survey.[11]

In England the Youth Justice and Criminal Evidence Bill 1999 proposes to make some inroad into this position in its explicit endorsement of the use of expert evidence to help determine the competence of witnesses,[12] and whether to make a special measures direction.[13]

C.   ULTIMATE ISSUE

A considerable body of authority once asserted that evidence of opinion may not be proffered on an ultimate issue. This rule was supposed to apply both to expert[14] and to

---

20   As in *R v Toner* (1991) 93 Cr App Rep 382 where starvation had induced hypoglycemia, though in Australia no comparable exception has been made for alcoholics, *R v Haidley and Alford* [1984] VR 229.

1   In *R v Robinson* [1994] 3 All ER 346, 98 Cr App Rep 370.

2   Citing *R v Raghip* (1991) Times, 9 December; *R v Ward* [1993] 2 All ER 577, [1993] 1 WLR 639 where expert psychiatric evidence was admitted to throw doubt upon the veracity of confessions made by mentally handicapped individuals. Though such an expert must rest his opinion on established fact: see *R v Lee* (1991) 42 ACR 393.

3   As in *Robinson* where the expert opinion was tendered to show that the complainant was too defective to have understood enough to be suggestible and insufficiently creative to be capable of fantasy about the incident in question.

4   See p 302 above.

5   [1996] 4 All ER 239, at 253h; *Re CB and JB* [1998] 2 FCR 313.

6   *R v P(C)* above.

7   *R v C(RA)* (1990) 78 CR (3d) 390.

8   *R v R(D)* [1996] 2 SCR 291.

9   *R v Manahan* (1990) 61 CCC (3d) 139.

10   *R v Barry* [1984] 1 Qd R 74.

11   *Ritz Hotel Ltd v Charles of the Ritz Ltd* (1988) 15 NSWLR 158, at 175. In England such evidence has been held not to be expert, nor even opinion: *Reckitt & Colman Products Ltd v Borden Inc (No 2)* [1987] FSR 407.

12   Clause 51(5).

13   Clause 20(6)(c).

14   See, for example, *North Cheshire and Manchester Brewery Co v Manchester Brewery Co* [1899] AC 83, at 85.

lay[15] opinion, and both to civil[16] and to criminal cases.[17] So far as the rule is justified upon the basis that it prevents usurpation of the function of the trier of fact, it was condemned by Wigmore as 'a mere bit of empty rhetoric',[18] the point being that the trier of fact is always free to reject the guidance offered by the opinion. The justification appeared to confuse the admissibility of evidence with its having conclusive weight. It may be for this reason that some recent overseas authority has formulated the rule in different terms as excluding opinion only on the application of an essentially legal standard, such as that of negligence or incapacity to marry:[19]

> When a standard, or a measure, or a capacity has been fixed by law, no witness whether expert or non-expert, nor however qualified, is permitted to express an opinion as to whether the person or the conduct, in question, measures up to that standard; on that question the court must instruct the jury as to the law, and the jury draw its own conclusion from the evidence.

The rule has now been abandoned in England.[20] In civil cases its abolition was recommended by the Law Reform Committee in its 17th Report[1] and implemented by s 3 of the Civil Evidence Act 1972:

> (1)   Subject to any rules of court made in pursuance of Part I of the Civil Evidence Act 1968 or this Act, where a person is called as a witness in any civil proceedings, his opinion on any relevant matter on which he is qualified to give expert evidence shall be admissible in evidence.
>
> (2) It is hereby declared that where a person is called as a witness in any civil proceedings, a statement of opinion by him on any relevant matter on which he is not qualified to give expert evidence, if made as a way of conveying relevant facts personally perceived by him, is admissible as evidence of what he perceived.
>
> (3) In this section 'relevant matter' includes an issue in the proceedings in question.

The Criminal Law Revison Committee recommended a similar step for criminal proceedings,[2] but it has not yet been enacted.[3] The continuance of the rule was however questioned in *DPP v A and BC Chewing Gum Ltd*,[4] and in *R v Stockwell*[5] the Court of Appeal adopted the view expressed in a previous edition of this text that the expert

15   See, for example, *R v Davies* [1962] 3 All ER 97, [1962] 1 WLR 1111.
16   See above.
17   *R v Wright* (1821) Russ & Ry 456, at 458.
18   *Evidence* (Chadbourn rev) para 1920.
19   *Grismore v Consolidated Products Co* 5 NW 2d 646, at 663 (1942), approved in *R v Tonkin and Montgomery* [1975] Qd R 1, at 42. See also *R v Palmer* [1981] 1 NSWLR 209.
20   For explicit approval of this view in three quite different contexts see *Glaverbel SA v British Coal Corpn* [1995] RPC 255 (obviousness of 'invention'), at 277; *Re M and R* [1996] 4 All ER 239 (credibility of witnesses), at 250j; *Routestone Ltd v Minories Finance Ltd* [1997] 1 EGLR 123, at 127L (satisfaction of professional standard of performance).
1   Cmnd 4489 conclusions (1) and (2). On the basis that in the case of non-expert opinion the relaxation applied only to compendious statements of fact and opinion perceived by the testifying witness.
2   Clause 43 of the draft bill annexed to its 11th report (Cmnd 4491).
3   Section 30 of the Criminal Justice Act 1988 which deals with expert reports contains no such, or even similar, provision.
4   [1968] 1 QB 159, [1967] 2 All ER 504.
5   (1993) 97 Cr App Rep 260, at 265 (where the issue was the identity of a disguised man in a security video recording, and an expert in facial mapping was permitted to testify to his being the accused).

should be permitted to give his opinion on an ultimate issue,[6] subject only to a direction to the jury that it is not bound to accept the expert's opinion.[7] A similar approach prevails in North America.[8]

D. PROCEDURE

As a result of the scathing criticism of the system of expert witnesses in civil proceedings in the Woolf Report, procedure in civil cases has been revolutionised in the Civil Procedure Rules.[9] In very broad outline the thrust of the change is to attempt to limit the ambit and cost of expert evidence. It starts by stressing that[10] 'Expert evidence shall be restricted to that which is reasonably required to resolve the proceedings.' It seeks to promote this result by requiring the leave of the court before expert evidence can be tendered at all,[11] puts significant pressure upon the parties to agree to instruct a single joint expert,[12] and empowers the court to cap the fees which may be recovered.[13] Even if a single joint expert is not appointed there is provision for the exchange of information[14] and reports,[15] which can then be used by the other party,[16] and for the court to direct discussion between the experts.[17] It is envisaged that expert evidence will normally be tendered in the form of a written report,[18] that written questions will be addressed to, and answered by, the expert before the hearing,[19] and that, at least on the fast track, attendance for cross-examination will be ordered only if the court believes it to be necessary in the interests of justice.[20]

For similar reasons it has been provided[1] that advance notice must be given of the intention to adduce expert evidence in criminal proceedings, an opportunity provided to examine the factual basis for any such evidence of opinion,[2] and, even when avowedly independent, the chance to call expert evidence in rebuttal.[3] Such evidence of opinion may however be given in the form of a written report in derogation of the hearsay rule, whether or not[4] its maker attends to give oral evidence.[5] It is within the discretion of

6   Cp *R v Jeffries* [1997] Crim LR 819 where the old rule seems to have been applied; but see also the critical commentary by Birch.
7   Though this need not be in any particular form, and its omission is not an automatic ground for allowing an appeal: *R v Fitzpatrick* (1999) Times, 19 February.
8   United States, FRE 704; Canada, *Grant v R* [1982] 2 SCR 819.
9   Part 35.
10   Rule 35.1
11   Rule 35.4(1).
12   Rule 35.7.
13   Rule 35.4(4).
14   Rule 35.9.
15   Practice Direction 35 para 1(1) provides that expert reports are to be addressed to the court and not to the instructing party.
16   Rule 35.11.
17   Rule 35.12.
18   Rule 35.5(1).
19   Rule 35.6.
20   Rule 35.5(2).
1   Police and Criminal Evidence Act 1984, s 81; Crown Court (Advance Notice of Expert Evidence) Rules 1987 (SI 1987/70 (L 2)), as amended by SI 1997/700 (L 6); Magistrates' Courts (Advance Notice of Expert Evidence) Rules 1997 (SI 1997/705 (L11).
2   If no such notice or opportunity is given or afforded the evidence can be adduced only by leave of the court.
3   *R v Sunderland Justices, ex p Dryden* (1994) Times, 18 May.
4   Then only by leave of the court.
5   Criminal Justice Act 1988, s 30.

the judge in a criminal trial to determine that a given field of expertise is irrelevant or unhelpful, and accordingly to refuse to allow it to be called.[6]

SECTION 3.   EXCEPTIONS TO THE RULE

A.   EXPERT OPINION[7]

The courts have been accustomed to act on the opinion of experts from early times. As long ago as 1553 Saunders J said:[8]

> If matters arise in our law which concern other sciences or faculties we commonly apply for the aid of that science or faculty which it concerns. This is a commendable thing in our law. For thereby it appears that we do not dismiss all other sciences but our own, but we approve of them and encourage them as things worthy of commendation.

The learned judge's assertion was amply borne out by copious citations, but the early expert was often a member of the jury, and there was no question of his opinion being disregarded by that body. Expert witnesses began to play their modern role in the eighteenth century. In *Folkes v Chadd*[9] Mr Smeaton, the famous engineer, was allowed to testify concerning his opinion whether an embankment had caused the silting of a harbour.[10]

> Mr Smeaton understands the construction of harbours, the causes of their destruction, and how remedied. In matters of science no other witnesses can be called ... Handwriting is proved every day by opinion; and for false evidence on such questions a man may be indicted for perjury.

In the vast majority of cases, the witnesses will not have perceived the occurrences with which the case is concerned. It is for the court to determine which party's version of the occurrences in issue is to be accepted. This can be done by framing a series of hypothetical questions[11]—a procedure which, however necessary it may be, certainly complicates the issues in a particular case.

The facts upon which an expert's opinion is based must be proved by admissible evidence, and he should be asked in-chief what those facts are.[12] If he observed them, he may testify to their existence, but, when the facts in question are dependent upon ordinary human powers of perception, the expert may be contradicted by a lay witness, as when a police officer and a doctor give different accounts of the behaviour of someone accused of drunken driving when he was being questioned at a police station.[13] A

6   *R v Hersey* [1998] Crim LR 281.
7   See Learned Hand (1901) 15 Harv LR 40. For a statutory definition of an expert see Social Security Act 1998, s 6.
8   *Buckley v Rice-Thomas* (1554) 1 Plowd 118, at 124.
9   (1782) 3 Doug KB 157.
10 Per Lord Mansfield.
11 Although in Canada it has been denied, it is submitted wrongly, that any matter which it is not proposed to adduce in evidence can be used as the basis for such a hypothetical question, *R v Howard* (1989) 69 CR (3d) 193, at 201.
12 *R v Turner* [1975] QB 834, at 840. See also *R v Abbey* (1982) 138 DLR (3d) 202.
13 *Sutton v Prenter* [1963] Qd R 401. On the dual role of an expert witness see per Cooke J in *Seyfang v G D Searle & Co* [1973] QB 148, at 151. If an expert offers an opinion as a layman, and not as an expert, this must be brought to the attention of the jury, *R v Cook* [1982] Crim LR 670.

doctor may not state what a patient told him about past symptoms as evidence of the existence of those symptoms because that would infringe the rule against hearsay, but he may give evidence of what the patient told him in order to explain the grounds on which he came to a conclusion with regard to the patient's condition.[14] In these cases an opinion based solely upon uncorroborated statements by the patient is not automatically inadmissible, but is likely to be of very little weight, and the jury should be instructed appropriately.[15]

The functions of expert witnesses were succinctly stated by Lord President Cooper in *Davie v Edinburgh Magistrates*[16] when he said:

> Their duty is to furnish the judge with the necessary scientific criteria for testing the accuracy of their conclusions, so as to enable the judge or jury to form their own independent judgment by the application of these criteria to the facts proved in evidence.

The Court of Session repudiated the suggestion that the judge or jury is bound to adopt the views of an expert, even if they should be uncontradicted, because: 'The parties have invoked the decision of a judicial tribunal and not an oracular pronouncement by an expert'.[17] This case reaffirmed the view that an expert might adopt statements made in scientific works as part of his testimony, and portions of such works might be put to him in cross-examination. To this extent they may be used as evidence in the case, but the judge is entitled to form an opinion on the basis of other parts of the book.[18] Although the judge or jury is bound to come to an independent view, it may occasionally be necessary for a judge, having heard expert evidence and considered it to be evenly balanced, to decide on the basis of the burden of proof.[19] The judge must not however simply substitute his own view for that of an expert,[20] but if there is nothing in the case to contradict unanimous expert evidence in favour of the accused, the trier of fact is not entitled to reject it.[1]

The testimony of an expert is likely to carry more weight, and more readily relate to an ultimate issue than that of an ordinary witness. It is thus understandable that higher standards of accuracy and objectivity should be required.[2] The obligations of an expert witness in these respects were helpfully summarised by Cresswell J in *The Ikarian Reefer,*[3] in the course of which he remarked that 'An expert witness should provide independent assistance to the Court by way of objective unbiased opinion in relation to matters within his expertise....An expert witness in the High Court should never assume

---

14   A statement explicitly approved in *R v Bradshaw* (1985) 82 Cr App Rep 79, at 83. *Ramsay v Watson* (1961) 108 CLR 642; *Leis v Gardner* [1965] Qd R 181; *Leonard v British Colombia Hydro and Power Authority* (1965) 49 DLR (2d) 422.

15   *R v Bradshaw* above, ibid. See also *Lortie v R* (1986) 54 CR (3d) 228.

16   1953 SC 34, at 40.

17   1953 SC 34, at 40. See also *Re B (a minor)(care: expert witnesses)* [1996] 1 FLR 667 applying these remarks in the context of child care, but requiring reasons for disagreement with a unanimous expert view.

18   *Collier v Simpson* (1831) 5 C & P 73.

19   *Pickford v ICI plc* [1998] 3 All ER 462, at 473, [1998] 1 WLR 1189, at 1200; cp *Sewell v Electrolux Ltd* (1997) Times, 7 November.

20   *Dover District Council v Sherred* (1997) 29 HLR 864.

1   *R v Bailey* (1961) 66 Cr App Rep 31, see also *R v Hall* (1988) 36 ACR 362; *Towne Cinema Theatres Ltd v R* (1985) 18 DLR (4th) 1 (community standard of obscenity).

2   See Laddie J in *Autospin (Oil Seals) Ltd v Beehive Spinning* [1995] RPC 683.

3   *National Justice Compania Naviera SA v Prudential Assurance Co Ltd* [1993] 2 Lloyd's Rep 68, at 81. For some qualification of this statement, see Speaight (1997) 146 NLJ 1100.

the role of an advocate.'[4] These remarks would appear applicable a fortiori in relation to forensic scientific evidence tendered by the prosecution in a criminal case.[5] It has also been emphasised that an expert in a case involving children bears a heavy responsibility to be as objective as possible, and to make clear the extent to which his opinion was based on hypothesis, especially when it departs from a consensus view.[6] This view of the role of the expert has received emphatic expression in r 35.3 of the Civil Procedure Rules:[7]

(1) It is the duty of an expert to help the court on the matters within his expertise,

(2) This duty overrides any obligation to the person from whom he has received instructions or by whom he is paid.

No useful purpose would be served by an endeavour to enumerate the matters which have been treated by the courts as requiring a sufficient degree of specialised knowledge to render expert evidence admissible.[8] They have included medical and scientific questions, the meaning of technical terms, questions of commercial practice or market value, the provisions of a foreign system of law and the identity of a person's handwriting—a subject which is discussed in ch XVI. These areas are in constant flux. Some areas become commonplace, and judicial notice more appropriate than the requirement of expert testimony.[9] Once established fields may be made obsolete,[10] and new areas arise, with the progress of human knowledge and technological prowess. At one time a conservative approach requiring the field of expertise to have become generally accepted was widely adopted.[11] This is now regarded as too stultifying, that test having now been rejected in its jurisdiction of origin,[12] and increasingly disregarded elsewhere.[13] The better, and now more widely accepted, view is that so long as a field is sufficiently well-established to pass the ordinary tests of relevance and reliability[14], then no enhanced test of admissibility should be applied, but the weight of the evidence should be established by the same adversarial forensic techniques applicable elsewhere.

---

4   Nor should an advocate, such as a guardian ad litem, assume the role of an expert for the purpose of expressing an opinion on a child's veracity: *Re N (a minor)(sexual abuse: video evidence)* [1996] 4 All ER 225, at 236d.

5   See Ormrod [1968] Crim LR 240; Roberts and Willmore 'The Role of Forensic Science Evidence in Criminal Proceedings' Roy Com Res St No 11 (1993) ch 4.

6   *Re AB (a minor)* [1995] 1 FLR 181. The desirability of reference to the consensus view was also stressed in the context of medical negligence in *Sharpe v Southend Health Authority* (1997) 8 Med LR 299.

7   See also in Scotland, *Preece v H M Advocate* [1981] Crim LR 783; and in New Zealand *R v Tihi* [1990] 1 NZLR 540, at 548.

8   See *Re Pinion, Westminster Bank Ltd v Pinion* [1965] Ch 85, at 98, [1964] 1 All ER 890, at 891. See also *Scottish Shire Line Ltd v London and Provincial Marine and General Insurance Co Ltd* [1912] 3 KB 51, at 70 and *Carter v Boehm* (1766) 3 Burr 1905.

9   See, in relation to proof of the ordinary operation of computers, *R v Shephard* [1993] AC 380, at 387, [1993] 1 All ER 225, at 231.

10   See *R v Robb* (1991) 93 Cr App Rep 161 for an indication of the imminence of such a development in relation to auditory analysis unassisted by quantified analysis.

11   Heavily influenced by the American case of *Frye v US* 293 F 1013 (1923).

12   In *Daubert v Merrell Dow Pharmaceuticals Inc* 509 US 579 (1993). See also *General Electric Co v Joiner* 522 US 136 (1997); and for commentary on subsequent developments Slovenko (1998) 2 Int J Ev & Pr 190.

13   See eg in Canada *R v Diffenbaugh* (1993) 80 CCC (3d) 97, at 106; and in England *R v Robb* (1991) 93 Cr App Rep 161, at 166.

14   In *R v Mohan* [1994] 2 SCR 9 evidence of a novel and exclusive categorisation of sexual offenders fell at these fences.

Even if a field of expertise is well-established, the guidance it provides must also be sufficiently relevant to a matter in issue.[15] If the court comes to the conclusion that the subject of investigation does not require a sufficient degree of specialised knowledge to call for the testimony of an expert, evidence of opinion will be excluded, unless the case is one in which non-expert opinion is admissible.[16] Thus in *R v Mackenney*[17] a psychologist was not permitted to give evidence of his opinion of the likelihood of a witness telling lies. He was not medically qualified and, even if he had been, the only evidence he could have given related not to the incapacity of the witness to tell the truth,[18] but to his disinclination to do so, which the jury was able, and indeed bound, to decide for itself. Much the same approach is being increasingly taken towards questions of the application of standards well within the knowledge of the court, such as those to be expected of a solicitor,[19] though it is important for the court to preserve an open mind, and not to exclude the expert evidence inflexibly when it can be of help.[20]

It is for the judge to determine[1] whether the witness had undergone such a course of special study or experience as will render him expert in a particular subject,[2] and it is not necessary for the expertise to have been acquired professionally. In *R v Silverlock*,[3] for example, the Court for Crown Cases Reserved considered that a solicitor might be treated as an expert in handwriting even if he had acquired his knowledge as an amateur. Most of the reported cases on the subject of a witness's skill are concerned with evidence of foreign law discussed in ch XVII. Specialisation is a matter of degree, but the area of expertise should not be taken at too high a level of abstraction.[4] It is however not necessary for a doctor to have specialised in studies concerned with the rate at which the blood destroys alcohol before he can give evidence on such a subject based on analysts' tables,[5] a stenographer who has familiarised herself with the contents of a tape recording may be treated as a temporary expert,[6] and a police officer's experience in investigating traffic accidents may make him an expert for the purpose of

---

15   *R v Tilley* [1985] VR 505 accepted stylistic analysis as a sufficiently well-developed field but denied that it was appropriate to apply it to the material available. See also *R v Watson* [1987] 1 Qd R 440, at 465.

16   See *United States Shipping Board v The St Albans* [1931] AC 632, now further reinforced by the Civil Procedure Rules Part 35; but see on the qualification *R v Hersey* [1998] Crim LR 281 where lay opinion identifying a voice was admitted, but expert evidence relating to the difficulty of doing so, excluded.

17   (1981) 76 Cr App Rep 271. See also *R v Smith* [1987] VR 907 (where evidence of a psychologist was rejected on the question of the reliability of eye-witness identification); *Hersey* (above) (where the rejection related to the reliability of voice identification).

18   Which is permissible: *Toohey v Metropolitan Police Comr* [1965] AC 595, [1965] 1 All ER 506; see also *Re J (a minor)* (1984) 14 Fam Law 308.

19   See *Bown v Gould & Swayne* [1996] PNLR 130; and in Australia *O'Brien v Gillespie* (1997) 41 NSWLR 549.

20   See the especially helpful analysis of Evans LJ in *United Bank of Kuwait v Prudential Property Services Ltd* [1995] EGCS 190.

1   See *R v Bonython* (1984) 38 SASR 45 for a particularly clear exposition of the issues to be considered by the judge in determining the admissibility of expert opinion.

2   Under Civil Procedure Rule 35.4 identification of expert and relevant field of expertise must be made in advance.

3   [1894] 2 QB 766; *R v Bunnis* (1964) 50 WWR 422. Cf *Clark v Ryan* (above).

4   So membership of a similar, but different, profession may not be enough, see eg *Sansom v Metcalf Hambleton & Co* (1997) 57 Con LR 88 (evidence of structural engineer inadmissible against chartered surveyor).

5   *R v Somers* [1963] 3 All ER 808, [1963] 1 WLR 1306; *R v Richards* [1974] 3 All ER 696, [1975] 1 WLR 131.

6   *Hopes and Lavery v H M Advocate* 1960 JC 104. See also *R v Clare, R v Peach* [1995] 2 Cr App Rep 333 where a police officer acquired expertise in identifying those shown on a security video film by studying it, and was permitted to testify as an expert in the interpretation of that film.

reconstructing a particular motor accident [7] or for testifying to the normal dosage of a drug addict.[8] But experience in driving does not make a bombardier an expert on the subject of the capabilities of someone charged with dangerous driving.[9] Addiction to a drug may give sufficient experience to permit credence to be given to the addict's identification of a substance as that drug.[10]

B. NON-EXPERT OPINION

When, in the words of an American judge,[11] 'the facts from which a witness received an impression were too evanescent in their nature to be recollected, or too complicated to be separately and distinctly narrated', a witness may state his opinion or impression. He is better equipped than the jury to form it, and it is impossible for him to convey an adequate idea of the premises on which he acted to the jury:[12]

> Unless opinions, estimates and inferences which men in their daily lives reach without conscious ratiocination as a result of what they perceived with their physical senses were treated in the law of evidence as if they were mere statements of fact, witnesses would find themselves unable to communicate to the judge an accurate impression of the events they were seeking to describe.

There is nothing in the nature of a closed list of cases in which non-expert opinion evidence is admissible. Typical instances are provided by questions concerning age,[13] speed,[14] weather, handwriting and identity in general. Proof of handwriting is discussed in ch XVI, but a word may be said here about the question of identification. When a witness says, 'that is the man I saw the other day', pointing to someone in court, or 'that is the man whose wedding I attended', pointing to a figure in a photograph,[15] or, 'that is a copy of a picture of which I have seen the original',[16] there is clearly a sense in which it is true to say that he is expressing an opinion. He is not simply narrating what he has perceived in the past; but the perception on which his statements are founded cannot be conveyed to the jury in the same way that the premises for or against an inference of negligence can be narrated. In *Fryer v Gathercole*[17] in order to prove the publication of a libellous pamphlet to friends of a female witness she was allowed to swear that she received a pamphlet from the defendant, lent it to friends in succession and put her name on it when it was ultimately returned to her. She said that she believed the pamphlet returned by the last borrower to be identical with that received from the defendant, but she could not swear to this fact because it was possible that another pamphlet had been substituted for the original. Pollock CB disposed of an objection to the effect that her evidence was mere opinion by saying: 'There are many cases of

---

7   *R v Oakley* [1979] RTR 417; *R v Murphy* [1980] QB 434, [1980] 2 All ER 325.
8   *White v H M Advocate* 1986 SCCR 224. In Australia police evidence as to the sort of pipes used by drug addicts has been regarded as evidence of fact and not opinion at all, *R v Barker* (1988) 34 ACR 141.
9   *R v Davies* [1962] 3 All ER 97, [1962] 1 WLR 1111. See also *Seyfert v Burnaby Hospital Society* (1986) 27 DLR (4th) 96; *Gaudiuso v Walker* (1989) 56 DLR (4th) 355, above p 515.
10 *R v Chatwood* [1980] 1 All ER 467, [1980] 1 WLR 874.
11 Gibson J cited in VII *Wigmore* p 12.
12 17th Report of the Law Reform Committee, para 3.
13 *R v Cox* [1898] 1 QB 179.
14 Road Traffic Regulation Act 1984, s 89.
15 *R v Tolson* (1864) 4 F & F 103.
16 *Lucas v Williams & Sons* [1892] 2 QB 113.
17 (1849) 13 Jur 542.

identification where the law would be rendered ridiculous if positive certainty were required from witnesses', and Parke B said in the course of the argument; 'In the identification of person you compare in your mind the man you have seen with the man you see at the trial. The same rule belongs to every species of identification.' Every fact on which the identification is based cannot be satisfactorily given in evidence.

In some cases a non-expert witness has been allowed to give evidence of opinion on a subject on which expert testimony would have been admissible. Acquaintances of a person whose sanity is in issue may be asked whether they consider him sane, but this is not so much a demand for an opinion as a 'compendious mode of ascertaining the result of the actual observations of the witness'. Did the witness observe any action by the accused characteristically associated with persons of dubious sanity? Similarly, in *R v Davies*,[18] the Courts Martial Appeal Court held that on a charge of drunken driving, a non-medical witness might state that he formed the impression that the accused had been drinking but it was said that he must state the facts on which that impression was based, and it was also held that the witness ought not to have been allowed to add that he believed the accused to be unfit to drive, although an expert could have testified to this effect. In an interesting decision in South Africa[19] it has been held that lay eyewitness evidence of a collision between motor vehicles was to be preferred to expert evidence reconstructing the collision from physical traces alone,[20] unless it were completely incredible.

In *R v Beckett*,[1] the accused was charged with maliciously damaging a plate glass window worth more than five pounds. The fact that the window was worth more than five pounds was an essential ingredient of the offence, and it was held to have been proved by the statement of an assistant superintendent of the post office who swore that the window was worth more than five pounds. In cross-examination it became clear that his evidence was largely based on hearsay, but the Court of Criminal Appeal upheld the conviction on the footing that the case was proved by the witness's statement of his personal opinion as to the value of the window. The basis of the admissibility of this evidence was not considered by the court, and the decision is perhaps open to question on the ground that it raises insoluble problems of degree. Is it confined to non-expert opinion concerning the value of commonplace objects? If so, what are commonplace objects? Does it apply where the witness opines that the value of an article exceeds a specified sum by a considerable amount? If so, what is a considerable amount? But *R v Beckett* was cited in a South Australian case in which it was said that the court may always act on non-expert opinion as to value when no specialised knowledge is required.[2]

18   [1962] 3 All ER 97, [1962] 1 WLR 1111. See also *Croft v Jewell* [1993] PIQR P270; *Sherrard v Jacob* [1965] NI 151; *R v German* [1947] 4 DLR 68; *Burrows v Hanlin* [1930] SASR 54; *R v McKimmie* [1957] VLR 93; *R v Spooner* [1957] VLR 540; *R v Kelly* [1958] VLR 412; *A-G (Rudley) v James Kenny* (1960) 94 ILTR 185 (77 LQR 166); *Blackie v Police* [1966] NZLR 910; *Grant v R* [1982] 2 SCR 819.
19   *Motor Vehicle Assurance Fund v Kenny* 1984 (4) SA 432.
20   As noted above p 523 this is a subject sometimes thought only marginally of a sufficient status to be appropriate for the admission of expert testimony.
1   (1913) 8 Cr App Rep 204.
2   *Wise v Musolino* [1936] SASR 447. In some cases judicial notice may be taken that the value of an object exceeds the specified sum or evidence of its purchase price might suffice.

SECTION 4.   REFORM OF THE RULE

Reform of the rule in England was first considered in detail by the Law Reform Committee in its Seventeenth Report 'Evidence of Opinion and Expert Evidence'.[3] The Report was however somewhat conservative in its approach and rejected radical reform, for example, for a switch to a system of court experts.

Some further measures of reform were implemented, such as rules enabling the limitation of numbers of experts,[4] to direct that a 'without prejudice' meeting of experts take place in advance of the trial,[5] and those enabling expert reports to be used in criminal proceedings without the necessity for the expert to testify orally.[6]

As described above, despite such reform, pressure continued to build, and Lord Woolf in his interim report identified the cost and partisan nature of much expert evidence as one of the principal defects of the system of civil litigation,[7] finding concern about it second only to that relating to discovery.[8] He found however that recommendations designed to limit the use of expert evidence aroused more opposition than those in any other area,[9] especially in relation to the use of single experts.[10] The final recommendations[11] were accordingly somewhat more muted, and as seen still do not make the use of single experts mandatory. In relation to criminal proceedings the topic was considered by the Royal Commission on Criminal Justice,[12] and a special research report commissioned on one aspect of it.[13] Many of the Committee's recommendations were directed to administrative and procedural questions. It sought to assimilate the position in criminal proceedings as far as possible to that which operates in civil proceedings,[14] especially so far as it seeks to resolve dispute by negotiation between the parties before the trial. The proposal was even made for compulsory pre-trial hearings in relation to scientific expert evidence unless both parties certify such a hearing to be unnecessary.[15] In order to allay some of the disquiet felt by expert witnesses themselves the Commission further recommended measures to enable them to give evidence in written and graphical forms, and the provision of an opportunity for them to indicate a desire to amplify or clarify their evidence after it had been given. To date no legislation incorporating such proposals has been introduced. Some aspects of expert evidence were further considered by the Law Commission in relation to hearsay, and the Commission has recommended that advance notice be given of the name of those who have provided information to an expert upon which his report is based, and that where such notice has been given the statement of the assistant be admissible in evidence, unless the court direct otherwise.[16]

---

3   Cmnd 4489 (1970).
4   RSC Ord 38, r 4.
5   RSC Ord 38, r 38. Further encouragement to such meetings, and to the submission of agreed joint reports has been provided by the grant of immunity from suit to the expert in respect of such agreement: *Stanton v Callaghan* [1998] 4 All ER 961.
6   Criminal Justice Act 1988, s 30.
7   *Access to Justice: Interim Report* (1995) para 3.7.
8   Paragraph 23.1.
9   *Access to Justice: Final Report* (1996) para 13.5.
10   Paragraph 13.16.
11   Recommendations 156–173.
12   Cm 2263 ch 9.
13   Res St No 11 (1993) Roberts and Willmore 'The Role of Forensic Science Evidence in Criminal Proceedings'.
14   Although these proposals antedated the publication of the Civil Procedure Rules.
15   Rec 294, para 9.68.
16   Law Com No 245 *Evidence in Criminal Proceedings: Hearsay and Related Matters* (Cm 3670, 1997) para 9.29 rec 33.

It may be expected that pressure for reform will continue to be felt, as scientific knowledge and techniques continue to advance, and to become used ever more widely. It must necessarily be the case that the increase of knowledge of the average juror cannot be expected to keep up with such scientific progress, so the need for expert guidance will continue to grow. It may also be the case that with the provisions mentioned above for advance disclosure, that the role of experts in the conduct of legal proceedings will become more diversified, and some experts used not so much as witnesses whose reports will need to be disclosed, but simply as advisers to the parties whose work will attract litigation privilege,[17] and be immune from such disclosure.[18]

17   Although in England it may not be possible to recover costs if the prior approval of the court has not been secured.
18   This is already commonplace in the United States.

Chapter XIII

Hearsay in general

The hearsay rule has often been regarded as one of the most complex and most confusing of the exclusionary rules of evidence. Lord Reid said that it was 'difficult to make any general statement about the law of hearsay which is entirely accurate.'[1] Both its definition, and the ambit of exceptions to it were unclear. It led to the exclusion of much reliable evidence, and, on that account, exceptions were created ad hoc, often without full consideration of their implications. In this jurisdiction,[2] at long last, the situation is changing. Fundamental statutory reform has already occurred in civil proceedings,[3] and has been recommended for criminal.[4] This permits shorter and more simple discussion of the topic in a work of this nature. This chapter will consider some general matters relating to hearsay; a chapter on hearsay in civil proceedings,[5] and another on hearsay in criminal proceedings,[6] will then follow.

The first section of this chapter will consider, in outline, the definition, rationale, development and reform of the hearsay rule; the second section will examine more closely the scope of the rule, and its relation to such concepts as implied assertions, res gestae, the rule against narrative, and the extent to which admissions constitute an exception to the rule.

---

1 *Myers v DPP* [1965] AC 1001, at 1019, [1964] 2 All ER 881, at 884.
2 Not only in England, but in most Commonwealth jurisdictions. The United States alone among major common law jurisdictions seems more conservative; for recent discussion see 49 Hastings LJ 477 et seq (1998).
3 Culminating in the passage of the Civil Evidence Act 1995.
4 Law Com No 245 *Evidence in Criminal Proceedings: Hearsay and Related Topics* Cm 3670 (1997).
5 This will include those matters where the rule is to remain the same for both civil and criminal proceedings.
6 This will include also confessions, treated separately from admissions in general which will be treated in this chapter, but also extending more widely into non-hearsay issues involved in the overlapping area of police questioning and inferences from pre-trial silence.

SECTION I.   THE NATURE OF THE RULE

This section opens with a short statement of the hearsay rule, explains why such an exclusionary rule was thought to be necessary, and goes on to indicate the main lines of its development and reform.

A. STATEMENT

According to the rule against hearsay as formulated in ch I, a statement other than one made by a person while giving oral evidence in the proceedings is inadmissible as evidence of any fact stated. The rule applies to all kinds of statement, whether made orally, in writing or by conduct,[7] and equally to hearsay of all degrees.[8] It is less clear how far it extends to assumptions of fact inferred from words or deeds. This formulation conflates two common law rules, the rule that the previous statements of the witness who is testifying are inadmissible as evidence of the facts stated (sometimes spoken of as the 'rule against narrative', or the 'rule against self-corroboration'), and the rule that statements by persons other than the witness who is testifying are inadmissible as evidence of the facts stated (the rule against hearsay in the strict sense). At common law there is only one clear exception to the first rule, an informal admission proved against the party who made it.[9] In ch VI it was said that, at common law, the previous consistent statements of witnesses are usually inadmissible as evidence of consistency though inconsistent statements might be proved, not as evidence of the facts stated, but in order to cast doubt on the witness's testimony. It was also shown that previous consistent statements might be proved by way of exception to the general exclusionary rule in the case of complaints of sexual offences, statements forming part of the res gestae, statements rebutting a suggestion that the witness's testimony was a recent invention and sundry statements of the accused. In these cases the witness's previous statements were not, strictly speaking, received as evidence of the facts stated, and therefore not received under exceptions to the rule against hearsay. There were however many common law exceptions to the rule against hearsay in the strict sense.

The law of evidence distinguishes between a witness's statements of fact and opinion. This should be reflected in a complete formulation of the rule against hearsay. A full version of that adopted in this book should therefore read: any statement other than one made by a person while giving oral evidence in the proceedings is inadmissible as evidence of any fact or opinion stated. This chapter is primarily concerned with the rule against hearsay in the strict sense. It has never been fully formulated judicially,[10] but most authorities concur in the view that:[11]

---

7   *Chandrasekera (alias Alisandiri) v R* [1937] AC 220, [1936] 3 All ER 865 (signs made by woman dying as a result of her throat being cut).

8   Ie irrespective of the number of intermediate communicators between the original source and the testifying witness.

9   The exception of the admission has been described as the only 'clear' one because of the possibility that previous statements of witnesses received as part of the res gestae are received as evidence of the facts stated.

10   It is however defined for the purposes of the Civil Evidence Act 1995 by s 1(2)(a), and effectively, as indicated by the side heading, for the purposes of the draft Criminal Evidence Bill appended to Law Com 245 by cl 1(1). A definition similar to that proposed above which appeared in earlier editions of this work was explicitly approved by the House of Lords in *R v Sharp* [1988] 1 All ER 65, at 68, [1988] 1 WLR 7, at 11.

11   *Subramaniam v Public Prosecutor* [1956] 1 WLR 965, at 969; that approach was explicitly approved by the Supreme Court of Canada in *R v Abbey* [1982] 2 SCR 24.

Evidence of a statement made to a witness by a person who is not himself called as a witness may or may not be hearsay. It is hearsay and inadmissible when the object of the evidence is to establish the truth of what is contained in the statement. It is not hearsay and is admissible when it is proposed to establish by evidence, not the truth of the statement, but the fact that it was made.

This crucial distinction was overlooked by the trial judge in the case from which the above extract from the advice of the Judicial Committee of the Privy Council is taken. The appellant was charged with being in possession of firearms without a lawful excuse and his defence was that he was acting under duress in consequence of threats uttered by Malayan terrorists. The judge would not allow the accused to state what had been said by the terrorists and the Judicial Committee advised that the conviction should be quashed because the reported assertions were tendered as original evidence and ought to have been received as such.[12]

The rule against hearsay applies just as much to evidence elicited in cross-examination as to evidence in-chief. A deceased workman's statements to his widow on returning home after an accident have been held inadmissible at common law as evidence of its cause on a number of occasions.[13] If a widow narrates in cross-examination what her deceased husband told her about the cause of his injuries or illness, her assertion is no more admissible as evidence of that fact than it would have been if made in-chief.[14]

B. RATIONALE

The development of the hearsay rule coincided with the stabilisation of a recognisably modern form of trial. Whether the exclusion of hearsay was based upon distrust of the abilities of the jury to evaluate it, or upon faith in the power of cross-examination, or both,[15] it remains to be seen what frailties required such elaborate precautions.[16] Their examination may help to explain the basis for the development of the rule.

It is helpful to start by contrasting the reasoning process involved in the acceptance of direct testimony with that involved in the acceptance of hearsay.[17] If a witness testifies to a relevant event which he has himself observed, say 'that x existed', the jury is invited to accept that the witness did perceive x, that he has remembered correctly what he perceived,[18] that there is no ambiguity in his relation of x to the court, and that he is sincere in his testimony. Rules of competence may disqualify such direct testimony in extreme cases, and sincerity may be promoted by the sanction of the oath and the

12 For a similar oversight by a trial judge: see *R v Willis* [1960] 1 All ER 331, [1960] 1 WLR 55; and for one by magistrates: see *Woodhouse v Hall* (1980) 72 Cr App Rep 39.

13 *Gilbey v Great Western Rly Co* (1910) 102 LT 202; see also *Amys v Barton* [1912] 1 KB 40.

14 *Beare v Garrod* (1915) 113 LT 673; see p 292 above. In *R v Summers* (1986) 22 ACR 47 an appeal was allowed on account of cross-examination permitted to elicit such hearsay.

15 The history of the rule has generated significant debate and dispute. For a modern indication of thinking, from an American perspective, see Friedman [1998] Crim LR 697, especially 700–705.

16 Such frailties have led to convictions being regarded as obtained contrary to basic principles of justice even in jurisdictions with a totally different tradition and form of trial when dependent upon evidence from anonymous informants: *Kostovski v Netherlands* (1989) 12 EHRR 434.

17 For a graphic exposition of the basis of the hearsay rules see Graham 5 Un of Ill LR 887 (1982).

18 The results of considerable scientific investigation into these factors were presented and evaluated in the Australian Law Reform Commission's Research Paper No 3 'Hearsay Evidence' (1981) ch 2.

prospect of prosecution for perjury, but the principal guaranties for these factors are provided by the witness's availability for cross-examination to probe into them. At the end of the day the jury must be satisfied both that the witness believes that x existed, and that his belief is justified.

It is obvious that any danger in accepting these conclusions is multiplied when hearsay is tendered. In such cases the jury must be satisfied that the witness believes he heard a third party say 'x exists'; that the witness's belief was justified; that the third party believed that x existed; and that the third party's belief was justified. It must do this in the absence of any safeguard from the ordinary conditions of testimony[19] in relation to the third party; in the absence of any opportunity to probe the third party by cross-examination; and despite the diminution of the value of these safeguards in relation to the testifying witness on account of the severance of any direct link between his testimony and the proposition which the jury is invited to support as a result of it. A direct witness, who asserts that x existed can be cross-examined much more fruitfully about his perception and memory of x of which he claims experience, than the hearsay witness, who merely testifies that he heard a third party say 'x exists', can be cross-examined about what he claims he heard.

It is largely because of the increased dangers of impaired perception, bad memory, ambiguity and insincerity, coupled with the decreased effectiveness of conventional safeguards, that hearsay is regarded as so particularly vulnerable as to require a special exclusionary rule.[20] Because dangers of ambiguity and insincerity relate to the existence of belief while those of impaired perception and bad memory relate to its reflection of reality, some commentators explicitly utilise the difference between them in their definition of hearsay.[1] Because cross-examination is often supposed to be more effective in relation to perception and memory, the diminution of such dangers in particular circumstances is often used to help to justify special exceptions.[2]

In defining hearsay implicit reference is made to the existence of these dangers in applying the exclusionary rule only to situations in which the out-of-court assertion is tendered for the truth of that which it asserts. If it is tendered merely as direct evidence of the fact of its having been asserted, or as circumstantial evidence of the belief of its auditor in the truth of the matter asserted, no question arises as to the sincerity, memory or perception of utterance of the third party, and in many cases there is little possibility of ambiguity. All four dangers are much more potent if the assertion is tendered to prove the truth of the matter asserted. Definitions of the type advanced here have been categorised as assertion-based definitions because of their concentration upon the role played by the assertion.[3] Other definitions which stress the absence from the courtroom of the original source of the information have been categorised as declarant-based definitions.[4] The principal reason for adopting the former approach is to cater for the assimilation of the exclusion both of the out-of-court assertions of third parties, and of those of the witness who is testifying.

---

19 Namely that the third party did not speak on oath, and was not liable to prosecution for perjury if he were lying.

20 In *Teper v R* [1952] AC 480, at 486, [1952] 2 All ER 447, at 449, Lord Normand summarised the classic rationale for exclusion as being 'It is not the best evidence and it is not delivered on oath. The truthfulness and accuracy of the person whose words are spoken by another witness cannot be tested by cross-examination, and the light which his demeanour would throw on his testimony is lost.'

1   Lempert and Saltzburg *A Modern Approach to Evidence* (2nd edn, 1982) pp 357, 358.

2   See eg United States Federal Rules of Evidence, r 803 (24) and r 804(b)(6).

3   Park (1981) 65 Minn LR 423.

4   See eg in South Africa, Law of Evidence (Amendment) Act No 45, s 4.

It must also be remembered that if the hearsay rule is to be effective it must exclude circumstantial as well as direct inference. As Thayer put it:[5]

the hearsay rule operates in two ways: (a) it forbids using the credit of an absent declarant as the basis of an inference, and (b) it forbids using in the same way the mere evidentiary fact of the statement as having been made under such and such circumstances.

There would be little point in excluding testimony that a named third party said 'x exists' for the purpose of showing directly that x existed, if the same testimony were nevertheless to be accepted as evidence that the third party said that x existed, perhaps coupled with testimony as to the third party's general high reputation for credibility, and then to permit the jury to draw from these circumstances what conclusion it pleased. The analysis of testimony inviting this sort of circumstantial inference causes some difficulty in borderline cases. Occasionally it leads to the mis-classification of non-hearsay as hearsay.[6] More often hearsay goes unrecognised, and if the definition were more widely drawn hardly any piece of testimony would be completely free of its tentacles.

C.   DEVELOPMENT

Parts of the rule are very ancient,[7] but like much of the law of evidence it began to crystallise in the late seventeenth century. Although apparently disregarded in some contexts,[8] it had become well-established by the beginning of the nineteenth century, and was brought to prominence in the Dickensian saga of *Wright v Doe d Tatham*.[9] For some inexplicable reason[10] that case turned on the admissibility of some letters written to a testator long before his death, tendered to rebut suggestions that he was a congenital idiot incapable of managing his affairs. In the course of the elaborate series of arguments and judgments which constitute the saga many of the basic concepts and problems of hearsay[11] were ventilated. In the end the letters were excluded.[12] The technicality of much of that discussion seems to have inhibited further development of the rule at common law, and it spluttered to an end soon afterwards.[13] Although sporadic efforts were made to create explicit exceptions in more modern times, the door was slammed shut by the declaration of Lord Reid in *Myers v DPP* that:[14]

5   Thayer *Legal Essays* (1907) p 270. See also McHugh J in *Pollitt v R* (1992) 174 CLR 558, at 620, 'The hearsay rule would be meaningless in practice if it prohibited a statement being used directly to prove a fact contained in a statement but allowed the statement to be used circumstantially to prove a state of mind from which could be inferred the existence of the very fact which could not be proved directly'; but cp Dawson and Gaudron JJ in the same case.

6   See eg *R v Olisa* [1990] Crim LR 721; and more arguably *R v Irish* [1994] Crim LR 922.

7   The rule allowing evidence of dying declarations as proof of the truth of their contents was shown by Thayer to antedate the exclusionary rule itself by some centuries.

8   Such as low level criminal prosecutions, see Langbein 45 U of Chi LR 263, at 301 (1978).

9   (1837) 7 Ad & El 313; affd (1838) 5 Cl & Fin 670. Other stages in the drama are reported in (1832) 2 Russ & M 1, (1834) 1 Ad & El 3 and (1837) 7 Ad & El 359.

10   There was plenty of other much more direct evidence.

11   And its interaction with evidence of opinion.

12   Although in the final stages the strictly hearsay point was no longer being pressed.

13   The last strong statement of judicial ability to shape the rule came in *Sugden v Lord St Leonards* (1876) 1 PD 154, at 241; the first strong denial in *Sturla v Freccia* (1880) 5 App Cas 623, at 647.

14   [1965] AC 1001, at 1021, [1964] 2 All ER 881, at 885. The comment was made in full knowledge, and approval, of the recommendations of the Law Reform Committee for wholesale

If we are to extend the law it must be by the development and application of fundamental principles. We cannot introduce arbitrary conditions or limitations; that must be left to legislation: and if we do in effect change the law, we ought in my opinion only to do that in cases where our decision will produce some finality or certainty. If we disregard technicalities in this case and seek to apply principle and common sense, there are a number of parts of the existing law of hearsay susceptible of similar treatment, ... The only satisfactory solution is by legislation following on a wide survey of the whole field ... A policy of make do and mend is no longer adequate.

Legislative reform of the rule had begun just as judicial moulding ceased at the end of the nineteenth century.[15] At first it was limited to special situations, but when it was found that the results were acceptable, more general reform was mooted, at least in relation to civil proceedings, and the first broad relaxation was made by the Evidence Act 1938. It took some time for the judiciary and the profession to warm to such relaxation,[16] but by the 1960s it was generally recognised that more thoroughgoing reform was desirable,[17] as evidenced in the quotation above. Part of the reason for this was realisation that the rule had been established to deal with an environment which had wholly changed,[18] and to cater for a system of the administration of justice which had also undergone considerable change.[19] This led to the realisation that not all hearsay was unreliable, and that tribunals could cope with its assessment perfectly capably. Unfortunately the tension between the technical rigidity of the rule and the need to do justice led to rather strained interpretation of basic concepts,[20] tending to undermine the whole edifice.

D.   REFORM OF THE RULE[1]

Although Wigmore regarded the hearsay rule as the 'most characteristic rule of the Anglo-American law of Evidence—a rule which may be esteemed, next to jury trial, the greatest contribution of that eminently practical legal system to the world's methods of procedure',[2] not all views have been quite so complimentary, with for example both Lord Reid[3] and Lord Diplock[4] judicially categorising it as absurd.[5]

reform of the rule, and probably in the expectation of their adoption by the Criminal Law Revision Committee and speedy enactment thereafter. For more modern affirmation of this approach see Lord Bridge in *R v Kearley* [1992] 2 AC 228, at 251H, [1992] 2 All ER 345, at 361a.

15   A clear example is the Bankers' Books Evidence Act 1879.
16   Partly because of the cautious technicality of the 1938 legislation.
17   As noted above the matter was referred to both Law Reform Committees in the early 1960s.
18   Especially in reliance upon modern systems of record-keeping in business, or more prosaically in the mobility and aggregation of populations. *Myers v DPP* was itself a case where all turned on the accuracy of stored records, and where oral testimony from those who had once had personal knowledge would have been valueless.
19   Most notably by the demise of the jury in civil proceedings, and the disappearance of witnesses from the committal stage of criminal proceedings.
20   See especially Ashworth and Pattenden 102 LQR 292 (1986); Birch in Smith P (ed) *Essays in Honour of JC Smith* 24 (1987); Pattenden 56 MLR 138 (1993).
1   Different approaches to reform of the rule are extensively discussed in Law Reform Commission of Australia Research Paper No 9 Hearsay Law Reform—Which Approach (1982).
2   5 *Wigmore* Evidence 1364.
3   In *Myers v DPP* [1965] AC 1001, at 1019, [1964] 2 All ER 881, at 884.
4   In *Jones v Metcalfe* [1967] 3 All ER 205, at 208, [1967] 1 WLR 1286, at 1291.
5   See also *R v Gilfoyle* [1996] 1 Cr App Rep 302, at 325: 'Although, in our opinion, the making of the statements in the present case was relevant and admissible under the existing complex

As mentioned above, the hearsay rule developed alongside that of the newer form of trial by jury, and was concerned to prevent its being undermined by the introduction of evidence which could not easily be tested by cross-examination in open court. Both of these justifications are now much weaker than once they were. The overwhelming majority of trials are now conducted without a jury, and a more literate and technologically advanced society provides, and depends upon, more reliable methods of keeping track of what has happened than can possibly be provided by the unassisted recollection of witnesses, even though exposed to cross-examination by an opponent. It remains true however that in some circumstances such records are not available, and the hearsay rule can then be relied upon to prevent the deliberate dilution of proof by straining out the testimony of those with direct personal knowledge of relevant events, and by seeking to substitute for it the bland reportage of those who know only what they have been told by others. The business of reform thus seeks to prevent the rule from causing unnecessary difficulty, while at the same time preserving its efficiency.

This has become a cause for concern across the whole range of legal proceedings and in all common law jurisdictions.[6] This section will consider first the strategic choices for reform, then its accomplishment in this jurisdiction, subdivided into civil and criminal proceedings, and finally make some brief comparison with reform elsewhere.

1. Strategic choices

Once reform of some sort has been decided upon the major question is how extensive it should be; both as regards its width in terms of the types of proceeding it should affect, and as regards its depth in terms of the degree to which the rule should be changed. One of the defects of the rule as it developed in English law was that it became complicated by a patchwork of interpretation, modification and reform, not always fully implemented, which led to differences between the operation of the rule in higher and lower courts, in civil and criminal proceedings, and sometimes between different forms of proceeding within those categories.

In England the traditional approach has been to distinguish sharply between the operation, and reform, of the rule in civil proceedings and in criminal. This could be justified by differences in procedure, both pre-trial and in-trial. Thus pre-trial procedure was more developed in relation to civil proceedings, and was thought capable of supporting a scheme of pre-trial notices to a greater extent than was allowed by the more vestigial pre-trial procedure in criminal proceedings. Jury trial is now very rare in civil proceedings, but universal in serious criminal proceedings. It is none the less anomalous and inconvenient to have different rules of admissibility in the two categories since it is now becoming more common for civil proceedings to be brought in respect of criminal offences, and in modern law, as has been described,[7] findings in the one form of proceedings may be admissible in evidence in the other. It is unconvincing for the courts to find a matter proved for one purpose, but not for another; and, if anything even less palatable, for it to be proved in one proceeding, only if that proceeding had been preceded by a different type of proceeding. Despite such considerations the Law

---

hearsay rules, the fact that dubbing them "hearsay" sufficed to proscribe them from the jury's judgment is hardly likely to enhance public esteem of the criminal process'.

6   Even in the United States: see symposium on reform in 76 Minn LR 363–555 (1991).

7   Ch II part 4 above.

Commission has worked upon the assumption[8] that the rules should continue to be different in civil and criminal proceedings, with more radical reform reserved for the former.

On the other hand the Law Commission does envisage that the rules should, in principle, be the same for all criminal proceedings to which the strict rules of evidence apply,[9] whether before magistrates, stipendiary or lay, or judge and jury, and adduced by either prosecution or defence. It had hitherto been a matter of dispute whether civil proceedings before magistrates should be governed by the same rules as proceedings in the High Court.[10] The Civil Evidence Act 1995 provides for the same law to apply in both types of proceeding. There has been less explicit discussion in relation to reform in criminal proceedings as between those before magistrates and those before judge and jury.[11] Despite the absence of explicit discussion, both the argument and definition in the reports both of the Criminal Law Revision Committee[12] and the Law Commission[13] require proceedings before magistrates and before judge and jury to be governed by the same rules.

The problem of whether to apply the same rules within criminal proceedings to the defence in the same way as to the prosecution was the subject of explicit discussion by the Law Commission.[14] The view was taken that to have different rules[15] should be rejected since, given the high standard required for conviction, it might lead to more unjust acquittals by permitting falsely manufactured evidence to tip the balance. It was also felt that it might lead to the anomaly that the prosecution would be entitled to cross-examine defence evidence which it could not itself have adduced in-chief. Its final consideration was that any unfairness would be cured by the inclusionary residual discretion which it recommended. It should be remembered that both the common law exclusionary discretion, and its statutory counterpart,[16] operate only in favour of the defence.

These considerations relate only to *general* rule. It does not follow that the rule will apply in exactly the same way to all types of civil or criminal proceeding, to all types of evidence, to all types of issue or in respect of all sorts of witness. In all of these respects some exceptions exist. Thus the rule does not apply in the ordinary way to applications for interim remedies,[17] or to the use of transcripts in retrials of criminal proceedings ordered by the Court of Appeal.[18] Similarly there has always been some relaxation in

8   Law Com No 216 Cm 2321 (1993) para 1.2 stressed that its consideration was restricted to the reform of the rule in civil proceedings because a separate reference was then pending in relation to criminal proceedings. The report on that reference Law Com 245 Cm 3670 (1997) did not explicitly consider adoption of the civil rules as such, but rejection was implicit in its rejection of its radical options 2 and 3.
9   Draft bill, cll 1(1), 26(1).
10 See Law Reform Committee 13th Report *Hearsay Evidence in Civil Proceedings* Cmnd 2964 (1966) paras 48–52; Law Commission No 216 above paras 3.22–3.47.
11 Although some of the arguments in relation to civil proceedings relied upon the complexity of magistrates having to handle so many different versions of the rule, including one for criminal proceedings, see Law Com No 216, para 3.23.
12 11th Report Cmnd 4991, eg para 246 and draft bill, cll 30(1), 45(1).
13 No 245 Cm 3670, eg para 3.28 and draft bill, cll 1(1), 26(1).
14 Paras 5.24, 8.136, 12.2–12.8.
15 Different in favouring greater exclusion of prosecution evidence; no one seems to have suggested a converse imbalance.
16 Police and Criminal Evidence Act 1984, s 78.
17 Affidavits are permitted, and required in certain cases, by the Civil Procedure Rules Practice Direction 25, para 3.1; see under the old law *Savings and Investment Bank Ltd v Gasco Investments (Netherlands) BV (No 2)* [1988] Ch 422, [1988] 1 All ER 975; *Deutsche Rückversichering Aktiengesellschaft v Walbrook Insurance Co Ltd* [1994] 4 All ER 181, [1995] 1 WLR 1017.
18 Criminal Appeal Act 1968, Sch 2, para 1.

relation to some forms of evidence such as public documents.[19] In relation to different types of issue, statute now allows the admission of hearsay in connection with the upbringing, maintenance, or welfare of a child.[20] Numerous minor statutory exceptions apply to particular criminal proceedings.[1] The rule also applies differently to some types of witness, such as experts tendering the basis for their opinion.[2]

2.   Reform in civil proceedings

As indicated above general statutory change came first to civil proceedings in the form of the Evidence Act 1938 making some types of documentary hearsay admissible. The legislation was deliberately cast in cautious terms,[3] and effected no revolutionary change of attitude.[4] Such a change was however manifest in the proposal of the Law Reform Committee in its 13th Report which started from the premise of abolishing the hearsay rule, and to require a case to be made for any exception. It is also noteworthy that the Committee attached importance to the saving of cost, which in its view militated against a discretionary basis for the admission of hearsay, since any uncertainty would result in cost being incurred in providing direct evidence if the litigator could not be sure that the cheaper expedient of tendering hearsay would be allowed. Because of the piecemeal[5] approach of the Law Reform Committee it was possible to secure substantial and speedy enactment of its recommendations as the Civil Evidence Act 1968. The hallmark of this legislation was its radical approach in putting the admission of hearsay upon an overwhelmingly statutory basis.[6] The general approach was to place the matter more firmly in the hands of the parties allowing admission by consent, or in the absence of objection following the serving of notice. The Civil Evidence Act 1995 has built upon these foundations.[7]

Alongside these overt reforms of the rules of admissibility there has also been significant change in rules of procedure militating in favour of greater pre-trial disclosure of evidence.[8] To such an extent have these considerations influenced each other that it is now provided for the first time that the new Civil Procedure Rules Committee shall have the power to modify the rules of evidence in the higher civil courts.[9]

---

19   See eg *Sturla v Freccia* (1889) 14 App Cas 437; *R v Halpin* [1975] QB 907, [1975] 2 All ER 1124.
20   Children Act 1989, s 96, and SI 1993/621, building on the approach of the common law to adoption in *Official Solicitor v K* [1965] AC 201, [1963] 3 All ER 191.
1   See Law Commission Consultation Paper No 138 (1995) where App C contains a non-exhaustive list of thirty.
2   See eg *H v Schering Chemicals Ltd* [1983] 1 All ER 849, at 853; *R v Abadom* [1983] 1 All ER 364, 76 Cr App Rep 48.
3   See Lord Maugham LC 17 Can BR 475 (1939).
4   See Report of the Committee on Supreme Court Practice and Procedure Cmnd 8878 (1953) para 272; 13th report of Law Reform Committee Cmnd 2964 (1966) para 11.
5   So piecemeal that the admission of hearsay evidence of opinion was postponed for a separate report: 17th, Cmnd 4489 (1970); itself followed by separate legislation: Civil Evidence Act 1972.
6   Although much of the statute reproduced aspects of the common law, especially the exceptions enacted in s 9.
7   To be considered in more detail in ch XIV below.
8   See further, above pp 245.
9   Civil Procedure Act 1997, Sch I, para 4.

3.   Reform in criminal proceedings

There has, so far, been much less progress here, no doubt influenced to a considerable extent by concern not to prejudice the position of the accused. The matter was first considered from a general point of view by the Criminal Law Revision Committee in its Eleventh Report.[10] Unfortunately the method adopted by that Committee, of considering in one report the reform of the whole of the law of evidence in criminal proceedings, had two unfortunate consequences. First it delayed the presentation of the Committee's proposals for some years[11] and, second, by being united with all of the other recommendations of the Committee, many of them unacceptable to the legislature, the proposals have never been enacted in England[12] in the form envisaged by the Committee. One consequence of this was that the legislature adopted[13] the very sort of piecemeal reform deprecated by Lord Reid in *Myers v DPP*. Another was that when the legislature did attempt to enact parts of the recommendations of the Committee at a later date, the failure to enact them in their original context led to some confusion.[14] Nevertheless over the years it has proved possible for the legislature to expand the admission of hearsay, notably in the provisions of Part II of the Criminal Justice Act 1988, and for the Law Commission to recommend[15] still further movement in that direction.[16] It is however not yet certain that it will be feasible to enact those recommendations in their existing form, as it may be felt[17] that such legislation would fall foul of the provisions for a fair trial enshrined in art 6 of the European Convention of Human Rights, recently incorporated into English law by the Human Rights Act 1998.

4.   Reform elsewhere[18]

In a few jurisdictions it has been possible to progress without legislation, by liberal judicial departure from the old constraints. The Supreme Court of Canada has, in a string of cases,[19] thus adopted what it describes as a 'principled' approach to the admission of hearsay, admitting hearsay upon a sufficient showing of the reliability of, and necessity for, the evidence. It is noteworthy that this appears to be regarded as perfectly consistent with the Canadian Charter of Rights and Freedoms.[20] There were also signs[1]

10   *Evidence: General* Cnd 4991 (1972) especially paras 224–271.
11   Thus despite contemporaneous reference to the two, the Criminal Law Revision Committee's proposals on hearsay were first published six years later than those of the Law Reform Committee, and four years after their enactment.
12   Singapore was more receptive.
13   Ironically the first such legislation, the Criminal Evidence Act 1965, was enacted to reverse the decision in *Myers*.
14   For example in relation to the rules relating to the confessions of other accused persons.
15   *Evidence in Criminal Proceedings: Hearsay and Related Topics.* Law Com No 245 Cm 3670 (1997).
16   To be considered in more detail in ch XV below.
17   Despite the rejection of such a view by the Law Commission itself: see Part V passim, and especially para 5.41.
18   For a survey of some Commonwealth jurisdictions see Tapper 22 UWALR 31 (1992).
19   *R v Khan* [1990] 2 SCR 531; *R v Smith* [1992] 2 SCR 915; *R v B(KG)* [1993] 1 SCR 740; *R v Finta* [1994] 1 SCR 701; *R v U(FJ)* [1995] 3 SCR 764; *R v Hawkins* [1996] 3 SCR 1043; but cp *R v R(D)* [1996] 2 SCR 291.
20   At least in a case where there has been some provision for cross-examination at an earlier stage: see *R v Potvin* [1989] 1 SCR 525 which adopted such a view before this line of cases was subsequently approved in *R v Beck* (1996) 108 CCC (3d) 385.
1   See Mason CJ in *Walton v R* (1989) 166 CLR 283, at 293 'The hearsay rule should not be applied inflexibly....there will be occasions upon which circumstances will combine to render

of such a development in Australia before the passage of the Evidence Act (Cwth) 1995,[2] and in New Zealand.[3]

The most radical approaches to reform in most common law jurisdictions have been statutory, especially those implemented in South Africa and Scotland, and that recommended for New Zealand.

(i)   South Africa

The Law of Evidence Amendment Act No 45 of 1988 provided an interesting new approach to the reform of the hearsay rule making its admission in evidence in contested cases where the maker of the statement did not testify wholly discretionary.[4] The provision is sufficiently short, and clear, to be quoted in extenso,

'3.   Hearsay Evidence. (1) Subject to the provisions of any other law, hearsay evidence shall not be admitted as evidence at criminal or civil proceedings, unless,-
- (a)   each party against whom the evidence is to be adduced agrees to the admission thereof as evidence at such proceedings;
- (b)   the person upon whose credibility the probative value of such evidence depends, himself testifies at such proceedings; or
- (c)   the court having regard to -
  - (i)   the nature of the proceedings;
  - (ii)   the nature of the evidence;
  - (iii)   the purpose for which the evidence is tendered;
  - (iv)   the probative value of the evidence;
  - (v)   the reason why the evidence is not given by the person upon whose credibility the probative value of such evidence depends;
  - (vi)   any prejudice to a party which the admission of such evidence might entail;
  - (vii)   any other factor which should in the opinion of the court be taken into account,

is of the opinion that such evidence should be admitted in the interests of justice.

(2) The provisions of subsection (1) shall not render admissible any evidence which is inadmissible on any ground other than that such evidence is hearsay evidence.

(4) For the purposes of this section-
"hearsay evidence" means evidence, whether oral or in writing, the probative value of which depends upon the credibility of any person other than the person giving such evidence;

---

evidence sufficiently reliable for it to be placed before the jury for consideration and evaluation of the weight which should be placed upon it, notwithstanding that in strict terms it would be regarded as inadmissible hearsay'; and Kirby P in *R v Astill* (1992) 63 ACR 148, at 158 'Reform, including judicial reform, of the hearsay rule appears to be both necessary and inevitable'.

2   Rather conservative in its admission of hearsay.

3   See Cooke CJ in *R v Baker* [1989] 1 NZLR 738, at 741; Casey J in *R v Smith* [1989] 3 NZLR 405, at 410; but for a more conservative view opposing piecemeal judicial development see Thomas J in *Reddy v Police* [1994] 1 NZLR 48. The admission of hearsay is not necessarily regarded as incompatible with the Bill of Rights: see *R v Cheprakov* [1997] NZLR 169, at 173; although the absence of an opportunity to cross-examine requires strong justification: see *R v L* [1994] 2 NZLR 54; *R v J* [1998] 1 NZLR 20.

4   An approach which would have been welcomed by some distinguished American judges: see, for example, Justice Learned Hand as quoted in Wigmore *Evidence* Vol V para 1576 p 530.

"party" means the accused or party against whom hearsay evidence is to be adduced including the prosecution.'

As noted above the proposal is radical, at least in the British context in applying equally to criminal and civil proceedings,[5] in applying to oral and documentary hearsay, and in applying to hearsay in any degree. It appears also to abridge the common law exceptions to the hearsay rule, since the opening words seem to contemplate pre-existing statutory provisions only. It is also interesting in its definition of hearsay which makes no reference to the use to which the out of court statement is to be put, and in particular makes no reference to its being intended to prove the truth of the matters to which it relates. While it is just possible that this limitation may be construed from the reference to reliance upon the *credibility* of the out of court declarant, it is at least possible that it will be taken to encompass other out of court utterances, writings or actions the cogency of which depend upon the sincerity of speaker, writer or actor.

A most important feature of the provision is the list of factors which the court is instructed to take into account in exercising its discretion. This simple and straightforward list seems ideally suited to the purpose of insulating the discretion from reversal on appeal. It will be easy for the trial judge to advert to each in turn, and difficult if he does so for an appellate court to hold that he has not taken into account the factors which he is bound to take into account. The last provision even allows for further considerations to be added to the six explicitly listed. One of the problems of so far-ranging a legislative change in the approach to the admission of hearsay, is that it may be frustrated by an ultra-conservative judicial approach.[6] It will be interesting to see how this legislation settles down. Its principal disadvantage, of course, is that, at least until it has been in force for some time and has built up a shell of interpretation, its amorphous nature will provide no guidance in advance of trial of the evidence likely to be admitted, and will thus hamper pre-trial, advice, negotiation, settlement and preparation.

(ii)   Scotland

In the same year as the South Africans made the admission of hearsay discretionary, the Scots took the radical step of abolishing the rule altogether in civil proceedings.[7] It is interesting that the two jurisdictions to make such moves are both ones in which there is some admixture of civilian law. It is noteworthy that Scottish common law was also more liberal than English in having a general rule admitting statements of deceased persons.[8]

It is particularly interesting that the Scottish Law Commission proposed a less radical measure of reform than that enacted. It took the view that it would be preferable to qualify its recommendation of abolition by conferring a power upon the court to refuse

---

5   No doubt because juries are not used in South Africa either for civil or criminal proceedings.
6   First indications were unpromising: see *Hlongwane v Rector, St. Francis College* 1989 (3) SA 318 (civil proceedings), and *S v Cekiso* 1990 (4) SA 20 (criminal); but a more robust attitude was taken by the appellate division in *Mdani v Allianz Insurance Ltd* 1991 (1) SA 184.
7   There was no such intention in relation to criminal proceedings: see Scottish Law Commission Discussion Paper No 77 'Criminal Evidence: Affidavit Evidence, Hearsay and Related Matters in Criminal Proceedings' (1988) para 3.7.
8   See *Lauderdale Peerage Case* (1885) 10 App Cas 692; *Lovat Peerage Case* (1885) 10 App Cas 763.

to admit the hearsay where it was both reasonable[9] and practicable for the maker to be called as a witness.[10] It was, at least in part, in reliance upon that qualification that the Commission felt emboldened to include within its recommendations hearsay of any degree, however remote.[11]

The legislation that ensued was starkly simple. Its effective provision is contained in the Civil Evidence (Scotland) Act 1988, s 2(1),

'In any civil proceedings–
(a)   evidence shall not be excluded solely on the ground that it is hearsay;
(b)   a statement made by a person otherwise than in the course of proof shall be admissible as evidence of any matter contained in the statement of which direct oral evidence by that person would be admissible; and
(c)   the court, or as the case may be the jury, if satisfied that any fact has been established in those proceedings, shall be entitled to find that fact proved by the evidence notwithstanding that the evidence is hearsay.'

This appears to be the first legislation anywhere in the common law world to have abolished[12] the hearsay rule. The use of 'solely' in s 2(1)(a) ensures that the rule does not affect other exclusionary rules. The Act applies to statements of opinion as well as to those of fact,[13] and of whatever degree. 'Document' is defined as in the English Civil Evidence Act 1968, and clearly extends to records emanating from computers. Transcripts of such records are admissible as copies, and are presumed to be accurate in the absence of evidence to the contrary.[14] It departs from the recommendations of the Scottish Law Commission in dispensing with the elaborate notice procedure it required to try to preserve the testimony of a witness whom it was practicable and reasonable to call. There is however still one line of escape from so completely radical a change. Section 4 permits an additional witness to be called by either party before the start of closing submissions, so if the maker is available, his presence for cross-examination can be secured, though only with the leave of the court. If a witness is called then any previous statements whether consistent or inconsistent can be put to him, and as such become evidence in the case. Further provisions of the Act[15] provide for the automatic admissibility of the records of any business or undertaking.[16] Following the explicit recommendations of the Scottish Law Commission no distinction at all is made between the admissibility of records from computers, and those from any other devices. Rather oddly the Act explicitly preserves the admissibility of statements as evidence of the fact that the statement was made, though it is hard to see when this will be relied upon.[17] Provision is explicitly made for the admission of negative hearsay,

---

9   This is designed to cover both cases where it is unreasonable on grounds of cost and trouble, and those where it is unreasonable in terms of procedure, such as those where the witness is in some sense an opponent.

10   Scottish Law Commission No 100 *Evidence: Report on Corroboration, Hearsay and Related Matters* (1986) para 3.40.

11   Para 3.52.

12   This is the terminology deliberately adopted by the Scottish Law Commission for its own more qualified proposal.

13   Section 9.

14   Section 6.

15   Section 5.

16   Defined widely enough to include trades, professions and both local and national governmental institutions.

17   Perhaps if the maker would otherwise have been incompetent it would forestall an objection; for example an utterance by an insane person, dead by the time of trial, to show that at the time of utterance the person was alive.

but only in the case of business records,[18] so presumably if a private person keeps a meticulously detailed diary of appointments, the absence of an entry will not be evidence that there was no appointment as may have been claimed.

Part of the reason for taking so radical an approach was that it seemed to have caused little or no difficulty in those non-judicial proceedings where hearsay is admitted.[19] So far there is no evidence that this measure has caused such mischief either.

(iii)   New Zealand

The most recent discussion paper of all was produced by the Law Commission of New Zealand.[20] It favoured a result very like that achieved by the Scots, especially in eliminating the notice procedure, and in securing that available witnesses are called to testify, first by the informal pressure of costs, but then by explicit permission to call the witness, differing from the Scottish position only in relation to the practical matter of specifying whose witness such a person was to be,[1] and by specifying more precisely the circumstances in which a judge should exercise his discretion as to whether or not to accede to such a request. This Commission considered criminal proceedings as well as civil, and although not inclined to go quite so far in criminal proceedings nevertheless proposed considerable rationalisation, which would probably lead to a more liberal overall regime for hearsay in New Zealand than anywhere else.

SECTION 2.   THE SCOPE OF THE RULE

Because the rule has now become largely statutory and more relaxed, it might be expected that there will be less need, or opportunity, to exploit legal technicality in order to hold that the exclusionary rule does not apply to particular categories of utterance, document or conduct. It is submitted that this will largely turn out to be the case, but nevertheless some attention still has to be paid to the scope of the rule since statutory reform[2] has chosen to define hearsay for the purpose, using terminology which has acquired a substantial patina of interpretation.[3]

Nevertheless discussion can now be considerably curtailed, since it is submitted that it is inconceivable that the courts will in civil cases countenance a situation in which the clearest non-hearsay and hearsay statements are admitted, but statements falling into some indeterminate penumbra between these extremes are excluded. Although in criminal cases a basic exclusionary rule has been maintained, it has been tightly drawn, and there are extensive exceptions which may easily conduce to a similar approach to definition.

---

18   Section 7.
19   SLC No 100, para 3.14.
20   Prel Pap No 15 (1991).
1   They would be the witness of the party opposite in interest to that requiring them to be called.
2   This will be taken to include the reform in criminal cases recommended by the Law Commission, even though not yet enacted.
3   The Law Commission itself envisages that reference will continue to be made to existing authority defining the boundary of hearsay: Law Com No 216, paras 4.6, 4.35 (for the purposes of civil proceedings), and Law Com No 245, para 7.41 (for the purposes of criminal proceedings) stating only that boundary problems will be *reduced*, an implied assertion that they will not disappear entirely.

In this section a number of the old frontier areas will be reviewed, including statements admitted on the basis that they have been made,[4] statements forming part of the res gestae,[5] previous consistent statements, and admissions.

A. STATEMENTS AS FACTS

One of the most difficult issues in the old law was the determination of when statements were admitted not as evidence of the truth of what they stated as such, but as a basis for grounding a relevant inference, alleged not to depend upon their being true. It was on this basis that operative statements were admitted. A very clear example of the distinction was provided by the American case of *Johnson v Hansen*[6] where the rent for a farm was half of the crop, and the crop was stored in a barn divided into two equal segments. The tenant was heard to say to the landowner, indicating one end of the barn, 'that part of the crop is yours'. This was an operative statement when first made since it designated the part of the crop which was the landowner's, but any later statement of the same words, for example because the landowner had forgotten which end of the barn had been indicated, would have been hearsay. In other words the statement that one part of the crop was the landowner's *was made true* by its first utterance, but its *truth was affirmed* by any subsequent statement to the same effect.[7] In such cases the statement is itself in issue, but sometimes it is merely relevant to a fact in issue. In *Ratten v R* the accused was charged with the murder of his wife, and it became important to establish just when, to what effect, and by whom, a telephone call had been made from the house where the death took place. The disputed evidence was that of a telephone operator who testified to having received a call from the deceased, asking for the police in a distressed voice. Lord Wilberforce expressed the view that the evidence of the call having been made was not hearsay:[8]

> The mere fact that evidence of a witness includes evidence as to words spoken by another person who is not called is no objection to its admissibility. Words spoken are facts just as much as any other action by a human being. If the speaking of words is a relevant fact, a witness may give evidence that they were spoken. A question of hearsay only arises when the words are relied on 'testimonially', ie as establishing some fact narrated by the words.

The situation is more problematic when the statement is relevant to the state of mind of its auditor,[9] or of its speaker.[10] Disputes often arose as to the relevance of the state of mind, and the contiguity of hearsay exclusion seems sometimes to have led to a very

---

4 Including such issues as statements as real evidence, as operative facts and implied assertions.
5 To a considerable extent overlapping the previous category.
6 201 NW 322 (Min, 1924).
7 English parallels are provided by *Stobart v Dryden* (1836) 1 M & W 615 (attestation as fact rather than statement); *Re Wright, Hegan v Bloor* [1920] 1 Ch 108 (distinction between appointment being void because it was *said* to be a fraud on a power or because it *was* a fraud on a power).
8 [1972] AC 378, at 387, [1971] 3 All ER 801, at 805.
9 As in *Subramaniam v Public Prosecutor* [1956] 1 WLR 965 where the question was whether a man had been acting under duress, and it was proposed to adduce evidence of the threats made to him by terrorists.
10 As in *Woodhouse v Hall* (1980) 72 Cr App Rep 39 where the question was whether a statement offering immoral services was evidence that they were being supplied.

strict view of relevance, so as to permit exclusion of the evidence on that basis, without resolution of the more complex hearsay issues.[11]

A cognate problem exists with identifying statements. This may be illustrated with one of the less celebrated issues in *Myers v DPP*.[12] That was a car ringing case, and involved comparison between numbers stamped into cylinder blocks and other numbers. No question was raised as to whether the number stamped into the block was hearsay, since it identified the car to which the other numbers were merely attached. The problem arises when the identifying feature is itself a statement of fact, whether what it is identifying is the nature,[13] provenance[14] or ownership of goods,[15] the date of a document,[16] or the relationship[17] or identity[18] of a person.

This issue often overlapped with another problem which caused great difficulty, frequently categorised as the problem of implied assertions. This concerned the extent to which circumstantial inference could be based upon the statements of third parties without breach of the rule. This was considered in the leading case of *R v Kearley*.[19] In that case the police conducted a raid on premises from which it was suspected that the accused was dealing in drugs. While on the premises they intercepted ten telephone calls seeking the supply of drugs, some referring to past transactions, and opened the door to seven callers who were also seeking drugs. The prosecution proposed to adduce evidence of the fact of these calls, and the terms of what transpired during them in order to prove that the accused was in the business of supplying drugs from the premises. This evidence was admitted by the trial judge, and his decision upheld by the Court of Appeal. A further appeal to the House of Lords was allowed by a majority of three to two. The speeches of the majority all stressed the irrelevance of the calls as direct evidence of the state of mind of the callers, and Lord Ackner went so far as perhaps to make any question of hearsay obiter dictum:[20]

> An oral request for drugs to be supplied by the defendant, not spoken in his presence or in his hearing, could only be evidence of the state of mind of the person or persons making the request, and since his or their state of mind was not a relevant issue at the trial, evidence of such a request or requests, however given, would be irrelevant and therefore inadmissible. The jury would not be entitled to infer from the fact that the request(s) was made that the appellant was a supplier of drugs.

11   As in *R v Blastland* [1986] AC 41, [1985] 2 All ER 1095 where statements indicating the knowledge of a third party of the detail of commission of a murder, at that time not public knowledge, were held irrelevant to the issue of whether it was committed by him or by the accused.
12   [1965] AC 1001, at 1019, [1964] 2 All ER 881
13   In *R v Fizzell* (1987) 31 ACR 213 the court rejected a forensic scientist's evidence of analysis which she had performed because she had relied upon the sample having been correctly taken and labelled by an absent assistant prior to her analysis; cp *R v Orrell* [1972] RTR 14. See also *Holmden v Bitar* (1987) 47 SASR 509 (labels on tins of paté).
14   Compare *Patel v Comptroller of Customs* [1966] AC 356, [1965] 3 All ER 593 (label on sacks of coriander as 'Produce of Morocco'), with *Comptroller of Customs v Western Electric Co Ltd* [1966] AC 367, [1965] 3 All ER 599 (stamp on plastic implement 'Made in Denmark').
15   *R v Brown* [1991] Crim LR 835 (name in book).
16   *R v Cook* (1980) 71 Cr App Rep 205. There is considerable early authority on the use of postmarks to establish the date of posting.
17   *R v Benz* (1989) 168 CLR 110 ('my mother is sick').
18   *R v McCay* [1991] 1 All ER 232, [1990] 1 WLR 645 (at identification parade).
19   [1992] 2 AC 228, [1992] 2 All ER 345.
20   At 254, 363. See also Lord Bridge at 243, 353; and Lord Oliver at 263, 370.

It will be apparent from what I have already stated that the application of the hearsay rule does not, on the facts so far recited fall for consideration. The evidence is not admissible because it is irrelevant.

The acid test for this view is whether the evidence would have been admissible if testified to directly by the callers, and Lord Oliver in particular makes it crystal clear that it would not.

The hearsay point arises only if the calls are treated as implied assertions of the basis for the beliefs of the callers which led them to make their requests, namely that the accused was a dealer. All three members of the majority were clear that implied assertions were just as susceptible to the operation of the hearsay rule as express assertions. Lord Ackner thought it only reasonable:[1]

> If...the simple request or requests for drugs to be supplied by the appellant, as recounted by the police contains in substance, but only by implication, the same assertion, then I can find neither authority nor principle to suggest that the hearsay rule should not be equally applicable and exclude such evidence. What is sought to be done is to use the oral assertion, even though it may be an implied assertion, as evidence of the truth of the proposition asserted. That the proposition is asserted by way of necessary implication rather than expressly cannot, to my mind, make any difference.

Lord Bridge[2] and Lord Oliver[3] had more qualms about the policy, but nevertheless felt constrained[4] to come to the same decision. This result opened a chasm between the rather technical rule in England, and the position arrived at elsewhere in the Commonwealth in this context.[5] It is ironic that the situation in the United States, which is the same in its result as that in the rest of the Commonwealth, was used by Lord Bridge to justify his contrary view, on the basis that it had there been achieved only by express provision in the Federal Rules of Evidence.[6]

It remained to be seen just how far the courts would go in discerning an implied assertion in the absence of any express assertion to like effect. It is apparent from the facts of *Kearley* itself that the implication can be made from a statement which is not itself an express assertion. In *R v Rothwell*[7] it was necessary to show that the persons to whom packages were supplied were drug users, and a constable testified to that effect. After citation of *Kearley* it was held that the basis of such testimony must be direct observation[8] by the testifying witness. In other words it is not permissible to conceal a hearsay basis for belief behind a direct statement of the belief as a directly known fact. It was clear that the implications of the decision in *Kearley* might prove to

1   At 255, 364.
2   At 249, 359.
3   At 268, 375.
4   Induced by the tenor of the decision in *Wright v Doe d Tatham* (1837) 7 Ad & El 313, and less plausibly by that in *R v Blastland* above.
5   Largely in the context of betting where antipodean decisions such as those in *Davidson v Quirke* [1923] NZLR 552; *Lenthall v Mitchell* [1933] SASR 231; *Marsson v O'Sullivan* [1951] SASR 224; *McGregor v Stokes* [1952] VLR 347; *Marshall v Watt* [1953] Tas SR 1; *Gorman v Newton* [1958] Qd R 169; *Mathewson v Police* [1969] NZLR 218; *Police v Machirus* [1977] 1 NZLR 288; *Fingleton v Lowen* (1979) 20 SASR 312 were not accepted. The more recent case of *R v Firman* (1989) 52 SASR 391 was not mentioned in *Kearley*.
6   Citing *US v Zenni* 492 F Supp 464 (1950) in its construction of Rule 801(a).
7   (1994) 99 Cr App Rep 388. In Canada the more lenient view would probably fail to discern hearsay in such a situation: see *R v Litchfield* [1993] 4 SCR 333, at 359.
8   Or a close equivalent.

be far-reaching, difficult to analyse or to isolate, time-consuming and unpalatable.[9] Pending implementation of the recommendations of the Law Commission the decision remains binding on lower courts.[10]

No question of hearsay was thought to be involved if a statement was adduced as demonstrably false.[11] Thus in *A-G v Good* where a wife's untrue statement that her husband was away from home was received on the issue whether he intended to defraud his creditors, Garrow B said:[12]

> The doubt on the present occasion has originated in calling that hearsay evidence which has no approximation to it. The answer is received as a distinct fact in itself, to be compared and combined with other facts; ... Suppose an unreasonable time had intervened between the demand of entrance and the opening of the door ... is not that a circumstance to be inquired into with a view to the fact under investigation ...

Another situation in which a false statement could be adduced for the circumstantial inference to be drawn from it was, for example, one where the witness swears that he heard a person whose sanity is in issue claiming to be Napoleon, or one where in order to help fix the time of a person's death a witness swore that he heard the deceased asserting, at a relevant time, his innocence of possession of goods subsequently found to have been in his pocket.

Questions of implied assertion also arise when a negative is sought to be proved from failure to state a positive, in situations where one might be expected. In the old law the admissibility of such evidence was regarded as compatible with the exclusion of hearsay.[13] It is envisaged that such evidence will continue to be admissible under the new statutory regime,[14] even without explicit[15] general[16] provision.

Assertions may sometimes be made by conduct rather than in words, either because speech is impossible,[17] or because conduct is more graphic and effective.[18] Such assertions were, and remain,[19] hearsay. It may also be noted that conduct has occasionally been regarded as equivalent to a statement, and susceptible to the hearsay rule.[1] This view has rarely been applied in England,[2] and despite the general

---

9   See Law Com No 245, paras 7.1–7.41 where the proposal to reject it is justified. See further below p 565. For American discussion, see contributions to symposium on *Kearley* 16 Miss CLR 1 (1995).

10   See *R v Watson* [1997] Crim LR 680 where the facts were very similar.

11   These situations fall outside the statutory definitions: see Civil Evidence Act 1995, s 1(2)(a); Criminal Evidence Bill, cl 1(1).

12   (1825) M'Cle & Yo 286a, at 290. See also *Mawaz Khan v R and Amanat Khan* [1967] 1 AC 454, where it was alleged that a false alibi had been concocted by two co-accused, and Lord Hodson said of the statement at 462: 'they can without any breach of the hearsay rule be used, not for the purpose of establishing the truth of the assertions contained therein, but for the purpose of asking the jury to hold the assertions false and to draw inferences from their falsity.'

13   *R v Shone* (1982) 76 Cr App Rep 72; *R v Muir* (1983) 79 Cr App Rep 153; *R v Harry* (1988) 86 Cr App Rep 105.

14   See Law Com No 216, para 4.40; Law Com No 245, paras 7.10–7.12.

15   Such provision is made elsewhere: see Civil Evidence (Scotland) Act 1988, s 7; FRE, ss 803(7), (10).

16   Provision is made for the proof of the absence of entries in public and business records: Civil Evidence Act 1995, s 9(3).

17   As in *Chandresekara v R* [1937] AC 220, [1936] 3 All ER 865 where a woman, whose throat had been cut, used sign language to indicate the identity of her assailant.

18   As in *Li Shu-ling v R* [1989] AC 270, [1988] 3 All ER 138 where a crime was re-enacted.

19   Civil Evidence Act 1995, s 13; draft Criminal Evidence Bill, cl 2(2).

1   Most famously by Parke B in *Wright v Doe d Tatham* (1837) 7 Ad & El 313, at 387.

2   See eg *Manchester Brewery v Coombs* (1900) 82 LT 347 (voluntary conduct); *R v Turner* [1975] QB 834, at 840, [1975] 1 All ER 70, at 73 (involuntary conduct).

endorsement of *Wright v Doe d Tatham* in *Kearley v R* no reference was made to these dicta.[3] It is submitted that evidence of such conduct is admissible, if relevant, without reference to the hearsay rule.

B.   RES GESTAE STATEMENTS

Partly on account of the injustice caused by the inflexibility of the hearsay rule an unsatisfactory[4] inclusionary exception[5] was created at common law for statements so closely intertwined with the events in issue as to amount to part of what was going on. The general abrogation of the rule in civil cases has eliminated any need for it there, but it still applies in criminal proceedings, and the Law Commission has recommended its retention.[6] It should be noted however that the stricter definition of hearsay proposed should reduce the need for reliance upon this exception. Thus in *Teper v R* a bystander at the scene of a fire had been heard to exclaim at the oddity of the owner of the premises driving away. Such a statement would not fall within the limited definition of hearsay proposed by the Law Commission,[7] and there would be no need to rely upon an exception under this doctrine. The need for the exception will be still further reduced if the Law Commission's proposals to allow a general exception for the statements of deceased persons, or those unavailable to testify on account of illness are accepted.[8]

To the extent that reliance upon the exception will remain necessary the Law Commission explicitly[9] adopted the classification used in this work. It is, however, now possible to state the four elements of the exception more economically than before.[10]

I.   Statements relating to a relevant event

The reasoning here is that some statements are inspired by events to such an extent as to reduce substantially, the chance of error. It seems that the statement must be roughly contemporaneous[11] with the event, and made in circumstances of such involvement in it as to diminish the dangers of concoction,[12] mistake[13] or distortion.[14] This exception

3   Such conduct falls outside the statutory provision; see Civil Evidence 1995, s 1(2)(a), Criminal Evidence Bill, cl 1(1).
4   In *Ratten v R* [1972] AC 378, [1971] 3 All ER 801 Lord Wilberforce remarked at 388, 806 that 'The expression "res gestae," like many Latin phrases, is often used to cover situations insufficiently analysed in clear English terms.'
5   Not only to the hearsay rule, but to other exclusionary rules also, such as those relating to evidence indicating bad disposition.
6   Law Com 245, paras 8.114–8.129, recs 22–25, departing from its recommendation of abolition in its consultative paper. For criticism of this decision see Ormerod [1998] Crim LR 301.
7   Law Com 245, draft bill, cl 1(3), because it would not have been uttered with the intention of causing belief in its truth.
8   This would have removed the need to rely upon res gestae in such leading cases as *R v Bedingfield* (1879) 14 Cox CC 341; *Ratten v R* [1972] AC 378, [1971] 3 All ER 801; *R v Andrews* [1987] AC 281, [187] 1 All ER 513.
9   Law Com 245, para 8.114 fn 151.
10   For further detail see previous editions of this work.
11   *R v Newport* [1998] Crim LR 581. It may however be either earlier (as in *Ratten v R),* or later (as in *R v Andrews* [1987] AC 281, [1987] 1 All ER 513), than the commission of the crime charged.
12   *Ratten v R.*
13   *R v Nye and Loan* (1977) 66 Cr App Rep 252. The Law Commission rejected this form of disqualification: see Law Com 245, para 8.120.
14   *R v Andrews.* To which list *R v Lawson* [1998] Crim LR 883 appears to have added fabrication and dishonest motive, though it is hard to see why these were not covered by concoction.

has most often been used to indicate the identity of the criminal,[15] but is sometimes used for other purposes.[16]

It seems immaterial that the statement is elicited by questioning, so long as the principle of 'spontaneity' can be held to have been satisfied. Perhaps the analogy of the instigation of complaints in sexual cases may be thought apposite.[17] Spontaneity will partly be a function of the intrinsic excitement of the event, partly of the declarant's degree of involvement in it, and partly of the separation in time between the event and the declaration.[18] In one case,[19] where the event was no more than a collision causing damage to a coach driven by the declarant, his identification of the accused as the other driver some 20 minutes later was not regarded as sufficiently spontaneous. If these conditions are taken into account by the trial judge an appellate court is unlikely to interfere with his decision. It must be stressed however that where the declarant is available as a witness he should normally be called, and not only is the statement likely to be excluded if there is any suspicion of an attempt deliberately to shield a witness from cross-examination, but even when a witness is not present owing to the incompetence of the prosecution the same attitude is likely to be adopted.[20] On the other hand, the doctrine can be used when the prosecution has taken all reasonable steps to secure the attendance of a witness, but he has simply failed to appear.[1]

It has been suggested that the rationale of this exception is unconvincing, and that involvement in an exciting event is just as likely to lead to failures of perception as it is to eliminate dangers of insincerity.[2] The Law Commission found little contemporary support for this view, and accordingly included a special exception in its draft bill, if:[3]

the statement was made by a person so emotionally overpowered by an event that the possibility of concoction or distortion can be disregarded.

2.   Statements accompanying a relevant act

More than 150 years ago, Parke B spoke of 'proof of the quality and intention of acts by declarations accompanying them' as an exception to the rule against hearsay that

---

15   As in *R v Andrews; R v Turnbull* (1984) 80 Cr App Rep 104 (in both cases identification of the attacker by the victim who later died); *R v Glover* [1991] Crim LR 48 (where the statement emanated not from the victim but from the accused, and was reported by a third party).

16   As in *R v Bedingfield; Ratten v R* (to defeat defence of suicide, or accident); *R v Boyle* (6 March 1986, unreported) (to show that a clock was taken without victim's consent).

17   See above p 275.

18   In Canada proneness of the class of witness to concoct has been taken into account in relation to the acceptability of a given temporal separation between event and declaration: *R v Khan* (1988) 44 CCC (3d) 197, at 210.

19   *Tobi v Nicholas* (1987) 86 Cr App Rep 323. See also *Re Plumbers and Gasfitters* (1987) 72 ALR 415, at 434.

20   Ibid.

1   *Edwards and Osakwe v DPP* [1992] Crim LR 576.

2   Hutchins and Slesinger (1928) 28 Col LR 432, discussed in Australian Law Reform Commission Research Paper No 3 p 37.

3   Clause 6(5)(a). It is a common feature of this part of the draft bill that the formulation seems not to be definitive, but merely indicative of the relevant part of the existing common law invoked. If the formulations were intended to be definitive they would extend the common law exceptions considerably in the remaining three exceptions, though they would reduce its ambit here.

has been recognised from very early times on the ground of necessity or convenience.[4] The rule was stated by Grove J to be that:[5]

> Though you cannot give in evidence a declaration per se, yet when there is an act accompanied by a statement which is so mixed up with it as to become part of the res gestae, evidence of such a statement may be given.

Thus in *Walters v Lewis*[6] the defendant was allowed to call a witness to say that he had heard the defendant's wife say 'this money is to pay for the sheep' when handing it over to a servant. The purpose of the evidence was simply to explain the nature of the wife's act.[7] The danger of permitting the manufacture of evidence looms up at this point, and it may be thought that *Lister v Smith*[8] illustrated it by making no distinction between evidence of the statement of a testator, at the time of making a formally valid codicil and at other times, that he did not intend it to take effect.[9] The difference between the two situations is that when the words are uttered at the time of the act they explain, they can be regarded as part of that act which is independently relevant, but when they are uttered separately they can have no purpose other than to make an assertion about the quality of the earlier act. For this reason the exception has been strictly confined by conditions that the act be independently relevant,[10] that the words be contemporaneous,[11] and that they be spoken by the actor.[12]

The Law Commission decided to retain this exception in its draft bill on the basis that it appeared not to have created injustice. Its formulated the exception as applying if:[13]

> the statement accompanied an act which can be properly evaluated as evidence only if considered in conjunction with the statement.

3.   Statements of a relevant mental state

A person's declaration of his contemporaneous state of mind or emotion was admissible at common law as evidence of the existence of such state of mind or emotion. The reason for this exception to the hearsay rule was usually regarded as being that a person's statements are the best, and sometimes the only, means of demonstrating his state of mind. To that extent even direct statements of state of mind, comprehending such states as knowledge, memory, belief, opinion, intention and emotion, could be accepted

---

4   *Wright v Doe d Tatham* (1837) 7 Ad & El 313, at 384.
5   *Howe v Malkin* (1878) 40 LT 196.
6   (1836) 7 C & P 344.
7   It was regarded as irrelevant that the absent third party was an incompetent witness. See also *R v Lord George Gordon* (1781) 21 State Tr 485 (words uttered during riot); *Hayslep v Gymer* (1834) 1 Ad & El 162 (words accompanying delivery of money).
8   (1863) 3 Sw & Tr 282.
9   It is hard to reconcile the reasoning with that in *Stobart v Dryden* (1836) 1 M & W 615 or *Re Wright, Hegan v Bloor* [1920] 1 Ch 108, though the evidence would now be admissible under the Civil Evidence Act 1995.
10   See the rejection of an attempt to justify the admission of the words used in *R v Kearley* on the basis that they accompanied the act of telephoning.
11   See Lord Denman CJ in *Peacock v Harris* (1836) 5 Ad & El 449, '[A] contemporaneous declaration may be admissible as part of a transaction, but an act done cannot be varied or qualified by insulated declarations made at a later time.'
12   *Howe v Malkin* (1878) 40 LT 196.
13   Clause 6(5)(b).

notwithstanding any technical objection to such a means of proof as hearsay.[14] The danger of undermining the hearsay rule in this situation is plain, and the law's response was first to require fairly strict contemporaneity,[15] and second to impose strict limitations upon what the declaration was permitted to prove. Thus in *Thomas v Connell*[16] it was held on appeal that a bankrupt's statement that he knew he was insolvent was admissible to prove his knowledge of that fact at the time when he made a payment to the defendant, but not the fact of the insolvency, and this point was emphasised by Parke B when he said:

> If a fact be proved aliunde, it is clear that a particular person's knowledge of that fact may be proved by his declaration... and under the impression that such evidence was admissible after proof of the fact to which it related, I postponed the reception of such declaration in a cause of *Craven v Halliley* tried by me at York until after the fact was proved.

The converse was held in *R v Gunnell*[17] where it was decided that a statement that a fact exists is not admissible as evidence of the knowledge of the recipient of such a statement that the fact exists. In that case the issue was whether the fact of Gunnell's fraud was known before his examination in bankruptcy. If it had not previously been disclosed he could take advantage of a special statutory defence. The prosecution called one Marshall to testify that another, Andrews, had told him of Gunnell's fraud before the date of the examination, and that hence it had not been disclosed, in the sense of made known for the first time, during the bankruptcy proceedings themselves. It can be seen that the inference that it had been disclosed rested upon double hearsay, what Gunnell told Andrews, and what Andrews told the witness. It is not however clear why the exception to the hearsay rule cannot be applied twice. Each speaker is declaring or demonstrating his own state of mind, namely his 'knowledge' of Gunnell's fraud. It may be true that information acquired at third-hand is generally less cogent than information acquired at second-hand, but it is not clear that it is different in kind. The real question should have been whether on the construction of the statute it had become so remote as to be accounted rumour rather than knowledge. An unusual, but it is submitted correct, application of the rule in *R v Pangallo*[18] admitted evidence of the accused's statement that he had heard voices in his head, not to prove that they existed, but that he believed he had heard them.

Such questions are particularly acute in relation to the states of mind of knowledge, memory and belief. The court must be specially sensitive to avoid infringement of the hearsay rule, and scrupulous to inhibit inference of the underlying fact, known, remembered or believed. In some cases, such as *Thomas v Connell*, the issue directly involves the relevant state of mind. It is more tricky if it is merely argued that the state of mind is relevant to facts is issue. The problem is well illustrated by the case of *R v Blastland*.[19] The accused was charged with the murder of a young boy with whom he

14   In some situations the line between hearsay and original evidence is very fine in this area. In Australia a more relaxed view has prevailed in the aftermath of *Walton v R* (1989) 166 CLR 283: see eg *R v Matthews* (1990) 58 SASR 19; for New Zealand see *R v Baker* [1989] 1 NZLR 738.

15   *R v Vincent, Frost and Edwards* (1840) 9 C & P 275; *R v Petcherini* (1855) 7 Cox CC 79; *R v Kay* (1887) 16 Cox CC 292.

16   (1838) 4 M & W 267.

17   (1867) 16 Cox CC 154.

18   (1989) 51 SASR 254.

19   [1986] AC 41, [1985] 2 All ER 1095. See also *R v Roberts* (1984) 80 Cr App Rep 89, a case very similar on its facts. In Australia see *R v Zullo* [1993] 2 Qd R 572 (*Blastland* cited); in Canada see *R v Luke* (1993) 85 CCC (3d) 163 (*Blastland* not cited).

admitted having homosexual relations early on the evening of the boy's murder, though he denied otherwise harming him in any way. He claimed that a third man had been lurking near by, and so implied that another had the opportunity to commit the crime. His description of the man agreed with that of a local homosexual who was interviewed by the police, and in relation to whom statements were taken from others. Those statements were made available to the defence, and the accused wished to adduce evidence that the third man had made statements indicating his knowledge of the killing before it had become public. The House of Lords held evidence of such knowledge inadmissible, adopting a very narrow view of its relevance. It was suggested that because there were a number of innocent explanations of the acquisition of that knowledge it would be no more than speculative to infer that it had been acquired in the course of the commission of the crime, and it thus had insufficient relevance to any issue in the case. The court was further struck by the anomaly that would be created by the rule that a direct 'confession' of guilt by the third party would be inadmissible,[20] if such a statement were to be admitted. It would be tantamount to allowing evidence to prove indirectly that which could not be proved directly. This is the classic argument against allowing circumstantial undermining of the hearsay rule. It is however certainly arguable, especially in the case of someone accused of so heinous a crime, that little harm would have been done by admitting the evidence, allowing its cogency to be attacked by reference to the alternative innocent explanations, and leaving its ultimate weight to be determined by the jury.

Declarations of intention need special consideration because proof of intention is required in very many different legal contexts, and is generally regarded as being particularly difficult to establish without reference to its declaration by the person in question. This view was very clearly expressed by Mellish LJ in *Sugden v Lord St Leonards*:[1]

> wherever it is material to prove the state of a person's mind, or what was passing in it, and what were his intentions, there you may prove what he said, because that is the only means by which you can find out what his intentions are.

The concluding words are greatly exaggerated since intention very often is proved in the absence of any express declaration of it by the relevant party. It is a curious phenomenon that declarations of intention are more prone to be used to establish the performance of the act intended, than are declarations of knowledge, memory or belief, perhaps because the clash with the hearsay rule is less overt. The phenomenon is surprising because it can hardly be doubted that the inference to the commission of the act from a statement of intention to perform it is more precarious than the inference of commission from a statement of memory of having performed it. Given equal sincerity in either case, it is more likely that something will occur to frustrate a sincere intention to act than that memory of having acted will be mistaken. Of course in either case there will be considerable variation in reliability depending upon the distance in time between the statement and the act, and in relation to different degrees of detail of the act intended or remembered.

Since there is usually little question but that the existence of intention can be proved by way of express declaration, whether by exception to the hearsay rule or as original evidence, the focus of attention must again concentrate on the relevance of the

---

20   As hearsay not falling within any exception to the rule at common law. It is noteworthy that just such 'confessions' had been made at various stages by the third man, although subsequently retracted.

1   (1876) 1 PD 154, at 251.

utterance. In the case of declarations of intention questions may be raised in relation to the persistence of any such intention, and to its eligibility to prove the commission of the act intended.

In *Robson v Kemp*[2] Lord Ellenborough said: 'If the declarations of the bankrupt had been made before his act (a fraudulent assignment) they may show with what intention it was done', and in *Re Fletcher, Reading v Fletcher*,[3] Cozens-Hardy MR said 'It is common practice, particularly in criminal cases, to prove intention at a particular time by words and acts at a subsequent date'. A's declaration of intention on 1 January is received as testimonial evidence of that fact under an exception to the rule against hearsay, and the existence of the intention is then treated as an item of circumstantial evidence to prove the continuance of the intention up to 1 February, or its antecedent existence on 1 December. Obviously a point will be reached at which A's intention on 1 January is so remote as to be irrelevant to the question of his intention at another time, and, equally clearly, it is impossible to lay down rigid rules to determine when that point will be reached.

It remains to be considered whether a declaration of intention to perform an act is admissible to prove that the act was performed. It should first be noted that in criminal cases it seems that the prosecution can so prove statements of intent by the accused, for example on a charge of murder that the accused threatened to kill the deceased.[4]

In civil proceedings the problem was mainly discussed in relation to wills. The leading case was *Sugden v Lord St Leonards*[5] where the testator was known to have taken great care in drafting his will, but after his death all that remained in the box thought to contain it were a number of codicils and holograph notes apparently made at the time of drafting it. His daughter, who had acted as housekeeper, was however able to remember its terms, and her version of the will was accorded probate. On appeal the question arose of what use could be made of the pre-testamentary[6] declarations of the testator, principally deduced from his holograph notes. It was held by the majority[7] of the five judge court that such pre-testamentary declarations were admissible as proof of the contents of the will. This decision found little favour with the House of Lords, and was said in *Woodward v Goulstone* to have reached 'the very verge of the law, and was not to be extended'. Some support for it can be found in earlier decisions[8] relating to disputes about the terms of executed wills, and in the light of the criticisms of the House of Lords[9] its effects probably extended no further.

2   (1802) 4 Esp 233.
3   [1917] 1 Ch 339, at 342.
4   *R v Ball* [1911] AC 47, at 68; *R v Williams* (1986) 84 Cr App Rep 299. See also *Plomp v R* (1964) 110 CLR 234; *R v Andrews* [1987] 1 Qd R 21; *R v White* (1989) 41 ACR 237.
5   (1876) 1 PD 154.
6   He had in addition made post-testamentary declarations of the contents of the will, and these were also held admissible evidence of its contents. The pronouncements of the court as to both categories were however regarded as unnecessary for its decision, and thus strictly, no more than obiter dicta: see Lord Cockburn CJ, at 224, Jessel MR, at 243, and Mellish LJ, at 250.
7   Lord Cockburn CJ, with whom Baggalley JA and James LJ agreed; Jessel MR thought that even then they were admissible only as circumstantial evidence; and Mellish LJ was prepared to admit them only to corroborate other evidence.
8   See *Doe d Shallcross v Palmer* (1851) 16 QB 747; *Johnson v Lyford* (1868) LR 1 P & D 546.
9   (1886) 11 App Cas 469, at 485. Though there are a few cases where such evidence seems to have been admitted without argument on this point: see *Marshall v Wild Rose (Owners)* [1910] AC 486 (declaration that deceased workman was going on deck to get some air); *Tracey v Kelly* (1930) WC & Ins Rep 214 (declaration that leaving room to relieve nature). See also *Dobson v Morris* (1985) 4 NSWLR 681 (declaration of destination of journey); *Italiano v Barbaro* (1993) 114 ALR 21 (declaration of intention to stage car accident); where the question was considered.

In criminal cases the English authorities were in some disarray. Evidence of a declaration of intention to visit the accused, who was subsequently accused of murdering the declarant, was excluded in two Old Bailey cases, once[10] by Lord Cockburn CJ on the basis 'that it was only a statement of intention which might or might not have been carried out.' On the other hand in *R v Buckley*[11] a declaration by a policeman that he was going to observe the suspected criminal activities of the man accused of his murder was admitted by Lush J on assize.[12] In that case however no question of hearsay was raised. The issue has since been considered only sporadically. In *R v Thomson*,[13] an appeal against conviction for abortion on a woman who had died before trial, it was held that her statement of intention to perform the operation herself had been rightly excluded as evidence for the defence together with her later assertions that she had procured her own miscarriage. The reception of such later assertions as testimonial evidence of their truth would have been an obvious infringement of the hearsay rule, and it may have been felt, much as was argued in *Blastland*,[14] that it would be anomalous to allow in the declarations of intention to prove indirectly what more direct assertions were not allowed to prove.[15]

There is no more modern English case in which the issue has been squarely addressed.[16] It was considered by the High Court of Australia in *Walton v R*.[17] The accused was charged with the murder of his wife, after having lured her into meeting him in the local town centre. After receiving a telephone call in which she declared that the caller was her husband, she said that she intended to meet him in the town centre. The High Court admitted evidence of such declarations, despite any hearsay element, as original evidence of her intentions from which the jury could draw appropriate inferences, though they could not use them as direct testimonial evidence, of her having met her husband at the appointed place. In so admitting the declarations of intention the High Court appears to have accepted a famous line of American authority stemming from *Mutual Life Insurance Co v Hillmon*.[18] In that case insurance had been taken out on Hillmon's life, and a claim was made in respect of a man killed in the wilds of Colorado. The defendants claimed that the body was not that of Hillmon, but that of one Walters, who had written letters declaring his intention of accompanying Hillmon on the relevant trip. At the trial[19] the judge excluded these letters as hearsay, but the Supreme Court of the United States held[20] that they were admissible as relevant original evidence of Walters' intentions. Despite subsequent criticism of this decision by the Supreme

---

10   *R v Wainwright* (1875) 13 Cox CC 171, see also *R v Pook*, ibid 172.
11   (1873) 13 Cox CC 293.
12   After consulting his colleague Mellor J.
13   [1912] 3 KB 19.
14   Above p 550.
15   Considerations of just such an anomaly led the majority in *Sugden v Lord St Leonards* to apply the same rules as to both pre- and post-testamentary declarations.
16   In *R v Moghal* (1977) 65 Cr App Rep 56 dicta suggested that a declaration of intent to kill by the principal offender, as conceded by the prosecution despite her previous acquittal, would have been admissible at the trial of an alleged accomplice, though these dicta were doubted by the House of Lords in *Blastland* at 60, 1104.
17   (1989) 84 ALR 59, see Odgers (1989) 13 Crim LJ 201. See also *R v Hendrie* (1985) 37 SASR 581 where the victim's declaration of intention to have repairs done to her bedroom by the accused was admitted to explain the absence of a struggle in any other part of the house, her raped and murdered body having been found in the bedroom.
18   145 US 284 (1892).
19   In fact the third trial, the jury having disagreed at the first two, and there were a further three, the last of which also found in favour of the claimant only to be reversed by the Supreme Court. The issue was finally settled in the widow's favour by the insurance companies.
20   For an account of the genesis of this decision see Maguire (1925) 38 Harv LR 109.

Court,[1] and by other eminent American judges,[2] it has been extended to allow such declarations of intention to implicate second parties, and to permit proof of declarations as to past facts in interpretation of such declarations.[3] It is however generally recognised in the United States that the admission of declarations for such purposes can be permitted only by way of exception to the hearsay rule.[4] Such extensions were also involved in the reasoning accepted in *Walton*, though without the invocation of any special exception.

Despite the importance of this issue to criminal proceedings the Law Commission devoted little space[5] to its consideration, and its formulation[6] is very bland.

4.   Statements of a relevant physical state

A person's statements concerning his contemporaneous physical sensation were admissible at common law as evidence of that fact. In *Gilbey v Great Western Rail Co* Cozens-Hardy MR entertained no doubt that:[7]

> Statements made by a workman to his wife of his sensations at the time, about the pains in his side or head, or what not—whether the statements were made by groans, or by actions, or were verbal statements—would be admissible to prove these sensations.

The Master of the Rolls also held that the workman's assertion of the cause of his condition was inadmissible at common law, and his view of the law on both points is supported by a long line of authority.[8] For example, as long ago as 1846 it was said:[9]

> If a man says to his surgeon 'I have a pain in the head', or 'in such a part of my body', that is evidence, but if he says to the surgeon. 'I have a wound', and was to add 'I met John Thomas who had a sword and ran me through the body with it', that would be no evidence against John Thomas.

The statement must not relate to a past state of body, though a little latitude has to be allowed:[10]

> Surely 'contemporaneous' cannot be confined to feelings experienced at the actual moment when the patient is speaking. It must include such a statement as 'Yesterday I had a pain after meals'.

It has been held in Australia to be immaterial that the person who experienced and declared the symptoms at the time does not testify although available to do so.[11] There

---

1   By Cardozo J in *Shephard v United States* 290 US 96 (1933).
2   By Traynor J in *People v Alcalde* 148 P 2d 627 (Cal, 1944), at 633.
3   *United States v Annunziato* 293 F 2d 373 (2nd Circ, 1961).
4   See Federal Rules of Evidence, r 803(3).
5   Paras 8.125 and 8.126.
6   See below p 599.
7   (1910) 102 LT 202.
8   *Aveson v Lord Kinnaird* (1805) 6 East 188; *R v Johnson* (1847) 2 Car & Kir 354; *R v Conde* (1867) 10 Cox CC 547; *R v Gloster* (1888) 16 Cox CC 471.
9   *R v Nicholas* (1846) 2 Car & Kir 246, at 248 per Pollock CB.
10   Salter J in *R v Black* (1922) 16 Cr App Rep 118.
11   *R v Perry (No 2)* (1981) 28 SASR 95; *Batista v Citra Constructions Pty Ltd* (1986) 5 NSWLR 351.

is plainly force in Wigmore's view that in such a case the contemporary statements of the witness as to his symptoms are likely to be more reliable than his later recollection of them in the witness box.

Here again the Law Commission felt that the exception had caused no injustice, and ought to be retained, applying if:[12]

> the statement relates to a physical sensation or a mental state (such as intention or emotion).

C. PREVIOUS STATEMENTS BY TESTIFYING WITNESSES

As noted earlier in this chapter, and explained in more detail in ch VI above, at common law previous statements of witnesses, whether consistent or inconsistent with the witness's testimony, were normally inadmissible, and to the extent to which they were admissible, were not admitted as evidence of the truth of the assertions contained in them. These rules largely[13] reflected the common law's preference for oral trials. In civil proceedings this preference is now reflected only in procedural rules, designed to ensure the tendering of oral evidence when it is necessary, but not otherwise.[14] Although this pattern was recommended for criminal proceedings by the Criminal Law Revision Committee,[15] and largely[16] adopted in Scotland,[17] it was rejected by the Law Commission.[18] Its recommendations distinguish between the rules relating to previous statements inconsistent, and consistent, with the witness's testimony,[19] which it is thus helpful to reflect here.

I. Previous inconsistent statements

Here the Law Commission was prepared to accept the robust view that a previous inconsistent statement either accepted by the witness, or proved against the witness under the provisions of the Criminal Procedure Act 1865, should be admitted as evidence of the truth of its contents.[20] Although the effect of this recommendation relates primarily to the effect of the evidence, it also extends admissibility in the case of co-accused to previous statements of a testifying co-accused whose previous statement implicated his co-accused, even though his testimony does not. It should be further noted that a second order effect is that in such a case other previous statements consistent with the testimony, but ex hypothesi inconsistent with the previous inconsistent statement, will also become admissible as evidence of the truth of their contents.[1]

---

12 Clause 6(5)(c). No reference is made here to the requirement of contemporaneity, or to the need for the statement to relate to the condition of the speaker.
13 Other factors include the saving of time, cost and complication; and fear of concoction.
14 Now under the provisions of the Civil Evidence Act 1995, and rules of court: see further below ch XIV.
15 Eleventh Report Cmnd 4991, paras 236, 249, draft bill, cl 31(1)(a).
16 For documentary statements by competent witnesses, authenticated and adopted by the maker as evidence for the trial.
17 Criminal Justice (Scotland) Act 1995, s 18; Criminal Procedure (Scotland) Act 1995, s 260.
18 Law Com No 245, para 10.34.
19 Statements which are partly consistent and partly inconsistent are treated as if wholly inconsistent for these purposes.
20 Law Com No 245, paras 10.87–10.101, rec 40, draft bill, cl 7(1).
1 Draft bill, cl 7(2); though in such a case they will merely reinforce the testimony.

2.   Previous consistent statements

The Law Commission took the view that the general admission of previous consistent statements as evidence of their truth might lead to needless proliferation of evidence.[2] Instead it proposed to admit such statements only in a number of discrete situations.

(i)   Previous statements of complaint

As noted above[3] there was at common law an ancient and anomalous exception permitting proof of the terms of a recent complaint of a sexual offence. The Law Commission felt that there was virtue in widening the admissibility of previous complaints to apply to any form of offence, on the basis that the court would generally benefit from the ability to consider the terms of the earliest statement made by the complainant about the alleged offence. The Law Commission also proposed removal of the condition that the complaint be unassisted,[4] and required merely that it be made as soon as reasonably possible. When admitted such a statement would constitute evidence of the truth of its contents.[5] These proposals are encapsulated in cl 8(7) so as to apply if:[6]

(a)   the witness claims to be a person against whom an offence has been committed,
(b)   the offence is one to which the proceedings relate,
(c)   the statement consists of a complaint made by the witness (whether a person in authority or not) about conduct which would, if proved, constitute the offence or part of the offence,
(d)   the complaint was made as soon as could reasonably be expected after the alleged conduct,
(e)   the complaint was not made as a result of a threat or promise, and
(f)   before the statement is adduced the witness gives oral evidence in connection with its subject matter.

(ii)   Previous statements to rebut suggestions of fabrication

The Law Commission decided[7] that a further exception to the hearsay rule should be made in relation to previous consistent statements of witnesses designed to rebut any suggestion of subsequent fabrication, thus retaining the old common law exception, but altering the formal effect of such admission, bringing the law into line with that applicable in civil proceedings under the provisions of s 6(2) of the Civil Evidence Act 1995, and achieving coherence in this respect with its recommendations as to previous inconsistent statements. Clause 8(2) of the draft bill accordingly provides:

2   Despite the court's power to exclude irrelevant evidence, as applied to previous consistent statements in *R v Tooke* (1990) 90 Cr App R 417.
3   At p 273.
4   This is to become a matter of weight.
5   Although if in the form of a written statement, and as such an exhibit, it should be made available to the jury only with the leave of the court.
6   Subject to conditions relating to the maker testifying, the evidence being admissible if tendered in testimony, and acknowledged and authenticated by its maker.
7   Law Com 245, paras 10.41 -10.45, rec 34.

If a previous statement by the witness is admitted as evidence to rebut a suggestion that his oral evidence has been fabricated, that statement is admissible as evidence of any matter stated of which oral evidence by the witness would be admissible.

(iii) Previous statements of identification

Despite the dictum of Lord Morris in *Sparks v R*[8] that 'There is no rule which permits the giving of hearsay evidence merely because it relates to identity' the law had come very close to creating one in its treatment of previous acts of identification of persons either on identification parades,[9] or by way of assisting with graphic representations of a criminal.[10] It had however developed no comparable rules for the identification of objects.[11] The Law Commission has now recommended[12] as an alternative to the process of creative definition which had previously disfigured this area of the law, a special exception to the hearsay rule for previous statements of witnesses which identify or describe a person, object or place.

(iv) Previous statements of matters reasonably forgotten

The common law rules relating to the refreshment of memory were complex, technical, and applied inconsistently. In some cases previous statements which might well have refreshed the memory of the witness, or even without doing so would have had value, were excluded for technical reasons; in others similar such statements were admitted, even though they could not credibly have refreshed anyone's memory. There was inconsistency between the general run of cases dealt with under this rule, and the special case of identification mentioned above. The Law Commission has accordingly chosen to create a further exception for cases where a testifying witness made a statement when the matters stated were fresh in the memory of the witness,[13] is now able to assert that the statement was made and is believed to be true, and that the witness reasonably does not now remember the matter in sufficient detail to be able to testify to it.

It should be noted that there is still an illogicality in requiring the witness to testify to the likelihood of the truth of matters of which the witness has no present recollection at all.[14]

---

8   [1964] AC 964, at 981, [1964] 1 All ER 727, at 735.
9   As in *R v Osbourne and Virtue* [1973] QB 678, [1973] 1 All ER 649; *R v McCay* [1991] 1 All ER 232, [1990] 1 WLR 645. Cases where the rule has been invoked in this context seem to turn more on the acceptability of dock identification: *R v Fergus* [1992] Crim LR 363; *R v Hussain* [1998] Crim LR 820.
10   As in *R v Percy Smith* [1976] Crim LR 511; *R v Cook* [1987] QB 417, [1987] 1 All ER 1049; *R v Constantinou* (1989) 91 Cr App Rep 74.
11   See eg on the identification of cars *R v Kelsey* (1982) 74 Cr App Rep 213, *R v Townsend* [1987] Crim LR 411, and on the identification of objects *R v Fizzell* (1987) 31 ACR 213 (label on sample in forensic laboratory); cp *R v Orrell* [1972] RTR 14. In Scotland a remarkably cavalier approach has been tolerated: see eg *Dryburgh v Scott* 1995 JC 75; *Allan v Ingram* 1995 SLT 1086.
12   Law Com 245, paras 10.46–10.52, rec 35; draft bill, cl 8(5).
13   This phrase appears in Evidence Act (Cwth) 1995, s 64(3), and in Australia has been construed to connote a different standard from the contemporaneity required under the old res gestae rule: *Commonwealth v McLean* (1996) 41 NSWLR 389.
14   As in *R v Thomas* [1994] Crim LR 745 (cited by the Law Commission in fn 81 to para 10.67) where a little girl had no recollection at all of the events, and was not at all assisted in her recollection by reading her earlier statement. It might have been better to have imposed as a condition that the witness has no reason to believe the statement to have been false.

D. ADMISSIONS

Although admissions are often said to be received on account of the unlikelihood of a person saying something to his disadvantage,[15] it can also be argued that the adversarial nature of litigation plays a part and the reason resides rather in the absurdity of a party seeking to assert his own unreliability except when speaking on oath, or the fact that he had no opportunity to cross-examine himself.[16] The exception was extended to include inextricable exculpatory parts of otherwise inculpatory statements.[17] In general it operated only against the party making it,[18] and against him only in a representative capacity if so made.[19] If the party had no personal knowledge of the matter admitted, then the admission was worthless.[20] In civil proceedings no special rules are any longer required to cater for informal admissions against interest, and the common law has been expressly superseded by statutory provision.[1] In criminal proceedings the use of an admission against its maker, or a co-accused,[2] will mainly be considered in ch XV below. The only issues to be considered here relate to the use of informal admissions by third parties, as evidence in criminal proceedings. First, there is the question of the use of third party admissions of guilt to exculpate the accused and, second, the use of third party admissions to inculpate the accused on a theory of vicarious effect.

I. Exculpatory third party admissions

The long-established rule of the common law was that statements by third parties confessing to the crime with which the accused is charged are inadmissible hearsay, whether tendered in chief,[3] or put in cross-examination.[4] Indeed so strong was the rule that in *R v Blastland*[5] not only was leave to appeal against its application refused, but that result was then, as noted above,[6] used as a lever to exclude evidence of the accused's state of mind as circumstantial evidence. It should also be noted that even if the maker of the confession had died before the trial, the statement would not have

---

15   *R v Hardy* (1794) 24 State Tr 199, at 1093; *R v Sharp* [1988] 1 All ER 65, at 68, [1988] 1 WLR 7, at 11.

16   Morgan *Basic Problems of Evidence* (1962) at 266, cited by Smith [1995] Crim LR 280, at 282.

17   *Harrison v Turner* (1847) 10 QB 482. See also Birch [1997] Crim LR 416.

18   As in *Morton v Morton, Daly and McNaught* [1937] P 151, [1937] 2 All ER 470 (leading to the conclusion that it was proved that A had sexual relations with B, but not that B had them with A). The Civil Evidence Act 1995 would now prevent such a result in civil proceedings, but the same absurd conclusion might be necessitated in an incest prosecution today, if the parties were relevantly related.

19   *Legge v Edmonds* (1855) 25 LJ Ch 125, at 141 (statement in personal capacity not binding when suit in representative capacity); but oddly not conversely: *Stanton v Percival* (1855) 5 HL Cas 257 (statement in representative capacity did bind when sued in personal capacity).

20   *Comptroller of Customs v Western Lectric Co Ltd* [1966] AC 367, at 371, 1965 3 All ER 599, at 601. This applies where both a subjective intent and objective state of affairs need to be demonstrated, eg in a prosecution for handling where an admission may be capable of proving belief that the goods were stolen without proving that they really were: *R v Korniak* (1983) 76 Cr App Rep 145.

1   Civil Evidence Act 1995, s 7(1).

2   Despite the fact that in many such cases such an admission will not only inculpate its maker, but also exculpate the co-accused seeking its admission.

3   Reaffirmed in *R v Turner* (1975) 61 Cr App Rep 67.

4   *R v Windass* (1989) 89 Cr App Rep 258; *R v Gray and Evans* [1998] Crim LR 570.

5   [1986] AC 41, [1985] 2 All ER 1095.

6   At p 551.

been admissible as a statement against interest.[7] The one crack in the edifice was furnished by dicta in a thin trickle of cases[8] where it seems that a factor reinforcing the doubts about a conviction felt by the Court of Appeal was that a third party had confessed.

The Law Commission proposes no direct change in this rule,[9] although its takes the view that some of its other proposals will reduce the number of situations in which it will apply to those where the maker of the statement is available to testify and refuses to do so or, if he does, to confirm the admission.[10]

2. Vicarious admissions

The question of how far the admissions of one party can inculpate another is more a matter of substantive law and of relevance than anything else, and will be discussed here only in connection with admissions by co-conspirators.[11] The general rule was that admissions by those in privity with a party to litigation could be given in evidence against him. The phrase 'in privity' as used here was not a technical term. It included predecessors in title,[12] referees,[13] all manner of agents and a few miscellaneous cases.

Statements made by an agent within the scope of his authority to third persons during the continuance of the agency could be received as admissions against his principal in litigation to which the latter was a party.[14] So far as the reception of admissions was concerned, the scope of authority was a strictly limited conception. It was sometimes said that the agent must be authorised to make the admission, but that was a confusing statement for admissions were often received although no one was expressly or impliedly authorised to make them. A better way of putting the matter is to say that the admission must have been made by the agent as part of a conversation or other communication which he was authorised to have with a third party. The authority to have such conversations or make such communications was frequently not co-terminous with an authority to act on behalf of the principal[15]—a point which had an important bearing on the limited extent to which an employee's admissions concerning acts done by him in the course of his employment could as such be proved against his employer.[16]

---

7   *Sussex Peerage Case* (1844) 11 Cl & Fin 85. The rule has been changed by statute in Australia, see Evidence Act (Cwth) 1995, s 65(2)(d), 65(7)(b); see also *R v Bannon* (1995) 185 CLR 1; and in the United States by Federal Rule 804(3)(b) (although corroboration is required); see also *Chambers v Mississippi* 410 US 295 (1973). In Canada, see *R v O'Brien* [1978] 1 SCR 591.
8   *R v Cooper* [1969] 1 QB 267, [1969] 1 All ER 32; *R v Hails* (6 May 1976, unreported, CA); *R v Wallace and Short* (1978) 67 Cr App Rep 291. See also *R v Beckford and Daley* [1991] Crim LR 833 where the same approach was adopted in relation to the confession of a co-accused there held to be inadmissible.
9   Law Com 245, paras 8.97–8.99.
10 It does however envisage the use of its recommended inclusionary discretion in this situation.
11 For more detail see earlier editions of this work. See also *Bowstead on Agency* (16th ed, 1969) art 96; Morgan (1928) 42 HLR 461.
12 As in *Falcon v Famous Players Film Co* [1926] 2 KB 474.
13 As in *R v Mallory* (1884) 13 QBD 33.
14 But if such admissions are sought by questioning the agent in the course of such litigation an objection by the principal automatically terminates any authority: *Bond Media Ltd v John Fairfax Group Pty Ltd* (1988) 16 NSWLR 82.
15 See *Scott v Fernhill Stud Poultry Farm Pty Ltd* [1963] VR 12 holding a company not bound by a director's admissions; and *Shears v Chisholm* [1994] 2 VLR 535 for the converse.
16 Cp *Kirkstall Brewery Co v Furness Rly Co* (1874) LR 9 QB 468 with *Great Western Rly Co v Willis* (1865) 18 CBNS 748.

The statement of the agent which was tendered as an admission had, on the preponderance of authority, to have been made to a third person, not to the principal.[17] It was necessary to prove the existence of the agency before the admissions of the agent could be received against the principal.[18] It was sometimes possible to imply the existence of the agency from the surrounding circumstances,[19] especially if an incorporate entity was to be bound.[20] It was not sufficient, at common law,[1] to rely upon the agent's own statements of that fact, because they were hearsay.[2] The agent could, of course, give evidence of the making of any operative statement without infringing the rule.

The statement tendered as an admission must have been made by the agent during the continuance of his agency.[3] Relatively few agents have authority to speak about past transactions, and, once an agent's employment as such had ceased altogether, he could have had no authority to do so.

It seems that the same rules concerning the requirement of personal knowledge applied in the case of admissions by agents as in that of admissions by parties, but this was subject to the proviso that an agent, such as a solicitor, who was instructed to pass on information, need not have accepted it in any way, and yet his statement could be evidence against his principal.[4] It seemed to be the case if an agent for a principal gathered information from employees, and made an admission based on such information, that the principal would be bound unless there was some overt qualification or disclaimer.[5]

These old common law rules provided the background to the treatment of the statements of conspirators in criminal proceedings.[6] The admissions of one conspirator are receivable against the other if they relate to an act done in furtherance of the conspiracy, but not otherwise.[7] For example, in *R v Blake and Tye*,[8] the accused were charged with a conspiracy to pass goods through the customs without paying duty.

17   *Re Devala Provident Gold Mining Co Ltd* (1883) 22 Ch D 593.
18   *G(A) v G(T)* [1970] 2 QB 643, [1970] 3 All ER 546; *R v Evans* [1981] Crim LR 699. See also *Maxwell v IRC* [1959] NZLR 708.
19   *R v Turner* (1975) 61 Cr App Rep 67 (acting as barrister representing a party); compare *Wagstaff v Wilson* (1832) 4 B & Ad 339 (acting as party's attorney insufficient), and *R v Evans* (above) (acting as clerk to party's solicitor insufficient). See also *Smart v Popper and Casswell* (1987) 26 ACR 140 (solicitor representing client who was present in court).
20   Reply signed by employee in company's name to enquiry addressed to the company and delivered to its premises: *Barnet London Borough Council v Network Sites Ltd* [1997] JPL B90; cp *R v Natesan and Subramaniam* (1996) 88 ACR 444 (individual directors not bound by employee's admission).
1   In appropriate circumstances it is now possible to invoke the Civil Evidence Act 1968, see *G(A) v G(T)* (above) where the only reason for not doing so was that the proceedings took place in the magistrates' court.
2   *R v Evans* (above). *Edwards v Brookes (Milk) Ltd* [1963] 3 All ER 62, [1963] 1 WLR 795 cannot be supported to the extent of any inconsistency after *Myers v DPP* [1965] AC 1001, [1964] 2 All ER 881.
3   *Peto v Hague* (1804) 5 Esp 134; *The Prinses Juliana, Esbjerj (Owners) v Prinses Juliana (Owners)* [1936] P 139, [1936] 1 All ER 685.
4   *The Actaeon* (1853) 1 Ecc & Ad 176. See in New Zealand *R v Harris* [1998] 1 NZLR 405.
5   *Welsbach Incandescent Gas Lighting Co v New Sunlight Incandescent Co* [1900] 2 Ch 1. See also *Claiborne Industries Ltd v National Bank of Canada* (1989) 59 DLR (4th) 533.
6   See further Smith [1996] Crim LR 386, [1997] Crim LR 333.
7   Though it should be noted that in many cases out of court assertions and actions of conspirators may be admissible as circumstantial evidence of a conspiracy quite independently of reliance upon any admission, express or even implied, and so subject to the reach of *R v Kearley* [1992] 2 AC 228, [1992] 2 All ER 345 outside the operation of the hearsay rule.
8   (1844) 6 QB 126; see also *R v Hardy* (1794) 24 State Tr 1076; *R v Hunt* (1820) 3 B & Ald 566; *R v Whitaker* [1914] 3 KB 1283.

Tye had made entries incriminating Blake as well as himself in two books. In one case the entry was a necessary part of the fraud, in the other case it was solely for the purposes of record and for Tye's convenience. It was held that the first entry was admissible against Blake as something tending to the advancement of the common object, but the second merely constituted evidence against Tye because it was not concerned with the disposal of the plunder. In determining whether there is such a common purpose as to render the acts and extra-judicial statements done or made by one party in furtherance of the common purpose evidence against the others, the judge may have regard to these matters, although their admissibility is in issue, as well as to other evidence.[9] This doctrine is obviously liable to produce circularity in argument:[10]

> Since what A says in B's absence cannot be evidence against B of the truth of what was said unless A was B's agent to say those things, how can one prove that A was B's agent to say them by showing what A said?

The answer is that the agency may be proved partly by what A said in the absence of B, and partly by other evidence of common purpose. It makes no difference which is adduced first, but A's statements will have to be excluded if it transpires that there is no other evidence of common purpose; it is another instance of conditional admissibility.[11]

In England this view of the law was accepted without cavil, or much elaboration.[12] In other jurisdictions questions have arisen both as to the standard which the extrinsic evidence of conspiracy should reach, and whether the question, once having been decided by the judge so as to admit the evidence, should be subject to reconsideration by the jury. Since there is little difference here between the preliminary question and the final issue, namely whether the accused was party to the conspiracy, it would be futile to require the preliminary issue to be decided upon proof beyond reasonable doubt. The better view is that the judge should decide[13] the preliminary issue on a prima facie basis.[14] It is submitted that since the evidence has been admitted upon such a basis it is unnecessarily confusing for the jury to be given an opportunity to reject it upon the application of a different standard of proof from that which they will have to be instructed to apply to the ultimate question of guilt or innocence of

---

9   *Ahern v R* (1988) 165 CLR 87.

10 *R v Mayet* 1957 (1) SA 492, at 494.

11 *Tripodi v R* (1961) 104 CLR 1; *Ahern*, above, at 104.

12 *R v Donat* (1985) 82 Cr App Rep 173, at 179; *R v Governor of Pentonville Prison, ex p Osman* [1989] 3 All ER 701; *R v Windass* (1988) 89 Cr App Rep 258. It has however influenced attitudes against the use of convictions for conspiracy under s 74 of the Police and Criminal Evidence Act 1984: see, above, p 100.

13 In the United States the Federal Rules of Evidence permit hearsay, including the hearsay of the alleged co-conspirators, to be used in the determination of that preliminary question, Federal Rules of Evidence, rr 104(a), 1101(d)(1); *Bourjaily v US* 107 S Ct 2775 (1987).

14 Used for some other issues of fact upon which the admission of evidence depends: see *R v Robson and Harris* [1972] 2 All ER 699, [1972] 1 WLR 651. For an example of evidence too weak to meet even this undemanding standard see *R v Williams: R v Davies* [1992] 2 All ER 183, [1992] 1 WLR 380. In *Ahern v R* (1988) 80 ALR 161 the High Court of Australia preferred the term 'reasonable evidence' to 'prima facie case' but thought there to be no real distinction of meaning; see also *R v Masters, Richards and Wunderlich* (1992) 26 NSWLR 450. But see *R v Buckton* [1985] 2 NZLR 257 suggesting that the standard of the balance of probabilities be adopted at this stage; this is also the position in the United States: *Bourjaily v US*, above.

participation in the conspiracy,[15] although at that stage it will be appropriate to warn the jury of the dangers posed by any admissible hearsay.[16]

The rule under consideration is not confined to charges of conspiracy as it is based on implied agency, and would apply, for example, to charges of aiding and abetting, even though the secondary party was not charged, perhaps to all charges involving a common purpose,[17] and even to civil proceedings;[18] but it is in relation to conspiracy trials that the rule may operate most oppressively. If there is a series of counts charging separate offences and a concluding count alleging conspiracy, evidence may be admissible against all the accused on the last count, although it would not be admissible against more than one of them on any of the separate counts.[19] The evidence often takes the form of directions given and acts done by the other parties which can take a much broader form when there is a conspiracy charge than when the charge relates to one specific transaction.[20]

The Law Commission devoted little attention to this issue, and rather perfunctorily accepted the current law.[1]

---

15   This seems the predominant view in other common law jurisdictions, see *Ahern*, above (Australia); *R v Walters* [1989] 2 NZLR 33 (New Zealand, explicitly endorsing *Ahern*); and *Bourjaily*, above (United States). But Canada adopts a different view: *R v Carter* [1982] 1 SCR 938; *R v Barrow* [1987] 2 SCR 694.
16   *R v Jones* [1997] 2 Cr App Rep 119.
17   See in Australia, *Tripodi* above; in Canada, *Koufis v R* [1941] SCR 481; and in New Zealand *R v Tauhore* [1996] 2 NZLR 641.
18   *Italiano v Barbaro* (1993) 114 ALR 21.
19   *R v Griffiths* [1966] 1 QB 589, [1965] 2 All ER 448; but see criticism by Smith [1995] Crim LR 47.
20   See *R v Gray, Liggins, Riding, and Rowlands* [1995] 2 Cr App Rep 100, and the gloss put upon it in *R v Murray, Morgan and Sheridan* [1997] 2 Cr App Rep 136.
1   Law Com 245, paras 8.130–8.132, recs 26, 27, draft bill, cll 6(7), 6(8).

CHAPTER XIV

Hearsay in civil proceedings

As noted in the previous chapter the hearsay rule has little, or no, exclusionary effect in civil proceedings in the modern law. Section 1 of the Civil Evidence Act 1995 proclaims that:

> (1) In civil proceedings evidence shall not be excluded on the ground that it is hearsay.

This certainly permits discussion to be abbreviated, but it does not permit it to be abrogated altogether. Doubts have been raised as to whether the Act does achieve the result proclaimed in the quoted section, and on any basis there are procedural differences between the methods of adducing different forms of hearsay under the provisions of the Act. Consideration of the effect of the Act in changing the law will constitute the first, and more important, section of this chapter.

Section 1 of the Act goes on to provide:[1]

> (2) In this Act–
>   (a) 'hearsay' means a statement made otherwise than by a person while giving oral evidence in the proceedings which is tendered as evidence of the matters stated; and
>   (b) references to hearsay include hearsay of whatever degree.
>
> (3) Nothing in this Act affects the admissibility of evidence admissible apart from this section.
>
> (4) The provisions of sections 2 to 6 (safeguards and supplementary provisions relating to hearsay evidence) do not apply in relation to hearsay evidence admissible apart from this section, notwithstanding that it may also be admissible by virtue of this section.

These provisions indicate that some of the existing rules relating to the admissibility of hearsay in civil proceedings remain in force, and consideration of them will occupy the second section of the chapter.

---

1   The definition in s 1(2) is repeated as CPR 33.1.

SECTION I.   THE CIVIL EVIDENCE ACT 1995

This Act implements the recommendations of the Law Commission in its report *The Hearsay Rule in Civil Proceedings.*[2] Although the two previous pieces of general legislation[3] had attempted to revolutionise the admissibility of documentary hearsay in civil proceedings, they had been bedevilled by excessive caution and cumbersome procedures, with the result that hearsay was very often admitted only by agreement between the parties, and despite any formal difficulty, an approach, in part at least, inspired by judicial distaste for the exclusion of relevant evidence in civil proceedings on technical grounds alone.[4] The new approach of the Law Commission was to extend admissibility, while using procedural measures and considerations of weight to prevent abuse. This section will consider first the admissibility, and then the means of proof of hearsay in civil proceedings.

A.   ADMISSIBILITY

Notwithstanding the bold claim in the very first subsection of the Act quoted above, it has been argued[5] that the Act has failed to achieve that result on account of its restrictive definition of hearsay in s 1(2)(a) in terms of 'a statement'.[6] It is argued that words can be used to perform other tasks than to make statements, and that after the decision of the House of Lords in *R v Kearley*[7] assumptions of fact immanent in such other uses of words are excluded as hearsay, even though they are not statements. Hence if the Act admits only hearsay contained in statements as it appears on its face to do, it fails to affect, and especially to make admissible, all the hearsay not so contained, and it might be added this is quite indeterminate in amount, given the uncertainty of the reach of the decision in *Kearley.* This results both from its trigger, since it is unclear how far it applies to hearsay immanent in conduct, and from its means of operation, especially in how exactly the assumption of fact needs to relate to the relevant words or conduct. If the argument is accepted it means that obvious non-hearsay and obvious hearsay at either end of the spectrum is admissible, but dubious and obscure hearsay in the middle is inadmissible. This would be an indefensible result, which would cause

---

2   Law Com No 216, Cm 2321 (1993). The Act follows the draft bill appended to the report very closely, adding only a single clause relating to the admissibility of Ogden tables which had been recommended in a separate Law Commission Report *Structured Settlements and Interim and Provisional Damages* (Law Com No 224 (1994)).

3   Evidence Act 1938; Civil Evidence Act 1968.

4   See eg per Balcombe LJ in *Ventouris v Mountain (No 2)* [1992] 3 All ER 414, [1992] 1 WLR 887, at 426b, 899: 'The modern tendency in civil proceedings is to admit all relevant evidence, and the judge should be trusted to give only proper weight to evidence which is not the best evidence.'

5   By Ockleton in his annotation of the Act in *Current Law Statutes.*

6   Support might be enlisted: first from the formulation of s 1(4) which could be read to suggest that some hearsay may not be made admissible by the section, although it is submitted that the alternative of construing 'may' as the subjunctive equivalent of 'is' is preferable both as a matter of grammar and of policy; and second, from the definition of 'statement' in s 13 as 'any representation of fact or opinion', though this too is capable of being read as equivalent to 'representing any fact or opinion' subject to appropriate grammatical manipulation of the form of the definition.

7   [1992] 2 AC 228, [1992] 2 All ER 345.

nothing but confusion, and seems not to have been intended by the Law Commission.[8] It remains to be seen how it may be met.

It is submitted that a solution to such a technical problem will be welcome. First, it is clear that much evidence capable of being regarded as hearsay on an extended interpretation of *Kearley* is simply not recognised as raising a hearsay issue at all. Second, even to the extent that it is so recognised, the overwhelming instinct of the lawyers will be to eschew technical reasons to exclude the evidence, especially in civil proceedings where there is unlikely to be a jury. Analysis of the reasoning and context of the decision in *Kearley* may go some way to indicate a possible line of argument. It has already been argued that the force of the dicta relating to the hearsay character of the evidence there was weakened by the accompanying stress on the irrelevance of the opinion of those seeking to buy drugs, an argument which would have disqualified their direct testimony of no more than such a belief. Such force as it retained was largely derived from the difficulty of distinguishing as a matter of policy between statements of a fact, which were *inadmissible* as hearsay, and words used in other ways which were based upon an assumption of the very same fact. The force of that argument now works in the opposite direction. Direct hearsay statements are now *admissible* as a result of the Act, and if, as a matter of policy, other uses of words containing assumptions of fact should be treated in the same way, they should also be admissible. Still more remarkable would be the anomaly which the contrary view would set up between the position in relation to civil proceedings, where hearsay has been more readily admitted, and to criminal, which have been more resistant to it. The Law Commission has recommended that for the purposes of criminal proceedings, hearsay should be defined in such a way as to exclude such assumptions from being regarded as hearsay.[9] Acceptance of such recommendations would produce the unfortunate result, if this argument were correct, that the decision of the House of Lords in the criminal case of *Kearley* would not exclude hearsay in criminal proceedings, but would do so only in civil. It is submitted that such a result is unacceptable, and is unlikely to be accepted, either because the argument never gets raised,[10] or as a matter of construction of the statute,[11] or by way of determining that the dicta in *Kearley* were obiter,[12] or by simply overruling them in view of the changes that have been, and are continuing to be, made in the legal context within which they have to operate. Such a result would have the happy result of bringing the English definition of hearsay back into line with that adopted elsewhere in the common law world.[13]

The remaining aspects of general admissibility can be considered shortly. It is clear from the definition in s 1(2)(a), and from the terms of s 6, that the new rule of admissibility applies both to third party hearsay, and to previous statements of a witness. In the latter case as much as in the former, such admissibility operates to prove the truth of

---

8   See Law Com 216, para 4.1: 'Our policy is, therefore, to abrogate the rule of evidence whereby *evidence of a hearsay nature* may not be adduced in civil proceedings as evidence of the facts asserted' para 4.6; 'In proposing to include a definition it is *only intended to identify* that which would formerly have fallen within the exclusionary rule' (emphases supplied). Para 4.6 further asserts that the old definitional law will bite only in respect of choice of procedures, and not in respect of admissibility.

9   Law Com 245, para 7.40, rec 2, draft bill, cl 2(3).

10 Or if raised, is withdrawn upon discouragement from the bench.

11 It can be argued that s 1 must contemplate the admissibility of implied assertions since s 9(3) explicitly provides a means of proving one category of them (omissions from records).

12 As, interestingly, were those in *Wright v Doe d Tatham* (1837) 7 Ad & El 313 upon which it relied.

13 See eg in Australia, Evidence Act (Cwth) 1995, s 59; in the United States, FRE, r 801.

the matter stated.[14] Section 1(2)(b) makes it quite explicit that admissibility extends to hearsay of any degree.[15]

It is worth emphasising that one great advantage over the previous law in this respect is the treatment of information in electronic form so far as possible in exactly the same way as any form of information.[16] The extremely cumbersome procedures of the 1968 Act have been jettisoned without specific replacement, and expansive definitions of 'records,'[17] 'statement', 'document' and 'copy'[18] adopted, clearly with a view to including electronic forms, and even automatic generation and reproduction.

The rule of admissibility extends to all civil proceedings, including proceedings in the magistrates' court,[19] and in tribunals, but only so far as the court or tribunal applies the strict rules of evidence[20] either as a matter of rule, or by agreement between the parties.[1] Although as pointed out in ch I above there is a myriad of rules of evidence, applying in different combinations to different courts, types of proceeding and stages, the courts can be relied upon to find a sensible and satisfactory route through the maze, given that there appear to be no examples of such tribunals applying *stricter* exclusionary rules than the ordinary courts.

B.   MEANS OF PROOF

The scheme of the legislation is to distinguish between information, which is governed by notice provisions, and special procedures for assessing and testing weight, and documents containing such information, the means of proof of which are in some cases alleviated.

Since one of the main defects of the 1968 Act had been identified as the cumbersome nature of the notice procedure required under it, every effort has been made to simplify the procedure here. Section 2(1) requires no more than an informal notice of the intention to rely on hearsay evidence, and an obligation to provide further particulars upon request. This added little to the previous requirement upon a party under the old procedure to supply witness statements to an opponent,[2] and it is now explicitly provided that the delivery of a witness statement satisfies the notice requirement.[3] It is put further within the control of the parties by permitting them to exclude the obligation by agreement, or for the party in whose favour it is intended to operate to waive it. Provision is also made for rules excluding particular classes of proceedings from the obligation, and for varying the requirements.[4] The effect of failure to give notice is significantly weakened by the consideration that such failure will be visited not by inadmissibility, but by re-ordering proceedings, sanctions by way of costs, and by authorising adverse inference as to weight.

---

14   It would also be capable of being used circumstantially as before, though it is hard to conceive of a case where this would provide any extra advantage.
15   So eliminating the tortuous reasoning in *Ventouris v Mountain (No 2)* [1992] 3 All ER 414, [1992] 1 WLR 887 under the old law.
16   For a full account see Saxby (ed) *Encyclopedia of Information Technology Law* ch 11.
17   Section 9(4).
18   Section 13.
19   Unlike the Civil Evidence Act 1968 which was never generally commenced for such application.
20   So not in wardship proceedings in the High Court
1   Section 11. See also the reference in s 12 to arbitration proceedings.
2   RSC Ord 38, r 2A; see further above p 247.
3   CPR 33.2.
4   Section 2(2). It is not envisaged that these powers will be used to impose a more stringent set of requirements than those under the current law, although there is no formal prohibition on their doing so.

One further safeguard to be mentioned here is that s 3 makes provision for rules of court under which a party against whom hearsay is to be tendered may call the maker of the statement to attend as a witness, for his statement to stand as his evidence in chief, and for him to be cross-examined. It should be noted that the reference is only to the maker of the statement, and does not appear to extend to intermediaries in the chain of supply of remote hearsay.[5]

Although previous statements of witnesses to be used under the provisions of s 6 are not explicitly exempted from notice procedures, they are clearly less appropriate.[6] Fuller notice may be required in relation to the use of admissions as such under s 7(1), but none is required in relation to other common law exceptions preserved by s 7.[7]

The principal counter-balance for expansion of admissibility is intended to be closer attention to weight,[8] and the Act not only permits any relevant circumstance to be taken into account, but goes on to mention a number of particular considerations:[9]

(a)   whether it would have been reasonable and practicable for the party by whom the evidence was adduced to have produced the maker of the original statement as a witness;

(b)   whether the original statement was made contemporaneously with the occurrence or existence of the matters stated;

(c)   whether the evidence involves multiple hearsay;

(d)   whether any person involved had any motive to conceal or misrepresent matters;

(e)   whether the original statement was an edited account, or was made in collaboration with another for a particular purpose;

(f)   whether the circumstances in which the evidence is adduced as hearsay are such as to suggest an attempt to prevent proper evaluation of its weight.

Since these criteria are not exclusive, and relate to weight rather than to admissibility, there will be no attempt to construe them rigidly, and they should achieve their purpose of highlighting the sorts of considerations and weaknesses which the trier of fact should attempt to take into account.

This safeguard is further strengthened and clarified by the provisions of s 5 excluding hearsay where the maker of the statement would have been incompetent.[10] It is odd that this section is much more explicit in applying both to the original supplier of information, and to subsequent conduits of it, than that relating to attendance for cross-examination under s 3. It is worth noting that the proviso to s 5(2) prevents the admission of evidence relating to any matter as to which a denial by the declarant, if he had testified in person, would have been conclusive. This is,[11] and if the recommendations of the Law Commission[12] are accepted, will remain, different from the situation in criminal proceedings.

---

5   This appears to be borne out by the use of the same form of words in CPR 33.4 which implements the statutory provision.

6   Any necessary procedural steps will be handled under the provision of s 6(2)(a) requiring the leave of the court before such statements are adduced.

7   Namely published works, public documents, records, and evidence of reputation.

8   Including the contemplation of some relevant evidence having no weight at all: s 4(1). see also in Scotland, *TSB (Scotland) plc v James Mills (Montrose) Ltd (in receivership)* 1992 SLT 519.

9   Section 4(2).

10   A child is regarded as competent if he would have been permitted to testify unsworn.

11   Cp Criminal Justice Act 1988, s 28(2), Sch 2 para 1(b).

12   Law Com 245 *Evidence in Criminal Proceedings: Hearsay and Related Topics* Cm 3270 (1997), paras 11.19–11.22, rec 44, draft bill, cl 13(2)(b).

Where hearsay is contained in a document, then the means of proof are simplified by the provisions of s 8[13] which permits production of original or copy,[14] subject only to whatever form of authentication the court deems appropriate. In the case of records[15] of [16] businesses or public authorities[17] certification procedures are specified in s 9(2), though the court is also given full power to dispense with them if it thinks fit.[18] In the case of such records an omission may be received in evidence.[19]

SECTION 2.   OTHER PROVISIONS

As noted above the Act seeks to expand admissibility, and to that end has chosen not to affect existing relaxation of the rule.[20] It further specifically preserves a number of common law[1] and statutory rules[2] having such an effect. Some of these have accreted a body of authority and interpretation, and will briefly be mentioned below.

A.   PUBLIC DOCUMENTS

Section 7(2) provides that:

The common law rules effectively preserved by s 9(1) and (2)(b) to (d) of the Civil Evidence Act 1968, that is, any rule of law whereby in civil proceedings–
(a) published works dealing with matters of a public nature (for example, histories, scientific works, dictionaries and maps) are admissible as evidence of facts of a public nature stated in them,
(b) public documents (for example, public registers, and returns made under public authority with respect to matters of public interest) are admissible as evidence of the matters stated in them, or
(c) records (for example, the records of certain courts, treaties, Crown grants, pardons and commissions) are admissible as evidence of facts stated in them,
shall continue to have effect.

---

13   Following the form of s 27 of the Criminal Justice Act 1988 which appears to have worked perfectly satisfactorily.
14   At whatever remove.
15   Although the form of a 'record' is given a wide definition, no explicit attempt is made to resolve the dispute in the old law as to the definition of a record itself: see *Savings and Investment Bank Ltd v Gasco Investments (Netherlands) BV* [1984] 1 All ER 296, [1984] 1 WLR 271; itself approved in *R v Governor of Pentonville Prison, ex p Osman* [1989] 3 All ER 701, [1990] 1 WLR 277. Compare the more liberal approach in *Campofina Bank v ANZ Banking Group* [1982] 1 NSWLR 409.
16   In Australia a similarly phrased provision was construed liberally to include private records of an employee about his business activities: *Standard Chartered Bank of Australia Ltd v Antico* (1993) 35 NSWLR 588. See also *Duncan Davis Pty Ltd v Hurstbridge Abattoirs (Australia) Pty Ltd* [1995] 1 VR 279 where a personal diary containing prices was held to be a 'book of account' under the local legislation.
17   Broadly defined in s 9(4).
18   Section 9(5).
19   Section 9(3).
20   Section 1(3).
1   Sections 7(2), 7(3).
2   Section 14.

I.   Published works

Little need be said about the first of the above rules, which is also applicable to criminal proceedings. It is not difficult to think of historical facts which could be proved in a contemporary court of law only by recourse to the works mentioned and Lord Halsbury was merely stating the dictates of common sense when he said: 'Where it is important to ascertain ancient facts of a public nature, the law does permit historical works to be referred to.'[3] It was by analogy with those dictates that the report of the engineer responsible for the construction of the Thames tunnel, made in 1844, was admitted in 1904 as evidence of the nature of the soil above it in *East London Rly Co v Thames Conservators*,[4] but it is regrettably true that a higher degree of technicality has been allowed to creep into this branch of the law. In the case of old maps, for instance, great stress is laid on the existence of a public duty on the part of those who prepared them[5] and, in *Fowke v Berington*,[6] Habbington's *Survey of Worcestershire* was excluded on the issue whether a church was the old parish church. The book was tendered as evidence on the condition of the church when Habbington saw it in the 17th century and, because there was no reference to public repute, the court treated this fact as one which was not of a public nature. The exclusion of evidence of such obvious relevance has been the subject of judicial regret,[7] but the conversion of the common law rule into a statutory provision cannot of itself effect any change in this regard.[8]

2.   Public documents

Statements in public documents are generally admissible evidence of the truth of their contents.[9] The common law relating to statements in public documents still applies in criminal proceedings,[10] and its retention, in virtually identical terms to those set out above, has been recommended by the Law Commission.[11] But since the rule operates more often in civil proceedings than in criminal, and there seem no special considerations applying to its operation in criminal proceedings, it is principally considered here. It has been retained largely on account of being presupposed by some of the statutory provisions which are being also being retained.[12] Many of the statements contained in such documents would be admissible in civil proceedings under the provisions of s 1 of the Civil Evidence Act 1995, but the advantage of proving such a document under this exception, is that the notice and weighing provisions associated with proof under s 1 do not then apply. Its nature, rationale, and scope will be mentioned here.

3   *Read v Bishop of Lincoln* [1892] AC 644, at 653.
4   (1904) 90 LT 347. The report had become part of the technical expertise of the relevant witness.
5   Contrast *A-G v Horner (No 2)* [1913] 2 Ch 140 with *A-G v Antrobus* [1905] 2 Ch 188 where, however, the duty was statutory.
6   [1914] 2 Ch 308.
7   *A-G v Horner (No 2)*, above.
8   Civil Evidence Act 1968, s 9(6).
9   In the United States the matter is governed by the Federal Rules of Evidence, r 803 (8)(c) which has been held to encompass opinion as well as fact, if based upon factual findings: *Beech Aircraft Corpn v Rainey* 488 US 153 (1988).
10 As supplemented by the provisions of Part II of the Criminal Justice Act 1988.
11 Law Com 245, para 8.132, rec 27, draft bill, cl 6(2)
12 Law Com 216, para 4.32.

(i)   Nature

The most succinct formulation of this exception to the hearsay rule is that of Phillimore J in *Wilton & Co v Phillips*:[13] 'A public document coming from the proper place or a certified copy of it is sufficient proof of every particular stated in it.' In *Re Stollery, Weir v Treasury Solicitor*,[14] Scrutton LJ expressed the opinion that this was simply a restatement of the law laid down in the leading cases of *Irish Society v Bishop of Derry*[15] and *Sturla v Freccia*.[16] Some limit must, however, be placed upon the generality of Phillimore J's statement, in view of the explanation of *Bird v Keep*[17] adopted in *Re Stollery, Weir v Treasury Solicitor*. In *Bird v Keep* it was held that a death certificate was inadmissible evidence of the cause of death mentioned therein on information supplied by a coroner.[18] This conclusion was technically obiter dictum because the Court of Appeal considered that the cause of death was sufficiently proved by other evidence, but it was justified in *Re Stollery* on the ground that, as the registrar of births, deaths and marriages is bound by statute to record the verdict of a coroner's jury, and as that verdict was inadmissible evidence of the facts on which it was based, it would be absurd to treat the registrar's certificate as any proof of this particular fact. Such a certificate does, however, constitute evidence of the date, as well as the fact of the birth, marriage or death recorded,[19] and, as was decided by the Court of Appeal in *Re Stollery*, a birth certificate may constitute a link in the evidence relating to the marriage of the parents of the child whose birth is recorded. A birth certificate is likewise evidence of the paternity of the person named therein as the father.[20]

(ii)   Rationale

The rationale of this broad exception to the hearsay rule was explained by Parke B in *Irish Society v Bishop of Derry* as being that:[1]

> In public documents, made for the information of the Crown, or all the King's subjects who may require the information they contain, the entry by a public officer is presumed to be true when it is made, and it is for that reason receivable in all cases, whether the officer or his successor may be concerned in such cases or not.

To the extent that this reason rests upon the reliability of the documents, it was amplified by Lord Blackburn in *Sturla v Freccia*:[2]

13   (1903) 19 TLR 390.
14   [1926] Ch 284, at 318.
15   (1846) 12 Cl & Fin 641.
16   (1880) 5 App Cas 623.
17   [1918] 2 KB 692.
18   *Bird v Keep* was followed in *Chapman v Amos* (1959) 18 DLR (2d) 140.
19   *Wilton & Co v Phillips* (above); *Re Goodrich's Estate, Payne v Bennett* [1904] P 138; *Brierley v Brierley and Williams* [1918] P 257. Statements of opinion are now admissible under the Civil Evidence Act 1995, and would include a doctor's statement of the cause of death.
20   *Jackson v Jackson and Pavan* [1964] P 25, [1960] 3 All ER 621. See also *Carlton and United Breweries Ltd v Cassin* [1956] VLR 186 (statement of age on marriage certificate evidence of that fact).
1   (1846) 12 Cl & Fin 641, at 668, 669.
2   (1880) 5 App Cas 623, at 644. In *R v Halpin* [1975] QB 907, [1975] 2 All ER 1124 it was suggested that it would have been more accurate if Lord Blackburn had spoken of registers of baptisms, marriages and burials because the parish officer would not have had personal knowledge of births and deaths and was under no duty to enquire into their occurrence.

In many cases, entries in the parish register of births, marriages and deaths, and other entries of that kind, before there were any statutes relating to them, were admissible, for they were 'public' then, because the common law of England making it an express duty to keep the register, made it a public document in that sense kept by a public officer for the purposes of a register, and that made it admissible.

This reasoning is just as capable of applying to foreign public documents as to English, and it was so extended by Lord Selbourne in *Lyell v Kennedy:*[3]

> Foreign registers of baptisms and marriages or certified extracts from them are receivable in evidence in the courts of this country as to those matters which are properly and regularly recorded on them when it sufficiently appears (in the words of Mr Hubbock's learned work on evidence) that they 'have been kept under the sanction of public authority and are recognised by the tribunals of the country' (i e of the country where they are kept) 'as authentic records'.

If these reasons cannot be demonstrated to apply then the courts will reject the document as evidence of the truth of what it asserts. Thus in *Sturla v Freccia,*[4] the report of a committee appointed by the Genoese government on the fitness of a candidate for the post of consul which contained a statement of his age was rejected as evidence of that fact. The grounds on which the House of Lords held that the evidence should be rejected were that the report was not made under a strict duty to inquire into all the circumstances it recorded, it was not concerned with a public matter, it was not intended to be retained, and it was not meant for public inspection. A word must be said about each of these matters which may be treated as the usual prerequisites of a document's admissibility as a public document although the last appears in the forefront of Lord Blackburn's description which has been quoted on a number of subsequent occasions. He said he understood:[5]

> a public document to mean a document that is made for the purpose of the public making use of it, and being able to refer to it. It is meant to be where there is a judicial or quasi-judicial duty to inquire, as might be said to be the case with the bishops acting under the writs issued by the Crown.

This is probably the definition most often repeated, and it is worth amplifying some of its elements.

(a) Public duty to inquire and record. It has been said that the admissibility of a register depends on the public duty of the person compiling it to make an entry after satisfying himself of the truth of the statement.[6] The duty must be imposed on a public official in that capacity. Surveys made under private authority have been held to be admissible, although they were kept in a public office,[7] and baptismal registers kept by nonconformists or Quakers were inadmissible as evidence of the facts stated at common

3   (1889) 14 App Cas 437, at 448–9.
4   (1880) 5 App Cas 623.
5   At 643, 4.
6   Per Erle J in *Doe d France v Andrews* (1850) 15 QB 756. A gratuitous annotation to an official record is thus inadmissible: *Re Simpson* [1984] 1 NZLR 738 (annotation on death certificate that the deceased's issue had been adopted).
7   *Daniel v Wilkin* (1852) 7 Exch 429. The surveys would now be admissible under s 1 of the Civil Evidence Act 1995.

law.[8] Even if a duty to report to a public authority is imposed upon an official by statute, his report will not constitute proof of the truth of its contents if made solely in order to provide a check upon himself.[9] Nor is it enough to make a report in anticipation of an official request.[10]

(b)   Public matter. It was recognised in *Sturla v Freccia* that a matter may be public although it is not the concern of the entire community. Accordingly, the court rolls of a manor have been received as evidence of a custom,[11] but entries in a corporation's books were sometimes rejected at common law because they did not concern a public matter.[12] It is, however, doubtful whether this is something with regard to which any high degree of precision can be achieved. In *R v Halpin*[13] it was held that a company's file of statutory returns kept in the register of companies was admissible evidence that the appellant was a director at the material time because, under modern conditions, it is sufficient if one person (the officer making the return) has a duty to satisfy himself as to the facts stated and another (the registration officer) has a duty to record those facts.

(c)   Retention. If a document is brought into existence for a temporary purpose it cannot be received under this head. Thus, in *Heyne v Fischel & Co*,[14] it was held that records compiled by the post office showing the times at which telegrams were received were inadmissible as there was no intention that they should be retained for public inspection, and Crown surveys were rejected on account of their temporary purpose in *Mercer v Denne*.[15]

(d)   Public inspection. The possibility that the public may refer to the document undoubtedly enhances the credibility of its contents;[16] but the decision in *Lilley v Pettit*[17] which turned on this requirement may be thought to justify Professor Baker's comment that:[18]

> Accessibility of the public to documents should never have been raised from the status of an additional reason for admitting official records to that of a condition of admissibility.

8   *Re Woodward, Kenway v Kidd* [1913] 1 Ch 392. In so far as they are not admissible by virtue of some other statute they would now be admissible under s 1 of the Civil Evidence Act 1995 (*Re H's Estate* [1949] VLR 197).
9   *Merrick v Wakley* (1838) 8 Ad & El 170.
10   *Newbold v R* [1983] 2 AC 705, though such a report would now be admissible in England under s 24 of the Criminal Justice Act 1988.
11   *Heath v Deane* [1905] 2 Ch 86.
12   *Hill v Manchester and Salford Waterworks Co* (1833) 5 B & Ad 866.
13   [1975] QB 907, [1975] 2 All ER 1124. Applied in Australia to the Annual Report of a public company: *Residues Treatment and Trading Co Ltd v Southern Resources Ltd* (1989) 52 SASR 54, at 83.
14   (1913) 30 TLR 190.
15   [1905] 2 Ch 538; see also *White v Taylor* [1969] 1 Ch 150, [1967] 3 All ER 349. There is no requirement of permanence for the admissibility of statements contained in records under s 4 of the Civil Evidence Act 1968.
16   But if this were the reason for the rejection of certificates issued under the Drug Trafficking Act 1986 as evidence of their contents in *R v Boam* [1998] Crim LR 205 it is unconvincing since the accuracy of the statements derived from their resulting from judicial inquiry, which seems a much better guarantee of accuracy.
17   [1946] KB 401, [1946] 1 All ER 593. Cf *Andrews v Cordiner* [1947] KB 655, [1947] 1 All ER 777 an affiliation case in which regimental records were admitted under the Evidence Act 1938, as they would be under the Act of 1968.
18   Baker *The Hearsay Rule* 137.

Lilley v Pettit was a case in which a woman was prosecuted for making a false statement with regard to the paternity of her child in entering it as that of her husband. The prosecution tendered in evidence the regimental records of the army unit in which her husband had been serving abroad at all material times, but the Divisional Court held them to be inadmissible because they were not kept for the use and information of the public who had not got access to them. Accordingly the prosecution failed. The result is no doubt surprising, but the principle on which it was reached was already deeply embedded in our law,[19] and has since been adopted by the Privy Council.[20]

(iii) Scope

It is clear from the cases mentioned above that there are several different kinds of public document. Wigmore distinguished between registers, returns and certificates.[1] Apart from its convenience from the point of view of exposition, it may have practical significance because the general conditions of admissibility which have just been enumerated undoubtedly undergo some modification when applied to different species of public document. In the case of registers, it may be fatal to the reception of the entry to prove that it was not made promptly[2] or in accordance with the prevailing practice relating to the keeping of the register.[3] Any excess of jurisdiction would be fatal to some types of return.[4] There would, however, be no point in endeavouring to lay down hard-and-fast rules, inferred from the cases, concerning the further conditions of admissibility which may have to be satisfied in the case of certain public documents, for each decision is highly dependent on its specific facts.

3. Records

This rule, which is applicable also in criminal proceedings, requires no special comment.

B. REPUTATION

Section 7(3) provides that:

The common law rules effectively preserved by s 9(3) and (4) of the Civil Evidence Act 1968, that is any rule of law whereby in civil proceedings
(a) evidence of a person's reputation is admissible for the purpose of establishing his good or bad character, or
(b) evidence of reputation or family tradition is admissible–
  (i) for the purpose of proving or disproving pedigree or the existence of the marriage, or
  (ii) for the purpose of proving or disproving the existence of any public or general right or of identifying any person or thing,

---

19 See, for example, *A-G v Horner (No 2)* (above)
20 *Thrasyvoulos Ioannou v Papa Christoforos Demetrious* [1952] AC 84, [1952] 1 All ER 179; see also *R v Kaipianen* (1954) 17 CR 388.
1   V *Wigmore* para 631 f.
2   *Doe d Warren v Bray* (1828) 8 B & C 813.
3   *Fox v Bearblock* (1881) 17 Ch D 429; *Doe d Davies v Gatacre* (1838) 8 C & P 578.
4   *Evans v Taylor* (1838) 7 Ad & El 617.

shall continue to have effect in so far as they authorise the court to treat such evidence as proving or disproving that matter.

Where any such rule applies, reputation or family tradition shall be treated for the purposes of this Act as a fact and not as a statement or multiplicity of statements about the matter in question.

It is important to distinguish between the establishment of reputation and the use made of it when established. Reputation is established by a witness's evidence concerning the sayings and doings of a plurality of people. Accordingly it has been said that a witness may not narrate a single person's statement of either the fact reputed or reputation unless it is the pedigree declaration of a member of the family with regard to a genealogical issue.[5] There is therefore no question of an infringement of the rule against hearsay so far as the establishment of reputation is concerned, but that rule would be infringed whenever reputation were tendered as evidence of the facts reputed. If a witness depose to a tradition concerning the existence of a public right prevailing in the community, or the neighbourhood's treatment of a couple as man and wife, he is recounting the express or implied assertions of a number of other people in order to establish the truth of that which was asserted.

This distinction is recognised in the final sentence quoted above, so as to make it clear that the notice provisions do not apply to every statement relied upon by the witness to justify his testimony as to reputation.

Nothing need be said about evidence of character, but reference must be made to the matters of pedigree and public or general rights mentioned in s 7(3) because, at common law, they are the subject of technical requirements some of which will very probably be held to have survived the Act.

1. Pedigree

At common law there is an exception to the hearsay rule under which the oral or written declarations of deceased persons, or declarations to be inferred from family conduct, are, subject to the conditions of admissibility mentioned below, admissible as evidence of pedigree. The evidence often takes the form of direct assertions of fact, as in the old leading case of *Goodright d Stevens v Moss*[6] where the question was whether a child was the legitimate offspring of its parents (since deceased), and Lord Mansfield admitted the parents' declarations, proved by the persons to whom they were made, to the effect that the child was born before their marriage. Such declarations would now, like any other first-hand hearsay statement, be admissible under s 1 of the 1995 Act. Lord Mansfield said that tradition is sufficient in point of pedigree, and referred to the treatment of a child as illegitimate (a matter which is best regarded as original evidence), an entry in a family bible, an inscription on a tombstone and a pedigree hung up in the family mansion. Without any strain of language, the inscription on the tombstone, entry in the family bible and hanging pedigree could be proved under s 1 of the Act as statements made by persons otherwise than while giving evidence. Reliance on this provision would however dispense with the necessity to serve notice of intention to do so. Lord Eldon said that the tradition must prevail among persons having such a connection with the person to whom it relates that it is natural and likely, from their domestic habits and connections, that they are speaking the truth and could not be

5   *Shedden v A-G* (1860) 30 LJPM & A 217.
6   (1777) 2 Cowp 591; *Murray v Milner* (1879) 12 Ch D 845; *Re Turner, Glenister v Harding* (1885) 29 Ch D 985.

mistaken;[7] but this is a matter of weight rather than admissibility, although it is clear that, in order to be admissible, the tradition must be family tradition, and not, for example, that prevailing among the neighbours.

The common law conditions of admissibility of pedigree statements or, to employ the more usual word 'declarations', are that:

(i)   the declarant should have been dead;

(ii) the declarations should relate to a question of pedigree, ie have a genealogical purpose;[8]

(iii) the declarant should have been a blood relation, or the spouse of a blood relation, of the person whose pedigree is in issue;[9] and

(iv) the declaration should have been made before the dispute in which it is tendered had arisen.[10]

All these conditions are now irrelevant so far as declarations of fact, as distinct from reputation, are concerned, provided they can be rendered admissible under s 1. For example, the issue being A's legitimacy, A's mother writes to B from America to say that she has heard of the dispute and may as well state the truth, viz that she never married A's deceased father; the mother's statement is admissible under s 1 as of one otherwise than while giving evidence. If the issue is whether the defendant to a claim for breach of contract is an infant, an affidavit sworn by his deceased father in relation to another case is admissible, although the question is not one of pedigree.[11] If the issue is which of the twins C and D is the elder, the statement of a deceased nurse that she was present at the birth and marked C's foot as that of the first born may be proved under s 1.[12]

It is therefore only in a very restricted sense that s 7 can be said to have preserved this common law exception to the hearsay rule. A statement tending to establish family reputation or tradition which would, but for the Act, have been admissible for the purpose of proving pedigree is admissible by virtue of s 7 only if the common law conditions of admissibility are satisfied. Accordingly, if A could prove that B, a deceased retainer of the X family, had told him that, according to the family tradition, X's grandfather was illegitimate, it seems that, although the statement would be inadmissible by virtue of s 7, it would still be admissible if tendered under s 1.

2.   Public or general rights[13]

At common law an oral or written declaration by a deceased person concerning the reputed existence of a public or general right is admissible as evidence of the existence of such right provided the declaration was made before the dispute in which it is tendered

---

7   *Whitelocke v Baker* (1807) 13 Ves 510, at 514.

8   *Haines v Guthrie* (1884) 13 QBD 818; cf *Hood v Beauchamp* (1836) 8 Sim 26 and *Shields v Boucher* (1847) 1 De G & Sm 40.

9   *Johnson v Lawson* (1824) 2 Bing 86; *Shrewsbury Peerage Case* (1858) 7 HL Cas 1, at 23; *Berkeley Peerage Case* (1811) 4 Camp 401; on problems of legitimacy and legitimation see *Hitchens v Eardley* (1871) LR 2 P & D 248; *Re Jenion, Jenion v Wynne* [1952] Ch 454, [1952] 1 All ER 1228; *Re Perton Pearson v A-G* (1885) 53 LT 707; *Re Davy* [1935] P 1, followed in *Battle v A-G* [1949] P 358. See also *Monkton v A-G* (1831) 2 Russ & M 147 and *B v A-G* [1965] P 278, [1965] 1 All ER 62.

10   *Berkeley Peerage Case* above.

11   Cf *Haines v Guthrie*, above.

12   Cf *Johnson v Lawson*, above.

13   Except where admissibility under the Civil Evidence Act is being considered, what is said under this head could apply in criminal proceedings.

had arisen, and, in the case of a statement concerning the reputed existence of a general right, provided the declarant had competent knowledge.

A public right is one affecting the entire population, such as a claim to tolls on a public highway,[14] a right of ferry,[15] or the right to treat part of a river bank as a public landing place.[16] Declarations by deceased persons tending to prove or disprove the existence of such rights are admissible at common law, and evidence of this nature is received on cognate questions such as the boundaries between counties and parishes,[17] and the question of whether a road is public or private.[18]

A general right is one that affects a class of persons such as the inhabitants of a particular district, the tenants of a manor, or the owners of certain plots of land. Examples are rights of common,[19] the rights of corporations[20] and a custom of mining in a particular district.[1] The distinction from public rights is not precise and important, if important at all, only because it has been said that no evidence of competent knowledge of the subject-matter of the reputed right on the part of the declarant is necessary when the right is public because 'in a matter in which all are concerned, reputation from anyone appears to be receivable; but of course it would be almost worthless unless it came from persons who were shown to have some means of knowledge as by living in the neighbourhood, or frequently using the road in dispute'. If, however, the alleged right is a general one, such as a mining right under certain land; 'hearsay from any person wholly unconnected with the place in which the mines are found, would not only be of no value, but probably altogether inadmissible'.[2]

A far more crucial distinction is that between public or general rights on the one hand and private rights on the other hand, for the latter cannot be proved by evidence of reputation.[3] But here again the distinction is none too precise, all that can be said is that a public or general right must be enjoyed by the claimant as a member of the public or as a member of some clearly defined class. Evidence of a reputation is admissible when private and public rights coincide, as when the boundaries between two estates are coterminous with those between two hamlets.[4]

The common law conditions of admissibility of hearsay statements concerning reputed public or general rights are:
(i)   the death of the declarant;
(ii) that the declaration should have been made before the dispute in which it is tendered;[5] and

---

14   *Brett v Beales* (1830) 10 B & C 508.
15   *Pim v Curell* (1840) 6 M & W 234.
16   *Drinkwater v Porter* (1835) 7 C & P 181.
17   *Brisco v Lomax* (1838) 8 Ad & El 198; *Evans v Rees* (1839) 10 Ad & El 151.
18   *R v Bliss* (1837) 2 Nev & PKB 464.
19   *Evans v Merthyr Tydfil UDC* [1899] 1 Ch 241.
20   *Davies v Morgan* (1831) 1 Cr & J 587.
1   *Crease v Barrett* (1835) 1 Cr M & R 919.
2   *Crease v Barrett*, above; see also *Rogers v Wood* (1831) 2 B & Ad 245. Even in the case of a general right, the declarant need not be proved to have been resident in the neighbourhood: *Duke of Newcastle v Broxtowe Hundred* (1832) 4 B & Ad 273.
3   *R v Antrobus* (1835) 2 Ad & El 788; *Talbot v Lewis* (1834) 1 Cr M & R 495; *Lord Dunraven v Llewellyn* (1850) 15 QB 791 (see *Evans v Merthyr Tydfil UDC* [1899] 1 Ch 241 for the limits of this decision); *White v Taylor* [1969] 1 Ch 150, [1967] 3 All ER 349.
4   *Thomas v Jenkins* (1837) 6 Ad & El 525.
5   *Berkeley Peerage Case* (1811) 4 Camp 401; the fact that the declaration was made to provide against future controversy does not affect its admissibility, nor does the existence of a general motive to misrepresent (*Moseley v Davies* (1822) 11 Price 162) but see the judgment of Joyce J in *Brocklebank v Thompson* [1903] 2 Ch 344 where, however, the remarks about interested persons were obiter.

(iii) that the declaration should concern the reputed existence of the right as opposed to a particular fact from which the existence of the right may be inferred.[6]

This last requirement marks a great distinction between the admissibility of pedigree declarations and the admissibility of declarations concerning public or general rights. In the case of each the declarant must be dead, and the statement must have been made before the dispute arose; but, whereas proof of reputation is merely one way of establishing pedigree by hearsay at common law, it is the only way of doing so in the case of public or general rights.

All the above conditions must be fulfilled if evidence of the reputed existence of such rights is to be admissible by virtue of s 7 of the Civil Evidence Act 1995; but is this true of a statement which can, by virtue of s 7(3), be treated as a statement of fact and thereby rendered admissible by virtue of s 1? For example, if A, formerly the oldest inhabitant of a village, were to write from America, after a dispute had arisen concerning rights of common, stating that, according to the tradition which had prevailed in the village community, those rights were enjoyed only by the occupiers of certain lands, could A's statement be received under s 1 as one made otherwise than while giving oral evidence? It is submitted that the answer is in the affirmative because the exclusion of statements made after a dispute has arisen is a common law restriction on the reception of hearsay under a particular exception to the hearsay rule and it has suffered the same fate as other restrictions on the admissibility of hearsay evidence at common law. Evidence of reputation is second-hand hearsay and this is now admissible under s 1.

A further, and possibly more difficult, question relates to the effect of the Act on the third common law condition of admissibility, that the declaration should concern the reputed existence of the right as opposed to a particular fact from which it might be inferred. In the past this has produced decisions of breathtaking absurdity. For example, in *Mercer v Denne*[7] the issue was whether the fishermen of Walmer had a customary right of immemorial antiquity to dry their nets on part of the foreshore. In support of the contention that the custom could not have existed throughout the relevant period, a survey, depositions and old maps were produced. They showed that the sea had run over the portion of foreshore in respect of which the customary right was claimed, but they were rejected because they amounted to statements of particular facts and had nothing to do with the reputed existence of the custom. Is the condition of admissibility under consideration simply a common law restriction on the reception of hearsay under an exception to the general rule excluding such evidence, or is it an independent rule, which can equally well be described as one of evidence or substantive law, which has survived the partial abolition of the hearsay rule in civil cases? Perhaps it would be rash to predict the courts' answer to this question, but it is to be hoped that *Mercer v Denne* and the congeries of similar decisions have not survived the Civil Evidence Act 1995. The survey, depositions and old maps appear to have been documents in which statements were made by persons who could, if living, have given direct oral evidence with regard to the condition of the foreshore.

Whatever view may ultimately be taken by the courts on the matters mentioned above, some of the absurd results of past decisions will be avoided for the future, so far as rights of way are concerned, on account of the provisions of the Highways Act 1980, s 32. The section provides that any map, plan or history of locality is admissible to show whether a way has or has not been dedicated as a highway, or the date when such dedication took place. Such weight is to be given to the above documents as the

6   *R v Lordsmere (Inhabitants)* (1866) 16 Cox CC 65 (conviction for non-repair as evidence road public).
7   [1905] 2 Ch 538; see also *R v Bliss* (1837) 7 Ad & El 550; *R v Berger* [1894] 1 QB 823; and *A-G v Horner (No 2)* [1913] 2 Ch 140.

court considers justified by the circumstances, including the antiquity of the document, the status of the person by whom it was made, its purpose, and the custody in which it was kept or from which it was produced.

C. CHILDREN

In part to avoid anomaly by comparison with wardship proceedings, where the strict rules of evidence[8] did not apply, s 96 of the Children Act 1989 empowered the Lord Chancellor to make orders admitting hearsay in any civil proceedings in connection with the upbringing, maintenance or welfare of a child.[9] In 1993 he ordered[10] that:

> 2. In–
> (a) civil proceedings before the High Court or a county court; and
> (b) (i)   family proceedings, and
>   (ii) civil proceedings under the Child Support Act 1991 in a magistrates'
>   court,
> evidence given in connection with the upbringing, maintenance or welfare of a
> child shall be admissible notwithstanding any rule of law relating to hearsay.

Despite such provisions, anomalies will remain so long as the hearsay rule is retained in English law for any purposes at all.[11]

D. COMPANY LITIGATION

Under the old law hearsay was admissible only under the terms of the Civil Evidence Act 1968, by agreement of the parties or under a statutory provision. It was thus prima facie odd[12] that in proceedings to wind up companies the courts came to rely upon hearsay in reports made by inspectors, despite their fulfilling none of these criteria.[13] The use of such a report can be justified upon the basis of the professionalism of the compilers of such a report, despite their lack of first-hand knowledge, especially when it has been considered sufficient for an independent official to act upon, and when the defendant who does have such first-hand knowledge has had ample opportunity to attempt to refute any statements it contains. The fig-leaf relied upon to cover its technical inadmissibility was an *implied* statutory exception.[14] It extended both to applications to wind the company up, and to disqualify a director.[15] In the latter case it applied whether under s 7 of the Company Directors Disqualification Act 1986 the hearsay

---

8   Including the hearsay rule: see *Official Solicitor v K* [1965] AC 201, [1963] 3 All ER 191.
9   For a similar result in Ireland, see *Southern Health Board v CH* [1996] 1 IR 219.
10 SI 1993/621.
11 *Re C (hearsay evidence: contempt proceedings)* [1993] 4 All ER 690 revealed that anomaly
    remained even in relation to the evidence of children. The modern law still stops short of total
    abolition of the sort accomplished by the Scots in the Civil Evidence (Scotland) Act 1988, s 2:
    see Cm 2321 (1993).
12 See doubts expressed by Staughton LJ in *Re Rex Williams Leisure Ltd* [1994] Ch 350, at 369c,
    [1994] 4 All ER 27, at 42a.
13 *Re Koscot Interplanetary (UK) Ltd* [1972] 3 All ER 829.
14 Unconvincingly derived from the terms of the 1986 Act and the relevant rules made under it.
15 *Re St Piran Ltd* [1981] 3 All ER 270, [1981] 1 WLR 1300.

were adduced by the Official Receiver or the Secretary of State,[16] and whether the application were made under s 7 or under s 8.[17]

E.   AFFIDAVITS[18]

It has been long established that where evidence is given in the form of an affidavit, it may be based on information and belief. The urgency of applications so supported, often precludes the possibility of discovering, and obtaining access to, original sources of information. Even before the passage of s 1(2)(b) of the Civil Evidence Act 1995 applying its provisions to evidence of every degree, it had been held that such statements could themselves be based upon hearsay statements.[19]

---

16   *Re Rex Williams Leisure Ltd* above.
17   *Secretary of State for Trade and Industry v Ashcroft* [1998] Ch 71, [1997] 3 All ER 86.
18   See the Civil Procedure Rules, especially CPR 32.15.
19   *Deutsche Ruckversicherung AG v Walbrook Insurance* [1994] 4 All ER 181, [1995] 1 WLR 1017 (unaffected on this point by the dismissal of an appeal at [1996] 1 All ER 791), declining on this point to follow *Savings and Investment Bank Ltd v Gasco Investments (Netherlands) BV* [1984] 1 All ER 296, [1984] 1 WLR 271.

CHAPTER XV

Hearsay in criminal proceedings

The Police and Criminal Evidence Act 1984 and the Criminal Justice Act 1988 transformed this subject from one primarily determined by common law rules to one dominated by statute. Further far-reaching reform has now been recommended by the Law Commission,[1] endorsed by the government,[2] but not, at the time of writing, introduced as a bill. It is accordingly necessary to present the law in its existing state, but with extensive reference to the recommendations of the Law Commission.

In contrast to its proposals for civil proceedings the Law Commission has recommended retention of a basic rule excluding hearsay in criminal proceedings,[3] though subject to considerable relaxation[4] and clarification in various respects. The position of the accused, and especially the great importance, in criminal proceedings, of the huge exception from the exclusionary rule for confessions made by the accused, dictate a different approach, both to the reform and to the exposition of the law. This chapter will consider first the general statutory rules relating to the admissibility of hearsay in criminal proceedings, and then in the second section go on to consider the rules relating to confessions and closely related rules, such as those concerned with police questioning and the right of silence. It should be noted that some topics strictly speaking within the scope of the title of this chapter have been considered elsewhere. In particular some discussion of criminal cases in their bearing on the admissibility of res gestae statements and admissions appeared in chapter XIII, and of public documents in chapter XIV.

SECTION I.   THE GENERAL RULE

In *Myers v DPP*[5] Lord Reid recommended wholesale statutory revision of the law of hearsay. Such wholesale reform has yet to take place in relation to the admissibility of

---

1   In Law Com No 245 *Evidence in Criminal Proceedings: Hearsay and Related Topics* Cm 3670 (1997).
2   Official Record, House of Lords, 17 December 1998.
3   Law Com 245, para 6.53, rec 1, draft bill, cl 1.
4   Including admission by agreement of all of the parties to the proceedings, draft bill, cl 1(1)(c).
5   [1965] AC 1001, at 1022, [1964] 2 All ER 881, at 886. See further, above p 544.

hearsay in criminal cases, and instead a series of piecemeal measures has been adopted, especially in the field of business records, relating both to general documentary evidence and to the more specialised field of computer output. The recommendations of the Law Commission will, if accepted, extend admissibility for the first time[6] in criminal proceedings to oral hearsay. It is convenient to deal with these matters separately, before dealing with s 9 of the Criminal Justice Act 1967, which, however important it may be in practice, requires less attention here.

A. DOCUMENTARY EVIDENCE[7]

The first response to the decision in *Myers* was to legislate on a stop-gap basis in the Criminal Evidence Act 1965 so as to admit business records. That legislation was repealed and replaced by s 68 of the Police and Criminal Evidence Act 1984, which was itself immediately subjected to further examination by the Roskill Committee into the conduct of trials for fraud. Although an initial bill went some way towards the adoption of its proposals, the final version, subsequently enacted as Pt II of the Criminal Justice Act 1988, was more limited. It dealt separately with first-hand documentary hearsay, with business documents and with documents prepared for the purposes of criminal proceedings or investigations, as well as incorporating some general provisions. Special rules also apply to the output of computers.[8] Each of these topics requires separate consideration, before embarking upon consideration of the recommendations of the Law Commission.

1. First-hand hearsay

(i) The provision

This area is governed at present by s 23 of the Criminal Justice Act 1988[9] which provides that:

(1) Subject–
(a) to subsection (4) below;
(b) to paragraph 1A of Schedule 2 to the Criminal Appeal Act 1968 (evidence given orally at original trial to be given orally at retrial); and
(c) to section 69 of the Police and Criminal Evidence Act 1984 (evidence from computer records), a statement made by a person in a document shall be admissible in criminal proceedings as evidence of any fact of which direct oral evidence by him would be admissible if–
   (i) the requirements of one of the paragraphs of subsection (2) below are satisfied; or
   (ii) the requirements of subsection (3) below are satisfied.

  (2) The requirements mentioned in subsection 1(i) above are–

---

6   Apart of course from some of the old common law exceptions, such as that for oral confessions of guilt.
7   See Birch [1989] Crim LR 15; Smith [1994] Crim LR 426.
8   Police and Criminal Evidence Act 1984, s 69 and Sch 3.
9   Though it has been argued that no document admissible under s 23 is not also admissible under s 24: Ockleton [1992] Crim LR 15.

582   *Chapter XV.   Hearsay in criminal proceedings*

(a) that the person who made the statement is dead or by reason of his bodily or mental condition unfit to attend as a witness;

(b) that–
   (i) the person who made the statement is outside the United Kingdom; and
   (ii) it is not reasonably practicable to secure his attendance; or

(c) that all reasonable steps have been taken to find the person who made the statement, but that he cannot be found.

(3) The requirements mentioned in subsection 1(ii) above are–

(a) that the statement was made to a police officer or some other person charged with the duty of investigating offences or charging offenders; and

(b) that the person who made it does not give oral evidence through fear or because he is kept out of the way.

(4) Subsection (1) above does not render admissible a confession made by an accused person that would not be admissible under section 76 of the Police and Criminal Evidence Act 1984.

(ii)   General considerations

The Act is confined to statements made in documents,[10] tendered as evidence of fact.[11] An oral statement recorded in a document, and authenticated by its maker will suffice.[12] In some respects the conditions carry over improvements upon the drafting of earlier comparable provisions applicable in civil proceedings, for example in referring to the maker as being 'outside the United Kingdom'[13] and in making the relevant conditions in s 2(b) cumulative.[14] Like the comparable provision in the Police and Criminal Evidence Act 1984 this condition will be construed against the background of the whole history of the litigation and not judged simply on the basis of the situation at the moment when the issue arises.[15] The factual substratum of such conditions, whether or not the issue is raised by the witness alleged to have been in fear,[16] must be proved to the ordinary

---

10   Unlike s 1 of the Civil Evidence Act 1995, though 'document' is given an extended meaning by Sch 2, para 5 incorporating the definition contained in s 10 of the Civil Evidence Act 1968, which, while expanding the conditions of admissibility does so by categories rather than by general provisions. It has been applied to video recording, and generously interpreted in the case of an unintelligible statement to a composite form of evidence consisting of the recording and a transcript of an interpretation of it: *R v Duffy* [1999] 1 Cr App Rep 307.

11   Evidence of opinion has been admitted under some earlier legislation despite similar apparent restriction: see *Dass v Masih* [1968] 2 All ER 226 [1968] 1 WLR 756 under the Evidence Act 1938; and *Wallhead v Ruston & Hornsby Ltd* (1973) 14 KIR 285 under the Civil Evidence Act 1968. Explicit provision is made in Part III of the Criminal Justice Act 1988 for the admission of expert reports in derogation of the hearsay rule: see s 30.

12   *R v McGillivray* (1992) 97 Cr App Rep 232, though see *R Eleftheriou and Eleftheriou* [1993] Crim LR 947.

13   Rather than 'beyond the seas'; cp *Rover International Ltd v Cannon Film Sales Ltd (No 2)* [1987] 3 All ER 986, [1987] 1 WLR 1597.

14   *R v Serdeiro* [1996] 1 Cr App Rep (S) 251; cp *Piermay Shipping Co SA v Chester* [1978] 1 All ER 1233, [1978] 1 WLR 411.

15   *R v Bray* (1989) 88 Cr App Rep 354; *R v French and Gowhar* (1993) 97 Cr App Rep 421.

16   The issue may well be denied in a case where the witness subject to pressure has been so affected by it, as to seek to deny it, as in *R v Waters* (1997) 161 JP 249.

criminal standard[17] by admissible evidence[18] normally on oath[19] and subject to cross-examination whether called by prosecution or defence,[20] and cannot be inferred,[1] even though this often means that a voir dire must be held to avoid prejudice to the accused.[2] This provision corresponds to s 2 of the old Civil Evidence Act 1968, and as such goes beyond the previous provision in criminal proceedings which was limited to business records or those made pursuant to a duty. The shoulder note refers to 'First-hand' hearsay, and as in the 1968 Act this restriction is principally accomplished by insistence that direct oral evidence by the maker of the relevant statement should have been admissible. Since witnesses cannot generally adduce hearsay such terminology normally restricts the operation of this provision to first-hand hearsay. This is however subject to a qualification in that where an exception to the hearsay rule operates then a witness can testify to hearsay.[3] It has been held however that if such evidence is recorded in a document, that document must be proved by admissible evidence in the normal way, and cannot prove itself.[4] It is far from clear why s 27 cannot be employed for this purpose. It is certainly the case that the condition of absence can be applied twice, once in relation to inability to attend of the maker of the statement, and second in relation to the inability to attend of the witness testifying to that inability of that statement.[5]

Although it was emphasised in *R v Cole*[6] that the jury should be directed about the weaknesses of hearsay as opposed to direct, and cross-examined, testimony, more recent cases have been less censorious.[7] Some form of warning is nevertheless still required, at least where the evidence is vital to the prosecution case.[8]

17 *R v Acton Justices, ex p McMullen* (1991) 92 Cr App Rep 98, at 104; *R v De Arango* (1993) 96 Cr App Rep 399. Where the defence seeks to prove the satisfaction of such a condition the standard required is, as in other cases, proof on the balance of probabilities: *R v Mattey and Queeley* [1995] 2 Cr App Rep 409.

18 Not by hearsay: see *Neill v North Antrim Magistrates' Court* [1992] 4 All ER 846, [1992] 1 WLR 1220; *R v Fairfax* [1995] Crim LR 949; cp *R v Maloney* [1994] Crim LR 525 where this appears to have been overlooked.

19 But see *R v Jennings and Miles* [1995] Crim LR 810 where it was said to have been realistic for counsel not to have taken the point that the witness had not been sworn; and *R v Greer* [1998] Crim LR 572 where the court upheld a decision made upon such a basis despite the point having been taken. It is far from clear why this departure from normal methods should be tolerated, since it adds a further layer of denial of cross-examination which might make the exercise of the ultimate exclusionary discretions still more difficult.

20 *R v Wood and Fitzsimmons* [1998] Crim LR 213.

1 It has been suggested in New Zealand that fair trial considerations under human rights provisions require rigorous examination of conditions under which cross-examination of a key witness will be avoided: *R v M* [1996] 2 NZLR 659.

2 *R v Nicholls* (1976) 63 Cr App Rep 187; *R v Case* [1991] Crim LR 192; *R v Jennings and Miles* above.

3 The exception for statements of mental state is especially important in relation to an account of fear made to the witness by the person experiencing it: see *Neill* above.

4 *R v Belmarsh Magistrates' Court ex p Gilligan* [1998] 1 Cr App Rep 14.

5 *R v Castillo* [1996] 1 Cr App Rep 438.

6 [1990] 2 All ER 108, [1990] 1 WLR 865. No criticism was made of a particularly strong direction by the trial judge to that effect.

7 Eg *R v Greer* [1998] Crim LR 572.

8 *R v Curry* [1998] 2 Cr App Rep (S) 410. Munday pointed out in (1997) 141 JP 691 that the specimen direction in the Judges' Bench Book echoes the form of direction recommended in relation to s 13 of the Criminal Justice Act 1925 in *Scott v R* [1989] AC 1242, [1989] 2 All ER 305.

(iii)   Attendance

The reference to the maker's fitness to attend in s 23(2)(a) relates to ability to testify capably, rather than simply to ability to be present in court, so an amnesiac would qualify.[9] The two conditions in s 23(2)(b) operate cumulatively. It should be noted that the first is to be construed to apply to physical rather than jurisdictional presence outside the United Kingdom, and so does not apply to a resident diplomat.[10] On the other hand a witness physically outside the United Kingdom may be said to attend if his evidence is taken by video link, though not if his evidence is taken on commission abroad, even if the accused has the opportunity to cross-examine.[11] However the second condition refers not to inability to attend, but to *secure* attendance, and may be satisfied by the recalcitrance of a witness outside the United Kingdom.[12] Reasonable practicality implies assessing the likely effectiveness of taking normal steps to secure the attendance of the witness, and considering in relation to such a judgment the importance of the evidence, the degree of prejudice to the defence if it is admitted, and the expense and inconvenience involved in securing attendance.[13] Unavailability is more strictly confined than in relation to the business documents admitted under s 24, and for this reason sub-s (4) is likely to have a very limited effect.[14]

The impracticality required by s 25(2)(c) was held to be satisfied in *R v Lockley and Corah*[15] where testimony alleging a confession by one of the accused during an aborted trial was recorded in a transcript, and the witness then absconded from an open prison and could not be found by the police.

(iv)   Fear

Subsection (3) appears to have been designed to overcome the defects in the old law[16] exposed by *R v O'Loughlin and McLaughlin,*[17] whereby the pressure was required to have been exerted by or on behalf of the accused. The problem of intimidation is now better recognised,[18] and perceived to be growing.[19] Increased use of s 23(3) has been urged by the Court of Appeal.[20]

The two conditions in s 23(3)(b) are to be read disjunctively, with the result that the fear may arise spontaneously and, provided that it is genuine, it need not be reasonable.[1] The section makes no explicit requirement that the fear need relate to the maker himself,

---

9   *R v Setz-Dempsey* (1994) 98 Cr App Rep 23.
10   *R v Jiminez-Paez* (1994) 98 Cr App Rep 239.
11   *R v Radak* [1999] 1 Cr App Rep 187.
12   *R v French and Gowhar* (1993) 97 Cr App Rep 421.
13   *R v Castillo* [1996] 1 Cr App Rep 438.
14   The conditions under which confessions are admitted are generally incompatible with these conditions, except perhaps in a rare case involving more than one accused.
15   [1995] 2 Cr App Rep 554. The report exhibits some confusion between this condition and parts of those in sub-s (2)(b) and (3).
16   In Criminal Justice Act 1925, s 13(3), repealed by Criminal Justice and Public Order Act 1994, s 168(3), Sch 11. The Law Commission has recommended further reform in Law Com 245, rec 14.
17   [1988] 3 All ER 431, 85 Cr App Rep 157.
18   It has been addressed directly by s 51 of the Criminal Justice and Public Order Act 1994, and ss 54 and 55 of the Criminal Procedure and Investigations Act 1996.
19   See Home Office WP *Speaking Up for Justice* (1998) ch 4, Annex A pp 111–129; see also Youth Justice and Criminal Evidence Bill, Pt II providing for special support for intimidated witnesses.
20   *R v Holt* (1996) 161 JP 96.
1   *R v Acton Justices, ex p McMullen* (1991) 92 Cr App Rep 98.

nor that it need be related either to the accused,[2] or even to the offence being tried.[3] The provision applies even when the witness attends court and gives some evidence, if the testimony is deficient as a result of fear.[4] It should be noted that any statement admitted under this provision will also require the leave of the court under s 26, and that it may still be excluded at the discretion of the court[5] either pursuant to the new discretion conferred by s 25, or that conferred by s 78 of the Police and Criminal Evidence Act 1984, or any exclusionary discretion operating at common law, such as where its prejudicial effect exceeds the probative force of the evidence. This provision creates some difficulty for trial judges in informing the jury of what has happened.[6]

It should be noted that under s 97A of the Magistrates' Courts Act 1980[7] anyone who the magistrate holds to be capable of giving relevant evidence, and who will not do so,[8] may be summonsed[9] to have a deposition taken. Once taken such a deposition will become admissible at the trial under the provisions of Sch 2, para 2 to the Criminal Procedure and Investigation Act 1996, thus creating another route for the reception of the hearsay of those suffering from fear, even though available to testify.

(v) Children

Further special provision has been made to permit video recordings of pre-trial interviews with children in relation to trials for certain offences[10] to be adduced in evidence.[11]

2. Business documents

The Act repeals s 68 of the Police and Criminal Evidence Act 1984, and in its place provides in s 24 as follows:

(1) Subject–
(a) to subsections (3) and (4) below;
(b) to paragraph 1A of Schedule 2 to the Criminal Appeal Act 1968; and

---

2   *R v Wood and Fitzsimmons* [1998] Crim LR 213; *R v Rutherford* [1998] Crim LR 490.
3   *R v Martin* [1996] Crim LR 589.
4   *R v Ashford Justices, ex p Hilden* [1993] QB 555, [1993] 2 All ER 154 (where the witness broke off on account of fear); *R v Waters* (1997) 161 JP 249 (where the witness gave false evidence on account of fear). See also *R v Jennings and Miles*, above, (where, although present in court, the witness refused to testify at all on account of fear).
5   Explicitly preserved by s 28(1)(b). This discretion operates only at trial, and not at the committal stage: *R v Tunbridge Wells Justices, ex p Webb* [1997] CLY 1117.
6   Cp *R v Ricketts* [1991] Crim LR 915 where the judge suppressed from the jury the information that it had transpired before verdict that the witness had never been intimidated as held, but had innocently failed to appear in time, with *R v Churchill* [1993] Crim LR 285 where the judge failed to tell the jury that the absence of the witness was no reflection on the accused but did tell it that it was no reflection upon the witness herself, and in both situations an appeal was allowed.
7   Inserted by Criminal Procedure and Investigation Act 1996, Sch 1.
8   For whatever reason, including fear.
9   Or if recalcitrant, arrested for the purpose.
10   As specified in Criminal Justice Act 1988, s 32(2), principally offences against children, but including offences involving assaults or injury upon anyone.
11   Section 32A inserted by Criminal Justice Act 1991, s 54, and regulated by *Practice Note* [1992] 3 All ER 909, sub nom *Practice Direction* [1992] 1 WLR 839. See further above p 211.

(c)   to section 69 of the Police and Criminal Evidence Act 1984, a statement in a document shall be admissible in criminal proceedings as evidence of any fact of which direct oral evidence would be admissible, if the following conditions are satisfied–

    (i)   the document was created or received by a person in the course of a trade, business, profession or other occupation, or as the holder of a paid or unpaid office; and

    (ii)   the information contained in the document was supplied by a person (whether or not the maker of the statement) who had or may reasonably be supposed to have had, personal knowledge of the matters dealt with.

(2) Subsection (1) above applies whether the information contained in the document was supplied directly or indirectly but, if it was supplied indirectly, only if each person through whom it was supplied received it–

(a)   in the course of a trade, business, profession or other occupation; or

(b)   as the holder of a paid or unpaid office.

(3) Subsection (1) above does not render admissible a confession made by an accused person that would not be admissible under s 76 of the Police and Criminal Evidence Act 1984.

(4) A statement prepared otherwise than in accordance with section 29 below or an order under paragraph 6 of Schedule 13 to this Act or under section 30 or 31 below for the purposes–

(a)   of pending or contemplated criminal proceedings; or

(b)   of a criminal investigation, shall not be admissible by virtue of subsection
    (1) above unless–

    (i)   the requirements of one of the paragraphs of subsection (2) of section 23 above are satisfied; or

    (ii)   the requirements of subsection (3) of that section are satisfied; or

    (iii)   the person who made the statement cannot reasonably be expected (having regard to the time which has elapsed since he made the statement and to all the circumstances) to have any recollection of the matters dealt with in the statement.

This provision reverts to the categorisation of admissibility in this area by reference to business[12] rather than duty.[13] However, given the expansive definition, and the incorporation of s 23 to deal with first-hand hearsay, this is unlikely to cause any difficulty.[14] A potentially more significant change is from the terminology of 'record' to that of 'statement in a document'. It seems that this could free the law from the unduly restrictive interpretation attached to the notion of a record.[15] A further indication of liberalisation is that it is necessary now only that the document be received in the course of business, not that it be supplied or made in the course of business. It remains

12   As in the Criminal Evidence Act 1965. Defined widely enough to include court records, as in *R v Lockley and Corah* [1995] 2 Cr App Rep 554, at 559; police custody records, as in *R v Hogan* [1997] Crim LR 349; and perhaps even to foreign customs records, as canvassed in *R v Dyer* [1997] Crim LR 442.

13   As in s 68 of the Police and Criminal Evidence Act 1984.

14   All subsequent reference in this part to 'business' is intended to refer to the extended meaning. For an attempt to exclude police documents from the ambit of s 24(1) see McEvoy [1993] Crim LR 480, and further discussion with Smith at [1994] Crim LR 426.

15   In cases such as *R v Tirado* (1974) 59 Cr App Rep 80; *R v Jones and Sullivan* [1978] 2 All ER 718, [1978] 1 WLR 195; *R v Cunningham* [1989] Crim LR 435; *R v Governor of Pentonville Prison, ex p Osman* [1989] 3 All ER 701, [1990] 1 WLR 277; *R v Iqbal* [1990] 3 All ER 787, [1990] 1 WLR 756.

necessary that the supplier of the information have personal knowledge. It is submitted that these conditions must be met to the satisfaction of the judge,[16] to the requisite standard depending upon whether they are adduced by prosecution or defence. It is not however clear that the rigid distinction between the maker of the statement contained in the document[17] and the supplier of the information contained in it is satisfactory. For example it is far from clear why the condition in s 24(4)(b)(iii) relating to the absence of recollection of the matters dealt with in the statement should be applied to the maker of the statement rather than to the supplier of the information which it contains.[18]

Although the statement should have been admissible in the mouth of some witness at some stage, and must have been supplied by someone with personal knowledge, there is no restriction upon the length of the chain of supply so long as every subsequent reception takes place in the course of business. It should be noted that intermediate reception need not be in documentary form.

In contrast to the position in some other jurisdictions[19] no explicit provision is made in relation to statements of negative purport. It might be thought that this would cause difficulty in the light of the condition requiring personal knowledge, since the negative cannot be within anyone's personal knowledge. Such an argument was advanced in at least two cases under the old law. In *R v Patel*[20] the court did not need to decide the question, but seemed to think that the proper custodian of the records could testify to their mode of creation, leaving the jury to infer from the absence of the inclusion of a particular person's name as a legal immigrant that he had immigrated illegally. In *R v Shone*[1] the argument was rejected, and a custodian was allowed to testify that certain stock records did not contain an indication of the stock's having been used legitimately, from which the jury was permitted to infer that the stock had left the relevant premises as the result of an illegal act. If the suggestion is that such a use does not infringe the hearsay rule, but rather represents no more than a circumstantial use of the record, the argument seems to be inconsistent with the decision in *Myers v DPP*[2] since it should make no difference whether the inference is superficially positive or negative. In *Myers* itself, although the records were tendered to prove the positive association of a series of numbers, it was equally essential to the argument that no record contained the association of numbers actually found on the cars alleged to have been stolen. *Shone* seems to be one more example of failure to appreciate that the hearsay rule is undermined by circumstantial inference.[3]

Where a witness remembers, and can reasonably be expected to remember, some but not all of the details of a statement, those parts may be considered separately from the remainder and admitted under this provision.[4]

Here again evidence admitted under the provisions of s 24 may be excluded at the discretion of the court under the provisions of s 25, those of s 78 of the Police and Criminal Evidence Act 1984 or at common law.

16 It seems quite inadequate to sweep them aside as being something other than 'foundation requirements' mandated by the old law, as appears to have been suggested in *R v Ilyas and Knight* [1996] Crim LR 810, a view shared by Smith in his commentary to the case.
17 Presumably the maker of the document; but now see *R v Derodra* (1999) Times, 16 July.
18 See *R v Bedi and Bedi* (1992) 95 Cr App Rep 21, and commentary by Birch at [1992] Crim LR 300.
19 Such as Australia, under Evidence Act (Cwth) 1995, s 69; and the United States, by Federal Rules of Evidence, r 803(7).
20 (1981) 73 Cr App Rep 117.
1   (1983) 76 Cr App Rep 72.
2   [1965] AC 1001, [1964] 1 All ER 877.
3   The dangers of such an approach are graphically illustrated by *R v Muir* (1984) 79 Cr App Rep 153.
4   *R v Carrington* (1993) 99 Cr App Rep 376.

3. Documents prepared for criminal proceedings or investigations

In order to deal with the problem of manufacture and to preserve the general orality of the criminal trial special conditions are imposed by s 26 of the Criminal Justice Act 1988 for documents, otherwise admissible under the provisions of ss 23 or 24 which appear to the court to have been prepared for the purposes of criminal proceedings or investigations.[5] It is necessary to secure the leave of the court to give such material in evidence, and such leave may be obtained only if the court regards such admission as in the interests of justice, having regard to the contents of the statement and to the risk of unfairness to the accused if the statement cannot be controverted and its maker does not attend to give oral evidence. It is not enough that in the circumstances the only effective way of rebutting the statement is for the accused to testify.[6] Nor is it a sufficient reason to refuse to admit the evidence that there is live evidence to prove the same matter.[7] In exercising its discretion the court is entitled to take into account the strength of the evidence, for example where identity is in issue, that the circumstances were such that mistake was extremely unlikely,[8] or conversely that they made the evidence suspicious.[9] In other words the court is likely to focus upon the likelihood of cross-examination being effective, and whether the effect could be achieved in other ways.[10] It is certainly a relevant consideration that under different available procedures cross-examination by the accused could have been secured.[11] It seems likely that this explicit reference in the body of the Act to such statements will overcome the difficulty felt under the old law in considering proofs of evidence or depositions to qualify as documentary records,[12] and this view appears to have been confirmed by the cases.[13]

Although the legislation appears to require the judge to attend to the contents of the statement in order to decide how to exercise this discretion, it seems sufficient to do so in general terms without reading the statement in full.[14] It even seems possible to admit evidence on the basis of this discretion without ever expressly considering it at all.[15] It should be noted that this discretion may be exercised in favour of the defence if it is seeking the admission of a statement under s 23 or 24, and in such a case the conditions for the exercise of the discretion need be established only on the balance of probabilities.[16] It was further held there that in such a case it is not necessarily decisive

5   Expert reports admissible under s 30 are expressly excluded from the range of this provision. It seems that statements made during the course of a trial might qualify: *R v W* [1997] Crim LR 678.

6   *R v Price* [1991] Crim LR 707, especially if an adequate warning is given; *R v Moore* [1992] Crim LR 882 where it was said that decisions on the old law should not be applied automatically to the new.

7   *R v Greer* [1998] Crim LR 572, despite this being one of the specified conditions to be taken into account in relation to the overlapping discretion under s 25.

8   *R v Fairfax* [1995] Crim LR 949.

9   In *R v Lockley and Corah* [1995] 2 Cr App Rep 554 the statements consisted of a disputed cell confession, as reported by a woman who had a strong motive for ingratiating herself with the authorities, and who was self-confessedly dishonest.

10 In *R v Dragic* [1996] 2 Cr App Rep 232 it was suggested that disputed identification could be supported by an alibi, and in *R v Martin* [1996] Crim LR 589 that counsel would be just as effective by making criticisms of the quality of the evidence in argument. But see *R v Radak* [1999] 1 Cr App Rep 187 where it was said that procedural rather than substantive concerns should prevail

11 See *R v Radak* above, where the evidence should have been taken on commission abroad.

12 See *R v Martin* [1988] 3 All ER 440, [1988] 1 WLR 655; *R v Cunningham* [1989] Crim LR 435.

13 See *R v Cole* [1990] 2 All ER 108, [1990] 1 WLR 865; *R v Lockley and Corah* above.

14 *R v Ashford Justices, ex p Hilden* [1993] QB 555, [1993] 2 All ER 154.

15 *R v Acton Justices, ex p McMullen* (1990) 92 Cr App Rep 98; *R v Samuel* [1992] Crim LR 189.

16 *R v Patel* (1993) 97 Cr App Rep 294.

that the statement is of crucial importance to the defence. The result is that in some situations evidence which is relevant to the accused's defence will be excluded if the court fails to be satisfied that the interests of justice, including fairness to the prosecution, will not be promoted.[17]

These provisions have been drastically, if not dramatically,[18] reinforced by the provisions of Sch 2 to the Criminal Procedure and Investigations Act 1996.[19] Under that provision any written statement or deposition[20] used for the purposes of committal may be used in evidence at trial in the Crown Court, subject only to the unfettered discretion of the court to exclude, or to override an objection if in its opinion it is in the interests of justice to do so. It seems that the powers have been drafted more widely than was intended to achieve the government's purpose,[1] which appears simply to have been to create a simpler means of proving uncontested statements, subject to the normal operation of the discretion under ss 25 and 26 of the Criminal Justice Act 1988. There is however no trace of such restriction in the drafting,[2] and all will[3] depend upon the reaction of the courts.[4]

4. General provisions

The Act makes a number of useful improvements of a general nature. In particular it provides for the admission of copies of any document, whether admitted under the provisions of the Act or otherwise, at any remove from the original, and subject only to authentication in any manner approved by the court.[5] It also paves the way for rules to be made so as to provide for evidence to be furnished to the court in any form[6] notwithstanding the existence of evidence in original form from which the evidence tendered has been derived.[7] The whole aim is to improve the comprehensibility to the jury of the material tendered in evidence. It is to be hoped that any such rules will be astute to prevent the diversion of any dispute from the ascertainment of the facts themselves to the techniques of their presentation. It can hardly be denied that the simplification achieved by graphic, statistical or summary presentation can sometimes be achieved only at the cost of distortion induced by selective choice of scale, starting point or categorisation.

In relation to evidence admissible under ss 23 and 24 of the Act provision is made for a special exclusionary discretion in the interests of justice by s 25. The guidelines for the exercise of this discretion are set out in sub-s (2) as follows:

17   *R v W*, above. It is not hard to see the dangers and drawbacks of making such a determination a condition precedent to the reception of defence evidence.
18   The provisions were introduced at a late stage, little public discussion ensued, and the debate, which took place only in the House of Lords, was somewhat cursory.
19   Brought into effect by s 68.
20   And the powers to take depositions have themselves been greatly expanded by a new s 97A inserted into the Magistrates' Courts Act 1980 by Sch 1, para 8 to the Criminal Procedure and Investigations Act 1996.
1   573 HL Deb cols 949, 950. See Munday (1997) NLJ 821, 860.
2   Although it is fair to note that in *R v Cole* [1990] 2 All ER 108, [1990] 1 WLR 865 and *R v Pring* [1996] Crim LR 46 the courts seemed prepared to apply the s 26 discretion to admissibility under s 13(3) of the Criminal Justice Act 1925 without any formal authorisation.
3   At the time of writing no cases applying this provision could be discovered in the reports or on LEXIS.
4   The Law Commission's reaction in Law Com 245 was to recommend repeal of the power to overrule objection: paras 8.108–8.113, rec 21, draft bill, cl 20.
5   Section 27.
6   For example by the use of charts, statistical analysis or summaries.
7   Section 31.

Without prejudice to the generality of subsection (1) above, it shall be the duty of the court to have regard–
(a) to the nature and source of the document containing the statement and to whether or not, having regard to its nature and source and to any other circumstances that appear to the court to be relevant, it is likely that the document is authentic[8];
(b) to the extent to which the statement appears to supply evidence which would not otherwise be available;
(c) to the relevance of the evidence that it appears to supply to any issue which is likely to have to be determined in the proceedings;
and
(d) to any risk, having regard in particular to whether it is likely to be possible to controvert the statement if the person making it does not attend to give oral evidence in the proceedings, that its admission or exclusion will result in unfairness to the accused or, if there is more than one, to any of them.

It may be noted that these guidelines may on occasion clash with each other. Thus the more the evidence is necessary under (b) and relevant under (c) the more risk there is likely to be under (d). It seems that if a document admissible under s 23 or s 24 has been prepared for the purpose of criminal proceedings, it must satisfy the different requirements of both s 25 and s 26,[9] although it has been remarked that the interests of justice which occur in both provisions are likely to be interpreted in the same way in relation to each.[10] Nevertheless since s 26 requires leave to be obtained it would appear that it will be for the prosecution to satisfy the court of the absence of risk to the accused under s 26, rather than to leave it to the accused to persuade the court to exclude the document on such a basis under s 25, though s 25 is not formally subordinated to s 26.[11] It also remains the case that s 25 is much more explicit in its detail, and it is disturbing to find that in *R v Gregory and Mott*[12] in which s 26 should have been considered, the court made its decision to exclude because of prejudice to other defendants, on the basis of part of the wording of s 25 which is not reproduced in s 26.

If the accused tenders a document under s 23 or 24 it may be excluded by the operation of s 25.[13] This seems quite contrary to the general tenor of English law, and in particular to the considerations which moved the House of Lords in *Murdoch v Taylor*.[14]

Some detailed considerations relating to the weight to be attached to evidence admissible under these provisions are provided by Sch 2.[15] It makes admissible evidence which could have been used to discredit a witness testifying to the information

8   Surprisingly interpreted as relating to the likelihood of accuracy of the relevant document in *R v Dyer* [1997] Crim LR 442.
9   Though Munday, relying to some extent on the side-notes to the different sections, takes the view that the discretions operate exclusively, s 26 in relation to statements admitted under s 23(3), and s 25 to the rest: (1997) 141 JP 691.
10 *R v Lockley and Corah* [1995] 2 Cr App Rep 554.
11 *R v Jennings and Miles* [1995] Crim LR 810. In practice, given the conditions of the two sections, if the prosecution prevails under s 26, in the absence of further evidence it is impossible to see how the defence could then secure exclusion under s 25.
12 [1995] Crim LR 507. The mistake was made by the trial judge, and apparently unnoticed by the Court of Appeal. For further examples of confusion between the two sections see above.
13 *R v Buzalek and Schiffer* [1991] Crim LR 116.
14 [1965] AC 574, [1965] 1 All ER 406. If there is no discretion to exclude otherwise admissible defence evidence despite prejudice to another defendant, it is odd to find one recognised when the only beneficiary of preventing the jury from considering the evidence is the prosecution.
15 Which replaces Part I of Sch 3 to the Police and Criminal Evidence Act 1984 in a simplified form.

contained in a document whether in such a case it could have been adduced in chief or used only to cross-examine, and permits the use of inconsistent statements by such a witness to show contradiction.[16] Although it hardly seems necessary, explicit provision is made forbidding the use of a statement admitted under the Act from being used to corroborate the evidence of its supplier when such corroboration is required.[17] It is significant that para 3, which explicitly deals with the estimation of weight, is now cast in much more general terms than under the old law by permitting reference to any circumstances from which any inference can reasonably be drawn to its accuracy or otherwise. This seems to allow reference to matters bolstering as well as to those diminishing weight. A final matter relates to the universal importation of definitions from the Civil Evidence Act 1968 to the extent of the overlapping of terminology, and to the definition of 'confession' from the Police and Criminal Evidence Act 1984.

Since, unlike the Civil Evidence Act 1968, these provisions contemplate the use of documentary hearsay, only where the supplier of the information is unavailable to give evidence, there is no need for any notice procedure. This has made it possible for the provisions to apply to the lower courts as much as to the higher.

5. Computer records[18]

It was thought necessary to make special provisions for the admission of computer records in evidence in criminal proceedings just as in civil. Criticism of those provisions was heeded, and s 69 of the Police and Criminal Evidence Act 1984 was very different in form:

> (1) In any proceedings, a statement in a document produced by a computer shall not be admissible as evidence of any fact stated therein unless it is shown–
> (a) that there are no reasonable grounds for believing that the statement is inaccurate because of improper use of the computer;
> (b) that at all material times the computer was operating properly, or if not, that any respect in which it was not operating properly or was out of operation was not such as to affect the production of the document or the accuracy of its contents; and
> (c) that any relevant conditions specified in rules of court under subsection (2) below are satisfied.

Although it seemed at one time as though such special provision might be omitted from the Criminal Justice Act 1988, the principal enabling provisions[19] of that legislation were explicitly made subject to s 69 of the Police and Criminal Evidence Act 1984. This is a much clearer and more straightforward provision than its then civil counterpart, s 5 of the Civil Evidence Act 1968. It is supported by further supplementary provisions in Part II of Sch 3 to the Police and Criminal Evidence Act 1984, and provision was made for rules of court to be drafted. The Schedule is however more concerned with questions of procedure and weight than with amplifying the conditions for admissibility.

The operation of those provisions was clarified by the decision of the House of Lords in *R v Shephard*.[20] In that case the House was faced with the need to prove till

16 Though in such a case it would not apparently be admissible to show the truth of its contents.
17 Schedule 2, para 2. It seems unnecessary because it does not come from an independent source, and so could not corroborate at common law in any case.
18 See further Tapper in *Encyclopedia of Information Technology Law* ch 11.
19 Sections 23 and 24.
20 [1993] AC 380, [1993] 1 All ER 225.

rolls from a highly automated store, where some of the information on the document was derived from the central computer, some read in automatically from the goods, and some input by the till operator. The House of Lords held that the requirements of s 69 of the Police and Criminal Evidence Act 1984 had to be satisfied in relation to any statement in a document produced by a computer,[1] whether hearsay[2] or not.[3] It was however held that some evidence was necessary to show that the requirements of s 69 had been satisfied.[4] If this were to be attempted by certificate, then the person providing the certificate would have to satisfy the statutory requirement relating to the responsibility of his position. The House also contemplated proof of satisfaction by oral evidence, when this provision would not apply.[5] Indeed it suggested that in many simple cases it would become the norm:[6]

> Documents produced by computers are an increasingly common feature of all business and more and more people are becoming familiar with their uses and operation. Computers vary immensely in their complexity and in the operations they perform. The nature of the evidence to discharge the burden of showing that there has been no improper use of the computer and that it was operating properly will inevitably vary from case to case. The evidence must be tailored to the needs of the case. I suspect that it will very rarely be necessary to call an expert and that in the vast majority of cases it will be possible to discharge the burden by calling a witness who is familiar with the operation of the computer in the sense of knowing what the computer is required to do and who can say that it is doing it properly.

It is clear that this passage was intended to simplify matters of proof, and the House of Lords has given a lead in adopting a broadly functional view, eschewing technicality.[7] The courts have further indicated their willingness in this context to permit adjournment to remedy any formal failure.[8] It is likely that in many cases advantage will have to be taken in this context of the provision of s 24(4) of the Criminal Justice Act 1988 permitting the use of the document containing the statement when the maker of the statement cannot be expected to remember the information it contains.[9]

1   In *R v Blackburn; R v Wade* (1992) Times, 1 December it was suggested obiter that word-processed documents might not be so regarded, but rather as documents produced by a human being with the aid of a computer. It is submitted that such an approach might lead to further anomaly. There is however no need to comply with s 69 if the document is used simply as the basis for an expert's opinion without itself being put in evidence: *R v Golizadeh* [1995] Crim LR 232; not even if used to refresh memory: *Sophocleous v Ringer* [1988] RTR 52.

2   In this case in addition to the provisions of s 23 or s 24 of the Criminal Justice Act 1988.

3   Thus the requirements of s 69 had to be satisfied when computer-generated banking documents were adduced as real evidence in *R v Governor of Brixton Prison, ex p Levin* [1997] AC 741, [1997] 3 All ER 289. In some cases special statutory provision is made for real evidence: see *R v McCarthy* [1998] RTR 374.

4   An intoximeter record was excluded in *R v Medway Magistrates' Court, ex p Goddard* [1995] RTR 206 in the absence of any evidence that it was working properly, which could not be presumed.

5   On the basis that in such a case the witness would be present, and any incompetence could be probed in cross-examination. This would not, of course, permit oral evidence of the content of the computer printout without attempting to produce it: *R v Burr* [1996] Crim LR 324.

6   At 387, 231.

7   *DPP v McKeown* [1997] 1 All ER 737, [1997] 1 WLR 295 (rejecting an attempt to exclude evidence of alcohol content from an intoximeter when only the clock was malfunctioning).

8   *Yearly v CPS* [1997] CLY 101.

9   In Scotland where there has been no legislation comparable to the Police and Criminal Evidence Act 1984 or Criminal Justice Act 1988 it has been necessary to use the common law to overcome this problem: see *Lord Advocate's Reference (No 1 of 1992)* 1992 JC 179.

It is also worth noting that special provision is made in the Code of Practice for the Searching of Premises and the Seizure of Property issued under the Police and Criminal Evidence Act 1984 for requiring relevant information held in a computer to be supplied in a visible and legible form.[10]

The tide of opinion in this area, as in others, has moved decisively in the direction of wider admissibility, indicated by the general attitude of the Royal Commission on Criminal Justice, and now adopted in the specific recommendations of the Law Commission.[11]

6.   Criminal Justice Act 1967, s 9

Provided the conditions specified in s 9 of the Criminal Justice Act 1967, are fulfilled,[12] agreed statements of facts may be admitted in evidence at any criminal trial to the same extent and with the same effect as oral evidence.[13] The principal conditions are that the statement should be signed and contain a declaration of the maker's knowledge that it was made subject to penalties in the event of its being used in evidence if the maker knew it to be false or did not care whether it was true, that a copy should have been served on the opposite party, and that no notice of objection should have been received from that party within seven days. Where such evidence is admitted it has the same status as oral evidence, and the jury should not, because of no more than a conflict with oral evidence, be instructed to prefer the latter.[14] It is also possible for the parties to agree to the reception of such a statement at or before the trial, although the provisions with regard to service of a copy of the statement and non-receipt within seven days of notice of objection have not been fulfilled.

If a defendant wishes to challenge such evidence he should serve notice under s 9(2)(d), and if he challenges it at the trial without doing so, the court may order an adjournment, and may charge him with the costs.[15] It is important to preserve the orality of criminal proceedings, and maintenance of the rule in *Browne v Dunn*[16] that the defence case should be put to the witnesses for the prosecution in cross-examination wherever possible.

B.   MISCELLANEOUS COMMON LAW EXCEPTIONS TO THE HEARSAY RULE

Statements as to pedigree and statements concerning public or general rights were discussed in ch XIV.[17] Having regard to the restricted nature of the issues on which they are admissible, the number of criminal cases to which the law governing the reception of such statements is relevant at the present day is small. In practice, the

---

10   Paragraph 6.5.
11   Royal Commission on Criminal Justice Cm 2263 (1993) para 826, rec 189; Law Com No 245 Pt XIII, rec 50, draft bill, Sch 2. See further below p 598.
12   It is vital that they are fulfilled meticulously: *Paterson v DPP* [1990] RTR 329. If the conditions are not fulfilled the statement may nevertheless be admissible under s 23 of the Criminal Justice Act 1988, although in that case it would be subject to a warning as being of lesser weight than oral testimony: *R v Millen* [1995] Crim LR 568.
13   *Ellis v Jones* [1973] 2 All ER 893.
14   *R v Mitchell* [1995] Crim LR 146.
15   *Lister v Quaife* [1983] 2 All ER 29, [1983] 1 WLR 48; although if this is not done and the trial proceeds in the absence of the prosecution witnesses, the trier of fact is not bound to accept the truth of their statements.
16   (1893) 6 R 67; see p 292 above.
17   See pp 574 and 569 above.

number of criminal cases to which the law governing the admissibility of declarations of deceased persons against interest and in the course of duty is relevant is not much larger. These exceptions are rarely invoked in the modern law, given the wider admissibility of hearsay under the statutory provisions described above, and the Law Commission has recommended that all statements of deceased persons be admitted as proof of their contents.[18] There is no need for discussion here, and the topic will not be further considered.[19] There is a stronger chance of dying declarations being adduced[20] pending the implementation of the Law Commission's recommendations. Brief discussion of that will then be followed by similarly brief reference to the admissibility of testimony in former proceedings, and about evidence of age which seems to involve exceptions to the hearsay rule at certain points.

1.   Dying declarations[1]

(i)   Statement and rationale of the exception

The oral or written declaration of a deceased person is admissible evidence of the cause of his death at a trial for his murder or manslaughter provided he was under a settled hopeless expectation of death when the statement was made and provided he would have been a competent witness if called to give evidence at that time.[2]

In *R v Woodcock*,[3] a man was charged with the murder of his wife, and her statement concerning the cause of her injuries given on oath to a magistrate was received in evidence against the accused for although the deceased said nothing of her impending death, the court was satisfied that she must have known she was on the point of dying. Eyre CB said:

> The principle on which this species of evidence is admitted is, that they are declarations made in extremity, when the party is at the point of death, and when every hope of this world is gone; when every motive to falsehood is silenced, and the mind is induced by the most powerful considerations to speak the truth; a situation so solemn and so awful is considered by law as creating an obligation equal to that which is imposed by a positive oath administered in a court of justice.

The theory is that no one would wish to die with a lie on his lips. The exception has been held to have no application in a community such as the indigenous people of Papua New Guinea where the next life is believed to be spent in comfort on a neighbouring island and there is no sanction against lying when at the point of death.[4]

---

18   Law Com No 245, para 8.35, rec 10, draft bill, cl 5(2).
19   See previous editions for further detail.
20   Although Lord Steyn clearly regarded the exception as obsolescent in *Mills v R* [1995] 3 All ER 865, [1995] 1 WLR 511, and preferred to apply the more recently renovated res gestae exception, he refrained from declaring it obsolete; as did Lord Bingham CJ in a similarly overlapping situation in *R v Lawson* [1998] Crim LR 883.
1   See Munday [1993] 22 Anglo-American LR 42.
2   There is no requirement that such a statement need be corroborated: *Nembhard v R* [1982] 1 All ER 183, [1981] 1 WLR 1515.
3   (1789) 1 Leach 500.
4   *R v Madobi* (1963) 6 FLR 1.

(ii) Conditions of admissibility

The conditions on which dying declarations are admitted in evidence are the death of the declarant, that the trial should be for his murder or manslaughter, that his statement should relate to the cause of his death, that he should have been under a settled hopeless expectation of death and that he could have been a competent witness. Nothing need be said with regard to the first of these conditions.

(a) Trial for murder or manslaughter

The second is the outcome of restrictions placed at the beginning of the 19th century on what bade fair to become a general principle under which dying declarations might be received.[5] In *R v Mead*[6] the accused was charged with perjury. He obtained an order for a new trial and shot the deceased before it took place. A dying declaration made by the deceased concerning the transaction out of which the prosecution for perjury arose was rejected, Abbot CJ saying that dying declarations are admissible only where the death of the deceased is the subject of the charge, and the circumstances of the death are the subject of the declaration. This case really settled the law, but, as late as 1860, an unsuccessful attempt was made to obtain the reception of a woman's dying declaration on a charge against the accused of procuring her abortion.[7]

(b) Statement must relate to cause of declarant's death

The words of Abbott CJ indicate that the declaration is admissible only in so far as it relates to the cause of the deceased's death, and this is borne out by observations in *R v Murton*.[8] *R v Baker*[9] is to the contrary, for a statement made by a cook shortly before her death from poison believed to have come from a cake, to the effect that she had put nothing wrong in the cake was admitted on the trial of another servant for murdering the master of the house who had also eaten some of the cake. It is doubtful whether the case has much bearing on the law relating to dying declarations, for Coltman J took refuge in the language of res gestae by treating the two deaths as part of the same transaction. Perhaps the cook's remark is best regarded as a statement accompanying and concerning a relevant event—the death of the master of the house.

(c) Declarant must have settled hopeless expectation of death

In the *Sussex Peerage Case*[10] Lord Denman said:

> With regard to declarations made by persons in extremis, supposing all necessary matters concurred, such as actual danger, death following, and a full apprehension at the time of the danger of death, such declarations can be received.

This suggests that the danger of death and the apprehension of it are to be treated separately, but the cases are all concerned with the second, and, in the absence of any authority, there is no point in speculating on the course that would be adopted with regard to a statement made by someone who believed himself to be dying when this

---

5   See *Wright d Clymer v Littler* (1761) 3 Burr 1244.
6   (1824) 2 B & C 605.
7   *R v Hind* (1860) 8 Cox CC 300. There is no authority on causing death by dangerous driving or abetting suicide.
8   (1862) 3 F & F 492, at 494; *R v Buck* [1941] 1 DLR 302. Questions of remoteness of causation and the admissibility of deceased's statements of opinion could arise but have not been discussed in the English cases.
9   (1837) 2 Mood & R 53.
10   (1844) 11 Cl & Fin 85, at 112.

was not the case although death in fact followed shortly after the making of the statement.

A number of judgments insists on the necessity of proving the apprehension of a speedy end on the part of the declarant. The words 'settled hopeless expectation' come from the judgment of Willes J in *R v Peel*.[11] They were approved by the Court of Criminal Appeal in *R v Perry*,[12] where the suggestion that there must be a settled hopeless expectation of immediate death was criticised.[13] It is immaterial that the deceased should have entertained hopes of recovery after the statement was made, so long as he or she had abandoned all hope of life when it was made.[14] The absolute necessity of compliance with this latter requirement was vividly illustrated by *R v Jenkins*.[15] This was a murder case in which the deceased made a statement implicating the accused. The statement was written down by a magistrate's clerk who included the words that it was made 'with no hope of my recovery', and read it over to the deceased. Before signing the statement she caused it to be amended so as to read 'with no present hope of my recovery', and it was held that the statement could not be received in evidence on account of the suggestion that the deceased entertained a faint hope of recovery.[16] The express declaration of the deceased is treated as the best proof of settled hopeless expectation of death. But other considerations may also be taken into account, such as his having talked about the devolution of his property, the fact that he took leave of his family and the fact that he made arrangements about his funeral.[17] The courts have, however, been extremely reluctant to infer knowledge on the part of the deceased of his or her impending death from the surrounding circumstances. In *R v Morgan*,[18] for instance, the deceased's head was all but cut off, but Denman J held that he could not admit the dying declaration for this reason alone and the prosecution proceeded without it.

2. Testimony in former proceedings[19]

At common law[20] a transcript of a witness's evidence at an earlier trial is admissible for the truth of its contents if the evidence would have been for or against the same accused, in relation to substantially the same facts, by a witness unable to attend the trial through death or illness[1] but not, it seems, because of absence from the jurisdiction.[2] It has also been held at common law that the trial court may read a deposition taken at a coroner's inquisition when the deponent committed suicide after the inquest.[3]

11   (1860) 2 F & F 21.
12   [1909] 2 KB 697.
13   The suggestion came from the judgment of Lush J in *R v Osman* (1881) 15 Cox CC 1. It was queried by Charles J in *R v Gloster* (1888) 16 Cox CC 471.
14   *R v Hubbard* (1881) 14 Cox CC 565; *R v Austin* (1912) 8 Cr App Rep 27.
15   (1869) LR 1 CCR 187; see also *R v Kharsekin* (1992) 74 CCC (3d) 163.
16   But see in Australia *R v Arnott* (1992) 79 ACR 275 where the expectation was inferred despite strong and repeated affirmation by the deceased that she was not going to die.
17   *R v Spilsbury* (1835) 7 C & P 187, at 190.
18   (1875) 14 Cox CC 337; *R v Cleary* (1862) 2 F & F 850; *R v Bedingfield* (1879) 14 Cox CC 341; *R v Rogers* [1950] SASR 102.
19   Statutes permitting the use of such testimony have been held to be consistent with the Canadian Charter of Rights and Freedoms: *Potvin v R* [1989] 1 SCR 525.
20   *R v Hall* [1973] QB 496, [1973] 1 All ER 1. See also *R v McGregor* [1968] 1 QB 371, [1967] 2 All ER 267.
1   Finally confirmed by the Court of Appeal in *R v Thompson* [1982] QB 647, at 659, [1982] 1 All ER 907, at 914.
2   *R v Scaife* (1851) 17 QB 238, at 243.
3   *R v Cowle* (1907) 71 JP 152.

If a retrial is ordered by the Court of Appeal then a transcript of the evidence of an unavailable[4] witness is admissible by leave of the judge under Sch 2 to the Criminal Appeal Act 1968.[5] As noted above[6] a further extensive exception has been created[7] in respect of statements and depositions admitted in transfer proceedings. In cases falling outside these provisions, it may sometimes be possible to admit transcripts under the provisions of the Criminal Justice Act 1988, s 23.[8]

3. Evidence of age

One of the stock illustrations of the breadth of the hearsay rule is provided by cases in which it has been held that a witness cannot give admissible evidence of the date of his birth, and the same decision has been reached with regard to the witness's place of birth. Generally speaking, these cases give rise to no problem because age can be proved under a variety of well- recognised exceptions to the hearsay rule (notably that relating to statements in public documents), by appearance, or by the recollection of past events by the person whose age is in question. It seems, however, that hearsay is allowed to creep in, where no recognised exception to the rule under which it is prohibited applies, on account of the different methods of proving the identity of a person named in a birth certificate that have been permitted by the courts in civil and criminal cases. Let us assume that A's age is to be proved by production of a certificate referring to the birth of someone named A. Clearly it will be necessary for the court to be satisfied that the A mentioned in the certificate is the same person as the A whose age is to be proved, and the courts have admitted hearsay evidence on this point without stating that they are doing so.

In *R v Weaver*,[9] the evidence was that of a child's grandmother who, though present at its birth, was not present at the registration; in *Wilton & Co v Phillips*[10] the evidence was that of a brother of the person whose age was in issue, and he does not appear to have been present either at the birth or registration; in *Re Bulley's Settlement*,[11] there was only an affidavit sworn by the claimant to a fund stating that he had reached his majority, and in *R v Bellis*,[12] the clerk to a board of guardians simply deposed to the result of inquiries which he had previously made about the age of the prosecutrix. In each of these cases the court acted on statements which must necessarily have been based on information supplied to the makers by third parties. It is submitted that this kind of evidence of age should be expressly treated as received under an exception to the hearsay rule.

C. REFORM OF THE RULE

As noted above this whole area has been the subject of thorough reconsideration by the Law Commission, which has recommended substantial change. It is proposed here, first to consider in outline the principal changes recommended by the Law Commission,

4   Or if the parties agree.
5   Para 1, as amended by Criminal Procedure and Investigation Act 1996, Sch 2, para 5.
6   At p 589.
7   Criminal Procedure and Investigation Act 1996, Sch 2, paras 1 and 2.
8   As in *R v Lockley and Corah* [1995] 2 Cr App Rep 554.
9   (1873) LR 2 CCR 85.
10   (1903) 19 TLR 390.
11   [1886] WN 80.
12   (1911) 6 Cr App Rep 283.

and then separately the possibly inhibiting effect of the enactment of the Human Rights Act 1998.

1.   Recommendations of the Law Commission[13]

Upon the recommendation of the Royal Commission on Criminal Justice[14] reform of this topic with a view to extending the ambit of admissibility was referred to the Law Commission.[15] It published its consultation paper[16] in May 1995 and, after an impressive and generally supportive response, its final report[17] in June 1997. Some of the issues dealt with in the Report have been considered in other chapters,[18] and others have been mentioned above. Here particular attention will be paid to the Law Commission's recommendations on the definition of hearsay, its general approach to admissibility, its treatment of evidence of computer output, its attitude to the use of discretion, and its procedural recommendations.

(i)   Definition

Perhaps the most radical reform recommended by the Law Commission consists in its restrictive definition of hearsay. As noted above, little attempt was made to reconsider the definition in the course of the reform of the law in civil proceedings, perhaps because it was thought that the abolition of the exclusionary rule made it unnecessary. In the case of criminal proceedings abolition was regarded as too radical a step, so it was seen to be necessary to confront the definitional problems, which had indeed come to a head in a criminal case, *R v Kearley*.[19] The view rejected in that case by the House of Lords was that the definition of hearsay itself required that the maker of the statement intended to assert the truth of its contents, and that where there was no such intention the statement could be proved without reference to the hearsay rule. Such a view is reflected in the treatment of hearsay elsewhere.[20] Despite minor reservations it was adopted by the Law Commission in its consultation paper.[1] However it was persuaded on consultation that more elaboration was required to meet its reservations. It was particularly concerned by the effect of a chance formulation of a statement on its admissibility, and especially by the danger of anomaly in excluding statements formulated in terms of assertive statements, while admitting functionally equivalent statements when they happened not to take the form of assertions. The Law Commission's solution[2] has been to tighten the definition so as to require the statement

---

13   See commentary on both the earlier consultative paper by Zuckerman, Ormerod and Spencer in [1996] Crim LR 4 et seq; and on the final report by Jackson (1998) 2 Int J of Ev & Pr 166, Fulford (1997) 37(2) J Med Sci & Law 133, Tapper [1997] Crim LR 771, and Friedman [1998] Crim LR 697.

14   (1993) Cm 2263 ch 8 para 28, rec 189.

15   On 28 April 1994.

16   No 138.

17   No 245 *Evidence in Criminal Proceedings: Hearsay and Related Topics* (1997) Cm 3670.

18   Such as previous consistent statements as hearsay in ch VI, the hearsay basis for expert opinion in ch XII, and common law exceptions also applicable in civil proceedings in ch XIV.

19   [1992] 2 AC 228, [1992] 2 All ER 345. See further above p 544.

20   Eg in Australia, in the Evidence Act (Cwth) 1995, s 59(1); in the United States, in the Federal Rules of Evidence, r 801(a). In Scotland such a view was adopted at common law, see Scot Law Com 149 (1995) *Evidence: Report on Hearsay Evidence in Criminal Proceedings*, paras 5.8–5.13.

1   No 138, para 9.36.

2   Law Com 245, paras 7.24–7.41, rec 2, draft bill, cl 2(3).

to be intended by its maker[3] to cause the hearer to believe that the matter stated is true, or to act on the basis that it is true.[4] It is far from clear that the simpler approach of an intended assertion would not have been able to cope with any difficulties likely to occur,[5] but there is probably little harm in spelling out a tighter one. As noted above[6] such an approach will do much to eliminate many of the most contentious situations[7] from the ambit of the rule.

It should be noted that the Law Commission remained adamant in its opposition to the reception of multiple oral hearsay, that is, where the declarant did not himself have personal knowledge of the matters sought to be proved by the reception of his statement.[8]

(ii)   Admissibility

The tight definition of hearsay renders the retention of a basic rule of the exclusion of oral hearsay more acceptable.[9] The Law Commission rejected options including abolition of the exclusionary rule,[10] admission of hearsay whenever it was the best evidence, and admission of hearsay if considered to be reliable. It thought that the first placed too little value on cross-examination, and might deluge the court with material;[11] that the second would be difficult to police;[12] and that the third would be impractical.[13] Its solution was to expand admissibility by its restrictive definition, to expand and clarify exceptions, and to add an inclusionary discretion. It is submitted that such a solution is susceptible to many of the arguments which the Commission itself deploys against other solutions. In particular its hope for simplicity may be disappointed by the complexity of the verbiage of rule and exceptions; and its hope for consistency by the unpredictability of the operation, and interaction, of both exclusionary and inclusionary discretions. The editor's preference is for simple abolition of the exclusionary rule,[14] in the expectation that deliberate evasion of cross-examination of available sources could adequately be met by discrediting arguments of counsel, afforced by adverse comment from the judge; and that over-indulgence would be self-defeating in the face of the same sanctions, to which might be added the imposition of costs.[15]

---

3   This is, of course, quite different from the intention of the party adducing the statement to the court.
4   Or to cause a machine to do so.
5   There appears to have been no such difficulty in practice in any of the jurisdictions which currently adopt such an approach.
6   At p 565.
7   That in *R v Kearley, Teper v R* and the betting cases for example.
8   Law Com 245, paras 8.15–8.17, rec 6, draft bill, cl 3(a). It would however allow multiple hearsay where certain hearsay exceptions apply at one remove, for example those for business documents or previous consistent statements, but not for others, for example retained common law exceptions or for unavailability, ibid paras 8.15–8.26, rec 7, draft bill, cl 10.
9   Although not to many of the commentators on its proposals; none of those mentioned above has expressed unqualified support for this approach.
10   For detailed consideration of this option see Jackson (1998) 2 E & P 166.
11   Law Com 245, paras 6.8–6.14.
12   Ibid, paras 6.17–6.32.
13   Ibid, paras 6.33–6.37.
14   For reasons of consistency with the law in civil proceedings, and the reduction of opportunity for technical argument.
15   In appropriate cases imposed upon legal advisers themselves.

(iii)   Computer output

There was little doubt that the old law was too cautious in its treatment of this form of hearsay, and in particular in subjecting computer output to a special test of its own, additional to the hearsay rule. It was odd that courts were so reluctant to accept as evidence material which was increasingly becoming vital to the continuing operation of business, and which was accepted more widely in other comparable legal systems.[16] The Law Commission was persuaded by such considerations, and has proposed[17] the abolition of any special test for computer output additional to that which would apply to similar records if they happened to be in conventional form. The Law Commission did however qualify its view to the extent of expressing its expectation that any evidential burden of throwing doubt on the accuracy of the records produced by a computer would not be imposed without reference to the means available to the party contesting the evidence to challenge it.

(iv)   Discretion

The basic disadvantage of an admixture of discretion was perceived by the Law Commission to be the inconsistency and uncertainty which it would create, and the difficulty of its operation in the magistrates' courts where the evidence would be heard by the trier of fact in the course of determining its admissibility. For these reasons the Law Commission rejected options for reform based upon discretion. At the same time it felt that the exclusion of reliable evidence was another serious weakness of the current law, and given the imperfection of human foresight and indeterminacy of language, this danger would not disappear completely under any codified scheme consisting entirely of exclusionary rules and inclusionary exceptions. For this reason it proposed the introduction of a new overarching inclusionary discretion:[18]

> In criminal proceedings a statement not made in oral evidence in the proceedings is admissible as evidence of any matter stated if the court is satisfied that, despite the difficulties there may be in challenging the statement, its probative value is such that the interests of justice require it to be admissible.

The Law Commission has described this as a 'safety-valve' and as very *limited*.[19] In its Consultation Paper it was insisted that it would be 'very limited, and clearly defined so as to avert possible injustice.'[20] It is hard to detect these characteristics in the drafting of the provision, nor does there seem any indication that it will be applied in only a limited way. It seems indeed to subvert the whole enterprise of arriving at a more certain and consistent set of rules of admissibility. It should also be noted that it is a discretion which can be used to the disadvantage of the accused,[1] when it is the prosecution which seeks to tender otherwise inadmissible hearsay.

In addition the Law Commission has expressly recommended[2] in relation to hearsay retention of the existing exclusionary discretions of evidence which is more prejudicial

---

16   Especially that of the United States which combined the widest use of computers, with one of the most detailed set of evidential rules.

17   Law Com 245, Part XIII, rec 50, draft bill, cl 29 and Sch 2.

18   Draft bill, cl 9.

19   Law Com 245, para 6.49, original emphasis.

20   Law Com Con pap138, para 10.73.

1   It is frequently stressed that the interests of justice are by no means coincident with the interests of the accused in this context.

2   Law Com 245, para 11.5, draft bill, cl 15(2).

than probative, and of that which would have such an adverse effect on the fairness of the proceedings that it ought not to be admitted. To this it has proposed the addition of a further discretion to exclude evidence whose probative force is substantially outweighed by the undue waste of time which its admission would cause.[3]

(v)   Procedure

The principal justification for the exclusionary rule is that it is difficult to evaluate the strength of hearsay. As it was graphically put in *R v Radak* 'You cannot conduct an argument with, nor ask questions of, a piece of paper.'[4] If hearsay is to be admitted it is thus necessary to try to compensate as far as possible. A number of means have been employed in the past, and recommendations were made by the Law Commission. In particular, in the case of those whose statements are admitted because they are unavailable to testify[5] it is necessary as a preliminary condition, to identify the declarant. It is proposed that the procedural means of accomplishing this should for a party seeking to rely upon hearsay to serve a notice containing the witness statement of the witness seeking to adduce the hearsay statement in the case of oral hearsay, or the document itself in the case of written hearsay. It would then be for the party upon whom the notice was served to challenge it, and failure to do so would trigger admission under s 9 of the Criminal Justice Act 1967. If it were challenged then the matter could be resolved under the pre-trial procedure[6] provided by s 40 of the Criminal Procedure and Investigation Act 1996.

The Law Commission recommends that the existing means[7] of challenging the credibility of the absent declarant[8] be re-enacted.[9] This will often lead to the admission of evidence opening up collateral issues, and in this case the Law Commission recommends that rehabilitation of such declarants be permitted, subject only to the leave of the court to keep the examination of such issues within reasonable limits. This seems reasonable since in the case of absent declarants such evidence will naturally take on greater significance than it would in the case of witnesses testifying in person. It is accordingly recommended[10] that the draft bill provide that:[11]

> If as a result of evidence admitted under this section an allegation is made against the maker of a statement, the court may permit a party to lead additional evidence of such description as the court may specify for the purposes of denying or answering the allegation.

2.   Human Rights Act 1998[12]

It is a somewhat contentious matter to know how far the recommendations of the Law Commission for reform of the hearsay rule will be thought compatible with the provisions

3   Ibid, paras 11.16–11.18. rec 43, draft bill, cl 15(1).
4   [1999] 1 Cr App Rep 187, at 200G.
5   This is not recommended for application to makers of business documents, to makers of statements admitted under the inclusionary discretion, or to makers of res gestae statements.
6   Although provision will be required for the exceptional situation where the need to adduce hearsay arises during the course of the trial.
7   Criminal Justice Act 1988, s 28(2), Sch 2 cl 1. See above p 590.
8   Or of any necessary intermediary.
9   Law Com 245, paras 11.19–11.23, recs 44, 45, draft bill, cl 13(2).
10   Ibid, paras 11.24–11.25, rec 46.
11   Draft bill, cl 13(3).
12   See Ashworth [1999] Crim LR 261, at 268.

of the Human Rights Act 1998, and with the European Convention on Human Rights which it incorporates into English law. The relevant provisions of the Act have not yet come into force, but it is possible that this will occur before provisions enacting the Law Commission's recommendations are brought before Parliament. It is abundantly clear that the shadow of the European Convention affected the light in which the Law Commission considered its recommendations, as evidenced by its devotion of a separate chapter to its impact in both Consultation Paper[13] and final Report,[14] and in its endorsement and then rejection of one fundamental proposal.[15]

It is generally agreed that the key provision is art 6 of the Convention, headed *Right to a Fair Trial*, and more particularly art 6.3(d):

Everyone charged with a criminal offence has the following minimum rights.

...

(d) to examine or have examined witnesses against him and to obtain the attendance and examination of witnesses on his behalf under the same conditions as witnesses against him.

It is immediately apparent that this provision is loosely drafted, and gives rise to many ambiguities and matters of contention. The scheme of the Act requires[16] a court to take into account[17] opinions[18] of the European Court of Human Rights, opinions[19] or decisions[20] of the Commission, and decisions of the Committee of Ministers.[1] It is dubious how helpful, consistent and unequivocal such guidance is likely to be.

It is nevertheless clear that these minimum rights apply only to the accused in criminal proceedings, and so, in relation to the admission of hearsay, seem incompatible with the general approach of the Law Commission which favoured application of the same rules to prosecution and defence.[2]

Although the European Court of Human Rights had approved the general scheme of the exclusion of hearsay in English criminal proceedings,[3] it was apparent from the decisions before the incorporation of the Convention into English law that the English courts took the clear view that there was no presumptive incompatibility between the admission of hearsay against the accused under the exceptions to the rule in the Criminal Justice Act 1988 and the right to a fair hearing guaranteed by the Convention. The matter was considered at some length in *R v Gokal*.[4] The evidence there was that of an associate of the accused, obtained under an offer of an indemnity from prosecution. Some of its more damaging aspects involved accounts of meetings between the witness

13   Con Pap No 138, Part V.
14   Law Com No 245, Part V.
15   To disallow convictions based upon hearsay alone. See further below.
16   Section 2(1).
17   Which it should be noted does not impose an obligation to accept. See Mirfield *Silence, Confessions and Illegally Obtained Evidence* (1997) p 317 for an ingenious argument that obligations may be cast obliquely through acceptance of this jurisprudence by the European Court of Justice, so becoming part of European Community Law which is given binding effect by the European Communities Act 1972. It is however believed that the route is too indirect; that criminal proceedings fall outside the central focus of the 1972 legislation; and that the courts will be reluctant to do indirectly what seems plainly contrary to what has been provided directly (the last point was not available to Mirfield).
18   Judgments, decisions, declarations and advisory opinions.
19   Under art 31.
20   Under arts 26, 27(2).
1   Under art 46.
2   Law Com 245, paras 12.2–2.8. rec 48.
3   *Blastland v United Kingdom* (1987) 10 EHRR 528.
4   [1997] 2 Cr App Rep 266, esp at 278 et seq.

and the accused. It was argued that as the evidence was of crucial importance, stemmed from a man who, if believed was an accomplice with every incentive to minimise his own involvement, and was effectively capable of refutation only by the testimony of the accused,[5] its acceptance without the opportunity to cross-examine infringed art 6. After examination of some of the leading cases[6] in the jurisprudence of the European Court of Human Rights the court took the view that it was concerned only with the overall fairness of the trial,[7] and that as far as possible it left the detail of the admissibility of evidence to national courts.[8] The court felt that in this case the ability of the accused to testify as to the meetings with the absent witness, his ability to contest the credibility of that person, and the intimation by the trial judge that he would direct the jury both of the relative cogency of hearsay and direct testimony, and of the danger of the witness seeking to minimise his own involvement and to maximise that of the accused, would be sufficient to satisfy the requirements of a fair trial, whether considered by the European Court of Human Rights under the Convention, or by an English court adjudicating on the interests of justice in applying its discretion under s 26 of the Criminal Justice Act 1988.[9]

The final view of the Law Commission was that there was no incompatibility between its recommendations and the Convention, and on that basis withdrew[10] the recommendation[11] in its consultation paper that no conviction should be based on hearsay alone.

SECTION 2. CONFESSIONS, SILENCE AND POLICE QUESTIONING

This part of the chapter is mainly concerned with the single largest exception to the hearsay rule, that for confessions of the accused, in connection with which it is convenient to consider also the evidential value of inferences from the accused's silence, and in relation to both, the Codes of Practice relating to different aspects of police investigation, which is often a component in the exercise of the judge's discretion to exclude evidence.[12]

---

5   Thus chilling his right not to testify.
6   *Unterpertinger v Austria* (1986) 13 EHRR 175; *Kostovski v Netherlands* (1989) 12 EHRR 434; see also *Windisch v Austria* (1990) 13 EHRR 281; *Delta v France* (1990) 16 EHRR 574. To the contrary effect see *Hayward v Sweden*; *Isgro v Italy* (1990) Series A 194-A; *Asch v Austria* (1991) 15 EHRR 597.
7   It seems that on that basis it is more inclined to allow hearsay in the form of documentary records: see *Ludi v Switzerland* (1992) 15 EHRR 173, and previous statements of witnesses, whether testifying at the hearing as in *X v Germany* Application 8414/78, or not so testifying, if the evidence was taken in advance on commission, thus enabling cross-examination at that stage as in *X, Y and Z v Austria* Application 5049/71.
8   *Schenk v Switzerland* (1988) 13 EHRR 242, at para 46; reaffirmed in *Doorson v Netherlands* (1996) 22 EHRR 330. While this is true, it cannot be denied that the European Court of Human Rights does seem more concerned with the availability of other evidence than an English court would be, especially now that corroboration is no longer a significant concept in the English law of evidence: see eg *Liefveld v Netherlands* (1994) 18 EHRR CD 103.
9   See also to similar effect, *R v Rutherford* [1998] Crim LR 490; *R v Thomas, Flannigan et al* [1998] Crim LR 887.
10 Law Com 245, paras 5.26–5.41.
11 Con Pap No 138, para 9.5.
12 See also: generally on the exclusionary discretion p 191 above; on the discretion to exclude real evidence p 498 above; and for the conduct of identification parades p 678 below.

A. CONFESSIONS[13]

This part will concentrate upon the substance of the law embodied in s 76 of the Police and Criminal Evidence Act 1984.[14] The Law Commission did not propose[15] major reform of the rules relating to confessions, although it has recommended a fresh approach to the problem of confessions made by one of several co-accused.[16] Before examining s 76 in detail, it is may be helpful to consider briefly the development and rationale of the old law relating to confessions.

1. Development

The Police and Criminal Evidence Act 1984 defines a confession to include: 'any statement wholly or partly adverse to the person who made it, whether made to a person in authority or not and whether made in words or otherwise.'[17] When made otherwise than by a witness testifying in court it amounts to hearsay as defined in this work. The origin of the exclusionary rule is to be found in the mid-18th century, and achieved its first clear and authoritative formulation in the case of *R v Warickshall*:[18]

> a confession forced from the mind by the flattery of hope, or by the torture of fear, comes in so questionable a shape when it is to be considered as the evidence of guilt, that no credit ought to be given to it; and therefore it is rejected.

It is interesting to note that the court went out of its way to assert that the rationale of the rule was based entirely on considerations of credit, having first denied quite explicitly that it depended upon any 'regard to public faith'. In origin the rule has little or no connection with the privilege against self-incrimination either.[19] That doctrine had developed a century or so earlier, in reaction to the oaths required by the Courts of High Commission and Star Chamber. The line between judicial proceedings in which that doctrine came to flourish, and extra-curial investigations was however blurred by the investigatory functions of magistrates, which were not clearly, or finally, distinguished until after the establishment of a regular police force, and the passage of the Indictable Offences Act 1848.[20]

---

13   This enormous topic has in the past been the subject of a number of monographs, among them Joy *On Confessions* (1842) still an important historical source. For a stimulating and perceptive modern view of the whole area, see Mirfield *Silence, Confessions and Improperly Obtained Evidence* (1997); for a more practitioner-orientated approach, see Wolchover and Heaton-Armstrong *Confession Evidence* (1996).

14   Influenced by, but not wholly in accord with, the recommendations of the Eleventh Report of the Criminal Law Revision Committee *Evidence: General* Cmnd 4991 (1972) pp 34–47, draft Bill, cl 2. Although the topic was considered by two later Royal Commissions, *Criminal Procedure* Cmnd 8092 (1981) Ch 4 and *Criminal Justice* Cmnd 2263 (1993) Ch 4, the recommendations are rather general, but the latter is a useful source of information since of the 22 empirical studies it commissioned more than half dealt with the subject matter of this chapter.

15   Law Com 245, paras 8.84–8.92, rec 18.

16   Ibid, paras 8.93–8.96, rec 19, draft bill, cl 17 inserting a new s 76A into the Police and Criminal Evidence Act 1984.

17   Section 82(1).

18   (1783) 1 Leach 263, at 263, 264.

19   See Wigmore (1891) 5 HLR 71, and Morgan (1949) 34 Minn LR 1.

20   The form of caution established by that legislation had an impact upon the attitudes of the judiciary to confessions secured by the police: see *R v Baldry* (1852) 2 Den 430. There is a persistent tendency to formalise, and to judicialise, the rules applicable to the earlier stages of investigation; the current law relating to the Codes of Practice is the most recent example.

Between the end of the 18th century and the middle of the 19th the rules excluding confessions were elaborated in a series of judgments at first instance. The conditions of that period were described by Lord Hailsham as:[1]

a time when the savage code of the 18th century was in full force. At that time almost every serious crime was punished by death or transportation. The law enforcement officers formed no disciplined police force and were not subject to effective control by the Central Government Watch Committee or an inspectorate. There was no legal aid. There was no system of appeal. To crown it all the accused was unable to give evidence on his own behalf and was therefore largely at the mercy of any evidence, either perjured or oppressively obtained, that might be brought against him. The judiciary were therefore compelled to devise artificial rules designed to protect him against dangers now avoided by other and more rational means.

By mid-century, not without some grave judicial misgivings, it was accepted that, in the words of Baron Parke:[2]

By the law of England, in order to render a confession admissible in evidence, it must be perfectly voluntary; and there is no doubt that any inducement in the nature of a promise or of a threat held out by a person in authority vitiates a confession.

Thereafter the formulation of the rule remained relatively constant,[3] but became more and more rigid as a developing case-law filled out the interstices of the definition by the determination of particular disputes. In England this prevented the rule from extending beyond inducements in the shape of threats or promises,[4] though these were often construed with some ingenious generosity. This meant that in order to accommodate the exclusion of confessions obtained by the use of reprehensible police methods, not on any view involving the use of either promises or threats, it was necessary to develop rules of practice.[5] Since the evolution of such a rule of practice could hardly be left to the vagaries of dozens of unco-ordinated decisions, the scene was set for the promulgation of the English Judges' Rules attempting to encapsulate a set of rules of fair police practices, though without the sanction of automatic enforcement. It also meant that in order to provide for automatic exclusion in the most egregious cases of malpractice, it was ultimately necessary to amplify the formulation of the exclusionary rule to include a reference to oppression.[6] Conversely the

1   *DPP v Ping Lin* [1976] AC 574, at 600, [1975] 3 All ER 175, at 182. See also the remarks of Lord Diplock in *R v Sang* [1980] AC 402, at 436, [1979] 2 All ER 1222, at 1230.
2   *R v Baldry* (1852) 2 Den 430, at 444.
3   The leading authorities are *R v Thompson* [1893] 2 QB 12 and *Ibrahim v R* [1914] AC 599.
4   In Australia the courts were more prepared to take a wider and less blinkered view of the impediments to voluntariness: see *Cornelius v R* (1936) 55 CLR 235 where Dixon J made an explicit contrast with the position in England. See also *Wan v US* 266 US 1 (1924), for a similar statement of the American position by Justice Brandeis.
5   It seems that they had developed by 1905: see *R v Knight and Thayre* (1905) 20 Cox CC 711 per Channell J.
6   It was first introduced by Lord Parker CJ in his judgment in *Callis v Gunn* [1964] 1 QB 495, at 501, [1963] 3 All ER 677, at 680, and shortly afterwards incorporated as part of principle (e) of the introduction to the new Judges' Rules of 1964. It may seem difficult to accommodate confessions obtained by actual torture within the classical formulation of the rule, unless one implies a promise to desist if a confession should be made, as in *R v Gardner* (1932) 51 NZLR 1648, but see *DPP v Ping Lin* [1976] AC 574, at 606, [1975] 3 All ER 175, at 188 per Lord Salmon.

consequence of construing individual decisions on particular facts as rules of law was that some forms of words, which many felt could hardly have induced the most timorous of suspects to confess falsely, became automatic warrants for exclusion.[7] The basic roots of the technicality in which the modern law had become enmeshed were addressed in *DPP v Ping Lin*.[8] The effect was to emphasise that the question of the exclusionary test was one of fact, especially one of causation, to be construed on a commonsense basis and necessarily determined without reference to authority, just because everything depended upon the particular circumstances in which the particular suspect was placed. In this way the judge could approach the question just as it would be approached by a jury, whose function in this situation he was unusually, but unavoidably, assuming.

2.   Rationale

The House of Lords declined to speculate in *Ping Lin*[9] upon exactly what basis the exclusion of involuntary confessions was to be justified. A number have been suggested, both in relation to the rules excluding involuntary confessions, and to the exercise of exclusionary discretions which apply to confessional statements, and to other evidence obtained by illegal means itself sometimes regarded as being governed by analogous policies. The general ground for accepting admissions, that what a party says against his own interests may be presumed to be true, has not always been accepted in relation to confessions. Thus Wigmore cites the same eminent English judge asserting first in 1798 that 'confession is a species of evidence which, though not inadmissible, is regarded with great distrust',[10] and in 1820 that 'confession generally ranks high, or I should say, highest in the scale of evidence'.[11] This discrepancy is plausibly enough explained[12] on the basis that when satisfactorily established to have proceeded from a genuine motive and to have been accurately recorded, a confession may well be worthy of the highest esteem, but just because this is the case, such high regard will also be sought by the less scrupulous for statements which merely purport to satisfy these conditions. In contested criminal cases, given that the accused is present in court, has not pleaded guilty and has retracted his confession, there must always be a possibility that the statement falls into the latter category.[13] It is for this reason that some form of corroboration has been suggested,[14] and the need for a warning to the jury to take great care and to look for supporting evidence endorsed by the Royal Commission on Criminal Justice.[15]

The requirement that a confession be 'voluntary' may be regarded as demanding satisfaction of quite different rationales. As noted above, *Warickshall* stressed the need for the confession to be credit-worthy, and to that end distinguished sharply

---

7   Here too some jurisdictions avoided such consequences by robust intervention, thus the colony of Victoria as early as 1857 enacted a provision providing that only inducements 'really calculated' to cause untrue admissions were to lead to exclusion, now Evidence Act 1958, s 149.
8   [1976] AC 574, [1975] 3 All ER 175.
9   By Lord Morris at 595, 178, and by Lord Salmon at 607, 188.
10   Sir William Scott in *Williams v Williams* (1798) 1 Hag Con 299, at 304.
11   *Mortimer v Mortimer* (1820) 2 Hag Con 310, at 315.
12   See also *R v Maynard* (1979) 69 Cr App Rep 309, at 312.
13   See per Cave J in *R v Thompson* [1893] 2 QB 12, at 18.
14   And accepted by the High Court of Australia in *R v Mackinney and Judge* (1992) 171 CLR 468.
15   Cmnd 2263, paras 4.56–4.87, and recs 89–90. See also the Commission's Research Study No 13 'Corroboration and Confessions: The Impact of a Rule Requiring that no Conviction can be sustained on the Basis of Confession Evidence Alone'.

between the making of an oral statement which might or might not be false, and the finding of objects which it assumed to be automatically cogent, though it must be conceded that it is rare for evidence of the latter sort to prove very much without the assistance of testimony, or other circumstantial evidence. In *Baldry* the court was anxious to point out that involuntary confessions are not presumed to be false,[16] but that it is nevertheless dangerous from the point of view of the administration of justice to admit them. *Ibrahim* referred to the rule as one of policy, but abstained from elaborating the nature of that policy.

Some modern cases, at the same time as clarifying the operation of the rule, have suggested a more diffused basis for it in policy. Thus one further strand intertwined with reliability in the current approach, and to be discerned both in Lord Reid's speech in *Harz and Power*[17] and in Lord Diplock's in *Sang*,[18] is that of the basis for the privilege against self-incrimination, a vindication of the right of the individual not to be subjected to official pressure to condemn himself.[19] Two other members of the House, so far from contrasting the basis of this privilege with that of ensuring a fair trial, seemed to equate them.[20] Lord Salmon made no reference to the basis for self-incrimination, but referred only to the preservation by the judge of a fair trial by excluding involuntary confessions.[1] This rationale, concerned so closely with the rights of the accused at his trial, seems to exemplify what has been called the 'protective principle'.[2] It is clearly intended to be distinguished from what the Criminal Law Revision Committee referred to as the 'disciplinary principle', the thrust of which is more to deter improper police practices than to protect the rights of the accused. Yet this principle itself has found expression in recent decisions, for example in *Wong Kam-ming v R* Lord Hailsham said:[3]

> any civilised system of criminal jurisprudence must accord to the judiciary some means of excluding confessions or admissions obtained by improper methods. This is not only because of the potential unreliability of such statements, but also, and perhaps mainly, because in a civilised society it is vital that persons in custody or charged with offences should not be subjected to ill treatment or improper pressure in order to extract confessions.

The generality and instrumentality of these words suggest that Lord Hailsham's principal concern was with the control of police behaviour.[4] Indeed the rationale is sometimes put on a still higher plane, and, quite irrespective of the deterrent force of a decision upon police practice, related to the court's expression of abhorrence for the

16 In *Burns v R* (1975) 132 CLR 258, at 262, the High Court of Australia was equally insistent that voluntary confessions were not to be presumed to be true.
17 [1967] 1 AC 760, at 820, [1967] 1 All ER 177, at 184.
18 [1980] AC 402, at 436, [1979] 2 All ER 1222, at 1230. The passage is somewhat difficult to interpret since after mentioning the principle *nemo debet prodere se ipsum* in relation to the justification for modern confession law, Lord Diplock relates it to the discretion to exclude, going on to describe that as a sanction upon the improper conduct of the prosecution, contrasting it with the power only to secure a fair trial, and denying the existence of any comparable sanctioning power in relation to obtaining any other evidence.
19 See also *R v Keenan* [1990] 2 QB 54, [1989] 3 All ER 598, at 603 where the modern law under s 76 of the Police and Criminal Evidence Act 1984 is ascribed to such a rationale.
20 See Lord Fraser at 449–50, 1241, and Lord Scarman at 455, 1246.
1 Lord Salmon at 445, 1237.
2 See Ashworth [1977] Crim LR 723.
3 [1980] AC 247, at 261, [1979] 1 All ER 939, at 946.
4 For a still more explicit reference to this rationale see *R v Trump* (1979) 70 Cr App Rep 300, at 303.

methods used. Thus in *King v R* Lord Hodson expressed the view of the Privy Council by saying:[5]

> This is not, in their opinion, a case in which evidence has been obtained by conduct of which the Crown ought not to take advantage. If they had thought otherwise they would have excluded the evidence even though tendered for the suppression of crime.

This view has received even stronger support in Australia where the High Court has explicitly rejected a fair play rationale in favour of such a view: 'It is not fair play that is called in question in such cases but rather society's right to insist that those who enforce the law themselves respect it.'[6] It should be noted that in both of these cases the issue related to the discretion to exclude real evidence secured after a breach of proper procedure, and in *Bunning v Cross* was said 'not to entrench upon the quite special rules which apply to the case of confession evidence'. Yet it can hardly be argued today that a weaker justification is required to restrain the application of pressure to human beings to force them to confess, than is required to prevent intrusion into private property. The further step of explicit extension to disputed confessions was taken by the High Court of Australia in *Cleland v R*,[7] in accordance with the position that the discretion to exclude had always been wider in Australia, than in England,[8] but not so different in the result from the position in Scotland.[9] It should be noted that under modern English law discretionary exclusion under s 78 of the Police and Criminal Evidence Act 1984 extends to means of obtaining evidence having an adverse effect upon the fairness of the proceedings, a provision which has been explicitly held to extend to confessions.[10] In Canada this area, like so much of the law of evidence, has been affected by the advent of the Canadian Charter of Rights and Freedoms. Under art 24(2) of the Charter any evidence in breach of the rights guaranteed by the Charter must be excluded 'if it is established that, having regard to all the circumstances, the admission of it in the proceedings would bring the administration of justice into disrepute'. This will, in many cases, operate in relation to confessions by way of breach of the right to counsel guaranteed under the Charter.[11]

The explicit rejection of such rationales is as significant as the espousal of such a variety has been as an indication of the uncertainty of the law in this area. In *R v Warickshall* the court was clear that:[12]

> It is a mistaken notion that the evidence of confessions and facts which have been obtained from prisoners by promises or threats, is to be rejected from a regard to public faith: no such rule ever prevailed.

In stark contrast when, in *Wong Kam-ming v R*, counsel for the respondent began his argument by expressing the reliability principle he was sharply upbraided by Lord

5   [1969] 1 AC 304, at 319, [1968] 2 All ER 610, at 617.
6   (1978) 19 ALR 641, at 659.
7   (1982) 151 CLR 1.
8   Justified by Murphy J at 17 on the basis of the lower standard of proof for the voluntariness of a confession in Australia.
9   *Cleland v R* per Gibbs CJ at 8.
10   *R v Mason* [1987] 3 All ER 481, at 484, [1988] 1 WLR 139, at 143H.
11   *R v Manninen* [1987] 1 SCR 1233. A vast jurisprudence has already developed around the Charter in general, and this article in particular: see Paccioco *Charter Principles and Proof in Criminal Cases* (1987).
12   (1783) 1 Leach 263.

Diplock with the assertion that such an argument was contrary to authority.[13] Nor do the views in *R v Sang* support a general disciplinary policy in this area, for as expressed by Lord Diplock:[14]

> It is no part of a judge's function to exercise powers over the police or prosecution as respects the way in which evidence to be used at the trial is obtained by them. If it was obtained illegally there will be a remedy in civil law; if it was obtained legally but in breach of the rules of conduct of the police, this is a matter for the appropriate disciplinary authority to deal with. What the judge at the trial is concerned with is not how the evidence sought to be adduced by the prosecution has been obtained, but with how it is used by the prosecution at the trial.

It should be noted that by excluding confessions from this reasoning Lord Diplock was countenancing just that split between the rationales in respect of police methods in obtaining confessions and in obtaining other evidence which was rejected by the High Court of Australia in *Cleland v R*.[15] Lord Diplock's view distinguished sharply, and perfectly understandably, between police practice in inducing speech and in searching premises. It is less clear how Lords Fraser and Scarman, who extended discretionary exclusion to some searches, could subscribe to the same rationale. It is hard to see why it is so much worse for the police to search the accused's premises improperly than so to search those of anyone else. If anything, the former seems marginally less iniquitous. The current view was stated by Lord Griffiths in *Lam Chi-ming v R*:[16]

> the most recent English cases established that the rejection of an improperly obtained confession is not dependent only upon possible unreliability but also upon the principle that a man cannot be compelled to incriminate himself and upon the importance that attaches in a civilised society to proper behaviour by the police towards those in their custody.

3.   Police and Criminal Evidence Act 1984[17]

This legislation now governs the admissibility of confessions, and requires consideration in detail. Questions arise as to its extent, the conditions which it imposes for admissibility, and its effect.

(i)   Extent

Section 76 of the Police and Criminal Evidence Act 1984 establishes its extent by providing:

> (1) In any proceedings a confession made by an accused person may be given in evidence against him in so far as it is relevant to any matter in issue in the proceedings and is not excluded by the court in pursuance of this section.

13   [1980] AC 247, at 251.
14   [1980] AC 402, at 436, [1979] 2 All ER 1222, at 1230. See also *R v Delaney* (1988) 88 Cr App Rep 338, at 341.
15   (1983) 43 ALR 619.
16   [1991] 2 AC 212, at 220, [1991] 3 All ER 171, at 179.
17   For early appraisal of the operation of this legislation see Birch [1989] Crim LR 95.

This is supplemented by s 82 which states that:

(1) 'confession' includes any statement wholly or partly adverse to the person who made it, whether made to a person in authority or not, and whether made in words or otherwise.

Two sets of issues arise as to the extent of these provisions, the first relating to substantial, and the second to procedural, delimitation. These will be considered in turn.

(a)   Substantial delimitation

In the first category it is necessary to elucidate the notion of a 'statement', whether it extends to matters of opinion as well as those of fact, the precise extent of the phrase 'made in words or otherwise', and the vexed notion of how far, if at all, purely exculpatory statements are caught by the words 'wholly or partly adverse'.

There is, in this part of the Act, no further definition of 'statement', by contrast to the preceding part where it is defined in accordance with the definition in the Civil Evidence Act 1968.[18] That definition, as amended, now includes an expression of opinion, so it is reasonable to construe 'confession' here as excluding any expression of opinion.

It will be noticed that to amount to a confession any statement must be, at least in part, adverse to its maker. A question may arise as to the position with regard to a statement wholly exculpatory in intention and apparent effect when made, but which by the time of trial, has become damaging to the accused either because it can be shown to be false, or because it is inconsistent with the defence raised at the trial.[19] In *Piché v R*[20] the Supreme Court of Canada held, by a majority, that such an exculpatory statement must also satisfy the voluntariness test, adopting the reasoning of Chief Justice Warren in *Miranda v Arizona*:[1]

no distinction may be drawn between inculpatory statements and statements alleged to be merely 'exculpatory'. If a statement made were in fact exculpatory it would, of course never be used by the prosecution. In fact, statements merely intended to be exculpatory by the defendant are often used to impeach his testimony at trial or to demonstrate untruths in the statement given under interrogation and thus to prove guilt by implication. These statements are incriminating in any meaningful sense of the word.

Such a view derives some support from the reasoning in *Lam Chi-ming v R* where Lord Griffiths said that:[2]

it is surely just as reprehensible to use improper means to force a man to give information that will reveal he has knowledge that will ensure his conviction as it is to force him to make a full confession. In either case a man is being forced

18   Section 72(1).
19   In *R v Toothill* [1998] Crim LR 876 the statement, which may well have been false, was intended to exculpate, but because of lack of knowledge of the relevant branch of the criminal law in fact supplied one of the essential elements of the charge.
20   [1971] SCR 23. A persuasive argument is that such a view avoids the indubitable difficulties of determining whether or not a statement was adverse at the time it was made.
1   384 US 436, at 477 (1966).
2   [1991] 2 AC 212, at 222, [1991] 3 All ER 171, at 179. See also *R v Ismail* [1990] Crim LR 109.

into a course of action that will result in his conviction: he is being forced to incriminate himself.

This is consistent with the decision in *R v Treacy*[3] that an inadmissible confession cannot be used as a previous inconsistent statement for the purpose of discrediting its maker. The view has also attracted powerful academic support.[4]

Nevertheless there remain formidable bastions for the view that exculpatory statements are not caught by the Act. In the first place 'adverse' in s 82 is more naturally read as referring to the effect of the statement at the time it is made.[5] Second, there is plenty of authority[6] to this effect, including the blunt statement in *R v Pearce*[7] that 'a denial does not become an admission because it is inconsistent with another denial.' It too has attracted academic support.[8] It is based on the fundamental proposition that a statement is hearsay only when relied upon for the truth of what it asserts,[9] and from which false exculpatory statements were distinguished in *Mawaz Khan v R*.[10]

It could perhaps be argued that the decision of the House of Lords in *R v Kearley*,[11] in its departure from the view that the character of a statement as hearsay is governed exclusively by its assertive form, might be regarded as having undermined the rejection of exculpatory statements as confessional for the purposes of the Police and Criminal Evidence Act 1984. This may be met by the riposte that the decision does not extend so far as to turn into an implied assertion something that is on its face an assertion of the very opposite, and excluded rather than implied. The cases can largely be reconciled on the basis that the prosecution cannot use such a statement when it relies upon its truth, however indirectly, but may do so when it relies on its falsity, subject only to the possibility of exclusion by invocation of the discretion if the manner of obtaining it was sufficiently oppressive or unfair.[12]

The most likely relevance of the false denial is to show consciousness of guilt. Such consciousness may also be shown by such things as making false,[13] or evasive,[14] statements, remaining silent when speech could have been expected,[15] refusing to supply a sample of real evidence,[16] putting in a false notice of alibi,[17] attempting to suborn witnesses,[18] calling witnesses to give testimony known to be false,[19] or

3   [1944] 2 All ER 229.
4   Elliott and Wakeham [1979] Crim LR 428; Mirfield *Silence, Confessions and Improperly Obtained Evidence* pp 54–58 seems to prefer this view.
5   For an interesting qualification of this proposition see Smith [1995] Crim LR 280 arguing persuasively of the admissibility of a confession to one crime, offered by way of exculpation in relation to a second, if tendered as proof of guilt of the first.
6   See *R v Sat-Bhambra* (1988) 88 Cr App Rep 55, at 61; *R v Park* (1994) 99 Cr App Rep 270. See also *R v Coats* [1932] NZLR 401; *R v Doyle* [1987] 2 Qd R 732, at 746. Cp *R v Marijancevic* (1991) 54 ACR 431, at 444 suggesting that a palpably false denial might be enough.
7   (1979) 69 Cr App Rep 365, at 370.
8   See Smith [1988] Crim LR 455; Andrews and Hirst *Criminal Evidence* (2nd ed) para 19.04; and the two previous editions of this work.
9   *Subramaniam v Public Prosecutor* [1956] 1 WLR 965.
10   [1967] 1 AC 454, [1967] 1 All ER 80.
11   [1992] 2 AC 228, [1992] 2 All ER 345. See further above p 544.
12   *R v Jukov* (1994) 76 ACR 353 provides an illuminating, if depressing, example.
13   *R v Knight* [1966] 1 All ER 647, [1966] 1 WLR 230; and see *R v Lucas* [1981] QB 720, [1981] 2 All ER 1008.
14   *Woon v R* (1964) 109 CLR 529.
15   *R v Chandler* [1976] 3 All ER 105, [1976] 1 WLR 585; and a fortiori assaulting an accuser, *Parkes v R* [1976] 3 All ER 380, [1976] 1 WLR 1251.
16   *R v Smith* (1985) 81 Cr App Rep 286.
17   *R v Rossborough* (1985) 81 Cr App Rep 139.
18   *Moriarty v London Chatham and Dover Rly Co* (1870) LR 5 QB 314.
19   *R v Perera* [1982] VR 901.

fleeing.[20] It is submitted that unless the conduct can be regarded as indicating acceptance of an assertion made by another, consciousness of guilt derived from such statements or conduct can amount only to circumstantial evidence, and cannot amount to hearsay.[1] In such a case it is admissible if relevant, irrespective of its motivation, save in so far as that may so reduce the weight of such evidence as to suggest that it ought to trigger the exercise of the judge's discretion to exclude because the prejudicial effect is likely to exceed probative value, a particularly likely situation here when the conduct or statement may have many other plausible explanations besides consciousness of guilt.[2] If an accused person is subjected to improper pressure to confess, his running away may clearly stem from a desire to avoid the pressure, rather than from a consciousness of guilt. This is a matter of simple commonsense, and there is no need to achieve the exclusion of any adverse inference from such conduct by so tortuous a chain of reasoning as first categorising it as hearsay and in principle inadmissible, then as falling within an inclusionary exception for admissions implied from conduct, and finally excluding it as coming within the exception to that exception for involuntary admissions. It might be argued that this view deprives the second part of the expression 'in words or otherwise' of any meaning, on the basis that even an allegation accepted by conduct, remains a statement in words irrespective of its mode of adoption. Such an argument seems to place insufficient emphasis upon the mode of adoption by the accused which is what turns it into an admission, and which is hypothesised to be made otherwise than in words. It should also be noticed that the concluding words are undeniably apt to cover evidence of admissions deduced from the conduct of the accused in the course of a re-enactment of the crime, arranged by the police.[3]

(ii)   Procedural delimitation

These matters comprehend such issues as the extent to which the section applies to use of confessional material by the defence, and especially by a co-accused, how far it applies to statements made in other curial proceedings, to what extent it applies to magistrates, and the stage at which particular exclusionary rules apply.

At common law statements made by third parties confessing guilt were inadmissible as hearsay when adduced by the accused in chief.[4] If made in a document they may now be admissible if they satisfy the conditions established by Part II of the Criminal Justice Act 1988.[5] They were however admissible in cross-examination of their maker, if he should testify, as previous inconsistent statements.[6] Confessions by one sole accused are inadmissible against him when adduced by the prosecution in chief unless they satisfy the conditions of s 76 of the Police and Criminal Evidence Act 1976, whether

---

20   *R v Gay* [1976] VR 577.

1   There is of course no doubt that it falls outside the definition proposed by the Law Commission.

2   This is consistent with the approach adopted in *Lucas* above, and in *R v Dowley* [1983] Crim LR 168, an appeal was allowed because the dangers had not been clearly enough spelled out.

3   *Li Shu-ling v R* [1989] AC 270, [1988] 3 All ER 138. Also accepted elsewhere see *Collins v R* (1980) 31 ALR 257; *R v Robert* (1996) 104 CCC (3d) 480; *S v Sheehama* 1991 (2) SA 860; *People v Dabb* 32 Cal 2d 491 (1948).

4   *Sussex Peerage Case* (1844) 11 Cl & Fin 85. The same rule applies in Australia, see *Re Van Beelen* (1974) 9 SASR 163; but not in Canada, *R v O'Brien* (1977) 76 DLR (3d) 513, or the United States, Federal Rule 804(3)(b) requiring corroboration, and see *Chambers v Mississippi* 410 US 295 (1973).

5   See further above p 581.

6   See further above p 294. Not as evidence of the truth of their contents, but only to discredit his inconsistent testimony.

or not they are made in a document. They are equally inadmissible if sought to be put in cross-examination of him by the prosecution.[7] Confessions made by a co-accused are inadmissible against him when adduced in chief by the prosecution unless the conditions of s 76 have been satisfied, whether or not they are made in a document.[8] This applies a fortiori to their inadmissibility when adduced in chief against another co-accused.[9] The substance of such a confession can however be adduced by cross-examination of a testifying co-accused by the prosecution in order to criminate another, so long as no reference is made to any earlier statement.[10] In the same way the substance of such a statement may be used in cross-examination of its maker by a co-accused in order to exculpate himself, once again whether or not the statement would be inadmissible.[11]

The wording of s 76 of the Police and Criminal Evidence Act 1984 seems to distinguish between its general extent which is to all confessions made by an accused person, and the special restrictive conditions which apply only to those put in evidence by the prosecution. The result might appear to be that one co-accused may himself adduce the confessions of another without regard to the restrictive conditions laid down, but, since such a confession would fall within the terms of s 76(1), can secure the advantage of the effects given by the Act. This interpretation was however rejected by the Court of Appeal in *R v Beckford and Daley*[12] on the basis that the provision was not sufficiently explicit[13] to overturn the common law rule that statements by third parties[14] admitting the commission of crimes are in principle inadmissible hearsay.[15] This reasoning was undermined by the later decision in *R v Campbell and Williams*,[16] and rejected by the House of Lords in *R v Myers*.[17] In the former one co-accused was allowed to adduce in chief a confession by another despite the hearsay rule. The confession had been obtained by stealth by the co-accused, and was not sought to be adduced by the prosecution since it had not known of it in advance.[18] *Beckford and Daley* was distinguished on the basis that there the confession could have been excluded if adduced by the prosecution. In *R v Myers* also the co-accused's confession could

---

7   *R v Treacy* [1944] 2 All ER 229.
8   Criminal Justice Act 1988, ss 23(4), 24(3). Cp *R v England* [1978] Tas SR 79.
9   Though it is not necessarily a misdirection that the judge fails so to direct the jury: *R v Turpin* [1990] Crim LR 514.
10   *R v Rice* [1963] 1 QB 857, at 868, [1963] 1 All ER 832, at 839. This applied irrespective of whether or not such a statement were inadmissible because obtained by any inducement, and so a fortiori to statements merely excludable by judicial discretion. It was regarded as very much a matter for the discretion of the judge that the evidence was then adduced after the prosecution had closed its initial presentation of its case.
11   *R v Rowson (Peter)* [1986] QB 174, [1985] 2 All ER 539 (where the earlier statement was excludable by discretion); *Lui Mei-lin v R* [1989] AC 288, [1989] 1 All ER 359 (where the earlier statement was inadmissible by rule).
12   [1991] Crim LR 833 (where it was sought to put the contents of the co-accused's inadmissible confession to a police witness). See Mirfield (1992) 108 LQR 34. Still less can a co-accused complain that because of separation of trials he has been deprived of an opportunity to cross-examine on such an exculpatory statement: *R v Clare* [1995] Crim LR 726.
13   The reference to 'any matter in issue in the proceedings' was construed as being restricted to an issue between the Crown and the maker of the confession.
14   See eg *R v Blastland* [1986] AC 41, [1985] 2 All ER 1095, and the authorities cited in n 4, p 612.
15   Whether proposed to be put by the co-accused to a police witness in cross-examination as in *Beckford and Daley* itself, or adduced by the co-accused in chief, as in *R v Marviadi and Ghanchi* [1992] Crim LR 733.
16   [1993] Crim LR 448.
17   [1998] AC 124, [1997] 4 All ER 314.
18   Although in the circumstances it would have been admissible if adduced by the prosecution, a slight variation in those circumstances under which the police had themselves been complicit in the means of obtaining the confession might have led to a different result: see above p 505.

have been excluded under the s 78 discretion for breaches of the Code of Practice, and for this reason was not adduced by the prosecution.[19] It was held that this confession could be adduced by the exculpated co-accused, over the objection of the other. So in the case of a confession which falls foul of s 78, it seems currently to be clear that a co-accused will be entitled to adduce, or to cross-examine on the basis of, such a confession, despite the objection of the inculpated co-accused, and however much prejudice it causes that co-accused. But what if it falls foul of s 76 ? On this point the House of Lords was divided in *Myers*. The point is most clearly addressed in the speech of Lord Hope,[20] where the view was taken that breach of s 76 rendered the confession worthless for all purposes. A further technical bolster to this argument was that even if s 76, contrary to the view taken in *Beckford and Daley*, does not apply to confessions adduced by the defence, the same result would follow at common law since such a confession would be hearsay, and not saved by the common law exception for admissions, because the breach of s 76 would render it involuntary.[1] The majority seemed more prepared to apply the same rule of admission to confessions excludable under either provision, whether by rule or discretion.

Although there is no discretion to exclude evidence which is otherwise admissible tendered by the defence,[2] it was held in *R v Rogers and Tarran*[3] that the discretion to exclude evidence tendered by the prosecution at a joint trial can be invoked on account of prejudice to the co-accused other than the one against whom it is tendered.

The Law Commission considered this matter while *Myers* was under consideration by the House of Lords. It recommended[4] the insertion of a new s 76A in the Police and Criminal Evidence Act 1984 which effectively applies exactly the same rules to confessions adduced by the co-accused to those adduced by the prosecution, subject only to the application of the lower standard of proof on the balance of probabilities to matters to be proved by the defence. The effect may however be different, since the discretion to exclude evidence at common law, and that under s 78 apply only to confessions upon which the prosecution proposes to rely.[5]

---

19   It is less clear why a confession in identical terms to a third party, not in any way governed by the Code, was not adduced.

20   In which Lord Mustill concurred.

1   This argument seems more clearly applicable to breach of s 76(2)(a) than to breach of s 76(2)(b), though as pointed out by Mirfield in *Silence, Confessions and Improperly Obtained Evidence* at p 220 (in a passage written before the decision of the House of Lords in *Myers*) this distinction seems to operate in the wrong direction in terms of the worthlessness of the confession.

2   *R v Miller* [1952] 2 All ER 667, at 669, 36 Cr App Rep 169, at 171; *Murdoch v Taylor* [1965] AC 574, [1965] 1 All ER 406. Or even if tendered by the prosecution if its effect is to exculpate one of the co-accused, and he objects to the invocation of discretion for this purpose, *Lobban v R* [1995] 2 All ER 602, [1995] 1 WLR 877. This is a strong decision since there was no case to answer against the co-accused, and it was only by accident that he had not already been excluded from jeopardy, and in such a case the confession would clearly be inadmissible as in *R v Campbell* [1995] 1 Cr App Rep 522.

3   [1971] Crim LR 413.

4   Law Com No 245, paras 8.93–8.96, rec 19, draft bill, cl 17.

5   It might just be possible to argue that such a confession, if in writing and made for the purposes of legal proceedings, would be subject to the discretions under ss 25 and 26 of the Criminal Justice Act 1988, although this would depend on taking the view that such a confession was *admissible by virtue of* s 23 or 24 of the Act despite not having been *rendered admissible* by that section (on the basis that although by compliance with the conditions of ss 23 or 24 and thus admissible, in the sense of capable of being admitted, under them, it was separately *admissible*, and indeed admitted, under the new cl 76A of the Police and Criminal Evidence Act 1984). This argument is weakened by the fact that if it were correct it would apply even more clearly to confessions adduced by the prosecution under s 76, and s 26 (s 25 would add little to the existing discretions) never seems so much as to have been invoked in that connection.

The next point to be made on the extent of the section relates to the question of the admissibility of confessions made in other proceedings, or at earlier stages of the same proceedings.[6] There is nothing in the wording of s 76 to suggest that it does not apply to statements made in the course of judicial proceedings just as much as to those not so made. It would follow that the common law rules admitting statements made in other proceedings,[7] pleas of guilty to associated offences,[8] and pleas of guilty which have been withdrawn,[9] will remain applicable since it is inherently unlikely that the conditions for exclusion will be capable of being established in such situations.[10]

The admissibility of statements on the voir dire has been more controversial. As noted earlier[11] the position at common law seems to have been changed in some respects by the section. It is best to consider the matter in two stages, first to consider to what extent admissions can be extracted on the voir dire, and then to what extent they can be adduced at the trial. Section 76 makes no explicit reference to the propriety of asking about the truth or falsity of a confession on the voir dire,[12] so the matter is left to the common law. This is in a somewhat uncertain state. In the case of such an issue being initiated by the prosecution there was conflict between a decision of the Court of Criminal Appeal that such questioning was permissible,[13] and one of the majority of the Privy Council, that it was not.[14] In the case of the issue's being initiated by the defence the House of Lords seems to have held that such questioning was proper.[15] This would probably have remained an academic issue at common law in view of the further finding that no reference could be made to such an admission at the trial. On ordinary principles of statutory interpretation however this happy result seems to have been overturned by the new statutory provisions. Section 76 applies to confessions in unrestricted terms, and makes them admissible at the instance of the prosecution in all cases, unless the conditions of sub-s (2) cannot be disproved.[16] But as noted above, there is, in the case of an admission on the voir dire every reason to suppose that such conditions will be held to be disproved. It would seem to follow that judicial confessions made at whatever stage are thus admissible. This effect appears to resurrect the conflict between *Hammond* and the majority view in *Wong Kam-ming*. In the first draft of the Bill, as noted above, such a conflict was to have been resolved by a specific provision in favour of *Hammond* and the minority in *Wong Kam-ming*, but that provision was withdrawn, and the Act is now silent on the propriety of questions as to the truth or

6   The editor has relied heavily in this section upon Pattenden (1983) 32 ICLQ 812.
7   *R v McGregor* [1968] 1 QB 371, [1967] 2 All ER 267.
8   *R v Bastin* [1971] Crim LR 529.
9   *R v Rimmer* [1972] 1 All ER 604, [1972] 1 WLR 268.
10   In *R v Scott* (1856) Dears & B 47, at 58, Lord Campbell CJ said 'Such an objection [involuntariness] cannot apply to a lawful examination in the course of judicial proceedings'. In *McGregor* also the vigour of Lord Parker CJ's repudiation of the notion of the inadmissibility of a statement on oath in judicial proceedings points in the same direction. But see *Seymour v A-G for Commonwealth* (1984) 53 ALR 513; *Clyne v R* (1985) 81 FLR 197.
11   At pp 165-168.
12   The Bill, as introduced, included a subsection specifically permitting such questioning, but it was withdrawn.
13   *R v Hammond* [1941] 3 All ER 318, 28 Cr App Rep 84.
14   *Wong Kam-Ming v R* [1980] AC 247, [1979] 1 All ER 939.
15   *R v Brophy* [1982] AC 476, [1981] 2 All ER 705. It is left unclear to what extent the questioning there did relate to an extra-judicial confession, and to what extent its adduction by the defence would permit cross-examination by the prosecution. In any event the situation there was atypical in that it was the defence which was alleging the confession to be true.
16   Above. The same result was reached by the Supreme Court of Canada in *Boulet v R* [1978] 1 SCR 332, at 350, and in none of *Hammond, Wong Kam-Ming* nor *Brophy* was the question so much as raised. The regressive effect of voir dires into voir dires is surely to be avoided if at all possible.

falsity of a confession on the voir dire.[17] On balance it seems, notwithstanding the strict doctrine of precedent, more likely in the circumstances that the views of the majority of the Law Lords in *Wong Kam-ming* will prevail, especially as no disapproval of that decision was expressed by the House of Lords in *Brophy*.[18] It does seem however that the general intention of *Wong Kam-ming* and *Brophy* to protect the accused from damaging use at the trial of proceedings on the voir dire has been frustrated by the drafting of the new statutory provisions[19] so as to exclude confessions, only upon the satisfaction of conditions which judicial proceedings will rarely, if ever, satisfy in the United Kingdom.

'Proceedings' are defined by s 82(1) to mean criminal proceedings,[20] though no indication is given of whether that expression is meant to comprehend all stages of such proceedings at which evidence might be tendered.[1] It is clear that they comprehend proceedings before magistrates, and s 76(2) in its mandatory terms seems to have imposed an obligation upon magistrates to consider the admissibility of a confession as a separate preliminary matter in summary proceedings,[2] and perhaps also in committal proceedings.[3] A different view was however taken in respect of an application to consider discretionary exclusion under s 78 as a preliminary matter.[4] The reasoning was based upon a supposed difference between the obligation under s 76(2) to take a decision on admissibility in advance of the evidence being tendered, and the decision under s 78 which could be taken at any time. It is doubtful however whether this view can survive the interpretation of ss 76 and 78 of the Police and Criminal Evidence Act 1984 in *R v Sat-Bhambra*[5] as referring only to the future, so that once the evidence has been adduced their direct effect has been spent. The effect of any such view is however slight, since the judge may still discharge the jury, or direct it to disregard the confession, under his general discretionary powers, preserved by s 82(3) of the Police and Criminal Evidence Act 1984. In the case of summary trial it has also been held that if the accused's claim on s 78 involves nothing more than questions relating strictly to the disputed evidence, and does not otherwise introduce the substance of the charge, that fairness might dictate the claim being dealt with as if on a voir dire in the way applicable to a claim under s 76.[6]

---

17   Commentators are not so much silent as divided, compare Murphy [1979] Crim LR 364 with Arvay (1981) 23 Cr LQ 173.

18   It seems still permissible to ask the question in Australia: see *Frijaf v R* [1982] WAR 128; but not in South Africa: *S v De Vries* 1989 (1) SA 228.

19   Mirfield argues in [1995] Crim LR 612 that the policies have been further frustrated by the pressures put upon the accused to testify by the Criminal Procedure and Investigation Act 1996.

20   It seems that a police caution will not be invalidated if it is based on a confession which would have been inadmissible in proceedings in court: *R v Chief Constable of Lancashire, ex p Atkinson* (1998) 162 JP 275.

1   Compare Criminal Evidence Act 1898, s 1.

2   *R v Liverpool Juvenile Court, ex p R* [1988] QB 1, [1987] 2 All ER 668. See also *Police v Macklin* [1989] 3 NZLR 600.

3   *R v Oxford City Justices, ex p Berry* [1988] QB 507, [1987] 1 All ER 1244. Though in most cases refusal to consider the admissibility of a confession will not be sufficient to justify judicial review of the decision to commit, such remedies being discretionary.

4   *Vel v Owen* (1987) 151 JP 510, see also *Carlisle v DPP* (1987) Lexis, 9 November.

5   (1988) 88 Cr App Rep 55, intimating that the 1984 legislation had altered the procedure determined by *R v Watson* [1980] 2 All ER 293, [1980] 1 WLR 991.

6   *Halawa v FACT* [1995] 1 Cr App Rep 21.

4. Conditions

Confessions were made admissible under the conditions set out in s 76:

> (2) If, in any proceedings where the prosecution proposes to give in evidence a confession made by an accused person, it is represented to the court that the confession was or may have been obtained–
> (a) by oppression of the person who made it; or
> (b) in consequence of anything said or done which was likely, in the circumstances existing at the time, to render unreliable any confession which might be made by him in consequence thereof,
> the court shall not allow the confession to be given in evidence against him except in so far as the prosecution proves to the court beyond reasonable doubt that the confession (notwithstanding that it may be true) was not obtained as aforesaid.

> (8) ... 'oppression' includes torture, inhuman or degrading treatment, and the use or threat of violence (whether or not amounting to torture).

It is convenient to discuss these conditions under four headings, oppression, unreliability, causation and burden of proof.

(i) Oppression

This term which seems to have entered English case law in this context only in the early 1960s,[7] was expansively construed in a number of cases,[8] and criticised for its imprecision.[9] It nevertheless received the endorsement of the legislature as indicated above, though it provided only an inclusive definition repeating the substantive form of the old Judges' Rules.[10] Its construction was considered by the Court of Appeal in *R v Fulling*.[11] In that case a woman accused of fraud at first refused to make a statement to the police. At one point during an interview she alleged that she was told by her interrogator that her lover had been engaged in a sexual affair with another woman, who was incarcerated in the next cell. She claimed that this upset her, and that in her anxiety to get away from the police station she then confessed. She contended that the confession should be excluded under s 76(2)(a) as having been obtained by oppression. The trial court rejected this view, and was upheld by the Court of Appeal on the basis that the Police and Criminal Evidence Act 1984 was a codifying Act, and to be construed without necessary reference to the old law. This was explained upon the basis that the newly extended grounds of exclusion on the basis of unreliability were sufficient to cover many of the situations previously within the wider old ambit of 'oppression'. It is perhaps the more surprising that no reference was made to the partial definition in s 76(8). Instead the court applied a dictionary definition:[12]

---

7   *Callis v Gunn* [1964] 1 QB 495, at 501, [1963] 3 All ER 677, at 680.
8   Among them *R v Prager* [1972] 1 All ER 1114, [1972] 1 WLR 260 citing Sachs J in *R v Priestley*; but see (1967) 51 Cr App Rep 1.
9   By the Royal Commission on Criminal Procedure, Cmnd 8092, paras 4.71 and 4.72.
10 Although the Criminal Law Revision Committee had proposed to use the phrase 'oppressive treatment'.
11 [1987] QB 426, [1987] 2 All ER 65, see commentary in [1987] All ER Annual Review 120.
12 Oxford English Dictionary third definition.

Exercise of authority or power in a burdensome, harsh or wrongful manner; unjust or cruel treatment of subjects, inferiors, etc; the imposition of unreasonable or unjust burdens.

and drew attention to one of the quotations, 'There is not a word in our language which expresses more detestable wickedness than *oppression.*'[13] The conclusion drawn from this reasoning was that it would be rare to establish oppression without some impropriety on the part of the interrogator. In this respect it should be noted that the first phrase of the partial definition in s 76(8) appears also in Article 3 of the European Convention on Human Rights, which must now[14] be interpreted so as to conform with the accepted construction of that Convention.[15] The term 'violence' does not appear in the Convention, nor is it a term of art in English law. It seems possible that it will, because of its connection with the notion of torture in s 76(8), be construed as connoting a substantial application of force. It must certainly indicate more than a mere battery as the legislature would presumably have used a term of art if to do so would have implemented its intention, and the requirement of so small a degree of force would be prone to cause disputes in far too many perfectly reasonable and acceptable situations. It has been remarked that a procedure, such as compulsory interrogation, expressly instituted by the legislature, is unlikely to be regarded as oppressive.[16]

It is somewhat uncertain how far the effect of the conduct on the particular individual is to be taken into account under this head.[17] In the case of a mentally disturbed suspect it seems that the fact that questioning might disturb him is irrelevant to the operation of the exclusionary conditions of s 76(2)(a), unless the asking of such questions was a deliberate attempt to exploit the suspect's mental condition,[18] though it may still aggravate other factors.[19] It is clear from the context that more than mere incarceration or interrogation in a police station is required to constitute oppression. The difficulty is to know exactly how much more. It seems that if a deliberately unpleasant and uncomfortable technique is used in order to sap the will of the suspect it will be held inherently oppressive.[20] Under the old law such factors sometimes led to the exclusion of a confession as involuntary, especially if the actions of the police were unlawful.[1] Much may depend upon the notion of 'wrongful' in the dictionary definition adopted in *Fulling*. It seems that it is capable of applying to breaches of the Code of Practice for the interrogation of offenders, provided that they are sufficiently numerous and serious.[2] In *R v Davison*,[3] as in *Hudson*, they were further aggravated by failure to

---

13   Original emphasis.
14   Human Rights Act 1998, s 3.
15   *Republic of Ireland v United Kingdom* (1978) 2 EHRR 25.
16   *R v Seelig* [1991] 4 All ER 421, at 429, [1992] 1 WLR 148, at 159.
17   It seems to have been decisive in *R v Gardner* [1986] CLY 1499, but that was decided before *Fulling*, and may have been over-influenced by the old law.
18   *R v Miller* [1986] 3 All ER 119, [1986] 1 WLR 1191.
19   As in *R v Paris* (1992) 97 Cr App Rep 99, at 105.
20   *Burut v Public Prosecutor of Brunei* [1995] 2 AC 579, [1995] 4 All ER 300, at 593, 309e (where the suspects were manacled and hooded while being interrogated). The unreported Hong Kong case of *Chan Lau* (1996) NLJ 1031 involved a suspect being suspended by his feet from a 16th storey window until he confessed.
1   *R v Hudson* (1980) 72 Cr App Rep 163 (uncomfortably hot); but cp *R v Hughes* [1988] Crim LR 519 (uncomfortably cold) where it was thought more appropriate to consider the s 78 discretion.
2   For a particularly flagrant example, see *R v Paris* (1992) 97 Cr App Rep 99. Cp *R v Beales* [1991] Crim LR 118; *R v Emmerson* (1991) 92 Cr App Rep 284 where the misbehaviour of the police was more venial, and held not to amount to oppression.
3   [1988] Crim LR 442.

charge for the offence with which the interrogation was principally concerned, and the ground of oppression was held not to have been disproved.

(ii)   Unreliability

Although, as noted above,[4] the danger of unreliability has always been regarded as one of the factors underpinning the development of the exclusionary rule for confessions in English law, it had never previously played a part in the formulation of the test for admissibility which had been traditionally cast in terms of 'voluntariness'.[5] The introduction of this notion into the English test for exclusion was recommended by the Criminal Law Revision Committee in its 11th Report.[6] It was not however endorsed by the Royal Commission on Criminal Procedure as a test for admissibility, but was simply to be regarded as an important matter going to the weight of those confessions obtained otherwise than by 'oppressive treatment'.[7] The Police and Criminal Evidence Act 1984 adopted the principle proposed by the Criminal Law Revision Committee, doing no more than broaden the nature of the conduct affecting reliability from 'threat or inducement'[8] to 'anything said or done'. Neither version limits such conduct to that performed by persons in authority. The Criminal Law Revision Committee stressed that the test was not to be based upon the actual, but the potential, unreliability of a confession made in the relevant circumstances, which took into account such matters as the seriousness of the offence. It will be noted that s 76(2) refers explicitly to the 'circumstances existing at the time'. This seems to reflect the concern of the Criminal Law Revision Committee that the judge should try to recreate in his mind the conditions as they seemed to the accused at the moment of interrogation, though the Royal Commission was sceptical of the feasibility of such an exercise.[9] It seems that this provision will be interpreted in a manner similar to those already in force in New Zealand and Victoria where despite minor differences of phraseology the Court have regarded their respective provisions as referring to potential rather than to actual unreliability, and as requiring consideration of all the circumstances.[10]

In an apparent effort to encourage such an interpretation s 76 makes explicit reference to the possibility of the confession's being true despite its potential unreliability, and this view is further strengthened by the absence from the section as enacted of any authorisation to ask about the truth or falsity of a confession. The reason for such concern was unease about the danger of the preliminary test for admissibility before the judge becoming one of whether or not a given confession is reliable, and, given such a test, that the jury would then infer that any confession proved before it had already been considered by the judge to be reliable. Given the lack of sophistication of some criminal proceedings, and the drafting of the section which requires all relevant circumstances to be taken into account, it was inevitable that the subtle difference

---

4   At p 604.
5   The state of Victoria has however had a test formulated in such terms since 1857, and New Zealand since 1895.
6   Cmnd 4991, para 65.
7   This term is here used to connote the gamut of conduct regarded by the Royal Commission as justifying automatic exclusion.
8   Draft bill, cl 2(2)(b).
9   Cmnd 8092, para 4.72, although uttered in the context of oppression it is just as applicable here.
10   *Cornelius v R* (1936) 55 CLR 235; *R v Coats* [1932] NZLR 401, suggesting that the change in terminology in New Zealand in 1905 to 'in fact likely' from 'really calculated' was specifically designed to prevent an interpretation forcing admissibility upon the court whenever it believed the confession true.

between the tests to be imposed by judge and jury would become blurred. This was noted in *R v Tyrer* [11] where the Court of Appeal considered the trial judge to have come close to confusing these matters by taking into account on the voir dire in relation to the confession of one co-accused, evidence given at the trial proper in relation to another co-accused which indicated that the confession was probably true. It was however held that the voir dire should not be conducted in a vacuum. In some cases[12] appeals have been allowed because trial judges have overtly posed the test in terms of reliability, as opposed to potential unreliability. It is asking a lot of a judge to hold that even though he is quite sure that this confession made by this accused in these circumstances was reliable, it might upon some hypothesis not have been, and should therefore, despite its actual reliability be rejected, and the jury prevented even from considering it.

It should be noted that in Victoria and New Zealand the courts regard an unreliability test as in no way antithetical to the continued existence of a wide discretion to exclude on the ground of unfairness.[13] The Police and Criminal Evidence Act 1984, s 82(3) explicitly retained the existing discretion in England, but it was less generously interpreted than in Australia.[14] Two interlocking factors seem to have influenced subsequent development in England, first the much more ready application of the discretion in s 78 to exclude evidence on the ground of 'unfairness', which was explicitly extended to apply to confessions,[15] and second the extremely detailed guidance for the behaviour of the police provided by the Codes of Conduct given statutory force by Pt VI of the Police and Criminal Evidence Act 1984. The general tendency has been to take the Code as a rough guide to the likelihood of reliability, so that failure to comply is some indication of potential unreliability,[16] and compliance some indication of potential reliability. In some cases[17] even though the relevant provision in the Code seems to relate only to reliability, and despite its breach not being held to have had sufficient potential to create unreliability for the purposes of s 76(2)(b), it has nevertheless been held to be sufficient to trigger discretionary exclusion under s 78.

Although in *R v Fulling*[18] it was stated that impropriety by the police is not a necessary condition to the establishment of potential unreliability under s 76(2)(b), the operation of this head is conditioned upon 'anything said or done'[19] which is likely in the circumstances to induce unreliability. It should be noted that the test is objective in the sense that it is immaterial that the police are unaware of the factors inducing the potential unreliability,[20] or that they acted in perfect good faith.[1] If the mental condition[2]

11   (1990) 90 Cr App Rep 446.
12   Eg *R v Cox* [1991] Crim LR 276; *R v Kenny* [1994] Crim LR 284.
13   *R v Gardner* (1932) 51 NZLR 1648; *R v Lee* (1950) 82 CLR 133; *Cleland v R* (1983) 43 ALR 619; *R v Larson and Lee* [1984] VR 559. In those jurisdictions however reliability operates positively to admit involuntary confessions which would otherwise be excluded, and in such cases the discretion seems not to have been applied, indeed in the ACT where there is a similar provision legislation has been enacted to provide such a power, see ACT Evidence Ordinance 1971, s 68(3); and similar legislation has been recommended for New Zealand.
14   See above p 193.
15   *R v Mason* [1987] 3 All ER 481, at 484, [1988] 1 WLR 139, at 144.
16   But by no means conclusive (see *R v Delaney* (1989) 88 Cr App Rep 338) or exclusive (see *DPP v Blake* [1989] 1 WLR 432, 89 Cr App Rep 179).
17   Eg *R v Howden-Simpson* [1991] Crim LR 49.
18   [1987] QB 426, at 432, [1987] 2 All ER 65, at 70. See also *R v Brine* [1992] Crim LR 122; *R v Walker* [1998] Crim LR 211.
19   It is immaterial that the crux of the stimulus is constituted by an omission, such as failure to allow a period of rest: *R v Trussler* [1988] Crim LR 446; or to allow access to a solicitor: *R v McGovern* (1991) 92 Cr App Rep 228.
20   *R v Everett* [1988] Crim LR 826.
1   *DPP v Blake* (1989) 89 Cr App Rep 179.
2   Which may amount merely to a personality disorder: *R v Walker* above.

of the suspect is such that any statement he makes is likely to be unreliable, it might be thought that even the most innocuous remark might satisfy this requirement. Such a view was rejected by the Court of Appeal in *R v Goldenberg*,[3] in respect of the interviewing of a drug addict who might have been desperate for release in order to satisfy his addiction, where it was emphasised that the stimulus must be external[4] to the suspect,[5] and likely to have an effect upon him.[6] On the other hand it seems that in the case of such a suspect very little pressure may take the case over the line, and into the area of potential unreliability.[7] It appears indeed that where there is an inherent mental disorder this may be enough to take any questioning by the police over the line of potential unreliability.[8] As noted above breaches of the Codes of Practice may influence a court in deciding that oppression has not been disproved. It will, if anything, be easier to contend that potential unreliability under this head has not been disproved.[9]

It should finally be noted that the unreliability in question is the unreliability of the confession itself, and not of any recording of it which raises different questions best dealt with under s 78.[10]

(iii)   Causation[11]

Under the previous law one way of avoiding the artificial construction of particular forms of words as automatically amounting to an inducement was to require a convincing demonstration that they had in fact caused the accused to confess. Thus in *Ping Lin* Lord Hailsham remarked that:[12]

> It is the chain of causation which has to be excluded by the prosecution and not the hypostatisation of any part of it.

---

3   (1989) 88 Cr App Rep 285.
4   It need not however emanate from the police, but can come from a third party: *R v Harvey* [1988] Crim LR 241. See also *R v Walker* above where an inherent condition may have been aggravated by the voluntary act of the accused.
5   This was thought to stem from the requirement of a causal link between stimulus and reaction, but it is not clear why self-stimulus cannot be causally linked to reaction, for example, by taking hallucinogenic drugs.
6   See also *R v Maguire* (1989) 90 Cr App Rep 115 where statements made by a child questioned innocuously by a police officer, but in the absence of a responsible adult, were not rejected; *R v Crampton* (1991) 92 Cr App Rep 369 where a heroin addict was suffering withdrawal symptoms, and despite police evidence that they would not have continued the interview if they had realised it.
7   See *R v Delaney* (1989) 88 Cr App Rep 338, where while interviewing an educationally subnormal and emotional youth accused of a horrific assault on a small child the police officers underplayed the seriousness of the matter, and emphasised the suspect's need for psychiatric help; in *R v McGovern* (1991) 92 Cr App Rep 228, at 232 such factors were said to be the 'background' to any submission.
8   *R v Everett* [1988] Crim LR 826; *R v Raghip* (1991) Times, 9 December; *R v Ward* [1993] 2 All ER 577, at 641, [1993] 1 WLR 619, at 690. It should be noted that medical evidence of the accused's condition is not only admissible in determining the factual basis for such a submission, but positively required (*R v Ham* (1995) 36 BMLR 169) and to be strong enough to be truly relevant (*R v Heaton* [1993] Crim LR 593).
9   See eg *R v Doolan* [1988] Crim LR 747.
10   See the helpful commentary by Birch in [1991] Crim LR 624 upon the decision in *R v Chung* (1991) 92 Cr App Rep 314.
11   See Mirfield [1996] Crim LR 554.
12   [1976] AC 574, at 602, [1975] 3 All ER 175, at 184.

Given the difficulties to which the notion of causation has led in other areas of the law,[13] it might have been feared that such concentration might prejudice the simplicity of the test for admissibility aimed at in *Ping Lin*, but such fears were allayed by the decision of the Court of Appeal in *R v Rennie*.[14] In that case the accused claimed that he had confessed because he was under stress, had been threatened by the police and wanted to prevent the rest of his family being charged with complicity in the frauds of which he was suspected. His evidence to this effect had received some support from one of the police witnesses who had testified that he believed that the accused had confessed in order to prevent the involvement of his family. Nevertheless the Court of Appeal while recognising that in most cases there are mixed motives for confessing, and that some of them may be inspired by something said or done by the interrogator, felt that it would be wrong to apply 'any refined analysis of the concept of causation'. The judge should instead apply the spirit of the test in much the same way as it would be applied by a jury. In a mixed motive case this would appear to require a determination of the dominant motive. Exactly the same approach is appropriate to the conditions imposed by s 76(2).[15] It should perhaps be noticed that there is a slight difference in the drafting of the two conditions in that the first relating to oppression is introduced by the word 'by', whereas the second which relates to unreliability is introduced by the phrase 'in consequence of'. If anything should turn on that difference, it would presumably be to require less in the way of the demonstration of a causal link in the case of oppression, which may perhaps more readily be inferred, and where the law will be more anxious to mark its disapproval. Thus in *Burut v R*[16] the Privy Council required positive evidence from the prosecution to prove that the inherently oppressive first interrogation had not had a continuing effect on subsequent confessions.

It is important to note that in order to qualify for exclusion a causal link must always be established between something said or done by the interlocutor and the person making the confession.[17] It may often be necessary to determine whether an admission is made as a result of whatever has been said or done, or rather in recognition of the implausibility of previous statements, perhaps revealed by what has been said or done.[18] A spontaneous confession seems admissible, however unreliable it may be in the light of the accused's mental or emotional state. It may, however, in such circumstances, be excluded by the judge at his discretion,[19] and even if it be admitted, the weight to be attached to the confession of a person in such a state would obviously be small. It had become well-established in the old law that a confession which, considered in isolation, appeared to satisfy the conditions for being voluntary, might nevertheless be excluded if preceded by an earlier involuntary confession. It would be so excluded if either the factors tainting the earlier confession continued to apply, or if the fact of having made such a confession could itself be regarded as precipitating its successor.[20] The situation has been elaborated in a series of cases. The question is one of fact. An early confession obtained in breach of the Police and Criminal Evidence Act 1984 or the Codes of Practice

---

13   See Hart and Honoré *Causation in the Law* (2nd edn 1985).
14   [1982] 1 All ER 385, [1982] 1 WLR 64.
15   And has been so applied, see *R v Phillips* (1987) 86 Cr App Rep 18; *R v Crampton* (1991) 92 Cr App Rep 369; *R v Weeks* [1995] Crim LR 52.
16   [1995] 2 AC 579, [1995] 4 All ER 300.
17   *R v Goldenberg* (1988) 88 Cr App Rep 285, at 290. This appears to have been rejected by the Supreme Court in Canada after the Charter, *Brydges v R* [1990] 1 SCR 190.
18   As in *R v Tyrer* (1989) 90 Cr App Rep 446.
19   See p193 above.
20   *R v Smith* [1959] 2 QB 35, [1959] 2 All ER 193. See also *Darryl R v R* [1994] 1 SCR 881, and *HM Advocate v Docherty* 1981 JC 6.

may well taint a later one,[1] but is less likely to do so if any breach was more accidental than deliberate,[2] or if legal advice were taken after the interview in respect of which the breach occurred,[3] or perhaps that a later interview still were barren.[4] It militates in favour of exclusion of the later confession if it were obtained without the presence of a legal adviser and succeeded an interview at which a legal adviser were present and at which no confession were made. The principle has been said to depend upon whether the accused has at the later interview an informed and independent choice as to whether or not to repeat, retract or remain silent.[5]

(iv) Burden of proof

At common law it was for the prosecution to prove beyond reasonable doubt that a confession was voluntary.[6] Section 76(2) explicitly retains both incidence and standard. It also provides that the matter is to be tested whenever 'it is represented to the court' that one of the conditions has been satisfied. It has been held that merely to cross-examine so as to suggest the satisfaction of the invalidating conditions of s 76 is not sufficient.[7] This might have appeared to suggest that the court could no longer[8] take the point of its own motion, but any such argument has been pre-empted by explicit provision allowing such a course.[9] In most cases, of course, the defence will itself raise the point, usually with the prosecution informally and before the trial, so that a disputed confession will not be opened before its admissibility has been tested. Breach of the provisions of the Codes of Practice requiring the documentation of action by the police may operate to prevent the prosecution from being able to negate the exclusionary conditions of s 76.[10] While it has been held that the prosecution bears no burden of disproof of unfairness for the purposes of s 78,[11] it seems that if breaches are significant and substantial then there is a prima facie breach of the standards of fairness set by Parliament.[12]

5. Effect

The principal intended effect of the legislation is to exclude confessions as evidence of the truth of their contents, but this effect is qualified by further provisions also set out in s 76 as follows:

1   *R v McGovern* (1991) 92 Cr App Rep 228, at 234; but the conclusion is not inevitable *R v Gillard and Barrett* (1990) 92 Cr App Rep 61, at 65; *R v Geddis* (1992) Times, 28 December.
2   *Y v DPP* [1991] Crim LR 917.
3   *R v Hoyte* [1994] Crim LR 215 (a strong case since it was merely presumed that legal advice would have been taken). It is not enough that there was merely an opportunity to take legal advice if it were not, in fact, taken: *R v Glaves* [1993] Crim LR 685.
4   See *Y v DPP*, above.
5   *R v Neil* [1994] Crim LR 441.
6   See *DPP v Ping Lin* [1976] AC 574, at 597, at 599, [1975] 3 All ER 175 at 178 and 180. The standard of proof had however been considered doubtful by the Criminal Law Revision Committee (Cmnd 4991, Annex 2 p 213).
7   *R v Liverpool Juvenile Court, ex p R* [1988] QB 1, [1987] 2 All ER 668.
8   See the guidance provided in *Ajodha v The State* [1982] AC 204, at 222, [1981] 2 All ER 193, at 202
9   Section 76(3), in accordance with the Criminal Law Revision Committee's recommendation and draft Bill: Cmnd 4991, para 54, cl 2(3).
10   *R v Delaney* (1988) 88 Cr App Rep 338, at 342.
11   *Vel v Owen* (1987) 151 JP 510.
12   *R v Walsh* (1989) 91 Cr App Rep 161, at 165.

(4) The fact that a confession is wholly or partly excluded in pursuance of this section shall not affect the admissibility in evidence–

(a)   of any facts discovered as result of the confession; or

(b)   where the confession is relevant as showing that the accused speaks, writes or expresses himself in a particular way, of so much of the confession as is necessary to show that he does so.

(5) Evidence that a fact to which this subsection applies was discovered as a result of a statement made by an accused person shall not be admissible unless evidence of how it was discovered is given by him or on his behalf.

These sections raised three matters which require to be mentioned, the admissibility of subsequently discovered facts, the limited circumstantial use which can be made of confessions, and the extent to which any part of an excluded confession may be given when it is confirmed by finding real evidence which it mentions. All three of these matters have already been considered.[13]

B.   SILENCE[14]

At common law[15] it was clear that a suspect could remain silent in the face of police questioning;[16] it was however not at all clear that such silence could be used as evidence, or made the subject of comment at a subsequent trial.[17] Following a recommendation originally made in the Eleventh Report of the Criminal Law Revision Committee,[18] and despite rejection by two subsequent Royal Commissions,[19] the current position was established by s 34 of the Criminal Justice and Public Order Act 1994:[20]

(1)   Where, in any proceedings against a person for an offence, evidence is given that the accused–

(a)   at any time before he was charged with the offence, on being questioned under caution by a constable trying to discover whether or by whom the offence had been committed, failed to mention any fact relied on in his defence in those proceedings, or

(b)   on being charged with the offence or officially informed that the might be prosecuted for it, failed to mention any such fact,

---

13   See ch XI, section 3, above.

14   For judicial dissection of the concept of the right to silence see *R v Director of the Serious Fraud Office, ex p Smith* [1993] AC 1, at 30, 31, [1992] 3 All ER 456, at 463, 464. For academic commentary see Easton *Right to Silence* (1991); Greer (1990) 53 MLR 709.

15   For specific statutory modification see eg Criminal Justice Act 1987, s 2 abridging this right in cases of allegations of serious fraud.

16   *Rice v Connolly* [1966] 2 QB 414, [1966] 2 All ER 649.

17   Such controversy continues to trouble superior courts elsewhere: see, in Australia, *Pavic v R and Swaffield* (1998) 192 CLR 159; in Canada, *R v Crawford* [1995] 1 SCR 858.

18   Cmnd 4991, paras 28–52, draft bill, cl 1. Consolidated by the Report on Right to Silence Home Office 13 July 1989: see Zuckerman [1989] Crim LR 855; and promoted by Lord Lane CJ in *R v Alladice* (1988) 87 Cr App Rep 380, at 385.

19   Royal Commission on Criminal Procedure (1981) Cmnd 8092, para 5.13; Royal Commission on Criminal Justice (1993) Cm 2263, rec 82.

20   Reinforced by further sections relating in a broadly similar way to failure to account for ostensibly incriminating objects, substances and marks (s 36); and failure to account for ostensibly incriminating presence in a particular place (s 37). For commentary see Pattenden (1998) 2 E & P 141; Mirfield *Silence, Confessions and Improperly Obtained Evidence* pp 238–281 (1997).

being a fact which in the circumstances existing at the time the accused could reasonably have been expected to mention when so questioned, charged or informed, as the case may be, subsection (2) below applies.

(2) Where this section applies–
(c) the court, in determining whether there is a case to answer; and
(d) the court or jury, in determining whether the accused is guilty of the offence charged,
may draw such inferences from the failure as appear proper.

(3) Subject to any directions by the court, evidence tending to establish the failure may be given before or after evidence tending to establish the fact which the accused is alleged to have failed to mention.

This section applies to all those charged with the duty of investigating offences, and complements rather than replaces the inferences available to be drawn at common law. It has itself subsequently been supplemented by the provisions of Part I of the Criminal Procedure and Investigation Act 1996[1] which introduced a general obligation upon the accused to disclose the general nature of the defence, and details of any alibi.[2] Failure to do so is also sanctioned by the possibility of adverse comment, and inference.[3]

To a considerable extent s 34 mirrors recommendations earlier introduced in Northern Ireland.[4] It has been necessary to devise a new, and longer, form of caution.[5] It remains to be seen how these new provisions will be interpreted. It is arguable that little has been lost since the consensus of empirical research[6] established that very few of those questioned in police custody did remain wholly[7] silent.[8] It has indeed been suggested that the new law has provided an opportunity to improve the lot of the suspect since the discretion to exclude on the ground of fairness may extend to inferences from silence, if it is conditioned by defective or non-disclosure of the police case which the accused is required to meet.[9]

Under the old law appeals were heard upon the ground that the trial judge went too far when commenting in his summing up on the accused's silence when charged.[10] The upshot of most of those decisions was that, although the accused's silence could

1   See also Ch VI above.
2   Section 5.
3   Section 11(3).
4   Criminal Evidence (NI) Order 1988 (SI 1988/1987 (NI 20)); see Jackson [1991] Crim LR 404.
5   The current form still reminds the suspect of his right to remain silent while warning him of the dangers of doing so. This can cause problems in cases where the suspect is at the same time being interviewed in respect of a special statutory offence which carries different consequences if he remains silent, as in *R v Comrs Customs and Excise, ex p Mortimer* [1998] 3 All ER 229, [1999] 1 WLR 17.
6   Previous studies are summarised in Leng *The Right to Silence in Police Interrogation: A Study of Some of the Issues Underlying the Debate* (1993) Royal Commission Res St No 10. But see Williams (1997) 141 Sol Jo 566 for a survey showing that the new legislation has decreased the incidence of no comment interviews.
7   Answering some questions did not invest failure to answer others with special significance: *R v Henry* [1990] Crim LR 574.
8   Silence is a more opaque concept than is generally assumed, and certainly does not equate to failing to make a sound when questioned. Both making and failing to make sounds, may be quite unrelated to the questioning. See *Yisrael v District Court of New South Wales* (1996) 87 ACR 63, at 67.
9   Zuckerman 144 NLJ 1104 (1994).
10   The principal authorities included *R v Tate* [1908] 2 KB 680; *R v Feigenbaum* [1919] 1 KB 431; *R v Littleboy* [1934] 2 KB 408; *R v Hoare* [1966] 2 All ER 846, [1966] 1 WLR 762; *R v Sullivan* (1966) 51 Cr App Rep 102; *Hall v R* [1971] 1 All ER 322; *R v Gilbert* (1977) 66 Cr App Rep 237; *R v Raviraj* (1987) 85 Cr App Rep 93.

be treated as something which had a bearing on the weight of his evidence, it was not something which could support an inference that the story told by him in court was untrue, and still less that it amounted to corroboration of, or support for, the evidence given against him:[11]

> It is one thing to make an observation with regard to the force of an alibi, and to say that it is unfortunate that the defence was not set up at an earlier date so as to afford the opportunity of its being tested; it is another thing to employ that non-disclosure as evidence against the accused person, and as corroborating the evidence of an accomplice.

After those words were spoken s 11 of the Criminal Justice Act 1967[12] made special provision with regard to notice of alibis in the case of trials on indictment,[13] and it was held that the judge should not comment on the accused's failure to mention an alibi when arrested.[14]

Although said to be very fine,[15] the distinction made in the quotation above was applied to other defences[16] but the dominant view remained that the judge should generally make no comment on the accused's pre-trial silence when charged or questioned by someone in authority.[17]

It should however be noted that in certain situations the stringency of the prohibition was mitigated. For example if the accused and the person questioning him could be said to be on equal terms, a summing-up on the lines of Lord Atkinson's speech in *R v Christie*[18] might be appropriate. It is arguable that the presence of a solicitor equalises the terms,[19] and this may provide a partial explanation of the decision in *R v Smith*[20] where the Court of Appeal allowed comment on the accused's refusal during such an interview to permit a sample of his hair to be taken for comparison with hair found on an incriminating object. It was also sometimes felt to be incumbent upon the court to make some comment in connection with a different rule, such as the presumption of knowledge arising from possession of recently stolen property.[1] Nor was it improper for the judge to emphasise both the nature of possible adverse inferences and the prohibition upon drawing them.[2]

It should be noted that the conditions under which s 34 operates to permit an adverse inference are somewhat confined. It applies only to failures at interviews with those charged with the duty of investigating offences,[3] and then only when the interview is conducted under caution with a view to discover whether a crime has been committed,[4] and if so by whom.[5]

---

11   Lord Hewart CJ in *R v Littleboy*, above, at 413.
12   Repealed and superseded by the Criminal Procedure and Investigation Act 1996.
13   See p 29 above.
14   *R v Lewis* (1973) 57 Cr App Rep 860.
15   Lord Salmon in *R v Sullivan*, above, at 105; apparently on the basis that it was too favourable to the accused.
16   See *R v Ryan* (1964) 50 Cr App Rep 144, at 148.
17   *R v Gilbert*, above, and further above; see also *R v Coombs* [1983] NZLR 748.
18   [1914] AC 545. See also *R v Horne* [1990] Crim LR 188.
19   *R v Chandler* [1976] 3 All ER 105, [1976] 1 WLR 585.
20   (1985) 81 Cr App Rep 286.
1   *R v Aves* [1950] 2 All ER 330, 34 Cr App Rep 159; *R v Raviraj*, above.
2   *R v McNamara*, (1988) 87 Cr App Rep 246, at 253.
3   Section 34(4) expands the scope of s 34(1) in this respect, Cp the Police and Criminal Evidence Act 1984, s 67(9) below p 631.
4   Section 34(1)(a). It also applies to similar failures upon being charged, or informed of possible prosecution: s 34(1)(b). It seems however that the police are entitled to suspend their belief that there is sufficient evidence to charge the accused pending his response to questioning, otherwise C11.4 of the Code of Practice would compel them to charge and desist from questioning: *R v McGuinness* [1999] Crim LR 318.
5   The person interrogated need not be the principal, still less only, suspect.

It applies also only if the accused fails to mention a fact *relied on in his defence.* The concept of reliance is not intrinsically clear, and in *R v N*[6] was strictly construed to exclude the accused's explanation of a fact which was itself adduced as part of the prosecution's case.[7] It is a consequence of this limitation that the normal time for raising the matter has been held to be only after all the evidence is in.[8] It is hard to reconcile so restrictive a construction of this condition with the permission explicitly offered by s 34(2)(c) to take the failure to mention such a fact into account in determining whether or not the accused has a case to answer. If it is to be so used, it must be determined before the matter comes before the jury, which implies that the accused must seek exclusion of evidence of the silence altogether, yet the Court of Appeal has regarded this as applicable only in a quite exceptional situation.[9] It has been recommended that the prosecution should content itself initially with establishing that the accused did remain silent during interview,[10] and wait for the case to develop before arguing for an adverse inference.

A more generic condition may be implied from the considerations that the matter must be one which it would have been reasonable for the accused to mention, and that only *proper* inferences can be drawn. As yet the boundaries of reason and propriety remain to be clarified. It has, nevertheless, emerged that merely to assert that refusal to mention facts was maintained on legal advice, will not, by itself, be sufficient, even though offered for other than merely tactical reasons.[11] The accused is put in something of a dilemma in this situation since it has been held both that it will rarely be sufficient to refer only to legal advice in the abstract, but that any elaboration of the basis of the advice will amount to a waiver of legal professional privilege,[12] which might well have fatal consequences.[13] Nor is it necessarily sufficient that the police hold back some information[14] in their possession from the suspect.[15] It has indeed been stated[16] that the only obligation is that the police should not actively mislead the suspect. In *R v Condron and Condron* the court approached the problem of what was reasonable from the opposite direction, and held that the jury should be directed that an adverse inference should be drawn only if subsequent fabrication of the fact relied upon were the *only* rational explanation for such failure. This seems remarkably generous to the suspect, since it requires little ingenuity to suggest some possible alternative

6   (1998) Times, 13 February.

7   It is immaterial whether the fact is put in evidence as part of the prosecution case, or as part of the defence case, including reliance by the defence on a fact elicited in cross-examination of a prosecution witness. But if no such fact is put in evidence, then there is nothing upon which the section can bite: *R v Moshaid* [1998] Crim LR 420; *R v Bowers, Taylor and Millan* [1998] Crim LR 817.

8   *R v Condron and Condron* [1997] 1 WLR 827, [1997] 1 Cr App Rep 185, at 837C, 196G.

9   Ibid at 837A, 196E; see also *R v Argent* [1997] 2 Cr App Rep 27, at 31D-F.

10   Although in *R v Griffin* [1998] Crim LR 418 the Court of Appeal somewhat surprisingly felt that it was not necessarily more prejudicial than probative for the prosecution to read, even at that early stage, the questions to which no answer had been vouchsafed.

11   *R v Condron and Condron* at 833, 192. In this respect following the Northern Irish approach, see Jackson [1995] Crim LR 587.

12   It seems unlikely that the accused will be prevented from testifying to the advice on account of the hearsay rule: see *R v Davis* [1998] Crim LR 659.

13   *R v Bowden* [1999] 1 WLR 823; *R v Roble* [1997] Crim LR 449. In *R v Condron and Condron* this prospect was regarded as so dire that the defence should be warned of its impending danger by the judge.

14   Including information about the status of an undercover officer: *R v Edwards* [1997] Crim LR 348.

15   In *R v Roble* an extreme failure to disclose was posited, and although in *R v Argent* above the court seemed more sympathetic to the argument that the accused was reasonable in meeting silence with silence, it still felt, and indeed held, that an adverse inference was justified despite less than full, or usual, disclosure there by the police.

16   *R v Imran and Hussein* [1997] Crim LR 754, the line between actively misleading and deliberately failing to disclose seems somewhat chimerical.

explanations, and it is hardly surprising that it has now been reined back.[17] It is clearly difficult to generalise in this area, and in *R v Argent* Lord Bingham CJ was anxious to stress the wide range of factors to be taken into account, and the balance between the subjective elements of factors peculiar to the particular accused, and the objective element of what is in principle reasonable.

If the conditions for drawing an inference are not satisfied, either at common law or under the Act, then it is desirable that the jury should be so instructed.[18] Such a direction must be especially sensitively drafted when the accused has been advised to remain silent by his lawyer.[19] It may also need to be very strong if the evidence of silence has been in some way prejudicial.[20] It seems however that the judge need not instruct the jury of other possible reasons for silence than those consistent with guilt. This seems very odd by comparison with the obligation to do so if the accused does not remain silent, but instead tells lies.[1]

Section 34 is supplemented by ss 36 and 37 of the Criminal Justice and Public Order Act 1994. These sections were not recommended in the Eleventh Report of the Criminal Law Revision Committee, and find their origin in the Republic of Ireland.[2] In broad and crude outline they permit adverse inferences against a suspect[3] who fails, when taxed by an investigator, to offer an explanation of objects or marks, on his person, on his clothes, in his possession or at the place of his arrest,[4] or under similar conditions[5] fails to offer an explanation of his presence at the scene of the crime at about the time of its commission.

Some safeguard is afforded by s 38(3) which provides that a case to answer or a conviction may not be based *solely*[6] on adverse inferences under the scheme. As noted above[7] it is only in relation to s 35 that the inference cannot count towards a case to answer.

It has been questioned how compatible these provisions are with the European Convention of Human Rights.[8] Although the European Court of Human Rights upheld a conviction supported by adverse inferences from silence under the comparable Northern Ireland provisions, in the course of its judgment it took the opportunity to refer to the right of silence and privilege against self-incrimination as 'generally recognised international standards which lie at the heart of a notion of fair procedure

---

17   *R v Daniel* [1998] Crim LR 628, by adding to subsequent fabrication such broad reasons as reluctance to be questioned further, or to respond to enquiry about prima facie embarrassing features of the case.

18   *R v McGarry* [1998] 3 All ER 805, [1999] 1 Cr App Rep 377; *R v Bowers, Taylor and Millan* [1998] Crim LR 817.

19   *R v Moshaid* [1998] Crim LR 420.

20   As it was held to have been in *R v Griffin* [1998] Crim LR 418. See also *R v Pointer* [1997] Crim LR 676.

1   Cp *R v Lucas* [1981] QB 720, [1981] 2 All ER 1008. The apparent anomaly was however rejected in *R v Napper* (1996) 161 JP 16, at 23 (s 35 was there being considered).

2   Criminal Justice Act 1984, ss 18, 19. They came into English law via Northern Ireland, but it should be noted that in origin they were confined to trials for a limited range of offences; that they are subject to a constitutional guarantee of proportionality: *Heaney v Ireland* [1996] 1 IR 244; and that proposals to apply them generally, as in England, have encountered significant resistance in the Republic.

3   Who must under these two provisions have been arrested.

4   Section 36.

5   There is however an enigmatic difference in the tense of the opening words.

6   It is not absolutely clear that the prosecution cannot add together adverse inferences from more than one of the sections, see Mirfield *op cit* p 269, but it is submitted that the better view is that it may not. The same presumably applies to the cumulation of inferences from different instances of silence within the same category.

7   At p 385.

8   Munday [1996] Crim LR 370.

under article 6.'[9] The Court also takes a very strong position on access to legal advice, and indeed allowed Murray's appeal on that basis. It is not inconceivable that in a less strong case than that of *Murray*, and one in which access to legal advice was more significant in its consequences the Court would find the regime of the Criminal Justice and Public Order Act 1994 unpalatable. It certainly seems odd to elevate the privilege against self-incrimination, the right to silence and access to a lawyer as among the most fundamental of human rights, and then to condone the exercise of those rights on the advice of the lawyer as grounds for conviction.

C. QUESTIONING SUSPECTS[10]

This topic was put on a new footing by the Police and Criminal Evidence Act 1984 and the Codes of Practice issued thereunder.[11] Their application and interpretation have generated a considerable amount of modern case law.[12] The whole subject was reviewed by the Royal Commission on Criminal Justice in 1994,[13] and some of its recommendations implemented in the Criminal Justice and Public Order Act 1994. It is proposed to give here first a brief account of the development of the modern law, and then a short summary of its operation, distinguishing special rules which apply to questioning children and the mentally impaired.

1. Development

During the nineteenth century the police gradually assumed the major responsibility for the detection, apprehension, and questioning of those suspected of the commission of crimes. They were also expected to collect evidence for, and to initiate, most prosecutions in England and Wales. Statutory authorisation for many of these functions was often absent, and its absence sometimes created problems, especially in relation to questioning, given the strict limitations on compulsory questioning by judicial tribunals,[14] and given the combination of stringency and uncertainty surrounding the exclusion of incriminating statements made to persons in authority. After being highlighted by a number of inconsistent decisions, and failing any direct legislative intervention, the matter was regulated by the judges who issued a set of rules to guide the police in 1912. These rules were supplemented from time to time by Home Office circulars, and in 1964 replaced by a further set of Judges' Rules.[15] The general scheme was that admissibility continued to be governed by the general law relating to confessions, but it was still possible for the trial judge to exclude evidence obtained as a result of a breach of the Judges' Rules at his discretion.[16] The Police and Criminal Evidence Act 1984, as noted above, in s 76 adopted a less stringent test for inadmissibility, but in s 66 prescribed the publication of Codes of Police Practice in relation to search and seizure, and to detention, treatment, questioning and

9   *Murray v United Kingdom* (1996) 22 EHRR 29, at 60, where the rest of the case against the accused was very strong.
10   For much valuable background to the current position see Gooderson (1970) 48 Can BR 270.
11   As recommended by the Royal Commission on Criminal Procedure (1981) Cmnd 8092.
12   Already described in *R v Keenan* [1990] 2 QB 54, [1989] 3 All ER 598, at 59, 601 as a 'flood'.
13   Cm 2263.
14   See Indictable Offences Act 1848 and Criminal Evidence Act 1898.
15   Issued as a *Practice Note* by the Court of Criminal Appeal [1964] 1 All ER 237, [1964] 1 WLR 152, and supplemented by Administrative Directions in Home Office Circular No 31/1964.
16   See above p 620.

identification.[17] Since then, as noted above,[18] the situation has been directly affected by the imposition of formal sanction upon failure to mention when questioned matters later relied upon at trial, or to explain suspicious marks or presence at the scene of a crime. It has also been affected indirectly by the new obligation[19] to disclose the nature of the defence and any alibi in advance of trial.

2.   Operation

The Codes of Practice are designed to regulate the rights of a suspect to communication with third parties, rights to legal advice and to medical treatment; and to provide guidance to the police on such things as the conduct of searches, the administration of a caution, the provision of interpreters, and in all cases the compilation of adequate documentation of what occurs. It is worth considering in more detail the questions of access to legal advice, to whom and when the Codes apply, their guidance, and the effects of breach of their provisions by the police.

(i)   Access to legal advice[20]

The right of access to a solicitor in a police station[1] is so fundamental a part of the scheme of the Police and Criminal Evidence Act 1984[2] that a court is highly likely to exercise its discretion to exclude a confession obtained after wrongful refusal of such access,[3] and to construe the grounds[4] for proper refusal of such access narrowly.[5] In *R v Alladice*[6] however the court was able to disregard a breach of these provisions on the basis that the suspect asserted, on the voir dire, not that in the absence of legal advice he had spoken instead of remaining silent, but that he had not confessed at all. It will be rare for that to be regarded as a sufficient reason as the accused might still be

---

17   Supplemented by Home Office circulars 22/1992 of 20 February 1992 and 7/1993 of 27 January 1993 announcing the availability of two training booklets on interviewing practice. The value of a legislative scheme has been endorsed in New Zealand: *R v Mitchell* [1996] 3 NZLR 302, at 305. In some jurisdictions the courts have themselves had to construe the principles from case law; see eg the encapsulation of the rules applicable in New South Wales into eleven (non-exhaustive) propositions in *R v Plevac* (1995) 84 ACR 570, at 580.

18   At p 624.

19   Under the Criminal Procedure and Investigation Act 1996, see above p 29.

20   See Police and Criminal Evidence Act 1984, s 58; Code C esp paras 3.1(ii), 6 passim. The need for such access is well illustrated by the Canadian case of *R v Burlingham* [1995] 2 SCR 206 where the accused misunderstood the legal implications of the offer made to him by the police to induce him to confess. It is also necessary in Canada to readvise the suspect of his right to legal advice if he indicates the possible commission of other offences: *R v Sawatsky* (1997) 150 DLR 4th 750.

1   But not necessarily at home: *RSPCA v Eager* [1995] Crim LR 59.

2   It is not a common law right, and does not exist in Northern Ireland: *R v Chief Constable of the RUC, ex p Begley* [1997] 4 All ER 833, [1997] 1 WLR 1475.

3   Which includes failure to inform the accused of the presence in the station of a solicitor called on his behalf: *R v Franklin* (1994) Times, 16 June. But see *R v Oliphant* [1992] Crim LR 40. In *Mohammed (Allie) v State* [1999] 2 WLR 552 the Privy Council even held that breach of a constitutional guarantee of a right to be informed of the right to consult a lawyer did not automatically lead to the exercise of the judge's discretion to exclude a confession made as a result.

4   As set out in Police and Criminal Evidence Act 1984, s 58(8), Code C para 6.3 and Annex B, as amended.

5   *R v Samuel* [1988] QB 615, [1988] 2 All ER 135.

6   (1988) 87 Cr App Rep 380.

prejudiced in the subsequent proceedings since he will be less able to corroborate his account of what has taken place.[7] If the refusal of access does not influence the accused's decision to speak, then the discretion to exclude will not be exercised.[8] Provision of access may indeed assist the prosecution since legal advice can neutralise otherwise effective breaches of the Codes.[9]

(ii) Range of application

If these provisions conferring a right to legal advice are to be effective it becomes increasingly important to regulate any other contact between the police and the suspect. Two issues need to be considered, first whether the investigator is a person to whom the provisions of the Code apply, and second whether the occasion is one to which they apply. They will be considered separately.

(a) Person

Although the Codes of Practice address themselves to 'police officers',[10] s 67(9) of the Police and Criminal Evidence Act 1984 extends their ambit to other persons 'charged with the duty of investigating offences or charging offenders'.[11] Code C has thus been applied to other investigators, both official[12] and private.[13] Nor is it possible to evade the provisions of the Code merely by acting under cover,[14] or through an 'agent or stooge.'[15] On the other hand it does not apply to foreign investigators,[16] to psychiatrists when attempting to determine whether the accused is fit to plead,[17] or to headmasters.[18] In such cases the only question is one of the effect of the procedure on the fairness of the proceedings, though the Code may nevertheless be used as an indicator of this.[19] Even where the Code does apply this remains the decisive question,

7   *R v Parris* (1988) 89 Cr App Rep 68.
8   *R v Alladice*, above; *R v Dunford* (1990) 91 Cr App Rep 150; *R v Chahal* [1992] Crim LR 124; but cp *R v Walsh* (1989) 91 Cr App Rep 161.
9   *R v Dunn* (1990) 91 Cr App Rep 237 (presence inhibits fabrication); *R v Hoyte* [1994] Crim LR 215 (advice about inadmissibility of earlier statement following breaches frees subsequent repetition from taint).
10   Whether or not at the time acting in the roles mentioned in s 67(9): *R v Sparks* [1991] Crim LR 128 (policeman sitting in station with eventual accused, but as friend).
11   A similar limitation applies at common law in Australia where it was determined that private citizens who had arrested children for stealing from a supermarket need not follow the procedures which bound the police in interviewing children: *H v Hill* (1993) 112 FLR 353.
12   See *R v Seelig* [1991] 4 All ER 429, [1992] 1 WLR 149 (inspector under Companies Act 1985); *R v Okafor* [1994] 3 All ER 741, 99 Cr App Rep 97; *R v Weerdesteyn* [1995] 1 Cr App Rep 405; *R v Courtney* [1995] Crim LR 63 (Customs officers); *R v Souter* [1995] Crim LR 729 (military police).
13   See *R v Twaites and Brown* (1990) 92 Cr App Rep 106 (company's internal investigators); *R v Bayliss* (1993) 98 Cr App Rep 235 (store detective); *Joy v Federation Against Copyright Theft Ltd* [1993] Crim LR 588 (Federation's investigator); *RSPCA v Eager* [1995] Crim LR 59 (RSPCA inspector), apparently equating having a duty with being charged with a duty.
14   *R v Bryce* [1992] 4 All ER 567, 95 Cr App Rep 320.
15   *R v Roberts* [1997] 1 Cr App Rep 217, at 232D. See in Australia, *R v O'Neill* (1995) 81 ACR 458.
16   *R v Quinn* [1990] Crim LR 581 (Irish police); *R v Konscol* [1993] Crim LR 950 (Belgian customs). See also in Canada *R v Terry* [1996] 2 SCR 207 (US police).
17   *R v McDonald* [1991] Crim LR 122.
18   *G v DPP* [1997] 2 All ER 755, [1997] 2 Cr App Rep 78.
19   Thus in *R v Smith* [1994] 1 WLR 1396, 99 Cr App Rep 233 it was held that although the Bank of England's supervisor of a banking institution fell outside the ambit of s 67(9) a statement was nevertheless to be excluded because of shortfalls from Code C even though it was not strictly applicable.

and failure to observe some aspects is unlikely to lead to exclusion. Thus neither an undercover policeman,[20] nor a customs officer on first encounter,[1] is required to administer a caution, nor is a private investigator, working in a private residence, bound to follow minutely the provisions as to recording which apply to police officers interrogating suspects in a police station.[2]

(b)   Interview

Any questioning[3] of a suspect designed to obtain admissions of guilt will constitute an 'interview' and require the suspect to be cautioned,[4] however informal and unpremeditated the situation,[5] even if it encompasses no more than one question.[6] The sequence of questions is to be treated as a whole for this purpose.[7] It has been said[8] not to be within the spirit of Act or Code to give 'interview' a restricted meaning. Code C has indeed been revised so as to apply some of its requirements, such as those relating to recording,[9] outside even this extended sense of 'interview'.[10] It may be preferable to adopt such an approach rather than to adopt an unduly rigid approach to the interpretation of the Code.[11] It should further be noted that the revised form of the Code was designed to clear up some of the confusion that had been created by the original provisions.[12] Although the structure and terms of the amendment are far from clear, it has been held that their general tenor is to enlarge rather than to constrict the concept of an 'interview'.[13]

(iii)   Conduct of questioning

As noted above the Code starts to govern questioning as soon as the police officer has grounds for suspecting the person questioned of having committed a crime;[14] thereafter as soon as the police officer decides to arrest the suspect he must normally

---

20   *R v Christou* [1992] QB 979, [1992] 4 All ER 559 (so long as this is not used as a subterfuge to evade the restrictions of the Code) ; nor need he follow the provisions of the Code if his aim is not so much the investigation of past offences, as to secure evidence of future plans: *R v Lin, Hung and Tsui* [1995] Crim LR 817.

1   *R v Shah* [1994] Crim LR 125, unless he already has reasonable grounds to suspect the commission of an offence: *R v Nelson and Rose* [1998] 2 Cr App Rep 399. See in Australia, *R v Raso* (1993) 115 FLR 319.

2   *Stilgoe v Eager* (1994) Times, 27 January.

3   If no questions are asked but the police merely listen and note down information then it is not an interview within the Code, *R v Menard* [1995] 1 Cr App Rep 306. This seems likely to be a rare occurrence, and any suggestion that it has occurred will need rigorous scrutiny.

4   See Code C note 11A; *Batley v DPP* (1998) Times, 5 March.

5   *R v Absolam* (1988) 88 Cr App Rep 332; *R v Keenan* [1990] 2 QB 54, [1989] 3 All ER 598. Code C para 11.1 requires interviews after arrest normally to take place in a police station.

6   *R v Ward* (1993) 98 Cr App Rep 337.

7   *R v Weekes* (1993) 97 Cr App Rep 222.

8   *R v Matthews* (1989) 91 Cr App Rep 43, at 47, 48.

9   As in *R v Miller* [1998] Crim LR 209 in respect of spontaneous remarks.

10   Code C, para 11.13. It should be noted that the Court regards changes to the Code as indicative of a new standard of fairness for the purposes of s 78: see *Ward*, above.

11   As indicated in *R v Marsh* [1991] Crim LR 455, though such flexibility seems more appropriate not so much to the question of breach, as to the consequences of any such breach.

12   See eg *R v Maguire* (1989) 90 Cr App Rep 115. The problem of impracticality identified in *R v Parchment* [1991] Crim LR 626 was solved by the re-drafted para 11.10.

13   *R v Cox* (1992) 96 Cr App Rep 464, at 470. See also *R v Goddard* [1994] Crim LR 46.

14   Para 11.1A. But not to preliminary questioning before this stage has been reached: *R v Nelson and Rose* above (whether bag being carried through Customs is the property of its carrier); especially if there are grounds to infer the answers to the questions in any event: *Whelehan v DPP* [1995] RTR 177 (whether person in driving seat of car at the roadside had driven there).

conduct any further questioning only at a police station,[15] and once the police officer believes that a prosecution should be brought, and that there is sufficient evidence for it to succeed, he must cease questioning.[16] Some of the most beneficial features of the Codes are its insistence upon the provision of documentation of what has occurred between the police and the accused[17] as much, if not more, outside, as within the confines of the police station. It has been said that the importance of these rules can scarcely be over-emphasised.[18] Despite doubts in some quarters as to its efficacy,[19] automatic recording of interviews relating to indictable offences has been made mandatory.[20] The Code contains detailed guidance as to the care and treatment of suspects, and in many ways guarantees the observation of these rules by allocating supervision to separate custody officers, and as noted above by provision for documentation. Even so complaints of breach of the provisions of the Codes are often made, and the sanctions for any such breach are considered below.

(iv) Effects of breach

The Royal Commission on Criminal Procedure was unhappy about reliance upon the use of an exclusionary discretion as the primary sanction for breach of the Code, and the early drafts of the Police and Criminal Evidence Bill contained no explicit reference to any such discretion, although *R v Sang* provided common law authority for its existence in relation to 'admissions and confessions and generally with regard to evidence obtained from the accused after the commission of the offence'.[1] At a late stage in its passage new and explicit provision was made in the 1984 Act for such a discretion:[2]

> (1) In any proceedings the court may refuse to allow evidence on which the prosecution proposes to rely to be given if it appears to the court that, having regard to all the circumstances in which the evidence was obtained, the admission of the evidence would have such an adverse effect upon the fairness of the proceedings that the court ought not to admit it.
>
> (2) Nothing in this section shall prejudice any rule of law requiring a court to exclude evidence.

It should be noted that sub-s (2) is designed to preserve the exclusionary rule set out in s 76. This was necessary because this section, unlike the clause it replaced, is of general application, and applies across the whole range of the law of evidence in criminal

---

15 Para 11.1, subject only to delay on account of danger to evidence or persons, the risk of alerting others or hindering the recovery of property. For criticism of any attempt to abuse this exception see *R v Khan* [1993] Crim LR 54.
16 Para 11.4, apart from asking whether the suspect has anything else he wants to say at that point.
17 Recording has been required of spontaneous remarks at the conclusion of a formal interview after the tape has been turned off: *R v Scott* [1991] Crim LR 56. See also in Australia on the value of recording, *R v Stewart* (1993) 2 Tas R 274; *R v Smith* (1996) 86 ACR 398.
18 *R v Canale* [1990] 2 All ER 187, at 190, 91 Cr App Rep 1, at 5.
19 Extending to video as well as to audio recording, see McConville [1992] Crim LR 532.
20 SI 1991/2686. In Australia some difficulty has arisen in construing the comparable provisions: see *Pollard v R* (1992) 176 CLR 177.
1 [1980] AC 402, at 437, [1979] 2 All ER 1222, at 1231.
2 Section 78.

proceedings.[3] Nor does this new discretion derogate from the common law discretion[4] discussed in *Sang*, since s 82(3) provides that:

> Nothing in this Part of this Act shall prejudice any power of a court to exclude evidence (whether by preventing questions from being put or otherwise) at its discretion.

Section 78 was expressed in such vague terms that it was hard to anticipate how it would be applied.[5] There was indeed some warrant for regarding s 76 as constituting an exclusive new codification of the rules relating to confessions, but as noted above any such view was rejected at an early stage in *R v Mason*.[6] Although, as also noted, the Codes of Practice have been accepted as providing some indication of the satisfaction of the conditions of admissibility under s 76, their implementation has mainly been by way of triggering the exercise of the discretion to exclude conferred by s 78.

In many, if not most, cases discretionary exclusion is held in reserve in case a claim under s 76 should fail.[7] The principal differences between the two sections are that exclusion under s 76 is by rule,[8] and that under s 78 by discretion. In the case of s 76 the burden of disproof of the relevant conditions is always on the prosecution, whereas under s 78 the incidence of burden of persuading the court to exercise its discretion is equivocal.[9] It has been held that it is not for the judge to exclude under s 78 on his own initiative in the absence of argument by the defence that he should do so.[10] Procedurally s 78 presents serious difficulties to the judge who has to exercise his discretion before all the evidence and relevant information is before him, and in particular in ignorance of the line of defence to the main charge, and how the accused will react, so far as himself testifying is concerned, whichever way the discretion is exercised.[11] This presents further problems on appeal when the court has to put itself in the position of the trial judge, and ignore any such matters even though they have by then been revealed.[12]

The relationship between breaches of the Codes and the operation of s 78 have come before the Court of Appeal in two main contexts; first, where the trial judge has found no breach of the Codes, and has not otherwise excluded the evidence under his discretion and, second, those where the trial judge has found breach of the Codes, but has exercised his discretion against excluding the evidence. The Court of Appeal is in principle more likely to intervene in the former situation in which the judge may not

---

3   'Proceedings' are defined as criminal proceedings by s 82(1).
4   Indeed in *Thompson v R* [1998] AC 811 the Privy Council approved the remarks of Lord Taylor CJ in *R v Christou* [1992] QB 979, [1992] 4 All ER 559 that there is no difference between them in this context.
5   See remarks to this effect in *R v Keenan* [1990] 2 QB 54, [1989] 3 All ER 598, at 62, 603.
6   [1987] 3 All ER 481, at 484, [1988] 1 WLR 139, at 144.
7   See, for example, *R v Delaney* (1989) 88 Cr App Rep 338, at 340; *R v McGovern* (1991) 92 Cr App Rep 228, at 235.
8   In *R v Chung* (1991) 92 Cr App Rep 314, at 323 the Court of Appeal declared its greater readiness to review the decision because it had been arrived at under s 76 as well as s 78.
9   In *R v Keenan* [1990] 2 QB 54, at 63, [1989] 3 All ER 598, at 605 it appears to be suggested that it varies according to the circumstances, though in *Vel v Owen* (1987) 151 JP 510 it was said not to be borne by the prosecution. In Australia it is borne by the accused: see *MacPherson v R* (1981) 147 CLR 512, at 519, 520; *Cleland v R* (1982) 151 CLR 1, at 19, 20 where Deane J applied the same principle to the *Bunning v Cross* discretion.
10   *R v Raphaie* [1996] Crim LR 812.
11   These difficulties are explained at some length in *R v Keenan* [1990] 2 QB 54, [1989] 3 All ER 598.
12   *R v Parris* (1988) 89 Cr App Rep 68.

have addressed his mind to the exercise of the discretion at all,[13] or only upon a hypothetical basis.[14]

In either case review of the trial judge's exercise of discretion is a limited exercise, determined by *Wednesbury* principles, and not by those appropriate to wrong determinations of law or fact.[15] It might also have been thought that in no case could unfairness not resulting in unreliability of outcome be regarded as sufficient to allow an appeal after the amendment of the Criminal Appeal Act 1968, but this awaits final resolution.[16]

In *R v Walsh*[17] the Court of Appeal took the view that any breach of the Codes impairs the fairness of the proceedings, though it also pointed out that s 78 seems by the use of the phrase 'such an adverse effect' to contemplate some situations of venial unfairness insufficient to justify the exclusion of evidence thereby obtained because the effect is not adverse enough.[18] Any breach should be 'significant and substantial', and while bad faith might exalt into that category behaviour which might otherwise fall short, the converse did not follow. If there was significant and substantial unfairness, directed against the complainant,[19] then it would be sufficient to justify discretionary exclusion whether or not there were bad faith. The basic problem is that the Codes of Practice cover a multitude of topics, occurring at different stages in the investigation and prosecution of crime, and it is far from obvious that all can be brought within the precise terms of s 78. Conversely there may well be other matters which are not dealt with under the Codes which should trigger such an exclusionary discretion.[20] It has been held in Australia that such a discretion should be employed to exclude from the record of a confession any lengthy argumentative assertions of guilt made by the interrogators.[1]

13 In *R v Parris* above the trial judge appears to have been under the impression that he was obliged to consider s 78 only if satisfied that a breach of the Code had been shown.
14 See *R v Samuel* [1988] QB 615, [1988] 2 All ER 135.
15 *Thompson v R* [1998] AC 811. See further above p 176. In Scotland fairness plays a larger role, and appeals have been allowed on the basis that the issue of fairness ought not to have been left to the jury: *Harley and Roche v HM Advocate* 1995 SCCR 595.
16 Cp *R v Mullen* (1999) Times, 15 February allowing pre-trial acts not leading to an unreliable outcome at trial to be sufficient, with *R v Callaghan* (5 March 1999, unreported), CA holding that where an erroneous decision on admissibility of evidence led to a plea of guilty an appeal would not be allowed on the basis of being unsafe, in the absence of unreliability of outcome. See further above p 200.
17 (1989) 91 Cr App Rep 161, at 163.
18 See also *R v Parris* (1988) 89 Cr App Rep 68, at 72; *R v Rajakuruna* [1991] Crim LR 458. But see *R v Fennelley* [1989] Crim LR 142 where it is hard to see why failing to tell a man why he was being searched so impaired the fairness of the proceedings as to lead to the exclusion of the real evidence so found. For a clear case of a breach regarded as insignificant see *R v Courtney* [1995] Crim LR 63 (note of answer not shown by Customs officer to accused when clear that he would make no further statement)
19 *R v Roberts* [1997] 1 Cr App Rep 217.
20 See *R v Woodall* [1989] Crim LR 288 where there appears neither to have been a breach of the Code nor any unfairness in obtaining the admission, but its use was nevertheless regarded as making subsequent proceedings unfair since it had been volunteered 'off the record', and no subsequent reference had been made to it until the first day of the trial; in *R v Pall* (1992) 156 JP 424 it was indicated that a caution should be given after arrest but before a voluntary statement even though the Code is silent as to this situation.
1   *R v Kallis* [1994] 2 Qd R 88.

3.   Special cases

The Code of Practice is also concerned to prevent statements being taken from juveniles, the mentally ill, the mentally handicapped, those incapacitated by drink or drugs, non-English speakers, or the deaf, except upon the satisfaction of appropriate conditions, just because they may be unreliable.[2] Accordingly breach of the Code in relation to such matters has led to discretionary exclusion under s 78.[3] The discretion conferred by s 78 also provides a means whereby statements spontaneously[4] blurted out by those so disadvantaged may be excluded.[5] Special mention may be made of the rules relating to children and the mentally impaired.

(i)   Children[6]

In the case of children Code C makes special provision for the presence during the interview of an appropriate adult,[7] who may be a parent, social worker or failing them any responsible adult over 18 and not a police officer or person employed by the police.[8] The appropriate adult[9] should act as more than an observer, and should be informed of his role in advising the child of any unfair conduct by the police and in assisting communication.[10] It should be recognised that children are likely to be especially vulnerable, and that unfairness may be triggered at an earlier stage than in the case of an adult.[11]

(ii)   The mentally impaired[12]

Code C also prescribes a special regime for such persons,[13] requiring the attendance at interview of an appropriate adult,[14] except in situations of urgency.[15] Despite this apparently mandatory requirement, s 77 of the Police and Criminal Evidence Act 1984

---

2   See Cmnd 8092, para 4.133.
3   *R v Fogah* [1989] Crim LR 141 (juvenile, and no appropriate adult); *Timothy v DPP* [1989] Crim LR 893 (drunkenness, though a note of a request for a specimen of breath was not excluded); but see *R v Clarke* [1989] Crim LR 892 (deaf, but discretion not exercised because the condition was not known to the police).
4   A wholly spontaneous statement has been held not to amount to an 'interview': *R v Menard* [1995] 1 Cr App Rep 306.
5   Compare *R v S and J* (1983) 32 SASR 174.
6   Described as 'juveniles', and defined in para 1.5 as those persons who appear to be under the age of 17 in the absence of evidence to the contrary.
7   And in para 3.7 for the person responsible for the welfare of the child to be informed of his arrest and whereabouts.
8   Para 1.7(a).
9   Exceptionally there may be more than one.
10 Para 11.16, though if he does so act it is not fatal that he has not been so informed: *H and M v DPP* [1998] Crim LR 653. For the position in Australia see *R v H* (1996) 85 ACR 481.
11 See *Codona v HM Advocate* 1996 SLT 1100.
12 This term is used descriptively rather than as a term of art; different categorisations and more specific terminology apply in different situations.
13 Para 1.4, referring to the mentally disordered or handicapped, and to those mentally incapable of understanding questioning and replies. Para 3.10 requires diagnosis to determine whether this condition applies to be conducted as soon as possible.
14 Para 1.7(b) see also note 1E. For appraisal see Hodgson [1997] Crim LR 785.
15 Para 11.1 and Annex C.

prescribes, in the case of the mentally handicapped,[16] a special warning to the jury against convicting on the basis wholly or substantially[17] of a confession, if it was made otherwise than in the presence of an independent person.[18] This seems to contemplate not only the tendering of statements obtained in breach of the Codes,[19] but also in that situation judicial abstinence from the exercise of any exclusionary discretion.[20] Indeed in *R v Bailey*[1] the court went further[2] and prescribed a more detailed warning of the reasons for the mentally handicapped confessing falsely, and an examination of their possible effect in the light of the detailed facts of the case. It may sometimes be necessary to call evidence as to events at a relevant interview with a mentally impaired suspect to determine whether any confession made in the absence of an appropriate adult is reliable.[3]

16 Defined by s 77(3) as those 'in a state of arrested or incomplete development of mind which includes significant impairment of intelligence and social functioning.' This has been interpreted as relating more to susceptibility to pressure than in terms of abstract ability as enumerated in tests: *R v Raghip* (1991) Times, 5 December; *R v Kenny* [1994] Crim LR 284.

17 So not if the effect of the confession is swamped by the rest of the evidence: *R v Campbell* [1995] Crim LR 157.

18 Not necessarily the same as an appropriate adult for the purposes of the Code: see *R v Lewis* [1996] Crim LR 260.

19 In *R v Lamont* [1989] Crim LR 813 the Court of Appeal insisted upon such a warning being given in an appropriate case, and because it had not, was able to abstain from deciding whether the evidence should have been excluded altogether.

20 There is some suggestion in *R v Moss* (1990) 91 Cr App Rep 371 that the discretion would more readily be exercised in relation to a series than to one interview in isolation. The suggestion that discretionary exclusion is mandatory in these circumstances was specifically rejected in *R v Law-Thompson* [1997] Crim LR 674.

1 [1995] 2 Cr App Rep 262.

2 As s 77(1) explicitly allows.

3 *DPP v Cornish* (1997) Times, 27 January.

CHAPTER XVI

Documentary evidence[1]

Darling J once said that a document is 'any written thing capable of being evidence' and he added that it is immaterial on what the writing may be inscribed.[2] This was sufficient to dispose of the issue with which he was concerned, the question whether a writing inside a sealed envelope was a document for the purposes of a subpoena duces tecum, but it is clear that the word may have a broader meaning in many contexts. These were not confined to cases, such as the Civil Evidence Act 1995[3] where there is an enlarging statutory definition.[4] For the purposes of the old[5] Rules of the Supreme Court concerning discovery the word was held to include a tape-recording,[6] a facsimile transmission,[7] and an electronic version residing[8] in a computer.[9] On the authority of the first, a majority of the Court of Appeal held that a film was a document for the purpose of the County Court Rules governing the same subject.[10] Some legislation defines a document to include other forms, but permits conventional forms to be required for production.[11] It seemed however that films, tapes and video recordings were not regarded as documents for the purposes of excluding authenticated copies as evidence of their contents, even though the original might have been in existence.[12] So too, it

---

1   See generally Style and Hollander *Documentary Evidence* (6th ed, 1997).
2   *R v Daye* [1908] 2 KB 333, at 340.
3   See Sch 1 para 12 making a comparable amendment to the definition in Part II of the Criminal Justice Act 1988 for the purposes of criminal proceedings.
4   See p 566 below.
5   The new CPR 31.4 reproduces the definition in the Civil Evidence Act 1995.
6   *Grant v South Western and County Properties* [1975] Ch 185, [1974] 2 All ER 465.
7   *Hastie and Jenkerson v McMahon* [1991] 1 All ER 255, [1990] 1 WLR 1575.
8   Including in Canada a file which had been deleted but remained recoverable: *Prism Hospital Software Ltd v Hospital Medical Records Institute* [1992] 2 WWR 157.
9   *Derby v Weldon (No 9)* [1991] 2 All ER 901, [1991] 1 WLR 652; *Alliance & Leicester Building Society v Gharemani* [1992] RVR 198. Some doubt has however been expressed in relation to a screen display on an electronic speed measuring device: *Darby v DPP* [1995] RTR 294.
10 *Senior v Holdsworth, ex p Independent Television* [1976] QB 23, [1975] 2 All ER 1009.
11 Eg Companies Act 1989, s 56. For a comprehensive survey of the terminology of statutory provision in this context see Reed *Digital Information Law* (1996).
12 *Kajala v Noble* (1982) 75 Cr App Rep 149.

was held,[13] and enacted,[14] that photocopies[15] of documents could be admitted without accounting for the absence of the original provided that they were authenticated[16] to the satisfaction of the court.[17] The advent of electronic systems capable of reproducing and storing an exact digitised 'image' of a document, spawned special rules to promote the use of such devices.[18] The Civil Procedure Rules have now clarified some of these issues with wide definitions of 'document' and 'copy'.[19]

If a litigant wishes to rely upon the provisions of a document, he must render the court conversant with its terms. To this end it used to be generally incumbent upon him to produce the original, but the situation has been transformed as described in section 1. In some cases the court will require to be satisfied that the document was duly executed before admitting it in evidence, and this is discussed in section 2. Finally, difficult problems may arise with regard to the extent to which extrinsic evidence is admissible when it relates to the terms of a transaction embodied in a document, or the meaning of the words used in a written instrument. The principal rules are mentioned in section 3.

SECTION I.   PROOF OF THE CONTENTS OF A DOCUMENT

The old law contained arcane provisions as to the proof of the contents of documents of various sorts.[20] The modern law[1] has become much more straightforward, largely as a result of statutory intervention. The process started in the nineteenth century with the Bankers' Books Evidence Act 1879, and has largely kept pace with successive statutory inroads into the exclusionary effects of the hearsay rule, culminating in the Civil Evidence Act 1995. This Act contains wide definitions of documents and copies:[2]

> 'document' means anything in which information of any description is recorded, and 'copy', in relation to a document, means anything onto which information recorded in the document has been copied, by whatever means and whether directly or indirectly.

It should be noted that in this respect the criminal law has sometimes moved ahead of the civil, and for the purposes of criminal proceedings the current position is contained in the provisions of the Criminal Justice Act 1988, which now incorporate the definitions

---

13   *R v Wayte* (1982) 76 Cr App Rep 110, at 116.

14   Police and Criminal Evidence Act 1984, s 71. See also Administration of Justice Act 1982, s 66; Criminal Justice Act 1988, s 27.

15   Including in Australia microfiche: *State Bank of South Australia v Heinrich* (1989) 52 SASR 596.

16   Authentication is no longer required for microfilm or other documents produced before examining magistrates: Criminal Procedure and Investigation Act 1996, Sch 1, paras 24, 31.

17   They are also discoverable if, exceptionally, this should be advantageous: *Dubai Bank Ltd v Galadari (No 7)* [1992] 1 All ER 658, [1992] 1 WLR 106.

18   See eg South Australian Evidence Act Amendment Act 1990. There is already a British Standard for the production of such images, BS 7768 (1994). See generally 5th Report of House of Lords Select Committee on Science and Technology (1998) *Digitised Images as Evidence.*

19   CPR 31.4 which adopts generally the definitions in Civil Evidence Act 1995, s 13: see below 642.

20   See previous editions of this work.

1   See also in Australia the simplifying provisions of Evidence Act 1995 Parts 2.2 and 4.3, and for commentary see Magner (1995) 18 UNSWLJ 67.

2   Section 13.

quoted above.[3] It has also been held that any deficiencies in these definitions may be remedied by invocation of the old common law rules, so in *R v Nazeer*[4] oral secondary evidence of the contents of records held on a computer was held admissible on the basis that there are no degrees of secondary evidence.

The main transformation has come in an increasingly liberal attitude towards the reception of copies as sufficient proof of the contents of an original document. As noted in ch XIV above, the rules relating to the admissibility of documentary hearsay continue to distinguish in some respects between business and public records, and others. This is mirrored in the provisions for the means of proof, although it should be noted that these provisions supplement rather than supplant existing means of proving documents.[5] The simplicity of the new methods may however gradually render recourse to the older means unnecessary. This section will consider, separately: proof under the new provisions of statements in documents generally; proof of business and public records; procedure under the Civil Procedure Rules; and some special considerations applying to public documents and to bankers' books.

A.   PROOF OF STATEMENTS IN DOCUMENTS

The means of proving such documents is now to be found for criminal proceedings in s 27 of the Criminal Justice Act 1988, and for civil proceedings in s 8 of the Civil Evidence Act 1995:[6]

(1)   Where a statement contained in a document is admissible as evidence in civil proceedings, it may be proved–
(a)   by production of that document, or
(b)   whether or not that document is still in existence, by the production of a copy of that document or of the material part of it, authenticated in such manner as the court may approve.

(2)   It is immaterial for this purpose how many removes there are between a copy and the original.

One of the main reasons for the liberalisation of the old rules was the development of new technology under which copies were in effect duplicate originals, and the possibilities of erroneous transcription were non-existent. The reform is not however limited to this situation, and it would be possible, if the court were satisfied of authenticity, for documents to have been copied from memory at intermediate stages. The Law Commission considered the less open-ended authentication provision to be found in the Scottish legislation,[7] but since the 1988 provision had caused no difficulty, forbore to recommend any change.[8] This seems sensible since the Scottish provision would cause difficulty in the case of long chains, old copies, and unidentifiable copiers, and for this reason has had to be made subject to contrary direction.

---

3   Civil Evidence Act 1995, Sch 1, para 12.
4   [1998] Crim LR 750.
5   Civil Evidence Act 1995, s 14(2).
6   The only difference between this provision and that of s 27 is that in the former the two numbered parts are combined into one composite provision.
7   Civil Evidence (Scotland) Act 1988, s 6 requiring the authentication to be by the person responsible for making the copy.
8   Law Com No 216 *The Hearsay Rule in Civil Proceedings* (Cm 2321, 1993), para 4.37.

Although the contrary has been suggested[9] it is submitted that these provisions apply not only to cases where the statements in the documents are to be used for the purpose of proving their truth, but also when they are operative, or require to be used for some other purpose.

In view of the modelling of the provisions of the 1995 Act upon the precedent set by s 27 of the Criminal Justice Act 1988,[10] it is surprising to find the same Commission recommending a rather radical change in the wording of the relevant provision in association with its new recommendations on the admissibility of hearsay in criminal proceedings.[11] The draft bill appended to the Report retains the basic form[12] of definition of 'document' and 'copy', but, without any argumentation or justification in the body of the report, its draft statute completely omits all reference to the immateriality of the number of removes between the original and the copy.[13] It is, of course, possible that this was simply thought unnecessary in view of the width of the definitions, and of the discretion as to authentication, but it is somewhat disturbing to find the hostage of formal deviation offered to the fortune of litigious desperation.

B. PROOF OF BUSINESS OR PUBLIC RECORDS

Although the Civil Evidence Act 1995 removed the distinction between statements and records for the purposes of admissibility, it retained it in relation to means of proof. It provides in s 9 that:

(1) A document which is shown to form part of the records of a business or public authority may be received in evidence in civil proceedings without further proof.

(2) A document shall be taken to form part of the records of a business or public authority if there is produced to the court a certificate to that effect signed by an officer of the business or authority to which the records belong. For this purpose— (a) a document purporting to be a certificate signed by an officer of a business or public authority shall be deemed to have been duly given by such an officer and signed by him; and (b) a certificate shall be treated as signed by a person if it purports to bear a facsimile of his signature.

(3) The absence of an entry in the records of a business or public authority may be proved in civil proceedings by affidavit of an officer of the business or authority to which the records belong.

(4) In this section– 'records' means records in whatever form; 'business' includes any activity regularly carried on over a period of time, whether for profit or not, by any body (whether corporate or not) or by an individual; 'officer' includes any person occupying a responsible position in relation to the relevant activities of the business or public authority or in relation to its records; and 'public authority' includes any public or statutory undertaking, any government department and any person holding office under Her Majesty.

---

9   Commentary to Current Law Statutes.
10   Law Com No 216 above last sentence of para 4.37.
11   Law Com No 245 *Evidence in Criminal Proceedings: Hearsay and Related Topics* (Cm 3670, 1997).
12   Merely abstaining from running them together as s 13 of the Civil Evidence Act 1995 had done.
13   There is a small number of other minor alterations of form.

(5) The court may, having regard to the circumstances of the case, direct that all or any of the above provisions of this section do not apply in relation to a particular document or record, or description of documents or records.

This provision is intended to allow the documents falling within it to prove themselves; that is, not to require even the open-ended process of authentication demanded of 'statements' in other forms of document. It was intended as a means of simplification,[14] justified positively by routine reliance upon regularly recorded documents of this character by those most affected by them, and negatively by the difficulty of providing authentication by human beings when the whole aim of modern business methods is to reduce the amount of human involvement in such documentation. Its reach is enhanced by the broad definitions in s 9(4).

It must be stressed that this provision merely secures admission of the documents; their effect will depend upon their weight, and that in its turn will depend upon the cogency of the evidence demonstrating the efficiency of the system of recording adopted. In an extreme case of unreliability the court will be able to invoke the provisions of s 9(5) to exclude a document altogether.

In criminal proceedings most difficulties of proof were eliminated by s 27 of the Criminal Justice Act 1988. The principal remaining obstacle is the necessity, when the document constitutes the output of a computer, of compliance with s 69 of the Police and Criminal Evidence Act 1984.[15] The Law Commission has now recommended the repeal of this provision, without replacement.[16] It notes that it will be succeeded by revival in this context of the common law presumption of the regular operation of mechanical devices,[17] but anticipates that this will be applied with some flexibility so as to permit ready questioning of the reliability of the operation of the machine, and of its output.

C.   THE CIVIL PROCEDURE RULES

These rules supplement the existing law by providing a simplified procedure which may reduce the need to rely upon older methods. Section 14(2) of the Civil Evidence Act 1995 preserved all existing exceptions to the older rules restricting proof of the contents of documents, and in s 14(3) endorsed a number of specific statutory provisions.[18] Those exceptions were discussed in earlier editions of this work.

The basic scheme of the new rules is to provide a much more liberal scheme for the disclosure and inspection of documents in advance.[19] CPR 31.6 imposes a duty[20] upon a party to disclose:

(a)   the documents on which he relies; and
(b)   the documents which–
    (i)   adversely affect his own case;
    (ii)   adversely affect another party's case; or
    (iii) support another party's case; and

---

14   Law Com No 216 supra, para 4.38.
15   Incorporating reference to Sch 3, Part II.
16   Law Com No 245 supra, para 13.23.
17   Above p 33.
18   Section 2, Documentary Evidence Act 1868; s 2, Documentary Evidence Act 1882; s 1, Evidence (Colonial Statutes) Act 1907; s 1, Evidence (Foreign, Dominion and Colonial Documents) Act 1933; and s 5, Oaths and Evidence (Overseas Authorities and Countries) Act 1963.
19   In Part 31. There are variations in relation to the different 'tracks'.
20   In the standard case.

(c) the documents which he is obliged to disclose by a relevant practice direction.

This applies to documents which are, or have been under his control,[1] and which, in the case of those falling into the latter two categories listed above, he has discovered after making a reasonable search.[2] Only one copy of each document need be disclosed.[3] Disclosure is to be made by list, and any documents indicated for which a claim to withhold inspection is being made.[4] Rights are conferred to inspect in addition documents mentioned a statement of case, witness statements or summaries, affidavits and subject to the provisions of CPR 35.10(4) expert reports.[5] Such a right entitles a party to a copy upon request.[6] It should be noted that provision is made for disclosure before proceedings start,[7] and from third parties.[8] Where documents have been disclosed to a party he is taken to admit the authenticity of such documents unless he serves a notice requiring the document to be proved at the trial.[9]

It has already been remarked that the new rules amalgamate notices of reliance upon hearsay, and service of a witness statement.[10] It should however be mentioned that in the case of other broadly documentary evidence, importantly including that which is receivable without further proof under s 9 of the Civil Evidence Act 1995, notice must be given of intention to use the evidence.[11] This is designed to give the other party a suitable opportunity to inspect the document,[12] and to agree to its admission without the necessity of formal proof and, in default of such notice, the evidence is not admissible.[13]

It must be stressed that the precise mode of operation of the new rules is, at the time of writing, uncertain, largely because of the wide discretionary power conferred upon the courts, especially by CPR 32(1)(c) which authorises directions as to 'the way in which evidence is to be placed before the courts'. It is neither fruitful to speculate, nor possible to anticipate, just how these sweeping powers will be exercised.

D. PUBLIC DOCUMENTS

In *Mortimer v M'Callan*,[14] it was held to be unnecessary to cause the originals of the books of the Bank of England to be produced. Alderson B said that if they were not removable on the ground of public inconvenience, that was upon the same footing in point of principle as in the case of that which is not removable by the physical nature of the thing itself.[15] At common law, the contents of numerous public documents[16] could be proved by copies of various kinds on account of the inconvenience that would

1 CPR 31.8.
2 CPR 31.7.
3 CPR 31.9, unless reliance is to be placed upon a different version.
4 CPR 31.10.
5 CPR 31.14.
6 CPR 31.15(c).
7 CPR 31.16.
8 CPR 31.17. See also CPR 34.2(4)(b) authorising the production of documents to the court in advance of the hearing on the direction of the court.
9 CPR 32.19. See also CPR 34.2 which is directed to witnesses rather than to parties.
10 CPR 33.2(1).
11 CPR 33.6, specifically referring to plans, photographs and models.
12 See CPR 33.6(8).
13 CPR 33.6(3), using the expression not *receivable at a trial.*
14 (1840) 6 M & W 58.
15 See also per Pollock CB in *Sayer v Glossop* (1848) 2 Exch 409, at 441: 'If in point of law you cannot compel a party who has the custody of a document to produce it, there is the same reason for admitting other evidence of its contents as if its production were physically impossible.'
16 See p 571 above for a definition of a public document.

have been occasioned by production of the originals. The mode of proving public documents is now governed by a host of statutes and, in a work of this nature, it is possible to mention only a few that are of more or less general application.

Private Acts of Parliament are, where necessary, proved by the production of a Queen's Printer's or Stationery Office copy.[17] Royal proclamations may be proved by production of a Queen's Printer's copy or of the gazette containing them, or of a copy certified to be correct by the appropriate official.[18] Orders in Council and statutory instruments are proved in the same way.[19] Journals of either House of Parliament are proved by production of a Queen's Printer's copy.[20]

Byelaws are proved under s 238 of the Local Government Act 1972, by the production of a printed copy endorsed with a certificate purporting to be signed by the proper officer containing details concerning the making and confirming of the byelaw and certifying that the document is a true copy.

Proclamations, treaties and other acts of state of any foreign state or British colony may be proved either by examined copy or by a copy authenticated with the seal of the foreign state or British colony.[1]

Records of the Supreme Court may be proved by production of any document sealed or stamped with the seal or stamp of the court.[2]

Records preserved in the Public Record Office are proved by copies certified by the Keeper of the Public Records,[3] and entries in registers which may be held on computer, kept in the Patent Office, are proved by copies certified by the Comptroller,[4] like those relating to companies which may also be held on computer[5] and may be proved by copies signed or sealed by the Registrar.[6]

Finally, two more general provisions may be noted: the effect of s 1 of the Evidence Act 1845 is that when a statute permits a document to be proved by certified or sealed copy, it is unnecessary to prove certification or sealing, the mere production of the certified or sealed copy sufficing. Under s 14 of the Evidence Act 1851, whenever any book or other document is of such a public nature as to be admissible in evidence on production from proper custody and no statute exists which renders its contents provable by means of a copy, it may be proved by certified or examined copy. The upshot of these two provisions, together with those of numerous special statutes, is that a very large number of copy documents may be put in evidence on mere production to the court, without there being any question of accounting for the original or proving the accuracy of the copy.

---

17 Evidence Act 1845, s 3; Documentary Evidence Act 1882, equating Stationery Office copies with those of the Queen's Printer or Government Printer referred to in other statutes. Under s 3 of the Interpretation Act 1978, every Act is a Public Act to be judicially noticed as such, unless the contrary is expressly provided by the Act; it applies to Acts coming into force after 1890 and re-enacts an earlier provision applying to Acts passed since 1850. Generally speaking, therefore, it is unnecessary to produce any particular copy of a modern statute.

18 Evidence Act 1845, s 3; Documentary Evidence Act 1868, s 2.

19 *R v Clarke* [1969] 2 QB 91, [1969] 1 All ER 924. Cp *Snell v Unity Finance Ltd* [1964] 2 QB 203, [1963] 3 All ER 50, suggesting judicial notice may be taken of all statutory instruments. In *R v Koon Cheung Tang* [1995] Crim LR 813 the Court of Appeal disapproved of objection to informal copies in the absence of any suggestion that they were wrong.

20 Evidence Act 1845, s 3.

1   Evidence Act 1851, s 7. Despite some technical difficulty it appears that s 7 applies to the Republic of Ireland, as it applies elsewhere: see *R v McGlinchy* [1985] 9 NIJB 62.

2   Supreme Court Act 1981, s 132.

3   Public Records Act 1958, s 9.

4   Patents Act 1977, s 32, as substituted by the Patents, Designs and Marks Act 1986, Sch 1.

5   Companies Act 1985, s 723.

6   Ibid, s 709(1) as substituted by Companies Act 1989, s 126.

E. BANKERS' BOOKS

At common law, bankers' books, other than those of the Bank of England, are private documents; but the inconvenience which would have been occasioned by the necessity of producing the originals as and when required for the purposes of any litigation has been avoided by the Bankers' Books Evidence Act 1879. Provided that the book is one of the ordinary ones of the bank, the entry was made in the ordinary course of business, the book is in the custody of the bank, and the copy has been examined against the original (all of which matters can be proved by the affidavit or the testimony of an officer of the bank),[7] a copy of an entry in a banker's book shall, in all legal proceedings, be received as prima facie evidence of such entry, and of the matters, transactions and accounts therein recorded.[8] The application of these provisions has been very sensibly extended to modern forms of book-keeping such as microfilmed and computerised records.[9] This reform does not, however, extend beyond the form of the records to their substance, and it seems that copies of letters sent by the bank,[10] or of cheques and paying-in slips,[11] would still not be covered by the provisions. Under s 7 any party to a legal proceeding can apply, if necessary without notice, for an order that he be at liberty to inspect and take copies of any entries in a banker's books for the purpose of such proceedings. This section, like the rest of the Act, applies to both civil and criminal proceedings.[12] In civil proceedings it is well-established that the provision is to be applied according to the ordinary rules of disclosure,[13] and in particular that it cannot be used to compel the revelation of incriminating matters.[14] There was no discovery in criminal proceedings, and for many years the application of the Act in such proceedings was left untested. In *Williams v Summerfield*[15] it was however held that to apply the same ban on self-incrimination would frustrate the operation of the Act to criminal proceedings, and that an application could be granted upon conditions analogous to those applying to search warrants. The order is such a serious invasion of privacy that it should not be made without the most careful consideration, and the court granting it should satisfy itself that there is other evidence to support the charge,[16] and that the order is limited to entries strictly relevant, especially temporally, to the charge.[17] It is generally desirable that notice be given to anyone affected by an order,[18] though it should be noted that the account need not be that of a party to the proceedings, and

7   Sections 4–5.
8   Section 3. The section creates an exception to the hearsay rule as to the transactions to which the entry relates (*Harding v Williams* (1880) 14 Ch D 197, questioned in argument in *Arnott v Hayes* (1887) 56 LJ Ch 844, at 847; but see *Myers v DPP* [1965] AC 1001, at 1028 and 1033). See also *Elsey v Taxation Comr of Commonwealth of Australia* (1969) 121 CLR 99.
9   A new definition clause, s 9, substituted by the Banking Act 1979, Sch 6, has applied since 1982, although *Barker v Wilson* [1980] 2 All ER 81, [1980] 1 WLR 884, had already indicated the capacity of judicial intervention to achieve the same result. See also *ANZ Banking Group Ltd v Griffiths* (1988) 49 SASR 385; *R v Saffron* (1988) 36 ACR 262, at 290.
10 *R v Dadson* (1983) 77 Cr App Rep 91.
11 *Williams v Williams* [1988] QB 161, [1987] 3 All ER 257.
12 Which in Scotland include a criminal petition: *Carmichael v Sexton* 1986 SLT 16n.
13 *Re Bankers' Books Evidence Act 1879, R v Bono* (1913) 29 TLR 635.
14 *Waterhouse v Barker* [1924] 2 KB 759.
15 [1972] 2 QB 512, [1972] 2 All ER 1334.
16 *Re v Nottingham City Justices, ex p Lynn* (1984) 79 Cr App Rep 238. The court will be wary of a situation in which the charge is laid simultaneously with the application for the order so as formally to satisfy the requirements of the section.
17 In *R v Marlborough Street Stipendiary Magistrate, ex p Simpson* (1980) 70 Cr App Rep 291, orders were quashed, largely on this basis. A party cannot necessarily prevent an order being made by proclaiming an intention to plead guilty: *Owen v Sambrook* [1981] Crim LR 329.
18 *R v Grossman* (1981) 73 Cr App Rep 302.

may even be that of a person incompetent to testify.[19] These safeguards may in some circumstances lead courts to approve of action under these provisions in preference to those under less fastidious statutory provisions[20] and in others to construe such provisions with particular care to avoid inconsistency.[1] It remains to be seen how far the provisions of the Civil Evidence Act 1995 will be permitted to supplant these provisions.[2]

SECTION 2.   PROOF OF THE EXECUTION OF PRIVATE DOCUMENTS

The statutes which enable the contents of public documents to be proved by means of copies also dispense with the necessity of proving that the documents have been properly executed. In the case of a public document, therefore, the mere production of the appropriate copy will suffice to put it in evidence, but something more than production is required in the case of a private document. The court will require to be satisfied by evidence that it was duly executed, unless it is more than 20 years old and comes from the proper custody, in which event there is a presumption of formal validity. The due execution of a private document is proved by showing that it was signed by the person by whom it purports to have been signed and, when attestation is necessary, that it was attested. Accordingly, proof of handwriting and attestation will be discussed before various presumptions applicable to documents are considered.[3] The section concludes with a brief reference to the Stamp Acts.

A.   PROOF OF HANDWRITING

There are three types of evidence of handwriting which call for discussion – testimonial evidence, opinion and comparison.

1.   Testimonial evidence

Testimonial evidence may take one of the following forms: the testimony of the person whose handwriting is to be proved; his admissible hearsay statement; the testimony of someone who saw the document executed (whether he be an attesting witness or a bystander); and an admissible hearsay statement of someone other than the person whose handwriting is in question. Nothing need be said with regard to any of these forms of testimonial evidence except that it is usually unnecessary, in the first instance, for a witness to the signature to do more than swear that he saw someone sign in a particular name. The name will, in itself, be sufficient evidence of the identity of the signatory with the person whose handwriting is to be proved,[4] unless there are

---

19   *R v Andover Justices, ex p Rhodes* [1980] Crim LR 644, where this was, in fact, regarded as a further reason for making the order.

20   See *R v Epsom Justices, ex p Bell* [1989] STC 169; *R v Crown Court at Southwark, ex p Bowles* [1998] AC 641, [1998] 2 All ER 193.

1   *R v Crown Court at Lewes, ex p Hill* (1991) 93 Cr App Rep 60.

2   The provisions of para 7(1)(b) of Sch 3 to the Prisoners and Criminal Proceedings (Scotland) Act 1993 were permitted to do so in *Lord Advocate's Reference (No 1 of 1996)* 1996 JC 152.

3   The authenticity of documents which have been disclosed in civil proceedings is governed by CPR 32.19, see above p 643. The due execution of a document might be formally admitted in a criminal case under s 10 of the Criminal Justice Act 1967.

4   *Roden v Ryde* (1843) 4 QB 626.

circumstances calling for investigation, or unless, perhaps, the name is a very common one.[5]

2. Opinion

Witnesses who have not seen the document in question written or signed may depose to their opinion that the writing is that of a particular person. Such opinion may be based upon the witness's acquaintance with the handwriting of the person in question through having seen him write on former occasions. It makes no difference whether these occasions were many or few, and whether the signature was merely that of the signatory's surname without the addition of the Christian names appearing on the document before the court,[6] although these matters will affect the weight of the evidence.

It is unnecessary that the witness who thus deposes to his opinion should have seen the person whose writing is in question write at all, for it will be sufficient if he has received documents purporting to be written or signed by him,[7] and the capacity in which he has done so is immaterial, although this may affect the weight of the evidence.[8]

> The clerk who constantly read the letters, the broker who was ever consulted upon them, is as competent to judge whether another signature is that of the writer of the letters, as the merchant to whom they were addressed. The servant who has habitually carried letters addressed by me to others has an opportunity of obtaining knowledge of my writing though he never saw me write or received a letter from me.

There must, however, have been a sufficient opportunity for the witness to acquire such knowledge of the handwriting in question as to make it worthwhile receiving his evidence.[9]

3. Comparison

There is a general sense in which it is true to say that:[10]

> All evidence of handwriting, except where the witness sees the document written, is in its nature comparison. It is the belief which a witness entertains on comparing the writing in question with an example in his mind derived from some previous knowledge.

but, under s 8 of the Criminal Procedure Act 1865, handwriting may also be proved by comparison in a more specific sense of the word. A document which is proved[11] to

5   *Jones v Jones* (1841) 9 M & W 75.
6   *Lewis v Sapio* (1827) Mood & M 39.
7   *Harrington v Fry* (1824) 1 C & P 289.
8   *Doe d Mudd v Suckermore* (1837) 5 Ad & El 703, at 750 per Lord Denman CJ.
9   *R v O'Brien* (1911) 7 Cr App Rep 29; *Pitre v R* [1933] 1 DLR 417 (sight of two letters and two postcards insufficient).
10   *Doe d Mudd v Suckermore* (1837) 5 Ad & El 703, at 739 per Patteson J.
11   The section applies to civil and criminal cases and in both instances the standard of proof is the one normally appropriate to those proceedings: *R v Ewing* [1983] QB 1039, [1983] 2 All ER 645. See also *R v Sim* [1987] 1 NZLR 356.

have been signed or written by the person whose handwriting is in issue is first produced, and this is compared with the writing[12] which is being considered by the court.[13] On the basis of such a comparison, an expert in these matters may give evidence.[14] The rigour of the old law restricting a witness to testifying to points of comparison rather than to the identity of two pieces of handwriting has probably not survived s 3 of the Civil Evidence Act 1972.[15]

Although the evidence may be thought to be of less weight, an opinion with regard to the handwriting of the two documents may be given by a witness who is not an expert, or the document may be submitted to the court in order that the handwriting on each of them may be compared. The document which is thus submitted to the jury for comparison with the one in dispute need not be relevant to the issues in the case in any other way,[16] and, if he gives evidence, the person whose handwriting is under consideration may be asked to write in court so that his writing may be compared with that on the document in question.[17]

Conclusions based on comparison of handwriting by those who are not experts must obviously be treated with considerable caution, and there are several instances in which the Court of Criminal Appeal has quashed a conviction after examining two specimens of handwriting which had been submitted to the jury at the trial.[18] It is wrong[19] for a judge to invite the jury to make a comparison without the guidance of an expert although, where they have to be allowed to consider exhibits, he cannot do more than warn them of the risks of comparison.[20] In Australia the question has been raised of possible prejudice to the accused as a result of counsel asking the accused to provide a specimen by writing in court during cross-examination.[1] It has been held that a policeman who induced a prisoner to write while under arrest in order that his handwriting might be compared with that on a threatening letter which he was alleged to have written, was a biased witness and that his evidence of opinion based on a comparison ought not to have been submitted to the jury,[2] and, in *R v Harvey*,[3] it was said that the jury ought not to act on a comparison of the handwriting in books found in the possession of the prisoner with that on a document alleged to have been forged by him. These decisions may have turned on their special facts, for it appears to have been ruled in a later case that evidence by a policeman that he had seen the accused write for his own purposes pending trial was admissible.[4]

12   If the original has been lost, a facsimile may be used: *Lockheed–Arabia Corpn v Owen* [1993] QB 806, [1993] 3 All ER 641.
13   Which must itself be the document in dispute: *R v Nicholas* [1988] Tas SR 155.
14   *R v Silverlock* (1894) 2 QB 766. It may be necessary to establish the basis of such expertise on a voir dire, though questions of methodology go to weight rather than to admissibility: *R v Bonython* (1984) 15 ACR 364.
15   See also *R v Mazzone* (1985) 43 SASR 330, at 339.
16   *Birch v Ridgway* (1858) 1 F & F 270; *Adami v R* (1959) 108 CLR 605. It may even be an otherwise inadmissible confession, see *S v Duna* 1984 (2) SA 591.
17   *Cobbett v Kilminster* (1865) 4 F & F 490.
18   *R v Smith* (1909) 2 Cr App Rep 86; *R v Rickard* (1918) 13 Cr App Rep 40.
19   The rule is less stringent in Australia, see *Adami* above; *Daley v R* [1979] Tas SR 75; *Grayden v R* [1989] WAR 208; *R v Medina* (1990) 3 WAR 21.
20   *R v O'Sullivan* [1969] 2 All ER 237, [1969] 1 WLR 497; *R v Tilley* [1961] 3 All ER 406, [1961] 1 WLR 1309; *R v Smith* (1968) 52 Cr App Rep 648.
1   *R v McCarthy and Martin* (1984) 14 ACR 73.
2   *R v Crouch* (1850) 4 Cox CC 163. Perhaps this case is best regarded as turning on an analogy with those in which the answers to questions improperly put by policemen to prisoners in custody were rejected.
3   (1869) 11 Cox CC 546.
4   *R v McCartney and Hansen* (1928) 20 Cr App Rep 179. For further cases turning on the proof of handwriting see *Lucas v Williams & Sons* [1892] 2 QB 113 and *R v Hope* (1955) 39 Cr App Rep 33. See also *R v Day* [1940] 1 All ER 402.

In spite of the variety of the methods by which handwriting may be proved, there might be great difficulty in employing them to authenticate handwriting of any antiquity, and that is why the presumption of due execution to which reference will be made shortly is of the utmost utility.

B. PROOF OF ATTESTATION

For historical reasons to be mentioned at the end of the discussion, it is convenient to deal separately with proof of the attestation of wills and other documents required by law to be attested.

I. Wills

If it becomes necessary to prove the due execution of a will, it is essential to call one of the attesting witness if any are available. Before other evidence is admissible, it must be shown that all the attesting witnesses are dead, insane, beyond the jurisdiction or that none of them can be traced. This requirement holds good even if the execution can be proved by those who saw it though they were not attesting witnesses, but the witness is treated as if he had been called by the court so he may be cross-examined by the party seeking to prove execution,[5] professional privilege cannot be claimed in respect of his previous statements to solicitors concerning execution,[6] and any other evidence may be given if he denies execution or refuses to testify.[7]

If none of the attesting witnesses can be called for the reasons indicated in the previous paragraph, steps must be taken to prove the handwriting of at least one of them. This constitutes secondary evidence of attestation.

If evidence of handwriting is unobtainable, evidence of those who saw the will executed, or any other evidence from which an inference of due execution can be drawn becomes admissible, but it seems that every effort must first be made to prove the handwriting of one of the attesting witnesses.[8] If a will is proved to have been in existence after the testator's death, a copy may be admitted to probate on proof that the original was signed by the testator and bore the signature of two attesting witnesses, although the person giving this evidence is unable to recollect their names.[9] It should perhaps be added that, when probate is sought in common form, the rigorous requirements as to proof of due execution to which reference has just been made do not apply.

2. Other documents required by law to be attested

In the case of the comparatively few documents, other than wills, to the validity of which attestation is essential, it may be proved by the testimony of one of the subscribing witnesses, but it is unnecessary to call any of them if the person wishing

---

5   *Oakes v Uzzell* [1932] P 19; *Re Webster, Webster v Webster* [1974] 3 All ER 822n, [1974] 1 WLR 1641 (general cross-examination by both parties permissible).
6   *Re Fuld's Estate (No 2), Hartley v Fuld* [1965] P 405, [1965] 2 All ER 657.
7   *Bowman v Hodgson* (1867) LR 1 P & D 362; *Re Ovens's Goods* (1892) 29 LR Ir 451, *Re Vere-Wardale, Vere-Wardale v Johnson* [1949] P 395, [1949] 2 All ER 250.
8   *Clarke v Clarke* (1879) 5 LR Ir 47.
9   *Re Phibb's Estate* [1917] P 93; *Re Webb, Smith v Johnson* [1964] 2 All ER 91, [1964] 1 WLR 509.

to prove due execution does not desire to do so. He may content himself with proving the handwriting of an attesting witness, and, if he is unable to do this, he may have recourse to other evidence.

3.   History of the present law

The rule that one of the subscribing witnesses of an attested document must be called unless they were all unavailable used to apply to all attested documents, whether attestation was required by law or not. Lord Ellenborough said that the rule was 'as fixed, formal and universal as any that can be stated in a court of justice'.[10] It probably originated in the ancient requirement that the witness to a deed should, where possible, be summoned to sit with the jury in the days when that body was composed of witnesses rather than triers of fact. In more modern times, the rule was justified on the ground that the parties to a document must be taken to have agreed that the document should not be given in evidence unless the attesting witness was called when possible,[11] but, by virtue of s 7 of the Criminal Procedure Act 1865 (which applies to civil and criminal cases), instruments to the validity of which attestation is not necessary may be proved as if there had been no attesting witnesses thereto, and s 3 of the Evidence Act 1938 provides that in any proceedings, civil or criminal, an instrument to the validity of which attestation is requisite may, instead of being proved by an attesting witness, be proved in the manner in which it might be proved if no attesting witness were alive. The only exception is the case of testamentary documents to which the section is expressly stated to be inapplicable. Section 7 of the Criminal Procedure Act 1865, and s 3 of the Evidence Act 1938, are the authorities for the foregoing treatment of the proof of attestation.

C.   PRESUMPTIONS RELATING TO DOCUMENTS

Attestation, like handwriting, would not be easily proved in the case of a document of any antiquity, but practical difficulties are, in the main, obviated by the presumption of due execution that attaches to a document proved or purporting to be not less than twenty years old, provided it is produced from proper custody. 'Proper custody' is that which was reasonable and natural under the circumstances of the particular case. Expired leases may be expected to be in the custody of either lessor or lessee and those claiming under them, a family Bible may properly be in the custody of any member of the family. Proper custody in this context does not mean the most appropriate custody possible. Papers relating to a bishopric have been held to come from proper custody when found among the family papers of a deceased bishop and not, as they should have been, in the possession of the bishop for the time being,[12] but, in the absence of further explanation, the parish clerk's house is not a place of proper custody for the parish registers.[13] The other basic fact of the presumption—the age of the document— is prescribed by s 4 of the Evidence Act 1938, for criminal and civil cases. At common law the period was thirty years.

Several other useful presumptions relating to documents may be mentioned. A document is presumed to have been executed on the date it bears;[14] alterations in a

---

10   *R v Harringworth (Inhabitants)* (1815) 4 M & S 350. See Stephen *Digest of the Law of Evidence* (12th edn) n XIII.
11   *Whyman v Garth* (1853) 8 Exch 803 per Pollock CB.
12   *Bishop Meath v Marquess of Winchester* (1836) 3 Bing NC 183.
13   *Doe d Lord Arundel v Fowler* (1850) 14 QB 700.
14   *Aderson v Weston* (1840) 6 Bing NC 296.

deed are presumed to have been made before execution, otherwise the entire deed might be avoided, but alterations in a will are presumed to have been made after execution because they would not invalidate the entire testament.[15] It is sometimes said that there is a presumption that a deed, even when less than twenty years old, was duly sealed, but this is not a presumption which is at all clearly established by the authorities.[16]

D. THE STAMP ACT 1891

In civil proceedings, stamp objections are taken by the court and cannot be waived by the parties.[17] If the original of a document is lost, or not produced after notice, it is presumed to have been duly stamped. If a document is shown to have been unstamped at a particular time, the ordinary provisional presumption of continuance applies, and there is evidence on which the court may find that the document was never properly stamped, but there is at least one case where language is used which suggests that the court must find that a lost document was duly stamped when the question is left doubtful by the evidence.[18]

SECTION 3. ADMISSIBILITY OF EXTRINSIC EVIDENCE

Having dealt with what may be called the 'exclusiveness' of a document as evidence of its terms, it is now necessary to consider its conclusiveness. The general effect of the rule considered in section 1 was that the contents of a document may be proved only on production of the original. The major problems with which this section is concerned are first, whether, once a transaction has been embodied in a document, evidence may be given of terms other than those it mentions, and, second, the extent to which evidence may be given of the meaning of the terms used in the document. In each instance, the problem is one of the admissibility of 'extrinsic evidence', an expression which means any evidence other than the document the contents of which are under consideration. It is often said to be 'parol evidence', no doubt because it usually takes the form of oral testimony, but it may consist of other documents.

A. THE CONCLUSIVENESS OF A DOCUMENT AS EVIDENCE OF THE TERMS OF THE TRANSACTION IT EMBODIES

1. Statement and illustrations of the rule

(i) Statement

Extrinsic evidence is generally inadmissible when it would, if accepted, have the effect of adding to, varying or contradicting the terms of a judicial record, a transaction required by law to be in writing, or a document constituting a valid and effective contract or other transaction.[19] Most judicial statements of the rule are concerned with its

---

15   *Doe d Tatum v Catomore* (1851) 16 QB 745.
16   *Re Sandilands* (1871) LR 6 CP 411; *National Provincial Bank of England v Jackson* (1886) 33 Ch D 1, at 11 and 14; *Re Balkis Consolidated Co Ltd* (1888) 58 LT 300.
17   *Bowker v Williamson* (1889) 5 TLR 382. Unstamped documents may be proved in criminal proceedings.
18   *Closmadeuc v Garrel* (1856) 18 CB 36.
19   The position is similar in Scotland: *Smith v Mackintosh* 1989 SCLR 83.

application to contracts, and one of the best known is that of Lord Morris who regarded it as indisputable that:[20]

> Parol testimony cannot be received to contradict, vary, add to or subtract from the terms of a written contract or the terms in which the parties have deliberately agreed to record any part of their contract.

Another well-known statement is that of Lord Denman when he said:[1]

> If there be a contract which has been reduced into writing, verbal evidence is not allowed to be given of what passed between the parties, either before the written instrument was made, or during the time that it was in a state of preparation, so as to add to or subtract from, or in any manner to vary or qualify the written contract.

Statements of this nature are best regarded as statements of the effect of the substantive law of merger which is now based on the presumed intention of the parties.[2] If the court is satisfied that they effectively agreed to be bound by a written instrument, they are bound by its terms though unacquainted with them,[3] even though one of the parties believes that something said in the course of the negotiations is still binding. In such circumstances, it would be pointless to admit extrinsic evidence with regard to those negotiations because it is irrelevant.[4] It is for the same reason that evidence that one of the parties to a written agreement did not intend to be contractually bound is inadmissible.[5] In areas like conveyancing where certainty is at a premium parol evidence is particularly unwelcome.[6] Evidence of antecedent negotiations is relevant and admissible if they retain their contractual effect or legal significance after the writing has been brought into existence. Such evidence is always admissible if tendered to establish the existence of a contract collateral to the writing, or the conclusion of a contract which is partly oral and partly in writing. Evidence of antecedent negotiations is likewise admissible when it is relevant owing to such provisions of the substantive law as the requirement of what is now s 14(3) of the Sale of Goods Act 1979, that the buyer should make known to the seller that he relies on his skill and judgment.[7]

20   *Bank of Australasia v Palmer* [1897] AC 540, at 545.
1   *Goss v Lord Nugent* (1833) 5 B & Ad 58.
2   The law of merger originated in deeds and the rules of pleading, but it had come to apply to written contracts as part of the substantive law by the eighteenth century; compare Bacon's *Maxims* (reg 25) with Viner's *Abridgement* (contract g 18); contrast *Countess of Rutland's Case* (1604) 5 Co Rep 25b with *Meres v Ansell* (1771) 3 Wils 275. See also Salmond (1890) 6 LQR 75 and Wigmore (1904) 4 Columbia Law Review 33–7. For further developments, see Wedderburn in [1959] CLJ 58.
3   *Parker v South Eastern Rly Co* (1877) 2 CPD 416, at 421.
4   *Lexmead (Basingstoke) Ltd v Lewis* [1982] AC 225, at 263, sub nom *Lambert v Lewis* [1980] 1 All ER 978, at 1002 (unaffected on this point by the subsequent decision in the House of Lords).
5   *Smith v Mansi* [1962] 3 All ER 857, [1963] 1 WLR 26.
6   *WF Trustees Ltd v Expo Safety Systems Ltd* (1993) Times, 24 May.
7   *Gillespie Bros & Co v Cheney Eggar & Co* [1896] 2 QB 59; *Manchester Liners Ltd v Real Ltd* [1922] 2 AC 74, at 85; *The Preload Company of Canada Ltd v The City of Regina* (1958) 13 DLR (2d) 305.

(ii)   Illustrations

(a)   Judicial records

Once it has been drawn up, the order of a court is conclusive evidence of that which was directed by the judge. Steps may be taken to have clerical errors corrected, and there may be an appeal, but, in any other proceedings, extrinsic evidence of the terms of the decision would be irrelevant.

(b)   Transactions required by law to be in writing

Even when a transaction is required by law to be in writing, extrinsic evidence is admissible in aid of the interpretation of the document, but that does not constitute an infringement of the rule under consideration. Additional or different terms may not be proved by extrinsic evidence. In *Re Huxtable*,[8] a testator bequeathed four thousand pounds to C 'for charitable purposes agreed between us'. It was held that, though evidence was admissible to show what purposes had been agreed, it was not permissible to adduce evidence tending to show that only the income of the bequest was to be devoted to these purposes. That would have contradicted the will, whereas proof of the agreed purposes did not have this effect. In *Re Rees*,[9] a testator left part of his estate 'to my trustees absolutely, they well knowing my wishes concerning the same'. The Court of Appeal affirmed the judge's decision, reached without resort to extrinsic evidence, that, as a matter of construction, the estate was given on trust, and accordingly evidence showing that, in the events which had happened, the testator intended his trustees to take it beneficially was inadmissible because it would contradict the terms of the will as construed by the court.

(c)   Written contracts

In *Angell v Duke*,[10] the defendant agreed in writing to let a house to the claimant together with the furniture therein. The claimant tendered evidence that, before the execution of the writing, the defendant had orally agreed to send in additional furniture, but it was held that such evidence was inadmissible because, having once executed the writing, without making the terms of the alleged parol agreement part of it, the claimant could not afterwards set up that agreement. It would have contradicted the restriction of the written document to furniture already in the house. In *Newman v Gatti*[11] an actress signed an agreement to understudy a named principal who left the employment of the defendant during the currency of the agreement. It was held that the actress could not give evidence of an oral undertaking that she should have the right to take the place of the principal because there was no evidence that this was to be a term of the contract. The Court of Appeal recognised that in some cases a collateral verbal contract for which the consideration was the entering into the principal contract might be proved, or it could happen that, after the written contract had been drawn up, the parties realised that it did not deal with a situation which might arise, and agreed to provide for that event, but the mere fact that a promise made during the negotiations preceding a written agreement is believed to be binding by the promisee when he signs the document does not prevent the doctrine of merger from operating.

The distinction between an addition, a variation and a contradiction has not been discussed by the courts. With the possible exception of *Angell v Duke* the cases

---

8   *Re Huxtable, Huxtable v Crawford* [1902] 2 Ch 793.
9   *Re Rees, Williams v Hopkins* [1950] Ch 204, [1949] 2 All ER 1003.
10   (1875) 32 LT 320, but see [1959] CLJ 65–6, *Kaplan v Andrews* [1955] 4 DLR 553.
11   (1907) 24 TLR 18; see also *Grimston v Cunningham* [1894] 1 QB 125 and *Aetna Factors Corpn Ltd v Breau* (1957) 10 DLR (2d) 100.

mentioned in the last paragraph were treated primarily as ones in which an effort was made to give extrinsic evidence of additional terms. A case which was treated as one of attempted variation is *Re Sutro (L) & Co and Heilbut, Symons & Co.*[12] A written contract having provided for the sale of rubber to be shipped to New York, evidence of a practice under which the goods were dispatched by rail for part of the journey was held to be inadmissible. The admissibility of evidence of a variation of a written contract which has once been concluded is plainly dependent on the substantive law. If, having regard to the rules of consideration, the variation is effective, and if, having regard to statutory provisions such as s 2 of the Law of Property (Miscellaneous Provisions) Act 1989, it is enforceable, evidence of its terms will be received. When these conditions do not apply, such evidence will be irrelevant.

> After the agreement had been reduced into writing, it is competent to the parties, at any time before breach of it, by a new contract not in writing, either altogether to waive, dissolve, or annul the former agreement, or in any manner to add to, or subtract from, or vary or qualify the terms of it, and thus to make a new contract, which is to be proved, partly by the written agreement, and partly by the subsequent verbal terms engrafted upon what will thus be left of the written agreement.

These words were spoken in a case[13] in which the claimant had agreed in writing to sell a number of lots of land to the defendant and tendered evidence of a subsequent oral agreement discharging him from the duty of making a good title to one of the lots. The evidence was held to be inadmissible on account of the Statute of Frauds 1677,[14] but the court was clearly of opinion that evidence of the subsequent contractual variation or discharge of a written agreement is admissible in the ordinary case.[15]

Decisions which primarily turned on the question whether extrinsic evidence could be received of terms contradicting those of a written agreement are *Henderson v Arthur*[16] and *Evans v Roe.*[17] In the first case, a lease having been executed under which rent was payable in advance, the lessee was not allowed to give evidence of a prior undertaking by the lessor to accept rent in arrears. In the second case, evidence of a contemporaneous oral agreement that a written contract of service from week to week was to last for a year was rejected. To the same effect are cases in which, when a person has signed an agreement as 'owner'[18] or 'proprietor',[19] evidence that he was acting as agent for an undisclosed principal has been held to be inadmissible, as contradicting the unambiguous statement in the agreement.[20]

---

12   [1917] 2 KB 348.
13   *Goss v Lord Nugent* (1833) 5 B & Ad 58 per Lord Denman CJ.
14   See now s 2 of the Law of Property (Miscellaneous Provisions) Act 1989.
15   A parol discharge as distinct from a variation was held effective in a case coming within s 4 of the Sale of Goods Act 1893 (now repealed), in *Morris v Baron & Co* [1918] AC 1.
16   [1907] 1 KB 10; see also *Goldfoot v Welch* [1914] 1 Ch 213.
17   (1872) LR 7 CP 138.
18   *Humble v Hunter* (1848) 12 QB 310.
19   *Formby Bros v Formby* (1910) 102 LT 116. This case, and *Humble v Hunter*, were said to be no longer law by Scott LJ in *Epps v Rothnie* [1945] KB 562, at 565, [1946] 1 All ER 146, at 147 (sed quaere). The cases are discussed below: *Humble v Hunter* was held to be good law in *Murphy v Rae* [1967] NZLR 103.
20   See the converse case of *Universal Steam Navigation Co v J McKelvie & Co* [1923] AC 492 and contrast *Automobile Renault Canada Ltd v Maritime Import Autos Ltd and Kyley* (1962) 31 DLR (2d) 592.

2. Exceptions to and cases falling outside the rule

The case of a subsequent variation or discharge of a written agreement to which reference has already been made may be treated as an exception to the rule under consideration. Transactions required by law to be in writing may be discharged or varied by a parol contract, subject, in the case of a variation, to the requirements of the relevant statutes such as s 3 of the Law of Property (Miscellaneous Provisions) Act 1989.[1] Evidence tending to establish such a contract may be regarded as evidence varying or contradicting the terms of the original document. The same can be said of evidence varying or discharging a contract embodied in a document when writing is not a necessary condition of its validity or enforceability. The cases about to be considered can be regarded as exceptions to the rule or as falling outside it according to taste.

(i) Public registers

Oral evidence has been received and accepted although it had the effect of establishing a different tonnage of a ship than that mentioned on the register of ships,[2] and a different proprietorship of a taxicab than that shown on the register of hackney carriages.[3] No reasons were given for the first of these decisions. In the second case, the judgments of the Court of Appeal were exclusively concerned with the construction of the relevant statutes. The upshot seems to be that, subject to the terms of the statute under which it is kept, the contents of a public register are not conclusive.[4] Extrinsic evidence affecting their truth is therefore admissible.

(ii) Cases concerning the validity or effectiveness of a written contract or other document

Extrinsic evidence is admissible to show that a written contract or any other document is void for mistake,[5] or illegality,[6] or for non-compliance with the provisions of a statute,[7] or voidable on account of a fraudulent or innocent misrepresentation.[8] It is also permissible to prove by extrinsic evidence that a deed or written contract, unconditional on its face, was delivered as an escrow or signed subject to a condition

---

1 *Morris v Baron & Co*, above.
2 *The Recepta* (1889) 14 PD 131.
3 *Kemp v Elisha* [1918] 1 KB 228.
4 See eg British Nationality Act 1981, s 45, which makes certificates merely prima facie evidence of the matters entered on the registers, but conclusive of other matters not so entered; see also *R v Secretary of State for the Environment, ex p Simms* [1991] 2 QB 354, [1990] 3 All ER 490 construing ss 53 and 56 of the Wildlife and Countryside Act 1981 to the effect that while a 'definitive' map was conclusive of its contents in independent proceedings such status does not preclude the admission of inconsistent evidence in proceedings designed to correct the map itself.
5 *Henkel v Royal Exchange Assurance Co* (1749) 1 Ves Sen 317; *Wake v Harrop* (1861) 7 Jur NS 710; *Cowen v Trufitt Bros Ltd* [1899] 2 Ch 309; *Roe v RA Naylor Ltd* (1918) 87 LJKB 958, at 968 (non est factum); *Craddock Bros Ltd v Hunt* [1923] 2 Ch 136; *United States of America v Motor Trucks Ltd* [1924] AC 196.
6 *Collins v Blantern* (1767) 2 Wils 341.
7 *Campbell Discount Co Ltd v Gall* [1961] 1 QB 431, [1961] 2 All ER 104.
8 *Dobell v Stevens* (1825) 3 B & C 623.

precedent to its effectiveness as in *Pym v Campbell*,[9] where the defendants agreed in writing to buy an invention from the claimant, subject to the oral stipulation that the transaction was conditional on the approval of the invention by the defendant's engineer. Extrinsic evidence was received concerning this stipulation and the fact that the invention had not been approved. Such evidence is also admissible to negative the implication of a warranty[10] or to raise an equitable defence.[11] The rule under consideration can hardly be said to be infringed in any of the cases mentioned in this paragraph because it applies only to valid and effective transactions.

(iii)   Consideration

The absence of consideration invalidates a simple contract in writing, and this may always be proved by extrinsic evidence. The fact that a bill of exchange contains the words 'for value received' does not render evidence that it was an accommodation bill inadmissible in cases where the fact is relevant. When a deed contains no reference to consideration, or mentions a nominal consideration, extrinsic evidence concerning a real consideration has been held to be admissible. Thus, in *Turner v Forwood*,[12] the claimant entered into an agreement under seal with a company and a director in which he assigned a debt due to him from the company for a thousand and fifteen pounds to the director in consideration of ten shillings, and it was held that oral evidence might be given of an antecedent agreement by the director to pay in full for the debt. The principle underlying such decisions appears to be that, as no consideration need, in general, be expressed in a deed in order that it should be effective, the parties may often be taken to have intended that their arrangements should be carried out, partly by a deed, and partly by parol. As a matter of conveyancing practice, it became usual to insert a nominal consideration in many deeds in order to avoid the implication of a use, so it was reasonable to infer that, so far as the intention of the parties was concerned, these cases were the same as those in which no consideration was inserted in a deed. There is no authority dealing with the admissibility of extrinsic evidence to vary a real consideration stated in a deed. In *Turner v Forwood*, Lord Goddard CJ was not prepared to say that the principle applied by him was confined to cases in which a nominal consideration was expressed in a deed, but, if the principle is extended, the question as to what undertakings are to be treated as part of the consideration would give rise to difficulty.

(iv)   The real nature of the transaction

When it is relevant, having regard to the principles of common law and equity involved, extrinsic evidence may be given of the real nature of any transaction, whether it is recorded in a document in pursuance of legal requirements or at the instance of the

---

9   (1856) 6 E & B 370; *Wallis v Littell* (1861) 11 CBNS 369; *Lindley v Lacey* (1864) 17 CBNS 578; *Davis v Jones* (1856) 17 CB 625; *Pattle v Hornibrook* [1897] 1 Ch 25, distinguished in *Smith v Mansi* [1962] 3 All ER 857, [1963] 1 WLR 26. See also *Frontier Finance Ltd v Hynes and Niagara Sewing Machine Co* (1956) 10 DLR (2d) 206. In *Re Tait* [1957] VLR 405, instructions for a will were admitted to show that a revocation clause was conditioned on the insertion of other clauses inadvertently omitted.

10   *Burges v Wickham* (1863) 3 B & S 669.

11   *Martin v Pyecroft* (1852) 2 De GM & G 785, followed in *Scott v Bradley* [1971] Ch 850, [1971] 1 All ER 583, *Wake v Harrop* (1861) 1 H & C 202.

12   [1951] 1 All ER 746; *Clifford v Turrell* (1845) 1 Y & C Ch Cas 138 (affirmed 14 LJ Ch 390); *Frith v Frith* [1906] AC 254.

parties. Thus evidence has been received to show that an apparent sale was really a mortgage,[13] and a secret trust could never be established without recourse to extrinsic means of proof.

(v)   Capacity of parties[14]

We have seen that, if someone signs a document as 'owner' or 'proprietor', extrinsic evidence of agency is inadmissible. This may be on the principle that only one person can comply with such descriptions, so the evidence would inevitably contradict the document. Extrinsic evidence of agency has been received in the case of such other forms of signatures as 'charterer,'[15] 'tenant'[16] and 'landlord'.[17] It is possible, however, that the true basis of the decisions excluding the extrinsic evidence was that it was a term of the contracts with which the court was dealing that the signatory should have been owner or proprietor. They were treated with reserve by Lord Shaw and said to be no longer law by Scott LJ.[18] Extrinsic evidence has been received of the fact that the successive endorsers of a bill of exchange were co-sureties,[19] and, in *Young v Schuler*,[20] where it was not clear whether the defendant had signed a guarantee as agent for a company or with the intention of making himself personally liable, evidence was received of his contemporaneous declaration to the latter effect. It might have been treated as an admission, but it seems to have been received on the principle, to be discussed later, under which declarations of intention are admissible in cases of equivocation.

(vi)   Collateral undertakings, contracts partly oral and partly in writing or subject to usage

We have seen that the Court of Appeal recognised in *Newman v Gatti*,[1] that a collateral oral contract might be proved when it was concluded in consideration of the execution of a written contract. In *De Lassalle v Guildford*,[2] for instance, the claimant made it plain to his landlord, the defendant, that he would not execute a lease unless the defendant gave a warranty concerning the healthy condition of the drains. Such warranty was given orally, and the lease was duly executed. The lease did not refer to the state of the drains, but it was held that this fact did not prevent the adduction of oral evidence concerning the warranty. A court may likewise come to the conclusion that the parties intended their contract to be partly oral and partly in writing, in which case the oral parts may be proved by parol testimony. In *Harris v Rickett*,[3] the defendant

---

13   *Re Duke of Marlborough, Davis v Whitehead* [1894] 2 Ch 133.
14   For the admissibility of extrinsic evidence to show who was purchaser and who vendor, see *Newell v Radford* (1867) LR 3 CP 52.
15   *Fred Drughorn Ltd v Rederiaktiebolaget Transatlantic* [1919] AC 203.
16   *Danziger v Thompson* [1944] KB 654, [1944] 2 All ER 151.
17   *Epps v Rothnie* [1945] KB 562, [1946] 1 All ER 146.
18   In *Drughorn's* case and *Epps v Rothnie* respectively; but see *Murphy v Rae* [1967] NZLR 103.
19   *Macdonald v Whitfield* (1883) 8 App Cas 733. See also *Rolfe, Lubell & Co v Keith* [1979] 1 All ER 860.
20   (1883) 11 QBD 651.
1   (1907) 24 TLR 18; see also *Bristol Tramways etc Carriage Co v Fiat Motors* [1910] 2 KB 831, at 838; and *Heilbut, Symons & Co v Buckleton* [1913] AC 30, at 47.
2   [1901] 2 KB 215; *Morgan v Griffith* (1871) LR 6 Exch 70; *Erskine v Adeane* (1873) 8 Ch App 756; *City and Westminster Properties (1934) Ltd v Mudd* [1959] Ch 129, [1958] 3 All ER 733. A possible distinction between this last case and *Angell v Duke* is that in *Angell v Duke* the lessee did not insist on the provision of further furniture being part of the consideration for his executing the lease. Cf *Couchman v Hill* [1947] KB 554, [1947] 1 All ER 103.
3   (1959) 4 H & N 1.

was allowed to prove that a written agreement for a loan was accompanied by an oral stipulation that a bill of sale would be given. The claimant contended that the effect of this evidence was to add to or vary the writing but Pollock CB said that: 'the rule relied on by the claimant only applies when the parties to an agreement reduce it to writing and agree or intend that writing should be their agreement.' A further example of the use of extrinsic evidence is provided by cases in which one party has been allowed to establish a trade usage provided it is not inconsistent with the writing.[4]

> In all contracts, as to the subject-matter of which known usages prevail, parties are found to proceed with the tacit assumption of these usages, they commonly reduce into writing the special particulars of their agreement but omit to specify these known usages, which are included, however, as of course, by mutual understanding, evidence therefore of such incidents is receivable. The contract in truth is partly express and in writing, partly implied or understood and unwritten.[5]

(vii)   Memoranda

In some cases, after an oral contract has been concluded, a memorandum relating to the whole or part of the transaction is prepared by one of the parties and handed to the other. The document may then be treated as a mere memorandum, and, as it has no contractual effect, additional matter may be proved. Whether the writing is to be treated thus, or whether it will be held to be, not a memorandum, but a contractual document, depends on the intention of the parties, which must, in the absence of direct evidence, be ascertained by means of the inferences which a reasonable man would draw from the terms of the document and the surrounding circumstances. In *Allen v Pink*,[6] the claimant bought a horse from the defendant who handed him a receipt for the purchase price, and it was held that this did not preclude the claimant from proving an oral warranty of the fitness of the animal. Lord Abinger CB concluded that the paper appeared to have been meant merely as a memorandum of the transaction, or an informal receipt for the money, not as containing the terms of the contract itself. This case may be contrasted with *Hutton v Watling*[7] in which a document providing for the sale of a business by the defendant to the claimant and containing an option to purchase the land on which the business was carried on was treated as contractual by the Court of Appeal with the result that the defendant's evidence, in a claim for specific performance of the option, that no option was given, was held to be inadmissible. The court treated the matter as one of construction, adding that:[8]

> The true construction of a document means no more than that the court puts upon it the true meaning, being the meaning which the other party, to whom the

---

4   The distinction between usages which add to and contradict a document is difficult. Contrast *Brown v Byrne* (1854) 3 E & B 703 with *Krall v Burnett* (1887) 25 WR 305.
5   Per Coleridge J in *Brown v Byrne* (1854) 3 E & B 703.
6   (1838) 4 M & W 140; as between the parties a bill of lading is a memorandum: *Ardennes SS (Cargo Owner) v Ardennes SS (Owners)* [1951] 1 KB 55, [1950] 2 All ER 517; cf *Leduc & Co v Ward* (1888) 20 QBD 475, turning on the point that the bill is conclusive evidence of the terms of the shipment as between shipowner and endorsee under the Bills of Lading Act 1855. Another case in which a post-contractual document was treated as a memorandum is *Bank of Australasia v Palmer* [1897] AC 540.
7   [1948] Ch 398, [1948] 1 All ER 803; *Stuart v Dundon* [1963] SASR 134.
8   Per Lord Greene MR at 403, 805 respectively.

document was handed or who is relying upon it, would put upon it as an ordinary intelligent person construing the words in a proper way in the light of the relevant circumstances.

The cases on collateral contracts, contracts partly oral and partly in writing, contracts subject to usage and memoranda raise the question whether, at least in its application to contracts, what is often called the parol evidence rule is anything more than an empty tautology.[9] If the law is simply that extrinsic evidence is inadmissible when the parties intended that a document should contain their entire contract, extrinsic evidence is naturally inadmissible because it is irrelevant. Cases like *Hutton v Watling* show that the rule is not a tautology because the parties are bound by the terms of a document if a reasonable man would have considered the document to be a contractual one. This is so even if one of them thought that the contract contained additional terms not mentioned in the document or that a clearly expressed term to which he had agreed bore a special meaning.[10]

(viii) Proceedings between strangers

There is little doubt that, in proceedings between strangers to transactions required by law to be in writing, the circumstances in which extrinsic evidence is admissible are the same as those in which such evidence is admissible in proceedings between the parties to the document, but there is some authority for the view that extrinsic evidence is always admissible when the document merely embodies a transaction to the validity of which the writing is not essential even if it has the effect of varying, adding to, or contradicting the terms of the writing. In *R v Inhabitants of Cheadle*[11] the parish was allowed to call a pauper whose settlement was in issue to swear that a deed of conveyance to which he was party was, contrary to its express terms, unsupported by consideration. In *R v Adamson*,[12] the accused was charged with obtaining money by false pretences as a premium payable under a deed of partnership executed by the prosecutor. It was held that the prosecutor could give evidence of a different consideration for the payment of the premium from that stated in the deed. Stephen treated these cases as authorities for a general exception to the rule prohibiting extrinsic evidence adding to, varying or contradicting the terms of a document,[13] but this rule certainly applies in some cases in which one of the parties to the proceedings was not a party to the writing. In *Mercantile Bank of Sydney v Taylor*,[14] for instance, the bank was not allowed to adduce evidence of an oral agreement between themselves and one of several sureties, of whom the defendant was another, that the guaranteed debt should not be included in a release from liability given by them. The evidence received in *R v Inhabitants of Cheadle* would now be admissible in proceedings between parties to the deed[15] and *R v Adamson* may

---

9   See the discussion of this point by Treitel in *The Law of Contract* (9th edn) p 183.
10   See the speech of Lord Denning in *London County Council v Henry Boot & Sons Ltd* [1959] 3 All ER 636, at 641. The parties may be bound by terms to which they have agreed although they both think the terms have a different meaning from that ultimately placed on them by the court.
11   (1832) 3 B & Ad 833. Contrast the operation of the rule that a document is exclusive evidence of its terms as illustrated by *Augustien v Challis* (1847) 1 Exch 279.
12   (1843) 2 Mood CC 286.
13   *Digest of the Law of Evidence* (12th edn) art 99.
14   [1893] AC 317.
15   See *Frith v Frith* [1906] AC 254.

simply indicate that the rule does not apply in criminal proceedings. The authorities are too scanty to be a convenient subject for any generalisation.[16]

The Law Commission, although at first inclined to recommend abolition of the rule, ultimately came to the conclusion that it had become too ineffective to cause serious difficulty, and that more disruption would probably be caused by formal abolition than by leaving it alone.[17]

B.   EXTRINSIC EVIDENCE IN AID OF INTERPRETATION[18]

It has been said that:[19]

> The admission of extrinsic circumstances to govern the construction of a written instrument is in all cases an exception to the general rule of law which excludes everything dehors the instrument.

But statements of this nature must be read with caution, for it would be impossible to interpret most documents if some extrinsic matter were not allowed to be proved. If a testator bequeaths 'my piano to my son John', evidence must perforce be received to show that there were in existence at his death a chattel and a person corresponding to these descriptions. In the words of James LJ: 'You must always, of course, have evidence who are the persons mentioned, and you must also have evidence of what are the things bequeathed'.[20] The main problem in relation to the construction of a will was the extent to which it was permissible to go beyond these matters in cases of disputed interpretation, and a similar problem arises with regard to the construction of other documents[1]—if there is a doubt concerning the persons or things to which the document refers, is it permissible to consider the surrounding circumstances and the extrinsic declarations of the parties in order to resolve the doubt, or must the document be held void for uncertainty? In some cases there may be no alternative to the adoption of the latter course. If a testator leaves his estate to 'Lady ', or to 'One or other of my daughters Joan and Jane', even if it is proved that he was acquainted with women of title, or the father of daughters named Joan and Jane respectively, no further evidence might be forthcoming, in which case there would hardly be a rational alternative to holding that he died intestate. There is, however, an infinite variety of degrees of doubt concerning the certainty with which a document may be interpreted. At the one extreme there are the cases of complete uncertainty to which reference has just been made, at the other there is the case of virtually complete certainty as where a man leaves

---

16   It has been held in South Africa that the rule does not apply between strangers (*Davies v Brooklands Car Sales* 1956 (1) SA 745).

17   Law Commission No 154 (Cmnd 9700) (1986) Part III. The term 'parol evidence rule' as used in this paper is confined to the rule so far discussed in this section. The paper is not concerned with the rules discussed in section 1 and in the remainder of this section.

18   Now that s 21 of the Administration of Justice Act 1982 has implemented the recommendations of the 19th Report of the Law Reform Committee on the Interpretation of Wills (Cmnd 5301), it has been possible to eliminate much of the discussion of the old case law to be found in early editions of this work. The position in Australia was stated by the High Court in *Codelfa Construction Pty Ltd v State Railway Authority of NSW* (1982) 149 CLR 337.

19   Per Plumer MR in *Colpoys v Colpoys* (1822) Jac 451.

20   *Sherratt v Mountford* (1873) 8 Ch App 928, at 929. For a modern illustration see *Freeguard v Rogers* [1999] 1 WLR 375.

1   The rules apply similarly to documents whether or not required to be evidenced or made in writing, and whether or not referring to future liabilities: *Perrylease Ltd v Imecar AG* [1987] 2 All ER 373, [1988] 1 WLR 463.

everything to 'my only son John', and it is proved that he had but one son and that son's name is John.

The extent to which a document may be treated as conclusive as to the meaning of its terms is thus a question of degree. It can hardly ever be completely so, because some extrinsic evidence must be received but the nature of such evidence, and the purposes for which it may be used in a case in which the meaning of a document is disputed, depends on the standard of interpretation by which the litigation must be decided.

1. Standards of interpretation

Wigmore[2] spoke of four possible standards—the popular, the local, the common and the individual. The popular standard refers to the ordinary meaning of words; the local standard refers to possible variations of the popular within a particular community, trade[3] or religious sect; the common standard covers the sense in which the words were understood by both parties to a contract, while the individual standard is that of one party to a transaction and is, in general, relevant only in cases of will construction. Subject to the need to resort to extrinsic evidence in order to ascertain the persons and things covered by the words used, the application of the popular standard is a matter of exegesis aided by judicial notice rather than evidence. Judicial notice may be taken of some local or trade usages, but these are matters which usually have to be proved.[4] The application of the common and individual standards calls, in the absence of anything in the nature of a formal admission, for extrinsic evidence which can be either circumstantial or testimonial. Assuming that no exclusionary rules apply, the fact that the parties to a contract have a common objective may warrant an inference concerning the meaning they attached to certain clauses, just as the speech habits of a testator may justify a particular construction of the words used by him. The meaning of the contracting parties and the testator could also, subject to exclusionary rules, be proved in the one case by their direct oral evidence and, in either case, by their out of court statements.

According to Wigmore, the application of each of the above standards should be, and to a large extent is, provisional. This means that extrinsic evidence in aid of interpretation may take a variety of forms and be adduced for a number of different purposes varying with the facts of the particular case, but Wigmore did not deny the existence of restrictions on its admissibility. Such restrictions may, as a matter of law, rule out one or more of the standards which have just been mentioned.

In the first place, there was a general rule (subject to very limited exceptions) excluding the statements of intention of the testator or contracting parties as evidence of the sense in which words were used by them in the will or written contract under consideration. In the case of wills, that general rule has been abrogated by s 21 of the Administration of Justice Act 1982 for wills taking effect after 1 January 1983.

Secondly, the individual standard must always be inapplicable when the court is concerned with the construction, as opposed to the existence, avoidance or rectification of a contract:[5]

---

2   Paras 2458 and 2460.
3   For an Australian example see *Homestake Australia Ltd v Metana Minerals NL* (1991) 11 WAR 435.
4   Sometimes by expert evidence: see *Davis v Temco* [1992] CLY 2064.
5   Per Lord Wilberforce in *Prenn v Simmonds* [1971] 3 All ER 237, at 241.

The words used may, and often do, represent a formula which means different things to each side, yet be accepted because that is the only way to get agreement and in the hope that disputes will not arise. The only course there can be is to try to ascertain the natural meaning.

But the most important of all the restrictions on the application of any standard of interpretation but the popular is the influence of the 'plain meaning' rule, according to which, if the words of a document apply exactly to a particular person or thing in their ordinary natural sense, extrinsic evidence cannot be received to displace it. In other words, if the document contains names or descriptive phrases which are wholly appropriate when the popular standard of interpretation is applied, resort cannot be had, in the case of a contract, to the common standard, and, in the case of a will, to the individual standard:[6]

> Suppose ... a testator left a legacy to his son John, and suppose he had a son John who had been living away from him, and there was another person named John living with him who was not his son, but whom he called his son, in such a case would any evidence be admitted that his son John was not the person intended to be benefited? How can the fact of a testator being in the habit of calling a person his son who is not his son be evidence of surrounding circumstances? It is really evidence of the intention of the testator...

2.   Interpretation of wills

Most of the discussion of the admissibility of extrinsic evidence in aid of interpretation has been derived from learning devoted to the rules governing the interpretation of wills. A number of principles, representing the common law of his day, was drawn up by Wigram in 1831. Wills created special problems because of the expectations and disappointments so often generated by death. The resolution of disputes so created is rendered particularly difficult because of the unavailability as a witness of the testator, who would have been the one to know most about the matters in issue. It was, of course, for such reasons that the law insisted upon strict formal requirements for the making, and proof, of a will. Much of the rigidity of the rules excluding extrinsic evidence in aid of the interpretation of wills was explained by the quite understandable desire to prevent the formal rules from being undermined. All extrinsic evidence was looked upon with suspicion, but none more than the testator's direct statement of his intentions. It would hardly have made sense to insist upon strict formal rules for making wills, but then allow any vague expression to be interpreted in the light of informal statements of the testator.

On the other hand a succession of cases exemplified the unsatisfactory nature of a system of rigid exclusionary rules, which often defeated the intentions of the testator completely. Thus in *Doe d Chichester v Oxenden*[7] the will referred to 'my estate of Ashton', and was construed so as to apply strictly to the testator's actual estate at Ashton, despite clear evidence that he was in the habit of including other nearby estates in his references to 'the Ashton estate'. The rigidity of these principles was further

6   Per Kay LJ in *Re Fish, Ingham v Rayner* [1894] 2 Ch 83, at 86. The Administration of Justice Act 1982, s 21, would now allow such evidence to be adduced.
7   (1816) 3 Taunt 147.

exemplified by a decision of the House of Lords in this century. In *Higgins v Dawson*[8] the question was whether pecuniary legacies were payable out of the entire residuary estate of a testator or only out of such estate after two sums due to the deceased on mortgages had been deducted. The testator had bequeathed 'all the residue and remainder' of these sums to named persons after 'payment of my debts, funeral and testamentary expenses'. In favour of the contention that the sums due on mortgage should be liable to bear their portion of the legacies, it was sought to adduce evidence that, when he made his will, the testator's estate, apart from these sums, was insufficient to meet the legacies so that he must have intended to charge them on the mortgage debts. It was held that the evidence was inadmissible because the language used by the testator clearly meant that the residue of the sums due on mortgage was to be calculated without deducting anything in respect of the legacies. In both of these cases the words bore on their face a plain, and apparently unambiguous, meaning. Similar difficulties are created by incomplete description or misdescription. Thus in one case[9] land was devised to John Hiscocks the eldest son of John Hiscocks. John Hiscocks had two sons: Simon, the eldest, and John, his second son, who was however his eldest son by a second marriage. It was held that this fact, and a number of other circumstances pointing to an intention that the second son should benefit, were admissible in evidence; but it was also held that the testator's declarations of intention were inadmissible.[10]

The old law distinguished such a situation from an equivocation where the description in the will clearly intends unique denotation, but is capable of applying to more than one instance. Here even the old law went a step further, and allowed use of the testator's informal declarations of intent to help resolve the ambiguity. In *Doe d Gord v Needs*[11] land was devised to 'George Gord, the son of Gord', and extrinsic evidence showed that there were two persons answering that description. Evidence was admitted of the testator's declarations of intention indicating which of the two he meant to benefit. In the words of Parke B:

> There is no blank before the name of Gord the father, which might have occasioned a doubt whether the devisor had finally fixed on any certain person in his mind. The devisor has clearly selected a particular individual as his devisee ... The evidence of the declarations of the testator has not the effect of varying the instrument in any way whatever; it only enables the court to reject one of the subjects, or objects, to which the description in the will applies; and to determine which of the two the devisor understood to be signified in the description in the will.

These rules were overlaid by further strata of learning devoted to such questions as whether the misdescription or equivocation was required to be patent, as in *Doe d Gord v Needs*, or could be discerned only after the reception of extrinsic evidence, as in *Doe d Chichester v Oxenden*. Then there were anomalies stemming from the reception of extrinsic evidence to show special meanings of particular terms, as in *Smith v Wilson*,[12] or even of particular names, as in *Re Ofner, Samuel v Ofner*[13] where the testator's

---

8   [1902] AC 1. A less rigid line was taken in *NSPCC v Scottish NSPCC* [1915] AC 207. *Higgins v Dawson* was distinguished by the New Zealand Court of Appeal in *Re Bell, Bell v Bell* [1964] NZLR 912 on the strength of *Re Knight, Re Wynn, Midland Bank Executor and Trustee Co Ltd v Parker* [1957] Ch 441, [1957] 2 All ER 252.

9   *Doe d Hiscocks v Hiscocks* (1839) 5 M & W 363.

10   See also *Charter v Charter* (1874) LR 7 HL 364.

11   (1836) 2 M & W 129.

12   (1832) 3 B & Ad 728 ('a thousand rabbits' held to mean 'twelve hundred rabbits').

13   [1909] 1 Ch 60.

declaration of intention to benefit a particular person was admitted merely to show his habit of misdescribing that person, and so indirectly to construe the use of the same misdescription in the will.

In addition there was some variation between the rules relating to the interpretation of wills and of other documents, such as contracts where extrinsic evidence was admissible, not only to resolve an ambiguity or uncertainty but also to raise one, as where the terms of a conversation were admitted to show that 'your wool' mentioned in the defendant's agent's written offer to buy included a quantity of wool produced by the claimant from other farms.[14]

For these reasons the whole question of the interpretation of wills was referred to the Law Reform Committee, which reported in 1973.[15] The entire Committee favoured an extension of the use of extrinsic evidence to resolve ambiguities, misdescription, partial description and equivocation. It was divided on how far to permit the use of direct evidence of the testator's dispositive intentions. The majority took the view that to allow it in all cases would go further than the rules applying to other documents, and would lead to uncertainty, expense and delay.[16] This view was accepted, and s 21 of the Administration of Justice Act 1982 embodies it:

(1) This section applies to a will–
(a)   in so far as any part of it is meaningless;
(b)   in so far as the language used in any part of it is ambiguous on the face of it;
(c)   in so far as evidence, other than evidence of the testator's intention, shows that the language used in any part of it is ambiguous in the light of surrounding circumstances.

(2) In so far as this section applies to a will extrinsic evidence of the testator's intention, may be admitted to assist in its interpretation.

This section should be read in conjunction with s 20 which extends the application of the equitable doctrine of rectification to wills, and thus allows words to be added to the probate, not, as before, merely to be omitted.

It is not intended that the section will enable a court to make a testator's will for him. Thus it will not allow complete blanks to be filled in, nor, it is submitted, will it allow vestigial coding to be expanded.[17] The use, and limitations, of the new law were demonstrated in *Re Williams, Wiles v Madgin*[18] where a letter written by a testatrix to her solicitor explaining her intentions was admitted to help construe her will, but was unable to remedy the deficiency, which there was the omission of words of gift. The instructions indicated an order of preference of potential beneficiaries, but was of too vague and preparatory a nature to be regarded as more than instructions for a draft. It was held however that the letter could be used only to attempt to resolve the ambiguity justifying its admission, and not for any other purpose. The admissibility of this letter under the new provisions may be compared with the inadmissibility of counsel's opinion to help construe a settlement drawn up in consequence of it.[19]

---

14   *Macdonald v Longbottom* (1860) 1 E & E 977, at 989 per Byles J.
15   19th Report (Cmnd 5301).
16   Para 54.
17   As in *Clayton v Lord Nugent* (1844) 13 M & W 200 where the letters K, L and M were used and a key made after the will was rejected.
18   [1985] 1 All ER 964.
19   *Rabin v Gerson Berger Association Ltd* [1985] 1 All ER 1041, [1985] 1 WLR 595.

The new section clearly retains the possibility of reference to the testator's direct statement of intention in cases of patent equivocation like *Doe d Gord v Needs*,[20] to resolve the problem of misdescription or incomplete description, thus adding to the evidence admissible if facts like those of *Doe d Hiscocks v Hiscocks*[1] or *Charter v Charter*[2] were to recur. It would be of still more assistance in cases like *Doe d Chichester v Oxenden*[3] or *Higgins v Dawson*[4] where anything except direct evidence of the testator's intention would be admissible to demonstrate the ambiguity, and then, even including such direct evidence of intention, to resolve it.

It seems likely, and is to be hoped, that these provisions will achieve the aim of the Law Reform Committee to make this branch of the law simpler and more logical. It has been seen that more satisfactory results would apparently have been achieved in the difficult problems thrown up by the old cases, and with the entry into force of these new provisions it seems that a complicated and confusing chapter of the law of evidence can now be closed.

20   (1836) 2 M & W 129.
1   (1839) 5 M & W 363.
2   (1874) LR 7 HL 364.
3   (1816) 3 Taunt 147.
4   [1902] AC 1.

Chapter XVII

Proof of frequently recurring matters

There is a sense in which this chapter is redundant, for almost every point made in it can be found elsewhere in this book. The collection under one head of the different ways in which evidence may be given of certain matters which frequently have to be proved in litigation may, however, be of some use to the student, if not to the practitioner. The proof of handwriting and certain kinds of document, both private and public was considered in the last chapter as well as the important provisions of the Bankers' Books Evidence Act 1879. It is now proposed to consider the proof of foreign law, identity, birth, death, age, marriage and legitimacy, judgments, convictions and other orders of the court and various other miscellaneous matters. Reference will from time to time be made to judicial notice and presumptions, although it is not customary to describe them as means of proof. The possibility of a fact being admitted formally or informally should always be borne in mind.

SECTION I. FOREIGN LAW[1]

We saw in ch IV that, so far as the English courts are concerned, foreign law is a question of fact[2] which since 1920 has to be decided by the judge.[3] We also saw in ch IV that, in this context, 'foreign law' comprises the law of Scotland, the law of the British dominions and colonies and, to some extent, the laws of Eire and Northern Ireland as well as the law of a foreign country in the strict sense of the term.

The general rule is that foreign law must be proved by an expert witness who will, in a disputed or complicated case, give his evidence on oath in the ordinary way. In simple routine cases it is not uncommon for the evidence to be by affidavit, or resort might be had to the Civil Evidence Act 1995.[4] The effect of the general rule is that foreign law

---

1   For a much fuller discussion and citation of authority see Dicey and Morris *Conflict of Laws* (12th edn) ch 9; Fentiman *Foreign Law in English Courts* (1998).
2   Though in some respects of a special character, see *Arab Monetary Fund v Hashim (No 8)* (1994) 6 Admin LR 348.
3   The same is true in Scotland: see *Armour v Thyssen Edelstahlwerke AG* 1989 SLT 182.
4   *Markes v Markes* (1955) 106 LJ 75 (a decision on the Evidence Act 1938); *Kirsh v Kirsh* [1958] SASR 258.

cannot usually be the subject of judicial notice,[5] or, at common law, inferred from previous English decisions on the same subject.[6] Before s 4(2), (5) of the Civil Evidence Act 1972 came into force it had to be proved afresh by an expert in each case. There are, however, certain cases in which foreign law is the subject of judicial notice or something taken to have been established by a previous English decision, and there are also some special statutory provisions governing the proof of foreign law. These matters will be considered before reference is made to the question of the qualification of the expert when testifying in cases to which the general rule applies.

The burden of proof rests on the party asserting that foreign law differs from English law. This is frequently expressed, rather infelicitously, by saying that there is a presumption that foreign and English law are the same.[7]

A. JUDICIAL NOTICE AND PREVIOUS DECISIONS

Chapter II noted that judicial notice may be taken of notorious facts, and, in some exceptional cases, the English courts have treated certain items of foreign law as matters of notoriety. The most famous instance is provided by *Saxby v Fulton*[8] in which judicial notice was taken of the fact that roulette is legal in Monte Carlo. Judicial notice might also be taken of the common law of Northern Ireland,[9] or of European Community law,[10] and the House of Lords will take judicial notice of Scots law.[11] Under the Maintenance Orders Act 1950, s 22(2), judicial notice must be taken of the law with regard to maintenance orders in every part of the United Kingdom. It also seems to be settled that once a statute passed in a British possession is properly before an English court, that court may construe the statute with the result that a body of case law on the subject may be created.[12] The principal statute is the Evidence (Colonial Statutes) Act 1907, which is confined to British possessions, and it is not clear how far the English courts will construe foreign legislation without the guidance of an expert witness. There are cases in which the English courts appear to have done this, and their decisions are then, presumably, binding on other courts within the limits of the doctrine of precedent.[13] In principle the function of an expert witness to foreign law is to provide an exposition of the foreign law, and not to apply it to the facts.[14]

5   *Brenan and Galen*'s Case (1847) 10 QB 492, at 498; *R v Ofori and Tackie (No 2)* (1994) 99 Cr App Rep 223, at 227.
6   *M'Cormick v Garnett* (1854) 23 LJ Ch 777.
7   See eg *University of Glasgow v Economist* (1990) Times, 13 July.
8   [1909] 2 KB 208; see also *Re Turner, Heyding v Hinchliff* [1906] WN 27.
9   *Re Nesbitt* (1844) 14 LJMC 30, at 33. See Nokes [1960] ICLQ 564.
10   European Communities Act 1972, s 3.
11   This is on account of the House's appellate jurisdiction in civil cases. It is doubtful whether the House of Lords would take judicial notice of Scots criminal law, should the question ever arise. The House would take judicial notice of the law of Northern Ireland.
12   *Re Sebba, Lloyds Banks, Ltd v Hutson* [1959] Ch 166, [1958] 3 All ER 393, following *Re Goetze, National Provincial Bank Ltd v Mond* [1953] Ch 96, [1953] 1 All ER 76. See also 22 MLR 317; 24 MLR 312. In *Mahadervan v Mahadervan* [1964] P 233, at 240, [1962] 3 All ER 1108, at 1113 it was said that an English court can construe a written foreign law once it is in evidence. Most of the decisions on this matter relate to countries to which the Evidence (Colonial Statutes) Act 1907 applies, although, in several instances, no reference is actually made to the Statute. See also *Shariff v Azad* [1967] 1 QB 605, [1966] 3 All ER 785.
13   In *Re Cohn* [1945] Ch 5, the English court appears to have construed a provision in the German Civil Code without expert evidence, and presumably its decision on the point constitutes a precedent.
14   *Di Sora v Phillips* (1863) 10 HL Cas 624, at 639. See also *Rouyer Guillet et Cie v Rouyer Guillet & Co* [1949] 1 All ER 244n. In Australia, see *United States Trust Co of New York v Australia and New Zealand Banking Group Ltd* (1995) 37 NSWLR 131.

Section 4(2) of the Civil Evidence Act 1972 permits the reception as evidence of foreign law of any previous determination by an English court of the point in question, provided it is reported in citable form,[15] and provided notice of intention to rely upon it has been given to the other parties to the proceedings.[16] The foreign law is to be taken to be in accordance with the determination unless the contrary is proved. It makes no difference whether the point was determined in civil or criminal proceedings, but foreign law may be proved in this way only in civil proceedings.[17]

B.   OTHER STATUTORY PROVISIONS

Under the Evidence (Colonial Statutes) Act 1907,[18] copies of Acts, Ordinances and Statutes passed by or under the authority of the legislature of any British possession shall be received in evidence by all courts of justice in the United Kingdom if purporting to be printed by the Government Printer[19] without any proof given that the copies were so printed. The term 'British possession' means any part of Her Majesty's dominions exclusive of the United Kingdom.[20] It is clear that this statute enables an English court to receive a statute or subordinate legislation of a British possession in evidence on the mere production of a Government Printer's copy, but the Act of 1907 would not be much use if this were all that it has achieved, and it has been held in a number of cases that the English courts may construe the statute, acting on its provisions as so construed without anything in the nature of expert evidence.[1]

There has long been provision for ascertaining foreign law by special reference to a foreign court. Within the Commonwealth this can be accomplished by the use of the British Law Ascertainment Act 1859.[2] Although the law to which it refers is strictly not 'foreign', of perhaps greater importance is the provision in art 130u of the Treaty of Rome that any subordinate court of a member country of the European Community may, if it considers it necessary to give judgment, refer any question of the interpretation of Community law to the European Court for its opinion, and that any final court must do so. In *HP Bulmer Ltd v J Bollinger SA*[3] the Court of Appeal set out guidelines to assist in determining when such reference was to be considered necessary, and for determining whether to exercise discretion to do so where it exists.

Although the Evidence (Foreign, Dominion and Colonial Documents) Act 1933 does not, strictly speaking, relate to the proof of foreign law, it contains useful provisions which should never be forgotten in cases involving a foreign element. Put very briefly, its effect is that Orders in Council may be made with regard to the proof, by authenticated copy, of extracts from public registers in the foreign country or dominion to which the order applies. The certificate is not merely evidence of the contents of the register, but

---

15   Ie in a report which could, if the question had been one of English law, have been cited as authority in any court in England or Wales.
16   See CPR 33.7.
17   There was a corresponding provision in the draft Bill attached to the 11th Report of the Criminal Law Revision Committee, but it was omitted from the Police and Criminal Evidence Act 1984 and from the Criminal Justice Act 1988.
18   See also the Colonial Laws Validity Act 1865, s 6.
19   Ie the Government Printer of the possession.
20   Quaere whether this statute still applies to all Commonwealth countries.
1   See the numerous cases cited in *Jasiewicz v Jasiewicz* [1962] 3 All ER 1017, [1962] 1 WLR 1426.
2   The comparable provision in relation to non-British law, the Foreign Law Ascertainment Act 1861, was never invoked, and consequently repealed in 1973.
3   [1974] Ch 401, [1974] 2 All ER 1226. See also *Customs and Excise Comrs v ApS Samex (Hanil Synthetic Fiber Industrial Co)* [1983] 1 All ER 1042.

also evidence of the facts stated. The statute is therefore of great utility[4] in connection with the proof of births, deaths and marriages occurring abroad. In the case of a marriage, it will generally dispense with the necessity of calling an expert in the relevant foreign law in order to swear that the certificate would be accepted as evidence of the marriage in question in the courts of the foreign country. A number of Orders in Council have been made under the Act.

C. EXPERT WITNESS

When a case falls within the general rule requiring proof of foreign law by an expert, the witness must be properly qualified. There has never been any doubt that a judge or regular practitioner in the jurisdiction whose law is in question is properly qualified,[5] but this was once thought to be both sufficient and necessary a condition. In *Bristow v Sequeville*[6] a jurisconsult, adviser to the Prussian consulate in London who had studied law in Leipzig and knew that the Code Napoleon was in force in Saxony was not allowed to give evidence concerning the Code. A number of cases departed from this rigid attitude over the years, and it seems that the Civil Evidence Act 1972, s 4(1) did no more than enact the common law in declaring that a person suitably qualified on account of knowledge or experience is competent to give evidence of foreign law irrespective of whether he has acted or is qualified to act as a legal practitioner in the country in question.[7]

This leaves open the question of what constitutes a suitable qualification. It seems that practical experience will suffice, even though gained as business man,[8] banker,[9] diplomat,[10] or Governor-General,[11] rather than as legal practitioner. A teacher of the law of the jurisdiction in question may be sufficiently qualified, though it is doubtful whether a student would be.[12] Conversely the evidence of a legal practitioner may be rejected if he cannot be shown to have practical experience.[13] There may indeed be room for argument as to what counts as practical experience.[14] A more lenient view used to be taken of the qualifications regarded as suitable, when there were particularly few witnesses,[15] though modern communications and relaxation of the hearsay rule should reduce the need for such leniency today.

---

4   Assisted in proceedings related to entitlement to social security benefits by a rule of European law that courts must accept certificates and similar documents from other member states, *Dafeki v Landesversicherungsanstalt Württemberg* [1998] All ER (EC) 452, ECJ.
5   *Baron De Bode's Case* (1845) 8 QB 208.
6   (1850) 5 Exch 275.
7   It is to be hoped that this is the case since the recommendation of the Criminal Law Revision Committee in Cmnd 4991 draft Bill, cl 44 that a similar provision be enacted for criminal proceedings seems not so far to have been implemented.
8   *Vander Donckt v Thellusson* (1849) 8 CB 812.
9   *Ajami v Customs Controller* [1954] 1 WLR 1405.
10 *Re Dost Aly Khan's Goods* (1880) 6 PD 6.
11 *Cooper-King v Cooper-King* [1900] P 65.
12 *Brailey v Rhodesia Consolidated Ltd* [1910] 2 Ch 95 (Reader in Roman-Dutch Law at Council for Legal Education); contrast *Bristow v Sequeville* (above) (a former student).
13 *Cartwright v Cartwright and Anderson* (1878) 26 WR 684 (English barrister as to law of Canada when he had appeared in the Privy Council on Canadian appeals, but not in the relevant area of law).
14 In *R v Brady* (1980) 57 FLR 198 the witness carried on a tax consultancy practice involving schemes operating under the law of Liechtenstein which he had studied only at second hand, and was held entitled to give evidence on the general basis of the law, but not of its detailed application.
15 See *Direct Winters Transport v Duplate Canada Ltd* (1962) 32 DLR (2d) 278.

The decision whether the proposed witness is properly qualified is made by the judge as a condition precedent to the admission of the evidence. In coming to a conclusion on a question of foreign law, the English courts may consider foreign statutes and decisions referred to by the expert witness, and if, but only if,[16] there is a conflict of expert testimony, the English judge must resolve it.[17] In cases where the relevant concepts of foreign law are sufficiently similar to those of English law for the judge to be able to employ his own legal training in determining their correct interpretation and application his decision is liable to reversal on appeal in much the same way as his determination of questions of domestic law.[18]

SECTION 2.   EVIDENCE OF IDENTITY

Identity must be proved[19] in a wide variety of situations. Most often it relates to the identity of persons, but sometimes relates to the identity of objects.[20] In a sense all litigation involves questions of the identity of persons, since the relevant order must relate to the same person as was implicated in the events upon the proof of which the order was made.[1] The most common situation however occurs in criminal cases where it can be established that a crime has been committed, and witnesses are prepared to testify that they observed the accused in circumstances making it likely that he committed it. Sometimes the presence of the accused[2] in a relevant place is controverted, but sometimes his presence may be admitted, and the question arises as to whether it was the accused or others of those also present who acted in a particular way.[3] Identity can, of course, be equally central in civil cases, for example, whether a particular claimant to an estate is the rightful heir.[4]

Evidence of identity is at its most vulnerable when it purports to be based upon the identification by a human being of the features of another human being, whether those features are identified by sight, hearing, smell or, just conceivably,[5] touch, based upon an evanescent contact in the past. Sometimes the past occasion has been captured in more permanent form, for example, on a video or tape recording, in which case the jury

16   *Bumper Development Corpn Ltd v Metropolitan Police Comr* [1991] 4 All ER 638, [1991] 1 WLR 1362 (judge must accept a unanimous expert view).

17   *Re Duke of Wellington* [1947] Ch 506, [1947] 2 All ER 854.

18   *Macmillan Inc v Bishopsgate Investment Trust plc (No 4)* (1998) Times, 7 December, rejecting the view that an appeal could be allowed only if the trial judge's view was an impossible one.

19   Mere coincidence of name, and appearance in the dock, does not justify failure to call evidence of identity: *R v Brennan* [1996] CLY 1381.

20   In *R v Browning* (1992) 94 Cr App Rep 109, at 122 the Court of Appeal noted the different considerations which apply and held a *Turnbull* direction inappropriate. Care is nevertheless very necessary, especially in relation to the identification of mass produced objects: see *Bond v MacFarlane* (1990) 102 FLR 38. In *Pfennig v R* (1995) 127 ALR 99 a witness was given the opportunity to listen to the sound of eight cars including the suspect one, and identified it; but still the trial judge urged the jury to use the evidence only to show that the witness had heard a sound *like* that made by the accused's car. A specific identification warning was required of a lorry in Australia in *R v Clout* (1995) 41 NSWLR 312.

1   For an expansive approach see *R v Andrews* [1993] Crim LR 590 where this feature is highlighted in Birch's commentary.

2   Slightly different considerations may apply to the identification of a third party accompanying the accused: see *R v Bath* (1990) 154 JP 849.

3   This has been regarded as not requiring the same consideration of caution as identification in the normal sense: *R v Oakwell* [1978] 1 All ER 1223, [1978] 1 WLR 32; and not necessarily the full *Turnbull* direction: *R v Slater* [1995] 1 Cr App Rep 584.

4   As in the famous 19th century case of the Tichborne claimant, a dispute which could probably by modern methods of genetic testing nowadays be settled with complete certainty.

5   Taste does seem inconceivable.

may make its own identification, perhaps assisted by identification testimony from witnesses who have greater familiarity with the accused,[6] or from experts in the interpretation of real evidence whether visual[7] or aural.[8] Identification may also be accomplished by the use of circumstances rather than testimonial evidence, or by presumption. This section will consider identification by direct, circumstantial and presumptive evidence separately, but the first is by far the most important.

A. DIRECT EVIDENCE

This part will first consider the reasons why direct evidence of identity poses particular problems, then the reactions of courts and law reformers to their perception of such problems. It will then go on to consider the modern law, mentioning in turn the different forms of identification, the question of the procedure for considering them, and finally the proper direction to be given to the jury.

I. Special problems[9]

It was stated by the Criminal Law Revision Committee in its Eleventh Report that:[10]

> We regard mistaken identification as by far the greatest cause of actual or possible wrong convictions. Several cases have occurred in recent years when a person has been charged or convicted on what has later been shown beyond doubt to have been mistaken identification.

This is far from being a new concern. It was because of the mistaken identification[11] of Adolph Beck that a Committee of Inquiry was set up, and, following receipt of its report,[12] that the Court of Criminal Appeal was established. Similarly it was concern over two miscarriages of justice on the basis of mis-identification that caused the government to set up a departmental committee under the chairmanship of Lord Devlin to review all aspects of the law and procedure relating to identification in criminal cases.[13] It has been established that the deficiencies of the old law sometimes led to the execution of those who should never have been found guilty.[14]

The reasons for such difficulty are apparent. A very substantial psychological literature[15] has demonstrated that the processes involved are riddled with weaknesses, from initial perception to eventual recall. Articulation is particularly difficult, and suggestibility, both in the sense of accepting externally inspired suggestions and in applying internal preconceptions, is high. These defects are compounded by the

---

6   *Kajala v Noble* (1982) 75 Cr App Rep 149; *R v Fowden and White* [1982] Crim LR 588; *R v Grimer* [1982] Crim LR 674; *R v Caldwell and Dixon* (1994) 99 Cr App Rep 73. But not if the witnesses have no more previous knowledge of the accused than the jury itself: see *R v Leaney* (1989) 50 CCC (3d) 289.

7   As in *R v Stockwell* (1993) 97 Cr App Rep 260; *R v Clarke* [1995] 2 Cr App Rep 425.

8   As in *R v Robb* (1991) 93 Cr App Rep 161.

9   See Jackson [1986] Crim LR 203.

10   Cmnd 4991 (1972) para 196.

11   By no fewer than fifteen different women.

12   Cmnd 2315 (1905).

13   HC Paper 338 (1976).

14   *R v Mattan* (1998) Times, 5 March.

15   Some of it is conveniently summarised in the Interim Report of the Australian Law Reform Commission No 26 Vol 1 paras 419–421 (1985).

inability of conventional cross-examination to reveal their weaknesses. Identification is a largely internal and isolated process so, unlike other evidence, it resists probing based upon its coherence with the rest of the surrounding evidence. It is also usually sincerely believed in by the witness,[16] and the witness's view is more likely to be reinforced than to be weakened by the passage of time and by challenge.[17] The courts are generally reluctant to allow challenge to evidence based upon abstract or theoretical studies divorced from the facts of the instant case, and in this context have refused to admit evidence designed to show the general weakness of evidence of identification.[18] The cumulative effect of these factors is to reduce the probative value of the evidence while at the same time increasing its prejudicial effect, given that in this context prejudice connotes adducing evidence which the jury[19] is likely to credit more than is warranted.

Problems are compounded when the variation between different situations is taken into account. For example if the person identified is well-known to the identifier, sometimes distinguished as recognition as opposed to identification, this might be regarded in many cases as decreasing the risk of mis-identification,[20] except that there is a known tendency for an identifier to assimilate a perception to someone who is already known. The procedure for initial identification may also be suggestive,[1] for example in using photographs, or may reinforce an initially uncertain perception, for example, by reference to an elicited description, or image. Quite apart from anything else physical conditions will vary greatly from one situation to another, and perceptive abilities from one person to another. Even in the case of a given individual it is unlikely to be obvious, or known, how distorted perceptive faculties may become as a result of the stress or trauma of perhaps being the victim of, or even an eyewitness to, a particularly distressing event like the commission of a brutal crime. It is sometimes suggested,[2] but by no means universally accepted,[3] that identification by trained observers, such as the police,[4] is likely to be more reliable than identification by others. Sometimes special factors in the situation aggravate the difficulty of identification, for example when it is necessary to distinguish between identical twins.[5]

While failure to identify a person may be mistaken for similar reasons, or perhaps even by appreciation of these dangers, it does not follow that it should be subject to similar directions to the jury, which might indeed have the effect of reversing the burden of proof.[6]

There are also technical problems with the use of evidence of previous identification, since if the testifying witness is able to recognise the accused in court as the criminal, then evidence of any previous act of identification might seem no more than a previous consistent statement, designed to bolster the testimony in court; while if the testifying

---

16   A factor emphasised in *R v Dickson* [1983] 1 VR 227, and echoed by the Privy Council in *Scott v R* [1989] AC 1242, [1989] 2 All ER 305 (where it was said to be 'fundamental') and *Reid v R* [1990] 1 AC 363, [1993] 4 All ER 95n.

17   See *R v Atfield* (1983) 25 Alta LR (2d) 97, at 98.

18   See *R v Smith* [1987] VR 907; cp Holdenson (1988) 16 Melb ULR 521.

19   Though the same factors apply to all human beings, and in Australia the same rules requiring careful direction have been held to apply to trial by judge alone: *Grbic v Pitkethly* (1992) 65 ACR 12.

20   See *R v Caldwell and Dixon* (1993) 99 Cr App Rep 73, at 77. See also *People v Stafford* [1983] IR 165.

1   The Code of Practice does not apply at this stage, but it has been strongly recommended that a new set of provisions should be devised for it: *R v Hickin* [1996] Crim LR 584.

2   See *R v Ramsden* [1991] Crim LR 295; *R v Tyler* (1993) 96 Cr App Rep 332; *R v Williams* (1994) Times, 7 October.

3   See *Reid v R* [1990] 1 AC 363, at 392; *Berrell v Gill* (1993) 113 FLR 333.

4   Or even bank clerks: *R v Hunter* [1969] Crim LR 262.

5   See *Sharrett v Gill* (1992) 65 ACR 44.

6   *R v Speede* (1991) Times, 4 April.

witness is unable to recognises the accused in court as the criminal, then evidence of any previous act of identification might seem no more than a previous inconsistent statement, and as such not, in principle, admissible as evidence of its truth.

2. Legal reaction

These problems have become better understood in modern times, especially as a result of the development of psychological research into perception and recall. This increased awareness was first translated into intervention at a high judicial level in *People v Casey (No 2)*[7] where the Supreme Court of Ireland took the view that a warning of the dangers of acting upon evidence of identification should always be given to the jury, and in the instant case ordered a retrial because no such warning had been given. It should be noted that in that case the purported identification was by a number of strangers to the accused, some of them victims or children or both, and in poor light and otherwise difficult conditions.

This approach was however rejected by the House of Lords in *Arthurs v A-G for Northern Ireland*,[8] significantly enough a case in which the accused was well-known to the identifying police witness. It was there held that there is no inflexible rule that a warning should always be given, still less a requirement that there should be corroborating material. The House of Lords appeared to leave open the question of whether a warning should be mandatory in a case where the accused was previously unknown to the identifying witness,[9] but in a subsequent case of that nature[10] the Court of Criminal Appeal rejected any such view, and the House of Lords refused leave to appeal.[11]

Although such an approach stressed the need for a proper direction to the jury in general terms on the strength of the prosecution case, many still felt this insufficient. Some groups felt the need for a corroboration requirement[12] and, in at least one case,[13] the still more stringent requirement that such corroboration should not itself consist of further identification evidence of the same character as that requiring corroboration. The Criminal Law Revision Committee in its Eleventh Report recommended a mandatory caution, but not any special form of words.[14] This recommendation was to apply whether or not the accused was previously known to the witness, and irrespective of the number of acts of identification. The Devlin Committee went further, impelled to some extent by the fact that in one of the cases which inspired its investigation[15] such a general direction had been given, but without being effective to prevent a demonstrably wrong conviction. The Devlin Committee was thus inspired to recommend something more radical. It resisted the suggestion of a corroboration requirement, partly because there frequently is corroboration in the evidence of other identifying witnesses, partly because corroboration had become enmeshed with technicality and partly because of the burden that it would impose in clear and simple cases.[16] Its recommendation was

7   [1963] IR 33.
8   (1970) 55 Cr App Rep 161.
9   A position endorsed by Hailsham LC in *DPP v Kilbourne* [1973] AC 729, at 740.
10   *R v Long* (1973) 57 Cr App Rep 871.
11   See also dicta of Gibbs J to the same effect in the High Court of Australia in *Kelleher v R* (1974) 131 CLR 534, at 551.
12   Submissions to this effect were received by the Devlin Committee from the Law Society, the British Legal Association and the National Council for Civil Liberties.
13   The submission of *Justice* to the Devlin Committee.
14   Cmnd 4991 (1972), para 199 and draft Bill, cl 21.
15   That of *Dougherty*, see Devlin Report, ch 2.
16   Paragraphs 4.36–4.42.

that the trial judge should in every case give a very strong direction to the jury that evidence of identification alone is not sufficient to satisfy the high burden of proof in criminal cases, and explain to it exactly why this is so. It recommended further that the jury be directed that only in a limited range of exceptional circumstances would a conviction depending upon identification evidence be justified.[17] Like the Criminal Law Revision Committee the Devlin Committee took the view that in the then state of the law it was necessary for any such change to be introduced by statute.

This view was however overtaken by the highly influential decision of the Court of Appeal in *R v Turnbull*.[18] Since the Court of Appeal took the view that the direction of juries was a matter of practice, it felt competent to prescribe the proper direction. It took its cue from the recommendations of the Devlin Committee, and in particular stressed the need for some explanation of the need for special caution in accepting evidence of identification.[19] It went on to require the judge to direct the jury in some detail about the quality of the evidence of identification. It was in this stress upon quality that the court departed from the Devlin recommendations. It was not to countenance an automatic direction to acquit upon the basis of identification evidence alone, even in the absence of exceptional features in the Devlin sense, provided that the quality was good. It was indeed felt that the concept of exceptional features was undesirable, and for the very reason which commended it to the Devlin Committee, namely that it would be likely to generate a considerable corpus of precedent. The Devlin Committee welcomed this as being indicative rather than definitive, but the Court of Appeal clearly feared the growth of excessive technicality, it is submitted, rightly.

These guidelines seem to have precluded statutory intervention. The Royal Commission on Criminal Procedure did however recommend that identification procedures be made the subject of statutory regulation.[20] Section 66(b) of the Police and Criminal Evidence Act 1984 accordingly required the issue of a Code of Practice for the identification of suspects by police officers. It should be noted that despite its title this code deals in detail with identification by lay witnesses under the supervision of the police. This Code regulates procedures in most of the common situations to be mentioned in the next section.[1]

3. Different procedures for identification

The most common situation is identification by a witness, but exceptionally identification may be accomplished by the jury directly.

(i) *Identification by witnesses*

There are many different procedures for identification by witnesses, depending upon the particular circumstances of a given case. Sometimes the witness is able to describe the criminal in sufficient detail for a suspect to be identified, and sometimes such description is taken beyond words and expressed by a drawing or amalgamation of pre-recorded features in a so-called 'photofit'. A different technique is to show the

---

17   For discussion of the Devlin Committee's Report see Glanville Williams [1976] Crim LR 407, and for a bibliography see Khan (1978) 122 Sol Jo 377.

18   [1977] QB 224, [1976] 3 All ER 549, endorsed by the Privy Council in *Reid v R* [1990] 1 AC 363, [1993] 4 All ER 95n.

19   The more sincere the witness, the greater the need for caution: *R v Devlin* [1997] CLY 1152.

20   Cmnd 8092 (1981) para 3, 138.

1   But not in all: see *R v Jones; R v Dowling* (1994) 158 JP 293.

witness a series of photographs or video film in the hope that the witness will be able to recognise one of those depicted as the criminal. Once a suspect has been initially identified by one of these methods, opportunity is often presented for confirmation of his identification by the relevant witness. Such confirmation is normally, and preferably, attempted by means of an identification parade, but may also take the form of a group identification where a number of people are presented to the witness otherwise than on a formal parade, or by individual confrontation with the witness, the least satisfactory form of such confrontation being one which takes place in court during the trial itself, frequently referred to as 'dock identification'. It will be helpful to say a little more about the evidential repercussions of each of these approaches, bearing in mind that breach of the appropriate procedure will result in the exclusion of the evidence only if the breach is so serious as to trigger the judge's discretion to exclude under s 78 because the breach has had a sufficiently adverse effect on the fairness of the proceedings.[2]

(a) Description

The Devlin Committee pointed out[3] that psychological research indicated that descriptions given by witnesses were likely to be a good deal more unreliable than acts of identification.[4] It nevertheless recommended that statutory provision be made for the police to secure a description from an identifying witness, and for the imposition of a duty to supply such description to the defence. In the case of a witness actually called by the prosecution to identify the accused it recommended that such a description should itself become admissible in evidence.[5] In *R v Turnbull*[6] the Court of Appeal recommended that any descriptions materially differing from the appearance of the accused should automatically be supplied to the defence, any other supplied upon request, and that the trial judge should specifically direct the jury as to any material discrepancy between such a description and the actual appearance of the accused.[7] The Code provides[8] that a description should be secured from an identifying witness, written down, and provided to the defence before any of the other procedures for identification is attempted. This is reinforced in relation to informal procedures for selection of suspects, but does not apply where it is impractical from the point of view of effective policing.[9]

(b) Drawings or photofit compilations[10]

These techniques are designed to overcome the difficulty frequently experienced in trying to describe a criminal. Instead an artist attempts to draw to the witness's description, or, given that adequately competent artists are in short supply, someone assembles drawings or photographs of parts of a face, in the hope that by trial and error a representation will be obtained more satisfying to the witness, and more readily

---

2   *R v Quinn* [1990] Crim LR 581; *R v Grannell* (1990) 90 Cr App Rep 149; *R v Khan* [1997] Crim LR 584.
3   Para 5.8.
4   Although they may sometimes be decisive and conclusive where there is a very small number of suspects, as in *R v Byron* (1999) Times, 10 March.
5   Para 5.15.
6   At 228, 552.
7   In *R v Nagah* (1991) 92 Cr App Rep 344 remarkable discrepancies contributed to quashing a conviction; in *R v Quercia* (1990) 60 CCC (3d) 380 they were decisive.
8   Code D, para 2.0.
9   Code D, para 2.17. In *R v El-Hannachi* [1998] 2 Cr App Rep 226 it was held not to be practicable in urgent situations where there is a danger of dispersion of possible suspects.
10   Although mentioned in Code D, there is no detailed regulation of this practice, presumably on the basis that it is usually a more investigative than evidential procedure. For a comprehensive collation of United States authority see the annotation at 42 ALR 3d 1217.

applied by investigators. In *R v Smith*,[11] one of the first English cases[12] to consider the point, it was argued that a sketch produced at the witness's behest was hearsay, just as much as would have been a dictated verbal description. This argument was rejected on the basis that the artist performed a purely passive function, acting no more independently than a pen in the witness's hand. Different results were achieved in 1982: one court rejected a 'photofit' as equivalent to a previous consistent statement by the identifying witness, though conceding possible use to refresh memory,[13] while another admitted it, though in that case the witness who had composed it had subsequently failed to identify the accused at a parade.[14] The matter was finally resolved in *R v Cook*[15] where the Court of Appeal held that such a photofit picture infringed neither the hearsay rule nor that against previous consistent statements, and was hence admissible, just like a photograph. It seems that here again the court must have taken the view that the composer of the photofit picture was acting purely passively. This may seem implausible, but, if accepted, disposes of the hearsay rule. It is far from clear that the rule against previous consistent statements can be surmounted. It seems that the victim was prepared to identify the accused at the trial, though she had during the investigation experienced some difficulty in doing so. The court's view was simply that a photofit representation is sui generis, and not being a statement at all, cannot amount to a previous consistent statement. At this point it really does seem to raise similar problems to those in *R v Smith*. If the analogy of a photograph is taken, it would be tantamount to saying that a photograph identified out of court by the witness as being that of the criminal would be admissible whether or not the witness testified. If the witness did not testify it is submitted that the photograph would be inadmissible because it could not be linked to the criminal except by hearsay. Similarly here the photofit can be linked to the criminal only by the initial statement of the witness that it resembled her attacker. If she testifies, it is that assertion, and not the photofit itself, which amounts to the previous consistent statement. She is in effect testifying that the accused looks like the criminal, and that she said so earlier as demonstrated by the photofit which is now produced. This regrettable line of reasoning has now been taken a stage further in *R v Constantinou*[16] by holding that even where such a photofit constitutes the only evidence of identification it is unnecessary to give the normal 'Turnbull' warning, though one would think that in these circumstances it was more, rather than less, necessary.

(c)   *Photographs*

The problems of using photographs to assist the identification of offenders were thoroughly analysed by the High Court of Australia in *Alexander v R*.[17] A distinction was made between their use as an aid to detection by the police, and their use as evidence of identification in court, recognising that their use for the former purpose might infect their use for the latter. It was pointed out that identification from photographs suffers from three defects; first, because it happens in the absence of the accused there is no opportunity to see whether or not it has been conducted fairly, without prompting; second, because the act of picking out a photograph as resembling the criminal can subtly crystallise into firm recognition of the subject of the photograph as the criminal

---

11   [1976] Crim LR 511.
12   Though a drawing was admitted as early as 1817: see *R v Watson* (1817) 32 State Tr 1, at 125.
13   *R v O'Brien* [1982] Crim LR 746.
14   *R v Okorodu* [1982] Crim LR 747.
15   [1987] QB 417, [1987] 1 All ER 1049. Apparently accepted by Brooking J in *R v Hentschel* [1988] VR 362.
16   (1990) 91 Cr App Rep 74.
17   (1981) 145 CLR 395. See also *Pitkin v R* (1995) 130 ALR 35.

at a subsequent stage; and, third, because any revelation of initial identification by reference to photographs in the possession of the police may suggest the possession of a criminal record.[18] These defects work to some extent in a cumulative fashion, since it is difficult for the defence to expose the frailties of the procedure employed without at the same time drawing attention to the provenance of the photographs, and by inference to the accused's record.[19]

The proper procedure for the use of photographs in England is now set out in Annex D to Code D of the Codes of Practice made pursuant to s 66 of the Police and Criminal Evidence Act 1984.[20] It provides that any showing of photographs must be supervised by an officer of the rank of at least sergeant, that only one witness at a time is to be shown the photographs, and that no fewer than 12 should be shown in a batch.[1] Even then such a procedure must be recognised to weaken the strength of subsequent identification despite a properly conducted parade.[2] It seems however that failure to comply with such practices will not itself automatically lead to the inadmissibility of such evidence.[3] Nor does it seem that a judge is necessarily bound to warn the jury of the danger of inferring a criminal record from the use of photographs,[4] or of the weakening of other identification evidence because of initial photographic identification, though such matters might well affect the general fairness of the direction to the jury on the question of identification.

Although there have been strong statements as to the inadmissibility of identifying photographs adduced in evidence, especially when they indicate possession of a criminal record,[5] it seems that such photographs are not in all circumstances inadmissible,[6] especially where the conduct of the defence had incited,[7] invited,[8] or agreed to,[9] it. It is however likely that a judge would normally exercise his discretion to exclude unduly prejudicial evidence in many such cases, even as a matter of common law,[10] and quite apart from any breach of the Code of Practice, at least in relation to photographs clearly indicating the accused's possession of a criminal record.[11] If the photographs come from police custody, but not because the accused has a criminal record, a good character direction is appropriate.[12] On the other hand, if the photographs, even though coming from police custody, do not indicate their provenance, and have relevance, for example, as explaining the failure of the identifying

---

18 See *R v Kitchen* [1994] Crim LR 684.
19 For an account of, and justification for, a different method of using photographs which has some advantages over an identification parade: see *R v Murphy* (1995) 85 ACR 286.
20 Some internal inconsistency in these provisions was criticised in *Kitchen* above.
1   Similar procedures have been approved in New Zealand in *R v Tamihere* [1991] 1 NZLR 195 where the law was said to be very similar to that in England; and in Australia in *R v Britten* (1988) 51 SASR 567.
2   *R v Dwyer and Ferguson* [1925] 2 KB 799.
3   *R v Seiga* (1961) 45 Cr App Rep 220, and as decided in *Alexander* itself.
4   *R v Lawrenson* [1961] Crim LR 398; *R v Seiga* above.
5   *R v Lamb* (1980) 71 Cr App Rep 198.
6   *R v Maynard* (1979) 69 Cr App Rep 309.
7   In *R v Bleakley* [1993] Crim LR 203 the accused attacked the reliability of identification at a parade subsequent to a successful identification by the witness from photographs.
8   In *R v Crabtree* [1992] Crim LR 65 where the accused put the photographs in himself.
9   *R v Allen* [1996] Crim LR 426 where the accused adduced evidence of his own bad record.
10   In Australia it seems that the *Bunning v Cross* discretion may also apply: see Gibbs CJ and Stephen and Murphy JJ in *Alexander v R* above; *R v Burchielli* [1981] VR 611; *R v Shannon* (1987) 29 ACR 434.
11   *R v Governor of Pentonville Prison, ex p Voets* [1986] 2 All ER 630, [1986] 1 WLR 470. See also *R v Coleman* (1987) 87 FLR 175.
12   *Guevara v R* [1996] CLY 1386, PC.

witness to pick out the accused on account of a recent change of appearance, then they may well be both admissible, and admitted.[13]

(d)   Video film

There are two principal situations in which such films may be used. First, the use of security cameras is becoming increasingly common, and the film may be useful to detect the individuals depicted on it by being shown to those who might recognise them, such as the police.[14] It has been suggested that specific provision should be made to regulate this situation.[15] Second, a special video film may be prepared showing different people but including a suspect so as to serve a function like that of a conventional identification parade. This procedure is regulated by Code D of the Code of Practice.[16] The advantages of this technique are that it eliminates any possibility of intimidation by the suspect, and may help surmount the problems of assembling enough suitable volunteers to attend ad hoc. It is also far preferable to the practice condemned in *R v Johnson*[17] of allowing the investigating officer to show the victim a video taken of the accused in the vicinity around the time of the crime.[18]

It should be noted that the procedures prescribed by the Code apply as much to police witnesses as to others,[19] and a warning should be given of the danger of identification even by the police from a security video seen only 10 minutes before the relevant arrest.[20]

(e)   Identification parades

A properly conducted identification parade is generally accepted as being the least unsatisfactory method of confirming the identity of a suspect.[1] The parade is conducted impartially, the accused is able to see what takes place, and choice is made from a number of persons of similar general appearance. The Code of Practice in England sets out elaborate regulations governing the conduct of a parade.[2] These apply only to cases of disputed identification, and the court is reluctant to define this condition too closely,[3] though it has affirmed that it is not to be read literally, and that it does not include a situation where the accused denies what appears to be a satisfactory prior act of identification.[4] They give the suspect some control. In particular they appear to provide

---

13   *R v Byrne and Trump* [1987] Crim LR 689.
14   Sometimes the position is reversed and the film shown in advance to facilitate recognition at the scene of the crime, as in *R v Crabtree* [1992] Crim LR 65. In *R v Clare; R v Peach* [1995] 2 Cr App Rep 333 there were two videos, one taken of football supporters arriving for a match taken in good conditions, and one of a fracas taken in bad conditions by a security camera, the first used by the police to identify those shown in the second.
15   In *R v Caldwell and Dixon* (1994) 99 Cr App Rep 73, at 78.
16   Paras 2.10–2.12, and Annex B.
17   [1996] Crim LR 504.
18   Especially when accompanied by prejudicial remarks from the investigating officer about previous dealings with the person depicted.
19   Code D, note 2A.
20   *R v Campbell* (1996) Times, 20 February.
1   But see McKenzie [1995] Crim LR 200.
2   Annex A to Code D. These do not apply where someone is found near the scene of the crime, and shown to witnesses there: *R v Oscar* [1991] Crim LR 778; *R v Rogers* [1993] Crim LR 386; *R v Malashev* [1997] Crim LR 587.
3   *R v Montgomery* [1996] Crim LR 507. Such reluctance is not always extended to provisions of the Codes.
4   *R v Popat* [1998] 2 Cr App Rep 208, described in *R v El-Hannachi* [1998] 2 Cr App Rep 226, at 235F as providing a definitive analysis of the area.

that he can normally[5] insist that a parade take place,[6] provided only that it is practicable to hold one.[7] This apparent entitlement[8] has caused problems. It has been attacked at both ends, sometimes it is claimed that a parade would be inappropriate because the relevant witnesses would certainly be unable to identify the accused, and at others that it would be inappropriate because they would be certain to identify the accused. The former situation arises when the witness has seen no more than the clothing of the accused,[9] or for some other reason is unable to be unlikely to identify the accused.[10] In such situations the prosecution may choose to rely upon other evidence to identify the accused with the criminal,[11] and so avoid any adverse consequences from failure to provide a parade.[12] The latter situation has occurred when the witness has presented the suspect to the police, or the police have themselves witnessed the crime. It began to seem that everything depended upon the quality of the initial means of selecting the suspect. If those means were in some way unsatisfactory[13] a parade within the regulations of Code D was required, but if they were unimpeachable, then it was held that denial of a parade might not be in breach of the Code.[14] Even if it was, it was unlikely to have any adverse effect on the fairness of the proceedings, so as to trigger exclusion under s 78 of the Police and Criminal Evidence Act 1984, or cause the conviction to be quashed as being unsafe.[15] This view has now been abandoned, and the law has reverted to the simpler, and more straightforward position that the Code must prevail, and a parade be held in this situation.[16]

5   Code D, para 2.10 provides for the use of a video film where that is deemed by the investigating officer to be the most satisfactory procedure, and it seems that it is then used in substitution for a parade.
6   Code D, para 2.3.
7   Code D, para 2.4; see *R v Conway* (1990) 91 Cr App Rep 143. The burden of showing that it is impracticable is borne by the prosecution, and the police officer responsible for the decision should normally testify: *R v Penny* (1991) 94 Cr App Rep 345.
8   It has been held in a number of cases that a parade is designed to benefit the defence as well as the prosecution: see *R v Graham* [1994] Crim LR 212; *R v Wait* [1998] Crim LR 68; *R v Popat* at 213F.
9   As in *R v Oscar* above and *D v DPP* (1998) 142 Sol Jo LB 254.
10 As in *R v Montgomery* above.
11 As in *R v Rutherford and Palmer* (1994) 98 Cr App Rep 191.
12 But see *R v Walker* (14 November 1994, unreported) where expert evidence based upon a security film was held insufficient to deprive the accused of the benefit of having a parade attended by eye-witnesses.
13 As they may have been in *R v Conway* above (no prior *visual* identification at all); *R v Brown* [1991] Crim LR 368 (witnesses in the same car may have influenced each other); *R v Macmath* [1997] Crim LR 586 (witnesses identified accused as member of a group, only some of which committed the crime); *R v Wait* [1998] Crim LR 68 (witness professed to being unable to distinguish one white man from another).
14 *R v Popat* above (where the witness identified the accused in clear light and without any police prompting during one of a series of observations of men in a particular area); nor is it absolutely necessary to hold a parade for other witnesses if informal identification by one is sufficiently satisfactory: *R v El-Hannachi* above; nor apparently where some members of a group were unimpeachably identified and the only issue was as to the truth of the accused's story of having joined the group after the event, *R v Bell* [1998] Crim LR 879. These cases do seem to dilute the requirement unnecessarily: despite the requirement in *R v Bell* that the jury be warned of the adverse effect on the accused.
15 *R v Rogers* above (witness present during chase of suspect and at arrest); *R v Hickin* [1996] Crim LR 584 (very large number of men detained, and not all strong suspects); *Williams v R* [1997] 1 WLR 548 (off-duty policeman witness who then participated in arrest, but in jurisdiction where Code not directly applicable); *R v Malashev* [1997] Crim LR 587 (accused in identical clothing close to scene of crime soon afterwards, and apparently no request for a parade); *R v Anastasiou* [1998] Crim LR 67 (police witness arrested suspect in premises which he had been seen entering ten minutes after commission of crime).
16 *R v Forbes* (1999) Times, 5 May approving of *R v Brown*, and overruling *R v Popat* to the extent of any inconsistency.

The Code also allows the suspect to refuse to participate,[17] though he will then be at risk of identification by confrontation with the identifying witness. They also permit him to object to the constitution of the parade. It seems that if the police have assembled enough persons of similar general appearance the suspect may not insist upon the inclusion of persons of his own choice.[18] If the police are, however, unable to assemble enough such persons then the defence should be allowed a reasonable time to find sufficient to make up the number.[19] It has been remarked that where members of particular groups refuse to participate in identification parades suspects who are also members of such groups may be prejudiced.[20] While breach of the Code does not lead automatically to inadmissibility,[1] here as elsewhere cumulative breaches are more likely to do so,[2] sometimes on the basis of an *appearance*[3] of injustice.

The prescribed procedure requires the witness to identify the suspect clearly during the course of the parade. Difficulty can occur if this is not done, or if the witness is subsequently unable or unwilling to identify the accused. As noted above, one of the advantages of a parade is that the suspect has an opportunity to monitor the fairness of the procedure. This is reduced to the extent that evidence may be admitted of events occurring out of his presence, especially when they are relied upon to contradict what did apparently occur. Thus in *R v Creamer*[4] the accused objected to evidence that a witness, having apparently failed to identify him at the parade, subsequently told the investigating officer that she had done so, but had been frightened to speak. The Court of Appeal accepted that this diminished the value of the evidence, but felt that to exclude the evidence would encourage intimidation. The problem of witnesses failing to make a clear identification at a parade is illustrated by the facts of *R v Osbourne and Virtue*.[5] Two ladies attended an identification parade, and allegedly identified the accused in the normal way. At the trial however one of them said that she could not remember identifying anyone, and the other said that the man she identified was not the accused. The officer supervising the parade was then called, and testified that they had, in fact, both identified the accused. His evidence was objected to, not on hearsay grounds, but as contradicting the evidence of the ladies. This was unfortunate since the evidence does raise very difficult hearsay problems.[6] Although in *Sparks v R*[7] Lord Morris had declared that 'There is no rule which permits the giving of hearsay evidence merely because it relates to identity', it is hard to resist the view that there is such a rule, at least in relation to acts of identification at an identity parade,[8] as indicated

---

17   The suspect must be asked to stand on a parade, and mere refusal to be interviewed should not be construed as refusal to participate: *R v Johnson* above.

18   *R v Thorne* [1981] Crim LR 702.

19   *R v Britton and Richards* [1989] Crim LR 144.

20   *R v Campbell* [1993] Crim LR 47 (rastafarians).

1   See eg *R v Jones (Terence)* [1992] Crim LR 365 (investigating officer accompanying witness to parade); *R v McEvoy* [1997] Crim LR 887 (no parade when requested and no good reason for denial, but case otherwise very strong).

2   See eg *R v Finley* [1993] Crim LR 50 (selection of participants inter alia).

3   See eg *R v Gall* (1989) 90 Cr App Rep 64 (opportunity for investigating officer to speak to witness just before parade); cp *R v Andrews* [1996] CLY 1380 (conversation between witnesses in uninterpreted Amharic shortly before parade); *R v Khan* [1997] Crim LR 584 (where the investigating officer not only took advantage of the opportunity but was also carrying in his pocket a current photograph of the accused, and the defect was held capable of correction by direction).

4   (1984) 80 Cr App Rep 248.

5   [1973] QB 678, [1973] 1 All ER 649.

6   See Libling [1977] Crim LR 268 and Weinberg (1980) 12 Melb ULR 543.

7   [1964] AC 964, at 981, [1964] 1 All ER 727, at 735.

8   A similar approach would apply to other disputed out-of-court identification exercises such as perusal of photographs: see *R v Barbaro* (1993) 32 NSWLR 619.

by the admission of the evidence in *Osbourne*'s case.[9] It can hardly be argued that there is any difference between touching a man on the shoulder, and saying 'He is the man who did it'. If a third party testified to the latter it would appear to be a clear assertion, and in cases where the principal identifier does not testify, not capable of being regarded simply as supporting the credibility of a witness, but instead used as evidence of the truth of what it asserts. This is recognised more frankly in the United States.[10]

The Code of Practice provides for the possibility that a witness may require more than the opportunity to inspect a static and silent line of human beings. In particular it provides for them to be required to adopt a particular posture, to move or speak.[11] It does however require the witness first to attempt to identify the criminal by appearance alone, since the parade has been assembled on that basis. Identification by voice[12] alone is particularly contentious[13] since the human ear is generally less discriminating than the eye, and the aural abilities of people differ greatly, and the area, not being regulated by Code D,[14] is governed by the common law. It is most useful in recognition cases, and where there is visual and circumstantial support has been held to require a less stringent direction.[15] On the other hand identification of the voice of a stranger is a slim basis upon which to justify the reception of prejudicial similar fact evidence in confirmation.[16] It may be especially prejudicial if the police claim to recognise the voice of the accused on the telephone on account of their extensive dealings with him.[17]

(f) Group or street identification

This involves the witness seeing the suspect among a group of other people, but not on a formal parade. Sometimes the accused is assembled with others, and sometimes the witness observes a succession of individuals in a particular situation over a period of time. By comparison with a parade there are disadvantages in the discrepancies between the attitudes, angles of view and lighting of different people, and in the second case the haphazard characteristics of the other people observed; an advantage is that people are seen behaving more naturally. Under the Code of Practice group identification

9   In *R v McCay* [1991] 1 All ER 232, [1990] 1 WLR 645 the admission of such evidence was said to have statutory authorisation as a result of s 66 of the Police and Criminal Evidence Act 1984 and the terms of the Code of Practice governing identification, and especially Annex A, para 7. Such evidence is now widely admitted both as to visual and aural identification: see above p 544; and has been said to constitute a special exception: see *R v Cook* [1987] QB 417, at 425, [1987] 1 All ER 1049, at 1051, 1052; see also *Frew v Jessop* 1990 SLT 396. In *R v Collings* [1976] 2 NZLR 104, at 114 the Court of Appeal drew a distinction between statements part of the act of identification which were admissible, and those not part of it which were rejected as inadmissible hearsay.
10   A specific provision in the Federal Rules of Evidence, r 80(d)(1)(C) redefined hearsay to exclude such statements. See also IV *Wigmore* para 1130.
11   It is undesirable to require those present to speak their names: *Ricketts v R* [1998] 1 WLR 1016.
12   In *Pfennig v R* (1995) 127 ALR 99 the possibility of identifying a car by its sound was treated still more cautiously.
13   *R v Robb* (1991) 93 Cr App Rep 161; *R v Deenik* [1992] Crim LR 578. Different approaches have been taken by different states in Australia, see *R v Milandinovic* (1992) 109 ACTR 11. See also in Scotland, *Lees v Roy* 1990 SCCR 310; and in New Zealand *R v Waipouri* [1993] 2 NZLR 410.
14   Although the requirements of the Code should be applied suitably adapted: *R v Hersey* [1998] Crim LR 281.
15   In *R v Marijancevic* (1993) 70 ACR 272; *R v Heuston* (1995) 81 ACR 387.
16   *R v Johnson* [1995] Crim LR 53 where the police played tapes of interviews with a number of different men to the victims of a masked man. Cp *Pfennig* above.
17   Although this did not prevent reception of such evidence in Canada in *R v Williams* (1995) 98 CCC (3d) 160.

is suggested in cases where the suspect refuses or fails to participate in a parade, or if the supervising officer thinks it advisable so as to avoid intimidation. It is wrong for the police to pre-empt a parade by contriving a street identification despite the accused having agreed to a parade,[18] or by using as arresting officer a constable, who had secured no more than a fleeting glance, to confirm his impression.[19] If however the accused agrees to a street identification,[20] or if it occurs quite accidentally,[1] then it is unlikely that the evidence will be excluded for that reason. The Code provides that so far as possible the conditions applying to the composition of parades shall be applied to group identification.[2] It further disapproves of conducting such a form of identification in a police station.[3] The Code is less specific about the conduct of a street identification, but evidence derived from it will clearly be strengthened the closer its conditions approximate to those of a parade or group identification.[4] In some circumstances a video recording may be taken of a group or street identification, but it seems wrong to use it as evidence of identification made on such an occasion, and worse to use it after committal proceedings to try to improve the quality of the evidence of the identifying witness.[5]

(g)   Confrontation[6]

A confrontation between the witness and the suspect will be arranged only as a last resort if parade or group identification is impracticable.[7] So strong is the objection that the evidence is liable to be rejected even if the confrontation has been insisted upon by the accused.[8] The reason for this is that a confrontation in which the witness is asked 'Is this the man?', is somewhat analogous to a leading question. Partly for this reason it is desirable here, as elsewhere, for a description to be made by the witness in writing prior to the confrontation.[9] Provision is made in the code for confrontation through a one-way screen if necessary, though in such cases only if the suspect is represented at the confrontation, or a video recording is made of it. If the accused succeeds on an objection to confrontation evidence it is not open for him to attempt to reinstate it in respect of some witnesses, but not all.[10]

---

18   *R v Nagah* (1991) 92 Cr App Rep 344. In Australian see *R v Shannon* (1987) 29 ACR 434.
19   *R v Kensett* (1993) 157 JP 620.
20   *R v Penny* (1991) 94 Cr App Rep 345.
1   *R v Quinn* [1990] Crim LR 581; *R v Long* [1991] Crim LR 453.
2   This appears to have been overlooked in *R v Ladlow* [1989] Crim LR 219 where the judge seems to have thought it permissible to include more than two suspects in a group, but not in a parade, and still more in *Tomkinson v DPP* [1995] Crim LR 60 where this possibility was regarded as justifying the conduct of such an exercise rather than a parade.
3   Code D, para 2.9. Though the foyer of a magistrates' court may be acceptable: *R v Tiplady* (1995) 159 JP 548.
4   See *R v Wright* (1992) 60 ACR 215.
5   *R v Smith and Doe* (1986) 85 Cr App Rep 197. It is interesting that no reference was made to *R v Cook* above where Watkins LJ also delivered the judgment of the court.
6   A confrontation is sometimes engineered otherwise than by the police: see *R v O'Leary* (1988) 87 Cr App Rep 387. If it is entirely accidental, then the evidence will be admitted: *R v Campbell* [1996] Crim LR 500.
7   *R v Ladlow* above indicates the court's distaste for this method of identification since the correct conduct of parades would have required some 231 parades over a bank holiday, and the conditions for a group identification could not strictly have been fulfilled, but still the convictions were quashed because confrontation had been preferred to either of these options; see also *R v Samms* [1991] Crim LR 197; in Ireland, *People v Duff* [1995] 1 IR 296; and in Canada, *R v Miaponoose* (1996) 110 CCC (3d) 445.
8   *R v Joseph* [1994] Crim LR 48 (confrontation in cells and no better than dock identification).
9   *R v Vaughan* [1997] NLJR 852 (the circumstances here were particularly suggestive).
10   *R v Campbell* [1993] Crim LR 47.

(h) Dock identification

The least satisfactory method of all is to ask the witness to identify the man in the dock as the criminal. It has all the disadvantages of a confrontation, and compounds them by being still more suggestive.[11] For these reasons the Devlin Committee recommended that dock identification should become a purely formal matter, allowed only where identification had been made by a parade unless the judge took the view that to hold a parade would be impractical or unnecessary.[12] It has been allowed when the accused has refused a parade.[13] While in cases of genuine recognition it might seem unnecessary to hold a parade and sufficient simply to allow identification by the witness in court, this might depend upon how familiar the witness was with the accused before the offence took place,[14] and upon the strength of the supporting circumstantial evidence.[15] Where a witness does identify the accused in his evidence at the trial it seems that evidence of a prior identification by him can be led.[16] A majority of their Lordships seem to have regarded such evidence as bolstering that of the witness, 'What was done and said out of court goes to show that the witness was able to identify at the time and to negative anything in the nature of an afterthought'.[17] It would be more consistent with principle to wait for some such attack to take place before permitting rebuttal in this way.

(ii) Identification by jury

If a crime has been recorded on film, video or sound recording, or by a still photograph, it may be possible for the jury[18] to make its own identification of the criminal with the man on trial before them,[19] for example in *Kajala v Noble*[20] where the incident had been captured on a television camera as part of a news broadcast. In such cases it is permissible for a witness to depose to the identity of the person depicted on the film, if for some reason or another it is desirable to supplement it.[1] This may even be done

---

11 *R v Tricoglus* (1977) 65 Cr App Rep 16 where the witness identified the accused in the dock despite having picked out someone else on a parade. See also *Davies and Cody v R* (1937) 57 CLR 170.

12 The alternative of permitting the accused to stand elsewhere in the court before the attempt at identification was rejected as likely to be ineffective (such a technique had been adopted in one of the cases which had led to the Committee's being set up). The Criminal Law Revision Committee in its 11th report had recommended that it be allowed only after successful identification at a parade: Cmnd 4991, para 201.

13 In *R v John* [1973] Crim LR 113. It seems more likely to be permitted in a magistrates' court: *Barnes v Chief Constable of Durham* [1997] 2 Cr App Rep 505.

14 In *R v Fergus* [1992] Crim LR 363 one previous encounter together with hearsay as to the name of the person was held insufficient to make a dock identification satisfactory; cp *R v Brennan* [1996] CLY 1381 where it seems two meetings together with hearsay would have done so.

15 *R v Demeter* [1995] 2 Qd R 626 (accused was overnight guest at house where the offence took place).

16 *R v Christie* [1914] AC 545.

17 Lord Haldane LC at 551.

18 In *R v Nikolovski* [1996] 3 SCR 1197 this was extended to a judge sitting as trier of fact, despite the failure of an eye-witness to accomplish the identification. It is submitted that it would have been better if an expert witness had been called in support, if only for the purposes of cross-examination.

19 Although it seems that the accused is equally entitled not to present himself so as to prevent such an identification from being made: *R v McNamara* [1996] Crim LR 750.

20 (1982) 75 Cr App Rep 149. See also in Ireland *People v Maguire* [1995] 2 IR 286; in Australia *R v Smith* (1983) 33 SASR 558.

1 *R v Fowden and White* [1982] Crim LR 588; *R v Grimer* [1982] Crim LR 674; *R v Caldwell and Dixon* (1993) 99 Cr App Rep 73. See also *Bowie v Tudhope* 1986 SCCR 205.

by an expert in the interpretation of photographic evidence who can then testify to the identity of the accused despite having had no previous familiarity with him, and despite such identification being 'an ultimate issue'.[2] Discrimination of sound is much more difficult, and it will be rare for a court to leave a sound recording to the jury to compare with the voice of the accused.[3] If however the sound recording has been analysed by an expert, then it may be right for the recordings used by the expert to be submitted to the jury so as to assist their evaluation of his testimony.[4]

4. Procedure

Two procedural questions may arise in relation to evidence of direct identification, first whether the evidence should be allowed to go to the jury at all, and second, if it is, the question of the proper direction to be given to the jury. The first involves the issue of whether a voir dire should be used in such cases, and the second of what, if any, warning should be given.

(i)   Voir dire

Under the old law it was determined that a voir dire should never be held in relation to evidence of identity.[5] This followed from the analysis undertaken by the Court of Appeal in *R v Turnbull*[6] which had determined that such evidence was either of such poor quality that the case should be withdrawn from the jury in the absence of any support, but if of better quality, or if supported, then the only question was one of weight rather than of admissibility, and there was no need for a voir dire. It was suggested in *R v Beveridge*[7] that the passage of s 78 of the Police and Criminal Evidence Act 1984 had transformed this situation in its enactment of a statutory discretion to exclude evidence likely to operate unfairly. Such a view was received coolly by the court, and apparently rejected by it in the subsequent case of *R v Flemming*[8] on the basis that identification evidence still differed from evidence of a confession admitted under s 76 where a voir dire was appropriate, since s 76 imposes a persuasive burden of proof upon the prosecution in relation to admissibility, while s 78 does not. Given the unpopularity of holding a voir dire, this view seems likely to prevail in England.[9]

It has been emphasised that there is no incongruity between the decision in *R v Turnbull* that if the evidence of identification is too poor the issue should not be left to the jury, and that in *R v Galbraith*[10] that the judge should not usurp the function of the jury and himself determine whether evidence is to be believed or not. In *Daley v R*[11] Lord Mustill reconciled these decisions on the basis that identification evidence is

---

2   *R v Stockwell* (1993) 97 Cr App Rep 260.
3   See *Bulejcik v R* (1996) 185 CLR 375 for very full consideration of the problem.
4   *R v Bentum* (1989) 153 JP 538.
5   *R v Walshe* (1980) 74 Cr App Rep 85, though it seems that voir dires were, in fact, sometimes held: see, for example, *R v Maynard* (1979) 69 Cr App Rep 309.
6   [1977] QB 224, [1976] All ER 549.
7   (1987) 85 Cr App Rep 255.
8   (1987) 86 Cr App Rep 32, rejecting the contrary practice adopted in *R v Leckie and Ensley* [1983] Crim LR 543.
9   But see *R v Kitchen* [1994] Crim LR 684 where one was held. The situation may be more flexible in Australia: see *R v Hallam and Karger* (1985) 42 SASR 126; cp *R v Rowley* (1986) 23 ACR 371.
10   [1981] 2 All ER 1060, [1981] 1 WLR 1039.
11   [1994] AC 117, [1993] 4 All ER 86.

unreliable not because of insincerity which a jury can assess for itself; but, despite total sincerity, because of inherent weaknesses not necessarily appreciated, or capable of evaluation, by the jury.

(ii) Direction to the jury

As noted above the framework for such a direction was provided by *R v Turnbull*.[12] A judge should always warn the jury of the special need for caution in relying on evidence of identification,[13] and instruct them of the reason for giving such a warning. There is something to be said for summarising all of the identification together,[14] though in this, as elsewhere, the judge must have flexibility to mould the direction to the contours of the case.[15] This applies even though the evidence of identification is left unchallenged by the defence.[16] It seems that a *Turnbull* warning is highly desirable even if the only issue is whether the identifying witness is sincere, and there is no real danger of a mistake.[17] In cases of direct identification some of the features of a *Turnbull* direction will be inappropriate, but it should nevertheless be followed so far as possible, since all forms of identification are so hazardous.[18]

Turnbull requires the judge to direct the jury to examine closely the circumstances in relation to each act of identification. He should also remind the jury of any specific weaknesses in the evidence,[19] and of any breaches of the Code of Practice in the conduct of the technique of identification.[20] If, in his view, the quality of the evidence of identity is good he can leave it to the jury even in the absence of supporting evidence, subject always to the warning of the need for caution having been given. If, in the judge's view, the quality of the evidence is poor he should withdraw the case from the jury unless there is some other evidence to support its correctness. The judge should identify what evidence can be relied upon as providing such support, and which cannot,[1] and draw to the attention of the jury any significant discrepancy between the witness's original description of the criminal, and the appearance of the accused.[2] In particular he should explain that the accused's absence from the witness box can prove nothing,[3]

12 Its purport was approved by the High Court of Australia in *Domican v R* (1992) 173 CLR 555, at 561.
13 Including recognition: *R v Bentley* (1994) 99 Cr App Rep 342; *R v Bowden* [1993] Crim LR 379.
14 See *R v Pattinson and Exley* [1996] 1 Cr App Rep 51.
15 *R v Mussell and Dalton* [1995] Crim LR 887.
16 *Beckford v R* (1993) 97 Cr App Rep 409; see also *R v Courtnell* [1990] Crim LR 115; but cp *R v Bath* [1990] Crim LR 716.
17 *Beckford v R* above; *Shand v R* [1996] 1 All ER 511, [1996] 1 WLR 67. Cases without a vestige of an identification issue will be very rare; but see *R v Courtnell, Shand v R*; *R v Cape, Jackson and Gardner* [1996] 1 Cr App Rep 191. *R v Beckles and Montague* [1999] Crim LR 148 is an unusual case in which the witness was wrong about two of the persons involved in an attack, but was regarded as incapable of being mistaken about three others, because they had admitted involvement.
18 *R v Dodson; R v Williams* [1984] 1 WLR 971, 79 Cr App Rep 220 ; *R v Blenkinsop* [1995] 1 Cr App Rep 7.
19 Is not absolutely necessary to group all the weaknesses together, nor to deal with the weaknesses in relation to all of the accused together: *R v Qadir* [1998] Crim LR 828.
20 *R v Quinn* [1995] Crim LR 56.
1 Though a failure to direct in this way, while to be deplored, is not necessarily fatal: *R v Akaidere* [1990] Crim LR 808.
2 *Ricketts v R* [1998] 1 WLR 1016.
3 Especially if a co-accused has testified: *R v Duncan* (1992) Times, 24 July, although, after the advent of s 35 of the Criminal Justice and Public Order Act 1994 it was regarded in *R v Kelly* (1998) Times, 23 February as weakening the accused's argument that failure to hold a parade was fatal to the safety of the conviction.

though it may leave prosecution evidence uncontradicted,[4] and that a false alibi may be put forward for reasons unconnected with consciousness of guilt.[5] Such a direction should be given whether or not the Crown has sought to rely upon the failure of the alibi.[6] Where lies are relied upon to support evidence of identification the direction recommended in *R v Lucas* should normally be given.[7] The guidance could perhaps be criticised for not indicating more clearly just how poor the evidence needed to be before a case should be withdrawn from the jury by the judge, and when a warning was sufficient.[8] It also failed to indicate whether further visual identification evidence could be relied upon as support. The answer to this was supplied in *R v Weeder*[9] where it was held that only high quality identification evidence could provide support.

These guidelines have been accepted in many Commonwealth jurisdictions,[10] but not in all.[11] Two situations which do not seem to require the full *Turnbull* treatment are first those where the real question is not whether or not someone was present on a particular occasion, but whether they were performing a particular act,[12] and second those where the issue is not one of personal identification, but rather circumstantial identification. This is well illustrated in *R v Bartels*[13] where the witnesses saw the accused running close to their apartment shortly after they had seen a crime committed some way off. They could not have made out the features of the criminal at the distance, and they did not have the man continuously in their sight. However no one else appeared to be in the vicinity, and the obvious way for the criminal to run was in their direction. The accused admitted that he was the man they saw, but denied that he had committed the crime, and suggested that the real criminal must have run off in a different direction.

It has been stressed that when the jury is cautioned it is wrong either to weaken the caution by putting counter-arguments,[14] or by the judge failing to make it clear that he is himself endorsing, and not merely recapitulating, cautionary arguments put by the defence.[15] On the other hand the judge is free to give a 'reverse' *Turnbull* direction in relation to false identification at a parade.[16]

It has been said[17] that 'It would be wrong to interpret or apply *Turnbull* inflexibly'. It purports, after all, to offer no more than guidelines, and so flexible has this interpretation become that there are examples both of appeals being allowed despite an impeccable

---

4   The judge should be slow to emphasise this, especially where the rest of the evidence is weak: *R v Allan* (1990) Times, 2 January.
5   This was further emphasised in *R v Keane* (1977) 65 Cr App Rep 247; *R v Duncan*, above. See also *R v Vincec* (1990) 50 ACR 203; *R v Dunn* (1990) 56 CCC (3d) 538.
6   *R v Pemberton* (1993) 99 Cr App Rep 228.
7   *R v Goodway* [1993] 4 All ER 894, 98 Cr App Rep 11.
8   It was so criticised by Wilson J in the Supreme Court of Canada in *Mezzo v R* [1986] 1 SCR 802.
9   (1980) 71 Cr App Rep 228.
10   For example in Australia, see *Domican v R* (1992) 173 CLR 555; in Canada, *Mezzo v R*, above; and in New Zealand, *Auckland City Council v Brailey* [1988] 1 NZLR 103.
11   For example New South Wales: see *R v De-Cressac* (1985) 1 NSWLR 381.
12   As in *R v Oakwell* [1978] 1 All ER 1223, [1978] 1 WLR 32 (which in a crowd was the assailant); *R v Curry and Keeble* [1983] Crim LR 737 (a similar situation); *Auckland City Council v Brailey* [1988] 1 NZLR 103 (which of two people in a car was driving it); *Sharrett v Gill* (1992) 65 ACR 44 (a similar situation).
13   (1986) 44 SASR 260.
14   *R v Keane* (1977) 65 Cr App Rep 247.
15   *Davis and Cody v R* (1937) 57 CLR 170, at 182, *Domican v R* (1992) 173 CLR 555, at 564.
16   *R v Trew* [1996] Crim LR 441 (the report in [1996] 2 Cr App Rep 138 does not include this issue).
17   By Scarman LJ in *R v Keane*, above, at 248; by the Privy Council in *Mills v R* [1995] 3 All ER 865, [1995] 1 WLR 511.

Turnbull direction,[18] and disallowed despite a quite inadequate *Turnbull* direction,[19] or without one at all.[20]

It should be noted that the judge's discretion to exclude evidence pursuant to s 78 of the Police and Criminal Evidence Act 1984 may be applied in respect of evidence of identification,[1] and occasionally the judge will feel inclined to exercise his discretion only after initially permitting the evidence to be adduced. In such a case he should do no less than direct the jury to disregard the evidence altogether. This might be thought too drastic a measure where the breach of Code D is considered venial, and in such cases it seems that the judge is entitled not to direct the jury to disregard the evidence,[2] but rather to explain to them the reasons for regarding it with suspicion.[3]

B. CIRCUMSTANTIAL EVIDENCE OF IDENTITY

When there is no doubt that an act has been done, and the question is whether it was the act of a particular person, all relevant evidence is normally admissible in order to prove or disprove that fact. Obvious instances are afforded by cases in which the criminal has left traces behind him. The fact that the crime was probably committed by a left-handed man and that the accused was left-handed, or any other physical or mental peculiarity exhibited by the criminal may be shown to have been exhibited by the accused. This is, however, a branch of the law in which it is often necessary to have regard to the general prohibition on evidence which merely goes to show criminal tendencies, or a disposition to commit particular crimes on the part of the accused. From the point of view of relevancy, these should often be admissible because they go to show that the accused was a member of a comparatively small class of which the criminal was also a member, but the prejudicial nature of the evidence will render it inadmissible unless the tendency or disposition is of sufficient weight and particular relevance to a matter in issue in the proceedings.

There is, of course, a variety of other factors which will go to prove membership of a restricted class. On a charge of bigamy, it is necessary for the prosecution to prove that the accused duly went through a ceremony of marriage with the first spouse. Since 1914, the latter has been a competent witness for the prosecution, and the necessary identification can often be accomplished by his or her direct evidence. But, where this is not forthcoming and where there is no other direct proof of the first marriage, such as that of a witness who was present at its celebration, it may be established by circumstantial evidence of which a material item would be the identity of the accused's name with that of the person named in a marriage certificate produced by the prosecutor. Standing by itself it would probably be insufficient in any case, but a conviction for bigamy has been upheld by the Court of Criminal Appeal on such evidence coupled with the fact that the accused cohabited with a woman of the same name as the other person mentioned in the marriage certificate and referred to her as his wife.[4]

---

18   *R v Pope* (1986) 85 Cr App Rep 201 (where the court seemed remarkably unaware of black vernacular usage).
19   *R v Clifton* [1986] Crim LR 399.
20   *Freemantle v R* [1994] 3 All ER 225, [1994] 1 WLR 1347; *Shand v R* [1996] 1 All ER 511, [1996] 1 WLR 67.
1   See *R v Quinn* [1990] Crim LR 581.
2   Though he must give some explanation for admitting the evidence despite breach of the Code: *R v Allen* [1995] Crim LR 643.
3   *R v Khan* [1997] Crim LR 584 (where the investigating officer interviewed identifying witnesses before the parade, carrying in his pocket a photograph of the accused).
4   *R v Birtles* (1911) 6 Cr App Rep 177.

Personal identity may be established by many other factors than that of name, obvious instances are provided by occupation, education, and mental or physical idiosyncrasies. In the *Lovat Peerage Case*,[5] it was held that the fact that an ancestor was reputed to have been guilty of manslaughter coupled with the fact that a similar tradition prevailed with regard to the lineage of one of the claimants was some evidence that the latter was the descendant of the former. The sole question with regard to the admissibility of circumstantial evidence of this nature is whether a particular characteristic is sufficiently rare, or a class sufficiently small, to make it worthwhile for the court to hear evidence tending to show possession of that characteristic or membership of that class.[6]

The most cogent circumstantial evidence of identity is likely to be evidence of fingerprints, or of DNA traces in relevant tissue.[7] In practice such evidence is likely to be conclusive.

C.   PRESUMPTIVE EVIDENCE OF IDENTITY

Although it is highly exceptional for presumptions to operate against the accused in criminal cases at common law, such a presumption was made in Scotland in *Rollo v Wilson*[8] where the accused sought acquittal on the basis that the prosecution had failed to prove that he was the person summoned to appear in court, despite his having so appeared in answer to the summons. In England there might be more difficulty, since it has been held necessary to adduce evidence that the accused who bore the same name and appeared in court was indeed the criminal,[9] and to show that a conviction really did relate to the accused as it appeared to do, at least once that had been denied.[10]

SECTION 3.   BIRTH, AGE, DEATH, MARRIAGE AND LEGITIMACY

A.   BIRTH

There are four methods of proving birth. Far and away the most usual at the present day is the production of a certified copy of an entry in the register of births which may be received as evidence of the facts stated under the exception to the rule against

---

5   (1885) 10 App Cas 763.
6   'Where a certain circumstance, feature or mark may commonly be found associated with a large number of objects, the presence of that feature or mark in two supposed objects is little indication of their identity, because, on the general principle of relevancy, the other conceivable hypotheses are so numerous, ie the objects that possess that mark are numerous and therefore two of them possessing it may well be different. But where the objects possessing the mark are only one or a few, and the mark is found in two supposed instances, the chances of their being different are nil, or are comparatively small ... Suppose there existed a parent named John Smith whose heirs are sought, and there is also a claimant whose parent's name was John Smith. The name John Smith is associated with so many persons that the chances of two supposed persons of that name being different are too numerous to allow us to consider the common marks as having appreciable probative value. But the chances may be diminished by adding other common circumstances going to form the common mark. Add, for instance, another name-circumstance, – as that the name of each supposed person was John Barebones Bonaparte Smith, here the chances of there being two persons of that name in any district however large are instantly reduced to the minimum' (II *Wigmore* p 386).
7   Though some doubts have been expressed: see further above p 43.
8   1988 JC 82.
9   *R v Brennan* [1996] CLY 1381.
10   *Bailey v DPP* (1998) 142 Sol Jo LB 198.

hearsay relating to statements in public documents.[11] The court will require some evidence identifying the person whose birth is in question with the person referred to in the birth certificate. This might take the form of a direct statement by the person in question if he were testifying to the date or place of birth, though the evidence is at best hearsay and at worst pure guesswork. It could also be provided by someone who was present at the birth, or by the informant to the Registrar; but, more often than not, the evidence of identity will be supplied by an affidavit in which the deponent, usually a member of the family of the person whose birth is in question, will depose to his or her belief that the person is or was the same person as the one referred to in the exhibited birth certificate. The testimony of someone present at the birth to that fact, its place or date is a second and separate method of proving these matters. They may also be proved, in civil proceedings, by statements admissible by virtue of the Civil Evidence Act 1968, and, in criminal proceedings, under exceptions to the hearsay rule relating to the declarations of deceased persons,[12] or perhaps under the provisions of Part II of the Criminal Justice Act 1988.

B.   AGE

There are four ways in which a person's age can be proved; two of them depend on direct evidence and two on the exceptions to the hearsay rule relating respectively to statements in public documents and declarations of deceased persons.

I.   Direct evidence

A person's age may be proved by direct evidence (a) by the testimony of those present at his birth and (b) by inferences from his appearance which are permitted in special cases by certain statutes.[13] In the nature of things, it is not often that resort can be made to the first of these methods, and, in many instances, its use would, to some extent, involve reliance on hearsay. For example, A's grandmother was present at his birth, and she sees a child whom she believes to be A once a quarter for the next ten years, after which she testifies to A's age in court. It cannot be said that she knows that A is the child at whose birth she was present exclusively by means of her own observation. Even the mother's evidence of the child's age might well be based on hearsay evidence of identity at the earliest stages of the child's life. The court is authorised to act on inspection with regard to questions of age by several statutes, but quite apart from these provisions the general effect of which is to make the result of the inspection prima facie proof of age, such result would presumably be evidence of age in every case.[14] It would be a kind of real evidence, though, in many instances, it would not be sufficient for the court to act on it without more.

---

11   Births and Deaths Registration Act 1953, s 34. See ch XV, section 1. As to certified extracts from foreign registers, see the Evidence (Foreign Dominion and Colonial Documents) Act 1933 and as to births on board ship the Merchant Shipping (Returns of Births and Deaths) Regulations 1972, made under s 75 of the Merchant Shipping Act 1970.
12   Ch XVI, section 2.
13   Children and Young Persons Act 1933, s 99; Criminal Justice Act 1948, s 80(3); Magistrates' Courts Act 1980, s 150(4); Sexual Offences Act 1956, s 28(5).
14   *Wallworth v Balmer* [1965] 3 All ER 721, [1966] 1 WLR 16.

2. Hearsay

Probably the most usual way of proving age is the production of a birth certificate as evidence of the date of the birth specified therein under the exception to the hearsay rule relating to statements in public documents.[15] Evidence of the identity of the person whose age is in question with the person named in the certificate will be required.

In criminal cases age may be proved by declarations by deceased persons against interest or in the course of duty, and, when a genealogical issue is involved, by the pedigree declaration of a deceased relation. In these cases too, it may be necessary to find some evidence identifying the person referred to in the statement with the person whose age is in issue.

C.   DEATH

There are six heads under which a person's death may be proved. It is not necessary to refer to any of them in detail. The first and most usual way to prove death is to rely on a death certificate coupled with some evidence identifying the person named therein with the person whose death is in question.[16] Second, in a criminal case, reliance may be placed on the declaration of a deceased person made against interest or in the course of duty or, when a genealogical question is in issue, the pedigree declaration of a deceased relation. Evidence of identity may also be necessary in these cases. Third, death may be proved by statements admissible under the Civil Evidence Act 1968 or the Criminal Justice Act 1988. Fourth, reliance may be placed upon the presumption of death.[17] Even where the presumption is inapplicable, the court may feel warranted in inferring death from a protracted period of absence the length of which will vary according to the facts of each case. The fifth and sixth methods of proving death are to rely either on the evidence of someone who was present at its occurrence, or else on the evidence of someone who, though not present at its occurrence, was able to identify the corpse as that of the person whose death is in issue.

D.   MARRIAGE

When a marriage is in issue, the first thing that has to be proved is the celebration of a marriage ceremony. In certain cases, this may be presumed from proof of cohabitation and repute. Subject to this further possibility, the person seeking to prove a marriage ceremony may rely on the same methods as those discussed in connection with the proof of birth. Evidence may be adduced from someone who was present at the wedding[18] and this is the method of proof almost invariably adopted in matrimonial cases.[19] Declarations that a couple were married may be received, in criminal cases, under exceptions to the hearsay rule relating to the statements of deceased persons as being against interest, or in the course of duty, or as to pedigree in cases involving a genealogical issue; and in civil cases, under the Civil Evidence Act 1995 or in criminal

---

15   Births and Deaths Registration Act 1953, s 34 and, as to foreign registers, the Evidence (Foreign, Dominion and Colonial Documents) Act 1933. See also Merchant Shipping (Returns of Births and Deaths) Regulations 1979.

16   Births and Deaths Registration Act 1953, s 34; Merchant Shipping (Returns of Births and Deaths) Regulations 1979.

17   See above p 123.

18   This includes a party to the marriage.

19   Statements may be received under the Civil Evidence Act 1995.

cases, under the Criminal Justice Act 1988. The third and most usual method consists in the production of a marriage certificate coupled with evidence identifying the persons mentioned in the certificate with those whose marriage is to be proved. When he or she is available, such evidence will generally be supplied by one of the parties to the marriage. Whenever a certificate is available, the courts require it to be produced in addition to receiving the evidence of the parties as to the ceremony.

The second thing to be proved by someone who is seeking to establish a marriage is that the ceremony constituted a formally valid marriage. Generally speaking, it will have to be shown that a form recognised by the law of the place of celebration was adopted, but there are exceptions in the case of marriages celebrated abroad.[20] If the ceremony took place in England or Wales, the certificate is evidence of the marriage to which it relates,[1] but, in other cases, it will be necessary to produce expert evidence by a witness or by affidavit of formal validity according to the local law. This could be a costly requirement, and there are accordingly eight exceptions the last two of which will no doubt supersede the others. These exceptions relate first to marriages celebrated in Scotland and Northern Ireland, certificates of which are recognised by the English courts as evidence of the facts stated under various statutory provisions.[2] Second, if the marriage took place in a British possession under a statute proved by virtue of the provisions of the Evidence (Colonial Statutes) Act 1907, it is not the practice of the courts to require expert evidence of the validity of the marriage according to the local law, although such evidence may be required if there is any doubt whether the statute in question in still in force.[3] Third, if the marriage took place in a country to which the Evidence (Foreign, Dominion and Colonial Documents) Act 1933, has been applied by Order in Council, a certificate produced under that Act is evidence of the marriage to which it refers, and the English courts will require no further evidence of the formal validity of the marriage, although they will of course require the usual evidence of identity. A further exception to the requirement of proof of formal validity according to the local law is provided by the Foreign Marriage Act 1892. All that is required is evidence that a marriage celebrated under that statute complied with its requirements. The fifth and sixth exceptions relate to marriages celebrated abroad according to the rites of the Church of England and it is unnecessary to go into details in a work of this nature.[4]

In spite of the numerous exceptions to the requirement of proof of formal validity under the local law, the general rule remained and it was often necessary to procure the attendance of an expert witness, or to obtain leave to read an affidavit by him to the effect that the certificate of the marriage would be recognised in the courts of the country in question. It was, for instance, held to be necessary in the case of an Irish marriage,[5] even in an undefended divorce, as neither the Evidence (Colonial Statutes) Act, nor the Evidence (Foreign, Dominion and Colonial Documents) Act, applied to Eire.

20 For details see Dicey and Morris *Conflict of Laws* (12th edn).
1 Marriage Act 1949, s 65.
2 Registration of Births, Deaths and Marriages (Scotland) Act 1854; *Drew v Drew* [1912] P 175 (Scotland); Evidence Act 1851; *Whitton v Whitton* [1900] P 178 (Eire before 1921, and Northern Ireland).
3 The authorities are comprehensively reviewed in *Jasiewicz v Jasiewicz* [1962] 3 All ER 1017, [1962] 1 WLR 1426.
4 Marriages celebrated according to the rites of the Church of England in the Channel Islands are recognised on production of a certificate with evidence of identification because they are in the diocese of Winchester (*Pritchard v Pritchard* (1920) 37 TLR 104). According to *Ward v Dey* (1846) 1 Rob Eccl 759, marriages celebrated according to the rites of the Church of England in any British possession may be recognised on production of a certificate with evidence of identity, but it is not clear how far this doctrine extends today.
5 *Todd v Todd* [1961] 2 All ER 881.

It is because of such possibilities that the seventh and eighth exceptions to the requirement of proof by testimony or affidavit of the legal validity of a foreign marriage are of great importance. Under r 40(1) of the Matrimonial Causes Rules 1977, the celebration and validity of a marriage, which took place outside England and Wales may be proved, in any matrimonial proceedings in which the existence and validity of the marriage is not disputed, by the evidence of one of the parties and the production of the foreign marriage certificate or a certified copy of an entry in a foreign register of marriages. In other cases in which the existence and validity of the marriage is not disputed, reliance may be placed on the evidence of one of the parties and the production of such a certificate or certified copy as a statement or record admissible by virtue of the Civil Evidence Act 1995 or the Criminal Justice Act 1988. Before this Act came into force, it was becoming increasingly common for the courts to accept a foreign marriage certificate as evidence of the validity of the marriage under the Evidence Act 1938,[6] and it could be given in evidence, even without the evidence of one of the parties under the Act of 1995, as prima facie evidence both of the celebration of the marriage and of its validity according to the relevant foreign law.

E.   LEGITIMACY

In order to establish a child's legitimacy, reliance may be placed on the presumption of legitimacy. For this purpose it is simply necessary to prove that the child was born or conceived during its mother's marriage to her husband, after which it is incumbent on those denying legitimacy to prove illegitimacy. Legitimacy may also be proved, in criminal cases, under exceptions to the rule against hearsay, notably that relating to pedigree declarations by deceased persons perhaps under the Criminal Justice Act 1988; and, in civil cases, by statements admissible under the Civil Evidence Act 1968. It might also be proved by a statement in a public document, for the statements as to paternity in birth certificates are evidence of their truth. Finally, reliance might be placed on a declaration of legitimacy which is a judgment in rem and therefore binding on the whole world.

SECTION 4.   JUDGMENTS AND CONVICTIONS

If the proof of judgments and convictions were not exhaustively covered by statutory provisions, it would be necessary to produce the actual record of the court and to call evidence identifying the relevant parties with the person mentioned in the record. The different statutory provisions may be summarised under the heads of civil and criminal cases.

A.   CIVIL CASES

A judgment of the House of Lords may be proved by production of the journal of the House. Judgments of the Court of Appeal and High Court may be proved by production of an office copy made in the central office or district registry.[7] Judgments of the County Court may be proved by a certified copy of the entry in the registrar's book.[8] Judgments

---

6   *Henaff v Henaff* [1966] 1 WLR 598.
7   Supreme Court Act 1981, s 132.
8   County Courts Act 1984, s 12(2).

of the magistrates in civil matters are also proved by the production of a certified extract from the court book.[9] There are special statutory provisions relating to proceedings in bankruptcy.[10] Foreign or colonial judgments may be proved by production of an examined copy[11] or a copy sealed with the seal of the court under the provisions of s 7 of the Evidence Act 1851. In all the above cases, production of the relevant document will usually be sufficient to establish its authenticity because the court will take judicial notice of the seal or certificate attached to the document, but oral evidence may be required to identify the parties to the judgment with the person whose rights the court is considering, or those through whom such persons claim. Evidence of this nature is, however, often rendered unnecessary by some kind of formal admission.[12]

B. CRIMINAL CASES

Proof of convictions in criminal cases has been revolutionised by the passage of the Police and Criminal Evidence Act 1984, s 73, which must be rendered in full:

(1) Where in any proceedings the fact that a person has in the United Kingdom been convicted or acquitted of an offence otherwise than by a Service court is admissible in evidence, it may be proved by producing a certificate of conviction or, as the case may be, of acquittal relating to that offence, and proving that the person named in the certificate as having been convicted or acquitted of the offence is the person whose conviction or acquittal of the offence is to be proved.

(2) For the purposes of this section a certificate of conviction or of acquittal—

(a) shall, as regards a conviction or acquittal on indictment consist of a certificate, signed by the clerk of the court where the conviction or acquittal took place, giving the substance and effect (omitting the formal parts) of the indictment and of the conviction or acquittal; and

(b) shall, as regards a conviction or acquittal on a summary trial, consist of a copy of the conviction or of the dismissal of the information, signed by the clerk of the court where the conviction or acquittal took place or by the clerk of the court, if any, to which a memorandum of the conviction or acquittal was sent; and a document purporting to be a duly signed certificate of conviction or acquittal under this section shall be taken to be such a certificate unless the contrary is proved.

(3) References in this section to the clerk of a court include references to his deputy and to any other person having the custody of the court record.

(4) The method of proving a conviction or acquittal authorised by this section shall be in addition to and not to the exclusion of any other authorised manner of proving a conviction or acquittal.

This provision was recommended by the Criminal Law Revision Committee, and is adopted almost verbatim from the Bill annexed to its Eleventh Report.[13] Although stated to be in addition to other methods of proving convictions or acquittals, it has permitted

---

9   Magistrates' Courts Rules 1981, rr 66 and 68.
10 Bankruptcy Act 1914, ss 137(2), 139 and 148(2).
11 An examined copy is one examined against the original. As evidence of the examination is usually necessary, proof by examined copy is rare. Some cases are governed by separate statutory provision eg Child Abduction and Custody Act 1985, s 22.
12 Which is equally admissible in a criminal court: *R v Stokes* [1988] Crim LR 110.
13 Cmnd 4991, Annex 1 cl 26.

the repeal or modification of a number of now obsolete provisions in relation to criminal proceedings.[14] It is unclear why s 14 of Perjury Act 1911 has been retained since it seems to add little to these provisions. There does however seem to have been a quite deliberate decision to retain as additional methods written statements admitted under the Magistrates' Courts Act 1980, s 102 or Criminal Justice Act 1967, s 9, admissions under Criminal Justice Act 1967, s 10, and proof by means of fingerprints under Criminal Justice Act 1948, s 39. The former provisions have been mentioned earlier, the last requires evidence of the previous conviction and that the fingerprints of the person convicted are the same as those of the person against whom it is sought to prove the conviction. This evidence may take the form of three certificates. First there is the certificate of conviction signed by or on behalf of the Commissioner of Metropolitan Police exhibiting copies of fingerprints and stating that they are the finger-prints of the person who was convicted. Second there is a certificate signed by or on behalf of the prison or remand centre where the person against whom it is sought to prove the conviction was detained in connection with any criminal proceedings; this certificate states that the exhibited fingerprints were taken from the person in question while he was detained. Last there is another certificate signed by or on behalf of the Commissioner of the Metropolitan Police stating that the fingerprints exhibited to the two previous certificates are identical.

Under s 31 of the Road Traffic Offenders Act 1988, the endorsement of a licence is prima facie evidence of a conviction. This provision is in addition to the other statutory provisions dealing with the proof of previous convictions which have just been mentioned; but its object is to enable justices to determine sentence and it does not supersede the other methods of proving convictions at the trial.[15]

If the apparent subject of the relevant conviction should deny that it relates to him, then this denial must be rebutted by evidence.[16]

SECTION 5.   MISCELLANEOUS

It would obviously be possible to protract a chapter of this sort indefinitely, but proof of most other frequently recurring points are dependent on special statutory provisions such as those of the Companies Act 1985, and the Insolvency Act 1985. It will be convenient to conclude with the proof of custom and ownership, two matters which are dependent on widely differing branches of the common law of evidence.

A.   CUSTOM AND USAGE

There are four ways in which the existence of a custom or usage may be proved. They constitute direct, circumstantial and hearsay evidence. The first method consists of the testimony of a witness who deposes from his personal knowledge to the actual existence of the custom or usage. He states that he is well aware of the fact that lessees in a given locality have been in the habit of removing 'way-going' crops, that is crops sown by the tenant before the termination of his lease,[17] or of any other custom or

---

14   Evidence Act 1851, s 13; Criminal Procedure Act 1865, s 6; and Prevention of Crimes Act 1871, s 18.
15   *Stone v Bastick* [1967] 1 QB 74, [1965] 3 All ER 713, also requiring a certificate of disqualification to refer only to the offence in respect of which the disqualification was imposed.
16   *Bailey v DPP* (1998) 142 Sol Jo LB 198. The same requirement would presumably apply to judgments.
17   Cf *Wigglesworth v Dallison* (1779) 1 Doug KB 201.

usage. The evidence may be based on the observation of many instances, and it may sometimes be based on reputation or hearsay. A second method of proving custom which also comes into the category of direct evidence is for a witness to testify to particular instances of its exercise. He refers to cases in which he or someone observed by him exercised the custom, but he does not generalise on the subject. The third way of proving a custom or usage depends on circumstantial evidence. It consists of evidence of a comparable custom in other localities similar to the one in question. Finally, what is probably the most typical way of proving a custom is to rely on the declaration of a deceased person concerning public or general rights,[18] admissible, in criminal proceedings, under a common law exception to the hearsay rule and, in civil cases, under the Civil Evidence Act 1968.

B.   OWNERSHIP

There are also four main ways in which ownership of real or personal property may be proved. The first consists of production of the documents of title which must, of course, be duly authenticated in the sense that their due execution must be proved unless they are produced from proper custody in circumstances giving rise to the presumption in favour of due execution in the case of documents more than twenty years old.

Possession is prima facie evidence of ownership, and a second way in which ownership may be proved is by proof of possession of the property in question. In the case of real estate, proof of connected property in circumstances rendering it probable that the owner of such connected property would, in addition, be the owner of the property in question may rank as a third means of proving ownership. Finally ownership may be proved by admissible hearsay statements.

---

18   See p 575 above.

Index